# Encyclopedia of the
# MODERN WORLD

## 1900 TO THE PRESENT

*Encyclopedia of the*
# MODERN WORLD
## 1900 TO THE PRESENT

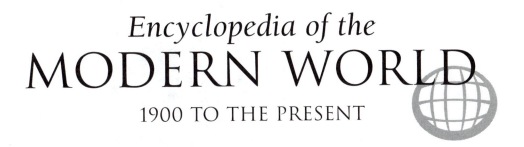

## VOLUME II
## G–O

William R. Keylor
GENERAL EDITOR

Michael McGuire
ASSOCIATE EDITOR

Facts On File
*An imprint of Infobase Publishing*

Encyclopedia of the Modern World: 1900 to the Present

Facts On File, Inc.
An imprint of Infobase Publishing
132 West 31st Street
New York NY 10001

**Library of Congress Cataloging-in-Publication Data**

The encyclopedia of the modern world: 1900 to the present / William R. Keylor, general editor ; Michael McGuire, associate editor.  p. cm.
ISBN 0-8160-4872-X (HC. : alk. paper)
1. History, Modern—20th century—Encyclopedias. 2. World politics—20th century—Encyclopedias. 3. Twentieth century—Encyclopedias. I. Keylor, William R., 1944– II. McGuire Michael (Michael E.), 1976–
D419.E53 2005
909.82′03—dc22          2004061975

Facts On File books are available at special discounts when purchased in bulk quantities for businesses, associations, institutions, or sales promotions. Please call our Special Sales Department in New York at (212) 967-8800 or (800) 322-8755.

You can find Facts On File on the
World Wide Web at http://www.factsonfile.com

Text design by Dorothy M. Preston
Cover design by Nora Wertz
Illustrations by Dale Williams

Printed in the United States of America

VB Hermitage 10 9 8 7 6 5 4 3 2 1

This book is printed on acid-free paper.

*To James Arthur Keylor*
*with brotherly love*

# Contents

# Entries G to O

# G

**Gable, Clark (William Gable)**
*(1901–1960)* Legendary American film actor. Born in Cadiz, Ohio, Gable began his show business career as a backstage handyman for a number of touring companies. He entered the HOLLYWOOD arena with bit performances in silent films during the 1920s, and by the early 1930s was a star. Cast mainly in he-man roles, he nonetheless won an ACADEMY AWARD for his sparkling comic performance in Frank CAPRA's *It Happened One Night* (1934). His best-known performance is undoubtedly that of Rhett Butler in the Civil War epic *GONE WITH THE WIND* (1939). Dubbed "the King of Hollywood," he appeared in some 65 films including *Red Dust* (1932), *Mutiny on the Bounty* (1935), *San Francisco* (1936), *The Hucksters* (1947), *The Tall Men* (1955) and *Run Silent, Run Deep* (1958). His rugged, straightforward style was last seen in *The Misfits* (1960), completed shortly before his death. Gable was married to the acclaimed comic actress Carole LOMBARD.

**Gabo, Naum** *(1890–1977)* Russian sculptor, painter and architect. Brother of Anton PEVSNER, he was born in Bryansk, Russia, lived in Germany and Norway during the RUSSIAN REVOLUTION and returned to his native country in 1917. While abroad, he studied medicine in Munich, but abandoned that career to study with the great art historian Heinrich Wolfflin. During this period he also met Wassily KANDINSKY and other modern artists and decided to devote himself to painting and sculpture. With his brother, he wrote the *Realist Manifesto* (1920), which stressed a new dynamism and proposed the inclusion of time and space into works of art. In Russia, Gabo was one of the founders of CONSTRUCTIVISM. His Constructivist sculptures are elegantly delicate abstract compositions, often employing plastic, nylon or metal in complicated geometric configurations. Gabo's nonpolitical aesthetics clashed with Soviet art dogma, and he left Moscow in 1922. Gabo taught at the BAUHAUS in Berlin, until forced to flee by the Nazis in 1932. He moved first to England, then to the U.S., where he settled in 1946. Examples of his work can be found in many leading contemporary art museums, and he is known for a number of major architectural commissions, such as the U.S. Rubber Company Building in New York City.

**Gabon (Republic of Gabon)** Nation located on the west coast of Africa

| GABON | |
|---|---|
| 1960 | Gabon is formally proclaimed an independent nation, with Leon M'Ba as prime minister. |
| 1961 | M'Ba is elected president |
| 1964 | The military leads a successful coup; French troops intervene and restore M'ba to office |
| 1967 | M'Ba is reelected president but dies within months; Vice President Albert-Bernard (later, Omar) Bongo succeeds to the presidency. |
| 1973 | Bongo is reelected president. |
| 1979 | As sole candidate in national presidential election, Bongo is reelected for a second seven-year term. |
| 1990 | After much social unrest and increasing pressure from disgruntled workers, President Bongo legalizes opposition. |
| 1993 | Omar Bongo is reelected president, a post held since 1967. |
| 1998 | Bongo is reelected, gaining two-thirds of the vote. |
| 2005 | Bongo is reelected to another seven-year term. |

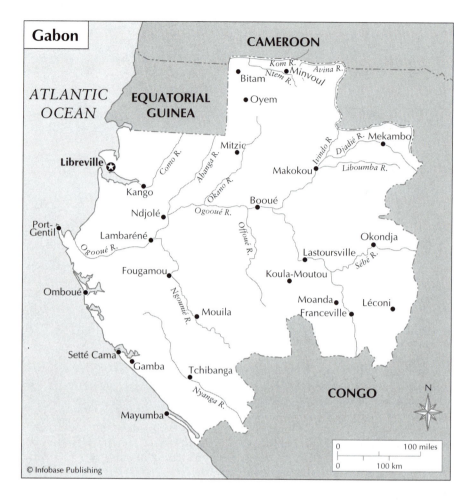

Gabon

in the equatorial zone. Gabon covers an area of 103,062 square miles. A French colony, Gabon achieved full independence in 1960. Leon M'ba was elected president in 1961, deposed by the military in 1964 and reinstated as president after French intervention. His successor, Albert-Bernard (later, Omar) Bongo, established a single-party government and maintained political and economic stability until the 1980s, when opposition groups formed a government in exile. In 1990 strikes, protests and continued opposition pressure pushed the government toward constitutional reform. Although a 1991 constitution legalized opposition parties, the governing Gabonese Democratic Party continued to control the national legislature. Bongo managed to retain power through reelection in 1993, 1998, and 2005, despite allegations by his opponents of voter fraud.

**Gabor, Dennis** *(1900–1979)* Hungarian-born British physicist. Gabor was educated in Budapest and Berlin, where he obtained his engineering doctorate (1927). After Adolf HITLER rose to power, he immigrated to Britain and became a British subject. In 1948 he jointed the faculty at the Imperial College of Science and Technology in London. He was later a staff scientist for the CBS. Gabor invented holography, a photographic method of reproducing three-dimensional images. He developed the system in 1948 by improving the resolution of the ELECTRON MICROSCOPE. (In 1960, other scientists achieved the same effect using laser beams.) For this invention, Gabor was awarded the 1971 NOBEL PRIZE for physics. He patented more than 100 other inventions.

**Gagarin, Yuri** *(1934–1968)* Soviet cosmonaut and the first human being in space. Gagarin stunned the world on April 12, 1961, when he successfully orbited the Earth. Remaining in orbit for 89.1 minutes and traveling at a velocity that reached 17,400 miles an hour, Gagarin opened the door to space travel for humans. Although in a few short years his historic achievements would be eclipsed by a series of epic space voyages, he was truly the world's first space traveler. The son of a carpenter born on a collective farm, Gagarin had lived with his family under German occupation for several years during World War II. While attending industrial technical school and studying to become a factory worker, he became interested in flying and joined an amateur pilot's club. Recommended for air force duty by one of the club's instructors, he joined the Orenburg air force school in 1955. For two years Gagarin served as a pilot with the Northern Fleet, based north of the Arctic Circle, then joined the cosmonaut corps and began training in October 1959.

After his historic spaceflight Gagarin found himself a popular and inspiring speaker. As a spokesman for the Soviet space program and its many successes, he charmed listeners around the world with his simple style and humility. Appointed commander of the cosmonaut team in 1961, he became deputy director of the cosmonaut training center in 1964. Yearning to get back into space, he managed to get himself assigned as a backup pilot for *Soyuz 3* and had just finished when he was tragically killed in an aircraft accident on March 27, 1968. Today, a bronze statue of Gagarin welcomes visitors to Star City near Moscow, a symbol of the man, his accomplishment and his hold on the hearts of the Soviet people.

*Soviet cosmonaut Yuri Gagarin, the first person to orbit Earth* (LIBRARY OF CONGRESS, PRINTS AND PHOTOGRAPHS DIVISION)

**Gaitskell, Hugh Todd Naylor** *(1906–1963)* British Labour politician. Gaitskell was educated at Winchester and at New College, Oxford, where he became a socialist, influenced by the events surrounding the GENERAL STRIKE OF 1926. A lecturer in political economy at University College in London, Gaitskell was elected Labour M. P. in 1945. He served in the ATTLEE government as minister of fuel and power (1947–50), minister of economic affairs (1950) and chancellor of the exchequer (1950–51). In 1955, Gaitskell defeated Aneurin BEVAN and Herbert MORRISON for the leadership of the LABOUR PARTY, succeeding Clement Attlee. Gaitskell was a skilled parliamentarian and representative of the tradition of the Labour Party, although his alterations of the NATIONAL HEALTH SERVICE alienated some of the party's left. He also opposed the party's position in favor of unilateral nuclear disarmament, and in 1961 persuaded the party to reverse its decision. Gaitskell died suddenly in 1963, but his enthusiasm had revitalized the Labour Party and it prevailed in the 1964 elections.

**Galbraith, John Kenneth** *(1908–2006)* Noted economist and author. Born and educated in Canada, Galbraith was a Harvard professor when he was brought to Washington, D.C., to serve in various government posts during World War II. An active liberal Democrat, he was an adviser to both Adlai STEVENSON and President John F. KENNEDY, who appointed him ambassador to INDIA during a critical period of Chinese-Indian border conflict. Galbraith was a prolific author throughout his career and is best known for three books: *American Capitalism* (1952), *The Affluent Society* (1958) and *The New Industrial State* (1967). Galbraith, trained as a Keynesian (see KEYNES, John Maynard), argued that the free-enterprise system had its limits. Unlike many traditional economists Galbraith also emphasized the importance of political decisions in shaping the economic system. He said that the American government should assume responsibility for health, housing and other segments of the economy that were not effectively providing basic services for many Americans.

**Gale, General Sir Richard** *(1896–1982)* British military officer. As commander of the Sixth Airborne Division,

*Economist and ambassador John Kenneth Galbraith* (LIBRARY OF CONGRESS, PRINTS AND PHOTOGRAPHS DIVISION)

he was one of the leaders of the Allied parachute troops at the INVASION OF NORMANDY during WORLD WAR II. For his role in the invasion, he was awarded the British Distinguished Service Order (DSO) and the American Legion of Merit. He also played an important role in the Allied counter-attack during the BATTLE OF THE BULGE (December, 1944). After the war he commanded British forces in PALESTINE and in Egypt. He was aide-de-camp to Queen ELIZABETH II in the 1950s and was deputy supreme Allied commander in Europe for NATO (1958–60).

**Galili, Israel** *(1911–1986)* Israeli politician. Galili was a leader in establishing ISRAEL's arms industry, and was long active as a behind-the-scenes policy maker and conciliator in the Labor Party. He was said to have been especially influential in the government headed by Golda MEIR. In 1980, he was the principal architect of a compromise peace plan with JORDAN.

**Gallant, Mavis** *(1922–   )* Canadian author. Born in Montreal, Gallant later lived in Paris. Her short story collections include *The Other Paris* (1956), *Overhead in a Balloon: Twelve Stories of Paris* (1987) and *In Transit: Twenty Stories* (1989). Novels include *Green Water, Green Sky* (1959) and *A Fairly Good Time* (1970). Gallant has been a frequent contributor to THE NEW YORKER, where many of her short stories first appeared.

**Gallant Fox** *(1927–1954)* Thoroughbred racehorse. The 1930 Triple Crown winner, Gallant Fox won 10 of 11 races during that campaign. The race he lost was responsible for one of the biggest payoffs in racing history, as he was upset as heavy favorite on a muddy track by 100–1 shot Jim Dandy in the Travers, who returned $20,000 on a $2 bet. Gallant Fox's stud career was perhaps even more outstanding, as his progeny included the 1935 Triple Crown winner Omaha and 1936 Horse of the Year, Granville.

**Gallegos, Rómulo** *(1884–1969)* Venezuelan novelist and statesman. In self-imposed exile from the Venezuelan dictatorship (1931–35), he returned home and became minister of education. He was elected president of the nation in 1947, but was ousted in a coup less than a year later. He fled to Mexico, returning to VENEZUELA in 1958. As a novelist, Gallegos used modernist methods to portray the landscape of his homeland. An extremely prolific author, he began writing novels with *El último solar* (1920, *The Last Manor*). His best known work is the novel *Doña Bárbara* (1929, tr. 1931), a work about the Venezuelan plains. His other works include *Cantaclaro* (1931) and *Canaima* (1935).

**Gallipoli Peninsula** In European TURKEY, a long and narrow point of land, aimed southwestward and lying athwart the DARDANELLES; perennially important because of its strategic position commanding the maritime commerce between the Mediterranean Sea and the Black Sea. In WORLD WAR I Allied British, Australian, French and New Zealand land and sea forces unsuccessfully stormed the Turkish forts in this area in 1915–16. Contemporaries, and later historians, blame First Lord of the Admiralty Winston CHURCHILL for the military disaster.

**Galloway, William "Bill"** *(1877–1952)* U.S. industrialist and catalog marketer. He put himself through college by selling pencils. This sales experience enabled him to become one of the first marketers through catalog solicitation. With his brother James he started Galloway Company at Waterloo, Iowa, to produce a complete line of farm machinery. Bill Galloway pioneered in marketing through catalog display and selective direct mailing. The company's manufacturing operations expanded quickly and encompassed a line of buildings almost a mile long, but internal disputes eventually brought the business down. The brothers started another business of manufacturing and distributing automatic humidifiers for furnaces. Galloway Park in Waterloo pays tribute to the pioneer Iowa industrialists.

**Gallup, George H.** *(1901–1984)* The American father of modern public opinion polling techniques. Gallup gained fame by predicting that Franklin D. ROOSEVELT would beat Alf LANDON in the 1936 presidential election, even though other pollsters predicted otherwise. Gallup survived a notable lapse when he incorrectly forecast that Thomas DEWEY would beat Harry S. TRUMAN in the 1948 election. Gallup's American Institute of Public Opinion, and later the Gallup Organization, came to set the standards for the polling industry around the world. He made polling a key tool of politics and business.

**Gallup Poll** Public opinion poll originated by statistician and market research expert George GALLUP (1901–84). In 1935 Gallup, who was an advertising agency market researcher (1932–47), founded the American Institute of Public Opinion, and in 1939 he set up the Audience Research Institute, both with headquarters in Princeton, New Jersey. Based on sound scientific sampling methods developed by American business in the 1920s and refined by later pollsters, the Gallup Poll interviews a representative group of 1,500 people regarding their views on a given issue and, from their responses, extrapolates American public opinion on the question. The poll is supported by approximately 140 newspapers and some 20 surveys a year are conducted. The best known are the preelection surveys carried out by the American Institute, which have been conducted yearly since 1936.

**Galsworthy, John** *(1867–1933)* British novelist, playwright and poet. Galsworthy was born in Surrey and educated at Harrow and New College, Oxford. Though called to the bar, he never practiced law. With a private income, Galsworthy was free to travel; during the course of one of his trips he became acquainted with Joseph CONRAD, who became a life long friend, and of whose work Galsworthy was an early champion. Galsworthy's first collection of short stories, *From the Four Winds,* was published in 1897; his first novel, *Jocelyn,* appeared in 1898. Both were published under the pseudonym John Sinjohn. These were followed by the short stories, *Villa Rubein,* in 1900, at which time Galsworthy became acquainted with the publisher Edward Garnett, who greatly encouraged Galsworthy in his work. Another source of encouragement was his future wife, Ada. Married unhappily when they met, she and Galsworthy lived together covertly until she was able to obtain her divorce. Her story and their relationship was the inspiration for Galsworthy's first major success, *The Man of Property* (1906), which was to become the first novel of THE FORSYTE SAGA, Galsworthy's best known work. The book not only tells the story of Irene and Soames Forsyte's unhappy marriage, but satirizes upper-middle-class life in Victorian England with its portrayal of the entire Forsyte family and their strict adherence to convention. It established Galsworthy's reputation. The other novels included in *The Forsyte Saga* (1922) are *In Chancery* (1920) and *To Let* (1921); and the short stories, "The Indian Summer of a Forsyte" (1918) and "The Awakening" (1920). However, Galsworthy published many other works of fiction between 1906 and 1920, including *Fraternity* (1909) and *The Dark Flower* (1913). Galsworthy's first play, *The Silver Box* (1906), established him also as a playwright of note. His realistic plays revolve around themes of social injustice. *Strife* (1909) examined the suffering of striking Welsh workers, while *Justice* (1910) reflected Galsworthy's crusade against solitary confinement of prisoners, and influenced Winston CHURCHILL's policy on prison reform. Galsworthy was offered a knighthood in 1917 which he refused. He was the founder of PEN in 1921. He was the recipient of the NOBEL PRIZE in literature in 1932. Galsworthy's work, though continually popular, has often been criticized as middlebrow, and he has been accused of inwardly admiring the very values his works purport to satirize. Other of his many works include the novels *The White Monkey* (1924), *The Silver Spoon* (1926) and *Swan Song* (1928), which further chronicle the Forsytes; and the plays *The Skin Game* (1920), *Loyalties* (1922) and *Old English* (1924).

**Galtieri, Leopoldo Fortunato** *(1926–2003)* Argentinean military officer, president of ARGENTINA. General Galtieri was leader of the controlling military junta in Argentina from 1979 to 1982, and was responsible for Argentina's seizure of the FALKLAND ISLANDS in 1982. Britain responded militarily, decisively defeating Argentina in the FALKLANDS WAR. Galtieri and other junta members were deposed by Argentinean democrats, accused of human rights violations and court-martialled. Galtieri was sentenced to 12 years in prison in 1986. In July 2002 he was arrested for human-rights abuses during the junta and died months later.

**Gambia, The (Republic of Gambia)** Nation located on the west coast of

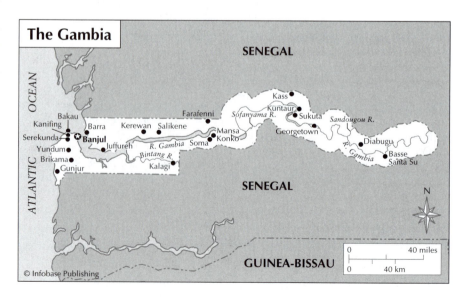

The Gambia

---

## GAMBIA

| 1965 | Gambia attains full independence within the Commonwealth. |
|------|----------------------------------------------------------|
| 1970 | Gambia becomes a republic, with Sir Dawda Jawara as first president. |
| 1982 | The Confederation of Senegambia comes into being, with Jawara as vice president of the new federation. |
| 1987 | Jawara is reelected president. |
| 1989 | The Senegambian Confederation is officially dissolved. |
| 1994 | A military junta seizes power under Lieutenant Yahya Jammeh. |
| 1996 | Jammeh is elected president of the country over three other candidates. |
| 2001 | Jammeh is reelected president. |

---

Africa. Gambia is a separate enclave within the country of SENEGAL and occupies an area of 4,359 square miles. A British colony since 1888, the country achieved independence in 1965 and became a republic in 1970. Its president, Sir Dawda Kairaba Jawara (1965–94), formed a Senegambian Confederation with Senegal in 1982, primarily for economic reasons, but it was dissolved in 1989. Although Gambia experienced greater democratization after the 1994 overthrow of Jawara, culminating in a 1996 multiparty constitution, its democratic system has been impeded by the government's refusal to recognize three major opposition parties and by its strained relationship with some humanitarian nongovernmental organizations. The elections that put current president Yahya Jammeh—who helped to overthrow Jawara—into power in 1996 and again in 2001 have been widely criticized for possible fraud.

**Gamow, George** *(1904–1968)* Soviet-American physicist. Gamow, the son of a teacher, was educated at the University of Leningrad, where he obtained his doctorate in 1928 and later served as professor of physics (1931–34). Before his move to the U.S. in 1934 he spent long periods at Göttingen, Copenhagen and Cambridge, England, the major centers of the revolution then taking place in physics. In America he spent his career as professor of physics at George Washington University (1934–68) and then at the University of Colorado (1956–68).

Gamow made many contributions to nuclear and atomic physics, but is mainly noted for his work on interesting problems in cosmology and molecular biology. In cosmology he revised and extended the BIG BANG THEORY of the creation of the universe and first announced it in his famous "alpha beta gamma" paper in 1948, which he wrote in collaboration with Ralph ALPHER and Hans BETHE. A fuller account was later published by Gamow in his *Creation of the Universe* (1952). Gamow later moved from showing how the universe began to the no less interesting question of how life began. He was quick to see the significance of the DNA model proposed by James WATSON and Francis CRICK in 1953. The problem was to show how the sequences of the four nucleic acid bases that constitute the DNA chain could control the construction of proteins, which may be made from 20 or more amino acids. Gamow had the insight to see that the bases must contain a code for the construction of amino acids. Gamow also produced convincing arguments to show that the code was not overlapping. Gamow was widely known as one of the most successful popular science writers of his day. He wrote many books that conveyed to the general public much of the excitement of the revolution in physics that he lived through.

**Gance, Abel** *(1889–1981)* French film director and writer, one of the most important figures in the early de-

velopment of the cinema. Gance was born in Paris to a physician father who wanted him to pursue a career in law. After abandoning early studies, however, Gance turned to acting and writing for the stage and for the medium still in its infancy, the motion picture. In 1911 he formed his own movie production company and made his first film, *La Digue*. Between 1915 and 1918 he made many films for the prestigious Film d'Art company, including the experimental *La Folie du Docteur Tube* (which distorted images through the use of mirrors and lenses). His first masterpiece, *J'accuse* (1919), was a pacifist statement made during WORLD WAR I with real soldiers under fire. (He remade it as a sound film in 1938 on the eve of World War II.) The two films upon which his reputation rests followed in the 1920s: *La Roue* (*The Wheel*) in 1923 and *Napoléon* in 1927. The first was a melodrama set against a railyard background. Technically astounding, it liberated the camera from the tripod and created a vast mosaic of thousands of shots intercut at times with dizzying rapidity. *Napoleon* may be regarded as the culmination of the era of SILENT FILM. An unabashed glorification of French spirit and art, it refined Gance's camera technique and presented an innovation, the Polyvision system, a triptych employing triple screen projection that anticipated Cinerama by 25 years. Excepting a few projects in the 1930s like *Beethoven* (1938), in which he experimented with montages of sound, Gance was tied to commercial projects and did little wholly creative work until his last original project, *Cyrano et d'Artagnan* (1963). Gance was a visionary whose finished work sometimes fell short of his grandiose ambitions. A member of the French movement known as The Seventh Art, he saw cinema as the marriage of feelings and machine.

**Gandhi, Indira** *(1917–1984)* Prime minister of INDIA (1966–77, 1980–84). The daughter of Jawaharlal NEHRU (and unrelated to Mohandas K. GANDHI), she joined the CONGRESS PARTY in 1939. Minister for broadcasting and information from 1964 to 1966, on the death of Prime Minister Lal SHASTRI (1966) she was elected leader of Congress and became prime minister. Her premiership was marked by significant social

*Indira Gandhi, prime minister of India. (1966–77. 1980–84)* (LIBRARY OF CONGRESS, PRINTS AND PHOTOGRAPHS DIVISION)

and economic progress, but also by tension with PAKISTAN (see INDO-PAKISTANI WAR OF 1971) and increasing internal discontent over her assumption of almost dictatorial powers on the declaration of an emergency in 1975. In 1977 Congress was defeated for the first time by the Janata coalition, united only in their opposition to Mrs. Gandhi (see Mararji DESAI). Within a few months she was on the road back to power, winning the election of 1980 with a promise of firm government, and demonstrating her popular appeal with ordinary people. She was assassinated in 1984 by Sikh extremists.

## Gandhi, Mohandas K(aramchand) (Mahatma, or "great soul") (1869–1948)
Indian national leader who helped INDIA achieve independence through a campaign based on nonviolence and civil disobedience. Born at Porbandar on the western coast of India, Gandhi studied law in London in the late 1880s and returned home to practice as a barrister in Bombay. In 1907 he went to South Africa, where he conducted passive resistance campaigns in protest of the Transvaal government's discrimination against Indian settlers, who formed a minority in the region. He returned to India in 1915

and eventually emerged as leader of the CONGRESS PARTY, which called for India's independence from the UNITED KINGDOM. Shedding his Anglicized demeanor (both figuratively and literally) Gandhi adopted a simple, ascetic way of life. He organized a boycott of British goods (both as a symbolic protest of India's colonial status and in order to stimulate India's local industries). His nonviolent campaigns of civil disobedience to British rule provoked the British to imprison him on four different occasions (1922, 1930, 1933, 1942); he also went on hunger strikes to focus attention on, and gather sympathy for, his cause.

Gandhi worked with Britain's last two viceroys of India (WAVELL and MOUNTBATTEN) to plan his country's independence, which was granted in 1947. Acknowledging the demands of JINNAH and the Muslim minority, Gandhi accepted the partition of the colony into two separate nations, India and PAKISTAN. The following year Gandhi was assassinated by a Hindu fanatic who viewed Gandhi's acceptance of partition as a betrayal of the Hindu population. Many of Gandhi's followers regarded him as a saint; his doctrine of nonviolence had a direct and profound influence on Martin Luther KING Jr., leader of the CIVIL RIGHTS MOVEMENT in the U.S.

## Gandhi, Rajiv (1945–1991)
Indian politician, prime minister of INDIA (1984–90). The grandson of Jawaharlal NEHRU and son of Indira GANDHI, Rajiv Gandhi was educated at Cambridge University and was subsequently a pilot in India. Following the death of his elder brother Sanjay in 1980, Indira Gandhi persuaded Rajiv to enter politics, hoping to groom him as her successor. Following her death in 1984, he won a record majority in the elections that year. Rajiv Gandhi identified domestic strife as his major problem and attempted to reduce tensions in Punjab, Assam and Gujarat, but was minimally successful, particularly in the Punjab, where Sikh militants revived their campaign for greater autonomy in 1986. Defeated in the 1990 elections, he was assassinated while campaigning in 1991.

## Gang of Four
Four radical Chinese leaders—Wang Hongwen, Zhang Chungqiao, Yao Wenyuan, and CHIANG CH'ING, Mao's widow—who were publicly denounced following the triumph of moderates in 1976. A show trial was held following a PROPAGANDA campaign and the arrest of the four on a charge of trying to take control of the army. Jiang Qing was given a suspended death sentence in 1981. In Britain, the name "Gang of Four" was popularly to given to four ex–LABOUR PARTY members—Roy JENKINS, Shirley WILLIAMS, William RODGERS, and David OWEN—whose decision to leave the party coincided with attacks on the Chinese Gang of Four. They formed the SOCIAL DEMOCRATIC PARTY in 1981.

## Gao Xingjiang (Kao Hsing-chien) (1940– )
Author, director and artist, winner of the NOBEL PRIZE in literature (2000). Born in Ganzhou, in the Jiangxi province of China, Gao obtained a B.A. in French literature and language from the Department of Foreign Languages at Beijing University in 1962 and began working as a translator and art critic. During the CULTURAL REVOLUTION (1966–76) Gao was one of many Chinese artists forced by the government to relocate to "reeducation" camps. During this period Gao burned an entire suitcase of his essays, plays and other writings for fear of its discovery by government officials.

In 1981, five years after the end of the Cultural Revolution, Gao published *A Preliminary Discussion on the Art of Modern Fiction* in Chinese, English and French, followed in succession by the novel *A Pigeon Called Red Beak* (1985), *Collected Plays* (1985) and the essay *In Search of a Modern Form of Dramatic Representation* (1987). During the 1980s he wrote several Chinese plays that were performed throughout Beijing, such as *Alarm Signal* (1982) and *The Bus Stop* (1983), although the government quickly labeled the latter performance an example of "intellectual pollution" and ended its run after a few weeks. Three years later it banned his play *The Other Shore*. In an effort to escape government harassment, Gao began a 10-month journey from the head of the Yangtze River to its mouth on the coast of China. Gao's experiences on this trek formed the basis for his 1990 novel *South Mountain*. In 1987, after he completed his journey, he emigrated from China to

France, where he has continued to live in self-imposed exile. In response to the 1989 TIANANMEN SQUARE MASSACRE, Gao resigned from the Chinese Communist Party (CCP) and began work on the play *Fugitives* (1992), which was based on events in China immediately following the Tiananmen massacre. In response, the Chinese government banned publication and performance of all Gao's writings. Since then he has composed two plays—*Between Life and Death* (1993) and *Weekend Quartet* (1996)—and one autobiographical work, *One Man's Bible* (1999), discussing his experiences in China after the Cultural Revolution. In 2000 Gao received the Nobel Prize in literature.

**Gapon, Father Georgi Apollonovich** *(1870–1906)* Russian priest. He believed in police socialism and founded the Assembly of Russian Factory and Mill Workers in St. Petersburg in 1903, which was financed by police funds. A strike at the Putilov works in St. Petersburg began because of alleged victimization of assembly members and soon spread. Gapon decided to make an appeal to the czar. He promoted a petition that was revolutionary in its demands, and organized an illegal march of 200,000 to the Winter Palace. The police fired on the demonstrators, killing 130 people, and January 9, 1905, became known as BLOODY SUNDAY and saw the start of a year of revolutionary unrest. Evidence suggests that Gapon was an agent provocateur. He was murdered by his fellow revolutionaries.

**Garang, John** *(1945–2005)* Officer in the Sudanese army and leader of the largely Christian southern Sudanese rebel group the Sudanese People's Liberation Army (SPLA). By the mid-1990s Garang's SPLA had taken control of the southern half of SUDAN. Garang refused to follow the lead of smaller rebel groups by signing peace accords with the northern, Muslim-dominated government and declared that he would continue to fight until southern Sudan became an independent state. By 1998 Garang had changed his position and agreed to participate in negotiations with the government for the creation of a new national government through an international supervised election. However, the negotiations never established a timetable for the elections; both sides refused to enter into peace negotiations, and the guerrilla war between the SPLA and the Sudanese government continued. When a peace agreement was finally signed in January 2005, Garang was appointed vice president in the Sudanese government. After only three weeks in office he was killed in a helicopter crash.

**Garbo, Greta (Greta Louisa Gustafsson Garbo)** *(1905–1990)* Legendary Swedish-born movie star of the SILENT FILM era and the early years of TALKING PICTURES. Throughout her 19-year, 27-film career she specialized in playing glamorous seductresses who often became involved in tragic love affairs. Her movies included the silent *Flesh and the Devil* (1927) with leading man John Gilbert, with whom she was romantically involved; and the sound films *Anna Christie* (1930), *Mata Hari* (1931), *Grand Hotel* (1932), *Queen Christina* (1933), *Camille* (1936) and *Ninotchka* (1939). Garbo was one of the highest-paid and most highly regarded stars of the 1930s; her performances generated acres of purple prose from writer-admirers attempting to explain her sphinx-like appeal. In the early 1940s, when WORLD WAR II cut off her European box-office (where much of her films' profits came from), Garbo took what was planned as a temporary sabbatical from films. The sabbatical eventually became permanent, and Garbo, who had always valued her privacy, became a famous recluse until her death.

**Garcia, Jerry (Jerome John)** *(1942–1995)* American ROCK and roll songwriter, vocalist and guitarist. Garcia, who is best known as the lead guitarist and primary public spokesman for the GRATEFUL DEAD, has been one of the most admired and influential rock guitarists of the past two decades. In the early 1960s, Garcia played guitar in folk, bluegrass and jug band styles before forging the blend of blues and psychedelic chord questing for which he became known in the late 1960s as the San Francisco–based Grateful Dead achieved national popularity. Garcia and lyricist Robert Hunter formed the primary songwriting team for the band. Garcia has combined his involvement with the Grateful Dead with outside solo projects and collaborative work with, among others, the bluegrass band Old and In the Way and with jazz saxophonist Ornette COLEMAN. In the early 1980s, Garcia successfully battled heroin addiction to return to top form in the Grateful Dead album *In the Dark* (1987), which featured the Garcia-Hunter hit *Touch of Grey*.

**García Lorca, Federico** *(1898–1936)* Spanish poet and playwright. García Lorca is widely considered to be the most significant figure in Spanish literature of the 20th century. Born in Granada, Spain, to a wealthy family, García Lorca showed himself early on to be gifted not only as a writer but as a painter and a musician as well. His first published book of verse, *Book of Poems* (1921), established him as an astonishingly evocative lyric poet with a gift for plain and moving utterance. García Lorca also became a leading figure in the Spanish theater with plays such as *The Butterfly's Curse* (1920), *Mariana Pined* (1927), *The Shoemaker's Amazing Wife* (1930), *Blood Wedding* (1933), *Yerma* (1934) and the posthumously published *House of Bernarda Alba* (1945). García Lorca's plays frequently dealt with the village-rooted lives of Andalusian peasants and the conflict between passion and honor. García Lorca traveled abroad to New York and Argentina, among other locales, before returning to Spain in the early 1930s. He was murdered in 1936, during the SPANISH CIVIL WAR, by Nationalist partisans.

**García Márquez, Gabriel** *(1928– )* Colombian author. García Márquez was born in Aracataca and was raised in early childhood by his grandparents, the source of much of the Latin American myth and folklore which would later find its way into his writing. He was educated at the University of Bogotá and worked as a journalist beginning at the age of 18, moving to Bogotá in 1954 to write full time for *El Espectador*. Eventually, he settled in Mexico City. García Márquez's first important work of fiction, *La hojarasca*, (published in English as "The Leaf Storm," and included in *Leaf Storm and Other Stories*, 1972) was published in 1955, but it was not until *Cien años de soledad*, (1967; *One Hundred Years of Solitude*) that he received international acclaim. The novel describes the decaying village of Macondo as a metaphor for Latin America, and follows the descendants of the Buendía family over seven generations. The novel, with its flights into the supernatural and straightforward descriptions of magical events, is a hallmark of MAGIC REALISM. It also evidences the influence of William FAULKNER and reflects García Márquez's left-leaning political beliefs and his disgust at the manipulation of and corruption in Latin American politics. A personal friend of Fidel CASTRO, García Márquez has nonetheless expressed reservations about the government in Cuba. Following the publication of *El otoño del patriarca* (*The Autumn of the Patriarch*, 1975), a depiction through varying points of view of the decline of a despotic Latin American dictator, and *Crónica de una muerta anunciada* (*Chronicle of a Death Foretold*, 1981), the story of a murder, again portrayed through various viewpoints, García Márquez was awarded the NOBEL PRIZE in literature in 1982. Other works include *In Evil Hour* (1979) *Love in the Time of Cholera* (1988), *The General in His Labryinth* (1991), *Strange Pilgrims* (1992), *Love and Other Demons* (1995), *News of a Kidnapping* (1996) and the first volume of his memoir, *Living to Tell the Tale* (2003).

**Garden, Mary (Mary Davidson)** *(1874–1967)* Scottish opera singer. Born in Scotland, Mary Garden grew up in Chicago and made her operatic debut in the title role of *Louise* in Paris in 1900. A member of the Opéra-Comique from 1900 to 1907, she created the role of Mélisande in the world premiere of Claude DEBUSSY's *Pelléas et Mélisande* in 1902, a role which became her signature piece. She was principal soprano for the Manhattan Opera House (1907–10), then became prima donna with the Chicago Opera (1910–30), serving briefly as the company's artistic director (1921–23). After a return to the Opéra-Comique (1930–35), she gave recitals, served as vocal adviser to METRO-GOLDWYN-MAYER in HOLLYWOOD, and gave master classes in voice at the Chicago Musical College. She was renowned for her command of the French repertory, and achieved particular acclaim in the title roles in *Manon, Thaïs,* and *Salome.*

**Gardiner, Muriel** *(1901–1985)* Psychoanalyst who specialized in the treatment of children. While studying medicine in Vienna in the 1930s, she joined the antifascist underground and helped hundreds of Austrians escape from the Nazis. The publisher of her 1983 memoirs suggested that she had been the model for the title character in the movie *Julia*, based on a key figure in Lillian HELLMAN's memoir *Pentimento.* Hellman denied the connection.

**Gardner, Ava (Lavinia)** *(1922–1990)* American actress. A farmer's daughter from North Carolina, Gardner was one of HOLLYWOOD's best-known stars from the 1940s through the 1960s. Early roles relied purely on her auburn-haired, green-eyed beauty, but she later won critical acclaim in such films as *Show Boat* (1951), *Mogambo* (1953), *The Barefoot Contessa* (1954), *On the Beach* (1959) and *The Night of the Iguana* (1964). Her marriages to actor Mickey ROONEY, band leader Artie SHAW and singer Frank SINATRA garnered widespread media attention. Such attention led her to move to Europe, where she continued to act in movies and television films.

**Gardner, Erle Stanley** *(1889–1970)* American mystery writer. The most published American author of his time, Gardner had worked for two decades as a lawyer in California before beginning to publish short stories and novels. No prose stylist, Gardner's principal contribution to his craft was to redirect the mystery genre away from amateur sleuths and toward professionals. His most enduring character was lawyer Perry Mason. Gardner also published under various pen names, including A. A. Fair.

**Gardner, John** *(1933–1982)* American novelist, critic and teacher. Among Gardner's novels were *Grendel* (1971), *The Sunlight Dialogues* (1973) and *October Light* (1976; National Book Critic's Circle Award, 1976). In his controversial nonfiction book *On Moral Fiction* (1978) Gardner argued that "almost all modern work is tinny, commercial and immoral." He founded and headed the creative writing department at the State University of New York at Binghamton. He also wrote poetry, children's books, fairy tales and criticism. He was killed in a motorcycle accident.

**Gargallo, Pablo** *(1881–1934)* Spanish sculptor. Studying art in Barcelona, he visited Paris in 1906 and 1911–14, meeting PICASSO and falling under the influence of CUBISM. Gargallo began sculpting in stone, but soon turned to working in iron, becoming one of the first modern artists to use this medium for sculpture. From 1917 to 1924, he taught at the Escuela Superior de Artes Oficios in Barcelona, returning to Paris in 1924.

**Garland, Hamlin** *(1860–1940)* U.S. novelist who wrote about the difficult lives of farmers of the Midwest region. His early stories were published in 1891 as *Main-Travelled Roads*, followed by his first novel in 1893, *Prairie Folks*. His other novels include *Wayside Courtship* (1897) and his first autobiography *A Son of the Middle Border* (1917). He won the PULITZER PRIZE in 1922 for his second autobiographical novel *A Daughter of the Middle Border*. He also published a number of politically oriented works, collections of essays and verse, and occult fiction.

**Garland, Judy (Frances Gumm)** *(1922–1969)* U.S. actress and singer. She started singing as a preschooler, and later became a stage actress. In 1935 she went under contract to METRO-GOLD-WYN-MAYER and remained at MGM until 1950. She appeared in many films between 1936 and 1962, but perhaps is best remembered for her role in *The Wizard of Oz* (1939), for which she received a special ACADEMY AWARD. The tensions, demands and pressures of her acting career led to the cancellation of her MGM contract. She returned to the screen in 1954 with one of her greatest successes *A Star Is Born*. She was also involved in singing and concert tours, and is considered by many as one of the truly great personalities of the entertainment world.

**Garland, William "Red"** *(1923–1984)* American JAZZ pianist; was an influential figure during the 1950s. Garland accompanied such renowned musicians as Charlie PARKER, Miles DAVIS and Coleman HAWKINS.

**Garner, John Nance** *(1868–1967)* American politician, vice president of the UNITED STATES (1933–41). Born in Red River County, Texas, Garner served in the Texas legislature (1898–1902) and House of Representatives (1903–33) and won election as speaker of the House in 1931. Garner served as vice president during Franklin D. ROOSEVELT's first two terms, helping push through much of the early NEW DEAL legislation. He opposed Roosevelt's third-term candidacy and ran unsuccessfully against Roosevelt for the 1940 Democratic presidential nomination. He retired from politics in 1941.

**Garvey, Marcus** *(1887–1940)* The Jamaican-born Garvey was a flamboyant and controversial figure in black American politics from the end of WORLD WAR I through the mid-1920s. In 1914 he founded the Universal Negro Improvement Association, a black nationalist organization, in Jamaica. Moving to the U.S. a few years later, he established the association's new headquarters in the HARLEM district of NEW YORK CITY. Unlike W. E. B. DUBOIS (who believed in radical political action to solve racial and economic problems facing blacks) or Booker T. WASHINGTON (who believed in black self-improvement through education), Garvey saw little hope for blacks to achieve social and economic justice in the U.S. Rather, he advocated a "back-to-Africa" movement; at a 1920 convention he was elected president of the "Republic of Africa"—his name for the proposed African nation for black American settlers. By the early 1920s, he had gained several million followers, many of whom sent him money to help fund the movement. However, in 1925 Garvey was convicted of mail fraud. After two years in prison he was deported to Jamaica. His influence quickly declined, and he spent his final years in Britain.

**Gascon, Jean** *(1920–1988)* Canadian actor-director, a leading figure in both French and English theater in Canada. A native of Montreal, Gascon founded that city's influential Théâtre du Nouveau Monde in 1951 and National Theater School in 1960. In 1969, he became the first native-born Canadian to be named artistic director of the Stratford (Ontario) festival, a post he held until 1974. From 1977 until his death, he was head of the theater program at Ottawa's National Arts Center.

**Gass, William H(oward)** *(1924– )* American author. Gass, a professor of philosophy, established himself with his acclaimed first novel, *Omensetter's Luck* (1966), which takes place along the Ohio River. Gass's work explores the nature of good and evil. Other works include the short stories *In the Heart of the Heart of the Country* (1968), and the essay collections *The World within the Word* (1978) and *Habitations of the Word* (1985). Gass's later works include *The Tunnel* (1995) and *Cartesian Sonata and Other Novellas* (1998). In 1990 he was named director of the International Writer's Center.

**Gasser, Herbert Spencer** *(1888–1963)* American physiologist. Gasser, the son of a country doctor, was educated at the University of Wisconsin and at Johns Hopkins University, qualifying as a physician in 1915. He then moved to Washington University, St. Louis, to take up an appointment as professor of pharmacology. Here he joined his old teacher Joseph ERLANGER in a famous collaboration that resulted in their sharing the 1944 NOBEL PRIZE in physiology or medicine for work on the differentiated function of nerve fibers. In 1931 Gasser was appointed to the chair of physiology at Cornell Medical School. Finally, in 1935, he was made director of the Rockefeller Institute in New York, a post he retained until his retirement in 1953.

**Gastev, Alexei Kapitonovich** *(1882–1939)* Russian poet and labor theorist. Gastev's poetry deals with industrialization, the necessity of building an "iron state," for which sacrifices are called. In his prose writings, Gastev expounded his theory of "mechanized collectivism," in which the workers synchronize their movements with the movements of machines, thus making individual thinking and a "normalized psychology" impossible. His reputation as a poet rests on his *Shockwork Poetry* (1918) and *A Stack of Orders* (1921). Gastev directed the Central Institute of Labor, but disappeared during the GREAT PURGE.

**Gates, Bill (William Henry Gates III)** *(1955– )* American businessman, cofounder of Microsoft Corporation. Born in Seattle, Gates learned BASIC, Fortran and LISP, all computer programming languages in high school. In 1972 Gates and his friend Paul Allen formed a company named Traf-O-Data, which built computers that counted automobiles for private and public organizations interested in analyzing traffic flow.

After enrolling in Harvard University in 1973, Gates again worked with Allen to develop a version of the BASIC language for the world's first personal computer (PC), the Altair 8800. Rather than selling the copyright to Micro Instrumentation and Telemetry Systems (MITS), the developer of the Altair series, they licensed the software to the company, keeping all copyrights as the property a company called Microsoft that they founded that year. The success of this endeavour convinced Gates that his time would be better spent working on Microsoft projects rather than continuing his studies at Harvard, so he dropped out in his junior year.

In 1980 Microsoft agreed to produce and provide IBM computers with an operating system called Disk Operating System (DOS). As with MITS, Microsoft retained the copyright to the software. When DOS proved a successful system for IBM PCs, other companies began to produce PCs for consumer and business demand. Because it owned the license to DOS, Microsoft was able to create similar business deals with these producers of PC "clones" throughout the 1980s and 1990s. In 1986 Microsoft became a publicly traded company. A year later the spectacular increase in the stock's price, largely due to the high demand for PCs and DOS, led to Gates's becoming the world's youngest self-made billionaire. Microsoft also developed Windows, an operating system for the personal computer that replaced DOS as the tool of choice for PCs.

Although Gates's career with Microsoft was full of commercial successes, he became the target of an antitrust lawsuit filed by the U.S. government alleging that Microsoft deliberately made its software incompatible with web browsers such as Netscape in order to force customers to employ Microsoft's own web browser, Internet Explorer. In 2000 a federal court ruled that Microsoft was guilty of violations of the Sherman Antitrust Act and decreed that Microsoft be divided into two new companies. Although a federal appeals court reversed the second half of the initial ruling, Gates later removed himself from the presidency and CEO position of Microsoft, taking on the title of chief software architect.

Along with his business successes, Gates established a philanthropic foundation, the Bill and Melinda Gates Foundation, which (among other things) funds Gates Millennial Scholarships that enable students to study the natural sciences and prepare teachers for primary and secondary education. Gates has also written two books, *The Road Ahead* and *Business @ the Speed of Thought,* both of which discuss his vision of the present and future role of technology in private and public life.

**Gate Theatre** Dublin theater company founded in 1928 by Hilton EDWARDS and Micheal MACLIAMMOIR that first performed in the Peacock Theatre, an adjunct of the ABBEY THEATRE, before establishing itself in the Rotunda Buildings in 1930. The aim of the Gate company was to create a world class theater, and it differed from the Abbey in that it presented international works as well as Irish drama. Following World War II, Lord Longford, and later his widow Christine, countess of Longford, ran the theater, overseeing several renovations. The theater continues to present the works of various small companies from Ireland and elsewhere.

**GATT (General Agreement on Tariffs and Trade)** An international body, established in 1948, aimed at reducing tariffs and other restrictions and fostering free trade. In 1993 GATT was superceded by the WORLD TRADE ORGANIZATION (WTO), an international body that promulgated rules of international trade and was empowered to impose sanctions on countries found to be in violation of those rules.

**Gaudí i Cornet, Antonio** (1852–1926) Spanish architect. Gaudí was trained at Barcelona University, and his best-known works are found in that city; they include his Casa Batlló (1906), Casa Milá (1910) and Park Güell (1914), all of which have fantastical and highly complex elements. His monumental Church of La Sagrada Familia, begun in 1883 and continued throughout his career, remains incom-

plete. After World War II Gaudí's work received renewed attention, and in 1957 the MUSEUM OF MODERN ART mounted an exhibit of his designs.

**Gaudier-Brzeska, Henri** (1891–1915) French sculptor and artist. Gaudier-Brzeska, who added to his own the name of his beloved wife Sophie Brzeska, was a brilliant sculptor whose career was cut tragically short by his death in WORLD WAR I. His work was ardently championed by the American poet Ezra POUND, of whom Gaudier-Brzeska made a number of drawings and a famous bust. Gaudier-Brzeska emphasized that the beauty of a sculptural work is intimately related to the materials from which it is made. His sculptures, which did not adhere to the fixed credos of any artistic school, combined a number of contrasting geometric forms to produce a jarringly energetic whole that Pound termed a "form-fugue."

**Gaulle, Charles de** (1890–1970) French general and statesman, first president of the Fifth Republic (1959–69). The man who was to become the symbol for French RESISTANCE to the Nazis during WORLD WAR II was born in Lille and attended the St. Cyr military academy. In WORLD WAR I he served with distinction under PÉTAIN, was wounded at VERDUN and taken prisoner by the Germans in 1916. After the war, de Gaulle served in the French military mission to Poland, in the forces occupying Germany and the Middle East. He also taught at the École Supérieure de Guerre, becoming expert in the use of tanks and aircraft. As the commander of an armored division, he engaged in one of the few successful sorties against invading German forces in May 1940. He was appointed a member of Paul REYNAUD's government before he was forced to flee to London. There in June 1940 he broadcast to his countrymen, calling for resistance, and there he organized the FREE FRENCH forces. Winning the support of CHURCHILL, ROOSEVELT, STALIN, in 1943 he established a provisional government in Algeria, and a year later he returned to FRANCE. De Gaulle was formally elected president of the Fourth Republic in November 1945 but resigned soon after because of the failure of the constituent assembly to give him

sufficient executive power. In 1947 he became head of a new anticommunist party, the Rassemblement du Peuple Français.

In 1958, the crisis in ALGERIA caused the French government to call the general from retirement and to make him premier. He assumed temporary emergency control, oversaw the drafting of a new constitution that provided for broad presidential power, and in December 1958 was elected president of the Fifth Republic. In this position, he first dealt with the Algerian question, calling for self-determination against the strong opposition of ex-Gaullists who opposed Algerian independence. After an independent Algeria was established in 1962, de Gaulle set out to reestablish France as a great world power. At home, he stabilized the currency by devaluing the franc, established a more favorable balance of trade, asserted his right to the development of a specifically French nuclear deterrent and worked toward full employment and economic well-being. In foreign policy, he called for a dynamic and independent France. Reelected in 1965, he came into conflict with America regarding France's stature in NATO. In 1966 he withdrew French forces from the organization and a year later closed NATO installations in France. A vigorous member of the Common Market, he vetoed Britain's entry into the alliance in 1967. He also strengthened France's ties with West Germany, the USSR, China and the Third World. In the wake of the 1968 student protest demonstrations in France, he resigned as president. An austere, aloof and even Olympian figure, de Gaulle was undoubtedly France's greatest 20th-century leader.

**Gaullists** Political followers of General Charles de GAULLE, although there is no precise definition of **Gaullism.** A mass movement under the Fourth French Republic centered on the **Rassemblement du Peuple Français** (RPF), an authoritarian anticommunist party, this movement enjoyed its greatest success in the late 1940s and early 1950s. The **Union de la Nouvelle République** (UNR) was formed from various Gaullist groups after the establishment of the Fifth French Republic in 1958. Gaullism survived the general's retirement in 1970, and provided a basis for support for his presidential successor, Georges POMPIDOU, and later Jacques CHIRAC.

**Gavaskar, Sunil Manohar** *(1949– )* Indian cricketer. Gavaskar holds the all-time Test cricket records for most runs scored and most games played. He scored 10,122 runs for India from 214 innings in 125 Test matches from 1971 to 1987. Gavaskar also holds the record for most centuries (100 runs scored) in Test cricket, with 34. From 1976 to 1985, Gavaskar captained India 47 times, and in 1983 he led the team to its first World Cup victory.

**Gavin, James Maurice** *(1907– 1990)* U.S. army officer. Gavin was one of the U.S.'s top combat leaders in WORLD WAR II. During the war he served in and eventually led the famous 82nd Airborne Division. Following the war, he rose to become the army's chief of research and development. He was, however, a critic of several key army policies, including its failure to pursue long-range missile technology and an overreliance on advanced hardware at the expense of conventional forces. He retired in 1958 with the rank of Lt. General and became a consultant with the Cambridge, Mass.-based industrial research firm of Arthur D. Little, Inc. In the early 1960s, he served a brief term as ambassador to FRANCE under President John F. KENNEDY. He was also the author of several books, including *War and Peace in the Space Age* (1958) and *Crisis Now* (1968).

**Gaye, Marvin** *(1939–1984)* African-American soul singer, popular from the early 1960s until his death. His string of hit records included "Can I Get a Witness" (1963), "Heard It Through the Grapevine" (1968), "What's Going On?" and "Sexual Healing" (1983 Grammy Award). Many of his songs featured social themes. Gaye was shot and killed by his father in a domestic dispute.

**Gayoom, Maumoon Abdul** *(1937– )* President of MALDIVES (1978– ). Gayoom is considered an Islamic scholar and was educated at Cairo's al-Azhar University before serving as a research assistant in Islamic history at the American University of Cairo (1967–69). After his return to Maldives he served as minister of transportation and permanent representative of Maldives to the United Nations in the administration of Amin Ibrahim Nasir. As president, Gayoom has worked to diversify and modernize the economy, and has given high priority to improving the standard of living outside the capital. His extensive travels and active participation in numerous international forums have increased the nation's profile on the international scene. Gayoom was reelected to a sixth five-year term in 2003, with more than 90% of the vote.

**gay rights movement** Political and social movement that seeks to win legal equality and economic opportunities for homosexuals. Since the 1960s the gay rights movement has campaigned to win societal acceptance of homosexuality as an "alternative lifestyle." The movement uses many of the same techniques, and was largely inspired by, the CIVIL RIGHTS MOVEMENT and WOMEN'S MOVEMENTS of the 1960s and '70s. The gay rights movement is sometimes dated from a police raid on a gay bar, the Stonewall Inn, in New York City in 1969, which led to increased political activism by gays. The advent of AIDS, which struck many gays in the 1980s, radicalized much of the gay community. Gay organizations such as Act-Up have held marches and demonstrations to demand government action. An annual "Gay Pride" march is held in San Francisco, and openly declared homosexuals and lesbians have been elected to political office. In 1989, Denmark became the first nation to allow civil marriage between homosexuals. In the U.S., the issue of gay rights became prominent as a result of the state of Vermont's decision in 2000 to recognize state-administered civil unions between homosexual couples, the Supreme Court's 2003 decision to declare unconstitutional all anti-sodomy laws, the 2003 ruling by the Massachusetts Supreme Court that denying gay couples a marriage license is unconstitutional and the 2004 decision by the mayor of San Francisco to issue marriage licenses to gay couples despite California law prohibiting such actions.

**Gaza Strip** A strip of land (146 sq. miles) extending northeast from EGYPT and bordered by ISRAEL and the Mediterranean Sea. Temporarily occupied by Israel in the 1956 SUEZ CRISIS, and occupied again during the 1967 SIX-DAY WAR, it remained an Israeli possession until 2005, when Israel removed Jewish settlers from the territory and turned over control to the PALESTINIAN AUTHORITY.

**Gdańsk** (German: Danzig) Polish seaport on the Baltic Sea, just west of the mouth of the Vistula River; capital of Gdańsk province. After WORLD WAR I the TREATY OF VERSAILLES restored its ancient status as a free city with its own legislature. But to provide a seaport for the newly re-created nation of POLAND, Danzig was made part of a Polish customs union under the jurisdiction of a high commissioner designated by the LEAGUE OF NATIONS—part of a strip of land barely 50 miles wide (the so-called **Danzig corridor**), with GERMANY proper to the west and the German province of East Prussia to the east. With the erosion of league authority after 1935, Danzig came under the influence, if not the control, of Nazi Germany. HITLER's call for the return of Danzig to Germany was a principal excuse for the German attack on Poland and a cause of the outbreak of WORLD WAR II. Danzig was annexed to Germany as the Hanseatic City of Danzig on September 1, 1939 (a small Polish garrison resisted until September 7). Retaken by the Soviets early in 1945, Danzig was soon returned by the Allies to Poland and its original name restored. Gdańsk, largely destroyed during the war, has since been rebuilt; with nearby Gdynia, barely 20 miles away, it is one of the world's principal shipbuilding centers. In late 1970 rioting by workers here led to the fall of Polish premier GOMUŁKA. By 1980 serious food shortages and labor discontent brought a strike at Gdańsk's Lenin shipyards that led to the formation of the SOLIDARITY Labor Union, headed by Lech WALESA, movements to reform the Polish economy and political system—and, after a Gdańsk Solidarity Congress (December 1981) called for a national vote of no-confidence in the government, the breakup of the union and the imposition of martial law.

**Gehrig, Lou (Ludwig Heinrich Gehrig; The Iron Horse)** *(1903–1941)*

*Baseball legend Lou Gehrig* (PHOTOFEST)

American baseball player. There is little dispute that Lou Gehrig was the greatest first baseman in history. He began his Yankee career at the age of 20, but his career began in earnest three seasons later when he filled in for an ailing Wally Pipp. Gehrig soon had a lock on the position that lasted 16 years and 2,130 consecutive games, a record that was broken by Cal Pepkin Jr. of the Baltimore Oreoles in 1995. He posted a lifetime batting average of .340 with 493 home runs and 1,990 runs batted in. He led the league in home runs and runs batted in several seasons and was a six-time All Star. He retired in 1939 after being diagnosed with amyotrophic lateral sclerosis, which came to be known as **Lou Gehrig's Disease.** His farewell address to fans at Yankee Stadium was one of the most moving and memorable events in baseball. Because of Gehrig's ill health, the entry requirements to the Hall of Fame were waived, and he was admitted that year. His life was recounted in the 1942 motion picture, *Pride of the Yankees,* starring Gary COOPER.

**Gehry, Frank O.** (*1929–  *) American architect, known for his postmodernist buildings and use of common building material in structures and sculptures. Born Ephraim Goldberg in Toronto, Gehry and his family moved to Los Angeles where he studied architecture at the University of Southern California, and worked at Victor Gruen Associates, an architectural firm. At age 27 Gehry enrolled in the Harvard School of Design to study urban planning. After graduating from Harvard he returned to Victor Gruen, where he worked until 1960. Leaving Los Angeles again, Gehry traveled to Paris, where he worked for a year under the French architect André Remondet. In 1962 he returned to Los Angeles to open his own firm.

During the following decade Gehry's work began to resemble less and less his original inspiration, the Swiss-French architect LE CORBUSIER, and more and more his own preference for the adoption of nontraditional building designs crafted out of common construction materials (such as corrugated metal). Gehry exhibited these pillars of his design both in his work for others, such as the Ron Davis house he remodeled in California between 1970 and 1972, and the remodeling of his own house and corrugated metal and angular roofs.

In addition to his work on private houses, Gehry sketched and supervised work on a variety of public buildings. The Loyola Law School's new campus (1981–84), the California Space Museum (1982–84), the University of Toledo (Ohio) Art Museum (1990–92), the Vitra Design Museum in Weil and Rhein, Germany (1997) and the Guggenheim Museum in Bilbao, Spain (1997), are some of the examples of his public *oeuvres.* All of the above designs reveal the same preference for angular, nontraditional geometric layouts that characterized his housing commissions. In recognition of his unique designs and design aesthetic, Gehry was awarded the Pritzker Architecture Prize for excellence in architecture.

**Geiger, Hans Wilhelm** (*1882–1945*) German physicist; studied physics at the universities of Munich and Erlangen, obtaining his doctorate (1906) for work on electrical discharges in gases. Geiger then took up a position at the University of Manchester, where he worked with Ernest RUTHERFORD from 1907 to 1912. In that year he returned to Germany, and from then until his death held a series of important university positions, including director of the Physikalisch Technische Reichsanstalt in Berlin (1912) and professor of physics at Kiel University (1925). A pioneer in nuclear physics, Geiger developed a variety of instruments and techniques for detecting and counting individual charged particles. In 1908 Rutherford and Geiger, investigating the charge and nature of alpha particles, devised an instrument to detect and count these particles. The instrument consisted of a tube containing gas with a wire at high voltage along the axis. A particle passing through the gas caused ionization and initiated a brief discharge in the gas, resulting in a pulse of current that could be detected on a meter. This prototype was subsequently improved and made more sensitive; in 1928 Geiger produced, with W. Muller, a design for what is now known as the *Geiger-Muller counter.*

**Gell-Mann, Murray** (*1929–  *) American theoretical physicist; graduated from Yale University in 1948 and gained his Ph.D. from the Massachusetts Institute of Technology in 1951. Gell-Mann spent a year at the Institute of Advanced Study in Princeton before joining the Institute for Nuclear Studies at the University of Chicago, where he worked with Enrico FERMI. In 1955 he went to the California Institute of Technology, where he became a full professor in theoretical physics in 1956. Gell-Mann's chosen subject was the theoretical study of elementary particles. His first major contribution in 1953 (at the age of only 24) was to introduce the idea of "strangeness." The concept came from the fact that certain mesons were "strange particles" in the sense that they had unexpectedly long lifetimes. Strangeness, as defined by Gell-Mann, is a quantum property conserved in any "strong" interaction of elementary particles. The search for order among the known elementary particles led Gell-Mann and Israeli physicist Yuval Ne'eman to advance, independently, a mathematical representation for the classification of hadrons (particles that undergo strong interactions). Gell-Mann felt that it should be possible to explain many of the properties of the known elementary particles by postulating even more basic particles (later to be called QUARKS, the name taken from *Finnegan's Wake* by James JOYCE). Quarks, together with their antiparticles, would normally be in combination as constituents of the more familiar nucleons and mesons. This idea challenged established thinking and has greatly influenced the direction of high-energy theory and experiment. Gell-Mann received the 1969 NOBEL PRIZE in physics, being cited for his "contributions and discoveries concerning the elementary particles and their interactions."

**Gemini program** American space program that launched 10 piloted flights in 1965–66, after two unmanned tests in 1964 and 1965. Called Gemini because of the two-man crew, this program followed the MERCURY PROGRAM and preceded the APOLLO PROJECT. It was designed to test the endurance of men in space (in preparation for lunar flights), to test the maneuvering ability of orbital spacecraft and to develop docking and rendezvous techniques needed for the later Moon missions. The Gemini spacecraft consisted of two modules, a reentry or command module and a service module. The bell-shaped command module measured 11 ft. high, had a base diameter of 7.7 ft. and weighed just under 6,000 lbs. It was launched by a two-stage Titan 2 rocket with four retro-rockets, each with a thrust of 11,100 newtons (2,500 lbs.).

Highlights of the Gemini program include *Gemini 3,* the first piloted mission, flown by Virgil I. (Gus) GRISSOM and John W. YOUNG and launched on March 23, 1965. During almost five hours of flight, it circled the Earth for three orbits. *Gemini 4,* launched on June 3, 1965, was flown by Edward H. WHITE II and James McDIVITT. During the two-day flight, White made the first U.S. space walk. *Gemini 6,* launched on December 15, 1965, with Walter M. SCHIRRA and Thomas P. STAFFORD aboard, made the first U.S. space rendezvous, with *Gemini 7,* launched on December 4 with Frank BORMAN and James A. LOVELL aboard. The two capsules rendezvoused on December 15, coming within one foot of each other. *Gemini 8,* with Neil ARMSTRONG and David Scott, launched on March 16, 1966, was the first to dock with another craft in space (an Agena target rocket). Later Gemini missions lengthened the time spent in space and the duration of space walks and vehicle dockings, and accomplished increasingly automated reentries.

**Genda, Minoru** *(1904–1989)* Japanese military and political leader. Genda was the general who planned JAPAN'S December 7, 1941, attack on U.S. naval forces at PEARL HARBOR, Hawaii, that brought the U.S. into WORLD WAR II. He was widely credited with originating attacks by low-flying torpedo bombers, which caused extensive damage to the U.S. fleet during the battle. Following the end of the war, he was made a general in the Japanese air force and served as chief of staff (1959–62), after which he was elected to the upper house of Japan's parliament. In 1962, U.S. president John F. KENNEDY presented him with the Legion of Merit, the nation's highest foreign honor, for his role in rebuilding the Japanese air force and cooperating with the U.S. Genda made a controversial lecture tour of the U.S. in 1969; during the tour, he said that if Japan had possessed the ATOMIC BOMB during WORLD WAR II, it might have used it against the U.S. The remark sparked an uproar in Japan that forced him to resign as chief of the ruling Liberal Party's defense policy board, although he remained a member of parliament until 1986.

**General Agreement on Tariffs and Trade** See GATT.

**General Motors** American and international corporation (the largest manufacturing company in operation), primarily a builder of automobiles and related transport products. General Motors (GM) was founded in 1908 and gradually acquired various smaller automobile makers, including Chevrolet, Pontiac, Oldsmobile, Buick, and Cadillac. The diverse approaches to design by these firms were gradually brought together in an overall design program that was headed after 1925 by Harley EARL. Earl organized an intricate plan for sharing body components among the different brand names, with varied trim and detail giving each brand individuality. Changes in styling on an annual basis encouraged "planned obsolescence," leading consumers to buy new cars in greater numbers and at shorter intervals than might be required by actual wear. From 1959 to 1978, Bill Mitchell took over Earl's role and directed GM styling. Although overwhelmingly successful commercially, the GM approach to design has been criticized for what is seen by some as its neglect of functional and economic values in favor of size and glitter as sales features. The competition of European and Japanese imports has forced some adjustment in GM styling practice. Some GM products are now joint Japanese-American efforts. General Motors is also a major manufacturer of household appliances under the Frigidaire brand name, of trucks and buses, and of diesel railroad locomotives through its electromotive division. In 2000 General Motors began purchasing shares in the Italian automobile company Fiat and eventually signed an agreement to buy the

*NASA's* GEMINI VII *spacecraft. 1965* (LIBRARY OF CONGRESS, PRINTS AND PHOTOGRAPHS DIVISION)

Italian company. But in early 2005 GM backed out of the deal. In November 2005 General Motors announced a 25% reduction in its workforce over a three-year period and closure of nine plants, in a restructuring effort aimed at avoiding bankruptcy.

## General Strike of 1926

British labor strike of May 1926. The general strike was a culmination of several years of labor unrest, during which the miners' unions had garnered support from other industrial unions. It was triggered by the Samuel Report, a study of the mining industry by a royal commission released in March of 1926 which rejected nationalization and recommended a cut in wages. At the same time, mine owners supported longer hours for the workers. On May first, at a special meeting of the TRADES UNION CONGRESS (TUC), it was agreed to call out transport workers, printers, builders, heavy industrial workers and later engineers in support of the miners. Prime Minister BALDWIN's government responded by organizing volunteers to fill essential posts, recruiting special constables and using troops to maintain food supplies. Nine days later the TUC called off the strike. The miners unions stayed out until the following August. In July of 1927, the Trade Disputes Act was passed, which made general strikes illegal. It was repealed in 1946.

## general theory of relativity

See Albert EINSTEIN.

## Generation of 1927

Group of Spanish poets who were active between 1923 and the beginning of the SPANISH CIVIL WAR in 1936. United mainly by friendship, a tendency toward SURREALISM, an attitude of anguish over the contemporary world and an emphasis on aesthetic purity, they were a diverse group of individuals with distinct poetic styles. Among the members of the Generation of 1927 were Federico GARCÍA LORCA, Rafael ALBERTI, Vicente ALEIXANDRE, Luis CERNUDA and Jorge GUILLÉN. Many of their works were collected in the 1932 anthology *Poesía española contemporánea*.

## Genet, Jean

*(1910–1986)* French novelist and playwright; one of the major French authors of this century.

Genet is also an unusual figure in the history of French literature due to his background as a convicted felon and a homosexual. He wrote his first novel, *Our Lady of the Flowers* (1944), while serving a jail sentence. This novel, which explores the complex psychological nature of homosexual relations within prison confines, won the attention of French intellectuals such as Jean-Paul SARTRE, who clamored successfully for Genet's parole. Other novels by Genet include *Miracle of the Rose* (1946) and *Thief's Journal* (1949). Genet also became a major figure in the THEATER OF THE ABSURD movement by virtue of his plays *The Maids* (1948), *The Balcony* (1956) and *The Blacks* (1958). He was also the subject of a full-length literary study by Sartre, *Saint Genet* (1952), which argued that Genet was the archetypal existential hero due to his having lived by his own value system.

## genetically modified foods

Artificially produced strains of produce (vegetables and fruits) and grains (wheat, etc.) designed to result in greater agricultural yields than those of naturally occurring strains. Examples of companies producing such genetically modified foods are Cargill Incorporated, which focuses on fruits and vegetables, and Holden's Foundation Seeds, which specializes in the production of altered corn and wheat seeds. Genetically modified foods have both proponents and detractors. Advocates of such products note that the increased bounties they make possible can lead to reduced famines in the developing world if its farmers are given access to the modified seeds. Critics are concerned that, over time, the germination of such modified grains, fruits and vegetables will adversely affect the cultivation of naturally bred produce, and argue that it is too soon to tell if the consumption of such products is harmless to humans.

## genetic engineering

Popular term for various techniques that manipulate DNA, the nucleic acid (contained in the nucleus of cells) that transmits the inheritance of characteristics. Recombinant DNA is produced through gene-splicing, a technique in which molecules of DNA are removed from one organism and introduced into the genetic material of another organism.

When inside a host cell, this recombinant DNA molecule replicates itself when the host divides, producing cloned cells with identical DNA structure. Gene-splicing is usually practiced on *Escherichia coli,* a common intestinal bacterium. A foreign gene is spliced into the plasmid, a circular piece of DNA that is the bacterial equivalent of a chromosome, and the *E. coli* goes on to produce cloned cells with the new genetic information. This technique has been used not only to study gene structure, but also to produce larger quantities of substances that are normally available only in extremely limited amounts. Substances produced by gene-splicing techniques include INSULIN, human growth hormone and INTERFERON. Other techniques of genetic engineering include nuclear transplants and cell fusion. It is hoped that one or more of the various genetic engineering techniques may ultimately be applied to the cure of human genetic diseases, and genetic engineering is one of the fastest-growing research fields in contemporary medicine.

## Geneva Conventions

A series of international agreements reached to provide for the humane treatment of individuals in wartime. Those protected include the wounded, the sick, prisoners of war and civilians. The first of these treaties was signed by representatives of 16 countries convened in Geneva, Switzerland, in 1864, and was recognized by all European nations, the U.S. and a number of countries in Asia and South America. Other such conventions were added in 1899, 1906, 1929, 1949 and 1977. The earliest agreements dealt mostly with combatants and with the international recognition of the role of the RED CROSS. Prompted by the phenomenon of total world war, later conventions extended the general laws of war and attempted to further protect civilians. They also forbade many kinds of racial and religious discrimination as well as such practices as the taking of hostages and the use of torture.

## Gennadios, bishop of Paphos

*(1910–1986)* Cypriot Orthodox church leader. His support for the Greek Cypriot guerrilla movement and opposition to Cypriot president Archbishop MAKARIOS III helped pave the way for the Turkish invasion of CYPRUS in 1974.

Gennadios (also referred to as Yennadios) and two other bishops were defrocked in 1973 after they had proclaimed the defrocking of Makarios.

**Gennep, Arnold van** *(1873–1957)* French ethnographer and folklorist; a pioneer in the development of structured, analytical methods for the collection and preservation of folk material in France. Van Gennep devoted himself to field work and produced a large number of collections in his lifetime while influencing an entire subsequent generation of university-trained folklorists. Works by Van Gennep include *Rites of Passage* (1909), *Folklore of the Dauphine* (1933), *Folklore of Bourgogne* (1936) and the multivolume *Manual of Categories of French Folklore* (1943–58). The methods of van Gennep exercised an influence on STRUCTURALISM.

**Genovese, Vito** *(1897–1969)* American gangster. Genovese began his career in crime early, working in the shadow of "Lucky" LUCIANO as a relatively minor MAFIA functionary in the 1920s. Charged with murder, Genovese fled to Italy in 1937, worked for the U.S. Army in 1944 and returned to New York in 1945. For the next decade he consolidated his position, engineering assassinations and emerging as a full-fledged Mafia don. Extremely important in the organized crime's narcotics operations, Genovese was implicated in a minor drug deal, arrested, tried and in 1959 sentenced to prison for 15 years. He allegedly continued to direct mob activities from his jail cell. He died while still in prison.

**Gentile, Giovanni** *(1875–1944)* Italian philosopher. Gentile is best remembered as the principal intellectual supporter of Italian FASCISM and the government of Benito MUSSOLINI. Gentile began his philosophical career as a neo-Hegelian theorist who emphasized the ideal nature of truth in *The Theory of Mind as Pure Act* (1916). He also worked closely with fellow Italian philosopher Benedetto CROCE and contributed to Croce's journal, *Critica*. In the 1920s, after Mussolini had assumed power, Gentile became politically active as a senator and as a minister of public instruction entrusted with major responsibility for

the development of a revised Italian educational system. Gentile outlined his ideas in this sphere in *The Reform of Education* (1922). He met his death at the hands of anti-fascist partisans.

**geodesic dome** See R. Buckminster FULLER.

**George V** *(1865–1936)* King of Great Britain (1910–36). George V was the second son of EDWARD VII and Queen ALEXANDRA, and became heir to the throne when his elder brother, Albert Victor, died in 1892. In 1893, George V married his brother's fiancee, Mary of Teck, later Queen Mary. Their eldest son, later EDWARD VIII and Duke of Windsor, was born in 1894. Although torn by WORLD WAR I, and unsettled by the deposition of many European monarchs, the reign of George V was marked by an increasing affection between the British people and their sovereign, due in part to such gestures as his broadcasts in later years, but also because of his respect for the constitutional monarchy. George V dealt with restraint with the Parliament Act of 1911, the Irish Crisis of 1913–14, BALDWIN's succession to the prime ministry in 1923 and the formation of the NATIONAL GOVERNMENT in 1931. He was also the only British emperor of INDIA to visit there while sovereign. His Silver Jubilee in 1935 was the occasion of a moving display of popular loyalty to him. He died eight months later at Sandringham.

**George VI (Albert Frederick Arthur George)** *(1895–1952)* King of the UNITED KINGDOM of Great Britain and Northern Ireland (1936–52). The second son of King GEORGE V and Queen Mary, he trained as a naval cadet. During WORLD WAR I he saw action at the Battle of Jutland as a Royal Navy officer. His service was interrupted by illness; however, before the war's end he joined the RAF and became a pilot. In 1920 he assumed the title of Duke of York. He married Lady Elizabeth Bowes-Lyon (later Queen Elizabeth the Queen Mother) of Scotland in 1923. Second-in-line to his brother David, the Prince of Wales (later EDWARD VII), he was seldom in the public eye during the first 41 years of his life. Shy and awkward, he was affected by a stammer which he eventually over-

came. In 1936, when his brother (then king) abdicated the British throne to marry Mrs. Simpson, the Duke of York suddenly became king. Thrust into a role for which he had been thought unprepared, he quickly adapted to his new responsibilities and won the affection of the British people. Upon his coronation (1937) he assumed the name George. In 1939, on the eve of WORLD WAR II, he and his wife made an important state visit to Canada and the U.S. to win support for Britain; he thus became the first reigning monarch to visit the U.S. During the war he, the queen and their two daughters, Elizabeth and Margaret Rose, remained in London and shared the hazards of the Blitz with their subjects. (Buckingham Palace was hit several times by German bombs.) In the course of the war, he periodically visited British forces in North Africa, Italy, Malta, and Normandy. From the late 1940s he suffered from various illnesses, including lung cancer, and was forced to curtail his activities. Upon his death his elder daughter inherited the crown as ELIZABETH II.

**George, Stefan** *(1868–1933)* German poet and literary critic; exercised a considerable influence on the German poets who emerged in the first decades of this century. George championed the classical poets of ancient Greece as a lasting standard for poetic excellence. He also applied the philosophical ideals of his countryman Friedrich Nietzsche in calling for a revived German humanism that would look to the poet as a central figure of societal guidance and inspiration. In his own verse, George dealt frequently with esoteric intellectual themes, as well as with his homosexual love affairs. His major volumes of poems include *Year of the Soul* (1897), *The Seventh Ring* (1907–11), and *The New Reich* (1928). While George was an ardent German nationalist, he was also a fierce opponent of NAZISM. In 1933, he chose exile in Switzerland after the rise of HITLER.

**George-Brown, Alfred, Baron (George Alfred Brown)** *(1914–1985)* British politician. The son of a truck driver, Brown worked as a union organizer before being elected to the House of Commons in 1945. In the 1950s, he was a member of the LABOUR

PARTY's shadow cabinet, rising to deputy leader of the party under Hugh GAITSKELL. After Gaitskell's death in 1963, Brown was narrowly defeated by Harold WILSON in the contest for Labour leadership. Brown then served for two years as secretary for economic affairs before being named foreign secretary in 1966. He resigned in 1968 over a lack of consultation during a gold crisis. In 1970, he lost his seat in Parliament. In 1976, angered by legislation proposing closed shops, Brown resigned from the Labour Party. In 1981, he became a member of the centrist SOCIAL DEMOCRATIC PARTY.

**Georgia, Republic of** Territory of the Russian Empire (1878–1918), independent state (1918–21, 1991–   ), and Soviet Republic (1921–91). Fully annexed by Russia in 1878, Georgia remained a territory of the Russian czar until the Russian Civil War began between the Bolshevik "Reds" and the anti-Bolshevik "Whites." In May 1918 moderate socialist politicians in Georgia called Mensheviks used the opportunity to establish an independent state of Georgia. However, by the end of the civil war, Bolshevik troops had captured Georgia and returned it to Russian rule. In 1921 Georgia was united with ARMENIA and AZERBAIJAN in the Transcaucasian Soviet Federated

| GEORGIA | |
|---|---|
| 1918 | Independence is established after the Russian Revolution. |
| 1921 | The region is invaded by the Red Army; a Soviet republic is established. |
| 1922–36 | Georgia is linked with Armenia and Azerbaijan as the Transcaucasian Federation. |
| 1930s | Industry develops rapidly, but resistance to agricultural collectivization and violent political purges are instituted by the Georgian Soviet dictator Joseph Stalin. |
| 1936 | Georgia becomes a separate republic within the USSR. |
| 1953 | Stalin dies; Nikita Khrushchev becomes first secretary of the Communist Party of the Soviet Union and begins a process of de-Stalinization throughout the Soviet Union. |
| 1985 | Mikhail Gorbachev becomes leader of the Soviet Union and initiates policies of glasnost (openness) and perestroika (restructuring), which inadvertently fuel the nationalistic sentiment of Georgia. |
| 1991 | On April 9 the Georgia Supreme Soviet formally declares Georgia's independence from the Soviet Union; in May Gamsakhurdia is elected Georgia's first president. |
| 1992 | With military and Russian backing, Gamsakhurdia is ousted in January; the presidency is abolished and Shevardnadze is named acting chairman of the State Council, the new national legislature; elections confirm Shevardnadze as chairman of the State Council. |
| 1993 | Georgia joins CIS. |
| 1994 | The United Nations brokers a cease-fire between the government of Georgia and Abkhazi separatists. |
| 1995 | Georgia adopts a new constitution reinstating the office of president, and Shevardnadze is named president |
| 2000 | Shevardnadze is reelected president, receiving nearly 80% of the vote. |
| 2001 | Clashes in Abkhaz with Georgian paramilitaries backed by fighters from the North Caucasus. Public outcry follows a raid by government forces on an anti-Shevardnadze TV station. Shevardnadze responds by dismissing the government. |
| 2004 | Mikhail Saakashvili wins the presidential election. The autonomous region of Ajaria does not recognize his authority and procedes to blow up all the bridges connecting the region to the rest of Georgia. The Ajarians comply with Saakashvili's orders to stand down. |
| 2005 | Fighting continues between Georgian forces and South Ossetian separatists. |

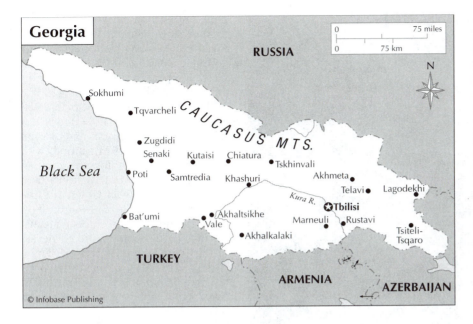

**Georgia**

RUSSIA

Sokhumi
Tqvarcheli

*C A U C A S U S   M T S.*

Zugdidi
Senaki    Kutaisi    Chiatura
Tskhinvali
Akhmeta

*Black Sea*

Poti    Samtredia    Khashuri
Telavi    Lagodekhi

*Kura R.*    ⊗ Tbilisi

Bat'umi    Akhaltsikhe
Vale    Marneuli    Rustavi

Akhalkalaki    Tsiteli-
Tsqaro

TURKEY

ARMENIA    AZERBAIJAN

© Infobase Publishing

0 ——— 75 miles
0 ——— 75 km

N

---

Socialist Republic (TSFSR), one of four political entities that in December 1922 formed the UNION OF SOVIET SOCIALIST REPUBLICS (USSR). In 1936 this political entity was dissolved and Georgia, Armenia and Azerbaijan each became Soviet Socialist Republics. When nationalist movements emerged in Georgia, Soviet leaders such as Vladimir LENIN and Joseph STALIN brutally suppressed them.

Although Stalin's death reduced the repression of Georgians, little changed in the Soviet republic until Soviet leader Mikhail GORBACHEV implemented his political philosophy of GLASNOST, or "openness." Using the increased civil liberties allowed under glasnost, Georgian nationalists pressed for independence from the Soviet Union. In April 1991 the nationalist head of the Georgian Supreme Soviet, Zviod Gamsakhurdia, declared Georgia independent. A month later Gamsakhurdia was elected Georgia's first president. But as the Soviet Union was collapsing in December 1991, opponents of Gamsakhurdia's increasingly dictatorial rule besieged his headquarters and forced him into exile in January 1992. Later that year Eduard SHEVARDNADZE, the former Soviet foreign minister was elected the country's chief of state.

Shevardnadze promptly obtained Russian assistance in combating separatist movements in South Ossetia and Abkhazia, which were demand-ing independence from Georgia. These secessionist threats prompted Shevardnadze to bring Georgia into the COMMONWEALTH OF INDEPENDENT STATES (CIS) in 1993. In February 1994 he arranged for Russian troops to be based near Abkhazia and to train the young Georgian military. By February 1995 diplomacy and military force resulted in an agreement between Abkhazia and Georgia for the creation of a confederation. Later that year Shevardnadze won election as president under a new constitution, and was reelected in 2000. However, his failure to establish a lasting settlement between Georgia and separatist groups in Abkhazia and Ossetia, together with popular dissatisfaction with his autocratic methods, resulted in nationwide protests in late 2003 that forced Shevardnadze to resign. In a new election Mikhail Saakashvili was chosen as his successor in 2004.

The autonomous region of Ajaria does not recognize his authority and proceeds to blow up all the bridges connecting the region to the rest of Georgia. The Ajarians complied with Saakashvili's orders to stand down, and Russia plans to start withdrawing troops from the area. Soon after, the South Ossetia region held elections that were not recognized by the Georgian government. Fighting continues between Georgian forces and South Ossetian separatist forces.

**Georgians** A term generally applied to authors who wrote during the reign of GEORGE V, 1910–36, and specifically referring to the poets included in the five volume anthology *Georgian Poetry* (1912–22). The name was coined by Edward Marsh, editor, who along with Rupert BROOKE, a contributor, conceived the series. Georgian poetry is traditional in form, and often celebrated nature and pastoral England. Critics—among them, the BLOOMSBURY GROUP—assailed its naivete and its irrelevance to the mood of post–World War I Britain, and the term took on a pejorative sense. Characteristic Georgian poets include Lascelles ABERCROMBIE, Walter DE LA MARE, John DRINKWATER, and Gordon Bottomley.

**German colonial wars in Africa** *(1903–1908)* Promoting white settlement to gain self-sufficiency for their African colonies, the Germans often dislodged native tribes by force. In 1903 the Hottentots revolted in German South West Africa (NAMIBIA), and the Herero tribe in 1904. Troops from Germany suppressed the rebels with much difficulty and bloodshed by 1908, killing 80 percent of the Herero and 50 percent of the Hottentots. Africans also revolted in German East Africa (now TANZANIA) and in CAMEROON in West Africa; all were brutally repressed and reduced to virtual slavery.

**German Democratic Republic** See EAST GERMANY.

**German-Soviet Nonaggression Pact** Also known as the Nazi-Soviet Pact and the Hitler-Stalin Pact, an agreement between Germany and the USSR signed in Moscow on August 23, 1939, by Joachim von RIBBENTROP and Vyacheslav MOLOTOV. Its public provisions included pledges of neutrality if either country were to go to war, and a trade agreement. A secret clause defined spheres of interest for both countries in eastern Europe and the Baltics. A surprising agreement for the committed anticommunists of Germany and the equally committed anti-fascists of the Soviet Union, the pact was used by Germany to isolate Poland in preparation for its invasion of the country on September 1, 1939.

*Soviet foreign minister Molotov signs the German-Soviet Nonaggression Pact in Moscow as Joachim von Ribbentrop and Joseph Stalin look on. 1939.* (LIBRARY OF CONGRESS, PRINTS AND PHOTOGRAPHS DIVISION)

many rebuilt its military machine, then began to demand and gain territorial concessions from neighboring countries, notably CZECHOSLOVAKIA. German-speaking AUSTRIA was also annexed in the ANSCHLUSS (1938). Hitler's invasion of POLAND in 1939 started WORLD WAR II. Germany initially won quick victories and overran and occupied much of Europe, with dire consequences for the civilian populations. However, Hitler's fatal invasion of the Soviet Union and the entry of the U.S. into the war brought overwhelming forces to bear against Germany. The nation suffered devastating Allied bombing raids, while Hitler's war policy drained the country both economically and spiritually. Even while suffering military defeat, however, the Nazi regime was carrying out a horrific policy of genocide toward the JEWS of occupied Europe (see FINAL SOLUTION, HOLOCAUST). Germany's unconditional surrender (May 7, 1945) resulted in a four-power (USSR, U.S., UK, France) oc-

The pact was honored by Hitler until June 1941, when German forces attacked the USSR.

**Germany** Germany is located in north-central Europe and since 1990 covers an area of 138,003 square miles. The country entered the 20th century in a dangerous economic and political rivalry with Britain and France that culminated in WORLD WAR I, when the German empire fought against those countries and their allies. After Germany's defeat, Kaiser WILHELM II abdicated and a new government, the WEIMAR REPUBLIC, was formed with Friedrich Ebert (1919–25), then Field Marshal von HINDENBURG (1925–34), as president. The harsh terms of the VERSAILLES peace treaty (1919), coupled with the political weakness of the Weimar government and the effects of the world recession after 1929, led to the emergence of Adolf HITLER and his National Socialist German Workers' Party (Nazis), which embraced extreme nationalism and ANTI-SEMITISM (see also NAZISM). Hitler became leader of the new Third Reich, which replaced the Weimar government in 1933. During the next few years Ger-

| GERMANY | |
|---|---|
| 1911 | Agadir Crisis exacerbates tensions between Germany and Britain. |
| 1914–18 | Germany loses 1.7 million dead and 4.2 million wounded in World War I. |
| 1918 | Allied breakthrough on the Western Front leads to collapse of German forces; (Nov. 9) Kaiser Wilhelm II abdicates, German republic is declared; (Nov. 11) armistice ends World War I. |
| 1919 | (January) Left-wing uprising of "Spartacists" led by Rosa Luxemburg and Karl Liebknecht is put down; (June) Treaty of Versailles imposes harsh terms on Germany, including loss of territory, demilitarization and reparations; (July) Weimar constitution adopted. |
| 1923 | "Beer Hall Putsch" in Munich: Adolf Hitler leads unsuccessful attempt to seize power. |
| 1925 | Dawes Plan eases German reparations payments; Paul von Hindenburg becomes president. |
| 1926 | Germany joins the League of Nations. |
| 1932 | Nazis win 37% of the vote in national elections. |

| | |
|---|---|
| 1933 | (Jan. 30) President Hindenburg appoints Hitler chancellor of Germany; (March) Hitler assumes emergency powers following Reichstag fire, suspends Weimar constitution; Germany withdraws from League of Nations. |
| 1934 | (June) Hitler purges Nazi rivals in "Night of the Long Knives"; (August) death of Hindenburg; Hitler takes title of "Fuehrer." |
| 1935 | Nuremberg Laws deprive German Jews of civil rights. |
| 1936 | German forces occupy Rhineland; Germany forms "Axis" alliance with Italy, signs Anti-Comintern Pact with Italy and Japan. |
| 1938 | Germany demands and gains control of Sudetenland region of Czechoslovakia in Munich Pact (September); (Nov. 9–I0) Nazis launch violent anti-Jewish pogrom on "Kristallnacht." |
| 1939 | (August) German foreign minister von Ribbentrop signs German-Soviet Non-aggression Pact with Soviet foreign minister Molotov; (Sept. I) German blitzkrieg invasion of Poland begins World War II. |
| 1941 | (June) Hitler launches surprise invasion of Soviet Union. |
| 1942 | (January) Wannsee Conference: systematic killing of Jews in concentration camps becomes official policy, unleashing the Holocaust; (October-November) German forces in North Africa decisively defeated by British. |
| 1945 | (May 7) Germany signs unconditional surrender; Germany partitioned into four zones of Allied occupation; (Nov. 20) war crimes trials open in Nuremberg. |
| 1948–49 | Soviets blockade Berlin; Western Allies supply city in Berlin Airlift. |
| 1949 | (May 23) British, French and U.S. occupation zones become Federal Republic of Germany. (Oct. 7) Soviet occupation zone proclaimed German Democratic Republic. |
| 1990 | (Oct. 3) East and West Germany reunited under the banner of the Federal Republic of Germany. |
| 1998 | Social Democratic Party forms governing coalition with Green Party. |
| 2000 | Kohl is forced to resign as his party's honorary chairman because of a campaign finance scandal. |
| 2002 | Germany adopts the euro as its national currency. |
| 2005 | Christian Democrat Angela Merkel becomes the first female chancellor in a coalition with the social Democrats. |

cupation government and in the NUREMBERG WAR CRIMES TRIALS that eradicated the Nazi leadership. The Soviet Union's opposition to Western plans for eventual self-government led to the division of Germany into two states (1948–49): the Federal Republic of Germany, aligned with the West, and the German Democratic Republic, aligned with the Soviet Union. Germany was reunited as one country in October 1990 under the name Federal Republic of Germany. In 1991, the Bundestag narrowly voted to restore Berlin as the nation's capital. Chancellor Kohl warned Germans against a resurgence of rampant nationalism. Kohl and the Christian Democrats remained in control of Germany until 1998 when they lost to Gerhard SCHROEDER and the Social Democrats, who formed a governing coalition with the Green Party and replaced Kohl as chancellor. Germany continued to cultivate close relations with France and became an ardent champion of greater political integration in the EUROPEAN UNION (EU). In 2005 the Social Democrats performed poorly in nationwide elections and Christian Democrat Angela MERKEL formed a coalition government to become the country's first female chancellor. (For a history from 1949 to 1990, see GERMANY, EAST and GERMANY, WEST.

**Germany, East (Deutsche Demokratische Republik—DDR, or German Democratic Republic—GDR)**
East Germany was located in north-central Europe and covered an area of 41,817 square miles, excluding West Berlin. At the end of WORLD WAR II, Soviet armies occupied the eastern part of GERMANY. Determined to prevent the reemergence of a large and possibly hostile German nation, the Soviets turned their treaty-ratified zone of occupation (intended, as were the American, British and French zones, to be only temporary), into the German Democratic Republic (GDR) in 1949, with Walter ULBRICHT as leader (until 1971). France, Britain, the U.S. and the new Federal Republic of Germany (WEST GERMANY) refused to recognize the GDR. Ulbricht embraced COMMUNISM and suppressed antigovernment uprisings in 1953. The GDR became a

founding member of the WARSAW PACT in 1955. Tensions between the GDR and the Western powers, as well as increased escapes by East Germans into West Berlin, led to the construction of the BERLIN WALL (1961). A similar barrier was eventually extended along the entire border between East and West Germany. During Erich HONECKER's leadership (1971–89), the country joined the UNITED NATIONS (1973) and solidified its borders through treaties. However, Honecker's resistance to reform led to mass protests in 1989. Tens of thousands of East Germans fled to the West via Hungary, which had reopened its border with Austria. After Honecker's resignation, interim leader Egon KRENZ opened the Berlin Wall in November 1989, allowing East Germans free passage into the West. The wall was torn down during the next year and East Germans voted for German reunification in March 1990. The GDR ceased to exist as a separate country after the reunification of Germany on October 3, 1990.

**Germany, West (Bundesrepublik Deutschland—BRD, or Federal Republic of Germany—FRG)** Located in north-central Europe, West Germany had an area of 96,001 square miles, with West Berlin as a separate entity within the territory of EAST GERMANY. The Federal Republic of Germany (FRG) was established in

| EAST GERMANY (GERMAN DEMOCRATIC REPUBLIC) | |
|---|---|
| 1949 | (Oct. 7) German Democratic Republic proclaimed in Soviet-occupied zone of Germany. |
| 1951 | Walter Ulbricht becomes head of ruling Socialist Unity (Communist) Party. |
| 1953 | Antigovernment worker riots suppressed with Soviet help. |
| 1955 | (May) GDR becomes founding member of the Warsaw Pact. |
| 1961 | (August) Construction of Berlin Wall. |
| 1971 | Walter Ulbricht resigns; succeeded by Erich Honecker. |
| 1973 | (September) GDR admitted to United Nations. |
| 1989 | Mass protests and exodus to the West force Honecker's resignation; Berlin Wall opened. |
| 1990 | (Oct. 3) Reunification of Germany; GDR absorbed into the Federal Republic of Germany. |

## WEST GERMANY

| 1949 | Federal Republic of Germany created from three Western occupation zones. |
|------|------|
| 1961 | (August) Construction of Berlin Wall. |
| 1963 | (January) FRG signs friendship treaty with France. |
| 1968 | Baader-Meinhof terrorist group formed. |
| 1972 | (September) "Black September" massacre of Israeli athletes at Munich Olympics. |
| 1989 | Mass exodus of East Germans into FRG; Berlin Wall opened; Chancellor Kohl proposes reunification of Germany. |
| 1990 | Reunification of Germany (Oct. 3); Kohl elected chancellor in first nationwide election since 1933 (Dec. 2). |

## WEST GERMANY: CHANCELLORS

| 1949–1963 | Konrad Adenauer (Christian Democrat) |
|-----------|------|
| 1963–1966 | Ludwig Erhard (Christian Democrat) |
| 1966–1969 | Kurt Kiesinger (Christian Democrat) |
| 1969–1974 | Willy Brandt (Social Democrat) |
| 1974–1982 | Helmut Schmidt (Social Democrat) |
| 1982–1990 | Helmut Kohl (Christian Democrat) |

May 1949 and granted partial sovereignty by Western occupation forces. Konrad ADENAUER became the first federal chancellor (1949–63), guiding the country to full sovereignty on May 5, 1955. During the 1950s and 1960s rapid economic recovery from postwar devastation occurred, and West Germany became a member of the EUROPEAN ECONOMIC COMMUNITY and NATO. An influx of East Germans, coupled with Adenauer's refusal to recognize the East German government and its desire to absorb all of BERLIN, led to the erection of the BERLIN WALL (1961) by East Germany. From 1966 to the late 1970s the country experienced social unrest, with protests and terrorism sponsored by the leftist BAADER-MEINHOF GROUP; its offshoot, the Red Army Faction; and the German Socialist Students' Union (SDS). In 1972 Arab BLACK SEPTEMBER guerrillas attacked Israeli quarters at the Munich Olympics, resulting in tragedy (see MUNICH OLYMPICS MASSACRE). The chancellorship of Willy BRANDT (1969–74) and his OSTPOLITIK policy brought treaties with the Soviet Union and East Germany and membership in the UN (1973). Controversy erupted during the chancellorship of Helmut SCHMIDT (1974–82) over the deployment of U.S. nuclear (INF) missiles in the country, leading to huge peace marches in 1982–83. Christian Democrat Helmut KOHL, who became chancellor in 1982, orchestrated the unification of East and West Germany in October 1990. The new nation kept the official name Federal Republic of Germany.

**Gershwin, George** (1898–1937) American composer who combined classical and jazz idioms to create enduring musical works. Gershwin was one of the great composers of popular and concert music in the 20th century. Gershwin published his first song in 1916 and achieved national recognition for his song "Swanee" (1919), as performed by Al JOLSON. He quickly rose above the run-of-the-mill, tin pan alley compositions of the day. Gershwin wrote the songs for five editions of *George White's Scandals* (1920–24), then composed the scores for several Broadway musicals, in collaboration with lyricist Ira GERSHWIN, his brother. Their musical plays included *Oh Kay!* (1926), *Funny Face* (1927) and *Of Thee I Sing* (1931). After the arrival of TALKING PICTURES, the Gershwin brothers also wrote songs for the movies, such as the Fred ASTAIRE films *Shall We Dance* (1937) and *A Damsel in Distress* (1937). Gershwin established his reputation as

*Composer George Gershwin (left) and his brother, lyricist Ira Gershwin (LIBRARY OF CONGRESS, PRINTS AND PHOTOGRAPHS DIVISION)*

a composer of serious music with such works as *RHAPSODY IN BLUE* (1924), the symphonic poem *An American in Paris* (1928) and the folk opera *PORGY AND BESS* (1935), all of which have become musical classics. Among his enduringly popular songs are such standards as "Love Walked In," "But not for Me," "They All Laughed," "Embraceable You" and "The Man I Love."

**Gershwin, Ira** *(1896–1983)* American song lyricist, noted for his distinguished collaboration with his brother George GERSHWIN during the 1920s and 1930s. Ira Gershwin put words to the music composed by his brother, creating such classic songs as *I Got Rhythm, Summertime, The Man I Love, S'Wonderful* and *Embraceable You,* among many others. The brothers' musical *Of Thee I Sing* (1932) was the first musical to win a PULITZER PRIZE for drama, and Ira Gershwin was the first lyricist to receive that honor. Their other musical collaborations included the Broadway show *Lady Be Good* (1924) and the operatic *Porgy and Bess* (1935). Gershwin also worked with his brother on a number of HOLLYWOOD films, and with other notable composers such as Harold ARLEN and Kurt WEILL, writing lyrics for *A Star Is Born, Cover Girl,* and *Lady in the Dark.* He is a member of the Songwriters Hall of Fame.

**Gerstenmaier, Eugen Karl Albrecht** *(1906–1986)* German diplomat. Gerstenmaier was postwar leader of WEST GERMANY's Christian Democrats and the architect of that country's reconciliation with ISRAEL. He was jailed under the Third Reich for his involvement in the 1944 army plot to kill Adolf HITLER. From 1954 to 1969, he was president of the lower house of West Germany's parliament.

**Gesell, Arnold L(ucius)** *(1880–1961)* American psychologist. In the 1930s and 1940s, Gesell was a dominant figure in American psychology by virtue of his systematic studies of the nature and timing of intellectual and emotional development in children. In 1911, Gesell founded the highly influential Yale University Clinic of Child Development, which he served as director until 1948. Two of his major works, coauthored with F. L. Ilg, were *Infant and Child in the Culture of Today* (1943) and *The Child from Five to Ten* (1946). Subsequent generations of psychologists have criticized Gesell's findings due to his exclusive reliance on white, middle-class children as experimental subjects and his rigid insistence on developmental patterns that took little account of individual variations.

**gestalt psychology** Originating in Germany in the early 1920s, gestalt psychology is a "school" that emphasizes "wholes"—that is, the organization, shape and unity of one's perception, behavior and experience. The German term *gestalt* means "pattern" or "form." Published studies on the organization of perception and the "phi phenomenon" by German psychologist Max WERTHEIMER (from 1912) established the gestalt school. Other leading gestaltists are Wolfgang KOHLER, Kurt KOFFKA, and Fritz and Laura PERLS. Gestalt psychology has had a profound impact on theories of learning because of its emphasis on perception as a dynamic system involving the interaction of all elements and human beings as active problem-solvers, not just passive responders to stimuli.

**Gestapo** Secret state police in Nazi GERMANY, officially known as the Geheime Staatspolizei. It was organized in 1933 by Hermann GÖRING as a Prussian political police force. Over the next few years the Gestapo came under the influence of Heinrich HIMMLER, who expanded it and took official control in 1936, the year it was absorbed into Himmler's ss (Schutzstaffel), which had been created as HITLER's personal guard. Three years later the Gestapo was combined with the SS's intelligence branch, the SD (Sicherheitsdienst), supervised by Reinhard Heydrich and, after Heydrich's assassination in 1943, by Ernst Kaltenbrunner. The Gestapo's daily operation was headed by Heinrich Mueller. Together, the SS, the SD and the Gestapo had enormous powers. The Gestapo's basic task was to eliminate all opposition to NAZISM in Germany and, after the start of WORLD WAR II, in occupied countries, a task it handled with ruthless and brutal efficiency. With virtually absolute power to arrest, torture, imprison in CONCENTRATION CAMPS or execute any person, its six sections handled all areas of possible opposition, from the religious to the political. Among its duties was the extermination of the JEWS, a subsection headed by the infamous Adolf EICHMANN. Gestapo membership from 1943 to 1945, the years of its greatest activity, has been estimated as between 30,000 and 50,000.

**Getz, Stan** *(1927–1991)* American jazz musician, considered jazzdom's foremost tenor saxophone lyricist. Influenced by the following melodicism of Lester YOUNG, who had achieved fame with Count BASIE's band in the early 1940s, Getz fashioned an inimitable style marked by a light, vibratoless sound and a sophisticated, indeed, elegant, diatonically based harmonic sensibility. A child prodigy, Getz made his first recording at the age of 16 as a sideman with trombonist Jack TEAGARDEN; important big band stints included Stan KETON (1944–45), Benny GOODMAN (1945–46) and Woody HERMAN (1947–49). Getz's translucent and virtuosic ballad solo on Ralph Burns's "Early Autumn" (with Herman) established the young tenorist as a major figure and led to his dominance of the important jazz polls during the 1950s and 1960s; historically, by sustaining his lyrical approach in the face of the comparatively extroverted BEBOP revolution, Getz became a "leader" of the so-called cool approach that became centered in Los Angeles. In 1961, Getz achieved notable success with "Focus" (1961), a "third stream" amalgam of jazz improvisation and classically oriented scoring. A year later, he scored another hit with his adroit adaptation of the insinuating bossa nova rhythm from Brazil with composer/pianist Antonio Carlos Jobim, guitarist João Gilberto and singer Astrid Gilberto; their version of Jobim's "Girl from Ipanema" even made the pop music charts. Getz continued as one of jazzdom's most distinctive and satisfying soloists working primarily in small-group, acoustic settings. He also gained notoriety because of his widely publicized drug addiction and a landmark divorce case that went to the U.S. Supreme Court in 1990.

**Ghana (Republic of Ghana)** The nation of Ghana is located on the West

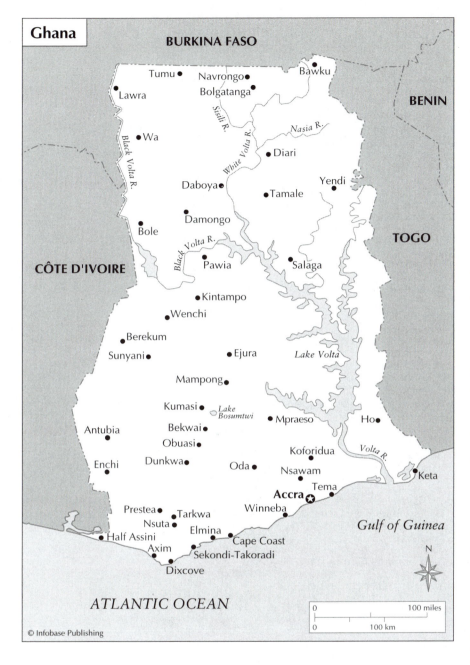

**Ghana**

BURKINA FASO

BENIN

TOGO

CÔTE D'IVOIRE

Tumu • Navrongo • Bawku
Lawra • Bolgatanga •
Wa •
Sisili R.
Nasia R.
White Volta R.
Diari •
Daboya • Yendi •
Tamale •
Damongo •
Bole •
Black Volta R.
Pawia • Salaga •
Kintampo •
Wenchi •
Berekum •
Sunyani • Ejura • Lake Volta
Mampong •
Kumasi • Lake Bosumtwi
Antubia • Bekwai • Mpraeso • Ho •
Obuasi •
Enchi • Dunkwa • Koforidua • Volta R.
Oda • Nsawam • Keta •
Accra ☆ Tema
Prestea • Tarkwa • Winneba •
Nsuta • Elmina • Gulf of Guinea
Half Assini • Cape Coast
Axim • Sekondi-Takoradi N
Dixcove •

ATLANTIC OCEAN

© Infobase Publishing

0          100 miles
0          100 km

African coast and covers an area of 92,133 square miles. Originally governed by Great Britain as the Gold Coast Colony, the country became independent in 1957, merging with British Togoland to form present-day Ghana. Under its first president, Dr. Kwame NKRUMAH, Ghana became a republic in 1960 and a socialist state in 1964. A military coup in 1966 brought successive military and civilian governments, none of which could maintain political or economic stability. Flight-Lieutenant Jerry Rawlings led a successful coup in 1981 and established a Provisional National Defense

Council to bring about a democratization of the country. Though challenged by several coup attempts, a planned attack by American mercenaries and Ghanaian exiles in 1986, and student and labor protests, Rawlings had held on to power and continued to move toward economic and political reform. Despite attempts at reconciling the government and opposition parties through a multiparty constitution in 1992, violence continued to erupt sporadically until the end of Rawlings's eight years as president in 2000. Term limits precluded his running for a third time, and John Kufuor

of the New Patriotic Party was elected president. Kufour was reelected in 2004.

**Ghelderode, Michel de** (1898–1962) Belgian playwright. Ghelderode's plays were among the first works to point toward the dramatic movement that ultimately became known as the THEATER OF THE ABSURD. Ghelderode was especially well known for his adept black humor. He wrote over 50 plays, most of which were in a comic vein. Most notable among them were *Les Viellards* (1919), *Escurial* (1927), *Barabbas* (1928), *Fastes d'enfer* (1929), *Pantagleize* (1929), *Hop! Signor* (1935) and *Mademoiselle Jaire* (1934).

**Gheorghiu-Dej, Gheorghe** (Gheorghe Gheorghiu) (1901–1965) Romanian communist leader, prime minister (1954–61) and president (1961–65) of ROMANIA. Gheorghiu began his career as a railway worker and became active in the outlawed Romanian Communist Party (1929). He was arrested and imprisoned in 1933 at Dej in northern Transylvania. Escaping in 1944, he added the suffix "Dej" to his name. He quickly became involved in national politics. He was made secretary general of the Communist Party, and in March 1945 became economic minister in the new coalition government. After the communists proclaimed Romania a "People's Republic" (Dec. 30, 1947), Gheorghiu-Dej jockeyed for position within the party and ultimately eliminated his chief rivals in a 1952 purge. He was an early communist supporter of Soviet premier KHRUSHCHEV's call for PEACEFUL COEXISTENCE between the East and West. While favoring close relations with the Soviet Union, he managed to steer an independent course for Romania. On his death the mantle of leadership passed to his protege, Nicolae CEAUȘESCU.

**Ghia, Giancinto** (1887–1944) Italian designer and builder of automobile bodies. Ghia learned his skills in a Turin body shop and became known for his custom designs for luxury and sports cars. Since Ghia's death, his firm has carried on under the direction of Mario Boana. Ghia bodies have been developed for exotic Italian cars including the Maserati, but the best-known

## GHANA

|  |  |
|---|---|
| 1901 | Britain absorbs northern remnants of Ashanti empire into its Gold Coast Colony. |
| 1903 | First railroad completed. |
| 1920 | Gold Coast exports one-half of world's cocoa; spread of cocoa farming encourages breakup of tribes' communal land holdings into private plots. |
| 1928 | First deepwater port built at Takoradi. |
| 1947 | Moderate nationalists found Gold Coast Convention. |
| 1949 | Kwame Nkrumah founds radical Convention People's Party; campaigns for independence. |
| 1957 | Independence and merger with former British Togoland creates Ghana; Nkrumah first president. |
| 1960 | Ghana sends troops to Congo to assist Patrice Lumumba. |
| 1961 | Black American scholar W. E. B. DuBois assumes chair at university after renouncing American citizenship. |
| 1964 | Nkrumah declares "socialist single party state." |
| 1965 | Falling price of cocoa cripples economy. |
| 1966 | While on visit to China, Nkrumah ousted by military; completion of huge Akosambo hydroelectric project. |
| 1969 | Kofi Busia elected prime minister. |
| 1972 | Military coup. |
| 1975 | Economy worsens; migration to Nigeria increases; food imported as cocoa production continues. |
| 1977 | Doctors and lawyers go on strike; military agrees to elections. |
| 1981 | Second coup by Flight Lt. Jerry Rawlings results in revolutionary government. |
| 1982 | Rawlings seeks ties with Cuba and Libya. |
| 1983 | Almost one million people forced back to Ghana from Nigeria. |
| 1986 | Exiles plot to overthrow Rawlings with American mercenaries. |
| 1990 | Ghana joins first modern inter-African peacekeeping force to end Liberian civil war. |
| 1992 | New constitution goes into effect. |
| 2000 | End of Rawlings's term as president; John Kufuor is elected president. |
| 2004 | Kufuor is reelected president. |

and most widely visible Ghia design is the special sport body developed for the VOLKSWAGEN Beetle chassis and engine, known as the Karmann Ghia. The firm was absorbed by Ford in 1972.

**Giacometti, Alberto** (1901–1966) Swiss sculptor and painter. Son of the impressionist painter Giovanni Giacometti (1868–1933), he studied at the École des Art-set-Metiers in Geneva (1919). Traveling with his father to Italy in 1920, he spent two years there studying various historical art styles. Settling in Paris in 1922, he studied with the sculptor Antoine Bourdelle. Becoming associated first with CUBISM, then with SURREALISM, he produced his first important sculptures, such as the surrealist-tinged *Palace at 4 A.M.* (1933, Museum of Modern Art, N.Y.C.). In the 1930s, Giacometti began to create the ghostly, elongated human figures with scarred and pitted surfaces, usually cast in bronze, for which he became famous. These strange and haunting sculptures project a kind of existential aloneness and, as such, have been hailed as emblems of 20th-century alienation. Monumental in feeling, whatever their size, these works have had a great influence on modern sculpture. Among them are *Walking Man II* (1960, Rijksmuseum Kroller Muller, Otterloo) and *Head of a Man* (1961,

Hirshhorn Museum and Sculpture Garden, Washington, D.C.).

**Giacometti, Diego** (*1902–1985*) Swiss-born furniture designer and sculptor. For some 40 years, in a collaboration unique in 20th-century art history, Diego Giacometti harnessed his own creative energies to those of his older brother, world-renowned sculptor Alberto GIACOMETTI, who died in 1966. Diego sat constantly for his brother, and his head became almost a signature of Alberto's art. After his brother's death. Diego won fame in his own right as a creator of rough-hewn bronze furniture ornamented with bird and animal heads and foliage.

**Giaever, Ivar** (*1929–   *) Norwegian-American physicist. Giaever studied electrical engineering at the Norwegian Institute of Technology. He did service with the Norwegian army (1952–53) and worked as a patent examiner in the Norwegian Patent Office (1953–54). In 1954 he immigrated to Canada to take up the post of mechanical engineer with the Canadian General Electric Company, transferring to General Electric's Research and Development Center in Schenectady, New York, in 1956. He gained his doctorate in 1964 from Rensselear Polytechnical Institute.

At General Electric, Giaever worked on tunneling effects in SUPERCONDUCTORS, a phenomenon explored by Leo ESAKI. In 1960 he performed experiments with metals separated by a thin insulating film through which electrons tunneled, and found that if one of the metals was in the superconducting state, the current-voltage characteristics of such junctions revealed much about the superconducting state. This laid the foundation for Brian JOSEPHSON's important discovery of the **Josephson effect**. Giaever, Josephson and Esaki shared the 1973 NOBEL PRIZE in physics for their various contributions to knowledge of the phenomenon of tunneling and superconductivity. Their work has had important application in microelectronics and in the precise measurement of electromotive force. Subsequently, Giaever has also published work in the field of visual observation of the antibody-antigen reaction.

**Giamatti, A(ngelo) Bart(lett)** (*1938–1989*) American scholar who served as president of Yale University and as commissioner of Major League Baseball. Originally a noted literature professor, Giamatti became the youngest man in 200 years to be named president of Yale when he was selected to succeed Kingman Brewster in 1978 at the age of 40. He confronted a series of challenges ranging from a $10 million debt (which he eventually overcame) to a rancorous strike by members of a newly formed union of clerical and technical workers. A longtime baseball fan, he readily accepted an offer to serve as president of the National League upon his retirement from Yale in 1986. In September 1988, baseball owners voted to select him as commissioner of baseball, a post he took up on April 1, 1989. His five months as commissioner were dominated by the controversy surrounding Cincinnati Reds manager (and former superstar player) Pete ROSE, who was accused of betting on baseball. Eight days before his death Giamatti suspended Rose from baseball for life. Giamatti was widely admired for his commitment to honesty, fairness and excellence.

**Giancana, Sam "Momo"** (*1908–1975*) American gangster. He began his criminal career early, first attracting notice as a gun runner for Al CAPONE in the mid-1920s. An active but not particularly slippery mobster, Giancana was arrested over 70 times and served a number of terms in jail. He rose to become an infamous MAFIA boss in Chicago, and was alleged to be involved in CIA plots to assassinate Fidel CASTRO during the 1960s.

**Giannini, A(madeo) P(eter)** (*1870–1949*) American banker who revolutionized the banking industry and instituted practices that became standard in the 20th century. Of Italian heritage, Giannini was a resident of San Francisco, California. In 1904 he founded a new bank, designed to serve ordinary citizens—Italian immigrants as well as others—in San Francisco. Loans from the Bank of Italy helped citizens rebuild after the 1906 SAN FRANCISCO EARTHQUAKE. Giannini was the first banker to open branch offices of his bank, and the first to advertise his services. By offering farm mortgages at reasonable interest rates, Giannini helped spur California agriculture; his loans to movie studios also helped the film industry. In 1930, the Bank of Italy was renamed the Bank of American National Trust and Savings Association. Giannini handed control of the bank to his son Lawrence Mario Giannini in 1936. Shortly after World War II, the Bank of America became the world's largest bank, with 538 branches and over $8 billion in assets by 1954. As Bank America Corp., it was still ranked number one in 1979, with $92 billion in assets, but if fell on hard times as THIRD WORLD nations defaulted on loans.

**Giap, Vo Nguyen** (*1912–   *) North Vietnamese general and minister of defense. Giap was born in 1912 in the French protectorate of Annam, which later became part of North Vietnam. Active in the communist underground, he was recruited into the VIET MINH movement in the early 1940s. During the FRENCH INDOCHINA WAR OF 1946–54, Giap was the Viet Minh's leading military commander, and he directed the stunning victory over the French at DIEN BIEN PHU. With independence, he became North Vietnam's minister of defense. During the war with South Vietnam, Giap advocated direct clashes with American forces, a strategy that cost North Vietnam more than half a million soldiers from 1964 to 1969 (see VIETNAM WAR). In 1972, Giap convinced the government that, with the heavy withdrawals of U.S. forces, the time had finally come to launch a massive invasion of the South, which again proved disastrous. Thereafter, Giap was replaced as commander by Van Tien Dung, who planned and executed the final offensive that brought North Vietnam ultimate victory in 1975. In 1980, Van Tien Dung also replaced Giap as minister of defense. In 2003 Giap greeted Cuban president Fidel Castro on his visit to Vietnam.

**Gibbs, Sir Humphrey Vicary** (*1902–1990*) British diplomat. The last British governor of Rhodesia (now ZIMBABWE), he was appointed to the post by Queen ELIZABETH II in 1959 and served until 1969. He spent the last four years of his tenure as a recluse in the governor's residence, following a unilateral declaration of independence by the white minority government of Prime Minister Ian D. SMITH in 1965.

He was unable to leave the residence until 1969, when Smith declared Rhodesia a republic. He then retired to his 6,500-acre farm there.

## Gibbs, William Francis (1886–1967)

American naval architect, the primary designer in the firm of Gibbs and Cox. Gibbs was responsible for a large number of naval and merchant ships including the OCEAN LINERS *America* and, his last great achievement, the *United States*. Gibbs was known for his obsessive concern with excellence and with matters of safety in passenger ships. His concern for fire safety led to many innovations in ship interiors aimed at the elimination of inflammable wood and textiles. The *United States* was the largest and most successful American passenger ship ever built. It established speed records for trans-Atlantic crossings that have never been exceeded. It was withdrawn from service and eventually scrapped when ship transportation declined as a result of the success of postwar airplanes, particularly jets, which made even the fastest ships seem unreasonably slow.

## Gibraltar

The British colony of Gibraltar, which covers only 2 1/3 square miles, is a peninsula connected to SPAIN and jutting southward between Algeciras Bay on the west and the Mediterranean Sea on the east. Because it guards the narrow strait (Strait of Gibraltar) that links the Mediterranean and the Atlantic Ocean, Gibraltar has had tremendous strategic importance throughout history. Its harbor became a key naval base for the Allies during World Wars I and II. Friction over Spanish claims to the colony intensified during the 1960s, culminating in Spain's closing of the international land frontier between Spain and Gibraltar in 1969. Improved relations between Britain and Spain resulted in the 1985 reopening of the border and the scheduling of talks concerning the issue of sovereignty over Gibraltar. The talks, which continued sporadically ever since, did not result in a resolution of the long-standing dispute. In 2002 Gibraltar's residents voiced their displeasure at British-Spanish bilateral negotiations for the cession of the colony to Spain by rejecting the territory's joint rule from London and Madrid.

## Gibraltar dispute

The British territory in southern SPAIN commanding the entrance to the Mediterranean, captured by Britain in 1704 and formerly a strategically important naval base, was claimed by Spain in 1939. The UN recognized the claim in 1963, with Britain asserting the wish of the population expressed overwhelmingly in a referendum was to remain British. The Spanish government closed the frontier in 1969, but, following discussions (1977–80), ended the blockade. Gibraltar continued to represent a minor obstacle to greater British cooperation with Spain, a fellow member of the EUROPEAN UNION (EU). The Gibraltar constitution of 1969 required that any transfer of the territory's control reflect the inhabitants' wishes. In 2002 Gibraltar's residents, who opinion polls showed preferred by a large majority to remain under British authority, voiced their displeasure at the ongoing negotiations between London and Madrid.

## Gibran, Kahlil (Jubran Kahlil Jubran) (1883–1931)

Lebanese poet, novelist, essayist, and painter. Gibran won an enduring worldwide fame for *The Prophet* (1923), a volume of inspirational poetry and prose in a highly spiritual vein. *The Prophet* has remained steadily in print over the decades and has been translated into over 20 languages. Gibran studied art with Auguste Rodin in Paris before immigrating to the U.S. in 1912. He wrote in both Arabic and English. Gibran's works were especially influential in the American popular culture of the 1960s. Other books include *The Earth Gods* (1931), *The Garden of the Prophet* (1933), *The Death of the Prophet* (1933), *Tears and Laughter* (1947) and *Nymphs of the Valley* (1948).

## Gibson, Bob (1935– )

American baseball player. One of the most dominant pitchers of the modern era, Gibson was named the National League's Most Valuable Player in 1968, a year in which he turned in 13 shutouts and 15 consecutive wins for the St. Louis Cardinals. His postseason play was consistently stellar, and he won the deciding game in two World Series. He is second only to Whitey Ford in World Series wins and strikeouts. An excellent all-around athlete and fierce competitor, he won nine Gold Gloves for his fielding, and was also a rarity in that he was a good-hitting pitcher, with 24 home runs to his credit. He was named to the Hall of Fame in 1981.

## Gide, André (1869–1951)

French novelist and essayist. Gide, who won the NOBEL PRIZE in literature in 1947, remains one of the most widely read French authors of the 20th century. He was raised as a Catholic, and his work is filled with the tension that stemmed from his own rejection of traditional religious belief and his simultaneous discomfort with the absence of absolute values that was the hallmark of secular society. In his first major novel, *The Immoralist* (1902), Gide described, in a North African setting, the decadent embrace of sensuality by a protagonist who had left behind the psychological anchors of religion and marriage. *Strait Is the Gate* (1909) further explores the conflict between Catholic belief and sensual temptation. In *Corydon* (1924), Gide defended his own homosexuality with reference to Greek societal ideals. *The Counterfeiters* (1926), his most famous novel, explores the nature of artistic creation and societal ethics. In *Return from the USSR* (1936), Gide rejected the communist beliefs that had tempted him during the depression era. *If It Die* (1936) is his autobiography.

## Gideon v. Wainwright (right to counsel on arrest) (1963)

The 1963 landmark criminal case that established a constitutional right to counsel for all persons tried for a crime in the U.S., in both state and federal courts. Gideon was accused and convicted of breaking into and stealing money from a poolhall in Florida. He could not afford a private attorney and had none at trial; at the time, only persons accused of capital crimes received free court-appointed counsel. On appeal the U.S. Supreme Court held that in any criminal case, in either state or federal court, indigent parties must be provided with free counsel. Gideon's appeal was funded by the ACLU and was handled by Abe FORTAS, who was himself appointed to the Supreme Court a few years later. Because of the favorable appeal Gideon was retired and this time—with the help of an attorney—he was acquitted of all charges.

**Giedion, Sigfried** (1894–1968) Swiss-American architectural and design historian who played a significant role in the development and recognition of modern concepts in all aspects of design. Giedion studied art history in Zurich and Berlin and earned his doctorate under Heinrich Wolfflin at Munich. His 1938 lectures at Harvard formed the basis for his 1941 book, *Space, Time and Architecture,* one of the first works to place modern architecture in an historical context. It also created a new understanding and appreciation of the role of Baroque design in relation to MODERNISM. His *Mechanization Takes Command* of 1948 takes a similarly serious historical view of the development of utilitarian objects and is recognized as a basic work of design history. A number of other Giedion books deal with various aspects of art and architectural history. Giedion was among the founding members of the CIAM (International Congress of Modern Architecture).

**Gielgud, (Sir) (Arthur) John** (1904–2001) English stage and film actor and stage director. Gielgud was one of the most acclaimed stage actors of the 20th century. He is especially well-known for his Shakespearean portrayals, in which he utilized his elegant profile and mellifluous voice to great effect. A great nephew of the famous English actress Ellen Terry, he was trained at the Royal Academy of Dramatic Art. He first won international fame for his portrayals of Hamlet and other Shakespearean leads while performing with the London-based Old Vic Company in the 1920s and 1930s. Gielgud also proved himself a deft comedic actor in the role of John Worthing in a 1930 performance of the Oscar Wilde classic, *The Importance of Being Earnest.* Gielgud remained active in the theater as both an actor and director in the decades that followed. From 1956 to 1964, he appeared worldwide in his one-man performance of Shakespearean soliloquies, *The Ages of Man.* In later life Gielgud appeared frequently as a film character actor. He won a best supporting actor ACADEMY AWARD for his comedic role in *Arthur* (1981).

**Gierek, Edward** (1913–2001) Polish Communist Party leader (1970–80).

Following food riots in 1970, Gierek replaced Władysław GOMULKA as party leader. He attempted to raise living standards through production of more consumer goods. However, he encountered increasing opposition from dissident students and from the Catholic Church, which was encouraged by the election of Cardinal Wojtyla of Kraków as pope in 1978 (see JOHN PAUL II). The emergence of the independent trade union SOLIDARITY in 1980 and further strikes raised doubts about his leadership, and he retired following a heart attack.

**Gieseking, Walter** (1895–1956) German pianist. Born in Lyon, France, of German parentage, Gieseking studied at the Hanover Conservatory, graduating in 1916. He made his debut in London seven years later, toured widely in Europe, and made his American debut in 1926. Thereafter, he made many successful tours, concertizing throughout the world. Noted for his rigorous precision, his brilliant technique and his wide repertoire, he was particularly skilled at performing French Impressionist works and was a great interpreter of the music of Claude DEBUSSY.

**Gigli, Beniamino** (1890–1957) Italian opera singer. Considered one of the great Italian tenors of the 1920s through the 1940s, Gigli first gained international attention when he won a vocal competition in Parma in 1914. Successful appearances throughout Europe followed, and eventually led to his American debut at the Metropolitan Opera as Faust in *Mefistofele* in 1920. After Enrico CARUSO's death in 1921, Gigli was principal tenor of the Met until 1932. Thereafter, he sang mostly in Europe, primarily as La Scala in Milan. Noted for the natural beauty of his voice and his technical mastery, he was best known for the title role in *Andrea Chenier,* Cavaradossi in PUCCINI's *Tosca* and Des Grieux in *Manon Lescaut,* and Nemorino in *L'Elisir d'Amour.*

**Gilbert, Cass** (1859–1934) American architect of major importance in the era of eclecticism. His best-known work in the Woolworth building (1911–13) in New York, for many years the tallest building in the world (760 feet). It is a modern office building of steel-frame construction, but its

exterior design is based on medieval Gothic forms typical of the great cathedrals. Its lobby, rich with pseudo-Byzantine mosaics, is ornamented with "gargoyle" portraits of Woolworth and Gilbert. It was designated "the cathedral of commerce" and represented an outstanding effort to make the Gothic style applicable to tall, modern buildings. In contrast, one of his last works, the Supreme Court building in Washington, D.C. (1935), is modeled on a Roman Corinthian temple.

**Gilels, Emil Grigoryevich** (1916–1985) Soviet concert pianist, widely regarded as one of the giants of the keyboard in the decades after World War II. Gilels was one of the first outstanding Soviet musicians to be allowed to perform in the West. His 1955 U.S. debut was preceded by several European engagements. After that, he appeared regularly in both the U.S. and Europe, performing in solo recitals and with leading Western orchestras and conductors. Gilels combined a powerful technique with refined musical intelligence and sensitivity. He was especially noted for his performances of the masterworks of Beethoven and Brahms, and made numerous recordings.

**Giles, Warren** (1896–1979) American baseball executive. As general manager of the Cincinnati Reds (1936–48), Giles led the team from last place in the National League to the pennant in 1939 and World Series championship in 1940. He was later president of the Reds (1948–51) and president of the National League (1951–69).

**Gilford, Jack (Jacob Gellman)** (1907–1990) American actor. A comic actor in theater, films and television, he was blacklisted in the years following World War II. In an appearance before the HOUSE UN-AMERICAN ACTIVITIES COMMITTEE in 1956, he refused to answer questions as to whether he was a communist. He later said that it was 10 years before he was offered another film or television job. One of his best known roles was that of Hysterium in the theater and film versions of *A Funny Thing Happened on the Way to the Forum.* His other films included *Enter Laughing* (1967), *Catch-22* (1970) and *Cocoon* (1985). He was nominated for an ACADEMY AWARD for his performance in *Save the Tiger* (1973).

**Gill, Arthur Eric Rowton** *(1882–1940)* English artist, sculptor and type designer best known for his design of several modern typefaces. Gill studied at the Central School of Arts and Crafts in London and became known as an illustrator and book designer, working in a restrained and craftsmanly vocabulary within the developing idiom of MODERNISM. He was also a craftsman carver of architectural lettering on stone and so came to the design of typefaces for the Monotype Corporation. His Gill Sans, a modern sans serif face of 1928, has become a widely used modern typeface. Gill was also a religious and sociological thinker who combined concern for art and design with interest in social theory.

**Gillespie, John Birks "Dizzy"** *(1917–1993)* American jazz musician, bandleader and composer. Born in Cheraw, S.C., the son of a part-time musician, Gillespie played in the early part of his career with Teddy Hill, Edgar Hayes, Benny Carter and Cab CALLOWAY. At Minton's Playhouse in Harlem, Gillespie jammed with Charlie PARKER, Thelonius MONK and others, helping to invent the jazz style called BEBOP, a term that Gillespie is credited with coining. In the 1940s he composed many bebop and other modern standards, and he guest-starred with the bands of Lionel HAMPTON, Duke ELLINGTON and others. He formed and headed Billy ECKSTINE's orchestra in 1944, led his own big band from 1946 to 1950 and continued to perform in a variety of venues for the next four decades. Lauded as a virtuoso performer, a musical innovator and a great entertainer, Gillespie is recognized as the father of the modern jazz trumpet and one of the all-time jazz greats.

**Gilliatt, Penelope** *(1932–1993)* British novelist, story writer, film critic and screenplay writer. Gilliatt, an accomplished and versatile writer, remains best known in the U.S. for her long stint (1967–79) as film critic for THE NEW YORKER, a position she shared with Pauline Kael. She has also published a number of critically acclaimed novels including *One by One* (1965), *A State of Change* (1967), *The Cutting Edge* (1978), and *Moral Matters* (1983). Her most noteworthy screenplay was for *Sunday Bloody Sunday,* a British film directed by John Schlesinger, which starred Peter Finch and Glenda JACKSON.

**Gilmore, Mary Jean Cameron** *(1865–1962)* Australian poet. One of the premier poets of Australia, Gilmore also taught and helped found an experimental socialist community in Paraguay in 1893. Her poetry collections include *Marri'd and Other Verses* (1910), *The Disinherited* (1941), *Pro Patria Australia and Other Poems* (1945) and *Verse for Children* (1955), one of many collections of juvenile poetry. Gilmore also wrote two volumes of autobiography, *Old Days, Old Ways: A Book of Recollections* (1934) and *More Recollections* (1935). She was named Dame Commander of Order of the British Empire in 1936.

**Gil-Robles, José María** *(1899–1980)* Spanish politician. A Christian Democrat, Gil-Robles led a conservative political coalition in the years before the SPANISH CIVIL WAR. At age 33 he was elected head of the Spanish Confederation of the Right. In 1935 he became minister of war. He was abroad when General Francisco FRANCO led the uprising against the Spanish republic. Gil-Robles remained in self-imposed exile for 17 years before returning the establish himself as a prominent critic of the Franco government.

**Gilroy, (Sir) Norman T(homas)** *(1896–1977)* Australian, Roman Catholic cardinal. Gilroy was elected to the college of cardinals in 1946, thereby becoming the first Australian-born cardinal in the history of the Catholic Church. He served in the Australian armed forces during World War II, then pursued theological studies in Rome and was ordained a Roman Catholic priest in 1923. From 1940 through 1971, Gilroy was the archbishop of Sydney, Australia. In 1969, he was knighted by Britain's Queen ELIZABETH II.

**Gilruth, Robert Rowe** *(1913–2000)* U.S. engineer and space scientist. Director of NASA's Project MERCURY from 1958 to 1961 and director of the Manned Spacecraft Center (now Johnson Space Center) at Houston from 1961 to 1972, Gilruth played a key role in shaping the early U.S. program for human spaceflight. An aerospace engineer with five doctoral degrees and numerous awards in his field, Gilruth continued to serve as a consultant to NASA after his retirement from the Manned Spacecraft Center in 1973. He was named to the National Space Hall of Fame in 1969 and the International Space Hall of Fame in 1976.

**Ginastera, Alberto** *(1916–1983)* Argentinian composer, known for his modern eclectic style. Ginastera's early nationalistic work in the late 1930s and 1940s combined folksong and dance with characteristic cultural rhythms. His later work was described as "neo-expressionist" (see EXPRESSIONISM). His operas, particularly *Bomarzo* and *Beatrix Cenci,* received wide attention for segments that were considered violent and sexually explicit. Ginastera also composed concertos, vocal and chamber music, and film scores. He received Argentina's national prize in 1940.

**Ginsberg, Allen** *(1926–1997)* American poet and diarist. Ginsberg is one of the most famous poets of modern times. He remains best known for his highly visible position of leadership—along with friends and fellow writers William BURROUGHS and Jack KEROUAC—in the BEAT GENERATION literary movement that burst into prominence in the 1950s. Ginsberg produced his best poems in that era, most notably *Howl and Other Poems* (1956), the title poem of which was unsuccessfully prosecuted as obscene. *Howl,* with its long, free-verse lines reminiscent of Walt Whitman, exemplifies Ginsberg's poetics of spontaneous composition with attention paid to the natural wanderings of the mind and the rhythms of breathing. Ginsberg was a key figure in the political protest and psychedelic exploration of the 1960s. His other major books of verse include *Kaddish and Other Poems* (1961), *Reality Sandwiches* (1963), *Airplane Dreams* (1969), *The Fall of America, Poems of These States* (1973), *Collected Poems* (1984) and *White Shroud* (1986). With Burroughs he wrote *The Yage Letters* (1963).

*Beat poet Allen Ginsberg (left) with LSD guru Timothy Leary (center) and Ralph Metzner (right) at the Village Theater, New York, c. 1965* (LIBRARY OF CONGRESS, PRINTS AND PHOTOGRAPHS DIVISION)

**Ginzburg, Alexander** *(1936–2002)* Writer and dissident. An employee of the State Literary Museum, Ginzburg edited the journal *Syntaxis*, which expressed discontent with the Soviet way of life. In 1960 Ginzburg was prosecuted by the KGB in connection with this, and was convicted and given a sentence of two years in corrective labor camps. In 1964 the KGB charged Ginzburg with possessing "anti-Soviet" literature, but the case was dismissed. In 1967 Ginzburg and Yuri Galanskov were arrested on the grounds of anti-Soviet agitation and propaganda, and tried in 1968. Despite massive support at home and abroad, Ginzburg was sentenced to five years and Galanskov seven years hard labor.

**Ginzburg, Natalia** *(1916–1991)* Italian novelist and dramatist. Ginzburg published her early work under the pseudonym Alessandra Tournimparte. Her first book, *La strada che va in città* (The road of the city, 1942), consisted of two novellas—the title work and "The Dry Heart." It was with her third work, the novel *Tutti i nostri ieri* (1952, translated as *A Light for Fools,* 1956), noted for its ruefully comic treatment of tragic themes, that she began to receive international attention. Her dispassionate, contained style drew comparisons to that of Chekhov. Of her plays, perhaps best known is *The Advertisement,* first produced at the Old Vic in London in 1968 and winner of the Marzotto Prize for European Drama. Other works include the novels *Caro Michele* (1973, translated as *No Way* in 1974, and as *Dear Michael* in 1975) and *All Our Yesterdays* (1985).

**Giolitti, Giovanni** *(1842–1928)* Italian statesman, five-time premier (1892–93, 1903–05, 1906–09, 1911–14, 1920–21). Born in Mondovi in the Piedmont region, Giolitti was educated in Turin and began his career as a civil servant. He entered parliament as a Liberal in 1882, serving there until his death. As prime minister for a total of 11 years, longer than any other Italian ex-cept MUSSOLINI, he favored progressive reforms, introducing universal male suffrage (1912), social security and a variety of liberal agrarian, labor and social policies. In foreign policy, he led his nation into the Italo-Turkish war to conquer LIBYA (1911) and opposed Italy's entry into WORLD WAR I. By allowing Fascist candidates to stand for election in 1921, he opened the door to the rise of Mussolini, whom he at first supported but publicly condemned in 1924.

**Giovanni, Nikki (Yolande Cornelia Giovanni)** *(1943– )* American poet. Giovanni became an activist in the CIVIL RIGHTS MOVEMENT while attending Fisk University in the 1960s. Her early poetry, such as *Black Feeling, Black Talk* (1968) and *Re: Creation* (1970), reflects her political views and her anger at society's rejection of them, as well as the more universal themes of love and self-discovery. Her later works, while less embittered, continue to explore the search for one's identity. These include *Cotton Candy on a Rainy Day* (1978), which, as she has done with much of her poetry, Giovanni recorded; *Those Who Ride the Night Winds* (1983) and *Sacred Cows and Other Edibles* (1988). Giovanni has also written *Gemini: An Extended Autobiographical Statement on My First Twenty-five Years of Being a Black Poet* (1971), and published dialogues with James BALDWIN and Margaret Walker.

**Gippius (Hippius), Zinaida Nikolayevna** *(1867–1945)* Russian symbolist poet. Gippius was a member of the Religious and Philosophical Society and wrote in a metaphysical vein. Leaving Russia in 1919 after the Russian Revolution, she continued writing poetry, plays, novels and and short stories, many of which displayed bitter opposition to Bolshevism. Her most important novel is *The Devil's Puppet* (1911).

**Giraud, Henri-Honoré** *(1879–1949)* French general. A career military man, Giraud served in WORLD WAR I and was later (1922–25, 1930–36) a commander in MOROCCO. Early in WORLD WAR II he was captured by the Germans during the invasion of FRANCE in 1940. He made a bold escape in 1942, fleeing to unoccupied France, Gibraltar and finally North Africa, where he

*French general Henri-Honoré Giraud. (1940) (LIBRARY OF CONGRESS, PRINTS AND PHOTOGRAPHS DIVISION)*

participated in the Allied landing and became commander in chief of French forces. After the assassination of Admiral DARLAN in December, 1942, he was also made French high commissioner in Africa. He and de GAULLE cofounded the French Committee of National Liberation in June, 1943, but his deeply rooted conservatism earned Giraud the distrust of most of the FREE FRENCH. Pressured by de Gaulle, he retired as commander in chief in April 1944. After the war, he served in the Constituent Assembly.

**Giraudoux, Jean** *(1882–1944)* French playwright and novelist. Giraudoux, who also enjoyed a long and distinguished career as a diplomat, was one of the leading figure in French theater of this century. He began his writing career as a novelist, producing works including *Suzanne and the Pacific* (1921). But it was as a playwright that he made his real mark. Giraudoux combined an optimistic view of human nature with a subtle poetical style to produce works of warmth and humor that are still widely performed. His major plays include *Amphitryon 38* (1929), *Tiger at the Gates* (1937) and *The Madwoman of Chaillot* (1945).

**Giri, V(arahagiri) V(enkata)** *(1894–1980)* President of INDIA (1969–74). A militant trade unionist and pacifist, Giri organized and headed the Bengal-Nagpur railwaymen's union, which grew into a large national working-class movement. As president, between 1969 and 1974 he worked closely with Prime Minister Indira GANDHI. He endorsed several of her government's measures, including nationalizing the country's banks and ending the practice of paying stipends to the country's princes. However, his own radical proposals for ending poverty and unemployment in India went largely unheeded.

**Giroux, André** *(1916–1977)* French-Canadian novelist and story writer. One of the major French-language writers to emerge from Canada, Giroux was educated in the Quebec Academy and served in the provincial civil service before being named to the Quebec mission in Paris in 1963. Key themes in the fiction of Giroux include the hypocrisy of societal values and the psychological isolation of the individual. His major works include the novels *Au delà des visages* (1948, winner of the Prix David) and *La gouffre à toujours soif* (1953), and the story collection *Malgré tout, la joie* (1959, winner of the Governor General's Award).

**Giscard d'Estaing, Valéry** *(1926– )* President of FRANCE (1974–81). A member of the National Assembly from 1956 to 1974, Giscard was leader of the Independent Republican Party, which supported the GAULLISTS after 1959 but retained its independence. Minister of finance under three successive prime ministers from 1962 to 1974, on the death of POMPIDOU (1974) Giscard was elected president, beating Gaullist and left-wing opponents. Though supported by Gaullists in the National Assembly, growing friction within the majority and alleged scandals, notably over gifts from Emperor BOKASSA of the Central African Empire, weakened his campaign for re-election in 1981 and led to his defeat by François MITTERRAND. Since 1989, Giscard has remained actively involved in the politics of the EUROPEAN COMMUNITY (EC) and EUROPEAN UNION (EU), serving as a deputy to the European Parliament (1989–93), and president of the Council of European Municipalities and Regions (1997– ). In 2002 he was named the head of a commission that drafted a constitution for the EU. French voters rejected the constitution in 2005.

**Gish, Lillian (Lillian de Guiche)** *(1896?–1993)* American actress. Known as "the first lady of the silent screen," Gish had a long and illustrious career in films, spanning more than eight decades. Her film debut was in D. W. GRIFFITH's two-reeler *An Unseen Enemy* (1912), and her association with the great director continued for more than 20 films, including the landmark *The Birth of a Nation* (1915), *Broken Blossoms* (1919) and *Orphans of the Storm* (1922). Gish struggled to find film roles in the 1920s and 1930s, due in part to salary disputes, the advent of sound films and a lack of interest on the part of the moviegoing public, which seemed to prefer the aggressively "modern woman" characterizations of Greta GARBO, Bette DAVIS and Joan CRAWFORD. But Gish found roles on Broadway and managed to win back her acclaim in films such as *Duel in the Sun* (1946) and *The Night of the Hunter* (1955). In the 1970s and '80s she continued to appear on screen, in *A Wedding* (1978) and *The Whales of August* (1987), among other films. In 1970 Gish was awarded a special ACADEMY AWARD "for her superlative and distinguished service in the making of motion pictures." Her sister and sometime costar Dorothy (who died in 1968) was also a respected film actress, although she never met with Lillian's phenomenal success.

**Giuliani, Rudolph "Rudy"** *(1944– )* Mayor of New York City (1993–2001). Born in Brooklyn and trained as a lawyer, Giuliani was chosen to head a federal investigation into charges of police corruption in New York City in 1973. His work in this endeavor led to his appointment as the third-ranking official in the Department of Justice during the first three years of the Reagan administration. At the end of 1983 Giuliani was named U.S. district attorney for the Southern District of New York. He promptly established a reputation as an active prosecutor of MAFIA figures, corrupt politicians and stock traders who violated the rules of the Securities and Exchange Commission.

After an unsuccessful campaign for the mayoralty of New York City in 1989, Giuliani defeated the incumbent, David Dinkins, in large part because of the widespread perception that New York City was suffering from a failing municipal bureaucracy, a soaring crime rate and a faltering local economy. As mayor, Giuliani worked to restructure police patrols and postings to those areas experiencing the highest crime rates. Within two years crime had dropped by a third, and murders in New York were cut in half. While the NYPD's tactics such as random strip searches and alleged racial profiling did not prevent Giuliani from easily winning reelection in 1997, the department's alleged mistreatment of members of the African-American community regularly caused controversy.

In early 2000, prohibited constitutionally from running for a third term as mayor, Giuliani prepared to announce his candidacy for the U.S. Senate seat soon to be left vacant by the retiring senator Daniel Patrick MOYNIHAN. While gearing up to combat Democratic nominee and then first lady Hilary Rodham CLINTON, he pulled out of the race after he was diagnosed with prostate cancer.

After the terrorist attacks on the WORLD TRADE CENTER on SEPTEMBER 11, 2001, Giuliani exuded calm, poise and dignity, and, for many people throughout the country, became an emblem of national resolve in the aftermath of the tragedy. For his efforts at restoring calm and confidence to the people of New York, *Time* magazine chose Giuliani as its "Man of the Year" in 2001. He campaigned on behalf of President George W. BUSH and other Republicans in 2004, further raising his profile throughout the U.S.

**Giulini, Carlo Maria** *(1914–2005)* Italian-born opera and symphonic conductor known primarily for interpretations of the standard repertory. Giulini was born in Barletta in southern Italy. He studied the violin and played in many opera orchestras in the 1930s under such conductors as Richard STRAUSS, Wilhelm FURTWÄNGLER, and Bruno WALTER. In the early years of WORLD WAR II his anti-fascist sympathies drove him into hiding with the arrival of the Nazis in Italy. In 1950 he became conductor of the Milan Radio Orchestra and performed operas throughout Italy and abroad, making his first appearances in Britain and the U.S. in 1955. A number of appointments followed: permanent guest conductor of the Chicago Symphony Orchestra in 1969, principal conductor of the Vienna Symphony Orchestra in 1973–76, and conductor of the Los Angeles Philharmonic Orchestra from 1978 to 1984. In later years he maintained a relatively limited repertoire and showed little interest in new composers. Giulini brings an almost mystical attitude to his interpretations, which critics have sometimes described as wayward and self-indulgent. He has been particularly praised for his performances of Mozart and Verdi operas and choral works and the symphonies of Bruckner and MAHLER.

**Givenchy, Hubert Taffin de** *(1927– )* French fashion designer known for quality design in a classic tradition stemming from Cristóbal BALENCIAGA and emphasizing elegance over innovation. Hubert de Givenchy studied at the École des Beaux-Arts and worked for designers Jacques Fath, Lucien Lelong, Robert Piguet, and Elsa Schiaparelli before opening his own house in 1952. His design was invariably refined and understated but perfectly cut, relying in part on a staff taken over from Balenciaga when his house closed in 1968. The ready-to-wear line designated Nouvelle Boutique has been added to Givenchy's couture production and is distributed throughout the world. The Givenchy name is now also attached to lines of eyeglasses, furs, home furnishings, men's shirts, perfumes, and sportswear under extensive licensing arrangements. Givenchy retired from the fashion industry in 1995.

**Gjellerup, Karl** *(1857–1919)* Danish novelist and playwright. Gjellerup was a student of theology and philosophy, and his works evolved from naturalistic novels to contemporary dramas reflecting the influence of Ibsen. He is best known for the verse drama, *Brunhild* (1884), which was inspired by Richard Warner's *Ring* cycle. In what is considered to be a politically motivated move to strengthen allegiance between Denmark and Sweden and to emphasize the latter's neutral stance, Gjellerup was awarded the NOBEL PRIZE in literature along with Henrik PONTOPPIDAN in 1917. Gjellerup's other works include the play, *Die Opferfeuer* (The Sacrificial Fires, 1903), and the novels *Der Pilger Kamanita* (The Pilgrim Kamanita, (1906), and *Die Weltwandere* (The World Travelers, 1910).

**Glackens, William James** *(1870–1938)* American painter. Born in Philadelphia, he studied at the Pennsylvania Academy of the Fine Arts and subsequently became a successful illustrator for newspapers and magazines in his native city and New York City. He gained recognition as a member of the EIGHT or ASHCAN SCHOOL, painting extremely realistic genre scenes and landscapes in a rather dark palette. Glackens traveled to Paris in the 1890s; taken with the work of the French Impressionists, particularly Renoir, he adopted a lighter, brighter color range after his return to the U.S. Characteristic of his later work is *Chez Mouquin* (1905, Art Institute of Chicago) and *Parade Washington Square* (1912, Whitney Museum, N.Y.C.).

**Glaser, Milton** *(1929– )* Highly successful American graphic designer. Glaser studied at Cooper Union in New York and, on a Fulbright scholarship, with the Italian artist Giorgio Morandi in Bologna. His professional career began with the founding of Push Pin Studios (with Seymour Chwast and Edward Sorel) in New York in 1954. He established a reputation for the graphic redesign of magazine and newspaper formats, setting the standards for layout and typography at *New York* magazine, *Paris-Match*, *The Village Voice*, *New West* and *Esquire*. In addition, he has developed a wide variety of corporate identity programs (for Grand Union supermarkets, among others), packaging, and graphic materials. He is particularly known and highly visible through his design of posters for varied products, organizations and events.

**glasnost** Russian word that has been variously defined as "openness" or "speaking out." Glasnost, a policy initiated in the USSR during the 1980s by Soviet leader Mikhail GORBACHEV, brought with it many new political, social and artistic freedoms. Under glasnost, censorship and repression of personal liberties were relaxed, bringing a new sense of openness to Soviet society. Contrary to Gorbachev's original intentions, glasnost helped to promote the formation of nationalist groups throughout the Soviet Union, such as in LITHUANIA and UKRAINE, whose demands for independence for their peoples contributed to the Soviet Union's disintegration in December 1991.

**Glass, Philip** *(1937– )* American composer; highly influential and eclectic, best known for his role in establishing MINIMALISM as an important modern school of composition. But Glass has also shown the marked influence of JAZZ and ROCK AND ROLL themes in his more recent compositions. He graduated from the Juilliard School of Music in 1962 and studied with Nadia BOULANGER in Paris from 1964 to 1966. His pioneering involvement with minimalist compositions—which featured highly intricate and repetitive rhythms and frequently employed electronic synthesizers—won Glass international acclaim in the 1970s. He also achieved popular acclaim on the Broadway and London stage for his innovative musicals—*Einstein on the Beach* (1975), written in collaboration with Robert Wilson, and *Satyagraha* (1980), a portrayal of the difficult years spent by Mohandas K. GANDHI in South Africa.

**Gleason, Jackie** (**Herbert John Gleason**) *(1916–1987)* American actor, comedian, musician, entertainer and television producer. Gleason was one of the leading show business figures of the 1950s and 1960s and a seminal figure in the new medium of television. Born into a poor Irish-American family in Brooklyn, New York, he began to pursue a career in small-time variety shows and nightclubs during the 1930s. In 1952, he inaugurated the weekly *Jackie Gleason Show,* which ran on television until 1959 and then again from 1962 to 1970. On the show, Gleason excelled at creating comic characters, from the pompous Reginald van Gleason to the pathetic mute known as the Poor Soul. His classic television comedy series *The Honeymooners* (1955–56) began as a sketch on the show and is still viewed by millions in reruns. In it, Gleason portrayed Ralph Kramden, a blustery, self-important but ultimately lovable New York City bus driver who was always looking to rise above his humble origins through some wildly improbable get-rich-quick scheme. Kramden shared his spartan tenement apartment (the main setting for most of the episodes) with his complaining, long-suffering, but devoted wife Alice (Audrey Meadows). Ralph's sidekick, sewer worker Ed Norton (Art Carney), often got the best of him through sheer good nature and luck. The show was notable for its memorable dialogue, inventive comic situations, improvisatory spirit and rich sense of humanity. It set a standard that few subsequent television "situation comedies" (among them, *I LOVE LUCY, ALL IN THE FAMILY* and *M\*A\*S\*H*) have been able to match. Gleason later won a best-actor award for his performance in the Broadway play *Take Me Along* (1959) and an ACADEMY AWARD nomination for his portrayal of pool shark Minnesota Fats in the film *The Hustler* (1961). The versatile Gleason, who epitomized the term bon vivant, was also a band leader and trumpeter. Although unable to read music, he composed a number of popular tunes, including his theme song, "Melancholy Serenade."

**Gleiwitz incident** Attack on a German radio broadcasting station in the German (now Polish) border city of Gleiwitz (Gliwice) on August 31, 1939, by 12 men in Polish military uniforms. All 12 attackers were killed in the ensuing firefight. This incident, occurring some six miles from the Polish border, served as a pretext for HITLER's invasion of POLAND the following day. It was later revealed that the attackers had been prisoners from a German CONCENTRATION CAMP ordered to perform the suicidal assault by the Nazi SS.

**Glenn, John Herschel, Jr.** *(1921– )* U.S. astronaut, the first American to orbit the Earth. Glenn flew 59 Marine missions in the WORLD WAR II Pacific Theater during 1944 and 1945, and won several distinguished awards for his services in World War II and the KOREAN WAR. He completed test-pilot training in 1954 and made the first transcontinental supersonic flight in 1957 as a test pilot. After three years of rigorous training as part of Project MERCURY, Glenn circled the Earth three times in 4 hours and 36 minutes on February 20, 1962. Greeted by President Kennedy on his arrival at CAPE CANAVERAL and given one of New York's largest ticker-tape celebrations, Glenn became a national hero and was elected to the Senate in 1974 from his native state, Ohio. He was reelected in 1980 and 1986. In 1998 Glenn returned to space on a NASA mission to determine the effects of spaceflight on aging individuals. Glenn retired from the Senate in January 1999.

**Glennan, T. Keith** *(1905–1995)* U.S. space administrator. Glennan became the first administrator of the National Aeronautics and Space Administration (NASA) when it was established October 1, 1958, and served in that position until January 20, 1961, when he was replaced by James E. Webb. He came to NASA from Case Institute of Technology, Cleveland, which he had headed since 1947; under his direction, Case had become one of the top engineering schools in the country. After leaving NASA, Glennan returned to Case and stayed there until 1969. From 1970 to 1973, he served as U.S. ambassador to the International Atomic Energy Agency in Vienna. Early in his career, after receiving a degree in electrical engineering from Yale in 1927, he was studio manager of Paramount Pictures, Inc., and Samuel Goldwyn Studios.

**Glière, Reinhold Moritzovich** *(1875–1956)* Russian composer. He studied in Kiev and Moscow and became professor of composition (1913) and director (1914) at the Kiev Conservatory, and professor of composition at the Moscow Conservatory (1920). He taught PROKOFIEV, KHACHATURIAN, Knipper and MYASKOVSKY. A prolific composer, his works include several symphonies, of which the best known is his number three, *Ilya Mouromets* (1909–11), the ballet *The Red Poppy* (1926–27) and a cello concerto. In his later works he used folk music from the USSR.

**globalization** A late 20th-century international phenomenon in the fields of communication, culture, economics, politics and transportation. Globalization is the post–COLD WAR process that vastly expanded the interaction of most nations with each other. It is characterized by an increase in the ability of goods, capital and individuals to travel more freely and rapidly from one nation to another, an increase in the means of communication (via such innovations as the CELLULAR TELEPHONE, COMPUTERS and the Internet) among individuals and societies, and an increasing influx of foreign cultural influences into countries. Some political scientists have argued that globalization has been conducive to the spread of democratic institutions throughout the world. According to this argument, the global proliferation of ideas and values and the increasing worldwide adoption of Western economic practices (such as free trade and market capitalism) through the WORLD TRADE ORGANIZATION (WTO) will eventually persuade nondemocratic governments of the need to adopt the Western political system of representative democracy in order to compete economically in the world. Critics have noted that countries such as CHINA have modernized their economies and introduced Western economic principles without introducing similar levels of democratic reform into their more authoritarian governments.

In the post–cold war era, efforts at increased globalization have depended largely on the willingness of nations to abide by rulings of international organizations. In world trade, organizations like the WTO have proven largely successful in reducing tariffs and regulating patents among its participants. However, the WTO has encountered opposition from European, Japanese and American governments, which have prevented the organization from curb-

ing government subsidies to their farmers and ending quotas imposed on the importation of certain agricultural products. In matters of communication, no organization has emerged capable of ensuring access to communication between individuals of different nations. As a result, authoritarian governments such as China's continue to restrict citizens' access to such media as the Internet and television. International travel is similarly regulated by nations, although many of them have followed the travel restrictions suggested by the WORLD HEALTH ORGANIZATION, as occurred during the 2003 outbreak of sudden acute respiratory syndrome in China.

**global warming** In the 1980s a series of unusually hot summers gave rise to fears that the Earth's climate was gradually becoming warmer. Some attributed this trend to carbon dioxide emissions from industrial plants and AUTOMOBILES and from the burning of RAIN FORESTS. If true, the global warming trend could lead to droughts, the melting of polar ice caps and a rise in sea levels. Although there were sustained efforts to formulate an international response to global warming at the Rio Summit in 1992 and the Kyoto Summit in 1997, neither meeting of industrialized nations produced an accord that was implemented by the major nations of the world.

**Glubb, Sir John Bagot** (*1897–1986*) British army officer. Glubb built JORDAN's Arab Legion into one of the most effective fighting forces in the Middle East during WORLD WAR II. He joined the Arab Legion as second in command in 1930 and took formal command of it in 1939. He became known as Glubb Pasha, a title conferred upon him by Jordan's King ABDULLAH IBN HUSSEIN. He served as a close confidant to Abdullah until the king's assassination in Jerusalem in 1951, and remained commander of the legion until 1956. Growing militant Arab nationalism led to Glubb's dismissal by Abdullah's successor, King HUSSEIN, who expelled him from the country. After returning to England, he wrote many books about the Arab world.

**Glushko, Valentin Petrovich** (*1906–1989*) Soviet rocket pioneer.

He became interested in the use of rockets for space travel while he was barely in his teens, and wrote to the Russian rocket pioneer Konstantin TSIOLKOVSKY about the subject in 1923. In 1929 he urged the Soviet government to develop a rocket propelled by liquid fuel. During the 1930s he worked on various rocket designs. After World War II he helped design a series of rocket engines that represented a major lead forward for Soviet missile technology. Among his achievements were the engine for the R-7, the world's first intercontinental ballistic missile, and engines for early Soviet manned and unmanned spaceflights.

**Glyndebourne Festival** Held annually from May to early August at the Glyndebourne estate in Lewes, Sussex, England, the festival is devoted exclusively to opera, and is especially noted for performances of operas by Mozart and Richard Strauss. The estate owner, John Christie, built an opera house amid the celebrated gardens at a suggestion from his wife, soprano Audrey Mildmay; in 1934 the festival was inaugurated with a performance of Mozart's *The Marriage of Figaro*. A succession of distinguished conductors have guided the performances: Fritz Busch (1934–51), Vittorio Gui (1951–60), John Pritchard (1960–77) and Bernard Haitink (current). Since 1984 Sir Peter HALL has been the producer. Many of the world's great opera singers, such as Luciano PAVAROTTI, have performed there. The festival is also known for exciting productions of such recent operas as Oliver Knussen's *Where the Wild Things Are*.

**Gmeiner, Herman** (*1919–1986*) Austrian humanitarian. Gmeiner's SOS Children's Village became a haven for thousands of orphaned and abandoned children throughout the world. The movement grew from one village, which he founded in 1949 in the Tyrolean region of Austria, to more than 225 "children's villages" in 85 countries on five continents.

**Gnessin, Michael Febianovich** (*1883–1957*) Composer. Gnessin studied at St. Petersburg Conservatory and helped to found the Don Conservatory, becoming director in 1920.

Later he was a professor at the Moscow and Leningrad conservatories. His compositions include an opera-poem *The Youth of Abraham* (1921–23), works for chorus and orchestra, including *Symphonic Monument, 1905–17* (1925), incidental music and folk song arrangements. After the revolution he set a poem by Sergie ESENIN to music for chorus and orchestra to commemorate the revolutions of 1905 and 1917.

**Gobat, Albert** *(1843–1914)* Swiss lawyer, politician, educator and peace advocate. He was active in the Inter-parliamentary Union in the 1890s. At the turn of the 20th century he worked for arbitration as a means of solving international disputes. For this work he shared the second NOBEL PEACE PRIZE with Elie DUCOMMUN in 1902. In 1906 he urged U.S. president Theodore ROOSEVELT to attend a peace conference at The HAGUE, which Roosevelt did in 1907. Gobat directed the International Peace Bureau from 1906 to 1909 and unsuccessfully advocated French and German disarmament.

**Gobbi, Tito** *(1913–1984)* Italian opera singer. A baritone, Gobbi possessed great expressive range in both dramatic and comic roles and was considered one of the finest operatic actors of his generation. He made his debut in Rome in 1938 but did not achieve full recognition until the 1950s. He appeared regularly at New York's Metropolitan Opera from 1956 to 1976 and was also featured at Milan's La Scala and other leading European opera

houses. Among his roles were Iago (in Verdi's *Otello*), Figaro (in Rossini's *Barber of Seville*) and the title characters in Mozart's *Don Giovanni*, Verdi's *Falstaff*, PUCCINI's *Gianni Schicci* and BERG's *Wozzeck*. His portrayal of Scarpia in Puccini's *Tosca* was considered definitive; he often played the role opposite Maria CALLAS and sang with her in a legendary 1953 recording of the work. After retiring from the stage he directed operas and was an influential singing teacher.

**Godard, Jean-Luc** *(1930– )* French filmmaker and critic, a leader (with François TRUFFAUT, Claude CHABROL and Jacques Rivette) of the NOUVELLE VAGUE in the late 1950s. Although he was educated in Switzerland and later at the Sorbonne, it was time spent watching films at Paris's Cinemathèque Française that decided his future. After working as a critic, actor and writer in the circle of young enthusiasts grouped around André Bazin and the *CAHIERS DU CINÉMA*, Godard created a sensation with his first feature, *À Bout de Souffle* (*Breathless*, 1959). With a script by Truffaut, this hommage to the gangster film was an iconoclastic experiment in loose-limbed film form and nervous, jump-cut continuity. Godard's mixture of leftist ideological polemic and comic-book slapstick made him the Bad Boy of the New Wave and the overnight darling of the cinema avant-garde. While critics John Simon and Susan SONTAG disagreed over his films ("infantile self-indulgence" and "nearly perfect work"), audiences were assaulted by the explicit atrocities of the

Algerian war in *Le Petit Soldat* (1960), moved by the intensely personal feminist statement of *Vivre sa Vie* (*My Life to Live*, 1962), amused by the satiric comments on rebellious youth in *Bande à Part* (*Band of Outsiders*, 1964), scandalized by the explicit lyric sensuality of *Une Femme mariée* (*The Married Woman*, 1964) and puzzled by the Marxist image/word games of *La Chinoise* (1967). Sometimes he abandoned the "bourgeois" conventions of subject and story altogether, photographing words or punctuating his shots with gunshot sounds. Many critics feel that his later work abandoned the humor of his early films.

**Goddard, Paulette** (**Marion Levy**) *(1911–1990)* American actress. A HOLLYWOOD film star of the 1930s and 1940s, Goddard was noted for her beauty and vivaciousness. Her two most memorable films were *Modern Times* (1936) and *The Great Dictator* (1940), made with her second husband. Charlie CHAPLIN. She eventually made more than 40 films, but her movie career began to fade in the early 1950s. In 1958, she married Erich Maria REMARQUE, author of *ALL QUIET ON THE WESTERN FRONT*, and retired to Switzerland, thereafter making only occasional film and television appearances.

**Goddard, Robert H.** *(1882–1945)* The "Father of American Rocketry," Goddard graduated from Worcestor Polytechnic Institute in 1908. He took his Ph.D. at Clark University three years later. An instructor in physics at

*Robert Goddard, inventor of the rocket, 1935* (LIBRARY OF CONGRESS, PRINTS AND PHOTOGRAPHS DIVISION)

Princeton (1912–13), he joined the Clark faculty in 1914 and was associated with the university until 1943. Fascinated with rockets all his life, he began testing them as early as 1908 and by 1914 had experimented with a two-stage rocket and various fuels. Highly individualistic and something of a loner, Goddard was a favorite target of the press, which saw his rocket experiments as fodder for sensational stories. After receiving a grant in 1916 from the Smithsonian Institution on the basis of a monograph outlining his ideas and research, he went on to publish his best-known work, "A Method of Reaching Extreme Altitudes," in 1919. A "hands-on" experimenter, he continued his work with the use of liquid fuels for rocket propulsion throughout the 1920s, settling on a combination of gasoline and liquid oxygen. After firing his first liquid-fueled rocket in March 1926, he continued to work on improvements in their design. However, complaints from his New England neighbors and hurried visits by the local fire department every time he made a test were getting on Goddard's nerves.

In 1929, with the help of Charles LINDBERGH, he received a grant from the Guggenheim Foundation and moved his equipment to a testing range in New Mexico. Continuing to build his rockets and work on everything from combustion chambers to steering systems, Goddard launched a series of rockets from 1930 to 1935 that reached speeds of up to 550 miles an hour and heights of over a mile and a half. In a 1936 publication, *Liquid-Propellant Rocket Development,* he summarized his work up to that point. Still the U.S. government showed little interest other than to seek his assistance briefly during World War II to help in developing systems for jet-assisted takeoffs (JATO) of airplanes from aircraft carriers.

Largely unrecognized at the time of his death, he received a knowing tribute from German rocket scientist Wernher von BRAUN when, surprised at questions put to him about rocketry upon his arrival in America, von Braun wondered why the questioners had not asked Goddard. "Don't you know about your own rocket pioneer?" the German asked. "Dr. Goddard was ahead of us all." In 1960, government

neglect came to an ironic end when the U.S. paid $1 million to Goddard's estate and the Guggenheim Foundation for infringements on many of the 200 patents dealing with rockets that Goddard had received during his lifetime. And, on July 17, 1969, as the APOLLO II astronauts prepared for their historic moon landing, *The New York Times* printed a formal retraction of its 1920 editorial ridiculing Goddard's claim that rockets would fly someday to the moon. Today, the Goddard spaceflight Center in Maryland bears his name.

**Godden, Rumer** *(1907–1998)* British novelist and poet. Born in Sussex, Godden spent much of her childhood in India, which was to figure prominently in her writing, along with the influence of her Roman Catholic upbringing. Godden is perhaps best known for the novel *The River* (1946), which she later adapted for film with the director Jean RENOIR for release in 1951. Of her many enormously popular works of fiction, several were adapted for film, notably, *Black Narcissus* (1939, filmed 1947). Other novels include *The Greengage Summer* (1958, filmed as *Loss of Innocence,* 1961), *The Battle of Villa Fiorita* (1961, filmed 1965), also *Five for Sorrow, Ten for Joy* (1979), and her 21st, *Cromartie vs. the God Shiva.* Godden wrote several children's books and her autobiography, *A Time to Dance, No Time to Weep* (1987).

**Godel, Kurt** *(1906–1978)* Austrian-American mathematician. Godel initially studied physics at the University of Vienna but soon turned to mathematics and mathematical logic. He obtained his Ph.D. in 1930 and the same year joined the faculty at Vienna. He became a member of the Institute of Advanced Study, Princeton, in 1938 and in 1940 immigrated to the U.S. Godel was a professor at the institute from 1953 to 1976 and received many scientific honors and awards, including the National Medal of Science in 1975. In 1930 Godel published his doctoral dissertation, the proof that first-order logic is complete—that is, that every sentence of the language of first-order logic is provable or its negation is provable. The completeness of logical systems was then a concept of central importance owing to the various attempts that had been made to reveal a

logical axiomatic basis for mathematics. Completeness can be thought of as ensuring that all logically valid statements, which a formal (logical) system can produce, can be proved from the axioms of the system, and that every invalid statement is disprovable.

In 1931 Godel presented his famous incompleteness proof for arithmetic. He showed that in any consistent formal system complicated enough to describe simple arithmetic there are propositions or statements that can be neither proved nor disproved on the basis of the axioms of the system—intuitively speaking, there are logical truths that cannot be proved within the system. Moreover, he showed (in his second incompleteness theorem) that the "consistency" of any formal system including arithmetic cannot be proved by methods formalizable within that system, consistency can be proved only by using a stronger system—whose own consistency has to be assumed. This latter result showed the impossibility of carrying out David HILBERT's program, at least in its original form.

Godel's second great result concerned two important postulates of set theory, whose consistency mathematicians had been trying to prove since the turn of the 20th century. Between 1938 and 1940 he showed that if the axioms of (restricted) set theory are consistent, then they remain so upon the addition of the axiom of choice and the continuum hypothesis, and that these postulates cannot, therefore, be disproved by restricted set theory. (In 1963 Paul Cohen showed that they were independent of set theory.) Godel also worked on the construction of alternative universes that are models of the general theory of relativity, and produced a rotating-universe model.

***Godfather* trilogy** Acclaimed saga of a criminal MAFIA dynasty (although the term *Mafia* is avoided), directed by Francis Ford COPPOLA from stories by Mario Puzo. The narrative thread running through all three films (1972, 1974 and 1990) is the violent assumption of power by three generations of the Corleone family. Ambitions to "legitimize" the family's gangland activities preoccupy the aging Don Vito (Marlon BRANDO, in an Oscar-winning role) and then his son Michael (Al Pacino); but outside powers and in-

ternecine conflict displace family loyalties with greed and violence. The action ranges broadly over space and
time, from Sicily and the poor immigrant neighborhoods of New York in
the 1900s, to postwar America's posh
estates and Nevada casinos, and finally
to Vatican City. The tone is a counterpoint between the bright festivity of
family ceremonies and a bitter chiaroscuro of treachery and deceit. But
what had been fresh and fast in the
first installment becomes brooding
and complex in the second, and, in
the opinion of many, terminally elegiac
in the third. To date the trilogy has
won 10 ACADEMY AWARDS and a place
in the national vocabulary. Aside from
Coppola's guiding hand, credit must
also go to Ennio Morricone's music
score, the performances by Pacino,
Brando, James Caan and Robert Du-
vall (to name only a few), and the
stunning cinematography by Gordon
Willis.

**Goebbels, Paul Joseph** (*1897–
1945*) German NAZI. Born at Rheydt
in Westphalia, Goebbels attended the
University. of Heidelberg, receiving a
Ph.D. in literature and history. Rejected
from service in World War I because of
a congenital foot defect, he began to
write articles for periodicals as well as
several unsuccessful novels. Meanwhile, in 1922 he joined the National
Socialist (Nazi) Party, and in 1926
HITLER appointed him Berlin's party
leader. He was elected to the Reichstag
in 1928, and when Hitler seized power
five years later, Goebbels was named
PROPAGANDA minister. This enormously
powerful position gave him complete
control over German media and arts,
and with a singularly vicious shrewdness he dictated the content of the
press, radio, literature, film, theater
and the visual arts with the purpose of
glorifying the Third Reich, pursuing
the war effort and stressing Nazi ideology. A mesmerizing orator and a master of mass psychology, he staged huge
rallies and candlelight marches where
the Aryan myth was extolled and JEWS
and intellectuals were excoriated.
Goebbels remained completely loyal to
Hitler until the fuehrer's suicide. Shortly
thereafter as Russian troops entered
Berlin, he and his wife poisoned their
six children and the two then shot
themselves. (See also NAZISM.)

**Goeritz, Mathias** (*1915–1990*)
German-born architect and sculptor.
Goeritz was educated as both a sculptor and an architect in his native Germany before leaving the country prior
to World War II out of disapproval of
the Nazi regime. He finally settled in
1949 in Mexico, where many of his
greatest architectural works—which
are frequently accompanied by his own
large-scale abstract sculptures—now
reside. These include the massive and
sharp-edged *Towers of Satellite City*
(1957, in collaboration with fellow architect Luis Barragan) and the cone-
shaped *Automex Towers* (1967).

**Goethals, George Washington**
(*1858–1928*) American civil engineer.
Goethals graduated from the U.S. Military Academy at West Point in 1880.
He served at various posts in the Army
Engineer Corps (1882–05) and Army
General Staff (1903–07) before being
appointed chief engineer of the
PANAMA CANAL in 1907. Despite numerous difficulties involving engineering problems, labor troubles, climate
and yellow fever, he completed the
project ahead of schedule. Goethals
was the first governor of the Canal
Zone (1914–16). Although retired
from active duty in 1916, he was recalled in 1917. He served briefly as
general manager of the Emergency
Fleet Corporation (1917) and as acting
quartermaster general and director of
purchase, storage and traffic.

**Goffman, Erving** (*1922–1982*)
Canadian-American sociologist. Goffman studied the hidden meanings of
ordinary activities and transactions.
In his books he argued that even an
individual's most casual actions were
actually performances calculated to
establish a certain positive impression.
Goffman held a Ph.D. from the University of Chicago (1953) and later taught
at the University of California (1958–
68) and the University of Pennsylvania (1968–82). Among his books are
*Behavior in Public Places: Notes on the
Social Organization of Gatherings*
(1966), *Encounters* (1961) and *The
Presentation of Self in Everyday Life*
(1959).

**Gogarten, Friedrich** (*1887–1967*)
German Protestant theologian; much
influenced in his theological works

by the writings of Karl BARTH and
Martin BUBER. Gogarten began his career in 1917 by serving as a pastor at
Stelzendorf. In 1931 he became a
professor of theology at the University of Breslau, then moved on in
1935 to a similar position at the University of Göttingen, where he taught
for nearly two decades. Gogarten
held that true historical events were
created only when an individual, in
an attitude of unconditional faith,
confronted the divine "Thou." His
works include *Fichte als Religiöser
Denke* (1914) and *Von Glauben und
Offenbarung* (1923).

**Golan Heights** Strategically important high ground in southern SYRIA overlooking Israeli territory, captured by
ISRAEL in the Arab-Israeli War of 1967
(SIX-DAY WAR) and occupied since.

**Gold, Herbert** (*1924–  *) American author. Gold's novels chronicle
contemporary American life, often
highlighting the difficulties in relations between men and women, and
he is noted for his ability to reproduce
idiom and spoken language. His early
novels, such as *Birth of a Hero* (1951),
are set in his native Midwest. Later
novels shrewdly capture the mood of
the West Coast. These include *He/She*
(1980), *A Girl of Forty* (1986) and
*Dreaming* (1988). Gold has also written the autobiographical novels *Fathers: A Novel in the Form of a Memoir*
(1967) and *My Last Two Thousand
Years* (1972).

**Goldberg, Arthur J.** (*1908–1990*)
Associate justice, U.S. Supreme Court
(1962–65). A graduate of Northwestern University and its law school,
Goldberg became a well-known labor
lawyer who represented the United
Steelworkers and the Congress of Industrial Organizations (CIO) as well as
other unions. In 1955 the CIO merged
with the older American Federation of
Labor to become the AFL-CIO; Goldberg was a leading participant in the
negotiations leading up to this historic
merger. He subsequently served as special counsel to the AFL-CIO. He became President John F. KENNEDY's
secretary of labor in 1961. In 1962
Kennedy nominated Goldberg to replace Felix FRANKFURTER on the
Supreme Court, continuing the prac-

tice of appointing one Jewish member of the Court. Goldberg occupied the seat briefly. President Lyndon B. JOHNSON persuaded him to resign in 1965 to become U.S. ambassador to the UNITED NATIONS after the death of Adlai STEVENSON II. Goldberg later admitted that his resignation from the Court had been a mistake. After serving for three years he resigned as UN ambassador. After an unsuccessful run for governor of New York state he returned to private law practice until his death.

**Goldberg, Rube** *(1883–1970)* American cartoonist. Goldberg was born in San Francisco and worked for the *Chronicle* and *Bulletin* in that city before moving to New York in 1907 to draw for the *Evening Mail*. His whimsical, convoluted slapstick cartoons won him tremendous popularity, and his name entered the language as a term for a wacky, overly complex contraption for performing a simple task. Some of the many cartoon features and strips originated by Goldberg include *The Look-A-Like Boys, Foolish Questions, I'm the Guy* and *Boob McNutt*. Throughout the 1940s, Goldberg also drew political cartoons for the *New York Sun;* he won the PULITZER PRIZE in 1948 for his cartoon "Peace Today," which dealt with the issue of atomic weapons.

**Golden Temple Massacre** On June 6, 1984, in an effort to suppress uprisings by extremist Sikh separatist groups, the Indian army invaded the Golden Temple, the holiest Sikh shrine, in Amritsar, Punjab. Between 800 and 1,000 were estimated killed, among them Jarnail Singh Bhindranwale, the fundamentalist leader of the Sikh extremists, and 48 Indian troops. The militant Sikhs, who had been using the temple as a bastion and refuge, had vowed in May to blockade all grain, water and power supplied from Punjab to the rest of INDIA. On June 1, 11 people had been killed in battle at the temple, and on June 2 the Indian government declared the state of Punjab a restricted area and brought in some 50,000 troops. Sikh uprisings, which had intensified that April, had since become increasingly violent, and Indian authorities applauded the attack. But it triggered a violent backlash by militant Sikhs in India and protests from Sikhs worldwide. The Indian

government reopened the temple on June 25, and later announced a plan to overhaul the Punjab state administration to maintain peace. The assassination of Prime Minister Indira GANDHI by Sikh extremists on October 31 was regarded as an act of revenge for the Golden Temple Massacre.

**Goldie, Grace Wyndham** *(1905?– 1986)* BRITISH BROADCASTING CORPORATION producer. Goldie was a BBC television producer from 1944 to 1965 and played a key role in the development of political and public affairs broadcasting in Britain. She set the pattern for general election nights on BBC-TV in the general election of 1950 and was responsible for the development of such programs as *Press Conference, Monitor* and *Panorama.*

**Goldin, Daniel S.** *(1940–   )* National Aeronautics and Space Administration (NASA) administrator (1993–2001). Born in the South Bronx neighborhood of New York City, Goldin graduated with a B.S. in 1962 from the City College of New York, where he had expressed a strong interest in the scientific aspects of space exploration, and began working for NASA at its Lewis Research Center in Cleveland, Ohio, on designing and improving propulsion systems for the rocket-launched missions that NASA utilized in its APOLLO program. In 1969 he left NASA to work at the TRW Space and Technology Group located near Redondo Beach, California, where his supervisory work improving communication devices on Earth and in outer space led to his promotion to vice president and general manager of the company. President Bill CLINTON appointed Goldin NASA administrator in 1993. Goldin overhauled the NASA budget and trimmed $40 billion from its expenditures by decreasing the use of the more expensive manned missions by 10% and by cutting the NASA's payrolls by a third while improving productivity by 40 percent. He also increased the U.S. commitment to unmanned scientific expeditions to the moon and Mars, intensified the use and transfer of NASA funds toward the International Space Station and improved the images gathered by the HUBBLE SPACE TELESCOPE by having a shuttle mission install a more focused lens on the device. After leaving

NASA in 2001 Goldin joined the research and development division of the Neurosciences Institute in La Jolla, California. In 2003 he was chosen by the Boston University Board of Trustees as the institution's new president, but the offer was revoked shortly before he was to take office because of concerns about his management style and his stated plans for the university.

**Golding, William Gerald** *(1911– 1993)* British novelist. Born in Cornwall, Golding was educated at Marlborough Grammar School and Brasenose College, Oxford, and published *Poems* (1934) while still a student. He worked for a time as a social worker, meanwhile writing plays and acting in a small London theater. In 1939 he began teaching English and philosophy at Bishop Wordsworth's School in Salisbury, where he remained, except for the years of World War II until 1961. Golding served in the Royal Navy during the war, and his experiences shaped his pessimistic view of human nature which is apparent in his writing. Golding's best-known work, THE LORD OF THE FLIES (1954, filmed 1963), a mythic tale of a group of boys abandoned on an island where they revert to savagery, was an immediate success and is still a part of most English curricula. Golding continued to explore the theme of man's inherent cruelty in the novels *The Inheritors* (1955), *Pincher Martin* (1956), *Free Fall* (1959) and *The Spire* (1964). Golding was awarded the NOBEL PRIZE in literature in 1983. Other works include the novels *Rites of Passage* (1980), which won the Booker Prize; *The Paper Men* (1984) and the essays *A Moving Target* (1982).

**Goldman, Emma** *(1869–1940)* Anarchist and social reform. She left Russia for the U.S. in 1885 and was politically active from about 1890 to 1917. She was imprisoned in 1893 for inciting a riot. After meeting Alexander Berkman in 1906, she became an active anarchist, was imprisoned in 1916 and in 1917; after two years in prison she was deported to Russia. She later lived in England and Canada and was involved in the SPANISH CIVIL WAR. Her writings include *Anarchism and Other Essays* (1911), *My Disillusionment in Russia* (1923) and an autobiography, *Living My Life* (1931). (See also ANARCHISM.)

Author and anarchist Emma Goldman. with Alexander Berkman. 1917 (LIBRARY OF CONGRESS, PRINTS AND PHOTOGRAPHS DIVISION)

## Goldman, Nahum (1894–1982)

Zionist leader who helped create the state of ISRAEL. Born in Lithuania, during his lifetime Goldman lived in several nations but never in Israel. He represented the Jewish Agency at the LEAGUE OF NATIONS in the 1930s. In the 1950s he was instrumental in negotiating the agreement under which WEST GERMANY paid Israel $827 million in postwar reparations. He headed the World Jewish Congress (1949–77) and the World Zionist Organization (1956–68). He was often outspoken in his opposition to Israeli government policies, and called on Israel to negotiate with the PALESTINE LIBERATION ORGANIZATION (PLO).

## Goldmark, Carl Peter (1906–1977)

Hungarian-American engineer and inventor. Although RCA Victor had demonstrated and released several 33.3 RPM, long-playing records in 1931, Goldmark conceived and invented the first commercially successful long-playing phonograph records (1948), utilizing the superior vinyl plastic instead of shellac; he was also instrumental in the development of color television. Born in Budapest, he immigrated to the U.S. in 1933 and joined the Columbia Broadcasting System (CBS) in 1936 as a technical engineer. Working in the CBS laboratory, he was credited with developing the first practical color television system, which was demonstrated in 1940. Goldmark's work in developing the modern long-playing record stemmed from his own interest in listening to recordings. The existing 78 RPM records could accommodate only four or five minutes of music per side. An entire symphony recording required several records, and the listener had to change the sides every few minutes. By contrast, a 33.3 LP could accommodate up to a half-hour of music on each side. Goldmark conceived a new stylus capable of cutting finer grooves on the long-playing 33.3 RPM disk, as well as the necessary turntable, tone arm and pick-up cartridge. All of these innovations became standard features and remained in use even after the advent of compact discs in the 1980s. Retiring from CBS in 1971 at the company's mandatory retirement age of 65, Goldmark formed Goldmark Communications Corp. in Stamford, Connecticut. Less than three weeks before his death in a car accident, Goldmark was awarded the National Medal of Science for developing communications sciences for education, entertainment and culture.

## Goldwater, Barry Morris (1909–1998)

American politician, 1964 U.S. presidential candidate and spokesman for the conservative wing of the REPUBLICAN PARTY. The heir to his family's Phoenix, Ariz. department store, Goldwater entered politics after service in World War II and was elected to the U.S. Senate from Arizona in 1952. Building a reputation as a vigorous anticommunist and an opponent of big domestic social programs, he became a key spokesman for conservatives in the American South and West. By the fall of 1963 he was the leading contender for the Republican Party's 1964 presidential nomination, although he was reluctant to run. He officially announced his candidacy in January 1964. Opposing what he regarded as the liberal tendencies of most Democratic and Republican leaders, Goldwater insisted that he offered "a choice, not an echo." A bitter fight for the nomination against Nelson ROCKEFELLER split the Republican Party between its liberal and conservative wings. Answering his critics, Goldwater declared "extremism in the defense of liberty is no vice, and moderation in the pursuit of justice is no virtue." During the campaign, however, President Lyndon B. JOHNSON's forces successfully painted Goldwater as a dangerous extremist who would abolish Social Security and threaten world peace. Goldwater lost the election to Johnson in a landslide, with only 38.4% of the popular votes and six states. Although largely disavowed by the Republican Party and the country at large, Goldwater remained active in national politics and reentered the Senate in 1968. He was a HAWK on the VIETNAM WAR, but called for an end to the draft in favor of a volunteer army. During the WATERGATE scandal, he at first supported president Richard M. NIXON. However, after the release of the White House tapes showing Nixon's involvement, Goldwater was instrumental in persuading the president to resign. The election of conservative Republican Ronald REAGAN as president in 1980 seemed to vindicate the views that Goldwater had espoused 16 years earlier. Ironically, Goldwater criticized Reagan on a number of issues. From being viewed as an extremist in many circles in the 1950s and

Senator Barry Goldwater. 1964 (LIBRARY OF CONGRESS, PRINTS AND PHOTOGRAPHS DIVISION)

1960s, Goldwater grew into an elder statesman of the Republican Party in the 1970s and 1980s, earning the respect of his allies and opponents alike for his integrity and independence. He retired from the Senate in 1986. His biography is *Goldwater* (1988).

**Goldwyn, Samuel (Samuel Goldfish)** *(1882–1974)* American motion picture producer, one of the best known of the HOLLYWOOD moguls. Born in Warsaw, Poland, he immigrated to the U.S. as a teenager. By age 30 he was in Hollywood, where he coproduced the first full-length feature, *The Squaw Man* (1913). He teamed with the two Selwyn brothers to form Goldwyn Pictures (a name formed by combining the first syllable of his last name, Goldfish, and the last syllable of Selwyn); Goldfish subsequently adopted the name as his own. The name Goldwyn is best known as part of METRO-GOLDWYN-MAYER studios, but Goldwyn himself left MGM the year after it was founded to run his own production company. Among the films he produced are *Wuthering Heights* (1939), *The Best Years of Our Lives* (1946) and *Guys and Dolls* (1955).

**Golkar** Official political party in IN-DONESIA during the SUKARNO era.

**Gollan, Dr. Frank** *(1909–1988)* American medical scientist. A polio victim, he was determined to find a cure for the disease. Gollan's isolation of the polio virus in 1948 aided other researchers in developing a vaccine. In the early 1950s, he invented the heart-lung machine for use in open-heart surgery.

**Gollancz, Victor** *(1893–1967)* British publisher, author, philanthropist. Although he founded a successful publishing house, Victor Gollancz, Ltd., in 1928, Gollancz is best known for his many campaigns to aid victims of injustice worldwide and for his political activities. In 1936 he founded the Left Book Club, which had a major impact on the development of the Labor political party. Establishing a committee to aid victims of the Nazis was just one of his humanitarian endeavors. He also wrote many books on religion, politics and music, and spearheaded campaigns for the abolition of capital pun-

ishment and for nuclear disarmament; he was knighted in 1965.

**Gómez, Juan Vicente** *(1857–1935)* Venezuelan dictator (1908–35). A meztizo from a cattle ranch in the Andes, Gómez became a guerrilla leader in support of the revolutionary Cipriano Castro. He was Castro's vice president, seizing control of the government for himself in 1908 while the erstwhile strongman was abroad. Sometimes assuming the title of president (1910–14, 1922–29, 1931–35), sometimes relinquishing it to others Gómez nonetheless retained the reins of powers for the next 27 years. His cunning and tyrannical rule was marked by absolute suppression of dissent by a ruthless secret police totally controlled by Gómez. However, the rule of "El Benemérito" ("The Meritorious One") was also characterized by political and economic stability. Gómez was able to pay VENEZUELA's huge debts and was instrumental in developing his nation's petroleum resources. He was also successful in setting up an array of public works projects that included a network of roads and railways. While amassing enormous wealth for himself and his large family, many of whom were made public officials, he was also responsible for bringing Venezuela into the modern world.

**Gompers, Samuel** *(1850–1924)* American labor leader. Born in London, he immigrated to the U.S. with his parents in 1863, becoming a cigarmaker that year and joining the local union a year later. He served as president of the Cigarmakers' Union (1874–81), before helping to found the Federation of Organized Trades and Labor Unions. Reorganized in 1886, the group was renamed the American Federation of Labor, and Gompers served as its first president (with the exception of the year 1895) until his death. Essentially conservative in his philosophy, Gompers built the AFL into the country's largest labor organization, encouraging improvements in wages, working conditions and hours, but avoiding political involvements and pronouncements. During World War I, he headed the War Committee on Labor and was a member of the Advisor Commission to the Council of National Defense, stressing the need for labor's loyalty to the war effort. His vigor and integrity made

him the most influential and widely respected labor leader of his day.

**Gomułka, Władysław** *(1905–1982)* Leader of POLAND's Communist Party from 1956 to 1970, Gomułka spearheaded the resistance to Soviet dominance of the Polish communist government. Active in the Communist Party from 1926, he organized the People's Guard RESISTANCE group during the WORLD WAR II German occupation. He was first secretary of the Communist Party from 1945 to 1949 but was imprisoned (1951–55) as the result of one of Joseph STALIN's purges. He returned to power in 1956 and initiated several reforms. However, widespread rioting over food prices coupled with his increased leaning toward more orthodox Marxism led to Gomułka's downfall in 1970.

**Goncourt Prize** French literary award. The Académie Goncourt was established in the will of Edmond Goncourt (1822–96), a 19th-century literary figure, to award the annual Prix Goncourt for prose. The Académie consists of 10 individuals whose purpose is to recognize innovative, independent fiction. The first award was made in 1903 to John-Antoine Nau for *Force Ennemie* (1903).

***Gone with the Wind*** Novel and popular motion picture, set during and after the American Civil War. Margaret MITCHELL's novel was published in May of 1936; by September it had made publishing history as the fastest-selling book of all time, with 370,000 copies in print. A mammoth work, it spanned the South of Civil War and Reconstruction, presenting vivid characters like the dashing Rhett Butler and the (ultimately) indomitable Scarlett O'Hara. On January 13, 1939, HOLLYWOOD producer David O. SELZNICK ended months of suspense when he selected the virtually unknown British actress Vivien LEIGH to play Scarlett in his film version of the book opposite Clark GABLE's Rhett. Thirteen days later director George CUKOR yelled "Action." At year's end, on December 15, at a cost of $4.25 million, the finished film went into release through MGM and premiered at Loew's Grand Theater in Atlanta. It grossed an unprecedented $945,000 in a single week. It garnered 10 ACADEMY

AWARDS, including best actress to Leigh, best supporting actress to Hattie McDaniel, best screenplay to Sidney Howard (with an uncredited assist from Ben HECHT) and best director to Victor Fleming (who had replaced George Cukor and who in turn was temporarily replaced by Sam Wood). The movie was a triumph of the studio system and stands today as a monument to Hollywood's Golden Age. In particular, the luxurious Technicolor photography (much of it shot by Lee Garmes) and the extensive use of stunning matte paintings and optical effects enabled a handful of incomplete sets to bloom into the improbable sumptuousness of everybody's dream of the Old South.

**González, Julio** *(1876–1942)* Spanish sculptor. Born in Barcelona, González was trained in metalworking by his goldsmith father. The family moved to Paris in 1900, and González soon met Pablo PICASSO, who introduced him to CUBISM and who was, in turn, tutored in ironworking techniques by the young Spaniard. He was a cubist painter throughout the 1920s, turning to sculpture in the early 1930s. From the period on, he created the cubist and constructivist-influenced iron sculptures for which he is famous (see CONSTRUCTIVISM). Conceived as drawings in space, these semi-abstract works often suggest human figures. Considered one of the most innovative sculptors of the 20th century, he was important in the development of such contemporary artists as David Smith and Anthony Caro. Among his best known works are *Woman Doing Her Hair* (1936, Museum of Modern Art, N.Y.C.) and *Montserrat* (1936–37, Stedelijk Museum, Amsterdam).

**Gonzalez, Richard Alonzo "Pancho"** *(1928–1995)* U.S. tennis player. Gonzalez dominated men's professional tennis throughout the 1950s. He won two U.S. singles titles and led the U.S. to a Davis Cup victory before turning professional in 1949. Speedy of both foot and serve, he won the U.S. professional title a record eight times, and was still able to defeat much younger opponents until he retired at the age of 41 in 1969.

**González Márquez, Felipe** *(1942– )* Premier of SPAIN (1982–96). In 1964, while still at university, González joined the then-illegal Spanish Socialist Workers Party (PSOE). In 1966, he graduated from Seville University Law School, and in 1970 he became a member of the executive committee of the PSOE, succeeding to the leadership of the party four years later. In 1977 the PSOE was legalized and became the largest party in the country. Following its landslide victory in the 1982 elections, González became premier. Known as a moderate, he decentralized the government, improved social programs and brought Spain into the EUROPEAN ECONOMIC COMMUNITY. He was elected to a second term in 1986 and a third term in 1989. Gonzalez's government fell in 1996 after it was plagued by several scandals, and he was replaced by the conservative government of José María AZNAR.

**Goodall, Jane** *(1934– )* British zoologist known for her ground-breaking studies of the behavior of chimpanzees. Since the 1960s, Goodall has spent much time in Africa living in close contact with chimpanzees and observing their behavior. Her discoveries have greatly increased human knowledge of primates. Goodall's work became widely known through *National Geographic* magazine (see NATIONAL GEOGRAPHIC SOCIETY), and she is widely considered the world's foremost authority on these animals. In April 2002 Goodall accepted appointment as a UN messenger of peace to work with nongovernment agencies to call attention to environmental and humanitarian issues. (See also Dian FOSSEY.)

**Goodhue, Bertram Grosvenor** *(1869–1924)* America architect whose work developed from eclecticism toward a creative proto-MODERNISM, who is also known as a graphic and type designer of some importance. Trained as a draftsman in the offices of James Renwick (1818–95) in New York and in the Boston office of Ralph Adams CRAM (1863–1942), Goodhue became a specialist in Gothic-style eclecticism. Promoted to a partner in Cram, Goodhue & Ferguson, he remained with that firm until 1913. His major work during that period was St. Thomas Church in New York (1914), a large, handsome neo-Gothic work. He was chief architect for the 1915 Panama-Pacific exhibition in San Diego, California, working there in an eclectic Spanish style. His St. Bartholomew's Church (1919) in New York is an outstanding work in eclectic Byzantine style. As a graphic designer, Goodhue was influenced by the Arts and Crafts movement and the ideas of William Morris. Goodhue's last major work in architecture was the Nebraska State Capitol building (1922) in Lincoln, Nebraska.

**Goodman, Benny** *(1909–1986)* The "King of Swing"; one of jazzdom's transcendent figures. Acknowledged as the single most important force in popularizing the uncompromising big band jazz style that coalesced as the SWING ERA in 1935, Goodman's flawless clarinet solos and his highly disciplined big bands set still-peerless standards. Goodman was also the first prominent white band leader to feature black artists such as pianist Teddy WILSON, vibraphonist Lionel HAMPTON and guitarist Charlie Christian. Goodman received his first important training in his hometown of Chicago, from classical clarinetist Franz Schoepp, and is significant as the first jazz musician to attain unqualified success as a classical performer. In 1938, he recorded Mozart's Clarinet Quintet with the Budapest String Quartet. Goodman commissioned "Contrasts" by Béla BARTÓK, which he premiered at CARNEGIE HALL in 1939; other clarinet concerto commissions were filled by Aaron COPLAND (1947) and Paul HINDEMITH (1947). Goodman's greatest recognition, however, was a jazz artist whose small

*Clarinetist and big band leader Benny Goodman* (LIBRARY OF CONGRESS, PRINTS AND PHOTOGRAPHS DIVISION)

groups (the trios and quartets) and big bands were models of precision and virtuosic interplay. In spite of the swing era's demise in the mid-1940s, Goodman remained a highly successful performer whose ad hoc combos and bands reached audiences throughout the world during the postwar decades. *The Benny Goodman Story* (1956), starring Steve ALLEN, is a better than average HOLLYWOOD movie, with Goodman's clarinet swinging throughout the soundtrack. Goodman's papers and recordings are housed at Yale University.

**Goodman, Paul** *(1911–1972)* American author and social critic. Goodman's espousal of New Left causes won him a large following among American college students in the late 1960s. He was an early opponent of American involvement in the VIETNAM WAR (see ANTIWAR MOVEMENT). He published hundreds of articles and books in a wide range of intellectual disciplines.

***Goon Show, The*** A comic British radio show that aired on the BBC from 1949 to 1960, the program was the brainchild of comedians Peter SELLERS, Spike MILLIGAN, Harry Secombe and Michael Bentine. The show was the most influential comedy program in British radio history, paving the way for such later comedy hits as the stage revue BEYOND THE FRINGE and the television program MONTY PYTHON'S FLYING CIRCUS. With its zany, off-the-wall humor, the show became a phenomenal success, achieving cult status.

**Goossens, Leon Jean** *(1897–1988)* English oboist. Goossens's career, spanning seven decades, helped redefine the potential of the oboe. Among the composers who dedicated works to Goossens were Benjamin BRITTEN, Francis POULENC and Sir Edward ELGAR. In the 1960s a serious car accident injured his teeth and lips, but within two years he returned to the concert stage after developing a new technique of lip control. His family included noted conductor Sir Eugene Goossens and the harpists Marie and Sidone Goossens.

**Gorbachev, Mikhail Sergeyevich** *(1931–  )* Soviet political leader. Born near Stavropol, he studied law in Moscow, joined the Communist Party

at the age of 20 and became a party leader in his native province. Coming to the attention of national party leaders, he was named to the party's Central Committee in 1971 and was put in charge of Soviet agriculture in 1978, A protégé of Yuri ANDROPOV, he became the USSR's economic planner after his mentor was named Communist Party general secretary in 1982. After the death of Andropov (1984) and of his successor, Konstantin CHERNENKO (1985), Gorbachev became secretary general of the party—and, as such, leader of the Soviet Union. In 1988, he became chairman of the Presidium, functioning as president of the USSR. Later that year, the powers of the presidency were greatly expanded as a result of constitutional amendments proposed by Gorbachev himself, and in 1989 he was elected president (officially, chairman of the Supreme Soviet).

Nothing in his background could have prepared the people of the USSR for the sweeping changes Gorbachev would bring to the nation. Faced with a moribund economy, he instituted revolutionary changes in the communist system, announcing a restructuring (PERESTROIKA) and moving toward decentralization and privatization. At the same time, he called for an openness in government operation, a policy known worldwide as GLASNOST, and moved toward a more open and less repressive system of handling domestic affairs and matters of dissidence. This policy was extended to individuals and to the USSR's restive constituent republics, who were given widely increased autonomy (but some of whose calls for independence were met with violence in the early 1990s).

In international affairs, Gorbachev moved to improved relations with Western nations. Reducing defense spending and trying to bolster the failing economy, he called for increased trade and financial interaction, and in a series of meetings with U.S. president Ronald REAGAN (1985, 1986, 1988) successfully sought closer ties with the U.S. In 1987 Gorbachev and Reagan signed a treaty calling for the elimination of intermediate-range missiles, and in the following two years he withdrew Soviet troops from AFGHANISTAN. For these efforts, Gorbachev was awarded the 1990 NOBEL PEACE PRIZE.

His domestic and foreign policy initiatives provoked criticism from both hard-liners, who opposed any deviations from classic communist ideology and any rapprochement with the West, and reformers, such as Boris YELTSIN, who called for more rapid and revolutionary change and for greater freedom in the constituent republics. As he entered the 1990s, Gorbachev was faced with ever-increasing economic problems and with independence movements in the Baltic and other republics that threatened to split the nation. His use of force in LITHUANIA and LATVIA early in 1990 brought wide condemnation, and his leadership fell under increased criticism as the USSR tottered on the brink of economic and political collapse.

With progressives like Foreign Minister Eduard SHEVARDNADZE quitting Gorbachev's government in protest of his shifting policies, it was uncertain whether or not the Russian leader might be drifting toward the old style of repressive dictatorship. On the international front, he continued to maintain close relations with the West, joining in the UN resolution (1990) that condemned his former ally, IRAQ, and calling for the use of force in the Persian Gulf. In August 1991 Gorbachev was briefly overthrown in a coup, but he returned to power following popular opposition to the rebellious cabal. However, the fact that some of his closest political associates had been involved in the plot severely damaged his reputation. Moreover, his government was beset by nationalist agitation in several of the republics of the USSR. Bowing to the inevitable, he resigned as president and witnessed the dissolution of the USSR in December 1991.

**Gordimer, Nadine** *(1923–  )* South African author. Gordimer's novels and short stories reflect her concern with South African politics and their effect on the human spirit. She was an active opponent of APARTHEID. Her works include the short stories in *The Soft Voice of the Serpent* (1953), and the novels, *A Guest of Honor* (1970), *The Conservationist* (1974), which was awarded the Booker Prize jointly; and *Sport of Nature* (1987). In 1991 Gordimer received the NOBEL PRIZE in literature.

**Gordon, Dexter** *(1922–1990)* An American JAZZ tenor saxophonist, Gordon was one of the pioneers of the BE BOP style. Throughout the 1940s, he played with the bands of Lionel HAMPTON, Louis ARMSTRONG and Billy ECKSTINE. In the 1950s, he became addicted to drugs and served a brief prison sentence before moving to Europe and becoming part of the American jazz community there. In 1986, he played the semi-autobiographical role of an aging jazz musician in the film *'Round Midnight*. The performance won him an ACADEMY AWARD nomination.

**Gordon, Max** *(1903–1989)* Founder of the Village Vanguard in New York City, one of the most influential JAZZ clubs in the U.S. After establishing the club in 1935, he helped promote the careers of many jazz greats and other performers, including the young Judy Holliday, Barbra STREISAND, Lenny BRUCE, and Woody GUTHRIE.

**Gordon, Ruth (Ruth Gordon James)** *(1896–1985)* A respected actress later in life, Gordon was in fact a highly successful playwright and screenwriter in the 1940s and 1950s. Between minor acting stints on Broadway and in film, she wrote—frequently in collaboration with husband Garson KANIN—*A Double Life* (1948), *Adam's Rib* (1949), *Pat and Mike* (1952) and several others. But it wasn't until she was 72 years old that she won public acclaim, winning the ACADEMY AWARD for best supporting actress for the occult-suspense film *Rosemary's Baby* (1968). This was followed in the 1970s and '80s by a string of "eccentric old lady" roles in films such as *Harold and Maude* (1971), *Where's Poppa?* (1978) and *My Bodyguard* (1980).

**Gore, Albert, Jr.** *(1948– )* American politician, member of the House of Representatives, (1977–85), U.S. senator (1985–93), vice president of the United States (1993–2001) and presidential nominee (2000). The son of former U.S. senator Albert Gore Sr., Gore graduated from Harvard University in 1969 and spent five months in South Vietnam serving as an army journalist. Gore was elected to his father's old House seat in 1976 on a conservative platform that included criticism of homosexuality, public

*Former Vice President Al Gore* (OFFICE OF THE VICE PRESIDENT)

funding of abortion clinics and restrictive gun-control measures.

Gore was elected to the U.S. Senate in 1984 and promptly developed an interest in the nation's evolving computer network. In 1986 he introduced a bill designed to encourage investment in more rapid information transfer between computers. This improved the development of fiber optic cables—thin, flexible glass pipes that use light pulses on specific light frequencies to transmit information rapidly, which paved the way for the development and extension of the INTERNET.

After launching an unsuccessful presidential campaign in 1987, Gore became the vice presidential running mate of Arkansas governor Bill CLINTON, in 1992. In November 1992, the Clinton-Gore ticket triumphed over Bush and Vice President Dan QUAYLE. At the beginning of the Clinton administration, Vice President Gore appeared to receive the de facto powers of "coexecutive" that Clinton had promised during the campaign. He attempted (unsuccessfully) to implement a new national energy policy, and worked to push the NORTH AMERICAN FREE TRADE AGREEMENT through the Senate.

The impeachment of President Clinton in December 1998 seriously hampered Gore's presidential aspirations.

But, in 1999 Gore made his second bid for the White House. After defeating his principal opponent in the Democratic primaries, former New Jersey

senator Bill Bradley, Gore chose Connecticut senator Joseph LIEBERMAN as his vice presidential running mate, making Lieberman the first Jewish-American vice presidential candidate of a major party. During the campaign against the Republican ticket of George W. BUSH and Dick CHENEY, Gore denounced Bush's proposed budget and tax plan as a threat to the Social Security system and the nation's economic growth. In the closest presidential election in U.S. history, Gore won the popular vote but lost the electoral vote (see FLORIDA BALLOT CONTROVERSY). When the U.S. Supreme Court finally ruled in favor of Bush, Gore conceded the election to his opponent. In 2002 Gore announced he would not seek the Democratic nomination in 2004.

**Gore, Sir (William) David Ormsby**
See HARLECH, Lord.

**Goremykin, Ivan Longinovich** *(1839–1917)* Russian minister of the interior under Czar NICHOLAS II from 1895 to 1899 and chairman of the council of ministers in 1906 and again from 1914 to 1916. He was considered to have taken little action against RASPUTIN and was forced to resign.

**Gorgas, William Crawford** *(1854–1920)* American physician. Gorgas was born in Toulminville, Ala., and received his medical degree from Bellevue Medical College in New York (1879). He was appointed to the U.S. Army Medical Corps the following year. In 1898, following the U.S. occupation of Havana in the Spanish-American War, he became the city's chief sanitary officer. Once Walter REED established the cause of yellow fever, Gorgas permanently rid the city of the disease by destroying mosquito breeding grounds and segregating patients. Gorgas became chief sanitary officer of the PANAMA CANAL Commission in 1904 and, despite administrative difficulties, successfully controlled malaria and yellow fever in the area, thus ensuring completion of the canal. He was appointed surgeon general of the army in 1914 and, after 1916, was attached to the International Health Board.

**Göring, Hermann Wilhelm** *(1893–1946)* German Nazi leader. Born of a distinguished family in Rosenheim,

Bavaria, Göring was a much-decorated WORLD WAR I hero and served as the last commander of Manfred von RICHTHOFEN's legendary air squadron. He studied briefly at Munich University (1920–21) and was an early convert to the National Socialist (NAZI) Party, joining in 1922. A year later he was wounded in the Munich BEER HALL PUTSCH. Escaping to Sweden for four years, he returned to Germany and was elected to the Reichstag in 1928, becoming the legislature's president in 1932. After HITLER's accession to power in 1933, Göring became second only to his leader in the hierarchy of the Third Reich. His posts included German air minister, Prussian prime and interior minister and founder-head of the dreaded secret police, the GESTAPO. In 1936 he took over the direction of the four-year economic plan, becoming virtual dictator of all aspects of the nation's economy. In 1939 he was officially designated Hitler's successor and a year later he was awarded the specially-created rank of Reichmarshal. A vainglorious figure, enamored of smart uniforms and endless pageantry, he ultimately succumbed to morphine addiction and became increasingly reclusive. Responsible for Germany's total air war, he lost popularity as Allied bombings took their toll, and by 1943 he had lost much of his authority. In May 1945 Göring surrendered to U.S. forces. Found guilty of war crimes at the NUREMBERG TRIALS, he was sentenced to death but managed to cheat the hangman by poisoning himself hours before his scheduled execution.

**Gorkin, Jess** *(1913–1985)* American magazine editor. As editor of *Parade* magazine from 1949 to 1978, he guided it from a small Sunday magazine to the most widely circulated Sunday supplement in the U.S. Gorkin is credited with having originated the idea of a telephone **Hot Line** between Moscow and Washington; he proposed the idea in a *Parade* editorial in March 1960.

**Gorky, Maxim (Aleksey Maximovich Pyeskov)** *(1868–1936)* Russian novelist, autobiographer and essayist. Gorky, who first emerged as a major literary talent in the Imperial Russia of the 1900s, ended his career as the preeminent spokesman for culture

*Russian author and theorist Maxim Gorky* (LIBRARY OF CONGRESS, PRINTS AND PHOTOGRAPHS DIVISION)

under the Soviet regime of Joseph STALIN. Gorky left his family home at age 12 and devoted long years to wandering, odd jobs and diverse human encounters. These years were recounted in his three-volume autobiographical series, *My Childhood* (1913), *My Apprenticeship* (1916) and *My Universities* (1922). Gorky, who as a young man was a protege of Anton CHEKHOV, scored his first major success with the play *The Lower Depths* (1902), which recounted the hardships of peasant life in realistic colloquial language and thus broke new ground in Russian theater. Gorky was a friend of Vladimir LENIN and enjoyed protected status after the RUSSIAN REVOLUTION of 1917. But his dissatisfaction with the new communist regime led to his voluntary exile from his homeland during the 1920s. In 1931 he returned to Russia, rendered praise to Stalin and articulated the theory of SOCIALIST REALISM that was to set the standard for publishable Soviet literature through the 1980s. In 1932, Gorky became the first president of the Union of Soviet Writers. The circumstances of Gorky's death remain unclear; there is a suspicion that he may have been a victim of Stalin.

**Gorodetsky, Sergei Mitrofanovich** *(1884–1967)* Russian poet. His first book, *Yar* (1907), demonstrated his considerable promise as a symbolist poet. His later work was disappointing. In 1912 Gorodetsky repudiated Symbolism, and together with Nicholas GUMILEV founded the Acmeist school (see

ACMEISTS). After Gorodetsky had joined the Communist Party, he denounced any connection with the Acmeists, largely as a result of Gumilev's execution. His later collections of verse, *The Sickle* (1921) and *Mirolom* (1923), idealize the life of the Soviet workers.

**Gorshkov, Sergei G(eorgievich)** *(1910–1988)* Soviet admiral. As commander in chief of the Soviet Navy from 1956 to 1985, he transformed the USSR from a nation with only a small coastal defense force into a nuclear-era sea power rivaled only by the United States. Many Western military experts regarded Gorshikov as a major contributor to modern naval strategy. His views were given seminal expression in his 1976 book *The Sea Power of the State.*

**Görz-Gradisca (Italian: Gorizia)** Former county and crownland of Austria, now Italy's Gorizia province, in the Friuli-Venezia Giulia region. The scene of severe fighting during the Isonzo River campaign of WORLD WAR I, it was taken by the Italians in 1916, recaptured during the Austro-German Karst Drive of 1917, was taken again by Italy in 1918—and ceded to Italy by the 1919 Treaty of St. Germain. Following World War II, eastern Friuli was ceded to Yugoslavia (in 1947) but Gorizia remained Italian.

**Gosplan** Acronym for State Planning Commission, founded in 1921, a group of government departments that planned and coordinated economic activities in the USSR. The Gosplan consisted of three types of departments, according to regional differences and branches of the economy. The party leadership disapproved of Gosplan's first FIVE-YEAR PLAN, which provoked a wave of terror against some of those in charge. Since then, Gosplan was directed by people from the party leadership. In 1960 responsibility for long-term economic planning was transferred to the *Gosekonomsoviet,* or state scientific economic council.

**Gottwald, Klement** *(1896–1953)* Czechoslovak communist leader, president of CZECHOSLOVAKIA (1948–53). Born into a peasant family in Moravia, Gottwald served in the Austrian army in WORLD WAR I. He joined the Czech Communist Party in 1921, becoming its secretary-general in 1928. The following year he was elected to the Czech parliament. Gottwald spent WORLD WAR II in Moscow, where he edited a newspaper for Czechs in the Soviet army. He became vice premier of Czechoslovakia after the war. When the Communist Party won 38% of the vote in the Czech elections of May 1946, Gottwald became premier, heading a coalition government. Two years later, with Soviet backing, he effected a coup d'état and forced President Edvard BENEŠ to accept a government composed entirely of Communists and their collaborators. In 1952 Gottwald purged his communist rival, party chief Rudolf Slansky, after charging him with treason and holding a show trial (see SLANSKY TRIAL). Gottwald was a strict Stalinist; ironically, he died after contracting pneumonia at Josef STALIN's funeral in Moscow (see STALINISM). Gottwald's rise to power has acquired notoriety in Czechoslovakia as a betrayal of democracy.

**Goubau, Georg** *(1906–1980)* German-born electronics engineer. A pioneer in microwave circuits, in the late 1940s Goubau developed an important message-transmission system for television and radio calls. This system enabled a single stand of wire to carry large volumes of messages to isolated areas otherwise reached only by a coaxial cable. The invention was a milestone in the communications technology and foreshadowed the later development of FIBER OPTICS transmissions systems. Goubau wrote more than 60 scientific articles and received several awards for his scientific work.

**Goudsmit, Samuel A(braham)** *(1902–1978)* Dutch-born physicist. Goudsmit received his Ph.D. from the University of Leiden (1927), then immigrated to the U.S. He taught at the University of Michigan (1932–46) and Northwestern University (1946–48) before moving to Brookhaven National Laboratory (1948–70). In 1925 Goudsmit and George Uhlenbeck discovered that electrons in the nucleus of the atom rotate, thus becoming charged and creating a magnetic field. This discovery was important in understanding the structure of the atom. During WORLD WAR II Goudsmit worked on

RADAR. In 1944 he became head of Project **Alsos**, a top-secret mission to find out if the Germans were making an ATOMIC BOMB. Goudsmit went to Europe with U.S. forces and inspected newly-captured areas for any evidence that the Germans were working on a bomb. He determined that they would not have an atomic bomb before the end of the war. Goudsmit was awarded the Medal of Freedom, and also received the National Medal of Science for his work.

**Goudy, Frederic W.** *(1865–1947)* American printer, typographer and type designer known for a number of traditional roman typefaces. In 1903 Goudy set up the Village Press in a barn in Park Ridge, Illinois, where, with Will Ransom as a partner, he began to produce hand-printed books with bindings by his wife. His Goudy Old Style typeface of 1916 designed for American Type Founders is probably his best-known achievement, a classically elegant Roman face still frequently used. Garamont, Kennerly and Goudy Trajan are other successful Goudy faces, the last based on the carved inscriptions on the Column of Trajan in Rome. Goudy was the author of a number of books on type and lettering and founded the magazine *Ars Typographica*. He won the Gold Medal of the American Institute of Graphic Arts (AIGA) in 1920.

**Gould, Chester** *(1900–1985)* American cartoonist. In 1931, while living in Chicago, Gould created DICK TRACY, the best-known of all comic strip detectives. The character was born out of Gould's hatred of such PROHIBITION-era gangsters as Al CAPONE. The strip was the first to present graphic violence. In the late 1950s, it was carried by close to 1,000 newspapers worldwide and read by 65 million people. Gould retired from drawing the strip in 1977.

**Gould, Glenn** *(1932–1982)* Canadian pianist and musical theorist, noted for his devotion to the music of J.S. Bach and for his musical and personal eccentricities. Some listeners believe Gould to have been one of the greatest musicians of the 20th century; others dismiss him as a crackpot. Born in Toronto, Gould was educated at the Toronto Royal Conservatory of Music, from which he graduated (the institu-

tion's youngest graduate ever) with high honors. He made his concert debut in 1947 playing Beethoven's Piano Concert No. 4 with the Toronto Symphony Orchestra; his first American performance was in Washington, D.C., in 1955. In 1956 he became the first North American pianist ever to play in the Soviet Union. Over the following decade, Gould built a substantial reputation through his concert appearances and recordings. However, increasingly ill at ease in the concert hall and convinced that a "perfect" performance could not be achieved in a "live" performance, after 1964 Gould refused to play in public. Thereafter, he made only recordings. The reclusive Gould also produced a documentary for Canadian television, "The Idea of North."

Gould's playing was marked by distorted tempi and idiosyncratic phrasing. He reportedly remarked that sound only interfered with music; his interpretations were attempts to get at the truth that he perceived behind the notes. At one early concert, conductor Leonard BERNSTEIN told the audience that he disagreed with Gould's interpretation of the piece they were about to play but thought that it deserved to be heard. Conductor George SZELL's remark about Gould was perhaps most telling of all: "That nut's a genius!" Gould's last recording was of Bach's *Goldberg Variations*—the first work he had ever recorded (1955).

**Gould, Stephen Jay** *(1941–2002)* American biologist and paleontologist. Born in New York City, Gould was educated at Antioch College and Columbia University. A working scientist with a clear and graceful prose style, he has been one of the country's most successful science popularizers. He has taught biology, geology and the history of science at Harvard since 1967, and is also the author of columns and essays that have appeared in many large-circulation magazines. In 1972 Gould and fellow-scientist Niles Eldredge posited a theory of evolution that suggested for numerous species a rapid evolution followed by a long period of relative genetic stagnation. This development, termed punctured equilibrium, remains a subject of intense scientific interest. Gould was the author of a number of books, some of them collections of his popular essays.

Among his works are *Ontogeny and Phylogeny*, *The Panda's Thumb*, *The Flamingo's Smile* (1985) and *Wonderful Life* (1989). Gould continued to publish until his death, producing the monumental *Structure of Evolutionary Theory* (2002) in addition to other important works.

**Gowon, Yakubu** *(1934–   )* Head of the federal military government in NIGERIA (1966–75). An army officer involved in the successful coup against Tafawa BALEWA in 1966, Gowon succeeded the coup's initial leader, Major General Ironsi, who was killed a few months later. Between 1967 and 1970 Gowon's rule was dominated by civil war with the predominantly Ibo Eastern Region, which had proclaimed itself as independent BIAFRA. Economic difficulties led to another military coup in 1975, led by Brigadier Murtula Mohammed while Gowon was out of the country. Gowon retired to exile in the U.K.

**GPU (Gosudarstvennoye Politicheskoe Upravleniye)** Abbreviation for "State Political Administration Soviet Security Service," which was founded in 1922, replacing the CHEKA. Its work was directed against the church, private entrepreneurs, KULAKS, the old intellectuals and former members of opposition parties. The GPU was also concerned with conflict within the party. In 1924 its name was changed to OGPU and in 1934 to NKVD before becoming the KGB in 1953. (See also SECRET POLICE.)

**Grable, Betty (Elizabeth Grable)** *(1916–1973)* One of HOLLYWOOD's great glamour queens in the 1940s, Grable began performing at an early age. She studied ballet and tap dancing and—having lied about her age (she was only 13)—found work as a chorus girl in films and on Broadway. After being fired from four movie studios and a failed marriage with actor Jackie COOGAN, Grable suddenly became a national sensation as American servicemen's favorite pin-up girl during WORLD WAR II; she was also perhaps the prime beneficiary of the perfected Technicolor process in a string of successful musicals for 20th CENTURY–FOX. Among her box-office smashes were films such as *Down Argentine Way*

(1940), *Coney Island* (1943), *Pin-Up Girl* (1944), *The Dolly Sisters* (1945) and *How to Marry a Millionaire* (1953). In 1943 Grable married band-leader Harry JAMES.

**Grace, Princess of Monaco (Grace Kelly)** *(1928–1982)* American-born film and stage actress. Grace Kelly began her career as a model, then acted on Broadway before turning to the movies and becoming one of the premier leading ladies of the American cinema in the 1950s. She projected a cool blonde elegance while bringing subtle emotionality to her roles. She remains especially well known for her roles in the Alfred HITCHCOCK films *Dial M for Murder* (1954), *Rear Window* (1954) and *To Catch a Thief* (1955) and won an ACADEMY AWARD as best actress for her role as the embittered wife of an alcoholic (played by Bing CROSBY) in *The Country Girl* (1954). Other films include *Fourteen Hours* (1951), *High Noon* (1952), *Mogambo* (1953), *The Bridges at Toko-Ri* (1955), *The Swan* (1956) and *High Society* (1956). In 1956 she left the cinema to marry Prince Rainier III of MONACO and became Princess Grace. She died in an auto accident in 1982.

**Grade Lew, Baron Grade of Elstree (Lewis Winogradsky, Baron Grade of Elstree)** *(1906–1998)* British impresario. The founder and chairman of Associated Television in Britain, Baron Grade created a show-business dynasty with his brothers Bernard and Leslie. After emigrating from Russia, he entered show business as a dancer, winning a World Charleston Competition (1926). A period as a talent agent led to his becoming a producer and establishing his own production company, now called the Grade Company (from 1985). He has produced such acclaimed films as *The Boys from Brazil* (1978) and *On Golden Pond* (1981), and such award-winning television specials as "Jesus of Nazareth" and "The Julie Andrews Show."

**Graebe, Herman** *(1901–1986)* German engineer. As a civilian contractor for the Third Reich's Railroad Administration, he hired and protected hundreds of Jewish workers from the Nazis (see NAZISM) in WORLD WAR II. He subsequently became the only German to

volunteer to testify for the prosecution at the NUREMBERG TRIALS. His testimony made his family's life in GERMANY untenable, and they moved to the U.S. in 1948. The Israeli government bestowed its highest honors on him in 1965.

**Graf, Steffi** *(1969–   )* German tennis player. Graf became the first woman to permanently break the Evert-Navratilova domination of women's tennis. In 1982 she became the second-youngest player ever to reach the computer ranking system established in 1975. In 1986 she won her first singles championship and went on to win seven more that year, including victories over EVERT and NAVRATILOVA. In 1987 she won the French Open, her first grand-slam title. In 1988 she became only the third woman to complete a grand slam in a single season. She also won the 1988 Olympic championship. In 1991 and 1992 Graf won the Wimbledon tournament, and in 1993 she dominated the 1993 French, U.S. and British Open championships. Graf retired from professional tennis in 1999. She married U.S. tennis player **Andre Agassi** in 2001.

*Graf Spee* See Battle of the River PLATE.

**Graham, Billy (William Franklin Graham)** *(1918–   )* American Baptist clergyman and evangelist. Graham's personal charisma, religious fervor and skill at preaching have made him one of the most admired men in America and the best-known evangelist worldwide. Ordained a Baptist minister in 1939, he gained national recognition during his 1949 crusade in Los Angeles. In 1950 he organized the Billy Graham Evangelistic Association and has conducted successful crusades around the world since then. Graham's message has also reached millions through radio, television and film programs, as well as through the print media. His many books include *Peace with God* (1953) and *How to Be Born Again* (1977). Graham received an honorary knighthood from Britain in December 2001.

**Graham, Katharine** *(1917–2001)* American newspaper publisher. Born Katharine Mayer to Agnes and Eugene Mayer, Graham's association with the

*Washington Post* began while she was still in high school, when at age 17 she began working as a copy girl for the Washington, D.C., area newspaper that her father had purchased in 1933. After graduating from the Madeira School in Washington she enrolled at Vassar College, but transferred to the University of Chicago after her second year, graduating in 1938. She was hired as a reporter by the *San Francisco News*, where she worked for a year before transferring to Washington and joining the *Post*'s journalism bureau. In 1940, after her return to her father's newspaper, she married Phillip Graham, then a clerk for the U.S. Supreme Court, with whom she had four children. Six years after their marriage Katharine Graham's husband succeeded her father as publisher of the *Post*. In 1963, 11 years after the birth of their fourth child, Stephen, Philip Graham committed suicide. Katharine then assumed the duties of president of the *Post*.

Along with mastering the challenging administrative tasks of president and later publisher, Graham became famous for her strong support for the publication of damning information about the VIETNAM WAR and Richard M. NIXON's reelection campaign. In 1971 she permitted the *Post* to print the stolen Pentagon documents on the Vietnam War that later became referred to as the "Pentagon Papers." The following year, Graham supported the investigative journalism of Carl Bernstein and Bob Woodward (see WOODWARD and BERNSTEIN) in the WATERGATE crisis that eventually led to the resignation of President Nixon. In 1973 the *Post* won the Pulitzer Prize for its coverage of the Watergate affair, and Mrs. Graham, named chief executive office of the newspaper that year, received the Zenger Award for Freedom of the Press. Graham ran the *Post* for 20 years before retiring in 1993 in favor of her son, Donald. While continuing to serve on the *Post*'s executive committee, Graham wrote *Personal History* (1997), an autobiographical account of her experiences in news journalism. The book was awarded the Pulitzer Prize the following year. On July 14, 2001, while attending a media conference in Sun Valley, Idaho, Graham suffered head injuries in a fall. She died of complications stemming from those injuries three days later.

**Graham, Martha** (*1894–1991*) American dancer, choreographer, teacher and company director. Graham has been a major force in the founding and development of modern dance in America. She studied and danced with the Denishawn Dancers (1916–23), appeared in musical revues in New York City and taught at the Eastman School of Music before giving her first solo performance in 1926. She founded her School of Contemporary Dance in 1927, then formed her company and began regular performances in 1929. She developed a specific dance technique to express her "dance plays" which revolved around American and European myths. Often in collaboration with designer/sculptor Isamu NOGUCHI, composer Aaron COPLAND and musician Louis Horst, she has created over 160 works (dancing the lead role in many), including *Primitive Mysteries* (1931), *Letter to the World* (1940), *Appalachian Spring* (1944), *Seraphic Dialogue* (1955), *Clytemnestra* (1958), and *Lucifer* (1975). In 1973 she retired from dancing and thereafter focused on running her school and company. Such well-known dancers as Erick Hawkins and Merce CUNNINGHAM were trained by her. In 1976 Graham was awarded America's highest civilian honor, the Medal of Freedom.

**Graham, Sheila (Lily Shiel)** (*1908?–1988*) American writer. Born into poverty in a London slum, she immigrated to the U.S. in 1933 and became a newspaper columnist. Together with Louella Parsons and Hedda Hopper, Graham was one of a trio of Hollywood's most powerful gossip writers. Her affair with F. Scott FITZGERALD, who died in her arms in 1941, was the inspiration for her first book *Beloved Infidel*, published in 1958. She was the model for Kathleen, the heroine of Fitzgerald's novel *The Last Tycoon*.

**Grainger, Percy Aldridge** (*1892–1961*) Australian-American pianist and composer. Born in Melbourne, he was educated in Frankfurt. Greatly influenced by his friend Edvard Grieg, he took an interest in folk music, which was to become the abiding passion of his musical life. Grainger began his concert career in England in 1901, touring South Africa and Australia before settling in the U.S. (1914) and becoming a citizen. Grainger's light and spontaneous music is almost always based on folk themes, and he is best known for his settings of folk tunes from the British Isles. Among his works are *Irish Tunes from County Derry* (1909), *Song of Democracy* (1917) and *Suite on Danish Folksongs* (1937).

**Gramsci, Antonio** (*1891–1937*) Italian Marxist and political theorist. Educated at the University of Turin (1911–14), Gramsci was an associate of Palmiro Togliatti and became involved with the socialist politics of the 1920s. He was a cofounder of the newspaper *L'Ordine Nuovo* (1919) and of the Italian Communist Party (1921), which he headed from 1924. He served in the Italian Chamber of Deputies from 1924 to 1926, when he and other communists were arrested and jailed by the fascists. Remaining in prison until months before his death, Gramsci wrote the influential *Letters from Prison* (1947, tr. 1973) and *Prison Notebooks* (1948–57, tr. 1971).

**Grand Coalition (German: *grosse Koalition*)** Term used in Central European politics to denote a coalition of two major parties, as opposed to a small coalition (*kleine Koalition*) of one major party and a minor party. Such a coalition, between the conservative Christian Democratic Union/Christian Social Union (CDU/CSU) and the Social Democratic Party (SPD) governed WEST GERMANY (1966–69) following the failure of the small coalition of CDU/CSU with the center-right Free Democratic Party (FDP). In 1969, the SPD and the FDP formed a small coalition and the Bundestag elected Willy BRANDT as chancellor. A grand coalition of the conservative OVP and the social democratic SPO governed AUSTRIA from 1945 to 1966.

**Grandi, Dino** (*1895–1988*) Italian fascist politician. He served as ambassador to Great Britain, justice minister and foreign minister under Benito MUSSOLINI. In 1943, he helped orchestrate Mussolini's downfall.

**Grandma Moses (Anna Mary Robertson Moses)** (*1860–1961*) American "primitive" landscape painter whose greatest measure of fame came during the last two decades of her long life. Actually, Moses despised the label, "primitive." "People come by the farm to look at the 'savage,'" she would laugh. "But my children are not amused." To put her longevity in perspective, she was five years old when President Lincoln was assassinated and 101 when astronaut Alan SHEPARD made his first manned spaceflight in 1961. She was a living link with a rapidly vanishing rural tradition. The titles of her more than 1,200 paintings told the details of her idyllic childhood in Greenwich, N.Y., her years as farmwife and mother in the Shenandoah Valley, Va., and her last years in the tiny village of Eagle Bridge, N.Y.—*Bringing in the Maple Sugar, The Mailman Has Gone, Joy Ride, The Black Horses.* "This whole paintin' business commenced when my arthritis flared up," she said in an article, "How I paint" (1947). "I switched from yarn to paint for one reason only—you see, a needle is hard to hold. But you can get a good grip on a brush." Independent art agent Louis Calder one day found three of her tiny paintings in a local drugstore near Eagle Bridge, showed them to New York dealer Otto Kallir, and in 1940 Grandma had her first one-woman show in New York. The critics argued, the viewers were delighted, she appeared on the covers of *Time* and *Life* magazines, Edward R. MURROW interviewed her on television in 1956, she met President TRUMAN, and she generally was astonished and delighted at all the fuss. When asked how she painted, she said simply, "From the top—down." However, there was no denying the masterful sense of form and organization and color.

**Grange, Harold "Red"** *(1903–1991)* Legendary American football player for the University of Illinois in the 1920s. Grange was popularly known as the "Galloping Ghost." In one of his most notable exploits, he scored four touchdowns and ran for 265 yards in the first 12 minutes of a game (against the University of Michigan in 1924). Grange joined the National Football League's Chicago Bears in 1925, giving the NFL a credibility it had lacked in its first few seasons. After a stint as a coach, he retired from the game in 1938 because of injuries. Grange tried a number of other pursuits (and even acted in a movie serial called *The Galloping Ghost* [1932])

and later became a radio and television commentator. He was a charter member of the Professional Football Hall of Fame in 1963.

**Grant, Cary (Archibald Leach)** *(1904–1986)* British-born actor, one of the most popular film stars of the 20th century. In a HOLLYWOOD career that spanned more than three decades, Cary Grant was known as the personification of charm, wit and style. Born in Bristol, England, during the 1920s he alternated between British and American theater, mostly in musical comedy and vaudeville. He made his screen debut in 1932, and in 1933 was chosen by Mae WEST to play opposite her in *She Done Him Wrong.* The last of his 72 films was *Walk, Don't Run* (1966). Grant was equally adept as a leading man in screwball comedies as he was in suspense thrillers. He worked with most of the leading actresses of his time (he was especially effective opposite Katharine HEPBURN) and gave memorable performances directed by George CUKOR, Frank CAPRA, Howard HAWKS and Alfred HITCHCOCK. His most popular films included *The Awful Truth* (1937), *Bringing Up Baby* (1938), *His Girl Friday* (1940), *The Philadelphia Story* (1940), *Suspicion* (1941), *Arsenic and Old Lace* (1944), *Notorious* (1946) and *North by Northwest* (1959). Grant retired at the height of his popularity and remained a legend. In 1970 he was given an ACADEMY AWARD for his "unique mastery of the art of screen acting."

**Grant, Duncan** *(1885–1978)* British artist and designer known for highly decorated work much at odds with the mainstream trend toward MODERNISM in the 1930s. Grant's work turned to textile and ceramic designs around 1912. In the 1920s and 1930s, he designed interiors, furniture and such graphic materials as book jackets—always in an elaborately florid decorative vocabulary. Grant was associated with the BLOOMSBURY GROUP.

**Grant, Maxwell** See Walter GIBSON.

**Grant, William T.** *(1876–1972)* American businessman and retailer, founder of Grant's department store chain. Grant opened his first department store in 1906 with fast-selling merchandise priced at 25 cents. In 1966, when he retired as chairman of

the board at age 90, Grant's stores operated in 44 states and grossed $839.7 million. However, in the 1970s, new competition and financial loses forced W.T. Grant's to go out of business.

**Granville-Barker, Harley** *(1877–1946)* British theatrical actor, playwright, director and Shakespearean scholar. Granville-Barker was one of the leading forces in the British theater in the first decades of the 20th century. He first gained wide attention as an actor through his portrayal of Marchbanks in the premiere of *Candida* (1900) by George Bernard SHAW. From 1904 to 1907, Granville-Barker directed a number of premieres of Shaw's plays at the Royal Court Theatre in London. He also scored successes with his own plays, most notably *The Voysey Inheritance* (1905) and *The Madras House* (1910). Granville-Barker was also well-known for his productions of the works of Shakespeare, in which he insisted on a close adherence to the original text.

**Grass, Günter** *(1927– )* German novelist, poet, playwright and essayist. Grass is one of the most prominent German authors of the latter half of the 20th century. He achieved international fame with his first novel, *The Tin Drum* (1959), which depicted the chaos and shame that dominated GERMANY during WORLD WAR II. That work drew from Grass's own difficult experiences as an adolescent boy attempting to survive in wartorn Germany. Other novels by Grass include *Cat and Mouse* (1961), *Dog Years* (1963), *Local Anaesthetic* (1969), *The Flounder* (1977) and *The Meeting at Telgte* (1979). Grass also achieved success as a playwright with *The Plebeians Rehearse the Uprising* (1966). *In the Egg and Other Poems* (1977) contains a representative selection of his verse. In 1999 Grass received the NOBEL PRIZE in literature. Grass has been active in postwar German politics as a supporter of the Social Democratic Party.

**Grasso, Ella T.** *(1919–1981)* American politician who was the first woman ever to be elected governor of a U.S. state without succeeding her husband in office. A Connecticut Democrat, Grasso held various state offices (1952–70) and served in the U.S. House of Representatives (1971–75). As governor of Connecticut (1975–80), she was in the mainstream of the Democratic political establishment, advocating liberal social programs while holding down state spending. She resigned from office halfway through her second term when she fell ill with cancer.

**Grateful Dead, The** American rock and roll band. Since its formation in the mid-1960s in San Francisco during the rise of the psychedelic music era, the Grateful Dead has remained a powerful force in American ROCK. Indeed, the Dead—as the band is known by its fans—is one of the most popular live acts in rock history, and draws fans both young and old to its perpetually sold-out shows. While certain Dead personnel have changed over the years, the principal band members have remained guitarist and vocalist Jerry GARCIA, drummers Mickey Hart and Bill Kreutzmann, bassist Phil Lesh, and guitarist Bob Weir. Lyricist Robert Hunter has collaborated frequently with Garcia on Dead songs, while lyricist John Barlow has done the same with Weir. While live performance—and not recordings—remain the strength of the Dead, the band has produced a large number of albums. Notable among them are *Anthem of the Sun* (1968), *Live/Dead* (1970), *Workingman's Dead* (1970), *American Beauty* (1970), *In the Dark* (1987) and *Dylan and the Dead* (1988), a collaboration with Bob DYLAN.

**Graves, Michael** (*1934– *) American architect and designer known for his leading role in the development of the design direction generally called POSTMODERNISM. Graves was trained as an architect at the University of Cincinnati and at Harvard, graduating in 1959. He worked for a time in the office of George Nelson in New York and then, in 1960, went to Rome for two years at the American Academy on a Prix de Rome fellowship. In 1962 he returned to Princeton, N.J., to take a teaching post at Princeton University and to establish a practice. In the 1970s he became known as one of the New York Five (also informally called "The Whites"), a group recognized for their abstract and puristic work in a Late Modern vocabulary. Toward the end of the 1970s, raves pulled away from this group. Graves has completed a number of residential projects, shops, and showrooms and has been at work on designs for the expansion of the Whitney Museum in New York, which involves a major addition to the existing structure by Marcel BREUER. He has received many honors and awards, including seven Honor Awards from the American Institute of Architects and the Brunner Memorial prize from the American Academy and Institute of Arts and Letters. Two volumes titled *Michael Graves: Buildings and Projects* published in 1983 and 1988 document his work.

**Graves, Morris** (*1910–2001*) American painter. Born in Fox Valley, Oregon, he studied with Mark Tobey, who introduced him to the delicate calligraphic "white writing" he later employed in his ethereal paintings. Interested in the philosophies of the Orient, with an emphasis on Zen Buddhism, Graves traveled widely in the East and in Europe before settling in the wilds of Washington state. His first one-man show was held in Seattle in 1936. Graves's most memorable paintings contain the beautifully drawn, ghostly birds that have become emblematic of his enigmatic work. Among his characteristic works are *Bird Singing in the Moonlight* (1938–40), *Blind Bird* (1940), both in the collection of New York's Museum of Modern Art, and *Spirit Bird* (1954).

**Graves, Robert von Ranke** (*1895–1985*) British poet. Graves spent most of his life on the Spanish island of Majorca, taking up residence there in 1929. He was considered by many to be second only to William Butler YEATS among 20th-century authors of love poetry in English. Although he considered himself primarily a poet, Graves was also a distinguished prose stylist and a noted classical scholar, translator and historical novelist. He wrote well over 100 individual volumes. Some 40 years after their first publication, his two novels about the Roman emperor Claudius, *I, Claudius* (1934) and *Claudius the God* (1934), became the basis for an extremely successful BBC miniseries in the 1970s. Among the best known of his other books were his 1929 autobiography *Goodbye to All That* and his highly speculative and controversial 1948 study of poetic myth, *The White Goddess*.

**Gray, Eileen** (*1878–1976*) Irish-born interior, furniture, and architectural designer whose Paris-based career spanned a stylistic range from ART DECO to the MODERNISM of the INTERNATIONAL STYLE. Gray studied at the Slade School of Art in London before moving to Paris in 1902. After World War I, her work was extended to include the design of carpets in abstract patterns and interior design and decoration. She opened her own Paris gallery in 1922 to show her furniture, lamps, carpets and lacquer work. Her work was admired by such leading modernists as J.J.P. Oud and LE CORBUSIER. Her furniture design used glass, mirror, ALUMINUM and CHROMIUM-plated metal in geometric forms typical of the modernism of the 1930s. In spite of her outstanding work, Gray was largely forgotten after World War II; her name scarcely figures in most histories of the period. She was rediscovered in the 1960s and is now viewed as a significant figure in the development of modern design. Her designs are still manufactured. Gray was a lively figure, known as a great beauty as well as an adventurous personality—an aviation enthusiast who made an English Channel crossing in a balloon in 1909 with the Hon. C. S. Rolls of Rolls-Royce fame.

**Gray, Francine du Plessix** (*1930– *) Franco-American journalist and author. Gray started her journalistic career working for United Press International, and later became a columnist for THE NEW YORKER. Grey's first books were nonfiction and include *Divine Disobedience: Profiles in Catholic Radicalism* (1970) and *Hawaii: The Sugar-Coated Fortress* (1972). Her first novel, *Lovers and Tyrants* (1976), is a highly autobiographical collection of chronological pieces following the life of the heroine, Stephanie. The novel's theme, that women are held back by those who profess to love them, struck a feminist chord of the time, and was praised for its intelligent writing (see FEMINISM). Later works include the novel *World without End* (1981) and the nonfiction *Soviet Women: Walking the Tightrope* (1990). In 1999 she published a highly acclaimed study of the marquis de Sade's relations with the women in his life, *At Home with the Marquis de Sade*. Six years later she brought out an affectionate memoir of her Russian émigré mother and step-father titled *Them* (2005).

**Graziano, Rocky (Thomas Rocco Barbella)** *(1921–1990)* American boxer. For much of the 1940s and 1950s Graziano reigned as middle-weight boxing champion, compiling a record of 67 wins, 10 losses and six draws from 1942 to 1952. Although he was not noted for his boxing skills or finesse, his brawling style made him a fan favorite. Three of his bouts, with Tony Zale in 1946, 1947 and 1948, were considered classics. In 1956, his autobiography *Somebody Up There Likes Me* was made into a film starring Paul Newman. Graziano went onto a successful career as an entertainer and commercial spokesman. He was elected to the Boxing Hall of Fame in 1971.

**Great Books Program** A foundation organized in Chicago in 1947 with Dr. Robert Maynard Hutchins, former president of the University of Chicago, as its chairman to promote the reading of a list of classics compiled by Mortimer J. Adler. Groups formed across the country to read and discuss the works. The foundation, in conjunction with the *Encyclopaedia Britannica* Educational Corp. and the University of Chicago published a series, *Great Books of the Western World,* which was sold with a two-volume Syntopicon index. The series was edited by Hutchins and Adler.

**Great Depression** A worldwide economic crisis during the 1930s. In its magnitude and effects, the Great Depression is considered the 20th century's most severe peacetime crisis. Millions of people lost their jobs, their homes and their savings, and large segments of the economy came to a virtual standstill. The Stock Market Crash of 1929 is generally considered to mark the beginning of the Great Depression, while the onset of World War II is regarded as its end point. The causes of the Great Depression are not easily understood. Unsound business practices (notably, a widespread reliance on easy credit without the backing of actual wealth), high tariffs and agricultural dislocation as early as the boom period of the 1920s helped set the groundwork for economic depression. At the onset of the depression, U.S. president Herbert

*Unemployed workers sell fruit in New York City during the Great Depression of the 1930s.* (Library of Congress, Prints and Photographs Division)

Hoover believed that the American economy would recover on its own without government intervention. As the depression deepened, he created the Reconstruction Finance Corporation to provide loans to distressed banks and businesses. In 1932, Franklin D. Roosevelt was elected president of the U.S. on his promise to take decisive action to end the depression. In his first Hundred Days in office he prompted Congress to enact far-reaching legislation—known collectively as the New Deal—to provide public relief, create new jobs and stimulate business. Although the New Deal policies did help many Americans, the depression continued through the 1930s, affecting virtually every country in the world. In many areas economic weakness bred political turmoil. In Germany, the chaos of the Great Depression created conditions that brought Adolf Hitler to power, while in Japan the military gained strength. Thus, the anxieties of the Great Depression helped sow the seeds of World War II.

**Great Gatsby, The** Novel of 1925 by F. Scott Fitzgerald, considered a classic of 20th-century American literature. The novel is narrated by Nick Carroway, who tells the story of Jay Gatsby, who has mysteriously amassed a fortune and bought a Long Island estate, and is intent upon pursuing Daisy Buchanon, a distant cousin of Carroway. The novel depicts the extravagance and self-destruction of the wealthy during the Jazz Age in the U.S., and culminates in a murder. Many critics considered *Gatsby* to be Fitzgerald's best and most fully realized book.

**Great Leap Forward** Chinese slogan for a series of radical changes in social and economic policy between 1958 and 1961 under Mao Zedong. Private consumption was cut and material incentives withdrawn. Massive agricultural communes were set up and services by light industrial and construction projects. The program failed following bad harvests and the withdrawal of Soviet technical aid. It is estimated that at least 10 million people died of starvation or diseases related to malnutrition as a result of this spectacular policy failure.

**Great Purge** A repressive wave of terror (1934–38) by which Joseph Stalin aimed at eliminating the opposition. It was followed by a number of show trials that resulted in the arrest, exile or death of about 8–10 million people. In 1934, following the death of Sergei Kirov, which was used as the pretext for the purge, only former political opponents were arrested; but the number and range increased and the arrests became almost indiscriminate. Guilt was established by extracting confessions through torture. The charges made against "the enemies of the people" ranged from treason to sabotage and espionage. NKVD tribunals sentenced the prisoners to death or to long terms of imprisonment in corrective labor camps. Stalin justified the purge by stating that, as progress toward full socialism is realized, the class struggle must be intensified. The result of the purge was to give Stalin supreme power.

**Great Society** Term for the 1960s U.S. domestic programs of the John-

SON administration. The phrase comes from a speech delivered by President Johnson on May 23, 1964. Some Great Society legislation included: in 1964—the CIVIL RIGHTS ACT; the Revenue Act, which reduced taxes; the Food Stamp Act; the Economic Opportunity Act (also called "the War on Poverty"). In 1965—MEDICARE and MEDICAID; the sweeping Elementary and Secondary Education Act; the Higher Education Act, which provided student aid; the creation of the Department of Housing and Urban Development; and the VOTING RIGHTS ACT OF 1965. In 1968—the Housing and Urban Development Act.

**Great Train Robbery** Popular name for the robbery of a Glasgow-to-London mail train on August 8, 1963. The robbery was executed by a gang of 20 to 30 masked robbers some 35 miles northwest of London and netted more than $7 million, making it the largest armed robbery to date. Detectives investigating the crime discovered the robbers' hideout, an isolated rural English cottage, on August 13. In 1964, 12 Britons were found guilty of involvement in the robbery and sentenced to prison terms ranging up to 30 years. However, only about $1 million of the stolen money was ever recovered.

**Grechaninov, Alexander Tikhonovich** *(1864–1956)* Russian composer. He studied at the St. Petersburg Conservatory under Rimsky-Korsakov and at the Moscow Conservatory with Vassily Ilich Safonov. In 1922 he made his first European tour. He lived in Paris from 1925 and finally settled in the U.S. His works comprise operas, including *Dobrynya Nikitich* (1902) and *Sister Beatrice* (1912), five symphonies, chamber music, Catholic church music, piano pieces, songs and folk songs. He intended his *Missa Oecumenica,* which was performed in Boston in 1944, to unite all creeds, both Eastern and Western.

**Greco, José** *(1919–2000)* Spanish dancer. Greco studied Spanish dance with "La Argentinita" (Encarnación López Julvez) and partnered her from 1943 to 1945. He subsequently partnered her sister Pilar López from 1946 to 1948, before forming his own Spanish dance company in 1949. His company has toured the world, and he has appeared in many films and television productions. Greco has become one of the most influential and popular Spanish dancers in America as well as worldwide. He retired in 1974 and established the Foundation for Hispanic Dance.

**Greco-Turkish War of 1921–22** Turkish resistance to Allied dismemberment of the OTTOMAN EMPIRE, led by Mustapha Kemal ATATÜRK, included expelling the Greek army from western Anatolia. Granted the Smyrna (Izmir) region by the Treaty of SÈVRES (1920), the Greeks attempted to gain Thrace and much of Anatolia. Despite inadequate supplies, Greek forces advanced on Eskisehir, were repulsed (January and March, 1921), but moved toward Ankara. Seriously defeated at Sakarya River (August 24–September 16, 1921), they began a year-long retreat to Smyrna, which Atatürk's forces besieged and captured September 11, 1922, killing thousands of Greeks. The Treaty of LAUSANNE (July 24, 1923) ended the war, forcing Greece to remove all occupation forces, return eastern Thrace and Turkish islands, and exchange Greece's Turkish minority people for Greek inhabitants of the Ottoman Empire.

**Greece (Hellenic Republic)** Greece is located on the southern end of the Balkan Peninsula in southeast Europe and covers a total area of 509,930 square miles, including over 1,400 Aegean and Ionian islands. During the BALKAN WARS (1912–13) the country

| GREECE | |
|---|---|
| 1913 | Greece acquires additional territory in Macedonia and Thrace following the Balkan Wars. |
| 1917 | Abdication of King Constantine I; Greece enters World War I on side of Allies. |
| 1935 | Restoration of monarchy under King George II. |
| 1936 | General Metaxas, named prime minister by George II, establishes fascist-style dictatorship. |
| 1940 | Greece repels attempted Italian invasion in World War II. |
| 1941 | Germany invades and occupies Greece. |
| 1944–49 | Civil War between communists and royalists; communists defeated. |
| 1952 | Greece joins NATO. |
| 1964 | Ascension of King Constantine II. |
| 1967 | Military coup brings right-wing colonels to power; constitutional rule suspended; Constantine II goes into exile after his failed attempt to depose the colonels. |
| 1973 | Monarchy formally abolished. |
| 1974 | War with Turkey over Cyprus leads to fall of military government; democratic government restored under Prime Minister Constantine Karamanlis. |
| 1975 | New constitution establishes a democratic republic. |
| 1981 | Greece joins European Community; socialist George Papandreou becomes prime minister. |
| 1989 | Papandreou steps down amid personal and political controversy. |
| 2000 | President Stephanopoulos is reelected; Turkey and Greece sign agreements pledging more cordial relations. |
| 2001 | Greece adopts the euro. |
| 2004 | Greece hosts Olympic Games in Athens. |

acquired Crete to the south and the eastern Aegean islands. After fighting with the Allies during World War I, Greece entered a period of political turmoil, swinging from a monarchy under George II (1922–24) to a republic (1924–35) to restoration of the king (1935–40). German occupation of Greece during WORLD WAR II gave way to the GREEK CIVIL WAR between communists and pro-democracy forces, which ended with the restoration of the monarchy in 1946. Subsequent elections brought power struggles, military coups and the eventual exile of King CONSTANTINE II (1967). TURKEY's invasion of CYPRUS in 1974 brought the end of military rule in Greece and in 1975 the adoption of a new constitution declaring a democratic republic. In 1981 Greece elected its first socialist government and joined the European Communities. Controversy over U.S. bases in Greece, a financial scandal involving government officials and another scandal surrounding powerful political leader George PAPANDREOU in 1988, plus a worsening economy, dominated the political scene in the last two decades of the 20th century. In January 2001 Greece replaced its currency, the drachma, with the new currency of the EUROPEAN UNION, the EURO. In the summer of 2004 it hosted the Olympics in Athens.

**Greek Civil War** War of 1944–49 between communists and pro-Western royalists in GREECE. In December 1944–January 1945, toward the end of WORLD WAR II, Greek communist guerrilla forces attempted to take over Greece, but were defeated. A British-arranged truce between leftists and moderates ultimately resulted in the restoration of the monarchy. In late 1946, communists reopened the war with support from ALBANIA, BULGARIA and YUGOSLAVIA. The Greek government, with British and American aid (the latter under the TRUMAN DOCTRINE), drove out the communist rebels with UNITED NATIONS support. The Greek communists announced the end of the war on October 16, 1949. About 50,000 combatants died in this conflict. The Greek Civil War was viewed as the first U.S. effort to halt the spread of COMMUNISM in the post–World War II era; it marked the opening phase of the COLD WAR.

**Green, William** (1873–1952) American labor leader. Born in Coshocton, Ohio, Green was a coal miner and a local miners' union leader while still a teenager, rising to become secretary-treasurer of the United Mine Workers of America (1912–24). In 1924 Green was elected to succeed the recently deceased Samuel GOMPERS as president of the AMERICAN FEDERATION OF LABOR (AFL), a post he held until his death. During Green's period of leadership a rift between craft and industrial unions deepened, provoking a 1935 schism that resulted in the formation of the CONGRESS OF INDUSTRIAL ORGANIZATIONS (CIO). Green's labor movement philosophy is expressed in his book Labor and Democracy (1939).

**green belt** Term, used in town planning, that describes a large tract of land around a city, on which building is not permitted. The green belt concept originated in the UNITED KINGDOM and was first put into practice after the end of

World War II. British planners realized that cities ought not to spread out into the surrounding countryside through unlimited building, and that rural areas ought to be preserved. Relatively small NEW TOWNS were built in and around green belt areas to help relieve overcrowding in large existing cities, notably LONDON.

**Greenberg, Hank (Henry Benjamin Greenberg)** *(1911–1986)* American baseball player. Greenberg led the American League in home runs five times while playing first base and outfield for the Detroit Tigers in the 1930s and 1940s. He was voted the American League's most valuable player in 1935 and 1940. In 1938 he hit 58 home runs, two shy of the 1927 record set by Babe RUTH. His career was plagued by injuries and interrupted by World War II, but his lifetime home run total was 331, with a lifetime batting average of .313. After his retirement in 1947, he held front-office jobs with the Cleveland Indians and Chicago White Sox. In 1956 Greenberg became the first Jewish player elected to the Baseball Hall of Fame.

**Greene, Graham** *(1904–1991)* British novelist and man of letters. Greene is perhaps the preeminent British writer of the second half of this century. He is, beyond question, one of the most prolific and versatile writers of modern times, having created both serious novels and what Greene calls "entertainments," as well as screenplays, film criticism, political analyses, travel books, literary biographies, critical essays and an autobiography. Educated at Oxford, Greene converted to Roman Catholicism in 1926. The travails of political conscience and religious doubt are two recurring themes in his works. Major works of fiction by Greene include *Orient Express* (1933), *England Made Me* (1935), *The Power and the Glory* (1940), *The Quiet American* (1955), *Our Man in Havana* (1958), *The Honorary Consul* (1973), *The Human Factor* (1978), and *Monsieur Quixote* (1982). Greene has written two volumes of autobiography, *A Sort of Life* (1971) and *Ways of Escape* (1980). Greene was reportedly a candidate for the NOBEL PRIZE in literature on numerous occasions but never received the award.

**greenhouse effect** Term used to explain the theory of GLOBAL WARMING. According to many scientists, the greenhouse effect is caused by the buildup in the atmosphere of carbon dioxide from industry, agriculture and the burning of fossil fuels. The carbon dioxide causes heat from the sun to be trapped near the Earth's surface, much in the way that glass traps heat in a greenhouse. Scientific opinion as to whether there actually is a greenhouse effect is mixed. A UN report in 1990 concluded that the Earth's surface and lower atmosphere had warmed by 0.3 to 1.1 degrees Fahrenheit in the last century and could be expected to warm by another 2.7 to 8 degrees Fahrenheit in the next century. However, according to a study published in *Science* (March 30, 1990), microwave temperature data collected by U.S. weather satellites from 1979 through 1988 showed no evidence of a global warming from the greenhouse effect. If the "effect" proves valid, it may have dire consequences for the Earth and its inhabitants in the next century.

**Greenland** Bounded on the north by the Arctic Ocean and on the west, south and east by various arms of the North Atlantic, including Baffin Bay and the Greenland Sea, the island of Greenland covers 839,782 square miles—only 131,896 square miles of it free of ice. Ancient claims to the island by Denmark and Norway were resolved by the International Court of Justice in 1933, granting Denmark sovereignty. Greenland became an integral part of Denmark in 1953 and joined the various European Communities (EC), though its populace was opposed to this. Internal autonomy was achieved in 1979, resulting in the island's withdrawal from the EC in 1985. Recently, Greenland has been divided over the status of U.S. bases, established on the island during World War II.

**Greenpeace** International organization known for its active efforts to protect the ocean environment and aquatic wildlife. Founded in Canada in 1969, Greenpeace has been at the forefront of the "save the whales" movement and worked for a worldwide ban on whale hunting. The group also attracted international attention in its efforts to stop the annual "cull" of baby seals off the coast of Newfoundland in the 1980s. Greenpeace does not rely solely on publicity to achieve its aims, but confronts hunters directly with its own fleet of boats. For example, in its "save the whales" campaign, Greenpeace boats mingle with boats of the hunting fleet and try to disrupt the hunt. Greenpeace became involved in an international incident in 1985 when one of its ships, the *Rainbow Warrior,* was sunk in Auckland harbor, New Zealand. The ship was about to sail into a nuclear test area in an effort to disrupt French atomic weapons testing in the South Pacific. It was subsequently revealed that French frogmen had sunk the ship on the orders of the French government, and the French defense minister was forced to resign.

**Greens** Originally and principally, the German (originally West German) Ecology Party, which first emerged as a political force in Bremen in 1979, when environmentalists and antinuclear groups won 5.9 percent of the seats in the Land (federal state) parliament. Greens were subsequently elected to other Land parliaments and to the BUNDESTAG, and similar parties had success in other West European countries. In 1998 the German Green Party entered in a coalition government with the Social Democrats, and one of its leaders, Joschka FISCHER, became Germany's foreign minister. The **British Ecology Party** changed its name to the Greens in 1985.

**Greenspan, Alan** *(1926– )* American economist, chairman of the Council of Economic Advisors (1974–77) and of the Federal Reserve Board (1987– ). Born in New York City, Greenspan studied economics at Columbia University under future Federal Reserve chairman Arthur BURNS and taught economics classes at that institution (1953–55). After leaving Columbia, Greenspan formed a consulting firm that he ran until his departure from the private sector in 1974.

One of the profound ideological influences in Greenspan's life was his friendship with the novelist and philosopher Ayn RAND, whose fictional and nonfictional works promoted "objectivism," a value system that trumpeted free-market capitalism and an individualistic lifestyle. Ayn Rand helped persuade Greenspan to join Richard NIXON's 1968 presidential campaign. Six years later, after several informal consultations with the president, Greenspan became chairman of the Council of Economic Advisors. When Nixon resigned in 1974, Greenspan remained in office during the Gerald FORD administration. When Ford's brief tenure as U.S. president ended in January 1977, Greenspan left the public sector and subsequently served on the boards of several American corporations. He returned to government service when President Ronald REAGAN appointed him chairman of the Federal Reserve in 1987. During his years as chairman, Greenspan sought to use his position to reduce government involvement in the economy and promote greater deregulation of the national banking industry. Although a Republican, Greenspan openly supported Democratic president Bill CLINTON's plan to reduce the federal deficit by cutting government spending and using the savings to pay off part of the national debt. When Clinton left office in 2001, Greenspan remained chairman under the presidency of George W. BUSH. Although early on in the Bush administration he agreed that Bush's proposed 2001 tax cut would stimulate greater economic growth, he disagreed with the president over the general health of the economy. In particular, Greenspan had earlier (in the 1990s) expressed concern over the "irrational exuberance" that investors and observers had demonstrated in buying up speculative shares in unproven companies, particularly in the high technology sector. When stock market prices declined in 2000, and especially after the terrorist attacks on SEPTEMBER 11, 2001, Greenspan responded by reducing interest rates in order to stimulate lending to businesses that would generate increased consumer spending and promote confidence in the economy. Over the course of his career as chairman of the Federal Reserve, Greenspan presided over the longest period of uninterrupted economic growth in American history. He retired in 2006 and was replaced as Fed chairman by Ben Bernanke.

**Greenwich Village** Bohemian residential district of lower Manhattan in the U.S.'s NEW YORK CITY; extending south from 14th St. to Houston St. and west from Washington Square to the Hudson River. In recent decades "Greenwich Village" has come to signify three distinct areas: the West Village, roughly west of Seventh Avenue; Greenwich Village proper, west of Broadway; and the East Village, east of Broadway. An influx of foreign immigrants settled here and nearby on the Lower East Side after 1880, and by 1901 it was already famous as a hotbed of avant-garde artists, radicals and freethinkers. Its longtime reputation was reinforced in the Beat era of the 1950s (see BEAT GENERATION) and the Flower-Power 1960s when the artists, poets and writers were joined by musicians, religious cultists, HIPPIES, homosexuals and just about anyone that the larger society considered different—all of it supported by cafés, galleries and clubs for jazz, folk and every other kind of music. Among the district's 20th-century residents were writers MILLAY, WHARTON, O'NEILL, DOS PASSOS, AUDEN, Dylan THOMAS; painters HOPPER and SLOAN; and journalist John REED.

**Greer, Germaine** *(1939– )* Australian author and feminist. Greer's controversial first book, *The Female Eunuch* (1971) brought her instant international celebrity and made her reputation as a leading figure in FEMINISM and the WOMEN's MOVEMENT. The book argued that women's sexuality has been denied and misrepresented as passivity, and that the stereotypical feminine behavior societally imposed on women is essentially that of a eunuch. Her subsequent and varied works include *Sex and Destiny* (1984), *Shakespeare* (1986) and *Daddy, We Hardly Knew You* (1989). An English scholar, Greer was latterly a special lecturer at Newnham College, Cambridge.

**Gregory, (Isabella) Augusta, Lady (née Persse)** *(1852–1932)* Irish playwright and patroness of the arts. An Irish nationalist instrumental in the IRISH LITERARY REVIVAL, Lady Gregory was a cofounder of the ABBEY THEATRE along with W. YEATS and J. M. SYNGE. Her many plays, which include *Spreading the News* (1904), *The Goal Gate* (1906) and *Dervorgilla* (1906) were written in Irish dialect and celebrated Irish tradition and folklore. She also translated the works of Molière for the Irish theater and collaborated with Yeats on numerous plays, including *Cathleen ni Houlihan* (1902). She successfully fought the censorship of Synge's *PLAYBOY OF THE WESTERN WORLD* and G. B. SHAW's *The Shewing up of Blanco Posnet*. Her house at Coole Park in County Galway was for many years a second home for some of IRELAND's leading literary figures. Lady Gregory recorded her memoirs of the early days of the Abbey in *Our Irish Theatre* (1913).

**Gregory, Cynthia** *(1946– )* American ballerina. Known for her technical skill and purity of line in such classical ballets as *Swan Lake,* Gregory first danced with the San Francisco Ballet (1961–65). She joined AMERICAN BALLET THEATRE (ABT) in 1965 as a principal dancer and created roles in many ballets, including Alvin AILEY's *The River* (1971) and Rudolph NUREYEV's production of *Raymonda* (1975). Acclaimed as one of America's outstanding prima ballerinas, she dances in works from ABT's modern repertory, such as *Dark Elegies* and *Theme and Variations,* as well as in the classical ballets. In 1991 Gregory gave her farewell performance dancing opposite Fernando Bujones as Odette-Odile in *Swan Lake.*

**Grenada** The most southerly of the Windward Islands in the eastern Caribbean Sea, Grenada has a total land area of 132.8 square miles, which includes the dependent islands of the Southern Grenadines to the north-northwest. Grenada attained full independence from Britain in 1974, and Sir Eric Gairy became premier. His corrupt regime was overthrown in a bloodless coup in 1979 by left-wing rebels led by Maurice Bishop. Bishop's failure to draft a new constitution or to hold elections, as well as his growing alignment with CUBA, resulted in another coup in 1983 during which Bishop and his associates were murdered by extremist elements in his movement. This led to the invasion of Grenada by troops from the UNITED STATES in October 1983. Afterward, the constitution was restored, and elections were held in 1984. Since the end of the COLD WAR in 1991, Grenada has attempted to improve relations with foreign countries, particularly the U.S., by forming a series of centrist coalition governments. However, repeated alle-

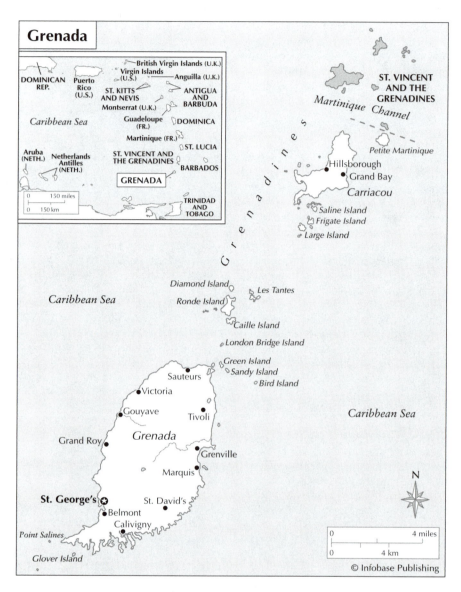

Grenada

gations of Grenada's complicity in money laundering schemes resulted in strained relations between the island and states such as Canada, China, France and the U.S. until Grenada began cooperating with international financial investigations in 2002.

**Grenfell, Joyce (Joyce Irene Phipps Grenfell)** *(1910–1979)* British actress and film comedienne. For more than 40 years, Grenfell was a popular fixture on stage, screen, radio and television. Her career included appearances in numerous revues, plays, one-woman shows, radio and television programs and international tours to Australia, Canada and the U.S. She also entertained Allied troops during WORLD WAR II. She used her long, toothy visage to create the character of a dotty, upperclass English spinster whom she made vastly popular with her audiences.

**Gresley, Sir Herbert Nigel** *(1876–1941)* British engineer known for the design of railroad locomotives, including streamlined types that achieved outstanding performance and speed. Gresley was in charge of locomotive design for the Great Northern Railway, and after World War I when British railway systems were reorganized, he became chief mechanical engineer for the newly created London & North Eastern Railway. In 1923, his design for a Pacific locomotive (with 4-6-2 wheel arrangement) became a new standard for both

### GRENADA

| | |
|---|---|
| 1974 | Grenada proclaims independence, as riots against Prime Minister Eric Gairy rock the island. |
| 1979 | Gairy is overthrown in a coup led by Maurice Bishop. The constitution and parliament are retained. A two-year technical pact is signed with Havana. |
| 1983 | Bishop is ousted, placed under house arrest, and later executed. U.S. and Organization of Eastern Caribbean States (OECS) forces invade the island and, after heavy fighting, capture General Austin, Bernard Coard, and other coup leaders. |
| 1984 | Elections are held |
| 1985 | The House of Representatives validates all laws enacted during the suspension of the constitution from March 1979 to November 1983. |
| 1991 | Grenada joins the OECS. |
| 1996 | Grenada signs two treaties with the U.S. |
| 2004 | Hurricane Ivan devastates the island. More than 90% of homes are damaged or destroyed. |

freight and passenger service. Beginning in 1932, a drive for speed records developed in English railroading, and in 1934, a Gresley Pacific pulling the *Flying Scotsman* reached a peak speed of 100 mph. The first streamlined Gresley Pacifics were of the A4 class of 1935, with the famous MALLARD setting a record speed of 126 mph in 1938. These locomotives were also notable for their reliability and performance in routine service in which they maintained high speeds over long runs in regularly scheduled service. Gresley was knighted in recognition of his achievements.

**Gretzky, Wayne** *(1961–    )* Canadian ice hockey player. Born in Edmonton, Alberta, Gretzky is considered possibly the greatest player in the history of the game. He entered the National Hockey League in 1979 and played center for eight seasons for the Edmonton Oilers, leading them to four Stanley Cup championships. In 1988 he was traded to the Los Angeles Kings. On October 15, 1989, playing against his former team in his 780th game, he broke the NHL's all-time record for scoring points set by Gordie HOWE. Gretzky's lifetime record at the end of that game stood at 642 goals and 1,210 assists for a total of 1,852 points. Gretzky was the NHL's scoring leader every season from 1981 through 1987 (an NHL record) and won the Hart Trophy for most valuable player each of those years as well as in 1989, also a record. In the 1995–96 season the Kings traded Gretzky to the Saint Louis Blues, but Gretzky became a free agent at the end of the season and signed with the New York Rangers, where he finished his career in April 1999. In that same year Gretzky was voted into the Hockey Hall of Fame. In 2000 he became part-owner of the Phoenix Coyotes NHL team and in 2004 became their head coach. Gretzky also helps manage Canada's national hockey team, leading them to a gold medal in the 2002 Winter Olympics.

**Grey, Sir Edward (Viscount Grey of Fallodon, 1916)** *(1862–1933)* British statesman. Educated at Oxford, he was elected to Parliament as a Liberal in 1885, becoming foreign secretary in the years preceding WORLD WAR I (1905–16). During this period, he supported France in the Moroccan crises

of 1905 and 1911, concluded the ANGLO-RUSSIAN ENTENTE of 1907 and convened the London Peace Conference (1912–13) to negotiate an end to the BALKAN WARS. While hating the idea of war, the German violation of Belgian neutrality caused Grey in 1914 to urge Britain's entrance into WORLD WAR I. After the war, he championed the LEAGUE OF NATIONS and served as a special ambassador to the U.S. from 1919 to 1920.

**Grey, Zane** *(1875–1939)* American author of popular western fiction and nonfictional works on deep-sea and freshwater fishing. After graduating from the University of Pennsylvania in 1896, Grey practiced dentistry before turning to writing. He published his first novel, *Betty Zane,* in 1904 and his famous *Riders of the Purple Sage* in 1912. Grey swiftly became a staple on national bestseller lists and his works have remained continuously in print.

**Grierson, John** *(1898–1972)* Motion picture producer, director and prominent leader in the British and Canadian documentary film movements. The son of a Scots schoolmaster, he studied philosophy at Glasgow University and social sciences in Chicago. Convinced that cinema presented an unparalleled mode of rhetoric and persuasion, he produced films about British trade and unity for the Empire Marketing Board (EMB). *Drifters* (1929) his first film, eschewed the romantic approach to picturesque fishing villages and replaced it with a contemporary "epic of steam and steel," depicting the modernization of the fishing trade. With his EMB Film Unit, an important group of rising young filmmakers, he produced over a hundred such films between 1930 and 1933. (After 1934 the Film Unit moved to the General Post Office and became known as the CROWN FILM UNIT.) In 1938 Grierson relocated to Canada, where he became film commissioner and the founder of the world-renowned Canadian Film Board. He continued throughout the postwar years to work tirelessly on behalf of the documentary film, forming International Film Associates in 1945, the Mass Communications and Public Information Department for UNESCO, and producing television documentaries in Scotland. By contrast to colleague Robert

FLAHERTY (with whom he worked for a brief period in the early 1930s), Grierson placed document and ideology ahead of poetry and entertainment. "I look on cinema as a pulpit," he said in his numerous treatises and theoretical writings, "and use it as a propagandist." The working person was his constant subject and his sympathies with labor issues and problems frequently ran him afoul of the government agencies that employed him. It was Grierson who first coined the term "documentary"—in a 1926 review of Flaherty's *Moana.*

**Griffes, Charles Tomlinson** *(1884–1920)* American composer. Born in Elmira, N.Y., Griffes studied in Berlin, where he was a pupil of Engelbert Humperdinck, who encouraged his work as a composer. After returning to the U.S., Griffes taught music in a Tarrytown, N.Y., boys school until his death. Influenced by French and Russian music, he developed an impressionist style that later matured into an extremely individualistic mode of expression. His numerous compositions include the *Roman Sketches* (1915–16), piano pieces that include the well-known *White Peacock;* the orchestral work *The Pleasure-Dome of Kubla Khan* (1920) and the piano sonata (published 1921). Among his other works are chamber music, pieces for the theater and songs.

**Griffin, John Howard** *(1920–1980)* American author. In 1959 Griffin decided to get a firsthand picture of the treatment of blacks in the American South by posing as a black man. He temporarily altered his skin color by using chemicals and ultraviolet light, then traveled throughout the South for six weeks. He chronicled his experiences in the book *Black Like Me,* which sold more than a million copies over the next several years and was made into a film.

**Griffith, Arthur** *(1872–1922)* Irish statesman and nationalist. Griffith was a pivotal figure in the Irish HOME RULE movement. In 1905 he helped found SINN FÉIN, a political party that advocated a separate Irish Parliament. When in 1916 he was elected to Parliament (British), he refused to serve. Instead he helped found the Irish revolutionary assembly, the DÁIL ÉIREANN.

He was imprisoned by the British several times (1916–18). In 1921 Griffith lead the delegation that negotiated the Treaty of Westminster, which created the Irish Free State.

**Griffith, D(avid) W(ark)** *(1875–1948)*. America's greatest filmmaker during the SILENT FILM period and one of the most important influences on the course of international cinema. Raised in Louisville, Ky., under the influence of his father, a Civil War veteran, Griffith was steeped in the romance and chivalry of the Old South. Under the stage name of Lawrence Griffith he unsuccessfully tried acting and writing for the stage. Reluctantly, he turned to the new medium of motion pictures and gained a featured role in an Edwin S. Porter film, *Rescued from an Eagle's Nest* (1907). However, it was as a director, not an actor or writer, that Griffith soon made his way. From 1908 to 1913 he directed virtually all the short films for the popular BIOGRAPH COMPANY, forging a stock company that included Lillian GISH and her sister Dorothy, and consolidating most of the technical and stylistic advances in the medium—dramatic use of close-ups, parallel editing, moving camera, historical reenactments, multiple-reel narratives and flashbacks. He brought a stinging satiric lash to the traditional forms of melodrama he knew from his itinerant years on the stage. His greatest international success and his most ambitious films come from the 1913–24 period. He released through Mutual, UNITED ARTISTS, and PARAMOUNT classics like *THE BIRTH OF A NATION* (1915), *Intolerance* (1916), *Broken Blossoms* (1919), *Way Down East* (1920), *Orphans of the Storm* (1922), *America* (1924) and *Sally of the Sawdust* (1924); in 1919 he moved to his own production facility in Mamaroneck, N.Y. Often working from sketchy scripts and frequently with his favorite cameraman, G. W. ("Billy") Bitzer, Griffith produced a body of work that vaulted American cinema into worldwide prominence and prestige. Griffith's last years, however, saw a decline in his personal fortunes and an increasingly sophisticated audience impatient with his by-now "old-fashioned" style. Viewers laughed at his last film *The Struggle* (1931), a creaky drama of alcoholism. Except for an "honorary" ACADEMY AWARD in 1935 for his "distinguished creative achievements," Griffith spent his last years in relative obscurity. He died, bitter, lonely, and virtually forgotten, from a cerebral hemorrhage in a Hollywood hotel room at age 73.

**Grigorenko, Pyotr Grigorevich** *(1907–1987)* Soviet military hero and dissident. Grigorenko won distinction in WORLD WAR II, but was later critical of the Soviet establishment. In 1961 he was stripped of his rank of major general, and was later committed to a series of mental hospitals—standard punishment for political dissidents in the USSR at that time. After being allowed to go to the U.S. for medical treatment in 1977, he was stripped of his Soviet citizenship.

**Grimes, Martha** *(1931–  )* American novelist. Like P. D. JAMES, Grimes followed the model established earlier in the century by Dorothy SAYERS, writing detective novels of literary merit. Her first 11 novels, whose titles are the names of pubs featured in the text, are set in an England both real and imagined. Rich in geographical and psychological detail, as well as wit, they explore human fallibility, familial relationships, childhood and the nature of good and evil. Grimes shows that trust is the basis of social order, although it can be exploited. She taught writing at Johns Hopkins University. Her books include *The Man with a Load of Mischief* (1981), *The Old Fox Deceived* (1982), *The Old Silent* (1989) and *The Old Contemptibles* (1991). *The End of the Pier* (1992) marked a departure for Grimes, as the novel is set in western Maryland in the U.S.

**Grin, Alexander** (**Alexander Stepanovich Grinevsky**) *(1880–1932)* Russian writer. As a schoolboy Grin read avidly, although he was at times suspended from school for laziness. After a short time in the merchant marine he led a tramp's existence, and finally started a career as a writer. After fighting with the Red Army, ill and penniless he was rescued by Maxim GORKY. A chronic alcoholic, he spent the last few years of his life as a failed writer and geography teacher, turned to carving for a living, and died in poverty. His stories, frequently romantic and exotic in flavor, are underestimated by Soviet critics, but they convey the turmoil the Soviet Union was undergoing. His best known works include *The Ratcatcher* (1924), *Fantastic Tales* and *The Road to Nowhere* (1930).

**Gris, Juan** *(1887–1927)* Spanish painter. Gris was a key figure in the artistic school of CUBISM and was heavily influenced by Pablo PICASSO. Gris first came to Paris in 1906 and lived for a time as Picasso's neighbor. But Gris did not begin to paint until 1910. His first major painting, *Hommage à Picasso,* was shown at the influential Salon des Indépendants exhibition of 1912. Gris is considered representative of the "synthetic" phase of cubism that followed after the initial "analytic" phase developed by Picasso and Georges BRAQUE. For Gris, the primary function of the artist was to transform the general concepts of the intellect and the imagination into unique yet comprehensible concrete forms. He was fond of comparing painting to mathematics and architecture in that it was a systematic means of representing the world and the evolving nature of human truth.

**Grishchenko, Anatoly** *(1935–1990)* Soviet aviator. He became a hero by flying his helicopter repeatedly over the site of the 1986 CHERNOBYL nuclear power plant disaster and dumping tons of sand and cement over the smoldering reactor. His actions were credited with helping to limit the effects of the disaster. He was given the SOVIET UNION's highest award for heroism. His death from leukemia was believed to have been radiation-induced.

**Grissom, Virgil "Gus"** *(1926–1967)* U.S. astronaut; one of the seven original MERCURY astronauts selected by NASA in April 1959. Grissom died in America's first major space tragedy, the APOLLO 1 fire on January 27, 1967—a tragedy waiting to happen. Grissom, who had flown a suborbital flight aboard *Liberty Bell 7* (July 21, 1961) as part of the Mercury-Redstone series and a GEMINI flight with John YOUNG (March 23, 1965), had been apprehensive about *Apollo 1.* More than 20,000 test failures of the spacecraft cabin and engines had been recorded—and did not inspire confidence. A week before the fatal accident that took the lives of Grissom and fellow astronauts Roger CHAF-FEE and Edward WHITE, Grissom had hung a lemon inside the cabin, signifying his opinion of the craft. Tragedy struck—sudden and deadly—during a routine simulated flight. With the three astronauts sealed inside the Apollo command module, a fire broke out, turning the cabin into a blazing, smoke-filled death trap, killing the three men in a matter of minutes. A board of inquiry confirmed the late Grissom's fears. Five factors, the board found, led to the tragedy: an abundance of inflammable materials that produced toxic gases inside the cabin; poorly designed and unprotected electric cables; unprotected tubing, which contained inflammable and corrosive coolant; lack of a suitable escape system for the crew; and the unsettling fact that no fire or emergency crews were even on duty at the time of the accident.

**Griswold v. Connecticut** *(1965)* U.S. Supreme Court case legalizing contraception for married adults. A Connecticut statute imposed an outright ban on the sale of contraceptives. The law was challenged all the way to the U.S. Supreme Court, which struck it down as contrary to the Constitution. Although there is no explicit language regarding sexual practices in the Constitution, the Court, through Justice William O. DOUGLAS's opinion, reasoned that the Bill of Rights created a right of personal privacy. Accordingly, the Court held that a state may not legally impose an outright ban on the sale or use of contraceptives by married adults. The Court later applied this right of privacy to legalize ABORTIONS in the controversial case *ROE V. WADE* (1973).

**Grivas, George** *(1898–1974)* Commander of the Greek Cypriot National Guard. A right-wing Greek army officer, Grivas initiated the guerrilla campaign in CYPRUS in 1953, creating a terrorist movement, EOKA. He was later given command of the Greek Cypriot National Guard, against Archbishop MAKARIOS's wishes. Recalled to Athens in 1971, where he regarded Makarios's acceptance of Commonwealth membership as treason, Grivas later secretly returned to Cyprus (1971–74) and reorganized his followers against Makarios. His divisive legacy contributed to the disastrous coup and subsequent partition of Cyprus in the summer of 1975. (See also Greek-Turkish CYPRIOT WAR OF 1974.)

**Grofé, Ferde** *(1892–1972)* Popular American composer of *The Grand Canyon Suite* and architect of the modern "jazz orchestra" sound. His earliest musical training came from family members in his native New York City. Later in California he wrote arrangements of popular songs in JAZZ idioms for the Paul WHITEMAN Orchestra. His orchestration of George GERSHWIN's *RHAPSODY IN BLUE* was performed (with Gershwin at the piano) in the legendary Whiteman concert, "An Experiment in Modern Music," in New York's Aeolian Hall, February 12, 1924. His remaining years were devoted to a handful of movie scores—including an early talkie epic, *King of Jazz* (1929); *Minstrel Man* (1944), for which he won an ACADEMY AWARD; and a science fiction thriller, *Rocketship X-M* (1950). He also wrote many popular orchestral suites, notably *The Mississippi Suite* (1925) and *The Grand Canyon Suite* (1931). (Several other suites, particularly the *Hudson River Suite* and *The Atlantic Crossing Suite,* are kitschy concoctions marred by the sound effects, respectively, of bowling balls and radio loudspeakers!) His most popular original composition was "On the Trail," from *The Grand Canyon Suite.* It was later adopted as the musical theme for Philip Morris cigarettes.

**Gromyko, Andrei Andreyevich** *(1909–1989)* Soviet diplomat and political figure, foreign minister of the USSR (1957–85). Gromyko served under every Soviet leader from Joseph STALIN to Mikhail GORBACHEV and played a leading role in the conduct of Soviet foreign policy in the post–World War II era. Born to a peasant family in Byelorussia, he joined the COMMUNIST PARTY in 1931 and quickly rose to become a diplomat in the foreign ministry. He was ambassador to the U.S. from 1943 to 1946 and headed the Soviet delegation to the 1944 DUMBARTON OAKS CONFERENCE on the foundation of the UNITED NATIONS. He was subsequently chief permanent Soviet delegate to the UN (1946–48), ambassador to Britain (1952–53) and deputy foreign minister. Named foreign minister in 1957, he played a largely subservient role to the outspoken Soviet leader Nikita KHRUSHCHEV. Under Khrushchev's successor, Leonid I. BREZHNEV, he began to exercise greater control over foreign policy, particularly after he was made a full member of the Politburo in 1973. He helped engineer detente agreements with the U.S. in the 1970s and defended the Soviet invasion of AFGHANISTAN in 1979 and POLAND's martial-law crackdown on SOLIDARITY in 1981. Gromyko played a crucial role in Gorbachev's 1985 rise to power by nominating him as general secretary to the Soviet Communist Party. However, after assuming power, Gorbachev replaced Gromyko with the younger, more flexible Eduard A. SHEVARDNADZE, and relegated Gromyko to the largely ceremonial post of president. On Gromyko's death Gorbachev issued a lukewarm tribute and did not attend the funeral.

**Gronchi, Giovanni** *(1887–1978)* President of ITALY (1955–62). In 1915 Gronchi helped found the Italian Popular Party, the forerunner of the Italian Christian Democratic Party. He was an early proponent of the "opening to the left" in the early 1950s.

**Grooms, Red (Charles Roger Grooms)** *(1937– )* American artist. Born in Nashville, Tennessee, he studied at the Peabody Institute and Chicago Art Institute as well as with Hans Hofmann. His first one-man show took place in 1958, the same year he was involved in the HAPPENING *Burning Building.* Related to POP ART, his work is playful, figurative and often riotously funny. His large three-dimensional constructions of painted papier mâché and wood are witty tableaux of various contemporary scenes filled with expressively distorted characters and their surroundings. They include *Discount Store* (1970), *Ruckus Manhattan* (1975) and *Tut's Fever* (1988), an ironic look at the motion picture on permanent display at the Museum of the Moving Image, New York City.

**Gropius, Walter** *(1883–1969)* German architect who founded the BAUHAUS school. Along with LE CORBUSIER and Ludwig MIES VAN DER ROHE, Gropius was the creator of architectural MODERNISM and the INTERNATIONAL STYLE. The son of a Berlin architect, he studied architecture in Munich and Berlin (1903–07), then worked with Peter BEHRENS (1908–10). After serving in WORLD WAR

I, he became director of the schools of fine arts and applied arts in Weimar. Pursuing his theories about the relationship between art and design, Gropius merged the two schools to form the Bauhaus. He himself designed the Bauhaus building in DESSAU in 1925 and hired many of the faculty members. He directed the Bauhaus until 1928, when he resigned to set up a private practice in Berlin. After HITLER came to power, Gropius moved to England (1934), where he collaborated with Maxwell FRY in designing private houses and schools. In 1937 Gropius immigrated to the U.S., where he became a professor at Harvard. In this post he had an enormous influence on an entire generation of young American architects. Gropius was a prolific author and lecturer; among his best known books is the seminal *New Architecture and the Bauhaus* (1935).

**Gropper, William** *(1897–1977)* American painter and cartoonist. Born in New York City, Gropper was influenced in the development of his bitingly realistic style by his studies with Robert HENRI and George BELLOWS. In 1919 he began his career as a cartoonist for the New York *Tribune*. His left-wing views were soon illustrated by cartoons in such radical periodicals as *Rebel Worker* and *New Masses*. During the 1920s and 1930s he became a leading American realist, often treating themes of social injustice and class conflict. During this period, he created a number of important murals, including a series at the Department of the Interior Building, Washington, D.C. Intensely political and scathingly satirical, he also skewered the pompous and the corrupt in such paintings as *The Senate* (1935, Museum of Modern Art, N.Y.C.).

**Groppi, James E.** *(1931–1985)* American Roman Catholic priest. During the 1960s, Groppi served in a largely black neighborhood in his native Milwaukee, Wis. He drew national attention as a crusader for open housing. He led more than 200 marches and was arrested more than a dozen times. Later Groppi became active in advocating the rights of welfare recipients and American Indians. He was removed from the priesthood in 1976 for getting married.

**Gross, Henry** *(1895–1986)* American crime boss. Kingpin of a vast illegal gambling operation in the 1940s, Gross was convicted in 1951 of heading a multimillion dollar bookmaking ring. That case also led to the conviction of 22 policemen and the dismissal or resignation of 240 others. The scandal, which prompted major police reforms, also saw the departure of Police Commissioner William O'Brien and the resignation of Mayor William O'Dwyer. He committed suicide rather than go back to prison after his arrest on a heroin trafficking charge.

**Grossman, Vasily Semyonovich** *(1905–1964)* Russian writer. Grossman worked as an engineer in Donbas and Moscow. In 1934 his novel *Glyukauf* attracted the attention of Maxim GORKY, who published it. From 1941 to 1945 Grossman wrote stories and sketches for *The Red Star,* mostly about the war. After the war he turned his attention to writing a novel concerning the defense of STALINGRAD, and his play *If We Were to Believe the Pythagorians* (1946) was banned by authorities.

**Grosz, George** *(1893–1959)* German-American painter and graphic artist. Born in Berlin, Grosz attended the academies of Dresden and Berlin, where he became an illustrator of magazines and books. During WORLD WAR I he produced drawings and caricatures that depicted the brutality of war. Directly after the war (1919) he joined the DADA movement, and organized (1920) the First International Dada Fair. In the postwar years, he also attacked the degradation of German society and skewered the hypocritical bourgeoisie with jagged pen-and-ink drawings and (from 1924 on) scathing, acid-colored paintings unmatched in their satirical savagery. Among his best-known graphic portfolios is *Ecce Homo* (1923), containing incisive studies of high-and low-life in a morally repugnant German society. Faced with the rise of NAZISM, Grosz immigrated to the U.S. in 1932. He became a teacher at New York's Art Students League in 1933 and achieved U.S. citizenship in 1938. His work became more mellow and realistic for a while, but he again turned to subjects of corruption and ravaged humanity after the outbreak of World War II. His work is well represented in American museums. His autobiography, *A Little Yes and a Big No,* was published in 1946.

**Grotewohl, Otto** *(1894–1964)* German communist politician, first prime minister of the German Democratic Republic (EAST GERMANY) from 1949 to 1964. A politician during the WEIMAR REPUBLIC, Grotewohl kept a low profile during the Nazi period. He refounded the German Social Democratic Party in 1945, joined the communists under Soviet pressure and became prime minister in 1949.

**Grotowski, Jerzy** *(1933–1999)* Polish theatrical director. Grotowski has been one of the most influential directors of the post-World War II era, due to his striking theories as to experimental theatrical performance. He studied at the Cracow Theater School and first came to international prominence as a result of his work with actors in the 1960s at the Polish Theater Laboratory. Grotowski's approach elucidated in his book *Towards a Poor Theater* (1968), focused upon an intensity of dramatic presentation that was heightened through encouragement of improvisation on the part of the actors, as well as free-form participation by the audience itself. Settings and costumes were to be minimally utilized. In the 1970s Grotowski worked with the Theater Laboratory in Poland. His theories much influenced the LIVING THEATER and the work of British director Peter BROOK.

**Grottrup, Helmut** *(1916–1981)* German rocket engineer. Of the group of rocketeers who had developed Germany's V-2 rocket at PEENEMÜNDE, Grottrup was the only principal scientist to surrender to the Soviets instead of to the Americans at the end of World War II. After working for the Russians in Germany for a time, he was taken to the Soviet Union in the autumn of 1946. He returned to Germany in 1953, disappointed in the level of opportunity given him and feeling that his work for the Soviets had been neither appreciated nor worthwhile.

**Group of Seven** Group of Canadian painters formed in 1920. They attempted to create a national art by depicting the grandeur of their nation's northern landscapes. Members of the

Group of Seven included Frank Carmichael, Lawren HARRIS, A. Y. Jackson, Frank Johnson, Arthur Lismer, J. E. H. MacDonald and Frederick Varley. Influenced by the techniques of modern European art but rejecting the dominance of European subject matter, these artists created large canvases that are vividly colored and expressively painted. The group disbanded in 1931 but continued to influence later generations of Canadian painters.

**Group Theatre** American theater movement headed by directors Harold CLURMAN, Cheryl Crawford and Lee STRASBERG. The goal of the Group Theatre, which was established in 1931 in New York City, was to present serious modern plays on the basis of quality alone, without regard to Broadway commercial concerns. Among the playwrights produced by the Group Theatre were Paul Green, Sidney Kingsley, Clifford ODETS and William SAROYAN. In 1941, due to funding difficulties and internal dissension, the Group Theatre disbanded. A similar theatrical movement, also called the Group Theatre, emerged in London in 1933, with Rupert Doone serving as principal director. The British Group Theatre staged plays by W. H. AUDEN, T. S. ELIOT, and Stephen SPENDER and often featured scores by composer Benjamin BRITTEN. It ceased production during World War II but was revived for a short time in the 1950s.

**Grove, Robert Moses "Lefty"** *(1900–1975)* American baseball player. An over-powering fastball pitcher, southpaw "Lefty" Grove finished his career with 300 wins. Over the course of 17 seasons with the Philadelphia Athletics (1925–33) and the Boston Red Sox (1934–41), he led the league in strikeouts seven consecutive times, earned-run average nine times and victories four times. In his early years he was famous for his inability to control either his pitches or his temper, and intimidated teammates and opponents alike. He was named to the Hall of Fame in 1947.

**Groves, Leslie R(ichard)** *(1896–1970)* American military engineer and administrator. Educated at the Massachusetts Institute of Technology and the U.S. Military Academy at West Point, by 1941 Groves was overseeing all U.S. military construction. From 1942 to 1947, he was the executive officer of the MANHATTAN PROJECT, responsible for coordinating the thousands of separate ultra-secret projects undertaken by the military, private corporations and universities that were necessary to the construction of the ATOMIC BOMB. In 1945 Groves was instrumental in the decision to drop the bomb, choosing the Japanese targets and training crews to perform the mission. In 1947 he organized the Armed Forces Special Weapons Project, which trained officers in the military aspects of atomic energy. He retired from the army in 1948 and became a business executive.

**Gruen, Victor (Victor Gruenbaum)** *(1903–1980)* Austrian-born architect and community planner. Gruen pioneered the design for American suburban shopping centers in the 1950s. His major projects set the pattern for large-scale shopping mall development in the U.S. He later disavowed the shopping mall concept and blamed land developers for corrupting the idea by promoting uncontrolled suburban sprawl and automobile traffic congestion. Gruen also founded one of the U.S.'s leading architectural, planning and engineering firms.

**Gruentzig, Andres** *(1939–1985)* German-born physician. In 1977, while working at a Zurich hospital, Gruentzig developed the revolutionary balloon catheter technique for cleaning arteries of fatty deposits. In 1980, the year he became a U.S. citizen, he also became a professor of cardiology and radiology at Emory University.

**Grumiaux, Arthur** *(1921–1986)* Belgian violinist. Grumiaux achieved world-wide fame through his stylish recordings and concert appearances. He often performed with pianist Clara Haskill, and their recordings of sonatas by Beethoven and Mozart came to be prized by collectors.

**Grumman Corporation** American aircraft and aerospace manufacturer and defense contractor. It was founded by Leroy Grumman (1901–82) in 1929 as an aircraft-repair shop in a converted basement. The company expanded rapidly and was the first to make aircraft with folding landing gear. It also pioneered in the development of the collapsed wing. It manufactured the Hellcat fighters and Avenger torpedo bombers that played a pivotal role in the American victory in WORLD WAR II IN THE PACIFIC. The company later diversified; by the 1970s, it was largely dependent on defense and aerospace contracts, and in the 1980s was a major supplier of buses to American municipalities. The company is headquartered on Long Island, N.Y. In 1994 Grumman was acquired by Northrop Corporation.

**Grundgens, Gustav** *(1899–1963)* German theatrical actor and director. Grundgens was a star of the German stage as a romantic actor in the 1930s, appearing in numerous plays by George Bernard SHAW and winning acclaim for his 1938 lead portrayal in *Hamlet*. Grundgens's startling successes at so early an age formed the inspiration for the novel *Mephisto* (1936) by Klaus Mann (the son of renowned German novelist Thomas MANN). After World War II, Grundgens worked both as a director and as an actor, starring as Mephistopheles in a touring production of Goethe's *Faust* in 1957–58. His death was an apparent suicide.

**Grundig, Max** *(1908–1989)* West German electronics pioneer. Grundig founded one of Europe's largest radio, television and high-fidelity stereo equipment manufacturing companies, Grundig AG. The firm was regarded as a symbol of WEST GERMANY's post–World War II economic success. However, sales began declining in the late 1970s, due to increased competition from cheaper Japanese exports, and Grundig was forced into an alliance with N. V. Philips Gloeilampenfabrieken of the Netherlands.

**Gruppe 47 (*English: Group 47*)** Gruppe 47 was created in post–World War II GERMANY in 1947 by a diverse group of German writers who met initially to consider the founding of a literary journal. While the journal never came into being, Gruppe 47 achieved prominence as a vital source of encouragement—through its annual autumn meetings in which manuscripts were read and discussed—for the postwar generation of German writers. Prominent writers who attended Gruppe 47 meetings regularly or sporadically included NOBEL PRIZE–winning novelist Heinrich BÖLL, poets Günter Eich and Hans Magnus Enzersberger, and novelists Günter GRASS, Siegfried Lenz, and Martin Walser.

**Guadalcanal** Volcanic island in the western Pacific Ocean, 100 miles southeast of New Georgia; a part of the Solomon Islands. A protectorate of Great Britain's since 1893, it was captured by JAPAN in 1942 (see WORLD WAR II IN THE PACIFIC). U.S. Marines seized a newly built Japanese airfield on August 7, 1942, in the first of a hardfought series of land and naval battles known as the **Battle of Guadalcanal**, from August 7 to November 13, 1942. Henderson Field, the bone of bitter contention, is now an international airport.

**Guadeloupe** Guadeloupe is a group of islands, including the larger islands of Basse-Terre and Grand-Terre, in the Caribbean Sea. Granted departmental status by France in 1946, the islands became a region of France in 1974 and were given greater autonomy in 1982.

**Guam** Island and unincorporated U.S. territory in the western Pacific Ocean; largest and southernmost of the MARIANA ISLANDS group. Discovered by Magellan in 1521 it was a Spanish possession until captured by the United States in 1898, during the Spanish-American War. The Japanese captured the island in 1941, at the beginning of WORLD WAR II in the Pacific; retaken by U.S. forces in 1944, Guam became a base for air assaults on the Japanese home islands. In the 1960s the U.S. used it for air operations against VIETNAM and LAOS.

**Guantánamo (Guantánamo Bay)** Harbor city in southeastern CUBA; the town is about 10 miles north of Guantánamo Bay. U.S. naval units landed here in 1898 during the Spanish-American War and have yet to leave. Often called the PEARL HARBOR of the Atlantic, "Gitmo" was leased by the U.S. in 1903 as a strategic naval station. Since 1960 it has been a bone of contention with the CASTRO government of Cuba, which has refused the token $5,000 annual rent from the U.S. and has pressed for surrender of

the base. Following the U.S. invasion of AFGHANISTAN in October 2001 to overthrow the TALIBAN government and destroy the terrorist organization AL QAEDA, the U.S. has utilized part of its facilities at Guantánamo as a detention area for individuals it has termed enemy combatants.

**Guarnieri, Johnny** *(1917–1985)* American musician; one of the major JAZZ pianists of the SWING ERA. A prolific recording artist, in 1940 he made a series of recordings with Artie SHAW on which he played what were considered to be the first jazz harpsichord solos. Guarnieri also played with such noted musicians as Benny GOODMAN and Jimmy DORSEY.

**Guatemala (Republic of Guatemala)** Covering an area of 42,031 square miles, Guatemala is located in Central America, just south of Mexico. The repressive government of General Jorge Ubico (1931–44) was followed by that of Juan José ARÉVALO BERMEJO, who initiated social, political and economic reforms. His successor, Colonel Jacobo ÁRBENZ GUZMÁN, confiscated land owned by the U.S. Fruit Company, which resulted in a successful U.S.-backed coup in 1954. All reforms were rescinded. Since then Guatemala was plagued by military coups and intense left-wing guerrilla activity, which has resulted in extreme military repression, massacre of suspected guerrilla supporters in the 1980s and international criticism for widespread human-rights violations. The government of President Mario Vinicio Cerezo Arévalo opened talks with the guerrilla leaders in 1987, but no solution to the conflict was reached until 1996, when the Guatemalan government signed a peace accord with the rebels, ending 36 years of civil war. In December 1999 Alfonso Portillo Cabrera was elected president. Cabrera's administration was plagued by accusations of theft and money laun-

# GUATEMALA

| | |
|---|---|
| 1906 | United Fruit Company develops banana plantations. |
| 1917 | Massive earthquake damages Guatemala City. |
| 1920 | Unionist Party overthrows dictator Estrada Cabrera after 22 years of rule. |
| 1921 | Liberal Party overthrows Unionists. |
| 1925 | Semi-feudal coffee plantations spread into highlands to be near Indian labor. |
| 1930 | Military coup. |
| 1931 | Jorge Ubico becomes dictator. |
| 1938 | Border with El Salvador defined. |
| 1944 | Revolution ousts Ubico; elections lead to progressive government under José Arévalo. |
| 1951 | Progressive programs expanded under President Jacobo Árbenz; huge redistribution is begun of unused land, including major holdings of United Fruit Company. |
| 1954 | U.S. backs and participates in coup placing Colonel Castillo Armas in place; Arbenz programs are cancelled and all land returned to United Fruit Company. |
| 1956 | New constitution ratified. |
| 1957 | Military coup. |
| 1963 | Relations broken with Britain over claim to territory of Belize. |
| 1965 | New constitution. |
| 1966 | Elections held; Julio César Méndez elected. |
| 1967 | Miguel Angel Asturias wins Nobel Prize in literature for stories based on Indian traditions. |
| 1968 | Church takes stand on social issues; Archbishop Casariggo kidnapped by right wing; violent leftist guerrillas active. |
| 1976 | Earthquake levels much of Guatemala City; 22,000 die. |
| 1978 | Leftist guerrilla activity increases; military mounts counterterror campaign, massacring rural villages; massive migration of Indians results. |
| 1979 | Government announces "Four Year Development Plan." |
| 1982 | Military coup by Efraín Ríos Montt voids elections. |
| 1983 | Military coup. |
| 1984 | Eugenia Tejada becomes first woman member of cabinet. |
| 1986 | Elections and new constitution. |
| 1989 | Guatemala City doubles in population since 1980. |
| 1990 | U.S. suspends military aid because of death squad activity by army. |
| 1991 | Election of Jorge Serrano Elías reflects growing political power of conservative evangelical Christian movement. |
| 1996 | Government and leftist rebels sign peace agreement ending civil war. |
| 1999 | The UN Historical Clarification Commission issues a report citing widespread human rights abuses by the Guatemalan government and the U.S. government during the civil war. |
| 1999 | President Bill Clinton apologizes for the role of the United States during Guatemala's civil war. Alfonso Antonio Portillo Cabrera is elected president (December). |
| 2003 | Óscar Berger Perdomo is elected president. |

dering. In 2003 Óscar Berger was elected president.

**Gucci, Guccio** *(1881–1953)* Italian leather worker and designer, the founder of the present firm that carries his name. Gucci opened a shop in Florence in 1904 producing saddles and, eventually, luggage. His sons enlarged the business and opened a shop in Rome in 1939. Shops in Paris, London and American cities followed. Gucci products are of generally high quality and distinguished design. In recent years Gucci has taken a strong turn toward high fashion and status appeal. The use of a monogram logotype and a decorative motif of thin red and green stripes makes Gucci products easily recognizable.

**Guchkov, Alexander Ivanovich** *(1862–1936)* Leader of the moderate liberals in Russia (1905–17). Founder and chairman of the Octobrist Party and president of the third state DUMA. In World War I he was chairman of the duma committee on military and naval affairs, and subsequently chairman of the nongovernmental central war industries committee. He became the minister for war and navy in the provisional government. He was a critic of the imperial regime and in March 1917 went to Pskov and secured the abdication of the czar. He left for Paris after the OCTOBER REVOLUTION.

**Guderian, Heinz** *(1888–1954)* German general. A career officer, trained in the Prussian tradition, he was commissioned in the infantry in 1908 and served with distinction in World War I. Specializing in armored fighting, he developed the highly mobile Panzerwaffe (tank corps) that allowed GERMANY to pursue its devastating BLITZKRIEG attacks on Poland, Belgium and France in the early years of WORLD WAR II. He commanded a panzer army during the invasion of Russia in 1941, but was dismissed by HITLER for his failure to take Moscow. He was appointed inspector general of armored troops in 1943 and head of the general staff in 1944. In March 1945, as the Red Army advanced on Berlin, Guderian was finally relieved of his duties by Hitler.

**Guernica (Guernica y Luno)** Town in Spain's Vizcaya province, near Bilbao. Once the seat of the Basque parliament, Guernica was bombed in 1937 by German planes, acting on behalf of FRANCO's Nationalists during the SPANISH CIVIL WAR. The bombing indiscriminately killed men, women and children and was an early use of blanket air attacks on civilian targets with no other purpose than to terrify the enemy into submission. It shocked the world. The destruction was the subject of the great painting of the same name by Pablo PICASSO. By the artist's will, the painting was returned by New York City's MUSEUM OF MODERN ART in September 1981 to the Prado Museum in Madrid.

**Guevara, Ernesto "Che"** *(1928–1967)* Latin American revolutionary. Born into an upper-middle-class family in Argentina, Che became radicalized after witnessing American intervention in GUATEMALA in 1954. Guevara accompanied Fidel CASTRO to CUBA and played a prominent part in the guerrilla campaign (1956–59) that led to BATISTA's downfall. Minister for industries in Cuba (1961–65), he resigned and returned to the jungles of BOLIVIA to test his revolutionary the-

*Marxist revolutionary and guerrilla Che Guevara in a poster protesting the Vietnam War*
(RESISTANCE PUBLICATIONS. LIBRARY OF CONGRESS. PRINTS AND PHOTOGRAPHS DIVISION)

ory. He was killed while leading a band of guerrillas against American-trained Bolivian troops in 1967. Che's rejection of both capitalism and orthodox communism made him a symbolic martyr for radical students throughout the world.

**Guggenheim, Peggy (Marguerite Guggenheim)** *(1898–1979)* American art collector and socialite. An expatriate millionaire who was the niece of philanthropist Solomon Guggenheim, Peggy Guggenheim assembled one of the foremost collections of modern art in her home on the Grand Canal in Venice. The collection included more than 250 works by BRAQUE, KLEE, MIRÓ, MONDRIAN, PICASSO, POLLOCK and other modern artists. It was valued at over $35 million at the time of her death. Guggenheim was also known for her flamboyant lifestyle.

**Guild, Lurelle** *(1898–1986)* American industrial designer, one of a group active in the 1930s who provided styling for manufacturers eager to boost sales in the difficult years of the GREAT DEPRESSION. A 1920 fine arts graduate of Syracuse University, Guild first worked in magazine illustration. He later claimed to have designed as many as a thousand products in a year. Such products as a Norge refrigerator and a May oil-burner, each styled in the manner known then as "modernistic," are typical of Guild's innumerable designs of the 1930s. His willingness to admit to "styling down" to a supposedly low level of public taste sets Guild apart from most of his competitors, who generally believed they were elevating public taste. His Electrolux vacuum cleaner of 1937 is probably his most famous design, with many thousands still in regular use.

**Guillén, Jorge** *(1893–1984)* Spanish poet, critic and teacher. Guillén was born in Castile and educated at the universities of Madrid and Granada. Like other members of the GENERATION OF 1927, he supported the Loyalist cause in the SPANISH CIVIL WAR. Imprisoned in 1936, he went into exile in 1938. He taught at Wellesley (1941–57) as well as McGill, Harvard, Princeton and Yale. Guillén devoted 47 years of work to *Antología: Aire nuestro* (1968), which incorporated *Cántico* (Canticle, four editions between 1928 and 1950), *Clamor* (Clamour, a trilogy published between 1957 and 1963) and *Homenaje* (1967, Homage). He received almost every international award except for the NOBEL PRIZE and was acknowledged in his lifetime as Spain's greatest poet. In 1972 the government of Madrid honored him with the first Cervantes Prize, the highest literary award of the world's Spanish-speaking nations. Guillén returned to Spain in 1977, two years after General FRANCO's death.

**Guillén, Nicolás Batista** *(1904–1989)* Cuban writer. Widely considered CUBA's national poet, Guillén was deeply concerned with the black experience in the Caribbean. A communist, he fought on the Loyalist side in the Spanish civil war. He later supported Fidel CASTRO, was a deputy in the Cuban assembly and served as president of the National Union of Writers and Artists of Cuba. His 12 books of verse began with *Motivos de son* (1930, Motifs of sound). Sensuous and rhythmic in character, his work incorporates elements of popular culture, incantations, dances and street cries. Other volumes of verse include *Sóngoro cosongo* (1931) and *Obra poética 1920–1958* (his complete poetry, published in 1973).

**Guinea** **(Republic of Guinea)** Located on the west coast of Africa, Guinea covers an area of 94,901 square miles. A French colony since 1890, Guinea became independent in 1958. The elected president, Ahmed Sekou Touré, governed from 1958 to 1984, putting down an attempted coup by Guinean exiles in 1970. Upon his death the military seized power, and Col. Lansana Conté became president. He foiled a coup attempt in 1985, which resulted in numerous executions, and was forced to endorse a return to a two-party system with an elected president and National Assembly after countrywide riots in 1988. In 1990 a new constitution was adopted. Guinea's first multiparty national elections in 1993 confirmed the continued rule of Conté and his Party of Unity and Progress. Despite Conté's success in 1993, as well as similar electoral successes in 1995, 1998, 2001 and 2003, opposition to his rule has increased from political opponents, such as Alpha Condé and his Guinean People's Rally Party, and from military officials, as seen in the 1996 mutiny of the Guinea armed forces.

| | GUINEA |
|---|---|
| 1958 | The Republic of Guinea is proclaimed, as Guineans overwhelmingly reject the French Community in a national referendum. Ahmed Sekou Touré is elected president. |
| 1970 | Portuguese-backed Guinean dissidents mount a seaborne invasion of Conakry. The invasion is foiled. In the aftermath of the invasion, mass purges are ordered by Touré. Nearly 10,000 are arrested. Over 100 persons are sentenced to death. More than 250 are convicted and sentenced to life imprisonment, including the Roman Catholic archbishop of Conakry. |
| 1984 | President Touré dies, and the army seizes power and installs the Military Committee for National Redressment (CMRN), with Col. Lansana Conté as head. The CMRN suspends the constitution and the National Assembly and releases all political detainees. |
| 1985 | Diarra Traoré leads an unsuccessful coup. He is arrested and immediately executed. |
| 1989 | Conté promises a return to a two-party system. |
| 1990 | A new constitution authorizing the transitional government is adopted. |
| 1993 | Facing seven opponents, Conté is reelected president, with 51% of the vote. |
| 1995 | Parliamentary elections are finally held after more than two years' delay. The ruling Party for Unity and Progress wins a majority of seats. |
| 1996 | Nearly a quarter of the military riots in the streets of Conakry, demanding higher pay and better working conditions. Thirty are killed, and the presidential palace is set ablaze in the melée. Conté dismisses his defense minister and negotiates with the protesters. |
| 1998 | Conté is reelected. Immediately thereafter Conté jails Alpha Condé, the leader of the opposition Guinean People's Rally (RPG), raising public criticism. |
| 2001 | In a poll that is boycotted by the opposition, voters approve President Conté's proposal to extend the presidential term from five to seven years. |
| 2003 | Conté wins a third presidential term in elections boycotted by the opposition. |

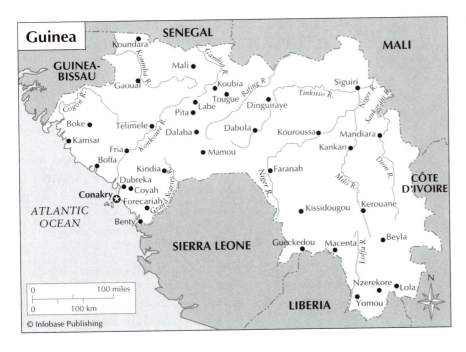

**Guinea-Bissau** Small country on the west coast of Africa, between Senegal and Guinea; formerly known as Portuguese Guinea. Guinea-Bissau was a part of Portugal's colonial empire from the time explorers first reached its coastline in 1446. Five hundred years later, in the early 1960s, a rebellion against colonial rule began. By 1974, independence had finally come—as a result of the 1974 Happy Revolution in Portugal. Guinea-Bissau was the first Portuguese colonial possession in Africa to become free. Since that time the nation has been trying to deal with the legacy of its colonial past, develop its health care and educational system, and make the infrastructure improvements that are desperately needed. In 1994 João Bernardo Vieira was elected president in a free election. Vieira was overthrown by General Ansumane Mane in 1998. Mane established a six-month interim government (under former speaker of Parliament Malan Bacai Sanha) that administered Guinea-Bissau until the 2000 election of Kumba Yalá. Yalá was overthrown in September 2003 and was replaced by Henrique Rosa, who faced severe economic problems and political instability. (See also GUINEA-BISSAUAN WAR OF INDEPENDENCE.) In 2005 João Bernardo Vieira was elected to the presidency, replacing Rosa.

**Guinea-Bissauan War of Independence** (*1962–1974*) Amilcar Cabral (1921–73), after founding the African Party for the Independence of Guinea and Cape Verde (PAIGC), attempted unsuccessfully to negotiate independence from the Portuguese. The PAIGC subsequently began a guerrilla campaign in late 1962. Bands established bases in the forest, while the Portuguese retaliated by bombing and raiding them. Tribalism and witchcraft threatened the rebels' unity until Cabral called a council and explained that the PAIGC was waging a dual revolution: against colonialism and outmoded beliefs. By 1973 it controlled two-thirds of Portuguese Guinea, and proclaimed independence as the Republic of GUINEA-BISSAU. Portugal refused recognition until 1974 when a military coup in Lisbon installed a new government. Luis de Almeida Cabral (b. 1931) became president after his brother Amilcar was assassinated in early 1973. Cape Verde Islands became an independent republic in 1975.

**Guinness, Sir Alec** (*1914–2000*) British theatrical and film actor. Known for his rich voice and for his ability to don the guises of varied characters, Guinness is one of the most acclaimed actors of modern times. He won fame both on the legitimate stage and in British and HOLLYWOOD films. Guinness began his career on the London stage in the 1930s, winning notice in productions by the Old Vic Company including a lead portrayal of Shakespeare's *Hamlet* (1938) in modern dress. After World War II, Guinness made notable appearances in his own stage adaptation of *The Brothers Karamazov* (1946), from the novel by Dostoyevsky, and in *The Cocktail Party* (1949) by T. S. ELIOT. Guinness began his film career in earnest in the late 1940s, appearing in a number of acclaimed movies, including the comedy *Kind Hearts and Coronets* (1949), and *The Bridge on the River Kwai* (1957), directed by David LEAN, for which he won an ACADEMY AWARD as best actor. His later projects included the *Star Wars* film trilogy (1977–83) and the role of spy George Smiley in television adaptations of the works of John LE CARRÉ.

**Guinness Book of Records** The *Guinness Book of Records* is an annual

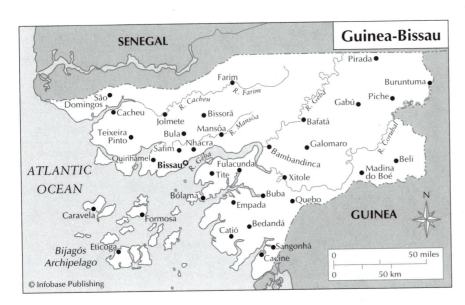

<table>
<tr><td colspan="2" align="center">GUINEA-BISSAU</td></tr>
<tr><td>1974</td><td>By formal agreement Portugal acknowledges independence of Guinea-Bissau and withdraws all Portuguese troops from the territory.</td></tr>
<tr><td>1980</td><td>A coup led by Prime Minister (Principal Commissioner) João Bernardo Vieira is successful.</td></tr>
<tr><td>1984</td><td>President Vieira is elected president for a five-year term.</td></tr>
<tr><td>1994</td><td>Vieira defeats seven opponents to retain the presidency of the country.</td></tr>
<tr><td>1997</td><td>Vieira is reelected prime minister.</td></tr>
<tr><td>1998</td><td>Former army chief of staff Ansumane Mane attempts to overthrow the government led by Vieira.</td></tr>
<tr><td>1999</td><td>The country again erupts into civil war.</td></tr>
<tr><td>2000</td><td>In presidential elections, Kumba Yalá defeats incumbent Malan Bacai Sanhá.</td></tr>
<tr><td>2003</td><td>Yalá is overthrown by a military coup. Henrique Rosa takes his place.</td></tr>
<tr><td>2005</td><td>Vieira wins the presidential election.</td></tr>
</table>

authoritative compendium of facts, feats and exploits of the world and its inhabitants. Conceived by Sir Hugh Beaver (1890–1967), managing director of Guinness Ltd., it was first published in the United Kingdom in 1955. Norris and Ross McWhirter edited the first edition as well as many subsequent editions. The first U.S. edition was published in 1956. In 1974 *The Guinness Book of Records* gained a place within its own pages as the top-selling copyrighted book in publishing history, with sales of 23.9 million copies. Sales passed 60 million copies by 1989. By 1990 there were 262 editions in 35 languages; the first Soviet edition was also published that year. By 2004 *Guinness* had published more than 100 million copies of the book in 37 languages.

*Gulag Archipelago, The* Three-volume history of Soviet prison camps from 1918 to 1956 (published between 1973 and 1976) by Alexander SOLZHENITSYN, the 1970 recipient of the NOBEL PRIZE in literature. Solzhenitsyn, who was himself a longtime prisoner in Siberia during the reign of STALIN,

created a unique blend of historical testimony and literary imagination in *The Gulag Archipelago*. Solzhenitsyn asserted in this work that a standard history of the camps was impossible, as too many of the millions who had suffered within them had died or were too afraid to recount their experiences. Thus Solzhenitsyn employed not only his own memories and the personal testimonies he had collected, but also literary metaphors and meditations on the meaning of so great a horror. *The Gulag Archipelago* was first published in Paris, after a copy of the manuscript had been smuggled out of the USSR. As a result of writing it, Solzhenitsyn was deported in 1974.

**Gumilev, Nikolai** *(1886–1921)* Russian poet. The son of a doctor, Gumilev studied at the University of St. Petersburg and the Sorbonne. He inaugurated two literary magazines. *Sirius* (1908) and *Apollon* (1909), the latter serving as a house organ for the ACMEISTS, a group of poets including Anna AKHMATOVA and Osip MANDELSTAM who opposed the neoromanticism

of the Russian Symbolist school. Gumilev's first book of poetry was *The Path of Conquistadors* (1905). Other major collections include *Romantic Flowers* (1908), *Pearls* (1910) and *Foreign Skies* (1912). His poetry is characterized by regal flourishes of love, heroism and death. He attempted suicide in 1908. Then in 1910 he married Akhmatova, but they were divorced eight years later. Gumilev was shot by Soviet authorities in 1921 for "counterrevolutionary activity."

**Gunnarsson, Gunnar** *(1889–1975)* Icelandic novelist. A well-known figure in Iceland, Gunnarsson also lived in Denmark for many years, writing in Danish as well as Icelandic. He resettled in Iceland in 1939. Gunnarsson is best known for the tetralogy, *The Family Borg,* first published in 1927 which follows four generations of an Icelandic farm family, and for his historical novels of Iceland, such as *The Sworn Brothers* (1920). Other works include *Blackbird* (1929) and a five-volume autobiographical series, *The Church on the Hill* (1923–28).

**Gunther, John** *(1901–1970)* American author. Gunther, who began his career as a news reporter, is best known for his "Inside" books, which include *Inside Europe* (1936), *Inside Latin America* (1941), *Inside U.S.A.* (1947) and the unfinished *Inside Australia* which was completed by William Forbis and published in 1972. The books are accessible, informative works combining history and journalism. Other nonfiction includes *Death Be Not Proud: A Memoir* (1949), *Inside Europe Today* (1961) and *Procession* (1965). Gunther has also written novels, including *The Lost City* (1964) and *The Indian Sign* (1970), which were not well received critically.

**Gurdjieff, Georgei Ivanovitch** *(c. 1877–1949)* Russian philosopher and spiritual teacher. Gurdjieff was one of the most fascinating and controversial spiritual teachers of this century. His written works, such as *Meetings with Remarkable Men* (1963), were all published posthumously. But Gurdjieff exercised his primary influence by face-to-face teaching encounters with his disciples and students, who included such eminent figures as the New Zealand short story writer Katherine MANSFIELD, the British essayist A. R. Orage, and the Russian philosopher P. D. Ouspensky. Gurdjieff was born at Alexandropol near the Russo-Persian border. As a youth, he traveled to Central Asia and other remote regions and came in contact with various spiritual masters who taught Gurdjieff a mode of personal development strongly influenced by Sufism. In the 1920s, Gurdjieff established himself at Fontainebleau, France, and attracted a number of disciples. Gurdjieff employed such means as verbal paradox, music, and disciplined physical labor to compel his followers to come to terms with their personality weaknesses and to attain to their higher selves.

**Gurney, Ivor** *(1890–1937)* English poet and composer. Born in Gloucester, Gurney studied with Sir Charles Stanford at the Royal College of Music (1911–14). He showed much promise as a composer, but WORLD WAR I interrupted his studies. Serving as a private on the Western Front, he was wounded in the arm and later gassed at PASSCHENDAELE (see WORLD WAR I ON THE WESTERN FRONT). In 1918, after suffering a nervous breakdown, he was discharged with "deferred shell-shock." Gurney published two wartime poetry collections, *Severn and Somme* (1917) and *War's Embers* (1919), but a third collection was rejected by his publisher. Returning to the Royal College of Music, he studied with Ralph VAUGHAN WILLIAMS but was unable to concentrate; he left the college and returned to an irregular life in Gloucestershire. During this time (1919–22) he wrote many fine poems and also composed songs, but he suffered increasingly from delusions, and in 1922 was committed to Dartford insane asylum, where he spent the rest of his life. Gurney's poetry was influenced by his wartime experiences and by his love for the Gloucester countryside; it is marked by subtle use of rhyme and by great imaginative resourcefulness. Largely unpublished during his lifetime, Gurney's work was rediscovered during the 1970s and 1980s. Gurney is now recognized as one of the most original British poets of the 20th century. His songs also have found a place in the repertoire.

**Guro, Elena (Eleonora Genrikhovna von Norenberg)** *(1877–1910)* Russian Futurist poet. She was a professional painter who had graduated from the school of the Society for the Encouragement of the Arts, and was interested in French, German and Scandinavian literature. Guro is one of the most neglected of the early Russian Futurists. Her literary career started with *Early Spring* (1905), followed by *The Hurdy-Gurdy* (1909), *The Autumnal Dream* (1912), *The Baby Camels of the Sky* (1914) and other works. Her work remains unjustly overlooked.

**Gusinsky, Vladimir** *(1953– )* Russian media tycoon. Gusinsky studied petroleum engineering during the Soviet era and worked as a cab driver and a theater director in Moscow. In 1989, capitalizing on Soviet leader Mikhail GORBACHEV's economic liberalization program of PERESTROIKA, Gusinsky created MOST Bank, which profited due to its loan speculation, funds management and close association with Moscow mayor Yuri Luzhkov. In February 1993 Gusinsky began to involve himself in the media business when he launched *Segodnya*, a national newspaper, using funds he borrowed from MOST Bank, a lending institution of which he was chief executive officer. Eight months later he established NTV, a small television station also funded largely with loans from MOST that broadcast programs throughout the St. Petersburg area; NTV represented Russia's first privately owned television station. Four years later Gusinsky left his position as CEO and establish Media MOST, a new banking company that held sizable shares of his television station and newspaper.

As a rising media mogul Gusinsky evoked his share of critics and admirers. In the early 21st century the government of President Vladimir PUTIN initiated legal proceedings against Gusinsky. His defenders claim that this was retaliation for the criticism of the government on NTV, Gusinsky's BONUM-1 satellite network and the pages of *Sogodnya*. In 2001 the government-controlled gas corporation Gazprom purchased NTV. Critics of Gusinsky argued that his exposés on Putin and the Russian government served only to distract attention from his embezzlement of approximately $250 million in loans from Gazprom to Media MOST, for which he was first arrested in Moscow in 2000 and then rearrested—in 2003.

**Gustav Line** Stretching across Italy south of Rome, it was set up by the Germans as a main line of defense in WORLD WAR II. Bitterly defended, the key position of CASSINO, with the valley of the Liri River behind it, was reached by the attacking Allies in February 1944 but not taken by them until May.

**Guthrie, Arlo** *(1947– )* American folk and rock musician. The son of renowned folk singer Woody GUTHRIE, Arlo Guthrie burst into national prominence in 1967 due to the success of his album *Alice's Restaurant*. Its wry and rambling title song tells the story of a diffident 1960s rebel who refuses to kill for the U.S. Army and is ultimately arrested for littering. *Alice's Restaurant* became one of the anthems of the ANTIWAR MOVEMENT, and a film by the same title, directed by Arthur Penn and with Guthrie in a starring role, was produced in 1969. In the past two decades, Guthrie has recorded a number of albums, including a tribute to his father, and has joined with folk singer Pete SEEGER in a number of river clean-up campaigns. In 1995 Guthrie released *Alice's Restaurant 2: The Massacre Revisited*.

**Guthrie, Tyrone** *(1900–1971)* English stage director. Noted for his inventiveness, Guthrie became famous for his direction of Elizabethan drama, especially the plays of Shakespeare. Initially, he was a director of the Scottish National Players (1926–27), then became director at the Cambridge Festival Theatre (1929–30) and the Old Vic (1933–34; 1936–37; 1951–52). In 1953 he founded the Shakespeare Festival in Stratford, Ontario, and subsequently served as one of the directors. In addition, he directed drama and opera in London and New York, and established a theater in Minneapolis in 1962, which bears his name and continues his theatrical legacy. Among his most important productions were *Hamlet* (Old Vic, 1938) and *Troilus and Cressida* (Stratford, Ontario, 1954).

**Guthrie, Woody (Woodrow Wilson Guthrie)** *(1912–1967)* American folksinger and political activist; widely

*Folksinger Woody Guthrie* (LIBRARY OF CONGRESS, PRINTS AND PHOTOGRAPHS DIVISION)

considered the preeminent American folksinger of the 20th century. Certain of his songs of the 1930s—"This Land Is Your Land," "Hard Traveling," and "So Long, It's Been Good to Know Ya"—have become enduring classics of American popular music. Guthrie was born in Indian territory in Oklahoma and traveled widely during the 1920s and the GREAT DEPRESSION era. For a time he worked for a California radio station on which he performed his songs. Moving to New York City in the late 1930s, he performed with fellow folk singer Pete SEEGER, contributed pieces to the socialist *Daily Worker* and recorded a number of DUST BOWL ballad albums—containing both original material and old folk songs collected by Guthrie—for the Archive of American Folk Song. Guthrie died after a painful 13-year struggle with Huntington's chorea. *Bound for Glory* (1943) and *Bound to Win* (1965) are autobiographical volumes; *Woody Says* (1975) is a posthumous collection. Singer Arlo GUTHRIE is his son.

**Guttuso, Renato** *(1912–1987)* Italian painter and Communist. He was perhaps the most commercially successful Italian painter of his generation. Most of his mature work was realistic or expressionistic in nature. Much of it dealt with political themes, from the execution of Spanish poet Federico GARCÍA LORCA in 1936 to the student uprisings of 1968. Guttuso also served in the Italian Senate.

**Guyana** Republic on the Atlantic coast of northeastern South America, bounded on the east and southeast by SURINAME, on the south and southwest by Brazil and on the northwest by VENEZUELA; formerly known as British Guiana. Its boundary with Venezuela, long a subject of controversy, became a serious issue in 1895, when U.S. secretary of state Richard Olney took a threateningly "American" view in Venezuela's dispute with Britain. An arbitration award in 1899 upheld most British claims; and the boundary with Brazil was similarly arbitrated in 1904. With the outset of World War II, the U.S. leased sites for military and naval bases on the Demerara River and near Suddie. By 1966 the colony had achieved independence, and in 1970 it became a republic. Throughout the 1960s tension between East Indians, who control commerce, and blacks led to clashes and bloodshed, which subsided in the 1970s. International tensions were eased with the signing in 1970 of a 12-year truce with Venezuela and a mutual troop withdrawal agreement with Suriname. The Venezuela border controversy still simmers. In 1978 Guyana gained international notoriety as the scene of a mass suicide committed at JONESTOWN by followers of the U.S.-originated religious cult of the Reverend Jim Jones.

© Infobase Publishing

---

### GUYANA

| | |
|---|---|
| 1966 | Guyana becomes a self-governing dominion within the Commonwealth. Venezuela occupies Anakoka Island and asserts a claim to land west of the Essequibo River. |
| 1969 | Government suppresses Rupununi rebels trying to establish an independent state. Border clashes with Suriname revive old border dispute. |
| 1978 | Jonestown, Guyana, is the scene of the bizarre and grisly suicide-murder of more than 900 members of the People's Temple Commune, led by U.S. cultist Jim Jones. |
| 1980 | Guyana adopts presidential form of government as new constitution is approved. |
| 1991 | Guyana becomes a member of the Organization of American States (OAS). |
| 1992 | Dr. Cheddi Jagan is elected president. |
| 1997 | President Jagan dies. Jagan is succeeded by his wife, American-born Janet Rosenberg Jagan, who wins 55 percent of the votes. |
| 1999 | President Janet Jagan resigns due to poor health. Bharrat Jagdeo becomes president. |
| 2000 | Guyana and Suriname resolve their border dispute. |
| 2001 | Bharrat Jagdeo reelected president in March. |

The government continually proved unstable, and in the 1980s the nation faced severe economic problems. In the country's first entirely free election in 1992, Cheddie Jagan was elected president. After his death in 1997, he was succeeded by his wife, Janet, who resigned two years later for reasons of health. Her successor, Bharrat Jagdeo, was reelected in 2001.

**Guyanan Rebellion of 1969** Rebel bands invaded from Brazil, seized the towns of Lethem and Annai in southwestern Guyana (January 2, 1969), but were driven out by Guyanese Army forces within several days. Several policemen lost their lives. The invasion was apparently sponsored by Americans owning large cattle ranches in the region, wishing to establish a state they could control.

**Gysi, Gregor** (*1948–   *) East German lawyer, leader of the East German Socialist Unity (Communist) Party following the ouster of Egon KRENZ, who in October 1989 replaced Erich HONECKER. A popular member of the reform wing of the party, he was nonetheless defeated by noncommunists who favored reunification with WEST GERMANY in March 1990 in the first free elections in EAST GERMANY.

# H

**Habibie, Baharuddin** *(1937– )* President of INDONESIA (1998–99). On May 21, 1998, when the country's longtime dictator SUHARTO resigned, Vice President Habibie succeeded him in office. As president of Indonesia, Habibie is perhaps best known for his efforts to resolve the issue of EAST TIMOR, a province of Indonesia that sought independence. He agreed to a UN-sponsored and observed election that would allow the residents of East Timor to determine whether they would return to their traditional status as an autonomous region within Indonesia or secede and form an independent nation. In addition to the separatist agitation in East Timor and the region of ACEH, Habibie inherited a debilitated economy suffering from currency devaluation, high inflation and massive unemployment.

In an attempt to avert another round of the prodemocracy protests and violent street clashes that had precipitated Suharto's last days in office, Habibie promised that free presidential elections would be held in 1999. After he withdrew from the race, he was succeeded by Abdurrahman Wahid, a moderate Muslim and member of the National Awakening Party.

**Habré, Hissène** *(1943– )* Defense minister and president of CHAD (1982–90). In 1980 Habré launched a rebellion against the government of Goukouni Oueddei and immediately encountered opposition from Libyan forces sent to support the Oueddei regime. When the Libyans left the fol-lowing year, Habré returned to the offensive, eventually capturing the town of N'Djamena from Oueddi in mid-1982. By 1988 the political, economic and military support that Oueddei received from Libya and Habré obtained from France had produced a stalemate. Both leaders then conceded the permanence of the situation by normalizing relations between the two entities they had carved out of Chad. However, in November 1990 the Patriotic Salvation Movement, a pro-Libyan insurgent group led by General Idriss Deby (a former cohort of Habré) overthrew Habré and replaced him with Deby, who assumed the presidency a year later. Habré fled into exile in Senegal, from where in 1992 he mounted an unsuccessful attempt to overthrow Deby. Although the Senegalese government criticized Habré's policies as president of Chad, it refused to charge him with the war crimes many critics have alleged he committed, or to revoke its offer of asylum.

**Haddad, Wadi** *(c. 1928–1978)* Palestinian pediatrician, terrorist and cofounder (1966) of the Popular Front for the Liberation of Palestine. Haddad directed several prominent airliner hijackings, including the hijacking of an El Al plane to Algeria (1968) and the hijacking of a Lufthansa jet to Somalia (1977); he was also behind the hijacking of four airliners that resulted in three of the planes being blown up on a runway in Jordan (1970). He was also apparently linked to the Tel Aviv airport attack by the Japanese Red Army (1972).

**Haganah** Protective force secretly formed by JEWS in PALESTINE in 1936 for defense of their communes against Arab attacks. Unlike purely terrorist organizations, it later became the nucleus of the Israeli army.

**Hagen, Walter** *(1892–1969)* U.S. golfer. He helped eliminate golf's elitist amateur image and turn it into a popular professional sport. A charismatic character who occasionally arrived at tournaments in a tuxedo, he was the leading golfer of the early 20th century, winning the U.S. Open in 1914 and 1919, the British Open four times between 1922 and 1929 and the PGA championship five times.

**Hague, The (Den Haag; 's Gravenhage)** Capital city of the Netherlands' South Holland province; 4 miles from the North Sea and 33 miles from Amsterdam. Developed as a permanent site for negotiation between sovereign nations, it saw peace conferences in 1899 and 1907 that unsuccessfully attempted to solve the problems of fin de siècle Europe. In the 1920s The Hague became the seat of the **World Court** (now the **International Court of Justice**) as well as of various Dutch governmental bodies. During WORLD WAR II, Germans occupied the city from 1940 to 1945, in January 1945 launching V-1 rocket-bombs against advancing Allied troops. In 1993 the Hague became the site for the International Criminal Tribunal for the Former Yugoslavia (see HAGUE WAR CRIMES TRIBUNAL FOR THE FORMER YUGOSLAVIA).

**Hague Conventions** International conferences convened by Czar NICHOLAS II; met May 18 to July 19, 1899, and June 15 to October 18, 1907, with the aim of "a possible reduction of the excessive armaments which weigh upon all nations" by "putting a limit on the progressive development of the present armaments." The first convention's achievements were limited but did include agreement on the use of gas, expanding bullets, the banning of explosives launched from balloons and the creation of a court of arbitration. The second convention reached agreement on a number of naval matters and on the employment of force to recover debts. A further convention was planned for 1915 but because of WORLD WAR I did not meet. The two conventions did influence the form of the LEAGUE OF NATIONS.

**Hague War Crimes Tribunal for the Former Yugoslavia** Also known as the International Criminal Tribunal for the former Yugoslavia (ICTY). Established on May 25, 1993, by UN Security Council Resolution 827, the ICTY was established to evaluate war crimes charges alleged to have been committed by individuals in the former YUGOSLAVIA since 1991. It is often referred to as the Hague War Crimes Tribunal because it has operated in the Dutch city of The HAGUE. As outlined by Resolution 827, the ICTY has investigated violations of the 1949 Geneva Convention on Warfare and other well-established wartime rules and regulations as well as alleged instances of genocide and crimes against humanity. While ICTY officials and judges acknowledge that the crimes they have investigated often fall under joint jurisdiction with national courts in the former Yugoslavia, Resolution 827 has given it a stronger claim to judge these alleged crimes. In an effort to maximize the impartiality of its decisions, the ICTY's judges have been selected from a variety of countries throughout the world, including the U.S., Britain, Italy, Germany, China, France, Guyana, Zambia, Australia, Jamaica, Turkey, Egypt, Malta, the Netherlands, South Korea, Argentina, the Czech Republic, Japan, Canada, Colombia, the Ukraine, Finland and Spain. Two of the judges serving on the ICTY had prior experience evaluating war crimes on the International Criminal Tribunal for Rwanda. In an effort to ensure that no bureaucratic organ of the ICTY contains national or cultural biases that would prejudice the institution's decisions, the more than 1,200 personnel assigned to the ICTY have come from 82 different countries. Since its creation the ICTY has passed judgment on more than 25 cases involving alleged war crimes committed during the course of the conflicts in Yugoslavia since 1991, including the trial of former Serbian president Slobodan MILOŠEVIĆ.

**Hahn, Otto** (1879–1968) German chemist. After obtaining his doctorate at the University of Marburg in 1901 Hahn studied abroad, first with William Ramsay in London and then at McGill University, Montreal, Canada, with Ernest RUTHERFORD. Hahn returned to Germany in 1907, where he took up an appointment at the University of Berlin, being made professor of chemistry in 1910. Two years later he joined the Kaiser Wilhelm Institute of Chemistry, where he served as director from 1928 to 1945.

Most of Hahn's career was spent in research on radioactivity. With Lise MEITNER he discovered a new element, protactinium, in 1917. He went on to define (1921) the phenomenon that arises when nuclei with different radioactive properties turn out to be identical in atomic number and mass. Hahn's most important work however, was done in the 1930s when, with Meitner and Fritz Strassmann, he made one of the most important discoveries of the century, namely nuclear fission. One of the strange features about Hahn's work was that he was repeating experiments already done and formulating hypotheses already rejected as nonsense or due to some contamination of the materials used.

Thus, when in 1938 Hahn bombarded uranium with slow neutrons and detected some strange, new half-lives, he assumed that the uranium had changed into radium, a close neighbor, with some undetected alpha particles. But when he tried to remove the radium all he could find was barium. This Hahn simply could not understand, for barium was far too low in the periodic table to be produced by the transmutation of uranium; and if the transformation was taking place it should be accompanied by the emission of a prodigious number of alpha particles, which Hahn could not have failed to detect. The thought that the heavy uranium nucleus could split into two lighter ones was too outrageous for him to consider seriously. He did realize that something of importance was going on. Appropriately enough it was his old collaborator Meitner, in exile from the Nazis in Sweden, and her nephew Otto Frisch, who made the necessary calculations and announced fission to the world early in 1939. Hahn received the NOBEL PRIZE in chemistry in 1944.

**Haider, Jörg** (1950– ) Austrian politician, governor of the state of Kärnten and leader (1986–2000) of the FREEDOM PARTY. In 1986 Haider assumed control of the Freedom Party and began to orient it toward the far right of the Austrian political spectrum. Over the next 14 years, he increased the party's representation in the Nationalrat, the Austrian parliament, by campaigning on a platform calling for increasing restrictions on the influx of foreign workers into Austria. In his first year as governor of Kärnten in 1989 he praised the policies adopted by the Nazi regime in Germany to end unemployment provoking an outcry throughout Austria and abroad that forced him to resign later that year.

In 1999 Haider and the Freedom Party scored their greatest political triumph, winning 52 seats and becoming the second-largest party in the Nationalrat. A year later the Freedom Party and the center-right People's Party formed a coalition government, but Haider's pro-Nazi comments, together with his harsh criticism of immigration, prevented him from obtaining a position in the coalition government. When other EU members continued to treat Austria as an international pariah, Haider announced that he would step down as party leader on February 28, 2000, and focus exclusively on governing the state of Kärnten.

**Haig, Alexander Meigs** (1924– ) U.S. Army officer, presidential adviser and secretary of state (1981–82). A career army officer, Haig rose through the ranks and, as colonel, commanded a brigade in VIETNAM (1966–67). Military adviser to President Richard M. NIXON from 1969 to 1973, General Haig became Nixon's White House chief of staff after the resignation of Robert Halde-man during the WATERGATE crisis and was a key figure in the White House during the final days of Nixon's presidency. Haig was subsequently commander in chief of American forces in Europe (1974–79) and supreme commander of NATO. He retired from the army with the rank of full general (four stars) to enter political life in 1979. He was appointed secretary of state by President Ronald REAGAN in 1981. When Reagan was shot by a would-be assassin, Haig made his famous "I'm in charge here" statement to the nation. As secretary of state, Haig's policy was often at variance with that of the president and other members of the administration, and Haig resigned after further differences with the president. He made an unsuccessful bid for the Republican presidential nomination in 1988.

## Haig, Douglas (first earl Haig)
*(1861–1928)* British field marshal. Born in Edinburgh, he was commissioned in the cavalry in 1885. Posted to the Sudan in 1898, he later served in the BOER WAR from 1899 to 1902. He was appointed an army corps commander in France at the outbreak of WORLD WAR I, becoming commander in chief of the British Expeditionary Force in 1915. Leading British troops during the bloody First Battle of the SOMME (1916) and Third Battle of YPRES (1917), Haig was widely held responsible for the appallingly high toll of British casualties in these engagements. Opposed by Prime Minister

*British military commander Field Marshal Douglas Haig* (LIBRARY OF CONGRESS. PRINTS AND PHOTOGRAPHS DIVISION)

Lloyd GEORGE for wasting British lives, he nevertheless retained the loyalty of the British military. In 1918 Haig secured the appointment of Ferdinand FOCH as supreme Allied commander, and the two generals collaborated in the war's final campaigns. He was made a peer in 1919, and spent the rest of his life in activities for the British Legion and in soliciting aid for disabled veterans.

## Haile Selassie *(1892–1975)* Last emperor of ETHIOPIA. Haile Selassie ruled Ethiopia for half a century: as regent (1916), as king (1928–30) and as emperor (1930–74). His reign was interrupted for five years in May 1936 following the Italian invasion of Ethiopia, which forced him into exile (see ITALO-ETHIOPIAN WAR OF 1935–36). In June 1936 he appealed to the LEAGUE OF NATIONS for aid against the Italian invaders but was refused. Selassie returned to Ethiopia in 1942 and began a series of modernization projects, including administrative reform, economic and judicial reorganization, the abolition of slavery and feudalism and the establishment of educational institutions. In 1963 he summoned the first meeting of the ORGANIZATION OF AFRICAN UNITY and devised the charter for the 38–member body, whose headquarters were in Addis Ababa. At his suggestion, the UNITED NATIONS set up the UN Economic Commission for Africa, also in Addis Ababa. However, he was unable to solve Ethiopia's social problems, and radicals in the country grew increasingly dissatisfied with his rule. Haile Selassie was overthrown in a 1974 coup by left-wing army officers, and died soon after under house arrest.

## Haiti (Republic of Haiti) Covering an area of 10,712 square miles, Haiti comprises the western third of the Caribbean island of Hispaniola as well as several West Indian islets. Haiti has been plagued by dire poverty and political instability during most of the 20th century. The murder of President Guilliame Sam in 1915 led to U.S. intervention and administration of the country until 1934. Between 1946 and 1957 a succession of presidents were either deposed or overthrown during coups. In 1957 Dr. François "Papa Doc" DUVALIER (1907–71) became dictator, creating a personal militia (the Tontons Macoutes)

*Haile Selassie. last emperor of Ethiopia* (LIBRARY OF CONGRESS. PRINTS AND PHOTOGRAPHS DIVISION)

and declaring himself president-for-life (1964). Popular among a wide segment of the population, Duvalier brought a measure of stability; however, his personal charm belied his ruthlessness and corruption. Upon his death he was succeeded by his son, Jean-Claude "Baby Doc" Duvalier. The younger Duvalier was forced to flee the country in 1986 after food riots and increasingly violent demonstrations. A period of political upheaval followed until Rev. Jean-Bertrand ARISTIDE, a leftist priest, was elected president in December 1990 in the first truly democratic election in Haiti's history. More than 100 people died in the unrest that followed a failed attempt to overthrow the Aristide government in January 1991. A second 1991 coup, staged in September by General Raoul CÉDRAS, proved successful, but Aristide returned to power in 1994 after the U.S.-CLINTON administration forced the leaders of the military government to relinquish power. In February 2004, an uprising against Aristide's rule plunged Haiti into a bloody civil war. The George W. BUSH administration, supported by France, engineered Aristide's departure from the country. In June 2004 the UN put in place the UN Stabilization Mission in Haiti (MINUSTAH) to attempt to stem further civil unrest and pave the way for elections when calm was restored. In 2006 former president René Préval is again elected to the presidency.

## Haitian Revolt of 1915 With the country in chaos, Vibrun Guillaume Sam (d. 1915) seized control of HAITI's government in early 1915. A mob assassinated Sam, July 28, 1915, and in

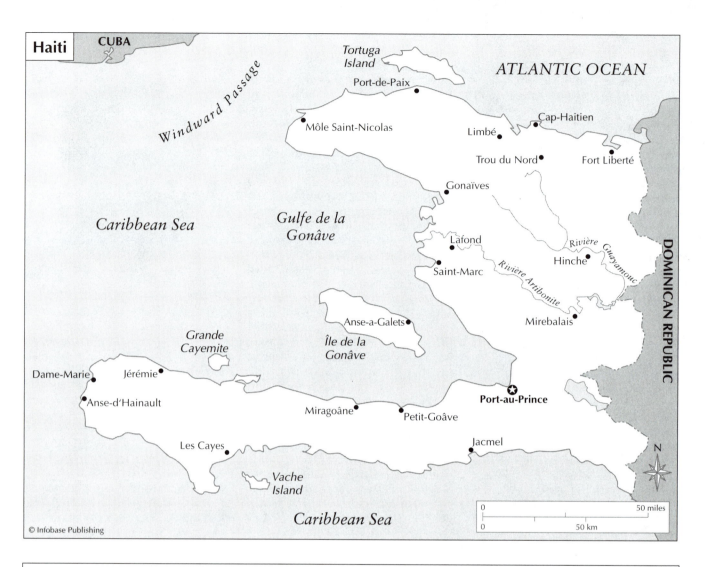

| Haiti | CUBA | | Tortuga Island | | ATLANTIC OCEAN |

## Haiti

| 1915 | U.S. Marines land to restore order after murder of President Guilliame Sam. |
| 1934 | U.S. Marines withdrawn. |
| 1957 | Dr. François (Papa Doc) Duvalier is elected president. |
| 1964 | Duvalier declares himself president-for-life. |
| 1971 | Papa Doc dies and is succeeded by his son Jean-Claude (Baby Doc) Duvalier. |
| 1985 | Food riots break out in Gonaives and spread rapidly to the capital, Port-au-Prince. |
| 1986 | Baby Doc flees the country. |
| 1990 | Supreme Court Justice Ertha Pascal-Trouillot assumes presidency; Jean-Bertrand Aristide wins landslide presidential election. |
| 1991 | A coup led by Tontons Macoutes attempts to prevent Aristide from assuming the presidency but is quickly crushed by the army; Aristide sworn in. |
| 1991 | Aristide overthrown by military coup. |
| 1994 | Aristide restored to office by U.S. pressure. |
| 1996 | René Préval becomes president with 88% of the vote. |
| 2000 | Aristide wins the presidential election with 91% of the vote. |
| 2004 | Aristide leaves country after severe political unrest. |
| 2006 | René Préval is again elected president. |

the subsequent anarchy U.S. Marines established order, protected foreigners and supervised elections. Philippe Sudre Dartiguenave (1863–after 1922), the new president enforced a treaty (September 16, 1915) in which Haiti became a political and economic protectorate of the United States, with customs and police under American control.

**Haitian Revolt of 1918–19** An American-supervised 1918 plebiscite adopted by the questionable vote of 98,225 to 768 established a new constitution in Haiti, since 1915 a 10-year protectorate of the U.S. Philippe Sudre Dartiguenave (1863–after 1922) remained as president, while American officers ran the government and the gendarmerie revived the labor draft. In late 1918 Haitians led by Charlemagne Péralte (d. 1919) and Benoît Batraville (d. 1919) rebelled against the corvee and U.S. occupation. Between 20,000 to 40,000 poorly armed rebels believing themselves invincible through voodoo potions terrorized the region and attacked the capital, Port-au-Prince. The gendarmerie crushed them with U.S. Marine and air support. Péralte and Batraville were executed and peace was restored. American occupation was later extended until 1934.

**Halas, George (Stanley) "Papa Bear"** (1895–1983) American athlete, football coach, and sports executive. Halas was a cofounder of the **National Football League,** owner of the **Chicago Bears** team franchise, and the winningest head coach in NFL history. After a brief stint with baseball's New York Yankees, Halas became player-coach of the Decatur (Ill.) Staleys of the American Professional Football Association. He bought the club and moved it to Chicago in 1921, renaming it the Chicago Bears. In 1922, he helped organize the NFL. He brought credibility to professional football by signing college star Red GRANGE in 1925. Halas coached for 40 years between 1920 and 1968, compiling a career record of 325 wins, 131 losses, and 31 ties. Under his leadership, the team also won six championships. Halas was inducted into the Pro Football Hall of Fame in 1963.

**Haldane, John Burdon Sanderson** (1892–1964) British geneticist. Haldane became involved in scientific research at an early age through helping in the laboratory of his father the physiologist John Scott Haldane. His interest in genetics was first stimulated as early as 1901, when he heard a lecture on Mendel's work, and he later applied this by studying inheritance in his sister's (the writer Naomi Mitchison) 300 guinea pigs. On leaving school he studied first mathematics and then the humanities at Oxford University. He served in WORLD WAR I with the Black Watch Regiment and was wounded at Loos and in Mesopotamia. Some work on gas masks, following the first German gas attacks, marked the beginning of his physiological studies.

In 1919 Haldane took up a fellowship at Oxford, where he continued research on respiration, investigating how the levels of carbon dioxide in the blood affect the muscles regulating breathing. He was next offered a readership in biochemistry at Cambridge, where he conducted some important work on enzymes. These experiments, and later work on conditions in submarines, aroused considerable public interest because he frequently used himself as a guinea pig.

In 1933 Haldane became professor of genetics at University College, London, a position he exchanged in 1937 for the chair of biometry. While at London he prepared a provisional map of the X sex chromosome and showed the genetic linkage between hemophilia and color blindness. He also produced the first estimate of mutation rates in humans from studies of the pedigrees of hemophiliacs, and described the effect of recurring deleterious mutations on a population. With the outbreak of the SPANISH CIVIL WAR, Haldane joined the Communist Party and advised the republican government on gas precautions. In the 1950s he left the party as a result of Soviet acceptance and promotion of Trofim LYSENKO. In protest at the Anglo-French invasion of Suez, Haldane immigrated to India in 1957, becoming an Indian citizen in 1961. He was director of the laboratory of genetics and biometry at Bhubaneswar from 1962 until his death. Haldane's books include *Enzymes* (1930), *The Causes of Evolution* (1932), and *The Biochemistry of Genetics* (1954); he also wrote a number of books popularizing science.

**Haldane, Richard Burden (Viscount)** (1856–1928) British statesman. Born in Edinburgh, Haldane attended Gottingen University in Germany. He served as a Liberal member of Parliament from 1885 to 1911. As war minister from 1905 to 1912, he increased the efficiency of the British army, creating a general staff, a territorial army, an officers' training corps and an expeditionary force. In 1912 he traveled on a mission to Berlin, where he was unsuccessful in halting German naval rearmament and rejected a plea for British neutrality. He served as lord chancellor from 1912 to 1915 but was forced from public life at the outbreak of WORLD WAR I when his knowledge of German affairs caused him to be unjustly branded as pro-German. He briefly served again as lord chancellor in Ramsay MACDONALD's first Labour government in 1924. Also a noted academic philosopher, Haldane was later the chancellor of the University of Bristol. His writings include a number of works on philosophy and an autobiography (1929).

**Halder, Franz** (1884–1972) German general. A career army officer, Halder succeeded General Ludwig Beck as chief of the German general staff in 1938, just after the MUNICH PACT. Although opposed to HITLER's plans for European conquest, Halder engineered the German BLITZKRIEG victories against Poland, the Netherlands, Belgium, Luxembourg and France in 1939 and 1940. Hitler relieved Halder of his command in 1942. Halder was later arrested and imprisoned for his involvement in the plot to assassinate Hitler (July 20, 1944). He was freed by the Americans in April 1945.

**Haley, Alex** (1921–1992) American author. Haley became famous with the publication of the novel ROOTS (1976), which traces his ancestry back to Africa and follows his ancestors as they are captured and taken as slaves to the U.S. The book was adapted for television, becoming the first "miniseries," and its popularity was something of a media phenomenon. The book sparked an interest in genealogy, particularly among black Americans, whose history was obfuscated by the practice of slavery. Haley's other works include *The Autobiography of Malcolm X* (1965, written with MALCOLM X) and *A Different Kind of Christmas* (1988).

**Haley, Bill** *(1927–1981)* American guitarist, singer, band leader, and pioneer of ROCK-and-roll music. With his group, the Comets, Haley recorded such early rock and roll hits as "Shake, Rattle and Roll" (1954), "Rock the Joint" and "Crazy, Man, Crazy." The group's biggest hit, however, was "Rock Around the Clock" (1955), which was the theme song to the film *The Blackboard Jungle*. It was written by Haley, and sold 22.5 million copies over the next 15 years. Haley's performances throbbed with energy and exuberance and helped make rock and roll a major part of the American music idiom in the 1950s. Along with Elvis PRESLEY, Haley and the Comets were an important influence on the BEATLES and other prominent rock performers of the 1960s and 1970s. Although they are primarily thought of as a 1950s group, Haley and the Comets continued to perform successfully during the next two decades.

**Haley, Sir William John** *(1901–1987)* British journalist. In a career of nearly five decades, Haley headed the *Manchester Guardian* (1939–43), the BBC (1944–52) and the *Times* of London (1952–66), as well as the *Encyclopaedia Britannica* (1968–69). While director general of the BBC, he broadened its cultural programming by instituting a Third Channel on radio in 1946. Perhaps his most memorable achievement as editor in chief of the *Times* was his banishment, in 1966, of birth, death and marriage notices from the front page; he replaced them with news.

**Halifax, Edward Frederick Lindley Wood** *(1881–1959)* British statesman. Lord Halifax began his political career as a Conservative member of Parliament (1910–25). He headed the Board of Education from 1922 to 1924 and the Board of Agriculture from 1924 to 1925, when he was created Baron Irwin. In the post of Viceroy of INDIA from 1926 to 1931, he negotiated with Mohandas GANDHI and advocated dominion status for the country. He succeeded his father as Viscount Halifax in 1934 and was appointed lord privy seal the following year. Serving as foreign

secretary (1938–40) under Neville CHAMBERLAIN, he was at first a lukewarm supporter of the APPEASEMENT policy toward Nazi GERMANY. Halifax was considered as a possible successor to Chamberlain as prime minister, but declined the appointment in favor of Winston S. CHURCHILL. He remained foreign secretary for several months under Churchill, then served as ambassador to the U.S. from 1941 to 1951. Halifax was created an earl in 1944. His autobiography, *Fullness of Days,* was published in 1957. Halifax was also chancellor of Oxford University from 1953 until his death in 1959.

**Hall, Edward T.** *(1914–    )* American anthropologist whose studies and writing had a direct influence on modern thinking about design and architecture. Hall's work became well-known with the publication of his books *The Silent Language* in 1959 and *The Hidden Dimension* in 1966. They reported on his studies of the ways in which human interactions are influenced by such physical circumstances as the size and shape of spaces, placement of furniture, quality of light, color, and similar elements of the environment. When related to human life, the concept of territoriality, first studied as an aspect of animal behavior, has led to an awareness of the problems created by crowding in modern cities, buildings and transport.

**Hall, Gus** *(1910–2000)* Secretary-general of the American Communist Party. The son of Finnish immigrants who were charter members of the American Communist Party, Hall himself joined the party at an early age. After serving in the Navy in World War II, he was imprisoned from 1949 to 1957 for conspiring to advocate the violent overthrow of the U.S. government. He was released in 1957, and in 1959 he became secretary-general of the party. In 1962, Hall refused to register the Communist Party with the federal government, as required by the McCarren Act, and in 1965 the United States Supreme Court ruled that the registration of individual members was unconstitutional. With the loosening of government restrictions, the party became more vocal throughout the 1960s, and Hall was nominated as the party's presidential candidate in 1972, 1976, 1980 and 1984.

**Hall, Joyce Clyde** *(1891–1982)* U.S. greeting card pioneer. He started selling postcards while still in school, and later started a wholesale business in postcards with his brother. In 1913 Hall became convinced that standard greetings could be printed to fit almost every occasion, and his philosophy provided the business pattern followed almost universally since. Hall devised marketing practices, such as the independent display rack. He invented the special occasion cards, and quickly Hallmark became the biggest name in the field. His company also sponsored quality radio and TV drama.

**Hall, Peter** *(1930–    )* British theatrical director. Hall attended Cambridge University, where he began his theatrical career. His earliest work was at the Theatre Royal, Windsor, and the London Arts Theatre. In 1957 he founded his own company, the International Playwrights' Theatre. At the same time, he established a reputation as a Shakespearean director with his version of *Love's Labour's Lost* at Stratford-upon-Avon. From 1960 to 1968 he was managing director of the new ROYAL SHAKESPEARE COMPANY, creating an incomparable ensemble and staging plays at Stratford and at the Aldwych Theatre, London. Among his most highly acclaimed productions were the *War of the Roses* cycle (1963) and *Richard III* (1964). Hall succeeded Laurence OLIVIER as director of the National Theatre in 1973, producing a wide range of plays until his departure in 1988. Among the best known were *Hamlet* (1975), Chekhov's *The Cherry Orchard* (1978) and Shaffer's *Amadeus* (1979). In 1988 Hall founded the Peter Hall Company, which has performed in both London's West End and New York's Broadway to critical acclaim.

**Halleck, Charles A(braham)** *(1900–1986)* American politician. A Republican from Indiana, Halleck was elected to 16 consecutive terms in the House of Representatives after winning a special election in 1935 to fill the remainder of the term of an incumbent who had died. He twice served as House majority leader, in 1947–48 and again in 1953–54. Although a conservative REPUBLICAN PARTY loyalist, he was frequently allied with conservative Southern Democrats. He parted company with them on the issue of CIVIL RIGHTS, supporting all major civil rights legislation in the late 1950s and early 1960s. Halleck became well known to U.S. television audiences in the 1960s as a participant with Illinois Republican senator Everett DIRKSEN in broadcasts attacking Democratic administration policies.

**Haller, Fritz P.** *(1924– )* Swiss architect and furniture designer known for the system of office furniture that bears his name. Haller has been in practice as architect and urban planner at Solothurn (near Basel), Switzerland, since 1949. He developed several steel-frame building systems currently used in Europe. In 1960 he developed a related system of office furniture using interchangeable steel tubes and connectors to form frames that carry shelves, work-tops, files and other storage elements. Haller has taught at the University of Southern California and at the University of Karlsruhe, West Germany. He is the author of *Integralurban; a Model,* a study of urban planning, and is the winner of several design awards.

**Hallinan, Hazel Hunkins** *(1891–1982)* American women's rights activist. She began her career as a member of the National Woman's Party in 1916, after chemical companies told her that they did not hire women. In 1917 she and other suffragists were arrested for chaining themselves to the White House fence and setting fire to its lawn. After the NINETEENTH AMENDMENT was passed in 1920 she moved to London, where she campaigned for British women's rights and wrote the "London Letter" column for the *Chicago Tribune.* (See also WOMEN'S MOVEMENTS.)

**Hallmark Hall of Fame** The most honored anthology series in the history of television. Hallmark Cards, Inc., had been founded by Mr. Joyce HALL in Kansas City in 1910. In the late 1930s and early 1940s he began sponsoring a radio series called *Tony Wons' Scrapbook.* The *Hallmark Playhouse* debuted on radio in 1948 and featured such notables as Ronald Colman in *Around the World in 80 Days* and Herbert Marshall in *Lost Horizon.* Hallmark moved to television in 1951 underwriting a series of 15-minute interviews hosted by

Sarah Churchill (daughter of British prime minister Winston); and then later on Dec. 24 of that year with the groundbreaking live telecast of the first original opera created for television, *AMAHL AND THE NIGHT VISITORS.* As the Hallmark-sponsored series moved into its "golden age" over the next 30 years—seen under a variety of names, such as *The Television Playhouse* and, finally, *The Hallmark Hall of Fame*—it garnered many "firsts" for the medium. *Hamlet* (1953) was the first full-length Shakespeare on any network. That same year a re-broadcast of *Amahl* was the first color transmission (aired just two days after the FCC approved NBC's patented "color tine" process). *Kiss Me Kate* (1958) was the first color video tape telecast. The 1960 version of *Macbeth,* filmed in Scotland, lays claim to being the first made-for-television movie. *The Tempest* (1960) was the first classic drama to rank in the Top 10 television ratings. Most of the great actors of stage and screen have appeared—including Julie HARRIS in 10 roles (including *Victoria Regina* in 1961), Katherine CORNELL in *There Shall Be No Night* (1957), James STEWART in *Harvey* (1972) and the team of Alfred LUNT and Lynne FONTANNE, in *The Magnificent Yankee* (1965). The series has won more than 56 Emmys, seven Peabody Awards, two Golden Globes, and numerous other distinctions. "I was convinced that the average American did not have the mind of a 12-year old," recalled Joyce C. Hall in his autobiography, *When You Care Enough* (1979), concerning his decision to sponsor these telecasts. "We wanted to reach the upper masses, not just the upper classes."

**Hallstein, Walter** *(1901–1982)* German lawyer and statesman. Hallstein was a key figure in the molding of WEST GERMANY's foreign policy after WORLD WAR II. He developed the doctrine of severing ties with any government (except the USSR) that recognized EAST GERMANY, but believed that it was important for West Germany to maintain diplomatic ties with the USSR. He was president of the commission of the EUROPEAN COMMUNITY from 1959 to 1967. In this post he worked for European unity.

**Halonen, Tarja Kaarina** *(1943–)* Finnish politician and Finland's first fe-

male head of state. Born in Helsinki, Halonen graduated from the University of Helsinki in 1968 and obtained a masters of law degree from the same institution. While working as a lawyer for the Central Organization of Finnish Trades Unions during the 1970s, she served as parliamentary secretary to the prime minister from 1974 to 1975 and then was elected to parliament as a member of the Social Democratic Party in 1979. She served as minister of social affairs from 1987 to 1990, minister of justice from 1990 to 1991, and foreign minister from 1995 to 2000. She was elected president of the country in 2000, becoming Finland's first female head of state.

**Halsey, William F(rederick, Jr.) "Bull"** *(1882–1959)* American admiral. Born in Elizabeth, N.J., Halsey graduated from Annapolis in 1904. During WORLD WAR I, he was a destroyer commander, and he was a naval aviator after 1935. During WORLD WAR II, the tenacious "Bull" Halsey commanded the Allied forces in the South Pacific (1942–44), successfully directing the Solomon Islands campaign. Commander of the U.S. Third Fleet in 1944–45, he was in charge of naval activities in the Philippines, defeated the Japanese fleet at Leyte Gulf in October 1944 and directed the sea-based bombardment of JAPAN in July 1945. He became a five-star admiral, the navy's highest rank, in 1945. He retired in 1947, the same year his memoirs, *Admiral Halsey's Story,* were published. (See also WORLD WAR II IN THE PACIFIC.)

**Halston (Roy Halston Frowick)** *(1932–1990)* American fashion designer. Halston first became famous as the milliner who created the "pillbox" hat worn by Jacqueline KENNEDY during her husband's inauguration in 1961. He showed his first clothing designs in 1966 and established his own couture line two years later. His ready-to-wear line was established in 1972. The simple, clean lines of his designs were immediately popular and won him such friends and clients as Liza Minelli, Elizabeth TAYLOR, and Bianca Jagger. He sold his business and his trademark name in 1973, leaving him with little say as to the products that bore his name.

**Hamas** A Palestinian Arab terrorist group formed in the late 1970s by its spiritual leader, Sheikh Ahmed Yassin, and which espouses a version of IS-LAMISM, a fundamentalist Muslim philosophy that calls for purging Islamic societies of all non-Muslim elements. Hamas first came to international attention for its use of violent rhetoric and of actions against the Israeli state during the first Intifada (see INTIFADA I), or uprising, in 1987. Hamas called for Palestinians to support its campaign to eliminate the state of ISRAEL and expel all Israelis from the WEST BANK and GAZA STRIP. The military branch, called the Izzedine al-Qassam Brigades, have concentrated on the use of homemade bombs, often carried by suicide bombers and detonated in areas of high Jewish population density, in an effort to create an atmosphere of terror in Israel. In addition to trumpeting its political goals in the Middle East and denouncing any Arab-Israeli peace process that recognizes the state of Israel's right to exist, Hamas has also engaged in humanitarian aid in Palestinian areas by establishing Muslim schools and hospitals. Some Israeli observers, however, have charged that these institutions serve largely as recruiting grounds for future soldiers and suicide bombers in the Izzedine al-Qassam.

The PALESTINE LIBERATION ORGANIZATION (PLO) originally supported Hamas's actions. But by 1997 the PLO's successor, the PALESTINIAN AUTHORITY (PA), had begun denouncing the suicide bombings and arresting Palestinian members of Hamas. In 2000, when a second Intifada (see INTIFADA II) broke out in Israel, Hamas was again at the forefront of the violence, along with another Islamist group called the Islamic Jihad. Since the outbreak of this second wave of terrorist attacks and suicide bombings, the Israeli government has initiated efforts to eliminate Hamas's capability to wage a war of terror on Palestinians and Israelis alike through the selective assassination of Hamas military and political leaders. In March 2004 an Israeli missile killed Sheikh Yassin. Hamas shocked the world in January 2006 by winning the legislative elections of the Palestinian Authority, thereby obtaining the right to form a government that would take control of the West Bank and the Gaza Strip.

**Hamburg** One of the largest ports in the world; a German cultural center and industrial city on the Elbe River, about 60 miles upriver from Cuxhaven, on the North Sea. The scene of communist rioting in 1923, since 1937 Hamburg has been coextensive with, and capital of, the state of Hamburg. During WORLD WAR II Hamburg was heavily bombed, so much so that much of the city today is brand new, while surviving buildings are identified as such by plaques. Many old churches were destroyed, but the baroque St. Michael's Church, built between 1750 and 1762, and the Church of St. Jacobi, begun in the 14th century, have survived. In 1989 Hamburg celebrated the 800th anniversary of its charter as a free city by Frederick Barbarossa.

**Hamilton, George Heard** (1910–2004) American art historian, teacher and museum director. Educated at Yale University, Hamilton taught art history there and was a curator at the Yale Art Gallery (1936–66). He was a professor at Williams College (1965–75), while serving as director of the Clark Art Institute, Williamstown, Mass. (1966–77). A specialist in European and American art of the 19th and 20th centuries, he is the author of such books as *Painting and Sculpture in Europe, 1880–1940* (1967) and *Nineteenth and Twentieth Century Art* (1970).

**Hamilton, Scott** (1958– ) American figure skater. The adopted child of university professors, Hamilton was diagnosed in early childhood with a growth-inhibiting disease. The disease abated when he took up skating at the age of nine. Never topping 5 foot 3 inches and 110 pounds, he won three consecutive world championships from 1981 to 1983. His ease with spectacular triple jumps made him a favorite entering the 1984 Winter OLYMPICS. While his performance in the short and long freeskating programs fell somewhat short, as he finished second to his longtime rival, Canadian Brian Orser, his compulsory figures were enough to give him the gold medal. After retiring from competition, Hamilton's insight into his sport led to a career as a skating commentator. In 1997 Hamilton was diagnosed with testicular cancer and immediately underwent a series of chemotherapy treatments and surgeries to eliminate the presence of cancerous cells.

**Hamm, Mia** (1972– ) American women's soccer player. Born Mariel Margaret Hamm in Selma, Ala., she played women's soccer in high school in Wichita Falls, Tex., before moving with her family to Virginia. While in high school, she played in a match against the Chinese national team in August 1987 and joined the U.S. National Women's Team in 1988. Accepting an athletic scholarship to the University of North Carolina (UNC), Hamm helped guide UNC to four championships in the 1989, 1990, 1992 and 1993 seasons. In addition to her four championships, she had her soccer jersey retired by UNC for becoming the Atlantic Coast Conference's all-time leader in goals (103), assists (72) and points scored (278). In her sophomore, junior and senior years she was named to the All-American Team of the National Soccer Collegiate Athletic Association (NSCAA).

After graduating from UNC in 1994 with a B.A. in political science, Hamm continued to play soccer and qualified for the U.S. Team for the 1995 Women's World Cup in Sweden. She started all five games the U.S. played in that year's competition, and helped the U.S. finish in a tie for first place with Norway. The following year she played with Team USA at the Olympics in Atlanta, Ga., where she helped the U.S. win the Gold Medal by defeating the Chinese national team. In 1999, after three years of regional and global women's soccer tournaments, including helping the U.S. team win a gold medal at the 1998 Goodwill Games, Hamm again joined the U.S. in the 1999 Women's World Cup held that year in the U.S. Over 26 games Hamm guided the U.S. to the World Cup Championship, where she helped Team USA defeat China by nailing the fourth penalty kick.

Since her success in the 1999 Women's World Cup, Hamm continued to play as both an amateur and a professional athlete. In 2000 she again joined the U.S. Women's Olympic

Team and helped lead it to the silver medal, losing the final game to China. The following year Hamm signed on as a player on the Washington Freedom, one of the eight teams comprising the Women's United Soccer Association (WUSA), the first female soccer professional league in the U.S., formed because the large turnout within the U.S. during the 1999 Women's World Cup made it appear that women's professional soccer could become a profit-making enterprise. In 2003 the Women's United Soccer Association suspended operations because revenues were insufficient to support a fourth season. Hamm retired in 2004.

**Hammarskjöld, Dag** *(1905–1961)* Swedish statesman, secretary-general of the UNITED NATIONS (1953–61). Hammarskjöld was Sweden's deputy foreign minister from 1951 to 1953. Elected secretary-general of the UN in 1953, he was reelected in 1957. The dignity and impartiality with which he conducted UN affairs, especially during the SUEZ CRISIS, enhanced the standing of the organization. In 1960 his handling of the Congo crisis provoked hostility from the USSR. While seeking peace between the Congo and the secessionist province of KATANGA, Hammarskjöld was killed in an airplane crash. He was awarded the 1961 NOBEL PEACE PRIZE posthumously.

**Hammer, Armand** *(1898–1990)* American industrialist and Soviet expert. Born in New York City and trained as a physician, Hammer made his first visit to the USSR in 1921 on a medical mission. Retaining an abiding interest in Soviet-American friendship, he had personal contacts with Russian leaders from LENIN to GORBACHEV. A gifted entrepreneur, he soon became involved in trading U.S. grain for Soviet furs and caviar. Over the years, Hammer headed successful businesses in fields ranging from whiskey to broadcasting, but his greatest fortune was made through his building of Occidental Petroleum Co. into a major international oil company. He was also a major philanthropist and noted art collector.

**Hammerstein, Oscar, II** *(1895–1960)* American song lyricist and librettist best known for his collaborations with Jerome KERN and Richard RODGERS. Hammerstein was born in New York into a musical theater family. After abandoning law studies at Columbia University he embarked upon a series of notable collaborations with Herbert Stothart (*Wildflower,* 1923); Sigmund ROMBERG (*The Desert Song,* 1926, and *New Moon,* 1928); and Jerome KERN (*Show Boat,* 1927). The historic partnership with Richard Rodgers began with *Oklahoma* (1943) and included such landmark musical shows as *Carousel* (1945), *South Pacific* (1949), *The King and I* (1951), *Flower Drum Song* (1958) and their last, *The Sound of Music* (1959). In contrast to Rodgers's previous collaborator, Lorenz HART (to whom he was frequently and unfavorably compared), Hammerstein had a positive and romantic style. To quote one of his songs, he was "stuck like a dope with a thing called hope." The style emerged at its best in "Oh, What a Beautiful Morning," "Younger Than Springtime," "Hello, Young Lovers" and "Billy's Soliloquy" (all with Rodgers); and at its worst in such saccharine ditties as "Happy Talk" and "Climb Ev'ry Mountain" (also with Rodgers). He wrote his autobiography, *Lyrics by Hammerstein,* in 1949, and died of cancer in 1960. He played an important part, wrote producer Max Gordon, in "laying the groundwork for what was to become America's undeniable contribution to the world's theatre."

**Hammer v. Dagenhart** *(1918)* U.S. Supreme Court decision striking down an early effort to ban child labor. During the early years of the century, young children were commonly employed in factories. Responding to popular outcries over this practice, Congress passed a federal Child Labor Law that outlawed the sale of goods produced by children working either more than six days a week or more than eight hours per day. The Supreme Court struck down the law as unconstitutional, however. The Court reasoned that manufacturing was not "commerce" and was outside the scope of Congress' regulatory authority. The case was not overruled until 1937 with the passage of the Fair Labor Standards Act, which severely limited the use of child labor in factories. (See also *BAILEY V. DREXEL FURNITURE CO.*)

**Hammett, Samuel Dashiell** *(1894–1961)* American novelist. Hammett's much-imitated fiction, beginning with *Red Harvest* (1929), is the origin of the tough, realistic genre of detective stories. His best known works include *The Maltese Falcon* (1930, filmed three times, most notably in 1941), which introduced the hardboiled detective Sam Spade; and *The Thin Man* (1934, filmed 1934), which features Nick and Nora Charles. Hammett's writing was based on his own experiences as a private detective in the late teens. Following 1934, Hammett worked as a screenwriter in HOLLYWOOD. Among his credits is the screen adaptation for *Watch on the Rhine* (1943) by Lillian HELLMAN, who became Hammett's companion in 1930. During the MCCARTHY era, Hammett was jailed for refusing to testify in 1951. He was ill when he was released, and later impoverished as a result of increased scrutiny by the Internal Revenue Service.

**Hammond, John** *(1910–1987)* American record producer. A JAZZ and BLUES aficionado, Hammond's legendary talent scouting abilities led him to such finds as Bessie SMITH, Billie HOLIDAY, Benny GOODMAN and Count BASIE. In 1933 he became American recording director of the English division of Columbia Records. There he used his private income as an heir to the Vanderbilt fortune to subsidize many recordings by such artists as Fletcher HENDERSON and Chick WEBB. A champion of racial equality, he was proud of his role in creating jazz's first integrated group—the Benny Goodman Trio. In later years, he signed Aretha FRANKLIN, Bob DYLAN and Bruce SPRINGSTEEN to Columbia Records.

**Hampshire, Sir Stuart** *(1914–2004)* British philosopher. Hampshire is one of the best-known British philosophers of the post–World War II era, although he has been a clarifier and synthesizer of past ideas rather than an originator of a new philosophic system. Educated at Oxford, Hampshire taught there as well as at University College, London, and at Princeton University. The fields on which he has written include epistemology, philosophy of mind, aesthetics and metaphysics. One of his key ideas has been that different conditions apply to the certainty of a statement, depending on the particular class of statement under consideration. Major works by Hampshire include *Spinoza* (1951), *Thought and Action* (1959), *Feeling and Expression* (1960) and *Freedom of the Individual* (1965) and the stage version of *Sunset Boulevard,* for which he won a Tony Award for Best Book of a Musical.

**Hampton, Christopher James** (*1946– * ) British playwright. Hampton's first play, *When Did You Last See My Mother* (1966), was performed by the English State Company at the Royal Court Theatre, where Hampton was resident playwright from 1968 to 1970. There he wrote *Total Eclipse* (1968) and *The Philanthropist* (1970). Perhaps his best known work is *Les Liaisons Dangereuses* (1986, filmed 1989), which depicts a manipulative contest of seduction between a nobleman and lady in prerevolutionary France. Hampton has also translated the works of CHEKHOV, Ibsen and Molière. Other works include *Savages* (1973) and *Tales from Hollywood* (1980).

**Hampton, Lionel** (*1909–2002*) American jazz musician and bandleader. Born in Louisville, Kentucky, Hampton performed in the early part of his career with Paul Howard, Les Hite, and Louis ARMSTRONG, playing drums, xylophone and vibraphone. He was a popular performer with Benny GOODMAN from 1936 to 1940, before founding his own band in 1941. One of the most popular and exciting big bands of the 1940s, Hampton's group survived until 1965, when he moved more into rhythm and blues and founded the Jazz Inner Circle sextet.

**Hamsun, Knut (Knut Pedersen)** (*1859–1952*) Norwegian novelist. Hamsun first achieved acclaim with the novel *Sult* (*Hunger* 1890). Based on his own travails, the novel depicts a starving young writer attempting to establish himself. With its intense prose and hallucinatory passages, the novel has come to be regarded as a seminal modernist work. Important subsequent fiction includes *Mysterier* (*Mysteries* 1892), *Pan* (1894) and *Markens grode* (*Growth of the Soil,* 1917) Ham-

sun was awarded the NOBEL PRIZE in literature in 1920. Although he continued to write throughout his life, Hamsun's later works never received the attention of his early novels. He was an avid supporter of NAZISM during the 1930s and WORLD WAR II. After the war he was arrested by the Norwegian government and tried in 1947.

**Hancock, Herbie** (*1940– * ) One of contemporary jazzdom's most visible and successful performers. While completing his education at Grinnell College in the late 1950s, Hancock returned to his hometown of Chicago on weekends to back such prominent jazz artists as Coleman HAWKINS. His successful recording debut as a leader in 1962 produced a hit song, "Watermelon Man," and an invitation to join Miles DAVIS's fabled quintet. With bassist Ron Carter and drummer Tony Williams, Hancock helped evolve a more open-ended and interactive approach to rhythm section playing that made the Davis fivesome one of the most influential groups of the 1960s. Following up the fusion experiments of Davis and groups like WEATHER REPORT, Hancock, since the late 1960s, has devoted much energy to various amalgams of rock, funk and jazz; his "Rockit" was a number-one pop hit in 1983. Hancock has made periodic returns to more conventional neo-bebop jazz settings, most significantly in his piano duos with Chick COREA. He has also scored feature films, including *Round Midnight* (1986), for which he won an ACADEMY AWARD. In 2004 he was the recipient of the National Endowment for the Arts Jazz Masters Fellowship, the U.S. government's highest award for jazz musicians. Among Hancock's original jazz standards are "Maiden Voyage," "Dolphin Dance," "Cantaloupe Island" and "Speak Like a Child."

**Hand, Learned** (*1872–1961*) American jurist. An honors graduate of both Harvard University and its law school, Hand was one of the best-known jurists of his day, although he was inexplicably never nominated to the U.S. Supreme Court. Hand favored the doctrine of judicial restraint, which requires courts not to substitute their views for those of the legislatures that make the laws. Under this doctrine courts should not make law or stretch laws beyond their

intended purpose. Perhaps his best-known opinion was in *DENNIS V. U.S.* (1949), in which he upheld the convictions of 11 leaders of the U.S. Communist Party under the SMITH ACT. Hand's opinion was later upheld by the Supreme Court, which adopted his view that the government could bar political speech even when it did not incite violence. Hand's brother Augustus was also a prominent federal appeals judge.

**Handke, Peter** (*1942– * ) Austrian playwright and novelist. Handke established himself as an unorthodox author with the plays, *Publikumsbschimpfung* (Offending the Audience, 1966), *Kaspar* (1968), which shows the influence of the philosopher Ludwig WITTGENSTEIN, and *Der Ritt bei den Bodensee* (1971). His works examine use of language and communication. His novels include *Across* (1986) and *Repetition* (1988). Handke continued to publish well-received novels throughout the 1990s, including *My Year in the No-Man's Bay* (1998) and *On a Dark Night I Left My Silent House* (1999). In 1996 Handke created political controversy with his essay "A Journey to the Rivers," which defended Serbian actions following the disintegration of YUGOSLAVIA in 1991. In 1999 he returned literary prize money that he had won in 1973 in protest against the NATO bombardment of the Serbian capital of Belgrade.

**Handl, Irene** (*1902–1987*) One of Great Britain's most beloved character actresses, Handl excelled in comic portrayals of eccentric Cockneys. Although she did not turn to acting until her late 30s, she achieved quick success and emerged as a star of stage, cinema and television. Her biggest theatrical hit was *Goodnight Mrs. Puffin,* which ran for three years in the early 1960s. She was familiar to TV viewers for appearances in such comedy series as "For the Love of Ada" (1970–73) and "Never Say Die."

**Handy, W(illiam) C(hristopher)** (*1873–1958*) Noted American jazz composer. Handy initially studied organ and music theory, then cornet. His first significant professional experiences occurred at the turn of the 20th century with Mahara's Minstrels, first as a cornet soloist, later as the group's leader. In

1917 he moved to New York, where he supplemented his playing career with song writing; he also enjoyed some success as a music publisher. Though he continued performing into the 1940s, Handy's greatest significance was as a composer and collector of BLUES; his "Beale Street Blues" and "Memphis Blues" are among the most popular songs of the standard jazz repertoire. In 1928, a 17-minute film dramatized Handy's most famous and enduring composition, "St. Louis Blues"; the film is significant for the only cinematic appearance of legendary blues singer Bessie SMITH, who in the 1920s had helped popularize Handy's immortal tune; also important is the short film's status as perhaps the first widely released sound film to be based on a popular song and therefore a proto-forerunner of the music-video phenomenon. In 1957, Nat "King" COLE starred in a highly fictionalized biography of Handy, *St. Louis Blues.* Handy's autobiography is *Father of the Blues.*

**Hanks, Tom** *(1956–   )* American television and movie actor. Born in Concord, Calif., Hanks began his acting career in theater performances in Ohio and California in 1977. His success in these theater pieces won him the attention of a team of television producers, who in 1980 cast him in *Bosom Buddies,* a sitcom about two men posing as women in order to live in an inexpensive apartment building reserved exclusively for women.

In 1984 Hanks debuted as a headlining motion-picture star in the film *Splash,* a comedic piece in which he starred as a man who falls in love with a mermaid (Daryl Hannah). In *Big* (1985), Hanks depicted the grown-up version of a 12-year-old who wished he could become adult overnight, and who then uses his childlike insight to create winning concepts for a toy industry giant. After receiving lukewarm receptions in reviews and at the box office in such films as *The 'Burbs* (1989), *The Bonfire of the Vanities* (1990) and *Joe Versus the Volcano* (1990), Hanks reversed this trend with his role as an alcoholic, misogynistic manager of a women's baseball team in *A League of Their Own* (1992). The following year *Sleepless in Seattle,* Hanks and Meg Ryan played two single people connected by Hanks's conversation with a radio psychiatrist, in which he un-

*Academy Award–winning actor Tom Hanks. 1988*
(PHOTOFEST)

knowingly describes himself as Ryan's soulmate, leading both to meet in New York. Hanks would team again with Ryan in *You've Got Mail* (1998), in which he played a bookstore executive who opens a shop near Ryan's children's bookstore, leading to competition between the two while they pursue an anonymous romance online.

His performance in *Philadelphia* (1993) a dark drama that chronicled the efforts of a successful lawyer (Hanks) to sue his employers for terminating his employment once they learned he had contracted the AIDS virus, won him a 1994 best actor award. The following year Hanks won the award again for his title role in *Forrest Gump,* a dramatic comedy in which he portrayed a mentally ill individual who navigated his way through life.

Hanks's later work generally has fallen into two camps, the dramatic and the comedic. The first category includes *Apollo 13* (1995), in which he costarred with Kevin Bacon and Bill Paxton as the three members of the doomed lunar mission; director Steven SPIELBERG's *Saving Private Ryan* (1998), in which he played an army Ranger captain sent to extract a soldier from battle in 1944 France; and *Cast Away* (2000), in which he appeared nearly alone throughout the film as a shipwrecked Federal Express executive. Hanks later provided the voice for Woody, a lanky cowboy, in the computer-animated films *Toy Story,* and *Toy Story 2,* which proved finan-

cial successes for Disney and Pixar Studios.

Hanks also moved into the producer's chair, with *From the Earth to the Moon,* a 1998 miniseries for HBO that traced the evolution of the American space program from its infancy to the first Apollo landing. Hanks reunited with Spielberg to produce *Band of Brothers,* a 2001 miniseries for HBO based on the book by historian Stephen Ambrose that chronicled the members of Easy Company of the 101st Airborne Division in WORLD WAR II.

**Hanley, James** *(1901–1985)* British author. Although Hanley never gained a large readership, he was regarded by some critics and fellow writers as one of the most important figures in 20th-century English literature. A number of his novels drew upon his youthful experiences as a seaman and led reviewers to compare him to Joseph CONRAD. Among the most acclaimed of his novels were *The Closed Harbor* (1952), *Levine* (1956), and *A Dream Journey* (1976). Although primarily a novelist, he probably achieved greater public recognition as a playwright. His plays were staged in London, New York and elsewhere.

**Hanoi**   Capital of VIETNAM; on the Red River, about 75 miles upriver from the Gulf of Tonkin port of Haiphong. Occupied by France in 1883, Hanoi was the capital of French INDOCHINA from 1887 to 1946, a period of industrial development; during WORLD WAR II its Japanese occupiers were frequently bombed. From 1946 to 1954 Hanoi was the seat of the unrecognized (by France) Democratic Republic of Vietnam and a scene of heavy fighting between the French and the VIET MINH. After France threw in the colonial towel, Hanoi became the capital of **North Vietnam** and experienced a period of great industrial expansion—until the VIETNAM WAR of 1965–73. Heavily bombed by U.S. forces, its factories were dismantled and moved elsewhere but were speedily reconstructed after the war.

**Hansberry, Lorraine** *(1930–1965)* American playwright. Hansberry is best known for the celebrated play *A Raisin in the Sun* (1959, filmed 1961), which depicts a black family facing a moral dilemma involving racial prejudice. The title of the play was taken from a poem by Nikki GIOVANNI. Hansberry's life was tragically short, and the only other of her works she was to see performed was *The Sign in Sidney Brustein's Window* (1964), which concerns Jewish life in New York City.

**Hanson, Duane** *(1925–1996)* American sculptor. An influential New Realist, Hanson is known for his life-sized figures of ordinary Americans caught in moments typical of their everyday lives. Among his uncannily realistic sculptures are the 1970 works *Hard Hat* and *Woman with Dog* (Whitney Museum of American Art, N.Y.C.).

**Hanson, Howard Harold** *(1896–1981)* American composer, conductor and educator. Hanson studied music at the University of Nebraska, the Juilliard School and at Northwestern University, Chicago. His 1920 composition earned him the Prix de Rome, for a three-year advanced study period in that city. In 1924, Hanson became director of the Eastman School of Music, Rochester (1924–64), and brought the school to national and international fame. He is considered one of the most influential teachers and composers of his time. Hanson founded the American Composers Concerts at Rochester, and wrote six symphonies, an opera and many other symphonic and choral works. He won a 1944 PULITZER PRIZE for his Fourth Symphony.

**Hapoel Hamizrachi (The Mizrach Worker)** In ISRAEL, a religious—moderately orthodox—center-left party. It joined with MIZRACHI in 1956 to form the **National Religious Party.**

**happening** Term for artistic event that emphasizes spontaneous developments. The term *happening* was coined in 1959 by conceptual artist Allan KAPROW to describe an artistic environment—whether in a public park or in a private art gallery—that allows participation by persons other than the artist in the creation of aesthetic works and moods. A key influence on the concept of a "happening" was the irreverent playfulness of the POP ART movement. Happenings featured artists painting, filming, and photographing on the spot; mass participa-

tion in the coloring of a canvas; dance and music; and any other activities that seemed to add to the joy and creativity of the situation. Happenings were as much philosophical statements on the stifled nature of societal behavior as they were aesthetic works of art. (See also BE-IN.)

**Haram al-Sharif (Temple Mount)** The site of a religious structure revered by both the Jewish and Muslim faiths. Haram al-Sharif, which means "Venerable Sanctuary," is the Muslim name for the Temple Mount. Situated in the Old City of Jerusalem, the Temple Mount was the site of the First Temple of Israel, constructed in the 10th century B.C.E. atop the hill where Jewish tradition holds that God made a covenant with Abraham. It was alongside the Temple Mount that Herod the Great constructed what later became known as the Western (or Wailing) Wall, a retaining structure designed to provide structural support to the Temple. Jews have long since journeyed to the wall, inserting in its chinks prayers written on paper and mourning at the site. The Wailing Wall is all that remains of the original First and Second Temple structures.

The site is also sacred to Muslims. According to Muslim tradition, Muhammad traveled to Jerusalem to visit the site of God's covenant with Abraham, and later ascended to heaven from the ground of the temple. To commemorate this event Muslims built the Dome of the Rock and the al-Aqsa Mosque on the Temple Mount area. Pilgrimages to it from Muslims all across the world have made it the third most holy Muslim site in the world after Mecca and Medina.

In the autumn of 2000 a visit by Israeli prime minister Ariel SHARON to the Temple Mount, and his participation in the Jewish ritual associated with the site, helped touch off the second Intifada, or uprising, by Palestinian Arabs against Israeli occupation of the WEST BANK and GAZA STRIP (see INTIFADA II).

**Harare (formerly Salisbury)** Capital city of ZIMBABWE (formerly known as RHODESIA); in southeastern Africa. The largest city in Zimbabwe was founded in 1890 as a fort by the Pioneer Column, a mercenary force organized by Cecil J. Rhodes, a diamond-rich British imperialist and entrepreneur. The out-

post was named for Robert Arthur Salisbury, then prime minister of Great Britain. Salisbury was the capital of the **Federation of Rhodesia and Nyasaland** from 1953 to 1963. In 1965, when Rhodesia unilaterally proclaimed its independence, Salisbury became the capital—and remained so when white political domination ended and the land was officially recognized as the African nation of Zimbabwe in 1979. In April 1982 Salisbury became Harare, to honor a 19th-century tribal chief.

**Harburg, Edgar Y. "Yip"** *(1896–1981)* American song lyricist. Harburg first gained notice with his words to the 1932 song, "Brother, Can You Spare a Dime," a poignant account of a man's dreams and hardships during the GREAT DEPRESSION. During his career he wrote the lyrics to more than 30 other well-known songs, which were often marked by touches of romantic imagination and strong feelings of social justice. He collaborated with some of America's leading popular composers on scores of stage and film musicals, including *Finian's Rainbow* and, most notably, *The Wizard of Oz,* which won him an ACADEMY AWARD in 1939. Undoubtedly his most acclaimed song was "Somewhere Over the Rainbow," which made a star of Judy GARLAND.

**hard-edge painting** Term for American painting developed in the late 1950s that uses large blocks of monochromatic color in sharp-edged geometrical forms. In these works, there is usually an interplay between positive and negative space, image and field. Artists who have used various forms of this style include Ellsworth KELLY, Alexander Liberman, Agnes Martin and Frank STELLA.

**Hardie, James Keir** *(1856–1915)* British labor leader and politician, revered as a major figure in the early history of the British LABOUR PARTY. The Scottish-born Hardie was a leading figure in the British labor movement from the 1880s until his death and was a co-founder of the Labour Party. He sat in Parliament from 1892 to 1895 and again (as M.P. for Merthyr Tydfil) from 1900 until his death. He was the first chairman (1906–07) of the parliamentary Labour Party and, more than anyone else, was responsible for establishing the party's identity and program in its early days. A committed pacifist and nonconformist, he opposed Britain's entry into WORLD WAR I.

## Harding, Field Marshal Lord John (Allan Francis) (1896–1989)
British army officer. Harding was the commander of British forces in North Africa during WORLD WAR II. As a brigadier general in 1940 he led Britain's Seventh Armoured Division, known as the "Desert Rats," in the battle of EL ALAMEIN, which turned the tide against the German forces in North Africa. After the war, he was appointed commander in chief of the British Army of the Rhine. He later served as governor of CYPRUS, where he was the target of death threats from a guerrilla group seeking unification with GREECE.

## Harding, Warren G(amaliel)
(1865–1923) Twenty-ninth president of the United States. Harding studied at Ohio Central College, began a journalistic career and built a strong Republican political base in Ohio. In 1899 he went to the state legislature and in 1904 became lieutenant governor. He lost a bid for the governorship but continued to rise politically. At the Republican National Convention in 1912, he was chosen to present the nomination of William Howard TAFT. In 1914 he was elected to the U.S. Senate, where he had an undistinguished term. However, a group of his fellow Republican senators proposed his name for president at the Republican convention of 1920. When the convention became deadlocked, Harding was thought of as an ideal compromise candidate. He received the nomination on the 10th ballot and ran against Democrat James COX. The election of Harding was the first to be reported by radio.

Harding had promised to form a cabinet of only the "best minds." In many instances he chose his administrative team well, but he also chose others with little civic responsibility. According to one source, "the [Harding] administration . . . was marked by one achievement, the Washington (naval) Conference" (1921–22). In August 1923, Harding became the first president to visit ALASKA. On this trip he received some notice of scandals in

*Warren G. Harding, 29th president of the United States* (LIBRARY OF CONGRESS, PRINTS AND PHOTOGRAPHS DIVISION)

his administration, which had been kept from him until that time. On his way home, at San Francisco, Harding died unexpectedly under circumstances still not entirely clear. He was not to be troubled by the humiliating scandals that plagued the administration he left behind, including, but not limited to, the TEAPOT DOME SCANDAL (involving Secretary of the Interior Albert B. FALL and Attorney General Harry M. DAUGHERTY). (See also Calvin COOLIDGE.)

## Hardwick, Elizabeth (1916– )
American author. Hardwick's fiction is noted for its insightful depictions of women and their roles within the family and for its cool, detached tone, which has been compared to that of Joan DIDION. Her novels include *The Ghostly Lover* (1945) and *Sleepless Nights* (1979). She has also published the collections of essays *Seduction and Betrayal: Women and Literature* (1974), *Bartleby in Manhattan* (1983) and a critical biography of Herman Melville (2000). Hardwick is a frequent contributor to THE NEW YORKER and other periodicals. She was the second wife of poet Robert LOWELL.

## Hardy, Oliver See LAUREL AND HARDY.

## Hardy, René (1912–1987)
French RESISTANCE leader during WORLD WAR

II. After the war, Hardy's reputation was besmirched by charges that he had betrayed top Resistance leader Jean MOULIN to Klaus Barbie, the GESTAPO chief of Lyon. Hardy was twice tried for treason and twice acquitted. Nonetheless, many of his former Resistance colleagues continued to insist that he was guilty. In 1972 Barbie, then living in sanctuary in South America, said that Hardy had been a collaborator. Hardy, meanwhile, had become a successful novelist.

## Hardy, Thomas (1839–1928)
English novelist, essayist and poet. Hardy is one of the unquestioned great figures in the history of English literature. Although born in the first half of the 19th century, his creative output and his influence extend well into the 20th. He earned his major renown for a series of intensely dramatic 19th-century novels set in his native Dorchester, which he renamed "Wessex" for fictional purposes. These include *Far from the Madding Crowd* (1874), *The Mayor of Casterbridge* (1886), *Tess of the D'Urbervilles* (1891) and *Jude the Obscure* (1896). In the late 1890s, spurred by bitter critical attacks on his novels but enjoying the financial security he had earned from them, Hardy resolved to devote the remainder of his writing career to poetry and poetic drama. He became, in the first three decades of the 20th century, a powerful practitioner in the standard metric forms of English verse, upholding tradition in the midst of the free verse literary revolution. The same pessimism and irony that pervades his fiction is also evident in his poetry. Among his key poetic works are the drama *The Dynasts* (1904) and the verse collection *Moments of Vision* (1917). Hardy's work has influenced many 20th century British poets and novelists, including the writers of the MOVEMENT of the 1950s, especially Philip LARKIN.

## Harkness, Georgia E(lma) (1891–1974)
American Methodist theologian and social critic; one of the most influential Methodist thinkers and educators of her era. Harkness emphasized the need for equal rights for women within the Methodist Church, although she did not herself seek ordination as a priest. In 1948 and 1954, Harkness served as a delegate to the

ecumenical World Council of Churches. Beginning in 1950, Harkness also became an active opponent of nuclear armaments. Her writings include *Dark Night of the Soul* (1945) and *Women in Church and Society* (1971).

**Harlan, John Marshall** *(1833–1911)* U.S. Supreme Court associate justice (1877–1911); grandfather of John Marshall HARLAN II, who was later a Supreme Court associate justice. The elder Harlan, son of a U.S. congressman and a native of Kentucky, studied law at Transylvania University. Although a slaveowner, Harlan served as an officer in the Union Army during the Civil War. He was elected Kentucky's attorney general after the war and became prominent in the Republican Party. He was instrumental in securing the presidential nomination for Rutherford B. Hayes at the 1876 Republican convention and was later rewarded with his appointment to the Supreme Court. On the Court Harlan was known as a rustic who chewed and spat tobacco during Court sessions. He was also dubbed the "great dissenter" because of his opposition to many notable decisions, including *Plessy v. Ferguson* (1896), which upheld "separate but equal" public services along racial lines. However, Harlan outlasted many of his detractors, serving a remarkable 33 years on the Supreme Court.

*Supreme Court associate justice John Marshall Harlan. engraved by Max Rosenthal* (LIBRARY OF CONGRESS. PRINTS AND PHOTOGRAPHS DIVISION)

**Harlan, John Marshall, II** *(1899–1971)* Associate justice, U.S. Supreme Court (1955–71). A graduate of Princeton University and a Rhodes Scholar, John Harlan was the grandson of John Marshall HARLAN, who served on the Supreme Court from 1877 to 1911. Harlan worked with a Wall Street law firm for many years, although he took leaves of absence to serve as an assistant U.S. attorney, special state assistant attorney general, and chief council of a state crime commission. He was appointed to the influential U.S. District Court for the Second Circuit in 1954. Several months later, President Dwight D. EISENHOWER nominated him to the Supreme Court. On the Court Harlan was generally known as a moderate. He resigned shortly before his death in 1971.

**Harlech, Lord** **(Sir [William] David Ormsby Gore)** *(1918–1985)* British diplomat. During the 1950s Sir David Gore led Britain's delegation at the UNITED NATIONS (UN). His career reached its peak when he served as Britain's ambassador to the U.S. during the administration of John F. KENNEDY. A close personal friend of the president, he reportedly exercised a restraining influence on Kennedy during the CUBAN MISSILE CRISIS (1962). In the 1970s he played a key role in British negotiations with its former colony RHODESIA. (See also ZIMBABWE.)

**Harlem** Part of New York City's borough of Manhattan, its name derived from the original Dutch settlers of New York. In the early part of this century the migration of southern blacks in search of better-paying jobs in the industrial North turned New York's Harlem into one of the largest black communities in the nation. From the 1920s through the 1940s, the HARLEM RENAISSANCE reflected black cultural life. After World War II the Hispanic population grew considerably in East Harlem. The area is the home of the Abyssinian Baptist church, established in 1808 and headed for many years by Adam Clayton POWELL Jr. Harlem's historic Apollo Theater stage still supports and encourages black theatrical talent. Poet Countee CULLEN, writer James BALDWIN and singer Billie HOLLIDAY, among others, were residents. In 2001

former president Bill CLINTON established his office in Harlem.

**Harlem Renaissance** Called by Langston HUGHES "that fantastic period when HARLEM was in vogue," the term *Harlem Renaissance* refers to an era of extraordinary artistic achievement by African-American writers and artists centered in the Harlem section of New York City. Ushered in by the JAZZ AGE and the successful black revue *Shuffle Along* (1921), the 1920s Harlem Renaissance saw the publication of important works by such authors as Hughes, Sterling BROWN, Countee CULLEN, Zora Neale HURSTON, Claude McKay, Jean Toomer, and many others. Harlem became a lively mecca for black artists and writers, and the movement symbolized a national mood of increased optimism and pride among black Americans. *The New Negro* anthology, edited by Alain Locke, remains an important document of the period and was mirrored in the "New Negro" social-political movement. There was increased activity by the NAACP under the leadership of W. E. B. DUBOIS, Marcus GARVEY's Universal Negro Improvement Association, and the National URBAN LEAGUE. The GREAT DEPRESSION of the 1930s sent Harlem into a decline, together with the rest of the country, and African Americans would not again capture such national attention until the CIVIL RIGHTS MOVEMENT of the 1950s and 1960s.

**Harlow, Jean (Harlean Carpenter)** *(1911–1937)* Hollywood's first "blonde bombshell," Harlow was the American film industry's greatest sex symbol of the 1930s. After running away from home at 16, Harlow became an extra in silent films in the late 1920s. Howard HUGHES caught sight of her beauty and cast her as the leading lady in his epic early talkie, *Hell's Angels* (1930). The hit led to several more films, at several more studios, including *Public Enemy* (1931, WARNER BROS.) and *Platinum Blonde* (1931, COLUMBIA). But it was in METRO-GOLDWYN-MAYER films such as *Red Dust* (1932) with Clark GABLE that she became a national sex goddess. Her magnificent career was cut short by tragedy, when she died of uremic poisoning during the filming of *Saratoga* (1937).

**Harmon, Ernest N.** *(1894–1979)* American military officer. Harmon was one of America's most decorated generals and among the U.S. Army's most daring and aggressive armored division commanders in WORLD WAR II. He commanded an invasion task force in North Africa and later led the "Hell on Wheels" 2nd Armored Division to victory in the BATTLE OF THE BULGE.

**Harmon, Thomas Dudley "Tom"** *(1919–1990)* American football player and commentator. While playing as a tailback with the Michigan Wolverines in the late 1930s, Harmon set a college record with 33 touchdowns, and scored 237 points in 24 games. He completed 101 of 233 passes for 1,399 yards and ran for a total of 4,280 yards, averaging 5.5 yards per carry. He won the Heisman Trophy, college football's highest award, in 1940 and was named the Associated Press male athlete of the year. After World War II he played professional football briefly for the Los Angeles Rams. He retired from the game in 1948, and went on to a successful career in radio and television sports broadcasting. He was the father of actor Mark Harmon.

**Harmsworth, Alfred Charles William** See Lord NORTHCLIFFE.

**Harnwell, Gaylord P.** *(1903–1982)* American atomic physicist and educator. During WORLD WAR II Harnwell headed the U.S. Navy Radio and Sound Laboratory at the University of California. In this post, he was responsible for the development of SONAR. He was president of the University of Pennsylvania from 1953 to 1970, expanding its enrollment, facilities and research programs.

**Harriman, W(illiam) Averell** *(1891–1986)* U.S. public official who advised Democratic presidents from Franklin D. ROOSEVELT to Lyndon B. JOHNSON, primarily as a diplomatic troubleshooter. Born in New York City, the patrician Harriman was heir to the Union Pacific Railroad fortune amassed by his father. By 1932 he had become chairman of the board of Union Pacific and had also embarked on a number of ventures in banking, shipbuilding and international finance.

Along with Armand HAMMER, Harriman was one of the first Americans to seek business concessions from the Soviet government. In 1941, President Roosevelt sent Harriman to the USSR, where he remained until 1946, first as minister and then as ambassador. After serving briefly as ambassador to the U.K. (1946), Harriman became secretary of commerce in the TRUMAN administration. From 1949 to 1950 he helped administer the MARSHALL PLAN. During the KOREAN WAR he served as Truman's National Security Advisor. Harriman was elected governor of New York in 1954 but was defeated in 1958 by Nelson ROCKEFELLER. He ran unsuccessfully for the Democratic presidential nomination in 1952 and 1956.

During the KENNEDY administration he served in several state department posts and in 1963 was a key figure in negotiating the NUCLEAR TEST BAN TREATY between the U.S. and the USSR. In 1965 President Lyndon Johnson appointed Harriman ambassador-at-large to handle Southeast Asian affairs. Harriman traveled around the world seeking international support for the U.S. policy in VIETNAM while sounding out the possibilities of a negotiated settlement of the war. When preliminary peace talks between the U.S. and North Vietnam opened in mid-1968, Harriman went to Paris as chief U.S. negotiator. He was succeeded by Henry Cabot LODGE after the election of Richard M. NIXON. Harriman subsequently criticized Nixon's handling of the war and the peace talks.

**Harrington, Michael** *(1928–1989)* American political scientist and writer. One of the most visible spokesmen for socialist ideals in the U.S., Harrington was co-chairman of the Democratic Socialists of America. His 1962 book *The Other America: Poverty in the United States* sparked a national debate on poverty with its assertion that there was an underclass of poor Americans who lived below the poverty line and who were ignored by government and society. The book was said to have inspired federal programs for the poor in the 1960s that became known as the War on Poverty. Harrington was widely respected by allies and opponents alike for his compassion, sincerity and eloquence.

**Harris, Arthur Travers "Bomber"** *(1892–1984)* Marshal of the Royal Air Force who headed RAF Bomber Command during WORLD WAR II and directed the saturation bombing of German cities. Harris earned a reputation as a contentious and stubborn man. He defended the saturation bombing strategy against charges that it was wasteful and even immoral. Harris rejected arguments favoring precision bombing and claimed that his methods forced a concentration of German forces that would otherwise have been sent to the Russian front. His policy climaxed in the bombing of DRESDEN (April 1945), which destroyed the city and may have killed as many as 50,000 people.

**Harris, Barbara** *(1951– )* Reverend Barbara Harris became the first woman consecrated as a bishop in the Episcopal Church (February 11, 1989). Harris, an African-American CIVIL RIGHTS activist, had been ordained for the priesthood in 1980. However, she held no undergraduate degree and underwent no seminary training in theology. The controversial ordination was denounced as sacrilegious by traditionalist members of the church. Bishop Harris retired from her duties in 2002.

**Harris, Frank (pen name of James Thomas Harris)** *(1856–1931)* Irish-born author and editor. Harris, who is best remembered for his sexually explicit three-volume autobiography, *My Life and Times* (1923–27), was born in Ireland but at age 15 came to the U.S., where he worked at a variety of odd jobs including a stint as a cowboy. Harris then went to England, where he earned a law degree and established himself as a successful editor of the British *Saturday Review* from 1894 to 1898, during which time he befriended George Bernard SHAW and Oscar Wilde. He then returned to America to edit *Pearson's Magazine,* but his sympathy with the German cause during WORLD WAR I led to public criticism and spurred Harris to move to Europe; he spent most of his final years in France. *My Life and Times,* which was banned in both the U.S. and Europe, no longer shocks readers but does stand as an interesting social portrait of the Edwardian era. Other works by Harris include a biography of Oscar Wilde (1920) and a five-volume essay series of *Contemporary Portraits* (1915–23) on famous friends and acquaintances.

**Harris, Julie (Julia Ann Harris)** *(1925– )* American stage actress. Harris first achieved critical acclaim for her role as the lonely tomboy in *The Member of the Wedding* (1950; repeating the role in the 1953 film version). Other major roles were Sally Bowles in *I Am a Camera* (1951; repeating the role in the 1955 film version) and Joan of Arc in *The Lark* (1955). Her most famous stage creation was the one-woman show *The Belle of Amherst* (1976), based on the life of Emily Dickinson. She also appeared on television and in other motion pictures, most notably *East of Eden* (1955). In 2001 Harris suffered a stroke and has since retired from the theater.

**Harris, Lawren** *(1885–1970)* An eminent Canadian landscape painter, Harris studied in Germany, returning to Toronto in 1907 to paint impressionist-style canvases. After a tour of northern Ontario in 1918, he began to paint large panoramas of the Canadian wilderness. A member of the Canadian GROUP OF SEVEN, he also painted dramatic, somewhat stylized landscapes of the Canadian Arctic and Rocky Mountains.

**Harris, Patricia Roberts** *(1924– 1985)* American lawyer, educator, administrator and CIVIL RIGHTS activist. Harris achieved a number of historic firsts for African-American women. In 1965 she became the first black woman to serve as a U.S. ambassador when President Lyndon B. JOHNSON named her ambassador to Luxembourg. Later she became the first black woman delegate to the UNITED NATIONS (UN). In 1969 she became the first black woman to serve as dean of a law school, a position she held briefly at Howard University. She was the first black woman member of a presidential cabinet when President Jimmy CARTER made her secretary of housing and urban development in 1977. She was later Carter's secretary of health, education, and welfare.

**Harris, Roy Ellsworth** *(1898–1979)* American composer. Harris started learning music while working as a truck driver, and then attended the University of California (1919–29). His *Andante* (1926) brought him a Guggenheim Fellowship in Paris. His *When Johnny Comes Marching Home* (1935), a Civil War overture, gained wide attention. The completion of his *Third Symphony* in 1939 marked Harris as a leading American classicist. He served on the faculty of Colorado College from 1948 to 1967. His work includes six symphonies, music for school bands, choruses, string and piano quintets, and piano solos. A recipient of numerous awards, he also won the prestigious Coolidge Medal for chamber music, from the Library of Congress in 1942.

**Harrison, Sir Rex (Reginald Carey Harrison)** *(1908–1990)* British-born actor. Harrison's 60-year career included more than 40 films and numerous plays. Among the films were *Blithe Spirit* (1945), *Anna and the King of Siam* (1946), *The Ghost and Mrs. Muir* (1947), *Cleopatra* (1963) and *Dr. Dolittle* (1967). He specialized in portraying urbane, sophisticated and somewhat eccentric characters and was best known for his portrayal of the waspish linguist Henry Higgins in *My Fair Lady.* Appearing in both the stage and film versions of the play, he won an ACADEMY AWARD and a Tony Award for his performances as Professor Higgins.

**Hart, Gary Warren (Gary Hartpence)** *(1936– )* American politician. Born in Ottawa, Kan., Hart attended Bethany Nazarene College, Yale Divinity School and Yale Law School. He entered public life as an attorney for the Justice Department in 1964. In private practice from 1967 to 1974, Hart served as campaign director for George MCGOVERN in his unsuccessful bid for the presidency in 1972. He served as a Democratic senator from Colorado from 1975 to 1986. During his unsuccessful bid for the Democratic presidential nomination in 1988, the press discovered that Hart was openly having an extramarital affair with a young model. Hart's personal judgment became a campaign issue, and Hart was forced to withdraw from the race. He later reentered the race briefly. His political career effec-

tively ended, he returned to Colorado with heavy campaign debts. In 1998 Hart worked on the bipartisan Hart-Rudman Committee to investigate U.S. domestic security procedure against terrorist threats, which called for the creation of a homeland security department. The committee's report was largely implemented following the terrorist attacks of SEPTEMBER 11, 2001.

**Hart, Herbert L(ionel Adolphus)** *(1907–1992)* British philosopher. Hart was one of the major thinkers on the philosophy of law in the 20th century. For decades he taught at Oxford University as its professor of jurisprudence. He defined his major task as a philosopher as the proper analysis of legal concepts. One of his major ideas is that all legal concepts are defeasible, that is, capable of being transformed and superseded if certain conditions exist. For example, a particular contract may meet all the standard legal criteria but is voidable if it is induced by fraud. Hart also argued that commonsense notions of causation should bear a great relevance to the exercise of punishment in the criminal law. Major works by Hart include *Causation in the Law* (1959), *The Concept of Law* (1961) and *Law, Liberty and Morality* (1963).

**Hart, Lorenz** *(1895–1943)* American song lyricist and librettist, best known for his musical shows with Richard RODGERS. While a student at Columbia University, Hart was already writing shows; and when he met a fellow Columbian, erstwhile composer Richard Rodgers, they immediately began working together—beginning with *Poor Little Ritz Girl* (1920) and ending with a revival of *A Connecticut Yankee* (1943). In all, the team wrote 28 shows and four film scores, including *Evergreen* (1930), *Jumbo* (1935), *On Your Toes* (1936), *Babes in Arms* (1937), *The Boys from Syracuse* (1938) and *Pal Joey* (1940). They ignored the stereotypes and hokum of Broadway formulas, injecting a full-scale ballet, "Slaughter on 10th Avenue," choreographed by George BALANCHINE, into *On Your Toes.* Hart's lyrics to *Pal Joey* were ahead of their time, so full of sex and illicit love that critics like Brooks ATKINSON rhetorically asked at the time, "Can you draw sweet water from a foul well?" While Hart's unpredictable, cynical nature lent an edginess to his finest songs, including "My Funny Valentine," "The Lady Is a Tramp" and "Falling in Love with Love," it may also have contributed to his chronic problems with alcohol. After a two-day drinking binge Hart died of complications from pneumonia in New York.

**Hart, Moss** *(1904–1961)* American playwright. Hart was a prolific writer for the theater who enjoyed steady popularity for over three decades. He remains best known for his comedy collaborations with fellow American playwright George S. KAUFMAN. These included *Once in a Lifetime* (1930), *Merrily We Roll Along* (1934), and two oft-performed classics—*You Can't Take It with You* (1936), which won a Pulitzer Prize, and *The Man Who Came to Dinner* (1939). Hart then moved on to a solo career in which he wrote, among other plays, *Winged Victory* (1943), *Christopher Blake* (1946), *Light Up the Sky* (1948), and *The Climate of Eden* (1952). Hart also contributed to the text of numerous musicals, most notably *My Fair Lady* (1956) and *Camelot* (1960).

**Hartack, William John "Bill"** *(1932– )* Hartack was one of the most successful—and temperamental—jockeys in the history of American thoroughbred racing. Only the second jockey ever to win five Kentucky Derbys, Hartack was named the nation's leading jockey three consecutive years (1955–57). He had both strong principles and a hot temper, which led him to resign from the Jockeys' Guild over its treatment of another rider. The only rider of any prominence not to belong to the Guild, he was the first rider to post $2 million in winnings and, soon thereafter, the first to win $3 million. Although he never had a Triple Crown-winning mount, Hartack rode such notables as NORTHERN DANCER and Majestic Prince to victory in the Kentucky Derby and the Preakness. At the age of 40, he became the first jockey to win 4,000 races.

**Hartal (Hind. "shop" "bolt")** Ceylonese (Sri Lankan) general strike organized by Marxists in 1953 in protest of rapid price rises, particularly of rice. Repressive measures were introduced, and there were clashes between gov-

ernment forces and strikers. Prime Minister Senanayake, of the United National Party, was forced to resign, and the opposition Sri Lankan Freedom Party won the 1956 election. (See also SRI LANKA.)

**Hartdegen, Stephen J.** *(1907–1989)* Franciscan scholar and renowned biblical scholar. From 1944 to 1970, Hartdegen served as editor in chief of a group of scholars who produced the *New American Bible*, a translation from the ancient Hebrew, Greek and Aramaic that supplanted the Douay Bible, the official bible used in Roman Catholic churches in the U.S.

**Hartford, John** *(1937–2001)* American bluegrass musician. Known for his skills as a singer, composer, performer and comedian, Hartford was not a child of the deep South, but was born in New York City. He developed his lifelong interest in bluegrass music and the riverboats near which it was performed as a result of growing up in St. Louis, Mo. By 1965 he had developed his own style and songs, modeled in part after those of Lester Flatt and Earl Scruggs. He went to Nashville, where he recorded his first album, *John Hartford Looks at Life,* in 1966. One of the individuals who heard Hartford's first record was Johnny CASH, who was impressed by the modesty and talent of the young artist. A year later Hartford followed his debut record with *Earthwords & Music* (1967), which contained the single "Gentle on My Mind"; the song, which won three Grammy Awards, described a homeless man's life and the pleasure brought to it by memories of an old lover, proved so popular that, by Hartford's death, 300 different artists had performed and recorded versions of it. Following the success of *Earthwords,* in 1968 Hartford traveled to California, where he found work as a writer and performer on *The Smothers Brothers Comedy Hour* and *The Glen Campbell Goodtime Hour.* He later returned to Nashville, recording *Aero-Plain,* an album highly touted for its acoustic rather than studio sound. However, save his Grammy Award–winning solo album *Mark Twang* (1976), Hartford disappeared from national attention until he recorded "Down from the Mountain" for the 2000 movie *O Brother, Where Art Thou?* In 2001 Hart-

ford died of cancer at a hospital in Nashville.

**Hartigan, Grace** *(1922– )* American painter. A member of the second generation of ABSTRACT EXPRESSIONISM, she was introduced to such seminal members of the movement as Willem DE KOONING and Jackson POLLOCK in the late 1940s, and had her first one-woman show in New York City in 1951. Her early work was sensuously abstract, and she soon turned to a style that incorporates figurative imagery into an abstract context. Her large canvases are usually characterized by vivid colors, strong lines and bold brushstrokes.

**Hartog, Jan de** *(1914–2002)* Dutch-born British novelist and playwright. Hartog, who was born in Haarlem, Holland, and ran away to sea at the age of 10, led an adventurous life that was frequently reflected in his fictional works. His earliest writings were in Dutch. During WORLD WAR II, Hartog served in the Dutch underground RESISTANCE, was badly wounded, and ultimately escaped to Britain, where he learned the English language so well that he began to write in it. His play *The Fourposter* won an Antoinette Perry Award during its Broadway run. Hartog remains best known for his popular and well-plotted novels, most notably *The Lost Sea* (1951) and *The Distant Shore* (1952).

**Hartung, Hans** *(1904–1989)* German-French painter. Born in Dresden, Germany, Hartung settled in Paris in 1935, fought with the Foreign Legion and became a French citizen. Influenced at first by German EXPRESSIONISM and KANDINSKY, Hartung evolved a distinctive abstract style that made him a leading figure in the School of Paris. Allied with COLOR-FIELD PAINTING, his untitled mature paintings feature cloud-like clusters of extremely thin calligraphic lines that seem to hover over luminously colored grounds.

**Hašek, Jaroslav** *(1883–1923)* Czechoslovakian novelist, story writer and journalist. Early in his career Hašek was active as an anarchist and published widely in Czech political journals. During WORLD WAR I Hašek was a peripatetic soldier who served at various times in the Czech, Russian and

Austrian armies. After the war Hašek composed a four-volume picaresque novel, *The Good Soldier Schweik* (1920–23), that has been acclaimed as one of the great satires in world literature. Schweik, an infantry everyman, survives his war experiences—and the foolish, callous orders of his own officers—through simple peasant warmth, humor and guile. To many critics, Schweik is the archetypal portrait of the Czech people. A later collection of Hašek's work is *The Red Commissar* (1981).

**Hasenclever, Walter** *(1890–1940)* German playwright, novelist and poet. Hasenclever is best remembered as a figure in the Expressionist movement that dominated German theater in the years following World War I (see EXPRESSIONISM). His first major play, *The Son* (1916), focused on the difficult relationship between a father and son. Subsequent works included an adaptation of *Antigone* (1917), by the Greek tragedian Sophocles, and *Der Retter* (1919), an antiwar drama. Hasenclever then wrote comedies such as *A Man of Distinction* (1926) and *Marriages Are Made in Heaven* (1928). He committed suicide while imprisoned by the Nazis in France during WORLD WAR II.

**Hassam, Childe** *(1859–1935)* American painter and printmaker. One of the foremost American impressionists, Hassam was born in Boston, Mass., and studied (1886) at the Académie Julien in Paris, where he was influenced by French impressionist works. He returned to the U.S. in 1889, settling in New York City and joining (1898) "The Ten," a group of American impressionists that included John Twachtman and Alden Weir. In 1913, Hassam exhibited in the ARMORY SHOW. His paintings include light-filled landscapes, people-filled cityscapes and lively interiors. Among his notable works are *Le Jour du Grand Prix* (1887, Museum of Fine Arts, Boston), *Isle of Shoals* and *Street Scene in Winter* (1901, both Metropolitan Museum of Art, N.Y.C.).

**Hassan II** *(1929–1999)* King of MOROCCO (1961–99). Born Moulay Hassan in Rabat to King Mohammed V of Morocco, Hassan was educated in Moroccan and French schools in Rabat and eventually qualified to practice law during the French protectorate (1912–56). In 1957, a year after France granted Morocco full independence, Hassan was designated crown prince and was selected by his father to become commander in chief of the Moroccan army. In conjunction with his military responsibilities he received additional appointments as minister of defense, and vice premier in 1960, performing these duties until his father's death in February 1961. With the passing of Mohammed V, Hassan was crowned Hassan II.

During his reign Hassan attempted to reform the traditional economy of Morocco, inject some modern concepts into the lifestyle of the North African state and coordinate his domestic and foreign policies with those of the other independent countries of the region. However, the monarchical and conservative nature of his rule antagonized leftist activists in ALGERIA and LIBYA, two states identified with a radical brand of Arab nationalism that condemned monarchical rule and accepted aid from the Soviet Union. These groups were allegedly behind the two unsuccessful assassination attempts made on Hassan's life in 1961 and 1972. Hassan's unpopularity among Algerians increased in 1976 when he annexed part of WESTERN SAHARA, and then all of it in 1979. Hassan's actions thwarted Algerian efforts to ensure that the Popular Front for the Liberation of Saguia el Hamra and Rio de Oro, a leftist independence movement, came to power when Spain left the region in February 1976. In addition to opposition from Algeria, the annexations exposed Hassan, his military and his country to guerrilla attacks from Saharan separatists.

Other than the Western Sahara, the main focus of Hassan's foreign policy was the Israeli-Palestinian conflict in the Middle East. Because of his close ties with Western governments (especially the U.S. and France), Hassan proved willing to meet with Israeli leaders and diplomats on numerous occasions in an effort to promote an Arab-Israeli peace settlement. In 1999 Hassan II died of a heart attack and was succeeded by his son, Mohammed VI.

**Hasselblad, Victor** *(1906–1978)* Swedish inventor and industrialist. In the 1940s Hasselblad devised the high-quality **Hasselblad camera**, which was used by professional photographers throughout the world. Hasselblad cameras were also used on all U.S. spaceflights.

**Hatch Act of 1939** U.S. legislation, sponsored by Senator Carl Hatch of New Mexico, that prohibited most federal officeholders in the executive branch from using their position to influence presidential or congressional elections. In 1940 the law was amended to include state and local employees whose salaries were derived even partially from federal monies. The amendment also limited the annual expenditures of political parties and the amount of individual campaign contributions.

**Hatem, Dr. George (Shaffick Hatem)** *(1910–1988)* American physician who devoted his career to public health efforts in China. Hatem arrived in China in 1933 and remained to treat venereal disease in Shanghai. After the communists took control in 1949, he helped organize the country's public health effort and was widely credited with eliminating syphilis and gonorrhea from China. The Chinese knew him as Ma Haide, meaning "virtue from overseas."

**Hauptmann, Gerhart** *(1862–1946)* German playwright, novelist and poet. Hauptmann, who won the NOBEL PRIZE in literature in 1912, is one of the major figures in the history of German theater. He first made his reputation for stark, naturalistic treatments of such issues as poverty, the effects of heredity and social pressures on individual freedom in plays such as *Before Dawn* (1889), *The Coming of Peace* (1890), *Lonely People* (1891) and *The Weavers* (1892), a study of an unsuccessful rebellion by the poor in the Silesian region of Germany in 1844. In his later work Hauptmann turned increasingly to fantastical Symbolist plots that utilized the supernatural. Noteworthy among these plays are *The Assumption of Hannele* (1893), *The Beaver Coat* (1893), *The Red Rooster* (1901) and *And Father Danced* (1906). Hauptmann was a fierce opponent of the Nazis, as evidenced by his four-part drama *Der Atriden* (1941).

**Hausner, Gideon** (*1915–1990*) Israeli politician. He served as ISRAEL's attorney general from 1960 to 1963, and led the prosecution of NAZI war criminal Adolf EICHMANN in 1961 and 1962. He later served in the Israeli Knesset (parliament) and as chairman of the Yad Vashem museum, which commemorated victims of the Nazi HOLOCAUST.

**Haut-Zaïre** Province (formerly Orientale) of northeastern Democratic Republic of the CONGO (formerly Zaire); a postindependence stronghold of Patrice LUMUMBA, who, with Antoine Gizenga, attempted to set up a government at Kisangani (Stanleyville). The central government at KINSHASA (Léopoldville) regained control in 1962, only to face further unrest in 1964, 1966 and 1967.

**Havel, Václav** (*1936– *) Czechoslovak playwright, poet and essayist; president of CZECHOSLOVAKIA (1989–92) and of the CZECH REPUBLIC (1993–2003). Havel has emerged as one of the leading intellectual figures of the late 20th century and a major literary, political and moral force in eastern Europe. He was born into a well-to-do family in Prague. Because of his "bourgeois" background, he was denied the right to attend university in communist Czechoslovakia. Instead, he served a stint in the military, then found work as a stagehand in Prague. Havel's interest in the theater quickly burgeoned; in 1963, at age 27, his first play was performed (*The Garden Party*, tr. 1969). He was subsequently enrolled at the Academy of Dramatic Arts in Prague, graduating in 1967. During the 1960s Havel satirized the communist bureaucracy and the politics of conformity in Czechoslovakia in a series of plays. His work of this time borrows from the THEATER OF THE ABSURD. Havel was an active supporter of the PRAGUE SPRING reform movement of 1968. After the movement was crushed by the SOVIET INVASION OF CZECHOSLOVAKIA that summer, his work was banned by the hard-line regime that replaced the reform government of Alexander DUBČEK. However, he continued to write; his manuscripts were circulated privately and also produced in western Europe. Havel was a founding member of the human rights organization CHARTER 77; because of his activities on behalf of this group, and because of his stature as a public figure who openly challenged the communist authorities, he was imprisoned from 1979 to 1982. He was rearrested during an anticommunist protest in January 1989 and released on parole that May. In November he formed a new opposition group, Civic Forum, and held talks on political reform and power-sharing with the Czechoslovak premier during a period of mass protest against communist rule. With the resignation of communist president Gustáv HUSÁK (December 10), the formation of an interim coalition cabinet and the promise of free elections, Havel announced his candidacy for the presidency.

On December 29 the Federal Assembly (parliament) unanimously elected Havel as Czechoslovakia's first noncommunist president in more than 40 years. During the first year of his presidency he was preoccupied with the difficult task of guiding Czechoslovakia's return to democracy. When the Czech and Slovak parliaments voted for the dissolution of Czechoslovakia in 1992, Havel resigned in protest. In March 1993 he was elected president of the Czech Republic and was reelected in 1998. Havel chose not to run in 2003 and retired from politics. Among Havel's plays are *The Memorandum* (1966; tr. 1967), *The Increased Difficulty of Concentration* (1968; tr. 1972), *Private View* (1975; tr. 1978) and *Protest* (1978; tr. 1980). *Disturbing the Peace: A Conversation with Karel Hvizdala* (published underground in Prague in 1986; tr. 1990) presents his thoughts on life, literature, politics and the Czechoslavak identity; *Letter to Olgo* (1988) contains his correspondence to his wife while he was imprisoned from 1979 to 1982.

**Havemann, Robert** (*1910–1982*) East German chemist and dissident. Havemann joined the Communist Party in 1932. During WORLD WAR II he took part in the RESISTANCE movement and was imprisoned by the Nazis. After the war he lived in East Germany but became an outspoken critic of TOTALITARIANISM. He was purged from the East German Communist Party in 1964, and was held under house arrest from 1979 until his death.

**Hawke, Robert James Lee** (*1929– *) Prime minister of AUSTRALIA (1983–91). Born in Bordertown, South Australia, Hawke was educated at the University of Western Australia, from which he received bachelor's degrees in law and economics. He won a Rhodes scholarship to Oxford University in 1953, taking a bachelor of letters degree there in 1955. Active since 1958 in the Australian Council of Trade Unions as research officer and advocate, he was its president from 1970 to 1980. Concurrently, from 1972 to 1980, he served on the governing body of the International Labor Organization. From 1973 to 1978 Hawke was president of the Australian LABOUR PARTY, which he had joined at age 17. In 1980 he was elected to parliament as representative of the federal electorate of Wills, later becoming the party's spokesman for industrial relations, employment and youth affairs. Early in 1983 Hawke was unanimously elected leader of the opposition. As Labour candidate for the office of prime minister, he led his party to victory and was sworn in on March 11, 1983. Hawke was reelected prime minister in 1984, 1987 and again in 1990 for a record fourth consecutive term. Hawke's tenure as prime minister ended in 1991. The following year he became an adjunct professor at the Australian National University.

**Hawking, Stephen William** (*1942– *) British astrophysicist, widely considered one of the most brilliant scientific minds since Albert EINSTEIN. A graduate of Oxford University, Hawking obtained his Ph.D. from Cambridge, where in 1977 he was appointed to the chair of gravitational physics. He subsequently held the seat of Lucasian Professor of Mathematics at Cambridge, a chair once held by Isaac Newton. Hawking has worked mainly in the field of general relativity and on the theory of BLACK HOLES. He is a leading authority on the BIG BANG THEORY. Hawking has been at the forefront of the search for a unified theory to account for, and reconcile, the general theory of relativity (which is concerned with the extraordinarily vast) and quantum theory (concerned with the extraordinarily tiny); such a theory, Hawking believes, would give "a complete description of the universe we live in." Hawking's book on the nature of time and the universe for the nonspecialist, *A*

*Brief History of Time* (1988), was a phenomenal bestseller.

Since the early 1960s, Hawking has suffered from motor neuron disease, known as Lou Gehrig's disease, which has confined him to a wheelchair. In 1985 he underwent a tracheostomy operation, which left him unable to speak. However, a speech synthesizer and specially designed personal computer have allowed him to communicate his brilliant and complex concepts to the rest of the world. Since *Brief History* Hawking has published several books designed to explain theoretical physics and astrophysics to the layman: *Black Holes and Baby Universes and Other Essays* (1993); *The Theory of Everything* (1996), which Hawking subsequently denounced for its allegedly unauthorized publication; and a sequel to *Brief History* called *The Universe in a Nutshell* (2001).

**Hawkins, Coleman** *(1904–1969)* A native of St. Joseph, Mo., Hawkins is significant for his pioneering role in establishing the tenor saxophone as a bona fide and primal voice in jazz. In the 1920s, during the early phase of his career with Mamie Smith's Jazz Hounds and Fletcher HENDERSON's big band, and then in the 1930s as an international jazz star in both Europe and the U.S., Hawkins perfected a robust sound, strong rhythmic drive and technical command that made his solos among the most exciting in jazz. His 1939 recording of "Body and Soul" was not only Hawkins's biggest hit, but also a declaration (and affirmation) that the tenor saxophone has arrived—an equal to the trumpet as the jazz world's most important "front-line" solo instrument. Throughout his career, Hawkins, unlike a number of his peers, welcomed innovations such as those spawned by the bebop revolution of the 1940s; but, although adapting newer elements that he deemed compatible with his overall style, Hawkins's rhythmic buoyancy, full-blooded tone and swinging inventiveness never faltered. Historically, Hawkins's muscular style is often contrasted to that of Lester YOUNG, whose lighter tone and more melodic improvisations had a profound influence on such 1950s "cool school" stylists as tenor saxophonist Stan GETZ. In actuality, virtually all saxophonists (and horn players) have been enriched by the contrasting yin and yang styles of Young and Hawkins, jazzdom's seminal pioneers of the tenor saxophone.

**hawks** Term coined in the 1960s to describe American politicians who wished to continue, intensify or escalate the VIETNAM WAR. The term came to be applied generally to politicians taking an aggressive stance on foreign policy issues.

**Hawks, Howard Winchester** *(1896–1977)* American motion picture producer, writer and director. Hawks gew up in California studying mechanical engineering, working in the PARAMOUNT prop department, racing cars and, during WORLD WAR I, flying planes in the Army Air Corps. He began directing films in the mid-1920s. In the next 45 years his best work depicted professional groups in dangerous occupations: flying aces and air mail pilots in *The Dawn Patrol* (1930) and *Ceiling Zero* (1938); wacky scientists and journalists in the "screwball comedies" *Bringing up Baby* (1938) and *His Girl Friday* (1940); cattle drovers and gunslingers in the westerns *Red River* (1948) and *Rio Bravo* (1959); bombshells and weightlifters in the musical *Gentlemen Prefer Blondes* (1953); and racketeers and convicts in the gangster films *Scarface* (1932) and *The Criminal Code* (1931). The character groupings and dialogue in his pictures displayed an interlocking, machinelike precision. *His Girl Friday,* perhaps the fastest-talking movie of them all, snaps briskly along like a class sports car. *Only Angels Have Wings* (1930), by contrast, rolls by with the well-oiled, lordly deliberation of a Rolls Royce. Hawks was not interested in flashbacks, skewed camera angels or decorative cutting, preferring to be head-on, direct and functional. Famous for his insistence on autonomy—he refused to shoot while a producer was on the set—he wrote or supervised the writing of most of his films. Although Hawks received only one ACADEMY AWARD nomination during his career (for *Sergeant York* in 1941), in 1975 he received a special Award for lifetime achievement.

**Hawley-Smoot Tariff Act** Protectionist legislation enacted in 1930 that brought U.S. tariffs to the highest level in history. Overall increases averaged approximately 5% but rates on agricultural raw materials increased from 30% to 50% in real terms. Sugar and textiles were given special protection. The act brought retaliation from other nations and led to a sharp decline in U.S. trade.

**Haxell, Frank** *(1913–1988)* British labor leader and the communist secretary general of one of Great Britain's most powerful labor unions, the Electrical Trades Union (ETU), forerunner of the Electrical, Electronic, Telecommunications and Plumbing Union (EETPU). Haxell headed the ETU from 1955 until his downfall in 1961, when he was removed from office after a High Court ruled that his election victory of 1959 had been rigged.

**Hay, Gyula** *(1900–1975)* Hungarian playwright. Hay scored his first major theatrical triumph with the play *Gott, Kaiser, Bauer* (1932), which was staged in Berlin by the renowned theatrical impresario Max REINHARDT. A politically controversial writer, Hay spent many years in exile from his native country. After his return, Hay was imprisoned in 1956 for his role in the 1956 HUNGARIAN UPRISING against Soviet authority. Other plays by Hay include *Tiszazug* (1945), *Das Pferd* (1964), a study of the Roman emperor Caligula, and *Gaspar Varros Recht* (1965), which featured an anticommunist theme.

**Haya de la Torre, Víctor Raul** *(1894–1979)* Peruvian statesman and major spokesman for democratic political movements in Latin America for half a century. In 1924 Haya de la Torre founded the American Popular Revolutionary Alliance (APRA). Although it was anti-capitalist and Marxist in outlook, it did not favor Soviet-style communism. APRA called for a program of land, tax and educational reforms for landless peasants, urban laborers, Indians and other disadvantaged groups. On three occasions the military prevented Haya de la Torre from taking the presidency of PERU. He spent much of his life in exile, hiding and imprisonment. Nonetheless, his writings on economics and political theory had great influence throughout Latin America.

**Haydée, Marcia (Marcia Pereira de Silva)** *(1937–   )* Brazilian-born ballerina and ballet director. One of the great dramatic ballerinas of the 1960s and 1970s, Haydée danced at the Rio de Janeiro Teatro Municipal before joining Grand Ballet deu Marquis de Cuevas in 1957. She became an internationally acclaimed prima ballerina after joining the Stuttgart Ballet (1961) where she created roles in John CRANKO's ballets, including Juliet in *Romeo and Juliet* (1962), Tatyana in *Onegin* (1965), and Kate in *Taming of the Shrew* (1969). She also has appeared with other companies, and created roles in Kenneth MACMILLAN's *Miss Julie* (1970) and Glen TETLEY's *Voluntaries* (1973), among others. In 1976 she was appointed artistic director of the Stuttgart Ballet and, in 1993, the Santiago Ballet. She retired from both in 1995.

**Hayden, Robert E.** *(1913–1980)* African-American poet. Hayden's work evoked Afro-American themes. He was the first black to hold the position of consultant in poetry to the Library of Congress (1978–80), and was also a member of the American Academy and Institute of Arts and Letters. He taught at the University of Michigan. His collections include *Words in Mourning Time* (1971) and *Angle of Ascent: New and Selected Poems* (1975).

**Hayes, Helen (Helen Hayes Brown)** *(1900–1993)* American actress. Born in Washington, D.C., Hayes made her stage debut there in 1905, first appeared in New York in 1908 and became a well-known child actress. She made her adult debut in *Dear Brutus* (1918). Her many notable performances have included roles in Kaufman and Connelly's *To the Ladies* (1922), SHAW's *Caesar and Cleopatra* (1925), ANDERSON's *Mary of Scotland* (1933) and the bravura title role in Laurence Houseman's *Victoria Regina* (1935–39). Hayes won an Academy Award in 1932 for *The Sin of Madelon Claudet*. She made her London debut in 1945, as Amanda in WILLIAMS' *The Glass Menagerie*. Other later roles included Norma Melody in O'Neill's *A Touch of the Poet* (1958) and Mrs. Antrobus in WILDER's *The Skin of Our Teeth* (1961). Among her films are *Arrowsmith* (1931), *A Farewell to Arms* (1933),

*Anastasia* (1956) and *Airport* (1969). A beloved and widely respected figure, she was long known as the First Lady of the American Theater.

**Hay-Herrán Treaty** See COLOMBIA.

**Haynes, Elwood** *(1857–1925)* American inventor. Haynes was one of the pioneers in the development of the automobile. In 1893–94 he designed and constructed a horseless carriage, the oldest American automobile in existence and now on exhibit at the Smithsonian Institution. He was the first to use aluminum in automobile engines and was the inventor and builder of a rotary engine in 1903. Haynes discovered tungsten chrome steel and developed an alloy of cobalt and chromium for making cutting tools. The Haynes Stellite Company manufactured tools from 1912 to 1920 and developed **stainless steel**, which was patented in 1919.

**Hays Code** Code of self-censorship adopted by the HOLLYWOOD film industry in self-defense against threatened government censorship. The Hays Code derived its name from Will H. Hays, a former chairman of the Republican National Committee who in 1922 was appointed by Hollywood studio owners to head a newly formed film standards organization, the Motion Picture Producers and Distributors of America, Inc. In the 1920s, Hays wielded little actual power over the content of films, but in the 1930s, as the public outcry over sexually suggestive movies (such as those starring Jean HARLOW and Mae WEST) and violent gangster films increased, the Hays Code took on real teeth: The new enforcement policy was that films that violated the Code would not be distributed by the powerful studios or exhibited by the theaters they owned. The Code strictly limited the sexual content of films, tacitly forbade any religious controversy and demanded that, if evil was depicted powerfully, it should be punished to an equivalent extent—thus encouraging a predictable happy ending in which good emerged triumphant. In the 1950s, directors such as Otto PREMINGER helped to weaken the artistic shackles imposed by the Code. In the 1960s, the Code was replaced by the current rating system, which focuses on excluding younger audience members from scenes of explicit sex and violence.

**Hayter, Stanley William** *(1901–1988)* British-born abstract artist and printmaker; his Paris studio, Atelier 17, was widely regarded as the most influential print workshop of the 20th century. Many major artists, including Pablo PICASSO, Marc CHAGALL and Jackson POLLOCK worked under Hayter either in Paris or in New York City, where Atelier 17 was based in the 1940s.

**Hayward, Max** *(1924–1979)* British scholar and translator. Hayward specialized in contemporary Soviet literature, translating works by Boris PASTERNAK, Alexander SOLZHENITSYN and other authors who were banned or banished in their own country. His colleagues at Oxford and elsewhere regarded him as "the custodian of Russian literature in the West."

**Hayworth, Rita (Margarita Carmen Casino)** *(1918–1987)* Mexican-American dancer and actress. Rita Hayworth was one of the most popular HOLLYWOOD film stars of the 1940s. Her career reached its peak in the years during and after World War II, when she shared pinup queen status with Betty GRABLE. She starred in a series of films that highlighted her lush beauty. Her screen persona was perhaps best realized in *Gilda* (1946), in which she played the title role, a seductress in black satin. Her second husband, Orson WELLES, directed her in another of her well-known films, *The Lady from Shanghai* (1948). In 1949 she left Hollywood to marry the third of her five husbands, Prince Aly Khan. She came back to Hollywood three years later, but never recaptured the glory of the war years. She suffered from Alzheimer's disease in the last years of her life.

**Hazam, Louis** *(1911–1983)* American television documentary writer and producer. Working for the National Broadcasting Company (NBC) from 1945 until 1966, Hazam was a pioneer in the field of broadcasting. He was credited with producing the first live telecast of a medical operation, the first telecast of the birth of a baby, and the first television report from the inside of a mental hospital. In 1956, his March of Medicine series became the first television program to receive an Albert Lasker Medical Journalism Award. He also received acclaim for his cultural productions, *Vincent Van Gogh: A Self-Portrait, Shakespeare: Soul of an Age* and *Michelangelo: The Last Giant.*

**Hazaras** An ethnic group inhabiting the central mountain ranges of AFGHANISTAN. Speaking an antiquated version of Farsi, the language of Iran, and hailing originally from northwestern China, the Hazaras largely earn their living from sheep husbandry and farming. Their confessional identity with the Shi'ite sect of Islam makes the Hazaras an oddity among the other groups in Afghanistan, the vast majority of which belong to the Sunni branch. During the late 1970s, Shi'ite practices resulted in severe repression of the Hazaras by the TALIBAN government, which espoused a fundamentalist brand of Sunni Islam and implemented Sunni Islamic law throughout the portion of Afghanistan it ruled.

**Head, Edith** (*1907–1981*) HOLLYWOOD costume designer. The most famous fashion designer in the history of the movies, Head was chief designer for PARAMOUNT PICTURES (1938–67) and UNIVERSAL (1967–81). During her long career she designed clothes for more than 1,000 movies and was nominated for 34 ACADEMY AWARDS. She won the award a record eight times, for *The Heiress* (1949), *All About Eve* (1950), *Samson and Delilah* (1950), *A Place in the Sun* (1951), *Roman Holiday* (1953), *Sabrina* (1954), *The Facts of Life* (1960) and *The Sting* (1973). She created screen wardrobes for such stars as Sophia Loren, Marlene DIETRICH, Elizabeth TAYLOR and Ingrid BERGMAN. Her clothes were also worn by the male and female leads in most of Alfred HITCHCOCK's Hollywood films.

**Healey, Denis Winston** (*1917–  *) British politician. Born in London of Irish parents, Healey rose to become a senior figure in the LABOUR PARTY from the 1960s through the 1980s. He was a major in the commandos during WORLD WAR II, and entered Parliament in 1952. He was defense minister (1964–70) in the cabinet of Harold WILSON and chancellor of the exchequer (1974–79) under Wilson and his

successor, James CALLAGHAN, who defeated Healey for the party leadership in 1976. In 1980 Healey again sought the leadership but was defeated by Michael FOOT. He served as deputy leader from 1980 to 1983. Although himself a leading moderate in the party, he was critical of the GANG OF FOUR moderates who left the party in 1981 to form the SOCIAL DEMOCRATIC PARTY (1981), and did not join them. Healey did not challenge Neil KINNOCK for the Labour Party leadership in 1983 but, as shadow foreign secretary, remained a respected and influential voice in the House of Commons. In 1992 Healey became a life peer in the House of Lords.

**Heaney, Seamus** (*1939–  *) Irish poet, critic, essayist and teacher. Heaney is widely considered to be the most important Irish poet since W. B. YEATS and one of the finest English-language poets of his generation. Born into a Catholic farming family in County Derry, NORTHERN IRELAND, Heaney was educated at Queen's University, Belfast, where his early work attracted favorable notice. His first book, *Death of a Naturalist* (1966), established him as an important poet; this reputation was confirmed by *Door into the Dark* (1969) and *Wintering Out* (1972). Full of closely observed details of Northern Irish country life, these books display the characteristic style and themes of his early period. With *North* (1975), Heaney addressed the ongoing civil strife in Northern Ireland, although in an oblique fashion. Around this time, partly to escape the turmoil and tensions of Belfast, Heaney moved to County Wicklow in Ireland, where he wrote most of the poems for his next book, *Field Work* (1979). In a country where the written word traditionally has had significant political implications, Heaney has been consistent in his refusal to reduce complex social and political issues to simple slogans or to endorse partisan causes. Heaney's more recent work, notably in *Station Island* (1985) and *The Haw Lantern* (1987), has often been allegorical and has drawn on the *Divine Comedy* of Dante and on the work of such contemporary central European writers as Czesław MILOSZ. Since the 1970s, Heaney has divided his time between Ireland and the U.S., where he teaches at Harvard University. In 1995 he was awarded the NOBEL PRIZE in literature.

**Hearst, Patricia Campbell** (*1954–  *) American heiress and kidnap victim. A scion of newspaper tycoon William Randolph HEARST, Patricia Hearst was kidnapped from her Berkeley, Calif., apartment on February 4, 1974, by the Symbionese Liberation Army (SLA), a radical, anti-capitalist terrorist organization. As ransom, the SLA demanded that her father, Randolph Hearst, provide $400 million worth of food for California's poor; he eventually initiated a $2 million program. Two months after her abduction, Hearst announced that she had joined the SLA and changed her name to Tania. She was later seen on film taking part in an armed bank robbery. In another incident, she fired on a store to free SLA members Emily and Bill Harris, and the three fled to San Francisco. After sending a final taped message on June 7, 1974, Hearst went underground. On September 18, 1975, the FBI captured Hearst and the Harrises in San Francisco. Celebrated attorney F. Lee BAILEY represented her at her trial, contending that she had been brainwashed and was not responsible for her actions as Tania. On March 20, 1976, she was found guilty and sentenced to a total of 35 years in prison. After several attempts to appeal her conviction, Hearst's lawyers petitioned for and received presidential clemency from President Jimmy CARTER in 1979. Hearst later described how she had been kept in a closet, tortured and given propaganda by the SLA, and general public opinion is that she was indeed brainwashed. Hearst detailed her ordeal in the book *Every Secret Thing* (1982), and a film of her story was made in 1988. She married her former bodyguard, Bernard Shaw, in 1979. In 2001 Hearst was pardoned by President Bill CLINTON in the final hours of his presidency.

**Hearst, William Randolph** (*1863–1951*) American editor and publisher. During the first half of the 20th century Hearst controlled one of the great communications empires in history. His first step in creating what would become the nation's largest newspaper chain was rebuilding the *San Francisco Examiner* (1887). His purchase of the *New York Journal* (1895) resulted in the famous newspaper war with Joseph Pulitzer's *New York World* during which the term *yellow journalism* was coined to describe their exaggerated journalistic style. Among the many magazines he owned were *Good Housekeeping, Cosmopolitan* and *Harper's Bazaar.* He bought or started papers in Chicago, Boston, Los Angeles and elsewhere. His empire also included Hearst News Service, King Features, radio stations and film companies. Hearst wielded power in politics, serving as New York representative to Congress (1903–07); he ensured Franklin D. ROOSEVELT's 1932 presidential nomination and used his papers for political propaganda.

**Heartfield, John** **(Helmut Herzfeld)** *(1891–1968)* German artist and graphic designer known for his early and successful use of photomontage. Heartfield was a Berlin artist who, in the 1920s, became an active member of the DADA movement. His special contribution was the development of a montage technique in which photographs and other image materials are cut up and reassembled using a technique similar to collage. In the late 1920s and early 1930s, he used this technique to create propagandistic works attacking HITLER and the rise of NAZISM. By 1933 he was forced to leave Germany, staying briefly in Czechoslovakia before relocating in England where he changed his name (translating his German name into English) and continued his graphic work. Heartfield's role in 20th century design is based on his development and exploitation of the montage technique, which has become a widely used part of the vocabulary of modern graphic design.

**Heart of Atlanta Motel, Inc. v. United States** *(1964)* Unanimous U.S. Supreme Court decision that banned racial discrimination in the provision of public accommodations in restaurants and hotels. Although discrimination at facilities operated by state and local governments was outlawed in the early 1950s, private discrimination was still common in the early 1960s. The CIVIL RIGHTS ACT OF 1964 contained a controversial provision outlawing racial discrimination in public accommodations that were privately owned. The law was challenged as an unwarranted governmental regulation of private business. A unanimous Supreme Court upheld the law,

reasoning that hotels and restaurants serve interstate travelers, and Congress also has the power to regulate local activities that may have a harmful effect on interstate commerce.

**Heart of Darkness** Novella of 1902 by Joseph CONRAD. Notable both for its literary subtlety and for its examination of the contemporary human condition, *Heart of Darkness* is considered one of the supreme masterpieces of English-language fiction of the 20th century. Narrator "Marlow" (who both is and is not Conrad) recounts his journey up the Congo to find the trader Kurtz, who had disappeared earlier. The journey is not only geographic but also metaphorical, from certainty into doubt and back into self-knowledge. Conrad examines the ambiguous relation between civilization and barbarism and addresses themes of greed and colonialism. Kurtz's dying words—"The horror! the horror!"—may indicate Conrad's apprehension about the 20th century.

**Heath, Edward** *(1916–2005)* British statesman, prime minister of the UNITED KINGDOM (1970–74). Born at Broadstairs, Heath was educated at Chatham House School and Balliol College, Oxford. He served as an artillery officer from 1940 to 1946 and left the territorials in 1951 as a lieutenant colonel. A member of the CONSERVATIVE PARTY, he was elected to Parliament in 1950 and has sat in the House of Commons continuously since then. From 1955 to 1959 he held the influential post of Conservative chief whip. He entered the cabinet of Alec DOUGLAS-HOME as minister for trade and industry (1963–64). In 1965, he defeated Reginald MAUDLING and Enoch POWELL for the Conservative Party leadership. He became prime minister with the Conservatives' general election victory in June 1970.

A lifelong champion of European cooperation and unity, Heath led Britain into the EUROPEAN ECONOMIC COMMUNITY in 1973—the capstone of his political career. However, his government was less successful in domestic affairs and was marred by labor strife. His Industrial Relations Act (1971), designed to democratize Britain's trades unions and regulate strikes, was denounced by the unions.

A coal miners' strike in late 1971–early 1972 led to power blackouts throughout Britain. Heath's attempt to impose limits on wage increases during an inflationary period led to further industrial action by the militant miners, and in January 1974 Heath put the nation on a three-day work week because of the resulting power crisis (see THREE-DAY WEEK). Seeking a mandate for his policies, Heath called a general election for February 1974 but failed to win a majority and resigned. The following year he was deposed as head of the party by Margaret THATCHER, who accused him of ineffectual leadership. After the Conservatives returned to power in 1979 he was a frequent critic of Thatcher's hard-line right-wing policies and allied himself with the so-called WETS within the party. Heath, a bachelor, was also known as a fine amateur conductor and yachtsman. In 2001 he retired from the House of Commons.

**Hébert, Anne** *(1916–2000)* Canadian poet and novelist. The daughter of a literary critic, Hébert was given a strict Catholic upbringing. Her struggles with the constraints of her faith are evident in her poetry, which includes *Le Songes en équilibre* ("Dreams in Equilibrium," 1942), *Le Tombeau des rois* (The Tombs of the Kings, 1953) and *In The Shadow of the Wind* (1984). Hébert has also written novels, which include *Kamouraski* (1970) and *Les Enfants du sabbat* (1975; Children of the Black Sabbath 1977); and plays, some of which are collected in *Le Temps sauvage, La Mercière assassinée, Les Invités au procès: Théâtre* (1967).

**Hecht, Ben** *(1893–1964)* U.S. writer. He worked for CHICAGO newspapers and was a correspondent in Germany and the Soviet Union between 1918 and 1920. He produced his most famous play, *The Front Page* (1928), with Charles MacArthur. In 1923 he founded and edited for two years the *Chicago Literary Times.* In addition to plays, he wrote novels and short stories, and produced and directed many motion pictures. Other well-known works include *Twentieth Century* (1933) and *A Child of the Century* (1954). *The Scoundrel* screenplay won Hecht and MacArthur an ACADEMY AWARD in 1935. Hecht was also active in his support of Jewish refugees.

**Hecht, Harold** (*1970–1985*) American film producer. As a pioneering independent HOLLYWOOD producer, Hecht was considered largely responsible for breaking the grip of the studio system. In the late 1940s, he and actor Burt LANCASTER formed a partnership that over 15 years was responsible for a number of hits, including the ACADEMY AWARD–winning *Marty*. After production costs forced the dissolution of their partnership, Hecht went on producing on his own. In 1965, he made *Cat Ballou*, for which Lee Marvin won an Academy Award as best actor.

**Heckel, Erich** (*1883–1970*) German painter. Born in Dobeln, Saxony, Heckel studied architecture in Dresden (1904). In 1905 he, Ernst Ludwig KIRCHNER and Karl SCHMIDT-ROTTLUFF cofounded DIE BRÜCKE. His earlier works are characterized by the slashing brushstrokes, angular forms, violent color and emotional drama of German EXPRESSIONISM. Heckel was a medical corpsman in World War I. He lived in Berlin from 1918 to 1934, when he was denounced by the Nazis and fled to Switzerland. He returned to Germany after the war and taught at the Karlsruhe Academy from 1949 to 1955. His later works often turned from figures, many of them nudes, to landscapes and became more gentle and meditative.

**Hedayat, Sadeq** (*1903–1951*) Iranian author and playwright. Hedayat's works, which include the novel *Buyf-i kur* (1936, translated as *The Blind Owl*, 1957) and the short story collections, *Zanda bi gur* (Buried Alive, 1930), *Se qatra kuhn* (Three Drops of Blood, 1932), and *Saage velgard* (Stray Dog, 1942), reflect his fundamentally hopeless and pessimistic worldview. A significant figure in Iranian literature, Hedayat has also translated some of the works of KAFKA, among others, into Persian. Hedayat committed suicide in Paris in 1951.

**Heidegger, Martin** (*1889–1976*) German philosopher. Heidegger was one of the most influential of 20th-century philosophers. He concerned himself primarily with metaphysical and ontological questions on the nature of being and of ultimate reality and helped to establish EXISTENTIALISM as a major philosophical movement. Raised as a Catholic, Heidegger was educated at the University of Freiberg where he studied under the phenomenologist Edmund HUSSERL. After a period of intense thought and retirement in the Black Forest, Heidegger produced his major work, *Being and Time* (1927), which posited categories of authentic and inauthentic being and argued for angst as a major motivating force in human development. Heidegger was a member of the Nazi Party from 1933 to 1945 and was named rector of the University of Freiberg by the HITLER government. His refusal to repudiate his Nazi political beliefs after the war caused much controversy. Other works by Heidegger include *An Introduction to Metaphysics* (1953) and *What Is Philosophy?* (1956).

**Heiden, Eric Arthur** (*1958–   *) American speed skater. In 1977 Heiden became the first American ever to win the men's all-around speed skating championship. His performances at the 1980 Lake Placid Olympics focused American attention on the little-watched sport of speed skating. He won gold medals in the 500-, 100-, 1500-, 5000- and 10,000-meter events, while setting a new record in each event. He retired after the 1980 Olympics to pursue a career in bicycle racing. Heiden's records held until they were broken in the 2002 Salt Lake City winter games.

**Heidenstam, Verner von** (*1859–1940*) Swedish poet and novelist. An important Swedish literary figure in his time, Heidenstam's reputation has not lasted, possibly, in part, due to the conservative and aristocratic bent of his later work. Heidenstam's lyric poetry includes, *Vallfart och vandringsar* (Pilgrimage: The wander years, 1888) and *Nya Dikter* (New poems, 1915). His fiction includes *Endymion* (1889); the stories, *Korolinerna* (The Charles men, 1897–98), and the two-volume novel *Folkunga Tradet* (The tree of the Folkungs, 1905–07). Heidenstam was awarded the NOBEL PRIZE in literature in 1916.

**Heifetz, Jascha** (*1901–1987*) Lithuanian-born violinist. Heifetz was one of the most renowned violinists of the 20th century. He achieved great success as a child prodigy in Europe be-

*Violinist Jascha Heifetz* (LIBRARY OF CONGRESS, PRINTS AND PHOTOGRAPHS DIVISION)

fore immigrating to the U.S. in 1917 with his parents at the onset of the RUSSIAN REVOLUTION. His October 1917 debut at New York City's CARNEGIE HALL became the stuff of musical legend. For the next 50 years he performed regularly in the U.S. and around the world. His playing was notable for tonal brilliance, technical perfection and fidelity to the written score. He recorded a memorable series of chamber music performances with pianist Artur RUBINSTEIN and cellist Gregor Piatigorsky. Heifetz retired from the concert stage in 1972, but continued to teach master classes at the University of Southern California until shortly before his death.

**Heijermans, Herman** (*1864–1924*) Dutch playwright and critic. Heijermans first achieved success with the play *Ahasverus* (1893), presented under the pseudonym Ivan Jelakowitch as he thought the Dutch favored foreign authors. Heijermans is best known for his later social dramas, which include *Ghetto* (1899), *Op van Zegen* (1900, *The Good Hope* 1903), and *Eva Bonheur* (1917, translated as *The Devil to Pay*, 1925). Heijermans was also a theatrical critic, and wrote novels under the pseudonym Koos Habema, and short sketches using the name Samuel Falkland.

**Hein, Piet** (*1905–1996*) Danish designer, mathematician and poet-humorist well known for his small books of poems and cartoon sketches called "Grooks." Hein's design reputation is largely based on his remarkable invention of a new geometric shape, the super-ellipse, a form sharing some of the characteristics of the true ellipse, the oval, and the rectangle—it might be called a somewhat squared ellipse. It has been used as the plan layout for a traffic "circle" in central Stockholm, as the form for the top of a table manufactured by Bruno Mathsson, and, in three-dimensional form, to make the super-egg—a solid that has the peculiar property of being able to stand on end as readily as on its side.

## Heinlein, Robert A(nson) (1907–1988)

One of the world's most popular, prolific and influential writers of science fiction, Heinlein was voted an unprecedented four Hugo awards for best science fiction novel of the year. The awards, voted on by science fiction fans who are voting members of each year's annual world convention, were given for *Double Star* (1956), *Starship Troopers* (1959), *Stranger in a Strange Land* (1961) and *The Moon Is a Harsh Mistress* (1966). The best selling *Stranger in a Strange Land* was regarded as a sort of "hippie bible" in the 1960s. In 1975 Heinlein was the first recipient of the Grand Master Award of the Science Fiction Writers of America, given for lifetime achievement. A graduate of the U.S. Naval Academy, Heinlein's navy career was cut short by illness and followed by graduate studies in physics and mathematics, then a raft of different jobs and in 1939 his first story sale, to *Astounding* magazine. From then until his last novel, *To Sail Beyond the Sunset* (1987), Heinlein's matter-of-fact integration of technological innovation with a pugnaciously American frontier attitude that challenged all social ideas, in fast-moving but sometimes rambling plots, the whole carried forward by competent, no-nonsense men and women, yanked science fiction forever out of its pulp fiction straitjacket.

## Heisenberg, Werner Karl (1901–1976)

German physicist. Heisenberg was educated at the universities of Munich (where his father was a professor of Greek) and Göttingen, where in 1923 he obtained his doctorate. After spending the period from 1924 to 1926 in Copenhagen working with Niels BOHR, he returned to Germany to take up the professorship of theoretical physics at the University of Leipzig. In 1941 Heisenberg moved to Berlin where he was appointed director of the Kaiser Wilhelm Institute for Physics and where he played the key role in the German atomic bomb program. After the war he helped establish the Max Planck Institute for Physics at Göttingen, serving as director and moving with it to Munich in 1955, where he was also appointed professor of physics.

In 1925 Heisenberg formulated a version of quantum theory that became known as matrix mechanics. It was for this work (later shown to be formally equivalent to the wave mechanics of Erwin SCHRODINGER) that Heisenberg was awarded the 1932 NOBEL PRIZE for physics. In 1927 he went on to explore a deeper level of physical understanding when he formulated his fundamental "uncertainty principle": It is impossible to determine exactly both the position and momentum of such particles as the electron. He demonstrated this by simple "thought experiments." Like Max BORN, Heisenberg had found it necessary to introduce a basic indeterminacy into physics.

After his achievements in quantum theory in the 1920s Heisenberg turned his attention to the theory of elementary particles. In 1932, shortly after the discovery of the neutron by James CHADWICK, Heisenberg proposed that the nucleus consists of both neutrons and protons. He went further, arguing that they were, in fact, two states of the same basic entity—the "nucleon." As the strong nuclear force does not distinguish between them, he proposed that they were "isotopes" with nearly the same mass, distinguished by a property he called "isotopic spin." He later attempted the ambitious task of constructing a unified field theory of elementary particles. Although he published a monograph on the topic in 1966 it generated little support.

Unlike many other German scientists, Heisenberg remained in Germany throughout the war and the whole Nazi era. He was not a Nazi but thought it essential to remain in Germany to preserve traditional scientific values for the next generation. In 1935, when he wished to move to the University of Munich to succeed Arnold Sommerfeld, he was violently attacked by the Nazi Party press for refusing to compromise his support for the physics of Albert EINSTEIN. Eventually, the post went to the little-known W. Muller. With the outbreak of war in 1939 Heisenberg was soon called to Berlin to direct a program to construct an atom bomb. Heisenberg's exact role in the program is a matter of controversy. He has claimed that he never had any real intention of making such a bomb, let alone giving it to HITLER. As long as he played a key role he was, he later claimed, in a position to sabotage the program if it ever looked like being a success. He conveyed such thoughts to Niels Bohr in 1941 in Copenhagen, hinting that Allied physicists should pursue a similar policy. Bohr later reported that if such comments had been made to him they were too cryptic for him to grasp; he was rather under the impression that Heisenberg was trying to find out the progress made by the Allies. At any rate, when talking to German audiences Heisenberg was more inclined to explain the failure of the German atomic bomb program by the comparative lack of resources in the wartime economy after 1942. But by 1957 he was declaring publicly that he would not "in any way . . . take part in the production, the tests, or the application of atomic weapons."

## Hejaz (Al-Hijaz)

Province along the Red Sea coast of western Saudi Arabia. Thousands of Islamic pilgrims visit its holy cities of Mecca and Medina annually. A railroad built from Damascus to Medina by the Ottoman Turks has been in disuse since the Turks lost their Arabian empire after WORLD WAR I. Husein ibn Ali, who gained independence for the province in 1916, was defeated by Ibn Saud of Nejd in 1924. The two provinces became a dual kingdom in 1926, and the single kingdom of SAUDI ARABIA in 1932.

## Hejiang (Ho-Chiang)

Formerly, a province of Chinese MANCHURIA created in 1945 by the Kuomintang (Guomindang) Nationalists. Hejiang became a part of Songjiang (Song-Chiang) province after the communist victory in the CHINESE CIVIL WAR OF 1945–49;

five years later it was incorporated into Heilongkiang province.

**Helgoland (Heligoland)** Resort island off the North Sea coast of Germany. Near the mouth of the Elbe River and the western end of the Kiel Canal (the great imperial naval base was at Kiel, on the Baltic Sea end of the canal) Helgoland was the almost inevitable site for several naval battles fought between Great Britain and Germany during WORLD WAR I. An early German defeat, on August 28, 1914, did much to discourage the Germans from leaving local waters to use their new, expensive fleet. The postwar TREATY OF VERSAILLES saw the dismantling of the island's fortifications, which were rebuilt under Adolf HITLER. Used by Germany as a naval base during WORLD WAR II, Helgoland was not surrendered to the Allies until May 5, 1945. In the British occupation zone, the island's fortifications were dynamited on April 18, 1947.

**Heller, Joseph** (1923–1999) American author. Heller achieved success with his iconoclastic first novel, *Catch-22* (1961, filmed 1970). Based on Heller's experiences as a bombardier in WORLD WAR II, the book depicts the absurdity of war and the system that promotes it. Its hero, Yossarian, who wants to be declared insane to get out of the war, is told that if he is sane enough to want to leave, he cannot be discharged for insanity, and that is the catch of the title. Heller maintained his reputation satirizing modern life in such novels as *Something Happened* (1974), *Good as Gold* (1979) and *Picture This* (1988). In 1984 he was stricken with a rare paralyzing disease, Guillan-Barré syndrome, that he chronicled in *No Laughing Matter* (1986). Heller also wrote plays and screenplays. Heller published *Closing Time* in 1994 a sequel to *Catch-22*, and his last novel, *Portrait of an Artist as an Old Man*, in 2000.

**Heller, Robert** (1899–1973) American industrial designer whose work of the 1930s carried streamlining and MODERNISM (as related to ART DECO) to an extreme. Heller's best-known work in a streamlined electric fan designed in 1938 for the A. C. Gilbert Company. Although his 1933 building for radio

station WCAU in Philadelphia has been destroyed, its interiors were a showcase of Art Deco interior design, while the street facade of blue cement with zig-zag trim in stainless steel symbolized the glamour of radio. However, conservative architects of that time and place found it offensive.

**Heller, Walter W(olfgang)** (1915–1987) American economist. Heller served as chairman of the Council of Economic Advisers under two presidents, John F. KENNEDY and Lyndon B. JOHNSON. He held the post from the start of the Kennedy administration until the end of 1964, but continued to serve as consultant to Johnson until 1969. Heller was regarded as the architect of the historic tax cut of 1964 that led to an unprecedented boom in the U.S. economy. After he left office, he helped develop the theory of **revenue sharing**, under which state and local governments were deemed more efficient spenders of federal tax revenues than the federal government itself. Heller was a professor emeritus at the University of Minnesota.

**Hellman, Lillian Florence** (1905–1984) American playwright and memoirist. The New Orleans–born playwright studied at New York University, Columbia and Tufts. She worked as a manuscript reader and reviewer before her first Broadway success, *The Children Hour* (1934). She began a tempestuous, lifelong relationship with mystery writer Dashiell HAMMETT in the early 1930s. Because she visited Russia in 1936 and 1945 and was active on the political left, she was called before the HOUSE UN-AMERICAN ACTIVITIES COMMITTEE in 1952 but refused to testify against her friends and colleagues. Her best-known plays include *The Little Foxes* (1939), *The Watch on the Rhine* (1941), *Another Part of the Forest* (1946) and *Toys in the Attic* (1960). Her memoirs appeared as *An Unfinished Woman* (1969), *Pentimento* (1973) and *Scoundrel Time* (1976). In her final years she engaged in a notorious public feud with novelist Mary MCCARTHY, who, in an interview on national television, had charged that Hellman was a liar.

**Helms-Burton Act** Formally known as the Cuban Liberty and Democratic Solidarity Act, the Helms-Burton Act of

1996 is a piece of congressional legislation sponsored by Republican senator Jesse Helms of North Carolina and Democratic congressman Dan Burton of Indiana that formalized the nature of U.S. sanctions against the regime of Fidel CASTRO in CUBA. It authorized the U.S. government to refuse to issue visas to individuals, shareholders and families of individuals who work for companies that have purchased or invested in property nationalized by Castro. The most controversial element of the act is Title III, which asserts that U.S. companies and individuals whose property was nationalized by the Cuban government after 1960 may sue, in a U.S. court, any foreign company that has purchased such property. This precipitated a wave of protests from nations such as Britain, Canada, France and Mexico—all countries with companies interested in investing in sectors of the Cuban economy that were nationalized. These four nations vowed to use the WORLD TRADE ORGANIZATION and the NORTH AMERICAN FREE TRADE AGREEMENT to compel the U.S. to revoke the law. However, since the act's passage, the U.S. has delayed implementation of Title III.

**Helpmann, Sir Robert** (1909–1986) Australian dancer, choreographer, actor and director. As the principal male dancer for the Vic-Wells Ballet (1930–50), Helpmann danced classical, dramatic and comic roles with equal command and formed a celebrated partnership with Margot FONTEYN that contributed to the development of the ROYAL BALLET Company. He has choreographed works for several companies, and is noted for the unified dramatic effect of his creations, which include *Comus* (1942), *Hamlet* (1944), and *Elektra* (1963). An accomplished actor as well as dancer, he played leading roles in several Shakespearean plays, receiving special acclaim for his Hamlet. In addition, he appeared in the films *The Red Shoes* (1948) and *The Tales of Hoffman* (1951). He became coartistic director of the Australian Ballet in 1965, and collaborated with Rudolph NUREYEV in filming the company's *Don Quixote* in 1973 in which he played the title role. Knighted by Queen ELIZABETH II in 1968, he retired in 1976 after producing the Australian Ballet's most popular work, *The Merry Widow*.

**Helsinki Accords** The Helsinki Accords, a result of the Conference on Security and Cooperation in Europe, were signed by 33 European nations plus the U.S. and Canada, on August 1, 1975. Although the agreement does not have the legal status of a treaty, it served as a keystone of DETENTE. The accords implicitly recognized Soviet dominance of Eastern Europe while guaranteeing human rights in those nations, facilitating trade within Europe and easing political and military tensions.

**Hemingway, Ernest** *(1898–1961)* Hemingway was one of the most famous American writers of the 20th century. Born in Oak Park, Ill., after high school he became a reporter in Kansas City. During WORLD WAR I he joined a volunteer ambulance unit in Italy, where he was wounded. Remaining in Europe after the war, he became part of the literary scene in Paris, associating with such American expatriate writers as Gertrude STEIN and F. Scott FITZGERALD. His first and perhaps most famous novel, *The Sun Also Rises* (1926), is a moving tribute to the "lost generation" of expatriate Americans whose beliefs were shattered by the war. Hemingway's World War I experiences inspired *A Farewell to Arms* (1929), considered a classic novel of the war despite its flaws. His writings reflected his many interests, including bullfighting and African big game hunting. After observing the SPANISH CIVIL WAR firsthand he wrote *For Whom the Bell Tolls* (1940). His WORLD WAR II reporting took him on many of the major Allied campaigns of WORLD WAR II IN EUROPE; his novel *Across the River and Into the Trees* (1950) is set during the war. Hemingway won a PULITZER PRIZE in 1953 for his novella *The Old Man and the Sea,* and the following year was awarded the NOBEL PRIZE in literature. Hemingway developed a type of laconic male character who typically faced violence and destruction with courage—what Hemingway called "grace under pressure." His deceptively simple prose style and his amoral outlook make Hemingway one of the leading figures of literary MODERNISM. He committed suicide by shooting himself at his home in Ketchum, Idaho.

**Hempel, Carl G(ustav)** *(1905–1997)* German philosopher. Hempel was trained in physics and mathematics and earned his doctoral degree at the University of Berlin in 1934. He was a member of the Berlin group of philosophers who contributed to the theories of the Vienna Circle—led by Rudolf CARNAP—that led to the formulation of the school of LOGICAL POSITIVISM. One of Hempel's key theories was that of a "translatability criterion" for truth: A statement was meaningful only if it was translatable into empiricist language. Hempel fled GERMANY and the Nazi regime in 1934 and ultimately came to the United States, where he taught at Princeton and Yale. Major works by Hempel include *Fundamentals of Concept Formation in Empirical Science* (1952) and *Aspects of Scientific Explanation* (1965).

**Hench, Philip Showalter** *(1896–1965)* American physician. Hench earned his M.D. from the University of Pittsburgh in 1920 and began work at the Mayo Clinic three years later. Over the course of his long career there, he researched a treatment for rheumatoid arthritis and was the first to use cortisone, developed by Edward KENDALL, to treat the condition. He shared the 1950 NOBEL PRIZE in physiology or medicine with Kendall and Tadeus Reichstein.

**Henderson, Arthur** *(1863–1935)* British statesman. Born in Glasgow, Scotland, at 12 Henderson was apprenticed to an iron molder. Becoming an iron worker, he was soon a leader in the labor union movement. In 1900 he was a cofounder of the Labour Representation Committee, the forerunner of the British LABOUR PARTY, and three years later he was elected to Parliament. He headed the 1906 conference that formally established the Labour Party, acting as the party's parliamentary leader from 1908 to 1911 and 1914 to 1917, and as its secretary from 1911 to 1934. He held various posts in ASQUITH'S WORLD WAR I coalition government and was home secretary (1924) and foreign secretary (1929–31) in the Labour government of Ramsay MACDONALD. Losing his parliamentary seat in 1931, he became president of the World Disarmament Conference the following year. For the rest of his life Henderson devoted himself to his party

and to the cause of world peace, and in 1934 he was awarded the NOBEL PEACE PRIZE. His books include *The Aims of Labour* (1917), *Consolidating World Peace* (1931) and *Labour's Way to Peace* (1935).

**Henderson, Edwin** *(1883–1977)* American educator. Henderson was the first black instructor of physical education in the U.S. (1904). He was also active in the NATIONAL ASSOCIATION FOR THE ADVANCEMENT OF COLORED PEOPLE (NAACP). During the 1950s he served two terms as president of the NAACP's Virginia chapter.

**Henderson, Fletcher** *(1897–1952)* American bandleader-arranger. like Duke ELLINGTON, Henderson was raised in an upper-middle-class family. He received early training in European classical music from his mother, a piano teacher who shunned blues, gospel and jazz forms as "unworthy." After graduation from Atlanta University as a chemistry major, Henderson moved to New York; unable to secure employment in his field because of racial prejudice, he became a song-plugger and music producer, putting together various acts for tour and club work. Soon, he became a bandleader. And by 1925, though he initially lacked any real jazz experience, his band featured such rising jazz talents as trumpeter Louis ARMSTRONG and saxophonist Lester YOUNG. Arrangements for Henderson's band, regarded as the prototype of the big swing bands that would dominate the 1930s, were made by Don Redman. When Redman departed, Henderson was forced to write much of his band's material. Fortuitously, Henderson's arranging gifts proved immense. Indeed, he was pivotal in establishing the basic format of the big band arrangement, featuring interplay between the reed and brass sections (sometimes in call-and-response dialogues, other times with one section playing background riffs behind the other), with improvised solos interspersed between the written passages. Though Henderson's lack of business acumen precluded his own large-scale success, his arrangements of tunes such as "King Porter Stomp" and "Down South Camp Meeting" helped catapult Benny GOODMAN to fame in the mid-1930s and, with Goodman, the entire big band swing phenomenon.

## Henderson, W(esley) Loy (1892–1986)

U.S. diplomat. Henderson was one of the first career officers in the U.S. foreign service, ambassador to India and Iran. He was prominent in Middle East diplomacy in the decade following World War II, and was credited with having played a major role in preventing the communist takeover of GREECE in the late 1940s.

## Hendrix, Jimi (James Marshall Hendrix) (1942–1970)

American ROCK guitarist and vocalist. Hendrix is widely regarded as one of the greatest guitarists in the history of rock and roll. Hendrix learned his musical craft in the early 1960s, when he performed as a backup musician for stars including B. B. KING, Little Richard and Ike and Tina Turner. It was Keith Richard, guitarist for the ROLLING STONES, who brought Hendrix to the attention of music industry people capable of making him a star. Hendrix signed a recording contract in 1967 and had immediate success with his classic single "Hey Joe" (1967). That same year he performed with his band the Jimi Hendrix Experience at the Monterey Pop Festival—a performance preserved in the film *Monterey Pop* (1969)—and riveted the audience by burning his guitar for his finale. Hendrix died from a drug overdose in 1970. His noteworthy albums include *Are You Experienced* (1967), *Axis-Bold as Love* (1967), *Electric Ladyland* (1968) and *Rainbow Bridge* (1971).

## Heng, Samrin (1934– )

Heng Samrin is president of CAMBODIA and leader of the country's official Communist Party. With little formal education, in the 1950s he became involved in illicit cattle trading across the Vietnamese border—the beginning of his contact with Vietnamese communists. He took up the revolutionary cause in 1959, then fled to the jungle in 1967 as Khmer communists escaped repression in Phnom Penh. Based in the eastern zone, near the Vietnamese border, in 1978 he joined the pro-Hanoi faction of the party. Samrin fled to Vietnam to escape POL POT's purges of cadres in the eastern zone. Shortly thereafter he returned to Cambodia with the Vietnamese invading force and became president of liberated Cambodia in January 1979. Heng resigned the presidency upon the return in 1991 of the Cambodian king Norodom SIHANOUK.

## Henie, Sonja (1912–1969)

Norwegian-born skater and film star. Born to one of Norway's wealthiest families, Henie won an unequalled three OLYMPIC figure skating gold medals, in 1928, 1932 and 1936. Her popularity became so great during her skating career that police had to provide crowd control wherever she appeared. After winning 1,473 skating trophies, she signed with 20th CENTURY–FOX. Her first film *One in a Million* (1936) was an enormous success, and a string of films whose plots revolved around skating followed. She retired from films in the 1940s. At her death she was worth an estimated $47 million.

## Henri, Robert (1865–1929)

American painter. Born in Cincinnati, Henri attended the Pennsylvania Academy of the Fine Arts, and continued his art studies in Paris from 1888 to 1891. Returning to teach in Philadelphia, he moved to New York City in 1900 and established his own school there nine years later. An advocate of a vivid and very American realism and an opponent of overly refined and mannered academic styles, Henri was a member of the group known as the EIGHT and its articulate spokesman. His bold, broad brushstroke was particularly effective in outstanding portraits, which include *Eva Green* (Wichita Art Museum), *Spanish Gypsy* (Metropolitan Museum, N.Y.C.) and *Young Woman in Black* (Art Institute of Chicago). At his school until 1912 and later at the Art Students League, Henri was an inspired and extremely influential teacher who numbered among his students George BELLOWS, William GLACKENS, Edward HOPPER, Rockwell Kent, George Luks and John SLOAN.

## Henson, James "Jim" (1939–1990)

Creator of the "Muppets" and a successful television and motion picture producer-director. Henson was born in Greenville, Miss., and after college landed his first television show, *Sam and Friends*, on WRC-TV in Washington, D.C. He referred to his hand-operated characters as "muppets"—a combination of the words "puppet" and "marionette." Such familiar characters as Kermit the Frog, Fozzie Bear, Miss Piggy and Cookie Monster were developed for the Children's Television Workshop program, *Sesame Street* (1969) and its spin-off *The Muppet Show*, which began in London in 1976. Henson then starred his Muppets in three motion pictures, *The Muppet Movie* (1979), *The Great Muppet Caper* (1981) and *The Muppets Take Manhattan* (1984). Meanwhile, his company, Henson Associates, Inc., began a successful licensing campaign, a Saturday morning children's show, *The Muppet Babies* (1984) and two "serious" movie fantasies, *The Dark Crystal* (1982) and *The Labyrinth* (1985). He sold the rights to the Muppets to Walt Disney Enterprises for a reported $150 million in 1989. Henson's style adroitly blended gentle, positive humor for children with a satiric edge finely honed for the adults. Henson died suddenly of pneumonia in 1990.

## Henze, Hans Werner (1926– )

German composer. Born in Gutersloh, he studied piano, percussion and composition, and was a student of Wolfgang Fortner and Rene Leibowitz. A British prisoner of war in World War II, he moved to Italy in 1953. Influenced by STRAVINSKY, HINDEMITH and BARTOK, he began writing twelve-tone music with his first violin concerto of 1947. Since the 1960s, Henze has modified that system into a more personal but no less dissonant style. He is probably best known for his operas, which include *King Stag* (1955), *Elegy for Young Lovers* (1961), *The Bassarids* (1965) and *La Cubana* (1973). In recent years Henze has composed a variety of musical works, including operas, such as *L'Upupa oder der Triumph der Sohnesliebe* (2003); solo concertos, such as Scorribanda Sinfonica (2001); and symphonies, such as his Symphony No. 10 (2002).

## Hepburn, Katharine (1907–2003)

Celebrated American stage and motion picture actress. Hepburn won four ACADEMY AWARDS, including for *Morning Glory* (1932), *Guess Who's Coming to Dinner* (1967) and *On Golden Pond* (1981). The Bryn Mawr–educated daughter of a distinguished New England family had the uncanny knack of

*Legendary actress Katharine Hepburn* (PHOTOFEST)

appearing in movies that paralleled her own life and temperament. *A Woman Rebels* (1936), the story of a 19th-century feminist leader, could also have been a portrayal of Hepburn's suffragist mother. The events in *Stage Door* (1937) resembled her own attempts to break into Broadway. (*Holiday* [1938] allowed her to take on a role that she had understudied on the stage a decade earlier.) The men's clothes worn by her title characters in *Christopher Strong* (1933) and *Sylvia Scarlett* (1935) suggested her own fashion predilections. Her liberal political views surfaced in the politician's wife she portrayed in Frank CAPRA's *State of the Union* (1947). Her personal and professional relationship with Spencer TRACY began with *Woman of the Year* (1942) and ended only with his death during the shooting of *Guess Who's Coming to Dinner?* (1967).

**Hepworth, Cecil** *(1874–1953)* Pioneering British motion picture director, producer and inventor at the turn of the 20th century. If first honors must go to Robert W. Paul as the Father of the British Film, Hepworth, lagging behind by only a few years, assumed the forefront of the British film industry for the first 15 years of the new century. The son of a noted lantern-slide lecturer, Hepworth designed and sold projector lamps. In 1898 he set up a company at Walton-on-Thames to process and make short films. Five years later at his own studio he began making short news films and trick films in the manner of MELIÈS and Paul.

His production in 1905 of the six-minute "Rescued by Rover" (directed by Lewin Fitzhamon) was a spectacular success and, like the American *The Great Train Robbery* (1903), helped establish the narrative film as the most important form of cinema entertainment. "I have never in my life before or since witnessed such intense enthusiasm as these short, crude films evoked in audiences who saw films for the first time," he recalled in his autobiography, *Came the Dawn* (1951). In 1910 he patented an early system for the synchronization of image and phonographic sound, the Vivaphone. However, after 1914 his career went into decline; new developments in the industry overtook him as his own films, including *Annie Laurie* (1916) and *Boundary House* (1918), lapsed into routine formulas. In 1924 Hepworth declared bankruptcy and after 1927 he made no more feature pictures. His last years were spend directing short advertising films and trailers.

**Hepworth, Dame Jocelyn Barbara** *(1903–1975)* English sculptor. She studied at the Royal College of Art, London and absorbed Romanesque and Renaissance styles as well as stone-cutting techniques in a 1924 study trip to Italy. Her work, carved directly in stone or wood, and later also cast in bronze, is simplified, abstract and organic. Often hollowed out and pierced, her sculpture has been compared to BRANCUSI, Henry MOORE and Jean ARP. After 1937, Hepworth often included color in her work and, after 1938, she also included string or wire into her compositions, giving the effect of abstract musical instruments. She is noted for several monumental public pieces, as in her work in the Royal Festival Hall, London, and she is particularly well represented in the Tate Gallery collection, London. Along with Moore and her husband Ben NICOLSON, she is considered one of the most important figures in British art (and in modern sculpture) in the 20th century.

**Herbert, Frank** *(1910–1986)* American science-fiction author. Herbert's epic novel *Dune* (1965) became an international bestseller and cult favorite. The lavish and expensive 1984 film version of the novel, although panned by U.S. critics, found success in Europe

and Japan. *Dune* was the first book in what began as a trilogy and grew to six novels. After his death two novels were published posthumously, *Man of Two Worlds* (with his son Brian Herbert) in 1986, and *The Ascension Factor* (with Bell Ransom) in 1988.

**Herbert, Victor** *(1859–1924)* Irish-American composer, conductor and cellist. Born in Dublin, he studied at the Stuttgart Conservatory. He came to the U.S. in 1886 as a cellist for the Metropolitan Opera, N.Y.C. Herbert conducted various military bands and orchestras and was the conductor of the Pittsburgh Symphony Orchestra from 1898 to 1904, after which he devoted most of his time to composing. Famous for his light-hearted, melodious operettas, he is best known for *Babes in Toyland* (1903), *The Red Mill* (1906), *Naughty Marietta* (1910) and *Sweethearts* (1913) and for such songs as "Ah! Sweet Mystery of Life" and "Gypsy Love Song." He also wrote the grand operas *Natoma* (1911) and *Madeleine* (1914), music for the ZIEGFELD FOLLIES, orchestral pieces and a cello concerto.

**Herbert, Zbigniew** *(1924–1998)* Polish poet, essayist and playwright. Herbert was one of the finest postwar Polish poets. His verse is noteworthy for its taut, austere style that deals movingly with themes of war, loss, love and the diminished meanings of faith and myth in a desacralized world. Herbert was born in Lvov, Poland, and

*Composer Victor Herbert* (LIBRARY OF CONGRESS. PRINTS AND PHOTOGRAPHS DIVISION)

fought against the NAZIS in the underground RESISTANCE during WORLD WAR II, during which time he also began to write poetry. After the war, Herbert studied economics, law and philology at the universities of Krakow and Torun. In the 1950s he traveled in western Europe, and he was Poet in Residence at the Free University of West Berlin in the late 1960s. His major volumes of verse include *The Chord of Light* (1956), *Hermes, Dog and Star* (1957) and *Study of the Object* (1961). *The Barbarian in the Garden* (1963) is a collection of travel essays. A volume of *Selected Poems,* including translations of Herbert's verse by NOBEL PRIZE laureate Czesław MILOSZ, was published in English in 1968.

**Hérelle, Félix d'** *(1873–1949)* French-Canadian bacteriologist. D'Hérelle, the son of a Canadian father and Dutch mother, went to school in Paris and later studied medicine at the University of Montreal. He worked as a bacteriologist in Guatemala and Mexico from 1901 until 1909, when he returned to Europe to take up a position at the Pasteur Institute in Paris. D'Hérelle moved to the University of Leiden in 1921 but after only a short stay resigned to become director of the Egyptian Bacteriological Service (1923). In 1926 d'Hérelle was appointed to the chair of bacteriology at Yale, a position he held until his retirement in 1933. He is best known for his discovery of the **bacteriophage**—a type of virus that destroys bacteria. This work began in 1910. A similar discovery of what d'Hérelle termed a "bacteriolytic agent" was announced independently by Frederick Twort in 1915. D'Hérelle published his own account first in 1917, followed by his monograph *The Bacteriophage, Its Role in Immunity* (1921). He spent the rest of his career attempting to develop bacteriophages as therapeutic agents. He tried to cure cholera in India in 1927 and bubonic plague in Egypt in 1926 by administering the appropriate phage to patients.

The importance of the bacteriophage as a research tool in molecular biology cannot be disputed. The so-called phage group, centered on Max DELBRÜCK, made many of the early advances in this discipline in the 1940s.

**Herman, Woody (Woodrow Charles Herman)** *(1913–1987)* American musician. A JAZZ clarinetist and big band leader, Herman's career spanned five decades. He led a series of ensembles, generally called his "Thundering Herd," in a wide range of styles that reflected the continually changing character of popular music. Alumni of various "Herds" included such popular musicians as Stan GETZ, Milt Jackson and Terry Gibbs.

**Herriot, Edouard** *(1872–1957)* French statesman. A moderate leftist, Herriot was an important figure in the political life of the Third and Fourth Republics and the leader of the Radical Socialist party of FRANCE. Elected mayor of Lyon in 1905, he held the office until 1941 and from 1945 until his death. Becoming a member of the senate in 1912 and of the chamber of deputies in 1919, he was a strong voice in opposing militarism and clericalism and promoting civil liberties and republicanism. Premier in 1924–25, he was responsible for withdrawing French forces from the Ruhr valley region and for recognizing the USSR. His unpopular stand in favor of paying war debts to the U.S. was the prime reason for the defeat of this government and for the failure of his next two terms as premier in 1926 and 1932. President of the Chamber of Deputies (1936–40), he opposed the VICHY government and was arrested in 1942. Deported to Germany in 1944, he was liberated the following year. Herriot served as president of the National Assembly from 1947 to 1954. Also a noted man of letters, Herriot was the author of literary studies and a biography of Beethoven.

**Herrmann, Bernard** *(1911–1975)* American composer. Herrmann, who was educated at the Juilliard School of Music in New York, established himself as one of most important composers of HOLLYWOOD film scores. He showed a special talent for eery and ominous scores that effectively blended with the visual imagery of suspense master Alfred HITCHCOCK. Herrmann's auspicious debut as a film composer was the score for *CITIZEN KANE* (1941), the masterpiece of director Orson WELLES. Hitchcock films for which Herrmann composed music include *The Man Who*

*Knew Too Much* (1956), *Vertigo* (1958), *North By Northwest* (1959) and *Psycho* (1960), the chilling score for which Herrmann remains best known. His last work was the score for *Taxi Driver* (1976) directed by Martin SCORSESE.

**Hersey, John Richard** *(1914–1993)* American journalist and novelist. Hersey was born in China, and spoke the language fluently. He began his career as an assistant to Sinclair LEWIS and later began writing for TIME and LIFE magazines, serving as a war correspondent for them during WORLD WAR II. Hersey is best known for his journalistic novels about various countries during the war. These include *Man on Bataan* (1942), *A Bell for Adano* (1944, filmed 1945), which won a PULITZER PRIZE in 1946; *Hiroshima* (1946), which first appeared in *The New Yorker,* and *The Wall* (1950), a study of Poland under the Nazis. Later works include *Aspects of the Presidency* (1980), *The Call* (1985) and *Blues* (1987).

**Hershey, Franklin Quick** *(1907–1997)* American automobile designer best known for his work on the original (1955) Ford THUNDERBIRD, although a major portion of his career was spent with GENERAL MOTORS. Hershey studied at Occidental College in California before going to work for the California custom automobile design firm of Walter M. Murphy in 1927, where he remained (except for a brief period in 1928 at General Motors in Detroit) until the firm closed in 1931. He was briefly with Hudson before joining GM in 1932 to take charge of styling for Pontiac and later for Buick and overseas GM divisions. After World War II he returned to GM to work on Cadillac design and in the firm's experimental design studio. In 1953 he was placed in charge of styling at FORD. In 1956 he left automotive design to work for KAISER Aluminum and then, until his retirement in 1978, for Wright Autotronics in California. Hershey's work spanned a wide range of automotive design concepts, extending from the peerless custom body of the early 1930s through GM models of the 1930s and early 1940s to the elegant and greatly admired 1955 Thunderbird, a sports car of simple form. Surprisingly, he also directed the design of other Ford cars, such as the 1957 Fairlane 500, which typified the trend toward oversized fenders and heavy CHROMIUM trim.

**Hertz, Gustav** *(1887–1975)* German physicist. The nephew of 19th-century physicist Heinrich Hertz, Gustav Hertz was born in Hamburg, Germany. He attended the universities of Berlin and Munich and afterward taught in Berlin and Halle. In 1925 Hertz shared the NOBEL PRIZE in physics with his colleague James Franck, for "discovering the laws governing the impact of an electron on an atom." Beginning in 1928, he worked as an instructor at the Technical University in Berlin. From 1935, when he was forced by the Nazis to leave his teaching position, until the end of WORLD WAR II, he worked as an industrial physicist for Siemens. In the decade following the war, Hertz helped to develop the Soviet atomic bomb. From 1955 until his retirement in 1961, he was a professor at the Physics Institute in Leipzig.

**Herut (Hebrew for "Freedom Party")** Extreme right-wing political group in ISRAEL, founded by Menachem BEGIN and a successor to the **Revisionist Party.** It was later a part of Gahal.

**Herzl, Theodor** *(1860–1904)* Founder of modern ZIONISM. A Hungarian Jew, Herzl studied law at the University of

*Theodor Herzl, founder of modern Zionism* (LIBRARY OF CONGRESS, PRINTS AND PHOTOGRAPHS DIVISION)

Vienna, receiving a doctorate in 1884. He became a journalist and was sent (1891) to Paris by the Viennese newspaper *Neue Freie Presse* and covered the Dreyfus Affair. His earlier experiences with anti-Jewish feeling coupled with the appalling ANTI-SEMITISM that he witnessed during the infamous trial turned Herzl against the idea of Jewish assimilation and convinced him that it was necessary for JEWS to have a nation of their own. He expressed this idea in the landmark work *The Jewish State* (1896), in which he suggested establishing this nation in the original Jewish homeland of PALESTINE. The following year Herzl convened the first World Zionist Congress in Basel, Switzerland, and he served as its president until his death. He worked tirelessly to promote Zionism and to secure both the necessary funding to realize his dream and the positive world opinion that would ease the way to a Jewish state. A year after the creation of ISRAEL, Herzl's body was moved from Vienna to Jerusalem.

**Herzog, Chaim** *(1918–1997)* President of ISRAEL (1983–93). Herzog was born in Belfast, Ireland. He studied at the Universities of Dublin, London and Cambridge and at Hebron's yeshiva. He moved to PALESTINE in 1935, served as a British major during World War II and then on the Allied General Staff in Germany. He headed the Jewish Agency's security section (1947–48) and served as director of military intelligence (1948–50, 1959–62) and, from June 1967, as first military governor of the West Bank. He was Israel's ambassador to the United Nations from 1975 to 1978, became a Labor Party member of the Knesset in 1981 and was made president in 1983. A lawyer by training, he is the author of *Israel's Finest Hour, Days of Awe, War of Atonement* and *Who Stands Accused.* He was awarded a KBE in 1970. Although Herzog has kept aloof from internal politics since becoming head of state in 1983, the series of presidential pardons he has granted to settlers and to members of the security service implicated in the killing of Palestinians has put him firmly on the right in Israel's political spectrum.

**Herzog, Werner** *(1942–   )* German film director. Herzog is one of the

most unique film directors of modern times. All of his films have an intensely visionary quality, and many critics have noted resemblances between his thematic concerns and those of the German Romantic writers of the 19th century. Herzog's first major film project, which was self-funded, was the satiric *Even Dwarfs Started Small* (1969). He achieved international fame for *Aguirre, the Wrath of God* (1975), which starred Klaus Kinski and dealt with greed and obsession in the age of the Spanish conquistadores. Subsequent films by Herzog include *Nosferatu the Vampire* (1979), *Woyzeck* (1979) and *Fitzcarraldo* (1982). During the 1990s Herzog worked on two documentaries: *Night of the Filmmakers* (1995), which examined German motion picture directors such as himself, Leni RIEFENSTAHL and Wim Wenders; and *My Best Fiend* (1999), which chronicled his partnership with Klaus Kinski in the 1970s.

**Hesburgh, Theodore M.** *(1917–   )* American educator. Hesburgh, who was ordained as a Roman Catholic priest in 1943, earned his doctorate from Catholic University in 1945. He was named president of Notre Dame University in 1952 and successfully transformed that institution from a strictly Catholic school to a secular university with a high academic standing. Hesburgh also entered the sphere of national politics through his appointment in 1957 by President Dwight EISENHOWER to the U.S. Commission on Civil Rights. Hesburgh remained on the Commission for fifteen years, served as its chairman from 1969 to 1972, and was instrumental in fostering the passage of major CIVIL RIGHTS legislation in the 1960s. Hesburgh was subsequently named by President Jimmy CARTER to the Overseas Development Council. In 1981 he was appointed by President Ronald REAGAN to the Select Commission on Immigration and Refugee Relief. Hesburgh continued to publish after his retirement, penning the autobiographical *Travels with Ted and Ned* (1992) and *The Challenge and Promise of a Catholic University* (1994).

**Hess, Dame Myra** *(1890–1965)* English pianist. Born in London, Hess studied at the Royal Academy of

Music, London. She became a major soloist with her brilliant debut in London in 1907, playing Beethoven under the baton of Sir Thomas BEECHAM. Concertizing throughout Europe, the U.S. and Canada, she was known for her sensitive interpretations of the classical repertoire, particularly the works of Bach, Mozart and Beethoven. During WORLD WAR II she organized the famous luncheon concerts at the National Gallery, London, playing in many of them herself. For these performances, some occurring while bombs fell on London, Hess was made a Dame of the British Empire in 1941.

**Hess, (Walter Richard) Rudolf** *(1894–1987)* German Nazi official. An early member of the Nazi Party, Hess was Adolf HITLER's first great admirer, and in 1920 he became Hitler's political secretary and closest associate. He participated in the Munich BEER HALL PUTSCH (1923). During their subsequent term in prison, Hitler dictated his political tract *MEIN KAMPF* to Hess. In 1934 Hess was named deputy party leader, and was officially second only to GÖRING behind Hitler in the hierarchy of the Third Reich. However, Hess was a naive man of limited intelligence and ability, essentially a dreamer rather than a doer. His influence waned with the rise of HIMMLER, GOEBBELS, and other more practical-minded Nazis. In 1941, on his own initiative, Hess made a solo flight to Scotland in a bizarre bid to end WORLD WAR II. He hoped that British leaders would negotiate with him and that this bold move would restore his flagging reputation in Germany. Instead, Hitler was infuriated by what he viewed as Hess's treason, while the British government refused to take Hess seriously. Hess was immediately imprisoned, and remained in British custody throughout the war. He was tried and convicted during the NUREMBERG WAR CRIMES TRIALS and sentenced to life imprisonment in SPANDAU PRISON in West Berlin. The last survivor of the 19 German officials convicted by the tribunal, by 1966 he was Spandau's only occupant, remaining there (at the insistence of the Soviet government) until his death, despite various appeals for his release. In the 1970s he became an object of international attention when a British doctor claimed that the

prisoner in Spandau was not Hess but a double. This charge was never proved.

**Hesse, Eva** *(1936–1970)* Born in Hamburg, Germany, in 1936, Hesse fled from the Nazis with her family to New York City. When she was 10 years old her mother committed suicide. After studying at Pratt Institute in Brooklyn and Cooper Union in Manhattan, she received a scholarship to the School of Art and Architecture at Yale University in 1957, where she studied painting with Josef Alhers. She graduated in 1959 and became a textile designer in New York City. Throughout the 1960s she had several solo shows of her art in New York and Germany, which included three-dimensional objects such as a costume made of chicken wire and soft jersey as well as drawings and latex and fiberglass sculpture. In 1969 she was diagnosed with a brain tumor and died the following year.

**Hesse, Hermann** *(1877–1962)* German-Swiss novelist, poet and essayist. Winner of the 1946 NOBEL PRIZE in literature, Hesse is known for his psychological probing of the dichotomy between spirit and flesh, art and life, emotion and intellect, independence and involvement, in his major works. His first successful novel, *Peter Camerzind,* was published in 1904. After World War I, Hesse produced his greatest works, which reflected his personal crises, his political views and his philosophical interests, especially in Confucianism and Buddhism. Important works include the novels *Siddhartha* (1922), *Der Steppenwolf* (1927) and *Das Glasperlenspiel* (1943); the poetry collection *Gesammelte Gedichte* (1952); and the volume of essays titled *Blick ins Chaos* (1920).

**Hewitt, Don** *(1922– )* American journalist and producer of television news programs. Born in New York City, Hewitt began his career in journalism in 1942 as a copyboy for the *New York Herald-Tribune.* During WORLD WAR II, he was a war correspondent for the *Herald-Tribune.* When the war ended in 1945, Hewitt found work as a nighttime editor at the Memphis, Tenn., bureau of the Associated Press, followed by a brief tenure (1946–47) as editor of the *Pellham Sun*

and the night telephoto editor for Acme News Pictures (1937–48). Hewitt began his career in television news with Columbia Broadcasting Systems (CBS) in 1948, working as an associate director (and later producer-director) for the weeknight news program *Douglas Edwards with the News.* In 1968 Hewitt created *60 Minutes,* an hour-long news program for CBS. Unlike other news programs, Hewitt patterned *60 Minutes* after variety magazines that contained exposé pieces, human interest stories and sports previews, along with the more traditional topics covered in news programs. For his work in developing *60 Minutes,* Hewitt received the President's Award for Lifetime Achievement from the Overseas Press Club in 1998 and was inducted into the National Association of Broadcasters Hall of Fame in 1993. He retired as executive producer of *60 Minutes* in 2004.

**Heston, Charlton (Charlton Carter)** *(1923– )* American film actor. Heston studied acting at Northwestern University and made his Broadway debut in *Antony and Cleopatra* (1947). Turning to the new media of television he became a respected actor in productions of *Julius Caesar* (1948), *Wuthering Heights* (1949), *Macbeth* (1949) and others. In the 1950s he starred in several films, including *The Greatest Show on Earth* (1952), but it wasn't until he portrayed Moses in Cecil B. DE MILLE's talkie remake of *The Ten Commandments* (1956) that he became known as America's leading actor in historical epics. Three years later he won the ACADEMY AWARD for best actor in the blockbuster remake of another silent hit, *Ben-Hur.* During his career Heston also had success in several off beat roles; he played a Mexican narcotics officer in Orson WELLES's masterpiece *Touch of Evil* (1958) and an astronaut stranded in the future in the science fiction classic *Planet of the Apes* (1968). Heston served as president of the NATIONAL RIFLE ASSOCIATION (NRA) from 1998 to 2003 before retiring because of Alzheimer's disease.

**Heyerdahl, Thor** *(1914–2002)* Norwegian anthropologist and explorer. Heyerdahl became an international celebrity when he made his 4,100-mile raft journey across the Pacific Ocean in

1947. He developed a theory that ancient peoples migrated by sea as well as by land routes. To prove the feasibility of this theory, Heyerdahl and five others built a balsa-wood raft, called the *Kon-Tiki*, which was like the type used by early South American Indians, and traveled from Peru to Polynesia (1947). His 1969 attempt to further test his theory, by crossing the Atlantic from Morocco to South America in a papyrus boat, had to be abandoned. In 1997 he published his memoir, *In the Footsteps of Adam*.

**He Yingqin (Ho Ying-ching)** *(1889–1987)* Chinese military leader. A longtime associate of Gen. CHIANG KAI-SHEK, he served as Chinese minister of war from 1930 to 1944. He was commander in chief of the Chinese army when 1 million Japanese troops surrendered at Nanjing in 1945. Ho fled to TAIWAN in 1949 with Chiang after the Communist victory in the CHINESE CIVIL WAR OF 1945–49. He served as Taiwan's defense minister until 1958.

**Heyse, Paul** *(1830–1914)* German writer, poet and playwright. Heyse is best known for his fiction, which includes the novellas *L'arrabbiata* (The Angry Girl, 1857) and *Bild der Mutter* (The Mother's Portrait, 1859), and the novels *Kinder der Welt* (*Children of the World*, 1873) and *Merlin* (1892). Heyse's romantic, lyric poetry was overshadowed by the Naturalists who followed him, and he is better remembered for his translations of Italian poets. His plays include, *Hans Lange* (1866) and *Maria von Magdala* (Mary of Magdala, 1899). Heyse was awarded the NOBEL PRIZE in literature in 1910, the first German writer to be so honored.

**Heywood, Eddie** *(1915–1989)* American JAZZ pianist, arranger and composer. Haywood's sextet was one of the most popular jazz groups of the 1940s. A bout of severe arthritis forced his retirement in 1947; he then turned to composing such hits of the 1950s as *Land of Dreams, Soft Summer Breeze* and *Canadian Sunset*. In his later years he suffered from Parkinson's disease and Alzheimer's disease.

**Hezbollah (Hizbollah)** Radical Shi'ite guerrilla group in LEBANON advocating the creation of an Islamic state in that country. Its name means "Party of God." During the 1980s Hezbollah received material support from the Iranian government, which hoped that Hezbollah's success would lead to a wave of Islamic governments in the Arab world and place ISRAEL in a precarious position. Generally, Hezbollah has restricted its actions to terrorist operations designed to undermine Israeli efforts to create a Lebanese state tolerant of Israel, for which Israel and the U.S. have repeatedly labeled it a terrorist organization. Hezbollah also conducted military raids from its bases in Lebanon on Israeli territory and on Lebanese territory controlled by Israeli allies. In addition, Hezbollah is a political party with representation in the Lebanese parliament. When the PALESTINE LIBERATION ORGANIZATION (PLO) and Israel made efforts to establish a working relationship between each other with the 1993 Oslo Accords and the 1995 Interim Agreement, Hezbollah denounced these efforts and insisted that the goal of all Arab Muslims was the destruction of the state of Israel. In January 2004 Israel and Hezbollah exchanged several prisoners as a result of negotiations sponsored by Germany. However, on July 12, 2006, armed Hezbollah forces shelled northern Israeli towns, crossed the border into Israel and captured two Israeli soldiers. Israel responded with air attacks and a naval blockade of Lebanon.

**Hidalgo del Parral (Parral)** Transportation and mining center in northern Mexico's Chihuahua state; a hotbed of Francisco Modero's revolt of 1917, Parral was also where popular hero Pancho VILLA was assassinated in 1923.

**Higashikuni, Naruhiko** *(1887–1990)* Japanese monk. A member of JAPAN's imperial family, he became the country's first premier after World War II. He was the first member of the imperial family to head a cabinet, which he formed two days after the Japanese surrender on August 15, 1945. His government lasted less than two months. In 1947 he was deprived of his title and became a Buddhist monk.

**Highsmith, (Mary) Patricia** *(1921–1995)* American novelist. Although they fall into the mystery genre Highsmith's novels have received acclaim from such critics as Brigid BROPHY for their psychological insight as well as their literary style. Perhaps best known in the U.S. is her first novel, *Strangers on a Train* (1950), which was filmed by Alfred HITCHCOCK in 1951. Highsmith's novels have a large following in Britain. Other of her many works include *The Talented Mr. Ripley* (1955, filmed as *Purple Noon* in 1961), the first of a series of novels featuring the repugnant anti-hero Ripley; *Found in the Street* (1986) and *The Animal Lovers Book of Beastly Murder* (1988). Highsmith originally published some of her early work under the pseudonym Clair Morgan.

**Hilbersheimer, Ludwig Karl** *(1885–1967)* German architect and town planner known as a teacher and writer who was influential in advancing BAUHAUS theory as it applied to urban planning. Hilbersheimer was trained in architecture and planning at the Institute of Technology at Karlsruhe in Germany and established his own practice thereafter in Berlin. From 1928 until 1932 he was at the Bauhaus, teaching architecture, construction, housing and town planning. In 1938 he emigrated to the U.S. to become a professor of city planning at Illinois Institute of Technology in Chicago and, after 1955, director of the department of city and regional planning there. He was the author of many articles and a number of books, including *Groszstadt Architektur* (1927), *The New City* (1950) and *The Nature of Cities* (1955). Hilbersheimer's writing emphasizes historical study of urban forms, while his own approach to planning is highly theoretical, leading to abstract, geometric forms generated by studies of prevailing wind directions in relation to industrial pollution output and to the logical study of density, land use and circulation patterns. Although his proposals now seem overly mechanistic, Hilbersheimer's basic concepts remain significant for all modern urban planning.

**Hilbert, David** *(1862–1943)* German mathematician, generally considered one of the greatest of the 20th century. Hilbert studied at the universities of Konigsberg and Heidelberg and also spent brief periods in Paris and Leipzig. He took his Ph.D. in 1885, by 1892 was a professor and in 1895 moved to Gottingen to take up the chair that he occupied until his official retirement in 1930. Hilbert's mathematical work was wide-ranging; there were few fields to which he did not make some contribution and many he completely transformed. From 1885 to 1888 he solved the central problems of the newly created theory of invariants. He created entirely new methods for tackling problems, in the context of a much wider general theory. The fruit of this work consisted of many new and fundamental theorems in algebra. Much of his work on invariants was later applied to the new subject of homological algebra.

Hilbert next turned to algebraic number theory and probably his finest work. He produced not only a masterly account of number theory but also a substantial body of original and fundamental discoveries. The work was presented in *Zahlbericht* (1897) with an elegance and lucidity of exposition that has rarely been equaled. Hilbert moved to another area of mathematics and wrote a classic work, *Grundlagen der Geometrie* (1899, *Foundations of Geometry*), an account of geometry as it had developed in the 19th century.

In mathematical logic and the philosophy of mathematics, Hilbert is one of the major proponents of the formalist view, which had a formative impact on the development of mathematical logic. Hilbert aimed at formalizing as much of mathematics as possible and finding consistency proofs for the resulting formal systems. It was soon shown by Kurt GODEL that "Hilbert's program" could not be carried out, at least in its original form; but Godel's own revolutionary meta-mathematical work would have been inconceivable without Hilbert. Hilbert's contribution to mathematical logic was important, especially to the development of proof theory.

Hilbert also made notable contributions to analysis, to the calculus of variations and to mathematical physics. His work on operators and on "Hilbert space" (a type of infinite-dimensional space) was of crucial importance to QUANTUM MECHANICS. His considerable influence on mathematical physics was also exerted through his colleagues at Gottingen, who included Minkowski, Weyl, SCHRODINGER and HEISENBERG. In 1900 Hilbert presented a list of 23 outstanding unsolved mathematical problems to the International Congress of Mathematicians in Paris. A number of

these problems remain unsolved, and the mathematics created in solving the others has fully vindicated his deep insight. Hilbert was an excellent teacher and during his time at Gottingen built the university into an outstanding center of mathematical research, which it remained until the dispersal of the intellectual community by the Nazis in 1933.

**Hill 60** Hill in Belgian province of West Flanders, about three miles southeast of YPRES—a bloody battle site during the first spring of WORLD WAR I, between April 17 and May 5, 1915.

**Hill 70** Hill in Pas-de-Calais department of northern France, 14 miles northeast of ARRAS. During WORLD WAR I occupied by Germany after fighting in September 1915; retaken by Canadian troops on August 15, 1917.

**Hill 102 (Mamai Kurgan)** Hill in Russian city of Volgograd (formerly Tsaritsyn; STALINGRAD). In WORLD WAR II, occupied by the invading Germans in the summer of 1942, it soon became the scene of intense combat. The Russians struggled in vain to recapture the hill on September 14, at the beginning of the German army's 66–day siege of Stalingrad.

**Hill 192** Strategically located hill in French province of NORMANDY, on the road from Saint-Lô to Bayeux; during the Allied invasion of France in WORLD WAR II, Hill 192 was part of a fierce U.S. offensive before capture on July 11, 1944.

**Hill 304** Hill in the Meuse department of northeastern France, 10 miles from VERDUN. During WORLD WAR I the Germans attempted an advance on Verdun by way of Hill 304, in May 1916. In August 1917 fighting resumed and the French pushed the Germans out of the area.

**Hill 516** See CASSINO.

**Hill 609** Hill overlooking Mateur in northern Tunisia. In WORLD WAR II, occupied by Germany in December 1942, it was regained by Allied forces on May 1, 1943, after several days of bitter combat.

**Hill, Lord Charles** (*1904–1989*) British physician, politician and administrator. Hill became a household name in Britain during WORLD WAR II as the "Radio Doctor" who discussed medical problems in a homespun manner. He also served as secretary of the British Medical Association during negotiations preceding the establishment of Britain's NATIONAL HEALTH SERVICE (NHS). He was elected to Parliament as a Conservative in 1950 and served in several cabinet posts. After being appointed chairman of the Independent Television Authority (ITA), he was named chairman of the BRITISH BROADCASTING CORPORATION (BBC) in 1967.

**Hill, Edwin C.** (*1884–1957*) American author and radio commentator. From 1904 to 1923 he worked as a reporter for the *New York Sun*. He was director of the Fox News Reel (1923–24) and scenario editor for the Fox Film Corporation (1925–26). Hill was a feature writer for the *Sun* from 1927 to 1932, when he became a syndicated feature writer and radio broadcaster known for his "Human Side of the News."

**Hill, Geoffrey** (*1932– )* British poet. Hill was raised in Bromsgrove, Worcestershire, where his father was a police constable. Hill's first poems, published in the early 1950s while he was a student at Keble College, Oxford, attracted critical attention. His subsequent collections—*For the Unfallen* (1959), *King Log* (1968), *Mercian Hymns* (1972), *Tenebrae* (1979) and *The Mystery of the Charity of Charles Peguy* (1984)—have consolidated his reputation as perhaps the most important British poet of the second half of the 20th century. In his relatively small but extremely concentrated body of work, Hill addresses the brutal forces of history and the savagery of the human condition. His dense, formal, highly learned and allusive poetry is in many respects the verse equivalent of Simone WEIL's prose; the two writers share a similar visionary and uncompromising religious consciousness. Hill has taught successively at Leeds, Cambridge and Boston universities. A recipient of the Gregory Award (1961), Hawthornden Prize (1969) and Heinemann Award (1972), he is a Fellow of the Royal Society of Literature. Hill was elected to the American Academy of Arts and Sciences in 1996 and received the 2000 T. S. Eliot Award, as well as the 2001 Heinemann Book Award for *The Triumph of Love* (1998). Other late collections include *Canaan* 1996, *Speech! Speech!* (2000), *The Orchards of Syon* (2000) and *Scenes from Comus* (2005).

**Hillary, Sir Edmund** *(1919– )* New Zealand explorer and mountaineer. Hillary became a mountain climber/explorer after WORLD WAR II, joining a New Zealand expedition to Garhwal, India, in 1951, then a British expedition to Cho Oyu, west of Mt. Everest, in 1952. During a 1953 expedition organized by the Royal Geographical Society and the Alpine Club, Hillary and his Sherpa guide Tenzing Norkay became the first people to reach the summit of Mt. Everest. He led the New Zealand contingent of the Commonwealth Trans-Antarctic Expedition, successfully completing the overland journey from the Ross Sea to the South Pole in 1958. Hillary's many books about his explorations include *No Latitude for Error* (1961). He became ambassador to India in 1985.

**Hillenkoetter, Roscoe Henry** *(1897– 1982)* American naval officer and first director of the CENTRAL INTELLIGENCE AGENCY (CIA) (1947–50). A graduate of the U.S. Naval Academy (1919), he was a diplomatic courier in Europe in the mid-1930s. Before the U.S. became officially involved in WORLD WAR II, he was a naval attaché to the VICHY government of France (1940–41), and also worked with the French RESISTANCE movement. Toward the end of 1941 he was transferred to the Pacific and was wounded in the Japanese attack on PEARL HARBOR (December 7, 1941). Later in the war he served as head of naval intelligence on Admiral NIMITZ's staff, then commanded a destroyer in the Pacific. In 1947 he was appointed director of the Central Intelligence Group, which evolved into the CIA, but was removed from his post by President TRUMAN in 1950. During the KOREAN WAR he commanded a navy task force. He retired from the navy in 1957 with the rank of vice admiral.

**Hillman, Sidney** *(1887–1946)* American labor leader. Hillman was born in Zagare, Lithuania, and immigrated to the U.S. in 1907, where he worked in the garment industry. He was the guiding spirit behind the formation of the Amalgamated Clothing Workers of America and became its first president in 1914. Hillman promoted union-management cooperation and pioneered in developing union health and welfare programs, cooperative housing and banking. An advocate of industrial unionism, he was one of the founders of the CONGRESS OF INDUSTRIAL ORGANIZATIONS and served as its vice president from 1935 to 1940. He was codirector of the Office of Production Management from 1940 to 1942. Hillman was a strong supporter of Franklin D. ROOSEVELT and an influential figure in the Democratic Party. He was the founder of the American Labor Party in 1944 and helped create the World Federation of Trade Unions in 1945.

**Hillsborough Accord** *(1985)* Agreement between the UNITED KINGDOM and the Republic of IRELAND regarding the governing of NORTHERN IRELAND. The accord set up an Anglo-Irish intergovernmental conference to deal with political, security, legal and judicial matters affecting Northern Ireland, and to promote cross-border cooperation. Both governments pledged not to change the status of Northern Ireland without the consent of the majority of the people of Northern Ireland. In return, the Irish republic was given a consultative role in Northern Irish affairs. The agreement followed 15 months of secret negotiations and was the first of its kind since Ireland was partitioned in 1922. Although the accord was denounced by loyalist (Protestant) and republican (pro-IRA) extremists, it was widely regarded as a major step toward solving the complex sectarian conflict in Northern Ireland.

**Hillsborough Stadium Disaster** On April 15, 1989, 95 British soccer fans were killed and nearly 200 injured when several thousand late-arriving fans surged into the stands at an important match between Liverpool and Nottingham Forest at Hillsborough Stadium in Sheffield. When 4,000 Liverpool supporters massed at one entrance to the already crowded stadium, orders were given to throw open an exit gate to allow the fans to enter. In the ensuing rush, fans already in the "terraces," or standing room, were pushed forward and those in the front were pushed up against metal fences. Eventually a gate to the field was opened and the injured and dying were treated on the field. Afterward both government and popular demands were made to eliminate standing room; but the expense of stadium renovation, and the pull of tradition, put the issue to rest.

**Hilton, Conrad Nicholson** *(1887– 1979)* Founder and chairman of Hilton Hotels Corp. and Hilton International. Conrad Hilton began in the hotel business in 1919, investing $5,000 in a Texas hotel. The business grew into a chain of hotels worldwide. At the time of his death, the business was valued at over $500 million. Located mainly in large cities and resorts, Hilton hotels generally provided a high standard of luxury, catering to executive business travelers and to well-off tourists. Many of Hilton's older hotels, such as the Waldorf-Astoria in New York, had been established by other owners; each of these hotels had its own distinct characteristic. However, after World War II, Hilton began the trend of building new hotels with identical architectural designs and standard features throughout the world.

**Hilton, James** *(1900–1954)* British novelist. Hilton is best remembered for the novels *Lost Horizon* (1933, filmed 1937), set in mystical Shangri-La in the Tibetan mountains, and *Goodbye, Mr. Chips* (1934, filmed 1939), the nostalgic story of a school master. In 1936 Hilton moved to HOLLYWOOD to work on screenplays. His film credits include the ACADEMY AWARD–winning *Mrs. Miniver* (1942). Hilton also wrote a mystery novel under the pseudonym Glen Trevor.

**Hilton Hotels** See Conrad HILTON.

**Himachal Pradesh** Himalayan state of northern INDIA, bordering on Tibet and China. Twenty-one former Punjab hill states were joined with it to form a union territory on April 15, 1948. Enlarged several times afterward, the territory became a state in 1970. Largely underdeveloped, its capital is at the hill resort of Simla.

**Himmler, Heinrich** *(1900–1945)* German Nazi leader, head of the notorious SS (Schutzstaffel). Himmler was

*Heinrich Himmler in Russia, 1941* (LIBRARY OF CONGRESS, PRINTS AND PHOTOGRAPHS DIVISION)

an early member of the Nazi Party, and took part in HITLER's failed BEER HALL PUTSCH in Munich in 1923. During much of the remainder of the 1920s he was a chicken farmer. In 1929 he was appointed head of the party's SS organization, which then consisted of only 300 men. During the early 1930s he consolidated his power. After helping to liquidate Brownshirt leader Ernst ROEHM and other of Hitler's Nazi rivals on the NIGHT OF THE LONG KNIVES (June 30, 1934), Himmler was assured a leading position in the Nazi hierarchy. Two years later he was made head of the unified police forces within GERMANY and given the title Reichsführer of the SS. Under his direction, the SS became virtually a state within the German state and made possible the Nazis' totalitarian control of all aspects of German life.

More than any other single individual, Himmler was responsible for putting into practice the so-called FINAL SOLUTION—the HOLOCAUST that saw the destruction of the JEWS of Europe. A cold and brutally efficient bureaucrat, Himmler administered the CONCENTRATION CAMPS from his Berlin headquarters. He was named minister of the interior in 1943. In the final days of the Nazi Reich, Himmler hoped to negotiate a peace settlement with the Allies and to succeed Hitler as leader of Germany at the war's end; however, his efforts were rebuffed by the Allies, who demanded Germany's unconditional surrender. Several weeks after the end of the war, Himmler was captured and arrested by British forces, on May 25, 1945. He committed suicide while in custody. (See also NAZISM.)

**Hindemith, Paul** *(1865–1963)* German composer. Born in Hanau, he studied at the Frankfurt Conservatory and began his career playing the viola and the violin. He was concertmaster for the Frankfurt Opera orchestra (1915–23), violist for the Amar Quartet (1922–29) and professor at the Berlin Hochschule (1927–37). When the Nazis came to power, his work was banned for its "decadent" modernism. Hindemith journeyed to the U.S. in 1937, becoming a professor of music theory at Yale University in 1940. He became an American citizen in 1946, but settled in Switzerland in 1953 to teach at the University of Zurich. One of the foremost composers of the early 20th century, he was extremely prolific and stylistically varied, usually employing the contrapuntal techniques of classical music in a contemporary idiom. His earlier compositions are usually atonal, while his later works display a tonality that has been dubbed **neoclassicism.** He is particularly known for his so-called *Gebrauchsmusick* music written specifically for performance by amateurs.

Hindemith composed in nearly all of the musical genres: opera, chamber work, instrumental music, orchestral work, song, choral and others. His best known composition is the symphony (1934) derived from his opera *Mathis der Maler.* Among his other important works are the song cycle *Das Marienleben* (1923, 1948), the viola concerto *Der Schwanendreher* (1935), the ballet *Nobilissima Visione* (1938), the piano interludes and fugues of *Ludus Tonalis* (1942) and the choral and orchestral treatment of Whitman's *When Lilacs Last in the Dooryard Bloom'd* (1946).

**Hindenburg, Paul von** *(1847–1934)* German military and political leader. The son of a Prussian officer, Hindenburg entered the Prussian Cadet Corps at the age of 11 and was commissioned in the army in 1866. He first saw service in the Franco-Prussian War (1870–71), was appointed to the general staff in 1878 and retired from active service as a general in 1911. Recalled to command the army in East Prussia at the beginning of WORLD WAR I (1914), he won decisive victories over the Russians at Tannenberg, the Masurian Lakes and the eastern front (see WORLD WAR I ON THE EASTERN FRONT). Acclaimed as Germany's leading war hero, Hindenburg was appointed a field marshal and commander of the German armies in the East in 1914, then succeeded General Falkenhayn as commander-in-chief in 1916, with LUDENDORFF serving as first quarter-master-general. Together, they virtually ran wartime Germany, controlling policies at home, imposing harsh terms on Russia, strengthening the HINDENBURG LINE and mounting the 1918 offensive on the western front. The entry of the U.S. into the war in 1917 together with the counteroffensive of FOCH caused severe German reversals, and Hindenburg was forced to seek an armistice in October 1918. Subsequently Kaiser WILHELM II abdicated, but Hindenburg remained in command of the army until his retirement in July 1919. A monarchist, he

*German military leader and president Paul von Hindenburg* (LIBRARY OF CONGRESS, PRINTS AND PHOTOGRAPHS DIVISION)

nonetheless supported the new republican government and was elected president in 1925. In 1932 the elder statesman was returned to office, but, unable to cope with his nation's enormous political, social and economic crises, he appointed Adolf HITLER chancellor in January 1933. Increasingly senile and losing all real power, he remained the figurehead president until his death, when Hitler abolished the office. Goldsmith, Margaret, *Hindenburg.* New York Ayer, 1972 (repr).

**Hindenburg disaster** Accident that destroyed the German dirigible *Hindenburg* at Lakehurst, N.J., on May 6, 1937. Designed by German aviation engineer Dr. Hugo Eckener and completed in 1936, the sumptuously outfitted *Hindenburg* was the world's first commercial aircraft to make regular transatlantic flights. Carrying over 70 passengers and a substantial cargo, and fitted out with private staterooms, lounges, a formal dining room and ship-like promenades, it made many 50–to–60–hour crossings during its almost two years of service. While most airships were inflated with helium, German airships at the time were filled with highly inflammable hydrogen gas because the U.S. refused to export helium to Nazi Germany. While landing at Lakehurst, the hydrogen ignited and the *Hindenburg* was destroyed in half a minute. Thirty-five passengers and crew and a member of the ground staff were killed in the conflagration. A radio news reporter covering the dirigible's landing captured the disaster in unforgettable commentary, and a motion-picture camera also recorded the event. Most authorities believe that electricity in the air was responsible (there was a lightning storm nearby), but some have claimed that the *Hindenburg* was sabotaged by anti-Nazi agents. In any case, the disaster destroyed public confidence in the dirigible and ended the commercial use of airships. The cause of the explosion has never been conclusively determined.

**Hindenburg Line** Named for Field Marshal von Hindenburg, this fortified German defense line extended across northeastern France during WORLD WAR I. Consolidated in 1916, it was a locus for heavy fighting, particularly in 1917 and when it was finally breached in the fall of 1918.

**Hine, Lewis** *(1874–1940)* American documentary photographer particularly known for his dramatic interpretation of machine and other 20th-century industrial forms. Hine's earliest work documented the experience of immigrants arriving at ELLIS ISLAND. From 1908 to 1916 he worked for the National Child Labor Committee documenting working conditions in factories, workshops, and mines, with the goal of exposing little-known abuses. After World War I, his reputation for outstanding photography of industrial locations led to assignments from industry that accentuated the beauty of many mechanistic subjects. For example, from 1930 to 1931 he documented the men constructing the EMPIRE STATE BUILDING in New York in hundreds of striking photographs. Whether documenting the abuses of child labor or the drama of industry, Hine's work was always of fine technical and artistic quality, making him an important figure in the development of modern documentary photography.

**Hines, Earl "Fatha"** *(1905–1983)* American JAZZ musician, known as the father of modern jazz piano playing. He created the "trumpet style" of playing jazz piano while working with Louis ARMSTRONG in the 1920s, and established a place for piano as a solo instrument in jazz. Hines led big and small bands intermittently until his death, including a Chicago big band that launched the careers of vocalists Sarah VAUGHAN and Billy ECKSTINE.

**Hinkle, Samuel F.** *(1900–1984)* American research chemist and business executive. Hinkle played a major role in the growth of the Hershey Foods Corp. He began as Hershey's director in 1924, when the company was still a small candy manufacturer. By the time he became chairman (1962), Hershey was a giant food-products conglomerate. He retired in 1965. Hinkle developed the K, C and D rations issued to U.S. soldiers in WORLD WAR II.

**hip-hop** American genre of music. Also known commercially as "rap music," hip-hop emerged in the 1970s among African-American and His-

panic-American minorities in large urban centers in the U.S. Originally it largely consisted of rhyming lyrics (sometimes improvised during a performance) set to percussion background music, and was usually accompanied by a form of dancing known as break dancing, in which performers would move acrobatically from a new-lying to a standing position. In later years, disco and "funk" music was used as background accompaniment to the "rapping" content of the artist's performance. In the early 1980s hip-hop performers included a variety of ethnicities, such as the all-white (and all-Jewish) Beastie Boys, who mixed rap with a certain amount of heavy metal musical accompaniment, and Grandmaster Flash, a musician largely influenced by funk. In 1990, hip-hop music had begun to go mainstream, with the first hip-hop single, M. C. Hammer's "U Cant Touch This," reaching number one on the pop music chart and staying there for a week. Hammer was followed the next year by a slightly longer stay of three weeks for Vanilla Ice's "Ice, Ice, Baby." However, it was not until 1992 when hip-hop music became a powerful force in the music industry with the popular national appeal of Dr. Dre and Snoop Doggy Dog (later Snoop Dog), two artists who collaborated regularly between 1992 and 1996. During the rise of these artists and others, such as Public Enemy, Run-DMC, and Jam Master Jay, Queen Latifah and Da Brat, hip-hop music developed an intranational rivalry between East Coast rappers coming from urban ghettos in cities such as New York, Philadelphia and Baltimore and West Coast rappers coming from the suburban ghettos in southern California. This rivalry derived from the style of the rappers and also from each faction's efforts to describe the other as not truly representing the mentality of a modern-day gangster. This conflict was fatally personified in the cases of Tupac Shakur and Notorious B.I.G., West and East Coast rappers, respectively, who belittled each other's claims to represent the true "gangsta" lifestyle, and both of whom were the victims of unsolved shootings. While hip-hop music in the early 21st century has evolved into a more mainstream genre, involving catchy beats from artists like P. Diddy and Nelly (neither of whom go to the extremes of Shakur and B.I.G. to prove the "gangsta" credibility), the genre still remains the target of allegations from political figures such as Lynne Cheney and Tipper Gore, who have campaigned against the artists EMINEM and Public Enemy, respectively, for their glorification of violence. Women's groups and gay rights groups have also complained that hip-hop music incites violence against their members through their lyrics.

**hippies** Name first given in the 1960s to long-haired members of the era's COUNTERCULTURE. The precise derivation of the word "hippie" remains unclear, but one theory has it stemming from "hip," which was one of the favorite words of praise of the Beatniks of the 1950s, who exercised a tremendous influence on the hippies of the next decade. Indeed, many of the literary heroes of the BEAT GENERATION—such as novelists William BURROUGHS and Jack KEROUAC and poets Allen GINSBERG and Gary Snyder—were highly popular with hippies as well. But the hippie phenomenon was based on more than a mere recycling of cultural trends. There were radically new factors at work in the 1960s. One of them was the research into the drug LSD being conducted by Harvard University psychology professor Timothy LEARY, who lost his academic position due to his enthusiasm for the drug's spiritual and psychological "benefits." Leary became a highly influential spokesman for hippies, who relished the Leary motto "Tune in, turn on, drop out." Hippies were also unique in their musical tastes, discarding the favored jazz of the 1950s beatniks for "psychedelic" rock such as that of the GRATEFUL DEAD, JEFFERSON AIRPLANE and other San Francisco–based groups. There were many superficial and faddish elements to the hippie phenomenon, such as love beads, day-glo posters and long hair.

Many hippie enthusiasms have transformed themselves, over the decades, into ongoing cultural influences in America, including: ecological awareness, nutritional consciousness and the value of organically grown foods, respect for Native American tribal traditions, widespread marijuana cultivation and use, and the entrepreneurial willingness to consider people-oriented forms of organizational structure in social and business contexts. Politically, hippies ranged from apolitical societal dropouts who went to live on isolated communes to fervent peace activists who contributed greatly to the strength of the ANTIWAR MOVEMENT. Hippie popularity in America and Europe reached its peak in the late 1960s with BE-INS in major urban parks that drew as many as 25,000 people in a single day. Hippies continue to carry on their freeform lifestyles—albeit in much smaller numbers—to the present day.

**Hirohito** (1901–1989) Emperor of JAPAN. The first member of the imperial family to travel abroad, Hirohito was appointed regent in 1921, shortly after a visit to Europe and the U.S. He succeeded to the Chrysanthemum Throne in 1926 upon the death of his father, Emperor Yoshihito (1879–1926). He married Princess Nagako Kuni in 1924, and his heir, AKIHITO, was born in 1933. A quiet, introspective and scholarly man, trained as a marine biologist, he apparently exerted little influence over political events in Japan during the 1930s and was not consulted during the military's drift toward WORLD WAR II or over its strategy during the war. However, in 1945 he was instrumental in

*Hirohito, the longest reigning emperor in Japanese history* (LIBRARY OF CONGRESS, PRINTS AND PHOTOGRAPHS DIVISION)

persuading Japanese officials to accede to unconditional surrender and thus save the nation from total destruction. In 1946 Hirohito renounced the concept of imperial divinity as well as claims to all but ceremonial authority. The new Japanese constitution of 1946 proclaimed him a "symbol of the state and of the unity of the people," and he remained a beloved figure to the Japanese public.

**Hiroshima** City and prefectural capital at the western end of Japan's Inland Sea. Founded in the 16th century, it grew in population and importance along with the railroad in the 19th century, also becoming a military headquarters. During WORLD WAR II it was devastated by the first ATOMIC BOMB dropped on an inhabited location (August 6, 1945). JAPAN surrendered eight days later, after another atomic bomb was dropped on NAGASAKI. Almost totally rebuilt, Hiroshima is a prosperous commercial center and hosts an annual world conference on the deterrence of nuclear weaponry.

**Hirshfield, Morris** (1872–1946) Polish-American painter. A self-taught primitive painter, Hirshfield began to paint when he was 65 years old. His entire output consists of 77 paintings, often of women or animals, created from 1937 until just before his death. His decorative, colorful, flat and highly patterned works are included in several museum collections, notably the Museum of Modern Art, N.Y.C.

**Hiss, Alger** See HISS-CHAMBERS CASE.

**Hiss-Chambers case** Confrontation between Alger Hiss (1904–96) and Whittaker Chambers (1901–61) over Hiss's alleged membership in the Communist Party and espionage activities. A distinguished public official, the Baltimore-born Hiss attended Harvard Law School and worked for the Agricultural Adjustment Administration (1933–36) and the Justice Department (1935–36) before joining the State Department. There he rose quickly, becoming a key adviser at many international conferences, most importantly YALTA. Leaving the government in 1947, he was appointed president of the Carnegie Endowment for International Peace. His steady rise to eminence was halted in 1948 when Whittaker Chambers, a New York-born magazine editor and self-confessed communist agent during the 1930s, in testimony before the HOUSE UN-AMERICAN ACTIVITIES COMMITTEE (HUAC) accused Hiss of having been part of a communist underground. This accusation marked the beginning of a decades-long drama of denunciation and denial.

Soon Chambers expanded his testimony to include accusations that Hiss had provided him with secret State Department documents destined for transmittal to the Soviet Union. To prove his assertions, Chambers produced microfilms of the documents, supposedly typed on Hiss's Woodstock typewriter and then hidden in a hollowed-out pumpkin. These so-called Pumpkin Papers were handed over to the anticommunist California congressman Richard M. NIXON. Throughout all this, Hiss denied knowing Chambers, insisted that he had never been a member of the Communist Party and claimed that the evidence against him had been fabricated by a psychopathic liar. The statute of limitations for the charge of espionage had run out, so Hiss was indicted on two counts of perjury in 1949. The first trial resulted in a hung jury; the second found Hiss guilty. Sentenced to five years in prison, Hiss served 44 months, from 1951 to 1954.

The controversial Hiss-Chambers case caused a furor in American political circles. Hiss supporters claimed that he had been railroaded by MCCARTHYISM and accused the FBI of evidence tampering. Chambers allies applauded his courageous anticommunism. Each principal pressed his case in print, Chambers in *Witness* (1952) and Hiss in *In the Court of Public Opinion* (1957). In 1992 a search of Soviet archives by Russian general Dimitry Volkogonov failed to confirm Hiss's service as a Soviet spy, although the evidence of his espionage activities from other sources was still compelling.

**Histadrut (Hebrew, Federation of Labor)** Organizational body of the Israeli trade-union movement.

**Hitchcock, Alfred (Joseph)** *(1899–1980)* British-born film director, known for his mastery of cinematic technique and screen suspense. In a career spanning half the century, Hitchcock directed scores of psychological thrillers, nightmares of menace and the macabre that became film classics. He became famous for planning every scene in advance, down to the smallest detail, and he pioneered new cinematic techniques. He made England's first talking picture, *Blackmail,* in 1929. Working in England in the 1930s, he won international acclaim for such spy thrillers as *The Man Who Knew Too Much* (1934), *The Thirty-nine Steps* (1935), and *The Lady Vanishes* (1938). In 1939 he moved to HOLLYWOOD, where he went on to make such stylish melodramas as *Rebecca* (1940), *Suspicion* (1940), *Lifeboat* (1944), *Notorious* (1946), *Strangers on a Train* (1951), *Rear Window* (1954), *Vertigo* (1958), and *North by Northwest* (1959). With *Psycho* (1960), Hitchcock's films became more overtly shocking and violent. He worked with such stars as Laurence OLIVIER, Ingrid BERGMAN, Cary GRANT and James STEWART. He was nominated for five ACADEMY AWARDS for best director, but never won. He also hosted a popular weekly television show in the late 1950s and early 1960s.

**Hitchcock, Henry-Russell** *(1903–1987)* American architectural historian and teacher. Beginning in the 1920s, Hitchcock was a leading advocate of the INTERNATIONAL STYLE in architecture. He is believed to have coined the term.

**Hitchings, George H(erbert)** *(1905–1998)* American pharmacologist. Born in Hoquiam, Washington, he attended Washington State University and Harvard. He taught at Harvard and at Western Reserve before joining the Burroughs Wellcome Laboratory, Tuckahoe, N.Y., in 1942. His distinguished career spanned some 50 years of research at this lab. Along with his longtime collaborator Gertrude B. ELION, Hitchings made discoveries that had a fundamental impact on the development of various disease-fighting drugs. The two developed a central principle of contemporary pharmacology that is based on blocking the workings of nucleic acids (the chemical substances that control heredity and cell function) in diseased cells while allowing it to function in healthy cells. This discovery came about through the two scientists' study of the chemical components of nucleic acids. They applied the principle to the creation of various forms of chemotherapy, achieving their first success in the 1950s when, working with researchers at the Sloan-Kettering Institute, they produced the first effective drug against leukemia. During the next decades they worked on drugs to treat autoimmune, viral and infectious diseases and to fight organ rejection. Their studies led directly to the development of various modern drugs, including AZT for the treatment of AIDS. Hitchings and Elion were awarded the 1988 NOBEL PRIZE in physiology or medicine with Sir James Black.

**Hitler, Adolf** *(1889–1945)* Chancellor of GERMANY (1933–45). Along with Joseph STALIN, Adolf Hitler ranks as the most heinous of all 20th-century dictators. He plunged Germany and the world into a war that saw the destruction of ancient cities, the dismemberment of entire nations and the deaths of millions of soldiers and civilians both in combat and through a calculated plan of extermination. Born at Brannau, Austria, across the Inn River from Germany, Hitler was the son of a minor government official and his young wife. He was raised near Linz, Austria. His father died when Hitler was in his early teens; soon thereafter Hitler left school. In 1907 he moved to Vienna with vague hopes of pursuing a career as an artist or architect. Rejected by the Vienna Academy of Fine Arts, he lived an aimless existence, living in doss houses and wandering the city as a malcontent. During this time he developed a fanatical belief in the superiority of the German-speaking people and a profound hatred of the JEWS (see ANTI-SEMITISM) and the institutions of bourgeois civilization. Obsessed by dreams of personal and national grandeur, he took to haranguing anyone who would listen to his ideas. He painted postcards to support himself but otherwise took no definite steps to improve his position in life. In 1913 he moved to Munich.

The outbreak of WORLD WAR I gave Hitler a focus for his discontented energy. He enlisted in the German army and served in the trenches on the western front (see WORLD WAR I ON THE

WESTERN FRONT). During the war he was wounded and was also temporarily blinded by mustard gas. He received two Iron Crosses and reached the rank of corporal. Germany's defeat and the harsh terms imposed on the country by the TREATY OF VERSAILLES gave Hitler another cause to claim as his own. His life took a fateful turn in 1919 when he was hired as a police informer and assigned to report on the fledgling German Worker's Party, a minor political organization in Munich. Hitler joined the group as its seventh member and soon found that it gave him a platform from which to express his discontent with the state of the world. By 1921 he had gained control of the group and transformed it into a disciplined organization whose political aims matched his. The party name was changed to National Socialist German Workers' Party (abbreviated as NSDAP in German); the group soon became better known as the Nazi Party. Discovering his considerable power as an orator, Hitler expounded his philosophy of NAZISM to ever larger audiences. In 1923 Hitler, joined by World War I hero General Erich LUDENDORFF and some 2,000 Nazi storm troopers, attempted to seize control of the Bavarian government in the BEER HALL PUTSCH. The event proved a fiasco for the Nazis; Hitler was arrested and sentenced to five years in prison. There he dictated his political gospel MEIN KAMPF to his aide Rudolf HESS. Hitler served only nine months of his sentence before being released. He spent the following decade rebuilding the Nazi Party.

The beginning of the worldwide GREAT DEPRESSION, which caused economic and political chaos in Germany, gave Hitler an opportunity to emerge as a formidable politician. National elections in 1932 gave the Nazis the largest share of the vote, although not an absolute majority. With this backing Hitler maneuvered for the post of chancellor, claiming that he was the only political leader able to deal with the Depression and with the perceived menace posed to the middle and upper classes by German communists. The aging President HINDENBURG was ultimately persuaded to name Hitler chancellor on January 30, 1933. Although the leaders of the conservative German political establishment distrusted

Hitler and indeed found him distasteful, they believed that they would be able to control him and, when necessary, remove him from office. The REICHSTAG FIRE (February 27, 1933) gave Hitler an excuse to suspend constitutional guarantees; he was, in effect, given dictatorial powers to cope with the perceived state of emergency. On the so called Night of the Long Knives (June 30–July 1, 1934) he eliminated his chief rivals within the party, the left-wing Nazi Gregor Strasser and the SA head Ernst ROEHM; he also dissolved the SA. Upon Hindenburg's death a month later, Hitler proclaimed himself "Führer" (leader) of the German people.

He quickly proceeded to suppress all remaining political opposition. This achieved, he worked to rebuild Germany's military might, ordering increased arms production, compulsory military service (March 1936) and the reoccupation of the Rhineland (March 1936)—all in violation of the Versailles Treaty. In the latter half of the 1930s, he systematically pursued his LEBENSRAUM foreign policy. He formed an alliance (the AXIS) with MUSSOLINI's ITALY in 1936, annexed Austria in March 1938 (see ANSCHLUSS) and demanded and won the annexation of the German-speaking SUDETENLAND region of CZECHOSLOVAKIA in the MUNICH PACT (September–October 1938). In March 1939 he annexed the Czech regions (Bohemia and Moravia) of Czechoslovakia.

The NAZI-SOVIET PACT (August 1939) gave Hitler a free hand to invade POLAND (September 1939) without Soviet interference. However, upon the invasion of Poland, the UNITED KINGDOM and FRANCE, which had pledged to support Poland's independence, declared war on Germany. During the early part of the war Hitler enjoyed success as the Germans won victory after victory. The BLITZKRIEG tactics that had defeated Poland led to the capitulation of BELGIUM, the NETHERLANDS, FRANCE and NORWAY in 1940; BULGARIA and ROMANIA also fell into the Nazi fold. These successes emboldened him to pursue further conquests. His assault on Britain, however, failed to yield the island's submission (see BATTLE OF BRITAIN). Frustrated, Hitler turned his attention to his erstwhile ally, and attacked the Soviet Union. The difficulty of supplying the

German forces over great distances, along with the tenacity of the Soviet defenders and the severity of the Russian winter, left the German armies in a fatal position. On December 19, 1941, Hitler made another costly mistake. Convinced of his genius as a military leader, he assumed direct command of Germany's army. From this point onward he ignored the advice of his generals, with dire consequences for Germany. Yet, even with military defeat inevitable, Hitler pursued his most terrible crime, the so-called FINAL SOLUTION to the Jewish problem—the extermination of Europe's Jews (see HOLOCAUST).

As Britain, the USSR and other allies (now joined by the UNITED STATES) rallied against the German forces, Hitler became increasingly withdrawn and isolated from reality. German staff officers led by Count Claus von Stauffenberg attempted to assassinate Hitler on July 20, 1944. The Führer was wounded but survived. Feeling betrayed by the German people who had failed to win the victories he expected of them, he decided that Germany deserved to be destroyed rather than surrender to the Allies. Trapped in his Berlin bunker as Soviet forces fought their way into the city, Hitler married his longtime mistress Eva Braun on April 30, 1945; shortly thereafter the couple committed suicide.

**Hitler-Stalin Pact** See GERMAN-SOVIET NON-AGGRESSION PACT.

**Hitler Youth (Hitler Jugend)** German youth organization of the 1930s and early 1940s. The Hitler Youth was formed to indoctrinate young Germans into the "ideals" of Adolf HITLER and to create the Nazis of the next generation. Like the Boy Scouts and other youth organizations in democracies, the Hitler Youth stressed outdoor and educational activities. However, it added the poison of NAZISM, crushing its members' individually into unquestioning loyalty to the state and the Nazi Party. As an auxiliary arm of the party, the Hitler Youth Organization was active even before Hitler became chancellor in 1933. At the end of 1932, there were 110,000 members; by the end of 1936, that number had swelled to six million. The organization was led by a young idealist, Baldur von Schirach, whose parents had been born in the U.S. As the German army collapsed toward the end of the war, many teenage members of the Hitler Youth were pressed into military service, and many died in combat.

**HIV** See AIDS.

**Hoaglund, Hudson** *(1899–1982)* American neuroendocrinologist. Hoaglund pioneered in the study of brain waves and the use of the electroencephalogram, or EEG. In 1944 he cofounded the Worcester Foundation for Experimental Biology in Massachusetts, which developed the birth control PILL.

**Ho Chi Minh (Nguyen Tat Thanh)** *(1890–1969)* Vietnamese communist and nationalist leader, president of North Vietnam (1954–69). Born Nguyen Tat Thanh in central VIETNAM, he left Vietnam as a ship's steward, traveling to London (1912), where he worked as a hotel chef, and Paris (1917), where he wrote articles for socialist newspapers and was a founder of the French Communist Party. He lived in the USSR from 1922 to 1925, becoming a member of the Comintern's Southeast Asia Bureau and studying Marxism and revolutionary techniques. He went on to China in 1925, organizing various communist groups. In China in 1938 he aided the communist revolution and planned his own country's struggle against colonialism, taking the name of Ho Chi Minh, "he who enlightens," in 1940. Ho returned to Vietnam at the beginning of WORLD WAR II after a 30–year absence and formed the VIET MINH, with which he began a guerrilla war against the Japanese. Taking HANOI in 1945, he declared Vietnamese independence and became president, serving in that office until his death. Ho was the chief spokesman for the nationalistic aspirations of the Vietnamese people and fought for an independent and communist-led Vietnam, first against the French (1946–54) and, after the Geneva conference split the country in 1954, against the South Vietnamese and the U.S. Becoming less involved in governing after 1959, he remained the symbol of Vietnamese communism. (See also VIETNAM WAR.)

**Ho Chi Minh Trail** Popular name for the jungle supply route by which North Vietnam sent soldiers as well as arms, ammunition, food and other materiel into the South during the VIETNAM WAR. Construction of the strategic route was begun in 1959 and included existing mountain trails, incorporating them into a large network of roads. It was the work of over 30,000 troops and various other workers and measured over 12,500 miles. Beginning in 1965, repeated raids by U.S. bombers slowed the flow of men and supplies, but the North Vietnamese repaired the road constantly and the trail was never completely closed.

**Hockney, David** *(1937– )* English painter. Born in Bradford, he studied at the Royal College of Art, London. Considered one of the major figures in contemporary British art, Hockney is noted for his witty, realistic imagery and masterful draftsmanship. The artist, who has lived in Southern California for some years, is known for sunny, stylized scenes of contemporary life where POP ART elements mix with a highly personal style. He has also created a number of print series and has designed stage sets, such as those for England's Glyndebourne Opera.

**Hodges, Gil** *(1924–1972)* American baseball player and manager. Hodges was an outstanding first baseman with the Brooklyn (and L.A.) Dodgers (1948–61). Beloved by Brooklynites, he continued to make his home there after the close of his career. He closed out his playing days with the New York Mets in 1963. During his career he had 370 home runs, 1,921 base hits, 1,274 runs batted in and a .273 lifetime batting average. Following his retirement as a player, Hodges managed the Washington Senators (1963–67) and the New York Mets from 1968 until his death. In 1969 he guided the once-lowly Mets, who became known as the "Miracle Mets," over the favored Baltimore Orioles to victory in the World Series.

**Hodgkin, Howard** *(1932– )* English painter. Born in London, Hodgkin lived in the U.S. from 1940 to 1943. He studied at the Camberwell School of Art, London and the Bath Academy of Art, where he taught from 1956 to 1966. He later taught at various institutions, and in the late 1980s was Kress Professor at the National Gallery, Washington, D.C. His first one-man show was held in London in 1962. His early works concentrated on the figure in an interior, blending the abstract and the figural in a flat and brightly colored geometry. His importance to English painting was recognized when he was chosen to represent Great Britain in the Venice Biennale of 1984. Hodgkin's paintings have always been relatively small in scale and most are worked on over a period of years. In his recent work elements such as the figure, the interior and the landscape are inferred rather than stated in swags, dots and arcs of vivid colors that cover the wood panel of the painting and its frame.

**Hodgson, William Hope** *(1877–1918)* British writer of maritime romances and supernatural horror. An important transitional figure between Edgar Allan Poe and H. P. LOVECRAFT, Hodgson translated the materials of the gothic romance into the modern forms of science fiction. The son of a clergyman, he ran away to sea as a boy. In 1899 after eight years and three voyages around the world, he returned to Blackburn to establish a body-building/physical culture academy and pursue a writing career. The bulk of his fiction, written in 1906–14, may be categorized into three groups. *The Boats of the "Glen Carrig"* (1907), *The Ghost Pirates* (1909) and the short-story collection *Men of Deep Waters* (1914) are all nautical horror tales. The great novels, *The House on the Borderland* (1908) and *The Night Land* (1912), are dystopian nightmares of a future Earth wracked by war, holocaust and extradimensional invasion by monstrous life-forms. The stories of a psychic detective named Carnacki pit 20th-century rationalism and technology against the traditional gothic apparatus of haunted houses and vengeful ghosts. Hodgson died in WORLD WAR I, killed in action near Ypres as an enlisted man in the Royal Field Artillery.

**Hoffa, James R(iddle) "Jimmy"** *(1913–1975)* American labor leader. Born in Brazil, Ind., Jimmy Hoffa moved to Detroit after his father's death and while still in his teens became actively involved in the teamster's union. Aligning himself with midwestern criminals, he strong-armed his way into enormous power in the union. In 1952 Hoffa became a vice president of the union, and five years later he succeeded Dave Beck as its president (see BECK CASE). Intensively investigated by federal agencies, he was tried and found guilty of jury tampering and pension fraud, beginning a 13-year prison sentence in 1967. In 1971 Hoffa was pardoned by President Richard M. NIXON. After his release, in spite of a court order to stay out of union affairs until 1980, he apparently attempted to wrest control of the Teamster's from union president Frank FITZSIMMONS. On July 30, 1975, Hoffa left his home in Detroit and disappeared. He was widely assumed to have been murdered; his body has not been found.

## Hoffman, Abbott Abbie (1936–1989)

Radical American protest leader of the 1960s ANTIWAR MOVEMENT and founder of the Yippies (Youth International Party). Hoffman rose to national prominence as a defendant in the raucous CHICAGO SEVEN TRIAL (1969–70). The seven defendants had been charged with inciting a riot during the 1968 Democratic National Convention in Chicago. Hoffman and four other defendants were convicted following a trial that featured antics such as Hoffman stomping on a judicial robe, but the convictions were later overturned. In 1973 he was arrested on charges of selling cocaine to an undercover narcotics officer; before the case came to trial, he went into hiding and spent six years (1974–80) working as an environmental activist in upstate New York and as a food reviewer in Europe, using an alias. He surfaced in 1980 for a nationally televised interview with Barbara WALTERS and eventually pleaded guilty to a lesser charge that netted him a brief prison sentence. His death was an apparent suicide.

## Hoffman, Dustin (1937– )

American film and stage actor. Hoffman has been a major film star since his acclaimed debut as the confused Benjamin Braddock in The Graduate (1967), directed by Mike NICHOLS. His consistent stardom has been unusual in that Hoffman has more often appeared in character roles than in standard romantic leads. Hoffman began his career on the New York stage in the 1960s, winning an Obie Award for his per-

formance in The Journey of the Fifth Horse. His successful films include Little Big Man (1970), in which he played a 112-year-old Indian survivor of Custer's last stand; Papillon (1973), in which he portrayed a nearsighted prisoner in a French penal colony; All the President's Men (1976), in which he appeared as reporter Carl Bernstein; and Tootsie (1982), in which he starred as a male actor who disguises himself as a female to get work. Hoffman won his first best actor ACADEMY AWARD for his role as a divorced father in Kramer Versus Kramer (1980) and his second for his performance as a man suffering from autism in Rain Man (1988). In 1997 Hoffman was again an Academy Award nominee for his role as a Hollywood producer in the drama Wag the Dog. Two years later, he received the Lifetime Achievement Award from the American Film Institute.

## Hoffman, Malvina (1887–1966)

American sculptor. Born in New York City, Hoffman studied with Auguste Rodin. She executed a number of realistic portraits of important figure of her day such as Jan PADEREWSKI and John MUIR, and is noted for her bronze figures of dancers, such as Pavlova gavotte, and monumental public commissions such as The Sacrifice at Harvard University's War Memorial. Hoffman is probably best remembered for a series of 100 anthropological portraits of the world's races she executed for the Hall of Man at the Field Museum in Chicago. She spent five years in travel and research preparing for this project and described it in her book Heads and Tales (1936). She was also the author of Sculpture Inside and Out (1939).

## Hoffmann, Josef (1870–1956)

Austrian architect and designer, a pioneer in the development of MODERNISM as expressed in the Werkstätte and Secession movements. Hoffmann was a pupil of Otto Wagner. After traveling in Italy, he returned to Vienna to work for Wagner from 1895 until 1899. He became a professor of architecture at the Vienna School of Applied Arts in 1899 and held that position until 1941. A member of the Secession, he helped found the Werkstätte in 1903. Hoffmann visited England in 1902 and was strongly influenced by the work of Charles Rennie

MACKINTOSH. His work moved away from the curvilinear forms typical of Wagner's work and became more rectilinear with squares, cubes and spheres appearing as favorite motifs. The Puckersdorf Sanatorium outside Vienna (1903–06) was a major example of the geometrically abstract direction in Hoffmann's work, while the special furniture designed for it carried the same themes. Hoffmann's major architectural masterpiece was the Palais Stoclet in Brussels (1905–11). It is a large town mansion in a geometrically austere style, with elaborate ornamentation inside and out. Much of its artwork is by Secessionist collaborators, including Gustav KLIMT and Carl CZESCHKA. Rich materials are used and detailing is elaborate, including special furniture, lighting fixtures, hardware and textiles. Hoffmann's designs included work for Werkstatte craftsmen and for factory production in great variety. Hoffmann was the designer of the Austrian pavilion at various exhibitions (Cologne in 1914, Paris in 1925, and Stockholm in 1930, among others), but it is his work of 1902 to 1910 that has attracted most interest in his career, particularly in recent years when the modernism of Secession work, with its characteristic ornamentation, has drawn increasing attention because of postmodern trends in both architecture and object design. Hoffmann remained active in both design and teaching, although few of his works were actually executed. Now much admired and collected, a number of his designs for furniture, metalwork, ceramics and textiles are currently produced in reproduction.

## Hofmannsthal, Hugo von (1874–1929)

Austrian playwright, story writer, poet and opera librettist. Hofmannsthal was a gifted and versatile writer who achieved his greatest successes as a playwright who combined a romantic sensibility with a deep moral intelligence. The first of his plays to win notice, Death and the Fool (1898), was a lyrical romance. The Adventurer and the Singer (1898) and several adaptations from classic Greek tragedies— Elektra (1903), Oedipus and the Sphinx (1905), King Oedipus (1907) and Alcestis (1909)—followed. His most acclaimed play was Everyman (1911), based on a famous medieval mystery play. Subsequent plays by Hofmannsthal include *The Difficult Man* (1921) and *The Tower* (1925), both of which deal with social issues. Hofmannsthal also won renown as a librettist for operas by Richard STRAUSS, including *Elektra* (1909), *Der Rosenkavalier* (1911), and *Ariadne auf Naxos* (1912). Hofmannsthal was a cofounder, in 1920, of the SALZBURG FESTIVAL.

**Hofstadter, Robert** *(1915–1990)* U.S. physicist. He won the NOBEL PRIZE in 1961 for his research into the size and structure of the particles that make up the nucleus of the atom. The Royal Swedish Academy praised him for providing the first "reasonably consistent" picture of the nuclear structure of the atom, and for determining the size and shape of the proton and neutron. He taught at Stanford University from 1950 to 1985.

**Hogan, William Ben(jamin)** *(1912–1997)* U.S. golfer. The winner of more than 60 tournaments, he is considered one of the finest players in golf history. Known as "Bantam Ben" (he weighed only 135 pounds) he was a four-time winner of the U.S. Open. His most memorable Open win came in 1950, less than a year-and-a-half after a serious automobile accident left his future in doubt. He also won the PGA tournament twice, the Masters title twice and the British Open once.

**Hogarth Press** See Virginia WOOLF.

**Holbrooke, Richard (Charles Albert Holbrooke)** *(1941– )* American diplomat. Born in New York City, Holbrooke graduated from Brown University with a B.A. in 1962. He joined the foreign service and, after a four-year stint in Vietnam, Holbrooke served in Paris with the U.S. negotiating team seeking a peace agreement with the North Vietnamese. Holbrooke left government service in 1969 to serve as a postgraduate fellow at the Woodrow Wilson School at Princeton University, where he remained until 1970, when he began a two-year stint as the director of the Peace Corps in Morocco. In 1972 Holbrooke became editor of *Foreign Policy,* a quarterly magazine devoted to international affairs. Four years later he joined the new Democratic administration of President Jimmy

Carter as assistant secretary of state for Asian and Pacific affairs, and remained in that post until Carter's defeat by Ronald REAGAN in 1980 sent him to the private sector.

in 1993 Holbrooke returned to government service when President Bill CLINTON nominated him as the U.S. ambassador to Germany, where he aided the administration in its efforts to redefine the U.S. relationship with its European allies under NATO and the emerging EUROPEAN UNION. In 1993 Holbrooke became assistant secretary of state for European and Canadian affairs. Holbrooke became well known for his role in attempting to persuade the Bosnian, Croat and Serb factions to suspend their military operations in the Yugoslav civil war (1991–95) and sit down at the negotiating table. In 1995 he brokered a cease-fire and a power-sharing arrangement that was incorporated in the DAYTON ACCORDS. Holbrooke left the State Department in 1996 to pursue a career as an investment banker at Credit Suisse First Boston. In 1999 he was confirmed by the Senate as the U.S. delegate to the United Nations after a long and better nomination process and served for the remainder of the Clinton administration.

**Holiday, Billie (Eleanora Fagan, Eleanora Gough)** *(1915–1959)* American jazz and blues singer, known as Lady Day; one of the great tragic figures in American jazz. The daughter of an unwed cleaning woman and a guitarist, Holiday was born in Baltimore, Md. She went to New York and by age 15 was singing in HARLEM nightclubs while living in poverty. Her rise was extraordinary; her talent was recognized almost immediately not only by the public but also by the greatest jazz musicians of the day. In the 1930s she sang with the bands of Benny GOODMAN, Count BASIE and Artie SHAW and performed with such greats as pianist Teddy WILSON and saxophonist Lester YOUNG; her partnership with Young ranks as one of the all-time great collaborations in jazz. Despite her professional success, her personal life was chaotic and insecure. Her later years were marred by heroin addiction and alcoholism, which took a sad toll on her health and her career.

At its peak, Holiday's voice was at once casual and yet haunting; her un-

canny phrasing and intonation, married to her life experience, gave her the ability to communicate the inner meaning of a given song. What Edith PIAF is to French ballad singing, Billie Holiday is to the blues. Among the songs for which she is best known are "I've Got My Love to Keep Me Warm," "The Very Thought of You," "These Foolish Things" and "Autumn in New York." Her autobiography is *Lady Sings the Blues.*

**Hollister Anabale, Gloria** *(1902–1988)* American explorer. In 1931, Hollister set a woman's world record for ocean descent in a bathysphere. She was the chief assistant of famed oceanographer William Beebe on many of his voyages in the 1920s and 1930s. She also served with other expeditions of the New York Zoological Society.

**Holloway, Stanley** *(1890–1982)* A beloved showman of the now-vanished British music halls, Stanley Holloway worked in a fish market before becoming a singer. In the 1930s his comic monologues as "Sam Small of Lancashire" made him as instant sensation, and he recorded several novelty tunes. In the 1940s and '50s he appeared in films, notably as the gravedigger in

*Jazz singer Billie Holiday. photographed by Carl Van Vechten* (CARL VAN VECHTEN COLLECTION. LIBRARY OF CONGRESS, PRINTS AND PHOTOGRAPHS DIVISION)

Laurence OLIVIER's *Hamlet* (1948) and costarring with Alec GUINNESS in *The Lavender Hill Mob* (1951). But it was onstage that Holloway had his greatest triumph, as dustman and philosopher/drunk Alfred Doolittle in the LERNER and LOEWE musical *My Fair Lady* (1956). The show (and film, in 1964) featured his classic renditions of "With a Little Bit of Luck" and "Get Me to the Church on Time." In 1960 Holloway was awarded the Order of the British Empire. In 1980, when he was 90 years old, Holloway gave a "royal command performance."

**Holly, Buddy (Charles Hardin Holley)** *(1936–1959)* Rock and roll composer, vocalist, and guitarist. Holly is one of the great founding figures of ROCK AND ROLL. In addition to his performing excellence as lead guitarist and vocalist of his band, Buddy Holly and the Crickets, he also stands as one of the foremost songwriters in the history of rock and roll. His classic hits, all of which were recorded between 1956 and 1959, include "That'll Be The Day," "Everyday, "Peggy Sue," "Oh Boy, "Words of Love" and "Raining in My Heart". Holly was born in Lubbock, Tex., in 1936 and learned the guitar at age 12. He formed his first band while in junior high school and won national fame when "That'll Be the Day" hit Number One on the Billboard charts in 1957. He died in a famous 1959 plane crash that also took the lives of rock stars "Big Bopper" (J. P. Richardson) and Richie Valens. Paul MCCARTNEY, who purchased the rights to most of Holly's songs, is among the many stars of contemporary rock music who was deeply influenced by Holly's work.

**Hollywood** A section of LOS ANGELES, CALIFORNIA, celebrated as the center of the American motion picture and television industries. In 1883 a Kansas prohibitionist, Harvey Wilcox, opened a real estate office seven miles from Los Angeles, subdivided a 120-acre tract and (at his wife's suggestion) filed the name "Hollywood" with the county recorded on February 1, 1887. Ten years later a post office was established, and the area became a sixth-class city. In 1910 it was annexed to Los Angeles, and its permanent boundaries were established in 1937: Doheny Drive on the west, the top of the Santa Monica

Mountains on the north, the Los Angeles River on the east and Melrose Avenue on the south. The consistent, sunny weather and the area's distance from the New York film trusts encouraged filmmakers to establish studios there as early as 1907, when the Selig Polyscope Company arrived to shoot scenes for *The Count of Monte Cristo*. Although every major studio built production facilities in the area within the next 20 years, only COLUMBIA, PARAMOUNT and RKO were located within city limits (today, only Paramount). During the film industry's peak production years in the late 1930s, an estimated 750 features were made annually in Hollywood and environs.

Popular landmarks include Grauman's Chinese Theater (with its courtyard of celebrity footprints and handprints), the Griffith Park Observatory, the Hollywood Bowl, the Hollywood Hotel and the Brown Derby (the last two now closed or relocated). Hollywood has survived the crises of Depression, three wars, air pollution, the growing presence of drugs and prostitution, and the competitive inroads of radio, television and the recording industry—and continues as a symbol of the hope and heartbreak of the American Dream. Much of Tinseltown's colorful past has perished over the years, through greed and neglect, but recently there have been encouraging signs of change. The "Walk of Fame," for example, was instituted in 1960—emblazoning the names of famous entertainers onto brass stars and implanting them into the sidewalks of Hollywood Boulevard and Vine Street. (At a rate of one name per month, by 2004 the total included 2,150 stars. In 1978 the legendary "Hollywood" sign, built on the side of Mt. Cahuenga in 1924, was restored. But there are still no holly and no woods in Hollywood.

**Hollywood at war** When the U.S. entered WORLD WAR II (Dec. 1941), the HOLLYWOOD film industry was eager, but ill-prepared, to play a major role in the war. Working under the restrictions of the PRODUCTION CODE had forced filmmakers to eliminate most social and political commentary from films. The war called for Hollywood to be a soldier in a PROPAGANDA campaign to convince people that democracy was worth fighting for.

Hollywood stood at the peak of its influence in 1941, averaging some 85 million paid admissions in the U.S., and dominated the world market. In June 1942 the U.S. created an official propaganda agency, the **Office of War Information,** and appointed Elmer Davis as its director. OWI immediately opened a Hollywood office, the Bureau of Motion Pictures, and began to work with studios to ensure that films complemented U.S. war policy. A government manual asked studios: "Will This Picture Win the War?" Films were to emphasize the war as a "people's war" against FASCISM, stress unity among the Allies and point out the strengths of democratic society. At the behest of the government the industry churned out films praising America's allies. *Mission to Moscow* (WB, 1943) was the industry's tributes to STALIN, and *North Star* (Goldwyn, 1943) a salute to the heroic Russian people; *The White Cliffs of Dover* (MGM, 1944) portrayed the British war effort; *Casablanca* (WB, 1943) united U.S. and French citizens; even China emerged as a great democracy in *Dragon Seed* (MGM, 1944).

Some of Hollywood's finest directors left the comfortable confines of Hollywood to make documentary and propaganda films for the War Department. William WYLER's *The Memphis Belle* (1944), John FORD's *The Battle of Midway* (1942) and John HUSTON's *The Battle of San Pietro* (1945) and *Let There Be Light* (1945) stood out. Perhaps the finest combination of documentary and propaganda film to emerge from the war was Frank CAPRA's series of films, *Why We Fight,* which told military recruits why America was fighting Germany, Japan and Italy and what they were preserving by so doing. Hollywood stars such as James STEWART, Tyrone Power, Douglas Fairbanks, Jr., Robert Montgomery and Clark GABLE entered the service and many others gave freely of their time to entertain troops and help raise money for the war effort. Hollywood emerged from the war as the premier mass entertainment force in the world, but would soon see its position collapse from the challenge of television and the rise of worldwide film production.

**Hollywood Ten** Term coined to describe a group of American screenwriters and directors who were imprisoned and blacklisted following allegations before the HOUSE UN-AMERICAN ACTIVITIES COMMITTEE of communist affiliations. The committee had begun an "investigation" of HOLLYWOOD in the fall of 1947. Refusing to answer questions under the freedom of speech guaranteed by the First Amendment rather than the self-incrimination clause in the Fifth, they were voted in contempt of Congress on November 24, 1947. The following year they were tried in federal court, found guilty, and each sentenced to a year in prison. After the Supreme Court refused to review the convictions, they went to prison in the spring of 1950. The Ten were screenwriters Alvah Bessie, Herbert Biberman, Lester Cole, Ring LARDNER, Jr., John Howard Lawson, Albert Maltz, Samuel Ornitz, Adrian Scott, Dalton Trumbo, and director Edward Dmytryk. After their release, many were blacklisted by the film industry. Some could gain work only by using pseudonyms. The best-known example was Trumbo's "Robert Rich," the name under which he won an ACADEMY AWARD for best screenplay for *The Brave One* (1956). Ironically, those went to the Federal Correctional Institution in Danbury, Connecticut, found that J. Parnell Thomas, former head of the HUAC committee that had condemned them, was also there, serving time for taking kickbacks.

**Holm, Hanya** *(1898–1992)* German-American dance teacher and choreographer. Through her teaching and lecture-demonstrations, Holm became one of the molders of the modern dance movement in America. She danced with Mary Wigman's company (1921–30), then opened the New York City branch of the Wigman School (1931), which became the Hanya Holm Studio (1936–67), one of the most important modern dance schools. In 1941 she founded the influential Center of the Dance in the West in Colorado Springs. She gained popular acclaim as a choreographer of such Broadway musical as *Kiss Me Kate* (1948), *My Fair Lady* (1956) and *Camelot* (1960).

**Holman, M. Carl** *(1919–1988)* American poet, activist, editor and scholar described as the godfather of the CIVIL RIGHTS movement. President of the National Urban Coalition from 1968, Holman was noted for his adeptness at forming coalitions among diverse groups and individuals. He emphasized to blacks the importance of education, warning them that without it the next generation would become economically superfluous.

**Holmes, Oliver Wendell, Jr.** *(1841–1935)* Associate justice U.S. Supreme Court (1902–32). Arguably the greatest justice of the 20th century, Holmes was the son of the author-physician, Oliver Wendell Holmes, who was not only a leading poet, essayist and novelist but also a professor of anatomy at Harvard Medical School. Young Holmes was educated at Harvard, where he was class poet of 1861. After graduation he joined the Union Army, served in the Civil War and was wounded several times. After the war Holmes again enrolled at Harvard, but instead of following medicine, as had his father, he enrolled in the law school. A practicing lawyer, Holmes also taught law at Harvard. In 1881 his slim volume, *The Common Law*, containing a series of his public lectures, was published and immediately established Holmes as a legal philosopher of international reputation. He became an associate justice of the Massachusetts Supreme Court after Louis BRANDEIS was appointed to the U.S. Supreme Court, and he was later elevated to be the state's chief justice. Twenty-three years after, President Theodore ROOSEVELT tapped him for the U.S. Supreme Court. Justice Holmes was famous for short, well-reasoned majority and dissenting opinions. He applied the law equitably without favoritism or agenda. He served 29 years with distinction, retiring at age 90.

**Holmes à Court, Michael Robert Hamilton** *(1937–1990)* South Africa-born financier. He built a business empire in AUSTRALIA that made him that country's wealthiest man. He started out with a small textile mill and an ailing road haulage and engineering concern in 1973. By 1987, through a series of shrewd business and stock deals, his company was worth A$1.3 billion. He lost much of his fortune in the worldwide stock market crash of 1987, but had rebuilt it to A$700 million by 1990.

**Holocaust** Name commonly used to describe the systematic mass murder of millions of JEWS in Nazi-dominated Europe, and the period when this took place. For Jews and many non-Jews alike, the Holocaust is regarded as the most horrific event in modern history. The Holocaust was more or less simultaneous with WORLD WAR II, but constitutes a separate event. It served no military purpose, but rather grew out of Adolf HITLER's intense ANTI-SEMITISM and his desire to "purify" the German Reich. Hitler's book *MEIN KAMPF* had outlined his contempt for the Jewish people; this virulent antisemitism became a cornerstone of NAZISM. Hitler's repeated insistence that the Jews were responsible for Germany's and the world's ills found a responsive chord among many Germans who sought a scapegoat for their problems. In the early 1930s, acts of intimidation against Jews in Germany became widespread. Nazis urged boycotts of Jewish businesses, and paramilitary storm troopers frequently attacked Jews, beating them and destroying Jewish property. After Hitler became chancellor in early 1933 many Jews, fearing the worst, fled Germany for the U.S., Britain and other countries. The majority, however, remained behind. In 1935 the Nazis enacted the **Nuremberg Laws** (1935), depriving German Jews of many of the rights of German citizens. On the evening of Nov. 9, 1938—**Kristallnacht** ("Night of Broken Glass")—Nazi thugs began a deliberate campaign of violence against Jews throughout Germany. Synagogues were burned, Jewish shops were looted and thousands of Jews were arrested. The German occupation of much of Europe during World War II brought millions of other Jews under Nazi jurisdiction. Initially, many of these Jews were confined to ghettos in the occupied countries. They were then systematically rounded up and transported to concentration camps, there to be used for slave labor or killed. Hitler's policy of exterminating the Jews—designated as "the FINAL SOLUTION to the Jewish problem"—was formalized at the **Wannsee conference** in January 1942. German killings of Jewish civilians continued up to the last days of the war. Although many of the Jews of Western Europe died, many were also sheltered or helped to escape by sympathetic gentiles in those countries, themselves victims of German occupation. The more numerous Jews of Eastern Europe—particularly in Poland and Ukraine—were virtually wiped out. More than 90% of Poland's 3.5 million Jews died in concentration camps; at the war's end, only 4,000 Jews remained in Poland. Altogether, an estimated 6 million Jews died during the Holocaust; their suffering and the suffering of those who managed to survive this dark period cannot be measured.

**Holst, Gustav** *(1874–1934)* English composer. Born in Cheltenham, Gloucestershire, Holst was the son, grandson and great-grandson of musicians. He studied at the Royal College of Music, London, and later taught there from 1919 to 1924. At various times a church organist, trombonist and music school administrator, he organized British army musical activities in Greece and Turkey during WORLD WAR I. Early in his career, Holst was influenced by composers Richard STRAUSS and Ralph VAUGHAN WILLIAMS and folklorist Cecil Sharp; the latter two aroused his interest in English folk music. A composer of brilliant harmonic inventiveness, Holst is best known for his orchestral suite *The Planets* (1914–16), in which each movement corresponds to a planet of the solar system. The immense popularity of *The Planets* has tended to obscure the excellence of many of Holst's compositions. These include the choral *Hymn of Jesus* (1917), the opera *A Perfect Fool* (1920–22), the *Choral Symphony* (1923–24), the symphonic poem *Egdon Heath* (1927) and the orchestral *Hammersmith* suite (1930).

**Holt, John** *(1923–1985)* American educator. Holt's landmark book *How Children Fail*, a diary based on his experience as a teacher, touched off a national debate on the failings of American education during the 1960s. The book and its sequel, *How Children Learn*, sold well over a million copies and were translated into 14 languages. Based on his conclusions, he founded the magazine *Growing without Schooling* (1977), which was designed to help parents educate their children at home.

**Holt, Victoria (Eleanor Burford Hibbert)** *(1906–1993)* British novelist. Holt was best known for her gothic novels filled with plot twists and intrigue. *Mistress of Mellyn* (1960), *The Demon Lover* (1982) and *The Captive* (1989) were popular ones. Under the pseudonym Jean Plaidy she wrote historical novels, which received critical and popular acclaim. These include *Beyond the Blue Mountains* (1947), *Queen of the Realm: The Story of Elizabeth I* (1985) and *Victoria Victorious* (1986). Notable for her extraordinary prolificacy, Holt also was published under her maiden name, Eleanor Burford, and the pseudonyms Philippa Carr, Elbur Ford, Kathleen Kellow, and Ellalice Tate.

**Holtby, Winifred** *(1898–1935)* British author and feminist. Holtby left Oxford to serve with the WAAC in WORLD WAR I. Her experiences led her to a more international political stance, which, along with FEMINISM, figures in her journalism and novels. Her novels include *Anderby World* (1923), *The Land of Green Ginger* (1927) and *South Riding* (1936), which takes place in her native Yorkshire and is perhaps her best-known work. Holtby was a frequent contributor to the *Manchester Guardian, Time and Tide* and many other British periodicals. She is the subject of *Testament of Friendship* (1940), written by her friend Vera BRITTAIN.

**Holyoake, Keith Jacka** *(1904–1983)* Prime minister of NEW ZEALAND (1957, 1960–72). Holyoake was a farmer who then entered parliament as a Nationalist Party member in 1932. He later served as deputy prime minister and minister of agriculture from 1949 to 1957, when he briefly took over as prime minister when Sir Sidney Holland became ill. He was elected prime minister in 1960 serving until 1972. Holyoake was an advocate of multiracialism, and outspoken against APARTHEID in SOUTH AFRICA and the regime of Ian SMITH in Rhodesia. He maintained close ties to the United States, and backed it by sending troops to VIETNAM in the 1960s. He was instrumental in the creation of the special trade relationship with Australia (NAFTA). Holyoake was governor-general from 1977 to 1980 when he became New Zealand's first knight of the garter.

**Home, Lord** See Alec DOUGLAS-HOME

**Home Rule** Movement in IRELAND, backed by the Liberals in Great Britain, seeking to establish a parliament in Dublin responsible for internal Irish affairs. The Home Rule Association was founded in 1870 by Isaac Butt (1813–79) and gained momentum under the leadership of his successor Charles Parnell. Home Rule bills introduced in the British Parliament under Gladstone (1886, 1893) were defeated. A third bill introduced in 1912 was opposed by Ulster Protestants, who feared potential domination by the Roman Catholic majority in the south of Ireland. By 1914 the issue of Home Rule had brought Ireland to the brink of civil war and led to the EASTER REBELLION (1916). In May 1921 six counties in northern Ireland obtained Home Rule with a parliament at Stormont, Belfast, forming the loyalist state of NORTHERN IRELAND. The remaining 26 counties negotiated for the status of a dominion with control over foreign affairs as well as internal and representation in the LEAGUE OF NATIONS, which was agreed to in December 1921. (See also DE VALERA.)

**Honduran Civil War of 1909–11** Former Honduran president, Manuel Bonilla led his conservative supporters in revolt against liberal president Miguel R. Davila, who was placed in office by Nicaraguan dictator José Santos Zelaya after the HONDURAN-NICARAGUAN WAR OF 1907. The ensuing civil war was inconclusive, and in an armistice February 8, 1911, both sides agreed to abide by the forthcoming elections. Bonilla was elected president October 29, 1911.

**Honduran Guerrilla War of 1981–90** Thousands of Salvadorans, Miskito Indians and anti-Sandinista Nicaraguans took refuge in Honduras, which feared conflict in their nations would exacerbate leftist struggle against the government. Cuban-trained Marxist guerrillas carried out urban terrorism, and police and military forces increased efforts to suppress them, prompting the U.S. to increase its military aid. The Honduras-based Nicaraguan Democratic Force (FDN) rebels continued raids into Nicaragua, heightening tensions with that country.

In 1990 the contras left Honduras, ending the guerrilla war.

**Honduran-Nicaraguan War of 1907** José Santos Zelaya, who became president of NICARAGUA through a liberal revolt in 1893, ruled as a dictator and meddled in the affairs of his neighbors. In 1903 Honduran conservative Manuel Bonilla overthrew the Honduran liberal government supported by Zelaya. Honduran rebels in 1906 attempted to oust Bonilla, getting Zelaya's support. Honduran troops invaded Nicaragua in pursuit of rebels, and Zelaya demanded war reparations. Honduras refused, and Nicaraguan forces invaded Honduras and on March 18, 1907, won the Battle of Namasigue, the first battle fought in Central America with machine guns. Nicaraguans occupied the Honduran capital, Tegucigalpa, Bonilla fled, and Zelaya named Miguel R. Dávila as president. (See also HONDURAN CIVIL WAR OF 1909–11.)

**Honduras** (**Republic of Honduras**) Nation located on the Central American isthmus. Honduras covers an area

| | HONDURAS |
|---|---|
| 1900 | American fruit companies establish huge holdings; build railroads and docks. |
| 1903 | U.S. Marines intervene to end political strife; install Miguel Dávila as president. |
| 1923 | Civil war; Marines return; U.S. sets policy of nonrecognition of revolutionary governments; government formed by military-dominated PNH Party holds power for 31 years, despite challenges. |
| 1931 | "Sigatoka" blight damages banana crop; attempted revolution. |
| 1943 | Death of Froilán Turcios, novelist. |
| 1948 | PNH President Andino steps down. |
| 1957 | Liberal government elected; begins land reforms and social security programs. |
| 1963 | Military coup. |
| 1969 | Football war; border disputes with El Salvador erupt into two-week war after fans riot at a soccer match. |
| 1971 | First major north-south paved highway completed. |
| 1974 | Hurricane Fifi destroys three-quarters of banana crop. |
| 1975 | United Fruit Company admits $1.25 million bribe to "high government official" for relaxation of export duties. |
| 1976 | Continued border conflict with El Salvador seriously damages foreign trade; President López overthrown by young officers who restart land reform. |
| 1978 | Political parties resume activity. |
| 1980 | Military government effectively ended by assembly elections. |
| 1982 | Liberal government elected; new constitution removes control of military from president; country joins in forming Central American Democratic Community. |
| 1983 | Contra rebels use Honduras as base to strike in Nicaragua; CIA conducts anti-Sandinista operations from Honduras. |
| 1986 | First succession of one elected government to another since 1929. |
| 1987 | Sixty percent of arable land owned by government, United Brands and Standard Fruit. |
| 1990 | "Banana War"; 600,000 workers threaten general strikes, win pay raise; UN troops disarm contras; conservative Callejas elected president. |
| 2001 | Ricardo Maduro is elected president. |
| 2006 | Manuel Zelaya takes office as president. |

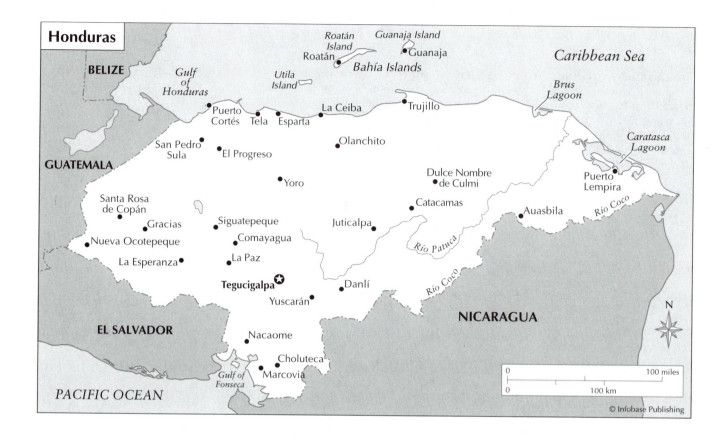

of 43,266 square miles, including several islands off its Caribbean Sea coast and 288 islands in the Gulf of Fonseca off its Pacific coast. Politically unstable, Honduras was under the control of the military almost continuously from 1923 to 1975. Power was gained through numerous coups and maintained through rewritings of the constitution. The so-called Soccer War with EL SALVADOR, which began in 1969, was ostensibly over the outcome of a football (soccer) match but in reality was over economic issues. A 1980 treaty resolved the conflict but left Honduras weakened politically and economically. A return to a democratic government occurred in 1982 with the election of Roberto Suazo Córdova as president; all military political power was ended in 1984. Elections in 1990 brought Rafael Leonardo Callejas to the presidency, continuing the democratic process. Throughout the 1990s Honduras made strides toward a democratic society, such as electing a Liberal Party candidate president in 1993 and 1997, ending compulsory military service in 1995 and placing the armed forces under civilian control in 1999. In 2001 Ricardo Maduro become the

sixth democratically elected president since the end of the military dictatorship in 1992. José Manuel Zelaya Rosales of the Liberal Party of Honduras was elected president in 2005.

**Hone, Evie** *(1894–1955)* Irish painter and stained-glass designer. Born in Dublin, Hone studied in London with Walter Sickert and in Paris with Andre Lhote and Albert Gleizes. Her early work consisted mainly of abstract paintings executed in deep, jewel-like colors. Hone was strongly influenced by Georges Rouault in her painting and in the stained glass she created from 1933 until her death. Her most celebrated works are the *Crucifixion* and *Last Supper* windows at the Eton College Chapel (1942–52).

**Honecker, Erich** *(1912–1994)* East German communist political leader, secretary-general of the Socialist Unity (Communist) party (1971–89). Honecker joined the German Communist party in his teens, was arrested under HITLER in 1935, sentenced to 10 years in prison in 1937 and released at the end of WORLD WAR II. He was first secretary of the party's youth organization

from 1946 to 1955. He joined the Central Committee in 1946 and the Politburo as candidate member in 1950 and as full member in 1958. Honecker succeeded Walter ULBRICHT as party leader in 1971. His policy was aimed at strengthening EAST GERMANY economically while repressing any challenges to the party's authority. He presided over East Germany's transformation into an industrial and military power second only to the USSR in the WARSAW PACT. His hardline leadership was successfully challenged in 1989 as East Germany's economy declined, tens of thousands of East Germans fled to the West and hundreds of thousands more took to the streets demanding an end to Communist rule. Honecker was ousted from his post on Oct. 10, 1989. Subsequent investigations revealed that he had led a lavish, privileged lifestyle at the expense of the East German people; he was put under house arrest, but because of ill-health he had not been formally tried for corruption as of March 1991. He later fled to the USSR.

**Honegger, Arthur** *(1892–1955)* French composer. Born in Le Havre of Swiss parents, he studied at the Zurich

Conservatory and the Paris Conservatory. With Darius MILHAUD, Francis POULENC and three other young French composers, Honegger was a member of the 1920s group known as the SIX. Often polyphonic and polytonal, his music is strongly rhythmic and sharply dissonant. He is particularly noted for his theatrical works, such as the ballet *Judith* (1926), the oratorio *King David* (1921–23) and the film music for *Mayerling* (1935). His other works include the tone poem *Pacific 231* (1923), five symphonies, piano works, chamber music and songs.

***Honeymooners, The***   See Jackie GLEASON.

**Hong Kong**   Former British Crown colony located on the southeast coast of China. The territory of Hong Kong included Hong Kong island (ceded to Britain in 1841) and adjacent islands, the Kowloon Peninsula (ceded in 1860) and the New Territories (acquired by 99-year lease in 1898), which consist of a mainland area adjacent to Kowloon and 235 islands. Hong Kong covers a total area of 414 square miles and was administered by Great Britain. The Japanese occupied Hong Kong during WORLD WAR II (1941–45), after which British rule resumed. Long a major center of trade, in the last third of the 20th century Hong Kong also became a leading center of manufacturing and international finance; along with JAPAN, it has taken a lead in the production of computers, radios, television sets, audio-video equipment and cameras. Historically an important center for refugees, Hong Kong experienced problems in the 1970s from increased illegal emigration from China, and in the 1980s from the arrival of huge numbers of Vietnamese BOAT PEOPLE. In 1989 Britain began a forced repatriation of the boat people to alleviate some of the problems. The Sino-British Joint Declaration of 1985 provided for China to regain sovereignty over Hong Kong on July 1, 1997. Fears over Hong Kong's future under Chinese rule led to increased emigration from the territory and pressure on Britain to admit the millions born in Hong Kong who can claim British passport rights under the British National (Overseas) category of immigration. In 1997 Great Britain re-

turned Hong Kong to China. It is now a Special Administrative Region of China, under the country's "one country, two systems policy." Hong Kong retains its economic system and a large measure of autonomy on local matters.

**Hood, Raymond M.**   *(1881–1934)* American architect, one of many to work on the design of ROCKEFELLER CENTER, who moved toward MODERNISM at a time when eclecticism was the dominant direction in architecture in the U.S. A graduate of MIT, Hood was associated with J. Andre Fouilhoux and John Mead Howells. Together they won a competition for the design of the Chicago Tribune Building (1922), a neo-Gothic skyscraper with useless flying buttresses at its top. Under the influence of European modernism, Hood moved toward a noneclectic, modern style with details relating to ART DECO. His vertically striped Daily News and horizontally banded McGraw-Hill buildings (1930 and 1934), designed with Fouilhoux, exemplify this shift. Hood played a major role in the Art Deco design characteristics of Rockefeller Center (begun in 1932).

**Hook, Sidney**   *(1902–1989)* American social philosopher. Hook was a prolific writer on politics, public policy and education. He described himself as a socialist and a "secular humanist," which he defined as someone who considered morality to be linked to human nature and separate from religious belief. Although a staunch anticommunist, he was also an early critic of the anticommunist crusade of Senator Joseph MCCARTHY in the 1950s. Hook taught at New York University from 1927 to 1969. In 1973 he became a senior research fellow at the Hoover Institution on War, Revolution, and Peace at Stanford University. His best-known books included *Toward the Understanding of Karl Marx: A Revolutionary Interpretation* (1933), *The Hero in History* (1943), and *Pragmatism and the Tragic Sense of Life* (1974).

**Hoover, Herbert Clark**   *(1874–1964)* President of the United States (1929–33). One of the great humanitarians of the 20th century, Hoover had the misfortune to preside over the beginning of the GREAT DEPRESSION of the 1930s. Born into a Quaker family in

*Herbert Hoover. 31st president of the United States* (LIBRARY OF CONGRESS, PRINTS AND PHOTOGRAPHS DIVISION)

West Branch, Iowa, Hoover was orphaned at the age of eight and thereafter lived with various relatives. He attended Stanford University, graduating with a degree in geology (1895), and joined a London-based mining firm. During the next 20 years he worked as a mining engineer in some 14 countries, including Australia and China, where he supervised important mining projects and introduced new mining techniques. He formed his own consulting firm in 1908 and became a millionaire.

In London at the outbreak of WORLD WAR I, Hoover turned to public service and played a major role in humanitarian relief efforts. Heading the American Relief Committee and the Committee for the Relief of Belgium, he organized food relief for 11 million refugees in war-torn Belgium and northern France. When the U.S. entered the war in 1917, President Woodrow WILSON appointed him chairman of the Food Administration Board, responsible for food rationing and conservation efforts in the U.S. Hoover continued his overseas relief work after the war, helping to avert famine in defeated Germany and the massive famine in the USSR in 1921.

As secretary of commerce (1921–28) under Presidents Warren G. HARDING and Calvin COOLIDGE, Hoover modernized the Commerce Department. He reformed the bureaus of Foreign and Domestic Commerce and the Bureau of Fisheries. He declared the radio airwaves public property, and introduced radio station licensing. During his tenure, the number of commercial radio stations in the U.S. increased from two to several hundred. Hoover also called the first commercial aviation conference (1922) and the first national conference on highway safety (1923), promoted uniform manufacturing standards and supported child health and welfare activities and conservation programs.

One of the most energetic but self-effacing figures of the 1920s, Hoover was also one of the few high officials who were not implicated in the scandals of the Harding administration. With a reputation for integrity, brilliant administrative abilities and wide practical experience, Hoover was selected as the Republican presidential candidate in 1928. He defeated Al SMITH by the second-largest popular vote margin up to that time.

Hoover promised to bring high standards to government and pledged to end poverty and hunger in America. However, the STOCK MARKET CRASH OF 1929 intervened. Hoover established the Reconstruction Finance Administration to make loans to stricken businesses, adopted a budget designed to stimulate the economy, and urged the Federal Reserve Board to ease the money supply and lower interest rates. However, he refused to involve the federal government in direct relief, believing that the efforts of private business and individual initiative would best revive the economy. As his administration progressed, Hoover was severely criticized for appearing to favor big business while ignoring the plight of the ordinary citizen. His apparent lack of concern was reinforced by his cold, humorless manner and his inability to communicate his ideas convincingly to the people. His claim that "prosperity is just around the corner" was not taken seriously by the majority of voters, and he was soundly defeated by Democrat Franklin D. ROOSEVELT in the election of 1932.

Hoover remained a vocal critic of Roosevelt and the NEW DEAL, claiming that FDR's big-government programs threatened individual liberty and stifled initiative. He initially opposed the U.S. entry into WORLD WAR II, believing that the war was not America's concern. At war's end in 1945, acknowledging Hoover's expertise, President Harry S TRUMAN asked Hoover to again undertake famine relief efforts. In 1946

Hoover traveled over 50,000 miles, visiting 38 countries to determine how food could be distributed to the areas where it was most needed. His efforts helped save millions of Europeans and Asians from starvation. Hoover continued as an adviser to Truman. His Hoover Commission (1947–49) studied the organization of the executive branch of government and issued 273 recommendations to improve its efficiency; the majority of these recommendations were adopted. Hoover also advised President Dwight D. EISENHOWER on a number of issues, and won new respect as the elder statesman of the REPUBLICAN PARTY.

For more than a generation after his 1932 electoral defeat, Hoover was largely viewed as a heartless reactionary and do-nothing, a villain in 20th-century American history. However, historians have reevaluated Hoover's presidency and acknowledged his substantial positive accomplishments.

## Hoover, J(ohn) Edgar (1895–1972)

American government administrator, director of the Federal Bureau of Investigation (FBI). Born in Washington, D.C., Hoover studied law at George Washington University, joined the U.S. Department of Justice in 1917, and from 1919 to 1921 worked extensively on the PALMER RAIDS. In 1924 he began his lifelong career as director of the Bureau of Investigation, which was renamed the FBI in 1935. During these years Hoover personified the FBI, both in its successes and its failures. At the time he took it over, the Bureau was inefficient and scandal-ridden. Hoover

*J. Edgar Hoover, director of the FBI for 48 years*

quickly turned it into a crack policing agency, doing away with political appointments and recruiting improved staff, establishing centralized fingerprint and statistical files, developing a crime laboratory and founding a training academy. In the early 1930s he launched a war on "public enemies," engineering manhunts for high-profile criminals such as John DILLINGER, "Pretty Boy" FLOYD and "Baby Face" NELSON. This proved a highly successful public relations ploy but did little to dislodge the hold of organized crime, which Hoover had been criticized for largely ignoring. During WORLD WAR II, he was given the responsibility of protecting the U.S. from sabotage or subversion by enemy agents. In the COLD WAR era he renewed his earlier campaign against COMMUNISM by pursuing what he perceived as left-wing organizations and sympathizers with an obsessive tenacity that brought him charges of civil-rights violation and the prosecution of personal vendettas. During his many years in office serving under eight presidents, Hoover amassed tremendous personal power and became the subject of enormous controversy.

## Hoover Dam

Formerly known as Boulder Dam, this immense engineering wonder was erected on the Colorado River, between Nevada and Arizona, between 1931 and 1936. Built by the U.S. Bureau of Reclamation, it is still one of the largest and most important hydroelectric power sources in the world and contributed greatly to the postwar growth of the southwestern U.S. Project workers founded Boulder City, Nev.

## Hope, Bob (Leslie Townes Hope) (1903–2003)

American entertainer, comedian and film star. Born in England, he moved with his family to Ohio at the age of four. One of the most popular entertainers on radio during the 1930s and 1940s and on TV beginning in the 1950s, he gained world renown for his seven "Road" movies (1940–53) costarring Bing CROSBY and Dorothy Lamour. During his career he made over 50 films. One of the most charitable figures in the performing arts, he made annual trips overseas to entertain American troops during WORLD WAR II, the KOREAN WAR, the VIETNAM WAR and in peacetime. He continued to work in commercials and TV specials and occasionally entertained troops. A personal friend of several U.S.

Bob Hope entertaining troops in Korea (LIBRARY OF CONGRESS, PRINTS AND PHOTOGRAPHS DIVISION)

Harry Hopkins, FDR's personal adviser (LIBRARY OF CONGRESS, PRINTS AND PHOTOGRAPHS DIVISION)

presidents, he was awarded the Presidential Medal of Freedom in 1969. He also received the Hersholt Award, an Emmy and an honorary ACADEMY AWARD.

**Hopkins, Anthony** (1937– ) British film, stage and television actor. Born in West Glamorgan, Wales, Hopkins began acting at age 17 at the local YMCA. Entranced by the theater, in 1960 he enrolled in the Royal Academy of Dramatic Art (London). That year he made his stage debut in *The Quare Fellow.* For four years, Hopkins worked in regional repertory theaters before he won recognition for his London performance in *Julius Caesar.* He made his inaugural performance as a film actor in *The White Bus* (1967); he received greater notice for *The Lion in Winter,* a

British actor Sir Anthony Hopkins during the filming of SELECTED EXITS. 1993 (PHOTOFEST)

picture released the following year in which he played one of the sons of King Henry II (Peter O'Toole) and Eleanor of Aquitaine (Katharine HEPBURN). The role for which he is best known is Hannibal Lecter, a cannibalistic psychologist who aides and evades the FBI, in *The Silence of the Lambs* (1990), *Hannibal* (2000) and *Red Dragon* (2002). For his first depiction of the deranged genius, Hopkins won the Oscar for best actor. Hopkins also garnered critical review in the Merchant-Ivory picture *The Remains of the Day* (1993), in which he portrayed the butler of a British aristocrat who sympathizes with the Nazi regime, and the Oliver Stone film *Nixon* (1995), in which he played the American president. *Nixon* also gained Hopkins another Academy Award nomination for best actor. In all, he has starred in over 60 films. Hopkins received a knighthood from Queen ELIZABETH II in 1993, which he later renounced to become a U.S. citizen.

**Hopkins, Harry Lloyd** (1890–1946) American public official and presidential adviser. Born in Sioux City, Iowa, Hopkins was trained as a social worker, and after college he settled in New York City. There, in 1931, he was appointed by then-governor Franklin D. ROOSEVELT as director of the Temporary Emergency Relief Administration. After Roosevelt became president, he made Hopkins chief of the Federal Emergency Relief Administration and the Civil Works Administration. Hopkins subsequently headed the WPA (1935–38) and served as secretary of commerce (1938–40). He was the key figure in administering NEW DEAL public assistance programs and in supplying jobs to some eight million workers. A close

friend of Roosevelt, Hopkins was called on frequently by the president to serve as an emissary, confidant and adviser, particularly during WORLD WAR II. Administering the LEND-LEASE program in 1941, he also went on many wartime missions in London and Moscow. Despite ill health, he accompanied the president to all the major conferences of the war and helped shape peacetime alliances. After Roosevelt's death, at the request of President TRUMAN, the gravely ill Hopkins held talks with STALIN in 1945 regarding the UNITED NATIONS.

**Hopkins, Sam "Lightnin"** (1912–1982) American country BLUES singer. Hopkins began his career in 1920 as a minstrel at Texas country fairs. He subsequently performed throughout the South and built a national reputation. After a hiatus of 15 years he regained prominence through appearances at New York's CARNEGIE HALL and the Village Gate club. Hopkins was one of the greatest and the last of the original blues performers. He was widely acclaimed by critics for his imaginative guitar playing, which exerted a major influence on ROCK guitar players.

**Hopman, Harry** (1906–1985) Australian tennis player; captain of Australia's Davis Cup team in 1938 and 1939 and again from 1950 to 1969. During the latter period, known as the golden age of Australian tennis, he worked with such great players as Rod Laver and John Newcombe. Hopman helped Australia capture the Davis Cup 15 times. He moved to Florida in the late 1970s to open an international tennis camp for young players.

**Hopper, Edward** *(1882–1967)* American painter. One of 20th-century America's finest realists, Hopper was born in Nyack, N.Y. He studied in New York City, with Robert HENRI, George Luks, Arthur B. Davies and others from 1900 to 1906. Hopper gained his first recognition through his early etchings. He traveled to Europe a number of times from 1906 to 1910, but was little affected by the new movements he encountered there. Hopper lived in New York City, exhibited at the ARMORY SHOW (1913), had his first one-man show at the Whitney Studio Club in 1919 and his first retrospective at the Museum of Modern Art in 1933. Hopper's paintings fall within the tradition of his teacher Henri and of the Ashcan School, but with a very personal approach. Painting his native New York or the landscapes of New England, he depicted slices of streets in cities or small towns strongly lit and shadowed with a cold light, often peopled with solitary figures, nearly always evoking a sense of profound loneliness and isolation. Unsentimental and starkly geometric, his best known works include *From Williamsburg Bridge* (1928, Metropolitan Museum, N.Y.C.), *House by the Railroad* (1925, Museum of Modern Art, N.Y.C.), *Early Sunday Morning* (1930, Whitney Museum, N.Y.C.) and *Nighthawks* (1942, Art Institute of Chicago).

**Horenstein, Jascha** *(1898–1973)* Russian-born conductor. Born in Kiev, Horenstein and his family moved to Vienna in 1904. He studied music there and in Berlin. In 1929 he was appointed director of the Düsseldorf Opera and conducted the company. In the 1930s he traveled and conducted throughout Europe. He settled in the U.S. in 1941, became an American citizen, and conducted in the U.S. and Latin America. After World War II Horenstein settled in Switzerland. A thoughtful and meticulous conductor, he was particularly known for his interpretations of the symphonies of Anton Bruckner and Gustav MAHLER.

**Horne, Lena** *(1917– )* American singer and actress. Known for her stylish interpretations of jazz and pop standards, Horne was born in Brooklyn, New York. While a teenager, she sang in a chorus at the famous Cotton Club in HARLEM. In the early 1940s she went to HOLLYWOOD, where she was featured in several all-black movies, most notably *Stormy Weather* (1943), whose title song became her signature tune, and also in several all-star musicals, where her own numbers could be neatly cut from the films when they played theaters in the South. The first black woman vocalist to be featured with a white band, Horne faced and fought discrimination for much of her career. She toured Europe and frequently appeared in nightclubs and on television variety shows in the 1950s and '60s. In 1981 Horne made a triumphant return to Broadway in a one-woman show, *Lena Horne: The Lady and Her Music*. In 1996 Horne won a Grammy Award for the best vocal jazz performance for *An Evening with Lena Horne* (1995).

**Horney, Karen** *(1885–1952)* German-American neo-Freudian psychoanalyst. Born in Hamburg, Germany, Karen Horney received her M.D. in Berlin in 1915. After World War I, she began work at the Berlin Psychoanalytic Institute. Horney took exception to many of the negative aspects of FREUD's theories, particularly those regarding women, and, like Alfred ADLER, went on to develop her own theories of personality and neurosis and to question key Freudian concepts and methods. Her books *Our Inner Conflicts* and *Neurosis and Human Growth* are considered landmark publications. Horney moved to the U.S. in 1932, and in 1941 she resigned from the New York Psychoanalytic Society and founded the Association for the Advancement of Psychoanalysis and the American Institute of Psychoanalysis.

**Horniman, Annie Elizabeth Fredericka** *(1860–1937)* British theatrical patron. A champion of modern drama, the wealthy Horniman founded Miss Horniman's Company of Actors. She financed a permanent home for the Irish National Theatre Company in the ABBEY THEATRE, Dublin. Though an admirer of W. B. YEATS, she had a difficult relationship with Lady GREGORY. Horniman

withdrew her funding of the Abbey in 1910 when the theatre was kept open on the day of King EDWARD VII's funeral. She then focused on the Gaiety Theatre in Manchester, in which she had begun to invest in 1907. There she promoted new plays by local playwrights until 1921.

**Hornsby, Rogers** *(1896–1963)* American baseball player. Hornsby is a legend among baseball players and fans. He was the batting champion in the National League from 1920 to 1925, and again in 1928. Considered one of the greatest hitters of all time, his 1924 batting average of .424 still stands as a modern-day league record. He was player-manager for the St. Louis Cardinals in 1925 and 1926, leading the team to a winning World Series in 1926. He maintained a lifetime batting average of .358 from 1915 to 1933, won the most valuable player awards in 1925 and 1928, and was elected to the Baseball Hall of Fame in 1942.

**Hornsby-Smith, Margaret Patricia, Baroness** *(1914–1985)* British politician; a prominent figure in the British House of Commons as Conservative MP for Chislehurst. Appointed parliamentary secretary to the ministry of health in 1951, she was, at 37, the youngest woman to hold office in any government. Hornsby-Smith held that post until 1957. When sworn of the Privy Council in 1959, she was the youngest woman ever to have received that honor.

**Hornung, Paul Vernon** *(1935– )* American football player. A stand-out running back at Notre Dame, Hornung was named winner of the prestigious Heisman Trophy in 1956. He turned professional with the Green Bay Packers and in 1960 set a season scoring record with 176 points. Under coach Vince LOMBARDI, he helped lead the team to three consecutive NFL championships (1960–62). Known for his relaxed approach to training, Hornung was suspended for the 1963 season for gambling on football games, although he never bet against his own team. His most memorable performance came in 1956, when he ran for five touchdowns.

**Horowitz, Vladimir Samoylovich** *(1903–1989)* Russian-born pianist whose technical brilliance and idiosyncratic interpretations placed him in the fore-front of modern keyboard virtuosos. Born in Kiev, Horowitz studied with Felix Blumenfeld, a pupil of Anton Rubinstein. His friendship with the composer Alexander SCRIABIN confirmed his ambitions to specialize in music of the late Russian romantics. He left the USSR in 1925 and three years later made his sensational CARNEGIE HALL debut with the Tchaikovsky 1st Piano Concerto (Thomas BEECHAM on the podium made his U.S. conducting debut). He immediately assumed his place among a galaxy of keyboard luminaries in New York including his great friend, Sergei RACHMANINOFF. He became best known for the speed and terrifying intensity of his Liszt and Rachmaninoff performances, although he also championed the icy fire of Scriabin and the poised clarity of Muzio Clementi and Domenico Scarlatti. His concert career, which made him the highest paid classical pianist in history, was frequently interrupted by "retirements" due to ill health and a high-strung temperament. His return to Moscow in 1986 was a spectacular media event and was broadcast live worldwide. He made more than 150 records and won more than 20 Grammy Awards. Since 1933 he was married to Wanda Toscanini, the daughter of conductor Arturo TOSCANINI.

**Horrocks, Sir Brian** *(1895–1985)* British military officer. Horrocks fought in WORLD WAR I. As a general in WORLD WAR II, he helped the British take North Africa from the Germans at the crucial battle of EL ALAMEIN (1942). He also played a major role in the June 1944 D day INVASION OF NORMANDY. He retired from active duty in 1949 and was knighted and given the important ceremonial post of Black Rod in the House of Lords. He was also a historian and a well-known British television personality.

**Horthy de Nagybányai Miklós** *(1868–1957)* Hungarian admiral and political leader. An aide-de-camp to Emperor FRANZ JOSEPH from 1911 to 1913, Horthy de Nagybányai commanded the Austro-Hungarian fleet during WORLD WAR I. After Béla Kun became head of the Hungarian government in 1919, Horthy led a counter-revolution that ousted the Marxists. In 1920 he became regent and headed a nationalistic and conservative regime, guiding the country in the years between the two world wars and helping to recover some of the lands lost by HUNGARY in post–World War I settlements. He reluctantly joined WORLD WAR II on the side of GERMANY but continued to maintain ties with the Allies. In 1944, after Russian troops entered Hungary, Horthy unsuccessfully sued for a separate peace with the USSR and was soon imprisoned by the Germans. Freed by U.S. troops, he testified at the NUREMBERG TRIALS (1946), and in 1949 he settled in Portugal, where he died.

**Horvath, Odon von** *(1901–1938)* German novelist and playwright. Horvath was one of the most critically admired German writers of his generation prior to his untimely death. He enjoyed a series of successes on the stage with socially poignant and romantic plays, including *Revolte auf Cafe* (1927), *Sladek* (1929), *Italienische Nacht* (1931), *Hin und Her* (1934) and *Der Jungste Tag* (1937). His novels include *Der Ewige Spiesser* (1930), *Ein Kind Unserer Zeit* (1938) and *Jegend Ohne Gott* (1938).

**Houdini, Harry (Ehrich Weiss)** *(1874–1926)* Legendary American magician and escape artist. Born in Hungary, he later changed his name in honor of the French magician Houdin. In 1922 he went to New York City as a trapeze artist, and later began a magic act with his brother. On a trip to England, he mystified Scotland Yard with a staged escape and earned a wide reputation. He was particularly noted for his ability to escape from almost any seemingly impossible situation. He left instructions that, after death, he would return to a specific bridge in Chicago, and his followers have kept their vigil on that day each year—without result. He left his library of magic to the Library of Congress.

**Hounsfield, Godfrey** *(1919–2004)* British engineer who developed the first commercially successful CAT SCAN machines in Britain. For this work, Hounsfield shared the 1979 NOBEL PRIZE in physiology or medicine with Alan Macleod CORMACK.

*Magician and illusionist Harry Houdini* (LIBRARY OF CONGRESS, PRINTS AND PHOTOGRAPHS DIVISION)

**Houphouët-Boigny, Félix** *(1905–1993)* African statesman, president of the Republic of the Ivory Coast (see CÔTE D'IVOIRE). Born in Yamoussoukro, Houphouët-Boigny was the son of a chief in the French colony of the Ivory Coast. He studied medicine in Paris, and returned to Africa to supervise his family's cocoa plantation and practice (1925–40). He entered politics and became chairman of the powerful African Democratic Rally in 1946. He served in the French National Assembly from 1946 to 1958. When the Ivory Coast attained autonomy within the FRENCH COMMUNITY in 1958, Houphouët-Boigny assumed the duties of president of the constituent assembly, and in 1959 he became the prime minister. Leading the country to full independence in 1960, he became president and was returned to that office in subsequent elections. He maintained close ties to France in commercial and cultural affairs.

**House, Edward Mandell** *(1858–1938)* U.S. diplomat. A political adviser to several Democratic Texas governors (1892–1904), House was given the honorary title of "colonel." He assumed a major tole in Woodrow WILSON's 1912 presidential campaign, and refused a cabinet post, choosing instead to help Wilson in a variety of political and administrative functions. As Wilson's chief agent in foreign affairs, he helped explore mediation alternatives with European countries in WORLD WAR I. As head of the U.S. mission, he was one of the signers of the TREATY OF VERSAILLES in June 1919. Because of disagreements about ratification of the treaty, and possible U.S. entry into the LEAGUE OF NATIONS, Wilson and House separated, never seeing each other again.

**Houseman, John (Jacques Haussman)** *(1902–1988)* American actor and producer. In the 1930s he teamed with Orson WELLES on a series of projects. Their most famous collaboration was the 1938 radio production "War of the Worlds." He was best known for creating the role of Professor Kingsfield in the movie and television versions of *The Paper Chase.* Houseman's portrayal of the crusty law professor won him an Oscar in 1974 and led to a series of television ads for the Smith Barney investment firm. He also helped establish the Juilliard drama school and the Acting Company repertory group.

**House Un-American Activities Committee (HUAC)** Special committee of the U.S. House of Representatives established in 1938. At first called the Dies Committee, for its chairman, Texas Democrat Martin Dies, Jr., it was formed to investigate fascist, communist and other "subversive" organizations in the U.S. It became a standing committee in 1945. For 30 years after the end of World War II, HUAC concentrated on ferreting out communists and left-wingers in a variety of American institutions and industries. In 1947 it investigated the film industry and condemned the HOLLYWOOD TEN. The following year, it shifted its efforts to investigating the State Department and conducted hearings regarding the HISS-CHAMBERS CASE. In 1950 HUAC sponsored a bill that became the McCarren Act, which, until some provisions were overturned by the courts, necessitated the registration of American communists as foreign agents, severely limiting their travel and preventing them from serving in government and certain strategic industries. As the RED SCARE of the 1950s lessened in intensity, HUAC gradually became less powerful. Re-

named the Internal Security Committee in 1969, it was abolished in 1975.

**Housman, A(lfred) E(dward)** *(1859–1936)* English poet and scholar. Housman remains one of the most widely read of English poets. While he was by no means a prolific poet, a number of his rhymed, elegiac verses—reflecting as they do the sunset of Victorian England—have taken their place as beloved classics of the language. Poems from *A Shropshire Lad* (1896), *When I Was One-and-Twenty* and *To an Athlete Dying Young* have been memorized by generations of English schoolchildren. *Last Poems* (1922) is a representative collection of Housman's verse. Housman led a quiet, academic life, serving for most of his adult years as a Latin professor at Cambridge University.

**Houston, Whitney** *(1963–   )* American pop musician. Born in Newark, N. J., Houston's familial connections placed her in an advantageous situation to develop her talents. Her mother Cissy was both a member of a gospel music choir and backup singer for Elvis PRESLEY; her cousin Dionne Warwick was a female pop music legend in her own right. When she turned 11 Houston began to refine her vocal talents by following in the footsteps of her mother, singing in her church choir, and singing backup for Chaka Kahn and Lou Rawls. In 1985 Houston's first album, *Whitney Houston,* debuted and soon reached the top of the pop music charts, with one of its songs, "Saving All My Love for You," earning her a Grammy in 1986. In 1987 her second album, *Whitney,* premiered, with another single, "I Wanna Dance with Somebody (Who Loves Me)," resulting in another Grammy (1988) for the young singer. Her critical and commercial success on both albums, which sold 10 million copies each, established her as a powerhouse in pop music.

In the 1990s Houston began to diversify her talents by pursuing parts on the silver screen. In 1992, two years after the premier of her third album, *I'm Your Baby Tonight,* and a year after her marriage to R&B singer Bobby Brown, she starred with Kevin COSTNER in *The Bodyguard,* a film describing the budding relationship between a former Secret Service agent turned bodyguard (Costner) and an award-winning

singer and actress (Houston) whom he agrees to protect from a deranged fan bent on killing her. Houston's remake of "I Will Always Love You," a song originally written and performed by Dolly Parton, for the movie's soundtrack was hugely successful. In 1994 Houston won four Grammys for the performances associated with the *Bodyguard* soundtrack. However, her attempt to mirror her *Bodyguard* character's critical success remained elusive. While *Waiting to Exhale* (1955) and *The Preacher's Wife* (1996) were popular movies, neither garnered her much praise from reviewers.

**hovercraft** Invented by British engineer Sir Christopher Cockerell in 1955, the hovercraft is an air-cushion vehicle that can travel over water or flat terrain. It is technically an aircraft but resembles a boat. The hovercraft is lifted several feet off the ground by air pressure generated under the hull by propellers. The pressure is contained by a flexible rubber "skirt" around the hovercraft's hull. Following his patent of the hovercraft, in 1956 Cockerell formed his own company, Hovercraft Limited, and interested the British government in his invention. The first practical hovercraft was flown in 1959. Further refinements were made, and in 1968 the largest hovercraft ever built, the SR.N4, was introduced. This model, which can carry up to 600 passengers as well as automobiles, is in regular commercial service on the English Channel between Dover and Calais.

**Hovhaness, Alan** *(1911–2000)* American composer. Hovhaness, of Scottish and Armenian parentage, is noted for the variety of international influences in his musical compositions. Born in Massachusetts, Hovhaness studied at the New England Conservatory and at Tanglewood. From 1948 to 1952 he taught at the Boston Conservatory, after which he moved to New York and devoted many years to extensive travel. His compositions, which are often intensely melodic with a modal foundation, sometimes feature Eastern musical touches such as a repetition of single notes within a limited pitch and range. Major works by this prolific composer include *Lousadzak* (1944), *Khaldis* (1951), *Meditation on Orpheus* (1958),

*Mountains and Rivers without End* (1968) and Mount Saint Helens (Symphony no. 50 [1982]).

**Howard, Leslie** *(1893–1943)* British film and stage actor and director. Howard was a gifted and sensitive leading man who made his mark in a number of memorable films of the 1930s. Howard served in the British Army in World War I and afterward suffered from shell-shock, which led him to pursue an acting career on the stage to distract him from his difficult memories. He rapidly achieved renoun and made his Broadway debut in *Just Suppose* (1922); Howard's film debut came in *Outward Bound* (1930). He achieved stardom as the victimized lover of Bette DAVIS in *Of Human Bondage* (1934). Subsequent successes included *The Scarlet Pimpernel* (1935), *The Petrified Forest* (1936), *Pygmalion* (1938) and *Gone With the Wind* (1939), in which he played Confederate gentleman Ashley Wilkes. Howard disappeared at sea in 1943 during WORLD WAR II, when the plane he was flying in was shot down while he was on a diplomatic mission for Britain.

**Howard, Robin Jared Stanley** *(1924–1999)* British dance patron. Howard founded the London Contemporary Dance Theatre and helped popularize modern dance in England. He also established the Contemporary Dance Trust and the London Contemporary Dance School. In 2001 the theater at the school was renamed the Robin Howard Dance Theatre in his honor.

**Howard, Roy** *(1883–1964)* American newspaper reporter, editor and publisher. He began his career as a news reporter in 1902 for the *Indianapolis News,* and later worked in St. Louis, Cincinnati and New York. In 1907 he became the New York manager of United Press International Association, and finally its president from 1936 to 1952. In 1925 he became chairman of the Scripps-McRae newspaper chain, which later became Scripps-Howard—a leading newspaper conglomerate with over 30 papers. Founder of the conglomerate *New York World-Telegram and Sun,* he was its editor until 1960 and its president until 1962.

**Howard, Trevor** *(1916–1988)* British actor. Howard made the transition from theater to film in 1944 and appeared in more than 70 films, including such classics as David LEAN's *Brief Encounter* (1946) and Carol REED's *The Third Man* (1950). In 1962, he portrayed Captain William Bligh opposite Marlon BRANDO's Fletcher Christian in a remake of *Mutiny on the Bounty.*

**Howe, Sir Geoffrey (later: Baron Howe of Aberavon)** *(1926–   )* British politician. A Conservative MP, Howe served as solicitor-general (1970–72) and minister for trade (1972–74) under Edward HEATH. Howe was a senior figure in the cabinet of Margaret THATCHER (1979–90). As her first chancellor of the exchequer (1979–83), he introduced strict monetarist policies (see MONETARISM). He served briefly as home secretary before becoming foreign secretary in 1983. In 1988 Howe was promoted to the nominal post of deputy prime minister, but his influence in the cabinet waned as a result of disagreements with Thatcher's European policy. Howe's dramatic resignation from the cabinet in October 1990 followed by his open criticism of Thatcher in the House of Commons led to Thatcher's ouster as leader of the CONSERVATIVE PARTY and as prime minister. Howe was the longest-serving member of Thatcher's cabinet. In 1990 Howe resigned from Thatcher's cabinet over her policies toward Europe and the adoption of a single European currency. Howe retired from politics in 1992 and was made a life peer. He published his memoirs, *Conflict of Loyalty* in 1994.

**Howe, George** *(1886–1955)* American architect whose work moved from eclecticism to MODERNISM and who exercised considerable influence as an educator and spokesman for modern architecture. Howe was educated at Harvard and at the École des Beaux-Arts in Paris. He joined the Philadelphia firm of Mellor, Meigs & Howe where he produced a variety of traditional houses and other buildings. After meeting William LESCAZE in 1929, Howe converted to modernism ideas and designed, with Lescaze as a partner, the Philadelphia Savings Fund Society building (PSFS 1932), the first excellent example of modern skyscraper design in America. Independently, Howe designed a handsome house with a strikingly cantilevered deck at Bar Harbor, Maine (1939), which was included in the MUSEUM OF MODERN ART exhibit and book *America Builds.* From 1950 to 1954 Howe was chairman of the architecture department at Yale University where he introduced Louis I. KAHN as a teacher and brought about reforms that made Yale a leading architectural school.

**Howe, Gordon "Gordie"** *(1928–   )* Canadian athlete. Perhaps the greatest ice hockey player of all time, Howe retired holding every major record for scoring, endurance—and penalties. He was named the National Hockey League's Most Valuable Player six times and was leading scorer six times. Known for his quick and sneaky use of his elbows to intimidate lesser players, Howe was a complete athlete who amazed teammates and rivals alike with his stickhandling ability. He spent the first 25 years of his incredible career with the Detroit Red Wings. He was named to the Hockey Hall of Fame in 1972, but emerged from retirement in 1973 to join the WHA's Houston Aeros, where, at 45, he skated alongside his sons, Mark and Marty. Howe returned to the NHL with the Hartford Whalers in 1977 and finally retired in 1980.

**Howe, Irving** *(1920–1993)* American writer. A leftist social and literary critic, he is the author of such works as *William Faulkner: A Critical Study* (1952), *Politics and the Novel* (1957), *Decline of the New* (1970) and *Celebrations and Attacks* (1978). Winner of the National Book Award, his *World of Our Fathers* (1976) is an evocative history of New York's immigrant Jewish community. Howe has played a prominent role in liberal American periodicals as the founding editor (1953) of *Dissent* and writer for *The Partisan Review, The New Republic* and *The New York Review of Books.* Also a prolific editor, Howe is the author of the 1982 autobiography *A Margin of Hope.*

**Hoxha, Enver** *(1908–1985)* Albanian communist leader, first secretary of the Albanian Communist Party (1941–85). Hoxha was the longest-ruling communist leader of the 20th century. Educated in France, he became a communist in the early 1930s. After his return to ALBANIA, he was a cofounder of the Albanian Communist Party and became its first secretary. During WORLD WAR II he was active in the RESISTANCE movement against the Italian occupation of Albania. With the establishment of a communist regime at the end of the war, he became Albania's premier and foreign minister. He held these posts until the early 1950s, when he resigned them to consolidate his power as party head. A strict Stalinist, Hoxha remained loyal to the USSR until STALIN's death in 1953 (see STALINISM). He then severed diplomatic ties with Moscow and joined Peking in its ideological struggle against the Soviets. After the death of Chairman MAO ZEDONG he drifted away from China, though without severing diplomatic ties. He subsequently turned Albania into an even more isolated and secretive nation than it had been.

## Hoyle, Sir Fred (1915–2001) British astronomer. Hoyle studied at Cambridge University, graduating in 1938. Hoyle lectured in mathematics at Cambridge from 1945 to 1958 when he became Plumian Professor of Astronomy. He also served as director of the Cambridge Institute of Theoretical Astronomy from 1967; he left Cambridge in 1973. He has held numerous research and visiting posts at such institutions as the California Institute of Technology, Cornell University, Manchester University and the Royal Institution in London. From 1954 to 1948 he was a staff member of the Mount Wilson and Palomar Observatories. He was one of the first to adopt the steady-state theory of Thomas Gold and Hermann BONDI and did much to introduce it to a wider audience in such works as *The Nature of the Universe* (1950); he was also one of the last to support the theory. He argued that violations found in the homogeneity of both space and time in the universe were more apparent than real, for they could be simply small-scale effects, whereas the steady-state theory was concerned with uniformities on the order of a billion light-years or more. Hoyle's contributions to cosmology and astrophysics have been numerous, deep and extensive. One of his main achievements was to show how elements heavier than hydrogen and helium could have been produced. With W. A. Fowler and

Margaret and Geoffrey BURBIDGE, Hoyle gave in 1957 the first comprehensive account of how the elements are produced in the interior of stars.

A prolific writer on a wide variety of subjects, Hoyle wrote a number of science fiction novels beginning with *The Black Cloud* (1957), on the history of astronomy in *Copernicus* (1973), on archaeoastronomy in *From Stonehenge to Modern Cosmology* (1972), on the origin of disease in *Lifecloud* (1978) with Chandra Wickramnsinghe, and on questions of social policy in *Commonsense in Nuclear Energy* (1980). Such works are noted for their originality, rigor and a willingness to speculate and to argue in new and unexpected fields. He also wrote a prodigious number of lectures, papers, textbooks and monographs, of which some of the most significant are his *Frontiers of Astronomy* (1955), *Astronomy and Cosmology* (1975) and, with J. V. Narlikar, various papers on gravity.

## Hua Guofeng (1920– ) Chinese political leader. A communist functionary and political disciple of MAO ZEDONG, he was minister of public security and deputy premier until the death of ZHOU ENLAI, becoming premier in 1976. When Mao died later that year, Hua also became the Communist Party chairman and head of the Military Affairs Commission. Responsible for the arrest of CHIANG CH'ING and the GANG OF FOUR, he was nonetheless criticized for his own political errors and personal cult of personality. In conflict with Deputy Premier DENG XIAOPING, he gradually lost leadership and power. In 1980 he was ousted as premier, the following year he lost the post of party chairman, and the year after that he was stripped of his seat on the Politburo. Hua continued to serve on the Central Committee of the Communist Party until November 2002. In October 2001 allegations surfaced that Hua had left the Communist Party for health reasons.

## Huai-Hai, Battle of Important engagement from November 1948 to January 1949, at the end of the CHINESE CIVIL WAR OF 1945–49. The battle is named for the two main defensive positions held by the Nationalists, the Huai River and the Lung Hai railway. The defeat of the Nationalist armies by

overwhelming communist forces led to the fall of Suchow on December 1. Destroying massive amounts of Nationalist supplies and severely undermining Nationalist morale, this battle opened the invasion route to Nanjing and Shanghai, which were conquered by communist forces in the spring of 1949 and helped to seal the communist victory in the war.

## Huang, Kechang (1903–1986) Chinese communist military officer. A survivor of the LONG MARCH of 1934–35, Huang was made chief of staff of CHINA's People's Liberation Army in 1958, although he was demoted the following year in a political struggle. In 1967 during the CULTURAL REVOLUTION, he was denounced as a rightist and remained in hiding for a decade.

## Huang He (Hwang Ho; Yellow River) Almost 3,000 miles long and of immense historical importance, this river rises in China's Qinghai province and flows eastward through Kansu and Inner Mongolia, then south along the northern border of Henan. Its lower course has changed many times over the centuries and is vital to the farmlands of the Great Plains. In 1938 the Chinese diverted its course southward to deter Japanese invasion during the second SINO-JAPANESE WAR—a shift that cost nearly a million lives and was not rectified until 1947. Its perennial floods have earned it a reputation as "China's Sorrow."

## Huascaran Site of one of the worst natural disasters of this century. This mountain in the Ancash department of western Peru is the highest in the country and one of the highest in the Andes. In 1962 an avalanche rolled down its slope, burying the village of Ranrahirca, situated at its foot. But the worst was yet to come: In 1970 earthquakes destroyed 10 villages.

## Hubbard, L. Ron (1911–1986) American writer. Hubbard's best selling 1950 book, *Dianetics: The Modern Science of Mental Health*, became the basis for the Church of **Scientology**, founded by Hubbard in 1954. The church was based on a form of psychotherapy called "auditing" and not on the worship of a god. Hubbard lived on a huge yacht from 1968 to 1975, avoiding var-

ious law enforcement officials who had accused him of fraud and other crimes. In 1975 his church was the target of investigations by both the Internal Revenue Service and the Federal Bureau of Investigation.

**Hubbell, Carl Owen** *(1903–1988)* American baseball player. A star pitcher famed for his screwball, Hubbell won 253 games for the New York Giants between 1928 and 1943. He hurled five consecutive 20-win seasons and led the New York Giants to the World Series three times. Hubbell was named the National League's most valuable player in 1933 and 1936 and was an eight-time all star. In a legendary feat in the second All-Star Game (1934), he struck out in succession five of the game's greatest hitters: Babe RUTH, Lou GEHRIG, Jimmie FOXX, Al Simmons and Joe CRONIN. He was elected to the Baseball Hall of Fame in 1947.

**Hubble, Edwin Powell** *(1889–1953)* American astronomer and cosmologist. Hubble was educated at the University of Chicago where he was influenced by astronomer George Hale. A good athlete, he was offered the role of Great White Hope in a match against black heavy-weight champion Jack JOHNSON. Instead, he accepted a Rhodes scholarship to Oxford where, between 1910 and 1913, he studied jurisprudence, represented Oxford in athletics and fought French boxer Georges Carpentier. He practiced law briefly in America, but in 1914 returned to the study of astronomy at the Yerkes Observatory of the University of Chicago; he earned his Ph.D. in 1917. After being wounded in France in World War I he took up an appointment in 1919 at the Mount Wilson Observatory in California, where Hale was director and where he spent the rest of his career.

Hubble's early work involved studies of faint nebulae, which in the telescopes of the day appeared as fuzzy, extended images. After the powerful 100-inch telescope went into operation at Mount Wilson, he produced some of the most dramatic and significant astronomy of the 20th century. In 1923 he succeeded in resolving the outer region of the Andromeda nebula into "dense swarms of images which in no way differ from those of ordinary stars." Several of them were cepheids,

which allowed him to determine their distance as the unexpectedly large 900,000 light-years. Between 1925 and 1929 he published three major papers showing that the spiral nebulae were at enormous distances, well outside our own galaxy, and were in fact isolated systems of stars, now called spiral galaxies.

In 1929 Hubble made his most significant discovery, announcing what came to be known as **Hubble's Law.** Using his own determination of the distances of 18 galaxies and the measurements of radial velocities from galactic red shifts carried out by Vesto Slipher and Milton Humason, he saw that the recessional velocity of the galaxies increased proportionately with their distance from us. It was this work that demonstrated to astronomers that the idea of an expanding universe, proposed earlier in the 1920s by Alexander FRIEDMANN and Georges LEMAITRE, was indeed correct. The expansion of the universe is now fundamental to every cosmological model. Hubble's Law was soon seen as containing the key to the size, age and future of the universe. Hubble also made a major contribution to the study of galactic evolution by producing the first significant classification of galaxies, a scheme that is still used as the basis for galactic classification.

***Hubble Space Telescope*** Astronomical instrument designed and constructed in the 1980s to orbit the Earth and, with its 94.5-inch mirror, to peer deeper into space and with a clarity 10 times greater than ever achieved by an Earth-based telescope. Launched by the space shuttle *Discovery* and deployed into an orbit 381 miles above Earth on April 25, 1990, the *Hubble* at first experienced problems with its antennas. After this was solved, the telescope began to send its first images back to Earth—pictures that were blurred due to an improper curvature in *Hubble's* primary mirror. Images from *Hubble* were still clearer than those from Earth-based astronomy but were only one-third as sharply focused as had been intended. The unexpected defect dashed hopes that *Hubble* might soon search for BLACK HOLES, distant quasars and possibly begin a calculation of the size of the universe, one of the telescope's chief objectives. In the early 1990s scientists used computers to im-

prove the resolution of *Hubble's* images. For the next 15 years, the *Hubble Space Telescope* took more than 700,000 photos of celestial objects such as galaxies and dying stars, providing spectacular images to the general public and valuable information to astronomers. Its photos have helped to prove the existence of dark energy, tracing gamma-ray bursts to distant planets and providing sample images of their atmosphere.

**Hudson, H. Claude** *(1886–1989)* African-American leader who helped found the NATIONAL ASSOCIATION FOR THE ADVANCEMENT OF COLORED PEOPLE (NAACP). Born to a family of former slaves in rural Louisiana, Hudson later went on to become the first black student to receive a law degree from Loyola University. He moved to Los Angeles in 1923 and eventually became one of the city's most respected black leaders.

**Hudson, Rock (Roy Scherer Jr.)** *(1925–1985)* American actor. Hudson's rugged good looks led him to superstardom under the old HOLLYWOOD studio system. He was twice voted the top box-office draw in the United States. His best-known films were *Giant* (1956), for which he received his sole ACADEMY AWARD nomination, and *Pillow Talk* (1959), one of three romantic comedies in which he starred with Doris Day. In the 1970s, he became one of the first movie stars to make a successful transition to television when his series *MacMillan and Wife* ran for six seasons. His disclosure that he had been diagnosed as having AIDS helped to build worldwide awareness and increased public support to fight the disease.

**Hudson, William H(enry)** *(1841–1922)* Argentine-born English writer. Hudson was born into a family of Americans (of British descent) who had immigrated to Argentina to start a ranch. His early, active years in the Argentina countryside were to leave a lasting influence on Hudson, who at age 15 contracted rheumatic fever and was thereby compelled to adapt to the more secluded life of a writer. He moved to London in 1874 and lived in poverty for more than two decades until his writings—natural history essays, memoirs and fiction—began to win him first a critical and then a popular following. His best books include the story collection *The Purple Land* (1885), the novels *Green Mansions* (1904) and *A Shepherd's Life* (1910) and the nature study *Adventures among Birds* (1913).

**Hue (Hué)** Ancient capital of the Annamese kings of INDOCHINA. This agricultural city, near the mouth of the Hue River in central Vietnam, was badly damaged during the FRENCH INDOCHINA WAR OF 1946–54, and was again a scene of heavy fighting in 1968, during the TET OFFENSIVE of the VIETNAM WAR, when most of the city, including the palaces and tombs of the old kings, was destroyed.

**Hufnagel, Charles Anthony** *(1916–1989)* Heart surgeon, Hufnagel developed and implanted the first artificial human heart valve in 1952. He also participated in the first human kidney transplant operation (1947) and made a major contribution to the development of the heart and lung machine. In 1974 he was part of a three-doctor team that evaluated the health of President Richard M. NIXON (who was suffering from complications from an operation to treat his chronic phlebitis) and concluded that Nixon was too ill to testify at the WATERGATE conspiracy trial. Ironically, Hufnagel died of heart, lung, and kidney disease.

**Hughes, Charles Evans** *(1862–1948)* American statesman, presidential candidate, associate justice, U.S. Supreme Court (1910–16), chief justice (1930–41). A graduate of Brown University and Columbia University Law School, Hughes spent several years in private practice and later was special council to a state commission investigating business fraud. His success in this role led to his election as governor of his native New York (1907–10). A Republican, he was appointed to the U.S. Supreme Court in 1910 by President William Howard TAFT. However, he resigned in 1916 to run for president against Woodrow WILSON, who defeated him. Hughes served as secretary of state (1921–25) in the HARDING and COOLIDGE administrations. When Hughes was nominated for chief justice by President Herbert HOOVER, the nomination was opposed

because of Hughes's past representation of big businesses. Despite his pro-business leanings, Hughes voted in favor of much of the NEW DEAL legislation. He retired in 1941 after serving as chief justice for 11 years.

**Hughes, Howard Robard** *(1869–1924)* American inventor and industrialist. After working in the oil drilling business, Hughes invented a revolutionary cone-shaped drill bit (1908). He later founded the successful Hughes Tool Company, which manufactured his bits and other tools. He was the father of multimillionaire aircraft pioneer Howard HUGHES.

**Hughes, Howard Robard** *(1905–1976)* American industrialist, aviator and film producer. Hughes studied at Rice Institute of Technology and California Institute of Technology, and inherited the family fortune at his father's death in 1924. He went to California to produce motion pictures. His *Two Arabian Knights* won an ACADEMY AWARD in 1928. He brought to fame stars like Jean HARLOW, Paul MUNI and Jane Russell. He founded Hughes Aircraft Company in 1933. In one of his personally designed planes he set a world speed record in 1935, flying at 352 miles per hour. In 1938 he completed a flight around the world in record time. Later he designed the world's largest airplane, which made only one short flight (1947), with Hughes at the controls. He also acquired controlling interest in Trans World Airlines (1959), and purchased major stock interest in Northeast Airlines. He bought enormous tracts of land in and around Las Vegas in the late 1960s, and was instrumental in development of that resort community.

Becoming a recluse in later life, he moved to Nicaragua and England and was widely followed by the media as one of the world's wealthiest and most mysterious figures. He was being flown from Mexico to Houston for medical treatment in early April 1976, when he died en route of liver failure.

**Hughes, Langston** *(1902–1967)* American author. Hughes dropped out of Columbia University and was traveling in Europe when his verse was discovered by Vachel LINDSAY in 1925. Subsequent praise for his work en-

abled him to graduate from Lincoln University in Pennsylvania in 1929, and he worked in New York City as a prominent member of the Harlem literary revival. His free-verse poetry is especially noted for its colloquial rhythms, as in "The Negro Speaks of Rivers" (1926) and "Weary Blues" (1926). His writings include novels and autobiographical works.

**Hughes, Richard** *(1906–1984)* Australian foreign correspondent, historian and Far East expert. Based in Hong Kong, he covered the area for the London *Sunday Times* and wrote articles for *The Economist,* the *Sun* and *Herald* of Melbourne and the *New York Times.* He was one of two journalists permitted to interview British turncoat spies Donald MacLean and Guy BURGESS when they surfaced in Moscow in 1956. Hughes was a model for characters in spy novels by Ian FLEMING and John LE CARRÉ.

**Hughes, Richard Arthur Warren** *(1900–1976)* British author, poet and playwright. After a youth spent traveling and sometimes begging or performing for his keep, Hughes established his reputation with his first novel *The Innocent Voyage* (1929, published in Great Britain as *A High Wind in Jamaica*), which was adapted as a play in 1943 and a film in 1965. This novel and his second, *In Hazard* (1938, published in Great Britain as *In Hazard: A Sea Story*) was a popular work. Critics consider *Human Predicament* a series that consists of *The Fox in the Attic* (1961) and *The Wooden Shepherdess* (1973), his most important work. Volume three was unfinished at Hughes's death. His other works include the poetry *Lines Written Upon First Observing an Elephant Devoured by a Roc* (1922), *Confessio Juvenis: Collected Poems* (1926), and the plays collected in *The Sisters' Tragedy and Other Plays* (1924, reprinted as *Plays,* 1966).

**Hughes, Ted** *(1930–1998)* English poet. Born and raised in Yorkshire, Hughes is perhaps the most prominent poet to have emerged in postwar England. He was named Poet Laureate in 1984, succeeding John BETJEMAN. Educated at Cambridge University, Hughes was married from 1956 to 1963 to poet Sylvia PLATH. Hughes's free verse style is marked by a taut, energetic use of language. He frequently employs violent imagery drawn from the struggle for survival in nature. His major volumes of poems include *The Hawk and the Rain* (1957), *Crow* (1970), *Gaudete* (1977) and *New and Selected Poems* (1982). Hughes also wrote numerous children's stories and has translated a number of East European poets.

**Hughes, William Morris** *(1864–1952)* Prime minister of AUSTRALIA (1917–23). Born in London, Hughes immigrated to Australia in 1884. He founded the Waterside Workers' Federation in Sydney in 1893. In 1894 he was elected to the New South Wales parliament as a Labour MP and transferred to the first federal parliament in 1901. Hughes held office in the Labour government of 1904, and named attorney-general in 1910, and became prime minister in 1915. He left the LABOUR PARTY in 1917 after his military conscription proposals were rejected, but he continued to lead a National Coalition until 1923. Hughes was instrumental in establishing the United Australia Party in 1931. He subsequently served as minister for external affairs (1937–39), attorney-general (1939–41), and minister for the navy (1940–41). Hughes was an intelligent and gifted orator who often aroused controversy as prime minister with his opinionated and emotional stance. During WORLD WAR I, he was regarded as a strong wartime leader, but at the PARIS PEACE CONFERENCE in 1919 he offended many, particularly the Japanese, with his imperialistic attitudes.

**Huie, William Bradford** *(1910–1986)* American author and activist. An Alabama journalist and CIVIL RIGHTS CRUSADER, Huie wrote more than 20 books, including the novel *The Revolt of Mamie Stover* and *The Americanization of Emily* (filmed, 1964). He was also the author of *He Slew the Dreamer,* a controversial biography of Dr. Martin Luther KING Jr.'s convicted assassin, James Earl Ray, and *The Execution of Private Slovik,* about Eddie SLOVIK, the only U.S. serviceman put to death for desertion in the 20th century. During the 1960s Huie emerged as the arch-opponent of the segregationist policies of Alabama governor George C. WALLACE. Huie was often a target of harassment, including cross-burnings.

**Hull, Cordell** *(1871–1955)* American statesman. Born near Byrdstown, Tennessee, Hull became a lawyer and Democratic member of the state legislature before his election to the House of Representatives, where he served from 1907 to 1921 and 1923 to 1931. A supporter and confidant of President Franklin D. ROOSEVELT, Hull resigned from Congress in 1933 to become secretary of state, an office he held until 1944. He was particularly interested in international trade as a method of fostering worldwide accord, instituting the Reciprocal Trade Agreements of 1934 and the "good neighbor policy" toward Latin America. As WORLD WAR II broke out in Europe, Hull urged economic aid for the Allies. After the U.S. entered the war, he fostered coordination among the Allied powers, traveling to Moscow in 1943 to press for greater cooperation. An internationalist in the Woodrow WILSON mode, Hull was convinced that a new world peacekeeping organization was absolutely essential to the creation of a lasting peace. As a delegate to the 1945 San Francisco Conference, Hull was a prime architect of the UNITED NATIONS, a role that brought him the NOBEL PEACE PRIZE later that year.

**Hull, Robert Marvin "Bobby"** *(1939– )* Canadian hockey player. A left wing with the Chicago Black Hawks, Hull was the dominant scorer of the 1960s, leading the National Hockey League in goal-scoring seven times and points three times. His slapshot terrorized goaltenders, but his gentlemanly play won him the Lady Byng Trophy for good sportsmanship in 1966. A member of only one Stanley Cup winner, he lent instant credibility to the fledgling World Hockey Association by being the first name player to "jump" in 1972, signing with the Winnipeg Jets. When that league folded in 1979, he finished his career, with the NHL Jets and Hartford Whalers, retiring in 1980. He was named to the Hockey Hall of Fame in 1983.

**Hulme, T(homas) E(dward)** *(1883–1917)* British literary critic and poet. Although he wrote relatively little and died tragically young, Hulme exercised a major influence on literary MODERNISM. Both his critical essays and his poems were greatly admired by T. S. ELIOT and Ezra POUND, among the notables. Hulme was a literary critic with a philosophical bent and austere, classical standards of aesthetics. He argued against the rhetorical excesses of Romanticism and favored a spare style in both prose and poetry. Hulme's admiration of what he termed hard, dry imagery influenced the poetic school of IMAGISM. Five brief poems by Hulme were published in 1912 in the literary journal *The New Age* under the ironic title *The Complete Poetical Works of T. E. Hulme.* Hulme was killed in WORLD WAR I. His major essays, edited by Herbert Read, were collected in two volumes, *Speculations: Essays on Humanism and the Philosophy of Art* (1924) and *Notes on Language and Style* (1929).

**human engineering** One of several terms that describe the relationship of human users to mechanical and other industrial products. The fields of anthropometrics and ERGONOMICS, which emerged after World War II, overlap the concerns of human engineering, with the latter term increasingly used to describe all such studies.

**Human Genome Project** Scientific project designed to discern and comprehend the entire genetic structure of human beings, involving the identification of the approximately 31,000 genes in the nucleus of a single human cell and the mapping out of the locations of these genes on chromosomes. The genesis of the project stemmed from a series of conferences that occurred between 1985 and 1987, in which scientists from the U.S., Britain, France, Germany and Japan planned the endeavor and conferred about the general procedures they would use. In 1990 the project began in the U.S. under the direction of James WATSON (one of the three initial discoverers of the DNA structure) and financed by the National Institutes of Health and the Department of Energy. Private firms also participated in this effort: Celera Genomics, led by J. Craig Venter, began testing a genome sequencing method that differed from the nationally funded efforts in the hopes of identifying a human genome sequence. Both privately and publicly funded scientists completed their work, and published their results in February 2001.

The goal of the project is to use the knowledge of genetic sequences to determine which genes are associated with physical traits in human beings, particularly those that cause inherited diseases or predispositions to such diseases. Additionally, it is hoped that the knowledge gained and the advances made possible by the project will allow the development of new medicines that capitalize on knowledge of the genetic structure of humans to fight diseases and illnesses.

**Human Rights Watch** U.S.-based human rights group devoted to publishing impartial findings on human rights abuses committed by countries throughout the world. Founded in 1978, it originally was called Helsinki Watch, and served to monitor the compliance of the Communist governments in Eastern Europe with the human rights provisions contained in Basket Three of the 1975 Helsinki Final Act. During the 1980s it expanded its operation to include Americas Watch, which exposed human rights abuses by Latin American governments. By 1988, after similar regionally focused "watch" groups had sprung up for Africa and Asia, their leaders united the associations under the umbrella organization Human Rights Watch.

Since the end of the COLD WAR and the disintegration of the Soviet Union in 1991, Human Rights Watch has evolved into an international nongovernmental organization advocating the protection of civil liberties, women's and children's rights, academic freedom, prisoner's rights, worker's rights and the humane treatment of refugees. In addition to criticizing countries such as China, Serbia, Rwanda, Israel, Sudan and Indonesia for their violation of these rights, Human Rights Watch has also issued reports critical of the U.S., particularly for alleged mistreatment of prisoners and illegal immigrants, and issues relating to police brutality and capital punishment. In 1997 the organization won the NOBEL PEACE PRIZE for its role in organizing the International Campaign to Ban Landmines.

**Hume, George Basil** (1923–1999) Roman Catholic Cardinal. Hume, a prominent Catholic religious leader in modern day Britain, first undertook monastic studies in 1941 at the Benedictine Abbey of St. Laurence. He joined the Benedictine Order in 1945 and was ordained as a priest in 1950. From 1963 to 1976 Hume served as abbot of Ampleforth before being elevated in 1976 as the archbishop of Westminster. He was also made cardinal in 1976 with St. Silvestro in Capite, Italy, as his titular church. Hume holds a curial membership on the Council on Christian Unity.

**Hume, John** (1937–  ) Politician and activist in NORTHERN IRELAND, leader of the Social Democratic and Labour Party (SDLP), and winner of the NOBEL PEACE PRIZE (1998). Born in Londonderry into a blue-collar Catholic family, Hume initially intended to study for the priesthood and enrolled in Saint Patrick's College in Maynooth, Northern Ireland, to prepare for ordination. When his interest in the seminary waned, he became involved in efforts in his city to create a credit union that would enable residents to purchase their own homes.

Hume later participated in the various efforts by the Catholic community to ensure just and fair treatment of its members by Protestant government officials and citizens in Northern Ireland. As Londonderry became one of the leading centers of Catholic activism, Hume helped found and become the first chairman of the SDLP in 1970. In this role he worked to provide Catholics with a political organ to address their grievances at the local and regional level. His election to the parliament of Northern Ireland a year earlier provided the party with effective representation in the governing structure of Northern Ireland. Four years after the founding of the SDLP, Hume joined a coalition government for Northern Ireland, serving as minister of commerce until the short-lived coalition collapsed in 1975.

In 1979 Hume was elected a delegate to the European Parliament, where he attempted to ensure that as European integration increased, it would minimize the division of Northern Ireland from the Irish Republic. Four years later he was elected to the British House of Commons. Hume used all of these positions to further his goals of improving the status of Catholics in Northern Ireland, in reducing the consequences of Ireland's territorial division and in ensuring that the economic prosperity that was the goal of the EUROPEAN UNION would improve economic conditions in Northern Ireland. By the mid-1980s, when it was clear that Londonderry's economy was reviving under the initiatives supported by Hume. He used the rebirth of his district as a model to initiate discussions with SINN FÉIN, the political voice of the IRA, to arrange for a cease-fire in its struggle against the British and their supporters.

Three years after the cease-fire began in August 1994, Hume participated in multilateral peace negotiations among all the major political parties in Northern Ireland. Headed by former U.S. senator George Mitchell, the talks eventually resulted in an agreement between Ireland and Northern Ireland in which both entities agreed to share power in Northern Ireland. For his efforts as head of the SDLP in this endeavor, Hume shared the 1998 Nobel Peace Prize with David TRIMBLE, the leader of the Ulster Unionist Party. In December 2000 Hume left the Northern Ireland assembly for reasons of health. He resigned as chairman of the SDLP following the September 2001 Irish elections in which the SDLP lost heavily to the IRA.

**Humphrey, Hubert Horatio, Jr.** (1911–1978) U.S. senator, vice president of the United States (1965–69). Humphrey graduated from the University of Minnesota in 1939, earned an M.A. from Louisiana University in 1940, and worked on a number of jobs, before he became state campaign

*Senator Hubert H. Humphrey, Jr.* (LIBRARY OF CONGRESS, PRINTS AND PHOTOGRAPHS DIVISION)

director for Franklin D. ROOSEVELT'S 1944 presidential campaign. In 1945 he was elected mayor of Minneapolis, then served as a U.S. senator from 1948 to 1964 and again from 1971 to 1978. A progressive Democrat, he became assistant majority leader of the Senate in 1961, and was instrumental in passing the historic CIVIL RIGHTS ACT OF 1964. In 1964 he was Lyndon B. JOHNSON'S vice presidential running mate, then served as vice president from 1965 to 1969.

After Johnson declared his intention not to seek reelection in 1968, Humphrey announced his candidacy. He won the Democratic presidential nomination in 1968 in a race marred by violent protests against the VIETNAM WAR and the political establishment, and by the assassination of rival candidate Robert F. KENNEDY. He narrowly lost the election to Richard M. NIXON but continued to remain active in political life, later winning reelection to the Senate. Humphrey received numerous awards during his life. His protégé, Walter MONDALE, served as vice president under President Jimmy CARTER and was the Democratic presidential candidate in 1984.

**Hundred Days** The "Hundred Days" is a term used to denote the 1933 special session of Congress in which much of President Franklin D. ROOSEVELT'S NEW DEAL legislation was passed. When Roosevelt was inaugurated in March 1933 the U.S. economy had effectively ceased functioning and the country (with much of the world) was in the throes of the GREAT DEPRESSION. Roosevelt boldly called Congress into a special session that produced sweeping economic and social legislation, to aid victims of the depression, and installed economic reforms. Roosevelt's unofficial advisers—his BRAIN TRUST—developed many of these programs. Banks were closed for a "bank holiday" and only solvent institutions were permitted to reopen, which rebuilt confidence in the nation's banking system. Congress also passed the Securities Act of 1933, regulating the issue of corporate stock; the NATIONAL INDUSTRIAL RECOVERY ACT (which established the NRA, the NATIONAL RECOVERY ADMINISTRATION), regulating business, including minimum wages and maximum hours; the CIVILIAN

CONSERVATION CORPS (CCC), which put the unemployed to work in conservation projects; and the AGRICULTURAL ADJUSTMENT ADMINISTRATION (AAA) to aid farmers. In 1935 Congress approved another notable group of laws, including the WORKS PROGRESS ADMINISTRATION (WPA, later renamed the Work Projects Administration), the NATIONAL LABOR RELATIONS ACT and the SOCIAL SECURITY ACT. The 1935 session is known as the "Second Hundred Days."

**Hung, Rham (Pham Van Thien)** *(1913–1988)* Vietnamese communist political figure, premier of VIETNAM from June 1987 until his death. Hung had served for seven years as interior minister, supervising Vietnam's huge internal security system. He played key roles from 1960 to 1975 in the war against the U.S.-backed government of South Vietnam.

**Hungarian Civil War of 1921** Former Austro-Hungarian emperor CHARLES I, exiled in Switzerland since 1919, returned to regain his throne, calling on regent Miklós HORTHY DE NAGYBÁNYA I to step down in March 1921, but opposition to Charles was violent and he departed. He returned in October at Odenburg, Hungary, and marched with troops on Budapest. Government troops repulsed them and arrested Charles, who was exiled to Madeira while the Hungarian Diet nullified all Hapsburg claims to the Hungarian throne.

**Hungarian Revolution of 1918** Defeats and food shortages during World War I led Hungarian leftists and nationalists to agitate for independence from Austrian (Hapsburg) rule. The Hungarian diet called its troops home, Count Mihály Károlyi (1875–1955) headed a liberal national council and Hungarians demanded an end to the war. Emperor CHARLES I made Károlyi premier (October 31, 1918) and a radical-socialist coalition came to power. But the ethnic nationalism of Slovaks, Serbs and Romanians threatened the state and Károlyi accepted peace terms with France, withdrawing Hungarian troops; Serb troops occupied the south, Romanians moved into Transylvania and Czechoslovakian soldiers into Slovakia. The Austro-Hungarian

monarchy had collapsed, and on November 16, 1918, the national council declared HUNGARY a republic.

**Hungarian Uprising** Unplanned revolt by the people of Hungary against Soviet control of their nation and against their own communist government; occurred from October 23 to November 4, 1956. Hungarian students, workers and others gathered in Budapest on October 23 to demonstrate, demanding economic reforms, free elections, the withdrawal of Soviet forces and the reinstatement of Imre NAGY, the anti-Soviet premier who had been forced from office the previous year. Violence erupted when police fired on the peaceful demonstrators. As the uprising spread throughout the country, the Soviets at first seemed to favor cooperation with a new regime and a new party administration. Nagy was recalled as premier on October 24 and soon proclaimed his nation's neutrality, an end to Hungary's participation in the WARSAW PACT, an end to its one-party state and the release of the imprisoned anticommunist Cardinal József MINDSZENTY. János KÁDÁR became party secretary. Meanwhile, revolutionary councils formed throughout the country, seized its political institutions and factories in the name of the new Hungary, and Soviet forces began to withdraw. The changes were too drastic for Kádár, who left Budapest to form a new government in eastern Hungary, and for the Soviets, who, having massed their tanks, returned to the capital on November 4 and ruthlessly destroyed the revolution. While Nagy called in vain for United Nations support, Hungarians fought in the streets. Within weeks, many thousands were killed, wounded or imprisoned, and some 200,000 Hungarians fled the country. Kádár took over and did institute some political and economic reforms, but Hungary's ties to the Soviet Union were not to be severed for more than 30 more years.

**Hungary (Hungarian Republic)** A landlocked country in the Danube Basin of east-central Europe, Hungary today covers an area of 35,910 square miles. Once part of the Austro-Hungarian Empire, it was reduced to its present size after the empire's defeat in WORLD WAR I. Plagued by economic woes and ethnic and class struggles, in 1920 Hungary

## HUNGARY

| 1914 | As part of Austro-Hungarian Empire, Hungary enters World War I on the side of Germany and the Central Powers. |
|---|---|
| 1918 | Hungary becomes an independent republic after end of World War I. |
| 1919 | Béla Kun's Red Terror. |
| 1920 | Adml. Miklós Horthy becomes regent and refuses to allow King Karl to return to Hungary. |
| 1944 | Germans occupy Hungary and begin exterminating Hungary's Jews and Gypsies; Stalin authorizes the formation in Debrecen of a provisional government comprising all the non-fascist parties. |
| 1945 | The last German forces leave Hungary. |
| 1947 | Hungary signs peace treaty with Allied powers, giving up all territories acquired after 1937. |
| 1948 | The Social Democrats are forcibly merged with the communists to form the Hungarian Workers' Party. |
| 1949 | Opposition political parties are outlawed; Roman Catholic primate of Hungary, Cardinal József Mindszenty, sentenced to life imprisonment. |
| 1953 | Imre Nagy becomes premier and introduces liberal and political reform. |
| 1956 | Soviet army invades Hungary; Nagy is executed; János Kádár is made premier. |
| 1967 | Jenö Fock becomes premier. |
| 1968 | The regime initiates a series of reforms known as New Economic Mechanism, decentralizing authority. |
| 1989 | Law passed allowing formation of new political parties; (June) body of Imre Nagy exhumed and reburied after a state funeral on the 31st anniversary of his execution. |
| 1990 | Soviets agree to complete pullout from Hungary. |
| 1991 | Military alliance of the Warsaw Pact ends. |
| 1999 | Hungary joins NATO. |
| 2004 | Hungary joins European Union. |

was invaded by Romanian troops who overthrew a communist regime and placed in power Admiral Miklós HOR-THY. He aligned the country with Nazi GERMANY, which occupied Hungary in 1944. After WORLD WAR II the communists gained control of the government, promoting industrialization and collectivization of agriculture. Poland's defiance of Soviet authority in 1956 led to huge demonstrations in Hungary demanding Soviet withdrawal. The Soviet army intervened, killing thousands of Hungarians and setting up a puppet government under Janós KÁDÁR (see HUNGARIAN UPRISING). The previous reformist prime minister, Imre NAGY, was executed in 1958. Gradually the Kádár regime moved toward economic reforms and a loosening of repressive political controls, and by the 1970s Hungary was regarded as the most liberal country in the Eastern Bloc. Prodemocracy demonstrations in 1988–89 led to approval of the formation of a multiparty democratic system, and a transitional constitution was drafted. In Oct. 1989 Hungary was proclaimed a republic; Nagy was formally rehabilitated and his memory officially honored. After abandoning communism and leaving the Soviet orbit in 1990, Hungary oriented itself toward western Europe, joining the NORTH ATLANTIC TREATY ORGANIZATION (NATO) in 1999 and the EUROPEAN UNION in 2004.

**Hun Sen** (1952– ) Cambodian politician and prime minister (1985– ). Born in the province of Kâmpóng Cham, Hun Sen became interested in national politics in high school as a result of the 1970 military coup against Prince Norodom SIHANOUK, the ruler of CAMBODIA. Not long after Sihanouk's replacement by a pro-U.S. regime, Hun Sen entered the ranks of a pro-Sihanouk coalition including the KHMER ROUGE, a Communist guerrilla group that was backed by the government of North Vietnam. During the final assault by the KHMER ROUGE on the capital of Phnom Penh, during the final stages of the CAMBO-DIAN CIVIL WAR in 1975. Hun Sen was

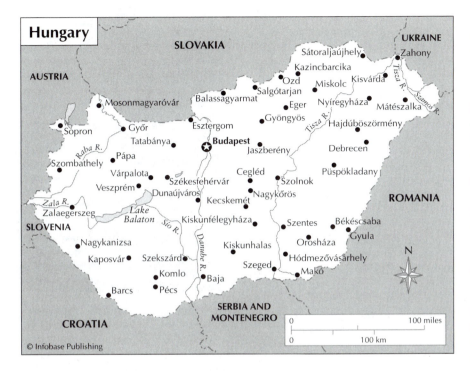

Hungary

severely wounded and lost the use of one of his eyes.

As a reward for his loyalty, the new Khmer Rouge government appointed Hun Sen a regimental commander and stationed him in eastern Cambodia. However, his unit's wartime affiliation with the Vietnamese marked him as suspect, causing him to flee to Vietnam to avoid arrest.

The Vietnamese government placed him in a leadership role in the Khmer National United Front for Salvation (KNUFNS), an anti–Khmer Rouge organization formed by Cambodian refugees who had also fled to Vietnam. By December 1978, when Vietnam invaded Cambodia, Hun Sen was named to the central committee of KNUFNS, which took control of Cambodia in January of 1979, when the Khmer Rouge were toppled. Hun Sen quickly moved to establish the People's Republic of Kâmpuchéa (PRK) in Cambodia, in which he initially served as foreign minister. Soon after renaming the country, he established the single national party that would control all facets of government—the Kâmpuchéan People's Revolutionary Party (KPRP), and began his advancement in the new regime, by 1981 he had ascended to the premiership.

When Vietnam withdrew its troops from Cambodia in 1989, the Khmer

Rouge fought PRK forces until both sides initialed a peace agreement two years later and transferred temporary control of the state to the UN and a national council representing all political factions in Cambodia. Hun Sen moderated his ideological position in 1990 by abandoning the pursuit of socialism and changing the name of the KPRP to the Cambodian People's Party (CPP). After the UN and the governing council had restored order to Cambodia, national elections were held in 1993 to select representatives to the Cambodian parliament. Eventually the CPP and FUNCINPEC, a monarchist party committed to restoring Sihanouk to power, agreed to form a coalition government with FUNCINPEC leader Norodom Ranriddh (the son of Prince Sihanouk) and Hun Sen sharing prime ministerial duties. In the division of governmental ministries, Hun Sen made certain that CPP officials obtained control of the Cambodian army, police force and key provincial posts throughout the country.

In 1997, after four years of deteriorating relations between the CPP and FUNCINPEC, Hun Sen deposed Ranriddh. In response to vigorous international protests, Hun Sen announced that national elections would be held in July 1998 under international supervision. As a result of those elections Hun

Sen joined a coalition government with his old foes in FUNCINPEC, this time without a power-sharing arrangement within the prime minister's position, which Hun Sen occupied by himself.

## Hunt brothers silver scandal

Commodities scandal in which the Hunt family of Texas attempted to manipulate the world's silver supply. The three wealthy Hunt brothers. Nelson, Herbert and Lamar, purchased silver commodities and made enormous profits as the price of silver skyrocketed. In March of 1980 the Hunts were either unwilling or unable to pay $100 million of margin calls from their commodity brokers, which caused panic selling in silver commodities. The price of silver dropped just as precipitously, from $52 to $10.50 an ounce, and the Hunts reportedly lost over $235 million. Although government investigations were conducted, no criminal charges were brought against the three brothers, who did, however, have to contend with lawsuits from a number of investors who claimed to have been harmed by their manipulations.

## Hunter, Evan (1926–2005) American novelist and screenwriter. Hunter achieved success with his second novel *The Blackboard Jungle* (1954, filmed 1955), which reflected his experiences teaching at an inner-city vocational school in New York. His popular novels—among them *Mothers and Daughters (1961)*, *Last Summer* (1968, filmed 1969), *Love, Dad* (1981) and *Lizzie* (1984)—often depict disenfranchised American youth. His screenplays include *Strangers When We Meet* (1960), based on his novel of the same name; *The Birds* (1963), based on a short story by Daphne DU MAURIER and directed by Alfred HITCHCOCK; and *The Chisholms* (1980). Hunter has written a successful series of detective novels under the pseudonym Ed McBain and has also published under the names Hunt Collins and Richard Marsten. The Mystery Writers of America awarded him its Grand Master Award for lifetime achievement in 1986, and in 1998 he received a Cartier Diamond Dagger from the Crime Writers Association of Great Britain, the first American to ever do so.

## Huntington, Anna Hyatt (1876–1973) American sculptor. Born in

Cambridge, Massachusetts, Huntington studied at the Art Students League in New York City. Huntington is noted for her realistic studies of animals, such as the Bronzes *Reaching Jaguar* (1926, Metropolitan Museum of Art) and *Fighting Elephants*. Among her public sculptures are an equestrian statue of Joan of Arc that stands on New York's Riverside Drive and a figure of El Cid, also in the city. Other large public pieces are located in Gloucester, Mass., Seville, Spain, and Buenos Aires, Argentina.

**Huntley, Chet (Chester Robert Huntley)** *(1911–1974)* American news commentator. Known for his serious, straightforward demeanor, Huntley worked as a newsman for CBS and ABC, but it was for his stint with NBC from 1955 to 1970 that he is best remembered. During this time he co-anchored the *Huntley-Brinkley Report,* an evening news program, with David BRINKLEY. Huntley was later the anchor for syndicated news commentaries for Horizon Communications (1970–74). At its peak, the *Huntley-Brinkley Report* reached an audience of over 17,000,000 viewers.

**Hurley, Patrick J.** *(1883–1963)* American lawyer and diplomat. Hurley served as secretary of war under President Herbert HOOVER from 1929 to 1933. Hurley was the personal representative of the United States to the Soviet Union in November–December 1942 and to Egypt, Syria, Lebanon, Iraq, Iran, Palestine, Saudi Arabia, India, China and Trans-Jordan in 1943. He was the American ambassador to China in 1944, where he strongly criticized the U.S. diplomats in that country for undermining the position of Generalissimo CHIANG KAI-SHEK. He negotiated an agreement between Mexico and five expropriated oil companies in 1940 and was the Republican candidate for U.S. senator from New Mexico in 1946 and 1948.

**Hurley, Ruby** *(1909–1980)* Black American civil rights activist. During the 1950s and 1960s, as an official of the NAACP, Hurley helped lead the CIVIL RIGHTS MOVEMENT in the American South. Known to her associates as "the queen of civil rights," she played a leading part in investigations of racial violence and in the legal struggles of

black students who sought to enter previously all-white Southern universities.

**Hurok, Sol (Solomon Hurok)** *(1888–1974)* American impresario and theatrical manager. Born in Russia, he immigrated to the U.S. in 1906. He worked at a number of menial jobs before arranging concerts for various labor groups, his first attempts (1911) at putting together performances. During his career, Hurok presented thousands of artists and companies in performances and tours. Among the artists whose work he sponsored were the dancers Anna PAVLOVA and Isadora DUNCAN, singers Jan PEERCE and Marian ANDERSON, musicians Artur RUBINSTEIN, Andres SEGOVIA, Benny GOODMAN and Van CLIBURN, and such companies as the Comédie Française, the Old Vic, the Royal Ballet and the Bolshoi Ballet. His 1946 autobiography is titled *Impresario.*

**Hurst, Fannie** *(1889–1968)* American novelist. Born in Hamilton, Ohio, she graduated from Washington University in 1909. She is known for her popular sentimental tales, often of women in distress over romance or marriage. He novels include *Stardust* (1919), *Lummox* (1923), *Back Street* (1931), *Imitation of Life* (1932) and *Anitra's Dance* (1934). Hurst was also the author of theater treatments and screenplays.

**Hurston, Zora Neale** *(1901–1960)* American author. Hurston began publishing short stories and essays while studying anthropology at Barnard College, in 1928 becoming that school's first black graduate. She then researched folk traditions and published ethnographic studies that include *Mules and Man* (1935) and *Tell My Horse* (1938). Winner of Rosenwald (1934) and Guggenheim (1936–37) fellowships, she became the most prolific black writer of the 1930s. Her novels include *Jonah's Gourd Vine* (1937) and *Seraph and the Suwanee* (1948).

**Husák, Gustáv** *(1913–1991)* President of CZECHOSLOVAKIA (1975–89). A leader of the 1944 Slovak uprising against the Nazis, after the war Husák held party and government posts until purged by Joseph STALIN. He was reha-

*Folklorist and author Zora Neale Hurston. 1935* (LOMAX COLLECTION, LIBRARY OF CONGRESS, PRINTS AND PHOTOGRAPHS DIVISION)

bilitated after a decade in prison; following the SOVIET INVASION OF CZECHOSLOVAKIA in 1968, he replaced the liberal Alexander DUBČEK as party secretary. A hardliner, he was made president of the country in 1975, holding the post until 1989, when he was succeeded by Václav HAVEL, the first noncommunist president of Czechoslovakia in four decades. In 1990 Husák was expelled from the Communist Party.

**Hussein** *(1935–1999)* King of JORDAN (1952–99). Educated at the Sandhurst military academy in Britain, Hussein succeeded his father, who had been forced to abdicate because of his mental illness. A moderate, pro-Western Arab with close personal ties to Britain and the U.S., he took steps to modernize his country. Although unsympathetic to the left-wing Arab nationalism of Egyptian president NASSER, he allied Jordan with EGYPT and attacked ISRAEL in the SIX-DAY WAR (1967). Badly defeated, Jordan lost the WEST BANK and Jerusalem to Israel. The country became a haven for Palestinian refugees, and the PALESTINE LIBERATION ORGANIZATION (PLO) used Jordan as a base from which they launched guerrilla attacks on Israel without Hussein's approval. Hussein's attempts to control the guerrillas led to the JORDANIAN *Civil* WAR OF 1970–71; nevertheless, he was able to expel the PLO. He refused to endorse the **Camp**

*King Hussein of Jordan. 1979* (Richard Mellou/
Corbis Sygma)

David accords (see Camp David Talks),
but sought to use his influence with
the PLO and other Arab nations to
work toward a peaceful solution of the
Arab-Israeli conflict. Kin Hussein supported Iraq during the Persian Gulf
War (1990–91). In 1994 Hussein
signed a peace treaty with Prime Minister Yitzhak Rabin of Israel. Before his
death in 1999, Hussein worked to improve Palestinian-Israeli relations and
aided in the negotiations for the **Wye
River Memorandum** in October 1998.

**Hussein, Saddam** *(1937– )* President of Iraq (1979–2003). A Sunni
Moslem, Saddam Hussein joined the
Ba'ath Party in 1957. He was involved
in the 1959 attempt on the life of Iraqi
leader Abd al-Karim Kassem. Sentenced to death, he escaped to Egypt,
returning in 1964 to organize the civilian wing of the Ba'ath. He rose to become deputy secretary-general of the
party in 1966 and vice chairman of the
Revolutionary Command Council in
1969. As president of Iraq, Hussein
followed an aggressive, militaristic policy aimed at making Iraq—and himself—the strongest power in the Arab
world. A territorial dispute with neighboring Iran led to Hussein's invasion of
Iran and the subsequent bloody eight-
year Iran-Iraq War, which ended in a
stalemate. In this conflict, Hussein
used poison gas on the Iranians and
also against the Kurds of his own country. On August 2, 1990, Hussein
launched a surprise invasion of Kuwait,
bringing that country under his control
in a matter of days (see Persian Gulf
War). Hussein was condemned by the
United Nations, and a multinational
coalition of Arab and Western nations,
led by the U.S. under President George
H. W. Bush, sent forces to prevent an

Iraqi invasion of Saudi Arabia. Comparing the Iraqi dictator to Adolf
Hitler, Bush repeatedly called on Hussein to withdraw from Kuwait; despite
a further buildup of U.S. and Allied
forces and a UN deadline for withdrawal (Jan. 15, 1991), Hussein refused. On Jan. 16, the Allies launched
a bombing campaign against military
targets (Operation Desert Storm). Hussein responded by launching Scud missile attacks on Saudi Arabia and Israel,
but to little avail. Suffering a swift and
humiliating defeat after the coalition's
ground invasion of Kuwait and Iraq in
late February 1991, Hussein was
forced to sue for peace. With his army
effectively destroyed and much of Iraq
in ruins, Hussein's future was uncertain. Various Iraqi groups—disaffected
soldiers, Shi'ite Muslims and Kurds—
openly rebelled against Hussein, but
Hussein quelled the rebellion and
maintained his grip on Iraq despite international sanctions. In 1998 Hussein
forced the departure of the United Nations Special Commission (UNSCOM),
an international team sent to verify that
Iraq had abandoned its efforts to acquire weapons of mass destruction
(WMDs). In March 2003, after U.S.
president George W. Bush insisted that
Iraq had WMDs, a U.S.-led coalition
invaded Iraq and occupied the country,
forcing Hussein to go into hiding. He
was caught near the city of Tikrit in
December 2003 and was put on trial in
2005 for war crimes.

**Hussein bin Dato Onn** *(1922–
1990)* Malaysian politician, Prime
Minister of Malaysia (1976–81). The
country's third prime minister since independence, Hussein had replaced his
brother-in-law, Abdul Razak, following
Razak's death in 1976. He resigned in
1981 and selected Mahathir Mohamad
to succeed him. The two men broke
with each other in 1988 over Mahathir's attempt to purge his opponents
in the ruling United Malays National
Organization.

**Husseini, Faisal** *(1940–2001)* Founder of the General Union of Palestinian
Students (GUPS, 1959), a member of
the Palestinian delegation to the Middle East Peace Conference in Madrid
and chief Palestinian Liberation Organization (PLO) representative in
Jerusalem. Born into a prominent Pales-

tinian Arab family. Husseini became involved as a teenager in Arab efforts to
expel the Israelis from what Arab nationalists regarded as Arab land in the
former British Mandate of Palestine.
While living in Cairo, he later founded
a group designed to educated Palestinian Arab students. After he left Cairo in
the mid-1960s Husseini studied military science at the Syrian Military College (B.A., 1967) and joined Fatah, a
militant faction of the PLO.

In 1964 he returned to Jerusalem
and became a prominent participant in
Palestinian protests against the creation
of new Israeli settlements in the West
Bank and Gaza Strip after Israel gained
those territories in the Six-Day War of
1967 and was repeatedly arrested by
Israel authorities. In 1987, when the
first Palestinian Intifada (see Intifada I)
or "uprising" began in an effort to end
the Israeli presence in the West Bank
and Gaza, Husseini emerged as the
chief spokesman of the PLO. Unlike
many PLO officials, Husseini tempered
his militancy with efforts to understand his Israeli foes and to convey to
them what he and his followers perceived as the injustice of the Israeli
presence in the West Bank and Gaza.
He learned Hebrew and regularly engaged Israeli leaders and media personalities on radio and television
shows in an effort to present the PLO
and Palestinian Arab perspective. He
headed a Palestinian delegation that
met with U.S. secretary of state James
Baker shortly after the 1991 Persian
Gulf War in an effort to jump-start the
Arab-Israeli peace negotiations the
U.S. had promised to promote at the
end of the conflict. On the other hand,
throughout the 1990s he defended
Palestinian suicide bombings as part of
"a war of independence." He died of a
heart attack on May 31, 2001.

**Husserl, Edmund** *(1859–1938)* German philosopher. Husserl is regarded as
the founder of the highly influential
20th-century philosophical school of
Phenomenology. Basically, phenomenology acknowledges that human
thought is capable only of subjective, ex-
periential analyses of reality—but it
seeks to heighten the validity of such
analyses by rigidly excluding personal
value systems. Husserl, who taught philosophy at the Universities of Göttingen
and Freiberg, wrote numerous books,

including *Logical Investigations* (1900–1901), *Ideas* (1913), *The Phenomenology of Internal Time-Consciousness* (1928) and *Formal and Transcendental Logic* (1929). His writings greatly influenced Martin HEIDEGGER, Jean-Paul SARTRE and the development of EXISTENTIALISM.

**Huston, John** *(1906–1987)* American film director, writer and actor. The son of actor **Walter Huston**, John Huston's early years were full of restless travels and unfulfilled ambitions. He toured in vaudeville, rode in the Mexican cavalry, boxed, and studied painting in Paris. He collaborated on several successful screenplays before directing *The Maltese Falcon* (1941), one of the great directorial debuts in screen history. The film's cynical tone, claustrophobic interiors and ill-fated characters prefigured such later Huston classics as *The Treasure of the Sierra Madre* (1948, for which he won the best writer and best director ACADEMY AWARDS), *Key Largo* (1948), *The Asphalt Jungle* (1950), *The Misfits* (1960) and *Wise Blood* (1979). Humphrey BOGART was the quintessential antihero in several of Huston's early films, and won his only Academy Award in Huston's *The African Queen* (1951). Huston served in the Signal Corps during WORLD WAR II, producing two classic wartime documentaries—*The Battle of San Pietro* (1943), one of the screen's finest antiwar statements, and *Let There Be Light* (1946), which chronicled the effects of battle fatigue on combat veterans, and which was suppressed by the government until 1980. Indeed, many of Huston's critical and box-office failures of the late 1950s and 1960s reveal inconsistencies of tone and technique. Yet he rebounded with a moving adventure film, *The Man Who Would Be King* (1975), adapted from a story by Rudyard KIPLING, and directed his daughter **Anjelica Huston** in an Academy Award–winning performance in *Prizzi's Honor* (1985). He spent his last years in Mexico and Ireland but continued to work despite increasing ill-health, directing a faithful adaptation of James JOYCE's *The Dead* (1987) shortly before his own death.

**Hutchins, Robert Maynard** *(1899–1977)* American educator. Appointed president of the University of Chicago at age 29, Hutchins revolutionized American higher education with his belief that college students should be taught not vocational skills but to reason. Over the next five decades he frequently commented on educational and public policy issues. Leaving the university in 1951, he founded (1954) and headed the Center for the Study of Democratic Institutions, an organization studying social and political questions.

**Hutton, Sir Leonard** *(1916–1990)* English cricketer. In a playing career that lasted from 1934 to 1956 (with a six-year interruption for World War II), he scored a total of 40,000 runs, including 129 centuries. In 1938 he scored 364 runs against the Australian team—a record that stood for 20 years, In 1952, he was appointed the first professional captain of the English national team. The following year he led the team in regaining the Ashes trophy from AUSTRALIA for the first time since 1938, and retained it in 1954–55. Upon his retirement in 1956, he became a cricket commentator for the *Observer* and wrote three books about his experiences.

**Huxley, Aldous** *(1894–1963)* British novelist, essayist and philosopher. Huxley was the descendant of an eminent British family that included the 19th-century Darwinian theorist Thomas Henry Huxley and the 20th-century biologist Julian Huxley. Huxley first gained literary renown for his witty, satiric novels of the 1920s, including *Crome Yellow* (1921), *Antic Hay* (1923), *Those Barren Leaves* (1925) and *Point Counter Point* (1928). During that decade he formed a close friendship with D. H. LAWRENCE with whom Huxley traveled in Italy and France. In 1932 Huxley published his most famous work, BRAVE NEW WORLD, which marked his shift to a more somber, philosophical, novelistic style, further developed in *Eyeless in Gaza* (1936) and *After Many a Summer Dies the Swan* (1940). Huxley, who moved to the United States in 1938, assembled an anthology of worldwide mystical writings, *The Perennial Philosophy* (1945), and an influential study of consciousness expansion through mescalin, *The Doors of Perception* (1954). Huxley died in Los Angeles in 1963.

**Huxley, Andrew Fielding** *(1917– )* English physiologist. Huxley, a grandson of T. H. Huxley and half brother of ALDOUS and JULIAN HUXLEY, graduated in 1938 from Cambridge University, receiving his M.A. there three years later. He is best known for his collaboration with Alan Hodgkin in elucidating the "sodium pump" mechanism by which nerve impulses are transmitted, for which they were awarded, with John Eccles, the NOBEL PRIZE in physiology or medicine (1963). He has also done important work on muscular contraction theory and has been involved in the development of the interference microscope and ultramicrotome. Huxley was reader in experimental biophysics at Cambridge (1959–60), and since 1960 has been Jodrell Professor of Physiology at University College, London. In 1980 he became president of the Royal Society, and in 1983 was admitted to Britain's Order of Merit.

**Huxley, Sir Julian Sorell** *(1887–1975)* English biologist. A grandson of noted Victorian biologist T. H. Huxley, and brother of novelist Aldous HUXLEY, Julian Huxley graduated in zoology from Oxford University in 1909. He did research on sponges at the Naples Zoological Station (1909–10) before taking up the post of lecturer in biology at Oxford (1910–12). From 1912 until 1916 he worked at the Rice Institute, Houston, Texas, where he met the famous American geneticist Hermann Muller. Before returning to Oxford to take up the post of senior demonstrator in zoology (1919–25) he saw war service in Italy. He was next appointed professor of zoology at King's College, London (1925–27), resigning from this post to devote more time to writing and research.

Huxley was a keen ornithologist. In the 1930s he was involved in the production of natural-history films, the most notable of which was the highly praised *Private Life of the Gannett* (1934). One of the leading popularizers of science of modern times (especially the years before and just after World War II), Huxley spent much of his life explaining advances in natural science to the layman and in advocating the application of science to the benefit of mankind. To many he is best remembered as a most capable and lucid educationalist, but Huxley was also eminent in many other fields.

In 1946 he was appointed the first director-general of UNESCO, a post he held for two years. As an administrator, he also did much to transform the Zoological Society's collections at Regent's Park (London Zoo). Viewing man as "the sole agent of further evolutionary advance on this planet," he caused considerable controversy by advocating the deliberate physical And mental improvement of the human race through eugenics. Huxley's biological research was also extensive, including work on animal hormones, physiology, ecology, and animal (especially bird) behavior as it relates to evolution. He was president of the Institute of Animal Behavior and the originator of the term *ethology,* now used to define the science of animal behavior. He also introduced several other scientific terms, such as cline and clade. Huxley was knighted in 1958.

**Hu Yaobang** *(1915–1989)* Chinese political leader. He joined the Communist Party in 1933 and, following the communist revolution in 1949, held a series of party posts. Purged during the CULTURAL REVOLUTION of 1966, he was rehabilitated in 1973, became a member of the politburo in 1978 and was named to the chairmanship of the Communist Party in 1980. Widely regarded as a protege of DENG XIAOPING, Hu supported Deng's reform policies and was expected to succeed him. However, the student rebellions of 1986 forced his resignation early in 1987.

**Hyde, Douglas** *(1860– 1949)* Irish playwright, author and first president of IRELAND (1938–45). A member of the Protestant Ascendancy, Hyde was a leading figure in the IRISH LITERARY REVIVAL, and committed to promoting the Irish language. He founded the Gaelic League in 1893 and was its president until 1915. His play *Casadh* (1901) was performed by the Irish Literary Theatre and was the first play in Irish professionally performed. Hyde served as vice president of the ABBEY THEATRE and often collaborated with Lady GREGORY and W. B. YEATS. Hyde's other works include *Love Songs of Connacht* (1893) and *A Literary History of Ireland* (1892). In recognition of his services to Irish language and culture, in 1938 he was elected Ireland's first president, a largely ceremonial but prestigious post.

**hydrogen bomb** By far the most destructive weapon developed during the 20th century, the hydrogen bomb (H-bomb) can produce an explosion much more powerful than that of an ATOM BOMB. Whereas the atom bomb releases energy by fission, splitting the heavy uranium atom, the H-bomb produces its destructive force through the fusion of hydrogen atoms, the lightest atoms. Scientists recognized the theoretical possibility of hydrogen atom fusion as early as 1922. During WORLD WAR II, U.S. and Allied scientists concentrated on developing an atom bomb using uranium, which presented fewer technical problems (see MANHATTAN PROJECT). The Germans did preliminary work on a hydrogen bomb, attempting to produce the "heavy water" needed for the bomb in Norway. After the war ended, expert opinion in the West was split over the issue of whether to develop a hydrogen bomb. After the USSR exploded its first atom bomb in 1949, President TRUMAN ordered work on the hydrogen bomb; the Soviets (whose research was led by physicist Andrei SAKHAROV) also raced to build a hydrogen bomb. The first H-bomb was tested by the U.S. on November 1, 1952, at the Pacific atoll of Eniwetok; it produced an explosion equal to 12 megatons (million tons) of TNT. The Soviets tested their bomb a few months later. Britain tested its first hydrogen bomb in 1957. American H-bomb tests during the 1950s at BIKINI atoll and other sites proved the immense destructive force of the bomb.

During the 1950s, there was great fear throughout the world that there might be a Third World War between the U.S. and USSR, in which the use of H-bombs could cause destruction on an unprecedented scale. Radioactive fallout from H-bomb tests proved that the initial explosion wasn't the only danger of atomic warfare; the fallout from such a war could result in millions of other deaths over a long period of time. There were at least 500 H-bomb tests before the NUCLEAR TEST BAN TREATY of 1963 ended aboveground hydrogen bomb testing by the two superpowers and Britain. China and France, however, developed their own H-bombs in 1967 and 1968, respectively, and continued to test bombs above ground. Despite the nuclear nonproliferation treaty (effective in 1970) banning the development or acquisition of H-bombs by other nations, several other nations may possess the

*Hydrogen bomb test* (LIBRARY OF CONGRESS, PRINTS AND PHOTOGRAPHS DIVISION)

bomb or have the technology and materials necessary to build it. The end of the COLD WAR brought new hope that the H-bomb will never be used. However, there are fears that the bomb could fall into the hands of international terrorists.

**Hyland, L(awrence) A. (Pat)** *(1897–1989)* Pioneer in RADAR technology and aircraft communications equipment. As vice president and chief executive of Hughes Aircraft Co. (1955–76), and president and chairman (1976–84) following the death of founder Howard HUGHES Hyland helped build the firm into the largest U.S. military electronics company and a leading builder of communications satellites.

**Hynek, J(osef) Allen** *(1910–1986)* U.S. astronomer. Hynek gained wide recognition during the more than two decades (1948–69) he served as a consultant to a U.S. Air Force research project regarding unidentified flying objects. He came to believe that reports of UFO's were to be taken more seriously than the air force was willing to take them. In his 1972 book *The UFO Experience* Hynek coined the phrase, "close encounters of the third kind." He subsequently served as technical adviser on the 1977 Steven SPIELBERG film of the same name.

# I

**Iacocca, Lee (Lido Anthony Iacocca)** *(1924– )* American automobile executive. An innovator in automotive engineering and marketing, Iacocca took over the financially distressed Chrysler Corporation in 1978 and was primarily responsible for transforming it into a profitable company by 1982. He began his career as a mechanical engineer, joined the Ford Motor Company and became a corporate vice president and general manager of the Ford division (1960) and president (1970). He introduced successful new models at Ford and introduced new fuel-efficient cars as head of Chrysler Corporation. In 1992 Iacocca retired from the Chrysler Corporation.

**Ia Drang** Valley in northwestern Vietnam, southwest of Pleiku, near the Cambodian border; site of the first major battle between the U.S. and North Vietnamese armies during the VIETNAM WAR. On November 14, 1965, 400 men of the U.S. 1st Batallion, 7th Cavalry, were surprised in the Ia Drang Valley by more than 2,000 North Vietnamese troops. Although heavily outnumbered at first, the Americans were successfully reinforced, and the North Vietnamese disengaged, some retreating across the border into Cambodia and others fleeing into the jungle. On March 10, 1975, the North Vietnamese army launched their final offensive against South Vietnam from a few miles south of the Ia Drang Valley.

**Ibárruri, Dolores Gómez** *(1895–1989)* Spanish Communist political figure and partisan known as "La Pasionaria." Ibárruri won fame with her impassioned oratory during the SPANISH CIVIL WAR (1936–39) in defense of the Republican cause. She was one of the founders of the Spanish Communist Party in 1920. With the outbreak of the 1936 revolt by army commander General Francisco FRANCO and his troops, Ibárruri gave a renowned radio speech in which she told Spaniards, "It is better to die on your feet than to live on your knees! They shall not pass!" The last phrase, borrowed from the French slogan at VERDUN in WORLD WAR I, became the rallying cry of the republic. She left SPAIN in 1937 shortly before the republic fell to Franco, and fled to the USSR, where she lived until 1977. After Franco's death she returned to Spain and was elected to the Spanish parliament. At her death she was honorary president of the Spanish Communist Party.

**Ibert, Jacques** *(1890–1962)* French composer. He studied at the Paris Conservatory, where he was a student of Gabriel FAURÉ. He won the Prix de Rome in 1919, later returning to the Italian city as director of its French Academy from 1937 to 1955. Thereafter (1955–57), he directed the Paris Opera and the Opéra-Comique. Lively and melodic in the French tradition, his music proved to be quite popular with the public. His best known piece is probably *Escales* (*Ports of Call*, 1924), an orchestral suite that evoked his life while a French sailor in World War I. Other popular works are the orchestral *Divertissement* and the woodwind quintet *Trois pièces brèves* (both 1930) and the concerto for saxophone (1935). Among his many other compositions are ballets, operas, songs, chamber music and symphonic poems.

**IBM (International Business Machines)** Leading American international corporation. IBM was founded in 1914 when Thomas J. Watson, Sr., a former executive of the National Cash Register Company, put together several small firms to create the Computing-Tabulating-Recording Company. The firm was a manufacturer of scales and time clocks, which gradually expanded into production of other types of business equipment. In 1924 the present name, International Business Machines Corp. (IBM), was adopted. Under Watson, IBM grew on strength of an aggressive sales and service orientation. IBM's involvement with design began when Thomas J. Watson Jr. returned to the company in 1945 after service in World War II. He became president in 1952 and chief executive officer in 1956. Watson's acquaintance with architect and industrial designer Eliot Noyes led to his being given various design assignments and, eventually, general responsibility for all IBM design. Noyes was the designer of postwar IBM electric typewriters, including the 1961 Selectric model that became a virtual universal standard, while the punch card (now commonly known as an "IBM card") became a standard format for data storage and manipulation. As IBM entered into computer development (with the 1943 Harvard Mark I), the visual design of the enclosures and consoles gave IBM products an identity and air of quality that helped push the firm into a leadership role. Noyes's advice and influence brought about an extraordinary level of design quality in all IBM products. Marcel Breuer, Ludwig Mies van der Rohe, Edward Larrabee Barnes, and Eero Saarinen are among the architects who have designed for IBM. Charles Eames was the designer of a number of IBM exhibits and produced a variety of educational films that aided understanding of the complex theories behind the function of IBM computer products. Although IBM failed to obtain to a position of dominance in the personal computer market in the 1980s and 1990s, it did develop server platforms to capitalize on the emerging business and consumer applications of the Internet.

**Ibn Saud, Abd al-Aziz** (*ca. 1880–1953*) Founder and king (1932–53) of Saudi Arabia. Born in Riyadh, Ibn Saud was an adherent of the Wahabi branch of Sunni Islam. During his youth, the Turkish-supported house of Rashid controlled most of Arabia, and he and his family were forced to live in exile in Kuwait (1891–1902). In 1902, Ibn Saud organized Arab resistance and, with his army, seized Riyadh. By 1912 he was in control of central Arabia, and in 1913 he expelled the Turks from eastern Arabia. In 1924–25, he defeated his rival Hussein Ibn Ali, captured the cities of Jedda, Medina and Mecca and proclaimed himself king of Hijaz and Najd. Solidifying his power over the Arabian Peninsula, he renamed his kingdom Saudi Arabia in 1932. Ibn Saud granted oil concessions to American companies in the 1930s, and the riches that flowed from his nation's oil wells made it one of the wealthiest countries in the world. During World War II, he was officially neutral but favored the Allied cause. At his death in 1953 he was succeeded by his son Saud.

**ICBM** An intercontinental ballistic missile (ICBM) is a land-launched missile that can deliver a nuclear warhead more than 3,000 nautical miles. American ICBMs include the Titan and Minuteman; Soviet ICBMs included the Sego, Sinner, Spanker, Satan, Stiletto and Sickle.

**Iceland** (**Republic of Iceland**) The volcanic island of Iceland, covering an

area of 39,758 square miles, is located in the North Atlantic Ocean approximately 186 miles east of Greenland, 559 miles west of Norway and 497 miles north of Scotland. In 1918 Iceland achieved full sovereignty but remained under the Danish Crown. After a friendly occupation by Britain and the U.S. during World War II, the country declared its independence in 1944, and Sveinn Bjornsson became the first pres-

ident. Iceland became a founding member of NATO in 1949. Conflict with Britain over fishing limits led to incidents at sea during the Cod War of 1972–76, which ended in compromise. Iceland declared itself a nuclear-free zone in 1985 after mounting opposition to the U.S./NATO base on the island. In 1994, through the European Economic Area agreement, Iceland gained full access to the European Union market.

| ICELAND | |
|---|---|
| 1918 | Iceland achieves full self-government under the Danish Crown. |
| 1940 | British forces occupy Iceland after Germany invades Denmark; U.S. troops take over in 1941. |
| 1944 | Iceland proclaims itself a sovereign republic with a new constitution. |
| 1949 | Iceland joins NATO. |
| 1975 | Iceland extends territorial limits to 322 km (200 mi), triggering third Cod War. |
| 1994 | The agreement on a European Economic Area (EEA) takes effect, giving Iceland full access to the internal market of the European Union (EU). |

**Ickes, Harold LeClaire** *(1874–1952)* American statesman and a leading figure in the NEW DEAL of the 1930s. Born in rural Pennsylvania, Ickes attended the University of Chicago, earning a law degree in 1907. A crusading reformer as a newspaper reporter and as a lawyer, he was extremely active in Progressive Republican politics in the midwest. In 1933 President Franklin D. ROOSEVELT appointed Ickes—an avid conservationist—secretary of the interior, a post he held for 13 years. "Honest Harold" reformed the notoriously corrupt department into a model of government efficiency, helping to conserve the nation's natural resources and opposing overexploitation by private industry. As head of the PUBLIC WORKS ADMINISTRATION he oversaw the spending of some $6 billion on various public works programs. Following a political dispute, Ickes resigned from President TRUMAN's cabinet in 1946. His books include *The New Democracy* (1934), *The Autobiography of a Curmudgeon* (1934) and *The Secret Diary of Harold L. Ickes* (3 vols., 1953–54).

**Idris Shah, Sultan** *(1924–1984)* Ruler of the Malaysian state of Perak from 1963 until his death. In 1983 Idris Shah joined with other sultans to force the elected government to alter constitutional amendments aimed at limiting the powers of the rulers of the nine Malaysian states. At the time of his death he was the frontrunner in the election of Malaysia's next king.

**Ilf and Petrov** Pseudonym of a literary partnership between Russian writers Ilya Arnoldovich Fainzilberg (1897–1937) and Yevgeny Petrovich KATAYEV (1903–42). In 1928 they published *The Twelve Chairs* and in 1931 *The Golden Calf,* both novels satirizing aspects of Soviet society. They also visited the United States and wrote *Little Golden America* (1936). Ilf and Petrov were frowned upon under STALIN, but their work later recovered its popularity.

**Illia, Arturo** *(1900–1986)* President of ARGENTINA (1963–66). A political moderate, Illia was elected in one of the freest elections in Argentina's history up to that time. He was overthrown by the military in a bloodless coup in 1966, however. He remained politically active thereafter, working to return Argentina to civilian government.

**Illich, Ivan** *(1926–2002)* Austrian-born educator and social critic. Illich, was ordained as a Roman Catholic priest in 1951, has become well known as a strident voice of dissent within the church, calling for increased social activism. Illich studied history and psychology at the University of Salzburg and earned his doctoral degree there in 1951. From 1951 to 1956, Illich was a priest in New York City, and from 1956 to 1960 served as vice-rector of Catholic University in Ponce, Puerto Rico. His major works include *Celebration of Awareness* (1970) and *De-Schooling Society* (1971).

*I Love Lucy.* Innovative American television comedy series starring Lucille BALL. In its first six years of weekly half-hour shows (1951 to 1957), it never ranked lower than third in popularity among all television programs. (During its remaining four years the series was reduced to several one-hour specials, later rerun under the title, *The Lucille Ball/Desi Arnaz Shows*.) The mix was unlikely—a Cuban bandleader (Desi), a redheaded, clownish wife (Lucy) and a mismatched married couple (Vivian Vance and William Frawley)—but superb scripts by writers Madelyn Pugh and Bob Carroll Jr. and Lucy's Chaplinesque antics captivated viewers in the 1950s as no show had done since Milton BERLE's *Texaco Star Theater* in the late 1940s. Among its innovations, largely at Lucy's insistence, was the decision not to broadcast live from New York but to film it in HOLLYWOOD with a three-camera process. Print quality was superior to that of kinescopes (film made from a picture tube image) and guaranteed the series a long life in syndication.

**Ilyushin, Sergei Vladimirovich** *(1894–1977)* Soviet aircraft designer. Ilyushin first became known for his Il-2 Stormovik, a dive bomber widely used by the Soviet Union during WORLD WAR II. He later worked on commercial aircraft, designing the jet airliner Il-62 (1962) and other airplanes used by the Soviet national airline Aeroflot. Altogether he designed more than 50 planes.

**imagism** American school of poetics, led by Amy LOWELL and Ezra POUND, which first emerged in the 1910s and has remained influential throughout the century. The central argument of imagism was that the poetry of the Victorian and Edwardian eras had become clogged with excess verbiage, which was inserted by poets into their lines of verse simply for the sake of metrical completion. This excess verbiage did result in a superficial musicality, but it also diminished the vividness of poetic metaphor—the presentation of new and powerful sensual images to the reader—due to its tendencies toward vagueness and conventionality. Imagism called for spare, evocative poetic compositions that relied on an exactitude of verbal presentation in a free verse form. Major poets such as T. S. ELIOT, D. H. LAWRENCE and William Carlos WILLIAMS were highly influenced by imagist theory.

**Imagists, Russian** A postrevolutionary literary movement. Russian imagism evolved more or less separately from Anglo-American IMAGISM. The imagists founded the movement in 1919 as a successor to FUTURISM. Characteristics of Imagism are the primacy of the image, coarse language and pessimism; these features can be seen in Sergei ESENIN's *Confession of a Hooligan* (1920). In the first manifesto or declaration of Imagism, signed by Esenin, Ivnev, Mariengov and Shershenevich (1893–1942), the image was defined as "the naphthalene preserving a work of art from the moths of time." The movement, although in agreement with the ethic of the October Revolution, found itself unable to maintain an apolitical stance during the Civil War, and by 1927 it had disintegrated.

**Ince, Thomas Harper** *(1882–1924)* Prominent producer, director and writer in the SILENT FILM era. After an itinerant life with his actor parents, he began his film career in 1910 in New York directing Mary PICKFORD films for Carl LAEMMLE's Independent Motion Pictures Company. Moving to Los Angeles in 1912, he built a studio he dubbed "Inceville" upon 20,000 acres of land. There, he contracted for the cowboys, Indians and equipment of the "Miller 101 Wild West Show" to make the westerns that soon made him famous. Epic two-reelers like *War on the Plains* (1912) pioneered the modern western movie. Releasing through several distribution outlets in the next 10 years, Ince featured his top stars, William S. Hart and Charles Ray, in some of the finest outdoor dramas of the day, including *On the Night Stage* (1914), *Hell's Hinges* (1916) and *The Coward* (1916). His most important contribution to the movies lay in developing the shooting script system still used today and in personally supervising his various projects. He was convinced that it was the writer/producer, not the director, whose personal stamp should go on every film. His epics, like *Civilization* (1916), are of less interest today than his smaller, social-problem films, like the remarkably tough and poignant *The Italians* (1915), a gritty drama of immigrants come to grief in the New World. Ince's mysterious death during a yachting party in 1924 has never been adequately explained.

**Inchon** City and port on the Yellow Sea coast of South Korea, 25 miles from SEOUL. Opened as a treaty port in 1883, it was expanded during the Japanese occupation (1904–45). In September 1950, during the KOREAN WAR, U.S.-led UN forces made a brilliantly successful amphibious landing here, following it up with an offensive northward.

**India** (**Republic of India**) Nation on the Indian subcontinent of southern Asia, covering an area of 1,222,396 square miles south of the Himalaya Mountains and between Pakistan and Myanmar; India is the seventh largest country in the world. Centuries of British influence and rule in India ended in 1947 when the predominantly Hindu country was granted independence, after Mohandas GANDHI had made the nationalist movement a powerful force through his civil disobedience campaigns (1920–46). The last British governor-general, Lord (Louis) MOUNTBATTEN, partitioned British India into two states, India and PAKISTAN, to avoid religious conflict between Muslims and Hindus. Nevertheless, war between India and Pakistan over the disputed Indian state of KASHMIR erupted in 1948 and ended in an unresolved cease-fire in 1949, only to explore again in 1965 (see INDO-PAKISTANI WAR OF 1947–48, INDO-PAKISTANI WAR OF 1965). A peace was achieved in 1966 through Soviet medi-

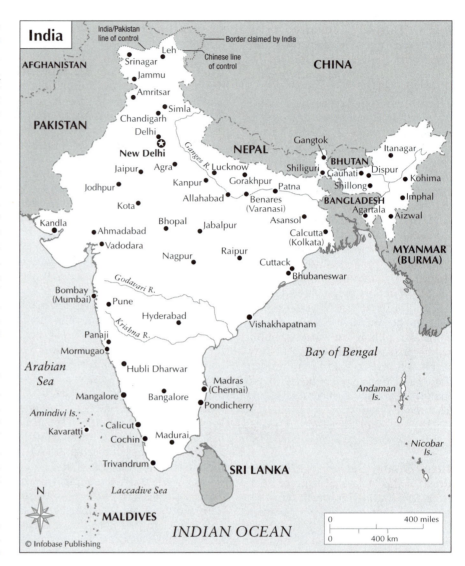

ation. Under Prime Minister Jawaharlal NEHRU's leadership (1947–64) India adopted a new constitution and became a republic (1950). During his daughter Indira GANDHI's ministry (1966–77, 1980–84) India again fought with Pakistan over its support of an independent BANGLADESH (East Pakistan) in 1971, while Sikh militancy in the state of Punjab culminated in Mrs. Gandhi's assassination (1984). Though her son and successor, Rajiv GANDHI, granted some Sikh demands, violence continued throughout the 1980s. Political crisis continued with the resignation of Prime Minister Chandra Shekhar in March 1991 and attempts by Rajiv Gandhi to regain the post. Gandhi was himself assassinated in 1991. After P. V. Narasimha Rao was sworn in as prime minister in June 1991, the Congress Party began a

sharp decline in popularity that culminated in a humiliating defeat in the 1994 parliamentary elections at the hands of the Hindu fundamentalist BHARATIYA JANATA PARTY (BJP). Acute political instability marked the next several years, with a succession of weak coalition governments. In 1998 the BJP's leader, Atal Bihari Vajpayee, became prime minister, and his party achieved a decisive majority in the 2000 parliamentary elections.

In the meantime, important changes had taken place in India. In May 1998 the government in Delhi announced that it had conducted five nuclear tests, which prompted India's arch-rival, Pakistan, to conduct two tests of its own later in the month. Tension between India and Pakistan further rose over the disputed region of KASHMIR and led to some hair-raising confrontations be-

## INDIA

|  |  |
|------|-------|
| 1906 | Muslim League formed. |
| 1913 | Poet Rabindranath Tagore wins Nobel Prize. |
| 1920 | Mohandas Gandhi launches first civil disobedience campaign for self-rule. |
| 1930 | Gandhi makes salt march, defying British. |
| 1931 | Gandhi represents Indian National Congress at Round-table conference on constitutional reform in London. |
| 1936 | Jawaharlal Nehru becomes president of Indian National Congress. |
| 1940 | Muslim League calls for independent status in Muslim majority areas. |
| 1942 | British offer dominion status in exchange for support of war effort; Gandhi launches Quit India movement. |
| 1947 | Independence; Pakistan divided from India, igniting religious war. |
| 1948 | (January) Gandhi assassinated; discrimination against untouchables banned. |
| 1952 | First international birth control organization founded in Bombay. |
| 1964 | Nehru dies. |
| 1965 | War with Pakistan over Kashmir. |
| 1984 | Army assaults Golden Temple of Amritsar to suppress Sikh uprising; Prime Minister Indira Gandhi assassinated by Sikh bodyguards; succeeded by her son Rajiv Gandhi; poison gas leak devastates Bhopal. |
| 1990 | Hindus storm Babri Masjid mosque, claiming site is birthplace of god, Rama; final episode aired of *Mahabharata*, most popular tv program ever. |
| 1991 | Former prime minister Rajiv Gandhi is assassinated. |
| 1996 | Congress Party is defeated in parliamentary elections, ushering in period of weak coalition governments. One is headed by Shri Atal Bihari Vajpayee from the Hindu nationalist party BHARATIYA JANATA (BJP). |
| 1998 | India conducts a nuclear weapons test. |
| 1999 | Vajpayee begins second consecutive term as head of coalition government. |
| 2000 | The BJP wins a decisive majority in parliament. |
| 2004 | Congress Party is returned to power after winning elections. Dr. Manmohan Singh, a Sikh, becomes first non-Hindu prime minister of India. |

tween these two newly nuclear-armed states. In the early 21st century India began to achieve an impressive record of economic growth facilitated by the government's export-oriented strategy. The outsourcing of employment to Indian companies by technology-intensive industries in the U.S. helped to promote a boom in the country's service industry. (See Also AMRITSAR MASSACRE; INDO-PAKISTANI WAR OF 1971; GOLDEN TEMPLE MASSACRE.)

**Indian Civil War of 1947–48**
During 1947 efforts to arrange independence of a unified Indian subcontinent from Great Britain foundered when the Muslim League and the Indian National Congress failed to agree to a federal formula. Riots between Muslims and Hindus, endemic since the "Great Calcutta Killing" (August 16–20, 1946), erupted into civil war when partition into INDIA and PAKISTAN was announced August 14, 1947. At least 5,500,000 refugees moved between West Pakistan and western India, and 1,250,000 between East and West Bengal; rioting took at least a million lives, in part because Indian prime minister Jawaharlal NEHRU prevented British troops from intervening. War between India and Pakistan over KASHMIR (1947–48) exacerbated refugee conflicts. Mohandas K. GANDHI, Indian spiritual and nationalist leader, attempting to calm Hindu-Muslim tensions, was assassinated by a Hindu extremist. The shock restored order and unified the Indian government.

**Indian Ocean earthquake, 2004**
See TSUNAMI DISASTER OF 2004.

**Indochina** Large peninsula in Southeast Asia, presently divided as the nations of BURMA, CAMBODIA, LAOS, THAILAND, VIETNAM and west MALAYSIA. The 19th-century struggle for colonial empire saw the British in control of the western and southern sections (Burma and Malaysia); while Thailand, in the center and then known as Siam, retained its independence with some difficulty. The eastern part became French Indochina and consisted of the colony of Cochin China (south Vietnam) and protectorates over Tonkin (north Vietnam), Annam (central Vietnam), Laos and Cambodia. WORLD WAR II put an end to

**Indochina**

CHINA

— Boundary of French Indochina

NORTH VIETNAM

Hanoi
Haiphong

Louangphrabang

*Mekong R.*

*Red R.*

*Gulf of Tonkin*

*Hainan (CHINA)*

Vientiane   LAOS

Hue

Danang

THAILAND

*South China Sea*

CAMBODIA

*Tonle Sap*

*Mekong R.*

SOUTH VIETNAM

Phnom Penh

Cam Ranh

Saigon

*Gulf of Thailand*

*Mekong Delta*

N

| 0 | | 150 miles |
| 0 | | 150 km |

© Infobase Publishing

France's colonial empire. Although most of the region was reoccupied by France after the Japanese surrender at the end of the war, Vietnamese demands for independence from France were soon backed up by military action. The climax came in 1954 at DIEN BIEN PHU, a French military base in the northwest that fell to insurgent forces on May 7. That same year Laos and Cambodia gained their independence; and Vietnam, formed out of Annam, Cochin China and Tonkin in 1949–50, was partitioned into north and south sections—a division intended to be temporary.

**Indonesia, Republic of** Vast archipelago-nation of more than 13,000 islands, off the coast of Southeast Asia. After hundreds of years under Dutch rule and exploitation, the Netherlands East Indies (or Netherlands Indies) saw the beginnings of Indonesian nationalism and the push for independence in the early 20th century. But it took the Japanese invasion of WORLD WAR II to disrupt Dutch rule. After the Japanese occupiers surrendered in 1945, nationalist leader SUKARNO proclaimed independence; a spontaneous revolution against the returning Dutch finally led

to the Europeans' relinquishing sovereignty to the U.S. of Indonesia late in 1949. Under Sukarno's leadership, Indonesia became a leader of the THIRD WORLD and by 1965 had developed close ties with China and the USSR. After an unsuccessful communist takeover attempt in 1965, Gen. SUHARTO led a right-wing coup, seized power and opened a campaign against the communists in Java and Bali, killing more than 100,000. In 1976 Suharto invaded Portuguese East Timor (also in the archipelago) and brutally eliminated all opposition. Since that unfortunate time, Indonesia enjoyed generally favorable relations with the West, as a member of the ASEAN economic and political alliance. In 1998 protests and riots occurred throughout Indonesia in response to the plummeting value of the rupiah, leading to the fall of Suharto. He was replaced by B. J. Habibie. In 1999, the country's first free multiparty elections since 1955, the Muslim leader Abdurrahman Wahid was elected as Indonesia's fourth president. In the same year the population of EAST TIMOR voted for independence setting off a wave of rioting by Indonesians on the island. In 2001 Wahid was removed from office for financial irregularities by the national assembly and was replaced by his vice president, Megawati Sukarnoputri, the daughter of former president Sukarno. Afer what was viewed as a mediocre term in office, she was defeated for reelection in 2004 by Susilo Bambang Yudhoyono. In May and July 2006 severe earthquakes on Java left more than 6,000 dead and over 40,000 people injured.

**Indonesian-Malaysian War of 1963–66** In 1963 Indonesian "Lifetime President" Achmed SUKARNO refused to recognize the democratic federation of MALAYSIA, and urged Indonesians to crush it. Britain aided Malaysia to fight infiltrating Indonesian guerrillas in Sabah and Sarawak and Indonesian paratroops in Malaya. The war was financially costly for INDONESIA, and Indonesian communists (PKI) attempted to seize power September 30, 1965. General SUHARTO squashed the coup and carried out a bloody anticommunist purge; at least 300,000 leftists were killed. Sukarno, who had been supported by the PKI and had been friendly with communist

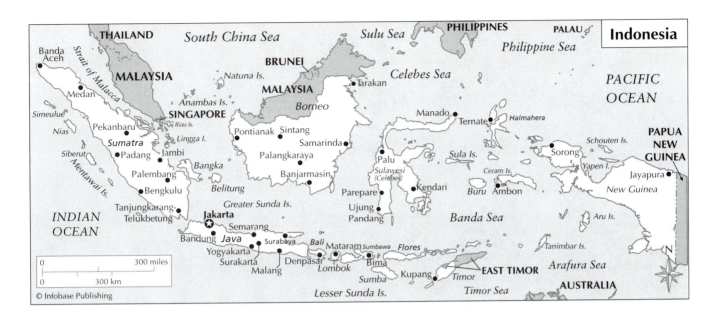

China, failed to regain government control. Eventually he had to surrender all authority to Suharto, who became acting president in 1967 and was elected president in 1968. Malaysia and Indonesia ended hostilities by a treaty signed at Djakarta on August 11, 1966.

## Indonesian War in East Timor

*(1975–1999)* Rival factions contended for power in Portuguese Timor (East Timor). (West Timor, formerly Dutch, had become part of INDONESIA in 1950.) The Revolutionary Front for the Independence of East Timor (FRETILIN) called for independence, another faction for merger with Indonesia, a third for remaining with PORTUGAL. Civil war erupted August 1975, the Portuguese governor left, and FRETILIN gained control. Opposing groups requested Indonesian intervention, and Indonesia eagerly complied, capturing Dili, the capital, December 7, 1975, and driving FRETILIN fighters into the mountains. Despite UNITED NATIONS condemnation of aggression, Indonesia annexed EAST TIMOR on July 17, 1976. FRETILIN guerrillas continued to resist, and East Timor lay in ruins with many of its people starving in internment camps. In a 1999 UN-sponsored referendum the people of East Timor voted for independence, and the region came under UN control for a transitional period.

## Indonesian War of Independence

Following the Japanese occupation (1942–45) of the Dutch East Indies (now INDONESIA) in WORLD WAR II, Indonesian nationalists proclaimed independence. Not recognizing the new government, Dutch and British soldiers landed at Djakarta to restore Dutch control. Fighting led to negotiations and the Cheribon Agreement (1946), creating the U.S. of Indonesia under the Dutch crown. Disagreements and disorder led to a large-scale Dutch police action arousing world opinion. The blockade of republican territory coincided with guerrilla warfare waged by Muslim extremists against both Dutch and republicans, and a communist uprising. The Dutch seized the republic's capital, Djakarta, and principal leaders, but resistance and United Nations condemnation continued. Indonesian and Dutch representatives met at The Hague (August 23–November 2, 1949), and the NETHERLANDS transferred full sovereignty to the U.S. of Indonesia with Achmed SUKARNO as president, Muhammed Hatta as premier. The state became the Republic of Indonesia in 1950.

## Indonesian Wars of 1957–62

Continued Dutch rule of West New Guinea angered Indonesian president Achmed SUKARNO. INDONESIA claimed the area as West Irian, asking without success for the United Nations to resolve the dispute. In December 1957 Sukarno began a strike against Dutch businesses, expelled Dutch subjects and expropriated Dutch holdings. While the Dutch prepared New Guinean natives for self-determination and defense, Indonesia obtained warships and planes from the USSR and in 1962 landed paratroops in West New Guinea to fight alongside rebel guerrillas against the Dutch. The U.S. and the United Nations sponsored negotiations to avert full-scale war. In an agreement of August 15, 1962, the NETHERLANDS transferred West New Guinea to UN control, which subsequently transferred it to Indonesia (1963).

## Indo-Pakistani War of 1947–48

The partition into INDIA and PAKISTAN left the status of Jammu and KASHMIR undecided. An independent, largely Muslim kingdom bordering West Pakistan, Jammu and Kashmir was ruled by a Hindu Maharaja. Demands for democracy and revolts by Pathan Muslims against Hindu landlords encouraged Pakistan to attack, seizing Muzaffarbad and Uri in October 1947, advancing toward the Kashmiri capital of Srinagar. The Maharaja asked for India's help, receiving it October 27, when he ceded the state to India. Sikh troops pushed the invaders back, and Pakistan was about to send troops until its British officers threatened to resign. Then Pakistan transferred "volunteers" into the invaded area to hold it as Azad (free) Kashmir. The turmoil exacerbated

## INDONESIA

| | |
|---|---|
| 1901 | "Ethical Policy" seeks better treatment of native populations under Dutch rule. |
| 1910 | Under the "Forward Movement," Dutch expand control through outer islands to reach present boundaries of Indonesia. |
| 1927 | Indonesians educated in Europe under Ethical Policy form groups of nationalist intellectuals; Sukarno founds Party National Indonesia. |
| 1942 | Japanese occupation; Sukarno cooperates, builds national power base. |
| 1945 | Three days after Japanese surrender, Sukarno declares independence; Dutch attempt at reentry meets guerrilla war. |
| 1949 | Federal republic established, with democratically elected parliament. |
| 1954 | Young officers mutiny in Sumatra. |
| 1955 | Afro-Asian conference at Bandung. |
| 1956 | Sukarno suspends parliament; begins "Guided Democracy" leading to martial law. |
| 1963 | Netherlands hands over West Irian (western New Guinea); Sukarno pursues friendship with China; influence of local Communists grows; economy falters. |
| 1965 | Sukarno leaves UN; young communists within military attempt coup; General Suharto crushes it, and becomes real power in nation; 500,000 communists killed as CIA assists in round-up. |
| 1967 | Sukarno stripped of office. |
| 1968 | Suharto assumes presidency; "New Order" signals turn to West. |
| 1969 | Separatist guerrillas acting in West Irian. |
| 1975 | Indonesia invades newly independent Portuguese East Timor; over 200,000 residents killed; oil boom brings relative prosperity. |
| 1976 | Government officials charged with taking bribes from U.S. corporations; government oil company collapses. |
| 1984 | Muslims violently protest Suharto's attempts to secularize society. |
| 1989 | FRETELIN guerrillas active in East Timor. |
| 1990 | Launches first communications satellite. |
| 1998 | General Suharto is forced from office. |
| 1999 | East Timor declares independence after UN-sponsored referendum. In the country's first free multiparty elections since the mid-1950s, Muslim leader Abdurrakman Wahid is elected president. |
| 1999 | Some 96% of 116 million registered voters cast ballots in the first free multiparty elections since 1955. Muslim leader Abdurrahman Wahid becomes Indonesia's fourth president, and PDI leader Megawati Sukarnaputri its vice president. UN peacekeeping forces mediate the rampage of paramilitary forces who oppose the popular 78.5% vote favoring East Timor's independence from Indonesia. |
| 2001 | National assembly removes Wahid from office for corruption and replaces him with his vice president, Megawati Sukarnoputri. |
| 2004 | Megwati Sukarnoputri is defeated by Susilo Bambang Yudhoyono in reelection bid. |
| 2006 | Severe earthquakes strike Java, killing over 6,000 people. |

Hindu-Muslim tensions in India, contributing to Mohandas K. GANDHI's (1869–1948) assassination by a Hindu extremist. Intervention by the United Nations resulted in a cease-fire and a de-facto boundary at the battle line; but Indo-Pakistani disputes over Kashmir continued.

**Indo-Pakistani War of 1965** Hostility between INDIA and PAKISTAN increased after 1958 when General Mohammed AYUB KHAN seized power in Pakistan, signing a treaty with China that put Kashmir's Chinese boundaries into question. Indian and Pakistani forces first clashed (April 9–30, 1965) in the Rann of Kutch. In August and early September both sides crossed the Kashmiri cease-fire line, and on September 6 India launched a drive toward Lahore with 900,000 troops. Four hundred-fifty Pakistani tanks were lost before the UNITED NATIONS arranged a cease-fire September 27, averting intervention by China. Mediation by Britain, the U.S. and the USSR led to a conference in Tashkent (1966) in which promises of friendship, cooperation and a Kashmiri plebiscite were made; but Prime Minister Lal Bahadur SHASTRI died within hours of the conference. His successor, Indira GANDHI, fulfilled most of the promises, but intervening events prevented the plebiscite from being held.

**Indo-Pakistani War of 1971** The Pakistani Civil War of 1971 forced more than 10 million refugees from East Pakistan (BANGLADESH) into West Bengal. INDIA appealed for international aid, but instead, the U.S., supporting PAKISTAN, cut off India's American credit. Pakistani warplanes attacked Indian airfields in Kashmir (December 3, 1971), and the next day India attacked both West and East Pakistan, recognizing Bangladesh's independence December 6. Indian forces captured Dacca, forced the surrender of Pakistan's forces in Bangladesh, and took 90,000 prisoners December 16; India established a cease-fire on both eastern and western fronts the following day. Pakistan lost over half its population and was on the verge of economic and military collapse. It finally recognized Bangladesh in 1974; the U.S. did so April 4, 1972.

**Industrial Party** In the Soviet Union, an allegedly subversive group of the technical intelligentsia that was said to be wrecking the first Soviet FIVE-YEAR PLAN at capitalist instigation. The members were tried and condemned in 1930, together with a number of those considered sympathetic to them. (See also PURGES.)

**Industrial Workers of the World (IWW)** Revolutionary union founded in 1905 by the Western Federation of Miners and other labor groups. Representing the principles of syndicalism, the organization was at first headed by Eugene DEBS and Daniel De Leon, with leadership soon passing to Vincent St. John and William Haywood. The IWW, whose members were known as Wobblies, aimed at organizing skilled and unskilled workers into one union, which, after a general strike, would topple capitalism and introduce a socialist industrial democracy. After 1908, it concentrated on organizing the unskilled. While meeting with strong opposition from local and federal government, the IWW amassed an impressive roster of membership, including agricultural, textile, dock, metal and lumber workers. It also made a special point of organizing both blacks and migrants. Membership reached a height of from 60,000 to 100,000 by the outbreak of World War I. Rejecting arbitration and collective bargaining, the IWW advocated direct action and conducted some 150 strikes. In the process, it was successful at achieving better working conditions and shorter hours for its members. In 1917 the Department of Justice arrested more than 200 Wobbly leaders for antiwar efforts. The RED SCARES of postwar America did much to discredit the IWW, and by the late 1920s it had ceased to be an important force in the American labor movement. After World War II the organization continued to lose membership amid the repressive measures of the McCarthy era and the general economic prosperity of the period. But it resumed its organizing activities and was involved in several struggles for workers' rights and free speech for the remainder of the century. In 2006 it moved its headquarters to Cincinnati, Ohio, as its membership had dwindled to about 2,000.

**Indy, Vincent d'** *(1851–1931)* French composer. He was a pupil and disciple of composer César Franck, succeeding his master as president of the Société Nationale de Musique. Also a follower of Richard Wagner, he did much to introduce the German composer's music to French audiences. He wrote noted biographies of both his mentors (1906 and 1930), as well as of Beethoven (1911). In 1894 d'Indy was one of the founders of the Schola Cantorum in Paris, teaching composition at the influential music school and directing it from 1911 until his death. His three-volume work *Cours de composition musicale* (1903, rev. 1950) embodies his teaching methods and philosophy. As a composer, he followed Franck's model in using recurring themes throughout various movements. His spare and contained compositions also employ plainsong and baroque elements. His most often-played works include the *Symphony on a French Mountain Air* (1887) and the symphonic variations *Istar* (1897). He also wrote three other symphonies, chamber music, piano pieces, choral works and the opera *Fervaal* (1897).

**INF Treaty** The Intermediate-Range Force (INF) Treaty, signed by the U.S. and the Soviet Union in December 1987, was the first agreement between the two nations that eliminated an entire class of missiles. Under its terms, the U.S. agreed to destroy all CRUISE and Pershing II missiles and the Soviet Union agreed to eliminate all SS-20s; both types of missiles were intended primarily for development in Europe. With the collapse of the Soviet Union in December 1991, the Russian Federation replaced the Soviet Union as a party to the INF Treaty and continued to abide by the treaty's provisions. In May 1994, an amendment to the INF Treaty made the U.S., Russia, Belarus, Kazakhstan and Ukraine parties to the INF Treaty and responsible for its continued implementation. The U.S. and Russia (together with the other parties) had the right to conduct 10 short-notice inspections per year of the other's former missile operating bases and former support facilities (more than 35 sites for the U.S. and over 125 for the other parties). These inspection rights ended on May 31, 2001. While no longer subject to inspection under INF, the parties remain obligated to observe the restrictions and prohibitions contained in the treaty, which are of indefinite duration.

## Inge, William Motter *(1913–1973)*

American playwright. Inge was noted for such "slice of life" dramas as *Come Back, Little Sheba* (1950), *Picnic* (PULITZER PRIZE, 1953), *Bus Stop* (1955) and *The Dark at the Top of the Stairs* (1957). Many of his plays were made into successful films. He won the 1961 ACADEMY AWARD for best story and screenplay (written directly for the screen) for *Splendor in the Grass.*

## Inge, William R(alph) *(1860–1954)*

British clergyman. Inge played a dominant role in the Anglican Church in the first half of the 20th century. Educated at Cambridge University, he taught there and at Oxford University before becoming dean of St. Paul's Cathedral in London, a position he held from 1911 to 1934. Inge achieved broad public recognition throughout Britain by virtue of his well-attended sermons and lectures, which frequently expressed a dour pessimism that earned Inge the nickname of "the gloomy Dean." Inge was also a prolific author. His major works include *Christian Mysticism* (1897), *Outspoken Essays* (1919), *Mysticism in Religion* (1948) and *Diary of a Dean* (1949).

## Ingersoll, Ralph McAllister *(1900–1985)*

American journalist and publisher. Ingersoll played a key editorial role in the development of magazines such as *The NEW YORKER, Fortune, TIME,* and *LIFE.* He was best known as owner of the New York City newspaper *PM* (1940–48). Noted for its in-depth coverage of various issues with a liberal standpoint and for its policy of carrying no advertising, *PM* was the first major American newspaper to advocate U.S. entry into WORLD WAR II.

## injection molding

Manufacturing technique in which PLASTIC in a semi-liquid state is forced into a hollow mold where it hardens into the shape determined by the mold. The finished part is ejected from the mold ready for use or for whatever further finishing and assembly steps are required. While automatic machines can produce small injection moldings at high speed at relatively low cost, the high cost of the molds tends to limit use of the process to the production of ob-jects and parts where demand can be expected to be high. Thermoplastics such as styrene and polyethylene are the usual materials used for injection molding to produce everyday objects such as plastic knives and forks, containers and toys.

## Inkatha

Zulu cultural and political organization in SOUTH AFRICA; led since 1975 by Chief Mangosuthu BUTHELEZI. Ostensibly, the group seeks to revive Zulu traditions and instill pride among Zulus. Some observers claimed that Inkatha was supported by the white minority government only to fracture the anti-APARTHEID movement in South Africa. In the late 1980s and early 1990s, Inkatha members were involved in violent clashes with blacks from other tribes and with members of the AFRICAN NATIONAL CONGRESS. After the end of apartheid in 1993, Inkatha emerged as one of the leading political parties in South Africa.

## Inner Mongolia (Inner Mongolian Autonomous Region)

Autonomous region of China bordering on Outer Mongolia and the USSR; the capital is at Hohhot. Nominally under Chinese rule until 1911, it then became part of the Chinese Republic; in 1947, the first autonomous region established by the Chinese communist government. (See also MONGOLIA.)

## İnönü

Village in Turkish province of Bilecik. During the GRECO-TURKISH WAR OF 1921–22, Greek offensives were twice halted at İnönü by Turks under Ismet Pasha, who, as a result of these victories, took the name of the village as his surname. As Ismet İNÖNÜ he became president of Turkey in 1938.

## İnönü, Ismet (Ismet Pasha) *(1884–1973)*

Turkish soldier and statesman. İnönü was born in Izmir. After a distinguished military career, he became ATATÜRK's chief of staff during the GRECO-TURKISH WAR OF 1921–22. He was first premier of the Republic of TURKEY (1923–38) and, after Atatürk's death, its second president (1938–50). He introduced free elections and a multiparty system in Turkey. After the 1950 elections, İnönü became leader of the parliamentary opposition. Under the Gursel government (1961–65), he was again premier, but resigned owing to lack of sufficient parliamentary support.

## Institutional Revolutionary Party (Partido Revolucionario Institucional; PRI)

Ruling political party in MEXICO from 1929 to 2000. Originally titled the National Revolutionary Party, the PRI was formed by President Plutarco Elías CALLES as a result of the assassination of President-elect Álvaro Obregón in 1928. The original purpose of the PRI was to end the rampant unrest in the army and the political, ideological and regional conflict that divided the country and unite the Mexican people under the banner of political reform and stability. A system developed in which the sitting president would select the PRI nominee shortly before national elections were to take place in order to avoid infighting within the party and the government. It also virtually guaranteed the election of the president's designee due to the PRI's total control of the country's political system.

Calles thought that the affiliation of a governing institution with the ideal of an ongoing national revolution would unite the key factions within Mexico behind it. In 1938 President Lázaro Cárdenas renamed it the Party of the Mexican Revolution to emphasize the influence of local organizations of white-collar workers, unionized labor and farmers, which he mobilized within the existing political structure. In 1946 the party was renamed the Institutional Revolutionary Party, to reflect the desires of its leadership to "institutionalize" the changes that it had enacted over the previous 18 years. In doing so it partly discarded its appeal to the workers, farmers and skilled professionals Cárdenas had embraced. Instead, it began to focus on modernizing the country's infrastructure and industrial system and promoting foreign investment.

The PRI used its position as the dominant political force in Mexico to gain control of the various branches of the federal, state and local government, as well as nongovernmental organizations. This process ensured that the head of the Mexican Workers Confederation (CTM), an association of all the country's labor unions supported by the government, was on the Central

Executive Committee of the PRI. PRI officials were also dispersed throughout the labor organization to ensure its cooperation with government policies.

Allegations of corruption that permeated President Carlos SALINAS DE GORTARI's six-year term in office, beginning in 1998, caused a decline in the PRI's popularity among Mexican voters. In March 1994, after the party's first candidate, Luis Donaldo Colosio Murrieta, was assassinated, he was replaced on the party ticket by his campaign manager, Ernesto Zedillo Ponce de Léon. Zedillo won with a bare majority of the popular vote, strengthening the position of the opposition parties in Mexico—the conservative National Action Party (PAN) and the leftist Party of the Democratic Revolution (PRD). In the July 1997 midterm elections, opposition parties won a majority of the seats in the lower house of the Mexican congress and opposition candidates won several state governorships. By 2000 the PRI had lost additional ground in the lower house as well as its control of the upper house. In the same year the PRI presidential candidate lost to the PAN candidate, Vicente Fox; for the first time in 71 years, the PRI was out of power. Despite its declining presence in national politics, party officials remained influential in many governmental bureaucracies and nongovernmental organizations.

**insulin** A natural substance produced by the pancreas and necessary for proper metabolism of glucose (sugar). Before the 20th century anyone whose pancreas stopped producing insulin developed diabetes mellitus and died. In 1921 Canadian Frederick BANTING extracted insulin from the pancreas of a dog and in January 1922 successfully treated a 14-year-old boy with diabetes mellitus. Insulin became commercially available by late 1922. A milestone 20th-century medical advance, insulin use has become routine and saved the lives of countless diabetes sufferers.

**Intel** American manufacturer of computer components, specifically microprocessors and integrated circuitry (see COMPUTERS). Founded in 1968 by computer engineers Gordon Moore and Bob Noyce, Intel was an abbreviation of *integrated electronics*, which Moore, Noyce and Andrew Grove (who joined

the company soon after its founding) hoped to develop for the burgeoning computer market. Intel's first task was the construction of a semiconductor that was cost-effective and could replace the large magnetic core memory units currently in use. In 1971 it developed the dynamic random-access memory circuit (DRAM) which kept information in the computer's memory through a constant recharging of the computer's random access memory (RAM) chips. In the same year engineer Ted Hoff, came up with the idea for installing a central processing unit (CPU) in computers that was condensed into a single computer chip. The result was the 4004, a one-sixth by one-eighth-inch computer chip with 2,300 transistors that equaled the output of ENIAC, the world's first computer. Eventually the 4004 and its successor, the 8080, became a vital component of a variety of machines such as calculators and the emerging personal computer (PC).

The increased speed of the Intel CPUs and the increasing popularity of the PC resulted in the installation of Intel units in an estimated 15 million machines by 1988. In 1989 Intel came out with a new CPU, the 486, followed by the first of four Pentium chips in 1993. This new model of CPU contained 5.5 million transistors, making it approximately 300 times more powerful than ENIAC. The continued improvement of CPU's with the development of the Pentium 2 (1997) 3 (2000) and 4 (2001) chips cemented Intel's reputation as one of the leaders in the development of computer hardware. In 1998 the U.S. Federal Trade Commission (FTC) accused Intel of attempting to force computer manufacturers to use Pentium chips by refusing to share technical information with them, making it difficult for these companies to produce hardware components compatible with Pentium chips or other products. Although dispute was settled out of court the following year. Intel remained in the sights of government agencies responsible for monitoring of antitrust violations.

**interferon** Any one of a naturally occurring protein family that functions as part of the body's defense mechanism by interfering with the multiplication of viruses within living cells. Discov-

ered in 1957 by English scientist Alick Isaacs and his assistant Jean Lindenmann, interferons were subsequently produced by cells cultured outside the body. Recombinant-DNA technology and chemical synthesis commercially produced human interferons used to treat such diseases as shingles and certain types of cancer.

**International** The first International was formed in London by Karl Marx in 1864; its aim was to coordinate working-class movements in different countries and thereby to establish international socialism. There were disputes between the Marxist and anarchist members, culminating in the final separation between Marx and Bakunin (1872). The movement was dissolved in 1876. The Second International was formed in Paris in 1889, comprising the radical parties of Austria, Belgium, Denmark, Germany, Spain, Sweden and Switzerland. A nonrevolutionary movement, it collapsed with the outbreak of World War I. The Third International (COMINTERN) was formed in Moscow by LENIN and the BOLSHEVIKS in 1917 and comprised the communist elements excluded from the Second International. Its aim was world revolution. A Fourth International was formed by TROTSKY in Mexico in the 1930s, and there was also a Fifth—the Situationist International—formed in 1954. There have been two revivals of the Second, nonrevolutionary Socialist International. The first (1923) ceased to operate in 1940. The second (1951) is the currently operative Socialist International. Its congress meets at least once every two years and its council, in which the Socialist Union of Central-Eastern Europe is represented, at least twice a year.

**International Atomic Energy Agency (IAEA)** Intergovernmental organization created to help its members develop nuclear power plants while preventing non-nuclear powers from developing nuclear weapons. Founded in 1957 and located in Vienna, Austria, the IAEA strives to improve the peaceful, economic and environmental state of the world by educating its members on the proper ways of using nuclear materials to generate electricity, as well as advocating research into alternate, non-fossil-fuel sources of energy. During the COLD WAR this organization failed to prevent international powers like France and China from developing nuclear weapons programs, although the U.S. and the USSR both used their superpower status to minimize the proliferation of atomic knowledge that could be used to develop nuclear weaponry. With the end of the cold war and the disintegration of the USSR in 1991, many international observers thought that the end of the bipolar rivalry would lead to greater cooperation among the U.S., Russia (the USSR's predecessor) and the other world nuclear powers to encourage countries to join the agency, acquire knowledge on how to build nuclear reactors and renounce efforts to obtain nuclear weapons. However, some countries, notably NORTH KOREA, IRAQ, and IRAN, have attempted to build reactors capable of producing weapons-grade plutonium. In 2003 the unwillingness of Iraqi president Saddam HUSSEIN to abide by the guidelines of the IAEA and submit to unrestricted inspections of suspected nuclear sites was one of the reasons cited by U.S. president George W. BUSH and British prime minister Tony BLAIR for invading Iraq and deposing Hussein. Three years later the IAEA reported Iran to the UN Security Council for its nuclear activities.

**International Bank for Reconstruction and Development** See WORLD BANK.

**International Committee of the Red Cross** A council of 25 Swiss citizens, with headquarters in Geneva, Switzerland, that acts as an administrative body coordinating the activities of individual Red Cross societies worldwide and of the Red Cross and wartime belligerents. The Red Cross grew from the work of Jean Henry Dunant, a Swiss humanitarian who aided the wounded in the battle of Solferino (1859). In 1863 the Geneva Public Welfare Society was formed and sponsored an international conference that laid the groundwork for the International Committee of the Red Cross (ICRC). The Red Cross became active in 1864, increasing its efforts in the Franco-Prussian War (1870–71) and the BALKAN WARS (1912–13). It grew in international scope, spreading to chapters around the world, including the founding of the American Red Cross in

1881. The organization assumed enormous importance with the outbreak of WORLD WAR I, when it trained volunteers, aided PRISONERS OF WAR and helped in repatriation. For its work the ICRC received the 1917 NOBEL PEACE PRIZE. The organization again played a great role in humanitarian efforts during and after WORLD WAR II, helping PRISONERS OF WAR and attempting to aid victims of the HOLOCAUST. It received its second Nobel Prize for peace in 1944. Today, the Red Cross has a membership of about 100 million, with affiliates in 74 countries. It continues to provide services for victims of war and to assure the carrying out of the GENEVA CONVENTIONS. In addition, its services have been extended to many peacetime activities, including running blood banks, caring for disaster victims, aiding refugees and offering first-aid training. In 1963, its centennial year, the ICRC received a third Nobel Prize, this time shared with the LEAGUE OF RED CROSS SOCIETIES. Its emblem of a red cross on a white field (the reverse of the Swiss flag, replaced in Muslim countries by a red crescent and in Israel by a red star of David) remains an international symbol of humanitarianism and neutrality.

**International Geophysical Year (IGY)** An international project (July 1, 1957–December 31, 1958) designed to study the geophysics of the Earth and its environment. The project was timed to coincide with increased sunspot activity. This enabled scientists to study the effects of sunspots on atmospheric magnetism and radio waves. More than 60,000 scientists from 60 nations were involved in research relating to the IGY. Some of the most important experiments were conducted by researchers stationed in ANTARCTICA. During the project, the first instrumented Earth satellites were launched, leading to the discovery of the VAN ALLEN radiation belts. Hugh Odishaw, the American scientist who coordinated the U.S. effort, called the IGY "the single most significant peaceful activity of mankind since the Renaissance and the Copernican Revolution."

**International Labour Organisation** Specialized agency, originally created in 1919 by the TREATY OF VERSAILLES and affiliated with the LEAGUE OF NATIONS. Its original purpose was to establish inter-

national guidelines for improving labor practices, working conditions and standards of living for workers worldwide. In 1946 the International Labour Organisation (ILO) became an agency of the UNITED NATIONS. In its mission to improve the lives of workers, the ILO promotes standards for working hours, adequate wages, safe and disease-free working conditions, vacations, unemployment insurance, protection of women and children and other such matters and provides technical assistance for vocational and management training. The ILO consists of a general conference of representatives of its 151 member states (in 1985), a governing body and an International Labour Office; it is financed by its member states. In 1969 it was the recipient of the NOBEL PEACE PRIZE. The U.S. withdrew from the ILO in 1977 because of the organization's criticism of ISRAEL and apparent favoring of leftist political movements; however, the U.S. rejoined the organization in 1980. By 2004 the ILO membership had grown to include 177 states.

**International Style** Term used to describe architectural design that is simple, functional, and unornamented, following the theoretical teaching of the BAUHAUS and the leading figures of MODERNISM of the 1920s and 1930s. While historic period design generally has been associated with national or regional traditions—as in French Gothic or Italian Renaissance styles—early modernism developed in France, Germany, the Scandinavian countries and elsewhere in similar patterns, so that all such work can be considered truly international in character. The term was used as the title for an exhibition and related book at the MUSEUM OF MODERN ART in New York curated by Henry-Russell HITCHCOCK and Philip JOHNSON in 1932. Most of the work shown shared such characteristics as flat roofs, large glass areas, plain white walls, and an emphasis on the use of steel and concrete as building materials. The term has come to be associated with and applied to such designs, whereas other types of modern work (that of Frank Lloyd WRIGHT, for example) are not described by this term.

**Internet** Global information network of computers, computer networks and servers joined by the transmission of data—information, files, text, graphics and sound—through satellites and/or fiber optic cables. It eventually developed into a very useful tool for personal, commercial, industrial and administrative tasks. However, its decentralized structure, which allows connections between any computer network regardless of transmission speed or computer model, has made it difficult for governments, businesses and citizens to regulate. To connect to one of these networks, an individual needs only a computer with a modem, a fiber optic cable and an Internet service provider (ISP). In some cases the ISP is a company or branch of government for which the individual works or a college/university in which the individual is enrolled. In others it is a commercial company, such as America Online (AOL), NetZero, MSN, Juno or Earthlink, which provides the connection to the Internet for a monthly fee.

The Internet was developed as a result of U.S. Defense Department research in the 1960s. The goal of the study was to create a communication system that would connect Defense Department posts after a nuclear attack, which would take information on one computer, and compress it into packets of coded data for electronic, cable-bound transfer to another computer. The result was the Advanced Research Projects Agency Network, or ARPANET, which produced ground- and satellite-based means of transferring such "packets" of information between computers. However, researchers quickly learned that the manner in which each of these ARPANETs were constructed made them incompatible with other ARPANETs, causing them to search for means of allowing connections between computer networks, hence the term *Internet*. The result of this additional research was the creation of Transmission Control Protocol and Internet Protocols, commonly abbreviated as TCP/IP, a series of computer communication rules that ensure that information packets transferred between different computers are communicated in a manner discernable to all types of computers, and that the information sent from one machine to another can be deciphered. The flexibility and rapid transfer of informa-

tion over the Defense Department's network made the system popular with other bureaucracies and institutions, such as the National Science Foundation's NSFNET and the Department of Energy's Magnetic Fusion Energy Network (MFENET).

By the 1980s the rapid communication that these networks afforded prompted private companies to develop similar networks within the firms, or intranets. Researchers working on the ARPANET also began to look for ways to transmit audio, video, and graphics over the evolving Internet. Another breakthrough came with the creation of a computer program that allowed its users to understand and utilize the full array of options, or menus, available as a result of a particular Internet connection. The computer program Gopher was one early effort to provide this service. By 1989 enough advances had been made in the transfer of information over the Internet that a new computer network, termed the World Wide Web, was created to facilitate rapid communication among physicists around the world and allow them to collaborate on research projects. Many businesses immediately saw the commercial applications of this computer network and began to petition the U.S. government to expand access to the Internet beyond the scientific and military communities. By the end of the 1980s the Internet was open for commercial ventures. By the middle of the next decade companies like AOL had vastly increased the appeal of the Internet among consumers, while Internet transmission technology allowed the packaging and reception of text, graphics, audio, visual and program files. Academic institutions, libraries, governments and businesses scrambled to reap the benefits of this new communication network.

Some problems with the structure and nature of the Internet became evident by the dawn of the 21st century. Foremost among them, for example, the methods of transmitting information were not originally designed to handle the high volume of Internet traffic that developed. As a result many small institutions, such as colleges, have developed Ethernets, which allow for more rapid connections and transmission of data between computers. Another response has been to utilize

BROADBAND connections, rather than those provided by telephone lines. Because broadband sends out information over a greater number of fiber optic cables than the connections established through telephone cables, this allows for a faster transmission and reception of information.

The issues that have raised the greatest concern are those involving security and content. As more users have transmitted personal information over the Internet, purchasing goods online with credit cards and opening seemingly harmless ELECTRONIC MAIL (e-mail) attachments, they have become the targets of hackers, viruses and moles that were previously confined to the large corporations with connections to the Web. The result has been a continued effort by government agencies and Internet Service Providers to ensure the secure transmission of all data over Internet connections. Also, recent efforts by the U.S. government to prohibit the transmission over the Internet of material it deemed indecent have been struck down by the U.S. Supreme Court (1997) and a federal court (1999). Both courts ruled that the 1996 Communications Decency Act and the 1998 antipornography Child Online Protection Act constituted violations of the First Amendment. In 2003 the state of Utah took aim at another Internet-related problem—spam, or unsolicited e-mail. In an effort to ensure their citizens were not the recipients of such messages, the state made it illegal for most businesses and agencies to send such e-mails without the consent of their recipients.

## Intifada I (1987–1993) (Arabic "shaking off")

An uprising among many parts of the Palestinian Arab population directed against the Israeli military occupation of the GAZA STRIP and the WEST BANK that began in December 1987 when the residents of the Gaza Strip rose up against the Israeli occupation. It resulted in the stoning of Israeli troops by Palestinian youths, and was fueled by incendiary statements by Muslim clergymen. It quickly spread to the West Bank, the other predominantly Palestinian territory occupied by ISRAEL since 1967. Though originally a spontaneous outbreak, the Intifada came under the control of the PALESTINE LIBERATION ORGANIZATION

*Child injured during Intifada I. 1990 (ELDAD RAFAELI/CORBIS)*

(PLO), HAMAS (the Islamic Resistance Movement) and ISLAMIC JIHAD. While all three groups initially demanded that the future state incorporate all of Mandate Palestine, the PLO began in 1988 to move toward the acceptance of an Israeli state with the pre-1967 borders and to advocate some form of coexistence with Israel, causing a split within the movement.

As a result, Hamas, Islamic Jihad and other more radical Palestinian organizations began to dominate the Intifada. These groups increasingly relied on terrorist tactics, such as the placing of bombs in Israeli shopping malls, markets, discotheques and restaurants. The intensity and frequency of these attacks, in addition to the stoning of Israeli troops by Palestinian youths, made it difficult for Israel to develop an effective counterinsurgency strategy. Israeli efforts to shatter the infrastructure of the uprising impeded but did not end the Intifada, because it was not a movement controlled by a rigidly defined hierarchy that was vulnerable to operations against specific individuals or locations. Rather, it was a loosely

controlled organization responding to individual initiatives as well as directives from Hamas and Islamic Jihad.

The first Intifada ended as a result of the opening of negotiations between Palestinians and the Israeli government. As a consequence of the 1991 PERSIAN GULF WAR, U.S. president George H. W. BUSH promised the Arab states that had joined the coalition against Iraq that the U.S. would take an increasingly active role in promoting a lasting settlement of the Palestinian issue. As a result of intensive negotiations begun under the Bush administration (1989–93) and resumed under the administration of President Bill CLINTON, the PLO and Israel signed a peace agreement in September 1993, effectively bringing the Palestinian uprising to an end.

**Intifada II** *(2001–2004)* A second uprising by the Palestinian Arab community that began after negotiations between Israeli prime minister Ehud BARAK and PALESTINIAN AUTHORITY (PA) leader Yasir ARAFAT to establish a Palestinian state composed of the Gaza Strip

and most of the West Bank broke down in late 2000. This second Intifada consisted largely of Palestinian militants with concealed explosives and metal projectiles blowing themselves up in densely populated areas of Israel and the occupied territories. Although these attacks on Israeli nightclubs, restaurants, buses, etc., were apparently the work of HAMAS and Islamic Jihad and Arafat publicly condemned them, the hard-line government of prime minister ARIEL SHARON, who defeated Barak in 2001, accused Arafat of duplicity in the uprising—of officially condemning the destruction in English but communicating approval in Arabic to Palestinian Arabs.

Israeli security forces responded to the violence with a harsh crackdown on suspected terrorists and their supporters. They eventually razed part of PA headquarters, including Arafat's living quarters, and placed Arafat under a virtual house arrest. The Sharon government also authorized military strikes on West Bank towns suspected of harboring Intifada militants. In July 2003 Sharon authorized construction of a tall barrier separating Israel and contiguous Israeli settlements from the West Bank, in order to prevent would-be suicide bombers from reaching Israeli population centers. Negotiations based on the U.S. "Roadmap to Peace" made little headway. After Arafat's death in 2004 and the subsequent election of Mahmoud ABBAS as Palestinian leader, both sides appeared to take a more conciliatory stance and to be willing to work toward a meaningful resolution.

**in vitro fertilization** Method of fertilizing a human egg outside the body of the mother, creating an embryo that can then be transplanted into the mother's uterus and develop normally. The child produced by this technique of fertilization has been popularly called a "test-tube baby." The technique was developed by British physician Patrick C. STEPTOE and Robert G. Edwards and was first used successfully in 1978. It was originally created for those cases of infertility in which the egg is produced normally but cannot be transmitted down the fallopian tube and into the uterus; it is now used in cases of low sperm count as well. The egg, or group of eggs, is removed from the mother's body, exposed to the father's sperm in a special culturing medium, fertilized and allowed to undergo several cell divisions before the tiny embryo is returned to the uterus. The technique has raised a number of ethical controversies but has provided an opportunity for thousands of previously infertile couples to have children.

**Ioffe, Adolf Abrahmovich** *(1883–1927)* Soviet revolutionary and diplomat, a supporter of TROTSKY. A member of the Menshevik Party, he joined Trostky in Vienna in 1908. They both joined the BOLSHEVIKS in 1917. After the revolution he was one of the negotiators of the Russian-German Treaty of BREST-LITOVSK, and he was made ambassador to Germany in 1918. He headed diplomatic missions to Geneva (1922) and China (1923). He remained a strong supporter of Trotsky in the power struggle after LENIN's death (1924). When Trotsky was defeated by STALIN, he committed suicide.

**Ionesco, Eugène** *(1912–1994)* French playwright and essayist. Ionesco, who won international fame with the premier of his very first play, *The Bald Soprano* (1950), was one of the leading figures of the THEATER OF THE ABSURD and the most gifted comic playwright to emerge from within that movement. Ionesco was a master at crafting absurdist, non sequitur dialogues that illustrated the fragility of language and of the social fabric itself. He adopted the existential outlook that society was based on arbitrary values and hence instilled a spirit of alienation in its citizens, who continued to hunger for meaning. This hunger was portrayed by Ionesco with a remarkably light touch, making his plays popular with theater audiences around the world. Other major plays by Ionesco include *The Lesson* (1951), *The Chairs* (1952), *Amedee, or How to Get Rid of It* (1954), *The New Tenant* (1955), *The Killer* (1959), *Rhinoceros* (1960), *Exit the King* (1962) and *A Stroll in the Air* (1963). *Notes and Counternotes* (1964) contains a selection of his essays on the theater.

**Ipatyeff, Vladimir Nikolayevich** *(1867–1952)* Russian chemist. He pioneered work on high-pressure catalytic reactions in hydrocarbons. He was made chairman of the government's chemical committee in 1914 and continued to work for the Soviet government after the revolution. He was, however, anticommunist and in 1927 he left the USSR to settle later in the U.S. He is best known for his work during World War II, when his process for manufacturing high-octane gasoline from low-octane fuels was used to produce aviation fuel.

**IRA** See IRISH REPUBLICAN ARMY.

**Iran (Islamic Republic of Iran)** Iran encompasses an area of 646,128 square miles in Southwest Asia. Known as Persia since ancient times, REZA PAHLAVI changed the country's name to Iran in 1935. For the first 26 years of the 20th century Persia was ruled by the Oajar dynasty, a period marked by chaos and foreign intervention. After the shah was crowned in 1926, he introduced a modernization program, but his close relationship with Germany led Britain and Russia to invade Iran in 1941, forcing the shah to abdicate in favor of his son. The new shah, MUHAMMAD REZA Pahlavi, pursued economic and social reforms (called the White Revolution). The continued Westernization and secularization of Iran brought increased opposition, spearheaded by exiled Islamic Shi'ite leader Ayatollah KHOMEINI. The situation became so volatile that the shah fled Iran in January 1979, and Khomeini assumed power. He started the Islamic Cultural Revolution that prompted the Revolutionary Guards to storm the American Embassy in Teheran (November 1979), resulting in a hostage situation that lasted until January 1981. Historical claims to Iranian territory led neighboring IRAQ to invade Iran in 1980. The eight-year IRAN-IRAQ WAR was devastating, and Iran sued for peace in 1988 under provisions of a UNITED NATIONS plan. The U.S.'s covert involvement in the war surfaced in 1986 as the IRAN-CONTRA SCANDAL, involving secret arms deals with Iran in exchange for Iranian intervention to free American hostages in LEBANON. Since Khomeini's death in 1989, his successor Hashemi Rafsanjani has pursued a more moderate

IRAN

| 1907 | Anglo-Russian agreement to protect foreign mineral interests effectively divides the country into three zones: Russian, British and neutral. |
|------|------|
| 1914 | Britain acquires controlling interest in the Anglo-Persian Oil Company. |
| 1920 | Gilan, an autonomous Soviet republic, is formed in the north of Iran. |
| 1921 | (Feb. 20) Col. Reza Khan takes over Gilan in a coup. |
| 1923 | Reza Khan becomes prime minister. |
| 1926 | Reza Khan is crowned Reza Shah Pahlavi. |
| 1935 | To curry favor with the Nazis, the shah changes the name of his country, Persia, to Iran—meaning "Aryan." |
| 1941 | Britain and Russia invade in 1941; Reza Shah Pahlavi abdicates in favor of his son Mohammad Reza. |
| 1946 | British and Russian occupation troops leave Iran; Azerbaijani dissidents establish independent republic and are put down by Iranian troops; Kurdish republic of Mahabad is proclaimed and suppressed by Iranian troops. |
| 1952 | With the support of Prime Minister Mohammad Mossadeq the Anglo-Iranian Oil Company is nationalized; relations with Great Britain are broken; shah dismisses Mossadeq but is forced to reinstate him; Mossadeq assumes complete control of the government; shah is forced to flee the country; in a countercoup, General Fazlollah Zahedi rallies army behind the shah and the shah is returned to power. |
| 1954 | Under a plan devised in Washington and London a consortium of oil companies is placed in charge of the AIOC (now called British Petroleum). |
| 1955 | Iran joins CENTO. |
| 1957 | SAVAK, the secret police, is established. |
| 1960 | Diplomatic recognition of Israel; Egypt breaks diplomatic relations as a result. |
| 1963 | Shah launches "White Revolution"; land reform and woman suffrage increased; Literacy Corps organized. |
| 1967 | Coronation of the shah. |
| 1969 | Dispute with Iraq over Shatt al-Arab erupts into open conflict. |
| 1970 | Iran accepts UN mediation on its claim to Bahrain. |
| 1973 | Oil industry is nationalized; Iran joins OPEC oil price hike. |
| 1975 | Restakhiz is made the sole political party. |
| 1977 | (October) Ayatollah Khomeini's son dies, sparking riots and strikes. |
| 1978 | (October) Khomeini's expulsion from Iraq to France highlights his position as opposition leader; strikes and demonstrations break out against the shah, country thrown into turmoil. |
| 1979 | (Jan. 16) The shah flees the country; (Feb. 1) Ayatollah Khomeini returns to Iran; (Nov. 4) Revolutionary Guards storm the U.S. embassy and take diplomatic personnel hostage. |
| 1980 | (Jan. 25) Abolhassan Bani Sadr elected as the first postrevolutionary president; Revolutionary Council disbands as Bani Sadr cabinet takes office; (March) nationalization of most |

| | |
|---|---|
| | medium- to large-size industries and financial institutions is begun; (Apr. 25) U.S. military attempt to rescue the embassy hostages fails; (Sept. 22) Iraq invades Iran, beginning bloody eight-year war. |
| 1981 | (Jan. 21) American hostages released; (June) impeachment proceedings commence against Bani Sadr; (July) Mohammed Ali Radjai named president; (August) Radjai and Prime Minister Bahonar killed in bomb attack launched by the Mujaheddin. |
| 1985 | U.S. offers arms deal to Iranians in an attempt to obtain release of American hostages in Lebanon. |
| 1988 | Iran sues for peace with Iraq on the basis of a UN resolution passed in 1987. |
| 1989 | (Feb. 14) Khomeini calls for the death of author Salman Rushdie for his book *The Satanic Verses*; (June) Khomeini dies; Hashemi Rafsanjani emerges as preeminent leader and is elected president. |
| 1990 | (Sept. 24) Iran states it will not violate UN trade sanctions imposed on Iraq for its invasion of Kuwait. |
| 1997 | Reformer Mohammed Khatami is elected president against the candidate of the hard-line clerics. |
| 2001 | Khatami is reelected president with 78% of the vote. |
| 2005 | Hard-line major of Teheran Mahmoud Ahmadinejad is elected to succeed Khatami as president. Negotiations continue between European powers and Iran over Iran's attempt to develop a nuclear program, which has drawn sharp criticism from the U.S. |
| 2006 | The International Atomic Energy Agency reports Iran to the UN Security Council for attempting to construct a nuclear bomb. |

course. He declared Iran's neutrality in the UN-backed war against Iraq for its invasion of Kuwait in 1990, and tried to act as peacemaker during the conflict. Moderate influences within the Iranian government increased with Mohammad KHATAMI's presidential election in 1997 and 2001, and the 2000 parliamentary election. But the reformist Khatami was continually reined in by the hard-line clerics under Supreme Leader Ayatollah Ali Khomenei, who maintained effective control of the country's political life. During the early years of the 21st century, Iran become the object of harsh criticism from U.S. president George W. BUSH for its alleged support of international terrorism and its efforts to develop a nuclear program. The power of the Islamic hard-liners was strengthened in 2005 when the conservative mayor of Teheran, Mahmoud Ahmadinejad, was elected to succeed Khatami as president. In 2006 the INTERNATIONAL ATOMIC ENERGY AGENCY reported Iran to the UN Security Council for allegedly trying to develop a nuclear bomb. (See also IRAN HOSTAGE CRISIS; PERSIAN GULF WAR.)

**Iran-contra scandal** Political scandal that rocked the second term in office of President Ronald REAGAN. When Reagan came to office in 1981, the U.S. and IRAN were bitter adversaries. After the IRANIAN REVOLUTION OF 1979, Iran had held more than 50 American hostages for over a year. Reagan denounced Iran because of its support of terrorism but later funded the "contra" movement, which was fighting a guerrilla war against the leftist Sandinista government of NICARAGUA. The Democrat-controlled Congress objected and voted to stop any financial support of the contras. In 1986 the press revealed that the U.S. government had secretly shipped arms to Iran and diverted the funds to a Swiss bank account controlled by the contras in violation of Congress' ban. Highly publicized congressional investigations revealed that the prime movers in the scandal were U.S. Marine Lieutenant Colonel Oliver North and his boss, Vice Admiral John Poindexter. Also implicated was Robert "Bud" McFarland, the national security adviser. The hearings caused a sensation. Although President Reagan denied involvement and was never directly

implicated, the scandal put his credibility and competence into question.

**Iran hostage crisis** After Mohammad REZA SHAH PAHLAVI of IRAN was forced to leave his country in January 1979, and was subsequently admitted to the U.S. for medical treatment, tensions between the U.S. and Islamic fundamentalists within Iran greatly increased. On November 4, 1979, Iranian students, with the support of fundamentalists in the provisional government, seized the U.S. embassy in Teheran and held 63 members of the embassy staff hostage. The students demanded the return of the ousted shah for trial. The crisis received almost continual television and press coverage in the U.S. and virtually paralyzed the administration of U.S. president Jimmy CARTER. An American military rescue attempt failed disastrously on April 25, 1980, further exacerbating matters. The crisis and Carter's handling of it became a major issue in the 1980 U.S. presidential election and contributed to Carter's defeat by Ronald REAGAN in November 1980. Behind-the-scenes diplomacy and the payment of a substantial sum of U.S.-held Iranian assets finally secured the hostages' release, which the Iranians timed to coincide with Reagan's inauguration. Most Americans viewed the crisis as a manifestation of anti-American feelings and a test of U.S. strength. However, many Middle East experts interpreted the hostage-taking as part of a power struggle between hard-line Islamic fundamentalists and pro-Western moderates within the provisional government. The fundamentalist faction (led by Ayatollah KHOMEINI) gained the upper hand and purged the moderates, establishing an Islamic republic.

**Iranian Revolution of 1979** IRAN's Shah Muhammed Reza PAHLAVI was opposed by Iranian liberals for his authoritarianism and by conservatives for his westernism. These groups collaborated in 1978 under exiled Muslim religious leader Ayatollah Ruhollah KHOMEINI until rioting forced the shah to flee in January 1979. Strikes, huge demonstrations, the neutrality of the army and the return of Khomeini to Iran brought down the government by February. Khomeini declared Iran an Islamic republic, establishing a revolutionary council to rule. Trials and executions of opponents ensued. The regime was approved overwhelmingly by a March 30, 1979, referendum, but the terror continued. Iran broke relations with the West and the Islamic world, and on November 4, 1979, militants seized U.S. embassy staff as hostage for the return of the shah's assets (see IRAN HOSTAGE CRISIS). Despite the shah's death (July 1980) the hostage crisis continued until Algerian mediation led to a U.S-Iranian agreement freeing the hostage as Ronald REAGAN was being inaugurated as U.S. president (January 20, 1981). Khomeini's Islamic revolution continued in Iran.

**Iran-Iraq War** Capping a long dispute over the Shatt-al-Arab waterway, and Ayatollah Ruhollah KHOMEINI's attempts to destabilize Iraq's government under President Saddam HUSSEIN, IRAQ invaded IRAN on September 21–22, 1980. With its well-equipped army it hoped for a quick victory. Iranian forces retaliated; Khomeini called for total mobilization and threatened oil shipments through the Strait of Hormuz. Despite massive offensives (Iraq

had a 500,000-man army, Iran had 2 million), neither side was able to occupy enemy territory, and the war settled into a vicious, costly stalemate until 1988. Iraqi air attacks against tankers in the Persian Gulf led the U.S. to initiate an international naval patrol tilted against Iran, which was held responsible for terrorist attacks. Iraq also employed chemical warfare, and, after many failed attempts the UNITED NATIONS arranged a cease-fire in August 1988. (See also PERSIAN GULF WAR.)

**Iraq (Republic of Iraq)** Iraq, encompassing the river valleys of the Tigris and Euphrates, was a birthplace of many of the civilizations of the ancient world. It is situated northwest of the PERSIAN GULF and is bordered by IRAN to the east, KUWAIT and SAUDI ARABIA to the south, JORDAN and SYRIA to the west and TURKEY to its north—an area of 167,881 square miles. Britain occupied the cities of BASRA and BAGHDAD during WORLD WAR I, and Iraq, carved out of the crumbled OTTOMAN EMPIRE, became a British

mandate in 1920. The growth of nationalist feeling led to the termination of the mandate in 1932 and Iraq's acceptance as an independent country in the LEAGUE OF NATIONS. Britain again occupied Iraq during WORLD WAR II. The corrupt pro-British government that ruled after the war was overthrown and the royal family executed during the revolution of 1958. The new government of Abd al-Karim KASSEM was overthrown in 1963. Five years of war with Iraq's Kurdish minority ended with another coup, which brought Ahmed Hasan al-BAKR to power (1968). When Bakr resigned in 1979, Saddam HUSSEIN became president. Hussein invaded Iran (September 1980), claiming Iraqi rights to the Shatt al-Arab waterway and the Iranian province of Khuzistan. The eight-year IRAN-IRAQ WAR was devastating for both countries and ended with a cease-fire in 1988. In August 1990 Hussein invaded and occupied Kuwait, at the head of the Persian Gulf, claiming historical rights to the territory. UN air forces, led by the

| | IRAQ |
|---|---|
| 1914 | (November) British occupy Shatt al-Arab waterway, removing it from control of Germany's ally, the Ottomans; modernize port at Basra. |
| 1917 | (March) British occupy Baghdad; promise postwar independence, encouraging a nationalist movement. |
| 1920 | San Remo Conference; League of Nations makes Iraq a British mandate; Faisal I installed as king. |
| 1923 | Oil discovered. |
| 1932 | Nominal independence granted; British keep military bases. |
| 1941 | "Golden Square" officers group attempts anti-British, pro-German coup; Britain reoccupies. |
| 1945 | Pro-British prime minister installed; corruption rises. |
| 1958 | "Free Officers" group under Abd al-Karim stages coup; royal family and prime minister killed; U.S. lands Marines in Lebanon in response to this and other Arab nationalist activity. |
| 1961 | Death of Jawid Salim, creator of huge modern sculpture, "Monument to Revolution," in Baghdad. |
| 1962 | Nationalists agitate for union with Nasser's United Arab Republic; communists oppose. |
| 1963 | Nationalist coalition seizes power; massacres communists; coalition includes Ba'athists, who favor a pan-Arab, secular socialist state. |
| 1964 | Civil war with Kurds in northern Iraq. |
| 1968 | Ba'athists seize power after Arab defeat in Six-Day War; under Ahmed Hasan al-Bakr, country turns toward Soviets. |
| 1972 | Oil companies nationalized; price boom brings great wealth to government. |
| 1974 | Civil war with Kurds. |
| 1978 | Shi'ite Muslims (majority of population) oppose secular policies of Ba'athists; violent oppression of Shi'ites results. |
| 1979 | Ayatollah Khomeini leaves exile to foment Shi'ite revolution in Iran; vows to carry it to Iraq; Saddam Hussein succeeds Bakr. |
| 1980 | Saddam Hussein invades Iran; bloody eight-year war follows. |
| 1988 | Cease-fire with Iran. |
| 1990 | Iraq overruns Kuwait and declares annexation; U.S. organizes large force in Saudi Arabia and Turkey; issues ultimatum that Iraq pull back. |
| 1991 | After the heaviest aerial bombardment in history, U.S.-led forces invade Iraq; infrastructure of the country is destroyed; Hussein fails to draw Israel into war (and hence drive out Arab members of U.S. coalition); he remains in power despite Shi'ite and Kurdish rebellions; Kurds begin disastrous exodus into mountains of Turkey, where thousands die. |
| 1998 | Hussein expel UN weapons inspectors from Iraq. |
| 2003 | U.S.-led, coalition invades Iraq and overthrows Hussein's regime. |
| 2005 | First free elections in 50 years lead to formation of Iraqi government dominated by Shi'ite and Kurd representatives. The new government begins work to prepare a constitution. |

U.S., attacked Iraq on January 16, 1991, after Hussein refused to withdraw from Kuwait. Six weeks of intensive high-precision bombing virtually destroyed Iraq's infrastructure; by the end of February 1991, Iraqi forces were in disarray and the nation was forced to accept a cease-fire on U.S. terms. Various rebel groups within Iraq subsequently turned against Hussein, and the country fell into civil strife. Hussein succeeded in suppressing rebellions by Kurds in the north and Shi'ites in the south. Iraq's repeated refusal to allow international weapons inspection teams such as UNSCOM and UNMOVIC full access to suspected sites of weapons of mass destruction resulted in a March 2003 U.S.-led invasion that deposed Hussein (see IRAQ WAR). The U.S. administration in Iraq after the fall of Hussein turned over political authority to the Interim Iraqi Governing Council composed of representatives from the Kurdish, Shi'ite and Sunni communities, and democratic elections were held in January 2005. The new government, with Kurdish leader Jalal Talabani as president and Shi'ite leader Ibrahim Jafare as prime minister, set out to write a new constitution for the country. After the overthrow of Hussein, the U.S.-led military occupation and its predominantly Kurdish and Shi'ite Iraqi allies faced a bloody insurgency dominated by Sunni militants. (See also PERSIAN GULF WAR.)

**Iraq War** (2003– ) In the aftermath of the terrorist attacks against New York City and Washington, D.C., on SEPTEMBER 11, 2001, U.S. president George W. BUSH began to criticize the Iraqi government of Saddam HUSSEIN for allegedly maintaining ties with radical Islamic terrorist groups, such as the one (al-QAEDA) that initiated the attacks. He also accused Hussein of undertaking a program to acquire weapons of mass destruction (WMDS; nuclear, biological, and chemical weapons) in violation of UN resolutions. Although the Iraqi government adamantly denied ties to Islamic terrorist groups and allegations that it was developing such weapons, U.S. and British intelligence agencies claimed to have evidence of an Iraqi WMD program. After failing to obtain authorization from the UN Security Council to

authorize a military operation against Iraq in the winter of 2002–03, President Bush assembled a "coalition of the willing" outside the auspices of the world body. While the original list of the coalition included 48 members, the U.K. and Australia were the only countries that supplied more than a token contingent of fighting forces. In March and April 2003, coalition forces drove into Iraq from a staging area in Kuwait, defeated the Iraqi army, overthrew the government of Hussein and occupied the country. The coalition was supported by an Iraqi Kurdish militia comprising more than 50,000 troops. The deposed Iraqi dictator went into hiding with several of his associates but was later captured and prepared for trial as a war criminal. On May 1, 2003, President Bush announced that major combat operations were over, but as the U.S.-led occupation set up an interim government to administer the country, a violent insurgency broke out in areas inhabited by Sunni Muslims, who felt marginalized by the Kurdish and Shi'ite groups that were jockeying for the political power that had eluded them under Hussein's Sunni-dominated regime. For the next several years U.S. forces worked to train Iraqi military and police units to take over the task of defeating the insurgency, as the American public lost its enthusiasm for a long military occupation and the costs and casualty figures mounted. In early 2005 nationwide elections in Iraq brought to power a government dominated by Shi'ite and Kurdish factions, which began to write a constitution for the country. The Sunni minority (bolstered by foreign fighters who slipped into the country across it porous borders with Syria and Iran) continued its violent insurgency, which resulted in horrific scenes of carnage as suicide bombers attacked Iraqi soldiers, police and civilians, as well as U.S. troops. After an intensive investigation, U.S. occupation authorities found no evidence of ties between the Hussein regime and Islamic terrorist groups or of Iraqi government programs to create WMDs. The Bush administration thereupon sought to justify the invasion on the grounds that the introduction of democratic rule in the Middle East would lead to political stability and economic progress in this volatile part of the world, which would in turn reduce the

appeal of terrorism to its disenfranchised and destitute inhabitants.

**Ireland** (Eire; Republic of Ireland) Island nation in the Atlantic Ocean, 50 miles west of Great Britain. The Republic of Ireland occupies the south, central and northwest regions of the island of Ireland. Ireland entered the 20th century as part of the UNITED KINGDOM, represented in the British Parliament. Intermittently throughout the 19th century, the Irish had agitated for independence. In the late 19th century, two bills proposing HOME RULE for Ireland were introduced in Parliament but defeated; a third was passed in 1914. Northern Protestants, led by Sir Edward CARSON, were determined to defend the union with Britain by force. However, Home Rule was deferred for the duration of WORLD WAR I. Moderate Irish nationalists supported the British war effort. In April 1916, militant nationalist and left-wing elements, including SINN FÉIN, launched the abortive EASTER REBELLION in DUBLIN under the leadership of Patrick PEARSE and James CONNOLLY; the British quickly suppressed the rebellion, but the subsequent execution of the 16 rebel leaders turned them into martyrs and led to increased public support for Irish independence. In the 1918 British general elections, Sinn Féin won 72 of the 105 Irish seats in the House of Commons; the Sinn Féin members refused to take their seats, but instead created a rebel Irish parliament, the DÁIL EIREANN, in Dublin (1919).

Several years of guerrilla war followed as the rebels battled the constabulary, which was reinforced by the "Black and Tans." Under the Government of Ireland Act (December 1920), the six Protestant-dominated counties of Ulster were given their own home rule parliament. An Anglo-Irish Treaty (December 1921) created the **Irish Free State** as a self-governing dominion within the British COMMONWEALTH. NORTHERN IRELAND opted to remain with the U.K. The new Irish Free State consisted of 26 of the 32 Irish counties. The IRISH CIVIL WAR (1922–23) followed in the Free State between those accepting the treaty and a majority of Sinn Féin, led by Eamon DE VALERA and supported by the IRISH REPUBLICAN ARMY (IRA), who opposed the

# Ireland

ATLANTIC OCEAN

SCOTLAND (U.K.)

North Channel

Dungloe
Letterkenny

NORTHERN IRELAND (U.K.)

Donegal

Donegal Bay

Sligo

Monaghan

Irish Sea

Ballina

Cavan    Dundalk

Achill I.

Castlebar    Carrick on Shannon

Erne R.    Blackwater R.    Boyne R.    Drogheda

Knock

Longford

Lough Mask    Roscommon    Lough Ree    Mullingar

Clifden

Lough Corrib    Ballinasloe    Athlone    Dublin    Dun Laoghaire
Bray

Galway

Liffey R.

Galway Bay

Tullamore

ARAN ISLANDS

Gort    Lough Derg    Portlaoise    Wicklow

Nore R.    Carlow    Arklow

Ennis    Nenagh    Barrow R.    Bann R.

Limerick    Kilkenny    Cashel

Listowel    Tipperary    Clonmel    New Ross

Tralee    Newmarket    Suir R.    Wexford

Dingle    Killorglin    Waterford

Dingle Bay    Blackwater R.    Dungarvan

Killarney    Blarney

Kenmare    Lee R.    Cork    Youghal    N

Kinsale    St. George's Channel

Kenmare Bay    Bantry    Ballinspittle

Bantry Bay

0    50 miles
0    50 km

© Infobase Publishing

partition of Ireland. The pro-treaty side prevailed, and in 1927 de Valera took his Dail seat as leader of the new FIANNA FÁIL party in opposition to a government led by the forerunner of the FINE GAEL party. Following Fianna Fáil's election victory in 1932, de Valera became prime minister and brought in a new constitution (1937), still largely in force, which described the national territory as "the whole island of Ireland" and enshrined Roman Catholic moral and social precepts. Ireland remained neutral during WORLD WAR II (officially known as "the Emergency") and maintained Irish neutrality in the postwar era.

The 1948 elections brought to power a four-party coalition. The country subsequently adopted the name Republic of Ireland and left the COMMONWEALTH (1949). In the same year,

British legislation guaranteed that Northern Ireland would not cease to be part of the U.K. without the consent of the Northern Irish parliament. De Valera was again prime minister (1951–54, 1957–59), then became president of the republic until his death in 1973. Under the Fianna Fáil government of Sean Lemass (1959–66), Ireland achieved significant economic progress and established free trade with the U.K. The Fianna Fáil government of Jack Lynch (1966–73) took the republic into full membership of the EUROPEAN COMMUNITY and the EUROPEAN ECONOMIC COMMUNITY, to the advantage of Irish agriculture. Successive Dublin governments sought a U.K.-Irish cooperative framework within which to address the conflict of aspirations between Protestants and Catholics in Northern Ireland,

where escalating violence from the late 1960s had impelled the U.K. government to impose direct rule in 1972–73 and again from 1974. In August 1979, Lord MOUNTBATTEN was murdered by the IRA while visiting Ireland, and 18 British soldiers in Northern Ireland were killed the same day in a separate IRA attack. As a result Lynch (who had succeeded Cosgrave as prime minister in 1977) agreed to strengthen border security. In 1979 Charles Haughey (whose career had survived allegations of gun-running for the IRA in 1970) became Fianna Fáil leader and prime minister, but elections two years later brought another Fine Gael/Labour coalition to power under Garett Fitzgerald. In November 1985 Fitzgerald and U.K. prime minister Margaret THATCHER signed an Anglo-Irish agreement (the HILLSBOROUGH ACCORD) giving Ireland a consultative role in Northern affairs in return of accepting that reunification could be achieved only with the consent of a Northern majority. Although Haughey had opposed the accord, he agreed to abide by it after he regained office in 1987.

Ireland faced serious economic problems in the 1980s—high inflation and unemployment. In the late 1980s, the new Haughey government intensified its predecessor's economic austerity program, seeking to reduce a huge budget deficit. In November 1990, Mary Robinson of the left-wing Labour Party became Ireland's first woman president (the official head of state) in an electoral upset.

In 1998 the major Catholic and Protestant factions in the struggle over Northern Ireland met with British and U.S. diplomats and signed the Good Friday Agreement, which created a joint power-sharing arrangement for the territory's rule. However, conflicts between and within the parties representing these sectarian groups have led to the repeated suspension of the agreement, despite the efforts of some Catholic and Protestant leaders, such as John HUME and David TRIMBLE, to make the settlement stick. Violent conflict decreased after the agreement, and in 2005 the Provisional IRA (PIRA) announced the end of its armed campaign. In the meantime Ireland experienced a remarkable spurt of economic growth in the early years of the 21st century. Its skilled and flexible workforce and

| IRELAND | |
|---|---|
| 1904 | W. B. Yeats and Lady Gregory found Abbey Theatre; Irish literary renaissance continues. |
| 1905 | Founding of Sinn Féin, independence movement; *Irish Independent* publishes first issue. |
| 1916 | Easter Uprising by Irish Republican Brotherhood crushed by British; 16 rebel leaders executed. |
| 1918 | After general election, Irish members of British Parliament refuse to report to London; convene as the Dáil in Dublin (1919). |
| 1920 | British offer limited autonomy to both Northern and Southern Ireland; the south rejects it. |
| 1921 | Anglo-Irish Treaty: British agree to Irish Free State, with expanded autonomy; six counties of Northern Ireland remain within United Kingdom. |
| 1922 | Civil war between factions accepting Free State compromise and those demanding full independence; Yeats wins Nobel Prize in literature; James Joyce's *Ulysses* published in Paris, banned in Ireland. |
| 1923 | Fighting ends but IRA continues guerrilla struggle for independence; IRa outlawed. |
| 1932 | Eamon de Valera elected prime minister; begins cutting ties to Britain. |
| 1937 | Dail adopts new constitution, embodying Catholic stance on many moral issues. |
| 1941 | Ireland remains neutral in World War II to show displeasure with Britain. |
| 1949 | Independence declared; republic established; Ireland withdraws from Commonwealth. |
| 1961 | First television station. |
| 1965 | Anglo-Irish free-trade treaty. |
| 1973 | Legal ban on contraceptives relaxed. |
| 1979 | Lord Mountbatten assassinated by IRA in Sligo; IRA continues terrorist campaign for independent Northern Ireland. |
| 1980 | Population at one-half the level of 1840. |
| 1985 | Prime Minister Garret FitzGerald signs Anglo-Irish Agreement (Hillsborough Accord) on Northern Ireland with British prime minister Thatcher. |
| 1990 | President Lenihan brought down by scandal; Mary Robinson elected as first woman president. |
| 1991 | Death of writer Sean O'Faolain. |
| 1995 | A national referendum legalizes divorce, effective in 1997. |
| 1998 | Irish prime minister Bertie Ahern and British prime minister Tony Blair sign the Good Friday Agreement, by which Ireland renounces all territorial claims to Northern Ireland and a North-South Ministerial Council composed of ministers from both governments is established. The agreement is approved by referenda in both countries and becomes effective in 1999. |
| 2001 | The IRA begins disarmament. |
| 2005 | The Provisional IRA (PIRA) announces the end of its campaign of violence. |

low corporate tax rates attracted a substantial amount of foreign investment. Agriculture, long the dominant sector of the economy was overtaken by the industrial and service sectors. Exports were the primary engine of the country's growth, which catapulted it to the second rank of per-capita grass domestic product among the EUROPEAN UNION's 25 members by 2005.

**Ireland, John Nicholson** (1879–1962) English composer. Ireland studied at the Royal College of Music, London, where he later taught. He also served as a church organist in Chelsea (1904–26). His many influences include the scenic beauty of the Channel Islands, folk music, German romanticism and Celtic myth. He is most admired for the simple beauty of his over

70 songs, many of them set to poems by writers such as John Masefield, A. E. HOUSMAN and Thomas HARDY. Ireland's other works include chamber music, piano works including a concerto (1930), choral pieces and orchestral music such as the *Symphonic Rhapsody* (1920–21) and the *London Overture* (1936).

**Irgun Zvai Leumi** Zionist terrorist organization founded in 1937. From 1943, Menachem BEGIN was its commander. Its most notorious act of terrorism was the blowing up of the KING DAVID HOTEL in Jerusalem on July 22, 1946. The British administration was housed in the southwest wing of the hotel, which was completely destroyed, and 91 people were killed. Irgun claimed responsibility for more than 200 terrorist acts against the British and the Arabs.

**Irian Barat** A province of INDONESIA that comprises the western half of the island of NEW GUINEA and approximately 12 nearby islands; formerly known as Dutch, or Netherlands, New Guinea. Occupied by the Japanese during WORLD WAR II, it was not returned to Dutch control until 1949. Indonesian claims to the region led to a Dutch handover of the territory in 1963; Indonesia's sovereignty was recognized following a plebiscite in 1969.

**Irian Jaya (West Papua)** Western half of the island of New Guinea belonging to INDONESIA. The largest Indonesian province, Irian Jaya is nearly three-quarters tropical jungle. Although sparsely populated, the western half of the island possesses large copper and oil reserves, and its nearby coves and bays are full of fish and shrimp. In an effort to reduce overcrowding on several of its other islands caused by excessive population growth, Indonesia resettled residents and migrants from Java, Bali and Sulawesi in Irian Jaya during the 1970s. By the mid-1980s these new residents and migrants were forced to enter the forested regions to carve out a niche for themselves, leading to poaching on national reserves, the transformation of forest land into farmland and commercial logging. Because the ethnic composition of Irian Jaya has changed drastically since the

1970s, the primary schools were flooded with students who lacked the necessary language skills to complete their education.

Following the example of EAST TIMOR, several indigenous movements have emerged in Irian Jaya to demand independence from Indonesia. The three most important independence movements are the Papuan Presidium Council (PDP), the Free Papua Movement (OPM) and West Papua Action (WPA). The Indonesian government has actively attempted to suppress these movements, but separatist agitation has continued.

**Irish Civil War** See ANGLO-IRISH CIVIL WAR OF 1916–23.

**Irish Free State** See IRELAND.

**Irish Literary Revival** A resurgence in nationalist Irish literature that began in the latter decades of the 19th century and continued into the 1920s. Some Irish nationalists favored a "Gaelic revival" but were unsuccessful in reintroducing the Gaelic language. Most writers supported W. B. YEATS, who felt that a national literature could exist even though written in English. The beginnings of the movement occurred with a renewed interest in Irish folklore and culture evidenced by works such as *Love Songs of Connaught* by Samuel Ferguson (1810–86) and *Literary History of Ireland* (1892) by Douglas HYDE. The same year Yeats's first play *The Countess Cathleen* (1892) appeared, thus launching a solely Irish drama separate from that of England. In 1899 Yeats and Lady GREGORY founded the Irish Literary Theatre to promote Irish drama. It became the Irish National Theatre Society, giving its first performance in 1902 of AE's *Deirdre* and Yeats' *Cathleen Ni Houlihan*. In the following year John Millington SYNGE's *In the Shadow of the Glen* and Padraic Colum's *Broken Soil* were presented. With the help of Annie HORNIMAN, the society found a home in the ABBEY THEATRE in 1904. Periodicals fundamental to the revival include *The Irish Statesman,* a literary review edited by AE, and the *Irish Review,* which was founded in 1911 by Colum, James STEPHENS, and Thomas MacDonagh. Other writers associated with the Irish literary revival include George MOORE,

Sean O'CASEY, George Bernard SHAW and James JOYCE.

**Irish Republican Army (IRA)** Nationalist organization whose goal is an independent and unified IRELAND. It was formed in 1919 by veterans of the 1916 EASTER REBELLION led by Michael COLLINS. Becoming the military arm of the SINN FÉIN party, it fought the British Black and Tans; after the partition of Ireland and the formation of the Irish Free State in 1922, it refused to recognize a separate NORTHERN IRELAND and, as a secret terrorist organization, continued an armed struggle against the new government. The IRA's hit-and-run bombings and street fights were quite successful for about 10 years, but it was significantly weakened after former IRA supporter Eamon DE VALERA became head of the Free State in 1932. Its violent tactics and pro-German activities during WORLD WAR II further lessened the IRA's popularity. After the war, it was outlawed by both Irish governments but continued to operate and to perpetuate terrorist attacks throughout the 1950s. After a comparatively peaceful time in the 1960s, the IRA broke into two groups (1969), forming a moderate or official wing, which pursued political means, and a radical or provisional wing, which continued to use violent techniques. Subsequently, the provisional mounted a campaign of terror in Northern Ireland, often concentrating on members of the British armed forces. In the early 1990s, the IRA continued to operate as an underground terrorist organization, and sporadic acts of violence perpetrated by its members continued in the two Irelands and England. In 1994 the IRA declared a cease-fire and Sinn Féin entered into talks with Britain, but the talks and the cease-fire ended in 1996. Sinn Féin did, however, accept the Good Friday Agreement of 1998 that established a power-sharing arrangement for Northern Ireland. In 2001 the IRA announced it had begun disarmament.

**Iron Curtain** Term used to denote the boundary between Soviet-dominated Eastern Europe and the democratic West during the COLD WAR. The Iron Curtain was not so much a physical barrier between two geographical areas as a metaphor for the constraints on the movement of people and ideas that the communist regimes imposed on their citizens. The term was coined by Sir Winston CHURCHILL during a speech he delivered at Westminster College in Fulton, Missouri, on March 5, 1946. "From Stettin in the Baltic to Trieste on the Adriatic, an iron curtain has descended across the continent." Denouncing the "people governments" that the USSR was establishing in Eastern Europe, Churchill added that "this is certainly not the liberated Europe we fought to build up." (See also BERLIN WALL.)

**Iroquois Theater fire** Disastrous fire of December 31, 1903, that killed more than 500 patrons at the Iroquois Theater in Chicago. A matinee audience at the sumptuous theater was engulfed in flames after the stage caught fire and the asbestos safety curtain failed to function. Some were burned to death or died of smoke inhalation, but most of those killed were crushed or suffocated in the hysterical dash for exists. The death toll made the fire the worst single-structure fire in American history.

**Irving, Clifford** (1930– ) American novelist and master literary forger. Irving began his writing career as a novelist and published three now-forgotten volumes of fiction. But he assured himself of a dubious immortality as the coauthor (with children's book writer Richard Suskind) of a forged autobiography of reclusive American billionaire Howard HUGHES, for which McGraw-Hill, the publisher of Irving's novels, paid Irving $765,000 in 1971. The autobiography manuscript (complete with notes in Hughes's handwriting, forged by Irving) was drawn both from library research and from illicit plagiarism of an unpublished work on Hughes's financial empire by journalist James Phelan, who was one of the first to point the finger at Irving as a forger. Deemed by many as the greatest literary hoax of the 20th century, the forged autobiography was never published and earned Irving, as well as Irving's wife (who deposited the advance check made out to Hughes in a false Swiss bank account) and coauthor Suskind, brief prison terms.

**Irving, John Winslow** (1942– ) American novelist. Irving had already written three fanciful novels when he drew critical acclaim and national atten-

tion with *The World According to Garp* (1978, filmed 1982), which tells the story of novelist T. S. Garp, son of an iconoclastic single mother, Jenny Field. The book presents a dark side of modern life, but not without humor; and like Irving's subsequent fiction, imbues contemporary situations with traditional, romantic values. His other works include *The Hotel New Hampshire* (1981, filmed 1984), *Cider House Rules* (1985) and *A Prayer for Owen Meany* (1989). Irving's screen adaptation of *Cider House Rules* won an Academy Award for best adopted screenplay in 2000.

**Irwin, James** (1930–1991) U.S. astronaut, popular public speaker and founder of the High Flight Foundation, a nonprofit religious organization. Irwin spent almost three days on the surface of the moon in 1971, but most recently has lead five expeditions to Mount Ararat in Turkey, searching for the remains of Noah's Ark. Irwin says that he experienced a religious revelation during his APOLLO 15 (July 26–August 7, 1971) flight; he resigned from NASA on July 1, 1972. Born in Pittsburgh, Pennsylvania, Irwin attended the U.S. Naval Academy at Annapolis, receiving a B.S. in 1951. After earning an M.S. in aeronautical engineering and instrumentation engineering from the University of Michigan, he entered the U.S. Air Force, serving as a fighter pilot. Irwin joined NASA in 1966, where he tested lunar module systems and served on the support crew for *Apollo 10*. As lunar command module pilot for *Apollo 15*, Irwin and fellow astronaut David Scott were the first astronauts to make use of the Lunar Rover, an electric car that carried them more than 18 miles on three moon excursions lasting a total of 21 hours.

**Isherwood, Christopher** (**William Bradshaw Isherwood**) (1904–1986) British-born author. Educated at Cambridge, during the 1930s Isherwood was closely associated with poet W. H. AUDEN. The two collaborated on three verse plays and a travel book about China. Isherwood immigrated to the U.S. in 1939 and settled in California. He was best known for the stories he wrote in the 1930s about pre-Nazi BERLIN, which became the basis for the play and film *I Am a Camera* and the stage and screen musical *Cabaret*. These adaptations enabled him to give up the

HOLLYWOOD screenwriting with which he had supported himself for a number of years. Isherwood was one of the first international figures to admit that he was homosexual, and in the 1970s became a leading spokesman for GAY RIGHTS. His autobiography, *Christopher and His Kind,* dealt candidly with homosexuality.

**Iskander, Fazil** (1929– ) Soviet writer. Although born in Abkhazia, Iskander's stories and poetry are written in the Russian language. The plots of his stories are simple, and the style is conversational and witty, although this does not weaken the strong satire. Iskander's best-known novel is *The Goatibex Constellation* (1966), in which bureaucrats aspire to crossbreed an ordinary goat with a mountain wild ox, thus resolving the problem of food production in the Soviet Union and affirming Michurinist genetics.

**Islamic Salvation Front (FIS)** Algerian political party (1989–92). The FIS was a political party formed in 1989 as a result of the newly revised Algerian constitution. Previously, politics in ALGERIA had been dominated by the National Liberation Front (FLN), a political organization formed in 1954 that led the country to independence from France in 1962. After independence, the FLN monopolized political power and established a secular state. When the new constitution provided for multiparty local and provincial elections in 1990, the FIS nominated a slate of candidates throughout the country who called for an end to secularization. These candidates trumpeted an Algerian version of ISLAMISM, a political philosophy calling for a return to Islamic practices as specified in the Koran and the transformation of the country into an Islamic republic modeled on the one in Iran. The FIS achieved a stunning political victory in the 1990 elections, winning a sizable majority of municipal and provincial offices. As the party entered the first round of the national elections in January 1992. The returns indicated that the FIS would win a majority in parliament and therefore would be in a position to create an Algerian theocracy. In response, a military and civilian cabal forced President Chadli Benjedid to resign, suspended the elections and created a high committee of state to govern the country.

This committee promptly attempted to suppress the FIS and its sources of support. After the nullification of the election and the suppression of the FIS, its militants mounted an insurrection against the secular government and its supporters—military officers, government officials, teachers, journalists and liberal members of the clergy. In 1994 FIS supporters seized hostages in an attempt to force the high committee to reverse its actions.

Although suppressed by the government, the FIS did attempt to restrain its more violent supporters. In 1997 it ordered all its members to observe a cease-fire, announcing that it had begun negotiations with the high committee to reach a settlement that would allow the FIS to remain a force in Algerian politics and society. However, by then the FIS faced a rival among fundamentalist Muslims—the Armed Islamic Group (GIA)—which planned and executed terrorist acts against the secular Algerian regime, such as a series of car bombings. By the end of the 20th century, it was estimated that more than 75,000 people had died as a result of the FIS and GIA's insurgency and the government's efforts to suppress it.

**Islamism** An extreme version of Islam that demands that Islamic governments strictly enforce the tenets of the Koran. Islamism originated in response to the dissolution of the OTTOMAN EMPIRE after WORLD WAR I and the emergence of increasing Western influences in the new Arab states that succeeded it in the Middle East. To preserve the Muslim heritage from the secular influences of Western life, some devout Muslims turned to a more extreme version of their faith. After the emergence of secular trends in the Arab world, Islamists also fought against secular Arab states, such as Gamal Abdel NASSER's EGYPT and FLN ALGERIA. Toward the end of the 20th century, Islamists made the U.S. a focus of their opposition: the stationing of its military forces near the holy sites of Mecca and Medina in SAUDI ARABIA, its continued support for the state of ISRAEL, and its support of secular regimes in predominantly Muslim countries made it an enemy of the basic tenets of Islamism.

Islamism was the major motivation behind various attempts to end what its adherents regarded as the corrupt, decadent influence of Western culture in Islamic societies. When the Ayatollah RUHOLLAH KHOMENI, a Shi'ite cleric, came to power in IRAN following the deposition of the shah (see MOHAMMAD REZA SHAH PAHLAVI) in 1979, he created a theocratic state dedicated to enforcing Muslim law throughout the nation that fulfilled the goals of Islamism. Other examples of Islamists include the TALIBAN, a fundamentalist Muslim group that ruled a large portion of AFGHANISTAN from 1994 to 2001, and AL-QAEDA, a paramilitary terrorist group given sanctuary by the Taliban. The Wahhabi sect in Saudi Arabia has had a powerful influence on the domestic affairs of that country, and the ISLAMIC SALVATION FRONT, a political party in Algeria, in 1992 attempted to take power through democratic elections, and then reverted to guerrilla warfare when the secular government nullified its electoral victory. In recent years, Islamism has been dealt a series of setbacks. The Taliban was forced out of power in Afghanistan by U.S. military forces in December 2001, and ruling clerics in Iran faced growing opposition from groups favoring an accommodation with Western nations and the secularization of Iranian society. Moreover, many governments in predominantly Islamic countries openly cooperated with the U.S. in its ongoing war on terror by keeping Islamists within their borders under surveillance to determine if they are directly or indirectly supporting al-Qaeda.

**isolationism** Diplomatic policy under which a nation maintains its rights and interests without alliances. The U.S. pursued a successful isolationist policy from 1800 until 1917, when it joined other countries to fight Germany in WORLD WAR I. After the war isolationism again dominated U.S. policy until WORLD WAR II and the ensuing COLD WAR made the policy untenable. The U.S. joined the UNITED NATIONS and established several defensive alliances, which have often entangled the country in foreign upheavals, such as the VIETNAM WAR. Cultural isolationism existed for much of the century in the USSR and China.

**Israel** Israel is situated in the Middle East along the eastern shores of the Mediterranean Sea; its area, as defined

| ISRAEL | |
|---|---|
| 1909 | Tel Aviv, the first modern all-Jewish city, is founded. |
| 1917 | British Balfour Declaration calls for national Jewish home in Palestine but respects rights of Palestinians. |
| 1922 | Britain given League of Nations mandate over Palestine. |
| 1929 | As a result of increased Jewish presence, bloody riots break out in Jerusalem, Hebron and Safed between Jews and the indigenous Palestinian Arabs. |
| 1946 | Israeli terrorist bomb King David Hotel in Jerusalem, kill 91. |
| 1948 | Britain leaves Palestine; State of Israel proclaimed in Tel Aviv; Egypt, Transjordan, Syria, Iraq and Lebanon invade Israel; Israel survives the war and adds territory to land granted by the UN; 780,000 Palestinians are displaced from their homes; Chaim Weizmann is elected first president and David Ben-Gurion first prime minister. |

*(Table continues)*

## Israel (*continued*)

| | |
|---|---|
| 1949 | Israel joins the UN. |
| 1956 | Suez War: Israel, with the backing of Britain and France, attacks Egyptian positions in Gaza and overruns the Sinai Peninsula, from which it withdraws after UN condemnation. |
| 1960 | Adolf Eichmann is kidnapped from Argentina and after a long trial is found guilty and hanged (1962). |
| 1964 | Palestine National Council is formed advocating armed struggle to liberate Palestine; the Palestine National Council establishes the PLO. |
| 1967 | Israel begins the Six-Day War; captures the Sinai Peninsula, Gaza, the West Bank and the Golan Heights; UN Resolution 242 passed, calling for Israeli withdrawal from captured territory and "mutual respect for the sovereignty of all states within secure boundaries." |
| 1969 | Golda Meir becomes prime minister. |
| 1972 | Palestinian terrorists kill 11 Israeli athletes at the Olympic Games in Munich. |
| 1973 | Yom Kippur War starts when Egypt and Syria attack Israel on the Jewish holy day. Cease-fire declared October 24. |
| 1974 | Golda Meir resigns and is replaced by Yitzhak Rabin. |
| 1976 | Israeli commandos free 110 hostages held at Entebbe Airport in Uganda by Arab terrorists. |
| 1977 | Rabin steps down and is replaced by Menachem Begin, who favors Israeli settlements of the occupied territories; Anwar Sadat becomes the first Arab leader to visit Israel, address the Knesset. |
| 1978 | Israel attacks PLO bases in Lebanon in retaliation for PLO raids on Israeli border settlements; Israel annexes the Golan Heights. |
| 1979 | Anwar Sadat of Egypt and Menachem Begin of Israel sign Camp David Accords. |
| 1982 | Israel invades Lebanon after an attempt to assassinate the Israeli ambassador in London; with Israeli complicity, Christian Falangist militiamen enter the Palestinian refugee camps of Sabra and Shatila and kill about 700; Israel begins phased withdrawal from Lebanon. |
| 1984 | Labor and Likud form a coalition, with Shimon Peres as prime minister. |
| 1986 | Yitzhak Shamir becomes prime minister. |
| 1987 | The Intifada (Palestinian uprising) begins. |
| 1991 | Israel hit by Iraqi Scud missiles during Persian Gulf War but does not enter conflict; U.S. secretary of state James Baker launches new Arab-Israeli peace plan. |
| 1995 | Israel and Palestinian Authority sign the Interim Agreement on the West Bank and the Gaza Strip providing for Palestinian self-government and the redeployment of Israeli security forces. |
| 1998 | Wye River agreement provides for continuation of the Interim agreement. |
| 2000 | Israeli forces withdraw from South Lebanon. |
| 2001 | U.S.-sponsored peace plan (the "Roadmap") fails. Second Intifada begins. Likud leader Ariel Sharon is elected prime minister. |
| 2003 | Prime Minister Sharon authorizes construction of a barrier separating Israel (and contiguous Israeli settlements) from the West Bank to protect against terrorist attacks. |
| 2005 | Israel begins the evacuation of Israel settlements from the Gaza Strip. |
| 2006 | A stroke forces Sharon from office. He is replaced by Ehud Olmert. Hezbollah partisans in Lebanon shell northern Israeli towns and kidnap two Israeli soldiers across the border, precipitating a wider conflict. |

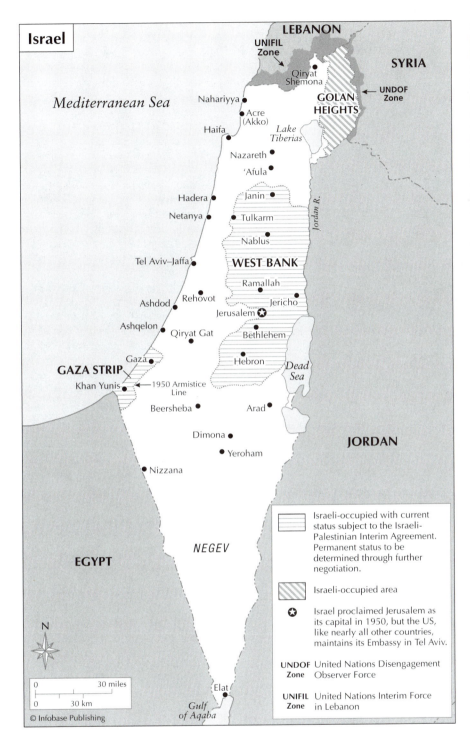

**Israel**

Mediterranean Sea

LEBANON

UNIFIL Zone

Qiryat Shemona

SYRIA

UNDOF Zone

GOLAN HEIGHTS

Nahariyya

Acre (Akko)

Haifa

Lake Tiberias

Nazareth

'Afula

Janin

Hadera

Tulkarm

Netanya

Jordan R.

Nablus

Tel Aviv–Jaffa

WEST BANK

Ramallah

Ashdod

Rehovot

Jericho

Jerusalem ✪

Ashqelon

Qiryat Gat

Bethlehem

Gaza

Hebron

Dead Sea

GAZA STRIP

Khan Yunis

1950 Armistice Line

Beersheba

Arad

Dimona

Yeroham

Nizzana

JORDAN

NEGEV

EGYPT

N

0      30 miles

0      30 km

© Infobase Publishing

Elat

Gulf of Aqaba

Israeli-occupied with current status subject to the Israeli-Palestinian Interim Agreement. Permanent status to be determined through further negotiation.

Israeli-occupied area

✪ Israel proclaimed Jerusalem as its capital in 1950, but the US, like nearly all other countries, maintains its Embassy in Tel Aviv.

**UNDOF Zone**  United Nations Disengagement Observer Force

**UNIFIL Zone**  United Nations Interim Force in Lebanon

by the 1949 Arab-Israeli armistice, is approximately 8,017 square miles. Excluded are occupied territories in the GAZA STRIP, the WEST BANK and the GOLAN HEIGHTS, acquired during the SIX-DAY WAR in 1967. Sacred to Judaism, Christianity and Islam, the land has been a battleground for millennia. Carved out of the post–World War I ruins of the OTTOMAN EMPIRE,

PALESTINE was administered by Britain under a LEAGUE OF NATIONS mandate (1922–47). Jewish immigration increased, as did Arab opposition; riots in 1929 progressed to sustained guerrilla warfare (1933 onward) between Arabs and JEWS. Attempts to partition the land into separate Arab and Jewish states failed (1937, 1947); Britain withdrew in 1947, leaving the coun-

try in a state of civil war. The state of Israel was proclaimed in 1948, with BEN GURION as the first prime minister. The problem of displaced Palestinian Arabs in the new state remained unresolved and led to the formation of the PALESTINE LIBERATION ORGANIZATION (PLO) in 1964. The PLO has launched repeated terrorist attacks against Israel and its primary ally the U.S. to force establishment of a Palestinian state. Israeli prime minister Menachem BEGIN signed the first peace treaty with an Arab country (Egypt) in 1979 (see CAMP DAVID TALKS). Israel invaded LEBANON in 1982 to destroy PLO bases but withdrew in 1986. Rapid Jewish settlement of the occupied West Bank led to the INTIFADA (Palestinian uprising), which began in 1987. Internal division within the current government led by Yitzhak SHAMIR has hampered resolution of the Palestinian question. During the PERSIAN GULF WAR between UN forces and Iraq (January–February 1991) Israel suffered Iraqi Scud missile attacks but remained uninvolved. After the war, U.S. president George H. W. BUSH announced a new peace initiative to resolve the ongoing Arab-Israeli dispute.

The Israeli government headed by Prime Minister Yitzhak RABIN attempted to resolve its differences with the Palestinian Arabs by signing the 1993 Oslo Accords, which allowed the PALESTINIAN AUTHORITY to govern part of the West Bank and Gaza Strip. However, the election of hard-liner Ariel SHARON as prime minister, and an outbreak of terrorist activities by Palestinian extremists (see INTIFADA II) damaged the peace process. International hopes for the "Roadmap to Peace"—a timetable for Israeli withdrawals, Israeli-Arab negotiations and Palestinian statehood proposed by the U.S. in 2001–02—was undermined by Sharon's 2003 decision to construct a 700-kilometer (420-mile) barrier between Israel and the West Bank (incorporating territory occupied by Jewish settlements in the West Bank) that was designed to prevent future Palestinian suicide bombers. In 2004 Sharon announced his decision to withdraw Israeli presence unilaterally from the Gaza Strip and areas of the West Bank by summer 2005, a promise he kept before a stroke forced him from office in 2006.

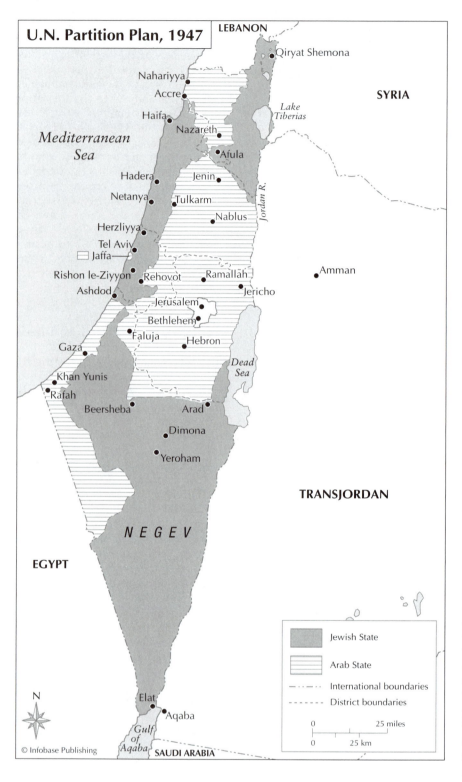

**U.N. Partition Plan, 1947**

LEBANON

Qiryat Shemona

Nahariyya

Accre

Haifa

*Lake Tiberias*

SYRIA

*Mediterranean Sea*

Nazareth

Afula

Hadera

Jenin

Netanya

Tulkarm

*Jordan R.*

Nablus

Herzliyya

Tel Aviv

Jaffa

Rishon le-Ziyyon

Rehovot

Ramallah

Amman

Ashdod

Jericho

Jerusalem

Bethlehem

Faluja

Hebron

Gaza

*Dead Sea*

Khan Yunis

Rafah

Beersheba

Arad

TRANSJORDAN

Dimona

Yeroham

N E G E V

EGYPT

N

Elat

Aqaba

*Gulf of Aqaba*

© Infobase Publishing

SAUDI ARABIA

Jewish State

Arab State

International boundaries

District boundaries

0    25 miles

0    25 km

**Israeli War of Independence** See ARAB-ISRAELI WAR OF 1948–49.

**Issigonis, Alec** (*1906–1988*) British automotive engineer and automobile designer whose work included some of the most important and inno-vative designs produced by the English motor industry. Issigonis was trained in London as an engineer and began work as a draftsman for Rootes Motors. He later joined Morris Motors and be-came that firm's chief engineer in 1961. His design (both engineering and ap-

pearance) for the Morris Minor of 1948 made it one of the most popular British cars of its era—it remained in produc-tion for 20 years. The Morris Mini of 1951 was an even more successful de-sign, introducing the modern trans-verse engine and front-wheel drive in a small car. The Mini offered surprising space and comfort along with excellent economy and mechanical simplicity in a way that has made it immensely pop-ular in a number of variations, includ-ing the sporty Mini Cooper. The Mini set a high standard for aesthetic design along with its technically advanced en-gineering. It remains in production in a somewhat updated form.

**Istanbul (Byzantium; Constantin-ople)** Partly in Europe and partly in Asia, this ancient city in northwestern TURKEY is located on both sides of the Bosporus. A busy port and Turkey's largest city, it was here that in 1908 a re-volt of the YOUNG TURKS called for a par-liament for the entire OTTOMAN EMPIRE. Turkey fought with the CENTRAL POW-ERS—the losing side—in WORLD WAR I, and Constantinople fell to the Allies in 1918. Its centuries-old empire shred-ded to pieces, Turkey was declared a re-public, and the capital was moved from Constantinople to Ankara by Kemal ATATÜRK in 1923. Istanbul (officially re-named in 1930) retains many notable signs of its past diversity and greatness, especially the church of Hagia Sophia, a masterpiece of Byzantine architecture.

**Itala Films** Important early Italian motion picture studio, which helped vault that country's cinema to world prominence in the years before World War I. Founded in Turin in 1905 under the name "Rossi," Itala developed under the management of Giovanni PASTRONE into a successful operation, producing numerous short action pic-tures and short comedies (especially slapstick farces featuring the French actor "Cretinetti," the pseudonym of André Deed). Its most significant pro-duction, the feature *Cabiria* (1914), be-came, along with rival studio Cine's *Quo Vadis* (1913), the most influential movie in the world. It confirmed that the feature-length film was the wave of the future and heavily influenced the epic ambitions of the American direc-tor D. W. GRIFFITH. Itala quickly fol-lowed up *Cabiria's* success with a series of historical vehicles for the strongman star, "Maciste" (Bartolomei Pagano), anticipating by decades the vehicles for later musclemen such as Steve Reeves and Arnold Schwarzenegger. At its height, Itala became part of the Unione Cinematografica Italiana, the most powerful film consortium in the world. The company went into decline when Pastrone retired and the Unione went bankrupt in 1923.

**Italian Somaliland** Now a part of SOMALIA, this former Italian colony in East Africa extended from Cape Asir to the Kenya border; its capital was Mogadishu. A small protectorate, set up by the Italians in 1889, was enlarged by subsequent additions, until it became a state of Italian East Africa (which included ETHIOPIA and ERITREA) in 1936. Invaded in 1941 by the British during WORLD WAR II, it remained under their control until 1950; in 1960 it was joined with British Somaliland to form the independent republic of Somalia.

**Italian Uprisings of 1914** A new, moderate conservative government being formed by Premier Antonio Salandra was faced with popular uprisings on June 7, 1914, in which radicals confronted strike-breakers, staged antidraft demonstrations, and began to take over Bologna, Ancona and other cities, with the Romagna declaring itself a republic. More than 100,000 soldiers were needed to restore order; but by July Italy was preoccupied with moves to declare neutrality, despite its alliance with Germany and Austria, in the imminent world war.

**Italo-Ethiopian War of 1935–36** As early as 1928, Benito MUSSOLINI, fascist dictator of ITALY since 1922, had planned to avenge the Italian defeat in the Italo-Ethiopian War of 1895–96. In a blatantly underhanded way, he sought to convince the world of Italy's right to ETHIOPIA, appealing to the LEAGUE OF NATIONS—after altering treaty documents of 1887, 1896 and 1900 and a great power agreement of 1908. His ploy worked: The League of Nations suggested partition, but Ethiopia rejected the Hoare-Laval plan, which would have given Italy most of the country. In 1934 a bloody clash occurred between Italian and Ethiopian

forces at Ualual, a disputed area on the Italian Somaliland border. As Italy slowly massed an invasion force, Ethiopia's Emperor HAILE SELASSIE pulled his troops back 20 miles from the Eritrean border; nonetheless, the Italians invaded Ethiopia, without declaring war, on October 3, 1935. Using aircraft and modern weapons, Italian forces slowly destroyed Ethiopia—so slowly, in fact, that it took seven months for the supposedly modern and superior armies of Generals BADOGLIO and Graziani to conquer the "inferior" Ethiopians. The Ethiopian capital of Addis Ababa was captured on May 5, 1936.

Haile Selassie fled and made a vain appeal for help to the League of Nations; Italy, however, had already called its own king "emperor of Ethiopia," had annexed Ethiopia and had united it with Eritrea and Italian Somaliland to form Italian East Africa. The Italians executed the archbishop of the Ethiopian Coptic Church, massacred monks and decimated Addis Ababa. Although it had failed to conquer the entire country, Italy occupied Ethiopia until 1941, when it was liberated by British, Free French and Ethiopian troops during WORLD WAR II. Haile Selassie regained his throne on May 5, 1941.

**Italy (Italia)** Republic of southern Europe; a long, boot-shaped peninsula, it is bounded on the north by France, Switzerland, Austria and Slovenia. But most of its border is a water-lapped coastline touched on the east by the Adriatic Sea and on the

## ITALY

| | |
|---|---|
| 1900 | Umberto I assassinated by anarchist. |
| 1907 | Prince Borghese wins Beijing to Paris auto race. |
| 1915 | Italy enters World War I on the side of the Allies. |
| 1919 | Vote granted to women; Mussolini publishes Fascist Manifesto. |
| 1922 | Mussolini leads fascist March on Rome; forms government. |
| 1926 | Mussolini abolishes all political opposition. |
| 1929 | The Lateran Treaties establish Italian recognition of the Vatican as a sovereign state. |
| 1933 | Toscanini boycotts German music festival to protest Nazi repression of artists. |
| 1936 | Italy conquers and annexes Ethiopia; Mussolini announces Axis pact with Germany. |
| 1939 | "Pact of Steel" with Germany. |
| 1940 | Italy enters World War II on Axis side; unsuccessfully attempts to invade Greece. |
| 1943 | Mussolini deposed; Italy signs armistice with Allies, declares war on Germany; Germans help Mussolini escape. |
| 1945 | Mussolini captured, tried and executed by partisans. |
| 1946 | King Victor Emmanuel III abdicates; Italian referendum narrowly rejects monarchy; Victor Emmanuel's son Humbert II also abdicates. |
| 1959 | Aldo Moro heads Christian Democrats. |
| 1966 | Floods devastate Florence. |
| 1972 | Michelangelo's *Pietà* vandalized. |
| 1978 | Red Brigade members kidnap and kill Aldo Moro. |
| 1981 | Pope John Paul II wounded in assassination attempt. |
| 1982 | Italy enjoys first World Cup Soccer victory; 100,000 demonstrate against Mafia. |
| 1985 | Rome airport bombed by terrorists. |
| 1990 | CIA-backed anticommunist network exposed; restoration of Sistine Chapel ceiling completed; Alberto Moravia dies. |
| 1991 | In Persian Gulf War, Italian forces fight in coalition to drive Iraq from Kuwait. |
| 1994 | Freedom Alliance, right-wing a coalition, forms government under media magnate Silvio Berlusconi, leader of the new Forza Italia Party, but Berluscioni soon resigns amid allegations of bribery. |
| 1999 | Italy participates in NATO air campaign against Serbia. |
| 2001 | Forza Italia wins legislative elections, and Berlusconi is named prime minister. |
| 2003 | Italy joins "coalition of the willing" in Operation Iraqi Freedom to topple the regime of Saddam Hussein. |
| 2006 | Romano Prodi wins narrowly over Berlusconi in national elections. |

west and south by the Mediterranean Sea. Also a part of Italy are the large islands of Sardinia and Sicily, the smaller islands of Capri, Ischia and Elba, and the Lipari Islands. After the late-19th-century occupation of Somaliland (now SOMALIA) and ERITREA on the Red Sea and an unsuccessful invasion of ETHIOPIA in 1896, Italy occupied LIBYA, across the Mediterranean on the coast of North Africa, in 1911. Italy joined the Allied WORLD WAR I effort in 1915, but only after a secret agreement that, if victorious, it would gain Austrian-held Trieste and desirable territories in Africa and the OTTOMAN EMPIRE (including more territory in Libya). A victorious postwar Italy saw the Christian Democrats and the Socialists develop into mass political parties that were largely ineffective in coping with postwar problems. Former socialist Benito MUSSOLINI (1883–1945) developed the theory of FASCISM and became leader of the movement. He and his BLACKSHIRTS marched on Rome in October 1922; King VICTOR EMMANUEL III named him premier, and by 1927 Mussolini ruled as dictator. Almost continuously at war in a barely pacified Ethiopia from 1935, Italy also intervened on the side of FRANCO and the FALANGE in the SPANISH CIVIL WAR.

As a partner in Adolf HITLER's AXIS, Italy entered WORLD WAR II, in June 1940, only to suffer humiliating defeats in Africa and in Greece, which was subsequently overrun by Germany. The Allies invaded Sicily on July 10, 1943. Mussolini was subsequently dismissed by King VICTOR EMMANUEL III and imprisoned, but he was rescued by German paratroops and established the Republic of Salo in northern Italy under German protection. As the war's devastation moved from south to north, all the way up the peninsula, many cities, including Naples, Rome, Genoa and Milan, suffered heavy bombing, although Rome was declared an open city and taken by the Allies without ground fighting. Mussolini was killed in April 1945 by partisans while trying to escape to Switzerland. Victor Emmanuel abdicated in May 1946 and Humberto II briefly became king, but on June 2 the Italians narrowly voted to replace the monarchy with a republic.

From 1948 until the early 1980s the Christian Democrats (a broad center-right party) were in power (with only two interruptions). Despite a proliferation of political parties, and numerous political crises resulting in frequent changes of prime ministers and cabinets, Italy's postwar democracy remained a stable force, enabling the country to rebuild after the war. The country has since enjoyed close cooperation with the rest of Western Europe and the U.S. In

1949 Italy was a founding member of the NORTH ATLANTIC TREATY ORGANIZATION (NATO). The country was also an original member of the EUROPEAN COAL AND STEEL COMMUNITY and, later, of the EUROPEAN ECONOMIC COMMUNITY (EEC). The long political monopoly of the Christian Democrats led to a measure of inertia and corruption in the late 1960s; the Italian Communist Party, the strongest communist party in western Europe, has consistently proved an attractive alternative for a sizeable percentage of the Italian electorate. The Christian Democrats formed coalitions with other parties, including the Socialist, in order to exclude the Communists from government. Extremist terrorism of the left and right in the late 1970s attempted to disrupt Italian society; trains and railroad stations were bombed, and in 1978 former premier Aldo MORO was kidnapped and murdered by the notorious RED BRIGADES. Terrorism abated in the 1980s. For four years after the 1983 elections, the Socialist Party headed the government. Italy joined the coalition against IRAQ in the PERSIAN GULF WAR (1990–91), and Italian pilots flew sorties from Saudi Arabia during Operation Desert Storm. Elections in March 1994 brought SILVIO BERLUSCONI and his Forza Italia center-right political movement to power. Berlusconi was defeated in 1996 elections following the collapse of his cabinet but regained primiership in 2001. His five-year government was the longest of the Italian Republic. In 2003 Italy was one of several nations that participated in the U.S.-led "coalition of the willing," that entered IRAQ and deposed Saddam HUSSEIN. In 2006 former prime minister and European Commission president Romano Pirodi defeated Berlusconi by a slim margin. Italy remains a center of the traditional arts and culture, a main attraction of world tourism. Rome is the capital, and other major cities are Naples, Milan, Palermo and Genoa.

**Iturbi, José** *(1895–1980)* Spanish-American pianist and conductor. Born in Valencia, he studied at the Paris Conservatory. Renowned for his interpretations of the music of Spain, he toured Europe and made his American debut in 1929, later settling in the U.S. He was a much sought-after concert artist, touring worldwide, playing with many of the foremost symphony or-

chestras and often performing with his sister, the pianist Amparo Iturbi (1898–1969). He conducted the Rochester Philharmonic Orchestra from 1936 to 1944. Iturbi was best known to the general public for his appearances in a number of American musical films during the 1940s.

**Ivanov, Vsevolod Vyacheslavovich** *(1895–1963)* Soviet writer. Ivanov is best known for his short stories and novels, notably *The Partisan* (1921) and *Armored Train 14–69* (1922), which described Soviet expansion into Siberia. A protégé of Maxim GORKY, he used his wide experience as partisan fighter, sailor, actor and circus performer in his writing. His plays include *The Compromise of Niab Khan* and *Twelve Young Lads from a Snuffbox*. He published his memoirs, *Meeting with Gorky,* in 1947. His early work, with its vivid, naturalistic description that attracted Gorky's attention, is considered to be his best.

**Ivanov, Vyacheslav Ivanovich** *(1866–1949)* Russian symbolist poet. In 1903 Ivanov published a volume of lyric poetry, *kormchie zvezdy,* which established him as leader of the St. Petersburg symbolist movement. *Cor Ardens* (1911) is considered his most important poetical work. He was also a philosopher and classical scholar. He was made professor of Greek at Baku University in 1921 and in 1924 immigrated to Italy, where he became a Catholic.

**Ivanov-Razumnik** *(1878–1946)* Pseudonym of Razumnik Valsilyevich Ivanov. He was a writer and critic and leader of "The Scythians," an intellectual group that believed in Russia's destiny as a part-Asian nation. Before the revolution he wrote populist and revolutionary works; after the revolution his even stronger inclination toward the Left eventually brought about his arrest in the 1930s, as a "populist ideologist." He left the Soviet Union for Germany during the war and died in Munich. He wrote an account of his life, including his imprisonments and exile.

**Ivens, Joris (Georg Henri Anton)** *(1898–1989)* Dutch film maker. Ivens specialized in documentaries portraying the social impact of revolution, particularly in communist countries. His masterpiece was considered to be

*The Spanish Earth* (1937), a documentary about the SPANISH CIVIL WAR that featured a commentary written and read by Ernest HEMINGWAY.

**Ives, Burl** *(1909–1995)* American folksinger and actor. Born in Illinois, Ives came out of a folksinging tradition. He traveled throughout the U.S., walking, hitchhiking and riding boxcars, before coming to New York City in 1937. Important in popularizing the folksong genre, he is remembered for his renditions of "The Foggy, Foggy Dew" and "The Wayfaring Stranger," which became the title of his radio show in 1940. Ives began acting in motion pictures in 1945, and won an ACADEMY AWARD for his performance in *The Big Country* in 1958. He is best known, however, for his role as Big Daddy in the Broadway production of Tennessee WILLIAMS's *Cat on a Hot Tin Roof* (1955) and in the film version that followed in 1958.

**Ives, Charles Edward** *(1874–1954)* America's first pioneer in modern musical expression. Because of his abhorrence of publicity and reclusive nature, Ives allowed few works to be published or performed in his lifetime; only in his last years did musicians like Leonard BERNSTEIN and Leopold STOKOWSKI present world premieres of some of his major works. Ives was born in Danbury, Connecticut, and received his musical training and inspiration from his father, a bandmaster in General Grant's army. He graduated from Yale in 1898 and began a long and prosperous career in life insurance, establishing his own successful firm, Ives and Myrick, in New York in 1906. For the next 20 years Ives lead a double life, working by day in his Manhattan office and at night composing music at his farm in Redding, Connecticut. By 1917 he had completed four symphonies, hundreds of songs, two piano sonatas, and numerous other miscellaneous works. After a heart attack that year, Ives reconsidered his publishing proscriptions and released a huge volume of songs; later, he published his massive *Concord Piano Sonata.* At a time when most American composers still depended heavily upon the traditions of European academies and conservatories, Ives turned to the vernacular music styles of the New England Yankees. As if in response to Ralph Waldo Emerson's charge that

American artists should "embrace the common," Ives evoked in his music the street bands of his youth. He quoted popular songs like "De Camptown Races" and "Old Black Joe." Years before the experiments by STRAVINSKY, BARTÓK and SCHOENBERG, Ives utilized modernist idioms in his work—double aural images, dissonance, polyrhythms and polytonalities. Ives composed little after 1918, choosing to live quietly at his farm with his wife of many years, Harmony Twichell. Only recently, it seems, has modern music caught up with Charles Ives. He died in New York City of complications following an operation in 1954.

**Ivory Coast**   See CÔTE D'IVOIRE.

**Iwo Jima**   Largest of the Volcano Islands; in the western Pacific Ocean, 660 nautical miles southeast of Tokyo. Iwo Jima was of strategic importance during WORLD WAR II because of its air base and its proximity to the Japanese main islands. The battle for control of the island—from February 19 to March 15, 1945—was one of the bloodiest in U.S. history. A memorable moment occurred on February 23, when men of the 28th Regiment of the

Fifth Division of U.S. Marines scaled Iwo Jima's heavily fortified **Mount Suribachi** and planted the American flag on its summit. Administered by the U.S. until 1968, Iwo Jima was then returned to Japan.

**Izetbegović, Alija** *(1925–2003)* Bosnian politician and president of BOSNIA AND HERZEGOVINA (1990–2000). Born in Bosanski Šamac, Izetbegović became involved early on in the predominantly Muslim community in the Yugoslav province of Bosnia. When YUGOSLAVIA became a communist country at the end of WORLD WAR II, his radical Islamic activities led to his arrest and imprisonment in 1946. After serving a three-year sentence, Izetbegović enrolled in the University of Sarajevo in 1949 to study law. After he obtained his law degree he practiced in Bosnia while campaigning for greater autonomy for the predominantly Muslim province. In 1983 he was arrested and sentenced to 14 years in prison.

After his early release from prison in 1988, Izetbegović plunged into the anticommunist activism that was sweeping Eastern Europe as a result of Soviet leader Mikhail GORBACHEV's policy of GLASNOST. In 1990 he helped found the

*The American flag being raised in victory at Iwo Jima. 1945*

Party of Democratic Action (PDA), a Bosnian nationalist party that, while representing the predominantly Muslim population in the province, called for an independent secular government. Six months after its creation the PDA won a plurality of votes in the country's first free election. Izetbegović joined six other party leaders in the creation of a collective presidency for Yugoslavia. The secession of Croatia, Slovenia and Macedonia from Yugoslavia in 1991 exacerbated tensions within Bosnia, with its large Croat and Serb minorities that began to clamor for their own autonomous districts within the autonomous province of Bosnia and Herzegovina. In a referendum in early 1992, a majority of the province's citizens were in favor of independence, while most Bosnian Serbs boycotted the referendum. Izetbegović declared Bosnia and Herzegovina independent in March 1992, unleashing a bloody civil war among Bosnians, Croats and Serbs.

After more than three years of bloodshed, Izetbegović met with his Croatian (Franjo TUDJMAN) and Serbian (Slobodan MILOŠEVIĆ) counterparts in Dayton, Ohio, at a peace conference cosponsored by the U.S. and the EURO- PEAN UNION. Signed in November 1995, the DAYTON ACCORDS established a power-sharing arrangement in Bosnia—between the Bosnian Muslim and Croat federation on the one hand and the Serbian Republic on the other—that brought peace to the troubled country. The accords also created a new three-member presidency that (along with a national legislature) would administer both the Bosnian Croat and the Bosnian Serb portions of Bosnia and Herzegovina. In September 1996 Izetbegović was elected by his constituents as the Muslim representative on the three-member presidency. He was reelected to that post in 1998. In 2000 Izetbegović resigned as president of Bosnia for reasons of health and withdrew from politics altogether the following year by relinquishing his post as head of the PDA.

***Izvestiya* (News)** Daily newspaper published by the Supreme Soviet Presidium; it was founded after the February 1917 Revolution as the organ of the Petrograd Soviet. It was published jointly by the central executive committee of Soviets and the Petrograd Soviet from August 1917, but became very similar to PRAVDA from October 1917. In 1918 publication was transferred to Moscow, and in 1957 the circulation stood at 1,550,000. However, under the editorship of Alexei Adzhubey (editor, 1959–64) the style of the newspaper changed, and it became an evening publication in 1960. It became popular and in the late 1970s the circulation was 8.6 million. A weekly supplement *Nedeliya* (The Week), as of 1980 sold separately, was also published. *Izvestiya* ceased publication after the disintegration of the Soviet Union in December 1991.

**Izvolsky, Count Alexander Petrovich** (*1856–1919*) Russian diplomat. As foreign minister he concluded a treaty with Britain resolving Anglo-Russian disagreements in the Middle East, but he was dismissed in 1910 following an unsuccessful agreement with Austria. In 1910 he was transferred to Paris, where he served as the Russian ambassador until 1917. He had sought Austrian help in 1908 in asserting Russia's right to use the DARDANELLES, but the resulting agreement strengthened Austria in the BALKANS at Russia's expense, and no aid was given in the Dardanelles question.

# J

**Jaccottet, Philippe** *(1925– )* French poet, diarist, translator and literary critic. Jaccottet is one of the finest of the post–World War II generation of French poets. In his often lyrical verse, Jaccottet rejects the linguistic obscurity and experimentation of SURREALISM and other abstruse schools of French poetics in favor of a more emotionally direct expressiveness that takes in the beauty of nature and the fragility of civilized values in the nuclear age. Born in Switzerland, Jaccottet was educated at the University of Lausanne and is married to the artist Anne-Marie Hassler. His major books of poems include *Requiem* (1947), *Airs* (1967) and *Pensées sous les nuages* (1983).

**Jackson, Glenda** *(1936– )* English actress. An outstanding actress of stage, screen and television, Jackson received international acclaim in the London and New York productions of Peter WEISS's play *Marat/Sade* (1964–65). Performing with the ROYAL SHAKESPEARE COMPANY she gained recognition for her roles in *Hedda Gabler* (1975) and *Antony and Cleopatra* (1978), among others. Title roles in Hugh Whitmore's *Stevie* (1977, about Stevie SMITH) and Andrew Davies's *Rose* (1980; Broadway, 1981) were personal triumphs. She has appeared in numerous films, receiving a best actress ACADEMY AWARD for *Women in Love* (1969). On television she triumphed as Elizabeth I in a BBC series. In 1992 she abandoned her acting career for politics, winning a seat in Parliament as a Labour representative of Hamp-

stead and Highgate. She became a vocal critic of the Conservative governments. In 1997, when the Labour Party was swept back into power, Jackson was named minister for transport in London. She later became an adviser to the mayor of London on homelessness.

**Jackson, Henry M(artin) "Scoop"** *(1912–1983)* U.S. senator. Jackson was born in Everett, Wash. After two years of private legal practice, he entered Democratic politics in 1935, was elected to the House of Representatives in 1940 and to the Senate in 1953. Thereafter, he served six terms. In domestic affairs, he was generally a liberal, maintaining close ties with organized labor and establishing a record as a dedicated environmentalist. In foreign affairs, he advocated large military expenditures from his seat on the Armed Services Committee, seeking to counter Soviet power. Jackson was a candidate for the Democratic nomination for president in 1972 and 1976.

**Jackson, Jesse Louis** *(1941– )* U.S. CIVIL RIGHTS leader and politician. Raised in the poor black section of Greenville, N.C., he starred on the basketball, football and baseball teams of all-black Sterling High School. An honor student and the college quarterback, he led the student protest in 1963 that resulted in the integration of Greensboro (North Carolina) theaters and restaurants. Jackson entered Chicago Theological Seminary in 1965. The same year he joined Dr. Martin Luther KING Jr. in

his civil rights actions in SELMA, Ala. Named head of the Chicago branch of Operation Breadbasket, he became its national director in 1967. He was ordained a Baptist minister in 1968. Jackson continued to gain national prominence and following, and in 1971 founded Operation Push (People United to Save Humanity) in Chicago.

He gained valuable support and experience in the field of politics in 1984 when he launched a campaign to win the Democratic presidential nomination. Again during the 1988 presidential primaries, Jackson received astonishing support, including from white voters, and received widespread press attention. Although Jackson has not run for political office since 1988, he was active in promoting voter registration, universal health care and corporate investment in poor communities. He also undertook several unofficial diplomatic assignments in world trouble spots. He brought hostages out of Kuwait and Iraq in 1990 before the PERSIAN GULF WAR and negotiated the release of U.S. soldiers held hostage in Kosovo in 1999. President Bill CLINTON awarded him the Presidential Medal of Freedom in 2000. Jackson's prestige was damaged shortly after the contested presidential election of that year when it was revealed that he had had an extramarital affair with a young staffer that resulted in the birth of a daughter. Allegations also surfaced that Jackson had used his influence and reputation to advance his family's financial interests.

*The Reverend Jesse Jackson leads a march for jobs in 1975. Washington. D.C.. photographed by Thomas J. O'Halloran* (U.S. NEWS AND WORLD REPORT MAGAZINE COLLECTION, LIBRARY OF CONGRESS, PRINTS AND PHOTOGRAPHS DIVISION)

**Jackson, Mahalia** *(1911–1972)* American gospel singer. She began making records in 1934, and later went on many concert tours in Europe and the U.S. She sang for President Eisenhower on his birthday in 1959, and at President Kennedy's inauguration in 1961. During the 1960s she became associated with the CIVIL RIGHTS MOVEMENT. She made eight records that sold over a million copies each.

**Jackson, Michael** *(1958–  )* American pop singer; began his career with his brothers as one of the Jackson Five. The group recorded four consecutive number-one hits, including "ABC" and "The Love You Save." He recorded three top-five solo singles during the early 1970s, including the number-one "Ben," a love song to a rat sung in Michael's trademark falsetto. He made his film debut in 1978 playing the scarecrow in *The Wiz,* an all-black version of *The Wizard of Oz.* In 1979, his career began to skyrocket, with the album *Off the Wall* providing four top-10 hits. His 1982 release, *Thriller,* set new music industry standards for success, with seven top-ten hits and sales topping 40 million. Jackson's child-like beauty and vulnerability have made him a teen idol in two decades, albeit that appeal is widely rumored to have been assisted by extensive plastic surgery. Jackson's subsequent albums, *Dangerous* (1991), *HIStory* (1995) and *Invincible* (2001), did not sell as well as *Thriller,* in part because of allegations of child abuse and molestation that surfaced in 1993 and again in 2003. Early in 2005 he went on trial in California, charged with 10 counts of child molestation but was acquitted in June on all counts.

**Jackson, Reggie** *(1946–  )* American baseball player. Born in Wyncote, Pa., Jackson attracted the attention of baseball scouts while a student athlete at Arizona State University (1964–66). The Kansas City Athletics (A's), signed him to a contract in 1966 and to insert him into their minor-league farm system. The A's called him up during the 1967 season, and by 1969 Jackson had established a reputation as a power hitter, finishing the season with 47 home runs and 118 runs batted in.

After nine seasons with the A's and with only one year remaining on his contract, Jackson was traded to the Baltimore Orioles. However, the team's lackluster performance that season convinced Jackson to test his free agency, and he signed the following year with the New York Yankees. It was with New York that Jackson experienced his greatest professional success, helping to steer the Yankees to two World Series titles, in 1977 and 1978.

In the race for his first Major League championship, Jackson performed an extraordinary feat in the fifth and sixth games against the Los Angeles Dodgers, hitting four consecutive home runs on the first pitch he received from four different pitchers. As a result of his role in the 1977 World Series, Jackson was labeled "Mr. October" (the month in which the Series occurs) for his ability to perform under great pressure. Jackson finished his career with the Yankees, retiring in 1987. In 1993 he was inducted into the Baseball Hall of Fame.

**Jackson, Robert H.** *(1892–1954)* Associate justice, U.S. Supreme Court (1941–54). Jackson did not attend college but spent one year at Albany Law School in addition to studying law in a lawyer's office. He first gained attention as general counsel of the Internal Revenue Service. A loyal Democrat, he served President Franklin D. ROOSEVELT as assistant U.S. attorney general, solicitor general and attorney general. In 1941, Roosevelt elevated Jackson to the Supreme Court. During 1945–46, Jackson served as chief prosecutor at the NUREMBERG TRIALS. Jackson is credited with charging the Nazis with crimes against humanity.

Jackson apparently did not always get along with his fellow justices on the high court. Reputedly, two justices threatened to resign if President TRUMAN elevated Jackson to the position of Chief Justice. Jackson died in 1954 while still a member of the Court.

**Jackson, Shirley** *(1919–1965)* American writer of contemporary fantasy and horror. Jackson's works have been frequently adapted to movies and television. She was born in San Francisco and early in childhood developed an absorbing interest in witchcraft and the occult. After placing several stories in *THE NEW YORKER* magazine, she became an international sensation with *The Lottery* (1947), a violent tale of ritualized murder in a New England farming community. Although she continued to write disturbing tales of madness and horror—notably, the extraordinary *The Bird's Nest* (1954), a story of a women with multiple personalities; *The Sundial* (1958), an evocation of imminent global apocalypse; and *The Haunting of Hill House* (1959), a truly terrifying novel of the psychic investigation of a "haunted house"—she also wrote delightful ac-counts of her own husband and children, amusing stories of family life collected under that titles, *Life among the Savages* (1953) and *Raising Demons* (1957). This duality is striking. She was, by turns, non-descript, thoroughly domestic, and essen-tially "normal;" and by others, withdrawn, paranoid, increasingly the victim of barbi-turates and alcohol. Only half-jokingly, she referred to herself late in life as the only practicing witch in New England. "The very nicest thing about being a writer is that you can afford to indulge yourself endlessly with oddness, and no-body can really do anything about it . . . ," she wrote. Shortly before her death from a heart attack she wrote in her unfinished autobiographical novel, *Come Along with Me:* "How can anyone handle things if her head is full of voices and her world is full of things no one else can see?" Her hus-band, Stanley Edgar Hyman, published two posthumous collections of her work, *The Magic of Shirley Jackson* (1966) and *Come Along with Me* (1968).

**Jackson State shootings** Killing of two black students at Jackson State College, Jackson, Miss., by state law-men on May 14, 1970. The shootings followed campus violence and were pictured as wanton killings by onlook-ers and as resistance to sniper fire by the police. A federal grand jury was convened later that year but failed to return any indictments. The shootings were viewed as emblematic of the cam-pus unrest and civil rights strife that occurred in the U.S. during the late 1960s and early 1970s.

**Jacobi, Lotte** (*1896–1990*) Ger-man-American photographer. Born in Berlin, she was influenced by the artis-tic movements of her youth, using sur-realist and cubist techniques in her many portraits. She was closely associ-ated with Berlin's theatrical world in the 1920s and 1930s, creating strik-ingly original portraits of such figures as Bertolt BRECHT, Kurt WEILL and Lotte LENYA. Fleeing Germany for the U.S. in 1935, she settled in New York. There she continued portrait photography and, in the 1950s, began experiments with abstract "photogenics" and with the photographs, called "photograms," taken without benefit of a camera.

**Jacobs, Walter L.** (*1896–1985*) Business executive who founded Amer-ica's first car-rental agency, which later became the Hertz Corp. In 1918, hav-ing acquired 12 Model T Fords, Jacobs started the Rent-A-Ford company in Chicago. In 1923 he sold the business to John D. Hertz, owner of a Chicago taxicab company. Jacobs remained with the company until 1960, serving as its president and chief operating officer.

**Jacob's Pillow Dance Festival** The world-renowned Jacob's Pillow Dance Festival, located on 150 acres near Lee, Massachusetts, became the first dance festival in the U.S. when it was estab-lished in 1941. In 1930 dancer Ted SHAWN bought the land as a summer re-hearsal place for the Denishawn Dancers, then his Men Dancers. An in-terested group purchased the land, started a school, and established the festival (1941), with Shawn as director (1942–72). In 1942 the Shawn Theatre was built; it was the first theater in the western hemisphere to have a stage constructed exclusively for dance. Since its inception, the Festival has wel-comed all kinds of dance. The Ameri-can debuts of many European dancers and companies have taken place at this annual summer Festival, and over 300 new works have been premiered there. Since Shawn's death (1972), the Festi-val has had several directors; as of 1990, the director was Liz Thompson. Thompson was succeeded as director by Samuel Miller (1990–94), Sali Ann Kriegsman (1995–97) and Ella Baff (1997–  ).

**Jaehn, Sigmund** (*1937–  ) Ger-man cosmonaut-researcher and the first German in space. Jaehn flew aboard *SOYUZ 31* (August–September 1978). An air force pilot, he had held an appointment at the Gagarin Air Force Academy in the USSR before be-coming an inspector for the general staff of the East German air force. After the reunification of Germany in 1993, he represented Germany at the Euro-pean Space Agency.

**Jagger, Mick (Sir Michael Philip Jagger)** (*1943–  ) British ROCK song-writer and vocalist. Jagger has achieved international fame as the lead vocalist for the British rock band the ROLLING STONES. Jagger was born in Dartford, Kent, to a middle-class family and en-rolled as a student in the London School of Economics in 1960. His love

for American blues and rock music, notably Chuck BERRY and MUDDY WA-TERS, led Jagger to take up singing in 1962. His early gigs included guest spots with Alexis Korner's Blues Incor-porated. In 1962 Jagger became a founding member of The Rolling Stones, and by 1963 he was a star in Britain. A 1964 Rolling Stones tour of the U.S. established Jagger on both sides of the ocean. Regarded as the "bad boy of rock and roll" because of his irreverent attitudes, Jagger is best known for his distinctive vocal style—insinuating and sneering, but also ca-pable of great emotive power. He has also teamed with Keith Richard to write the majority of the Rolling Stones's hit songs, including the classic "(I Can't Get No) Satisfaction" (1965). Five solo albums, including *She's The Boss* (1985), *Primitive Cool* (1987), *Goddess in the Doorway* (2001) and *Alfie* (movie soundtrack, written with Dave Stewart [2004]). In June 2002 Jagger was knighted by Queen ELIZA-BETH II for "services to popular music."

**Jajce Congress** Meeting held No-vember 29–30, 1943, in the Bosnian town of Jajce. Consisting of Yugoslavian delegates to the Anti-Fascist National Liberation Committee, the Jajce Con-gress agreed to the postwar creation of a federated republic of YUGOSLAVIA. The congress also established the commit-tee as Yugoslavia's provisional govern-ment and gave communist partisan leader Josip TITO the title of Marshal. Exactly two years later, the Federal Peo-ple's Republic of Yugoslavia was offi-cially proclaimed.

**Jakarta (Djakarta; formerly Batavia)** Capital city of INDONESIA; on the island of Java's Jakarta Bay, an inlet of the Java Sea. Known to its longtime Dutch occu-piers as Batavia, Jakarta is the largest city of Indonesia, as well as its leading commercial and industrial center. Dur-ing WORLD WAR II, the Japanese cap-tured the city in March 1942 and held it until 1945. In December 1949 Batavia was renamed and made the capital of the newly independent Indonesia.

**Jamaica** Island republic in the West Indies, south of CUBA and west of HAITI; capital is Kingston. As a British colony, Jamaica experienced civil strife caused by poverty and British racial policies. This came to a peak in violent rioting in

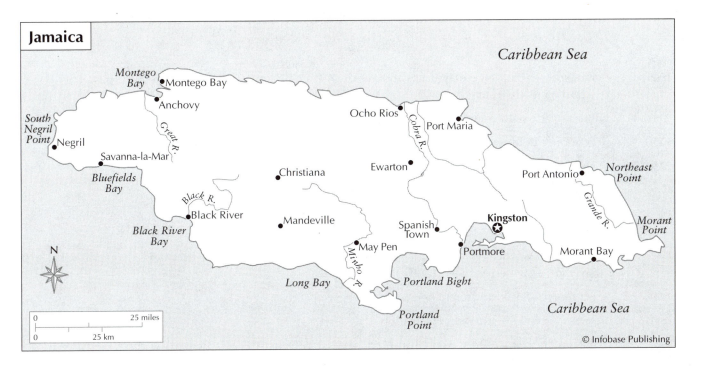

Jamaica

1938, which brought about universal adult suffrage in 1944. Jamaica regained internal autonomy in 1953, and in 1958 joined the WEST INDIES FEDERATION. A campaign led by nationalist labor leader Sir Alexander BUSTAMENTE led to Jamaica's withdrawal from the federation in 1961. In 1962, Jamaica became an independent member of the COMMONWEALTH with Bustamente as its first prime minister. Michael MANLEY of the People's National Party became prime minister in 1972 and instituted socialist reforms, but Jamaica's economy suffered, and some factions violently protested his government. In 1980, Edward P. Seaga, a conservative Labour Party member, defeated Manley and encouraged a return to capitalistic policy. Jamaica suffered in the recession of the early 1980s, but in 1984 Seaga responded with a series of reforms, including devaluation of the Jamaican dollar, which resulted in an increase in tourism, agriculture and manufacturing. Concurrent inflation, however, left many Jamaicans in poverty. In 1989, Manley was reelected, though on a more moderate platform than its previous administrations. The People's National Party continued to dominate the political scene throughout the 1990s and into the 21st century, despite a steep recession that began in 1999.

**Jamalzadeh, Mohammed Ali** *(c. 1895–1997)* Iranian short story writer. Jamalzadeh received a progressive, Western-style education in Dijon and Lausanne, where he studied law. His father was a leading figure in the Iranian national revival. During World War I, he joined emigrés in Berlin to fight against the Anglo-Russian occupation of Iran; thereafter he worked at the Iranian embassy in Berlin. In 1931 he took up permanent residence in Switzerland. His first book, *Yeki bud va yeki nabud* (1921, Once upon a time), gave a critical and realistic picture of Iranian life. He published no more books until 1941. *Dar ol-majanin* (1942, Lunatic asylum), *Qualtashan Divan* (1946, Dictator of the imperial office) and *Sar o tahe yak karbas ya Esfahanname* (1956, All of a Pattern, or the book of Isfahan) were longer works dealing with social themes. Jamalzadeh has also translated Schiller, Wilde and Anatole FRANCE.

**James, C(yril) L(ionel) R(obert)** *(1901–1989)* Trinidad-born political historian, literary critic and cricket writer who was a leader of the pan-African movement. After moving to London in the 1930s, James became a Marxist and involved himself in several left-wing political causes. He rejected STALIN's version of COMMUNISM, however, and allied himself with Stalin's exiled rival, Leon TROTSKY. After spending 15 years in the U.S., he was expelled in 1953 during a period of intense anti-

communism (see McCARTHYISM). He then traveled to Africa and became involved in the African independence movement. In 1958 he returned to Trinidad at the invitation of Chief Minister Eric WILLIAMS and later became secretary of the West Indies Federal Labour Party coalition. His books included *The Black Jacobins: Toussaint L'Ouverture and the San Domingo Revolution* (1938) and *Beyond the Boundary* (1963).

**James, Harry** *(1916–1983)* American trumpet player and bandleader. James began playing in bands at age eight. He played in the band of Benny GOODMAN from 1937 until 1939, when he started his own group. He added romantic ballad arrangements to his repertoire beginning in 1941 with *You Made Me Love You.* He helped launch the careers of singers Frank SINATRA, Dick Haymes, Helen Forrest, and Connie Haines. In 1943 he married film star Betty GRABLE and appeared in several films, which brought him more popularity. Along with Glenn MILLER, James developed and refined the big band sound known as swing, the most popular jazz style in the U.S. during World War II. (See also SWING ERA.)

**James, Henry** *(1843–1916)* American novelist whose works are remarkable for their subtlety, psychological penetration and stylistic care. One of the most influential figures in American

| | JAMAICA |
|---|---|
| 1907 | Kingston leveled by earthquakes; governor of British Crown colony resigns after misunderstanding leads to landing and rapid departure of U.S. Marines. |
| 1916 | Black Nationalist Marcus Garvey immigrates to U.S. |
| 1930 | Economic depression leads to rioting and strikes. |
| 1939 | Norman Manley founds People's National Party. |
| 1940 | U.S. granted military bases as part of Lend-Lease program. |
| 1944 | British allow internal self-government; first House of Representatives election is dominated by Jamaican Labour Party. |
| 1945 | Blight and wartime disruption of shipping discourage banana planting, lead to agricultural diversity and increased self-sufficiency. |
| 1954 | PLP purges leftist members and wins elections. |
| 1958 | Jamaica joins West Indian Federation. |
| 1962 | Full independence from Britain granted; secession from WIF; Bustamente of the JLP elected first prime minister; University of the West Indies chartered. |
| 1965 | International air routes make tourism an important industry. |
| 1969 | Jamaican dollar replaces the pound. |
| 1970 | Population down 15% from 1960, due to emigration. |
| 1972 | Michael Manley of the PNP elected; launches radical leftist programs, including land reform and ties to Cuba. |
| 1975 | Tourism slumps; oil prices rise; economy devastated. |
| 1979 | Prime Minister Manley refuses to accept conditions set by International Monetary Fund; denied desperately needed loans; middle-class emigration increases. |
| 1980 | Seven-hundred killed in election violence between PNP and JNP; Seaga of JNP elected. |
| 1981 | Seaga reverses Manley policies; seeks new ties with U.S.; encourages free enterprise; adopts IMF-backed austerity programs; singer Bob Marley dies; tourism up. |
| 1988 | Hurricane Gilbert leaves 20% of island's population homeless. |
| 1989 | Manley and the PNP, projecting a more moderate image, are reelected. |
| 1990 | Young & Rubicam, one of New York's leading advertising agencies, pleads guilty to bribing Jamaican officials in return for a large contact to promote tourism there. |
| 1992 | Manley retires for health reasons and is succeeded by Percival J. Patterson. |
| 1997 | Patterson leads the PNP to an unprecedented third consecutive term as governing party. |
| 1999 | Severe economic downturn leads to high unemployment and an enormous budget deficit. |
| 2005 | The murder rate in the country soars to 1,145, the highest in the island's recorded history. |

literature, James was born in New York and educated abroad and at Harvard Law School. His father was a theological writer, and his older brother, William JAMES, became an eminent philosopher. James began his career contributing to periodicals. His first major novel, *Roderick Hudson* (1876), appeared in *The Atlantic Monthly* in 1875. James settled in England in 1875, and much of his work insightfully contrasts European worldliness with American naivete. Such novels include *Daisy Miller* (1879), *Portrait of a Lady* (1881), *THE AMBASSADORS* (1903),

*American author Henry James* (LIBRARY OF CONGRESS, PRINTS AND PHOTOGRAPHS DIVISION)

and *The Golden Bowl* (1904). Some of his fiction, including *The Spoils of Poynton* (1897) and *The Awkward Age* (1899), focuses more specifically on the nature of the English. James was a mentor and close friend to Edith WHARTON; a volume of their correspondence was published in 1989. In addition to a number of other novels, James also wrote short stories, the best known being *The Turn of the Screw* (1898); travel sketches; and plays. James became a British subject shortly before his death. A four-volume biography of James was written by Leon Edel between 1953 and 1972.

**James, M(ontague) R(hodes)** *(1862–1936)* British medieval scholar and educator, commonly acknowledged as the 20th century's greatest master of the ghost story. The son of a Suffolk clergyman, James decided, after attending Eton and King's College, Cambridge, not to follow his father and brother into the Church. Rather, as Provost of King's College and, later, Eton, he pursued his scholarship of medieval manuscripts and architecture. He is best known today for his hobby—writing ghost stories for annual Christmas gatherings with his friends. The spectral tales first appeared in the collection, *Ghost Stories of an Antiquary* (1904) and in subsequent books, *More Ghost Stories of an Antiquary* (1911), *A Thin Ghost* (1919) and *A Warning to the Curious* (1926). Although the props and characters might

seem at first glance rather cliched— haunted wells, yawning graves, vampires and ghosts—he has added some novel effects of his own. These include witchcraft on a tram car (*Casting the Runes*), a pair of haunted binoculars (*A View from a Hill*), and an inexplicable, "face of crumpled linen" of some haunted bedsheets (*Oh, Whistle, and I'll Come to You, My Lad*). Yet the stories are set against careful and meticulous backgrounds of bookish, antiquarian lore; and they are written in a sober, refined narrative style. Notoriously reticent about his work, James best summed up his intent in the Latin inscription found on a certain ancient whistle in one of his stories: "Quis est este qui venit?" ("Who is this who is coming?") The answer was usually dreadful—and superbly memorable.

**James, P(hyllis) D(orothy) (baroness James of Holland Park)** *(1923– )* British novelist. Born in Oxford and educated at Cambridge University, she was an administrator in the NATIONAL HEALTH SERVICE from 1949 to 1968. In 1968 she transferred to the Home Office, where she worked as a senior civil servant in the police and criminal law departments. Her first book, *Cover Her Face* (1962), introduced readers to Scotland Yard detective Adam Dalgleish, who appears in most of her subsequent books. In 1979 she resigned from her job to write full time. James adapted the detective mystery genre (perfected in the 1930s by Dorothy L. SAYERS) to examine the social order in late-20th-century Britain. Her realistic novels transcend the customary limits of the mystery genre, and she is regarded as being in the mainstream of contemporary English literature. Several of her books have been adapted for television by the BBC. These include *The Black Tower* (1982), *A Taste for Death* (1986) and *Devices and Desires* (1989). In 1991 P. D. James was made a Dame of the British Empire and was elevated to the peerage as baroness James of Holland Park.

**James, William** *(1842–1910)* American philosopher and psychologist. James stands among the most original and influential thinkers that America has ever produced. He came from a remarkable New England family—his father, Henry James Sr., was a prominent theologian, and his brother Henry JAMES

was one of the greatest American novelists. William James earned a medical degree from Harvard University in 1869 and went on to teach anatomy, physiology, psychology and philosophy at Harvard. In 1884 James helped found the American Society for Psychical Research. His two-volume *Principles of Psychology* (1890) was a pioneering work in a then new field of social science. *Varieties of Religious Experience* (1902) remains a classic work on the nature and modalities of religious beliefs. James is best known for his formulation of the philosophy of **pragmatism**, which argues that we live in a pluralistic universe in which truth is relative and best measured by the extent to which it serves human freedom. James's key philosophical essays are contained in *Pragmatism* (1907) and *Essays in Radical Empiricism* (1912).

**James Bond** Fictional British secret agent ("007") with a "licence to kill"; created by novelist Ian FLEMING, Bond first appeared in the novel *Casino Royale* (1954) and was subsequently featured in numerous feature films, beginning in the 1960s and continuing into the 1990s. James Bond was an immensely popular character; his far-fetched adventures bore little resemblance to actual espionage work but rather reflected male fantasies. Bond was first portrayed by actor Barry Nelson, on American television; in the movies, Bond was first portrayed by Scottish actor Sean CONNERY and afterward by David Niven, George Lazenby, Roger Moore, Timothy Dalton, Pierce Brosnan and Daniel Craig.

**Jameson, (Margaret) Storm (Mrs. Guy Chapman)** *(1891–1986)* British novelist and feminist. As president of the English section of PEN from 1938 to 1944, Jameson worked tirelessly to rescue and assist writers from countries under Nazi occupation. Three of her finest novels stemmed from that period: *Cousin Honore, Europe to Let* and *Cloudless May*. Perhaps her most important postwar work was her two-volume autobiography, *Journey from the North* (1969–70).

**Janáček, Leoš** *(1854–1928)* Czech composer. Born in Moravia, his father was an organist, and his earliest musical experience was a choirboy. He began directing choirs at the age of 16 and later (1875–80) studied composition at Prague, Leipzig and Vienna. He moved to Brno in 1881, teaching and conducting there. He was a professor at Prague from 1921 to 1923. Janáček was an avid student and collector of Slavic folk music, and his work was influenced by its rhythms and melodies as well as by the inflections of the Czech language itself. He is particularly noted for his operas, including *Jenufa* (1904), *Katya Kabanova* (1921), *The Cunning Little Vixen* (1921) and *From the House of the Dead* (1930). Among his other works are the symphonic poem *Taras Bulba* (1915–18), the song cycle *The Diary of One Who Vanished* (1916–19) and the *Glagolitic Mass* (1926), as well as many orchestral, chamber, piano, vocal and choral compositions.

**Janco, Marcel** (*1895–1984*) Romanian-born Israeli painter and architect. Janco helped found the DADA movement in Switzerland in 1916. Together with Hans ARP, Tristan TZARA and other artists, Janco formulated an approach to art that abandoned traditional conventions in favor of art without preconceived ideas. This approach, DADAISM, was a forerunner of SURREALISM and modern ABSTRACT ART. Janco was best known for his abstract masks recalling the Japanese and Greek theater. In 1953 he founded Israel's first art colony, Ein Hod.

**Janet, Pierre Marie-Félix** (*1859–1947*) French psychiatrist. Janet was one of the pioneers of clinical psychiatry and a dominant figure in the administration of mental health programs in France. In the 1880s and 1890s, he served as the director of the prestigious Salpêtrière clinic. For the first four decades of this century, he taught at the Collège de France. In papers written in the 1880s, Janet anticipated certain theories of Sigmund FREUD as to the unconscious symptomology of hysteria and other mental disorders. Janet also conducted researches into hypnosis and the clinical classification of mental illness. His major works include *Neuroses and Fixed Ideas* (1898), *The Mental State of Hysteria* (1911) and *Psychological Medicine* (1923).

**Janson, H(orst) W(oldemar)** (*1913–1982*) American art historian and teacher. Born in Leningrad, Janson studied at the universities of Hamburg and Munich and at Harvard, where he began his teaching career. He also taught at the Worcester Art Museum, Iowa State University and Washington University before becoming a professor of art history at New York University in 1949. One of America's most distinguished art historians, he is best known for his comprehensive survey, *History of Art* (1962), which sold more than 2 million copies internationally. Janson was also the author of such works as *Apes and Ape Lore in the Middle Ages* (1952) and *The Sculpture of Donatello* (1957).

**Janssen, Werner** (*1899–1990*) U.S. conductor and composer. A specialist in 20th-century music, in 1934 he became the first American-born conductor appointed to lead the New York Philharmonic orchestra. He later moved to Los Angeles, where he led his own Janssen Symphony (1940–52). He wrote scores for such films as *Blockade* (1938) and *The General Died at Dawn* (1936).

**Japan** Japan entered the modern era in 1868 when young members of the military oligarchy installed Emperor Meiji on the throne and launched a vast program of industrialization and modernization. Japan opened its doors to Western influences and ideas, imported Western technologies and concluded friendship treaties with such countries as the U.S., Britain and the Netherlands. It was RUSSIA and CHINA, however, that were to play a major role in Japanese foreign affairs between the

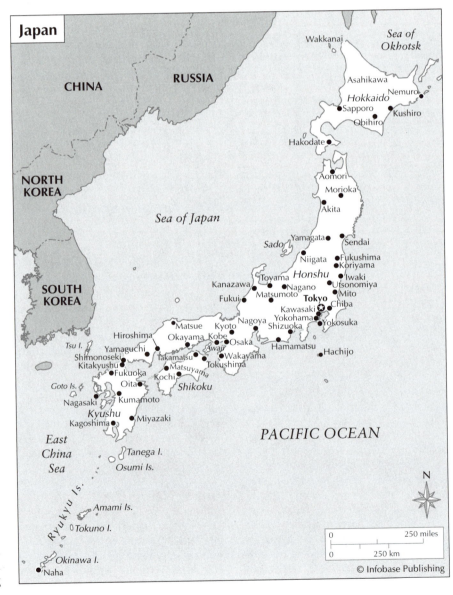

# JAPAN

| | |
|---|---|
| 1904 | (Feb.) Attacks Russia and declares war; wins territorial objectives in Korea and Manchuria. |
| 1926 | Accession of Emperor Hirohito. |
| 1931 | The Mukden incident of 1931, involving an explosion on the Manchurian rail line; results in annexation of Manchuria and army control of political power. |
| 1932 | (May) Prime Minister Takashi Inukai is assassinated, ending the last nonmilitary-controlled government. |
| 1936 | Japan joins the Axis powers in a pact against the Soviet Union. |
| 1937 | (July) War with China erupts after Marco Polo Bridge Incident. |
| 1941 | (Dec. 7) Japan attacks Pearl Harbor in the U.S. Hawaiian Islands; (Dec. 8) U.S. declares war on Japan. |
| 1942 | Defeats at Midway Island and the Coral Sea break Japanese sea power. |
| 1945 | Philippines reconquered; (Aug. 6) Atomic bomb dropped on Hiroshima; (Aug. 8) Soviet Union declares war on Japan; (Aug. 9) Atomic bomb dropped on Nagasaki; (Aug. 14) Japan accepts the unconditional surrender terms of the Potsdam Declaration; (Sept. 2) Formal surrender signed; Gen. Douglas MacArthur becomes supreme commander of Allied forces occupying Japan. |
| 1946 | Demobilization and demilitarization are completed; civil and land reform commence. |
| 1948 | War Crimes Tribunal sentences 25 to death or life imprisonment; (Dec. 23) General Hideki Tojo is hanged. |
| 1949 | San Francisco Peace Conference promises full sovereignty to Japan by April 1952. |
| 1952 | Security treaty is signed with the U.S. |
| 1955 | Industrial output meets peak prewar levels. |
| 1956 | Japan admitted to the UN. |
| 1960 | Hayato Ikeda begins four-year term as prime minister. |
| 1964 | Tokyo Olympics; Eisaku Sato begins eight-year term as prime minister. |
| 1970 | EXPO '70, the first world exposition held in Asia, is hosted by the city of Osaka; United States returns Okinawa and Ryukyu islands. |
| 1973 | Oil embargo causes Japan to shift industrial focus to high-tech areas such as consumer electronics. |
| 1974 | Prime Minister Kakuei Tanaka is implicated in the Lockheed scandal and is arrested for accepting a 500 million-yen bribe; Sato wins Nobel Prize for peace. |
| 1986 | To stem exports, Plaza Accord obliges Japan to accept a 40% upward valuation of the yen. |
| 1988 | Japan becomes the largest donor of foreign aid and largest supplier of foreign aid. |
| 1989 | (Jan. 7) Emperor Hirohito dies and is succeeded by his son Crown Prince Akihito. |
| 1993 | A coalition of eight opposition parties forms a government headed by Morihiro Hosokawa, ending the LDP's long rule. |
| 1994 | Tomiichi Murayama becomes Japan's first Socialist prime minister since 1948 as head of a coalition including the LDP. |
| 1997 | The Japanese economy slides into its longest recession since the end of World War II. |
| 2001 | Junichiro Koizumi becomes prime minister. |
| 2006 | Economic indicators show positive growth for the first time in eight years. Koizumi is succeeded as prime minister by Abe Shinzo. |

1890s and 1930s. The first Sino-Japanese War, over Korea, was fought in 1894–95; the RUSSO-JAPANESE WAR, over Manchuria, followed in 1904–05. Victorious in both encounters, Japan greatly increased its sphere of influence and gained tremendous military prestige. During WORLD WAR I, Japan was on the side of the Allies and became their major supplier of ammunition and ships. Its economic development was further enhanced by increasing demand from Asia and Africa, which could no longer rely on British and German exporters. The war also proved beneficial for Japan politically because, as an ally of Britain, it was asked to destroy German warships protecting German interests in China; this ultimately led to Japan's occupation of Shantung (now Shandong) province in China.

By 1922 Japan had been recognized as a major Asian power, and its navy had become the world's third largest after that of Britain and the U.S. The 1920s were a decade of rapid economic growth. An important step in the gradual democratization of Japan was taken in 1925 when the government enacted universal suffrage for males. Soon after the 1926 ascension to the throne of Emperor HIROHITO Japan was hit by the worldwide economic depression. The economic dislocations and discontent led to political violence (two prime ministers were assassinated in the early 1930s), to the rise of radical nationalistic groups and to the reemergence of the military, who felt that Japan should become "master of Asia." Without the knowledge of the country's political leaders, the Japanese armed forces took advantage of the political disarray in China and in 1931 invaded MANCHURIA. In 1932 the military proclaimed Manchuria an "independent" state, renamed MANCHUKUO, and installed a puppet government. The occupation of Manchuria was just the beginning of a protracted conflict between Japan and China, which escalated into another Sino-Japanese War in 1937 and lasted until 1945.

After signing military pacts with GERMANY and ITALY in 1940, Japanese military leaders began to plan an attack on the U.S. Pacific Fleet in order to prevent the United States from interfering with Japanese "liberation" of European colonies in East Asia (French INDOCHINA, British Malaya and BURMA

and the Dutch East Indies). In April 1941 Japan concluded a nonaggression treaty with the Soviet Union to postpone any military encounter with the country. On December 7, 1941, Japanese bombers attacked PEARL HARBOR on Oahu and destroyed or severely damaged most of the U.S. ships and aircraft anchored there. Other U.S. military installations in the Pacific, including two airfields near Manila in the Philippines and bases on GUAM, MIDWAY and WAKE, were successfully attacked the same day. In January 1942 Japan captured the PHILIPPINES, and by the following spring it had conquered a vast area stretching from Malaya eastward to the Pacific islands of Wake and Guam and southward to the Dutch East Indies (present-day INDONESIA). U.S. armed forces soon struck back, and in early May 1942, in the battle of the CORAL SEA off New Guinea, stopped the Japanese expansion. The next three years saw a number of fierce battles (at Midway, GUADALCANAL, LEYTE GULF) and a steady American advance. In January 1945 the Philippines were recaptured. Meanwhile, in May 1945 peace in Europe was concluded, and the U.S. decided to use the newly developed ATOMIC BOMB to force Japan to surrender. Two bombs were dropped in August 1945, on HIROSHIMA and on NAGASAKI, causing the death of about 340,000 people. On August 14, 1945, Japan unconditionally surrendered to the Allied powers.

The U.S. military occupation of Japan, headed by Gen. Douglas MACARTHUR, lasted from 1945 to 1952. It was a period of far-reaching changes in Japanese society, politics and economy. Japan had lost over three million people during the war, and when the hostilities ended it was economically devastated, with most of its industry in shambles. The American occupation administration, working through a capable Japanese bureaucracy, set up a massive rebuilding course for the country. With huge amounts of American aid, and the Japanese tradition of hard work, the economic recovery was fast and impressive. Recovery was also helped by the KOREAN WAR of 1950–52, when Japan became the major base for the U.S., providing airfields, harbors, repair and medical services, ships and other materiel. Politically, the aim of the U.S. occupation was the demilitarization and

democratization of Japan. After military leaders and others were executed for war crimes and acts of cruelty, the power of the military oligarchy was effectively broken.

In 1947 a new constitution was promulgated, renouncing war, abolishing the divinity of the emperor and proclaiming the sovereignty of the people. The Japanese started to transform their country. Relations with the West were codified in a peace treaty in 1951. At the same time Japan concluded a bilateral security treaty with the U.S., which stipulated that U.S. armed forces would retain military bases in Japan and would assist Japan in case of aggression. Japan also normalized relations with its Asian neighbors. In 1965 diplomatic ties with South Korea were established, and in 1972 Japan established full relations with the People's Republic of China. A treaty for economic aid and investment between Japan and China was agreed upon in 1988. When Prime Minister TAKESHITA announced in 1988 that his government would spend U.S. $5 billion in foreign aid over the next five years (and thus become the world's largest donor of foreign aid), it became clear that Japan intended to play a global economic role, as befits a nation with the second largest GNP in the world.

For a short period in 1947 socialists controlled the government; otherwise, postwar Japan has been governed by conservatives. Two leading conservative parties, the Liberals and the Democrats, merged into a single party in 1955; since that time the LDP has been the predominant political force in Japan. Eisaku SATO, who served as prime minister from 1964 until 1972, was awarded the NOBEL PEACE PRIZE in 1974 for his "reconciliation policy that contributed to a stabilization of conditions in the Pacific area." The first OLYMPIC GAMES to be held in Asia took place in Tokyo in the summer of 1964; six years later the Japan World Exposition was held in Osaka, and in 1972 Sapporo hosted the Winter Olympics. The thousands of visitors to these events were impressed by the highly developed Japanese technology, especially in transportation.

Kakuei TANAKA, Sato's successor, was in office during the first major oil crisis in 1973, which Japan withstood by making its industry more efficient and less energy-intensive. Politically, Tanaka fared worse. He had to resign in 1974; and in 1976 he was charged with, and later found guilty of, accepting bribes from the Lockheed Corporation. Tanaka was succeeded as prime minister by Takeo Miki, Takeo Fukuda, Masayoshi Ohira, Zenko Suzuki and in 1982 by Yasuhiro NAKASONE—who differed from the previous prime ministers by his forceful, almost flamboyant style, and his great international visibility. He visited the U.S., Australia, Southeast Asia and Europe, promoting political and economic ties. Domestically, he concentrated on restructuring government-run enterprises; on fiscal reform, aimed at eliminating the deficit; and on liberalization of the educational system. In 1987, Nakasone stepped down (after an unsuccessful bid for another term), and Noboru Takeshita became the new prime minister. Takeshita's political victory was overshadowed by a scandal involving many highly placed politicians and business executives who bought shares in a real estate company before they were publicly traded and thus made huge profits. The scandal eventually led to Takeshita's resignation. He was succeeded briefly by Sosuke Uno, who was himself forced to resign by another scandal.

Emperor Hirohito died in January 1989 and was succeeded by Crown Prince AKIHITO. In the 1993 national elections the LDP was forced from power by an eight-party coalition. The coalition collapsed the following year and was replaced by a government of LDP and Socialist politicians. Throughout the remainder of the 1990s and into the 21st century Japan was plagued by a persistent economic slowdown that showed signs of recovery only in 2006. In the early years of the 21st century, tensions between Japan and Asian victims of its aggression during World War II (such as China and South Korea) escalated, as Japanese government officials insisted on visiting shrines to convicted war criminals and refused to alter school textbooks that downplayed Japan's wartime atrocities.

## Japanese-Americans, internment of
Forced detention of Americans of Japanese ancestry and resident aliens at the beginning of WORLD WAR II. After the Japanese attack on PEARL HARBOR

*Japanese Americans in an internment camp in Turlock. Calif.. 1942* (LIBRARY OF CONGRESS, PRINTS AND PHOTOGRAPHS DIVISION)

(December 7, 1941), a wave of anti-Japanese sentiment swept the U.S. Lt. Gen. John L. DeWitt, security chief for the western U.S., alleged that Japanese Americans posed a security threat. Convinced congressmen urged internment on President Franklin D. ROOSEVELT, who signed an executive order early in 1942 authorizing army relocation and detention of anyone considered dangerous. DeWitt established a military area in western Washington, Oregon and California and decreed that all people of Japanese origin be removed from it. With only a few days notice, some 120,000 Japanese Americans were forced to sell what they owned and were removed to guarded barbed-wire-rimmed barracks in desolate parts of the West, where they were kept for two to three years. While most Americans were ignorant of this legal scandal, news of the internment gradually reached the public. In 1976 President FORD proclaimed that the detention had been wrong, and in 1988 a bill was passed that called for government apology and for the payment of $20,000 apiece to all survivors.

**Jaray, Paul** *(1889–1974)* Swiss engineer who pioneered in the development of automobile design using streamlined forms. As an engineer for the ZEPPELIN works. Jaray designed dirigible airships. In 1922 he patented an automobile design of streamlined form based on aerodynamics. Although he never designed a production car, his ideas have had a major influence on all modern automotive design.

**Jarrell, Randall** *(1914–1965)* American critic and poet. Born in Nashville Tenn., and educated at Vanderbilt University, Jarrell was known as a vitriolic and even cruel critic. His friend Robert LOWELL said he was "almost brutally serious about literature." He taught at many colleges and universities and contributed to prestigious literary journals. In 1961 *The Woman at the Washington Zoo* won a National Book Award for poetry. He was a master of the modern plain style, where poetry resembles a colloquial mode of speech. One of his favorite themes was war: His most famous poem is a five-line lyric, "The Death of the Ball Turret Gunner." His best-known critical work is *Poetry and the Age* (1953).

**Jarry, Alfred** *(1873–1907)* French playwright, novelist and poet. Although not a prolific writer, Jarry has exercised as great an influence on 20th-century theater as any playwright. Jarry's plays are the founding blocks of the THEATER OF THE ABSURD, and his overall oeuvre served to inspire both DADA and SURREALISM. Jarry, who began his literary career as a symbolist and an aspiring dandy, shocked Parisian theatrical circles with his raw absurdist play, *Ubu Roi*, which featured an obscenity-spouting monarch whose unending appetites and cynical lack of values made a mockery of all societal values. Riots broke out in the theater on the night of the first performance. Jarry's other works include a volume of poems *Days and Nights* (1897), the novel *The Supermale* (1902) and two further Ubu plays. Jarry coined the term **pataphysique**—loosely translated as the study of absurdity—which is still widely used in France.

**Jaruzelski, Wojciech** *(1923– )* Polish general and communist prime minister (1981–89) and president (1989–90) of POLAND. Jaruzelski took office to restore order following the unrest (1980–81) that had arisen in fear of Soviet intervention. As prime minister, he initially made further concessions to the independent trade union SOLIDARITY. However, having also become leader of the Polish Communist Party, he proclaimed martial law in December 1981 and arrested Solidarity leaders, including union leader Lech WAŁĘSA. Some relaxation occurred the following year, but tension between the government and Solidarity led to sporadic outbursts of unrest throughout the 1980s. In 1989 Jaruzelski agreed to the relegalization of Solidarity and far-reaching constitutional reforms, including free elections. He became president under the new government system (1989) but resigned at the end of 1990 after Walesa was elected president. In 1993 Jaruzelski was charged with criminal conduct in the 1970 deaths of demonstrating workers, but the trial was delayed because of technicalities. In 2005 Jaruzelski apologized for the participation of Polish troops in the Soviet-led invasion of Czechoslovakis in 1968.

**Järvi, Neeme** (1937–  ) Estonian conductor. Järvi was born in Tallinn, Estonia, and continued his music studies at the Leningrad State Conservatory, where he made his conducting debut at the age of 18. His first major appointment was Director of the Estonian Radio and Television Orchestra and the Tallinn Opera. A first prize at an international conducting competition in Rome in 1971 led to invitations to work with major orchestras throughout the world. He left the USSR in 1980 and became a resident in America where he made his Metropolitan Opera debut with *Eugene Onegin* in the 1978–79 season. His subsequent principal appointments include principal conductor of the Gothenburg Symphony Orchestra and musical director of the Scottish National Orchestra. A prolific performer and recording artist, Järvi has won special praise for his interpretations of composers once associated with his Gothenburg Symphony Orchestra, notably Jean SIBELIUS. A long-cherished project of great importance has been his recording of the complete orchestral works of fellow Estonian Edward Tubin. From 1989 to 2003 Järvi served as music director of the Detroit Symphony Orchestra. In 2003 he ac-

cepted the same position with the New Jersey Symphony Orchestra.

**Jarvik heart** Artificial heart designed by the American physician Robert K. Jarvik. The first heart replacement intended for permanent implantation into a patient, the air-powered system is fitted with a disk-shaped pump, a power system, two ventricles and a system of air tubes. The Jarvik-7 was first used in a human recipient in 1982, when it was implanted in Barney Clark, who survived 112 days. Subsequent recipients had the heart implanted as a temporary or permanent measure, but there were a number of serious problems with blood clots and stroke.

**Jarvis, Gregory** (1941–1986) American astronaut, one of seven killed in the explosion of the space shuttle *Challenger* (January 28, 1986). He was an engineer with the Hughes Aircraft Co.

**Jaspers, Karl Theodor** (1883–1969) German philosopher, psychiatrist and essayist. Jaspers was one of the leading influences upon the emerging philosophical school of EXISTENTIALISM. He began his career as a practicing psychiatrist at the University of Heidelberg hospital and produced a medical work, *General Psychopathology* (1913). But shortly thereafter Jaspers turned his primary attention to philosophy, which he believed represented man's unending search for ultimate reality. He emphasized the vital importance of individual freedom as opposed to socially conditioned values and behaviors. Forced into academic retirement by the Nazis, Jaspers continued his teaching career after World War II at the University of Basel in Switzerland. He forthrightly acknowledged a national German guilt for Nazi crimes and urged that serious attention be paid to the horrible lessons of recent history. Major works by Jaspers include the three-volume *Philosophy* (1932), *Reason and Existence* (1938) and *The Origin and Goal of History* (1949).

**Jaurès, Jean** (1859–1914) French socialist writer, orator and political leader. Born of middle-class parents in Castres, he studied at Toulouse University, where he subsequently taught philosophy. He served in the Chamber of

Deputies (1885–89, 1893–98 and 1902–14) and became a socialist; he was a leading supporter of Alfred Dreyfus. A noted writer and orator, he was founder (1904) and editor of the influential left-wing daily *L'Humanité*. In 1905, Jaurès was successful in uniting the various factions of the socialist movement into a unified French Socialist Party. His was an idealistic socialism; he advocated economic equality through peaceful revolution and the separation of church and state while denouncing nationalism and ANTI-SEMITISM. A noted historian, he is remembered for his *Histoire socialiste de la Revolution française* (1901–07). As World War I approached, Jaures favored arbitration as an alternative to armed conflict. He was assassinated by a nationalist fanatic in 1914.

**Java [Djawa]** Island in the Greater Sunda Islands group of Indonesia, southeast of Sumatra and south of Borneo. Two-thirds of INDONESIA's population lives on Java, although it is only the fifth-largest of the archipelago-nation's islands. The population includes Javanese, Sudanese, Madurese, Chinese and Arabs; people from India were the first colonizers and the Japanese were the last, occupying Java during WORLD WAR II. The Dutch tried to restore their rule after the war ended but had to fight Indonesian forces intent on winning independence, which they did by 1949. Jakarta is the nation's capital and largest city; Surabaja (Indonesia's major naval base) and Bandung (site of the BANDUNG CONFERENCE), both on Java, are the second- and third-largest cities.

**Java Sea** Arm of the western Pacific Ocean, between the islands of Java and Borneo. An important naval battle was fought here between Japanese and Allied forces on February 27, 1942, early in WORLD WAR II. The Allies were defeated and JAVA was laid open to Japanese attack.

**Javits, Jacob Koppel** (1904–1986) American politician. The son of Jewish immigrants, Javits became a leader of the liberal wing of the REPUBLICAN PARTY. A U.S. senator representing New York from 1957 to 1981, he played a part in the 1973 War Powers Act, the creation of the National Endowment for the Humanities, and the 1974 Pension Reform

Act. His age and ill health cost him his first and only electoral defeat in a 1980 primary contest.

**Jaworski, Leon** *(1905–1982)* American attorney. A graduate of Baylor University and the George Washington University and the George Washington University School of Law, Jaworski made his reputation as a lawyer in Houston. Among his clients was then-congressman Lyndon B. JOHNSON. Jaworski also served as a prosecutor at the NUREMBERG WAR CRIMES TRIALS after World War II, and as president of the American Bar Association. Jaworski may be best remembered for his role as the special prosecutor during the investigation of the WATERGATE scandal that eventually forced the resignation of President Richard M. NIXON. Jaworski was appointed to the post after Nixon ordered the previous prosecutor, Archibald COX, fired in the infamous Saturday Night Massacre. Jaworski's investigation revealed wrong-doing at the highest levels and forced the resignation of both the U.S. attorney general John MITCHELL and also President Nixon himself.

**Jayewardene, Junius Richard** *(1906–1996)* Jayewardene was elected the first president of SRI LANKA in 1978 and reelected in 1982. He led the country through the most difficult period of its postindependence, pursuing a carrot-and-stick policy toward Tamil moderates and militants until 1987. Under his rule military forces committed brutal atrocities against Tamil civilians. In 1987, in a remarkable change of policy, he signed an agreement with Indian prime minister Rajiv GANDHI, in which the Tamils were allowed a degree of regional autonomy and India effectively committed itself to maintain the unity of Sir Lanka. Jayewardene declined to seek a third term in 1988.

**Al-Jazeera** Arabic television news station. Meaning "the Island" of "the Peninsula" (referring to the Arabian Peninsula), it began its operations toward the end of 1996, broadcasting out of Qatar, largely because the BBC World Service closed its two-year-old Arabic TV station rather than continue to operate under the stringent censorship guidelines of Saudi Arabia. Stepping in to fill the void left by the BBC

(and hiring many of the former BBC employees), al-Jazeera premiered and heralded itself as the Middle East's only independent source of news. However, its repeated insistence of editorial objectivity has been somewhat impeded by the network being owned by the government of Qatar.

It came to prominence as a result of the terrorist attacks committed against the U.S. on SEPTEMBER 11, 2001. Not long after the attacks on New York and Washington, D.C., al-Jazeera broadcast video footage of Osama BIN LADEN and Sulaiman Abu Ghaith offering justification for the use of three airplanes to destroy the WORLD TRADE CENTER and to damage the Pentagon. Soon after this footage aired, the U.S. government developed a generally hostile stance toward the network, alleging that it served as a propaganda organ for bin Laden, Iraqi dictator Saddam HUSSEIN and the leadership of the TALIBAN, for whom Al Jazeera has aired statements between 2001 and 2003. Also, al-Jazeera repeatedly aired graphic videos of casualties in the U.S-led assault in Afghanistan (2001), and in Operation Iraqi Freedom (2003), during which they displayed footage of five captured American soldiers. During Operation Iraqi Freedom, U.S. units shelled and incapacitated an al-Jazeera news outlet in Baghdad, prompting criticism from the network of the U.S. pledge to limit civilian casualties and collateral damage during the war. However, there were efforts to bridge the gap between the Western government and the Arabic news agency. For instance, the U.S. offered to "embed" a reporter from al-Jazeera with one of its units during the fighting, thereby giving the station access to front-line footage along with CNN, NBC, ABC, CBS, and Fox News. Also, during Operation Iraqi Freedom, CENTCOM always had a journalist from al-Jazeera included in its briefings, and made certain to afford him a prayer room for the five times Muslims are required to pray each day. Al-Jazeera has also received criticism from some of its Arab and Muslim constituents for its willingness to air statements and interviews with Israeli statesmen, which was seen as giving legitimacy to the Israeli cause.

**jazz** Jazz is generally thought to have developed from a fusion of elements

present in the 19th-century musical heritage of southern culture, specifically along the Mississippi River. A blend of European, Creole and traditional African rhythms, jazz drew upon the black field work songs, and spiritual and special funeral music. Other influences were the BLUES and RAGTIME. The first jazz records were made in 1917. Concerts given in New York City in 1917 by the ORIGINAL DIXIELAND JAZZ BAND led to the first official, critical acknowledgment of jazz. This group also played in London, England, in 1919. Another famous jazz group was King OLIVER's Creole Band. Among the finest musicians who played with Joseph "King" OLIVER were saxophonist Sidney Bechet, and perhaps the greatest jazz soloist, cornetist Louis ARMSTRONG. From New Orleans, jazz spread to other cities like Memphis, St. Louis, Kansas City, Chicago, New York and to the West Coast. A number of styles emerged, often associated with a particular city or area. By the early 1930s, jazz had ceased to be strictly a southern phenomenon and had become a long-established national and international tradition.

**Jazz Age** Name commonly given to the 1920s, particularly in the U.S. and Britain. The jazz age generally coincides with PROHIBITION, the laissez-faire policies of Presidents HARDING and COOLIDGE, post–World War I prosperity and a hedonistic outlook on life prevalent among the leisured classes. The Jazz Age was largely a reaction to the cares engendered by the war and to the refined seriousness of the prewar era. For the wealthy, this period was marked by lavish parties and social events, fast cars and lighthearted liaisons—in short, a carefree attitude. The bouncy rhythms and flippant lyrics of contemporary jazz songs gave the era its name. The American novelist F. Scott FITZGERALD is regarded as the supreme chronicler of the Jazz Age; his novel *THE GREAT GATSBY* captures the high spirits and ultimate wastefulness of the age. The Jazz Age effectively ended with the STOCK MARKET CRASH OF 1929, which in turn brought on the GREAT DEPRESSION of the 1930s.

**Jebel ed Druz (Jebel Druze; Djebel-Druze)** Area in southwestern SYRIA, bordering on Jordan; formerly a subdivision of Syria. Its capital of Es Suweida lies on the site of an ancient Roman town, about 50 miles south of Damascus. A region of plateaus and mountains, Jebel ed Druz is inhabited by the Druse Muslims, who also dwell in Israel, Lebanon and Jordan. Druse beliefs differ radically from those of both the Sunni and Shi'ite branches of Islam. The Druse resisted France after the French were given a LEAGUE OF NATIONS mandate over Syria and LEBANON in 1920. Between 1925 and 1927, with the aid of Syrian nationalists, the Druse led a revolt against the French and captured Damascus. In 1944, with Syria about to obtain its independence from France, the Druse in Jebel ed Druz agreed to give up their autonomous rights. Since the late 1970s they have attempted to maintain their independence amid conflicts among Lebanese, Syrian and Israeli forces.

## Jeffers, (John) Robinson (1887–1962) American poet. Son of a Presbyterian minister and scholar of biblical literature, Jeffers was born in Pittsburgh and educated at several colleges in the U.S. and at the University of Zurich. He did graduate work in forestry and medicine. After 1924, he built a stone house and tower near Carmel, California, where he lived in seclusion with his family. He termed his pessimistic philosophy "Inhumanism"; it called for a "recognition of the transhuman magnificence" and detachment from human concerns. After two minor volumes he made his name with *Tamar and Other Poems* (1924); the title poem is a long narrative of passion and incest based on an Old Testament story. *The Women at Point Sur* (1927), *Cawdor and Other Poems* (1928) and *Thurso's Landing and Other Poems* (1932). *Hungerfield and Other Poems* won a PULITZER PRIZE in 1954. His reputation has been controversial, in part due to his wartime isolationist stance. Many readers find his philosophy repugnant; others see him as an American prophet.

## Jefferson Airplane American ROCK band. Jefferson Airplane was the most commercially successful of the so-called psychedelic bands to emerge from the psychedelic rock scene that centered in SAN FRANCISCO in the late 1960s. The original members of the band, which released its first album *Jefferson Airplane Takes Off* in 1966, were vocalist Signe Anderson, vocalist and guitarist Marty Balin, bassist Jack Casady, drummer Spencer Dryden and guitarists Paul Kantner and Jorma Kaukonen. Shortly after that album was released, vocalist Grace Slick replaced Anderson. The group's next album, *Surrealistic Pillow* (1967), reached number three on the Billboard pop album chart and featured two hit songs, "Somebody to Love" and "White Rabbit." Subsequent albums included *Crown of Creation* (1968) and *Volunteers* (1969). In the 1970s the group's name was changed to **Jefferson Starship** and issued an album that reached number one on the Billboard pop chart, *Red Octopus* (1975). With numerous personnel changes, Jefferson Starship issued recordings through the 1980s and 1990s and through 2000, including *Deeper Space/Extra Virgin Sky* (1995), *Windows of Heaven* (1999) and *Across the Sea of Suns* (2001).

## Jeffries, James J. (1875–1953) American prizefighter. Born in Carroll, Ohio, Jeffries began boxing in 1896. A powerful defensive fighter, he won the heavyweight championship in 1899 and defended his title six times before retiring undefeated in 1905. Touted by fight promoters as "the Great White Hope," he came out of retirement in 1910 to fight the black Jack JOHNSON; Johnson knocked Jeffries out in the 15th round of their championship bout at Reno, Nevada.

## Jelgava (Yelgava; Mitau (German); Mitava (Russian)) City on the Lielupe River in southern Latvia. Occupied by German forces during WORLD WAR I, in October 1919 it was a headquarters for BOLSHEVIK troops until they were driven out by a Latvian and Lithuanian army. A part of independent LATVIA between 1920 and 1940, it was taken by the Soviet Union in 1940, reoccupied by Germany from 1941 to 1944 and reoccupied by counterattacking Russian forces in 1944.

## Jellicoe, John Rushworth (first earl (1925)) (1859–1935) British admiral. A career naval officer, he entered the Royal Navy in 1872, was made a captain in 1897, vice admiral in 1910 and full admiral in 1915. In WORLD WAR I, he served as commander in chief of the Grand Fleet (1914–16), winning a Pyrrhic victory at the battle of JUTLAND. He was first sea lord (1916–17) and naval chief of staff at war's end. Jellicoe was governor general of New Zealand from 1920 to 1924.

## Jenkins, Herbert (1907–1990) U.S. police chief. He held the post of police chief at Atlanta from 1947 to 1973. His policy of accommodating CIVIL RIGHTS leaders in the 1960s helped Atlanta's image as a Southern city that cooperated in the civil rights movement. He maintained order during sit-ins at lunch counters and gave police protection to "freedom riders." In 1967, he was the only southerner appointed by President Lyndon B. JOHNSON to the National Advisory Commission on Civil Disorders. In 1968 he also provided a police escort for a KU KLUX KLAN march through one of the city's black sections, preventing conflict.

## Jenkins, Roy Harris (1920–2003) British politician. Born in Wales, Jenkins was the son of a miner who became a union organizer and later an M.P. After leaving Oxford Jenkins served as an army captain in WORLD WAR II. He was elected to parliament in 1948. Jenkins was on the executive committee of the FABIAN SOCIETY from 1949 to 1961. A leading figure in the British LABOUR PARTY, he served as minister of aviation (1964–65), home secretary (1966–67, 1974–76) and chancellor of the exchequer (1967–70). Jenkins left Parliament in 1976 to serve as president of the EUROPEAN ECONOMIC COMMUNITY until 1980. In 1981 along with Shirley WILLIAMS, David OWEN and William RODGERS, he co-founded the SOCIAL DEMOCRATIC PARTY and served as its first leader until 1983. In a 1982 by-election, Jenkins was reelected to the House of Commons. He was elevated to the House of Lords in 1987. Jenkins was the author of biographies of Clement ATTLEE, Herbert ASQUITH and Charles Dilke. In 1997 Jenkins was appointed to head a commission to recommend reforms of the British electoral system.

## Jensen, Alfred Júlio (1903–1981) Guatemalan-born abstract painter who developed a highly distinctive style in his lushly colored, intricate-patterned

canvasses. Jensen was first associated with the abstract expressionists, then with the American avant-garde movement and the so-called New York School. He began exhibiting in New York in 1952, and his paintings were displayed in major museums throughout the world.

**Jensen, Georg Arthur** *(1866–1935)* Best known of all Danish craft designers for his high-quality modern jewelry and silverware. Jensen was trained as a goldsmith and also studied sculpture at the Copenhagen Academy. Beginning in 1895 he worked in ceramics with Joachim Petersen. Some of his work was exhibited at the Paris Exhibition of 1900. In 1904 he opened a small shop in Copenhagen, offering jewelry and silver of his own design. As the business grew, it produced and sold designs of other Danish designers and craftsmen, eventually distributing a wide variety of Scandinavian products of high design quality, which combine the aesthetics of MODERNISM with traces of Nordic traditionalism. The firm is now international, with the New York shop well known as a primary showcase for Danish design.

**Jensen, Johannes** *(1873–1950)* Danish novelist. To support himself as a medical student at the University of Copenhagen, Jensen wrote a series of detective novels under the name Ivar Lykke. He also began work on his first serious novel, *Danskere* (Danes, 1896). With the publication of *Einar Elkoer* (1897), Jensen abandoned his medical studies. He first attracted critical acclaim with *Himmerlandsfolk* (Himmerland people, 1898), a collection of stories situated in his native Jutland, which he followed with several similar volumes. Jensen's best known work is the trilogy *Konages Fald* (*The Fall of the King*, 1901), which presents the life of Danish king Christian II, combining myth and realism. Between 1908 and 1922 Jensen published the six-volume *Den lange rejse* (*The Long Journey*, 1922–24), a fictional expression of his evolutionary theories, which begins in prehistoric Jutland, and ends with Columbus discovering the New World. Jensen then produced the 11-volume *Myter* (Myths) published between 1907 and 1944. Jensen was awarded the NOBEL PRIZE in literature in 1944. His other works include *Digte*

(Poems, 1906) and *Andens Stadier* (The stages of the mind, 1928).

**Jeritza, Maria** *(1887–1982)* Czech-Austrian opera singer. A dramatic soprano, Jeritza made her debut as Elsa in Wagner's *Lohengrin* in 1910 and went on to huge successes in major roles at the Vienna Opera and New York's Metropolitan Opera over the next 25 years. She was a favorite soprano of both Richard STRAUSS and Giacomo PUCCINI. Strauss wrote the roles of Ariadne in his *Ariadne auf Naxos* and the Empress in *Die Frau ohne Schatten* for her. Her performances in the title roles of Puccini's *Tosca* and *Turandot* were considered definitive. Known for her brilliant voice, dramatic stage presence, and glamorous star quality, Jeritza was not only one of the greatest singers of her day but also an international celebrity.

**Jersey** Largest and most southerly of the CHANNEL ISLANDS. In the English Channel, 15 miles from the coast of France's Normandy, Jersey was occupied by the Germans during WORLD WAR II, from 1941 to 1945; a part of the U.K. since the Norman Conquest, some 10,000 of its inhabitants had been evacuated to Britain. French is the official language of Jersey.

**Jerusalem** Ancient city, sacred to three religions and capital of ISRAEL; 35 miles inland from the coast of the Mediterranean Sea and 13 miles west of the Dead Sea. The city is venerated by JEWS, Christians and Muslims. Inspired by the Zionist movement in the late 19th century, Jews began to settle once more in and around Jerusalem, until by 1900 they were the largest group in the city (see ZIONISM). During WORLD WAR I the city was captured by the British (Dec. 1917) from the Ottoman Turks, longtime rulers of PALESTINE. From 1922 until 1948 the city was under British rule as part of a LEAGUE OF NATIONS mandate. Exasperated by continuous Jewish-Arab conflict, Britain handed over its mandate to the UNITED NATIONS in 1947; the UN planned to partition Palestine between Jewish and Arab states and guarantee Jerusalem as a neutral city. On the expiration of the mandate in 1948, the Jews (emboldened by the informal BALFOUR DECLARATION of

1917, which pledged British support for a new Jewish state) and the Arabs went to war. JORDAN seized Jerusalem's old city, and the Israelis the new city, which they declared the capital of their new state of Israel. During the SIX-DAY WAR (1967) the old city was captured by Israel and integrated with the new, or Israeli, sector. Jerusalem as a whole was formally made the capital of Israel in 1980; although international recognition of that status has not been accorded.

**Jessner, Leopold** *(1878–1945)* German theatrical director and producer. Jessner was one of the leading forces in German theater in the 1910s and 1920s, serving as a producer at prominent state theaters in Hamburg, Königsberg, and Berlin. In particular, he fostered the rise of EXPRESSIONISM in German drama, championing the works of playwright Frank Wedekind, among others. Jessner also won renown for his adaptations of classic theatrical works by Shakespeare and Lessing. A Jew, Jessner fled Nazi Germany in 1933, going first to Palestine and then to the U.S.

**jet engine** The jet engine is similar to the rocket engine, but takes oxygen from the atmosphere to burn its fuel, whereas the rocket engine carries its own oxygen. Jet engines generate greater thrust than piston-driven propellers; thus, jet planes can fly significantly faster. British engineer Frank Whittle patented the turbo-jet engine in 1930 and subsequently tested a successful jet engine on the ground. The first British jet aircraft, powered by Whittle's engine, flew in May 1941. German aviation engineer Ernst Heinkel developed a twin-engine jet fighter that flew in small numbers near the end of World War II. After the war, the British and Americans developed passenger jet aircraft. The late 1950s saw the dawning of the "jet age" with the introduction of long-distance passenger jets.

**Jet Propulsion Laboratory (JPL)** NASA research laboratory in Pasadena, California. It was transferred from U.S. Army jurisdiction to NASA in 1958 and operated in conjunction with the California Institute of Technology. JPL managed the unmanned RANGER and SURVEYOR missions to the moon, as well as many later planetary missions, such as PIONEER missions to Jupiter and Saturn and VOYAGER missions to Jupiter, Saturn, Uranus and Neptune. The laboratory's staff has continued to play vital roles in U.S. space missions such as the *Cassini* space probe sent in 2002 to examine Saturn and its moons, and the Mars *Global Surveyor* mission that in 2003 began to probe the planet's surface for indications that Mars once had water on its surface.

**Jews** Jews are descendants of the Hebrews, a term including many Semitic, nomadic tribes of biblical times. Jews are not a separate race, but rather members of a religious or ethnic community drawn together by centuries of persecution and a minority status wherever they settled. Most Jews can trace their ancestry to either the Ashkenazim, which includes the Jews of central and eastern Europe, or the Sephardim, who were expelled from Spain and Portugal at the end of the 15th century. Currently, there is also an informal distinction between people of Jewish ancestry who associate themselves with the political aims and culture of the Jews but are not religious, and those who strictly uphold the practice of Judaism. Of the approximately 18 million Jewish people in the world, some 6 million live in the United States, about 3 million in ISRAEL and about 3 million in the former Soviet Union. Other countries with significant Jewish populations include Argentina, Canada France and the United Kingdom.

A renewed wave of anti-Semitism swept Europe toward the end of the 19th century. In Germany and Austria-Hungary, many sought to prove the inferiority of the Jews to the Aryans. In Russia, where Jews already had a diminished legal status, many were massacred during the POGROMS. Some 2 million Jews immigrated to the United States where they found their rights legally protected, although they still faced discrimination. In France, the Dreyfus affair brought increased hostility toward the Jews. Theodor HERZL, a Jewish lawyer who reported on the Dreyfus case, was moved to form the World Zionist Organization and propose a separate Jewish homeland. In the early 1900s, Zionists began establishing colonies in PALESTINE. During WORLD WAR I,

Great Britain seized Palestine from Turkey, then in 1917 issued the BALFOUR DECLARATION, which gave British endorsement to the formation of a Jewish state in Palestine. The LEAGUE OF NATIONS approved the declaration, and Palestine was made a mandated territory of Great Britain in 1920. In the face of much Arab opposition, many Jews immigrated to Palestine in the 1920s and '30s.

In 1933 Adolf HITLER came to power in GERMANY. His Nazi Party began disseminating vicious propaganda blaming the Jews for Germany's economic woes and proclaiming the superiority of the Aryan people. In 1935, German Jews were deprived of their citizenship. Many fled Germany, but many others, their property seized by the Nazis, were sent to CONCENTRATION CAMPS. Some, like Anne FRANK and her family, went into hiding. In 1941, Hitler proposed the FINAL SOLUTION, a systematic plan to exterminate all European Jews. Nazi firing squads murdered thousands of Jews, and concentration camps were outfitted with gas chambers for the mass annihilation of Jews. Approximately 6 million European Jews were killed during the HOLOCAUST in Nazi Germany.

Following WORLD WAR II, the decimated Jewish population renewed its efforts to form a state in Palestine but met continual opposition from the Arabs. In 1947 Britain urged the UNITED NATIONS to intervene. The UN proposed that Palestine be divided into an Arab state and a Jewish one, ISRAEL, which became independent the following year. Arab hostilities did not subside, however, and Israel was at war with its Arab neighbors in 1948, 1956, 1967 and 1973.

In the Soviet Union, Jewish culture and the practice of Judaism continued to be suppressed and the emigration of Jews restricted. Following years of protest, emigration laws began to ease in the early 1970s, and with the advent of PERESTROIKA, Jews regained many rights of expression and movement. American Jews—in the 20th century, the most secure and successful—are concerned about the loss of their tradition and heritage as they become increasingly assimilated into American culture. Many maintain strong ties to Israel, which they consider their spiritual homeland. Jews continue to experience

anti-Semitism and fear such extremist organizations as the KU KLUX KLAN and Neo-Nazis in the U.S. and elsewhere.

**Jhabvala, Ruth Prawer** (*1927– *) British novelist and screenwriter. With her first novel, *To Whom She Will* (1955, published in the U.S. as *Amrita*, 1965), Jhabvala established her reputation as a perceptive chronicler of contemporary India, which she has maintained with a steady output of acclaimed fiction including, the novels *A New Dominion* (1972, published in the U.S. as *Travelers*, 1973), *Heat and Dust* (1975, filmed 1983), *Three Continents* (1987), and the short stories, *An Experience of India* (1971) and *How I Became a Holy Mother and Other Stories* (1976). In 1966 she became associated with the filmmaking team of director James Ivory and producer Ismail Merchant. She has adapted many of her novels for the screen and co-authored screenplays with Ivory. These include *Shakespeare Wallah* (1966) and *The Europeans* (1979), based on the novel by Henry JAMES. In 1992 Jhabvala won another Academy Award for best adapted screenplay for *Howards End* (1991).

**Jiang Qing (Chiang Ch'ing)** (*1914–1991*) Chinese political leader and wife of MAO ZEDONG. Born in Shandong province. Jiang Qing became an actress, touring China and settling in Shanghai. In 1933 she joined the Communist Party, meeting Mao in Yenan and marrying him. She stayed removed from politics until the 1960s, when she became an enormous force in the CULTURAL REVOLUTION, wielding great power over all aspects of Chinese culture and propaganda. In 1969 she was appointed to the Politburo. After Mao's death in 1976, Jiang and three colleagues, known as the GANG OF FOUR, were arrested and tried for crimes against the state. Convicted in 1981, she was sentenced to death, but she remained imprisoned after several reprieves.

**Jiang Zemin** (*1926– *) Chinese political figure, general secretary of the Chinese Communist Party (1989–2002) and president of CHINA (1993–2003). Born in Yangzhou, a city in eastern China, Jiang's association with the Chinese Communist Party (CCP) began soon after his uncle died fighting for the

CCP against the military forces of Japan in the SINO-JAPANESE WAR (1937–45). When news of his uncle's death reached Jiang's father, it was decided that Jiang would be adopted by his uncle's family: his uncle had no male heirs, and as it was considered a great misfortune to depart from life without leaving behind a son to carry on the family name and heritage. When the CCP defeated the Nationalist forces in 1949 to win the CHINESE CIVIL WAR OF 1946–49, Jiang became known to many as the adopted son of a Communist martyr who had died for the party in one of its darkest hours.

In 1946, when hostilities between the Communists and Nationalists broke out, Jiang joined the CCP. After graduating from Shanghai's Jiaotong University in 1947 with a degree in electrical engineering, he worked as an engineer for a local factory, and was promoted to factory manager.

After 24 years in the heavy-industry sector of China's centralized economy, Jiang's responsibilities shifted to managing the country's export-oriented enterprises created under the reformist leadership of DENG XIAOPING. In 1982 Jiang was designated vice minister of China's burgeoning electronics industry and appointed to the CCP's Central Committee. Three years later he was named mayor of Shanghai, one of the cities in the Special Economic Zones that was booming as a result of the massive influx of foreign capital and orders for Chinese products.

Following the governments' crackdown on the pro-democracy protesters in TIANANMEN SQUARE (June 3–4, 1989), Deng chose Jiang as the new general secretary of the CCP to replace ZHAO ZIYANG, who had opposed the repressive response to the unrest. In the same year Deng also named Jiang his successor as chairman of the Central Military Commission, the party organ that controlled the military. After Deng's retirement in 1993, Jiang was chosen by the Politburo as his successor.

At the 15th CCP Congress in 1997, Jiang began to unveil a new vision of China's economic future from that diverged from that of Mao and Deng (who had died earlier in the year.) While remaining committed to Deng's vision of adapting socialist principles to the Chinese way of life, he also announced that he would begin selling

off state-run companies to private individuals and corporations. This new policy led to the creation of a mixed economy that combined elements of free-market capitalism with a highly centralized state.

Jiang's foreign policy focused on economic concerns. He worked tirelessly for China's admission into the WORLD TRADE ORGANIZATION (WTO) and to ensure that the recently acquired former British colony of HONG KONG continued to enjoy its economic prosperity as a Special Administrative Zone. He cultivated a friendly relationship with the U.S., despite continuing American criticism of China's treatment of political prisoners, the persecution of groups such as the FALUN GONG and the government's coercive "one child" birth policy. Jiang proved less conciliatory on the issue of TAIWAN, authorizing a large naval exercise near the island and strongly condemning any talk of independence for China's "wayward province." In November 2003 Jiang selected vice president Hu Jintao to replace him as Communist Party general secretary and president of China.

**Jigme Singye Wangchuk** (1955– ) King of BHUTAN. As a 17-year-old, he ascended the throne when his father died in 1972. He followed his father's policy of working with the National Assembly and moved to increase popular participation in economic planning. In 2005 King Wangchuck announced his decision to abdicate the throne in 2008.

**jihad** Arabic word meaning a "spiritual struggle" constantly required of all Muslims. Generally, there are four ways in which individual Muslims may fulfill this duty: through their hearts by battling against vices and evil passions, through their tongues by acting as apostles of Islam throughout the world, through their hands by propagating good works and deeds throughout their daily lives and through the sword by waging war against non-Muslims.

It is the last of these four categories of jihad that has had international repercussions, generating controversy between the Muslim and non-Muslim world as well as within the Muslim world. It is the interpretation of Islamic law that has caused the greatest con-

cern in non-Muslim states. According to one interpretation of the Koran and Islamic law, Muslims are required to fight in jihads of the sword until all nations surrender to Islamic rule and are promised lavish rewards in heaven if they die in that struggle. It is in the context of this radical interpretation that some fundamentalist Muslim groups, such as AL-QAEDA, HAMAS and Islamic Jihad, have attempted to justify their attacks on the citizens of "infidel" countries such as the U.S., ISRAEL and on those who do not strictly follow the Koran. It is interesting to note that Islamic law requires the forced conversion or execution only of *kafir,* a term denoting practitioners of religions with no spiritual connection to Islam, such as Buddhists and Hindus. Jews and Christians, by contrast, qualify as "people of the book"—individuals not subject to execution if they refuse to convert to Islam provided that they acknowledge their subservience to an Islamic government. Moderate Muslim clergymen and practitioners emphasize their devotion to the three peaceful forms of jihad (the heart, tongue and hand), and denounce most of the actions undertaken by terrorist groups in the name of jihad as barbaric and against the teachings of Islam.

**Jiménez, Juan Ramón** (1881–1958) Spanish poet. Jiménez published his first poetry in *Vida nueva* (New Life) in 1899, where it attracted the attention of Rubén DARÍO, among other notable Spanish-language writers, after which he devoted himself to writing poetry and later helped found the literary journals, *Helios* (Helium) and *Renacimiento* (Renaissance). His first volumes of poetry, such as *Almas de violeta* (Violet souls, 1900) and *Ninfeas* (Water lilies, 1900), now dated in their sentimentality, were still unique in their form and lyrical sensuality. He continually evolved in his style and scope. *Dario de un poeta recién casado* (Dairy of a newlywed poet, 1917) is a hallmark in the use of free verse in Spanish poetry. Jiménez served as a cultural attaché in the U.S. at the outbreak of the SPANISH CIVIL WAR; following FRANCO's rise to power in 1939, Jiménez decided to remain abroad, finally settling in Puerto Rico. He was awarded the NOBEL PRIZE in literature in 1956. Other works include *Animals *de fondo* (Animal of depth, 1949) and *Tercera antología poética* (Third poetic anthology, 1957).

## Jinnah, Muhammad Ali (*1876–1948*)

Founder of PAKISTAN. Born in Karachi, Jinnah studied law in England and was admitted to the bar there. Returning to India, he practiced law and entered politics as part of the Indian National Congress Party in 1906. Opposing Hindu dominance of the party and disapproving of the tactics of Mohandas GANDHI, Jinnah joined the Muslim League in 1913, becoming its president in 1916 and finally breaking with the CONGRESS PARTY in 1930. He reshaped the league into an organization that at first promoted parity between India's Hindus and Muslims. By the mid-1930s all the Muslim members of the Congress Party had joined the league, and a disillusioned Jinnah was calling for the partition of India and the creation of the independent state of Pakistan. During WORLD WAR II, Jinnah was an active supporter of the British, increasing his standing in British eyes. Muslim pressure and the bloody Hindu-Muslim riots of 1946 helped convince the Congress Party to accept the establishment of Pakistan in August 1947. Jinnah became the first governor general of Pakistan and died in office a little over a year later.

## Jobs, Steve(n) (*1955–   *)

Founder of Apple Computer, a pioneering company in the creation of personal COMPUTERS. Jobs began his career in the computer industry as a high school student in Los Altos, California, while serving as a summer employee at Hewlett-Packard (HP), a company engaged in the construction of computers and other business-oriented machines. At HP Jobs met Stephen Wozniak, who was working on the development of new electronic machines for commercial use. In 1975, Jobs convinced Wozniak to help him build a computer for sale to individuals, which he named Apple I after a pleasant summer job experience Jobs had picking apples in Oregon. In 1976 the two formed Apple Computer Company and brought out the Apple I model, which sold more than 600 units at a price of less than $700. The next model, Apple II, proved extremely successful in the emerging personal computer market, prompting Jobs and Wozniak to incorporate the company in 1977 in order to raise capital to expand their operations.

By 1983 Apple had developed the basic computer format still in use today. Instead of a machine relying on keyboard-typed prompts to access programs and initiate functions, Apple's latest computer, Lisa, allowed its users to begin activities by moving a hand-operated "mouse" to icons displayed on the computer screen and clicking on those icons with a button on the mouse.

Shortly after developing Lisa, Apple developed Macintosh, the first personal computer (PC) designed and priced for the average consumer. In 1985, despite producing a popular machine at an affordable price, declining sales led shareholders to force Jobs to resign from the company in 1985.

After an unsuccessful attempt to form another computer company, Jobs raised funds to purchase Lucasfilm Ltd.'s computer special-effects division for $60 million. He then took this detached component, transformed it into Pixar Animation Studios and concentrated on the development of computer graphics and special effects for the film, television and computer software industries. The Pixar eventually succeeded in enhancing the quality of computer-generated images and graphics, as well as the animation of shapes generated by computers.

In the following year, Apple's executive board fired its CEO, Gilbert Amelio, and hired Jobs as interim CEO while the company sought to refine its consumer appeal, improve its hardware and software and raise investment capital. In 1997 the company unveiled the iMac, a new PC with a transparent design and fused into a single unit that came in multiple colors. Apple later developed a laptop version of the iMac, as well as the iPod, a device designed to download music from computers and record it in electronic form on a small, rectangular-shaped device that could be carried anywhere and could retain thousands of songs in its memory for over a month. As a result of his role in rescuing the company, Jobs was appointed CEO of Apple in 2000.

## Jochum, Eugen (*1902–1987*)

German conductor. Jochum held posts with various German orchestras between 1926 and 1949. Though he remained in Germany during WORLD WAR II, he did not join the Nazi Party. He founded the Bavarian Radio Symphony in Munich in 1949. After 1960 he concentrated on guest appearances with such major orchestras as the Berlin Philharmonic, Amsterdam Concertgebouw and London Symphony. His repertoire included the music of Bach, Mozart, Haydn, Schubert, Wagner, Richard STRAUSS, and Karl ORFF, among others. He recorded all the Beethoven and Brahms symphonies three times, and was the first conductor to record all of Anton Bruckner's symphonies. Jochum was one of the last representatives of the German romantic school of conducting. Like Wilhelm FURTWÄNGLER, he concentrated on the spiritual aspects of music, and his flexible tempos reflected a personal response to the composer rather than a literal reading of the score.

## Joffrey, Robert (Abdullah Jaffa Anver Beykhan) (*1930–1989*)

American dancer, choreographer and ballet director. Founder and artistic director of the popular Joffrey Ballet, he was born in Seattle of Afghan descent. He trained as a dancer and joined Roland Petit's Ballet de Paris as a soloist in 1948. However, he found his metier as an impresario, company manager and choreographer when he launched his own company, which began as a raggle-taggle group that toured the U.S. in a loaned station wagon in 1956. His vision of hip, young, lithe Americana became widely admired, and his company played an instrumental role in expanding the audience for ballet in general. Joffrey's style came to be known as strong, sleek, fast and sexy, with an athletic wit and a willingness to perform modern dance as well as ballet. His most important works include *Gamelon* (1962), *Astarte* (1967) and *Remembrances* (1973). In the 1980s Joffrey turned his attention to the past, embarking on ambitious revivals of rarely performed works of historical significance, by such choreographers as Vaslav NIJINSKY, Bronislava NIJINSKA and Frederick ASHTON. Following Joffrey's death, Gerald ARPINO became artistic director of the company.

**John XXIII (Angelo Giuseppe Roncalli)** *(1881–1963)* Supreme Pontiff of the Roman Catholic Church (1958–63). Born Angelo Giuseppe Roncalli into an Italian peasant family and ordained in 1904, he rose through the echelons of Vatican diplomacy, becoming the VATICAN's first permanent observer of UNESCO, patriarch of Venice and, finally, pope. As Pope John XXIII, he worked for world peace and favored the interchange of ideas with other religions. In 1962 he convened the SECOND VATICAN COUNCIL (also known as Vatican II), an ecumenical council that called for greater religious tolerance and Christian unity and brought about dramatic reforms within the Catholic Church.

**John, Augustus Edwin** *(1879–1961)* British painter. Born in Wales, he studied (1894–98) at London's Slade School of Art, where he was acclaimed for his phenomenal draughtsmanship. He journeyed to Paris and was influenced by the work of Puvis de Chavannes and PICASSO. John lived an exotic and bohemian life, from time to time tramping through Europe and living in gypsy caravans. He became a renowned portraitist, painting with verve and without flattery and numbering many of the important political, social, literary, artistic and theatrical figures of the day among his sitters. These included David LLOYD GEORGE, Queen ELIZABETH II, W. B. YEATS, Sir Jacob EPSTEIN, George Bernard SHAW and Tallulah BANKHEAD. Also a gifted etcher, John was the author of an autobiography, *Chiaroscuro* (1952).

**John, Sir Elton Hercules (Reginald Kenneth Dwight)** *(1947–  )* British singer and songwriter. Paired with lyricist Bernie Taupin, Elton John dominated the pop charts in the 1970s. A rock pianist with classical training, his hit single "Your Song" (1970) was the first in an unbroken string of top-10 hits, culminating in the first album ever to debut at number one, *Rock of the Westies* (1975). Among his more critically acclaimed works were the double album *Goodbye Yellow Brick Road* (1973), and the autobiographical *Captain Fantastic and the Brown Dirt Cowboy* (1975). His performances have often included outrageous costumes and spectacular spectacles. The first rock star ever to tour the Soviet Union, he continued to achieve popular success through the 1980s and 1990s, and played to a record-breaking 600,000 people in New York's Central Park on September 13, 1980. In 1997, several months after John's musical eulogy of DIANA, Princess of Wales, at her funeral ceremony, he was knighted by Queen ELIZABETH II. In December 2005 he entered a civil partnership with David Furnish, a former advertising executive. John scored the horror musical *Lestat*, which opened on Broadway in 2006 to tepid reviews.

**John Birch Society** Organization founded in the U.S. by Robert H. W. Welch Jr. in 1958. Named after Captain John Birch, who was killed by Chinese communists in 1945 and is considered the first hero of the COLD WAR, the society is strongly anticommunist and promotes ultraconservative causes. It has denounced most welfare programs and called for U.S. withdrawal from the UNITED NATIONS. The society is headquartered in Belmont, Massachusetts, and publishes several pamphlets and papers.

**John Paul I (Albino Luciani)** *(1912–1978)* Supreme Pontiff of the Roman Catholic Church. Pope John Paul I has left an enduring memory as a man of great kindness and piety, even though his 34-day reign as pope was the shortest since the 18-day rule of Pope Leo XI in 1605. Born Albino Luciani, he was raised in Forno di Canale (now Canale D'Agordo), a village in northeastern Italy. His father was a worker and a socialist, his mother a devout peasant. Luciani was ordained as a priest in 1936 and worked in the parish of his native village for a time before moving on to a teaching career. He served as vicar general from 1954 to 1958, when he was appointed bishop of Vittorio Veneto. In 1969 he became patriarch of Venice. One of his first acts in this prestigious office was to allow parishes to sell church jewels for the benefit of the poor and the handicapped. Throughout his years of service, Luciani emphasized the need to teach Christian truths simply, with respect for the needs of ordinary people. He was elected pope in 1978 but died shortly thereafter.

**John Paul II (Karol Wojtyla)** *(1920–2005)* Supreme Pontiff of the Roman Catholic Church. Karol Józef Wojtyła was born to a devout Catholic family in Wadowice, Poland, in 1920. He and his widowed father moved to Kraków in 1938, where he studied literature and philosophy at Jagiellonian University with the intention of becoming a priest. After the German occupation of Poland the following year, he studied at an underground seminary in Kraków and took theology courses at the university while working in a quarry and a chemical plant to support himself. He was ordained in 1946 and took two master's degrees and a doctorate before beginning service as an assistant pastor at a church in Kraków in 1949. In 1954 he became an assistant professor at the Catholic University of Lublin, the only Catholic university in the communist world, and commuted between the two jobs. In 1956 he was appointed to the professorial chair in ethics at Catholic University and two years later was designated as the auxiliary bishop of Kraków. He was chosen as archbishop of the city in 1964 and was named by Pope Paul VI to the college of cardinals in 1967. Throughout the 1960s Wojtyła wrote learned philosophical tracts about ethics and phenomenology that established his reputation as a deep theological thinker.

After the death of Pope John Paul I in September 1978, the college of cardinals elected Wojtyła on the eighth round of balloting. He chose the name of his predecessor, whose reign had been cut short by a heart attack after only 34 days on the papal throne. He was the first non-Italian pope since the Dutch-born Adrian VI in 1522–23 and, at 58, the youngest pope in 132 years. Eight months after his inauguration, John Paul III returned to his native Poland for nine emotional days, during which huge crowds cheered him as he urged his countrymen to fight for their human rights, to the embarrassment of the Communist regime in power. He frequently criticized the communist system in his public statements during the 1980s and publicly praised the underground Polish political movement Solidarity, emboldening Catholics in other eastern European countries to oppose their oppressive governments until the fall of communism at the end of the decade. The pope also spoke out against right-wing dictatorships in Latin America and elsewhere. On trips to the U.S. he did not hesitate to warn his hosts about the evils of materialism and the need to share their wealth with the poor people of the world. A fierce opponent of contraception, abortion and euthanasia, the pontiff accused the industrialized world of fostering "a culture of death" by tolerating such practices. John Paul II was criticized for his unbending insistence on theological conformity on the part of teachers in Catholic universities the world over. His strong views on priestly celibacy, homosexuality, and the role of women in the church also brought him into conflict with reformist elements. His staunch opposition to the use of contraceptives became particularly controversial after the outbreak of the AIDS epidemic in the 1980s.

John Paul II traveled more than any of his predecessors, visiting more than 100 countries and all of the continents. He spoke before crowds of admirers numbering in the millions and held audiences with many heads of state and of government, during which he forcefully expressed his views on a number of subjects. In 1981 a Turk named Mehmet Ali Ağca shot the pope twice in an assassination attempt, but he recovered from his wounds and resumed his globetrotting. In 2001 it became apparent that the pope was suffering from Parkinson's disease, but even this disability did not prevent him from following his packed schedule of foreign trips. He died in 2005 and was succeeded by Cardinal Joseph Ratzinger of Germany, who took the title BENEDICT XVI.

**Johns, Jasper** *(1930– )* American artist. A major figure in contemporary American art, he was born in Allendale, S.C., studied at the University of South Carolina and settled in New York City in 1952. He burst on the art scene with his first one-man show in N.Y.C. in 1958. Influenced in subject matter by the commonplace objects used by Marcel DUCHAMP and the DADAISTS and by the painterly techniques of ABSTRACT EXPRESSIONISM, Johns became a precursor of the POP ART movement with his paintings of flags, targets, maps, letters and numbers. In these works, he sought to explore the relationship between the object portrayed and the image that

portrays it, transforming ordinary subjects into art. His best known paintings include *Target with Four Faces* (1955, Museum of Modern Art, N.Y.C.) and *Flag on an Orange Field* (1957, Wallraf-Richartz Museum, Cologne). Johns is also noted for his graphics and for his brass castings of objects such as the beer cans portrayed in *Painted Bronze* (1964).

**Johnson, Amy** *(1903–1941)* British aviator. Johnson taught herself to fly and in 1929 became the first woman to hold an Air Ministry ground engineer's certificate. In 1930 she made a solo flight from Croydon, England, to Darwin, Australia, in 20 days, which brought her great celebrity. In recognition of this feat she was made a Commander of the British Empire. In 1931 she set a 10-day record flying from London to Tokyo, and in 1932, flew solo to Cape Town. From 1932 to 1938, she was married to the aviator Jim Mollison (1905–59) and flew with him from London to the U.S. in 1932. During WORLD WAR II Johnson served in the Air Transport Auxiliary as a ferry pilot, and died in the line of duty when she bailed out before her aircraft crashed in the Thames estuary.

**Johnson, Ben** *(1961– )* Canadian sprinter who lost his Olympic gold medal after it was revealed that he had cheated by using steroids. Johnson blazed to fame in 1987 when he set a new world record time of 9.83 seconds for the 100-meter sprint at the 1987 World Championships. After he won the 100-meter race at the OLYMPIC GAMES, a routine drug test revealed that he had used illegal steroids; he was stripped of his gold medal and disgraced. The use of steroids by athletes subsequently became a major subject of concern. In the Montreal international track meet of 1993 Johnson again tested positive for steroids and received another life suspension.

**Johnson, Dame Celia** *(1908–1982)* British stage and screen actress. Johnson trained at the Royal Academy of Dramatic Art (RADA). Her long and distinguished career included roles in some of the best contemporary British films, modern plays and the classical repertory. Her films included *Rebecca*

(1940), *In Which We Serve* (1942), *Brief Encounter* (1946) and *The Captain's Paradise* (1953). She gave acclaimed performances in plays by AYCKBOURN, CHEKHOV,, SHAW, and Shakespeare. She was awarded her title by Queen ELIZABETH II in 1981.

**Johnson, Clarence L. ("Kelly")** *(1910–1990)* American aeronautical engineer whose work had extensive influence on the design of modern aircraft and on all modern industrial design. Johnson was a graduate of the University of Michigan and began work for LOCKHEED in 1933. By 1938 he became chief engineer. The Lockheed P-38 fighter of 1941 was his first outstanding and original design. Later projects include the P-80 jet fighter, the U-2 spy plane and the C-130 Hercules military transport. His work is often credited with having had a strong influence on automotive design in 1952, when airplanelike tail fins appeared on American automobiles purely for style.

**Johnson, Earvin "Magic"** *(1959– )* American basketball player in the National Basketball Association (NBA; 1980–91, 1992, 1996). Born in Lansing, Michigan, he was nicknamed "Magic" after scoring 36 points, grabbing 18 rebounds and recording 16 assists in a high school game. In college he played basketball for Michigan State, which he guided to victory in the 1979 National Collegiate Athletic Association championship.

After being drafted by the Los Angeles Lakers the rookie point guard helped the Lakers win the NBA championship, the first of five he won with the team. During his 11-year career, Johnson became famous for his scoring and his passes as well as his rivalry with Larry Bird of the Boston Celtics, as the two teams fought each other for eight titles. In the autumn of 1991, after losing the NBA finals to the Chicago Bulls, Johnson retired after learning that he had contracted the AIDS virus. But he joined the 1992 U.S. Olympic men's basketball team (nicknamed the "Dream Team," because it was the first Olympics open to professional basketball players), which frightened players on several national teams, who feared that an on-court cut could expose them to infection. But

Johnson was warmly greeted by fans and the U.S. captured the gold medal. Johnson also worked to increase awareness about the AIDS virus and how to avoid it by writing a book and appearing on numerous television shows.

In 1992 Johnson announced he would return to basketball and signed a new contract with the Lakers. Several NBA players criticized Johnson's decision as endangering the lives of other players. After this cold reception and several disappointing performances, Johnson retired again at the beginning of the 1992–93 season and subsequently worked as a TV commentator for NBA games. The following year Johnson returned to the Lakers yet again, this time as their head coach, but resigned at the end of the season. Johnson made one final return as an NBA player in 1996 and played occasionally at the point guard and power forward positions before retiring permanently with a legacy that included 13 All-Star Game appearances, three season NBA MVP selections and NBA Finals MVP designations and a record as the second all-time career leader in assists.

**Johnson, Eyvind** *(1900–1976)* Swedish novelist. On his own from the age of 13, Johnson educated himself by reading. His early novels, such as *Timans och rattfardigheten* (Timans and justice, 1925), are strongly influenced by James JOYCE and Sigmund FREUD. Johnson began working a journalist, and during WORLD WAR II coedited *Et Handslag* (A handshake) with Willy BRANDT for the Norwegian RESISTANCE. In Sweden Johnson is perhaps best known for the tetralogy, *Romanen om Olof* (The novel about Olof, 1934–1937), which depicts the rise of the Swedish proletariat through one youth's development. Internationally, he is better known for *Strandernas svall* (1946), translated as *Return to Ithaca: The Odyssey Retold as a Modern Novel*, in 1952, which began a series of novels emphasizing the repetition of history. Johnson was awarded the NOBEL PRIZE in literature in 1974 jointly with Henry MARTINSON. Of Johnson's 30 novels, only four have been translated into English.

**Johnson, Hiram** *(1866–1945)* U.S. politician. Johnson won election as governor of California in 1910 on a platform of political reform. During his administration he smashed the Southern Pacific Railroad machine, which had long dominated the statehouse, and passed the Public Utilities Act, which created one of the most effective systems of railroad control in the country. A founder of the Progressive Party, Johnson ran as vice president on the 1912 ticket headed by Theodore ROOSEVELT. In 1916 Johnson was elected to the Senate on the Progressive ticket. In the upper house he developed a reputation as an independent, reluctantly supporting U.S. entry into WORLD WAR I but criticizing Woodrow WILSON's foreign policy. Although he initially supported President HOOVER, he became increasingly critical of the administration, blaming it for much of the distress of the Great Depression. Johnson backed Franklin ROOSEVELT in 1932 but later refused to support FDR's foreign and domestic policy. He was one of the Senate's most consistent isolationists. Johnson was a leading candidate for the Republican nomination in 1920. When he lost the nomination to Warren HARDING, he refused offers of the vice presidential nomination; he served in the Senate until his death.

**Johnson, Howard Deering** *(1896–1972)* American ice cream maker and entrepreneur. In 1924, Howard Johnson bought a soda fountain in Wollaston, Mass., and started to sell his famous "28 flavors" of ice cream. Five years later, he began to license his name and products, creating the chain of Howard Johnson's restaurants. The firm flourished in the postwar years, and by 1964, when Johnson retired, it had grown into the largest food distributor in the United States.

**Johnson, James Weldon** *(1871–1938)* American writer, diplomat and civil rights activist. A graduate of Atlanta University, he was the first African American admitted to the bar in Florida (1897). He also served as consul to Venezuela and Nicaragua. In 1901 Johnson moved to New York to collaborate with his brother on the lyrics for light operas and popular songs. Their "Lift Every Voice and Sing" was considered virtually a black national anthem. He taught creative literature at Fisk University from 1930 to 1938. His only novel, *The Autobiography of an Ex-Colored Man,* was published in 1912.

*The first African-American heavyweight champion. Jack Johnson* (GEORGE GRANTHAM BAIN COLLECTION. LIBRARY OF CONGRESS, PRINTS AND PHOTOGRAPHS DIVISION)

**Johnson, John Arthur "Jack"** *(1878–1946)* American boxer. Jackson fought his way through the ranks and, in 1908, became the first black world heavyweight champion. His flamboyant ways and lavish lifestyle led to his becoming the immediate subject of an outpouring of hate, which culminated in the search for a "great white hope" to take back the heavyweight crown. The searchers found former champion Jim JEFFRIES, whom Johnson decisively beat in 1910. In 1915 Johnson lost his title to Jess Willard in a bout held in the broiling sun of Havana, Cuba. Johnson's three marriages to white women aroused further racial prejudice, and he was harassed by federal authorities on a variety of trumped-up charges—including white slavery—that led him to flee to Europe to tour in theatrical shows. He returned to the U.S. in 1920, and served eight months of a one-year sentence at Leavenworth Penitentiary.

**Johnson, John Harold** *(1918–2005)* U.S. publisher. He started his Chicago-based publishing empire with emphasis on stories of black achievement. In 1942 he started *Negro Digest,* which changed its title to *Black World* in 1970. Other Johnson magazines include *Ebony* (1945) and *Jet* (1951). Johnson was named Publisher of the Year in 1972. The company ranks first nationally in earnings among black enterprises.

**Johnson, Lyndon Baines** *(1908–1973)* Thirty-sixth president of the UNITED STATES (1963–69). Born near Johnson City, Tex., the son of a farmer, Johnson worked his way through teachers college and was a high school teacher before entering politics in 1932 as secretary to a Democratic congressman from Texas. Committed to the principles of the NEW DEAL, he became a protégé of Sam RAYBURN, who successfully urged President Franklin D. ROOSEVELT to appoint him director of the National Youth Administration in 1935. He was first elected to the House of Representatives in 1937, serving there as an active supporter of Roosevelt's military and foreign policies until his election to the Senate in 1948. He was soon one of the nation's most powerful senators, becoming Democratic leader in 1953 and majority leader in 1954. A canny strategist and shrewd compromiser, he supported most of the programs of President Dwight D. EISENHOWER and was known for his moderate to conservative positions. He ran for the Democratic presidential nomination in 1960, but lost to John F. KENNEDY, who chose Johnson as his vice presidential running mate.

Johnson was sworn in as president after the assassination of President Kennedy on November 22, 1963. As president, Johnson energetically endorsed the social programs promised by his predecessor and used his considerable political skills to see them enacted. Persuaded by Johnson, Congress passed a broad tax cut and the landmark CIVIL RIGHTS ACT OF 1964. Calling for what he called a GREAT SOCIETY, Johnson pressed for a vigorous domestic program that included a war against poverty and sweeping economic and social reform and legislation.

His domestic achievements were largely overshadowed by his troubles abroad, as Johnson became increasingly enmeshed in the VIETNAM WAR. After passage of the TONKIN GULF RESOLUTION, Johnson began the massive bombing of North Vietnam in 1965 and increased U.S. troop levels from some 20,000 to over 500,000. War costs increased, and many Great Society programs proved too expensive. Riots soon broke out in America's black ghettos, and the ANTIWAR MOVEMENT gained momentum across the country. Ailing and increasingly unpopular, Johnson announced that he would not run for reelection in 1968. He remained a powerful force in Democratic politics and saw to it that his chosen successor, Vice President Hubert HUMPHREY, was nominated for the presidency. Humphrey lost by a narrow margin to Richard M. NIXON, and Johnson retired to his Texas ranch in 1969. His memoirs, *The Vantage Point,* were published in 1971.

**Johnson, Martin** *(1884–1937)* American explorer and writer. Johnson joined author Jack LONDON on the cruise of the *Snark.* He made well-known expeditions to the SOLOMON and NEW HEBRIDES islands (1914) and BORNEO (1917–19 and 1935). He and his wife Osa traveled around the world six times, wrote, lectured and gained a reputation as jungle experts, especially on Africa. They were famed for their motion pictures of their explorations, such as *Simba* and *Congorilla,* and also cowrote *Cannibal Land* (1917), *Camera Trails in Africa* (1924) and *Lion* (1929); Osa also wrote *I Married Adventure* (1940).

**Johnson, Pamela Hansford** *(1912–1981)* British novelist, playwright, and critic and wife of novelist C. P. SNOW. Although she did not achieve the same level of popularity as her husband, Johnson's work was highly regarded by critics. Among her 25 novels were *An Impossible Marriage* and *The Good Husband.*

**Johnson, Philip Cortelyou** *(1906–2005)* American architect. Born in Cleveland, Johnson attended Harvard University. He became one of the leading advocates of the new European architecture as the coauthor (with Henry-Russell HITCHCOCK) of *The International Style: Architecture since 1922* (1932) and as head of the department of architecture at the MUSEUM OF MODERN ART (1932–34, 1945–54). Johnson brought the INTERNATIONAL STYLE to the U.S. in his own buildings, designing a number of houses that were greatly influenced by MIES VAN DER ROHE. These include his own "glass house" (1949–50) and the Wiley house (1953), both in New Canaan, Connecticut. Johnson collaborated with Mies on the Seagram Building in New York City (1958), a great amber slab that is considered one of modern architecture's greatest skyscrapers. Johnson largely abandoned the International Style in the 1960s and produced such classically influenced buildings as the Sheldon Art Gallery, Lincoln, Nebraska (1963), and the New York State Theater at Lincoln Center (1964). In the 1970s he created innovative structures such as Pennzoil Place, Houston, Texas (1976), and the AT&T Building, New York City (1978), whose massive Chippendale-like broken pediment has been seen as an emblem of POSTMODERNISM.

**Johnson, Randy** *(1963–  )* American baseball player, winner of several Cy Young Awards (1995 American League; 1999–2002 National League). Johnson began his major league baseball career when he signed as a pitcher with the Montreal Expos of the National League (NL) in 1988. After being traded to the Seattle Mariners of the American League (AL) in May 1989, Johnson initially struggled as a pitcher. In 1995 his 2.48 earned run average and his 18-2 win-loss record secured him his first AL Cy Young Award for the best starting pitcher in the AL. In 1997 he set an AL game record for strikeouts by a left-handed pitcher (19) against the Oakland Athletics. In the same year he was traded to the NL Houston Astros, before signing with the newest NL team, the Arizona Diamondbacks, as a free agent.

As a Diamondback pitcher from 1999 to 2002, Johnson recorded 81 wins to 27 losses, threw 787 strikeouts, walked only 284 batters and won four consecutive NL Cy Young Awards. In 2001 he helped guide the Diamondbacks to the World Series, where he pitched and won the second and sixth games, helping to defeat the Yankees four games to three. In recognition of his performance on the pitching mound, Johnson was named co-MVP of the series along with his fellow pitcher Curt Schilling. He was traded to the New York Yankees before the start of the 2005 season.

**Johnson, Robert** *(1912–1938)* African-American blues composer, vocalist and guitarist. Johnson, who never reached a sizeable audience outside his native Mississippi during his lifetime, achieved a posthumous reputation as perhaps the greatest songwriter and performer in the history of the blues. Contemporary musicians who have sung his praises (and performed his songs) include Eric CLAPTON and Bob DYLAN. Johnson ran away from home at an early age to learn guitar from blues master Son House. In the 1930s, Johnson performed in Mississippi with fellow blues greats Howlin' Wolf and Elmore James. His greatest recordings, featuring Johnson's heartrending, moaning vocals, include "Hellhound On My Trail," "Milkcow's Calf Blues" and "Terraplane Blues." Blues guitarist Robert Jr. Lockwood is his stepson.

**Johnson, Walter** *(1887–1946)* American baseball player. Elected to the Baseball Hall of Fame in 1936, Johnson ranks as one of the greatest fastball pitchers in history. While pitching for the Washington Senators from 1907 to 1927, he won 416 games. He set a career strikeout record of 3,508, and in 1913 pitched 56 consecutive innings without allowing a run. In his career, he pitched seven opening-game shutouts.

**Johnson-Sirleaf, Ellen** *(1938– )* Liberian politician and the first elected female president of an African country. Born in Liberia, Johnson-Sirleaf was educated at Madison Business College, the University of Colorado, and Harvard University (from which he received a masters degree in public administration in 1971) before returning to her native country. After serving as minister of finance in 1972–73, she was imprisoned for criticizing the military regime of President Samuel Doe and was then exiled to Kenya. In exile she gained a great deal of experience in financial affairs, working for Citibank in Nairobi and holding the post of senior loans officer at the World Bank. Originally a supporter of President Charles Taylor, she returned to Liberia in 1997 to mount an unsuccessful campaign against him. A sharp critic of Taylor's corrupt practices and authoritarian rule, Johnson-Sirleaf headed the Governance Reform Commission that was formed in 2003 to bring the bloody civil war in Liberia to an end. Hailed by her supporters as the "iron lady" for her steely determination, she defeated the popular former soccer player George Weah in the presidential elections of 2005 and was inaugurated in January 2006. She declared that her foremost goal was to heal the wounds that still festered from the Liberian civil war.

**Johnson Space Center** NASA center at Clear Lake, Texas, near Houston. Originally known as the Manned Spacecraft Center, this site houses NASA Mission Control, which managed all manned spaceflights after lift-off from CAPE CANAVERAL Air Force Station (MERCURY, GEMINI and most unmanned missions) or from KENNEDY SPACE CENTER (APOLLO, SKYLAB and SPACE SHUTTLE missions). It was named for President Lyndon B. JOHNSON.

**Johore (Johor)** A state of MALAYSIA, on the southern extremity of the Malay Peninsula, opposite SINGAPORE; its capital is Johore Bahru. Occupied by Japan during World War II, Johore joined the Federation of Malaya in 1957 and became a part of Malaysia in 1963.

**Joliot-Curie, Frédéric** *(1900–1958)* French physicist. Frédéric Joliot, the son of a prosperous tradesman, was education at the School of Industrial Physics and Chemistry. In 1923 he began his research career at the Radium Institute under Marie CURIE, where he obtained his doctorate in 1930. He was appointed to a new chair of nuclear chemistry at the Collège de France in 1937 and, after World War II (in which he played an important part in the French RESISTANCE) was head of the new Commissariat à l'Energie Atomique (1946–50). In 1956 he became head of the Radium Institute.

In 1926 Joliot married the daughter of Marie CURIE, Irène, and changed his name to Joliot-Curie. In 1931 they began research that was to win them the NOBEL PRIZE for physics in 1935 for their fundamental discovery of artificial radioactivity (1934).

In 1939 Joliot-Curie was quick to see the significance of the discovery of nuclear fission by Otto HAHN. He confirmed Hahn's work and saw the likelihood of a chain reaction. He further realized that the chain reaction could be produced only in the presence of a moderator to slow the neutrons down. A good moderator was the heavy water that was produced on a large scale only in Norway at Telemark. With considerable foresight Joliot-Curie managed to persuade the French government to obtain this entire stock of heavy-water, 185 kilograms in all, and to arrange for its shipment to England out of the reach of the advancing German army.

**Joliot-Curie, Irène** *(1897–1956)* French physicist. Irène Curie was the daughter of Pierre and Marie CURIE, the discoverers of radium. She received little formal schooling, attending instead informal classes where she was taught physics by her mother, mathematics by Paul Langevin, and chemistry by Jean-Baptiste Perrin. She later attended the Sorbonne although she first served as a radiologist at the front during WORLD WAR I. In 1921 she began work at her mother's Radium Institute, with which she maintained her connection for the rest of her life, becoming its director in 1946. She was also, from 1937, a professor at the Sorbonne.

In 1926 Irène Curie married Frédéric JOLIOT and took the name Joliot-Curie. In 1935 the Joliot-Curies won the NOBEL PRIZE in physics for their discovery in 1934 of artificial radioactivity.

Irène later almost anticipated Otto HAHN's discovery of nuclear fission but like many other physicists at that time found it too difficult to accept the simple hypothesis that heavy elements like uranium could split into lighter elements when bombarded with neutrons. Instead she tried to find heavier elements produced by the decay of uranium.

Like her mother, Irène Joliot-Curie produced a further generation of scientists. Her daughter, Hélène, married the son of Marie Curie's old companion, Paul Langevin, and, together with her brother, Paul, became a distinguished physicist.

**Jolson, Al (Asa Yoelson)** *(1886–1950)* American stage and motion picture entertainer. A Russian immigrant, Jolson sang in a New York synagogue during his youth and also performed in VAUDEVILLE and blackface theaters. Popular entertainment won out, and at his peak in the early 1920s many people considered Jolson the greatest all-round performer in the world. It was his habit to interpolate into his shows any song that struck his fancy. Thus, during a performance of his hit show *Sinbad* (1918), he sang a little thing he had heard at a party, "Swanee"; the song's immediate success catapulted its composer George GERSHWIN into the big time. Jolson's film career did not spring full-blown from *The Jazz Singer.* He had been tested for the cameras many years previously; and he had made a sound short several months before beginning *The Jazz Singer.* His famous "throwaway" line—"You ain't heard nothing yet"—was actually a "signature" piece, already well known in his stage performances. And it was not *The Jazz Singer* so much as Jolson's immediate follow-up, *The Singing Fool* (1928)—with smash-hit songs "Sonny Boy," "There's a Rainbow Round My Shoulder" and "I'm Sittin' on Top of the World"—that really launched the TALKING PICTURES. In semi-retirement in the 1940s, Jolson found a new generation of admirers thanks to two less-than-truthful biographical films, *The Jolson Story* (1946) and *Jolson Sings Again* (1949), starring Larry Parks and utilizing Jolson's dubbed voice. Jolson died of a heart attack after a tour entertaining U.S. troops in Korea.

**Jones, Blanche Calloway (Blanche Calloway)** *(1902–1978)* American singer. Blanche Calloway first appeared in 1920 with the Earl "Fatha" HINES and Louis ARMSTRONG bands. In the 1930s she became the first woman to lead a major American dance band. After retiring as a singer in 1944, she became the first woman disk jockey in the American South. She was the sister of JAZZ bandleader and performer Cab CALLOWAY.

**Jones, Bobby** *(1902–1971)* U.S. golfer. His domination of the sport in the late 1920s and early 1930s was challenged only by Gene SARAZEN and Walter HAGEN. In 1930 he won the U.S. Open, British Open, British Amateur and U.S. Amateur titles, completing an unprecedented "Grand Slam." He won the U.S. Open a total of four times, the British Open three times and the U.S. Amateur title five times. Although he retired at the age of 28, his influence on golf continued as he cofounded the Augusta National Golf Club. In 1934 he

established the Masters Tournament, which rapidly became one of golf's most prestigious championships.

**Jones, David** *(1895–1974)* British poet, essayist and artist. Jones was born in Kent, England, but was strongly influenced by the Welsh ancestry of his family, an influence that shows in his poetic works. He served in the British army during WORLD WAR I, an experience that he drew upon in composing his literary masterpiece, *In Parenthesis* (1937), a haunting narrative blending of poetry and prose that explores wartime suffering along with the chivalric legends of King Arthur and the Welsh *Mabinogion.* Other works by Jones include *The Anathemata* (1952), *The Sleeping Lord* (1974) and *The Dying Gaul* (1978). Jones was also a gifted artist who produced engravings, watercolors and drawings to accompany his own writings as well as books by his contemporaries.

**Jones, James** *(1921–1977)* American novelist. During WORLD WAR II he served in the Pacific and fought at GUADALCANAL. His wartime experiences formed the background to his subsequent work as a writer. Jones is best known for his first—and many consider, his best—novel, *From Here to Eternity* (1951, filmed 1953) an expansive story that takes place on an army base prior to the bombing of PEARL HARBOR. This insightful, unsentimental study of masculine attitudes and interaction told in plain, blunt language won the National Book Award in 1951; the film won three ACADEMY AWARDS in 1953. Jones felt that the success of *From Here to Eternity* overshadowed his subsequent fiction, which includes *The Thin Red Line* (1962, filmed 1964), *The Ice-Cream Headache and Other Stories* (1968) and *Whistle,* edited by Willie Morris and published posthumously in 1978.

**Jones, James Earl** *(1931– )* American stage and film actor. Born in rural Mississippi, Jones attended the University of Michigan. He first came to public attention in the early 1960s as a member of the New York Shakespeare Festival playing, among others, Caliban in *The Tempest* (1962) and the title role in *Othello* (1964) and returning as Lear in 1973. He became a star in the role of

prizefighter Jack JOHNSON in *The Great White Hope* (1968; filmed 1970). Since then he has lent his superb acting skills and magnificent voice to such plays as *The Iceman Cometh* (1973), *Of Mice and Men* (1974), *Master Harold and the Boys* (1981) and *Fences* (1985) and to such films as *Star Wars* (1977, as the voice of Darth Vader), *Field of Dreams* (1989) and *The Hunt for Red October* (1990). He has also appeared in many television dramas, notably in the starring role of the early 1990s series *Gideon's Fire.* In 1991 Jones won an Emmy Award for best actor on the television series *Gabriel's Fire* and for best supporting actor for his part in the made-for-TV movie *Heat Wave,* which depicted the 1968 Watts riots.

**Jones, Spike (Lindley Armstrong)** *(1911–1964)* American musician and bandleader. Spike Jones enjoyed a major success in show business in the 1940s and 1950s, when his madcap style of comical musical performance led to appearances by himself and his band on radio and on a regular television series. Jones was born in Long Beach, Calif., and first came to national attention with his recording of *Der Fuhrer's Face* (1942), a satirical attack on Hitler that featured a loud Bronx cheer. Jones toured the U.S. for many years with his band, the City Slickers, which featured such extemporaneous instruments as doorbells, pistols, hammers and anvils, and the "Latrinophone"—a toilet seat with catgut strings.

**Jonestown massacre** Mass suicide on Nov. 18, 1978, of members of the People's Temple religious cult, in the agricultural commune of Jonestown, Guyana. The group, led by Rev. Jim (James Warren) Jones (1931–78), an Indiana-born minister, began in Indianapolis in the late 1950s. With a predominately black congregation, Jones preached equality of social and racial status, favored apocalyptic predictions and made himself absolutely central to his flock's well-being. He and his growing band of followers moved to California in 1965, settling in San Francisco. As membership grew to the thousands, Jones expanded his activities to include social programs for the city's poor. In 1976 the popular preacher was named chairman of the San Francisco Housing Authority.

However, word of his bizarre practices, including rigid and violent discipline, extortion of money and property, death threats and sexual misconduct, soon surfaced.

In 1977 Jones, together with several hundred cult members, fled to Guyana and settled on land Jones had acquired earlier. Some Temple members wrote relatives detailing the conditions of physical and psychological abuse under which they were forced to live abroad. On the basis of these complaints, Rep. Leo Ryan of California and an entourage of aides and press visited Jonestown in November 1978. After spending a night there, Ryan and his party, together with some residents who had decided to leave the commune, proceeded to the local airstrip, where they were set upon by an armed group of Jones's followers. In the ensuing gunfire, Ryan and four others were killed and a number wounded. After the ambush was revealed to Jones, he ordered his band to commit suicide by drinking a fruit punch laced with cyanide. Most followed the order without question; some resisted but were forced to consume the poison or were shot; some escaped. Jones and several top aides shot themselves to death. Altogether, 911 died in the massacre.

**Jong, Erica Mann** *(1942– )* American novelist and poet. A native New Yorker educated at Barnard College, Jong published a well-received book of poems in 1971 before she burst on the scene with *Fear of Flying* (1973). This erotic feminist bestseller introduced her fictional alter ego, Isadora Wing, whose sexual exploits, marriages and divorces were later chronicled in *How to Save Your Own Life* (1977) and *Parachutes and Kisses* (1984). *Fanny, Being the True History of Fanny Hackabout-Jones* (1980) is a picaresque novel in the style of Fielding, Defoe and Cleland. *Serenissima: A Novel of Venice* (1987) follows its 20th-century heroine through a time warp similar to that of Virginia WOOLF's *Orlando*. Jong has also continued to produce poetry of indifferent quality. She has been much praised for her lusty humor and liberated fantasies and much derided for her tawdriness. It is safe to say, however, that she occupies a unique place in American literature. In 1998 Jong

received the UN Award for Excellence in literature.

**Jooss, Kurt** *(1901–1979)* German choreographer. Jooss was the first choreographer to successfully combine elements of modern dance with classical ballet. He introduced his new concepts with his ballet company in Essen, Germany, in the late 1920s and early 1930s. He fled to Britain after Adolf HITLER's rise to power, and did not return to his homeland until 1951. His ballets were noted for their compassion and social consciousness. His most famous ballet, *The Green Table* (1932), was perhaps the most acclaimed anti-war ballet ever choreographed.

**Joplin, Janis** *(1945–1970)* American rock-and-roll vocalist. Joplin was perhaps the greatest vocalist to emerge from the psychedelic era of the 1960s. Born and raised in Texas, she moved to San Francisco in 1966 and became the lead singer for a band, Big Brother and the Holding Company, which soon won international acclaim due to the sheer power and emotion of Joplin's bluesy, throaty vocals. *Cheap Thrills* (1968) remains a classic album of the era and features the hit single "Piece of My Heart." In 1969 Joplin pursued a solo career and released two noteworthy albums, *I Got Dem Ol' Cosmic Blues Again* (1969) and *Pearl* (1971), the latter including the hit single "Me and Bobby McGee." She died in 1970 from a heroin overdose. Posthumously released albums include *In Concert* (1972), *Janis* (1974), *Farewell Song* (1982) and *Janis Joplin in Concert* (1987).

**Joplin, Scott** *(1868–1917)* American pianist-composer; the preeminent exponent and popularizer of RAGTIME, a corruption of "ragged time," the popular pianistic form of the late-19th century that originated in the South and Midwest of the U.S. As developed by Joplin, the style typically set a highly syncopated, or "ragged," right-hand melody against a comparatively straightforward rhythmic pattern in the left-hand or bass. After initial successes playing "sporting houses" (brothels) in his native Texarkana, Tex., Joplin traveled throughout the Midwest scoring impressive triumphs, including the 1893 Chicago World's Fair. Joplin was the undisputed king of ragtime musi-

cians. In addition to his spirited yet precise playing, Joplin became a prominent composer whose through-composed works included "Maple Leaf Rag," "The Entertainer" and "Gladiolus Rag." Royalties from his published rags enabled him to settle comfortably in St. Louis. However, a disastrous attempt to produce his ambitious opera *Treemonisha* (1911) broke Joplin's spirit, health and finances. In the 1970s, Joplin's rags enjoyed a huge revival by virtue of their use in the soundtrack of the hit motion picture, *The Sting* (1973), and due to the immensely popular recordings of pianist-musicologist Joshua Rifkin, who took to heart Joplin's admonition—"It is never right to play 'Ragtime' fast"—in performances clearly revealing the pristine, pre-jazz elegance of Joplin's original conception.

**Jordan** (**Hashemite Kingdom of Jordan**) Jordan is located in the region of southwest Asia known as the Middle East and covers an area of 37,129 square miles, of which 2,565 square miles (known as the WEST BANK) are currently occupied by ISRAEL. For centuries a part of the OTTOMAN EMPIRE, modern Jordan took form in 1920 as **Transjordan,** a British sphere of influence. Autonomy was granted under Emir Abdullah in 1923, and full independence achieved in 1946. Now a constitutional monarchy, Jordan has been led by King HUSSEIN Ibn Talal since 1952. As a result of the 1967 SIX-DAY WAR, Israel occupied the West Bank of the Jordan River and East Jerusalem, both formerly held by Jordan. Tensions between the Jordanian government and the PALESTINE LIBERATION ORGANIZATION (PLO) led to the expulsion of the PLO in 1970–71. Hussein reconciled with PLO leader Yasir ARAFAT in 1983, while Jordan and Egypt formed a moderate Arab bloc to work for a solution to the issue of a Palestinian homeland. During the PERSIAN GULF WAR (1990–91) King Hussein supported the initial UNITED NATIONS resolutions condemning IRAQ for its invasion of KUWAIT. However, the majority of Jordanians (including its sizeable Palestinian refugee population) opposed military action by the allied coalition against Iraq, and Jordan lent its vocal support to Iraq's president, Saddam HUSSEIN. As a result,

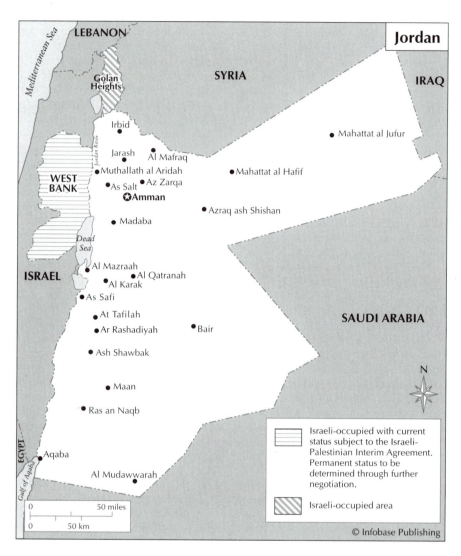

Jordan's ties with the U.S. and with other Arab nations who opposed Iraq were strained. Jordan joined the peace process in the Middle East by signing a peace treaty with Israel in 1994. Following the death of King Hussein in February 1999, his son Crown Prince Abdullah was sworn in as King ABDULLAH II. In 2002 a U.S. diplomat was gunned down outside his home in Amman. Eight Islamic militants were sentenced to death for the slaying in 2004.

**Jordan, Michael Jeffrey "Air"** *(1963– )* American professional basketball player (1984–93, 1995–98, 2001–03). Born in Brooklyn, N.Y., Jordan and his family moved to Wilmington, N.C., where in high school he attracted attention from college basketball coaches, who offered him full scholarships to play for their teams. After choosing the University of North Carolina, Jordan helped the Tar Heels win the 1982 National Collegiate Athletic Association (NCAA) Men's Basketball championship by scoring the game-winning shot. Jordan recorded impressive statistics at North Carolina and led the U.S. men's basketball team to a gold medal at the 1984 Olympics.

At the end of his junior year Jordan was drafted by the Chicago Bulls and promptly recorded impressive statis-

| JORDAN | |
|---|---|
| 1918 | Region of present-day Jordan gains independence from Ottoman Empire. |
| 1920 | Jordan east of the Jordan River administered by Britain as Transjordan, a part of Britain's League of Nations mandate for Palestine. |
| 1946 | Jordan gains full independence. |
| 1949 | Transjordan renamed Jordan; annexes West Bank and East Jerusalem. |
| 1952 | Mentally ill King Tallal is deposed; his son Hussein declared king. |
| 1967 | Jordan loses West Bank to Israel in Six-Day War; 200,000 Palestinians seek refuge in Jordan. |
| 1970 | Jordanian army routs Palestinian guerrillas in a civil war; Hussein and Arafat truce. |
| 1991 | King Hussein supports Iraq in Persian Gulf War; aid from U.S. placed under review. |
| 1994 | King Hussein signs peace treaty with Israel. |
| 1999 | King Hussein dies and is succeeded by his son Abdullah II. |
| 2002 | U.S. diplomat is shot dead in Amman. |
| 2004 | Eight Islamic militants are convicted of the 2002 shooting. |

tics—28.2 points, 6.5 rebounds, 5.9 assists and 2.4 steals per game—and won the NBA's Rookie of the Year Award and a position on the NBA All-Star Team in 1985.

From 1988 to 1993 Jordan led the Bulls under coach Phil Jackson to three NBA championships. At the end of the 1992 postseason Jordan added another honor to his career: two-time Olympic gold medalist on the U.S. men's basketball team, which swept the Olympic tournament, never losing a game, and always winning by at least 20 points, against the best basketball players in the world.

At the end of the 1992–93 season, Jordan retired from basketball, stating that after three NBA championships, three MVP awards, three NBA finals MVP selections and seven season scoring titles, he had nothing left to prove to himself and his fans. In 1994 he surprised everyone by signing with the Chicago White Sox, a Major League Baseball team. However, after several poor performances, he was sent down to the Sox's AA team, the Birmingham Barons, where he recorded a mediocre performance during the 1994 season.

The following year Jordan returned to the Bulls, whom he helped to advance to the second round of the 1995 playoffs, but he showed constant signs of fatigue and on occasion poor decision-making skills that contributed to the Bulls' postseason exit. In the 1995 off-season Jordan began a rigorous conditioning program to refine his basketball skills, that had become rusty during his retirement. Returning to his All-Star performance level, Jordan's 10th full year with the Bulls was one of the best for any franchise in NBA history. The Bulls stampeded to a 72-10 season, the best in the NBA, and the franchise's fourth NBA title. Jordan also picked up another scoring title, as well as regular and postseason MVP honors. During the next two years Jordan helped the Bulls win a fifth and sixth NBA championship and earned a fifth regular season MVP trophy. In 1999, Jordan again retired from the NBA. Then in 2001 Jordan announced he would again return to the basketball court and play two seasons for the Washington Wizards, an NBA franchise. After playing far below his past performance level, Jordan retired for what he said would be the final time at the end of the 2002–03 season.

**Jordanian Civil War of 1970–71**
After the SIX-DAY WAR 400,000 Palestinian refugees joined 700,000 others already in JORDAN. From Jordan some Palestinians conducted terrorist attacks against Israel. Adherents of Yasir ARAFAT's PALESTINE LIBERATION ORGANIZATION (PLO) claimed Jordanian law did not apply to them; Israel staged retaliatory raids. King HUSSEIN, his regime threatened, resolved to destroy PLO power in Jordan, and after Palestinian hijackers flew airliners to Amman, Jordan's capital ("Black September," September 6–9, 1970), he declared martial law September 16. His troops surrounded refugee camps, disarming guerrillas and deporting militant leaders. By September 25 a cease-fire had been arranged by Arab heads of state, but battles against guerrilla bands continued until July 1971, when Palestinian bases were destroyed. Palestinian organizations subsequently moved to LEBANON.

**Jorgensen, Christine (George Jorgensen)** (*1926–1989*) The first American transsexual to announce that she had undergone a sex-change operation. In Jorgensen's 1967 biography, the former army private said she had had a normal, happy childhood but, as an adult, had come to feel that she was a woman trapped in a man's body. Following the operation, which took place in Denmark in 1952, she became the focus of intense tabloid newspaper interest. She later starred in a nightclub act that featured her theme song, "I Enjoy Being a Girl."

**Josephson, Brian David** (*1940–  *) British physicist. Josephson was educated at Cambridge University, where he obtained his Ph.D. in 1964. He remained at Cambridge and in 1974 was appointed to a professorship of physics.

His name is associated with the **Josephson effects** described in 1962 while still a graduate student. The work came out of theoretical speculations on electrons in SEMICONDUCTORS involving the exchange of electrons between two superconducting regions separated by a thin insulating layer (**Josephson junction**). He showed theoretically that a current can flow across the junction in the absence of an applied voltage. Furthermore, a small direct voltage across the junction produces an alternating current with a frequency that is inversely proportional to the voltage. The

effects have been verified experimentally, thus supporting the BCS theory of superconductivity of John BARDEEN and his colleagues. They have been used in making accurate physical measurements and in measuring weak magnetic fields. Josephson junctions can also be used as very fast switching devices in computers. For this work Josephson shared the 1973 NOBEL PRIZE in physics with Leo ESAKI and Ivar GAIEVER. More recently, Josephson has turned his attention to the study of the mind.

**Jourdain, François** (*1876–1958*) French architect and interior designer whose career extended from the ART NOUVEAU era through the MODERNISM of the 1930s. Jourdain was trained as a painter but after 1909 worked only as an interior and furniture designer. He was interested in low cost, prefabricated furniture of simple design. His work and publications of the 1920s were well known and influential since he was a strong champion of the austere, undecorated design vocabulary of the time. After 1945 he focused on historical writings about art and design.

**Jouvet, Louis** (*1887–1951*) French theatrical actor, director and producer. Jouvet was a major force in the French theater in the years between the two world wars. He served as director of several theaters, including a stint at the Comédie des Champs-Elysée from 1924 to 1934. Jouvet was noted for his popular touch in direction and production and was instrumental in first bringing the works of French playwrights Jean GIRAUDOUX and Jules ROMAINS to the attention of the French public. Jouvet also appeared as an actor in many of his own productions.

**Joyce, James (Augustine Aloysius Joyce)** (*1882–1941*) Irish novelist, short story writer and poet. Best known for his novel ULYSSES (1922), he is one of the towering figures of 20th-century literature and of MODERNISM. Born in DUBLIN, he was educated in Catholic schools and graduated from University College, Dublin (1902). After briefly studying medicine in Paris, he returned to Dublin, where, on June 16, 1904—the date on which he later set the events of *Ulysses*—he met his future wife, Nora Barnacle. From 1905 on, he lived successively in Italy, Switzerland

*Irish author James Joyce* (LIBRARY OF CONGRESS, PRINTS AND PHOTOGRAPHS DIVISION)

and France—in self-imposed exile from Ireland, a country he felt had rejected him. Moreover, he believed exile to be necessary for his art, which he felt should transcend the ties of family, country and religion. His first book of poems, *Chamber Music* (1907), was followed by a volume of stories, *Dubliners* (1914), the autobiographical novel *A Portrait of the Artist as a Young Man* (1916), and a play, *Exiles* (1918). After *Ulysses,* Joyce devoted nearly two decades to *Finnegans Wake,* a STREAM-OF-CONSCIOUSNESS dream book in which he transformed the English language by way of elaborate puns, sound-play and immense erudition.

**Joyner, Florence Griffith** *(1959–1998)* American athlete. Joyner broke the world record for 100 meters (10.49 sec.) on July 16, 1988. At the OLYMPIC GAMES she won three gold medals: 100 meters, 200 meters (21.34 sec., another world record) and 4x100 relay. Her sister-in-law **Jackie Joyner-Kersee** (b. 1962) is also a world record-holder. She won the seven-event heptathlon in the 1988 Seoul Olympics with a record 7,291 points. Griffith Joyner won a second Olympic medal in the long jump and holds the U.S. records for heptathlon, long jump and 100-meter high jump. In 1995 Griffith Joyner was inducted into the U.S. Track and Field Hall of Fame. She died in 1998 of a heart seizure at the age of 38.

**József, Attila** *(1905–1937)* Hungarian poet. Born in Budapest, József spent his entire life in extreme poverty and used his poetry to protest the misery of the poor and express his own suffering. The influence of both Marx and Sigmund FREUD is evident in his work. At the age of three, he was abandoned by his father; at nine he attempted suicide; at 14 his mother died. His first volume, *Szepseg Koldusa,* appeared in 1922. In 1925 he was expelled from the University of Szeged for a revolutionary poem and left to study in Vienna and Paris. He joined the illegal Hungarian Communist Party in 1930 but was expelled in 1933 by Stalinists who attacked him as a fascist. Though he entered psychoanalysis in 1931 he was later hospitalized for severe depression. He committed suicide by throwing himself under a freight train. His poems began to be translated in the 1960s.

**Juan Carlos I** *(1938– )* King of Spain *(1975– )*. The grandson of King ALFONSO XIII, Juan Carlos was named by dictator Francisco FRANCO as future king in 1969. Crowned in 1975, shortly before Franco's death, he encouraged the restoration of democracy in Spain and established himself as a constitutional monarch, with effective power in the hands of a prime minister. Juan Carlos has been instrumental in developing and preserving Spain as a democracy, a function he began to exercise in 1981 when he helped avert a right-wing military coup.

**Jubaland (Transjuba)** Region of southwestern SOMALIA between the KENYA border and the Juba River. Once a province of Kenya, it was transferred by Britain to ITALY in 1925 and administered as a separate territory until July 1, 1926, when it was absorbed into Italian Somaliland.

**Judson, Arthur** *(1881–1975)* American impressario and concert manager. Judson was a major figure in the formative years of commercial recording and broadcasting in the U.S. He was a co-founder of the COLUMBIA BROADCASTING SYSTEM (CBS) and at one time was the sole owner of Columbia Records. From 1930 to 1935 he simultaneously managed the New York Philharmonic, the

Philadelphia Orchestra, several summer concert series and was president of Columbia Concerts Corp., a major booking agency.

**July Days** Period of July 16–18, 1917, after the FEBRUARY REVOLUTION when Russian soldiers and civilians, in sympathy with the BOLSHEVIKS, tried to seize power from KERENSKY's provisional government in Petrograd. LENIN considered their rising inopportune. They received no significant support and the attempt failed. Bolshevik involvement was ascribed to pro-German sympathies and Bolsheviks in general were accused of treason. Lenin fled to Finland.

**Jung, C(arl) G(ustav)** *(1875–1961)* Swiss psychologist. Jung was one of the most famous psychological theorists of the 20th century. His most famous concept, that of the **collective unconscious**—a reservoir 'of inherited' mental imagery and structure from which all members of the human race draw myth and meaning—has exercised a pervasive influence not only in psychology but also in philosophy and the arts. Jung received his medical degree in 1900 and began his professional career as a psychiatrist at the University of Zurich. In 1907 he met Sigmund FREUD and became closely associated with Freud's emerging school of psychoanalysis. But within a few years Jung broke with Freud over the latter's insistent emphasis on sexuality alone as the dominant factor in unconscious motivation. Jung subsequently developed his theories of the animus and the anima—the male and female elements of the unconscious psyche that must be brought into harmony. *Two Essays on Analytical Psychology* (1956) provides a useful introduction to Jung's thought. His *Memories, Dreams, Reflections* (1965) is a revelatory autobiography.

**"just-in-time" system** See Shigeo SHINGO.

**Jutland (Jylland)** A peninsula, about 250 miles long, projecting into the North Sea from Germany; comprised of continental Denmark and the German state of Schleswig-Holstein. The only major fleet action of WORLD WAR I was fought by British and German DREADNOUGHTS and supporting vessels on May 31 and June 1, 1916, approximately 60 miles off Jutland's northwest coast. Although the British suffered heavy casualties and the loss of many smaller vessels, their capital ships (and Germany's) were largely undamaged; the smaller German fleet was forced to retreat, and Britain retained control of the North Sea. Winston CHURCHILL said of the victorious Admiral JELLICOE that he was the only man who could have lost the Great War in a single day. In Germany the BATTLE OF JUTLAND is known as the battle of Skagerrak.

**Jutland, Battle of** (*1916*) Part of British strategy against Germany in WORLD WAR I was to maintain a naval blockade in the North Sea to keep all shipping from German ports. Germany tested Britain's navy when its High Seas Fleet under Admiral Reinhard Scheer (1863–1928) sailed into Skagerrak, the sea passage between Jutland (Denmark) and Norway, May 31, 1916. British scouting squadrons encountered it and sustained severe losses. The British Grand Fleet under Admiral John R. JELLICOE arrived by evening, nearly entrapping the High Seas Fleet, but the Germans managed to escape in darkness and fog, losing only nine warships (out of 103) to the British loss of 14. Despite the heavier losses, the battle maintained British supremacy of the seas.

# K

**Kabalevsky, Dimitri Borisovich** (*1904–1987*) Soviet composer, conductor and musicologist. He studied composition under Nicholas MYASKOVSKY and piano under SCRIABIN at the Moscow Conservatory. He taught at the conservatory from 1932, becoming a professor there in 1939. His works include the operas *Colas Breugnon* (1938), *Semya Tarasa* (1950) and *Nikita Vershinin* (1955). He has composed four symphonies, including his No. 1 in commemoration of the 15th anniversary of the Russian Revolution, three piano concertos, a violin concerto and a cello concerto, as well as many choral works, songs and piano works.

**Kabila, Laurent Désiré** (*1939–2001*) President of the Democratic Republic of the CONGO (1997–2001). Born in Jadotville when the Congo was still a colony of Belgium, Kabila strongly supported Patrice LUMUMBA, a Marxist and the state's first postindependence prime minister, Lumumba was overthrown and murdered a few months after assuming power, and Kabila went underground to train with supporters of Lumumba's philosophy (including the Argentine revolutionary Che GUEVARA). After Colonel Joseph MOBUTU, the organizer of the coup against Lumumba, installed himself as dictator of the Congo (renamed ZAIRE in 1971 by Mobutu), Kabila traveled to Tanzania, where in 1967 he founded the People's Revolutionary Party (PRP) and established a rebel "government" in the high country near Lake Tan-

ganyika in southeastern Zaire. When his rebel domain collapsed in the mid-1980s, Kabila returned to Tanzania and became a gold merchant.

In 1996 Kabila joined the insurrection initiated by the Tutsis, an ethnic group living in the eastern portions of the nation. Uniting Tutsi dissidents with veteran opponents of Mobutu under the Alliance of Democratic forces for the Liberation of Congo (AFDL). For seven months the AFDL fought Mobutu's supporters with substantial support coming from Rwandan and Angolan forces. By May 1997 the AFDL had marched on Zaire's capital, Kinshasa, ousted Mobutu and renamed the country the Democratic Republic of the Congo (DRC) with Kabila as president.

Not long after coming to power, Kabila was accused of being a front man for the Rwandan government, whose leader, Paul KAGAME, had been instrumental in the AFDL's victory. He also made many enemies by using military forces to disperse protesters against his administration. In 1998 Kabila's two major allies, RWANDA and UGANDA, turned against him and supported a rebellion against Kabila that began in the eastern portions of the DRC. Although managed to block the rebels' advance with help from Angola, Chad, Namibia and Zimbabwe. Kabila was assassinated in January 2001 and was succeeded by his son Joseph.

**Kabul** Capital city of AFGHANISTAN. In recent times Kabul has been engulfed in three bloody conflicts to determine

the leadership of the Afghan state. In 1979 it was occupied by Soviet military forces at the request of its government that was considered controlled by Communists subservient to Moscow. It remained under Soviet occupation until 1989, when Soviet president Mikhail GORBACHEV ended the 10-year war against Muslim fundamentalist guerrilla MUJAHIDEEN that had spearheaded the resistance to the Soviet occupation. Within three years of the Soviet withdrawal, Kabul had again became the focus of a conflict among the victorious mujahideen factions, each vying to ensure that it would dominate the post-Soviet Afghan state. These miniature wars subsided in 1996, when the TALIBAN, a guerrilla group championing the creation in Afghanistan of a Islamic state that strictly enforced the dictates of the Koran, managed to seize control of Kabul and establish its Islamist rule over much of Afghanistan. In 2001 the Taliban's rule in Kabul ended when, as a result of its refusal to hand over leaders of the Islamic terrorist organization AL-QAEDA residing in its borders, a U.S.-led military force entered Afghanistan and removed the Muslim fundamentalists from power.

**Kádár, János** (*1912–1989*) Hungarian communist leader; he came to power in the wake of the 1956 HUNGARIAN UPRISING against Soviet domination and remained Hungarian Communist Party leader until 1988. During the uprising, he had initially sided with popular reformist premier Imre NAGY but later negotiated in secret with Moscow and arranged to be installed as premier, supported by the Soviet invasion force. For years, Hungarians viewed him as a traitor to the uprising and to the reform movement. Nonetheless, in the early 1960s he initiated his own brand of economic and political liberalization, which made HUNGARY one of the most prosperous and tolerant members of the Eastern bloc and won Kádár a measure of grudging respect. His limited reforms eventually led to calls for more substantial changes, changes that Kádár was not prepared to make. As the Hungarian economy stagnated in the 1980s, he came to be viewed as an opponent of needed reform. He was replaced as party leader in May 1988 by Károly Grosz and was given the figurehead position of party president; in early 1989 he was removed from this position due to failing health.

**Kadet Party** Russian political party. The name was formed by the initials of the Constitutional-Democratic Party, which represented members of the bourgeoisie and petty bourgeoisie civil servants, army officers, shopkeepers and the like. It was founded in October 1905 and was headed by Pavel Miliukov, who advocated government on a constitutional basis to be attained by legal methods. He looked to Great Britain for a model of his ideas. Nearly all the ministers in the provisional government were Kadets. The party was suppressed in 1917.

**Kafka, Franz** (*1883–1924*) Austrian novelist and short story writer. Born in Prague (then a part of the Austro-Hungarian Empire) of a Jewish family, he studied law at the University of Prague and thereafter worked for most of his life in a government insurance office while writing in his off hours. Although his life was outwardly uneventful, he was tormented by phobias and dark obsessions. His novel *Amerika* (1927) was a fantasy of a country he never visited, and the novella *Metamorphosis* (1915) has its protagonist, Gregor Samsa, transformed into a giant cockroach. *The Trial* (1925) is a dreamlike novel of bureaucratic justice forever postponed, while *The Castle* (1926) concerns a royal summons that can never be fulfilled. Kafka also produced numerous other novellas, stories, parables and aphorisms. Most of his

*Austrian author Franz Kafka* (LIBRARY OF CONGRESS. PRINTS AND PHOTOGRAPHS DIVISION)

work was published only after his death, in spite of his request that his manuscripts be destroyed. His work prefigured that of such later writers as Albert CAMUS and Samuel BECKETT (see EXISTENTIALISM). The word "Kafkaesque" has become part of the vocabulary of the 20th century; it refers to the helplessness of the individual in the face of an absurd situation.

**Kagame, Paul** (*1957–  *) President of RWANDA (2000–  ). Born in Gitarama, a region in western Rwanda, he and his family left the country and traveled to UGANDA in 1961 because of growing sentiment in Gitarama against Tutsis, his ethnic group. In 1979 he joined the National Resistance Army (NRA) headed by Yoweri Museveni, and helped Museveni wage guerrilla war against the government of Uganda. In 1986 Kagame left the NRA to form a similar organization in Uganda in 1989 called the Rwandan Patriotic Front (RPF), which was dedicated to overthrowing the government of Rwanda. In October 1990 the RPF invaded Rwanda from its bases in Uganda. In July 1994, after four years of fighting against the Rwandan government of Juvenal Habyarimana, which had perpetrated a genocidal massacre of Tutsis, the RPF took control of the government, with Kagame serving as he took the posts of vice president and minister of defense under President Pasteur Biz-

imungu. In 2000, tensions between Kagame and Bizimungu over Kagame's suppression of opposition to the government prompted Bizimungu to resign. In response Kagame imprisoned the former president and repressed the Democratic Republican Movement (MDR), an opposition political party. In the national elections held in August 2003 Kagame was elected president of Rwanda for a seven-year term.

**Kaganovich, Lazar Moyseyevich** (*1893–1991*) Communist and disciple of LENIN. In 1911 Kaganovich joined the Bolshevik Party and played a prominent role in the leather workers' union. He assisted in organizing party affairs and rapidly advanced from post to post, including membership in the central committee from 1924, head of party organization in the Ukraine (1925–28) and, from 1930, membership in the Politburo. He was in charge of the collectivization of agriculture from 1929 to 1934 and the party purge in 1933–34. He became one of STALIN's chief lieutenants, but in 1957, as a member of the "anti-party group," Kaganovich was expelled from the central committee and the Presidium. (See also ANTI-PARTY GROUP CRISIS.)

**Kahn, Albert** (*1869–1942*) American architect best known for his work on industrial buildings, often of outstanding modernist design. Kahn was born in Germany but came to the U.S. as a child. He worked for a Detroit architectural firm for some years before establishing his own office in 1902. Much of his work was for automobile manufacturers in the Detroit area. While the work tended to be conservative in ornamental detail, it excelled in the functional parts of factories where large glass areas and roof skylights generated forms related to those of more doctrinaire European modernists. The firm of Albert Kahn, Inc., was at its best with such works as the Chrysler Motor Company truck assembly plant building of 1936 near Detroit, with its dramatic structural trusses, or the Kellogg grain elevators in Battle Creek, Michigan. Kahn built projects around the world; there are many in the USSR and even a few in China and Japan.

**Kahn, Herman** (*1922–1983*) American nuclear strategist, economic theorist and futurist. Kahn established a reputation as a strategist while working at the Rand Corporation in California from 1948 until 1961. He later founded and directed the **Hudson Institute,** a "think tank" in Croton-on-Hudson, N.Y., where a range of political, foreign policy and economic topics was explored. He believed that nuclear war was likely but survivable. He argued that nuclear deterrence was unworkable, and that policy planners must develop survival techniques. In economics he predicted that poverty and unemployment in the U.S. would disappear as a result of zero-inflation growth. He was consulted by every U.S. president from Harry S TRUMAN to Ronald REAGAN.

**Kahn, Louis Isadore** *(1901–1974)* American architect and architectural educator whose influence far outstrips the extent of his executed work. Kahn was born in Estonia and studied art and architecture, the latter at the University of Pennsylvania in Philadelphia from 1920 to 1924, when the program there was oriented toward classical Beaux-Arts design. He worked for several Philadelphia firms and turned toward MODERNISM while working with George HOWE and Oscar Stonorov. Kahn was asked to teach at Yale by Howe in 1947. He stayed until 1957 and became known for his Yale University Art Gallery addition (1953) with its triangular, trussed structure visible as gallery ceilings. His Richards Medical Research Laboratories at the University of Pennsylvania, with all the service elements grouped in external towers, followed in 1957–61. Although a controversial work disliked by many of its users, it established his international reputation. From 1957 until his death he taught at the University of Pennsylvania in Philadelphia, where he is credited with becoming a major influence in developing the "Philadelphia school" of modernism. Kahn came to have an almost mystical power as an educator and architectural theorist in a way that went far beyond the seeming modesty of such works as his Unitarian Church (1963) in Rochester, N.Y., and his Salk Institute Laboratories (1965) in La Jolla, Calif. His last works included government buildings in Dacca, Pakistan (under construction at the time of his death) and the Kimbell Art Museum (1972) in Fort Worth, Tex. Kahn's de-

sign was generally simple in detail but powerful in form and full of complexities and subtleties that have made him one of the most admired and studied of all modern architects.

**Kahn, Lord Richard Ferdinand** *(1905–1989)* British economist. Kahn introduced the concept of the "multiplier" in an article in the *Economic Journal* in 1931. An associate of John Maynard KEYNES, he contributed to the discussions that formed the basis of Keynes's general theory of employment, interest, and money. He was also the author of *Selected Essays on Economic Growth* (1973) and *The Making of Keynes' General Theory* (1984).

**Kahnweiler, Daniel-Henry** *(1884–1979)* German-born art dealer and art historian. Kahnweiler was an early champion of the cubist painters in his Paris gallery (see CUBISM). He met Pablo PICASSO in 1907 and was closely associated with him until Picasso's death in 1973.

**Kaifu, Toshiki** *(1931–   )* Japanese politician, prime minister of JAPAN (1989–91). Born in central Japan, Kaifu began his political career in 1960, when he was elected to the Japanese diet as a member of the governing Liberal Democratic Party (LDP). Kaifu's reputation for effectiveness and honesty earned him several high posts within the government, including deputy chief cabinet secretary (1974–76) and minister of education (1976–77, 1985–86). In 1989, as the government of Uno Sosuke faced repeated charges of corruption, causing a decline in support for the LDP among Japanese voters, Kaifu was chosen to succeed Prime Minister Uno Sosuke amid charges of corruption. Kaifu's success in combating corruption led the LDP to a victory in the diet elections of 1990. But, his government fell in September 1991 because of opposition from factions within the LDP and public dissatisfaction with economic decline that began in 1991.

**Kaiser, Georg** *(1875–1945)* German playwright. Kaiser was one of the leading figures in the rise of EXPRESSIONISM as a dominant force in German theater between the two world wars. His plays relied upon dramatic incident, sharp and rapid dialogue, and frequently

dealt with the clash between individual freedom and the economic and social demands of the machine age. A highly popular voice in the theater, Kaiser was no longer allowed, after the rise of the Nazis in 1933, to have his works publicly performed. Kaiser's major work is his dramatic trilogy *The Coral* (1917), *Gas I* (1918) and *Gas II* (1920).

**Kaiser, Henry John** *(1882–1967)* American industrialist. Born in Sprout Brook, New York, Kaiser began in the construction business in 1913, becoming a leader in the road-paving industry. He became known as a builder of dams and bridges, participating in the construction of the Boulder (HOOVER) DAM (1936), Bonneville and Grand Coulee dams and the San Francisco–Oakland Bay Bridge. An important contributor to the war effort in WORLD WAR II, he and his companies produced enormous numbers of ships, planes and other military vehicles. After the war he headed Kaiser Industries (1945–67), presiding over the company as it prospered and grew to include steel, aluminum, cement and home-building. One of his few failures was the postwar automobile called the Kaiser-Frazer.

**KAL 007** Early in the morning of September 1, 1983, a Korean Airlines Boeing 747 strayed from its normal flight path and was shot down by Soviet fighters. All 240 passengers and 29 crew members aboard the airliner, Flight 007 from New York to Seoul, Korea, were killed. The world was horrified; U.S. president Ronald REAGAN condemned the downing of the airliner and demanded an apology. The Soviets insisted that they had believed the plane was a military aircraft, and that the pilot had ignored their signals to identify himself. Some Americans speculated that flight KAL 007 had deliberately "strayed" into Soviet airspace to carry out a spying mission. The incident seemed to confirm President Reagan's assertion that the USSR was an "evil empire."

**Kaledin, Alexei Maksimovich** *(1861–1918)* Russian Cossack leader and soldier. Kaledin served from 1914 in command of a cavalry division but opposed the military reforms of the provisional government and in 1917 was forced to resign. Returning to the Don region, he was elected hetman of the Cossacks and organized an anti-Bolshevik campaign, but he suffered many defeats and shot himself in February 1918.

**Kaline, Al** *(1934– )* American baseball player. A 16-time All-Star, Kaline was known as Mr. Tiger, spending all of his 20-year career with Detroit. In 1955 he became the youngest player in American League history to capture the batting title. His average that year was .340, with 27 home runs and 102 runs batted in. Formidable on both offense and defense, his steady play in right field netted him 10 Gold Gloves. Kaline retired in 1974 and was named to the Hall of Fame in 1980.

**Kalinin, Mikhail Ivanovich** *(1875–1946)* Communist statesman, born at Tver (now Kalinin). An active revolutionary arrested many times after 1898, he became one of the first supporters of LENIN. He supported STALIN in the party struggle following Lenin's death. In 1919 he became chairman of the all-Russian executive committee of the Soviets and a member of the central committee. He was a member of the Politburo from 1926 and chairman of the Supreme Soviet of the USSR from 1938 to 1946.

**Kaliningrad** **(Königsberg)** Russian Baltic seaport on the Pregolya River, 80 miles east-northeast of Gdańsk. Before WORLD WAR II Königsberg was a part of German East Prussia and a major German naval base. Soviet troops captured it as they advanced toward Berlin at the end of the war. Under the POTSDAM agreement it was transferred to the USSR and renamed in honor of communist statesman Mikhail Ivanovich KALININ. With the breakup of the USSR in 1991, the Kaliningrad administrative district was cutoff from Russia. With the enlargement of the EUROPEAN UNION to include Poland and Lithuania in 2004, Kaliningrad became a geographical enclave within the EU.

**Kalmyks** **(Kalmucks)** Mongol people of the Tibetan Buddhist faith living in the Kalmyk Autonomous Soviet Socialist Republic. They migrated from western China to Russia (Nogay Steppe) in the early 17th century. In 1920 a Kalmyk autonomous oblast was established and in 1933 it became an autonomous republic. Occupied in part by the Germans in 1942, it was thought that the Kalmyks had collaborated with the enemy; as a result they were exiled to Soviet Central Asia. Rehabilitation of the Kalmyks was announced in 1957 and they returned to their homes. In 1979 Kalmyks numbered about 150,000.

**Kaltenborn, H(ans) V(on)** *(1878–1965)* Pioneering radio news reporter. Born in Milwaukee, Kaltenborn attended Harvard University, then became a newspaperman, working on the *Brooklyn Eagle* from 1910 to 1930. While on the *Eagle* (1922), he began delivering current events talks on a New York City radio station (a "local" station, as were all the primitively powered stations of the time). Eight years later he began work at CBS as a news commentator, and in 1936 he traveled to Spain to report the SPANISH CIVIL WAR. Returning to New York, he continued to broadcast news bulletins along with running commentary, and was particularly noted for his broadcasts on the 1938 Munich crisis. Kaltenborn became famous for his quick, clipped delivery in a somewhat nasal voice and for an encyclopedic knowledge that allowed him to discourse on nearly any subject without preparation. His autobiography, *Fifty Fabulous Years,* was published in 1950.

**Kamenev, Lev Borisovich** *(1883–1936)* Soviet political figure; a prominent leader of the Bolshevik movement before the revolution. Although he opposed LENIN's seizure of power in 1917 he remained prominent in the party. Initially he supported STALIN against TROTSKY and later he supported Trotsky and ZINOVIEV. He was expelled from the party several times. Finally, in 1935, he was sentenced to five years' imprisonment; at a retrial in 1936 he was again sentenced and was executed.

**kamikaze** Japanese for "divine wind," this term was used by the Japanese to describe the suicide air squadron that was formed toward the end of WORLD WAR II. It was an allusion to the typhoon that destroyed Kublai Khan's fleet before it could invade Japan in 1281. Kamikaze pilots attempted to crash their explosives-laden planes directly into Allied targets, mainly ships; a successful strike ensured their own deaths. The first attacks occurred at LEYTE GULF in November 1944, and they became a severe threat early in 1945. They were particularly devastating to Allied ships at OKINAWA. Largely because they came into use so late in the war, when Japanese defeat was all but assured, the kamikaze was of little importance in the outcome of the war.

**Kandinsky, Wassily** *(1866–1944)* Russian painter and art theorist. Widely considered the originator of purely ABSTRACT ART, he and his works have had enormous importance in the development of 20th-century painting. Born in Moscow, he was trained there as a lawyer, but abandoned the law to study painting in Munich in 1896. Traveling to Paris, he studied the work of the neoimpressionists, Gauguin and the Fauves. He exhibited at the Salon d'Automne (1904), at the Salon des Indépendants and with the German Expressionists of DIE BRÜCKE (1907); in 1910 he founded the New Association of Munich Artists. The following year he painted his first nonrepresentational painting and articulated his ideas about the power of pure color and the relationship between art and music in his theoretical book *Concerning the Spiritual in Art* (1912). In 1911, along with Franz MARC and other artists, he founded the BLAUE REITER group. Kandinsky returned to Moscow in 1914, teaching and organizing museums and other artistic enterprises.

He settled in Germany again in 1921, taught at the BAUHAUS (1925–33) and wrote *Point and Line* (1926), a study that concentrated on the geometric in art. His paintings of the period tend to change from the brilliantly colored improvisations of his earlier work to more linear and geometrical compositions. In 1933 the Nazis closed the Bauhaus and denounced Kandinsky's art as degenerate. He moved to Paris, where he remained until his death. Kandinsky's paintings and drawings are represented in important museums throughout the world. The Solomon R. Guggenheim Museum, N.Y.C., has an especially outstanding collection of his work.

*Two kamikaze aircraft hit the USS* Bunker Hill. *1945.* (LIBRARY OF CONGRESS, PRINTS AND PHOTOGRAPHS DIVISION)

**Kanellopoulos, Panayotis** *(1902–1986)* Greek politician. Kanellopoulous was briefly prime minister of GREECE in 1945 and again in 1967, when his caretaker government was overthrown after 18 days by the military coup that ushered in a period of rule by the GREEK COLONELS.

**Kanin, Garson** *(1912–1999)* American film and stage director, actor, playwright, screenwriter and novelist. Kanin enjoyed an unusually successful and eclectic career in show business. But he is best remembered for his directorial and screenplay work in HOLLYWOOD. After working as both an actor and director on Broadway, Kanin came to Hollywood in 1938 and directed comedies including *The Great Man Votes* (1939), *Bachelor Mother* (1939), *My Favorite Wife* (1940) and *Tom, Dick and Harry* (1941). During WORLD WAR II, Kanin directed military documentaries, including collaborations with Sir Carol REED and Jean RENOIR. His play *Born Yesterday* (1946) was adapted into a successful film (1951). With wife Ruth GORDON, Kanin wrote the ACADEMY AWARD–nominated screenplay for *A Double Life* (1948). Kanin, again with Gordon, coscripted films for Katharine HEPBURN and Spencer TRACY including *Adam's Rib* (1949) and *Pat and Mike* (1952).

**Kansas City Jazz** An influential style of American "Swing" jazz in the 1930s. Its major performers included Count BASIE, Pete Johnson, Mary Lou WILLIAMS, "Big Joe" TURNER and Jay MCSHANN. Many factors made Kansas City, Mo., an active jazz center in the late 1920s and 1930s. It was a key intersection of the routes of many of the traveling bands of the time. New Orleans jazz was spreading north from the Crescent City. Locally, the notorious Pendergast political machine had created a wide-open town with many clubs and ballrooms and a large black population. "The jam session tradition really started in Kansas City," recalled Jay McShann. "You got cats from the north, south, east, and west; and everytime a new cat came to town, everybody would bring him down to the session and let him blow. It made for good times. . . ." Things really began to jump when Kansas City's leading jazz figure, Bennie Moten, absorbed the nucleus of the Blue Devils, an Oklahoma City jazz band that included bassist Walter Page, vocalist Jimmy Rushing, and pianist Count Basie. After Moten's death in 1935, the band became the Basie Band. Other groups that flourished at the time included the Andy Kirk band, Twelve Clouds of Joy. Young musicians were everywhere, at the Subway, the Reno Club, the Lone Star, the Sunset, mostly in areas around 18th and Vine. "Basie, Johnson, Williams, McShann, Turner—even the young Charlie 'Yardbird' Parker—all forged a distinctive, upbeat blues," says McShann "and we'd play all night until about six o'clock in the morning when the porter would come in to clean up. We'd just move over, do a little tastin', and then we'd start playin' again. Fellows headin' for work at that hour would come in with their lunch buckets and stay awhile. . . ." With the end of the decade, the departure for New York City of Basie and McShann, and the approaching war, the music scene declined in Kansas City, although that famous sound was now being heard worldwide.

**Kapek, Antonín** *(1922–1990)* Czechoslovakian political leader. Kapek was the chief of CZECHOSLOVAKIA's Communist Party (1969–88) for the two decades following the Soviet invasion that crushed the PRAGUE SPRING reform movement. He rose to this post through the party ranks, at one point serving as a party boss in a machine factory. Kapek welcomed the Soviet invasion in 1968 and helped carry out the purges of reformers who had taken part in the Prague Spring movement under Alexander DUBČEK. In February 1990, following the "velvet revolution" that returned Czechoslovakia to democracy, Kapek was expelled from the Czechoslovak Communist Party. He apparently committed suicide.

**Kapitsa, Pyotr Leonidovich** *(1894–1984)* Soviet physicist. Educated at Leningrad and at Cambridge (under Lord RUTHERFORD), Kapitsa was assistant director of research in magnetism at the Cavendish Laboratory (1924–32) and Messel Research Professor at the Royal Society's Mond Laboratory (1932–35). He did important work on the magnetic and electrical properties of substances at low temperatures and also designed an improved plant for the liquefaction of hydrogen and helium. Kapitsa was detained in the USSR in 1935, but later became director of the Institute for Physical Problems at the Academy of Sciences in Moscow. He was awarded the Stalin Prize for physics (1941 and 1943), and held the Order of Lenin. He was elected a Fellow of the Royal Society of Great Britain in 1929, the first foreigner in 200 years to gain membership. Kapitsa received the NOBEL PRIZE in physics (1978) in recognition of his lifetime scientific achievements. He was a strong advocate of the free exchange of scientific information.

**Kaplan, Henry** *(1918–1984)* American radiologist. Kaplan's pioneering work in research treatment was responsible for making Hodgkin's Disease one of the most curable forms of cancer. He was coinventor, with Edward Ginzton, of the **linear accelerator,** which enabled patients with cancer to receive high-dose radiation therapy. In 1969 he became the first physician to receive the Atoms for Peace prize, and in 1972 he was the first radiologist elected to the National Academy of Sciences.

**Kapler, Aleksei Y.** *(1904–1979)* Soviet screenwriter. Kapler was best known for his prewar films about LENIN, *Lenin in October* and *Lenin in 1918.* In 1943 he was sent into internal exile by Joseph STALIN, spending five of those years in Soviet prison camps (see GULAG).

**Kapp Putsch** Nationalist conspiracy hatched by right-wing German politician and journalist Wolfgang Kapp (1868–1922), aimed at setting Kapp up as chancellor and restoring the monarchy. Supported by Erich LUDENDORFF and backed by General von Luttwitz (1859–1942) and his troops, the putsch occurred on May 13, 1920, when Luttwitz and his men took BERLIN and proclaimed a new government with Kapp at its head. The government of the WEIMAR REPUBLIC fled and quickly called a general strike, which, along with a lack of foreign support, soon destroyed Kapp's abortive regime. The putsch revealed the discontent and nationalism that seethed beneath the republican government's surface and was to find expression in the later triumph of Adolf HITLER.

**Karachi** Pakistani seaport. When the independent nation of PAKISTAN was created in 1947, Karachi was its first capital; in 1959, the capital was moved to Rawalpindi (later renamed Islamabad). The city was bombed and shelled during the INDO-PAKISTANI WAR OF 1971. Muhammad Ali JINNAH, the founder of Pakistan, is buried here.

**Karadžić, Radovan** *(1945–   )* Serbian politician and leader of the Bosnian Serbs. Karadžić graduated with a degree in psychiatry from the University of Sarajevo and eventually worked in local hospitals and as the sports psychiatrist for the Sarajevo soccer team.

At the end of the 1980s, Karadžić abandoned psychiatry for politics to found the Serbian Democratic Party, dedicated to defending the interests of Serbs within Bosnia and Herzegovina. Karadžić's party did well in the national elections held in November 1990, winning enough of the votes to be invited to form a coalition government under Alija IZETBEGOVIĆ, the head of a Muslim political party. But the coalition broke down in 1991 as CROATIA, SLOVENIA and Macedonia announced plans to secede from the federation and form independent states. When the Muslim community of Bosnia began to voice similar sentiments, Karadžić announced that if Bosnia and Herzegovina declared its independence, the Bosnian Serbs would secede and unite with Serbia. When a referendum held throughout the province in April 1992

favored independence from Yugoslavia, an ethnic-based civil war broke out among the Croats, Muslims and Serbs within Bosnia. By the end of that year Serb forces controlled approximately 70% of Bosnia and Herzegovina, and Karadžić became the self-appointed president of the Republika Srpska, a Serb republic within Bosnia's borders.

Karadžić's alleged maltreatment of Bosnian Muslims and Croats within the area he administered led to his indictment for war crimes in 1995 by a tribunal established by the UNITED NATIONS. Slobodan MILOŠEVIĆ, the leader of Serbia, promptly replaced Karadžić as the chief Bosnian Serb negotiator at the Dayton Conference in the U.S. that sought a negotiated settlement of the conflict in Bosnia. In July of 1996, a year after the DAYTON ACCORDS had established a power-sharing arrangement among the country's Muslim, Serb, and Croat factions, the war crimes tribunal issued an international warrant for Karadžić's arrest. Karadžić went underground to escape arrest, and has not been found.

**Karajan, Herbert von** *(1908–1989)* Austrian-born opera and symphonic conductor. Karajan's phenomenal musical gifts, flair for media exploitation, dramatic platform manner and controversial political associations made him into an international celebrity. Karajan was born in Salzburg and studied conducting under Bernhard Paumgartner.

*Conductor Herbert von Karajan* (LIBRARY OF CONGRESS, PRINTS AND PHOTOGRAPHS DIVISION)

From 1928 to 1935 he conducted at Ulm, and from 1938 to 1944 he served as music director at Aachen, the youngest appointed conductor in Germany. A member of the Nazi Party, he remained in Germany during WORLD WAR II, and his career was championed by GOEBBELS. He was "denazified" in 1947 but political opprobrium, particularly in the U.S. and in Israel, dogged him the rest of his days. His peak creative period came with the Berlin Philharmonic Orchestra from 1955 to 1989 and with his many operatic performances in Milan and Vienna. Alternating a staggering series of recordings with a globe-trotting lifestyle, he was astute in exploiting the possibilities of every available medium: stereo LP record, film, television, video, and compact disc. He brought the famous juicy string sound and the burnished brass timbres of his orchestra to many recorded sets of Beethoven and Brahms symphonies, numerous Italian operas, and the lush sonorities of Richard STRAUSS and Peter Tchaikovsky. Despite a notorious ego and driving temperament, he was totally devoted to music, molding the BPO into the front rank of world ensembles.

**Karamanlis, Constantine** See Constantine CARAMANLIS.

**Kardiner, Abram** *(1891–1981)* Pychoanalyst. A student-patient of Sigmund FREUD for six months in 1921, Kardiner cofounded the first psychoanalytic training school in the U.S., the New York Psychiatric Institute (1930). He was a leading proponent of the so-called environmental school of psychiatry, which stressed the importance of social conditions to human behavior. In addition to several scholarly works, he wrote a popular account of psychoanalytical apprenticeship titled *My Analysis with Freud* (1977).

**Karelia (Karelian Autonomous Soviet Socialist Republic)** Former autonomous republic in the USSR's RSFSR, stretching from Finland to the White Sea and from the Kola Peninsula south to the Vologdia and Leningrad oblasts. As a result of the RUSSO-FINNISH WAR OF 1939–40 the western part, which had shared Finland's history, had nearly all of its territory absorbed by the Karelo-Finnish Soviet

Socialist Republic (as it was known from 1940 to 1956). Finns and Germans occupied Karelia from 1941 to 1944 during WORLD WAR II, after which even more of the area passed to the Soviet Union. Following the Soviet Union's disintegration in December 1991, Karelia became an autonomous region of the Russian Federation.

**Karjalainen, Ahti** *(1923–1990)* Finnish politician. He was one of FINLAND's most prominent politicians in the years after World War II. Although he served as prime minister from 1962 to 1964 and again in 1970–71, he was overshadowed by the 25-year presidency of Urho KEKKONEN, who served from 1956 to 1981. Karjalainen was a leading expert on trade with the USSR. Convicted of drunk driving in 1979, he was forced out of government.

**Karlfeldt, Erik Axel** *(1864–1931)* Swedish poet. Karlfeldt's work, little known outside of Sweden, celebrates nature and the lore of the Swedish peasantry. His collections include *Vildmarks—och käleksvisor* (Songs of the wilderness and of love, 1895), *Fridolins visor* (Fridolin's songs, 1898) and *Fridolins lustgard* (Fridolin's pleasure garden, 1901). Beginning in 1907, Karlfeldt served on the Nobel Committee for literature and was subsequently offered the prize several times. He declined, becoming the first individual to do so. He was awarded the NOBEL PRIZE for literature posthumously in 1931.

**Karloff, Boris (William Pratt)** *(1887–1969)* British-born film and stage actor. One of the leading horror film actors of all time, Karloff has become indelibly identified with his role of the Monster in FRANKENSTEIN (1931), the film that made him a star. Karloff began his career on the Canadian stage and first came to HOLLYWOOD in 1921 where he worked as a bit actor in silent films throughout the decade. After his success in *Frankenstein,* Karloff became a ubiquitous figure in Hollywood horror films of the 1930s, including *The Mummy* (1932), *The Mask of Fu Manchu* (1932), the excellent *Bride of Frankenstein* (1935) and the disappointing *Son of Frankenstein* (1939). In the 1940s Karloff enjoyed a Broadway triumph as a killer on the run in the comedy *Arsenic and Old Lace.* His ca-

reer declined in the 1950s, but Karloff enjoyed a comeback in the 1960s through his roles in the Roger CORMAN films *The Raven* (1963) and *A Comedy of Terrors* (1964). His last film was *Targets* (1967).

**Karman, Theodore von** *(1881–1963)* Hungarian-American aeronautical engineer and physicist. The son of an educator, von Karman was educated at the Royal Polytechnic University at Budapest, at Göttingen and at the University of Paris. After viewing an airplane flight in Paris in 1908, he developed an interest in aeronautical engineering. Von Karman moved to the United States, accepting a post at the Guggenheim Aeronautical Laboratory at the California Institute of Technology in Pasadena, (GALCIT). He became director the following year, and with Frank MALINA in the late 1930s, he developed the facility into the beginnings of what is now NASA's JET PROPULSION LABORATORY. A pioneer in the theories of supersonic flight, von Karman later became chief consultant on the development of the Atlas, America's first operational intercontinental ballistic missile.

**Károlyi, Count Mihály** *(1875–1955)* Hungarian statesman. Born in Budapest, Károlyi was a member of an ancient aristocratic family. A liberal with a taste for reform, he entered parliament in 1905. During WORLD WAR I he was leader of the Independent Party, which supported the Allied cause. Appointed premier in 1918, he sought an armistice while attempting to mediate between political extremists of the left and right. When a republic was proclaimed in 1919, he was elected provisional president. Károlyi tried to initiate democratic reforms, but had little power. Finally, he was forced to cede the government to the communists and was supplanted by Béla KUN. He soon went into exile in England, returning to Hungary only after WORLD WAR II. He served as Hungarian ambassador to France from 1946 to 1949 but resigned in the face of disagreements with his increasingly totalitarian government. He spent his last six years as an exile in France.

**Karpov, Anatoly** *(1951– )* Soviet chess player. Karpov won the world individual championship for junior chess players in 1969, became an international grandmaster, and in 1975 became world champion. He held his title until 1985, when he was defeated by Gary KASPAROV. The two players resumed their rivalry in a championship match in 1990, and Karpov failed to regain his title. In 1993 Karpov regained the International Chess Federation title when the organization stripped it from Kasparov. Karpov lost the title in 1999 when he refused to defend it in tournament play.

**Karsavina, Tamara Platonovna** (*1885–1978*) Russian-born prima ballerina and star of Serge DIAGHILEV'S BALLETS RUSSES. The sister of **Lev Karsavin,** Karsavina made her debut in 1902 and became prima ballerina of the Maryinsky Theater in St. Petersburg. She joined the Ballets Russes at its inception in 1909 and remained closely associated with Diaghilev until his death in 1929. She had leading roles in the premieres of two of Igor STRAVINSKY'S works staged by Diaghilev in Paris. She was the first *Firebird* (1910) and the first ballerina-doll in *Petrouchka* (in which she danced with Vaslav NIJINSKY, 1911). She settled in London in 1918 and helped found the Royal Academy of Dance. After her retirement from the stage in 1933, she coached Margot FONTEYN and assisted the ROYAL BALLET.

**Karsh, Yousuf** (*1908–2002*) Armenian-born Canadian photographer. Karsh, who as a young boy survived the Turkish massacres of that country's Armenian population, immigrated to Canada in 1924 and established his first photographic studio in Ottawa in 1932. Karsh soon established himself as a leading portrait photographer of the great political, scientific and cultural figures of the age. In 1941, Karsh achieved popular fame for his striking portrait of a fierce-looking Winston S. CHURCHILL in *Life* magazine; Karsh elicited the expression from Churchill by snatching his cigar just before taking the picture. Karsh's photographs were collected in three volumes—*Faces of Destiny* (1946), *Portraits of Greatness* (1959), and *Karsh Portraits* (1976). *Search for Greatness* (1962) was his autobiography.

**Karzai, Hamid** (*1957–   *) Leader of AFGHANISTAN (2001–   ). Born in KANDAHAR, Karzai was the son of Abdul Ahad Karzai, head of the Popozai, a large Pashtun tribe, and legislator under the monarchy of Mohammed Zahir Shah. After the Soviet invasion of Afghanistan in 1979, Karzai's father moved his family to the town of Quetta in PAKISTAN. Karzai received his university education in India and returned to join the Popolzai resistance to the Soviet occupation.

After the Soviet withdrawal Karzai served as deputy foreign minister (1992–94) in the government in KABUL that attempted to unite the various MUJAHIDEEN rebel factions that had fought against the Soviet occupation. Initially, Karzai supported the TALIBAN'S efforts in the mid-1990s to unite the warlords throughout Afghanistan under one centralized government. However, he and his father soon became open critics of the Taliban, which he believed was controlled by the government in Pakistan. Following his father's assassination in 1999, which many believed was ordered by the Taliban, Hamid Karzai became chief of the Popolzai. In October 2001, following the terrorist attacks on the U.S. on SEPTEMBER 11, 2001, Karzai convened a "Loya Jirga," or grand council, in an effort to establish a new Afghan government independent of the Taliban. His activities brought him to the attention of the U.S. government as its military forces toppled the Taliban in 2001. After occupying the country, the Americans appointed Karzai interim leader of Afghanistan. In July 2002 the newly constituted Loya Jirga of Afghanistan elected him president for two years. He was reelected in a nationwide popular election in 2004. As leader of Afghanistan he has attempted to solicit substantial U.S. economic and military aid to rebuild the shattered country while attempting to avoid accusations of being subservient to American foreign policy interests.

**Kasavubu, Joseph** (*1910–1969*) President (1960–65) of the Republic of the Congo (now Democratic Republic of the CONGO). Mayor of Léopoldville (Kinshasa) in 1957, when the Belgian Congo became independent in 1960, Kasavubu became the first president, with LUMUMBA as prime minister. He remained in office during the civil war over the KATANGA secession until 1965, when he was replaced by MOBUTU following a military coup.

**Kasdan, Lawrence** (*1948–   *) American film director, producer and screenplay writer. Kasdan, who was educated at the University of Michigan, began his career as an advertising copywriter before selling his first screenplay in 1977. That same year, his screenplay for the film *Continental Divide* (1981) was purchased by Steven SPIELBERG, who recommended Kasdan to George LUCAS, who in turn hired Kasdan to write the screenplays for the blockbuster films *The Empire Strikes Back* (1980), *Raiders of the Lost Ark* (1981) and *The Return of the Jedi* (1983). Kasdan also emerged in the 1980s as a first-rate director with films including *Body Heat* (1981), *The Big Chill* (1983) and *The Accidental Tourist* (1988), all of which were written or cowritten by Kasdan as well. Throughout the 1990s Kasdan continued to direct dramas, such as *The Bodyguard* (1992), *Wyatt Earp* (1994) and *Mumford* (1999).

**Kashmir** Territory (approximately 85,800 square miles) located mainly in INDIA, bordering PAKISTAN, and whose control has long been disputed by those two states. In 1947 the region of Kashmir was partitioned between the newly created states of India (predominantly Hindu), which received about 38,800 square miles, and Pakistan (predominantly Muslim), which obtained a lesser portion of roughly 30,500 square miles. The division of this region was decided upon by the departing British colonial authorities to ensure that India would have adequate control over the Indus River, a vital waterway that flows through Kashmir. However, the separation from the Muslim state of Pakistan of the part of Kashmir assigned to India angered some fundamentalist Muslim residents, who demanded that they be allowed to secede and unite with Pakistan. Not long after the Hindu maharaja of Kashmir, Sir Hari Singh, refused their request, Pakistan attempted to take the region by force. The result was the first of many wars between India and Pakistan. While UN peace efforts secured a cease-fire by January 1949, they failed to produce a political settlement for Kashmir. The region suffered border skirmishes between the forces and supporters of both states in 1965, 1971, 1989 and 1990. A similarly violent response followed the Indian government's efforts in 1998 to hold elections in Jammu and Kashmir (as the Indian-controlled portion of the Kashmir region is called officially), as Muslim separatists responded to the scheduled vote with bombings throughout the regional capital of Srinagar and near polling stations. In response, the Indian government dispatched troops to the region and used coercive force to prompt many citizens to cast their ballots. In the 1996 election the National Conference, a party that advocated greater autonomy for Kashmir within India, acquired a decisive majority of the contested positions at the ballot box. However, even after the 1996 elections, violence continued to break out as a result of increasing Muslim-Hindu tensions, such as the seizing of the Srinagar Hotel in Kashmir by militant members of the pro-Muslim terrorist group Lashkar-e-Tabia, which took hostages in the hotel. In an ensuing gunfight that ended on August 28, 2003, the militants were forced from the hotel by Indian security forces in an engagement that killed two civilians and four terrorists.

**Kasparov, Gary (Garik Weinstein)** (*1963–   *) Russian chess master. Born in Baku, the capital of Soviet Azerbaijan, Kasparov took on a Russianized version of his maternal family's name after his father's death in 1970. A chess prodigy, he was solving complex chess problems at six and represented the USSR at chess tournaments abroad by the age of 13. He became Soviet champion at 18 and world champion at 22, beating his arch-rival, the Russian grandmaster Anatoly KARPOV. A bold, passionate player, Kasparov also brought his passion to bear as a political dissident, actively opposing Soviet communism in the late 1980s. His many championship matches with Karpov have been seen as contests between the old-style Soviet regime as represented by Karpov and the radical change sweeping the USSR as personified by Kasparov. In 1989 he and many of his family members were forced to flee the ethnic strife in Baku. Since then he has used Moscow as a home base. Traveling to various Western cities, he promotes chess in an attempt to make the game a popular international sport and continues to criticize the communist system. He again de-

feated Karpov in an international match in 1990–91. In 1993 the International Chess Federation stripped Kasparov of his title after he helped to create the rival Professional Chess Association.

**Kassem, Abdul Karim** (*1914–1963*) Iraqi general and political leader. Born in Baghdad, he was trained in military institutions and became a career officer. He distinguished himself by his bravery in warfare against the KURDS and in the Palestine war (1948). Kassem was instrumental in the coup of July 1985 that overthrew King FAISAL II, and he became prime minister of the new republic that replaced the monarchy. He put down a communist uprising the following year, but his powers steadily waned, and he was overthrown in the BA'ATH Party coup of February 1963 and subsequently executed.

**Kasserine Pass (Al-Kasrayn, Al-Qasrayn)** Mountain pass in Tunisia's Grand Dorsal chain, 130 miles southwest of Tunis, the scene of a decisive tank battle during the NORTH AFRICAN CAMPAIGN in WORLD WAR II. Driven westward into Tunisia after the German defeat by the British at EL ALAMEIN, German field marshal Erwin ROMMEL regrouped his forces and launched a daring counterattack. Tanks of his Afrika Korps captured the Kasserine Pass early on February 22, 1943. Four days later, however, U.S. forces under Gen. George S. PATTON dealt the Afrika Korps a mortal blow and recaptured the pass. This spelled the end of German domination of North Africa.

**Katanga Revolt** (*1960–1963*) On the granting of Congo independence by Belgium, the province of Katanga—encouraged by Union Minière, a company with exclusive mining rights in the copper- and uranium-rich province—seceded from Congo on July 11, 1960, under Moise TSHOMBE. Using a white mercenary army to resist United Nations attempts to restore order, the Katanga rebellion lasted until January 14, 1963.

**Kateyev, Valentin Petrovich** (*1897–1986*) Soviet novelist and playwright. Among members of the older generation of Soviet writers, Kateyev was un-

usual in that he generally managed to avoid trouble with the Soviet authorities, while at the same time winning the respect of Western critics of Soviet literature. His reputation in the West rested largely on his lively satirical works dating from the 1920s, before SOCIALIST REALISM had become firmly entrenched as the dominant literary mode.

**Katona, George** (*1901–1981*) Hungarian-born economist and psychologist. Often called the dean of behavioral economists, Katona was the first to apply the study of consumer attitudes to economic forecasting. He taught at the University of Michigan (1946–72) and wrote more than a dozen books, including *The Mass Consumption Society.*

**Katrina, Hurricane** The costliest natural disaster in the history of the U.S., and one of the deadliest as well, the 2005 hurricane crossed southern Florida before gaining strength over the Gulf of Mexico and eventually making landfall along the coastlines of Louisiana, Mississippi and Alabama. The resulting storm surge broke the levees that separated Lake Ponchartrain from New Orleans, resulting in a massive flood that covered 80% of the city and surrounding neighborhoods. Many were caught off guard by the seriousness of the situation, which in the aftermath included more than 1,600 people dead, thousands of homes destroyed or damaged, 3 million people without electricity and an estimated $75 billion in overall damages.

**Katyn** Village in west-central Russia, approximately 12 miles west of Smolensk. Katyn was captured by the Germans in August 1941, during WORLD WAR II. On April 14, 1943, they announced the discovery of a mass grave of approximately 4,250 Polish officers in the woods near the village; the officers had all been tied and shot through the head. The Germans accused the Soviets of having murdered the soldiers in 1940, when the area had been under Soviet occupation. In 1944 a Soviet commission accused the Nazis of the crime. The International Red Cross tried to investigate the incident but was denied access to the site. In 1951–52, a U.S. congressional commission concluded that the Soviets were indeed responsible; in

1990, during the era of GLASNOST, the Soviets finally admitted culpability for the Katyn massacre. The Poles had apparently been among the cream of the Polish officer corps and, as such, had been marked for liquidation by STALIN.

**Kauffer, Edward McKnight** *(1890–1954)* American artist and graphic designer best known for his posters, especially those designed while he was living in England from 1914 until 1940. Kauffer studied painting in Paris, but came to notice in the 1930s for his poster designs beginning with an assignment by Frank Pick for the London Underground (subway). His book *The Art of the Poster* appeared in 1924 and his work in the field, using strong typography along with abstracted but recognizable illustrative imagery, was widely exhibited and received a variety of awards. He also designed books and book jackets. In 1940–41 he produced several graphic designs for the New York MUSEUM OF MODERN ART. He became inactive after the early 1940s, having designed over 250 posters and 150 book jackets.

**Kaufman, George S.** *(1889–1961)* American journalist, playwright and director. A towering influence on the American theater, Kaufman is also remembered for his caustic wit evident in his writing and his participation in the legendary Algonquin Round Table. Kaufman's plays include *Jacques Duval* (1920), *The Forty-niners* (1922) and *The Butter and Egg Man* (1925). He also collaborated on many succesful plays with Edna FERBER and Moss HART, among others. His collaborations include *Dinner at Eight* (1932), *The Man Who Came to Dinner* (1939) and *Ninotchka* (1955). Kaufman was responsible for the production of 45 Broadway shows, many of which were adapted for film. He also directed classics such as *The Front Page* (1928), *Guys and Dolls* (1950), which he co-wrote and *Romanoff and Juliet* (1957).

**Kaunda, Kenneth** *(1924–  )* President of ZAMBIA (1964–91). Kaunda led the United Nationalist Independence Party in opposition to the Federation of Rhodesia and Nyasaland in 1960, which resulted in the end of the federation. Appointed prime minister of Northern Rhodesia in 1964 and having supervised the constitutional arrangements that won his country independence, he became president of Zambia 10 months later. Kaunda sought to hold in check militants opposed to the Ian SMITH regime in Rhodesia, but his strong hostility to racism led to periods of tension with Britain over this and other issues. He assumed autocratic powers in 1972 to prevent total breakup but, after a new constitution in 1973, his presidency was confirmed. He remained one of the most respected leaders of Africa and the Commonwealth, although by 1990 he faced significant internal opposition. In 1991 Kaunda yielded to calls for free presidential elections, which he lost to the Movement for Multiparty Democracy's candidate, Frederick Chiluba.

**Kautsky, Karl Johann** *(1854–1938)* German socialist theorist. Born in Prague, he joined the Social Democratic Party in Vienna in 1875 and became private secretary to communist theorist Friedrich Engels in 1881. A loyal Marxist, he was founder and editor of the left-wing journal *Die neue Zeit* (1883–1917). He was largely responsible for the Erfurt program (1891), which linked the German Social Democratic Party with revolutionary Marxism, and he was a consistent opponent of Eduard Bernstein and his revisionist theories. Opposed to Germany's entry into World War I, he and Hugo Haase formed the Independent Social Democratic Party (1917–22). He bitterly denounced the BOLSHEVIKS in Russia, condemning their revolution (1917) as undemocratic and anti-Marxist. Kautsky settled in Vienna, where he rejoined the Social Democrats, living there until the eye of the Nazi occupation, when he fled (1938) to Holland. He was a prolific writer whose works include *The Economic Doctrines of Karl Marx* (tr. 1925) and *Ethics and the Materialist Conception of History* (tr. 1907). He also edited a four-volume history of the origins of World War I (1919).

**Kawabata, Yasunari** *(1899–1972)* Japanese author and playwright. Kawabata early evidenced his literary talent as a founder of an avant garde literary journal, *Bungei Jidai*, an advocate of the Neo-Sensualist movement. He experimented with surrealistic techniques, but his best-known works are more traditional in style and characterized by a nostalgic despondency tinged with eroticism. Kawabata's numerous works include the novels *Izu no odoriko* (1925, translated as *The Izu Dancer* 1964), *Yaukiguni* (1937, translated as *Snow Country* 1957) and *Sembazuru* (1959, translated as *Thousand Cranes* 1959); he has also written short stories, plays and criticism. Kawabata was awarded the NOBEL PRIZE in literature in 1968. He committed suicide in 1972.

**Kay, Hershy** *(1919–1981)* American orchestrator, composer and arranger. Kay is best known for his ballet scores, many of which were commissioned by George BALANCHINE. He also made arrangements of Leonard BERNSTEIN's musicals and orchestrated popular Broadway shows such as *Evita, A Chorus Line* and *Barnum*.

**Kaye, Danny (David Daniel Kaminski)** *(1913–1987)* American comic actor and entertainer. Kaye became famous in 1940 in the Broadway show *Lady in the Dark*. His HOLLYWOOD film career began with *Up in Arms* (1944) and peaked with his acclaimed performance as *Hans Christian Andersen* (1952). His comic gifts were best displayed in *The Secret Life of Walter Mitty* (1947), in which he played a bumbling daydreamer. Beginning with a series of sold-out appearances at the London Palladium in 1948, he became perhaps the most popular American entertainer in postwar Britain. In the 1960s he hosted *The Danny Kaye Show* on U.S. television; later, he was known largely for his comic performances that raised millions of dollars for the United Nations International Children's Emergency Fund (UNICEF), and also for his burlesque conducting of symphony orchestras to benefit musicians' pension funds.

**Kaye, Nora (Nora Koreff)** *(1920–1987)* American ballerina. Kaye was the first American dramatic ballerina to acquire an international reputation. She joined the AMERICAN BALLET THEATER (ABT) at its inception in 1939, and was primarily associated with this company. She also danced with the NEW YORK CITY BALLET. During her career some two dozen ballets were created for her. Prominent among these were Antony TUDOR's *Pillar of Fire* (1942) and Agnes DeMILLE's *Fall River Legend* (1948). Kaye retired from the dance stage in 1961, but subsequently worked with her husband, director-choreographer **Herbert Ross,** on several dance films, including *The Turning Point* (1977).

**Kaye, Sammy** *(1910–1987)* U.S. bandleader. During the Swing Era of the 1940s, Kaye led one of the country's most popular "sweet bands." A bandleader for over 50 years, he had more than 100 hit records. His band was particularly popular during World War II, when it performed live on Kaye's long-running radio show *Sunday Serenade.*

**Kaysone Phomvihane** *(1925–1992)* Laotian communist leader, prime minister of LAOS (1975). The son of a Vietnamese civil servant and a Laotian woman, Kaysone Phomvihane attended a lycée and law school in Hanoi. He was reputedly taught by the Vietnamese revolutionary, General VO NGUYEN GIAP. In 1955 he was a cofounder of the Laotian Communist Party, which he has since led. During the American bombing of Laos (approximately 1964–73), a part of the VIETNAM WAR, and for a couple of years thereafter, he and other PATHET LAO leaders lived in caves near the Vietnamese border. In 1975 he became prime minister of the newly formed Lao People's Democratic Republic. Kaysone held the position of prime minister until his death in 1992.

**Kazakhstan** Predominantly Muslim territory of the Russian Empire (1880–1917), autonomous period under Bolshevik rule (1917–28), constituent member of the Union of Soviet Socialist Republics (USSR, 1928–91) and independent state (1991–  ). Originally acquired during the period of Russian imperial expansion in the 19th century, the area now encompassing Kazakhstan was conquered by Russia in an effort to expand its commercial influence and political control throughout Central Asia. In the early 20th century, Russian rule brought with it an influx of Slavic migrations and settlements, which soon began to constrict the nomadic lifestyle of the native Kazakhs. The friction resulting from the inevitable clashes of culture reached a crescendo in mid-1916 when, in an effort to improve industrial military output during WORLD WAR I, Russian authorities forced the recruitment of Kazakhs into work units. By August 1916, the Kazakhs, as well as the other peoples of Central Asia, had organized a revolt against this practice, and began to massacre nearby Russian settlers, prompting similar attacks by Russian forces against Kazakhs.

By November 1917, when the Bolsheviks seized power in Petrograd and began to create a state based on the rule of the Communist Party, the Kazakhs attempted to gain greater independence from Russian rule. The Alash Orda, a nationalist Kazakh political party formed to achieve this greater autonomy, collaborated with the "Red" Bolshevik forces in their struggle against the "White" anti-Bolshevik and anti-Communist state during the RUSSIAN CIVIL WAR (1918–20). In return the Alash Orda received promises that under Bolshevik rule, the Kazakhs would continue to enjoy the substantial autonomy they now exercised. When the war ended, the Bolsheviks drew borders for the Kazakhs similar to those now in existence, and established Kazakhstan as an Autonomous Socialist Republic. Two years later the borders were changed as Kazakhstan was amalgamated with other territories into the Kirgiz Autonomous Soviet Socialist Republic (ASSR), a founding member of the new USSR, renamed the Kazakh ASSR in 1925 and the Kazakh Soviet Socialist Republic in 1936. By 1928 the autonomy that the Kazakhs had experienced under Soviet rule began to disappear, as Soviet leader Joseph STALIN began to remove indigenous leaders from power, and later murdered many of them in the 1930s. Stalin also instituted collectivized agriculture in the region and forced the nomadic Kazakhs to settle on large combined farms. More than a million Kazakhs died of starvation because of the decline in food output under this system. Nikita KHRUSHCHEV ended the Stalinist purges and increased agrarian cultivation of land in the northern Kazakh region. But projects initiated under Khrushchev and his successor, Leonid BREZHNEV, such as the Baikonur Cosmodrome (the major Soviet space center) and the development of the region's industry, led to fresh arrivals of Russians into Kazakh society that caused a renewal of ethnic tensions.

In 1989, Soviet leader Mikhail GORBACHEV's policy of GLASNOST, or "openness," led to major changes in the Kazakh S.S.R. Gorbachev removed the Russian head of the Communist Party in Kazakhstan and replaced him with Nursultan A. Nazarbayev, an ethnic Kazakh. In December 1991 the Kazakh parliament voted to secede from the crumbling USSR, and establish Kazakhstan as an independent republic with Nazarbayev as president. In 1995 a conflict erupted between Nazarbayev and the parliament, the Supreme Kenges. When the country's Constitutional Court ruled that recent legislative elections were illegitimate, Nazarbayev dissolved the Supreme Kenges. Despite vigorous protests from the legislators, Nazarbayev eventually won the contest of wills when he gained an extension of his term in office from 1996 to 2000. He also won popular approval of his proposed new constitution, which increased the powers of the executive and created a bicameral legislature that soon came under the domination of Nazarbayev's supporters. Nazarbayev himself won reelection in 1999, despite complaints of noting irregularities in the earlier than expected election.

While Nazarbayev and his new constitution gained the support of most Kazakhs and the large Russian minority, a few extremists within both ethnic groups—those demanding Russia's annexation of northern Kazakhstan and those demanding the expulsion of all non-Muslims from the country—have caused several outbreaks of civil unrest. However, most of the country has favored cooperation with Russia, such as occurred with the transfer of Soviet-era nuclear weapons to Russian control in 1995 and with the Kazakh-Russian agreement jointly to develop and transport Kazakhstan's oil resources. Nazarbayev was reelected in a landslide victory in 2005.

**Kazan, Elia (Elia Kazanjoglous)** *(1909–2003)* American stage and film director. He was born in Istanbul, Turkey, to Greek parents. He immigrated to the U.S. in 1913, acted with New York's Group Theater in the 1930s and became a founding member

| KAZAKHSTAN | |
|---|---|
| 1920 | Kazakhstan becomes an autonomous republic within the USSR. |
| 1936 | Kazakh Autonomous Soviet Socialist Republic [ASSR] achieves status as full republic of the Soviet Union. |
| 1930s | More than a million in Kazakhstan die in Stalin's campaign of forced collectivization. |
| 1953–64 | "Virgin Lands" policy of Khrushchev brings more Russian settlers to cultivate former grazing lands. |
| 1955 | Baikonur launch site at Turatam for Soviet rockets is selected, and construction begins. |
| 1991 | With the fall of Soviet Union, Kazakhstan achieves independence. Nursultan Nazarbayev becomes president. |
| 1995 | Constitutional crisis after Constitutional Court declares 1994 elections void, suspending parliament. Nazarbayev rules by decree, obtains referendum approval extending his term to 2000, and pushes through a new constitution giving himself greater powers and replacing Kenges with a new bicameral legislature. Last of the nuclear warheads in Kazakhstan are transferred to Russia. |
| 1997 | Capital is moved from Almaty to Akmola. |
| 1999 | Nazarbayev wins 81.7% of the votes for presidency in an election whose conduct is denounced by Organization for Security and Cooperation in Europe. |
| 2001 | The first major pipeline for transporting oil from the region to world markets connects the Tengiz oil field in western Kazakhstan to the Russian Black Sea port of Novorossiysk. |
| 2005 | Nazarbayev is reelected president by a wide margin. |

of the Actors' Studio. Kazan was especially acclaimed for his powerful and realistic direction of the plays of Tennessee WILLIAMS, such as *A Streetcar Named Desire* (1947), and Arthur MILLER, such as DEATH OF A SALESMAN (1948). Among his many other stage successes were *The Skin of Our Teeth* (1942), *All My Sons* (1947) and *Tea and Sympathy* (1953). His films include *Gentleman's Agreement* (1947), *A Streetcar Named Desire* (1951), *On the Waterfront* (1954) and *East of Eden* (1955). Also a writer, he directed two films adapted from his own novels, *America, America* (1963) and *The Arrangement* (1969). More recently, he was the author of *The Anatolian* (1983), *An American Odyssey* (1989) and an autobiography, *A Life* (1988). KAZAN was criticized by some of his former friends and colleagues for naming former members of the Communist Party during a congressional investigation into subversive activities. In 1999 he received an honorary Oscar for his films from the Motion Picture Academy of America.

**Kazantzakis, Nikos** *(1883–1957)* Greek author. Considered modern Greece's greatest novelist, Kazantzakis was also one of the most controversial writers of his time. He was a philosophical writer greatly influenced by his teacher Henri BERGSON, Nietzschean theory and his birthplace of Crete. The latter became the central metaphor of his art, representing the dynamic of thesis, antithesis and final synthesis that he called the *Cretan Glance*. He gained international recognition with his novel *Zorba the Greek* (1946; tr. 1952). Other major works include the novels *Freedom or Death* (1954) and *The Last Temptation of Christ* (1960), and the epic poem *Odyseia* (1938; tr. *The Odyssey: A Modern Sequel,* 1958).

**Kazin, Alfred** *(1915–1998)* American critic. Born in Brooklyn, N.Y., he attended City College and Columbia University. His influential critical study of American prose, *On Native Grounds* (1942), established him as one of America's most important literary critics. Among his other critical works are *The Inmost Leaf* (1955), *Contemporaries* (1962), *Bright Book of Life* (1973) and *A Writer's America* (1988). A noted edi-

tor, teacher and memoirist, he is also the author of an evocative autobiographical trilogy, *Walker in the City* (1951), *Starting Out in the Thirties* (1965) and *New York Jew* (1978).

**Keaton, Buster (Joseph Francis Keaton)** *(1895–1966)* American motion picture actor and producer. Keaton is considered one of the Big Five SILENT FILM actor-comedians, with Charles CHAPLIN, Douglas FAIRBANKS, Sr., Harry LANGDON, and Harold LLOYD. He was born in Piqua, Kansas, to a family of medicine show performers. His skills at rough-and-tumble acrobatic comedy—magician Harry HOUDINI dubbed him "Buster"—led to his first series of one-reel films with rotund funnyman Roscoe "Fatty" ARBUCKLE in 1917. Two years later Keaton teamed up with producer Joseph M. Schenck and for the next decade produced his finest work, numerous shorts and feature films that rank among the greatest of all silent-screen comedies. Many of the important Keaton themes emerged at this time— the dogged determination and triumph of "the little man" (*Our Hospitality,* 1923); the world as reality, fantasy and dream (shorts like *The Playhouse,* 1921, and features like *Sherlock, Jr.,* 1924); and man's uneasy relationship with machines (*The Navigator,* 1925, and *The General,* 1927). Contrasting with the ready grin of Fairbanks and Lloyd and the eager pathos of Chaplin and Langdon, Keaton's face was a mutely expressive mask, with barely a twitch of an eyelash to betray inner thoughts and feelings. Coupled to that face was a superbly coordinated body that contributed to chases and falls and a hair-raising sense of speed and danger (see the long, concluding chase in *Seven Chances,* 1925). In 1928 Keaton relinquished his customary complete control over his work and began releasing his pictures through MGM. A long decline began, further troubled by alcoholism and emotional and marital instability. Aside from a few flashes of his comic genius—some gag writing on Red Skeleton films in the 1940s and a brief appearance with Chaplin in *Limelight* (1952)—he lapsed into obscurity. It was not until the late 1950s that a worldwide revival of interest in his work began at film festi-

vals and on college campuses. At the time of his death from cancer in 1966, he was again acclaimed one of the masters of motion picture comedy.

**Keck, George Fred** *(1895–1980)* American modernist architect who built a significant reputation in the 1930s before MODERNISM became widely accepted. Keck first won recognition as the designer of the futuristic House of Tomorrow in a village of model homes at the CENTURY OF PROGRESS EXHIBITION in Chicago in 1933. The house was a twelve-faceted, all-glass-walled circular pavilion placed on top of a base that included services, garage, and a hangar for the family airplane! At the 1934 fair Keck provided his Crystal House, also with walls of glass and a strikingly modern interior. His work thereafter for private clients was largely residential, including many midwestern houses of simple modern design. Most of his designs emphasized the concept of the solar house, which Keck developed by carefully studying patterns of the sun's path so that a maximum of winter sun aided heating and a minimum of summer sun penetrated the houses' windows. Orientation and placement of windows and overhangs for shading were planned to give maximum comfort and energy economy. It can be said that Keck is a precursor of the interest in solar heating that began in the 1970s.

**Keeling Islands** See COCOS ISLANDS.

**Kees, Weldon** *(1914–1955?)* American author, painter and composer. Though virtually unknown during his lifetime, Kees wrote jazz compositions, did some painting and wrote fiction and poetry. Among his best known poems are "The Beach in August," "Early Winter" and "River Song." His fictional satire of scholarly life, *Fall Quarter,* originally written in the 1930s, was published in 1990. He disappeared in 1955 and is presumed a suicide.

**Kefauver, Carey Estes** *(1903–1963)* American politician. A Democratic U.S. congressman from Tennessee (1939–49), he was elected to the U.S. Senate in 1948. He gained national fame with the Kefauver Crime Committee (1950–51). In 1956 Kefauver ran unsuccessfully as the Democratic vice presidential candidate (with Adlai STEVENSON). He was the author of *Crime in America* (1951).

## Kefauver investigation (1950–51)

Televised U.S. Senate hearings into organized crime, chaired by Senator Estes KEFAUVER of Tennessee. The Senate Special Committee to Investigate Crime in Interstate Commerce called hundreds of witnesses, including reputed mob bosses, corrupt policemen and politicians. The hearings, which gained wide attention because they were televised, made "taking the Fifth" part of the American vernacular after one witness refused to testify "on the grounds it might tend to incriminate me." The highlight of the hearings was the testimony of mob leader Frank Costello, who agreed to testify only if his face was not shown. The cameras focused on Costello's hands during his lengthy testimony. He was later sentenced to jail for contempt and tax evasion. Testimony also implicated former New York mayor William O'Dwyer in the corruption. After the hearings' revelations, the FBI formally became involved in the fight against organized crime.

## Keillor, Garrison (1942– )

American author, humorist and creator and host of the popular radio show *A Prairie Home Companion*. Born in Anoka, Minn., Keillor received his B.A. from the University of Minnesota in 1966. While studying at that institution he gained radio experience as a staff announcer for the university's radio station. Two years after graduation he began to host a classical music program on Minnesota Public Radio in which he would often create and recite farcical commercials for products and services in the fictional town of Lake Wobegon, Minn. His ability to blend music and humor seamlessly on his classical show and his careful study of Nashville's Grand Ole Opry eventually inspired him to develop his own variety show centered around the concepts of Lake Wobegon he had already developed. Keillor's new show, *A Prairie Home Companion*, debuted in 1974 with an audience among the Midwestern listeners of 30 radio stations. In 1979 Keillor's program received national attention when it was broadcast coast to coast during a national radio promotion.

The formation of American Public Radio (later renamed Public Radio International) propelled Keillor and his *Prairie Home* companion show to an even wider national audience. When the nationwide network of public radio stations was created in 1982, *Prairie Home Companion* was broadcast on more than 200 stations by the time of Keillor's brief retirement from radio in 1987, earning him a 1981 Peabody Award and a 1987 Grammy Award in the process. Two years later Keillor returned to radio with *American Radio Company of the Air,* a more cosmopolitan version of *Prairie Home* companion broadcast from New York City, until it moved to St. Paul, Minnesota, in 1993, resumed its original title and returned the focus of his show to the topics, music and venue he had pursued during his early days on Minnesota Public Radio.

In addition to his career in radio, Keillor also regularly writes short stories and books, including (*Lake Wobegon Days, WLT: A Radio Romance*), and *We Are Still Married.*

## Keitel, Wilhelm (1882–1946)

German field marshal. During WORLD WAR II, Keitel was chief of staff of the supreme command of German forces. On May 8, 1945, he signed the articles of surrender on behalf of the Wehrmacht. Keitel was condemned as a war criminal at the NUREMBERG TRIALS and was hanged.

## Kekkonen, Urho Kaleva (1900–1986)

Finnish diplomat and politician. A dominant figure in Finnish politics for five decades, Kekkonen was first named FINLAND's minister of justice in 1936. He later served as prime minister five times before becoming president, a post he held from 1956 to 1981. He was regarded as the chief architect of his nation's special brand of neutrality, which evolved after World War II in response to Finland's need to maintain cordial relations with the Soviet Union while forging ties with the West.

## Keldysh, Mstislav Vsevolodovich (1911–1978)

Soviet scientist and mathematician. Keldysh was president of the Soviet Academy of Sciences from 1961 to 1975. In this post, he had responsibility for development of the Soviet space program and for all national

scientific projects. His personal research was in computer science, rocketry and spacecraft.

## Keller, Charles Ernest "Charlie" (1916–1990)

American baseball player. Keller joined the New York Yankees in 1939 and quickly became their starting right fielder. Together with Joe DIMAGGIO and Tommy Henrich, he formed one of the most renowned outfields in baseball history. He later played for the Detroit Tigers. He appeared in the World Series four times, batting .306. He played 1,170 career games, with a .286 batting average. Retiring from baseball in 1952, Keller went on to a successful career as a horse breeder.

## Keller, Helen Adams (1880–1968)

American author. Keller lost her hearing and sight during an illness at 19 months of age. Under the tutelage of Anne Sullivan, she learned to speak, to use sign language, to read braille and to type. She graduated with honors from Radcliffe College in 1904. She wrote books, and made lecture tours to promote interest in the handicapped, and in the process became a world-famous inspiration for others. Her works include *The Story of My Life* (1903) and *Out of the Dark* (1913).

## Kellogg, Frank Billings (1856–1937)

American diplomat. A U.S. senator from Minnesota from 1917 to 1923, he became secretary of state in 1925 and served until 1929. He also served as special counsel for the United States and was a judge of the Permanent Court of International Justice from 1930 to 1935. He received the NOBEL PEACE PRIZE in 1929.

## Kellogg, Will Keith (1860–1951)

American philanthropist and food products manufacturer. At the age of 14 he started selling brooms for his father. Later, he and his brother, who operated the Battle Creek Sanitarium, started experimenting with prepared cereal products of different kinds. In 1906 Will began the Kellogg business in cereals and started the prepared food era in America. He retired from active participation in the firm in 1929, and established the W.K. Kellogg Foundation in Battle Creek, Michigan. He invested most of his fortune in the foundation and supported endeavors he judged to be helpful.

**Kellogg-Briand Pact** More formally known as the Pact of Paris, the agreement, signed August 27, 1928, renounced war as an instrument of national policy. The treaty, which arose out of negotiations between Aristide BRIAND, foreign minister of France, and Frank B. KELLOGG, U.S. secretary of state, called for the ratifying parties to use only peaceful means to settle disputes. By 1934 almost all the nations of the world had signed the pact, although many signed with certain limitations. Because it contained no provisions for enforcement, the pact proved ineffective. The treaty formed part of the basis for the war crime trials following World War II. (See also NUREMBERG TRIALS.)

**Kelly, Charles E.** (1920–1985) American World War II hero, popularly known as Commando Kelly. In 1943 he became the first enlisted man to receive the Medal of Honor in WORLD WAR II, for singlehandedly fighting off a German platoon in Italy in 1943. He wrote a book about his exploits, *One Man's War,* which was later made into a film.

**Kelly, Ellsworth** (1923–  ) American painter. Born in Newburgh, N.Y., Kelly studied at the Boston Museum School and the Académie des Beaux-Arts, Paris (1943–46), and continued to live in Paris until 1954. A leading exponent of HARDEDGE PAINTING, he is known for grandly proportioned canvasses composed of large areas of vivid, flat color in abstract geometric shapes. Often named for the colors they contain, his paintings include *Blue Red Green* (1962, Walker Art Center, Minneapolis) and *Green Blue Red* (1964, Whitney Museum, New York City).

**Kelly, Emmett** (1898–1979) The most familiar clown in America. Kelly's forlorn and wistful characterization of a tattered hobo delighted audiences for more than 40 years. He appeared with Ringling Brothers and Barnum & Bailey Circus from 1942 to 1956, and with the Brooklyn Dodgers baseball team in 1957. He also made numerous television appearances. He was best known for a pantomime of sweeping the spotlight away.

**Kelly, Gene** (1912–1996) American actor, dancer, choreographer, film director. Kelly was one of the great popular dancers and innovative choreographers in motion pictures. He first gained attention in the Broadway musical *Pal Joey* (1941). He starred in several film musicals, including *On the Town* (1949) and *Singin' in the Rain* (1952). His innovations as director/choreographer are best seen in the films *An American in Paris* (1951) and *Invitation to the Dance* (1956). In the latter, unsuccessful film his dance sequences with animated characters made movie history.

**Kelly, Grace** See GRACE, PRINCESS OF MONACO.

**Kelso** (1957–1983) Thoroughbred racehorse, widely considered the best racehorse of his time and one of the top American horses of the 20th century. A gelding, Kelso captured the Gold Cup and the Horse of the Year title five times, from 1960 through 1965, a record no other racehorse has ever matched. During his career, he started 63 times, won 39 races, finished second 12 times, and third twice. He retired in 1965. His total earnings held the record for 13 years; at his death, he ranked fifth on the all-time earnings list.

**Kempe, Rudolf** (1910–1976) German-born opera and symphonic conductor, one of the greatest musicians of his generation. By contrast to the high-profile gloss of Herbert von KARAJAN and the mannered technique of Leonard BERNSTEIN, Kempe was a model of consistency and technique, sublimating himself to the service of the music. He was born in Niederpoyritz near Dresden, educated at the Orchestra School of the Saxon State Orchestra, and debuted as an opera conductor in 1933 with the Leipzig Opera. After a brief service as an infantryman in WORLD WAR II, he was named to several posts, including general music director of the Saxon State Theater in Dresden (1949–52), conductor of the Bavarian State Opera in Munich (1952–54), artistic director of the Royal Philharmonic Orchestra in 1964 (after the death of Sir Thomas BEECHAM), and chief conductor of the BBC Symphony Orchestra (1975). Never as well known in the U.S. as in Europe (although he occasionally conducted at the Metropolitan Opera in New York City), he built an exemplary reputation for opera—particularly German and Italian works—and for the works of orchestral composers as various as Frederick DELIUS and Richard STRAUSS.

**Kendall, Edward Calvin** (1886–1972) American biochemist. Born in South Norwalk, Conn., Kendall earned his Ph.D. from Columbia University in 1910. From 1921 to 1951, he was a professor of physiological chemistry at the MAYO Foundation. Kendall isolated the adrenal hormone later known as cortisone, which his colleague Philip HENCH demonstrated to be effective in the treatment of rheumatoid arthritis. For this work, Kendall shared the 1950 NOBEL PRIZE for physiology or medicine with Hench and Tadeus Reichstein.

**Kendrick, Pearl L.** (1890–1980) American microbiologist. Kendrick helped develop a whooping cough vaccine in 1939. The vaccine led to the virtual eradication of this childhood illness. Kendrick also developed the standard DPT shot, which provided combined protection against diptheria, whooping cough and tetanus. She later worked as a consultant for the WORLD HEALTH ORGANIZATION (WHO) and started immunization programs in Mexico, India, Germany, the USSR, and South America.

**Kennan, George F.** (1904–2005) U.S. official and political analyst. Kennan graduated from Princeton University in 1925 and joined the diplomatic corps. After World War II, he was placed in charge of long-range policy planning for the State Department. In 1947, Kennan introduced the concept of "containment," the strategy of counteracting postwar Soviet expansionism with countermeasures aimed at preserving the status quo; Kennan believed that, in the face of vigilant, measured opposition from the West, the Soviet Union would eventually soften its foreign policy and liberalize its domestic controls. Many analysts believe that Kennan accurately predicted the outcome of the COLD WAR, more than 40 years later. Kennan went on to serve as U.S. ambassador to the Soviet Union and to Yugoslavia. In later years, he wrote and lectured widely on foreign policy. In 1989 he was awarded the Medal of Freedom.

## Kennedy, Anthony M. *(1936–   )*

Associate justice, U.S. Supreme Court (1989–   ). A native of California, Kennedy is a graduate of Stanford University, the London School of Economics and Harvard University Law School. After several years in private practice in Sacramento, California, Kennedy was appointed as a justice of the U.S. Court of Appeals for the Ninth Circuit. He was nominated to the Supreme Court by President Ronald REAGAN after Reagan's two previous nominees, Robert BORK and Douglas Ginsburg, failed to win approval. (Bork was rejected by the Senate based partly on his outspoken conservative views, while Ginsburg's nomination was withdrawn after it was revealed that he had smoked marijuana as a law student and professor.) In contrast, Justice Kennedy was confirmed without incident. On the bench Justice Kennedy was predictably conservative, generally helping to form a solid conservative bloc on the Court. However, in his first year on the Court he surprised many by siding with the liberal justices in overturning a Texas statute outlawing the desecration of the American flag on First Amendment grounds.

## Kennedy, Jacqueline (Jacqueline Kennedy Onassis; née Bouvier) *(1929–1994)*

Born into a wealthy New York family and educated at Miss Porter's School, Vassar, the Sorbonne and George Washington University, Jacqueline Bouvier was an ideal wife for politician John F. KENNEDY, whom she married in 1953. After her husband became president in 1961, the elegant First Lady, dressed in Oleg Cassini gowns, BALENCIAGA suits and the "Pillbox" hats, designed by HALSTON, was emulated by women all over the world. Utilizing her knowledge of art and antiques, she undertook a renovation of the White House that was televised in the famous "A Tour of the White House with Mrs. John F. Kennedy" in 1962. During her tenure, Mrs. Kennedy was also an able ambassador for the U.S. and traveled widely, winning support for the Kennedy administration with her youthful beauty and finishing school charm. In 1963 she was voted the most admired woman in America, suffered the death of a newborn child and the terrible assassination of her husband, shot before her eyes in Dallas, Tex. Her stoicism as a young widow with two small children, Caroline and John, further endeared her to the American public. Her subsequent marriage to the Greek shipping magnate Aristotle ONASSIS in 1968 surprised her loyal fans. After his death in 1975, she established herself as an editor at the Doubleday publishing house in New York City and then led a quiet life out of the public spotlight. She remained, however, a mysterious and fascinating figure to many and an enduring symbol of style and sophistication. She died of cancer in 1994.

## Kennedy, John Fitzgerald *(1917–1963)*

Thirty-fifth president of the UNITED STATES (1961–63). Born in Brookline, Mass., of Irish Catholic background, he was part of a well-known business and political family, the son of Joseph P. KENNEDY (1888–1969), a successful businessman and movie industry executive who had been ambassador to Great Britain, and the brother of Robert F. KENNEDY and Edward M. Kennedy. He attended Harvard University (1936–40) and enlisted in the navy in 1941, distinguishing himself during WORLD WAR II as the commander of a PT boat in the Pacific. Kennedy entered politics as a congressman from Massachusetts (1947–53) and was a supporter of President TRUMAN's domestic policies but a critic of his relationship with China. He was elected to the Senate in 1952, and the following year he married Jacqueline Bouvier. He suffered from severe, war-related back problems in 1954–55 that to some degree hindered his active role in the Senate. During this period he wrote *Profiles in Courage* (1956), a series of biographical sketches of courageous American leaders that won him a 1957 PULITZER PRIZE. Kennedy was narrowly defeated for the vice presidential nomination in 1956 but won reelection to the Senate by a landslide in 1958.

An anticommunist in foreign policy and a liberal in domestic affairs, the charismatic and popular senator became the Democratic nominee for president in 1960. With Texan Lyndon B. JOHNSON as his running mate, he narrowly defeated his Republican opponent, Richard M. NIXON, to become the first Roman Catholic to be elected president and the youngest man ever to hold the office. He quickly initiated a domestic program (the New Frontier) that included tax reform, federal aid to education, increased civil rights and medical care for the elderly. He barely had time to fight for these programs when he was embroiled in crises abroad. His support of the failed Cuban BAY OF PIGS INVASION (1961) was largely criticized, but he was widely lauded for his resolute stand against the Soviets in the CUBAN MISSILE CRISIS (1962). In 1963 Kennedy was successful in working out a limited NUCLEAR TEST BAN TREATY with the USSR. In other foreign policy decisions, he established the PEACE CORPS to help the needy in developing countries and the

*President John F. Kennedy conferring with his brother, attorney general Robert Kennedy, 1962* (NEW YORK WORLD TELEGRAM & SUN NEWSPAPER COLLECTION, LIBRARY OF CONGRESS, PRINTS AND PHOTOGRAPHS DIVISION)

ALLIANCE FOR PROGRESS to aid Latin America. He also increased the number of American advisers in South Vietnam from some 700 to about 16,000, thus adding to a U.S. presence that would soon escalate into the VIETNAM WAR. He continued to press for his domestic programs, proposing (1963) extensive civil rights legislation, but met with a good deal of resistance from Congress. Most of these programs were not acted upon until the Johnson administration.

Kennedy was shot to death in Dallas, Tex., on November 22, 1963. The apparent assassin was Lee Harvey OSWALD. While the Warren Commission concluded that Oswald had been the killer and had acted alone, conspiracy theories about Kennedy's death abounded and flourish to this day. The death of the vital and eloquent young president, who had yet to fulfill his promise, caused shock and grief throughout the U.S. and the world.

**Kennedy, Joseph Patrick** *(1888–1969)* U.S. ambassador to Great Britain. A successful businessman and movie industry executive, Kennedy served as chairman of the Securities and Exchange Commission (1934–35) and head of the U.S. Maritime Commission (1936–37) before his appointment as ambassador (1937–40). An opponent of U.S. intervention in European affairs, Kennedy supported Neville CHAMBERLAIN's negotiations with HITLER. He resigned in 1940 to return to business. Kennedy encouraged his sons to pursue political careers and was important in the election of John F. KENNEDY to the presidency in 1960.

**Kennedy, Robert "Bobby" F(rancis)** *(1925–1968)* American political figure. Born in Brookline, Mass., he was a younger brother of John F. KENNEDY. He attended Harvard University and the University of Virginia Law School. After graduation in 1951, he worked as a lawyer for the Justice Department before becoming campaign manager for his brother's successful congressional bid. He was an assistant counsel for Sen. Joseph MCCARTHY's communist-hunting subcommittee from 1953 to 1956 and gained wide recognition as chief counsel for the Senate Rackets Committee, where he was instrumental in bringing to light the corruption in the Teamsters Union and of its leaders, James HOFFA

and Dave BECK. He went to work for his brother again in 1960, this time managing the elder Kennedy's successful presidential campaign. A close adviser during his brother's administration, he was also appointed attorney general and won praise for his pursuit of organized crime and his enforcement of CIVIL RIGHTS legislation. After the president's assassination, he continued to serve in the cabinet but resigned to run for the Senate from New York in 1964. Elected, he was an outspoken advocate of social change and of the rights of the poor. From 1966 on, he also became a powerful critic of the VIETNAM WAR. He became a candidate for the Democratic nomination for president in 1968, winning a string of primary victories that culminated in the California primary of June 4. After a victory speech that evening, he was leaving a Los Angeles hotel when he was shot to death by a disaffected Jordanian immigrant named Sirhan Bishara Sirhan.

**Kennedy Round** Long, complex negotiations to encourage world trade through reduction of tariffs on industrial and agricultural imports, particularly in the U.S. and Europe. These negotiations were prompted by President John F. KENNEDY's message to Congress on January 25, 1963. A final compromise was reached in Geneva on May 15, 1967.

**Kenton, Stan** *(1911–1979)* American bandleader-pianist-composer. Kenton began his career playing and writing for various West Coast theater and dance bands. He formed his first band in 1941, the Artistry in Rhythm Orchestra, which gained prominence with its large orchestral sound and precise ensemble playing. With the addition of arrangers like Pete Ruggolo and outstanding soloists such as alto saxophonist Art Pepper, Kenton's band dominated the jazz polls of the mid-1940s organized by such publications as *Down Beat* and *Metronome*. In 1949 Kenton appeared with the 20-piece Progressive Jazz Orchestra, which gave its name to the modern big band approach it represented. Kenton's most ambitious undertaking came in 1950–51 with the 43-piece Innovations in Modern Music Orchestra, with strings and an expanded wind section; though scoring successes with such large-scale compo-

sitions as Bob Graettinger's "City of Glass," the venture proved too costly to sustain. Thereafter, Kenton led a series of highly competent but more conventionally sized big bands.

Kenton's place in jazz history is somewhat ambiguous: On the one hand, he attracted a large and faithful following; on the other, he was often dismissed by the critics, especially in his more epic endeavors, as pompous and vacuous. What is indisputable is the large number of highly talented jazzmen he helped nurture, such as Stan GETZ and Maynard Ferguson. Kenton is similarly secure in his justly earned reputation as a pioneering jazz educator whose summer jazz camps introduced a new generation to the improvisational muse.

**Kent State shootings** Shooting of student demonstrators protesting the VIETNAM WAR on the campus of Kent State University in Kent, Ohio, on May 4, 1970. Students had gathered to protest the U.S. invasion of CAMBODIA on May 1, holding rallies on the Kent State campus and in town. On May 2, a state of civil emergency was declared by the mayor, who called for Ohio National Guard troops. The troops arrived that night as the ROTC building was burned. Tensions between students and troops escalated until the morning of May 4, when some 1,000 students gathered on campus. Refusing to disperse, the students taunted the guardsmen and hurled stones at them while the troops lobbed tear gas canisters at the students. Apparently believing that they were being shot at by a sniper, some of the guardsmen opened fire at 12:25 P.M., killing four students (two men and two women) and wounding 11. The shootings shocked the nation and set off a wave of demonstrations on campuses throughout the U.S. and abroad.

**Kenya (Republic of Kenya)** Kenya, on the east coast of Africa, covers an area of 150,943 square miles. It became a British colony, but nationalist sentiment led to the formation of the Kikuyu Central Association (1928) with Jomo KENYATTA as leader. Pressure to restore land and political control to Africans brought about the violent MAU MAU uprisings from 1952 to 1960, during which the country was under a state of emergency. Kenya

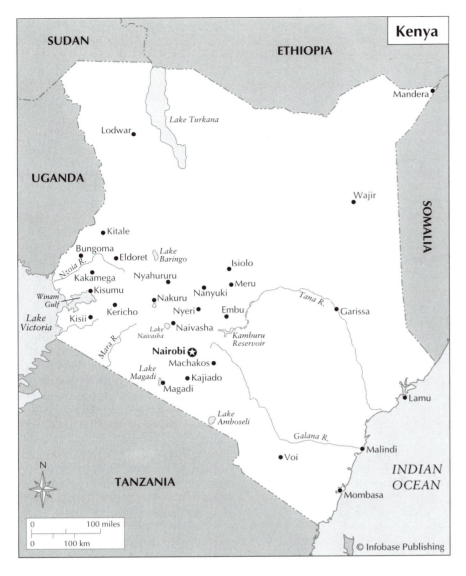

achieved independence in 1962, establishing a republic with Kenyatta as president (1963). Kenyatta's death brought Daniel arap Moi to the presidency in 1979. He maintained tribal balance in government and established close relations with the West. However, increased opposition to his policies led to an attempted coup (1982), student riots (1985, 1987), Muslim riots (1987) and detention of suspected rebels. Though Moi was reelected in 1988, the stability of the country continued to deteriorate, with the murder of a government minister in 1990 igniting antigovernment riots. Moi was reelected in 1992 and 1997, but his government was accused of human rights violations. In December 2002 Moi's rule of Kenya came to an end when opposition candidate Mwai Kibaki was elected to the office in a landslide. In 2004 Kenyan ecologist Wangari Maathai was the first African women to be awarded the Nobel Peace Prize. Severe drought has plagued Kenya in 2006, as it has other nations in the African Horn.

**Kenyatta, Jomo** (*1895?–1978*) Kenyan nationalist leader, first president of KENYA (1964–78). A member of the minority Kikuyu tribe, Kenyatta was educated in a Christian mission school and began his public career in 1922 when he joined the Kikuyu Youth Association in Nairobi, the capital of Kenya, which was then a colony of Great Britain. As

| KENYA | |
|---|---|
| 1920 | Kenya becomes a British colony. |
| 1952 | Formation of Mau Mau anticolonial terrorist movement; colonial government declares state of emergency, arrests nationalist leader Jomo Kenyatta. |
| 1956 | Mau Mau activity subsides; state of emergency lifted. |
| 1960 | Tom Mboya and Oginga Odinga form Kenya African National Union (KANU); British begin to prepare for Kenyan independence. |
| 1961 | Kenyatta released from detention. |
| 1963 | (June 1) Kenya gains self-government, with Kenyatta as prime minister. |
| 1964 | (Dec. 12) Kenya gains full independence, declared a republic with Kenyatta as president. |
| 1969 | Assassination of Tom Mboya. |

*(Table continues)*

| KENYA (CONTINUED) | |
|---|---|
| 1978 | Death of Kenyatta; Daniel arap Moi becomes president. |
| 1982 | Attempted air force coup against Moi is foiled. |
| 1990 | Kenya's foreign affairs minister, a top government official, is found murdered; government bans demonstrations. |
| 1992 | Moi reelected in multiparty elections. |
| 1998 | Bomb explodes at the U.S. embassy in Nairobi, killing 224 people. |
| 2002 | Mwai Kibaki replaces Moi as president. |
| 2004 | Kenyan ecologist Wangari Maathai wins the Nobel Peace Prize. |
| 2006 | Drought threatens millions with starvation in what the president calls a "national disaster." |

he rose in Kikuyu politics, he traveled to Europe in 1929 to protest British encroachment upon Kikuyu land. He returned to Europe in 1931 for a 15-year stay that included study at the London School of Economics. Upon his return to Kenya in 1946, Kenyatta became head of the New Kenya African Union, a nationalist group seeking political rights for blacks. Although he favored reform by legal means, he was connected in many people's minds with the underground MAU MAU movement, which was responsible for acts of terror against whites and blacks from 1952 to 1955. He was jailed by the British during the 1952 emergency in Kenya and he subsequently was sentenced to seven years imprisonment. At the end of his term, Kenyatta was confined to his tribal village. After his release, Kenyatta headed the Kenya African National Union (KANU), which won a majority in elections in 1962 for an independent Kenyan parliament. Kenyatta became prime minister upon Kenya's independence in December 1963. The following year he proclaimed Kenya a republic and became its president. Under Kenyatta's administration, KANU became the sole legal political party, and few figures rose to challenge the president's leadership. He outlawed the Kenya People's Union in 1969 and detained those members who did not join KANU. After the assassination in that year of Tom MBOYA, widely regarded as Kenyatta's successor, talk of the president's replacement was discouraged and finally declared illegal in 1976. Under Kenyatta's

leadership, the country followed a moderate, pro-West course, encouraging free enterprise and making Kenya one of the most prosperous countries in black Africa. While promoting foreign investment, Kenyatta also required that companies train and hire Africans, thus building up a native labor force capable of running the country's affairs. Despite great income disparity, urban unemployment and substantial corruption, Kenya's economic future was considered relatively promising compared with other African nations.

**Kepes, György** (1906–2001) Hungarian-American painter, designer and art theorist. Born in Hungary, Kepes studied at Budapest's Academy of Fine Arts from 1924 to 1928. During his student days, Kepes began his photogram experiments, creating abstract images on photographic paper without benefit of camera. Emigrating to the U.S., he and Lázló MOHOLY-NAGY cofounded the New Bauhaus in Chicago in 1937. In 1946 he went to the Massachusetts Institute of Technology where he became professor of visual design and director of the Center for Advanced Visual Studies. His works of art and his studies explored the emotional role of light and color in art, particularly in abstract images. His many books of art theory include *The Language of Vision* (1944) and *Structure in Art and Science* (1965).

**Keppel, Francis** (1916–1990) American educator. As U.S. commissioner of education from 1962 to 1966, he was a

strong supporter of programs to improve the education of children from poor families and encouraged rigorous enforcement of the CIVIL RIGHTS ACT OF 1964 as it applied to education. He also played a major role in the creation of the National Assessment of Educational Progress, which measured the effectiveness of education across the country. He later served as director of the education policy program of the Aspen Institute, and as an adviser to libraries, art centers, the WORLD BANK and developing nations.

**Kerensky, Alexander Fedorovich** (1881–1970) Russian statesman. A moderate socialist, Kerensky was elected to the fourth DUMA in 1912 and there led the Labor group of socialist peasant members. A brave opponent of the czarist government, he later joined the Socialist Revolutionary Party (see SOCIALIST REVOLUTIONARIES). He was a leading figure in the FEBRUARY REVOLUTION of 1917. During 1917 he held many government posts: minister of justice (February), minister of war and navy (May) and in July became prime minister. As prime minister he aimed to continue the war against Germany, but this undermined his popularity and in November he was ousted by the BOLSHEVIKS (see OCTOBER REVOLUTION). He lived the rest of his life in exile, first in France and then in Australia, and finally, from 1946, in the U.S.

**Kern, Jerome David** (1885–1945) One of the prime architects of American

*Russian revolutionary and émigré Alexander Kerensky* (LIBRARY OF CONGRESS, PRINTS AND PHOTOGRAPHS DIVISION)

popular song in the 20th century. As a boy in New York he preferred music studies at the New York College of Music to working in his father's business. Dividing his time between New York and London, he studied, worked for impresarios Charles Frohman and Florenz ZIEGFELD and finally had the chance to write his first musical score to a show, *The Red Petticoat* (1912). At a time when the American stage was dominated by European songs and shows, Kern wrote a series of small musicals for Broadway's Princess Theater, including *Very Good Eddie* (1915) and *Oh, Boy* (1917). He was soon an established figure in American musical theater, composing the songs and music for the landmark SHOW BOAT (1927). He moved to HOLLYWOOD in 1934 and wrote several original film scores, including *Swing Time* (1936), *High, Wide and Handsome* (1937) and *Cover Girl* (1944). His many collaborators were major figures in the business: Dorothy Fields, Johnny MERCER, E. Y. HARBURG, Ira GERSHWIN and Oscar HAMMERSTEIN II. Among his most distinguished melodies are "Look for the Silver Lining," "Make Believe," "Ol' Man River," "Smoke Gets in Your Eyes," "All the Things You Are" and "The Last Time I Saw Paris" (included in the score for the 1941 movie *Lady Be Good*, it won him an ACADEMY AWARD). Despite his classical training, Kern seldom strayed from song writing into the more traditional forms of "serious" music.

**Kerner scandal** In 1973 Otto Kerner, a U.S. Federal Circuit Court judge and former governor of Illinois (1961–69), was convicted on 17 counts of conspiracy, fraud, perjury, bribery and income tax evasion committed when he was governor. He was sentenced to three years in prison and fined $50,000.

**Kerouac, Jack** (*1922–1969*) American novelist. Born Jean Louis Kerouac in Lowell, Mass., he briefly attended Columbia University. A leader of the rebellious BEAT GENERATION of the 1950s, he is best known for the novel *On the Road* (1957), an autobiographical account of his travels throughout the U.S. in search of new sensation and a kind of drugged enlightenment. Similar in theme, his later works include *The Subterraneans* and *The Dharma Bums* (both 1958), *Big Sur* (1962) and *Desolation Angels* (1965). Kerouac also wrote poems and essays.

**Kerr, Deborah** (*1921– *) A veteran of 44 films between 1943 and 1969, Kerr was nominated for six ACADEMY AWARDS for Best Actress but never won. Born in Scotland, she achieved success in British films such as *Black Narcissus* (1947) before signing with METRO-GOLDWYN-MAYER in HOLLYWOOD. Although well known for her portrayal of poised, well-bred women, steamy love scenes such as the one on the beach with Burt LANCASTER in *From Here to Eternity* proved her ver-

*Beat novelist and poet Jack Kerouac (right). with Neal Cassady. the inspiration for* On the Road *protagonist Dean Moriarty* (PHOTOFEST)

satility. Other films include *The King and I* and *Tea and Sympathy* (1956), *Separate Tables* (1958), *The Sundowners* (1960) and *The Night of the Iguana* (1964). In 1994 Kerr received an honorary Academy Award for her contributions to the film industry.

**Kerr, Walter** (*1913–1996*) American drama critic and playwright. Kerr was a professor of theater at Catholic University in Washington before turning to criticism. He joined the *New York Herald Tribune* in 1951 and moved to the *New York Times* in 1966. His Broadway reviews influenced a generation of theatergoers. Other works include *How Not to Write a Play* (1956) and *Tragedy and Comedy* (1967). He also collaborated on the musical *Goldilocks* with his playwright-wife Jean Kerr.

**Kerry, John F(orbes)** (*1943– *) American politician. The son of a foreign service officer, Kerry was educated in private schools in the United States and Europe. He graduated from Yale University in 1966 and entered the U.S. Navy. Sent to Vietnam during the VIETNAM WAR, Kerry served as an officer on a gunboat that operated in the Mekong Delta. He won a Silver Star, a Bronze Star with Combat V, and three Purple Hearts for his performance in battle. On returning from Vietnam, Kerry cofounded Vietnam Veterans of America and became a leading member of the Vietnam Veterans against the War, testifying before the Senate Foreign Relations Committee in 1971 in opposition to the U.S. war effort in Southeast Asia. After obtaining a law degree from Boston College Law School in 1976, Kerry served as prosecutor in the Middlesex County District Attorney's Office in Boston. He was elected lieutenant governor in 1982, and two years later was elected United States senator despite Ronald REAGAN's landslide victory in the national presidential election. Kerry was an active and outspoken member of the Senate Foreign Relations Committee and worked with Senator John McCain of Arizona, a fellow Vietnam veteran, to promote the interests of veterans and campaign finance reform. Kerry was reelected in 1990, 1996 (in a closely watched race against the popular Republican governor, William Weld) and 2002. After a slow start in the Democratic presidential primary campaign of 2004, Kerry became the party's candidate against Republican president George W. BUSH in the November 2004 election. He was defeated by Bush and returned to the Senate.

**Kesey, Ken** *(1935–2001)* American writer. Born in La Junta, Colo., Kesey became a COUNTERCULTURE hero in the 1960s with the publication of his uproarious and iconoclastic novel *One Flew Over the Cuckoo's Nest* (1962, filmed 1975). His reputation was enhanced by his advocacy of psychedelic drugs and by the antics of his "Merry Pranksters," a group of likeminded rebels who toured the U.S. and Mexico in a converted school bus. Their activities were described by Kesey in the novel *Ken Kesey's Garage Sale* (1973) and chronicled in Tom WOLFE's *The Electric Kool-Aid Acid Test* (1968). Kesey was also the author of *Sometimes a Great Notion* (1964) and *Demon Box* (1987).

**Kesselring, Albert** *(1885–1960)* German field marshal. Kesselring served as an artillery officer in WORLD WAR I. In WORLD WAR II, he was an important Luftwaffe commander, at one time or another in charge of air operations in Poland, the Western Front, central Russia and the Mediterranean. In 1943 he became supreme commander of German forces in Italy, and later that year, commander in chief of the West. In 1947 Kesselring was convicted of war crimes and sentenced to death, but his punishment was commuted to life in prison. He was released in 1952.

**Keyes, Sidney Arthur Killworth** *(1922–1943)* English poet. Keyes was a shy and frail child, and his early education took place mostly at home. At Queens College, Oxford, he displayed great brilliance and promise and was associated with the poet John Heath-Stubbs. He edited a literary magazine and founded a theater group that performed his play "Hosea." Following the publication of *The Iron Laurel* (1942), Keyes was mobilized and stationed in Tunisia. Shortly before his 21st birthday, he was killed on a reconnaissance patrol. *The Cruel Solstice* was issued posthumously in 1943, *Collected Poems* appeared in 1945; Its introduction by Robert Penn WARREN praised Keyes for being the first English poet "to marry

Continental symbolism to the English romantic tradition." His major influences were W. B. YEATS and Rainer Maria RILKE. He was one of three important English poets killed in WORLD WAR II, the others being Keith DOUGLAS and Alun LEWIS.

**Keynes, John Maynard (first Baron Keynes)** *(1883–1946)* English economist. One of the most influential economic thinkers of the 20th century, he was born and educated at Cambridge. A member of the BLOOMSBURY GROUP, Keynes was a man of wide interests and great intelligence. He was a currency specialist in the India Office (1906–08) and served in the treasury (1915–19) before becoming the principal British financial representative to the PARIS PEACE CONFERENCE after World War I. He resigned in protest against the harshness of the terms imposed upon Germany, outlining his views in *Economic Consequences of the Peace* (1919), a book that won him international acclaim. While continuing to support a capitalist system, Keynes began to deviate from classical free economy concepts in 1929, supporting efforts by LLOYD GEORGE to create a program of government-sponsored public works and public employment. Keynes stressed full employment through cheap money, lowered interest rates and increased public and private investment.

His advocacy of active government intervention into the free play of the market and his belief that the unrestrained workings of that market would ultimately result in a depression were spelled out in his classic work *General Theory of Employment, Interest and Money* (1936). His economic and fiscal theories became generally accepted and were incorporated into such national policies as the American NEW DEAL. Keynes served as a consultant to the chancellor of the exchequer and was a director of the Bank of England during World War II. He was an important figure in the BRETTON WOODS CONFERENCE of 1944, establishing postwar monetary policies and creating a WORLD BANK (the INTERNATIONAL MONETARY FUND) to help developing countries. His many works include *Tract on Monetary Reform* (1923), *The End of Laissez Faire* (1926) and *Treatise on Money* (2 vols., 1930).

**Keyserling, Leon H.** *(1908–1987)* U.S. government consultant. Keyserling helped draft major NEW DEAL legislation and served as a high-ranking official in federal housing programs. In 1949 he was named chairman of President Harry S TRUMAN's Council of Economic Advisers, a post he held until the end of Truman's presidency. After leaving government in 1953, he worked as a private consultant and lawyer and founded the Conference on Economic Progress, a nonprofit group devoted to public interest projects.

**KGB** Acronym for Komitet Gosudarstvennoy Bezopasnosti (Committee for State Security). The KGB was the Soviet security service since 1953. It both enforced Communist Party rule at home and conducted espionage abroad. Despite the reforms of GLASNOST and PERESTROIKA under Mikhail GORBACHEV in the late 1980s, the KGB remained a powerful force in the USSR. Following the disintegration of the Soviet Union in December 1991, the KGB became the Federal Security Service (FSB), the intelligence agency of the Russian Federation. In 2000 a former KGB agent, Vladimir PUTIN, became president of Russia. (See also SOVIET SECRET POLICE.)

**Khachaturian, Aram Ilyich** *(1903–1978)* Soviet composer. Born in Georgia, he studied at the Moscow Conservatory (1923–34). His compositions were influenced by Armenian, Georgian and other folk tunes that he collected. His first symphony (1934) drew attention to his talent, and this was followed by a piano concerto (1936) and a violin concerto (1940). His best-known works are two ballets, *Gayane*, which includes the saber dance (1942), and *Spartacus* (1954, revised 1958). He also composed music for films and plays. For a short period he was under censure during the worst of the ZHDANOV "formalist" pressures. He received many awards, including the Order of Lenin.

**Khamenei, Ayatollah Seyed Ali** *(1939– )* Shi'ite Muslim cleric, ayatollah (1989– ) and president of IRAN (1981–89). Born in Mashhad to a Shi'ite cleric, Khamenei studied Islamic theology in the city of Qom under Ayatollah Ruhollah KHOMEINI.

Khomeini's teachings and interpretation of the Koran promoted an Iranian version of ISLAMISM, a strict application of Islamic law to everyday life, economics, society and national politics. Khamenei soon came to accept Khomeini's pronouncements, and in 1962 joined his instructor's fundamentalist Shi'ite movement against the ruler of Iran, Shah Mohammad Reza PAHLAVI. He was arrested by the Savak, the shah's secret police, in 1963.

In 1979 massive protests against the shah's rule led to a revolution that overthrew the Iranian monarchy and installed a theocracy directed by Khomeini. Khamenei helped found the Islamic Republican Party (IRP), the political organization that would ensure the application of Khomeini's teachings throughout the Iranian government, including the Majlis (the Iranian parliament). Khamenei later served in the Majlis as a representative of the IRP, a member of the Council of the Islamic Revolution, a commander of the Revolutionary Guard (the Iranian paramilitary group devoted to Khomeini), a deputy minister of defense and a member of the Supreme Council of Defense. In 1981 he was elected president of Iran, he won reelection in 1985. He retired from the presidency in 1989, as required by the Iranian constitution.

Following the death of his longtime mentor Khomeini in the same year, Khamenei assumed the Shi'ite title of ayatollah, a Persian word that means "gift of God" that designates the supreme spiritual leader of Iran under the Islamic state. As "Guide of the Islamic Republic," he continued to support the strict application of Islamic law throughout Iran. He and his clerical colleagues cracked down on the press that had supported reformist president Mohammed KHATAMI in the 1997 and 2001 elections, suspending more than 100 newspapers and arresting dozens of journalists.

In 2004 the Iranian Guard Council, dominated by Khamenei and his clerical allies, disqualified some 2,500 reformist candidates for election to the Majlis. The result was a victory for the hard-line supporters of Khamenei. In the following year they disqualified hundreds of candidates in the presidential election, which was won by the hard-line major of Tehran, Mahmoud Ahmadinejad.

**Khan, Ishmael** (?–  ) Warlord in control of the western region of AFGHANISTAN, operating from the city of Herat (2001–  ). During the 1979–88 campaign of the MUJAHIDEEN, a loosely organized group of Muslim rebels, to expel Soviet forces from Afghanistan and overthrow the pro-Soviet government, Khan served as a member of the Islamic guerrilla forces. After the departure of Soviet forces in 1989 Khan was jailed by the fundamentalist regime run by the TALIBAN from 1995 to 1999. In 1999 he was released from prison and sent into exile in Iran. Khan came to international attention following the overthrow of the Taliban government in Afghanistan by American forces. Following the Taliban's defeat Khan reentered the Afghan city of Herat, where he established himself as the military ruler of the western region.

Since the creation of a national Afghan government under President Hamid KARZAI, Khan's relationship with the president has been unusual. While he has acknowledged Karzai to be the official ruler of Afghanistan, Khan has continued to run his territory virtually as an independent country, collecting $800,000 per day in import duties from Iran, fielding a 50,000-man army and funding his own schools and hospitals. In his administration of the western region of Afghanistan, Khan has drawn criticism from HUMAN RIGHTS WATCH, an international group dedicated to drawing world attention to violations of international human rights.

**Khatami, Mohammed** (1943–  ) Iranian Shi'ite cleric and politician, president of IRAN (1997–2005). Born in Ardakan as the son of Ayatollah (a Shi'ite term that means "gift of God") Ruhollah Khatami, Khatami enrolled at the Iranian theological seminary at Qom in 1961, the same institution where Ayatollah KHOMEINI (a high-ranking Islamic cleric and long-time friend of Khatami's father) taught a version of ISLAMISM, a philosophy that calls for the strict application of Koranic and Islamic law within a society. Khatami supported Khomeini's efforts to overthrow Mohammed Reza Shah PAHLAVI, disseminating Islamist propaganda and organizing mass meetings while attending the University of Esfahan. After obtaining his B.A. at Esfahan

and a masters degree in education from the University of Tehran, Khatami returned to the Qom seminary, which eventually awarded him the midlevel rank of hojatolislam.

In 1979, when the shah was swept from power and Khomeini became the leader of the Islamic state, Khatami returned from West Germany (where he had organized Iranian emigrés against the shah's rule). After his election to the Iranian parliament in 1980, Khatami served as the minister of culture and Islamic guidance. In this he acquired a reputation as a liberal by allowing artists and authors more freedom of expression. When the real conservative clerics forced Khatami to resign as cultural minister in 1992, Khatami became director of the Iranian National Library, and served as a cultural adviser to moderate president Ali Akbar Hashemi Rafsanjani. When Rafsanjani left the presidency in 1997, reformists in Iran persuaded Khatami to run against the conservative candidate to succeed Rafsanjani. Khatami received nearly 70% of the popular vote in the 1997 elections. He was reelected president in 2001 with 77% of all ballots cast. As president, Khatami installed a moderate cabinet that included Iran's first postrevolution female minister and permitted the national press greater freedom. He also sought to improve Iranian relations with the U.S., but after President George W. BUSH declared Iran a member of the "Axis of Evil" in 2002, Khatami's efforts at rapprochement with the U.S. were blocked by the hard-line clerics. U.S. pressure to force Iran to abandon its nuclear program also strengthened the hand of the conservatives, weakening Khatami's position. He retired from the presidency in 2005 and was succeeded by the hard-line mayor of Tehran, Mahmoud Ahmadinejad.

**Khe Sanh** Site of U.S. Marine base in the extreme northern corner of South Vietnam, near the Demilitarized Zone and the Laos border. On January 21, 1968, the North Vietnamese army attacked the strategically located base and held it under siege, raising fears that Khe Sanh would become the military and public relations disaster for the Americans that DIEN BIEN PHU had been for the French. The siege was finally lifted on April 7, as the TET OFFENSIVE drew to a close, but the base was abandoned in June of that year as U.S. military plans changed. In the siege, 205 Americans had been killed, with official U.S. estimates of North Vietnamese dead placed at more than 10,000 men.

## Khlebnikov, Velemir Vladimirovich (1885–1922) Russian poet and Slavophile. He was the founder of Russian FUTURISM, which aimed at shocking the reader and made an attempt at breaking with past conceptions of the use of words by creating a "trans-sense" language.

## Khmer Rouge Radical and fanatical Cambodian Marxist revolutionary political organization. Under the leadership of POL POT, the Khmer Rouge ruled CAMBODIA from 1975 to 1979 and conducted a bloody reign of terror. Pursuing a policy of radical social change, the Khmer Rouge tried to destroy Cambodia's old way of life and dealt ruthlessly with any and all potential opponents. The entire population of the capital, PHNOM PENH, was taken from the city and forced to work in the countryside; tens of thousands were executed, and as many as a million died from starvation and mistreatment. Khmer Rouge guerrillas continued to terrorize thousands of refugees in western Cambodia and Thailand while seeking to overthrow the Vietnam-backed government in Phnom Penh. After the withdrawal of Vietnamese forces, the Khmer Rouge attempted to retain its political power in the face of UN-supervised elections. However, its membership continually declined throughout the second half of the 1990s, and its leader, POL POT, died in 1998.

## Khomeini, Ayatollah Ruhollah (Sayyid Ruhollah Moussavi) (1900 or 1902–1989) Imam (spiritual leader) of IRAN (1979–89). Khomeini studied Islamic theology and law at the provincial center of Arak and moved in the early 1920s to the holy city of Qom. He became a teacher, wrote poetry and over 20 religious books, and delved into Islamic mysticism and even Western philosophy. Khomeini became known as a leading scholar in the 1930s and earned the title of ayatollah in the late 1950s. But it was not until the early 1960s that he emerged as the leader of the Shi'ite clergy's opposition to the shah's regime

(see Reza PAHLAVI). He organized general strikes, boycotts and demonstrations to protest elements of the Shah's "White Revolution," or modernization programs, that the mullahs (clergy) deemed un-Islamic. Khomeini also led a campaign against diplomatic immunity for U.S. military personnel in Iran. Khomeini spent months in jail and almost a year under house arrest after calling in 1963 for the shah's overthrow. After a brief stay in Turkey, Khomeini settled in the Shi'ite holy city of Najaf in Iraq. Over the next 13 years he issued periodic proclamations against the shah that were widely circulated clandestinely in Iran. By 1970 he had broadened his attacks, speaking out against both the institution of the monarchy and constitutional republicanism and calling instead for an Islamic state ruled by religious authorities.

In early 1978 a government-controlled newspaper published an article attacking Khomeini's character and implying he was a tool of foreigners and communists. The tactic backfired, leading to Muslim riots that spread across the country. After Khomeini refused an offer of amnesty from the shah, Iran prevailed upon Iraq first to place the ayatollah under house arrest and then to expel him. The move was a further miscalculation by Tehran: Khomeini set up new headquarters in a Paris suburb, where he had access to the international news media and could coordinate activities with his followers in Iran by telephone. After the shah fled into exile on January 16, 1979, Khomeini returned to a tumultuous welcome in Tehran on February 1. Under Khomeini, "modernists" were gradually shunted aside as an Islamic republic was declared and a constitution was approved by national referendum that consolidated the power of the clergy and made Khomeini Iran's supreme religious and political leader for life. Western music was banned, women's rights were curtailed, religious minorities were persecuted and uncounted thousands of people were executed.

Two of Khomeini's most widely touted slogans were "Death to America" and "Neither East nor West." Although revolutionary Iran steered a nonaligned course in world affairs, Khomeini reserved his special venom for what he called the "Great Satan"—

the U.S. Khomeini's Iran provided the basis for the political humiliation of two successive American presidents. It was unclear if Khomeini gave prior approval to the militants who seized the U.S. embassy in Tehran and held its staff hostage for 444 days from November 4, 1979 to January 20, 1981 (see IRAN HOSTAGE CRISIS). But he refused to disavow the takeover, and did not consent to have the hostages go free until President Jimmy CARTER was leaving office. The seminal event of Iran under Khomeini was the IRAN-IRAQ WAR (1980–88), which helped rally mass popular support around the revolutionary regime. In July 1988 after suffering hundreds of thousands of dead, and its economy a wreck, Iran accepted a United Nations–sponsored cease-fire. In early 1989, Khomeini denounced British author Salman RUSHDIE and his allegedly anti-Muslim book *The Satanic Verses* and called for Rushdie's assassination.

## Khrennikov, Tikhon Nikolayevich (1913– ) Soviet composer. He was a pupil of Shebalin at the Moscow Conservatory from 1932. His works include an opera, *The Brothers*, two symphonies, a piano concerto, piano works, music for plays and films, including incidental music for *Much Ado About Nothing*, and many songs, including some to words by Robert Burns. In 1948, acting in his capacity as secretary of the Union of Soviet Composers, he condemned many of his colleagues, including PROKOFIEV and SHOSTAKOVICH, for "formalism." In 2003 Khrennikov received the Mozart Medal from the United Nations Educational, Scientific and Cultural Organization.

## Khrushchev, Nikita Sergeyevich (1894–1971) Soviet politician, first secretary of the Central Committee of the Communist Party of the USSR (1953–64). Khrushchev joined the party in 1918 while working as a locksmith in the Donets Basin. He became second secretary of the Moscow Party Organization in 1934, its first secretary in 1935 and first secretary of the Ukrainian Party Organization in 1938. Khrushchev took a prominent part in the GREAT PURGE. In 1939 he became a member of the Politburo and during World War II was an important political officer in the army. Toward the end of

*Soviet premier Nikita Khrushchev addressing the United Nations. 1959* (UNATIONS)

STALIN's rule Khrushchev was the party's chief agricultural expert, but his policy of "rural cities" was a disaster. After Stalin's death and Malenkov's brief tenure, Khrushchev became first secretary of the central committee, proving to be the most powerful member of the "collective leadership." After denouncing Stalin in a four-hour secret speech at the 20TH PARTY CONGRESS of the CPSU in 1956, he pursued a policy of DESTAL-INIZATION with a degree of inconsistency. His plans for greater industrialized state farming eventually resulted in lower agricultural production. While Khrushchev's reforms improved the standard and quality of life in the USSR, they did not win him much popularity. In his dealings with the West, Khrushchev alternated peaceful gestures with threats, and his decisions led to the CUBAN MISSILE CRISIS with the United States in 1962. Khrushchev was forced out of office in 1964.

**Kielce (Keltsy, Kel'tsy)** Polish city 85 miles north-northeast of KRAKÓW; a part of Russia from 1818, it was given to the new state of Poland in 1919. Kielce was a German-Russian battle site in 1914–15; during WORLD WAR II four German CONCENTRATION CAMPS were sited here.

**Kiel Mutiny** (*1918*) GERMANY began to discuss a possible armistice with the Allies near the end of WORLD WAR I. At that time, the German navy was in a

mutinous state. When the German High Seas Fleet was ordered to sail to the North Sea for a major battle against the British, the German sailors in Kiel refused to go and took up arms, setting off an open revolution throughout Germany (Oct. 29–Nov. 3, 1918). Only the U-boat crews remained loyal to Kaiser WILHELM II. Major revolts occurred in Hamburg, Bremen and Lübeck (Nov. 4–5) and spread to Munich (Nov. 7–8). Bavaria declared itself a democratic and socialist republic. The kaiser was forced to abdicate, and on Nov. 11, 1918, the armistice was signed and World War I ended.

**Kiesinger, Kurt Georg** (*1904–1988*) German politician, chancellor of WEST GERMANY from 1966 to 1969. As a Christian Democrat, Kiesinger led a government formed by a GRAND COALITION of Christian Democrats and Social Democrats. His past as a minor Nazi brought him much negative attention when he became a candidate for chancellor. He was slapped in the face by Nazi hunter Beate Klarsfeld at a conference in West Berlin in November 1968. After losing to Willy BRANDT in the 1969 election, he played only a minor role in West German politics, remaining a member of the Bundestag (Parliament) until 1980.

**Kiesler, Frederick** (*1890–1965*) Austrian theatrical designer who became part of the de STIJL movement in

Holland in 1923. Kiesler's *Cité dans l'Espace,* a de Stijl utopian city of the future, was part of the Austrian exhibit at the 1925 Paris exhibition. From 1923 to 1960 he worked on the concept of a futuristic "Endless House" with curving, biomorphic forms. The house was never built but often published and exhibited. After coming to the U.S. in 1926, he designed the Film Guild Cinema in New York in a style closely related to de Stijl thinking and established a reputation as both a sculptor and a designer of visionary and futuristic architectural projects. His *Art of this Century* gallery of 1942 was a strong expression of his personal aesthetic. From the 1940s until his death, Kiesler produced and regularly exhibited "Galaxies," sculptural works made by grouping flat, painted panels to form spatial environments. Lisa Phillip's 1989 book *Frederick Kiesler* is an inclusive survey of his achievements.

**Killebrew, Harmon Clayton** (*1936–  *) American baseball player. Killebrew was one of the most dominant players of the 1960s, but his chance to break Babe RUTH's home run record was spoiled by injuries. His steady defensive play with the Washington Senators—later the Minnesota Twins—allowed his managers to use him at virtually any position. His hitting power was legendary, as his home run shots hit upper decks and sailed out of even the largest stadiums. An All-Star throughout his career, he had his best season in 1969, with 49 home runs and 140 runs batted in. Killebrew spent 1975, his last season, with the Kansas City Royals, and was inducted into the Baseball Hall of Fame in 1984. He had 573 lifetime home runs.

**Killy, Jean-Claude** (*1943–  *) French skier. An Alpine racer with matinee-idol good looks and charm, Killy dominated international skiing during the late 1960s. He first came to prominence in 1964, when he won all three French Alpine championships—slalom, giant slalom and downhill—and led the French team to the world championship. During the 1968 Grenoble OLYMPIC GAMES in his native France, Killy became the focus of international media attention as he took all three Alpine gold medals. He retired from skiing after the games and turned to acting. Four years later, he began a career as a professional skier; he took the world professional championship in 1972. In 1992 he co-chaired the Albertville Olympics and in 1994 was named President of the Société du Tour de France.

**Kilmer, (Alfred) Joyce** *(1886–1918)* American poet. Born in New Brunswick, N.J., he worked on the *Standard Dictionary* before joining the U.S. Army at the outbreak of World War I. He is famous for the cloyingly sentimental poem "Trees" in *Trees and Other Poems* (1914). His other verse collections are *Summer of Love* (1911) and *Main Street and Other Poems* (1917). Kilmer wrote some powerful war poetry before being killed in action in France.

**Kim Dae Jung** *(1925–   )* South Korean politician, president of South Korea (1998–2002), and recipient of the 2000 Nobel Peace Prize. Born into an agrarian family in the southwestern region of the Korean Peninsula, he joined opposition to South Korea's authoritarian president SYNGMAN RHEE during the 1950s. At rallies and marches against Rhee, Kim established his reputation as an orator who articulated the progressive and democratic cause in South Korea.

In 1961 Kim was elected to the National Assembly, in parliament where he led the opposition to the strongman president PARK CHUNG HEE during the 1960s. After failing to defeat Park in the presidential elections of 1971, Kim was imprisoned in 1975 and was sentenced to death in 1980 for allegedly inciting an uprising in the town of Kwangju. Pressure from the U.S. government resulted in the 1982 release of Kim for three years of temporary exile in America, where he served as a visiting fellow at Harvard University.

On his return to South Korea in 1985, Kim resumed his political activism and was elected to the National Assembly in 1988. After two more failed bids for South Korean presidency, Kim finally won the office by a narrow margin in 1997, amid a severe financial crisis that caused a sharp drop of the South Korean currency, the won. After negotiating a massive loan from the INTERNATIONAL MONETARY FUND to stabilize the won, Kim Dae Jung launched a rapprochement with North Korea in 1998. He offered the Communist state humanitarian aid in an attempt to improve relations between the two states. Two years later, Kim Dae Jung held a historic meeting with his North Korean counterpart, KIM JONG IL in the northern capital of Pyongyang. The two leaders pledged to promote détente, particularly in the field of economic cooperation. Kim Dae Jung also participated in multilateral negotiations to thwart North Korea's efforts to develop a nuclear bomb, after acting as an intermediary between Kim Jong Il and American president GEORGE W. BUSH. Kim Dae Jung retired in December 2002 from the presidency and was succeeded by Roh Moo-Hyun.

**Kim Il** *(1910–1984)* Korean communist leader. A member of the inner circle of early Korean revolutionaries, Kim Il joined the then-underground Communist Party in 1932 and fought Japanese colonial occupation. He was appointed first deputy premier of NORTH KOREA in 1959, premier in 1972 and vice president in 1976. He was also a member of the Central Committee of the Communist Party and of the National Administration Council.

**Kim Il Sung** *(1912–1994)* Communist leader of NORTH KOREA (1948–94). Kim Il Sung joined the Communist Party in 1927. During World War II he was a guerrilla leader in Manchuria. After the war—and with Soviet support—he prevailed over opponents from other factions of the party and gradually became a supreme leader, the center of an extreme personality cult. He is extravagantly praised and called the "great leader," the "heaven-sent and talented leader" and so on. He also awarded himself a number of high orders and decorations, such as Hero of the Democratic People's Republic of Korea (two times) and the Order of National Flag First Class (three times). Kim Il Sung died on the eve of talks with the U.S. to end North Korea's diplomatic isolation. He was succeeded by his son, Kim Jong Il.

**Kim Jong Il** *(1942–   )* Ruler of the Communist state of NORTH KOREA (1994–   ). Born in Watsukoye, a military camp in the Soviet territory of Siberia, Kim Jong Il was the son of KIM IL SUNG, Kim Jong Il was carefully prepared to succeed his father. In 1990 Kim Jong Il was appointed as vice chairman of the North Korean National Defense Commission and succeeded his father as supreme commander of the Korean People's Army. Two years later he received the title of marshal of the Korean People's Army, the second-highest military rank behind the rank of grand marshal held by his father.

Just before his death on July 8, 1994, Kim Il Sung publicly declared that his son would succeed him as head of North Korea and assume all of his duties and offices. Once in power Kim Jong Il made symbolic efforts to reconcile with South Korea. In 2000 he met with his South Korean counterpart, KIM DAE JUNG, and accepted food aid from South Korea, to combat the problem of malnutrition that has regularly plagued his country. On the issue of nuclear energy and nuclear weapons, Kim Jong Il has proven less accommodating to international opinion. In 2001 North Korea violated an agreement with the U.S. to cease construction and operation of nuclear reactors capable of pro-

*North Korean president Kim Il-Sung with Chinese president Li Xiannian. 1987 (LIBRARY OF CONGRESS, PRINTS AND PHOTOGRAPHS DIVISION)*

ducing weapons-grade plutonium in exchange for shipments of oil to fuel North Korean power plants. Two years later North Korea formally acknowledged that it had developed the proscribed weapons and withdrew from the NUCLEAR NON-PROLIFERATION TREATY (NPT). Kim Jong Il continued to deny international inspectors access to his nuclear facilities and failed to reach a settlement with the U.S., despite repeated entreaties by South Korea and China to come to an understanding with Washington.

**Kiner, Ralph (Ralph McPherran)** *(1922– )* American baseball player. One of the great sluggers of the postwar years, Kiner led the National League in home runs from 1946 through 1952. The Pittsburgh Pirates tailored their left field line at Forbes Field to suit his (and Hank GREENBERG's) home run power, and that area of the park became known as "Kiner's Korner." The end of his career was hastened by back troubles, but he finished with 369 home runs, giving him a lifetime home run to at-bat ratio second only to Babe RUTH's. Kiner took the name "Kiner's Korner" for his talk and interview program when he began his successful broadcasting career with the expansion New York Mets in 1962. He was named to the Hall of Fame in 1975.

**King, Billie Jean** *(1943– )* U.S. tennis player. King's influence on and off the court is still felt in the world of tennis. A tireless fighter for the rights of women players, she brought the women's game to a wider audience and eventually helped to establish a separate women's tour. Winner of a record 20 Wimbledon titles, she won four U.S. Open singles titles, as well as an Australian and a French Open. Perhaps her best remembered match, however, was the super-hyped "Battle of the Sexes" in which she defeated the middle-aged tennis great and self-proclaimed "male chauvinist pig" Bobby RIGGS. King was active in AIDS charities and in organizations dedicated to raising awareness and education about homosexuality. The Gay and Lesbian Alliance Against Defamation (GLAAD) honored King for her work in these fields.

**King, Carole (Carole Klein)** *(1942– )* American singer-songwriter. With hus-

band Gerry Goffin, King was one of the most important pop/rock composers of the 1960s. Together they penned such hits as "Will You Love Me Tomorrow," "Locomotion," "Some Kind of Wonderful" and "A Natural Woman." After the dissolution of their marriage and their professional partnership, King turned to performing. Her second album release, *Tapestry,* sold more than 14 million copies and was named album of the year. Hit singles from the album included "It's Too Late" and "I Feel the Earth Move." King has rarely performed live, and although she continues to release records, none of her later releases have approached the success of *Tapestry.*

**King, Charles Glen** *(1896–1988)* American chemist and nutritionist. In 1932, while on the faculty of the University of Pittsburgh, King isolated vitamin C from the juice of lemons. He was a professor of chemistry at Columbia University from 1941 to 1947.

**King, Ernest** *(1878–1956)* U.S. military officer. King was born in Lorain, Ohio, and graduated from the U.S. Naval Academy at Annapolis in 1901. He became a rear admiral in 1933. In 1941 King became commander of U.S. naval forces and was appointed chief of naval operations the following year. He was the only officer in U.S. history to occupy both posts. As commander of the greatest naval fleet in history, he directed the strategy that lead to the defeat of the Japanese navy. He was made admiral of the fleet in 1944.

**King, Larry (Lawrence Harvey Zeiger)** *(1933– )* American radio and television personality and talk-show host. Born Lawrence Harvey Zeiger in Brooklyn, N.Y., he adopted the name Larry King in 1957, when he disk-jockeyed in Miami, Florida. In the next year he began hosting a four-hour morning show. Set in a Miami restaurant, King would mix question-and-answer sessions with roaming conversations with restaurant patrons. In 1963 he began a weekend television interview show and later began writing a syndicated newspaper column. In 1978 King reached a national audience with a nationally syndicated four-hour radio talk-show. After moving his broadcasting headquarters to Washington, D.C., and focussing on political subjects, he launched, in 1985,

the hour-long *Larry King Live* on then relatively new CABLE NEWS NETWORK (CNN). Larry King's national audience and broad appeal turned his shows into a popular venue for individual politicians across the American political spectrum. By the early 21st century the rise of Fox News and other cable outlets caused a decline in King's ratings, as his competitors hosted commentators on contemporary political and social issues.

**King, Martin Luther, Jr.** *(1929–1968)* American CIVIL RIGHTS leader. The son and grandson of black Baptist ministers in the Deep South, King was born in Atlanta, Georgia. He graduated from Morehouse College in 1948, then received a divinity degree from Crozer Theological Seminary in 1951 and a doctorate in 1955 from Boston University, where he met Coretta Scott, who became his wife. In 1954 King accepted a ministry at the Dexter Avenue Baptist Church in MONTGOMERY, Ala. By December 1955, racial tensions there, which had focused on segregated bus seating, led him to form the Montgomery Improvement Association, the first of many organizations he formed to pursue a nonviolent resistance modeled on that led by Mohandas GANDHI in India. His leadership and his methods brought about integration of the Montgomery buses in 1956.

*Civil rights leader Martin Luther King, Jr.* (LIBRARY OF CONGRESS, PRINTS AND PHOTOGRAPHS DIVISION)

To broaden his civil rights activities King formed the SOUTHERN CHRISTIAN LEADERSHIP CONFERENCE in 1957. In 1959 he moved to Atlanta, where he became assistant pastor to his father at the Ebenezer Baptist Church. King first gained national fame for his civil rights demonstrations in BIRMINGHAM, Ala., in 1963. There his followers were abused by police and King was arrested, leading to his *Letter from Birmingham Jail.* His most important demonstration was the MARCH ON WASHINGTON by 250,000 civil rights supporters on August 28, 1963, when he delived his "I Have a Dream" speech. For his nonviolent activities on behalf of civil rights, he was awarded the NOBEL PEACE PRIZE for in 1964.

In 1965 he led the Freedom March to SELMA, Alabama, for the cause of voting rights. The following year he brought his campaign to the North. During the later stages of his struggle, King opposed the VIETNAM WAR, arguing that it drained resources from the war on hunger and poverty. On the evening of April 4, 1968, King was assassinated in Memphis, Tennessee, where he had gone to lead a strike of sanitation workers. James Earl Ray, a white man, was later arrested and found guilty of the crime, although he has since claimed that a wider conspiracy was involved in the shooting. Despite later revelations of improprieties in King's personal life, for many people King remains one of the most revered Americans of the 20th century. His birthday, January 15, is celebrated as a legal holiday in most U.S. states.

**King, Riley B. "B. B."** (1925–   ) American blues singer. Like so many blues singers of his era, King developed his style in childhood as a gospel singer. King and his guitar, Lucille, toured blues clubs throughout the 1950s and 1960s, without being able to cross over to a mainstream audience. In the late Sixties, younger audiences who were ready to discover the roots of rock music "discovered" B. B. King, and he began to achieve popular success with such albums as *Confessin' the Blues* (1966), *Blues Is King* (1967) and his biggest hit, *Live in Cook County Jail* (1971). Throughout the 1990s King continued to win acclaim for his work, including four Grammy Awards—Best Traditional Blues Recording for *Live at the Apollo* (1991); Best Traditional Blues Recording for *Blues Summit* (1993); Best Rock Instrumental Performance for *SRV Shuffle* (1996), with collaboration by renowned guitarists ERIC CLAPTON and Bonnie Raitt; and Best Traditional Blues Album for *Blues on the Bayou* (1999). In 2000 King and Clapton recorded *Riding with the King,* an album containing both blues and rock music.

**King, Stephen Edwin** (1947–   ) American writer of the weird and the macabre, the most successful horror writer in the world. King was a struggling high school teacher in Maine living in a trailer when he published his first novel, *Carrie* (1974), a tale of a girl with telekinetic powers. Its modest success (13,000 copies sold in hardcover), coupled with the popular film adaptation by Brian DE PALMA in 1976 and the breakthrough publication of *Salem's Lot* in paperback that year (3,000,000 copies sold) quickly established King's preeminence in horror fiction. King is frankly derivative of the traditions in 19th-century gothic horror; and he peppers them with references to contemporary rock music and consumer culture. His dialogue is vulgarly realistic and his imagery is intentionally visceral and repellent, a modern extension of *grand guignol.* Some of his works, like *The Stand* (1978) and *It* (1986), are preoccupied with the cinematic effects of rapid crosscutting of scenes, shifts in points of view, alteration of time sequence, and so on; others like *The Shining* (1977) are authentic masterworks in the sheer excitation of terror; whereas others, like his best books, *The Dead Zone* (1979) and *Misery* (1987), are brooding psychological studies of psychotic states. In *Danse Macabre* (1981), a collection of essays on horror fiction, King described the writing process as a kind of "dance" in which the author searches out the private "phobic pressure points" of each reader. "We have emotional musculature just like we have physical musculature," he told an interviewer. "And our dark emotions need exercising, but society doesn't allow that. So, somebody has to take them for a walk and exercise them for you. And I guess I'm one of the guys who does that." Many of King's books have been adapted as motion pictures. In 1999 King suffered severe injuries when he was hit by a van near his home. After a lengthy period of recovery he returned to his work as a writer of fiction and nonfiction. King attempted, with limited success, to sell his fiction for download on the Internet.

**King, William Lyon Mackenzie** (1874–1950) Canadian statesman, prime minister of CANADA (1921–30; 1935–48). Born in Kitchener, Ontario, he was the grandson of the 19th-century Canadian rebel leader William Lyon Mackenzie. King studied at the universities of Toronto and Chicago and at Harvard, becoming an expert in political economy and labor affairs. He helped to establish the Department of Labour during the Liberal administration of Wilfrid LAURIER and served as its deputy minister (1909–11) and minister (1909–11). In 1909 he also became a Liberal member of Parliament. During World War I, he did research on industrial relations for the American Rockefeller Foundation. In

Canadian prime minister William Mackenzie King with Franklin Roosevelt and Winston Churchill (LIBRARY OF CONGRESS, PRINTS AND PHOTOGRAPHS DIVISION)

1919 he succeeded Laurier as leader of the LIBERAL PARTY and became prime minister in 1921 after his party's victory in the national elections. Except for a two-month period, King served until 1930. He was the leader of the opposition during the Conservative administration of Richard Bedford BENNETT (1930–35) and was prime minister again after the Liberal victory of 1935, serving until he retired in 1948. Between the wars, King maintained an essentially isolationist position and pressed for Canadian autonomy within the BRITISH EMPIRE, while mediating between the English- and French-speaking communities at home. He brought Canada into WORLD WAR II, forming a war cabinet, mobilizing public opinion in favor of the war and finally instituting conscription in 1944. Insisting upon the recognition of Canada's importance, he also maintained cooperation with Great Britain and signed joint defense agreements with the U.S. After the war, King was the head of the Canadian delegation at the 1945 San Francisco Conference that drafted the United Nations charter and at the 1946 Paris Conference.

**King David Hotel attack** *(July 22, 1946)* Jewish guerrillas of the IRGUN ZVAI LEUMI organization blew up the King David Hotel, which housed the British administrative headquarters in JERUSALEM. The explosion caused 91 deaths.

**King Kong** The giant ape King Kong made his first appearance in 1932, in a book of that title by Delos W. Lovelace, "novelized" from the screenplay of the forthcoming film *King Kong,* which was released in 1933. Directed by Merian C. Cooper and Ernest B. Schoedsack, the film starred Fay Wray as Ann, the woman Kong kidnaps in a variation on the beauty-and-the-beast theme. Featuring spectacular stop-motion special effects, the film was an instant sensation and is credited with saving the RKO studios from bankruptcy during the GREAT DEPRESSION. A remake of the film was made by Dino de Laurentiis in 1976, and a sequel, *King Kong Lives,* was released in 1986. In 2005 Peter Jackson directed another remake. Kong was also the star of two Japanese films, *King Kong vs. Godzilla* (1963) and *King Kong Escapes* (1967). An icon of popular cul-

ture, he has also been featured in a television cartoon show (1966–69), comic books and a variety of merchandise.

**Kingsley, Sir Ben** *(1943– )* British stage and film actor. Born Krishna Bhanji in Scarborough, North Yorkshire, England, his father was a physician of Indian descent and his mother was of English-Russian origin. Kingsley developed a passion for the theater soon after he saw a performance of Great Britain's prestigious ROYAL SHAKESPEARE COMPANY (RSC). After several stints in regional and touring theaters in Britain, he gained admission to the RSC, for which he performed in *A Midsummer Night's Dream* (1970), *Nicholas Nickleby* (1980) and *Othello* (1985). He participated in performances in the King's Head Theatre (1973's *Hello and Goodbye*) and the National Theatre (*Volpone* in 1975), in London.

During Kingsley's tenure on the RSC he also made his debut as a motion-picture actor in *Fear Is the Key,* a 1972 drama. However, it was not until 10 years later that he achieved international fame and recognition for his film performance of MAHATMA GANDHI in the film *Gandhi,* for which he won an Academy Award for Best Actor that year. He received universal acclaim for his 1993 role of Itzhak Stern in Steven Spielberg's *Schindler's List.* After many other successful performances on the stage and in films, he was knighted in 2001.

**Kinnock, Neil** *(1942– )* British politician. Born and educated in Wales, Kinnock worked for the Workers' Educational Association and was elected to Parliament as a Labour member in 1970 by a Welsh constituency. He served as shadow minister for education from 1979 to 1983. Despite his lack of government experience, Kinnock succeeded veteran Michael FOOT as leader of the LABOUR PARTY following the party's defeat in the 1983 general election. Originally in the left wing of the Labour Party, Kinnock was viewed as a compromise choice between the party's opposing factions and promised to follow a more moderate course. He instigated the ejection of the extreme left-wing Militant Tendency faction from parliament in 1986. Although a gifted orator, as leader of the Opposition, Kinnock proved an unequal opponent to Conservative

prime minister Margaret THATCHER, and there was doubt both in and out of the party that he could lead Labour to a general election victory. Kinnock received attention in the U.S. in 1988 when Democratic presidential hopeful Joseph Biden was found to have plagiarized one of his speeches and was forced to withdraw from the campaign. In 1992 Kinnock was replaced as Labour Party leader by John Smith. Since 1995 he has served on the EUROPEAN UNION's European Commission, becoming its vice president in 1999.

**Kinsey Reports** Research on human sexual behavior conducted by Professor Alfred Kinsey of Indiana University. Kinsey was a zoology professor who, in 1938, commenced what is regarded as the first major scientific study of the nature of human sexual preferences and patterns. The "Kinsey Reports" refers to the two publications that summarized the findings of Kinsey and his researchers—*Sexual Behavior in the Human Male* (1948) and *Sexual Behavior in the Human Female* (1953). These books were deemed as degenerate and even as communist by MCCARTHY-era conservatives and religious fundamentalists. The basis for this furor, which led to cessation of funding for Kinsey's work by the Rockefeller Foundation and other agencies, was the statistical evidence put forward in the Kinsey Reports that indicated that human sexual behavior differed greatly from supposed established norms. For example, 37% of males were said to have had at some point a homosexual contact leading to orgasm. In addition, Kinsey pointed to partner insensitivity rather than biological incapability as the most frequent cause of female frigidity. At the time of his death, Kinsey was working on a book that was critical of sex laws in the U.S. The Kinsey Reports are widely regarded as a pioneering effort toward an objective view of human sexuality. However, such notable public figures as anthropologist Margaret MEAD, theologian Reinhold NIEBUHR and critic Lionel TRILLING criticized the reports for ignoring the spiritual implications of sex.

**Kipling, Rudyard** *(1865–1936)* British poet and author. Born in Bombay, India, Kipling was sent to England to be educated. He chronicled his unhappy childhood spent in a series of foster

*British author Rudyard Kipling* (LIBRARY OF CONGRESS, PRINTS AND PHOTOGRAPHS DIVISION)

homes in the short story "Baa Baa, Black Sheep" (1888) and the novel *The Light That Failed* (1937). He completed his education at the United Services College in Devon. Unfit for military service because of poor eyesight, he returned to India to work as a journalist. His popular first collection of poems, *Departmental Ditties* was published in 1886; his first volume of short stories, *Plain Tales from the Hills* in 1888. Kipling continued writing prolifically and was received as a celebrity when he traveled to London in 1889. He married Caroline Balestier, with whose brother Kipling wrote the novel *The Naulahka* (1892). The Kiplings moved to Vermont where the Balestiers had property but returned to settle in England in 1896, though Kipling continued to travel throughout his life. Kipling's varied works depicted life in colonial India and reflected his conservative patriotism. *Barrack Room Ballads* (1892) includes the notable poems "Gunga Din" and "Mandalay." The poem "Recessional" celebrated Jubilee Day in 1897. *Kim* (1901), the novel considered to be his masterpiece, is an account of a boy and a Buddhist monk traveling in India. Kipling was the first English writer to receive the NOBEL PRIZE in literature, in 1907. He carried on a long correspondence with U.S. president Theodore ROOSEVELT and

was influential in shaping Roosevelt's outlook in foreign policy. Kipling's reputation went into decline, partly due to its nationalistic jingoism—he coined the term "white man's burden"—and also because of what many considered to be its lowbrow appeal. A resurgence in appreciation for his craftsmanship occurred when T. S. ELIOT edited a collection of his poetry for FABER & FABER in 1943. Later critics have also reevaluated Kipling's work and found more subtlety than he was earlier given credit for. Always popular were his works for children such as *The Jungle Book* (1894) and *Just So Stories* (1902). Other works include *Soldiers Three* (1890), *Captains Courageous* (1897) and an unfinished autobiography, *Something of Myself* (1937).

**Kipnis, Alexander** *(1891–1978)* Ukrainian-born operatic bass. Alexander Kipnis was best known for his Wagnerian roles and for his performances in Russian operas, particularly the title role in *Boris Godunov*. He was with the Chicago Civic Opera from 1923 to 1933, and sang over 100 performances at the Metropolitan Opera in New York from 1940 to 1945. He was a familiar figure in the great opera world of Europe and was also featured in numerous operatic and lieder recital recordings. His son **Igor Kipnis** (1930–2002) was a renowned harpsichordist and musicologist.

**Kirchner, Ernst Ludwig** *(1880–1938)* German painter and graphic artist, a leading exponent of German EXPRESSIONISM. At first a student of architecture, Kirchner began painting in Munich (1903–04) and Dresden (1905) and made a particular study of primitive art at the Dresden Museum of Ethnology. In 1905 he, Erich HECKEL and Karl SCHMIDT-ROTLUFF cofounded DIE BRÜCKE. Influenced by the intensity of feeling and line in the paintings of Vincent Van Gogh and the intensity of color in FAUVISM, Kirchner was also shaped by Dürer, Gothic woodcuts and Edvard MUNCH. His art exploits strong color contrasts and angular forms in the expressive portrayal of figures and landscapes. Moving from Dresden to Berlin in 1911, he captured the life of that city in acid-tinged portraits and street scenes. His paintings became increasingly bitter

and tortured in colors that went from bright and pure in the early 1900s to dark and shadowy in works painted into the 1920s. Kirchner was also a master printmaker, producing some 2,000 powerful and often savage etchings, lithographs and, most notably, woodcuts. Drafted into the German army, he suffered an emotional breakdown in 1914 and moved to a sanatorium in Davos, Switzerland, remaining in the area for the rest of his life. Condemned by the Nazis for his "degenerate" art and in failing health, Kirchner committed suicide in 1938.

**Kiribati** Republic in the western Pacific Ocean, on the equator and northeast of the Solomon Islands (see map page 957). Formerly known as the Gilbert Islands, the nation consists of the 16 former Gilbert islands, Ocean Island, some of the Line islands and some of the Phoenix islands. Great Britain proclaimed a protectorate over the Gilberts in 1892 and in 1915 combined them with the Ellice Islands into the Gilbert and Ellice Islands Colony. Ocean Island and some of the Line and Phoenix islands were then also included. In WORLD WAR II Japan occupied the Gilberts from 1941 to 1943. The U.S. Marines retook Tarawa atoll in a bloody battle in November 1943, while the army regained Makin Island the same month. In 1971 the colony was given self-government, and at the start of 1976 the Ellice Islands (now TUVALU) were separated from the colony. On July 12, 1979, the Gilbert Islands and the others named above became independent as Kiribati, a member of the Commonwealth of Nations. Its inhabitants are Micronesian, and its chief exports are copra and phosphates.

**Kirilenko, Andrei Pavlovich** *(1906–1990)* Soviet politician. A long-time associate of Leonid BREZHNEV, in the 1970s Kirilenko was widely thought to be a leading candidate to succeed the Soviet leader. A member of the Politburo, he retired from the body in 1982 and dropped from sight. Although the official explanation for his retirement was ill health, unofficial reports said that he had been disgraced by the defection of his son to the West.

**Kirillin, Vladimir Alekseyevich** *(1913–1999)* Soviet government offi-

| KIRIBATI | |
|---|---|
| 1892 | The Gilbert (Kiribati) and Ellice (Tuvalu) Islands are proclaimed a British protectorate. |
| 1916–39 | The uninhabited Phoenix Islands, Christmas Island, Ocean Island, and Line Island (Banaba) are added to the colony. |
| 1942–43 | While occupied by the Japanese, the island is the scene of fierce fighting with U.S. troops. |
| 1971 | The island group becomes autonomous. |
| 1976 | The mainly Melanesian-populated Ellice Islands separate to become Tuvalu. |
| 1979 | Kiribati becomes an independent republic within the Commonwealth of Great Britain. Kiribati and the United States sign an agreement under which the U.S. relinquishes all claims to territory in the Phoenix and Line Island groups, including Canton, Enderbury and Hull. |
| 1999 | Two of Kiribati's uninhabited islands, Tebua Tarawa and Abanuea, disappear beneath the waves, as global climate changes raise sea levels to new heights. |
| 2003 | Anote Tong wins presidential election against his elder brother, Harry. |

cial. A graduate of the power engineering institute, Kirillin gained membership in the COMMUNIST PARTY in 1937 and served in the Soviet army from 1941 to 1943. Kirillin's numerous posts include head of the department of science, high schools and schools (1954–55) and head of the ideologies department of the central committee (1955–63). From 1961 to 1966 Kirillin was a member of the central committee, and from 1963 to 1966 the chairman of the all-union society for the dissemination of political and scientific knowledge. In 1965 he became chairman of the Comecon committee for scientific-technological cooperation. Kirillin was decorated with various orders, medals and prizes.

**Kirk, Alan Goodrich** *(1888–1963)*
U.S. Navy officer and diplomat. A graduate of the Naval Academy, Kirk served as gunnery officer aboard several ships, and was promoted to chief of staff for the commander of naval forces in Europe early in WORLD WAR II. He commanded the 1,000 ships in the INVASION OF NORMANDY, France. Admiral Kirk retired from the Navy in 1946, and served as U.S. ambassador to Belgium (1946–49), the USSR (1949–52) and the Republic of China (1963).

**Kirk, Russell Amos** *(1918–1994)*
American political writer. Kirk was one of the most eloquent writers in defense of the conservative tradition to emerge

in postwar America. His first book, *The Conservative Mind* (1953), was his doctoral dissertation, but it won a wide readership by tracing a glowing intellectual tradition for CONSERVATISM that dated back to the 18th century and the English statesman Edmund Burke. Further, Kirk argued that the true basis of conservatism lay in defense of family, tradition and community, and not in the support of big business and the free market. This latter view made Kirk a controversial figure within conservative circles. Kirk taught at Michigan State and other universities and lectured frequently throughout the country. His other books include *A Program for Conservatives* (1954) and *Confessions of a Bohemian Tory* (1963).

**Kirkpatrick, Jeanne J.** *(1926–  )*
U.S. public official. Originally a liberal Democrat, in the 1970s Kirkpatrick became a leading neoconservative and anticommunist. Her views attracted the attention of Ronald REAGAN, who appointed her U.S. ambassador to the UN (1981–85) when he took office. She criticized many UN programs as contrary to U.S. interests. She helped develop the Reagan administration's policies toward Latin America, condemning the Sandinista government in NICARAGUA and urging support for the CONTRAS. In the late 1980s Kirkpatrick was mentioned as a possible candidate for high office, but her support was limited.

**Kirov, Sergei Mironovich Kostrinov** *(1886–1934)* Soviet politician. He became a Bolshevik in 1905. His first task after the revolution was to establish soviet power in the Caucasus. From 1926 he was party secretary in the Leningrad area, and he became a Politburo member in 1930. Kirov gave support to STALIN but opposed Stalin's personal rule after the 17th party congress in 1934. His assassination in December 1934 began the witch-hunt that developed into the GREAT PURGE, which resulted in the judicial execution of over 100 suspected opponents of Stalin's regime.

**Kirst, Hans Helmut** *(1914–1989)*
German author. One of West Germany's most popular novelists, Kirst wrote a total of 46 books, many of which dealt with the experiences of soldiers in WORLD WAR II. (He himself had served in the German army throughout the war.) The English translations of his novels *The Lieutenant Must Be Mad* (1951), *Night of the Generals* (1962, filmed 1967), and the trilogy *08/15* (published in the mid-1950s) were highly popular in the U.S. and Great Britain. Critics argued, however, over whether his works were criticisms of Nazi Germany or merely adventure-thrillers with a wartime setting.

**Kirstein, Lincoln** *(1907–1996)*
American writer and ballet director

who was influential on the American and international ballet scene for over 50 years. Kirstein was responsible for bringing George BALANCHINE to the U.S. and for forming the School of American Ballet with Balanchine and E.M.M. Warburg (1934). He established the Ballet Society in 1946, from which the NEW YORK CITY BALLET (NYCB) evolved. Kirstein served as general director for NYCB from 1948 to 1991; he wrote many acclaimed ballet books, including *The New York City Ballet* (1974) and *Nijinsky Dancing* (1975). He was awarded the Medal of Freedom in 1984.

**Kishi, Nobosuke** *(1896–1987)* Japanese politician. Kishi was the dominant figure in pre–World War II Japanese industrial planning. During much of the war, he served as minister of commerce and industry and was responsible for economic mobilization. After the war he was arrested as a war criminal and imprisoned without trial until 1948. He began his political comeback in December 1956 and two months later became prime minister. He was forced to resign in 1960 after the passage of a revised version of the U.S.-Japan Mutual Security Treaty triggered mass protests. In retirement he continued to exercise considerable influence over the ruling Liberal Democratic Party. He was the brother of another prime minister, Eisakyu SATO,

and the father-in-law of a leading prime ministerial contender, Shintaro Abe.

**Kissinger, Henry Alfred** *(1923– )* U.S. diplomat, foreign policy adviser and analyst and secretary of state (1973–77). Kissinger was arguably the most influential, and controversial, diplomat of his time. Born in Germany, he fled that country with his family and came to the U.S. when the Nazis came to power. Professor of government at Harvard from 1958 to 1971, he formed close ties with prominent U.S. politicians, including Nelson ROCKEFELLER, and was adviser to Richard M. NIXON during the 1968 presidential campaign. As White House national security adviser from 1969 to 1973, Kissinger played a more prominent role than the secretary of state, traveling on peace missions to the Middle East, Vietnam and southern Africa and negotiating with the USSR in the Strategic Arms Limitation Talks (SALT). In 1971 he made a secret trip to the People's Republic of CHINA, paving the way for President Nixon's visit the following year and the normalization of relations between the two countries. Kissinger was also involved in negotiations to end the VIETNAM WAR. His statement just before the 1972 presidential election that "peace is at hand" helped build support for Nixon's candidacy, but Kissinger's credibility was questioned as talks—

and the war—dragged on for another half-year. Kissinger was awarded the 1973 NOBEL PEACE PRIZE with LE DUC THO (who refused to accept it) for concluding the PARIS PEACE ACCORD that ended the Vietnam War; the award caused much controversy.

He was appointed secretary of state in 1973, holding that office for the remainder of Nixon's presidency and throughout President Gerald FORD's administration. Kissinger practiced a conservative but pragmatic brand of diplomacy, concentrating on relations between the superpowers in terms of realpolitik. Although U.S. foreign policy took a different turn during the CARTER presidency, Kissinger was an influential if background figure during the REAGAN administration, in which several of his protégés served. He was later accused of complicity in the military coup that overthrew Chile's Marxist president Salvador ALLANDE in 1973.

**Kistiakowski, George Bogdan** *(1900–1982)* Russian-born U.S. chemist. Kistiakowski emigrated to the U.S. in 1926 and worked briefly at Princeton before going to Harvard. He was named professor of chemistry at Harvard in 1937. During World War II he worked on the MANHATTAN PROJECT. As head of the Explosives Division at Los Alamos (1944–45), he developed the complicated trigger device used to detonate the first ATOMIC BOMB. After the war he was a leading member of the U.S. scientific establishment. He served as science adviser to President EISENHOWER from 1959 to 1961. Active in the movement for nuclear disarmament, he was later chairman of the Council for a Livable World and adviser to the U.S. Arms Control and Disarmament Agency.

**Kitchen Debate** See Richard M. NIXON.

**kitsch** Term used in design criticism to describe work of a deliberately tasteless, gross and foolish sort. The Gillo Dorfles book of 1969, *Kitsch*, is the definitive study of the subject. It explains the obvious, popular attraction of objects and design elements that are silly, ugly and insulting to both concepts of "high style" and serious theories of modernism. Gift and novelty shops thrive on the commercial distribution

*U.S. secretary of state Henry Kissinger with Indira Gandhi. 1974* (LIBRARY OF CONGRESS, PRINTS AND PHOTOGRAPHS DIVISION)

of kitsch trinkets, while kitsch themes often appear in housing, furniture and accessories intended for the mass market. Postmodern theory continues to struggle with pop or kitsch elements in an attempt to bring about an accommodation between popular taste and serious design theory.

**Kitt, Eartha** *(1928– )* American singer. Born in Columbia, South Carolina, Kitt sang in New York and Paris before attracting widespread attention for her appearance in the 1952 Broadway revue *New Faces*. Known for the sultry sexuality of her renditions, which was considered somewhat shocking early in her career, Kitt's best-known songs include "C'est Si Bon," "Santa Baby" and "An Old-Fashioned Girl."

**Kitty Hawk** Village in North Carolina, near Cape Hatteras. This otherwise obscure village became part of 20th-century history on Dec. 17, 1903, when the WRIGHT BROTHERS made the world's first successful flight in a powered heavier-than-air machine—the airplane. The Wright Brothers chose this part of the world for their glider and powered aircraft experiments because of the constant winds from the ocean; the deserted beaches and dunes were also ideal for such early aviation experiments.

**Klammer, Franz** *(1953– )* Austrian skier. Klammer is arguably the greatest downhill racer of all time. He won 22 races from 1974 to 1978, including six consecutive triumphs to best the old record held by Jean-Claude KILLY. His flying, wild run to win the downhill OLYMPIC gold in 1976 at Innsbruck in his native Austria may rank as one of the most thrilling moments in the history of any sport. Although Klammer was World Cup champion in 1977 and 1978, he was not selected to represent Austria in the 1980 Olympic games. He made a comeback in 1982–83, winning the World Cup championship once more.

**Klee, Paul** *(1879–1940)* Swiss painter. Combining sophisticated abstraction with an aura of childlike innocence, his delicate and dreamlike works are gentle monuments of 20th-century art. From a

musical family, Klee was a violinist but finally decided to study art, entering the Munich Academy in 1900. He settled in Munich in 1906, became friendly with Wassily KANDINSKY and Franz MARC, and exhibited with the BLAUE REITER group. A trip to Tunisia in 1914 awakened the young artist to the possibilities of color and gave his work a new radiance. He taught at the BAUHAUS from 1922 to 1931 and at the Dusseldorf Academy from 1931 to 1933, when he was dismissed by the Nazis who considered his work degenerate. Klee defined his approach to art in his *Pedagogical Sketchbook* (1925, tr. 1964). He left Germany in 1933, returning to Switzerland where he spent the rest of his life. An extremely prolific artist, Klee created over 9,000 works—paintings, drawings and graphics—that are included in virtually all of the world's great museums. Some of his best known paintings are *The Twittering Machine* (1922, Museum of Modern Art, N.Y.C.), *Fish Magic* (1925, Philadelphia Museum of Art) and *Revolutions of the Viaducts* (1937, Kunsthall, Hamburg). Klee's works display a whimsy and fantasy, a witty personal language of signs and a poetic sense of mystery that are unique in all of modern art.

**Kleiber, Erich** *(1890–1956)* Austrian-born opera and symphonic conductor. A fierce individualist, on several occasions he clashed with repressive political regimes. He was born in Vienna. After hearing Gustav MAHLER conduct, he decided to pursue that career, and he made his debut at the German Theater in Prague in 1911. A quick succession of appointments followed—at Barmen-Elberfeld (1919–21), Düsseldorf (1921–22), Mannheim (1922–23), and the Berlin State Opera (1923). His service to the cause of new music reached its peak in these years; and he presented premieres of new works by Darius MILHAUD, Max Reger, Igor STRAVINSKY, Arnold SCHOENBERG and Alban BERG.

His world premiere of Berg's WOZZECK in 1925 was a landmark event in the history of SERIAL MUSIC. Although not a Jew, he left Germany in 1935 protesting Nazi persecutions. He did not return until after the war and a number of guest posts in London, Prague, Amsterdam and Buenos Aires (becoming an Argentinian citizen in 1939). Dissatisfaction with the mix of

art and propaganda in East Berlin led him to resign his post at the Berlin State Opera. He spent his last years conducting in London, Vienna, Cologne and Stuttgart. In his last decade he made many recordings for the Decca label, including a magnificent set of the complete symphonies of Beethoven, a composer whom he revered. Kleiber could be a difficult and tough disciplinarian. "A conductor must live in his house like a lion," he said, "with its claws deep in its prey." His son **Carlos Kleiber** (b. 1930) is also a highly acclaimed conductor.

**Klein, Calvin** *(1942– )* American fashion designer, a graduate of the Fashion Institute of Technology in New York, who has built a major national and international "name" reputation. The Calvin Klein stylistic direction shows the influence of Yves Saint Laurent but tends to have a more colorful, less subtle character. After five years as an apprentice designer with several large firms, Klein founded his own business in 1968 and built a name for apparel design that is simple, functional and classic while at the same time recognizable and stylish. Klein designer jeans quickly became an international fad, and his name continues to make anything associated with it, such as Obsession perfume, a commercial success. He won a Coty design award in each of five consecutive years beginning in 1973. In 1995 one of Klein's ad campaigns was denounced by President Bill Clinton for depicting teenagers in sexually suggestive poses, which caused him to pull the ads. In 2003 he sold his company to Phillips-Van Heusen.

**Klemperer, Otto** *(1885–1973)* German-born orchestra conductor, one of the last titans in the Austro-German tradition; born in Breslau and later studied in Hamburg, Frankfurt am Main and Berlin with Hans Pfitzner. The young Klemperer was encouraged in his conducting ambitions by Gustav MAHLER. After numerous conducting assignments, he settled into his first important post as director of the Kroll Opera in Berlin in the late 1920s. In addition to many standard works he also performed new operas by STRAVINSKY, SCHOENBERG and HINDEMITH. Because of his Jewish heritage, he was dismissed from the Berlin State Opera in 1933. In his subsequent travels through Austria, Switzerland and the U.S., he incurred a skull injury during a fall; and in 1939 an operation for a brain tumor left him partially paralyzed. Psychological affective disorders further impaired him at periodic intervals. And he was severely burned in a fire in 1959. But Klemperer always fought back from misfortune. He conducted the Los Angeles Philharmonic from 1935 to 1939, organized the Pittsburgh Symphony Orchestra in 1939 and became principal conductor of the Philharmonia Orchestra (later the New Philharmonia Orchestra) of London in 1959. His reputation with the Austro-German symphonic tradition of Beethoven, Brahms, Bruckner and Mahler grew. His seriousness, his imposing, monumental appearance, his big orchestral sound, his majestic (to some, laborious) tempi and his utter lack of flamboyance made him the venerated heir to musical traditions rooted in the 19th century. His recordings after 1954 on the EMI label have preserved that style and that sound for new generations.

**Klimt, Gustav** *(1862–1918)* Austrian painter. A lifelong Viennese, he studied at Vienna's School of Decorative Art. He opened a mural studio with his brother in 1883, executing decorations at Vienna's Burgtheater and Kunsthistorisches Museum. Klimt was a cofounder of the Vienna secession, a group that rebelled against the academic art of the late 19th century, and served as its president from 1898 to 1903. The foremost exponent of *Secessionstil,* the Viennese version of ART NOUVEAU, he created works that were symbolic in theme, jewel-like in color, flatly decorative, richly patterned and rhythmically erotic. He continued to create works for public buildings, such as the ceiling murals at the University of Vienna, *Philosophy, Medicine* and *Jurisprudence* (1900–02)—whose sensual imagery caused a furor of criticism—and the mosaics for Josef HOFMANN's Palais Stoclet in Brussels (1905–09). However, his most celebrated works are his portraits and landscapes. Among his best known paintings are *The Kiss* (1907–08, Oesterreichische Galerie, Vienna, and 1909, Musée

d'Art Moderne, Strasbourg) and *Hope I* (1903, National Gallery, Ottawa).

**Kline, Franz** *(1910–1962)* American painter, one of the chief figures in ABSTRACT EXPRESSIONISM. Born in Wilkes-Barre, Pa., Kline studied at Boston University (1931–35) and the Heatherley School of Fine Art in London (1937–38) before settling in New York City in 1938. A struggling painter during the 1940s, his early works were humorous sketches and realistic still lifes and city scenes. In the 1950s Kline developed the style that was to make him world famous. In paintings such as *High Street* (1950), *Mahoning* (1956, Whitney Museum of American Art, New York City) and *Kupola* (1958) he filled huge canvases with heavy streaking black lines on a white field, developing a powerfully spare visual calligraphy that spoke of action, impulse, violence and disciplined gesture. Kline also taught at Black Mountain College (1952), Pratt Institute (1953) and the Philadelphia Museum School (1954). In the late 1950s he returned to color in large abstract works such as *Green Vertical* (1958) and *Copper and Red* (1959) that maintained much of the boldness and force of his earlier monochromatic compositions.

**Klint, Kaare** *(1888–1954)* Danish furniture designer and architect who had, as both teacher and designer, a broad influence on the development of the type of modern furniture called "Danish modern." Klint studied painting and architecture at the Copenhagen Academy. With his father P. V. Jensen Klint (1853–1930), Klint did extensive studies on human dimensions and developed storage furniture based on these studies. Beginning in 1924 he became a teacher of furniture design and craftsmanship at the Copenhagen Academy where he was also later a teacher of architecture. His teaching influenced a whole generation of Danish designers. His own work won many awards and appeared in a number of exhibitions. Klint's style was clearly modern but retained a respect for traditional values in structure and craftsmanship. His 1933 folding deck chair and knock-down Safari chair, both based on traditional models, are among his best-known works.

**Klyun, Ivan** *(1870–1942)* Russian artist. He was a minor suprematist and a close friend of Kazimir MALEVICH (see SUPREMATISM). His work is considered to show how the concern for ornamentation and beauty deteriorated into standard formulas after the Russian Revolution.

**Knave of Diamonds** Society of painters, founded in Moscow in 1909 for exhibition purposes, by Michael LARIONOV and others. For two years the Knave of Diamonds was the leading movement of the Soviet avant-garde.

**Knight, John S.** *(1895–1981)* American publisher, founder of the Knight newspaper publishing empire. Starting with one local newspaper inherited from his father in Akron, Ohio, in 1933, Knight went on to preside over Knight-Ridder Newspapers, which owned 33 daily newspapers nationwide, as well as three television stations and other subsidiaries. A fierce advocate of economic and editorial independence in journalism, he won the 1968 PULITZER PRIZE for distinguished editorial writing in his weekly "Editor's Notebook" columns.

**Knipper-Chekhova, Olga Leonardovna** *(1870–1959)* One of the most outstanding actresses of the first generation of the Moscow Art Theater. In 1901 she married Anton CHEKHOV. Knipper-Chekhova is especially remembered for her interpretation of the leading female roles of the plays of Chekhov, GORKY and Turgenev, as well as for her performance in plays by Molière, Gogol and Griboyedov. She was awarded the Order of Lenin and twice received the Order of the Red Banner of Labor.

**Knopf, Alfred Abraham** *(1892–1984)* American publisher, a pioneer in publishing translations of outstanding foreign authors, such as Knut HAMSUN, Franz KAFKA and Jean-Paul SARTRE, as well as in the publication of such influential American authors as Willa CATHER, John UPDIKE and H. L. MENCKEN. He founded Alfred A. Knopf, Inc., in 1915 and collaborated with assistant Blanche Wolf (who became his wife in 1916) to create a publishing house noted for high standards in the selection of titles, book design and printing quality. In 1924 he co-founded the *American Mercury* magazine with H. L. Mencken and George Jean Nathan. Though the Knopf company was sold to Random House in 1960, if has survived as a separate imprint. Knopf served as president of the company from 1918 to 1957 and as chairman of the board from 1957 to 1972. From 1972 until his death, he was chairman emeritus.

**Koch, Frederick Henry** *(1877–1944)* American dramatist and educator. A graduate of Harvard University, he joined the staff of the University of North Carolina in 1918. Considered the father of American folk drama, he founded the Carolina Playmakers. This group's playhouse became the first state-subsidized theater in America. Eleven volumes of folk plays appeared under his editorship.

**Kodak** Coined brand name for the cameras developed by George EASTMAN that made photography a popular hobby through the use of his invention of roll film. With the slogan "You push the button, we do the rest," Eastman relieved the average camera user of the complexities of darkroom work. With the introduction of inexpensive box and folding cameras, Kodak quickly became synonymous with camera. On this basis the Eastman Kodak Company became a major American and international corporation producing a vast variety of photographic and related and unrelated products.

**Kodály, Zoltán** *(1882–1967)* Hungarian composer. Educated at the Budapest Hochschule, Kodály later taught composition there and became its assistant director in 1919. As a lecturer at the University of Budapest (1931–33), a private music teacher and the author of books on musical pedagogy, he did much to improve the teaching of music in Hungary and introduced the "Kodály Method" to the world. Second only to Béla BARTÓK as Hungary's preeminent modern composer, like Bartók he was an avid collector of folk music and collaborated with his fellow-composer in its study. The melodies, rhythms and formal structure of this music is evident in his music, which is also strongly romantic in style. In addition to his most popular work, the opera (1926) and orchestral suite (1927) *Hary János*, Kodály composed a symphony, an orchestral concerto, piano works, chamber music, songs, *Missa Brevis* (1945) and other choral works, theatrical music and many other works.

**Kodama, Yoshio** *(1911–1984)* Wealthy right-wing Japanese power-broker who influenced major Japanese political figures. Kodama was the first person indicted by Japanese authorities in the LOCKHEED SCANDAL (1976). His conviction and prison sentence were being appealed at the time of his death.

**Koestler, Arthur** *(1905–1983)* Anglo-German author and journalist. Born in Budapest, Koestler was educated at the University of Vienna. He was a member of the German Communist Party from 1932 to 1938 and worked as a foreign correspondent. While reporting the SPANISH CIVIL WAR, Koestler was arrested and imprisoned under FRANCO, and in 1940 was arrested and interned under the VICHY government. After his release he moved to England and wrote his first book in English, *The Scum of the Earth* (1941), an autobiography. His best known work, DARKNESS AT NOON (1940), is a novel evidencing his rejection of COMMUNISM and TOTALITARIANISM, themes he elaborated on in his contributions to *The God That Failed: Six Studies in Communism* (1950). Koestler's later works, which include *The Roots of Coincidence* (1972), evidence his interest in philosophy and parapsychology. A lifelong advocate of euthanasia, Koestler, ill with leukemia and Parkinson's Disease, took his own life with a drug overdose. Other works include the political novels *Arrival and Departure* (1943) and *Thieves in the Night* (1946), and the nonfiction *The Trail of the Dinosaur and Other Essays* (1955) and *The Act of Creation* (1964).

**Koffka, Kurt** *(1886–1941)* German psychologist. Koffka, along with Wolfgang KOHLER and Max WERTHEIMER, was one of the key founders, in 1912, of GESTALT PSYCHOLOGY. The Gestalt school emphasized that human learning and perception was based upon the relatively rapid recognition and integration of structured wholes, as opposed to an instance-by-instance slow assemblage of isolated data. Gestalt psychology had a major influence on subsequent thinking in such diverse fields as psychotherapy, art criticism and aesthetics, and educational theory. Koffka taught at the University of Giessen from 1911 to 1924 before coming to America, where he served as a professor at Smith College from 1927 to 1941. His major works are *The Growth of the Mind* (1921) and *Principles of Gestalt Psychology* (1935).

**Kogan, Leonid Borisovich** *(1924–1982)* Soviet violinist. A graduate of the Moscow State Conservatory (1948), Kogan won first prize at the prestigious Queen Elizabeth International Competition in Brussels in 1951. He was acclaimed for his technical mastery and classical precision. He was a professor at the Moscow State Conservatory and performed frequently in the USSR as well as Western Europe and the U.S.

**Kohima** Battle site and capital of India's Nagaland state, 139 mi E of Shilleng. In March–June 1944 the Japanese took it, but the victory of Anglo-Indian forces here on June 30, 1944, stemmed the Japanese advance into India.

**Kohl, Helmut** *(1930– )* Chancellor of WEST GERMANY (1982–90) and of re-united GERMANY (1990–98). Born in Ludwigshafen in the German Rhineland, Kohl attended the University of Frankfurt and earned his doctorate in political science from the University of Heidelberg. He joined the conservative CHRISTIAN DEMOCRATIC UNION and was elected to the Ludwigshafen city council. He went on to win a series of political posts

*West German chancellor Helmut Kohl, 1987* (LIBRARY OF CONGRESS, PRINTS AND PHOTOGRAPHS DIVISION)

that he was the youngest person ever to hold. Elected to the state parliament of the Rhineland-Palatinate in 1959, he became minister-president of that state in 1969, and in 1973 was chosen as national chairman of the CDU. Elected to the Bundestag (national parliament) in 1976, Kohl served as leader of the opposition (1976–82) during the government of Helmut SCHMIDT.

Kohl was elected prime minister in 1982, forming a coalition government with the support of the Free Democrats. In his foreign policy, he was both pro-European and pro-American, keeping West Germany in the forefront of the EUROPEAN ECONOMIC COMMUNITY and NATO. Domestically, he followed a conservative economic policy favoring free enterprise, in contrast to the Social Democrats' emphasis on social programs. With the fall of the communist government of EAST GERMANY (1989–90), Kohl pushed for a quick reunification of the two Germanys under the existing West German constitution. In the first nationwide elections in the new, unified Germany (Dec. 2, 1990), he won an easy victory over his Social Democratic opponent, thus becoming the first chancellor of all Germany in more than 45 years. Kohl's critics have charged that he is unintellectual and unimaginative, but he has proven an astute, pragmatic and popular politician and a leading figure in the Western alliance. Because of the stagnant national economy during the 1990s, Kohl's CDU fared poorly in the 1998 national elections, and he was replaced as chancellor by the Social Democrats and GERHARD SCHROEDER. A year after leaving office, Kohl became implicated in a financial scandal involving illegal campaign contributions to CDU members. Criminal proceedings against him were dropped in exchange for a payment of 300,000 marks.

**Kohler, Wolfgang** (*1887–1967*) German psychologist. Kohler, along with Kurt KOFFKA and Max WERTHEIMER, was one of the key founders, in 1912, of GESTALT PSYCHOLOGY. The Gestalt school emphasized that human learning and perception was based upon the relatively rapid recognition and integration of structured wholes, as opposed to an instance-by-instance slow assemblage of isolated data. Gestalt psychology had a major influence on subsequent thinking in such diverse fields as psychother-

apy, art criticism and aesthetics, and educational theory. Kohler was the director of the Prussian Academy of Sciences in the Canary Islands from 1913 to 1920. His research on the learning capabilities of chimpanzees during this period was summarized in *The Mentality of Apes* (1917). Kohler fled Nazi GERMANY shortly after the rise of HITLER and came to the U.S. where he taught at Swarthmore College from 1935 to 1955. Other major works by Kohler include *Gestalt Psychology* (1929), *Dynamics in Psychology* (1940), and *The Task of Gestalt Psychology* (1969).

**Koizumi, Junichiro** (*1942– *) Japanese statesman and leader of the Liberal Democratic Party (LDP) (2001–06). Born in Yokosuka, Koizumi graduated from Keio University in 1967 with a B.A. in Economics. He began his political career in 1972 as a delegate of the LDP, the dominant political party in Japan, representing the cities of Yokosuka and Miura in Japan's House of Representatives. In 1979 he was appointed the state secretary for finance, chairman of the LDP's Finance Committee (1980–86), chairman of the House of Representatives Finance Committee (1986), and chief deputy chairman of LDP's Diet Affairs Committee. In 1988 he was appointed to his first ministerial position in the national government, as minister of health and welfare. He held cabinet posts again in 1992 and 1996–98. In 2001 he was elected president of the LDP on a platform that championed greater regulation of commercial banks and greater privatization of government to end Japan's 10-year economic decline. He became prime minister that year. In addition to his efforts to improve Japan's economy, Koizumi increased Japan's involvement in negotiations aimed at convincing North Korea to terminate its nuclear program. He drew criticism from China and South Korea by refusing to cancel visits to Japanese shrines that honored, among others, convicted war criminals. He stepped down from office in 2006.

**Kokkinaki, Vladimir** (*1904–1985*) Soviet aviator. During the pre-jet era Kokkinaki held a number of aviation records, including the world altitude record. He made world headlines in 1939 when, on what was supposed to be the first nonstop flight from Moscow to New York, he ended up on

Miscou Island in New Brunswick, Canada. The flight came to be known as "Moscow-Miscou."

**Kokoschka, Oskar** (*1886–1980*) Austrian painter, art theorist and dramatist. Kokoschka was a major figure in the Expressionist art movement. He became known for his psychologically intense canvases that evoked emotional depth through the use of uneven, nervous lines, formal distortion and jarring color contrasts. Kokoschka articulated his Expressionistic art theories in an influential essay, *On the Nature of Visions* (1912). He was influenced by the abstract art theories of Wassily KANDINSKY but continued to maintain that the objects and appearances of the real world were fundamental to painting. *Schriften 1907–1955* (1956) is a major collection of his writings on art.

**Kolbe, Georg** (*1877–1947*) German sculptor. Beginning as a painter, Kolbe met Auguste Rodin and turned to sculpture, continuing to be influenced by Rodin's style throughout his career. His impressionist nudes, mostly executed in bronze during the 1920s, are his most highly regarded works. Many of them, such as *Standing Nude* (1926, Walker Art Center, Minneapolis), can be found in American collections. During the Nazi period, Kolbe turned to the creation of monumental figures of soldiers and athletes that correspond to Aryan ideals of masculinity.

**Kolbe, Maksymilian Maria** (*1894–1941*) Polish priest and saint. Kolbe was ordained in 1918. During the early 1930s he was a missionary in India and Japan, then returned to Poland where he founded a religious community near Warsaw. Early in WORLD WAR II, after the German invasion of POLAND (1939), Kolbe was arrested by the Nazis and eventually sent to AUSCHWITZ. There, in 1941, Kolbe sacrificed his life by taking the place of a fellow prisoner, Franciszek Gajowniczek, who was one of 10 persons randomly chosen to die of starvation; Gajowniczek survived the war and lived into his 80s. In 1982 Pope JOHN PAUL II elevated Kolbe to sainthood.

**Kolchak, Admiral Alexander Vasilyevich** (*1873–1920*) Russian naval commander and explorer; served with distinction in the RUSSO-JAPANESE

WAR and with the Black Sea fleet during WORLD WAR I. Kolchak was leader of the anti-Bolshevik troops in Siberia (1918–20). He overthrew the Ufa Directory and was recognized by anti-Bolshevik organizations as representing a provisional government. Kolchak's early successes were followed by withdrawals; after the fall of Omsk in 1919 he retreated to Irkutsk and was taken prisoner, tried and executed.

**Kollek, Teddy** *(1911– )* Israeli politician, mayor of JERUSALEM (1965–93). Kollek was born near Budapest, was raised in Vienna and immigrated to Palestine in 1936. He worked as intelligence liaison officer for the HAGANAH until 1945 and headed Haganah's New York office from 1947 to 1948 as chief arms buyer. He served as Israeli minister plenipotentiary in Washington (1951–52) and as director-general of the prime minister's office (1952–64). Kollek was chairman of the Israeli Tourist Board from 1956 to 1965 and is a founder and chairman of Jerusalem's Israel Museum. He was elected mayor of West Jerusalem in 1965 as the candidate of the Rafi Party with the support of Herut and the religious parties—defeating the Labor Party incumbent. Since 1967 Kollek also administered East Jerusalem in place of Jordanian mayor Rouhi al-Khatib. Kollek is renowned for his ability to reach compromises that enable the Israeli government to carry out its plans for the city without exacerbating Israeli-Palestinian tensions. Thus, in 1968, he ordered the erection of a memorial to the Arab war dead in East Jerusalem, in exchange for the Muslim authorities' unofficial consent to shifting all the Muslim graves in the city, which obstructed Israel's construction projects. Kollek clashed with Jerusalem's Orthodox Jews, who held mass demonstrations against him for extending secular leisure facilities and allowing a Mormon university to be built in the city. Kollek ran for reelection in the 1993 Jerusalem municipal elections but was defeated by the Likud candidate, Ehud Olmert.

**Kollontay, Alexandra Mikhailovna** *(1872–1952)* Russian politician and propagator of "free love." A BOLSHEVIK in the 1890s, Kollontay subsequently became a MENSHEVIK "liquidationist." After 1903, she lived in exile and joined the International Bureau of Women Socialists. From 1915 Kollontay assisted LENIN, and after her return to Russia in February 1917 she became a member of the Bolshevik central committee. Her interest in women's affairs found its outlet in 1920–21 when she was head of the women's department of the central committee. In 1921–22 she was secretary of the International Women's Secretariat of the COMINTERN. She continued her political career as a diplomat in Norway (1923–26 and 1927–30), Mexico (1926–27) and Sweden (1930–45). She developed the Bogdanovist approach to the question of relations between the sexes, and advanced the "winged eros theory," in which individuals in a socialist society should be free to associate with different persons of the opposite sex. Although Lenin disapproved, this theory was popular with others, since by making the family appear an outmoded institution, family ties were weakened. Her works include *The Workers' Opposition in Russia* (1923) and *Free Love* (1932).

**Kollsman, Paul** *(1900–1982)* American aeronautical engineer. Kollsman revolutionized AVIATION in the late 1920s when he invented the altimeter, which measures a plane's altitude while in flight.

**Kollwitz, Kathe Schmidt** *(1867–1945)* German graphic artist and sculptor. A resident of BERLIN, she was a socialist and pacifist whose themes were strongly political and social: poverty, war, human suffering and death. Her powerfully compassionate images were first recognized in her etching and lithograph illustrations based on Gerhardt HAUPTMANN's *The Weavers' Uprising* (1895–98). Kollwitz's other print series include the woodcuts in *War* (1902–08) and *Proletariat* (1925). She also is recognized for her portrayals of mothers and children and for her self-portraits. As a sculptor, she is particularly noted for her war memorial in the Rogevelt Military Cemetery in Belgium. Kollwitz was the director of the graphic arts department at the Berlin Academy in the early 1930s, but was dismissed when the Nazis came to power. Evacuated from Berlin in 1943, she settled in a German mountain village, where she died.

**Kolmogorov, Andrei Nikolayevich** *(1903–1987)* Soviet mathematician. From 1931 he was a professor at Moscow University and, from 1939, a member of the Academy of Sciences. Kolmogorov was a leading international authority on the theory of probability, having put forward the widely accepted axiomatic theory, and was an authority on mathematical logic. He was also interested in cybernetics.

**Komarov, Vladimir M.** *(1927–1967)* Soviet cosmonaut. The first person to die during a space mission, Komarov plunged to his death on April 24, 1967, when the reentry parachute of his *Soyuz 1* space capsule failed to deploy properly. Chosen for his skill to pilot the first manned flight of the new spacecraft, the Soviet cosmonaut had previously piloted *Voskhod 1* on October 12–13, 1964, with design engineer Konstantin Feoktistov and aerospace physician Boris Yegorov aboard. His tragic death caused a delay in further SOYUZ flights for more than a year while an investigation ensued. Komarov graduated with honors from the Soviet Air Force secondary school in 1942 and was selected for cosmonaut training in 1960. A skilled parachutist who had made over 77 jumps, Komarov had once said "whoever has flown once, whoever has piloted an airplane once, will never want to part with either an aircraft or the sky."

**Komenda, Erwin** *(1904–1966)* German automotive engineer responsible for the body design of a number of famous, classic cars. Komenda worked for Daimler-Benz before joining PORSCHE in Stuttgart in the 1930s. He was the designer of the original VOLKSWAGEN Beetle, probably one of the most widely recognized automotive designs ever developed—however controversial. His design for the 1949 Porsche, a somewhat plump and bulging streamlined form, was developed through study of aerodynamics rather than through aesthetic concerns. Komenda continued to develop Porsche body designs through the model 911 of 1963. Many critics would argue that the Porsche design has not been of equal quality since that time.

**Komsomol (All-Union Leninist Communist Union of Youth)** A Soviet youth organization attached to and founded by the COMMUNIST PARTY in 1918, it catered to the 14–28 age range. The Komsomol worked closely with the party; Komsomol members participated in the RUSSIAN CIVIL WAR, collectivization and industrialization, and by the 1980s more than 70% of party recruits came from the Komsomol. Komsomol members were encouraged to play a full part in sociopolitical life; membership and service also enhanced employment and further education prospects. The Komsomol program ended with the collapse of the Soviet Union in December 1991.

**Konchalovsky, Peter** *(1876–1956)* Russian painter. Expelled from Moscow College in 1909 for leftism, Konchalovsky exhibited paintings in the first KNAVE OF DIAMONDS exhibition. His *Portrait of Georgy Yakulov* is reminiscent of MATISSE's style, although later Konchalovsky was to be more influenced by Cézanne, in that his former predilection for color was replaced by a monochromatic palette.

**Kondrashin, Kiril** *(1914–1981)* Soviet-born symphony conductor. Kondrashin studied at the Moscow Conservatory (1931–36) and was later permanent conductor at the Bolshoi Theater (1943–56). He conducted for the American pianist Van CLIBURN at the 1958 Tchaikovsky Piano Competition in Moscow, and subsequently won acclaim in the West when he accompanied Cliburn on his triumphant return to America. In 1960 he was appointed music director of the Moscow Philharmonic and helped revitalize it. Feeling that his artistic freedom was being restricted, he defected to the West in 1978 and settled in Amsterdam.

**Kondratenko, Roman Isidorovich** *(1857–1904)* General in the Russian army who fought heroically in the defense of Port Arthur in 1904. Prior to Port Arthur, Kondratenko commanded the Seventh East-Siberian Infantry. Once at Port Arthur, he greatly increased its fortifications. (See also RUSSO-JAPANESE WAR.)

**Koo, V(i) K(yun) Wellington** *(1887–1985)* Chinese diplomat. Koo's career in international relations spanned more than 50 years. He was chairman of CHINA's delegation to the 1919 PARIS PEACE CONFERENCE and delegate to the LEAGUE OF NATIONS. During the 1920s he was briefly China's foreign minister and prime minister. During WORLD WAR II he was China's ambassador to the U.K. and afterward was Nationalist China's ambassador in Washington. In 1945 he was acting chairman of the Chinese delegation at the San Francisco conference that created the UNITED NATIONS. A judge at the International Court of Justice at the Hague from 1957 to 1967, he was also the court's vice president (1964–67). For many years a senior adviser to CHIANG KAI-SHEK, he continued as senior adviser to the president of the Republic of China in the U.S. after Chiang's death in 1975.

**Kopelev, Lev Zinovyevich** *(1912–1997)* Soviet author, critic, translator and literary historian. Graduating from the Moscow Foreign Language Institute in 1938, Kopelev pursued his studies before serving in World War II. He was expelled from the party in 1945 and sentenced to 10 years' imprisonment and five years' exile, but was released prematurely and rehabilitated. However, Kopelev was criticized for his role in the Human Rights movement and expelled from the Writer's Union in 1965. His publications include *The Heart Is Always on the Left* (1960), *Myths and Truths of the American South* (1958) and *To Be Preserved Forever* (1976).

**Koppel, Edward James (Ted)** *(1940– )* American television journalist and host of the American Broadcasting Corporation (ABC) weeknight news show, *Nightline* (1979–2005). Born Edward James Koppel in Lancashire, England, Koppel arrived in New York when his family relocated to the U.S. in 1953. After completing his undergraduate and graduate education at Syracuse and Stanford universities, Koppel was employed as a news-writer at WMCA and WABC, radio stations located in New York City. In 1967 ABC hired him as a television journalist, and stationed him at their news bureau in South Vietnam to cover the VIETNAM WAR. As a result of his distinguished coverage of that conflict, ABC promoted Koppel as its bureau chief in Hong Kong in 1969, and subsequently as its chief diplomatic correspondent in 1971. In 1979, soon after Iranian extremists took hostages in the American Embassy in Tehran, Koppel began hosting a series of late-night news reports on the ongoing hostage situation. These programs were the origin of *Nightline,* a news program on ABC that summarized news developments and included commentary by Koppel, as well as debates between prominent spokespersons for various positions on national and international issues. Koppel later experimented with a "town meeting" format in auditoriums at varied locations, featuring a panel of experts on a particular topic who answered questions from Koppel and the audience. Koppel retired from *Nightline* in 2005.

**Korbut, Olga Valentinovna** *(1956– )* Soviet gymnast. Korbut captivated the sports world with her Olympic performances. In the 1972 Munich games, she won three gold medals and a silver, and became the first person ever to do a backwards somersault on the uneven parallel bars. She is perhaps best remembered for her charm as well as her athleticism, as she broke free of the stereotype of the stolid, unemotional Soviet athlete, working the crowd and the camera with her petite charm, dazzling smile and innovative choreography. In 1976 a more grown-up Olga was able to capture only one individual medal, a silver on the balance beam, as gymnastics' next doll-like star, the unsmiling Nadia COMANECI, had already taken center stage. Korbut lives in the U.S., where she teaches gymnastics and devotes much of her time to raising funds for victims of the CHERNOBYL nuclear disaster.

**Korchnoi, Victor** *(1931– )* Soviet chess player. He was Soviet champion in 1960, 1962 and 1964 and is an international grandmaster. He left the USSR in 1976. Korchnoi remains an impressive force on the world chess scene, winning events such as the 2004 Gyorgy Marx Memorial Tournament, and regularly representing Switzerland, his adopted country, at the World Chess Olympiad.

**Korda, Sir Alexander** *(1893–1956)* Hungarian-born film director and producer. Korda made films in Bonn, Vienna and HOLLYWOOD in the 1920s but achieved his greatest fame—as well as knighthood—for his work in Britain in the 1930s and 1940s. Korda was a major factor in bringing worldwide recognition to the British film industry through his direction of lushly produced and vividly acted historical epics such as *The Private Life of Henry VIII* (1933) and *Rembrandt* (1936), both of which starred Charles LAUGHTON in the title role. In subsequent decades, Korda turned his primary attention to producing films such as *Sinbad the Sailor* (1947), featuring Douglas Fairbanks, Jr., *The Third Man* (1949), directed by Sir Carol REED, and *Richard III* (1955), the Shakespearean adaptation by Sir Laurence OLIVIER.

**Korea** *(pre-1953)* Korea, a peninsula in Northeast Asia, covers an area of 84,543 square miles. In 1904 it was conquered by Japan and in 1910 became a Japanese colony. After World War II the Allies partitioned Korea, with territory north of the 38th parallel

## NORTH KOREA

| | |
|---|---|
| 1905 | Russo-Japanese War ends; at peace conference Theodore Roosevelt OK's Japanese takeover of Korea. |
| 1910 | Japanese annexation completed; emperor's abdication ends 518-year dynasty; use of Korean language banned; place names and surnames changed to Japanese; workers conscripted and property given away to Japanese citizens. |
| 1945 | Japanese driven out; land north of 38th parallel occupied by Soviets. |
| 1948 | Democratic People's Republic of Korea formed; division from South Korea formalized. |
| 1950 | North Korea invades South, overruns the country; American-led counterattack sweeps to Chinese border; Chinese enter war and driven UN forces back to 38th parallel. |
| 1953 | Cease-fire leaves heavily fortified border at 38th parallel; no North-South treaty signed. |
| 1958 | Kim Il Sung consolidates power within Communist Party; promotes "Juche" self-reliance for nation, begins creation of intense personality cult around himself, which approaches deification. |
| 1959 | Last land removed from private ownership. |
| 1965 | Kim Il Sung successfully avoids taking sides in Sino-Soviet rift; maintains ties but also independence. |
| 1967 | Kim Il Sung criticized during Cultural Revolution; relations with China cool. |
| 1968 | Seizure of U.S.S. *Pueblo*; crew imprisoned. |
| 1971 | Purchase of Western technology leads to heavy foreign debt. |
| 1975 | Fall of Saigon ends period of eased tension with South Korea. |
| 1976 | Default on foreign debt; two U.S. soldiers killed at border. |
| 1979 | Reunification talks deadlock. |
| 1984 | Kim Jong Il groomed to succeed his father as president. |
| 1990 | Japan apologizes for crimes of colonial period; signs agreement covering already active trade with North Korea. |
| 1994 | North Korea pledges to halt production of weapons-grade plutonium in exchange for deliveries of oil from the U.S. Kim Il Sung dies and is replaced by son Kim Jong Il. |
| 2003 | North Korea reveals that it had resumed production of weapons-grade plutonium. |
| 2003 | International Atomic Energy Agency passes a resolution demanding North Korea readmit UN nuclear weapons inspectors. Six-nation talks in Beijing on North Korea's nuclear program begin. North Korea withdraws from the nuclear Non-Proliferation Treaty. |
| 2005 | North Korea agrees to give up its nuclear activities and rejoin the nuclear Non-Proliferation Treaty. The U.S. affirms that it has no intention of attacking the country. Negotiations continue. |

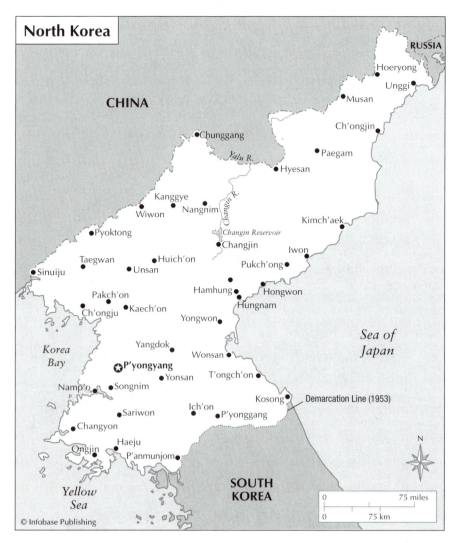

occupied by the Soviet Union and territory south of the line occupied by American forces. By 1948 the COLD WAR had destroyed prospects for reunification of Korea, and the division of the country into the Democratic People's Republic in the north and the Republic of Korea in the south was formalized. Withdrawal of foreign troops brought armed conflict between the two states in 1948–49, which led to war in July 1950 when North Korean forces began a massive invasion of South Korea. UNITED NATIONS armies, predominantly composed of U.S. personnel, pushed the North Koreans back. Eventually, following a massive intervention by Chinese troops, the frontline was stabilized near the 38th parallel, and an armistice was signed on July 27, 1953. (For history after 1953, see KOREA, NORTH and KOREA, SOUTH.)

**Korea, North (Democratic People's Republic of Korea)** North Korea, covering an area of 46,528 square miles, is located in the northern half of the Korean Peninsula in northeast Asia. The Communist Korean Worker's Party (KWP) established the Democratic People's Republic of Korea in 1953 after the signing of the armistice ending the KOREAN WAR. The country has been ruled since 1958 by KIM IL SUNG, who has kept control through a strong personality cult and a personally constructed communist

*Panmunjom cease-fire talks. 1951* (LIBRARY OF CONGRESS, PRINTS AND PHOTOGRAPHS DIVISION)

ideology known as Juche. During the first two seven-year plans, dependence on imports from the West for rapid development of heavy industry led to huge foreign debts by 1976. The third seven-year plan (1987–93) involved more realistic growth expectations. Good relations were maintained with China and the Soviet Union, but relations with South Korea remained tense.

In 1994 Kim Il Sung died and was succeeded by his son, KIM JONG IL. The new North Korean dictator has created intense international controversy with his repeated efforts to acquire atomic weapons and a ballistic missile system, confirming U.S. president GEORGE W. BUSH's determination to create a NATIONAL MISSILE DEFENSE system to defend against missiles launched from "rogue states" such as North Korea. In the meantime, South Korea sought to improve relations with the North, engaging in negotiations and providing food aid during famine in North Korea during the early 21st century.

**Korea, South (Republic of Korea)**
Covering an area of 38,015 square miles, the Republic of KOREA is located

| SOUTH KOREA | |
| --- | --- |
| 1904 | Japan annexes Korea. |
| 1910 | Formally made a colony of Japan. |
| 1945 | Following the defeat of Japan, Korean territory north of the 38th parallel is occupied by Soviet troops and southward by American forces. |
| 1948 | The country's division is formalized by formation of the Republic of Korea in the south and the Democratic People's Republic in the north with both governments claiming sovereignty over the entire peninsula; Syngman Rhee is elected president. |
| 1949 | Soviet and U.S. troops begin withdrawal. |
| 1950 | (July 25) North Korea invades South Korea; (September) UN forces land amphibious forces at Inchon, outflanking the North Koreans; (November) Chinese volunteers enter the war, driving UN forces back. |
| 1953 | (July 27) Armistice signed. |
| 1960 | (April) Rhee overthrown by popular revolt. |
| 1961 | (May 16) General Park Chung Hee emerges as leader. |
| 1963 | Park, as member of the Democratic Republican Party, is elected president. |
| 1972 | Park proclaims martial law and is elected to a six-year term by the new electoral body, the National Conference for Unification. |
| 1979 | (October 26) Park is assassinated by the head of his secret police; (Dec. 12) Military coup takes over government. |
| 1980 | (August) Presidency assumed by Chun Doo Hwan. |
| 1981 | (January) Martial law is lifted. |
| 1987 | (October) New democratic constitution is approved; (November) South Korean jetliner destroyed by agents of North Korea; (December 16) Roh Tae Woo is elected president. |
| 1988 | Summer Olympic Games held in Seoul. |
| 1991 | Soviet President Mikhail Gorbachev becomes first Soviet leader to visit South Korea. |
| 1998 | Kim Dae Jung becomes president, seeks better relations with North Korea. |
| 2000 | Kim Dae Jung wins the Nobel Peace Prize for efforts in improving the relationship between North and South Korea. |
| 2002 | Roh Moo-hyun is elected president. |
| 2004 | Roh is impeached by the National Assembly; several weeks later the impeachment is overturned |

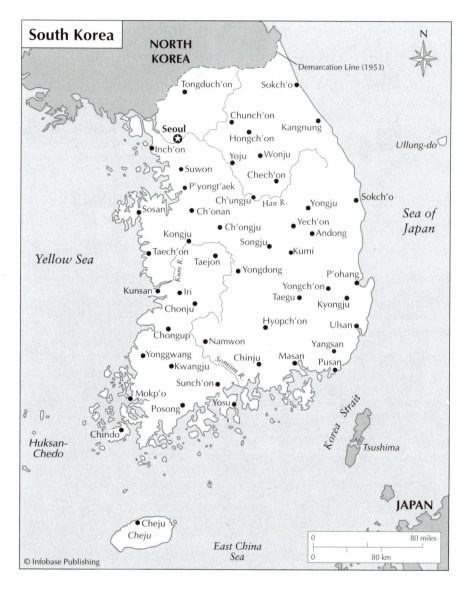

**South Korea**

NORTH KOREA

Demarcation Line (1953)

Tongduch'on • • Sokch'o

Chunch'on •

**Seoul** ★ • Kangnung

Hongch'on •

Inch'on •

Yoju • • Wonju

Suwon •

Chech'on •

*Ullung-do*

P'yongt'aek •

Ch'ungju • *Han R.* • Yongju • Sokch'o

Sosan • • Ch'onan

*Sea of Japan*

Ch'ongju • • Yech'on

Kongju • Songju • Andong

*Kum R.*

Taech'on • Taejon • Kumi

*Yellow Sea*

Yongdong • P'ohang

Kunsan • • Iri Yongch'on •

Chonju • Taegu • Kyongju

Hyopch'on • Ulsan •

Chongup • Namwon • Yangsan

Yonggwang • Chinju • Masan

*Somjim R.* Pusan

Kwangju •

Sunch'on •

Mokp'o •

Posong • Yosu

*Korea Strait*

Chindo •

*Tsushima*

Huksan-
Chedo

JAPAN

Cheju •
*Cheju*

*East China Sea*

| 0 | 80 miles |
| 0 | 80 km |

© Infobase Publishing

power. In the early years of the 21st century, North Korea's determination to develop nuclear weapons caused increased anxiety in South Korea and inhibited the earlier movement toward reconciliation.

**Koreagate** *(1977)* Political scandal involving illegal South Korean influence peddling and bribery on Capitol Hill. House and Senate Ethics Committee investigations revealed that a number of congressmen had accepted gifts and contributions from Tongsun Park, a South Korean rice trader and influence peddler. The funds allegedly were paid in return for votes in favor of U.S. aid and the continuing presence of U.S. troops in South Korea. The investigations led to the indictment of Congressmen Hanna (California) and Passman (Louisiana), although only Hanna was convicted of taking bribes. A number of other congressmen were censured, and all charges were dropped against Tongsun Park, who testified at the hearings and cooperated with investigators.

**Korean War** *(1950–53)* In order to disarm Japanese forces that had occupied KOREA since 1904, the victorious Allies at the end of WORLD WAR II established the 38th parallel as a "temporary" dividing line between Soviet-occupied NORTH KOREA and U.S.-occupied SOUTH KOREA; later efforts by the UNITED NATIONS to reunite the country failed. On June 25, 1950, North Korean troops suddenly and without warning invaded South Korea; within two months they had pushed south almost to the tip of the Korean Peninsula, where South Korean defenses were thrown up in a perimeter around Pusan. Two days after the invasion, the UN had called on its members to help South Korea, and 15 did so. The international force was under the command of U.S. general Douglas MACARTHUR, who planned and executed a successful amphibious landing behind the lines at the Yellow Sea port of INCHON (September 15, 1950) and cut enemy supply routes. The North Koreans were driven northward and eventually back to the Yalu River (November 24, 1950), the boundary between CHINA and North Korea. UN forces, in two columns on each side of Korea's central mountain spine, planned

on the southern half of the Korean Peninsula in northeast Asia. The corrupt government of South Korea's first president, Syngman RHEE (1948–60), was overthrown in 1960, but the unstable Second Republic that replaced it fell victim to a military coup in 1961, bringing to power General PARK CHUNG HEE (1962–79). Though his regime brought economic success, it also introduced an authoritarian constitution (1972) and practiced coercion. After Park's assassination in 1979, subsequent popular uprisings led to a declaration of martial law. Chun Doo Huan became president in 1980, lifting martial law (1981) and improving human rights in response to foreign pressure. His successor, ROH TAE WOO (1987–   ), undertook reforms and es-

tablished a new democratic constitution in 1987 in response to proposals to move the coming OLYMPIC GAMES (held in Seoul in 1988) because of unrest in Korea. In 1998 Kim Dae jung became president and initiated a "sunshine policy" toward North Korea, in which South Korea unconditionally offered North Korea economic and humanitarian aid, in the hopes of improving relations between the two states. In recognition of his efforts to restore peaceful relations between the two Kim Dae Jung received the Nobel Prize in 2000. Roh Moo Hyun won the presidency in 2002 but suffered a setback when he was impeached by the National Assembly in 2004. The country's Constitutional Court overturned the impeachment, and Roh was restored to

*Members of an American convoy in Korea* (LIBRARY OF CONGRESS. PRINTS AND PHOTOGRAPHS DIVISION)

to reunite Korea under southern control. But the plan was never realized because, on November 26, 1950, a large Communist Chinese army invaded the north in support of the North Koreans and helped them drive the UN forces south after much bitter fighting.

By January 1, 1951, a North Korean–Chinese army of about 485,000 men had forced MacArthur's 365,000 UN troops back to the 38th parallel. The South Korean capital of SEOUL fell into enemy hands, but a counteroffensive by UN forces retook the city on March

*The 38th parallel. which divides North and South Korea. 1950* (LIBRARY OF CONGRESS. PRINTS AND PHOTOGRAPHS DIVISION)

14, 1951. Both sides began a "talking war" to reach an accord; negotiations dragged on while fighting continued intermittently around the dividing line. MacArthur publicly advocated attacking and bombing Chinese bases in Manchuria, contrary to UN and American orders. On April 11, 1951, U.S. president Harry S. TRUMAN summarily dismissed MacArthur from command of UN and American forces in the Far East and appointed General Matthew B. RIDGWAY in his place. Offensives and counteroffensives were launched by both sides, which suffered heavy casualties.

Ridgway's truce negotiations, which hinged largely on the repatriation of prisoners, sick and wounded, broke down in October 1952; the UN forces had taken over 70,000 prisoners, and UN negotiators insisted that they be allowed to choose whether to return to the north or to stay in the south. The latter view ultimately prevailed, and three out of four prisoners remained in South Korea (21 American prisoners elected to stay with the communists). In April 1953, peace talks resumed and led to the signing of an armistice at PANMUNJOM on July 27, 1953; but no formal peace treaty has ever been concluded.

**Korngold, Erich Wolfgang** *(1897–1957)* Celebrated symphonic, opera and motion picture composer. When Austrian-born Korngold arrived in HOLLYWOOD in 1934, he had already written operas and ballets as a teenager, collaborated with impresario Max REINHARDT on several Johann Strauss vehicles, and been acclaimed a "genius" and a "second Mozart" by Gustav MAHLER and Richard STRAUSS. It was at Reinhardt's invitation in 1935 that Korngold scored his first film for WARNER BROS., *A Midsummer Night's Dream.* In his subsequent 12 years in Hollywood he wrote 18 scores of a consistently high quality and achieved the enviable status of highest paid composer in the business. His greatest wish, however, was to return to the classical music world in Europe after World War II. Sadly, productions in his beloved Vienna of his most famous operas, *The Dead City* and *Die Kathrin,* were unsuccessful, and he had to return to Hollywood. His lasting legacy must surely be his film music. Particularly memorable is the brassy splendor of *King's Row* (1942), the dashing bravado of *The Adventures of Robin Hood* (1938) and *The Sea Hawk* (1940) and the lush sentiment of *The Constant Nymph* (1943). When accused by a film producer that his music had degenerated in quality over the years, Korngold snapped, "When I first came here, I couldn't understand the dialogue—now I can." Upon his death in Hollywood of a heart attack, a black flag—the traditional Austrian mark of mourning—appeared over the Vienna Opera House.

**Kornilov, General Lavr Georgevich** *(1870–1918)* Russian soldier. Kornilov served in the RUSSO-JAPANESE WAR (1904–05) and in WORLD WAR I. He was captured by the Germans but made a spectacular escape. He was Petrograd military district commander in 1917 and was responsible for the arrest of NICHOLAS II and his family. As commander in chief of all Russian forces in August 1917, he believed that the provisional government was incapable of dealing with any threat from the BOLSHEVIKS. Mistakenly be-

lieving that Alexander KERENSKY was in agreement, he organized his troops to march on Petrograd but was arrested on Kerensky's orders. This action strengthened the Bolsheviks, and after the fall of Kerensky, Kornilov escaped to join the anti-Bolshevik forces of Anton DENIKIN on the Don, where he was killed in action.

**Kornilov's Revolt** *(1917)* Conservative Russian generals, backed by Alexander F. KERENSKY who had replaced Prince LVOV as premier in the provisional government, decided to form a military dictatorship to end the increasing anarchy and lack of army discipline after the FEBRUARY REVOLUTION. When Kerensky realized that General Lavr G. KORNILOV, whom he had appointed army commander in chief, aspired to become sole dictator, he declared him a traitor and dismissed him. In response, Kornilov dispatched his Cossack troops to Petrograd (now St. Petersburg), hoping to reform the soviet (revolutionary council) and the provisional government along more conservative lines. Kerensky withdrew his support for a rightist military takeover and sought help from the soviets' central committee and leftist forces. Workers, armed by the Bolsheviks and urged to resist Kornilov's threat to their revolution, persuaded the Cossacks to defect, and the counterrevolution collapsed after five days (September 9–14, 1917). Kornilov was arrested and jailed; he escaped from Petrograd after the BOLSHEVIK REVOLUTION, also called the October Revolution. (See also RUSSIAN REVOLUTION.)

**Korovin, Konstant** *(1861–1939)* Russian painter. Korovin is considered by many to be the first Russian artist to be influenced strongly by the impressionists, whose work he saw in Paris in 1885. Korovin's transposition of French Impressionist ideas brought about a complete change in theatrical design in Russia. Appointed professor of the Moscow College in 1901, he supervised the work of almost all the avant-garde of the first decade of the 20th century.

**Kosinski, Jerzy Nikodem** *(1933–1991)* Polish-American novelist. Kosinski's impactful first novel, *Painted Bird*

(1965), is a semiautobiographical account of his childhood in wartime Poland, when orphaned and homeless, he survived as he could. The book was published just eight years after he arrived in the U.S. having tricked the Polish authorities to emigrate. His next novel, *Steps* (1968), won the National Book Award in 1969. His work is often graphically brutal and violent. In 1982 Kosinski found himself at the center of controversy when *The Village Voice* published an article claiming that his books were written largely by assistants and secretaries. Kosinski denied the charges, and various members of the publishing community lined up on both sides. Other novels include *Being There* (1971, filmed 1979), *Pinball* (1982) and *The Hermit of 69th Street* (1988). Early in his career Kosinski also wrote anticommunist nonfiction under the pseudonym Joseph Novak.

**Kosovo** Autonomous region of SERBIA in the Federal Republic of Yugoslavia. Approximately 4,200 square miles, this forested and mountainous region briefly functioned as a district of ALBANIA in 1912, when the Muslim Albanians in Kosovo—who composed more than 90% of the region's population—united Albania to expel the forces of the Ottoman Empire from their domain. A conference of the major European powers, however, imposed a settlement that transferred control of Kosovo to the Kingdom of Serbia. Following the end of the WORLD WAR I, Kosovo became part of the newly formed Kingdom of the Serbs, Croats, and Slovenes, a multiethnic state ruled by the Serbian monarch that was later renamed YUGOSLAVIA. At the end of WORLD WAR II (1939–45), the Yugoslav government of Marshal TITO granted Kosovo a substantial degree of autonomy to the Kosovars, as the majority ethnic Albanians were called. After Tito's death in 1980, ethnic tensions broke out between the Muslim Albanian majority and the Serb minority in Kosovo. In 1989 the leader of the Serbian Communist Party, SLOBODAN Milošević, ended Kosovo's political autonomy within the federated Yugoslav state in response to efforts by the Kosovars to obtain even greater autonomy. Milošević placed the region under military control, suppressed all provincial media outlets and prohibited the use of the Albanian language in Kosovo's schools. The following year, Milošević disbanded the Kosovo parliament, which prompted the provincial leadership to flee to Macedonia, another autonomous region within Yugoslavia, to continue the struggle against the Yugoslav government. The dispute between Yugoslavia and Kosovo was transformed as a result of the fragmentation of the multiethnic state in 1992, when Croatia, Bosnia and Herzegovina, Macedonia and Slovenia all seceded from Yugoslavia. The breakup of Yugoslavia resulted in a civil war among Serbia, BOSNIA AND HERZEGOVINA and Croatia that ended with the 1995 DAYTON ACCORDS. When Croatia deported thousands of ethnic Serbs from the Krajina region it had recently wrested from Serb control, Milošević decided to settle these refugees in Kosovo. The influx of Serbs to Kosovo and the martial law imposed by the truncated Yugoslav state led to the formation of the KOSOVO LIBERATION ARMY (KLA), a paramilitary group that fought for the province's independence. Originally staging attacks on Serb forces in the region, the KLA began to defend Kosovars against Serb police and troops in March 1998. When Serb forces in Kosovo initiated attacks against Kosovars, forcing many of them to flee their homes, the NORTH ATLANTIC TREATY ORGANIZATION (NATO) launched a sustained air campaign against Serbia in March 1999. Serbia retaliated by increasing its assaults on Kosovar villages, leading to a massive exodus of approximately 640,000 Albanian Kosovars into Albania. The fighting and air strikes ended on June 3, 1999, when Milošević accepted the NATO-sponsored peace plan. After Yugoslavia finally began withdrawing its troops from Kosovo seven days later, the UN approved the dispatch of a 50,000 strong peacekeeping force, primarily to ensure that refugees in Albania could return to their homes if they so desired. As these Kosovars returned, the KLA and other pro-Kosovar paramilitary groups began reprisals against Serbs residing in the province, forcing many of them to flee. The continued tension between ethnic Albanians demanding independence for Kosovo and Serbian attempts to retain control of the region have complicated efforts to reach a formal settlement of the dispute.

**Kosovo Liberation Army (KLA)** A paramilitary group composed of ethnic Albanians, which account for more than 90% of the population in the Yugoslav province of KOSOVO. The KLA engaged in guerrilla fighting against the military and paramilitary forces of Yugoslavia for control of Kosovo since 1995. Although the Serb-dominated Yugoslav army left the province in October 1999 after the NATO bombing campaign against SERBIA, the KLA continued to mount a series of raids on ethnic Serbs within Kosovo in retaliation for Serb attacks on Albanians between 1995 and 1999.

**Koštunica, Vojislav (1944– )** Yugoslav author, professor, politician, president of the Federal Republic of Yugoslavia (2000–03) and prime minister of SERBIA AND MONTENEGRO (2004– ). Born in 1944 in the Yugoslav capital of Belgrade, Koštunica soon developed a reputation as a political and constitutional liberal and critic of the repressive rule of Marshal TITO.

In 1989 Koštunica began his political career by forming the Democratic Party and was elected to the Serbian provincial parliament in 1990. The following year, Koštunica left the organization to found the Democratic Party of Serbia, convinced that the Democratic Party had failed to recognize the dire consequences of the secession of Croatia and Bosnia and Herzegovina from Yugoslavia. Koštunica further defended Serbian sovereignty and policies in 1999 when he denounced NORTH ATLANTIC TREATY ORGANIZATION (NATO) air campaigns against Serbian cities to force an end to the Serb-led military and paramilitary actions in KOSOVO. As a result of popular dissatisfaction with the authoritarian aspects of Serbian president Slobodan Milošević's rule, Koštunica won the five-candidate contest for president in 1999 with more than 52% of the vote. When Milošević attempted to alter the outcome by tampering with the ballots cast, massive protests and general strikes forced him to step down in favor of Koštunica.

As president of Yugoslavia, Koštunica developed a reputation as a liberal committed to democratic and constitutional government, although some foreign commentators criticized his strident Serbian nationalism and his efforts to block full autonomy for Kosovo, increasing ethnic tensions between the majority ethnic Albanians and its Serb and Montenegrin minorities in the province. Yet, Koštunica seemed committed to the rule of law, as revealed in his willingness to allow the transfer of Milošević to the international war crimes tribunal at The Hague and in his refusal to resort to extraconstitutional methods to rule his country.

**Kosygin, Alexei (1904–1980)** Soviet politician, chairman (prime minister) of the Council of Ministers of the USSR (1964–80). A member of the Central Committee of the COMMUNIST PARTY of the Soviet Union in 1939, Kosygin was minister for economic planning in 1956–57, rising to chairman of the state economic planning commission and first deputy prime minister in 1960. A leading figure in the ouster of Soviet leader Nikita KHRUSHCHEV in 1964, he succeeded Khrushchev as prime minister. He collaborated closely with Leonid BREZHNEV, but the latter became increasingly dominant. Kosygin partially attained his objective of decentralizing the control of industry and agriculture, but his hopes of producing more consumer goods remained largely unfulfilled. Ill health forced his resignation in 1980, and he died a few weeks later.

**Koufax, Sandy (1935– )** American baseball player. Widely considered one of the greatest pitchers in the history of baseball, Koufax pitched in 397 games from 1955 to 1966, all with the Brooklyn and Los Angeles Dodgers. A left-hander, in his early years in the game his pitching was often wild, but in the 1960s he mastered his overpowering fastball and virtually unhittable curve. During his career he pitched four no-hitters, including a perfect game. He struck out 2,396 batters in 2,325 innings. In 1963, when he led the Dodgers to a memorable World Series victory over the New York Yankees, he was named the National League's Most Valuable Player. His career record was 165 wins and 87 loses with an earned run average of 2.76. Koufax's career was cut short by arthritis in 1996. In 1972, at the age of 36, Koufax became the youngest person ever elected to the Baseball Hall of Fame.

**Koussevitzky, Serge** *(1874–1951)* Russian-born orchestra conductor and leader of the Boston Symphony Orchestra. In his time he was the most important and arguably the greatest of all Russian conductors. Born at Tver, near Moscow, in his youth he became a widely known double bass performer at the Moscow Philharmonic Society. He studied conducting at the Berlin School of Music, traveled extensively through Russia with his own orchestra and founded a Moscow publishing house, Editions Russes de Musique, to promote new music by STRAVINSKY, SCRIABIN, and PROKOFIEV. In 1920 he and his wife left Russia after the revolution. After a notable series of "Concerts Koussevitzky" in Paris, he replaced Pierre MONTEUX as conductor of the Boston Symphony Orchestra. There, despite poor relations with some of the players, notoriety as a bad score reader, reluctance to perform operas and other problems, Koussevitzky elevated the Boston Symphony to unquestioned stature as one of the greatest orchestras in the world. For 25 years he was one of the "Big Three" American conductors, along with Arturo TOSCANINI and Leopold STOKOWSKI. Certainly no conductor of his time meant more to American musical development. He sponsored new music by Aaron COPLAND, Walter PISTON, William SCHUMAN, and Roy HARRIS, for example; he took over the Berkshire Music Festival in Tanglewood, Mass., in 1937 and created a music school there in 1940. He led an acclaimed conducting class from which emerged such figures as Leonard BERNSTEIN. His notable series of RCA recordings still convey his unique nervous energy and glow, the unique lyric sheen of his RAVEL and DEBUSSY scores and—above all—unparalleled interpretations of the Russian masters.

**Kovacs, Ernie** *(1919–1962)* Zany American television personality, program host, writer, and movie actor, credited with many innovations in video programming. Kovacs was born in Trenton, N.J., of Hungarian immigrant parents. His professional career, which spanned little more than the decade of the 1950s, began with local television shows in Philadelphia in 1950, continued nationally on the CBS, NBC, Dumont, and ABC networks, and extended briefly into movie

acting in HOLLYWOOD. He is best remembered for the series of Kovacs Specials, on ABC in 1961. By contrast with such other early television performers as Steve ALLEN and Sid CAESAR, who were still working essentially in a vaudeville tradition, Kovacs was defining the video medium itself, anticipating later video artists like Nam June Paix. He devised all manner of video chicanery from the very *effects* of the medium—the line-scan pattern, the "key" effects of camera switching and mats, picture compression and polarity reversals. He changed the nature of the television *event* as well. His first program, *3 to Get Ready* (1950), was the first morning talk show of its kind, defining television as an *audience-bound* event. He broke the medium's "fourth wall" for the first time, plunging beyond the studio set to the control room, outside corridors, the firescapes, and into the audience. His quick, pungent sketches, sudden noises, and satiric blackouts predated the formats of SATURDAY NIGHT LIVE and LAUGH-IN by a generation. An innovator, yes, but according to critic Jeff Greenfield, television's great subversive at the same time. Since his untimely death in a car crash in 1962, his work has been revived in tributes on public television in 1977 and at the Museum of Broadcasting in 1986. *Erratic,* is the word he used to describe himself in his autobiographical novel, *Zoomar* (1957). "His comedy is too extreme and too frequently he gets his punch line from the grisly side of life."

**Kozintsev, Grigory Mikhailovich** *(1905–1973)* Soviet film director and script writer. Kozintsev began his career in film in 1920 in Kiev. In 1924 he was the director of the Lenfilm Studio in Leningrad. One of his best-known works is the *Maksim Trilogy*, which he produced at Trauberg. During World War II Kozintsev worked in the theater and produced *King Lear* (1941) and *Othello* (1943).

**Kraft, Christopher C., Jr.** *(1924– )* U.S. flight director. The most frequently heard voice during the early years of the U.S. space program, Chris Kraft was flight director on all the Project MERCURY flights and most of the GEMINI missions. His was the responsibility for controlling each mission from

the ground, and he decided ultimately whether to launch or not and what to do if things went awry. Kraft began working for NACA in 1945, and in 1958 he became one of the original members of the space task group charged with developing the Mercury program. He was responsible for much of the mission and flight-control development and the design of the Mission Control Center at what is now the JOHNSON SPACE CENTER. Kraft also served as director of flight operations and became director of JSC in 1972, retiring in August 1982. (See also NASA.)

**Krag, Jens Otto** *(1914–1978)* Prime minister of DENMARK (1962–68; 1971–72). A Social Democrat, Krag led his country into the EUROPEAN ECONOMIC COMMUNITY (EEC) and resigned from office immediately after a referendum approved the step.

**Kramer, Jack** *(1921– )* American tennis player. Kramer won the U.S. National Doubles title while still a teenager (1940); he won again in 1941 and 1943. In 1946–47 he lead the U.S. Davis Cup team to victory. He won both the U.S. singles and doubles and the British singles and doubles that same year. In 1947 he turned professional and continued to win national and world titles until retiring as a player in 1954. Kramer then spent many years promoting the growth of professional tennis around the world.

**Kramer, Stanley** *(1913–2001)* American film director and producer. Kramer is best known as a creator of "message" films that take strong liberal stands on a range of social and political issues from racism to nuclear war. Born in New York City, Kramer worked as a B-movie screenwriter for METRO-GOLDWYN-MAYER studios before WORLD WAR II, during which he served in the armed forces. In 1948 he started Screen Plays, Inc., an independent production house that fostered memorable films including *Champion* (1949), *Cyrano de Bergerac* (1950) and *The Caine Mutiny* (1954). Kramer began directing his own films in 1955 and enjoyed a number of critical and popular successes including *On the Beach* (1959), a portrayal of a dying world after a nuclear war, and *Guess Who's Coming to Dinner* (1967), the story of an interracial marriage that featured Spencer TRACY's last film appearance. Kramer was less successful in the 1970s and ceased filmmaking.

**Krasin, Leonid Borisovich** *(1870–1926)* Russian communist. Having become a member in 1890 of one of the earliest social democratic organizations in Russia, from 1900 to 1903 Krasin was a leading member of *Iskra*. From 1904 to 1905, Krasin opposed LENIN's methods in the party and had him expelled from the central committee. In 1905, however, with Lenin reinstated in favor, Lenin, Krasin and Bogdanov led the Bolshevik faction of the revolution. In 1909 he broke with Lenin. Krasin's important political positions include membership in the presidium of the supreme council of national economy, commissar for foreign trade, and ambassador to Britain twice and to France once. His technical skills and business acumen helped him to play a leading part in reorganizing the Soviet economy.

**Krasner, Lee** *(1908–1984)* American painter. Krasner was a leading figure in the so-called New York school of ABSTRACT EXPRESSIONISM. Her use of draftsmanship and color to celebrate the natural world showed the influence of MATISSE and Pablo PICASSO, as well as of her husband, Jackson POLLOCK. After Pollock's death (1956) she was slow to gain recognition in her own right; however, by the 1970s her work had won much international acclaim.

**Krasnoye Selo** Formerly a town outside St. Petersburg; now part of the city. It was the summer residence of Czar NICHOLAS II and has two former palaces. The Germans occupied it from 1941 to 1944, while they had LENINGRAD under siege.

**Kraus, Lili** *(1905–1986)* Hungarian-born concert pianist renowned for her interpretations of the music of Mozart. Kraus had two careers, divided by three years during WORLD WAR II when she was held captive in a Japanese prison camp in the Dutch East Indies. A U.S. resident since the late 1960s, she retired from the concert stage in 1982.

**Krebs, Sir Hans Adolf** *(1900–1981)* German-British biochemist. Born in Germany, Krebs studied at the universi-ties of Göttingen, Freiburg, Munich, Berlin and Hamburg, where he obtained an M.D. in 1925. He taught at Berlin's Kaiser Wilhelm Institute and the University of Freiburg, where he researched the production of urea in the liver, until the rise of NAZISM caused him to immigrate to England in 1933. While serving as a professor at Sheffield University (1935–54), he discovered in 1937 the Krebs cycle (or citric acid cycle), the chemical reactions in the later stages of the metabolism of food that provide much of the energy for living organisms. For this discovery, he was awarded the 1953 NOBEL PRIZE in physiology or medicine (with F. A. Lipmann). Krebs became a professor at Oxford in 1954, was knighted in 1958 and retired in 1967.

**Kreisky, Bruno** *(1911–1990)* Austrian politician. Born to a Jewish family, he was a lifelong socialist who was jailed for his activities in the 1930s. After the takeover of AUSTRIA by Nazi GERMANY in 1938, he fled to Sweden, where he remained until after World War II. He returned to Austria, entered the diplomatic service and was named foreign minister in 1959. In 1970 he became chancellor, a post he held until 1983. His tenure was marked by strong economic growth and prosperity. He pursued an active role for Austria in international affairs, but was criticized by ISRAEL for his evenhanded approach to Israel's Arab neighbors.

**Kreisler, Fritz** *(1875–1962)* Austrian violinist and composer. Kreisler is one of the legendary violin performers not only of the 20th century, but in the history of classical music. Born in Vienna, he was a musical prodigy, becoming the youngest student at the esteemed Vienna Conservatory at the age of seven. Among his teachers was the famed composer Anton Bruckner. By his teens Kreisler was an international star of the concert stage, on which he reigned for over six decades. Kreisler was also one of the great composers for the violin, although he sparked controversy by passing off his own compositions—in the early decades of his career—as "transcriptions" from earlier masters, in the hopes of thereby gaining for them a more respectful hearing. Kreisler's most famous compositions

*Violinist and composer Fritz Kreisler* (LIBRARY OF CONGRESS, PRINTS AND PHOTOGRAPHS DIVISION)

include *Liebesfreud, Caprice Viennois* and *La Gitana*.

**kremlinology** Name derived from the Moscow Kremlin, where the Supreme Soviet of the USSR held its sessions. Kremlinology was the study of the policies of the Soviet government. It also implies gleaning information or clues about the conduct of Soviet politics, getting an indication of what goes on behind the facade of "monolithic unity" among the leaders. It lost its relevance with the dissolution of the Soviet Union in December 1991.

**Krenz, Egon** *(1937–   )* East German politician. Krenz was the communist leader who, on November 17, 1989, opened the BERLIN WALL and allowed East Germans free access to the West. Trained as a teacher, he spent most of his career as an administrator in the East German (GDR) Communist Party's youth movement. He was at the Soviet Communist Party's Central Committee College from 1964 to 1967. In November 1983 he was promoted to the East German Central Committee Secretariat and also became a full member of the Politburo. Upon the resignation of Erich HONECKER (October 18, 1989), he became secretary general of the party and president of the GDR, promising reforms, but resigned (along with the entire Politburo) on December 3, 1989, as a result of continuing protests by the East German people against communist rule. In 1990 Krenz's Party—in an attempt to improve its image—stripped Krenz of his membership. Krenz was sentenced in 1997 to six years in prison for crimes during the cold war, specifically the murder of people who tried to escape EAST GERMANY, election fraud and other crimes. He appealed the ruling in 1999 but lost and was confined to Spandau prison in Berlin. Krenz was released in 2003, having served only three years of his sentence.

**Kripalani, Jiwatram Bhagwandas** *(1888–1982)* Indian political leader. In 1919 Kripalani became a disciple of Mohandas K. GANDHI. Kripalani worked closely with Gandhi over the next 28 years in the nonviolent struggle for INDIA's independence from Britain. He was president of the CONGRESS PARTY when India achieved independence (1947), but later broke with the party over differences with Jawaharlal NEHRU. He became an independent in 1957 and helped form the Janata Party, which came to power in 1977, temporarily ousting Indira GANDHI.

**Krips, Josef** *(1902–1974)* Austrian conductor. Born in Vienna, Krips studied at the Vienna Academy of Music with Felix WEINGARTNER. He began his musical career as a violinist, making his conducting debut in 1921. He served as the conductor of the Dortmund Municipal Theater (1925–26), music director at Karlsruhe (1926–33) and conductor of the Vienna State Opera (1933–38), and was a professor at the Vienna Academy of Music (1935–38). Because Krips had Jewish grandparents, he was forced to abandon his musical career after the German occupation in 1938. After World War II, Soviet authorities chose him to reconstruct Vienna's musical structure, a task he accomplished from 1945 to 1950. He was later the conductor of the London Symphony (1950–54), the Buffalo Philharmonic (1954–63) and the San Francisco Symphony (1963–70). Noted for the warmth and lyricism of his performances, he had a large repertoire that included the great Viennese and German classics as well as works by such modern composers as BARTÓK, HINDEMITH and STRAVINSKY.

**Krishnamurti, Jiddu** *(1895–1986)* Indian philosopher and teacher. In 1929 Krishnamurti renounced all organized religions and ideologies, claiming that these tended to retard rather than advance self-awareness. With the aid of his supporters, he set up nonprofit foundations in California, England and India. He traveled around the world to deliver lectures stressing the importance of maximum self-awareness. Many of his 40-odd books were drawn from these lectures. He came to be regarded by many as an outstanding spiritual leader.

**Kristallnacht** Nazi-directed anti-Jewish violence throughout Germany on the night of November 9, 1938. On that day, Ernst von Rath, a German official in Paris, died after being shot by a young Polish Jew. Using the incident as an excuse, Josef GOEBBELS, Nazi propaganda minister, ordered Nazis to commit acts of violence against German JEWS. Over the following 24 hours, more than 30,000 Jews were arrested, nearly 100 were killed and 36 were seriously injured. Seven thousand Jewish businesses were destroyed, and nearly 300 synagogues were burned. The name Kristallnacht, or "Night of the Broken Glass," is a reference to the windows of the Jewish-owned buildings.

**Kroc, Ray A.** *(1902–1984)* Founder and chairman of McDonald's Corp. Kroc opened his first McDonald's hamburger stand in Chicago in 1955. By 1983 more than 7,500 McDonald's franchise restaurants in 32 countries displayed the famous golden arches. Kroc's automating and standardizing techniques revolutionized the fast-food business and the American way of eating. Kroc also owned the San Diego Padres baseball team.

**Kroeber, Louis and Theodora** American anthropologists. Alfred Louis (1876–1960) and Theodora Brown (1897–1979) Kroeber both wrote major works in the field of anthropology. Alfred exercised the broader influence, establishing the department of anthropology at the University of California in Berkeley in the early 1900s and teaching there until 1946. He wrote a widely used introductory text, *Anthropology* (1923), and did field work in Mexico and Peru. His later works include *The*

*Nature of Culture* (1952) and *Style and Civilization* (1957). Theodora wrote two stylish and influential works, *The Inland Whale* (1959) and *Ishi in Two Worlds* (1961). Their daughter is science fiction writer Ursula K. LE GUIN.

**Kronstadt Rebellion** An uprising among Soviet sailors in Kronstadt on the Gulf of Finland, March 7–18, 1921. The sailors, who had supported the BOLSHEVIKS in the OCTOBER REVOLUTION, demanded economic reforms and an end to Bolshevik political domination. The Red Army, led by Leon TROTSKY and Michael TUKHACHEVSKY, crushed the rebels, and Lenin's NEW ECONOMIC POLICY (1921) was introduced to relieve the privations that had given rise to the revolt.

**Kruchenykh, Alexei Yeliseyevich** *(1886–1970)* Futurist poet who began his career as a painter. Together with Velemir KHLEBNIKOV, Kruchenykh was the originator of "trans-sense" (or *zaumney*) verse. Although somewhat an outsider among postrevolutionary Futurists (see FUTURISM), he developed the Cubo-Futurist theory. His artistic output includes a "nonsense" play *Gli-Gli*, in which the senses of the audience were bombarded from all sides, and the opera *Victory Over the Sun* (1913), which—with its songs in Kruchenykh's language of the future, Kazimir MALEVICH's costumes and scenery representing partial objects and individual letters, and Matushin's quarter-tone music—constituted a landmark in theater.

**Krupa, Gene** *(1909–1973)* American JAZZ drummer and big band leader. Krupa is regarded as perhaps the greatest drum virtuoso in the history of jazz. His uniquely flamboyant style of playing emphasized his technical brilliance and unerring sense of rhythm. Krupa first gained national fame through his appearances in the 1930s with the Benny GOODMAN big band and trio. In 1938 Krupa formed his own big band, which continued—after a hiatus for World War II—through 1951. A Hollywood biographical film, *The Gene Krupa Story* (1959), featured actor Sal Mineo as Krupa.

**Krupskaya, Nadezhda Konstantinovna** *(1869–1939)* Russian communist educator and wife of LENIN.

*Jazz drummer Gene Krupa* (Library of Congress, Prints and Photographs Division)

Educated at the Women's College in St. Petersburg, she aided Lenin in his revolutionary work and married him in 1898, accompanying him in his exile. After their return to Russia, Krupskaya was a member of the commissariat of education and developed and expounded the party's plans for education. She was later to become vice commissar of education and a member of the Central Committee of the Communist Party and the Presidium of the USSR. She died in the Kremlin on February 27, 1939.

**Krutch, Joseph Wood** *(1893–1970)* American author. After receiving his doctorate from Columbia University (1923), he became an editor of *The Nation* (1924–52). A noted literary critic, his works include *Comedy and Conscience After the Restoration* (1924), *The Desert Year* (1952) and *The Voice of the Desert* (1955). His *Measure of Man* (1954) won him a National Book Award.

**Kubelík, Jan** *(1880–1940)* Czechoslovakian violinist. A prodigy, Kubelík entered the Prague Conservatory at the age of 12. He debuted in Vienna in 1898, and soon became a virtuoso performer throughout Europe. Beginning in 1901, he also made frequent tours of the U.S. Known for his brilliant, fiery style, he was acclaimed for his performances of the major violin concerto repertoire and for his superb interpretations of Paganini's compositions Kubelík

was also a composer, whose works include several violin concertos, a symphony and chamber music. He was the father of conductor Rafael KUBELÍK.

**Kubelík, Rafael** *(1914–1996)* Czechoslovakian conductor. The son of violinist Jan KUBELÍK, Rafael Kubelík studied at the Prague Conservatory (1928) and made his conducting debut in 1934. He was artistic director of the Czech Philharmonic Orchestra from 1942 to 1948. Immigrating to the U.S. in 1949 following the Communist takeover of CZECHOSLOVAKIA, he directed the Chicago Symphony Orchestra (1950–53) and became well known for his controversial introduction of new music to the orchestra's repertoire. He subsequently conducted the New York Philharmonic (1957–58) and the Royal Opera House orchestras, Covent Garden (1955–58). Chief conductor of the Bavarian Radio Symphony Orchestra from 1961 to 1979, he was briefly (1973) music director of New York's Metropolitan Opera. Kubelík is particularly known for his sensitive and lyrical performances of such Czech composers as Dvořák, Smetana and JANACEK, as well as for his performances of German orchestral classics and the works of MAHLER and BÁRTÓK. He made numerous recordings. Kubelík returned to Czechoslovakia for the first time in 1990, at the invitation of President Václav HAVEL.

**Kubrick, Stanley** *(1928–1999)* American film director. Kubrick is one of the most critically acclaimed film directors of the modern era, although his films have had a hit-and-miss record with film-going audiences. Born and raised in the Bronx, Kubrick was encouraged by his father to learn photography and became so skilled at it that he won a job with *Look* magazine upon graduating from high school. In the 1950s Kubrick made a series of self-funded small films before winning acclaim with the antiwar film *Paths of Glory* (1957), which starred Kirk DOUGLAS. Kubrick replaced director Anthony Mann to complete the filming of *Spartacus* (1962), which also starred Douglas. He then enjoyed a box office hit with *Lolita* (1962), based on the controversial novel by Vladimir NABOKOV. Kubrick's next project, *Dr. Strangelove or: How I Learned to Stop Worrying and Love the Bomb* (1964), re-

mains a classic black comedy. *2001: A Space Odyssey* (1968) was alternately praised and reviled by critics, but most agreed that it set a new standard for visual splendor in filmmaking. Subsequent films by Kubrick include the darkly futuristic *A Clockwork Orange* (1971), *Barry Lyndon* (1975), *The Shining* (1980) and *Full Metal Jacket* (1986). In 1999 Kubrick's last film, *Eyes Wide Shut,* was released shortly after his death.

**Kuiper, Gerard** *(1905–1973)* Dutch-American astronomer. Born in the Netherlands, Kuiper earned his Ph.D. at the University of Leiden. After moving to the United States in 1933, he became an American citizen in 1937. Best known for his studies of our solar system, he had a long association with Yerkes Observatory, twice holding the position of director (1947–49, 1957–60). From 1960 until his death in 1973, Kuiper worked in a similar capacity at the Lunar and Planetary Laboratory at the University of Arizona. His theories of the origins of the planets, including the idea that stars and planets are products of condensation from interstellar gas clouds, helped to spark a renewed interest in our solar system. During the 1960s and early 1970s, he was closely linked with the American space program, instigating many planetary research projects.

**Ku Klux Klan** American secret organization based on the idea of white supremacy. Organized in Pulaski, Tenn., in 1866 by Confederate veterans, its purpose was to oppose the former slaves. The organization spread throughout the South. Clad in long, hooded white robes, masked Klan members rode the countryside and employed violent measures in their suppression of blacks. In 1869 the KKK was disbanded, but local organizations continued, largely in rural areas. The Klan's violent and overzealous activities prompted congressional legislation in 1870 and 1871. In 1915 a new organization, largely anti-Catholic and anti-Semitic, was founded—with the name Ku Klux Klan—in Stone Mountain, Ga. This movement, active North as well South, used as its symbol a burning cross. It is estimated that the Klan's membership in the 1920s was between 2 to 3 million, but during the

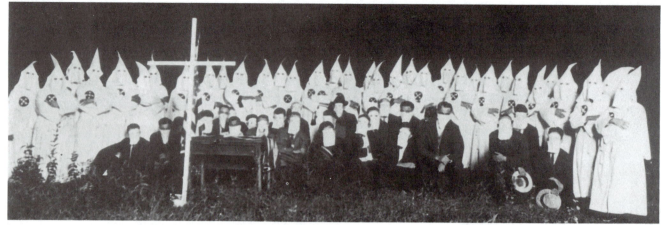

*A gathering of the Ku Klux Klan* (LIBRARY OF CONGRESS, PRINTS AND PHOTOGRAPHS DIVISION)

depression of the 1930s, it lost most of its dues-paying members; by the early 1940s the organization disbanded. In 1964, as a result of the CIVIL RIGHTS ACT, there was a resurgence of the Klan. There have been sporadic KKK rallies in both North and South, but Klan support is minimal.

**Kulakov, Fyodor D.** *(1918–1978)* Soviet communist politician. Kulakov was a member of the Politburo and an apparent protégé of Soviet leader Leonid BREZHNEV. Western Kremlinologists considered him a potential successor to Brezhnev, but he died before Brezhnev, at the relatively youthful age of 60.

**kulaks** Term for wealthy peasants in Russia around the turn of the 20th century and into the Stalinist era. Before the RUSSIAN REVOLUTION (1917) they were prominent in village affairs. After the revolution, they benefited from LENIN'S NEW ECONOMIC POLICY (NEP) until 1927, when STALIN raised their taxes and transformed their lands into collective farms. Stalin's collectivization program and his campaign against the kulaks resulted in the execution, starvation or exile of as many as 12 million of them.

**Kuleshov, Lev Vladimirovich** *(1899–1970)* Russian filmmaker and pioneering theoretician who founded the State Film School. Kuleshov was born in Tambov, Russia, and received early training as a painter at the Fine Arts School in Moscow. A growing fascination with the motion picture—especially the work of the Americans D. W. GRIFFITH and Mack SENNETT—turned his interests toward that medium, and in 1918 he began writing the first sub-

stantial body of criticism and theory in Russia. After making a film, *Proyekt inzhenera Praita* (Engineer Prite's project) in 1918, he began the formation of the First State Film School and in 1920 established the famous Kuleshov Workshop. Vsevelod PUDOVKIN and Sergei EISENSTEIN, among other important Soviet filmmakers, attended classes. Pudovkin conducted a series of "experiments" in montage theory and practice—the synthetic creation of events and ideas through the assemblage and alteration of film (scenes) Thus, his concepts of "creative geography," "creative anatomy," and "creative acting" (the "Mozhukin Experiment") were born. His most important films of the 1920s were *Neobychiniye priklucheniya Mistera Vesta v stranye bolshevikov* (The Extraordinary adventures of Mr. West in the land of the Bolsheviks, 1924), a satire on detective stories in the Sennett style, and *Pozakonu* (By the law, 1926), an emotional tale of murder adapted from novelist Jack LONDON. Although Kuleshov fell out of favor due to his supposed "formalism" with the STALIN regime in 1935, he continued to direct the State Institute of Cinematography in Moscow after 1944. Before his death in 1970 he was "rediscovered" in several major retrospectives in the West. "The shot is a sign, a letter for montage," wrote Kuleshov in his treatise, *The Art of the Cinema* (1929). With him began the consideration of film as an expressive language.

**Kulikov, Viktor Georgyevich** *(1921–   )* Soviet military official, and from 1942 a member of the COMMUNIST PARTY. Having served at the front during WORLD WAR II, Kulikov rose

through various positions and responsibilities, and was made a member of the central committee in 1971. In 1977 he was appointed commander in chief of WARSAW PACT forces and marshal of the Soviet Union.

**Kunayev, Dinmukhamed Akhmedovich** *(1912–1993)* Soviet official. Kunayev joined the party in 1939 after graduating from the Institute of Non-Ferrous and Fine Metallurgy in Moscow in 1936. He pursued his career in science, rising to the position of chief engineer at Altaypolymetall combine, and was director of Leninogorsk Ore Board from 1936 to 1942. In 1949, Kunayev was made a member of the central committee of the Kazakh Communist Party. He was then elected to various governmental posts and in 1971 was made a member of the Politburo central committee. In 1986 Soviet leader Mikhail Gorbachev forced Kunayev's resignation as first secretary of the Communist Party of the Kazakh SSR.

**Kundera, Milan** *(1929–   )* Czechoslovakian novelist. Kundera, who is one of the leading European writers of his generation, was a university student when the USSR established its Communist regime in CZECHOSLOVAKIA in 1948. After working as a manual laborer and as a jazz musician, Kundera studied film and became a professor at the Institute for Advanced Cinematographic Studies in Prague. The publication of his first novel, *The Joke* (1968), coincided with the brief period of liberalization in 1968 known as PRAGUE SPRING. Shortly thereafter, the SOVIET INVASION OF CZECHOSLOVAKIA took place and Kundera lost both his teaching post and the right to publish his works. He immigrated to France in 1975. His major works of fiction include *Laughable Loves* (1974), *Life Is Elsewhere* (1974), *The Farewell Party* (1976), *The Book of Laughter and Forgetting* (1980), *The Unbearable Lightness of Being* (1984, filmed 1988) and *Immortality* (1991). Kundera has continued to publish throughout the 1990s with such books as *Slowness* (1994) and *Identity* (1998). In 2000 he received the Herder Prize from the University of Vienna.

**Küng, Hans** *(1928– )* Swiss theologian. Küng, a Roman Catholic, emerged as one of the most brilliant and controversial theologians of the second half of the 20th century. Ordained a Roman Catholic priest in 1954, he became a professor of theology at the University of Tübingen. In the 1960s, Küng was appointed by Pope JOHN XXIII as an official theologian of the SECOND VATICAN COUNCIL and produced numerous tracts in favor of increased ecumenicism on the part of the church. But Küng subsequently issued a challenge to papal authority with his book *Infallible? An Inquiry* (1970). In *On Being a Christian* (1974), Küng spoke out in favor of increased dissent within the church. He followed this with a similarly challenging work, *Does God Exist?* (1978). In 1979 Küng was censured by the Vatican and forbidden to teach under church auspices. He was an outspoken critic of the traditionalist policies of Pope JOHN PAUL II.

**Kuniyoshi, Yasuo** *(1893–1953)* Japanese-American painter. Born in Okayama, Japan, Kuniyoshi emigrated to the U.S. in 1906, studying at the Los Angeles School of Art and the Art Students League in New York City, where he later taught from 1933 to 1953. He also taught at the New School and the Brooklyn Museum School. His richly figurative paintings, drawings and prints portray cityscapes, nudes and other human subjects in subdued tones and a style touched with SURREALISM and fantasy. His later works are brighter in color, but harsher in subject matter, concentrating on often grotesque figures in circus or carnival settings.

**Kun's Red Republic** *(1919)* Béla Kun established the Hungarian Communist Party December 20, 1918. When president Count Mihály KÁROLY (1875–1955) resigned (March 21, 1919), Kun formed a coalition government, soon establishing a Communist dictatorship. Kun appealed to Hungarian nationalism, formed a Red Army and reconquered Slovakia from the Czechs. However, promised Soviet aid never materialized, nationalization of landed estates alienated the peasantry, while terror estranged the bourgeoisie. The Allies forced relinquishment of Slovakia, counterrevolutionaries attempted Kun's overthrow, and Romania, invading HUNGARY to protect newly acquired Transylvania, advanced on Budapest, the Hungarian capital. When his army refused to fight, Kun fled to Vienna, August 1, 1918. The Romanians occupied and pillaged Budapest August 5–November 14. Admiral Miklós HORTHY DE NAGYBÁNYAI, leader of the counterrevolutionaries, entered Budapest and was appointed head of state, March 1920.

**Kuomintang** Chinese Nationalist Party, also known as the KMT, organized in 1912 by Song Jiaoren (Sung Chiao-ren) and led by SUN YAT SEN. A successor to the earlier revolutionary group, the Tongmeng Hui, its purpose was to promote democratic parliamentary government and social reforms. The KMT was suppressed by China's president, Yuan Shikai, and was returned to power on Yuan's death in 1916. As China's ruling party under Sun's leadership, the KMT accepted aid from the USSR, whose advisers exercised a great deal of control over the party's reorganization in the early 1920s. In a party congress held in Canton in 1924, the KMT officially adopted Sun's Three People's Principles: nationalism, democracy and a guaranteed livelihood. On Sun's death in 1925, leadership of the KMT was assumed by CHIANG KAI-SHEK (Jiang Jieshi), who led the NORTHERN EXPEDITION (1926) against the warlords in Beijing. He expelled Russian advisers and Chinese communists from the party in 1927, beginning the struggle that ended in China's civil war. KMT troops captured Beijing in 1928, and the party became the effective government of China during WORLD WAR II. By 1946 the KMT had betrayed its original democratic principles and had become a corrupt institution controlled by Chiang and his military oligarchy. It was defeated in the civil war, after which (1949) MAO ZEDONG and his Communist Party controlled China. When Chiang fled the mainland he brought his party with him, and the Kuomintang became the ruling party of TAIWAN. In March 2000 opposition candidate Chen Shui-bian defeated the Kuomintang candidate, ending the party's 50-year dominance of Taiwanese elections. Chen subsequently defeated the Kuomintang candidate in the 2004 elections. (See also CHINA.)

**Kuprin, Alexander Ivanovich** *(1870–1939)* Russian writer. Having served in the army for four years, he engaged in various professions before deciding to devote his life to literary pursuits. His first story, *Moloch*, was published in 1896, but *The Duel* (1916) was to bring him fame. Kuprin's novels include *Yama* (The Pit) (1927) and *Yunkera* (1933), although he is chiefly remembered for his collections of short stories, such as *The River of Life* (1916) and *Sasha* (1920). He was associated with GORKY's publishing enterprise, *Znanye,* and the Realist writers. Following the 1917 Revolution Kuprin lived in Paris, but he returned to the USSR in 1938.

**Kurds** Western Asian people who, with their neighboring Armenians, have suffered much throughout the 20th century. The Kurds are centered in Kurdistan, a region of mountains and plateau mainly in southeastern TURKEY, northwestern IRAN, northeastern IRAQ and northeastern SYRIA The tribal Kurds were subjects of the OTTOMAN EMPIRE until WORLD WAR I. After the war they were promised autonomy, but that promise was never carried out. Since then various Kurdish rebellions have occurred but have been forcefully put down in Turkey, Iran and Iraq. In the 1980s Iraq's dictator Saddam HUSSEIN pursued a particularly brutal policy against the Kurds, killing perhaps tens of thousands, many with poison gas. After the PERSIAN GULF WAR, there was another Kurdish rebellion in northern Iraq. The Turkish president, Turgut OZAL, expressed support for the Iraqi Kurds in 1991, and France urged UN action to stop their slaughter. The U.S. military subsequently provided shelter, food and protection for close to one million Kurdish refugees who had fled to the mountainous Iraq-Turkey border. Following the overthrow of Saddam Hussein in March 2003, Kurdish leaders were included by the U.S. in the Interim Iraqi Governing Council and in

**Kurile Islands** Island chain approximately 775 miles long, from the south Kamchatka Peninsula to northeast Hokkaido, Japan; the Kuriles are under the jurisdiction of the USSR. There are some 30 large islands and many smaller ones. In 1875 Japan exchanged SAKHALIN ISLAND (previously under joint Russo-Japanese control), for the Russian Kuriles. Shortly before the end of WORLD WAR II the Soviets occupied the islands. The Kuriles were granted to the USSR at the YALTA CONFERENCE, but Japan has disputed the Soviet claim. In 2002 Russia announced it would recognize the Soviet-era decision to return Shikotan and Habomai to Japan with the conclusion of a formal peace between both countries.

**Kuropatkin, Alexei Nikolayevich** (1848–1925) Russian general. Kuropatkin served in the Russo-Turkish War of 1877; following service in the Caucasus, he became minister of war in 1898. His campaigns in the early stages of the RUSSO-JAPANESE WAR were disastrous and brought about his resignation. He served in the first years of World War I, but in 1916 was appointed governor of Turkestan. He wrote *The Russian Army and the Japanese War* (1909).

**Kurosawa, Akira** (1910–1998) Japanese film director considered, with Kenji MIZOGUCHI and Yasujiro OZU, the greatest of that country's modern filmmakers. Kurosawa's work in the early 1950s helped "open up" Japanese cinema to the West. *Rashomon*, a tale of violence and rape told through multiple narrators, won the Grand Prix at the Venice International Film Festival in 1951. The most eclectic of the Japanese masters, Kurosawa has paid tribute to American western and gangster genres—*Shichinin no samurai* (*Seven Samurai*, 1954), *Yojimbo* (*The Body Guard*, 1960), and *Tengoku to jigoku* (*High and Low*), 1963; adapted Shakespeare's *Macbeth* (*Kumonosu-jo, Throne of Blood*, 1957) and *King Lear* (*Ran*, 1985); and ranged among subjects as diverse as martial arts (*Sugata Sanshiro*, 1943), nuclear war (*Ikimono no kiroku* [*I Live in Fear*], 1957) and police detectives (*Nora inu—Stray Dog*, 1949). He

shaped the early career of Japanese superstar Toshiro MIFUNE. Scorning the traditional Japanese *enryo* (ceremonial reserve), his films are dynamically edited and dramatically composed. His mastery of widescreen, as in *High and Low* and *Akahiga* (*Red Beard*) is unrivaled. The recipient of an American ACADEMY AWARD for lifetime achievement (1989), Kurosawa is reverently addressed by his colleagues at Toho Studios as "Tenno"—"Emperor."

**Kushner, Rose** (1929–1990) American journalist and psychologist. Kushner became a champion of the rights of breast cancer patients after discovering a lump in her own breast in 1974. She refused to undergo the then-standard procedure in which a cancerous breast was removed under general anesthesia before the patient was informed of the biopsy result. Her 1976 book *Why Me? What Every Woman Should Know about Breast Cancer to Save Her Life* described her experiences. Many of the controversial treatments she sought to implement, including less radical surgery and the use of hormonal therapy, later became common practice.

**Kuskova, Ekaterina Dmitryevna** (1869–1959) Russian journalist. She was the author of *Credo*, which advocated raising the living standards of the working people rather than following the main aim of orthodox Marxists, which was to overthrow the autocracy. In 1921 she was active in GORKY's famine relief committee, whose appeals to the world public resulted in the NANSEN and HOOVER relief missions. She was expelled from Russia in 1922, together with many leading intellectuals; she lived first in Prague and later in Geneva.

**Kuwait** Located in western Asia at the head of the Persian Gulf, Kuwait covers an area of 6,879 square miles, including nine Gulf islands. Ruled by an emir of the Al Sabah royal family, Kuwait began the 20th century as a protected state of Britain under the

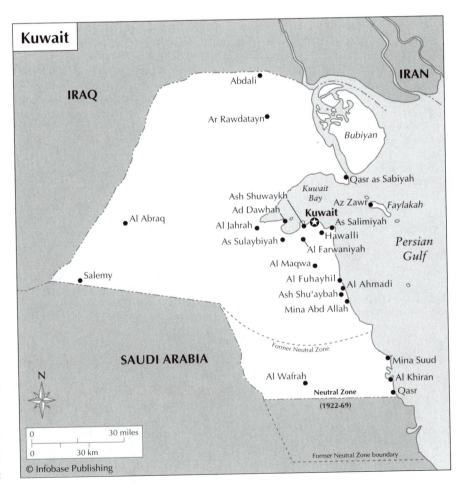

---

### KUWAIT

| | |
|---|---|
| 1899 | Britain signs a treaty with Kuwait, establishing a self-governing protectorate. |
| 1914 | Britain recognizes Kuwait as an "independent government under British protection." |
| 1938 | Oil is discovered; large-scale exploitation after World War II transforms the economy. |
| 1961 | Kuwait becomes a fully independent state. |
| 1962 | New constitution is promulgated. |
| 1963 | Kuwait is admitted to the United Nations. |
| 1973 | Iraqi troops occupy the Kuwaiti outpost at Samtah. |
| 1990 | Iraq invades and overruns the emirate, forcing the emir and most of the royal family to flee to Saudi Arabia. |
| 1991 | From mid-January to the end of February, Allied forces stage air, sea, and ground campaign that defeats Iraqi forces and liberates Kuwait. Al-Sabah family rulers return and retain firm hold on power. New cabinet in April retains Crown Prince Saad as premier. Emir promises parliamentary elections for 1992. |
| 1999 | Parliamentary elections are held in July. In May, Sheikh al-Sabah decrees that women can vote in the next elections, to be held in 2003. Parliament rejects this proposal in November. |
| 2006 | Sheikh Jaber dies and is succeeded by Crown Prince Sheikh Saad al-Abdullah al-Sabah. The parliament removes Sheikh Saad al-Abdullah due to his ill health, and replace him with Sheikh Sabah al-Ahmad al-Sabah. |

---

leadership of Emir Mubarak al Sabah (1896–1915). The discovery of oil in 1938 led to a more direct British involvement in Kuwaiti affairs, until Kuwait gained full independence in 1961. A constitution and national assembly were established in 1962, but the assembly was dissolved in 1976 and again in 1986. The current emir, Shaikh Jabir al Ahmad al Jabir al Sabah, rules by decree. A founding member of the ORGANIZATION OF PETROLEUM EXPORTING COUNTRIES (OPEC) in 1960, Kuwait joined the UNITED NATIONS in 1963. In the 1980s Kuwait was affected by the IRAN-IRAQ WAR, enduring Iranian bombing and several terrorist attacks. Territorial claims by neighboring Iraq led to clashes with Kuwait in 1961 and 1973–74 and Iraq's invasion of Kuwait in August 1990. (See PERSIAN GULF WAR.) Attempts to negotiate an Iraqi withdrawal failed, leading to war. On January 16, 1991, American-led UN forces initiated an air attack against Iraq to forcibly remove it from Kuwait. A UN ground offensive launched on Feb. 21, drove the Iraqis out of Kuwait

in less than a week. Kuwait suffered greatly during the Iraqi occupation; 600 Kuwaiti oil wells burned out of control, creating an ecological and economic disaster. Fulfilling a promise he had made during the Iraqi occupation, the emir permitted new elections for the National Assembly, which had been dissolved in 1981. In 1999 the emir granted women the right to vote, but this was rejected by the parliament.

In 2006 Sheikh Jaber, who had led the country since 1977, died after suffering a minor stroke in 2001. Soon after he was succeeded by Crown Prince Sheikh Saad al-Abdullah al Sabah, the Kuwaiti parliament removed Sheik Saad al-Abdullah on grounds of ill health and replaced him with Sheikh Sabah al-Ahmad al Sabah, who had been prime minister since 2003.

**Kuzmin, Michael Alekseyevich** *(1875–1936)* Russian poet. A member of the Symbolist group, although his work is not considered part of the Symbolist school because his poetry is less solemn. Kuzmin's poems are often

a blend of religious themes with a refined sensuality and are very carefully crafted. *Songs of Alexandria* (1906) is usually considered his best collection of verse. This was followed by *The Seasons of Love* (1907). Kuzmin also wrote scenarios for plays, ballets and operettas. In 1910 Kuzmin wrote *Concerning Beautiful Clarity,* a manifesto on poetry that marked the transition from Symbolism to ACMEISM.

**Kuznets, Simon** *(1901–1985)* Ukrainian-born economist. Kuznets immigrated to the U.S. in 1922 and did his most important work during a lengthy affiliation with the National Bureau of Economic Research. In 1971 while professor emeritus of economics at Harvard University, he was awarded the NOBEL PRIZE in economic science for his development of the concept of the gross national product (GNP).

**Kuznetsov, Vasily V.** *(1901–1991)* Soviet diplomat. He played a role in the negotiations surrounding several major international events of the 1960s, including the CUBAN MISSILE CRI-

SIS of 1962, the SOVIET INVASION OF CZECHOSLOVAKIA in 1968 and the Sino-Soviet dispute. He served as first vice president under Leonid I. BREZHNEV and was also a nonvoting member of the Politburo from 1977 to 1986.

**Kwangtung (Guangdong, Kuang-Tong)** Southernmost province of CHINA, on Liaoning Peninsula. The KUOMINTANG was formed here in 1912 by SUN YATSEN. was also the center of CHIANG KAI-SHEK's Nationalist forces in the 1920s.

**Ky, Nguyen Cao** (*1930–* ) South Vietnamese military officer and political leader. Ky was drafted into the Vietnamese National Army (raised by the French to combat the VIET MINH insurrection) in 1950. After serving as an infantry lieutenant, he volunteered for pilot training and, after advanced training in France and Algeria, graduated as a fully qualified pilot in 1954. Rising to the rank of lieutenant general in the newly formed South Vietnamese Air Force, he was one of the Young Turks who seized power in 1965 to end the near anarchy that had followed

the assassination of President Ngo Dinh DIEM two years earlier. Ky was elected by the Armed Forces Council to serve as prime minister. In 1966 Buddhists and other political factions demanded Ky's ouster; and protests, including immolations, took place in various cities, as they had under the Diem regime. The disturbances ended partly as a result of a government crackdown and partly because of a loss of support for the Buddhists among dissident elements of the military. Ky continued in the post of prime minister until the elections of 1967, when he became vice president of South Vietnam. He served in that position until 1971, when he chose not to run as an opposition candidate against President Nguyen Van THIEU. He reverted to the rank of air marshal in the air force. On April 29, 1975, during operation Frequent Wind, he flew from Saigon to join the U.S. evacuation fleet. (See also VIETNAM WAR.)

**Kyrgyzstan** Territory of the Russian Empire (1876–1921), the RUSSIAN SOVIET FEDERATED SOCIALIST REPUBLIC (RSFSR), the UNION OF SOVIET SOCIALIST

REPUBLICS (USSR, 1922–91), and independent nation-state (1991– ). Kyrgyzstan was one of several territories acquired by the Russian Empire in its expansion in Central Asia during the latter half of the 19th century. Under Russian rule the inhabitants of the area were incorporated into the territory of Turkistan, and had to cope with an influx of Russian settlers. After the Bolshevik Revolution of November 1917, the predominantly Muslim Kyrgyz attempted to gain their independence, but they were suppressed first by the remaining czarist forces in the region, and later their territory came under the control of the Bolsheviks following their victory in the RUSSIAN CIVIL WAR OF 1918–20. The new Communist government established modern-day Kyrgyzstan within the RSFSR as the Turkistan Autonomous Soviet Socialist Republic. Turkistan's area also included the current independent states of Tajikistan, Turkmenistan, Uzbekistan and a portion of Kazakhstan. Two years after the RSFSR reconstituted itself as the USSR, in 1922, the Soviet government redrew the borders of its Central Asian provinces and au-

| KYRGYZSTAN | |
| --- | --- |
| 1917–1924 | Kyrgyzstan is part of the independent Turkestan republic. |
| 1924 | Kyrgyzstan becomes an autonomous republic within the USSR. |
| 1930s | An agricultural collectivization program provokes *basmachi* resistance, and local "nationalist communists" are purged from the Kyrgyz Communist Party (KCP). |
| 1936 | Kyrgyz ASSR is granted full republic status. |
| 1990 | The conflict over land between Uzbeks and Kyrgyz in Osh region explodes into rioting, killing at least 320 on both sides. |
| 1991 | Kyrgyzstan asserts its independence on August 31 in the wake of Soviet Union's disintegration. Askar Akayev is confirmed in October as president of the new republic, which joins Commonwealth of Independent States. |
| 1995 | The Supreme Assembly vetoes Akayev's proposal to extend his term to 2001, forcing a presidential election in December, which Akayev wins. |
| 1996 | A second constitutional referendum further heightens the president's powers. |
| 1997 | Human rights groups report increasing instances of government repression and jailing of journalists and opposition figures. |
| 2005 | The "Tulip Revolution" forces Akayev to resign. The presidential election held soon after is won by Kurmanbek Bakiyev. |

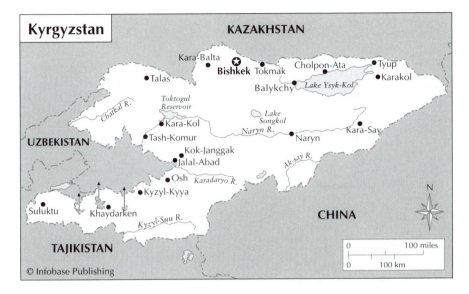

tonomous regions to reflect their ethnic composition. The Kara-Kyrgyz Autonomous Region was formed, comprising modern-day Kyrgyzstan. The following year, the region became an autonomous republic within the USSR and in 1936 it achieved the status of a constituent Soviet Socialist Republic (SSR). Under the rule of Joseph Stalin, the area was subjected to the forced collectivization of all arable land into state agricultural farms and grazing areas and the forced relocation of the largely nomadic Kyrgyz to work on these farms. During the COLD WAR (1947–91) Kyrgyz's sizable uranium reserves led to a large influx of Russian miners and engineers to extract the uranium for use in the Soviet nuclear weapons program. Russian workers were accompanied by an expansion of primary and secondary institutions in which Russian was the exclusive language of instruction.

The Russian cultural presence in Kyrgyz began to diminish in 1985 due to Soviet premier MIKHAIL GORBACHEV'S political policy of glasnost, or "openness," which permitted autonomy to the 15 SSRs of the Soviet Union. As a result of this increasing autonomy, the Kyrgyz began to form associations with political agendas.

The republic suffered from increased ethnic conflicts between the Kyrgyz and the Uzbeks (an ethnic group comprising about 14 percent of the province's population) in the city of Osh, located near the border between Kyrgyz and the Uzbek SSR, which led to an outbreak of urban violence between Uzbeks and Kyrgyz in June 1990. In October the province's Supreme Soviet designated the liberal and reform-oriented Askar Akayev as president. Akayev won widespread respect as an innovator and as one of two SSR presidents (the other being Boris Yeltsin) who immediately openly denounced the August 1991 coup attempt by reactionary members of the Communist Party of the Soviet Union. After the failure of the coup, the Kyrgyz Republic voted to secede from the Soviet Union and change its name to Kyrgyzstan.

Since declaring independence, Kyrgyzstan has attempted to balance the interests of Kyrgyz nationalism with efforts to remain linked economically with neighboring republics in Central Asia. The relationship between the state and its Russian minority has been particularly strained since 1991. Following the failed effort to make Russian the second official language of the republic (after Kyrgyz), Russian emigration from the republic continued at a high rate. In an effort to jump-start free-market reforms Akayev halted the circulation of the Russian ruble as the country's currency, and instead instituted its own currency, the som. In response, Russian president Yeltsin terminated continued Russian subsidies to formerly state-owned heavy industries in Kyrgyzstan. After Akayev won reelection as president in 2000 amid allegations of electoral fraud, his status as a symbol of Central Asian democracy was diminished. In 2001 Kyrgyzstan allowed the U.S. to use the country's territory during the military campaign against the Taliban regime in nearby Afghanistan. The following year construction began on a large U.S. airbase near the city of Bishkek as part of U.S. president George W. Bush's war on terror. In 2005 parliamentary elections criticized by international observers as fraudulent incited nationwide protests, dubbed the "Tulip Revolution," that forced Akayev to resign and flee into exile. Kurmanbek Bakiyev won the presidency in the 2005 election held soon after Akayev's ouster.

# L

**Labouisse, Henry R(ichardson)**
*(1904–1987)* U.S. diplomat. In the late 1940s, Labouisse was one of the principal organizers of the MARSHALL PLAN, the U.S.-backed program for the economic recovery of postwar Europe. From 1954 to 1958 he was director of the United Nations Relief and Works Agency for Palestinian Refugees. He was U.S. ambassador to Greece from 1962 to 1965. He returned to the United Nations in 1965 to head the United Nations International Children's Emergency Fund (UNICEF), a post he held until 1979.

**Labor Party (Israel)** Israeli political party formed in 1930. The Labor Party was originally called Maipai, from Mifleget Poalei Yisrael (Israel Workers Party). One of its organizers was David BEN-GURION, who became the first prime minister when ISRAEL became independent in 1948. He remained in power almost continuously until 1963, and Maipai repeatedly dominated the elections. In 1965 Ben-Gurion and his protégés, Moshe DAYAN and Shimon PERES, left Maipai to form Rafi, which advocated more technocratic efficiency in government. Rafi rejoined Maipai in 1968 along with Achdut Haavodah, another political party previously associated with Maipai, to formally create the Israel Labor Party under Prime Minister Levi Eshkol. Upon his death in 1969, he was succeeded as partly leader and coalition prime minister by Golda MEIR, who remained in office until 1974. The subsequent administration of Yitzhak RABIN was beset by corruption scandals and internal conflict. The Labor Party lost the 1977 elections and remained in opposition throughout the 1980s, except for a short-lived coalition with Yitzhak SHAMIR. The Labor Party returned to power from 1992 to 1996 under Yitzhak Rabin and Shimon Peres, and from 1999 to 2000 under EHUD BARAK. After its electoral defeat in 2000 by the Likud Party, headed by Ariel Sharon, the Labor Party struggled to redefine its political program and languished in opposition. In 2005 Shimon Peres announced he was leaving the party and planned to join Ariel Sharon's new Forward (Kadima) Party.

**Labour Party (New Zealand)**
NEW ZEALAND political party formed in 1916. The Labour Party entered its first general election in 1919. While it maintained policies favorable to farmers, the party gained prominence in the 1920s when New Zealand became increasingly urbanized. Labour won a majority in 1935 and remained in power until 1949 under the leadership of Prime Ministers Michael SAVAGE and Peter FRASER. During that time many relief and social welfare programs were instituted, including a state health care program in 1941. Labour came to power again in 1957 by a slim majority led by Prime Minister Sir Walter Nash, but he was unable to cope with a severe economic crisis, and the National Party was elected in 1960. From 1972 to 1975 Prime Ministers Norman Kirk and Wallace Rowling led Labour governments. After nine years of National administration, the Labour Party, led by David LANGE, was voted back into power in 1984. Led by Prime Minister Helen Clark, the Labour Party returned to power in 1999, and retained a governing majority in the elections of 2002.

**Labour Party (United Kingdom)**
British political party formed in 1906. Labour Party membership can be either individual or collective, and the party is comprised of a network of constituency associations overseen by 11 branch offices. At the national level are the national Executive Committee and the Parliamentary Labour Party (PLP) whose members act as shadow cabinet to the party.

Labour Party philosophy reflects its socialist origins. It is strongly supportive of trade unions, government health and social welfare programs, and generally shares the political stance of the liberal faction of the American DEMOCRATIC PARTY. At various times the Labour Party has advocated British withdrawal from the EEC, unilateral nuclear disarmament and abolition of the House of Lords and of private schools.

The Labour Party arose from the Labour Representation Committee that had been formed in 1900 by the FABIAN SOCIETY, the Independent Labour Party, and trade unions. Two Labour MPs were elected in 1900, and 30 in 1906. By 1922 it had become the second largest British political party. In 1924 and from 1929 to 1931, minority Labour governments held office with the support of the LIBERAL PARTY. In the 1945 elections Labour won a sweeping victory and Clement ATTLEE became prime minister. He instituted a broad range of social reforms, including the creation of the NATIONAL HEALTH SERVICE. By the 1950 elections, however, the Labour majority had dwindled, and the Conservatives returned to power in 1951. Subsequent Labour governments were from 1964 to 1970 under Harold WILSON and from 1974 to 1979, first under Wilson and then under James CALLAGHAN. The Labour Party has a history of factionalized squabbling between its left-wing and moderate elements. Beginning in the 1970s the party's left gained prominence, taking control in 1980 when Michael FOOT became leader. In 1981 several moderate members left to form the SOCIAL DEMOCRATIC PARTY. Following Labour's stunning defeat in the 1983 general elections, Neil KINNOCK became party leader. Initially a member of the left of the party, Kinnock became somewhat more moderate since 1983. Although the Labour Party failed to unseat the Conservatives in the 1992 national election, it defeated the Conservatives in May 1997 and retained a majority in 2001 under Prime Minister TONY BLAIR.

**Lacan, Jacques** *(1901–1981)* French psychologist, philosopher and literary critic. Lacan was a brilliant polymath who was jointly influenced by STRUCTURALISM, especially the works of linguistics theorists Roman Jakobson and Ferdinand de Saussure, and by the psychoanalytic theories of Sigmund FREUD. Lacan posed the theory that the structure of the unconscious resembled that of a language. He also argued that Freudian theory, while it discussed the nature of repression, had fallen victim to it by repressing its extreme significance. Lacan, who founded the Ecole Freudienne de Paris in 1963, was an unorthodox psychoanalytic practitioner who sometimes substituted 10-minute therapy sessions for the standard one-hour encounter. His major essays are collected in *Ecrits* (1966). Other works by Lacan include *The Four Fundamental Concepts of Psychoanalysis* (1978) and *Speech and Language in Psychoanalysis* (1983).

**Lacey, James Harry "Ginger"** *(1917–1989)* British World War II fighter pilot. During the BATTLE OF BRITAIN (1940) Lacey shot down 18 enemy aircraft, more than any other pilot. Throughout the war, he shot down a total of 28 German Luftwaffe aircraft, including one that was returning from a bombing raid on Buckingham Palace.

**Lachaise, Gaston** *(1882–1935)* French-American sculptor. Born in Paris, Lachaise learned classical sculptural technique at the Ecole des Beaux-Arts, Paris. Emigrating to the United States in 1906, he executed sculptural details for the artists H. H. Kitson and Paul MANSHIP, working on such commissions as New York's Telephone and Telegraph Building and RCA Building. Lachaise is best known for his monumental figures of women. Powerful and voluptuous, these nudes seem to float pneumatically on tiny feet. They include the famous *Standing Woman* in the collection of the MUSEUM OF MODERN ART, New York City.

**Lacoste, Robert** *(1898–1989)* French socialist politician. Lacoste was best known for his opposition to the concept of Algerian independence in the late 1950s. His strong nationalist support of a French-controlled ALGERIA put him at odds with his own socialist party and eventually contributed to the downfall of France's Fourth Republic.

***Lady Chatterley's Lover*** Novel by D. H. LAWRENCE first published in Italy in 1928. An edited version was published in England in 1932; the full text was not published there until 1960. The book tells the story of Constance Chatterley who is married to Sir Clifford, an enfeebled intellectual wounded in WORLD WAR I and confined to a wheelchair. Lady Chatterley develops a satisfying and passionate relationship with the gamekeeper, Oliver Mellors. She becomes pregnant, and the novel ends with she and Mellors both seeking divorces and hoping for a life together. Lawrence contrasts the effete upper classes with the potency and earthiness of the lower. The novel's frank treatment of sexuality caused it to be banned as obscene in England. Its publication in 1960 caused the publishers, Penguin, to be embroiled in a

prosecution under the Obscene Publications Act of 1959, and many authors, including E. M. FORSTER, spoke on behalf of the defense. Penguin was acquitted.

**Laemmle, Carl** *(1867–1939)* German-born motion picture producer and president of UNIVERSAL PICTURES. The diminutive Laemmle came to America in 1887 at age 13 and rose from errand boy at a New York drugstore to owner of his own company in 1907, a film distribution exchange called the Laemmle Film Service. Two years later, in defiance of the newly formed Motion Pictures Patents Company—a trust organized by Edison and others to put independent distributors and producers out of business—Laemmle founded the Independent Motion Picture Company of America (IMP), a forerunner of Universal Pictures. From his New York office he became one of the most powerful men in the film industry, not only defeating the trust in a court action in 1912, but also launching the "star system" and the feature-length film, among the most important innovations in film history. "Laemmle wasn't a brilliant aesthetic innovator," writes historian Neal Gabler, "but he had become a brilliant exploiter." After the opening in 1915 of the vast Universal City complex, a 230-acre municipality and studio facility in California's San Fernando Valley that cranked films out like a factory assembly line, he presided over operations until 1929, when he transferred power to his son, Carl Jr. The young Laemmle was one of 15 relatives eventually placed on the company payroll.

**Laetrile** **(also called vitamin B-17, amygdalin)** Controversial chemical substance, claimed by some people to be a cure for cancer and by others to be a quack remedy. Laetrile occurs naturally in apricot pits, peaches, bitter almonds and other plants. It contains small amounts of the poison cyanide. In the 1970s laetrile was legally available in many countries but was banned in the United States by the Food and Drug Administration. Laetrile's promoters claimed that since there was no evidence that it was harmful, it should be legally available in the United States to patients who wanted it. The FDA said that numerous tests had indicated that laetrile was therapeutically worthless. The agency warned that cancer patients who put their faith in laetrile might be risking their lives by failing to receive orthodox medical treatment. Some authorities felt that laetrile's promoters were taking advantage of desperately ill people. Many cancer patients went to Mexico to receive laetrile treatment, and others obtained laetrile illegally in the United States. In 1977 federal judges ruled that terminally ill patients should have the right to receive laetrile even if there was no proof that it could cure cancer. Most of the American medical establishment continued to question laetrile's effectiveness.

**La Farge, Oliver** *(1901–1963)* American author. La Farge won the PULITZER PRIZE in 1929 for his novel *Laughing Boy: A Navaho Romance,* which dramatized the painful effort of American Indians to adjust their age-old ways to the modern age. La Farge went on to serve as director for the Eastern Association on Indian Affairs (1930–32), and as president of the National Association on Indian Affairs (1933–37) and the American Association on Indian Affairs (1937–42).

**Lafayette   Escadrille** Renowned unit of volunteer American flyers in the French air service before the U.S. entered WORLD WAR I. It was reorganized in 1918 as the U.S.'s 103rd Pursuit Squadron. The escadrille (squadron) consisted of 38 flyers, only six of whom survived the war.

**La Follette, Robert Marion** *(1855–1925)* U.S. politician. A law graduate, he was elected district attorney and, later, to the Wisconsin House of Representatives as a Republican. In 1901 he was elected as the governor of Wisconsin; over a period from 1903 to 1905 many of his liberal reform policies were adopted. These included pensions for the blind, old age assistance, unemployment compensation and laws governing working conditions of children. He was one of the first to call on economic and other experts as government consultants. As a member of the U.S. Senate from 1906 to 1924, he became one of its most influential men. In 1909 he organized the National Progressive Republican League, from which Theodore ROOSEVELT adopted many of La Follette's liberal ideas.

Later, he opposed American entry into WORLD WAR I, but supported most of Woodrow WILSON's policies. He also opposed the LEAGUE OF NATIONS and the World Court. In 1924 he ran unsuccessfully for president on the Progressive Party ticket (but gathered almost five million votes).

**La Follette, Suzanne** *(1893–1983)* American author and editor. A prominent conservative, La Follette founded several magazines, most notably the NATIONAL REVIEW. Among her books was *Concerning Women,* which argued for civil rights for women. She was an early anti-Soviet activist and served as secretary to the commission that investigated the Soviet-ordered assassination of Leon TROTSKY. She was a cousin of Senator Robert M. LA FOLLETTE.

**Lagerkvist, Pär** *(1891–1951)* Swedish author and playwright. Lagerkvist first began publishing poetry in 1912, the same year his first novella, *Manniskor* (People) was published. His early works were strongly influenced by modern painting, and rejected naturalism. The expressionist poetry collection, *Angest* (Anguish, 1916) reflects his pessimism and despair wrought by the events of WORLD WAR I. His early plays, which include *Den sista manniskan* (The Last Man, 1917) and *Himlens hemlighet* (Secret of heaven, 1919) also evidenced an existential desperation. His later works were less stylized, humanistic outcries against FASCISM and evil. These include the poems, *Sång och strid* (Song and struggle, 1940), the drama *Lat Manniskan leva* (Let man live, 1949) and the novel *Barabbas* (1950, filmed 1952), Lagerkvist's acclaimed and best-known work. He was awarded the NOBEL PRIZE for literature in 1951. Later works include the novels, *Det heliga landet* (The holy land, 1964) and *Mariamne* (Herod and Meriamne, 1967).

**Lagerlöf, Selma** *(1858–1940)* Swedish novelist. Lagerlöf's first novel, *Gösta Berlings saga* (Gösta Berling's Saga, 1891), was published after it won a literary contest in a Swedish magazine. Its romantic style was unusual in a period of literary naturalism. Her many popular works, which include *Nils Holgerssons underbara resa genom Sverige* (The wonderful adventures of Nils, 1906), and *Tösen från Stormyrtorpet*

(The girl from the marsh croft, 1907), are rich in Swedish folklore and myth. Lagerlöf received the NOBEL PRIZE for literature in 1909. During World War II, she donated the gold medal to a fund to benefit Finland, and was also instrumental in helping German intellectuals, such as Nelly SACHS, escape from Nazi GERMANY.

**LaGuardia, Fiorello Henry** *(1882–1947)* American politician known for his three terms as reform mayor of NEW YORK CITY. Popularly known as the "little flower," LaGuardia spent much of his childhood in the western United States and in Europe but returned to New York City, his birthplace, and graduated from New York University Law School. A reform Republican in a city dominated by Tammany Hall Democrats, LaGuardia was elected to Congress in 1916 and served (with the exception of the years 1919–23) until 1933. He cosponsored the NORRIS-LAGUARDIA ACT (1932), a major labor law that protected the rights of striking workers. LaGuardia ran as a reformer for mayor of New York in 1929 but was defeated by Jimmy WALKER. In 1933, a year after he lost his congressional seat in the Democratic landslide, he was elected mayor of New York City on a "fusion" ticket after Walker resigned after investigations had exposed gross corruption in city government. Short, stout and often unkempt, LaGuardia was an energetic reform mayor who enjoyed broad support. He is popularly remembered for reading the comics on the radio during a prolonged newspaper strike.

*New York mayor Fiorello LaGuardia* (LIBRARY OF CONGRESS, PRINTS AND PHOTOGRAPHS DIVISION)

**Laika** Dog that became the first Earth creature to travel into outer space; the name Laika means "barker." On November 3, 1959, Laika was launched into orbit aboard Sputnik 2, the second artificial satellite launched by the Soviet Union (see SPUTNIK I). Laika lived in space for 10 days before dying when her oxygen ran out. Laika's vital signs were monitored from the ground, Sputnik 2 thus providing the first information about the effects of space travel on living creatures. The flight of Laika showed that the Soviets were serious about sending people into space—and that the Soviets were ahead of the United States in the space race. In August 1960 Sputnik 5 carried two dogs, Belka and Strelka, into space; they returned to Earth safely, the first creatures to do so.

**Laing, R(onald) D(avid)** *(1927–1989)* Scottish psychiatrist. Laing's unorthodox theories about mental illness, particularly schizophrenia, made him a COUNTERCULTURE hero in the 1960s. His theories first gained recognition in 1960 with the publication of his first book, *The Divided Self: An Existential Study in Sanity and Madness.* Laing argued that schizophrenia was not a genetic or biochemical aberration but rather an avenue of escape from a family situation fraught with conflicting emotional demands. An outspoken critic of standard psychiatric treatments, which he claimed did more harm than good, he experimented with various alternative approaches, including the use of psychedelic drugs. He put his theories into practice at Kingsley Hall, a therapeutic community he set up in London in the 1960s. Eventually he became disenchanted with much of his early thinking about mental illness and admitted that many of his treatment methods had failed.

**Laker, Edwin Francis** *(1910–1980)* American inventor. While serving as a major in the 82nd Airborne Division in WORLD WAR II, Laker developed the **Pathfinder** long-range bombing system. Bomber crews used this to find and mark targets with smoke or flares, which other aircraft then used as indicators to drop their bombs.

***L.A. Law*** Television drama series produced for the NATIONAL BROADCAST-ING CORPORATION (NBC) about a fictional law firm named McKenzie, Brackman, Chaney & Kuzak. Premiering at the start of the 1986–87 season, it focused on the civil and criminal cases taken by the law firm and the relationships of the firm's staff and its competitors, while the junior members of the firm competed against each other to become full-fledged senior partners. The show ran for eight seasons on NBC before filming its final episode in 1994. *L.A. Law* won four Emmys for Best Drama Series (1987, 1989–91). In May 2002 NBC released a made-for-TV *L.A. Law* movie.

**Lalique, René** *(1860–1945)* French glass and jewelry designer. Born in the Marne, Lalique studied drawing and goldsmithing in Paris. Traveling to London (1878–80), he returned to Paris as a jewelry designer, cofounding a business to market his designs in 1884 and purchasing a jewelry workshop the following year. In 1891 Lalique began to work in glass. Starting to show his work at exhibitions in 1894, he was the recipient of many important awards, his success capped by his own pavilion at the Paris exhibition of 1925. Early in the 20th century he diversified into textiles, mirrors and other products, beginning to use engraved glass in jewelry in 1905 and adding pressed-glass perfume bottles to his roster in 1906. He opened his first glass factory in 1909, founding another in 1918. Lalique's innovative designs included various tablewares and light fixtures, and he was particularly famed for the elegant salon he designed for the luxury ocean liner NORMANDIE. Working at first in the ART NOUVEAU style, he developed a sleek, geometric design mode (employing plant, animal and abstract forms) that was the epitome of ART DECO.

**Lamar, Joseph R.** *(1857–1916)* Associate justice, U.S. Supreme Court (1910–16). Lamar, a native of Georgia, and a graduate of Bethany College, studied law at Washington and Lee University before his admission to the bar. In private law practice, he was also involved in politics and was elected to the Georgia legislature before being appointed to the state Supreme Court. In 1910 Lamar was appointed to the U.S. Supreme Court by President William Howard TAFT. A hard worker, Lamar died while serving on the Court in 1916.

**L'Amour, Louis Dearborn** *(1908–1988)* American author best known for his westerns. L'Amour wrote 101 books—86 novels, 14 story collections and one work of nonfiction, with sales nearing 200 million. *Hondo,* published in 1953, was his first and perhaps best known novel; it was made into a film starring John WAYNE. Many of L'Amour's other works were also adapted as feature films, including *Shalako, Stranger on Horseback* and *How the West Was Won; The Sacketts* was adapted for television. He was the only novelist honored with both a congressional gold medal (1983) and a presidential Medal of Freedom (1984).

**Lampedusa, Giuseppi Tomasi Di** *(1896–1957)* Italian novelist. An upper-class Sicilian, Lampedusa is best remembered for the novel *Il gattopardo* (*The Leopard,* 1955–56; filmed 1963), which describes the reactions of a noble family to the social and political landscape following Sicily's appropriation by Garibaldi in 1860.

**Lancaster, Burt (Burton Stephen Lancaster)** *(1913–1994)* American film actor. Born in New York City, Lancaster attended New York University but left to become a traveling acrobat. He served in World War II before making his acting debut on Broadway (1945). Moving to HOLLYWOOD, he won a role in *The Killers* (1946, adapted from an Ernest HEMINGWAY short story) and soon became a genuine star. Handsome and muscular, he was at first identified with swashbucklers, westerns and other action pictures, such as *The Flame and the Arrow* (1950), *Jim Thorpe—All American* (1951), *Apache* (1954), *Trapeze* (1956) and *Gunfight at O.K. Corral* (1957); in all of these he performed his own stunts. He also scored a hit as a romantic leading man in *From Here to Eternity* (1953) and showed his versatility in challenging dramatic roles in *All My Sons* (1948), *The Rose Tattoo* (1955), *The Rainmaker* (1957), *Elmer Gantry* (1960, ACADEMY AWARD), *The Birdman of Alcatraz* (1962), *The Leopard* (1963) and *The Swimmer* (1968). As he aged, Lancaster made a successful transition to character roles, as in Louis MALLE's *Atlantic City* (1980). He also created memorable supporting characters in *Local Hero* (1983), *Field of Dreams* (1989) and other films. While his performances are often mannered, they show his complete dedication to, and his impressive command of, the actor's craft. Lancaster has gradually been acknowledged as one of the finest film actors of his generation.

**Lanchester, Elsa (Elizabeth Sullivan)** *(1902–1986)* British-born actress. After a successful stage career in London, Lanchester became one of Hollywood's most outstanding character actresses. Known for her talents in eccentric or comic parts, she scored a singular triumph in *The Bride of Frankenstein* (1935), a film in which she played both the title role and Frankenstein's creator, Mary Shelley. Her career was closely linked with that of her husband, Charles Laughton, to whom she was married from 1929 until his death in 1962. They made a number of films together, most notably, *Witness for the Prosecution* (1957). After his death, she revealed that their marriage survived numerous homosexual liaisons on his part and affairs on hers. Her last film was *Murder by Death* (1976).

**Land, Edwin Herbert** *(1909–1991)* American inventor, scientist and industrialist. Born in Norwich, Connecticut, he attended Harvard University, but dropped out in 1932 to pursue his scientific interests on his own. Fascinated with polarized light, he began a series of inventions involving polarization and in 1937 founded the Polaroid Corporation. In 1943 Land conceived the idea for what was to be the most famous and successful of his many inventions (he held 533 patents): an instant camera that captured an image and developed it in a single-step process. He began marketing this Polaroid Land Camera in 1948 and introduced a color version in 1963. Land served as Polaroid's chairman until his retirement in 1981. Land was also a military adviser to the federal government and was an early advocate of the use of reconnaissance SATELLITES.

**Landis, Kenesaw Mountain** *(1866–1944)* American judge, first commissioner of professional baseball. In the early years of the 20th century professional baseball and the World Series had

caught the imagination of the American public. That same public was dismayed when it was revealed that several members of the Chicago White Sox had taken bribes to throw the 1919 World Series. The affair became known as the BLACK SOX SCANDAL. Judge Landis, a U.S. district court judge from Chicago, was enlisted to become the czar of baseball with broad powers to regulate the sport and banish those whose actions were not in the best interests of the game. Landis barred the errant participants for life and imposed a strict ban on gambling by ballplayers. Landis and those who followed established a tradition of a strong commissioner with sweeping powers to maintain the integrity of the sport.

**Landon, Alf(red Mossman)** *(1887–1987)* American politician. A banker and an oilman, Landon served as governor of Kansas (1933–37). He was widely praised for economy in government operations during the GREAT DEPRESSION. Reelected in 1934, he gained national renown for his support of Kansas farmers in the depth of the Depression. He was the Republican nominee for president in 1936, but lost the election to the enormously popular Franklin D. ROOSEVELT. Landon's daughter, **Nancy Landon Kassebaum,** was later a U.S. senator.

**Landowska, Wanda** *(1877–1959)* Polish-French harpsichordist and pianist. Born in Warsaw, Landowska studied at the conservatory there and began her career as a pianist in 1891. She later taught piano at the Schola Cantorum, Paris (1900–12). Fascinated with the music of the baroque period, she turned her attention to the harpsichord, making her debut on the instrument in 1903. Landowska taught harpsichord at the Berlin Hochschule (1912–19) before establishing her own Ecole de Musique ancienne at Saint-Leula-Forêt near Paris in 1919. She taught and gave renowned concerts of early music there until 1940, when World War II caused her to settle in the United States. Here she continued her activities as teacher, performer and recording artist. The guiding spirit in the 20th-century revival of interest in the harpsichord, much admired for her Bach interpretations, she was also an inspiration to modern composers. Both Manuel de FALLA and Francis

POULENC wrote harpsichord concertos expressly for her. Landowska and her husband, Henry Lew, were the authors of *Music of the Past.*

**Landry, Tom** *(1924–2000)* American professional football player and coach in the All-American Football Conference (AAFC) and the National Football League (NFL). Born in Mission, Texas, Landry began his football career as a quarterback and a fullback for the University of Texas Longhorns. In a successful playing career as a cornerback/safety and a punter for the New York Giants of the National Football League, Landry averaged an impressive 31 interceptions on defense and compiled a 40.4-yard punting average on special teams.

In his last two seasons as a player for the Giants, Landry began to develop an interest in coaching professional football. Landry ended his playing days in 1956 and for the next four seasons, served as the Giants's defensive coordinator. Landry did so well in this post that an NFL expansion team, the Dallas Cowboys, named him head coach in 1960.

As head coach of the Cowboys, Landry compiled an impressive 250-162-6 regular season record, as well as a 20-16 postseason record that resulted in two Super Bowls (VI and XII). More important, Landry modified the manner in which professional football was played through his liberal use of player substitution on offense and defense and his willingness to use multiple offensive formations and defensive zones to confuse opponents and capitalize on their inadequacies. Although his record and his role in the 20 consecutive winning seasons gave Dallas a national fan base, Landry was forced to resign as head coach in 1988 by Jerry Jones, who had purchased the team in 1987. After leaving the Cowboys, Landry retired from professional football, and was inducted into the Pro Football Hall of Fame two years later.

**Lane, Sir Hugh Percy** *(1875–1915)* Irish connoisseur and art collector. Born in Cork, Lane worked for a number of art dealers in London before opening his own gallery. In 1901 he commissioned John Butler YEATS to paint portraits of contemporary Irishmen, a project that was completed by Sir William ORPEN. He also organized various exhibits of Irish art, and participated in the foundation of Dublin's Gallery of Modern Art. In recognition of his services to Irish art, Lane was knighted in 1909. He was drowned in the torpedo attack on the LUSITANIA in 1915. The provisions of his will caused a bitter controversy in IRELAND. His collection, now split into two parts, is rotated every five years for alternate exhibition in Dublin and London.

**Lang, Fritz** *(1890–1976)* German-born director of fantasy and suspense movie thrillers. Lang entered the film industry in Berlin as a screenwriter and director in 1918. With his wife, screenwriter Thea von Harbou, he made some of GERMANY's most famous films in the 1920s, including the expressionist fantasies *Der müde Tod* (*Destiny,* 1921), *Siegfrieds Tod* (Siegfried's Death, 1923), and *Metropolis* (1927); the visionary science fiction film *Die Frau im Mond* (*The Woman in the Moon,* 1929); the criminal conspiracy thrillers about "Dr. Mabuse" (1923); and the police procedural films *Spione* (*Spies,* 1928) and *M* (1931). After a hasty departure from Nazi Germany in 1933, Lang began a long career in America, where he became one of the architects of FILM NOIR, infusing the standard genres of the western (*The Return of Frank James,* 1940), romance (*Scarlet Street,* 1945) and gangster picture (*The Big Heat,* 1953) with his own unrelieved sense of darkness and paranoia. Disillusioned with HOLLYWOOD, Lang worked abroad after 1956, bringing the infamous "Dr. Mabuse" back for a final bow in *The 1000 Eyes of Dr. Mabuse* (1960).

Lang's central characters are usually victims or victimizers, either falling prey to their own obsessions (the child molester in *M,* the artist in *Scarlet Street*) or manipulating the world into their own insane images (the mad scientist Rotwang in *Metropolis* and Mabuse). In any case Lang's universe is closed to individual freedom—perhaps, significantly, like the motion picture set where Lang himself was able to exercise an almost despotic control.

**Langdon, Harry** *(1884–1944)* Generally regarded as one of America's greatest silent film comedians (along with CHAPLIN, KEATON and LLOYD), Langdon was born in Council Bluffs,

Iowa. Working in his teens as a ticket seller, circus clown, acrobat and ventriloquist, Langdon was noticed by producer-director Mack SENNETT. The collaboration produced a few amusing short films, but it was not until Langdon met gagwriter (later director) Frank CAPRA and director Harry Edwards that his comic character of the "child with adult desires" developed. The three went on to make dozens of two-reel and three-reel comedy hits, including *Picking Peaches* (1924), and features, including *Tramp, Tramp, Tramp* (1926) and *Long Pants* (1927). With success under his belt, Langdon fired Capra and Edwards in order to write and direct his own films. The result was a string of critical and commercial flops. Langdon was never able to resurrect his early success; he continued to work in the 1930s but only in occasional featured roles. In 1944 Langdon died of a cerebral hemorrhage; his films have largely been forgotten by the public, but his strong influence can be detected in the style of Stan Laurel (see LAUREL AND HARDY), as well as other comedy stars.

**Lange, David** *(1942–  )* Prime minister of NEW ZEALAND (1984–89). Born in Auckland, Lange graduated in law from the University of Auckland in 1966. He practiced as a lawyer, was a tutor at the University of Auckland and completed a postgraduate degree in law. Lange entered parliament at a by-election in 1977; became deputy leader of the LABOUR PARTY, then in opposition, in November 1979; and became leader of the party on February 3, 1983, upon the resignation of Sir Wallace Rowling. Following Labour's victory in the July 1984 election, he became New Zealand's youngest prime minister in this century. He stepped down as prime minister in mid-1989. In 1996 Lange retired from Parliament.

**Lange, Dorothea** *(1895–1965)* American photographer. Born in Hoboken, New Jersey, Lange took an early interest in photography and operated a portrait studio from 1916 to 1932. She became famous for her photographs taken during the GREAT DEPRESSION, stark works that record the time, place and character of the people portrayed with rare power. Photographs such as *Migrant Mother, Nipomo, California* (1936) reveal poverty and dignity in

one powerful image. This work was part of a series Lange and her husband, the economist Paul Taylor, executed for the state of California, documenting the life of migrant workers. This project resulted in their book *An American Exodus* (1939). She worked for the Farm Security Administration (1935–42), on projects that studied rural America. After the outbreak of WORLD WAR II Lange created a series of documentary photographs that recorded the internment of JAPANESE AMERICANS. She also contributed many photo essays to LIFE magazine.

**Langer, Suzanne K(naith)** *(1895–1985)* American philosopher. Langer was one of the rare academic philosophers of the modern era to find a substantial popular readership. Her major work, *Philosophy in a New Key* (1942), which argued that all intellectual ideas are ultimately expressed in a symbolic mode, was reprinted many times and became a standard text in numerous undergraduate philosophy classes. Langer was educated at Radcliffe College, where she studied under the eminent philosopher Alfred North WHITEHEAD. Her other major works include *An Introduction to Symbolic Logic* (1937) and the three-volume *Mind: An Essay on Human Feeling* (1967–82).

**Langley, Samuel Pierpont** *(1834–1906)* American scientist, inventor and aviation pioneer. In the 20th century, Langley is known for his efforts to fly the first motor-driven airplane. His interest in the possibility of powered flight dated to 1886, the year before he became secretary of the Smithsonian Institute in Washington, D.C. By 1903 he had designed and built a 60–foot-long aircraft with a wingspan of 48 feet. The plane was launched by catapult off a 70–foot ramp on the Potomac River, but crashed and was wrecked. Less than two months later (December 17, 1903) the WRIGHT BROTHERS made the first successful powered flight at Kitty Hawk, North Carolina. AVIATION experts have since recognized that Langley's plane crashed not because of any faulty design, but because of the catapult method of launching.

**Lanham, Charles Truman "Buck"** *(1902–1978)* A career U.S. Army officer, Lanham led the first American military unit to reach Paris (August 25, 1944) in WORLD WAR II. He was a friend of the writer Ernest HEMINGWAY and was said to be the model for the typical American soldier in Hemingway's novels. He retired with the rank of major general and was later chairman of Colt, the U.S. firearms manufacturer.

**Lanphier, Thomas G(eorge) Jr.** *(1890–1987)* American fighter pilot. In WORLD WAR II, Lanphier flew 112 missions in the South Pacific. In April 1943 he shot down the airplane carrying the commander in chief of the Japanese Royal Navy, Adm. Isoroku YAMAMOTO, known as the architect of the attack on PEARL HARBOR.

**Lansbury, George** *(1859–1940)* British LABOUR PARTY leader. Lansbury joined the Social Democratic Federation in 1892 and served as a Labour Party member of Parliament (1910–12 and 1922–40). An articulate reformer, he was active in fighting against poverty and unemployment, and he vigorously championed woman suffrage. A pacifist, he also opposed World War I. One of the founders (1912) of the *Daily Herald,* he edited the paper until 1922. Commissioner of works from 1929 to 1931, he led the opposition to Ramsay MACDONALD's National Government from 1931 to 1935, when he resigned as party leader. Attempting to promote Anglo-German understanding and avoid another war, Lansbury advocated British disarmament and visited HITLER in 1937.

**Lansing, Robert** *(1864–1928)* U.S. secretary of state. Born in Watertown, New York, Lansing graduated from Amherst in 1886. An authority on international law, he frequently served as counsel for the U.S. in international disputes. Lansing succeeded William Jennings BRYAN as secretary of state in 1915. Because Woodrow WILSON conducted foreign policy with his close adviser Edward M. HOUSE, Lansing had little influence on the decision to enter WORLD WAR I, although he advocated participation in the struggle. Lansing worked in harmony with Wilson until the PARIS PEACE CONFERENCE, when he lost the president's confidence because of his view that the LEAGUE OF NATIONS was not important. When Lansing conducted cabinet meetings during Wil-

son's illness, the president requested his resignation.

**Lansky, Meyer** *(1902–1983)* American organized crime figure. Born in Poland, Lansky was reputedly the financial mastermind of organized crime in the U.S. for more than four decades. He began his criminal career in the 1920s during PROHIBITION, and formed a notorious crime syndicate with gangster "Lucky" LUCIANO. Lansky was said to have amassed a multimillion dollar personal fortune through illegal operations in gambling, bootlegging, loansharking, stock manipulation and infiltration of legitimate businesses throughout the U.S. During his career, he was charged with many crimes, including tax evasion, assault and contempt of court; but he spent only two months of his life in prison.

**Laos (Lao People's Democratic Republic)** Laos covers an area of 91,405 square miles on the Indochinese peninsula in southeast Asia (see INDOCHINA). Under French control since 1907, Laos was occupied by Japan during WORLD WAR II, then became a free state within the FRENCH COMMUNITY in 1946. Full independence was granted in 1953. The country suffered political instability during the next 20 years due to conflict between pro-and anticommunist forces. The leftist political party's links with North Vietnam prompted the United States to initiate secret bombing raids into Laos to destroy North Vietnamese havens there (1964). In 1973 a cease-fire was signed; by 1975 the communists controlled the government and established the People's Democratic Republic. The ruling Lao People's Revolutionary Party (LPRP) is the only legal

| LAOS | |
|---|---|
| 1907 | Most of Laos under French administration as part of French Indochina. |
| 1940–45 | Japan occupies Laos, ruling through the Vichy French government. |
| 1950 | Prince Souphanouvong forms communist-inspired Pathet Lao after contact with Ho Chi Minh in northeast Laos. |
| 1954 | Geneva Accords establish Laos as an independent, neutral nation under the rule of royal government and allot two "regroupment" provinces, adjacent to North Vietnam, to the Pathet Lao. |
| 1960 | Civil war begins between troops of the pro-Western royal government and Pathet Lao. |
| 1964 | 14-nation Geneva conference sets up coalition government with Prince Souvanna Phouma, a neutralist, as prime minister, anticommunist Prince Boun Oum, and communist Prince Souphanouvong as cabinet ministers. |
| 1971 | South Vietnamese troops backed by U.S. bombers invade Laos to attack Ho Chi Minh Trail; CIA admits U.S. has 30,000-man army in Laos. |
| 1975 | Following American withdrawal and the subsequent fall of South Vietnam to the communists, King Savang Vatthana abdicates; Pathet Lao take control of Laos with the support of North Vietnamese troops. |
| 1988 | Two American MIA searchers arrested in Laos after offering $2.4 million for information; later claim that Laos still holds U.S. prisoners of war; charge is denied by Laotian authorities. |
| 1989 | First elections since 1975; Communists remain in power as all candidates must be approved by Lao People's Revolutionary Party (LPRP). |
| 1991 | New constitution in place. |
| 1994 | Bridge over the Mekong River linking Laos and Thailand opens. |
| 1997 | Laos becomes a member of the Association of Southeast Asian Nations (ASEAN). |
| 2003 | The Fact Finding Mission, a U.S.-based exile group, announces the start of a revolution by the Lao Citizens Movement for Democracy in 11 provinces. Government refutes the claim. |
| 2006 | President Khamtay Siphandon is succeeded by Vice President Choummaly Sayasone as head of the LPRP. |

political party. In 1997 Laos joined the Association of Southeast Asian Nations (ASEAN). In recent years bomb attacks against the government have occurred across Laos, attributed by some to revolutionary groups such as the Lao Citizens Movement for Democracy. In March 2006 the head of LPRP, President Khamtay Siphandon, was replaced by Vice President Choummaly Sayasone.

**La Pasionaria** See Dolores Gómez IBÁRRURI.

**Lardner, Ring(gold Wilmer)** (*1885–1933*) American short story writer and journalist. Lardner developed one of the unique voices in American literature—

wry, colloquial, subtly incisive as to nuances of character. His best known volume of stories, *You Know Me, Al: A Busher's Letters* (1916), remains perhaps the finest fictional portrayal of baseball and its impact on American life. Lardner began his writing career as a journalist, covering sports for several years for newspapers in Chicago and New York. In the 1920s, he became a close friend of fellow writer F. Scott FITZGERALD. His tongue-in-cheek volume, *How to Write Short Stories* (1924), was typical Lardner with its bemused humility as to the nature of literary creation. Lardner also collaborated with George S. KAUFMAN on *June Moon* (1929) and other theatrical works. *Some Champions*

(1976) is a posthumous selection of Lardner's stories.

**Lardner, Ring (Wilmer), Jr.** (*1915–2000*) American screenwriter and author. The son of noted sports and short story writer Ring LARDNER, Lardner began his film career as a press agent for David O. SELZNICK. His first screenwriting work came when he collaborated on rewriting *A Star Is Born* (1937). Other screenplays include *Woman of the Year* (1942), for which he won his first ACADEMY AWARD; *The Cincinnati Kid* (1965); and M*A*S*H (1970), for which he won his second Oscar. Lardner joined the U.S. Communist Party in 1937 and was among the HOLLYWOOD TEN who refused to testify to the HOUSE UN-AMERICAN ACTIVITIES COMMITTEE (HUAC) during its investigation of communist influence in Hollywood in 1947. Charged with contempt of court in 1950, he served 10 months in prison. Blacklisted, Lardner was unable to work in films again until 1965. In 1955 he published a book, *The Ecstasy of Owen Muir* in England, and in the late 1950s he wrote anonymously for television. In 1976 he published *The Lardners*, an account of his family.

**Larionov, Mikhail Fyodorovich** (*1881–1964*) Russian painter. Born in Teraspol, Larionov studied at the School of Painting, Sculpture and Architecture in Moscow. Interested in avant-garde art, he took an important part in the introduction of new ideas from FRANCE and ITALY into Russian painting. With his wife, Natalya Goncherova, he founded the Rayonist movement in 1912, advocating color expressed in radiating light as the "guiding principle" of painting. This early doctrine influenced the development of abstract art in Russia, particularly on Kasimir MALEVICH and SUPREMATISM. Larionov settled in Paris in 1914 and abandoned painting in 1915 when he began an association with Serge DIAGHILEV that started with set designing and ended with the artist's involvement in all aspects of the BALLETS RUSSES.

**Larkin, Philip** (*1922–1985*) English poet, novelist and critic; a leading figure of THE MOVEMENT. Although hardly prolific, Larkin was one of the best known and most widely read English poets of his generation. Born in Coventry, he attended St. John's College, Oxford, during WORLD WAR II, where he knew Kingsley AMIS. After graduating he became a librarian; from 1955 until his death he was the librarian of the University of Hull. His first book was a slender collection of poems, *The North Ship*, influenced by YEATS. His two novels, *Jill* (1946; revised 1963) and *A Girl in Winter* (1947), explore the theme of adolescent loneliness in wartime England with great sensitivity. Larkin's literary reputation rests almost entirely on three poetry collections: *The Less Deceived* (1955), *The Whitsun Weddings*

(1964) and *High Windows* (1974). Understated and carefully crafted, the poems in these books show the influence of Thomas HARDY. Moreover, they register the mood of provincial life in postwar England—a period of austerity and reduced expectations. Larkin's attitude to life is summed up in his famous statement, "deprivation is to me what daffodils are to Wordsworth." Larkin was also a noted jazz critic; his jazz reviews and articles were collected in *All What Jazz?* (1970).

**Larsen, Leif Andreas** (*1906–1990*) Norwegian sailor and WORLD WAR II hero. A member of the Norwegian RESISTANCE movement during the war, Larsen made 52 trips across the North Sea in fishing boats to smuggle arms, supplies and Allied agents into occupied NORWAY. He won 11 medals for bravery, making him one of the most highly decorated Allied naval officers of the war. His adventures were later retold in many books and films.

**Lartigue, Jacques-Henri** (*1896–1986*) French photographer. Little known until 1963, a retrospective at New York City's MUSEUM OF MODERN ART led to Lartigue being recognized as a major 20th-century photographer. His work provided a matchless chronicle of Parisian high society with photographs taken when he was a child being particularly memorable.

**Lashley, Karl** (*1890–1958*) American neuropsychologist. Lashley is best known for his research into the relationship between the brain's mass and its ability to learn. He taught at several universities between 1917 and 1955, including Harvard. He studied the relationship between behavior and brain damage in rats, and wrote *Brain Mechanisms and Intelligence* (1929).

**Laski, Harold Joseph** (*1893–1950*) British political scientist and economist. Laski attended Oxford University and had a distinguished teaching career at McGill University (1914–16), Harvard University (1916–20) and the London School of Economics (1926–50). A committed socialist, he was a member of the FABIAN SOCIETY and later became active in the British LABOUR PARTY, serving as its chairman in 1945 and 1946.

Also holding a number of government posts, he was a prime figure in moving his country toward a peculiarly British socialism. He is best known as a prolific and influential author. Among his books are *Political Thought in England from Locke to Bentham* (1920), *Karl Marx* (1921), *Communism* (1927), *Democracy in Crisis* (1933), *Faith, Reason and Civilisation* (1944) and *The American Democracy* (1948). Laski's lively correspondence with his friend Justice Oliver Wendell HOLMES was published as *Holmes-Laski Letters* (2 vols., 1953).

**Laski, Marghanita** (*1915–1988*) British novelist, critic and radio personality; widely known as a broadcaster on "The Critics" and its successor, "Critics' Forum." One of her novels, *Little Boy Lost,* was the basis for a 1953 film about the displaced peoples of postwar Europe that starred Bing CROSBY. She wrote critical studies of such authors as Jane Austen, George Eliot and Rudyard KIPLING. A passionate amateur lexicographer, she was said to have contributed about a quarter of a million quotations to the four-volume supplement to the *Oxford English Dictionary,* the fourth volume of which was published in 1986.

**Laskin, Bora** (*1912–1984*) Chief justice of the Supreme Court of CANADA (1973–84). Laskin was appointed to the Court in 1970. His written opinions, which often dissented from the more conservative opinions of his colleagues, were praised for their legal scholarship. In 1974 he wrote the unanimous opinion upholding the Official Languages Act, which upgraded the position of French in the Canadian government.

**Lasky, Victor** (*1918–1990*) American journalist and author. An outspoken anticommunist, Lasky was a newspaper reporter and columnist, a Hollywood screenwriter and a lecturer for conservative organizations. His first book, *Seeds of Treason* (written with Ralph de Toledano), was based on the Alger HISS spy case of the late 1940s and became a best seller. His other books included *J.F.K., the Man and the Myth* (1963), and *It Didn't Start with Watergate* (1977), in which he showed the Democratic administrations also had been guilty of "dirty tricks."

**Lassie** Perhaps the most famous canine star of all time, Lassie was featured in eight feature films and a long-running television series. Trained by Rudd Weatherwax, the first Lassie was a male collie named Pal, who appeared in *Lassie Come Home* in 1943, when the intended star, a female collie, was shedding too heavily to perform. Pal's male offspring later succeeded him in the role. The last Lassie movie, *The Magic of Lassie,* was released in 1978.

**late modernism** Term that has come into use to describe and criticize current architectural and design practice and to designate work that continues to develop the ideas of MODERNISM, particularly the austere work of the INTERNATIONAL STYLE. While POSTMODERNISM tends to turn away from the ideas of the modern movement, introducing more decorative elements and often returning to historicism, the modernist direction survives and has also moved in the direction of greater complexity of form. The works of architects such as Charles Gwathmey and Robert Siegel, Richard Meier, and I.M. PEI with their strong loyalty to the modernist ethic, characterize the late-modernist direction.

**Lattimore, Owen** *(1900–1989)* American China scholar and writer. Born in Washington, Lattimore was educated in England and at Harvard. He then worked and studied in China and elsewhere in Asia, becoming an expert on Asian affairs. He edited the *Journal of Pacific Affairs* (1934–41) and wrote a number of books on the Far East. During WORLD WAR II he served the U.S. government in several capacities, including adviser to CHIANG KAI-SHEK. In 1950 while he was director of the Walter Hines Page School at Johns Hopkins University, he was accused by Senator Joseph MCCARTHY of being "the top Soviet espionage agent in the U.S." A Senate Foreign Relations Subcommittee investigated the charges against Lattimore and concluded that they were "a fraud and a hoax." Nevertheless, he was indicted for perjury in 1952 in connection with his Senate testimony; a federal judge dismissed the indictment in 1955 for lack of evidence. His brother **Richard Lattimore** was a distinguished poet and classics scholar noted for his translations of Homer and other ancient Greek poets and dramatists.

**Lattre de Tassigny, Jean de** *(1889–1952)* French general. A prominent military figure during WORLD WAR II, Lattre de Tassigny commanded the Fifth Army in Alsace in 1939. The following year, he led the 14th Infantry in its attempt to repel the German invasion of France. He was arrested by the Germans in 1942, after having become the commander of the 17th Division in Montpellier, and sentenced to 10 years imprisonment. He escaped the following year, joining General GIRAUD and becoming a commander in French North Africa. In 1944 he led the First French Army in its landing in FRANCE, and fought northward until finally striking into GERMANY. Named inspector general of the army in 1945, he was posthumously granted the title of marshal of FRANCE.

**Latvia** One of the Baltic Sea republics of the USSR, Latvia is located between ESTONIA and LITHUANIA in northeastern Europe and covers an area of 24,704 square miles. The territory of modern Latvia was annexed to Russia by Peter the Great in 1709 and was controlled by German estate owners, called "Baltic Barons," who served the Russian czar. In 1918 Latvia declared its independence, but it did not gain international recognition until 1921. Karlis Ulmanis became dictator in 1934 after economic problems forced the suspension of democratic government. His failure to obtain German protection against Soviet encroachment led to Russian occupation and establishment of Latvia as a Soviet

| LATVIA | |
|---|---|
| 1918 | National Council proclaims an independent Latvia. |
| 1919–20 | Soviet troops invade Latvia and set up a government; following their eviction, Latvian independence is recognized. |
| 1940 | Soviet troops invade Latvia, which is incorporated into the USSR |
| 1941 | Latvia occupied by Nazi Germany. |
| 1944 | Red Army returns. |
| 1986 | Beginnings of anti-Soviet demonstrations. |
| 1991 | Declaration of independence of the Republic of Latvia; Latvia admitted to the UN. |
| 1993 | Constitution of 1922 restored and first independent elections to parliament. |
| 1999 | Vaira Vike-Freiberga is elected president, first woman president in eastern Europe. |
| 2004 | Latvia admitted to NATO and the European Union. |

**Latvia**

republic in 1940. Germany occupied the country from 1941 to 1944. The loosening of authoritarian control in the Soviet Union under the leadership of Mikhail GORBACHEV led to Latvia's declaration of sovereignty and achievement of full independence. In August 1991 during the abortive coup by Soviet hard-liners against Gorbachev, Latvia declared its independence from the USSR Latvia joined NATO and the EUROPEAN UNION in 2004.

**Latvian War of Independence** *(1919–1920)* After GERMANY's defeat in World War I, the Latvians proclaimed an independent state with Karlis Ulmanis (1877–1940) as prime minister. In early January 1919 Soviet forces invaded, seized the capital, Riga, and set up a Soviet government. German-Latvian troops with Allied approval forced the Soviets to withdraw in March 1919. By the TREATY OF VERSAILLES Germans were required to leave the area, but occupied Riga and were not expelled until November 1919, while the Soviets, again attempting a takeover, were evicted with Allied support by January 1920. By the Treaty of Riga, August 11, 1920, the Soviets recognized Latvian independence.

**Lauder, Harry** *(1870–1950)* Scottish entertainer. Primarily a comedian and singer, Lauder was one of the most popular music hall artists of the early 20th century and appeared widely in both Britain and the U.S. One of the most highly paid entertainers of his day, he was also a prolific songwriter as well as a novelist and short story writer. His popular songs included "I Love a Lassie" (1905), "Roamin' in the Gloamin" (1911) and "It's Nice to Get Up in the Morning" (1914). Lauder entertained British troops during WORLD WAR I and was knighted in 1919 for his aid to the war effort.

*Laugh-In* Zany American comedy-variety television series of the late 1960s. Its rapid-fire blackout sketches, burlesque gags and satiric pokes at contemporary America made it the number one program for two full seasons, 1968–70. It was a kind of "happening," a weekly push at the envelope of television propriety and censorship. Comedians Dan Rowan and Dick Martin presided over a cast of 40 regulars, each of whom appeared with a brief shtick, or tag, that became part of the national vocabulary: Arte Johnson had his guttural "Verrrry Interesting!"; Ruth Buzzi her ferocious umbrella; Lily Tomlin her nasal snort; Goldie Hawn her jiggle; and announcer Gary Owens his outrageously overmodulated tonsils. Catchphrases were everywhere: "Sock it to me!" and "Here come da judge!" and "You bet your bippy!" are just a few examples. The show was like a quick mosaic of interchangeable pieces that changed pattern from week to week. A "Jock Wall" concluded each program,

from which the faces of the cast popped in and out of little windows with quick one-liners. It ended its run in 1973. Six years later producer George Schlatter assembled a cast of unknowns and revived *Laugh-In* as a series of NBC specials. Although the show had grown stale and was dropped, at least one star was "discovered"— Robin Williams.

**Laughton, Charles** *(1899–1962)* British film and theatrical actor. Laughton was one of the most gifted character actors in the history of the cinema. Educated at the Royal Academy of Dramatic Arts, Laughton achieved successes on the London and Broadway stages before appearing in his first HOLLYWOOD feature, *The Old Dark Horse* (1932), a horror film. He won widespread fame for his title role in *The Private Life of Henry VIII* (1933), a British film directed by Alexander KORDA. Returning to Hollywood, Laughton gave memorable performances in *The Barretts of Wimpole Street* (1934), *Ruggles of Red Gap* (1935), and *Mutiny on the Bounty* (1935), in which he played Captain Bligh opposite Clark GABLE as Fletcher Christian. One of Laughton's finest performances was as Quasimodo in *The Hunchback of Notre Dame* (1939). Laughton directed only one film, the classic thriller *The Night of the Hunter* (1955), starring Robert Mitchum. His last film appearance came in *Advise and Consent* (1962). Laughton was married to the actress Elsa LANCHESTER.

**Laurel and Hardy** The team of **Stan Laurel** (born Arthur Stanley Jefferson, 1890–1965) and **Oliver Hardy** (1892–1957) stands alongside the MARX BROTHERS as one of the greatest comedic ensembles ever captured on film. Both Laurel and Hardy enjoyed independent careers as comic actors in silent films, and in the 1910s Laurel served as an understudy for Charlie CHAPLIN. But they were teamed together in 1926 by film producer Hal Roach and enjoyed immediate success as evidenced by a series of over 30 silent shorts directed in the late 1920s by Leo McCarey, George STEVENS and others. With the transition to sound, Laurel and Hardy turned eventually to feature films and Laurel himself took over artistic responsibilities. The basic premise in their films was simple but had universal appeal: The thin, woebegone Englishman Laurel and the rotund, blustery American Hardy found themselves in circumstances they could neither control or understand. For all their good intentions, they were eternal victims of fate. Their performances were memorable because they combined outrageous slapstick pranks with genuine human pathos. The team won an ACADEMY AWARD for *The Music Box* (1932), a live action comedy short. Their classic comedy features include *Sons of the Desert* (1933), *Fra Diavolo* (1933), *Babes in Toyland* (1934), *Way Out West* (1937), and *A Chump at Oxford* (1940). In 1960 Stan Laurel was awarded a Special Oscar for his pioneering excellence in screen comedy.

**Lauren, Ralph** (*1939–  *) American fashion designer whose career has vastly expanded from the introduction of wide necktie designs to designing clothing for men, women and children, as well as the environments they inhabit. Born in the Bronx, Lauren studied business at New York's City College at night while holding a wide variety of jobs in clothing stores, including Brooks Brothers, where he found an affinity for classic, sports-oriented clothing. There are overtones of belonging to upper-class circles in his relaxed styling and in his own lifestyle (he owns a 10,000-acre ranch in Colorado). In addition to clothing, his business now includes designs for fragrances, home furnishing and luggage. The restored Rhinelander mansion in New York serves as a flagship for his vast network of Polo/Ralph Lauren shops. He was the recipient of a 1970 Coty Men's Wear Award, the year before he began designing women's clothing. In 1992 Lauren accepted the Council of Fashion Designers of America's Lifetime Achievement award, the most celebrated award within the industry. Six years later, the Breast Cancer Research Foundation honored Lauren's contributions to research combating the disease by honoring him with its Humanitarian Award.

**Laurier, Sir Wilfrid** (*1841–1919*) Canadian statesman, prime minister of CANADA (1896–1911). Born in Quebec province, Laurier was educated at McGill University, became a lawyer and served in the Ottawa parliament as a Liberal member from 1874 to 1878. In the opposition to the Conservative government from 1878 to 1896, he was appointed Liberal leader in 1887. In 1896 Laurier became the first French-Canadian prime minister, and the following year he was knighted. His 15-year tenure has been called the "age of Laurier," an era in which a Canadian identity was forged. During this period the country grew enormously, its economy flourished and it opened its doors to some two million immigrants who helped develop the Canadian West and build the nation's huge railroad system. Laurier sought to create harmony between Canada's French and English-speaking citizens and to strengthen links with Great Britain and the U.S. His trade ties to the U.S. were central to his defeat in the 1911 elections. Leader of the opposition until his death, he supported Canada's 1914 entry into WORLD WAR I, but opposed conscription and resisted the formation of a coalition government in 1917. (See also LIBERAL PARTY–CANADA.)

**Lausanne, Treaty of** Treaty signed in Lausanne, Switzerland, in 1923 that established modern TURKEY's borders and settled a number of territorial problems that arose at the end of World War I. The earlier (1920) Treaty of SÈVRES had virtually destroyed the defeated OTTOMAN EMPIRE. However, its provisions were rejected by Turkish nationalists led by Mustafa Kemal (later known as ATATÜRK), who forced new negotiations when they drove Greek troops out of Smyrna and overthrew the sultan. According to the new treaty, Turkey recovered Smyrna, eastern Thrace and some islands in the Aegean and resumed its control of the DARDANELLES, which were demilitarized. Turkey also renounced claims on former Ottoman Empire territories. A separate agreement between Greece and Turkey arranged for the forced exchange of minority populations from each signatory country.

**Laval, Pierre** (*1883–1945*) French statesman. Born in the Auvergne, Laval became a lawyer and entered politics as a Socialist deputy in 1914. He held a number of governmental posts, began moving to the right politically and was elected as an independent senator in 1926. He served as premier from 1931 to 1932 and as premier and foreign minister from 1935 to 1936. In 1935 he and British foreign minister Sir Samuel Hoare formulated a plan to partition ETHIOPIA in order to stop the Italian invasion, a scheme that would have appeased MUSSOLINI by giving much of the country to its invader. Laval's government fell after public uproar over the plan caused its withdrawal. After the fall of FRANCE in 1940, Laval became vice premier in the VICHY government, supporting close ties with Nazi GERMANY. He was dismissed on suspicion of attempting to overthrow Marshal PÉTAIN, but was reinstated in 1942. Facilitating Nazi policy, he nonetheless attempted to retain some distance from the Germans, a task in which he was largely unsuccessful. After the Allied invasion, the fleeing Germans arrested Laval in 1944, but he escaped to Spain in 1945. He subsequently surrendered himself to the Allies, and was returned to FRANCE to face treason charges. Found guilty in a trial whose fairness was questionable and in which he eloquently defended himself, Laval was sentenced to death. After unsuccessfully attempting to commit suicide, he was executed.

**Laver, Rod(ney George)** (*1938–  *) Australian tennis player. Best known for his Davis Cup play, Laver may be the last player to have made a worldwide reputation as an amateur. He won Wimbledon twice before turning professional and led Australia to four Davis Cups, winning all six of his singles event in 1960, 1961 and 1962. He relinquished his amateur status in 1963 and went on to win 71 championships in 17 countries, including two additional Wimbledons, and a 1969 Grand Slam. Laver was the first player to break the $1 million mark.

**Lavin, Mary** (*1912–1996*) Irish author. Though born in the U.S., Lavin moved to Ireland at the age of nine, and her writing evokes her enchantment with the Irish ambience. Encouraged to write by the playwright and Irish revivalist Lord DUNSANY, Lavin published her first collection of stories, *Tales from Bective Bridge* in 1942. Lavin was widowed and left with the management of a farm and three children, and remarried in 1969 after which she lived in Dublin and Meath. Her perceptive writing examines relationships, depicting the lives of both the Irish peasantry and the middle classes. Other works include the novels *The House in Cluew Street* (1945) and *Mary O'Grady* (1950) and the short story collection *The Shrine and other Stories* (1977).

**Lavrenyov, Boris Andreyevich** *(1894–1952)* Soviet author. Lavrenyov joined the army in 1915 and served as a cavalry officer in World War I. In 1921 he began to write seriously. In the early stages of his literary career Lavrenyov was attracted to FUTURISM, but he later came under the influence of ACMEISM. He was a member of the Leningrad literary group *Sodruzhestvo*. Lavrenyov's stories are romantic and his plots dynamic. Among his stories are the collections *Crazy Tales* (1925) and *The Forty-First* (1924). He also wrote the plays *Smoke* and *The Debacle* (1928). Much of his work recounts incidents from the Civil War and the days of WAR COMMUNISM.

**Law, Andrew Bonar** *(1858–1923)* British politician, prime minister of the UNITED KINGDOM (1923). Born in New Brunswick, Canada, Law emigrated to Scotland at the age of 12 and was educated at Glasgow High School. He was a successful iron merchant in Glasgow when he was first elected to Parliament in 1900 as a member of the CONSERVATIVE PARTY. He served as parliamentary secretary to the Board of Trade from 1902 to 1906, and gained support from party members who considered party leader Arthur BALFOUR too remote. In 1911 he succeeded Balfour as the leader of the Opposition, strongly supporting the Ulstermen in the Irish crisis of 1912–14. At the outbreak of WORLD WAR I, Law supported the government and entered the ASQUITH coalition as colonial secretary, later becoming chancellor of the Exchequer and leader in the Commons under David LLOYD GEORGE from 1915 to 1919, and Lord Privy Seal from 1919 to 1922. Following Lloyd George's resignation in 1922, Law became prime minister, but was forced by an inoperable cancer to resign seven months later. Law's brief tenure set the pattern for British Conservatism between the two world wars.

**Lawler, Richard** *(1895–1982)* American surgeon who successfully performed the world's first kidney transplant operation (1950). Lawler performed the operation only once, saying that he "just wanted to get it started." He was nominated for the NOBEL PRIZE in 1970 for his pioneering surgery but did not receive the award.

**Lawrence, D(avid) H(erbert)** *(1885–1930)* English novelist, story writer, literary critic, travel writer, poet and painter. Lawrence is one of the greatest figures in 20th-century English literature. Indeed, there are few writers in the history of world literature who can equal Lawrence in terms of a versatility and excellence shown in so many writing genres. He was born in Eastwood, Nottinghamshire, the fourth child of a struggling coal miner who was a heavy drinker. Lawrence, who suffered from frail health for much of his life, was very close to his mother, who provided encouragement for his artistic career. He earned a scholarship to Nottingham University and briefly pursued a teaching career. The publication of his acclaimed first novel, *The White Peacock* (1911), launched him as a writer. His other major novels include *Sons and Lovers* (1913), *The Rainbow* (1915), *Women in Love* (1920) and the controversial *LADY CHATTERLEY'S LOVER* (1928), a frank and beautiful love story that was for a time banned in both Great Britain and the U.S. as pornographic. Lawrence also wrote vibrant short stories and lyric poetry, travel classics such as *Etruscan Places* (1932) and even attained posthumous renown for his expressionistic paintings completed in the 1920s. Lawrence married Frieda von Richthofen in 1914 and traveled with her through Europe, the U.S., Mexico and Australia in the final two decades of his life.

**Lawrence, Ernest Orlando** *(1901–1958)* American physicist. Born in Canton, South Dakota, Lawrence earned his Ph.D. from Yale University in 1925. In 1930, while a professor at the University of California at Berkeley, he began experiments that eventually led to his invention of the cyclotron, a device in which atomic particles are accelerated by means of an alternating electric field in a constant magnetic field. Lawrence received the 1939 NOBEL PRIZE in physics for this work. Later, he played a key role in the development of the atomic bomb. Element 103, lawrencium, is named for him.

**Lawrence, Gertrude** (Gertrud **Lawrence Klasen**) *(1898–1952)* British actress. Though she began her career performing in revues and musicals, Lawrence gained international acclaim in several Noel COWARD plays, most notably *Private Lives* (1930), which he wrote for her, and *Blithe Spirit* (1945). She also had personal triumphs in the Broadway musicals *Lady in the Dark* (1941) by Moss HART and Kurt WEILL and *The King and I* (1951) by Richard RODGERS and Oscar HAMMERSTEIN II.

**Lawrence, Jacob** *(1917–2000)* American painter. Born in Atlantic City, New Jersey, Lawrence studied at various schools and with various artists in New York City from 1932 to 1939. An African American, he has explored the black experience in the U.S. in many of

*Artist Jacob Lawrence at an exhibit of his work in Boston. 1945 (NEW YORK WORLD-TELEGRAM AND THE SUN NEWSPAPER COLLECTION, LIBRARY OF CONGRESS, PRINTS AND PHOTOGRAPHS DIVISION)*

his figurative paintings. Flat, angular and decorative in style, often using tempera as a medium, Lawrence's work includes a number of painting cycles including *Harlem* and *Migration of the Negro* (1940–41). Lawrence is a noted teacher, and his work is included in collections such as the Whitney Museum of American Art and Museum of Modern Art, New York City, and the Phillips Collection, Washington, D.C.

**Lawrence, T(homas) E(dward) (Lawrence of Arabia)** *(1888–1935)* British soldier, adventurer, author and WORLD WAR I hero. Educated at Oxford, he participated in archaeological expeditions to the Middle East while still an undergraduate. He stayed in the region from 1911 to 1914, learning Arabic and working as an archaeologist. After the outbreak of World War I, he was posted to Egypt as a member of the British army's intelligence staff. In 1916, he joined the forces of the Arabian sheik Faisal al Husayn (later FAISAL I), becoming a leader in the Arab revolt against Turkish rule. His guerrilla tactics, striking at the Damascus-Medina railroad and fringe areas, were extremely successful in expelling the much larger Ottoman army from western Arabia and Syria (see OTTOMAN EMPIRE; WORLD WAR I IN MESOPOTAMIA). After the Arab forces took DAMASCUS in 1918, Lawrence returned to England. A delegate to the PARIS PEACE CONFERENCE after the war, he vainly fought for Arab independence. Thereafter, he was a research fellow at Oxford (1919) and a Middle Eastern adviser at the Colonial Office (1921–22).

Whether out of a sense of failure in the Arab cause, or from a desire from anonymity, Lawrence resigned from his post and in 1922 enlisted under the name of Ross as a mechanic in the Royal Air Force. His identity was discovered a year later and he joined the tank corps, later rejoining (1925) the RAF under the name of Shaw. His account of his Arabian adventures was privately printed in 1926 under the title *Seven Pillars of Wisdom*, later abridged to *Revolt in the Desert*. He died in a motorcycle accident near his home in Dorset on May 19, 1935. A man of intense contradictions, Lawrence remains one of the most legendary and enigmatic public figures of the 20th

century. His exploits formed the basis of David LEAN's film, *Lawrence of Arabia* (1962).

**Laxness, Halldór (Halldòr Guojónsson)** *(1902–1998)* Icelandic novelist. Laxness's early fiction, which includes the short stories *Nokkrar sogur* (Some Stories, *1923*) and the novel *Verfarinn mikli frá Kasmír* (The Great Weaver from Kashmir, 1927), reflects his conversion to Catholicism in 1923 and the influence of the surrealist movement. Influenced by Upton SINCLAIR on a trip to North America in the late twenties, Laxness became a socialist, and it is for his subsequent political fiction depicting the lower classes of Iceland that he is best known. These include the two-volume novel, *Salka Valka* (1931–32), the first of his works to be translated into English; the two-volume *Sjolfstoett folk* (Independent People, 1934–35), and the tetralogy *Heimsljos* (World Light, 1937–40), which is considered his most important work. Laxness was awarded the NOBEL PRIZE for literature in 1955. Later works include the novel, *Brekkukotsannoll* (The Fish Can Sing, 1957) and the autobiographical *Skaldatimi* (Poetic Age, 1963).

**Leach, Bernard** *(1887–1979)* English master potter in the handcraft tradition, who reflected modernist directions in his works. Leach was born in Hong Kong and studied the traditional art and craftwork of China, Japan and Korea, before moving to England in 1920. He established his own pottery at St. Ives in Cornwall where he produced individual works of high quality in terms of both craftsmanship and design. He eventually developed a range of basic designs that were handmade in considerable quantity and available for practical use. His shapes were generally simple and functional in a way that matched the developing taste of MODERNISM; his brush-painted decorations, where they occur, suggest a more self-conscious orientalism. His book, *A Potter's Book* (1940), is a standard text and manual in the field.

**League of Arab States** See ARAB LEAGUE.

**League of Nations** International arbitration and peacekeeping organiza-

tion established in 1919. U.S. president Woodrow WILSON was the chief architect of the League of Nations, and its formation was one of his FOURTEEN POINTS. He was, however, unable to persuade the U.S. Congress of its merits, and the U.S. never became a member. The League of Nations constitution was adopted at the PARIS PEACE CONFERENCE and recognized in post–World War I peace treaties. The League's headquarters were established in Geneva; its first secretary-general was Sir Eric Drummond (1876–1951), a British diplomat and later Earl of Perth. The League consisted of three branches: a council, the main peacekeeping arm composed of between 8 and 10 members; the assembly, in which all members participated; and the secretariat, which was its administrative staff. There were 42 original member-nations, including UNITED KINGDOM, CHINA, FRANCE, ITALY and JAPAN. GERMANY was a member from 1926 to 1933 and the UNION OF SOVIET SOCIALIST REPUBLICS from 1934 to 1940.

The League's aim was to provide collective security to member countries, in that all would come to the aid of a country attacked or threatened by war. It had no armed forces and would instead rely on economic sanctions to coerce errant countries. Its successes included settling conflicts in Latin America and the Balkans and providing assistance to Russian and Turkish refugees in the 1920s, but it proved ineffectual against more powerful or determined countries. When the League failed to recognize Japan's annexation of MANCHURIA, Japan withdrew from the organization in 1933. ITALY withdrew in 1937 after the League imposed sanctions on it over the Abyssinian War, and the USSR was ejected in 1940 following its attack on FINLAND in 1939. As hostilities increased prior to World War II, most countries dismissed the League and operated independently. It was dissolved in 1946, and its functions were taken up by the UNITED NATIONS.

**League of Red Cross Societies** Federation of national Red Cross societies that administers worldwide relief efforts. Headquartered in Geneva, Switzerland, it was founded in Paris after World War I. From its inception, the League's purposes included the prevention of disease, the encouragement of new national Red Cross organizations, the spreading of information regarding science and medicine and the coordination of national and international relief work. During its years of operation the League has participated in hundreds of relief, rescue and disease-prevention programs. In 1963 it was awarded the NOBEL PEACE PRIZE, shared with the INTERNATIONAL COMMITTEE OF THE RED CROSS (ICRC). Today the League has a combined membership of some 250 million from approximately 144 national groups and is one of the three components of the International Movement of the Red Cross and Red Crescent, which also includes the ICRC and the various national Red Cross societies.

**Leakey, Louis S(eymour) B(azett)** (1903–1972) Anglo-Kenyan archaeologist and anthropologist. Born in Kenya to British missionary parents, Dr. Leakey is one of the best known anthropologists of the 20th century. His discoveries of early primate fossils in the Olduvai Gorge in east Africa helped shape the 20th-century view of human evolution. In 1959 he and his wife **Mary Leakey**, also a noted anthropologist, discovered fossils of *Zinjanthropus* (now called *Australopithecus boisei*), a close ancestor of humans. From 1961 to 1964 the Leakeys and their son **Jonathan Leakey** unearthed fossils of *Homo habilis*, the oldest known primate with human characteristics. Louis Leakey's theories about the age of humankind aroused much controversy. In 1972 his son **Richard Leakey**, who directed the National Museum of Kenya, reported the discovery of a 2.6 million-year-old skull that bore a close resemblance to the skull of modern humans. Richard Leakey suggested that modern humans evolved from this creature rather than from *Australopithicus*. This finding raised further controversy. In 1975 Richard Leakey discovered the skull of *Homo erectus* (estimated at 1.6 million years old), and in 1984 he and another paleontologist discovered a virtually complete *Homo erectus* skeleton.

**Lean, David** (1908–1991) British film director. Lean earned a reputation as one of the leading directors in the cinema, primarily due to the epic grandeur and scope he instilled in classic films such as *The Bridge on the River Kwai* (1957) and *Lawrence of Arabia* (1962), both of which won the ACADEMY AWARD for best picture. Lean began his directorial career in the 1940s, first as an assistant to Noel COWARD and then as a director on his own film versions of the Coward plays, *Blithe Spirit* (1945) and *Brief Encounter* (1945). Lean went on to adapt two works by Charles Dickens to the cinema, *Great Expectations* (1946) and *Oliver Twist* (1948). *Lawrence of Arabia* (about T. E. LAWRENCE) vaulted Irish actor Peter O'-Toole to world prominence. Subsequent films by Lean include *Doctor Zhivago* (1964), *Ryan's Daughter* (1970) and *A Passage to India* (1984). In the early 1990s he was working on a film version of Joseph CONRAD's novel *Nostromo*.

**Lear, Norman** (1922–    ) American television and motion picture producer/screenwriter, best known for ALL IN THE FAMILY. After serving with the U.S. Army Air Force in World War II, Lear worked for many years in television as a comedy writer; he and partner Bud Yorkin formed Tandem Productions, which produced a number of successful situation comedies depicting family life in the 1970s. *All in the Family* began its 12-year run in 1971 (with spinoffs *Maude*, 1972, and *The Jeffersons*, 1975). *Sanford and Son* debuted in 1972, and *Good Times* first appeared in 1974. Another Lear company, T.A.T. Communications, developed several additional series, including *One Day at a Time* and *Mary Hartman, Mary Hartman* (both beginning in 1975). After leaving television in 1978, Lear pursued political, environmental and spiritual concerns in activist organizations like People for the American Way, Business Enterprise Trust and a multimedia conglomerate, ACT III. He later produced a new comedy series about what he called "today's lack of spiritual values"; he also produced several motion pictures for director Rob Reiner, who had earlier portrayed "Meathead" in *All in the Family*.

**Lear, William Powell** (1902–1978) American industrialist and inventor. Lear held patents on more than 150 inventions. He devised the automatic pilot, which became a standard feature on military, commercial and private aircraft. He also designed the first practical automobile radio and the eight-track stereo player. His small Lear Jet was designed for the corporate market and replaced other small propeller-driven aircraft as the most popular airplane model owned by businesses.

**Leary, Timothy (Francis)** (1920–1996) American psychologist and drug experimenter. Born in Springfield, Massachusetts, he received a B.A. from the University of Alabama (1942) and a Ph.D. from the University of California, Berkeley (1950). Leary began teaching at Harvard in 1958. There he and a colleague initiated a series of experiments with the hallucinogenic drug LSD, often using themselves and their students as subjects. Leary soon became a psychedelics evangelist, touting their revolutionary, consciousness-altering properties and helping to introduce them to influential members of the 1960s generation. His experiments caused friction with Harvard's administration and he was fired from his post early in the '60s. Having converted to Hinduism in 1965, Leary founded the League for Spiritual Discovery the following year. In 1967 he delivered a version of the anthematic 1960s line "Turn on, tune in, drop out." He was first arrested on a drug charge in 1965, and a subsequent 1970 arrest and conviction sent him into exile abroad and caused his 1973–76 imprisonment. With a somewhat softened message on drugs, Leary remained a COUNTERCULTURE spokesman until his death in 1996.

**Leavis, F(rank) R(aymond)** (1895–1978) British author and critic. An enormously influential literary scholar and critic, Leavis was born in and educated at Cambridge, where he was influenced by I. A. RICHARDS, whose textual approach to literary criticism Leavis embraced and enhanced. He married Q. D. Leavis in 1929, another student of Richard's, whose *Fiction and the Reading Public* (1932) addressed the correlation between literature and literacy. From 1932 until 1953 Leavis was chief editor of *Scrutiny*, the controversial journal which was a forum for the NEW CRITICISM, and in which he attacked what he considered the dilettantish elitism of the BLOOMSBURY GROUP. Leavis's many groundbreaking works, which include *Mass Civilization and Minority Culture* (1930), *The Great Tradition: George Eliot, Henry James, Joseph Conrad* (1948), and *Dickens the Novelist,* written with Q. D. Leavis, (1970), purport that "ethical sensibility" is the most important criteria by which to judge an author. He offended many by criticizing literary lions such as Thomas HARDY and Charles Dickens. Leavis created additional furor by his caustic response to C. P. SNOW's lecture, Two Cultures, in *Two Cultures?: The Significance of C. P. Snow* (1962). Leavis taught at Cambridge until 1964.

## Lebanese Civil War of 1958

Elected president of LEBANON in 1952. Camille CHAMOUN oversaw a predominantly Christian (Maronite) government that stressed closer ties to Europe and the U.S. Lebanese Muslims, who made up about half of the country's population, favored stronger economic and political relationships with the surrounding Arab nations. On May 9–13, 1958, Muslim groups openly rebelled against Chamoun's regime, rioting and fighting in the streets of Tripoli and BEIRUT, Lebanon's capital. The newly formed United Arab Republic (a political union of Egypt and Syria) had allegedly instigated the violence against the pro-Western policies of President Chamoun, whose government seemed on the verge of collapse as rebels under several Muslim leaders and Druse (Druze) chieftain Kamal Jumblatt overcame army troops. Refusing to resign, Chamoun appealed to the U.S. for help; U.S. president Dwight D. EISENHOWER ordered American forces from the Sixth Fleet to land near Beirut to support the government, as well as to protect American lives and to guard against a possible Egyptian-Syrian invasion of Lebanon (July 16–20, 1958). Within a month the Lebanese government and army, assisted by more than 14,000 U.S. troops, had control of the situation. General Fuad Chehab, a Maronite Christian, succeeded Chamoun as president on September 23, 1958; a new cabinet of four Christians, three Muslims and one Druse was formed. The U.S. backed the new government and completely withdrew its troops from Lebanon by late October that year.

## Lebanese Civil War of 1975–90

LEBANON's various Muslim groups, principally the Shi'ite and Druse (Druze) sects, which make up about half the population, were never happy with the 1943 National Pact, which established a dominant political role for the Christians, especially the Maronites, in the central government. Further complicating the political climate was the presence of refugee Palestinian Muslims, living in camps or bases, particularly in the south, from which guerrillas of the PALESTINE LIBERATION ORGANIZATION (PLO) were carrying out attacks on neighboring Israel. Native Lebanese Muslims tended to sympathize with the PLO.

On April 13, 1975, a bus carrying many Palestinians was assaulted by Christian Phalangists and the passengers slain—triggering a long and bloody civil war. At first a leftist Muslim coalition fought rightist Christians; in early 1976, the PLO joined the Muslims after Christians raided a Palestinian refugee camp. ISRAEL supplied arms to Christians. With the backing of the ARAB LEAGUE of states, SYRIA sent 30,000 troops to restore order in Lebanon and to implement a peace plan (1976). Elias SARKIS, a Maronite Christian, was elected Lebanon's president and, with Syrian, Israeli, U.S. and Saudi support, attempted to establish authority. By 1977 Lebanon was divided into a northern section, controlled by Syrian forces, and a coastal section under Christian control, with enclaves in the south dominated by leftist Muslims and the PLO. Syrians and Christian militiamen were soon battling each other, and the Syrians shelled the Christian part of BEIRUT, Lebanon's capital. In retaliation for a Palestinian guerrilla terrorist attack on Israel, Israeli troops invaded southern Lebanon (March 14, 1978) to wipe out PLO bases and occupied the area as far north as the Litani River. The Israelis complied with a United Nations demand for their withdrawal from the area, then occupied by a UN peacekeeping force (1978).

In 1980 Syria concentrated forces in central Lebanon's Bekaa (al-Biqa) Valley and later moved Soviet-made surface-to-air (SAM-6) missiles there. When the Phalangists (Christians) occupied the hills around Zahle near the strategic Beirut-Damascus highway, Syria launched a major offensive against them; Israeli jets intervened and attacked the Syrians and also bombed areas of Beirut in retaliation for PLO rocket attacks from Lebanon into northern Israel. A cease-fire went into effect on July 24, 1981, but it was temporary. To dispel the PLO, invading Israeli troops reached the outskirts of Beirut and forced the evacuation of PLO guerrillas in 1982.

Lebanon's Phalangist president-elect Bashir Gemayel (1947–82), chosen to succeed the retiring Sarkis, was assassinated on September 14, 1982; his brother, Amin Gemayel (b. 1942), a more moderate Christian leader, became president—just days before 328 Palestinian civilians would be massacred by alleged Phalangists at the SABRA AND SHATILA refugee camps in west Beirut (September 16–18, 1982). Afterward U.S. Marines and British, French and Italian troops arrived in Beirut as a peacekeeping force. A bomb blast killed more than 50 people at the U.S. embassy in Beirut on April 18, 1983. Israeli forces withdrew from Lebanon's Shuf Mountains, which the Druse under their leader Walid Jumblatt (b. 1947) occupied after heavy fighting against Christians and the Lebanese army. On October 23, 1983, and without warning, 239 Americans and 58 French died in separate, suicidal bomb attacks on U.S. and French military headquarters in Beirut.

At Tripoli, PLO leader Yasir ARAFAT and his loyalists were attacked and besieged by PLO dissidents, supported by Syria, for six weeks until they were evacuated by a U.N.-flag-flying Greek ship on December 20, 1983. U.S. warships off the coast bombarded Syrian and Druse positions. Faced with his country's disintegration into multiple ministates, President Gemayel sought national reconciliation talks to settle differences among political leaders—Phalangist, Maronite, Druse, Sunni, Shi'ite and others—in order to stabilize the government. U.S. Marines left Beirut in February 1984, with Lebanon still occupied in part by Syrian and Israeli troops and still divided by bitter feuds and warring factions. After Gemayel left office in 1988, Christian general Michel Aoun refused to acknowledge the new Syrian-backed government. In March 1989 his forces began a bitter fight against the Syrians, and later, against Christian factions that supported the new government.

### Lebanon

| | |
|---|---|
| 1910 | Lebanon is governed as a semiautonomous province under shared French-Turkish control; internal power shared between representatives of Christian, Muslim and Druze communities. |
| 1920 | League of Nations formalizes French mandate in Lebanon and Syria. |
| 1926 | Detached from Syria and made semiautonomous republic by French, with Bechera al-Khoury as first president. |
| 1943 | Religious communities reach agreement to form government dominated by Christians, who are majority in population; independence granted. |
| 1948 | Lebanon joins Arab League attacks on Israel; accepts Palestinian refugees in large numbers. |
| 1952 | Corrupt al-Khoury forced to resign; Camille Chamoun assumes presidency. |
| 1958 | Nasserist Muslims revolt; U.S. president Eisenhower sends U.S. Marines at Chamoun's request to restore order. |
| 1964 | Under President Fuad Chebab, "Chebabist" Muslim-Christian alliance leads to period of calm; economic boom as Beirut becomes center of finance and trade in the Middle East. |
| 1967 | After the Six-Day War, PLO forces move to southern Lebanon, conduct raids on Israel. |
| 1975 | Despite new Muslim majority, Christians refuse to revise Agreement of 1943; frightened by Muslim demands and PLO strength, Christian militias attack Muslims; all-out civil war ensues. |
| 1976 | Syria and the Arab League intervene in Lebanese civil war. |
| 1978 | Israeli forces briefly occupy southern Lebanon; UN forces intervene after Israeli withdrawal. |
| 1982 | Israel again invades Lebanon, to wipe out PLO; Muslim refugees massacred by Israeli-backed right-wing Lebanese Phalangist militia; multinational peacekeeping force intervenes; country divided into areas of military control, with little real authority for central government. |
| 1984 | Peacekeeping force withdraws after losing hundreds of soldiers in bombing attacks; Christians and Muslims each begin fighting among themselves; government is powerless as anarchy prevails. |
| 1985 | Israeli forces complete their withdrawal. |
| 1990 | General Aoun of Christian Militia occupies presidential palace; Glias Hrawi forms second government with Muslim backing; Syrian forces destroy Aoun's base; Hrawi proclaims "Second Republic" with new constitution reflecting Muslim majority but guaranteeing Christian and Druze rights. |
| 1991 | Christian and Druze ministers quit new government and threaten new bloodshed. |
| 1992 | Rafik Hariri becomes prime minister; Western hostages still held by Shi'ite groups are released. |
| 1996 | Israel bombs Hezbollah bases in Beirut, southern Lebanon and the Bekaa Valley. |
| 1998 | Army head Emile Lahoud becomes president, succeeding Ilyas al-Hirawi. |
| 2000 | Israel withdraws from southern Lebanon; Rafik Hariri again becomes prime minister. |
| 2004 | UN Security Council resolution calls for foreign troops to leave Lebanon; Syria ignores the move. |
| 2005 | Former prime minister Rafik Hariri is killed in a car bombing in Beirut; calls for Syrian withdrawal from Lebanon escalate; Syria withdraws its troops. |
| 2006 | Armed Hezbollah factions kidnap two Israeli soldiers across the border and fire shells on northern Israeli towns, causing new Middle East crisis. |

This stage of the war consisted mostly of artillery shelling; the bloodshed continued and more areas of Beirut were reduced to rubble. Aoun finally surrendered in October 1990. In the following months, calm returned to Beirut, and Lebanon began to achieve a genuine peace.

## Lebanon (Republic of Lebanon)

Lebanon covers an area of 4,014 square miles in southwest Asia, along the east coast of the Mediterranean. Part of France's LEAGUE OF NATIONS mandate for Syria in 1920, Lebanon became a semi-autonomous republic in 1926 and achieved full independence in 1944. The country fought with the Arab League against ISRAEL (1948–49). Internal stability was achieved for a period (1958–70) by maintaining a balance of political power between Christian and Muslim populations. The increased presence of the PALESTINE LIBERATION ORGANIZATION (PLO) by 1967 led to Israeli reprisal raids and eventual civil war between the PLO-leftist Muslim alliance and the Christians. As a result, Syrian forces occupied northern and eastern Lebanon in 1976, and Israel occupied southern Lebanon, withdrawing in favor of a UNITED NATIONS peacekeeping force (1978). Under President Amin Gemayel (1983–88) reform attempts and proposals to remove foreign troops failed, and increasingly volatile factions within the Christian-Muslim schism proliferated. Militant Muslim groups began kidnapping Western nationals and holding them hostage (18 known hostages by 1987). There was a complete breakdown of government authority by 1988, resulting in Michel Aoun heading a transitional military government based in Christian east Beirut while a rival government formed by President Elias Hrawi was headquartered in Muslim west Beirut. Aoun finally surrendered in late 1990, and the civil war came to an end. Despite the end of the civil war, terrorist groups such as HEZBOLLAH continued to operate in southern Lebanon, provoking cross-border raids by Israel in 1993 and 1996. In 2000 Israel withdrew its military forces from the "security zone" in southern Lebanon that they had occupied since 1985. This Israeli withdrawal allowed Hezbollah to employ southern Lebanon as a haven for its fighters. In 2005 Lebanese prime minister Rafik Hariri, a critic of the Syrian presence in Lebanon, was assassinated. An explosion of anger in Beirut and other cities by demonstrators who blamed the Syrian government for the murder forced Syrian president Bashar al-Assad to comply with a UN Security Council resolution and withdraw the 14,000 Syrian troops from Lebanon. (See also LEBANESE CIVIL WAR OF 1975–90.)

## Lebedev, Peter Nikolayevich

*(1866–1912)* Soviet physicist. He studied at the Moscow Higher Technical School and at the universities of Strasbourg and Berlin and was appointed professor at Moscow University. He founded and built up the first large school of physics in Russia. Lebedev conducted research in Maxwell's electromagnetic theory and succeeded in proving the pressure of light on solids and gases. His *Experimental Research on Light Pressure* was published in 1901.

***Lebensraum*** German term meaning "living space," and the doctrine it described. The term *Lebensraum* was introduced as early as the 1870s, but the concept did not become part of German policy until the 1920s and 1930s, when Adolf HITLER argued that GERMANY's boundaries were too small to support the German population; therefore, Germany would have to conquer foreign territory in order to give the German people more "living space."

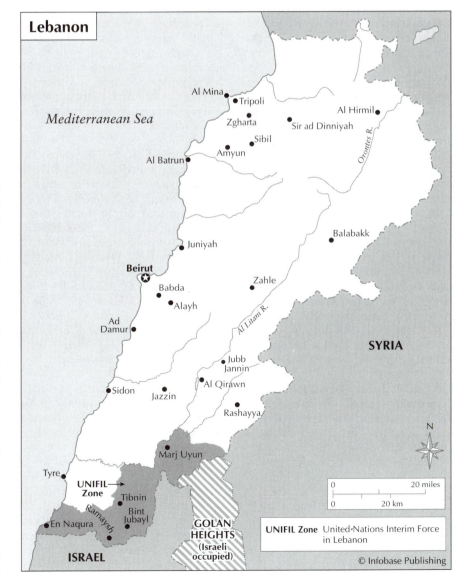

Hitler considered the Slavic countries to the east of Germany—namely, Poland and Russia—as Germany's destined "Lebensraum." In the NAZI mentality, the Slavic and Jewish people in these areas were inferior to the Aryan Germans. Germany thus had the right to occupy these lands and enslave or kill their people. The *Lebensraum* policy was carried out largely by Heinrich HIMMLER and the SS.

**Le Brocquy, Louis** *(1916–   )* Irish painter, graphic artist and book and textile designer. Le Brocquy is one of the leading Irish artists of modern times, having won acclaim not only in his native land but also in England, America and France. The latter country awarded him a Chevalier of the French Legion of Honor in 1975. Le Brocquy has painted tinkers and other figures out of Irish folklore, as well as numerous canvases devoted to children. He is also renowned for his portraits of literary figures including countrymen Samuel BECKETT, James JOYCE and William Butler YEATS. In 1992 *Aosdána,* an organization honoring literary, musical and visual artists in Ireland, recognized le Brocquy's artistic contributions by designating him with the rank of *Saoi* (meaning "magnanimous man"), which was bestowed on him in 1994 by Ireland's president Mary Robinson. Other recent awards include honorary PhDs awarded le Brocquy by Dublin City University (1999) and Queen's University Belfast (2002), the French rank of *Officier des Arts et des Lettres* (1999), and the Belgian *Officier de l'Ordre de la Couronne Belge* (2001). Le Brocquy was commissioned to paint a portrait of Bono, the lead singer in the Irish band U2. The portrait was unveiled in October 2003 at Ireland's National Gallery.

**le Carré, John (David John Moore Cornwell)** *(1931–   )* British novelist known for his complex spy thrillers set during the COLD WAR. Educated at Oxford and Berne University, during the late 1950s he taught school at Eton and in Switzerland before joining the British foreign service. Ostensibly a member of the diplomatic corps in West Germany, he was actually an intelligence agent (1959–64). While in the Foreign Office he published two novels under the pen name John le Carré. These books attracted little notice, but his third, *The Spy Who Came in from the Cold* (1963), won international acclaim as a classic of the genre. The novel concerns the efforts of a British agent, Lemas, to discredit an East German official. However, like many of his subsequent books, it can also be read as a gloss on cold war morality and the decline of Britain as a world power. Throughout his writing, le Carré debunks the myth of the glamorous spy popularized by Ian FLEMING. George Smiley, the hero (or antihero) of many of le Carré's books (believed to be based on Sir Maurice OLDFIELD), is the antithesis of Fleming's suave hero, James Bond. In le Carré's world, the distinction between good and evil is often a matter of degree. Although his plots are meticulously detailed, le Carré is not interested primarily in the technical aspects of spycraft. Rather, he is concerned with the larger issues of loyalty, betrayal and faith. In this, in his careful prose style and in the doom-laden atmosphere of his novels, le Carré is the direct successor of Joseph CONRAD and Graham GREENE. Among le Carré's other books are *A Small Town in Germany* (1968), *Tinker, Tailor, Soldier, Spy* (1974), *The Honourable Schoolboy* (1977), *Smiley's People* (1980), *A Perfect Spy* (1986), *The Russia House* (1989) and *The Secret Pilgrim* (1991). (See also Kim PHILBY.) With the end of the Cold War, le Carré's novels began to focus more on the clandestine nature of spycraft, as was the case in *The Night Manager* (1993), *Our Game* (1995), *The Tailor of Panama* (1996), *Single & Single* (1999), and *The Constant Gardener* (2000). In January 2003 the *London Times* published his essay entitled "The United States Has Gone Mad," which criticized U.S. plans to invade Iraq.

**Le Corbusier (Charles Edouard Jeanneret-Gris)** *(1887–1965)* Swiss-born architect. Le Corbusier was one of the most influential architects of the 20th century. He was equally renowned for his theoretical writings and for his unique architectural projects, which were constructed in locales around the world. These latter projects included the Unité d'Habitation, a "vertical city" in Marseilles, and the Punjabi capitol complex at CHANDIGARH, India. Le Corbusier was closely associated with numerous painters influenced by the Cubist movement, including Fernand LÉGER. In his writings Le Corbusier emphasized the need to plan for ideal cities of the future in which "modulor" man could function with efficiency and safety. His major works included *Towards a New Architecture* (1923), *The City of Tomorrow* (1925), and *When the Cities Were White* (1937).

**Ledbetter, Huddie "Leadbelly"** *(1888–1949)* American blues singer and composer. He started his career by playing guitar at dances. He was jailed three times for murder, attempted murder and assault charges between 1918 and 1939. Writer John A. Lomax met him in prison and assembled his songs into a book, *Negro Folk Songs as Sung by Lead Belly* (1936). After his release from prison, Ledbetter toured France in 1949.

**Le Duc Tho (Phan Dinh Khal)** *(1911–1990)* North Vietnamese diplomat. A member of the North Vietnamese Communist Party Politburo from 1955 until his retirement in 1986, he negotiated secretly in Paris with U.S. national security advisor Henry KISSINGER in an effort to end the VIETNAM WAR. Those negotiations produced a cease-fire agreement and a withdrawal of U.S. troops, but fighting between North and South continued. The two men were jointly offered the NOBEL PEACE PRIZE in 1973, but Tho declined on the grounds that "peace has not yet been established." He later directed the final military offensive by North Vietnam in 1975, which brought about the fall of the South Vietnamese government and the merger of the two nations under communist rule.

**Led Zeppelin** British rock-and-roll band (1968–80). Led Zeppelin is one of the most commercially successful and musically influential bands in the history of ROCK AND ROLL. While many critics disdain the band's music, the Led Zeppelin sound—throbbing guitar and thrashing rhythm section overlaid with melodramatic vocals—defined heavy metal in the 1970s and inspired a host of imitative bands who continue to perform to this day. The members of Led Zeppelin were John Bonham, drums; John Paul Jones, keyboards and bass; Jimmy Page, guitar; and

Robert Plant, vocals. All 10 Led Zeppelin albums went gold or platinum in total sales. The band's trademark anthem, "Stairway to Heaven" (1971), is considered one of the greatest rock-and-roll songs of all time.

**Lee, Ang** *(1954– )* Taiwanese film director and writer. Born in Taiwan, Lee first exhibited his interest in the performing arts when in 1978 he enrolled in the University of Illinois to study drama. While studying toward his B.A. in theater, Lee developed an interest in film and enrolled in the New York University (NYU) Film School, from which he graduated in 1984. After leaving NYU, he spent eight years searching for funding for his film scripts. Lee returned to Taiwan and won a script contest through which he obtained funding for *Pushing Hands* (1992), a film that depicted a Taiwanese father-son relationship. Lee followed *Hands* with *The Wedding Banquet* (1993) and *Eat Drink Man Woman* (1994). Both films portrayed the relationship between a traditional Taiwanese father and his cosmopolitan children and were also nominated for the Academy Award for Best Foreign Language Film. Following these critically acclaimed Chinese-language projects, Lee directed a screen version of *Sense and Sensibility* (1995), *The Ice Storm* (1997), and *Ride with the Devil* (1999), all of which received great critical praise. However, it was not until his Chinese-language adventure film *Crouching Tiger, Hidden Dragon* (2000) that Lee experienced both critical acclaim and box office success. *Crouching Tiger* won the 2001 Academy Award for Best Foreign Language Film, and proved one of the most lucrative films of 2001, despite its use of English subtitles. In 2006 Lee won the Academy Award for best director for *Brokeback Mountain* (2005).

**Lee, Gypsy Rose** *(1914–1970)* American entertainer. Born Rose Louise Hovick, Gypsy Rose Lee elevated the striptease to an art form and became the sophisticated queen of burlesque. Intelligent as well as beautiful, she became the toast of New York intellectuals. She starred in the ZIEGFELD FOLLIES in the 1930s and on Broadway (*Star and Garter*), in addition to publishing a ghostwritten novel (*The G-String Murders*) and hosting her

own national television talk show in the 1960s. A Broadway musical based on her life opened in 1959 (music by Jule STYNE and lyrics by Stephen SONDHEIM), was made into a film in 1962 and was revived on Broadway in 1990.

**Lee Kuan Yew (Lee Kwan Yu)** *(1923– )* Prime minister of SINGAPORE (1959–1990); educated at Raffles College, Cambridge University (double first in law with star for special distinction) and the Middle Temple, London. In the early 1950s he was legal adviser to a number of trade unions in Singapore. Lee Kuan Yew helped found the PAP People's Action Party in 1954 and was elected to parliament in 1955. Prime minister of Singapore since 1959, he was widely recognized both within and outside Singapore as a man of outstanding intelligence, political skill and vision; but he was also seen as a man of ruthless determination who has found it increasingly difficult to tolerate opposition to his views. He was the dominant figure in the political life of Singapore and one of Asia's most well-known political figures. In 1990 Lee left the premiership, though he remained in the Cabinet as senior minister.

**Lee Teng-hui (Li Denghui)** *(1923– )* Mayor of Taipei (1978–81), governor of Taiwan province (1981–84), vice president of Taiwan (1984–88), and president of TAIWAN (1988–2000). Born to a family of tea-leaf farmers, Lee worked on his family's farm in Sanchih and attended school on the Japanese-controlled island of Taiwan until 1941, when he qualified for several years of study at Kyoto Imperial University. After five years of studying at Kyoto, Lee returned to Taiwan in 1946, where he studied agricultural economics at the National Taiwan University and received a B.S. in 1948.

After 13 years directing the improvement of agricultural yields of Taiwanese farms, as an economist, on the Joint Commission on Rural Reconstruction (JCRR), Lee left the JCRR to enroll at Cornell University, where he studied the flow of capital investment within the agrarian sector in Taiwan. After receiving his Ph.D from Cornell in 1968, Lee returned to Taiwan where he eventually accepted an appointment in the Taiwanese Cabinet as a minister without portfolio. In 1978 Lee was ap-

pointed mayor of Taipei, the capital of Taiwan, and in 1981 became governor of Taiwan province. Because of his success as governor, President Chiang Ching-kuo (Jiang Jingguo), son of former president CHIANG KAI-SHEK (Jiang Jieshi), selected Lee as his vice president in 1984, making Lee the first native-born Taiwanese to hold that office. Together, Chiang and Lee worked to introduce more democratic elements into Taiwan, such as ending the state of martial law in 1987 that had been in force since the Chinese Nationalist regime established itself in Taiwan in 1949. When Chiang died in 1988, Lee became president of Taiwan as well as president of the Kuomintang (Guomindang). Lee continued to introduce liberal reforms in Taiwan by sanctioning the formation of opposition parties and the holding of free local and provincial elections. In 1990 the National Assembly elected Lee to a six-year term as president. Following his election, Lee modified the constitution to ensure that the presidential office would be filled through direct popular election and its term would be only four years. In 1996 he won the first presidential election with 55 percent of the vote. In 2000 Lee abstained from running for reelection and resigned as head of the Kuomintang.

During his elected terms as president, Lee's greatest challenge was the improvement of relations between CHINA and Taiwan. Still viewing Taiwan as a "renegade province," the People's Republic of China (PRC) vehemently protested Lee's 1995 private visit to the U.S. and scheduled a large naval exercise in Taiwanese waters during the election in an attempt to intimidate those opposition candidates who ran on platforms advocating the independence of the island.

**Left Socialist Revolutionaries** The heirs of the *narodnik* (see **Narodnaya Volya**) tradition, the Left Socialist Revolutionaries enjoyed the support of many of the peasants. One-time allies of the BOLSHEVIKS, their alliance foundered when the Bolsheviks strengthened the power of the army and police. The Left Socialist Revolutionaries, however, lacked clearly devised policies; although angered by the reintroduction of the death penalty, they kept their men in the CHEKA. They opposed LENIN over the Treaty of BREST-LITOVSK, in 1918; Muravev attempted to declare war on Germany and the Bolsheviks; and several groups of the Left Socialist Revolutionaries attempted to overthrow the Bolshevik leadership of the local Soviets in provincial towns. After the assassination of the German ambassador, Count Mirbach, Maria Spiridonova and other leading members were shot, and the Left Socialist Revolutionaries lost credibility and ceased to threaten the position of the Bolsheviks.

**Léger, Fernand** *(1881–1955)* French painter. Léger was deeply influenced by CUBISM, although he maintained a large degree of independence from all artistic movements during his lengthy career. He first came to prominence in the years prior to World War I after his canvasses were displayed at the *Section d'Or* exhibition of 1912, which also featured the work of numerous Cubist painters. Léger was fascinated with the possibilities of applying modern technology to artistic creation. He made a close study of architecture and became friends with LE CORBUSIER and the artists and craftsmen of the de STIJL movement. Léger's paintings also show the influence of the cinema and advertising art. His experience as an artilleryman during WORLD WAR I also showed itself in Léger's work and led him to theorize that machinery was the most successful and aesthetically significant of all human creations. In his later years Léger turned away from his abstract compositions to more figurative works.

**Legion of Decency** Formed in the U.S. in 1933 by the Catholic Church, the legion forced the film industry to adhere to a rigid moral code for all films; the church replaced it in 1966 with the National Catholic Office for Motion Pictures. Upset by what it considered to be an increasing number of immoral movies, like Mae WEST's *She Done Him Wrong* (1932), the Catholic Church launched its Legion of Decency campaign in 1933, led by Martin Quigley, owner of the industry trade paper *Motion Picture Herald,* and Archbishop John McNicholas of Cincinnati. The legion had two goals: to install a Catholic censor in Hollywood and to continue to pressure the industry to produce "clean" films. It achieved its first goal in 1934 when Will Hays, head of the Motion Picture Producers and Distributors of America (MPPDA), hired Joseph Breen, an active lay Catholic, as censor. Its second goal was successfully defended for almost 30 years.

From 1934 to 1936, legion activities were centered in Chicago, where a "C," or Condemned, rating was initiated, forbidding Catholics to attend such films as *Anna Karenina* (MGM, 1935), *Laughing Boy* (MGM, 1934), *Of Human Bondage* (RKO, 1934) and *Girl from Missouri* (MGM, 1934). In 1936 Legion offices were moved to New York. Films were reviewed by the International Federation of Catholic Alumnae. A new rating system was developed that gave films an A-1 (Morally Unobjectionable), A-II (Morally Unobjectionable for Adults), B (Morally Objectionable in part) or C (Condemned). Each year the legion "pledge" was given by 20 million Catholics, who promised to avoid condemned and objectionable films. For three decades the legion quietly pressured Hollywood to alter hundreds of films. After an initial flurry of "C" ratings, the legion issued few because the industry began to rigidly enforce the motion picture code. There were notable exceptions. Howard HUGHES incurred the wrath of the legion when he released *The Outlaw* (1943), an oversexed story of outlaw Billy the Kid. Roberto ROSSELLINI's *The Miracle* (Tinia, 1948) was condemned as "sacrilegious and blasphemous" in 1950; it was banned in New York, but the U.S. Supreme Court overturned the decision and declared films protected under the First Amendment.

In a postwar climate of growing freedom of expression, the legion was seen as an anachronism. When the industry began to restrict audiences and rate its films in 1966—G for anyone, M for mature audiences, R restricted and X for adults only—the legion's influence began to wane.

**Lego** Plastic construction toy developed in Denmark that has outstanding design quality along with very rich play possibilities. Lego is based on a modular plastic block studded on top with projecting disks that mate with a hollowed-out bottom so the blocks lock together. The system first appeared in 1947 and has gradually been expanded, with the addition of components in many shapes and sizes, all using the same connecting detail and all in modular sizes. In 1955 sets were introduced that make up particular toys (some very elaborate), but all using interchangeable components so that the toy can be used in a wide variety of ways as a child grows. The manufacturer, Lego System A/S of Billund, Denmark, does not give design credit to any individual, although the firm's founder, Godtfred Kirk Christiansen, appears to have developed the concept based on the children's wood blocks that the firm made previously. Many variations of Lego have appeared, and many imitations are now made. Lego is a truly educational toy in both technical and aesthetic terms.

**Le Guin, Ursula K.** *(1929– )* American novelist, story writer, poet and essayist. Le Guin is best known for her science fiction novels, the most famous of which is *The Left Hand of Darkness* (1969), which depicted an alien planet on which female cultural values were dominant. She is the daughter of two well-known anthropologists, Alfred and Theodora KROEBER; an anthropological approach to customs and morals is one of the hallmarks of Le Guin's fiction. She is one of the most highly honored of science fiction writers—having won numerous Hugo and Nebula Awards—and her work in that genre has won the praise of mainstream critics as well. Other novels include *Wizard of Earthsea* (1968), *The Dispossessed: An Ambiguous Utopia* (1974), *The Lathe of Heaven* (1975) and *The Word for World Is Forest* (1976). *Orsinian Tales* (1976) is her best known story collection. *Always Coming Home* (1985) is a representative selection of stories, essays and poems. Since 1991 le Guin has published 27 books on topics ranging from science fiction to poetry, and has received 28 awards, including the Asimov Readers Award (1995 and 2003), and the Nebula Award (1996).

**Lehar, Franz** *(1870–1948)* Austrian composer. Lehar was an extraordinarily popular composer of operettas during the early decades of the 20th century. His beautiful melodies and lilting waltzes typified the gaiety and joie de vivre of life in Vienna early in the century. His most well-known operetta, *The Merry Widow*, was first produced in 1905 and has enjoyed worldwide popularity with opera and light opera companies ever since.

**Lehmann, Lilli** *(1848–1929)* German singer. The greatest Wagnerian soprano of her time and one of the great performers of *Lieder*, Lehmann also excelled in the French and Italian repertories, demonstrating her musical versatility and dramatic ability by mastering 170 roles in 119 operas. After performing with the Berlin Royal Opera, she made her New York Metropolitan Opera debut as Carmen in 1885. She thrilled Met audiences when she created the roles of Isolde in *Tristan and Isolde* (1886), Brunnhilde in *Siegfried* (1887) and Brunnhilde in *Die Götterdammerung* (1888), for the first time in America. She gave *Lieder* recitals after 1909; among her students was future opera star Geraldine FARRAR. Lehmann also taught at the Mozarteum in Salzburg, Austria (from 1926). Her annual appearances as singer and director at summer performances in Salzburg (1905–10) gave the impetus for the establishment of the annual SALZBURG FESTIVAL in 1920.

**Lehmann, Lotte** *(1888–1976)* German-born opera singer, recitalist and voice teacher, considered one of the great dramatic sopranos and *Lieder* singers of the early 20th century. After appearing with the Hamburg Opera (1909–14), Lehmann gained international fame with the Vienna Royal Opera, establishing herself as a great Wagnerian soprano in such roles as Sieglinde in *Die Walküre* and Eva in *Die Meistersinger*. She also became the foremost interpreter of female roles in Richard STRAUSS's operas, creating the role of the Dyer's wife in *Die Frau ohne Schatten* (among others) and emerging as the greatest Marschallin in *Der Rosenkavalier* of her generation. In the 1920s she began giving *Lieder* recitals, which continued even after her retirement from opera. In addition, she became a well-known voice teacher, helping to establish the Music Academy of the West at Santa Barbara, California. The recipient of many awards and honors, she became an American citizen in 1945.

**Leica** Family of 33 mm cameras considered design classics, which are produced by the German optical firm of Ernst Leitz GmbH. of Wetzlar, Germany. The concept of the miniature camera using standard motion picture film was developed around 1913 by Oskar BARNACK, a technician employed by Leitz. In 1924 a commercial version of the camera was put into production, and improved versions were introduced in quick succession, adding refinements such as range-finder focusing, interchangeable lenses and a full range of fast and slow shutter speeds. The design of the Leica, based on the technical vocabulary of quality optical instruments (such as the microscopes made by Leitz) and on close adherence to the functional demands of the camera, reached its high point with the models F and G of the 1930s. Acceptance by a number of famous photographers, such as Henri CARTIER-BRESSON and Walker EVANS, combined with awareness of the camera's technical excellence, made it extremely popular, and early models are now collected by a cult of admirers. Later models, including the post–World War II series M versions, have maintained Leica's high level of design excellence. Many similar cameras were developed to compete with the Leica, but none have reached the same level of popularity.

**Leigh, Vivien (Vivien Mary Hartley)** *(1913–1967)* British screen and stage actress. Leigh, renowned as one of the most ethereally beautiful actresses of the 20th century, remains best known for her starring role as Southern heroine Scarlet O'Hara in the 1939 film GONE WITH THE WIND, for which she won an ACADEMY AWARD for Best Actress. Leigh first rose to prominence in the British cinema in the 1930s, most notably through her starring role opposite Laurence OLIVIER—whom she married after leaving her first husband—in *Fire Over England* (1937). She also appeared frequently on the British stage, including a 1937 role as Ophelia opposite Olivier's Hamlet. After *Gone With The Wind*, Leigh became an international star, though recurrent physical and emotional problems limited her roles in the final decades of her life. Her subsequent films included *Waterloo Bridge* (1940), *That Hamilton Woman* (1941), *Caesar*

*and Cleopatra* (1945), *Anna Karenina* (1948), a second Oscar-winning performance as Blanche du Bois in Tennessee WILLIAMS's *A Streetcar Named Desire* (1951), *The Deep Blue Sea* (1955), *The Roman Spring of Mrs. Stone* (1961) and *Ship of Fools* (1965).

**Leighton, Margaret** *(1922–1976)* British stage actress. Leighton came to prominence in the 1940s as an accomplished actress capable of playing the classic roles of the British theater. While a member of the renowned Old Vic company from 1944 to 1947, Leighton won acclaim for her roles as Raina in *Arms and the Man* by George Bernard SHAW, and as Regan opposite the Shakespearean King Lear of Laurence OLIVIER. Leighton subsequently appeared as Celia in *The Cocktail Party* (1950) by T. S. ELIOT and in three major Shakespearean roles—Rosalind, Ariel and Lady Macbeth—at Stratford-upon-Avon (1952). Leighton continued to be active in both London and Broadway theatrical productions until her death.

**Leinsdorf, Erich** *(1912–1993)* Austrian-born opera and symphonic conductor renowned for his affiliations with the Metropolitan Opera and the Boston Symphony Orchestra. Leinsdorf was a latter-day adherent to the objective, antiromantic school of conducting. He was born in Vienna, graduated from the Vienna Conservatory, and assisted Bruno WALTER and Arturo TOSCANINI at the Salzburg festivals in the mid-1930s. In 1938 he immigrated to the U.S., where he reigned supreme for 10 years at the Metropolitan Opera. He reached his zenith as Musical Director of the Boston Symphony in 1962–69 succeeding, chronologically, Serge KOUSSEVITZKY and Charles MUNCH. His mastery of large forces and relentless discipline with players made him an effective opera conductor. However, his methodical, calculating objectivity did not make him popular with many critics and performers. A man of great intellect with a thorough grasp of diverse subjects, he felt justified in altering or "adjusting" symphonic classics to his own standards. "I think these works should be edited in order to sound as well as they can sound," he told this writer. "They should not be done literally the way they have been orchestrated originally, because our orchestras are different, our halls are different, and our ears are different." He was well known for his advocacy of music of the so-called second Viennese school—Arnold Schoenberg, Alban Berg and Anton Webern.

**Lem, Stanisław** *(1921–2006)* Polish science fiction writer. Lem is the first major writer in this genre to have emerged from Eastern Europe. Currently regarded as one of the leading voices in science fiction, Lem was educated in his native Poland and earned a medical degree in 1946. He has enjoyed the rare distinction of seeing his science fiction stories published in mainstream literary periodicals such as *The New Yorker*. Lem has also been influential, through his essays in the Polish journal *Quarber Merkur,* as a stringent critic of the overall literary standards of the science fiction genre. Lem's major works of science fiction include *Solaris* (1970), *Memoirs Found in a Bathtub* (1977), *Memoirs of a Space Traveller* (1983) and *Imaginary Magnitude* (1984).

**Lemaître, Abbé Georges Edouard** *(1894–1966)* Belgian astronomer and cosmologist. After serving in World War I, Lemaître studied at the University of Louvain in Belgium from which he graduated in 1920. He then attended a seminary at Malines, and was ordained as a Roman Catholic priest in 1923. Before taking up an appointment at the University of Louvain in 1925, he spent a year at Cambridge, England, where he worked with Arthur Eddington and a year in America where he worked at the Harvard College Observatory and the Massachusetts Institute of Technology. He remained at Louvain for the whole of his career, being made professor of astronomy in 1927. Lemaître was one of the propounders of the big bang theory of the origin of the universe. Einstein's theory of general relativity, announced in 1916, had led to various cosmological models, including Einstein's own model of a static universe. Lemaître in 1927 (and, independently, Alexander Friedmann in 1922) discovered a family of solutions to Einstein's field equations of relativity that described not a static but an expanding universe. This idea of an expanding universe was demonstrated experimentally in 1929 by Edwin Hubble who was unaware of

the work of Lemaître and Friedmann. Lemaître's model of the universe received little notice until Eddington arranged for it to be translated and reprinted in the *Monthly Notices of the Royal Astronomical Society* in 1931. It was not only the idea of an expanding universe that was so important in Lemaître's work, and on which others were soon working, but also his attempt to think of the cause and beginning of the expansion.

If matter is everywhere receding, it would seem natural to suppose that in the distant past it was closer together. If we go far enough back, argued Lemaître, we reach the "primal atom," a time at which the entire universe was in an extremely compact and compressed state. He spoke of some instability being produced by radioactive decay of the primal atom that was sufficient to cause an immense explosion that initiated the expansion. This big bang model did not fit too well with the available time scales of the 1930s. Nor did Lemaître provide enough mathematical detail to attract serious cosmologists. Its importance today is due more to the revival and revision it received at the hands of George Gamow in 1946.

**LeMay, Gen. Curtis Emerson** *(1906–1990)* U.S. Air Force officer. In World War II, LeMay pioneered precision daylight bombing of Germany and Japan. It was he who received President Harry S. Truman's order to drop nuclear bombs on Hiroshima and Nagasaki in 1945. In 1948 he led the Berlin Airlift, which overcame a Soviet blockade of the city. He commanded the Strategic Air Command from 1948 until 1957, when he was named U.S. Air Force vice chief of staff. From 1961 to 1965 he held the position of U.S. Air Force chief of staff. Following his retirement, in 1968 he was the controversial running mate of presidential candidate George Wallace; he advocated the nuclear bombing of Vietnam.

**Lemmon, Jack (John Uhler Lemmon III)** *(1925–2001)* American actor. Educated at Harvard University, Lemmon served in the navy and returned to begin his acting career in Off-Broadway productions and television dramas. He made his movie debut

opposite Judy Holliday in the comedy *It Should Happen to You* (1954). He later appeared in a number of films, his performance in *Mr. Roberts* (1955), winning a supporting actor Academy Award. He became a major star through his association with director Billy Wilder, co-starring in *Some Like It Hot* (1959) and *The Apartment* (1960). His 1960s movies include the wrenching drama *The Days of Wine and Roses* (1962) and the hilarious comedy *The Odd Couple* (1968), the first of his many projects with actor Walter Matthau and writer Neil Simon. His later films included *The Prisoner of Second Avenue* (1975), *The China Syndrome* (1979), *Tribute* (1980) and *Mass Appeal* (1984). A kind of Hollywood "Everyman," Lemmon distinguished himself in a wide variety of roles, from farce to melodrama, and proved to be an enduring movie star.

**Lemnitzer, General Lyman L.** *(1899–1988)* U.S. Army commander. Lemnitzer, a World War II hero who also served as a diplomat, helped to negotiate the surrender of Italian and German forces in Italy and Austria. Lemnitzer later commanded United Nations forces during the Korean War. In 1957 he returned to Washington and in 1960 was named chairman of the Joint Chiefs of Staff. His last post was as supreme Allied commander in Europe, a job he held until he retired from active duty in 1969.

**Lemon, Bob** *(1920–2000)* American baseball player and manager. One of the most consistent pitchers of the postwar era, Lemon posted 20-win seasons seven times. A fastballer, he was part of the Cleveland Indians's fearsome pitching staff of the 1950s that included Bob Feller and Early Wynn. He led the American League in strikeouts in 1950. A solid hitter, he was occasionally used in pinch-hit situations, and finished his career with 37 home runs. Upon his retirement in 1958, he stayed in baseball as a coach and scout. He returned to the major leagues in 1970 with the Kansas City Royals, and won Manager of the Year honors in 1971. In the late 1970s and early 1980s, he managed the tumultuous New York Yankees, replacing the often-hired-and-fired Billy Martin, and later being replaced by him. Later yet, he returned to replace Gene

Michael, and was replaced by him in 1982. Lemon was named to the Hall of Fame in 1976.

**LeMond, Greg** *(1962–   )* American cyclist. LeMond became the first non-European and first American to win the 2,500-mile, 22-leg Tour de France, in 1986. In April 1987 he was accidentally shot while hunting, and many believed his career was over. Nevertheless, he came back to win the Tour again in 1989 and was named "Sportsman of the Year" by *Sports Illustrated* magazine. In 1990 he won it for the third time, prompting the French sports paper *L'Étoile* to dub him "roisoleil," the "sun king." In 1994 LeMond retired from professional cycling.

**Lendl, Ivan** *(1960–   )* Czechoslovakian-born tennis player. The son of two national tennis stars, Lendl became one of the top players of the 1980s. He won the U.S. Open singles championship three times from 1985 to 1987. He won the French Open twice and was Grand Prix Masters champion an unprecedented five times during the 1980s. His stern on-court demeanor prevented his ever becoming a crowd favorite, but tennis purists were enthralled by his powerful serve and forehand. Lendl moved to the U.S. in 1981. Lendl became a U.S. citizen in 1992 and retired from professional tennis in 1994.

**Lend-Lease** Act proposed by President Franklin D. ROOSEVELT and passed by Congress on March 11, 1941, while the U.S. was still a neutral party in WORLD WAR II. The Lend-Lease Act allowed the president to transfer, lend or lease war materials to "the government of any country whose defense the president deems vital to the defense of the U.S." It permitted the immediate supply of arms, ships, machinery, food and services to Great Britain and China. The lend-lease program was soon extended to the USSR and later to most of the Allied countries. It was also an important factor in pressing American industry to gear up for wartime production. From September 1942 the U.S. received "reverse lend-lease" from British COMMONWEALTH countries and the FREE FRENCH in goods and services supplied to U.S. troops abroad. By the time President Harry S TRUMAN ended

the program on August 21, 1945, some $50 billion of lend-lease aid has been supplied to the Allies, with some $8 billion in "reverse lend-lease" given to the U.S. After the termination of lend-lease, American overseas aid was continued through the MARSHALL PLAN. Settlements of lend-lease debts were negotiated after World War II. The final settlement with the USSR was concluded in 1972.

**Lenin (Vladimir Ilyich Ulyanov)** *(1870–1924)* Russian revolutionary, leader of the Bolsheviks and chief theoretician of Russian Marxism. He was born at Simbirsk into a middle-class family. His brother Alexander was hanged in 1887 for planning an attempt on Czar Alexander III's life, greatly influencing Lenin's early life. Lenin studied law at Kazan University, but was expelled for subversive activity. Having studied Marx extensively, he went to St. Petersburg and organized the League for the Liberation of the Working Class. As a result he was arrested in 1897 and exiled for three years to Siberia, where he married Nadezhda KRUPSKAYA. He continued his revolutionary activities abroad. In 1903, in London, Lenin became the leader of the BOLSHEVIK faction of the Russian Social Democratic Labor Party. He returned to RUSSIA for the 1905 Revolution. In 1907 he fled to

*Russian revolutionary Vladimir Lenin* (LIBRARY OF CONGRESS, PRINTS AND PHOTOGRAPHS DIVISION)

Switzerland, and by means of underground organizations continued to master-mind the Russian revolutionary movement.

He was living in Switzerland during World War I and in March 1917 the Germans clandestinely arranged for Lenin to return home in a sealed train. Once in Petrograd, he turned his attention to the overthrowing of Alexander KERENSKY's provisional government, and was appointed chairman of the Council of People's Commissars. The APRIL THESES were published, and during that summer he took refuge in Finland before returning to organize, with TROTSKY, the OCTOBER REVOLUTION. He secured peace with Germany by the Treaty of BREST-LITOVSK and in 1919 set up the COMINTERN to work toward world revolution.

Lenin and the Red Army fought until 1921 before defeating the WHITES. His position as chairman was strengthened, and Lenin became a virtual dictator. To restore the economy, he instituted the NEW ECONOMIC POLICY in 1921. Lenin's health, which had been failing since an assassination attempt in 1918, grew worse. Although he warned that STALIN should not be allowed to continue as secretary general of the COMMUNIST PARTY, Lenin's warning went unheeded. He died in 1924, and his body, now embalmed, lay in a mausoleum in Red Square during the Communist era.

**Leningrad** See ST. PETERSBURG.

**Leningrad, siege of** *(1941–1944)* Siege operation during WORLD WAR II. On June 22, 1941, the Germans put 500,000 troops over the Russian frontier, and by November 1941 elements of that army were outside Leningrad. The Soviet forces, weakened by the GREAT PURGE, were unprepared. Leningrad was besieged and 750,000 people eventually perished. On January 15, 1944, the Russians began to break out of the town, and on January 20 succeeded in cutting the German supply corridor to the Gulf of Finland. On January 27 the two-and-a-half-year siege—one of the most heroically defended in the history of warfare—ended.

**Lennon, John** *(1940–1980)* British rock and roll composer, vocalist and guitarist. Lennon, who remains best

*John Lennon and Yoko Ono. c. 1975* (LIBRARY OF CONGRESS, PRINTS AND PHOTOGRAPHS DIVISION)

known for his 1960s years in the BEAT-LES, was one of the greatest songwriters in the history of ROCK AND ROLL, as well as one of its most outspoken personalities. Born in 1940 to a working-class LIVERPOOL family, Lennon took up the guitar at age 14 and, in 1955, began to play with fellow Liverpool teenager Paul MCCARTNEY. In 1958 the two formed a band named Johnny and the Moondogs that would transform into the Silver Beatles and then simply the Beatles. In the 1960s, Lennon and Mc-Cartney formed a songwriting team par excellence, drawing on their shared 1950s rock roots and their passion for studio experimentation. From "I Want to Hold Your Hand" (1964) to "Let It Be" (1970), Lennon-McCartney songs dominated and transformed popular music. In 1969 Lennon married Yoko Ono, with whom he would collaborate, after the breakup of the Beatles in 1970, on numerous musical projects. In the late 1960s, Lennon became a fervent antiwar spokesman and his song "Imagine" (1971) became an anthem of the peace movement. Lennon's final solo album *Double Fantasy* (1980), featured a Billboard number one hit song, "(Just Like) Starting Over." It was released just before the tragic murder of Lennon in New York City on December 8, 1980, which provoked worldwide mourning.

## Leno, James Douglas Muir "Jay"

(1950–  ) Comedian; television talk show host. Born in New Rochelle, New York, in 1950, Leno grew up in Andover, Massachusetts. After obtaining his B.A. in speech therapy from Emerson College in 1973, he performed as a standup comic in many nightclubs during the 1970s and 1980s, using his sharp wit and evocative facial expressions to delight audiences. He also landed minor parts in films. But he discovered his true métier in comedy routines on late-night television. He made numerous appearances on the popular variety program *Late Night with David Letterman* and served for many years as the permanent guest host on Johnny Carson's *Tonight Show*. When Carson announced in 1991 his intention to retire the following year, Leno defeated David LETTERMAN in a spirited contest to succeed the popular Carson. After Letterman left NBC for CBS to create a new show titled *The Late Show with David Letterman,* Leno and Letterman dueled for the late-night audience for the rest of the decade and into the 21st century. Letterman's *Late Show* took an early lead in the ratings, but Leno overtook his rival in 1995 and has usually had higher ratings ever since. On *The Tonight Show's* 50th anniversary episode in September 2004, Leno announced his intention to retire in 2009, with the host of NBC's *Late Night,* Conan O'Brian, to replace him.

## Lenya, Lotte (Karoline Blamuer)

(1898–1981) Austrian born actress and singer. While acting in BERLIN in the 1920s Lenya met the composer Kurt WEILL, whom she married. She appeared in many plays on which Weill collaborated with Bertolt BRECHT, including *Die Dreigroschen Oper* (THE THREEPENNY OPERA, 1927), in which she created the role of the prostitute, Jenny. She and Weill fled to the U.S. after Adolf HITLER came to power in GER-MANY. After Weill's death she resumed her stage career on Broadway, winning a Tony Award for playing Jenny in a revival of *Threepenny Opera* (1955); she was also in *Cabaret* (1966). She also appeared in films, including *From Russia With Love* (1963), and supervised and sang on a series of recordings of Weill's music.

## Leonard, Hugh (pen name of John Keyes Byrne)

(1926–  ) Irish playwright, theater critic and television and screenplay writer. Leonard worked as a civil servant before achieving success as a playwright in the 1950s. His first play, *The Big Birthday* (1956), was produced at the ABBEY THEATRE in Dublin and dealt with the social fabric of Irish life, as did subsequent plays including *A Leap in the Dark* (1957), *Madigan's Lock* (1958) and *The Passion of Peter Ginty* (1961), an adaptation of Henrik Ibsen's *Peer Gynt.* In 1959 Leonard began to write scripts for the BRITISH BROADCASTING CORPORATION while maintaining an active involvement in the theater. *Stephen D* (1962) is a stage adaptation of the writings of James JOYCE. Leonard focused on Anglo-Irish relations in the play *The Au Pair Man* (1968). Other plays by Leonard include *Da* (1973), *A Life* (1978), *Moving Days* (1981) and *Scorpions* (1983). *Home Before Dark* (1975) is his autobiography. Leonard published his sole novel, *Parnell and the Englishwoman,* in 1992.

## Leone, Sergio

(1921–1989) Italian film director. Leone was best known for his "spaghetti westerns"—violent, low-budget movies set in the American wild west but produced in Italy and Spain. His westerns helped revive a genre that, at the time, was thought to be dead. He also made an international star of actor Clint EASTWOOD by featuring him in such films as *A Fistful of Dollars* (1964), *For a Few Dollars More* (1965) and *The Good, the Bad, and the Ugly* (1966). Leone maintained that his movie violence was exaggerated because he "wanted to make a tongue-in-cheek satire of run-of-the-mill westerns." In 1984 U.S. film executives severely cut his last major project, an ambitious homage to American gangster films titled *Once Upon a Time in America.* Although the film had won awards in Europe, the truncated U.S.

version received a lukewarm critical reception and popular response.

**Leoni, Raul** *(1905–1972)* President of VENEZUELA (1964–69). Leoni spent 30 years in exile after participating in the insurrection of 1921 while a student. He was later leader of the Accion Democratica party (1958–64). As president of Venezuela, he maintained the country's rapid economic growth and fostered political stability.

**Leonov, Alexei** *(1934– )* Soviet cosmonaut; an accomplished artist, the personable Leonov has been on two historic space missions. During his Voskhod 2 mission (March 18, 1965) he became the first human to walk in space when he spent 10 minutes outside the spacecraft commanded by fellow cosmonaut Pavel BELYAYEV. The successful Voskhod mission almost ended in disaster, when the cosmonauts missed their prime recovery area and were forced to land in the Ural Mountains, spending a freezing, snowy night aboard the spacecraft before rescuers could arrive. Leonov's second mission was as commander of the SOYUZ half of the historic APOLLO-SOYUZ Test Project (July 1975), which found the American and Soviet spacecraft linking up to share friendship and scientific experimentation in space. His flight engineer on the historic mission was Valery Kubasov, and after the mission the two Soviets joined their American counterparts in a worldwide speaking tour demonstrating the possibilities of U.S./Soviet cooperation in space. It was the only time that such a joint mission was flown. Following the disintegration of the U.S. space shuttle *Columbia* in 2003, Leonov insisted that the U.S. should provide the Russian space agency with all available information regarding its design flaws.

**Leonov, Leonid Maksimovich** *(1899–1994)* Russian novelist. Having served in the Red Army, Leonov settled in Moscow and had his first work published in 1922. At the outset of his career he was a member of the Serapion Brotherhood (see SERAPION BROTHERS). At the same time, he was profoundly influenced by the writings of Dostoyevsky. Much of Leonov's work reflects his concern for universal ethical

and moral problems and the fate of Russia. His novels include *The Badgers* (1924) and *The Thief* (1927). He was later obliged to conform to the demands of SOCIALIST REALISM, demands that he found easier to fulfill in plays rather than in novels. His psychological plays include *The Invasion* (1924) and *The Golden Carriage* (1954).

**Leontief, Wassily** *(1906–1999)* Born in Russia and educated in Germany, Leontief served as an adviser to the Chinese government before immigrating to the U.S. He joined the Harvard faculty in 1931. Leontief was best known for developing the input-output method of economic analysis used for national planning. He won the NOBEL PRIZE for economics in 1973.

**Leopold III** *(1901–1983)* King of the Belgians (1934–51). When the Germans invaded BELGIUM early in WORLD WAR II (1940), Leopold surrendered to the Nazis instead of fleeing and establishing a government in exile, as his ministers had urged. Many Belgians regarded Leopold as a turncoat and collaborator for this act, and he left Belgium after the war. He returned in 1951 after a national referendum indicated that he would be accepted by his people. However, violent protests convinced him to abdicate in favor of his son Baudouin later that year.

**Leopold, Aldo** *(1887–1948)* American conservationist. Iowa-born, Leopold was a pioneering environmentalist. As an official with the U.S. Forest Service in the 1920s, he was instrumental in developing the science of wildlife management and he drafted the plan to set aside America's first wilderness area, Gila National Forest in New Mexico. He also taught at the University of Wisconsin and in 1935 was a founding member of the Wilderness Society. His credo as a naturalist is set forth in the autobiographical *A Sand County Almanac* (1949) and in the essays collected in *The River of the Mother of God* (1991).

**Leopold and Loeb case** One of the most sensational murder cases of the 20th century. Two wealthy Chicago teenagers, Nathan Leopold and Richard Loeb, planned what they con-

ceived of as the "perfect murder" for the sheer excitement of committing the crime and getting away with it. On May 21, 1924, the two college students abducted and bludgeoned to death Loeb's distant cousin, 14-year-old Bobby Franks, and dumped his body in a drain pipe. Inept criminals, they were soon captured. In the widely publicized trial that followed, famous trial lawyer Clarence DARROW admitted their guilt but argued against putting them to death. Darrow was successful in his defense, and they were each sentenced to life plus 99 years for kidnap and murder. Loeb was killed in a prison brawl in 1926; Leopold was released in 1958 and died in 1971.

**Le Pen, Jean-Marie** *(1928– )* French politician and founder of the National Front. Born in the small town of La-Trinité-sur-Mer in Brittany, he joined the French Foreign Legion in 1954 where he served in that military unit's struggles against rebel forces in INDOCHINA and ALGERIA. Two years later, he left the Foreign Legion and was elected to the French National Assembly as a member of Pierre Poujade's Shopkeepers' Party. In 1965 Le Pen helped organize the unsuccessful presidential campaign of far-right politician Jean-Louis Tixier-Vignancour. In 1972 Le Pen created the National Front and used the party repeatedly to stage his own runs at the French presidency. During his presidential campaigns from 1974 to 2002, Le Pen's repeated warnings of the dangers represented by continued immigration into France from North Africa increased his share of the first-round popular vote from 0.74 percent to 17 percent. Along with his continued anti-immigration stance (directed mainly at Muslims from North Africa), Le Pen also antagonized Jewish voters by dismissing the HOLOCAUST as "a detail of history" in 1987.

In 1998 Le Pen's party suffered a serious setback when its leading technocrat, Bruno Megret, attempted to unseat Le Pen as the head of the party. Although Le Pen loyalists defeated the effort, the struggle fractured the National Front and reduced its effectiveness as a national political organization. However, the infighting did not prevent Le Pen from gathering 17 percent of the popular vote in the 2002 elections, the second highest of any candidate after the incumbent Gaullist president JACQUES CHIRAC. In the runoff election, Le Pen lost handily to the conservative Chirac who also drew votes from the left.

## Lepeshinskaya, Olga Vasilyevna
*(1916– )* Ballerina, graduated from the Bolshoi Theater School. One of the greatest Soviet dancers of her day, Lepeshinskaya's style is characterized by her virtuosity and strength. A member of the COMMUNIST PARTY since 1943, she served on numerous boards and committees.

## Lerner, Alan Jay *(1918–1986)* U.S.
lyricist and playwright. Lerner's greatest successes were the product of a longtime collaboration with composer Frederick LOEWE. Their hit Broadway musicals included *Brigadoon* (1947), *Paint Your Wagon* (1951) and *Camelot* (1960). Their most successful work of all was *My Fair Lady,* which opened on Broadway in March 1956 and ran for more than 2,700 performances. Another collaboration, *Gigi* (1958), is regarded as one of the most fully realized of all film musicals.

## Lescaze, William *(1896–1969)*
American architect born in Switzerland, who is credited with introducing the INTERNATIONAL STYLE in America. Lescaze had studied with Karl Moser before coming to the U.S. in 1920. His best known work (in partnership with George HOWE) is the 1932 Philadelphia Savings Fund Society (PSFS) building, the first fully modern skyscraper anywhere, and one of the first examples of MODERNISM in American architecture. Lescaze seems to have been the leader in the design of the building (Howe's earlier work had been quite traditional), so a major share of the credit for its success is his. After the partnership with Howe ended in 1934, Lescaze continued to practice architecture in New York, designing a number of modern townhouses (including his own on 48th Street), the Williamsbridge housing project in New York, and various other works including radio stations, office buildings and a pavilion for the 1939 NEW YORK WORLD'S FAIR. Lescaze also designed furniture, lighting and many small accessory products—all by-products of his architectural work.

## Les Misérables (musical) Stage
musical adaptation of the 1862 French novel by Victor Hugo. Inspired by the commercial success of a French musical adaptation of the book that premiered in September 1980, Cameron Mackintosh and Herbert Kretzmer began production of an English-language version of the musical. Their interpretation of *Les Misérables* premiered in 1985 in London and in 1987 on Broadway. It won eight Tony Awards its opening year in the U.S., including Best Musical, Best Score, and Best Director. On March 18, 2003, after 6,680 shows, *Les Misérables* ended its run on Broadway and became the second-longest running show in Broadway history after Andrew Lloyd Webber's musical, *CATS;* its performances in London continued through 2003.

## Lesotho (Kingdom of Lesotho) A
landlocked country within the Republic of SOUTH AFRICA, Lesotho covers an area of 11,715 square miles. Originally known as Basutoland, the country became a British Crown colony in 1884. Resisting incorporation into South Africa when that country was formed in 1910, Basutoland was granted a new

| | LESOTHO |
|---|---|
| 1966 | Lesotho is granted independence under the Independence Constitution. Moshoeshoe II is proclaimed king. In a trial of strength between the king and Prime Minister Leabua Jonathan, the king is forced to yield. |
| 1970, | Lesotho holds first national elections. When the electoral defeat of his Basotho National Party appears imminent, Prime Minister Jonathan proclaims an emergency and suspends the constitution. Opposition leaders are arrested. The king is placed under house arrest and is later exiled for nine months. |
| 1971 | All political prisoners are released under a general amnesty. |
| 1986 | Jonathan is ousted in a pro–South African coup led by General Justin Lekhanya, who is sworn in as head of government. |
| 1990 | Lekhanya strips King Moshoeshoe II of his power and sends him into exile. Moshoeshoe's son Prince Mohato is sworn in as King Letsie III. |
| 1995 | King Moshoeshoe II is restored to the throne but dies in a car accident and is again replaced by his son Letsie III. |
| 2004 | After a three-year drought the government declares a state of emergency and appeals for food aid. |
| 2005 | Lesotho starts a program that will test all its citizens for AIDS. |

**Lesotho**

SOUTH AFRICA

Libono

Butha-Buthe

Hlotse

Letseng-la-Tarea

Teyateyaneng

Malibamatso R.

Senqu (Orange) R.

✪ Maseru

Mokhotlong

Kornetspruit R.

Thaba-Tseka

Dinakeng R.

Caledon R.

Mafeteng

Senqu (Orange) R.

Qachas Nek

Mohales Hoek

SOUTH AFRICA

N

Quthing

Orange R.

| 0 | | 40 miles |
| 0 | | 40 km |

© Infobase Publishing

constitution in 1960 and achieved independence as the Kingdom of Lesotho in 1966. Political tensions between King Moshoeshoe II and Prime Minister Chief Lebua Jonathan led to the declaration of a state of emergency in 1970 and the eventual overthrow of Chief Jonathan in 1986 in a military coup led by Major General Justin Lekhanya. In 1990 the king's powers were reduced, consolidating power in the hands of a military council headed by Lekhanya. In 1995 Moshoeshoe II was restored as king, but he died later that year in a car crash and was succeeded by Letsie III. At the beginning of the 21st century, Lesotho finds itself plagued by severe drought and AIDS.

**Lesser, Sol** (*1890–1980*) Pioneer HOLLYWOOD film producer. Lesser started in the movie industry in 1907 as a producer of two-reel films. He went on to produce some 117 motion pictures, including a series of TARZAN films starring Johnny WEISSMULLER. Among his other credits were the ACADEMY AWARD–winning 1951 documen-

tary *Kon Tiki, Our Town, The Red House* and *Stage Door Canteen.* Lesser was also credited with introducing new ideas in film merchandising that became standard practice, including previews and personal appearances by the stars.

**Lessing, Doris** (*Doris May Tayler*) (*1919–* ) British author. Lessing emerged as one of the most important fiction writers since World War II. Her first novel, *The Grass Is Singing* (1950), achieved immediate critical and popular acclaim, and contains one of her recurring themes: the experience of living in Africa (she was raised in Southern Rhodesia, now ZIMBABWE). Other prominent themes include the individual's search for wholeness, FEMINISM, the battle of the sexes and, later, mental collapse and extrasensory perception. She most often uses a solitary, strong woman pushed to the breaking point as her protagonist. Among her many novels are *The Golden Notebook* (1962), considered one of her best, the five-volume series *Children of Violence* (1952–69) and *Memoirs of a Survivor*

(1974). She later embarked on a series of space-age fantasy books, such as *The Sirian Experiments* (1981), and was a guest of honor at the 1987 World Science Fiction Convention.

In 1995 Lessing published the first volume of her autobiography, *Under My Skin,* which narrated her life from childhood until 1949; the second volume, *Walking in the Shade,* was released in 1997. The book subsequently received the James Tait Black Prize for best biography. In 1996 Lessing published her first new novel in seven years, *Love Again,* which was followed by *Mara and Dann* (1999), *Ben, in the World* (2000), and *The Sweetest Dream* (2002). In 2001 she received Spain's Prince of Asturias Prize in Literature (2001).

**Lester, Richard** (*1932–* ) A controversial film director in the 1960s and '70s, Lester was born in Philadelphia, where he quickly advanced to director of a local television station. In the early 1950s he traveled throughout Europe and struggled to earn a living through writing and tuning pianos. Near starvation in 1955, Lester moved to England, where he met comedians Peter SELLERS and Spike MILLIGAN. Lester directed these two "Goons" in various shorts for British television, where he developed a reputation for broad comedy and satire. In 1964 and 1965 Lester's brand of humor clicked in two hilarious, off-the-cuff films featuring the BEATLES: *A Hard Day's Night* and *Help!* For the remainder of the decade Lester focused his creative energy on films with biting social satire, political commentary and black humor, such as *How I Won the War* (1967), *Petulia* (1968) and *The Bed-Sitting Room* (1969). Refusing to cater to studio demands, Lester struggled to find success in the early 1970s. But from the mid-1970s onward he returned to prominence with a series of entertaining adventure films, including *The Three Musketeers* (1974), *The Four Musketeers* (1975), *Robin and Marian* (1976), *Cuba* (1979) and *Superman II* (1980).

**Letelier, Orlando** (*1932–1976*) Chilean official. Letelier had been CHILE's ambassador to the U.S. and was serving as President Salvador ALLENDE's defense minister when Allende was overthrown in a military coup in September 1973. Letelier was arrested at the time and, after his release in 1974, was exiled. He moved to the U.S., where he was employed by the Institute for Policy Studies, a Washington, D.C., research group. Letelier had become outspoken in his criticism of the Chilean junta's civil rights violations under General Augusto PINOCHET. On September 10 Letelier's Chilean citizenship was revoked. On September 21 Letelier was killed when a bomb exploded under his car in Washington. In 1980 the Federal District Court in Washington concluded that members of DINA, the Chilean national intelligence agency, had assassinated Letelier; in 1978 former DINA agent Michael Towley had confessed to planting the bomb, and, in 1987, another former DINA agent, Armando Fernández, also admitted involvement in the crime.

**Letterman, David** *(1947– )* American comedian and television talk-show host. Born in Indianapolis, Indiana, Letterman graduated from Ball State University in 1978 and worked as a weatherman for a local television station (1970–74). In 1975 Letterman moved to Los Angeles with the ambition of becoming the next Johnny Carson, then the king of late-night television.

In 1982 NBC tapped him to headline *Late Night with David Letterman. Late Night* found a loyal audience

*Comedian and talk-show host David Letterman* (PHOTOFEST)

among young professionals and college students, who appreciated Letterman's off-beat sense of humor and his aggressive interview technique with media figures.

In May of 1993 Letterman ended his stay with NBC and *Late Night* and moved to CBS to start production in September. After its opening night Letterman's show, *The Late Show with David Letterman,* beat Jay LENO both in the ratings and in critics' reviews of both programs. It was not until late 1995 that Leno caught up with Letterman and began several consecutive years of higher ratings for the *Tonight Show.*

**Lévesque, René** *(1922–1987)* Canadian politician. Lévesque entered politics as a Liberal with his 1960 election to the Quebec Legislative Assembly. He held a number of ministerial posts before being expelled from the LIBERAL PARTY in 1967 over the issue of Quebec sovereignty, which he had come to champion. He then formed the PARTI QUÉBÉCOIS. He led the party to power in the 1976 election when he was elected prime minister of the province. In 1979 he pushed through a law, fiercely opposed by Prime Minister Pierre TRUDEAU, that formalized the status of French as Quebec's only official language and made English-language commercial signs illegal. Lévesque resigned from the Parti Québécois in 1985, ending his political career.

**Levi, Carlo** *(1902–1975)* Italian novelist, essayist and painter. Levi earned a medical degree before turning to writing as a career. In the 1930s, he was exiled by the fascist regime of MUSSOLINI—which was displeased at his outspoken left-wing politics—to an isolated Italian village. This experience inspired Levi to write the novel *Christ Stopped At Eboli* (1945), a sensitive portrayal of life in an impoverished Italian village, which became an international best seller. As a result, Levi became a major figure in the neorealism movement in postwar Italian literature. His subsequent novels included *The Watch* (1950) and *The Linden Trees* (1959). From 1963 to 1972 Levi served in the Italian Senate.

**Levi, Primo** *(1919–1987)* Italian Jewish author. Levi's autobiographical writings reflected his experiences as a survivor of the HOLOCAUST. During

WORLD WAR II he served in the Italian RESISTANCE but was arrested and deported to AUSCHWITZ in 1943. His experiences there gave rise to his 1947 memoir, *If This Is a Man,* which became an international best seller. Levi pursued his literary vocation while working as a chemist at a paint factory in Turin for 30 years. *The Periodic Table* (1975), one of his most highly regarded works, fused his two callings, using the analogy of the chemical elements to analyze people and events. Levi committed suicide.

**Levine, James** *(1943– )* American conductor. Levine is best known as the principal conductor (since 1972) and musical director (since 1976) of the New York Metropolitan Opera. With George SZELL as his mentor, he became an apprentice conductor, then assistant conductor (1964–70) of the Cleveland Orchestra. In 1971 he made his Met debut conducting *Tosca.* He has appeared regularly at the SALZBURG FESTIVAL (since 1975) and has been a guest conductor with orchestras worldwide. Specializing in the Italian opera repertory, Levine has made many records of operas and symphonies. Throughout the 1990s Levine conducted the Metropolitan Opera on its international tours through Spain, Japan and Germany, such as the 1994 tour commemorating the opera's 120th anniversary. He received numerous awards in the U.S. and Europe for his musical contributions. In 1999 he became chief conductor of the Munich Philharmonic Orchestra, and in 2001 was chosen to succeed Seiji OZAWA as music director of the Boston Symphony Orchestra. He took up his new post in Boston in 2004.

**Levison, Stanley** *(1912–1979)* American lawyer, businessman and Jewish civic leader who played a prominent role behind the scenes in the CIVIL RIGHTS MOVEMENT of the 1960s. Levison was a key adviser to the Rev. Dr. Martin Luther KING Jr. and influenced the financial policies, strategy and tactics used by King and the SOUTHERN CHRISTIAN LEADERSHIP CONFERENCE.

**Levi Strauss** American firm specializing in the production of utilitarian work pants, the famous "Levi's" that have become accepted as fashion items in modern times. The original Levi Strauss began his business in San Francisco during the 1850s' gold rush making tents for prospectors. In the 1960s Levi's became a popular form of informal dress and acquired a status that made the brand name important in the world of fashionable apparel.

**Lévi-Strauss, Claude** (*1908–* ) French anthropologist, the founder of STRUCTURALISM. Born in Brussels, Belgium, Lévi-Strauss studied law and philosophy at the University of Paris (1927–32). He taught sociology at the University of São Paulo from 1935 to 1937, at which time he began anthropological field work in Brazil, researches wich continued in 1938–39. He taught at the New School for Social Research, New York, from 1941 to 1945 and was France's cultural attaché to the U.S. from 1946 to 1947. Director of the Ecole Pratique des Hautes Etudes, Paris, from 1950, he was elected to the chair of anthropology at the Collège de France in 1959. He was honored with election to the Academie Française in 1973. In formulating structuralism, he sought to analyze myths and kinship systems through a system of complicated mathematical and linguistic-based methods. The underlying structures thus discovered suggest, he posits, universal patterns of cultural behavior and uniform attributes of human logic. His methods and conclusions have been extremely influential, not only in anthropology, but in sociology, linguistics and literary criticism as well. Among his many works are *Elementary Structures of Kinship* (1949, tr. 1969), *Structural Anthropology* (1958, tr. 1963 and 1976), *Totemism* (1962, tr. 1963) and *Mythologies* (1964–71, tr. 1970–79).

**Levy, Marv** (*1928–* ) National Football League (NFL) head coach. After serving as assistant coach at Coe College and the University of New Mexico, he became the head coach at New Mexico in 1958. He later served as head coach by the University of California (1960–64) and the College of William and Mary (1964–68).

In 1969 Levy entered the National Football League (NFL) as the special teams' coach for the Philadelphia Eagles, a position he later held with the Los Angeles Rams and the Washington Redskins. In 1973 he left the NFL for the Canadian Football League (CFL), where in five seasons he guided the Montreal Alouettes to two league championships (1974 and 1977). After four seasons as head coach of the NFL Kansas City Chiefs, Levy worked as a color commentator for telecasts of college and NFL football games. In 1986 he was hired as the head coach of the Buffalo Bills, an NFL team. In 12 seasons with the Bills, Levy compiled a 112-70 regular season record, and an 11-8 postseason record. He helped lead the Bills to four straight appearances in the NFL championship game, the Super Bowl (1990–93), but never won the championship game before his retirement in 1997. Levy was inducted in 2001 into the Pro Football Hall of Fame in Canton, Ohio.

**Lewin, Ronald** (*1914–1984*) British military historian. Critically acclaimed, Lewin was known for his books analyzing the leadership of Winston CHURCHILL and the strategies of field marshals Erwin ROMMEL of Germany and Bernard MONTGOMERY of Britain. Lewin served as chief of the BRITISH BROADCASTING CORPORATION's domestic radio service from 1957 to 1965. His most popular book was *Ultra Goes to War,* an account of Allied efforts to decode German secret messages during WORLD WAR II. (See also ENIGMA.)

**Lewis, Alun** (*1915–1944*) British poet. Lewis was born in Alberdare, a Welsh mining village, and educated at Aberystwyth University College and Manchester University. Lewis returned to Wales and taught for two years before deciding to enlist in 1940. His first volume of poetry, *Raider's Dawn,* was published in 1942. His first book of short stories, *The Last Inspection,* (1943), dealt with the tedium and drabness in the lives of soldiers in England waiting for assignment, themes which resurfaced in his most famous poem, "All Day It Has Rained." Lewis was posted to Burma in 1942, where he was killed in 1944. His lyrical poetry explores the themes of death and the fundamental isolation of the soldier and his resulting feelings of futility. Lewis's poetry shows the influence of Edward THOMAS. Other works include *Ha! Ha! Among the Trumpets* (1945), poetry; *In the Green Tree* (1948), a collection of letters and poetry; and *Selected Poetry and Prose* (1966), with an introduction by Ian Hamilton.

**Lewis, Carl (Frederick Carlton)** (*1961–* ) American track and field star. Both of Lewis's parents were track stars, and he was already a standout by high school. Like so many American athletes, politics forced him onto the sidelines for the 1980 OLYMPIC GAMES. A winner of innumerable NCAA titles, he reached the world stage in 1983 in Helsinki, winning World Championship gold medals in the 100-meter dash, long jump and as part of a 400-meter relay team. The 1984 Olympics saw him win four gold medals in the 100-meter dash, 200-meter dash, 400-meter relay and the long jump. Lewis won another gold medal for the 100-meter dash in 1988, two gold medals at the 1992 Olympics for the 4-x-100-meter relay and the long jump, and a gold medal for the long jump in 1996.

**Lewis, C(live) S(taples)** (*1898–1963*) British literary critic, scholar and author. Lewis was a fellow of Magdalene College, Oxford, and later a professor of medieval and Renaissance English at Cambridge. An eminent scholar, Lewis has written distinguished works of criticism including *The Allegory of Love* (1936), *English Literature in the Sixteenth Century* (1954) and *An Experiment in Criticism* (1961). Outside of literary circles, he is best known for his popular fiction, fantasy and science fiction novels, such as *Out of the Silent Planet* (1938), which shows the influence of J. R. R. TOLKIEN; *The Screwtape Letters* (1940) and *The Lion, The Witch and the Wardrobe* (1950), which is the first of a series of children's books known as the *Chronicles of Narnia.* Lewis's writing reflects his abiding Christianity. and explores moral dilemma in that context. He has also written *Surprised by Joy* (1955), an autobiography emphasizing his religious life.

**Lewis, Jerry (Joseph Levitch)** (*1926–* ) American comedic actor and film director. Lewis, who was a leading HOLLYWOOD box office draw in the 1950s and 1960s, is best known for his cinematic slapstick style that combines physically distorted movements with psychological naivete verging on idiocy. To certain European film critics—most notably in France—he is one of the great clowns of the cinema. To most American critics, Lewis seems unduly obvious and obnoxious. Lewis first achieved film stardom in 1949 after forming a comedy team with straight man/crooner Dean Martin. Their first film, *My Friend Irma* (1949), was followed by 15 more until Martin left in a highly publicized breakup in 1956. Lewis has since pursued a solo career in films, television and nightclubs. His most highly regarded films, which he wrote and directed, are *The Ladies' Man* (1961), *The Nutty Professor* (1963) and *The Patsy* (1964). In recent decades, Lewis has become best known for his Labor Day telethons raising money for muscular dystrophy research.

**Lewis, Jerry Lee** *(1935–  )* American rock-and-roll vocalist, pianist and composer. Lewis is one of the founding fathers of the ROCK AND ROLL sound that burst into prominence in the U.S. in the mid-1950s. Lewis is especially well known for a flamboyant performing style that features his trademark pumping barrelhouse piano. Born in Louisiana, Lewis was exposed to both black blues and gospel and white country music as a youth. In 1956 he was signed to a contract by Sam Phillips of Sun Records in Memphis, Tennessee. Lewis enjoyed two massive hits in 1957—*Great Balls of Fire* and *Whole Lotta Shakin' Goin' On*. Lewis followed these up with *Breathless* (1958) and *High School Confidential* (1959), but the adverse publicity that stemmed from his marriage to a 13-year-old cousin seriously hampered his climb to stardom. In the 1960s and after, recording for several record labels, Lewis made a comeback as a country and western performer. He remained a favorite among both rock and country audiences. The film *Great Balls of Fire* (1989)—made with Lewis's cooperation—portrays his early success and subsequent downfall in the 1950s. In 1995 Lewis and Bruce Springsteen both performed in a concert opening the Rock and Roll Hall of Fame in Cleveland, Ohio.

**Lewis, John L(lewellyn)** *(1880–1969)* American labor leader, president of the United Mine Workers of America (1920–60). Although highly controversial, Lewis was perhaps the single most important figure in the American labor movement in the 20th century. Born to Welsh immigrant parents in a coal-mining community in Iowa, he quit school after the seventh grade and entered the mines at age 15. A man of commanding presence with a talent for oratory and a fondness for Shakespeare, Lewis considered going on the stage before deciding to pursue a career in the labor movement. In 1909 he moved to the coal fields of central Illinois, where he began to rise rapidly in the local hierarchy of the United Mine Workers of America (UMW). In 1911 he became a field representative of the American Federation of Labor (AFL), a job that enabled him to travel widely through the minefields and to build strong personal support within the UMW. As a result, he became UMW vice president in 1917, acting president in 1919 and president of the UMW—the largest union in the AFL—the next year.

In the years following WORLD WAR I, Lewis emerged as a dynamic but ambiguous figure on the national labor scene. A champion of industrial unionism, he headed an unsuccessful challenge to the conservative leadership of AFL president Samuel GOMPERS in 1921. At the same time, Lewis exemplified a tough, pragmatic business unionism. A Republican and a strong believer in free enterprise capitalism, he crushed the strong radical faction opposed to his leadership. With the advent of the NEW DEAL, Lewis took advantage of the NATIONAL INDUSTRIAL RECOVERY ACT (1933) to launch a massive organizing drive in the coalfields, recruiting 300,000 miners to the UMW in two months. Unsuccessful in persuading the AFL to open its membership to unskilled and semi-skilled workers, Lewis brought together the leaders of 10 other unions under the Committee for Industrial Organization (CIO) in 1935. The CIO began a sweeping organizing campaign in basic industries. After conflicts with AFL craft unions, it became the independent Congress of Industrial Organizations in 1936.

As head of both the UMW and the CIO, Lewis lent vital support to President Franklin D. ROOSEVELT's 1936 reelection campaign. When WORLD WAR II began in Europe, Lewis opposed U.S. intervention and endorsed Wendell WILLKIE for president in 1940. Lewis resigned from the CIO presidency when Roosevelt won a third term. Following the Japanese attack on PEARL HARBOR, Lewis announced his support for the American war effort and joined other leaders in a no-strike pledge for the duration of the conflict. However, in 1943 he concluded that the government had taken advantage of the no-strike agreement to impose an unfair wage formula on workers, and he led a series of epic strikes in defiance of Roosevelt's threat to use federal troops to keep the mines in operation. Vilified by the press, Lewis nonetheless won a 35-hour work week and other benefits for UMW members.

After the war, Lewis was at odds with President TRUMAN's labor policies. Beginning in April 1946, after talks between the UMW and mineowners broke down, Lewis led a national strike. Within a month coal shortages forced a national brownout, to save fuel, and cutbacks in auto and steel production; the government seized control of the mines. After a series of proposals and countermoves, the government found Lewis and the union guilty of civil and criminal contempt and imposed the heaviest fine in American history up to that time. Lewis's bitter feud with Truman continued. During the EISENHOWER administration (1953–61) Lewis pursued cooperation rather than conflict with the coal industry. He never again seriously used the threat of a strike. Rather, he encouraged the largest mineowners to introduce mechanization and close inefficient mines, even at the expense of massive miner unemployment. Lewis resigned the leadership of the UMW in 1960 and became president emeritus.

**Lewis, Richard** *(1914–1990)* British tenor. He was one of the first British singers to achieve worldwide fame in opera and concert performances. He appeared as Troilus in the world premier of William WALTON's *Troilus and Cressida* (1955) and also sang leading roles in the first performances of *Midsummer Marriage* and *King Priam* by Michael TIPPETT.

**Lewis, Sinclair** *(1884–1951)* American author. He began his career as a newspaper reporter and later worked for the Associated Press. His first major work, *Main Street,* was published in 1920, and *Babbitt* appeared two years later. In 1926 he refused to accept the PULITZER PRIZE for his *Arrowsmith.* Residents of his hometown resented his depiction of small-town life, but accepted him after he won the NOBEL PRIZE for literature in 1930. His most notable later work was *It Can't Happen Here* (1935). His total output includes 22 novels and three plays.

**Lewis, Wyndham** *(1884–1957)* British writer and painter. Lewis, as both novelist and critic, was one of the key figures in the emergence of the modernist school of literature, which also included Lewis's friends T. S. ELIOT, James JOYCE and Ezra POUND. Lewis was also an important painter and the central theorist behind Vorticism, a school of British painting that flourished around the time of World War I. Lewis first gained attention as a writer in 1909 when his short stories were published in *The English Review,* an influential quarterly edited by Ford Maddox FORD. In the 1910s, Lewis edited *Blast,* which became the leading avant-garde journal of its time in Britain. His novels include *Tarr* (1918), *The Childermass* (1928), *The Apes of God* (1930), *The Vulgar Streak* (1941) and *Self-Condemned* (1954). As a critic, his most important works are *Time and Western Man* (1927), *Filibusters in Barbary* (1932) and *Men without Art* (1914). Lewis authored several autobiographical volumes including *Blasting and Bombardiering* (1937).

**Ley, Willy** *(1906–1969)* German-American engineer and rocket pioneer. Born in Berlin, Ley studied at the University of Berlin and was on his way to becoming a zoologist when he chanced upon an early book on rocketry. From that moment the direction of his life was decided. One of the founders of the German Rocket Society he was also a writer whose popular books on rocketry captured the public's imagination. Although it was

Ley who introduced Werner von BRAUN into the German Rocket Society, his conscience would not permit him to follow von Braun and others in their collaboration with the Nazis after Adolf HITLER came to power. After coming to the United States in 1935, he became a naturalized citizen in 1944. Although Ley had tremendous influence among science fiction writers and space buffs in the U.S., it was von Braun, bringing to the United States his experience with the V-2 rocket used by the Nazis, who became America's hope for a space future. Although he had fought for it and dreamed about it all of his life, Ley died three weeks before Neil ARMSTRONG and Edwin "Buzz" ALDRIN made their historic touchdown on the moon.

**Leyte Gulf, Battle of the** *(October 23–26, 1944)* The decisive naval battle of WORLD WAR II IN THE PACIFIC. In a series of engagements U.S. naval forces, with air support, destroyed the Japanese fleet that had attempted to prevent the Allied landings on Leyte in the PHILIPPINES. The Japanese lost three battleships, four aircraft carriers, 10 cruisers, nine destroyers and one submarine; the American naval losses were much lighter. Although fighting continued in the Pacific for another nine months, the U.S. victory at the Leyte Gulf gave the U.S. complete sea supremacy in the Pacific.

*Douglas MacArthur in the Philippines, 1944* (LIBRARY OF CONGRESS, PRINTS AND PHOTOGRAPHS DIVISION)

**Lhevinne, Josef and Rosina** Josef (1874–1944) and Rosina (1880–1976) Lhevinne were Russian-born pianists and music teachers. Both trained in piano in their native Russia—Josef earning a gold medal from the Moscow Conservatory in 1892 and Rosina winning a gold medal at the Kiev Conservatory in 1898. Josef also won the prestigious Anton Rubinstein piano competition in 1895. The two met when Josef was hired to give piano lessons to the young Rosina. They married in 1898. In subsequent decades, Josef became an internationally acclaimed piano soloist, while Josef and Rosina performed piano duets that established them as uniquely accomplished musical collaborators. In the 1910s the couple lived in Berlin, but in 1919 they moved to the U.S. and became founding members of the faculty of the Juilliard School of Music in New York City. After Josef's death, Rosina continued to teach at Juilliard to the end of her life. Among her most famous pupils was pianist Van CLIBURN.

**Li, Choh Hao** *(1913–1987)* Chinese-born biochemist. Li spent more than 50 years in the University of California system. In 1971 while at the University of California at San Francisco, he synthesized the human pituitary growth hormone, which he had discovered in the 1950s. In 1978 he discovered beta-endorphin, a powerful pain-killing substance produced in the brain. He was director of the laboratory of endocrinology at UCSF from 1983 until his death.

**Liaquat, Ali Khan** *(1896–1951)* First prime minister of PAKISTAN (1947–51). Liaquat was a leading member of the Muslim League in the 1920s and 1930s, working closely with Mohammad Ali JINNAH. After the partition of India and the creation of Pakistan in 1947, he became prime minister. Following Jinnah's death, he was the most powerful man in the new state. Criticized over his attempts to reduce tension with India and his refusal to declare Pakistan an Islamic state, he was assassinated by a fanatic in 1951.

**Libby, Willard F(rank)** *(1908–1980)* American chemist. Libby obtained his Ph.D. in chemistry from the

University of California at Berkeley (1933). During World War II he participated in the MANHATTAN PROJECT that developed the ATOMIC BOMB. He worked at Columbia University under Harold UREY on the gaseous-diffusion method of separating uranium isotopes. Shortly after the war, at the University of Chicago, Libby discovered that radioactive carbon decayed at a predictable rate. Since all living organisms naturally absorb minute traces of this carbon (carbon-14), this meant that by measuring this carbon in dead organic archaeological and geological remains, the age of these remains could be determined. This technique, known as radiocarbon dating or **carbon-14 dating**, had immense implications for extending knowledge about the past and helped revolutionize archaeology, anthropology, and geology. For his role in developing radiocarbon dating, Libby was awarded the 1960 NOBEL PRIZE for chemistry. In addition to his other work, Libby also served on the Atomic Energy Commission (AEC) (1954–59).

**Libedinsky, Yuri Nikolayevich** (*1898–1959*) Soviet author, one of the founders of the proletarian "October Group" in 1922. His short novel *A Week* (1922) won Libedinsky the party's favor, in spite of his nonproletarian origins. His next novel, *Tomorrow* (1923), implied that the Soviet Union should be rescued from the NEW ECONOMIC POLICY and was thus obviously less successful. Something of a political speculator, in his play *Heights* Libedinsky emphasized LENIN's warning that the party should not depend on officials trained by the czarist regime. He was expelled from the party in 1933 as a result of his novel *Birth of a Hero* (1930) but was later reinstated.

**Liberace (Wladziu Valentino Liberace)** (*1919–1987*) American pianist and entertainer. Liberace was known for his flamboyant showmanship and lavish costumes. Performing show tunes and popular arrangements of classical pieces, he became U.S. television's first matinee idol. In the 1950s his syndicated show was carried by a record number of stations. During this period he was said to have been the world's highest-paid entertainer, earning up to $400,000 a week in Las

Vegas night clubs. He continued performing in Las Vegas after his show went off the air; he also toured and made occasional TV appearances. His death was believed to have been from complications resulting from AIDS.

**liberalism** Philosophical and political doctrine that emphasizes individual freedom and stresses the goodness and rationality of human beings. In broad terms, liberalism is contrasted to CONSERVATISM. Supporting change in the status quo, liberalism traditionally upholds the idea of progress. In the U.S., political liberalism is generally associated with the DEMOCRATIC PARTY, although many Republicans have embraced the main tenets of liberalism, while there have also been conservative Democrats. Liberalism in the modern era has largely centered on government as provider of individual freedom, and has asked the state to prevent the oppression of the individual and to provide decent conditions for all members of society. By supporting a government that intervenes in the national economy, liberals seek to provide for the economic and social welfare of the populace. This doctrine was instrumental in the creation of the WELFARE STATE in early 20th-century Europe and in providing an impetus for welfare state reforms in the U.S. The central figure in 20th-century American liberalism was undoubtedly President Franklin D. ROOSEVELT. His NEW DEAL programs, which encompassed the minimum wage, social security, welfare programs and progressive taxation, are all reflective of liberal thinking and have all become staples of the American social system. The liberal agenda in the last quarter of the 20th century included racial and sexual equality, public education and equitable health care. While some liberals have embraced the principles of socialism, the degradation of individual rights that has been a feature of COMMUNISM in the 20th century makes many liberals extremely antagonistic to the principles and practice of Marxism.

**Liberal Party (Australia)** Australian political party established in 1945. The Liberal Party was formed primarily by Sir Robert MENZIES, who became its first leader. He brought the non-Labour members of Parliament to-

gether and formed a mass organization to sustain them. The Liberal Party joined the coalition government formed by the Nationalist and Country parties, and Menzies was prime minister from 1949 until 1966. The coalition remained in power until 1972. It was returned under Prime Minister Malcolm FRASER in 1975 following the controversial administration of Gough WHITLAM but was defeated in 1983.

**Liberal Party (Canada)** One of CANADA's two major political parties. The Liberal Party was formed when Canada gained dominion status in 1867. The party adopted free trade and anticolonial policies. In English-speaking Canada the party's supporters included anticonservative, free-trade Ontario English (Clear Grits) and anglophone farmers. In French Quebec the party was largely based on anticlericalism. The party has a tradition of alternating Anglophone and Francophone leaders, many of whom became prime ministers. Twentieth-century Liberal prime ministers include Sir Wilfred LAURIER (1896–1911), William Lyon Mackenzie KING (1921–30, 1935–48), Louis ST. LAURENT (1948–57), Lester PEARSON (1963–68) and Pierre Elliot TRUDEAU (1968–79, 1980–84). Although Laurier and King actively encouraged American investment, Trudeau sought a more independent Canada both economically and politically. In the second half of the century the party's power base was in central Canada, primarily Ontario. Led by Prime Ministers JEAN CHRÉTIEN (1993–2003) and Paul Martin (2003–   ), the Liberal Party returned to power in the 1990s.

**Liberal Party (New Zealand)** Former New Zealand political party. The New Zealand Liberal Party was dominant at the beginning of the 20th century under the leadership of Prime Minister Richard Seddon. He left office in 1906, but the Liberals retained power until 1911. The Liberal Party took part in the wartime coalition government between 1915 and 1919 but went into decline after the war. Its leader, Sir Joseph Ward, restyled the party as the United Party in an effort to broaden its support. He was prime minister between 1928 and 1930. In 1935 the United Party joined with the

Reform and Democratic Parties to form the NATIONAL PARTY.

**Liberal Party (United Kingdom) (Liberal Democratic Party from 1988)** British political party established in 1877, known as the **Liberal Democratic Party** after 1988. Liberal policies occupy the moderate ground between the LABOUR and CONSERVATIVE parties. The Liberal Democratic Party advocates governmental decentralization, proportional representation in the House of Commons, reform of the House of Lords, and a mixed economy of nationalized industries and private enterprise. It also supports British membership in the EU and NATO. The Liberal Party entered the 20th century as one of the two major British political parties, but began to decline early in the century due to its division on the question of Irish HOME RULE and to the advent of the Labour Party. Liberals came to power in 1906 under the leadership of Sir Henry CAMPBELL-BANNERMAN, whose government included David LLOYD GEORGE and Herbert ASQUITH, who succeeded him in 1908. The party was split by disputes between Lloyd George and Asquith during World War I, and its radical elements were absorbed by the Labour Party. The Liberal Party continued to dwindle between the wars, and has not held office since the National Coalition of World War II. Although it supported the minority Labour government in 1977 and 1978 (the so-called Lib-Lab Pact), Liberals held no cabinet seats in that government. In 1981 the Liberals formed an alliance with the new SOCIAL DEMOCRATIC PARTY, and they ran joint candidates in the 1983 general elections. Despite substantial support in the opinion polls, the Liberals failed to make significant inroads in the general elections. In 1988 the two parties merged to form the Liberal Democratic Party, with Paddy Ashdown as its leader. The Liberal Democrats improved their political position throughout the 1990s, obtaining 46 seats in Parliament in 1997 and increasing their presence in local governments throughout Great Britain.

**Liberation Theology** The radical position initiated by many Catholic priests against oppressive regimes, especially in Latin American. It evolved in the 1960s and was expounded during the 1970s and 1980s despite the disapproval of the Vatican.

**Liberia (Republic of Liberia)** Liberia is located on the west coast of Africa and covers an area of 42,988 square miles. The Republic of Liberia was established

### LIBERIA

|  |  |
|---|---|
| 1926 | Firestone Rubber Company begins operations in Liberia under the terms of a loan it made to the country; Liberian finances are brought under U.S. supervision. |
| 1944 | William Tubman inaugurated president; promotes foreign investment and local participation in government. |
| 1947 | Universal suffrage enacted. |
| 1952 | Firestone loan paid off 15 years before maturity. |
| 1971 | Tubman dies; William Tolbert ascends to the presidency. |
| 1980 | (April 12) Tolbert assassinated during coup led by Master Sergeant Samuel K. Doe; Doe suspends constitution and parliament and executes 13 leading officials of the former regime. |
| 1985 | (Oct. 15) Under allegations of election fraud Doe is elected president as head of the National Democratic Party of Liberia. |
| 1988 | (Oct. 10) William Kpolleh, leader of the Liberian Action Party, is imprisoned for plotting to overthrow the government. |
| 1990 | (July 30) Government troops massacre 300 to 600 men, women and children who have taken refuge in a Lutheran church in Monrovia; (Sept. 10) Doe is killed after being captured by rebel forces. |
| 1991 | A cease-fire is signed. |
| 1993 | A peace agreement is signed in Geneva, Switzerland. |
| 1994 | Groups excluded from transitional government reject peace agreement and resume violence. |
| 1997 | Charles Taylor is elected president. |
| 2001 | UN Security Council accuses Taylor of trading weapons for diamonds from rebels in Sierra Leone and reimposes embargo on weapons. |
| 2003 | Rebels battle for control of Monrovia; Nigerian peacekeepers arrive. Charles Taylor goes into exile and U.S. troops arrive (August) and depart (September–October). Interim government and rebels sign peace agreement. |
| 2004 | Riots in Monrovia blamed on former combatants. |
| 2005 | First elections held since end of civil war. Ellen Johnson-Sirleaf is elected president. |

Liberia

in 1847 by freed American slaves who had returned to Africa. Under President William Tubman (1944–71) foreign investment and citizen involvement in government were encouraged. His successor William R. Tolbert continued these policies but encountered protests when he instituted economic changes, resulting in riots that were violently suppressed (1979). In 1980 Tolbert was assassinated and army sergeant Samuel K. Doe assumed power, gaining recognition and support from the U.S. A new constitution providing for universal adult suffrage without the qualification of property ownership was approved in 1984. Doe, who was elected president in 1985, survived several coup attempts before he was confronted with a bloody armed rebellion in northern Liberia (1990). The rebellion resulted in the deaths of partisans on both sides of the confrontation, and of many civilian deaths at the hands of both government and rebel forces. The situation degenerated into anarchy despite the attempts of neighboring African nations to intervene

in the dispute. Doe himself was killed as the rebels moved into the capital. Afterward, tensions continued between two rival rebel factions. There was a mass migration of Liberians into GUINEA and CÔTE D'IVOIRE. Although CHARLES TAYLOR emerged as the strongest force in Liberia, winning the 1997 presidential election, a popular uprising by his opponents led to his resignation in 2003. In 2005 Ellen Johnson-Sirleaf was elected president of Liberia, making her the first elected female president of an African country.

**Libya (Socialist People's Libyan Arab Jamahiriya)** Libya, located on the Mediterranean coast of north Africa, covers an area of 679,182 square miles. Part of the OTTOMAN EMPIRE since the 17th century, Libya was invaded by ITALY in 1911. The Turkish sultan relinquished all rights to the country in the 1912 peace settlement, and Italy secured its position through the strong-arm tactics of Governor Giuseppe Volpi (1921–32) and colonization (1938–39). The British cap-

tured the capital of Tripoli during WORLD WAR II (1945). The victorious Allies permitted the Libyans to form an independent country, the United Kingdom of Libya, under King Idris in 1951. In 1969 a military coup led by Colonel Muammer el-QADDAFI deposed the king and set up a military regime with Qaddafi as head. He closed Western military bases (allowed by Idris since 1952) and espoused Arab nationalism. The new constitution of 1977 established the Socialist People's Libyan Arab Jamahiriya. During the 1980s Qaddafi was condemned for his assassination campaign against Libyan exiles and his promotion of worldwide terrorism. Tensions between Libya and the U.S. over Libyan support of terrorism culminated in the U.S. bombing of Tripoli and Benghazi in 1986. Despite continued hostility to U.S. foreign policy throughout the 1990s, such as protesting the Oslo Accords and the WYE RIVER MEMORANDUM, Libya and the U.S. improved their relationship in 2003 when Libya obtained an end to UN sanctions after pledging to abandon its campaign to develop weapons of mass destruction.

**Libya Raid** *(April 14, 1986)* On April 4, 1986, a U.S. serviceman was killed in a bomb explosion in a West Berlin discotheque. The attack was believed to have been carried out by Libyan-trained terrorists. In retaliation, U.S. President REAGAN ordered a military strike against suspected terrorist bases in Libya. U.S. F-111 bombers based in Britain carried out the mission. The raid was highly popular in the U.S., but international opinion was divided.

**Lichine, Alexis** *(1913–1989)* Russian-born wine expert. An internationally recognized authority, Lichine specialized in promoting French wines in the U.S. In 1951 he purchased the Château Prieure-Cantenac winery near Bordeaux, France, which he renamed the Chateau Prieure-Lichine. He also founded Alexis Lichine & Co., a wine shipping firm that he later sold to the British brewer Bass. His books *The Wines of France* (1951; later retitled *Alexis Lichine's Guide to the Wines and Vineyards of France*) and the *Encyclopedia of Wines and Spirits*

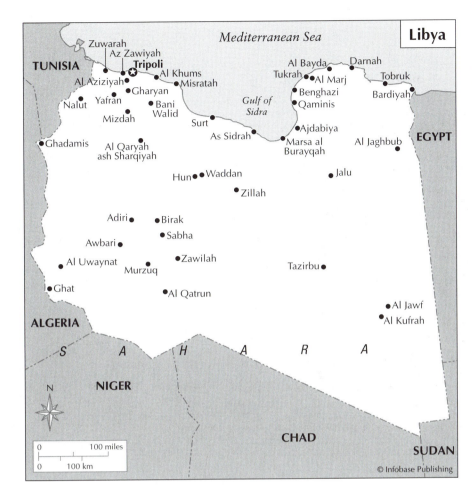

(1967) were considered landmark reference books.

## Lie, Trygve (1896–1968) Norwegian statesman, secretary-general of the UNITED NATIONS (1946–53). A Social Democrat, Lie served in every Norwegian government from 1935 to 1946. Elected the first secretary-general of the UN, he was an early but unsuccessful advocate of the admission of communist CHINA to the UN. At the outbreak of the KOREAN WAR (1950) he took the initiative in organizing UN forces to assist SOUTH KOREA in checking aggression by NORTH KOREA. He resigned in 1953 and later reentered Norwegian politics.

## Lieb, Fred (1888–1980) American sportswriter and baseball historian. Lieb started his career in journalism in 1911. Active for nearly 70 years, he wrote more than a dozen books on baseball and covered some 8,000 major league games. It was Lieb who called Yankee Stadium "the house that Ruth built" (see Babe RUTH). He was the first sportswriter to be inducted into the Baseball Hall of Fame.

## Lieberman, Joseph (1942–  ) U.S. senator (1970–  ) and Democratic vice presidential candidate (2000). Born in Stamford, Connecticut, Lieberman attended Yale University where he received his B.A. in 1964 and his law degree in 1967.

In 1988 Lieberman was elected to the U.S. Senate and was reelected in 1994, 2000, and 2006 (as an independent). Lieberman supported the 1991 Persian Gulf War launched by President George H. W. BUSH. In 1995 Lieberman began a three-year term as chairman of the Democratic Leadership Council, an organization charged with developing the national platform of the Democratic Party. In 1999, during President Clinton's Senate trial, Lieberman rebuked Clinton for his affair with White House intern Monica Lewinsky, but did not vote to convict Clinton. In 2000 Lieberman was selected by Democratic presidential candidate Al GORE as his running mate, the first Jewish vice presidential candidate in American history. The Gore-Lieberman ticket lost the campaign to Republicans George W. BUSH and Dick CHENEY (see also FLORIDA BALLOT CONTROVERSY (2000)). Following his defeat, Lieberman resumed his post in the Senate and supported the initial foreign policy actions of the second Bush administration. In 2002 Lieberman had been a candidate for the Democratic presidential nomination but left the race in February 2004 after losing the Delaware primary.

## Liebes, Dorothy (1899–1972) Leading American designer of textiles, known for her typically modernist use of strong colors and unusual materials. Liebes's education was primarily academic, but in the 1930s she established a studio in San Francisco where she produced custom handweaves of simple design for designers and architects. In 1940 she became a designer for the production firm of Goodall Fabrics. As her reputation grew, she became a designer and consultant to a number of larger firms, including Sears Roebuck and DuPont. For many years she was the only textile designer with national public recognition.

## Liechtenstein Liechtenstein is an alpine principality of central Europe, tucked between Austria and Switzerland and occupying a total area of only 61.8 square miles; it is the fourth smallest country in the world. Neutral

*UN secretary-general Trygve Lie* (LIBRARY OF CONGRESS, PRINTS AND PHOTOGRAPHS DIVISION)

## LIBYA

| 1911 | Italy seizes Libya from weakened Ottoman Empire. |
| 1938–39 | 30,000 Italian peasant farmers settled in Libya under Mussolini colonization policy. |
| 1940–43 | Italian and German forces use Libya as base of operations during World War II North African campaign. |
| 1949 | Libya is granted independence following Italy's defeat in World War II. |
| 1951 | United Kingdom of Libya proclaimed under King Idris (Muhammad Idris al-Mahdi al-Senusi). |
| 1960s | Discovery of oil brings foreign investment, new wealth and social change. |
| 1969 | Coup led by Col. Muammer el-Qaddafi deposes King Idris; new Arab nationalist regime closes Western military bases, confiscates property of Jews and Italians. |
| 1980 | Libyan forces enter Chad; Qaddafi announces merger of the two countries; Libyan troops withdraw the following year. |
| 1984 | Britain breaks relations with Libya after Libyans fire on a crowd from their London embassy, killing a British policewoman. |
| 1986 | U.S. bombers raid Tripoli and Benghazi in retaliation for Libyan terrorist bombings. |
| 1989 | (January) U.S. Navy fighters shoot down two Libyan MIGs off Libyan coast; U.S. asserts that Libya is building chemical weapons factory with German assistance. |
| 1991 | Qaddafi releases international terrorist Abu Nidal from house arrest. |
| 1992 | UN imposes sanctions for Libya's refusal to extradite two Libyans suspected on bombing Pan Am flight 103 over Lockerbie, Scotland. |
| 1993 | A failed army coup leads to mass arrests. |
| 1994 | International Court of Justice rules against Libya's claim to the Aozou Strip in Chad. Libyan troops are withdrawn. |
| 1996 | United States imposes additional sanctions against companies doing business in Libya following continuing Libyan refusal to extradite Lockerbie suspects. |
| 1998 | Qaddafi announces realignment of Libyan foreign policy toward Africa and away from the Arab world. |
| 1999 | Libya surrenders two suspects in the Lockerbie bombing to Scottish court; UN Security Council suspends economic sanctions. |
| 2001 | Special Scottish court in the Netherlands finds one of two Libyans charged in the Lockerbie bombing guilty and he is sentenced to life imprisonment. The other is found not guilty. |
| 2002 | United States and Libya announce they have held talks to mend relations. |
| 2003 | Libya announces end of programs to develop weapons of mass destruction. |

during both world wars of the 20th century, in 1919 Liechtenstein entrusted its external relations (previously handled by Austria) to neutral Switzerland, with which it established currency, customs and postal unions in 1921–24. Prince Franz Josef II succeeded his grand-uncle as ruler in 1938; the principality has since been governed by a coalition of the Patriotic Union (VU) and the Progressive Citizens' Party (FBP). Early in 1939 a plurality of 95% voted for continued independence and the Swiss link. In the postwar era Liechtenstein became increasingly prosperous as a financial center, achieving one of the world's highest per capita incomes. In August 1984 Prince Franz Josef transferred his executive powers to Crown Prince Hans Adam, while remaining titular head of state. Female suffrage was narrowly approved by referendum in July 1984; in February 1986 an environmentalist Free Voters' List (FW) just failed to win the 8 percent vote-share required for representation. Prince Franz Josef died in November 1989 and was succeeded by his son Hans Adam II. In 1990 Liechtenstein was granted UN membership. In 2003 Prince Hans Adam won sweeping new powers, allowing him to veto laws and select judges.

**Lifar, Serge** *(1905–1986)* Russian-born dancer and choreographer. He was the last world-famous dancer to emerge under the tutelage of Serge DI-AGHILEV. He joined Diaghilev's BALLETS RUSSES in Paris in 1923 and two years later became the company's principal male dancer. Before that company disbanded in 1929, he created roles in a number of early ballets by George BAL-ANCHINE, most notably *The Prodigal Son* and *Apollo*. He first tried his hand as a choreographer with Igor STRAVINSKY's *Le Renard.* From 1929 to 1945 and from 1947 to 1958, he served as ballet master of the Paris Opera Ballet. He greatly enlarged that company's repertory, restored technical standards and established the company's standards with the Parisian audience. He was also a prolific author of books on dance theory and dance history.

*Life* **magazine** American periodical. Started in 1936, *Life* magazine was conceived of by publisher Henry LUCE and his wife Clare Boothe LUCE. It was to be a large-format, inexpensive—its initial price was 10 cents an issue—photographic magazine. Its staff of photographers included Margaret BOURKE-WHITE and Alfred EISENSTADT, and it became known for its excellent photography, particularly for its stirring portraits of soldiers and war-torn Europe during WORLD WAR II. At its peak of popularity in the postwar years each issue sold 8 million copies worldwide. As the availability of televised images increased, the magazine foundered and eventually folded in the early 1970s but was later revived. In 2002 the Time Magazine Group announced that it was reviving *Life* magazine, and it would produce the publication at six-week intervals.

**Likud** Alliance of various right-wing Israeli parties, which, under the leadership of Menachem BEGIN, won the gen-

eral election of 1977, displacing the Israeli Labour Party for the first time in the country's history. Yitzhak SHAMIR later headed the Likud alliance. In the 1990s the Likud returned to power under Prime Ministers Benjamin Netanyahu (1996–99) and Ariel Sharon (2000–   ). In 2005 Prime Minister Sharon announced he was leaving Likud to start a new party, named Kadima.

**Lillie, Beatrice Gladys (stage name of Constance Sylvia Munston, Lady Peel)** *(1898–1989)* Canadian-born actress and comedienne, often called "the funniest woman in the world." Lillie emigrated to England in 1910 to study music, and soon began appearing in theatrical revues. During a 50-year career she appeared in numerous plays, musicals and films in the U.S. and Britain, including *Auntie Mame, Around the World in Eighty Days, Thoroughly Modern Millie,* and *High Spirits,* a musical version of Noel COWARD's *Blithe Spirit.* Her one-woman show *An Evening with Beatrice Lillie* won her a Tony Award in 1953.

**Lima Declaration** Document of Pan-American solidarity issued in Lima, Peru, on December 26, 1938, by representatives of North and South American governments. Prompted by fascist incursions in Europe and by Japanese expansionism, it stated that a threat to the peace, security or territorial integrity of any republic in the Americas would be viewed as a threat to all of the American republics.

**Limón, José** *(1908–1972)* Mexican-American dancer, choreographer and teacher. Limón studied with Doris Humphrey and Charles Weidman and joined their company in 1930. In 1946 he formed his own dance company with Humphrey as coartistic director. The company received immediate acclaim as one of the outstanding modern dance troupes. Limón, himself, is one of the most influential and admired modern dance figures. He choreographed his most famous work, *The Moor's Pavane,* in 1949. Other important works include *The Traitor* (1954) and *Missa Brevis* (1958). In addition to world tours with his company and yearly performances at the American Dance Festival at Connecticut College, he has taught at the Juilliard School of

Music and various other colleges. After his death the José Limón Dance Company was in residence at the New York 92nd Street YM-YWHA.

**Lin Biao (Lin Piao)** *(1908–1971)* Chinese communist soldier and MAO ZEDONG's designated successor. Lin was a veteran of the LONG MARCH (1934–35), during which he commanded a communist army. He gained victories over CHIANG KAI-SHEK's KUOMINTANG (Guomindang) troops in 1948 and carried the war victoriously into central CHINA in 1949. Created a marshal in 1955 and minister of defense in 1959, he assisted Mao in organizing the CULTURAL REVOLUTION of the mid-1960s. Marshal Lin was declared Mao's designated successor by the Ninth Party Congress in 1966 but was killed in an air crash in 1971 while fleeing from China after an unsuccessful attempt to seize power in Peking.

**Lindbergh, Charles Augustus** *(1902–1974)* American aviator. Born

*Charles Lindbergh with his plane.* The Spirit of St. Louis (LIBRARY OF CONGRESS, PRINTS AND PHOTOGRAPHS DIVISION)

in Detroit, Michigan, Lindbergh was named for his father, a Republican congressman. Lindbergh attended flying school in Nebraska and bought his first plane in 1923. He entered the U.S. Army Air Corps Reserve in 1925 and also flew as an airmail pilot. In 1927, enticed by a $25,000 reward being offered for the first nonstop solo transatlantic flight, Lindbergh won backing from a group of St. Louis businessmen, who funded the construction of a specially designed airplane, *The Spirit of St. Louis*. Lindbergh took off from New York's Roosevelt Field on the morning of May 20, 1927. Thirty-three and a half hours later he landed at Le Bourget, Paris, and was welcomed by a rapturous crowd. The flight brought Lindbergh worldwide fame. Upon his return to New York he was hailed as "the lone eagle" and given the largest ticket-tape parade ever held up to that time. A long series of speaking engagements and receptions followed. In 1929 Lindbergh married Anne Morrow, the daughter of noted American banker and diplomat Dwight W. Morrow. They attempted to settle into a quiet family life, but in 1932 their infant son was kidnapped and murdered. A highly publicized investigation and trial ensued (see LINDBERGH KIDNAPPING CASE). To escape the constant attention of reporters and the curious public, the Lindberghs moved to England (1935). In 1938 the German government invited Lindbergh to inspect the Luftwaffe. Lindbergh was highly impressed by Nazi GERMANY and its military forces. (Some authorities have suggested that Lindbergh was actually an American spy, reporting to the U.S. government on the German military buildup.) Returning to the U.S. (1939), he became an outspoken advocate of American ISOLATIONISM and made public appearances for the AMERICA FIRST Committee. His view that the new world war was strictly a European affair that America ought to ignore angered many of his previous admirers. After JAPAN attacked PEARL HARBOR, however, Lindbergh supported America's role in WORLD WAR II and flew combat missions in the Pacific. He became a brigadier general in 1954 and was a consultant to the Defense Department and an adviser to Pan American Airways.

His autobiography, *The Spirit of St. Louis,* won a PULITZER PRIZE in 1953. In his later years, spent in Hawaii, Lindbergh was an active conservationist. Among his many accomplishments, Lindbergh was also the co-inventor (1936, with Alexis CARREL) of a so-called artificial heart that could pump nutrients through the human body. Lindbergh remains one of the most complex and fascinating figures of the 20th century. A man of great personal courage, he was also intensely private. Almost universally admired for his achievements in AVIATION, he was also criticized by many for his unorthodox political views.

## Lindbergh kidnapping case (*New Jersey v. Bruno Hauptmann*) (*1932–1936*) Kidnapping and subsequent murder of the infant son of American aviator Charles A. LINDBERGH, followed by a sensational trial. Lindbergh became a national hero after his solo transatlantic flight in 1927 in *The Spirit of St. Louis*. Two years later, he married the writer Anne Spencer Morrow, and the couple settled in rural Hopewell, New Jersey. The couple's bliss was shattered when their infant son Charles Lindbergh Jr. was kidnapped from his nursery during the night of March 1, 1932. In the following weeks, Lindbergh and the police followed numerous false leads in the hope of recovering the Lindbergh baby unharmed. After paying a ransom and receiving a note about the baby's whereabouts, their hopes were dashed when the baby's body was discovered on May 12, not far from their home. The nation was stunned and a massive manhunt eventually led to the arrest of Bruno Richard Hauptmann, a German immigrant.

Although there was only circumstantial evidence and Hauptmann maintained his innocence, he was convicted. After a series of unsuccessful appeals Hauptmann was executed in the electric chair. However, controversy still lingers about the actual facts of the crime. The Lindbergh case was one of the most sensational of the 20th century, and the glare of publicity that followed the Lindberghs forced them to leave the U.S. for several years.

## Lindsay, Nicholas Vachel (*1879–1931*) American poet. Born in Springfield, Illinois, Lindsay attended Hiram College, the Art Institute of Chicago and the New York School of Art. During his early years, he walked the U.S. as a modern troubadour, selling his drawings and giving poetry readings to pay for his meals and his lodging. Lindsay's strongly musical and rhythmic poetry, often concerned with the American experience, is particularly effective when read aloud. Books that reflect his years of wandering include *Rhymes to Be Traded for Bread* (1912), *Adventures While Preaching the Gospel of Beauty* (1914) and *A Handy Guide for Beggars* (1916). Among his collected volumes of verse are *General William Booth Enters into Heaven* (1913), *The Congo* (1914) and *Collected Poems* (1930).

## Line of Control (Kashmir) A 700-kilometer border between India and Pakistan established by the Simla Agreement in 1972. According to the agreement, the Line of Control was supposed to function as a temporary solution to the ongoing dispute between INDIA and PAKISTAN over the province of KASHMIR until both sides reached a diplomatic solution to that territory's status. To help enforce the Line of Control, a UN observation force that had been stationed along the Indo-Pakistani border since 1949 agreed to maintain a small presence along the new frontier. However, both sides have disputed the exact location of the Line of Control, which has led to frequent border clashes during times of tension in Kashmir. Since its establishment, the Line of Control has remained the starting point for offensives conducted by India into Pakistan and Pakistan into India. It is also the territory from which India has shelled Pakistan following outbreaks of Islamic separatism in Kashmir, such as the Hizbul MUJAHIDEEN insurrection begun in 1990 against Indian rule of the province that had claimed over 25,000 lives by the end of the decade.

## Link, Edwin A. (*1904–1981*) American inventor. In the 1930s Link invented the flight stimulator, a mechanical device that simulated night conditions and was used for many years to train millions of military and commercial pilots, including some 50,000 WORLD WAR II pilots. He founded Link Aviation in 1935 and went on to design many other advanced aviation devices. Some of these were used to train the first astronauts. Link also developed equipment for deep-sea exploration, including the

first submarine with an underwater exit hatch, and "The Shark," a protected television camera that could be lowered to depths that divers could not reach.

**Lipatti, Dinu** *(1917–1950)* Romanian concert pianist. Born into a musical family, Lipatti developed into a child prodigy. Encouraged by his godfather, composer Georges ENESCO, he attended the Bucharest Conservatory. When he placed second in an international competition in Vienna (1934), one of the judges, Alfred CORTOT, resigned from the jury in protest and invited Lipatti to study with him in Paris. Lipatti's budding career was curtailed by WORLD WAR II, which he spent in Switzerland. From 1944 to 1948, Lipatti was professor of piano at the Geneva Conservatory; during this period, through his recitals, concerts and recordings he won international recognition as a major artist, and was particularly renowned for his interpretations of the music of J. S. Bach and Frédéric Chopin. In 1948 he was diagnosed as having leukemia; musicians around the world, including Yehudi MENUHIN and Igor STRAVINSKY, donated money for his treatment. Despite his illness, Lipatti remained active until his final months; his last recital was in the autumn of 1950. He died on December 2, 1950, at age 33. Many critics consider Lipatti's premature death a tremendous loss to 20th-century music and feel that, had he lived, he would have been one of the greatest pianists of the century. In the years since his death, his legend has grown.

**Lipchitz, Jacques (Chaim Jacob Lipschitz)** *(1891–1973)* Born in Lithuania, Lipchitz settled in Paris in 1909 and studied at the Ecole des Beaux-Arts. He soon became associated with cubist artists, reinterpreting the tenets of CUBISM in sculpted form in works such as *Man with a Guitar* (1916, Museum of Modern Art, New York City). In the 1920s he experimented with transparent sculptures and by the 1930s began to create monumental and powerful semi-abstract sculpture. Lipchitz lived in the U.S. during the early 1940s and returned to France after World War II. The large and rhythmic forms and the mingling of the allegorical and the contemporary in subject matter that characterize his mature style may be seen as early as *The Rape of Europe* (1941) and as late as *Peace on Earth* (1967–69). Lipchitz is widely considered to have played a pivotal role in the development of modern sculpture in the 20th century.

**Li Peng (Li P'eng)** *(1928– )* Chinese prime minister (1987–92). Born in Chengdu, his father was executed by the Kuomintang (Guomindang, ZHOU Enlai or Nationalists) in 1930. In 1939 he was adopted by CHOU EN-LAI, a leading member of the Chinese Communist Party (CCP). In 1941 Li attended the Institute of Natural Science in Yan'an. Six years later, he traveled the Soviet Union to study Soviet engineering techniques. In 1954 Li returned to China and began his long career as an electrical engineer and minister of the national electric power industry for the Communist Chinese government that defeated the Kuomintang in 1949. In 1982 he left the electrical industry to head the national water conservation agency and was named to the CCP's Central Committee. A year later, he was appointed vice prime minister and took control of the ministries of education, energy and transportation. In 1985 Li was inducted into the CCP's Politburo, the chief decision-making body in China. Following the resignation of ZHAO ZIYANG as prime minister of China in 1987, Li succeeded him and was appointed to a second term in 1992.

In June 1989 Li supported Chinese leader DENG XIAOPING's decision to use military force to brutally suppress the student-led movement in what became known as the Tiananmen Square massacre. Li had the responsibility to oversee Chinese efforts to deal with the harsh criticism of the government's actions from foreign powers, especially the U.S.

In March 1998 Li completed his second and final term as prime minister. He has remained active in Chinese politics through his continued participation in the Politburo and his appointment as chairman of the National People's Congress, the Chinese national legislature.

**Lipinski, Edward** *(1888–1986)* Polish economist. Lipinski twice served as director of POLAND's Institute of National Economy. In 1975 he resigned from the Communist Party and in 1976 helped found the Committee for Workers' Self-Defense. That group, known by its Polish initials KOR, was credited with helping pave the way for the formation of the SOLIDARITY free trade union confederation in 1980. At Solidarity's first national congress in 1981, Lipinski dissolved KOR, declaring it had outlived its usefulness.

**Lippmann, Walter** *(1899–1974)* American journalist. Winner of two PULITZER PRIZES (1958, 1962), Lippmann was a dominant intellectual figure for four decades. In 1914 he helped establish the NEW REPUBLIC, serving as associate editor until 1917. He served as editorial page chief (1923–29) then editor (1929–31) of the *New York World*. He wrote his famous column, *Today and Tomorrow*, for the NEW YORK HERALD-TRIBUNE (1931–62), then for the *Washington Post* (1962–67). The column appeared in more than 250 newspapers worldwide. Lippmann was also the author of several books, including *Public Opinion* (1922) and *U.S. Foreign Policy* (1943). He retired in 1967.

**Lippold, Richard** *(1915–2002)* American sculptor. Born in Milwaukee, Lipinski studied at the University of Chicago and the Chicago Art Institute (1933–37), becoming an industrial designer. His link with industry and architecture was clear in his elegant geometrical constructions of gleaming wire and sheet metal. Exquisitely engineered, these intricately constructed works are suspended in space and use the play of light as part of their design. Lippold created a number of pieces for architectural installation, including *Orpheus and Apollo* at Avery Fisher Hall in Lincoln Center, New York City. Among his best known pieces are *Variation No. 7: Full Moon* (1949–50, Museum of Modern Art, New York City) and *Sun* (Metropolitan Museum, New York City). Lippold taught art and was a professor at New York's Hunter College from 1952 to 1967.

**Lipset, Seymour M(artin)** *(1922– )* American sociologist. Lipset is one of the most admired and influential sociologists to have emerged in postwar America. He was raised in a working-class New York Jewish family and came to know well the workings of the local printer's union to which his father belonged. This knowledge came to bear in one of Lipset's major works, *Union Democracy* (1956), in which he argued that not all organizations necessarily created elite leaderships—equality could lead to better decision making when a healthy level of disrespect prevailed. Lipset, who taught at Berkeley, Columbia and Harvard universities, also sparked controversy in the 1950s by his analyses of the social origins of what he termed the "radical right"—a grouping of disaffected social groups who craved more status or feared losing what status they had and were thus deviant at root. *Political Man* (1960) argued that the delicate social and ideological balances necessary to maintain democracy were in danger of eroding. Lipset's later writings include *The Politics of Unreason* (1970). From 1992 to 1993 Lipset served as president of the American Sociological Association. In 1996 Lipset released two books—*American Exceptionalism: A Double-Edged Sword,* and *Jews in the New American Scene*—that he coauthored with Earl Raab. Lipset received the World Association for Public Opinion's Helen Dinnerman Prize in 1997 for his contributions to international policy issues. Lipset held a joint appointment as senior fellow at the Hoover Institution at Stanford University and Hazel Professor of Public Policy and professor of sociology at George Mason University.

**Lispector, Clarice** *(1925–1977)* Brazilian novelist and short story writer. Lispector was the daughter of Ukrainians who immigrated to Brazil shortly after her birth. She attended law school in Rio de Janeiro while working as a journalist. One year after graduation (1943) she published her first novel, *Perto de coracão selvagem* (Close to the savage heart). Because Brazilian writers of the 1940s were preoccupied with social problems and realistic fiction, critics were shocked by the poetic luminosity and introspectiveness of her prose; nevertheless, the book won the Fundacão Graca Aranha prize. Her finest novel was *A Mac no escuro* (1961; tr. 1967 and reissued 1986 as *The Apple in the Dark*). In all she produced 15 volumes of fiction. Despite her high reputation in Latin America, her work is still difficult to obtain in translation.

**Lissitzky, El(iezer Markovich)** *(1890–1941)* Russian painter, designer and architect. Born in Smolensk, Lissitzky studied engineering at Darmstadt (1909–14), returning to Russia in 1919 to teach at the Vitebsk art school and becoming a professor at the Moscow Academy of Arts in 1921. Working closely with other members of the Russian avant-garde, Lissitzky began (1919) to create abstract drawings and paintings using strong color and simple geometrical shapes that he named *Prouns*. When the Russian government manifested active disapproval of abstract art, he left the country and settled in Germany in 1922. There he helped to popularize Suprematism and Constructivism and added ideas from these movements to Bauhaus philosophy. He returned to Moscow in 1928. Well represented in European and American museums, he was the author of a number of volumes, including *Russia; The Reconstruction of Architecture in the Soviet Union.* (1930).

**List, Eugene** *(1918–1985)* American concert pianist. List gained international fame in 1945 when, while serving in the U.S. Army, he was asked to perform for Winston Churchill, Harry S Truman and Joseph Stalin at the Potsdam Conference. Later he championed the music of the 19th-century American composer Louis Moreau Gottschalk. He also toured in "monster concerts" featuring performances by 20 or more pianists at a time, seated two to a keyboard.

**Lithuania** One of the three Baltic Sea republics, Lithuania is located in Northeast Europe. After Lithuania declared its

| LITHUANIA | |
|---|---|
| 1918–20 | War for independence against Bolshevik Russia; Lithuanian independence recognized internationally. |
| 1922 | A new constitution is enacted. |
| 1940 | Soviet Union invades. |
| 1941 | Nazi Germany invades. |
| 1944 | Soviet Union reconquers Lithuania and begins mass arrests and persecutions. |
| 1956 | Russification campaign begins. |
| 1990 | Lithuania declares independence from the Soviet Union, but a military crackdown leads to numerous civilian deaths. |
| 1991 | Lithuania is granted independence. |
| 1992 | A new constitution is promulgated. |
| 1998 | Valdas Adamkus is elected president. |
| 2000 | Center-right coalition of the Lithuanian Liberal Union and the New Union wins parliamentary elections and form a government. |
| 2001 | Coalition collapsed and former president Algirdas Brazauskas becomes prime minister. |
| 2004 | Lithuania is admitted to NATO (March) and the EU (May); Valdas Adamkus is reelected president and general elections produce a new coalition under Algirdas Brazauskas as prime minister. |

the modern corporate conglomerate. The textile company Little founded in 1923 (which later became known as Textron, Inc.) showed little promise for expansion in the early 1950s, so Little branched out into other fields by acquiring a diverse range of companies. He stepped down as Textron chairman in 1960 and later founded a venture capital firm.

**Little America** U.S. base on ANTARCTICA. Located on the Ross Ice Shelf, south of the Bay of Whales, it was established in 1928 by Commander Richard E. BYRD. Some 30 miles east, another U.S. base (Little America IV) served as a research station during the INTERNATIONAL GEOPHYSICAL YEAR (1957–58).

*Little Review, The* American magazine. Founded in Chicago in 1914 by Margaret C. Anderson, the magazine was devoted to promoting the arts. Its home base was moved to San Francisco, New York and finally Paris before Anderson decided to cease publication in 1929. Foreign editors included Ezra POUND. The magazine presented reproductions of modern paintings and sculptures, and published the work of such writers as James JOYCE, Amy LOWELL, Sherwood ANDERSON, T. S. ELIOT, Marianne MOORE, Wallace STEVENS and W. B. YEATS.

**Litvinov, Maxim Maximovich (Meir Wallach)** (1876–1951) Soviet diplomat and politician. Of Jewish background, Litvinov joined the Social Democratic Labor Party in 1898 and its Leninist faction in 1901. Having taken part in the 1905 Revolution, in 1907 he moved to London where he worked as a clerk. Named representative of the Soviet government in Great Britain after the 1917 Revolution, he was arrested and later exchanged for the British ambassador. Deputy foreign commissar in 1921–30 and 1939–46, Litvinov was foreign commissar from 1930 to 1939. He made a considerable impression at the LEAGUE OF NATIONS by advocating disarmament. Removed from the post in 1939, shortly before the pact with HITLER, he was appointed deputy foreign minister (1941–46) and was ambassador to Washington (1941–43).

**Liu Shaoqi (Liu Shao-ch'i)** (1898–1974) Chairman of the People's

independence in 1918, invasion by Russian BOLSHEVIKS led to the Russo-Lithuanian War, which ended with the Treaty of Moscow in 1920. Recognized as a democratic republic in 1922, Lithuania continued to face conflict with GERMANY over the port of Memel (administered by Lithuania until HITLER's annexation in 1939) and with Poland over the city of Vilna (controlled by Poland until 1939). After the NAZI-SOVIET PACT of 1939, Lithuania's vulnerability to Soviet expansion led to a vote in 1940 to peacefully join the Soviet Union. Some liberalization under Soviet leader Mikhail GORBACHEV encouraged Lithuania to move toward independence (1988–89). However, a Soviet crackdown in late 1990 resulted in civilian deaths. On February 9, 1991, Lithuania voted overwhelmingly (in a nonbinding referendum) for independence, though Gorbachev refused to recognize the vote. Following the abortive coup by Soviet hard-liners against Gorbachev, Lithuania obtained its independence from the USSR in September 1991. It joined the EUROPEAN UNION (EU) in 2004.

**Lithuanian War of Independence** *(1918–1920)* Lithuania declared its independence (February 1918) when the Russian czar was overthrown. Soviet forces invaded, but were driven out by Germans. German troops withdrew after their World War I surrender, and Soviets invaded January 1919; the Poles intervened, driving the Soviets out. In December of that year the Lithuanian-Polish border, defined by the Allies, gave Vilnius to Lithuania. Fighting continued with the Soviets until they recognized Lithuanian independence in the Treaty of Moscow on July 12, 1920. Polish raiders, led by General Lucian Zeligowski (1865–1947) captured Vilnius, established a provisional government and by plebiscite demonstrated that a majority of its citizens wanted union with POLAND. Lithuanian relations with Poland were severed, but by 1922 Lithuania, minus Vilnius, had been recognized as a democratic republic.

**Little, Royal** *(1896–1989)* U.S. business executive, credited with inventing

Republic of CHINA (1959–69). Elected to the Central Committee of the Communist Party in 1927, Liu was appointed a political commissar during the LONG MARCH. A principal vice chairman of the party on the establishment of the Chinese People's Republic in 1949, Liu succeeded MAO ZEDONG as chairman (head of state) of the People's Republic. He lost his position as heir apparent to Mao during the CULTURAL REVOLUTION in 1966. Criticized for defending the importance of industrial workers instead of the primacy of the peasantry as a spearhead of the revolution, he was deprived of all his party offices in 1968. He disappeared from public life the following year.

**Living Theatre** *(1951–1970)* Avant-garde theater group founded in 1951 by Julian Beck and Judith Malina, who served as the principal theorists and directors of the group. The Living Theatre quickly established itself in New York City as one of the leading Off-Broadway troupes. Its many experimental productions, which featured improvisation and modern resettings of classic plays, included stagings of *The Connection* by Jack Gelber (1959) and a VIETNAM WAR–era version of *Antigone* by the Greek dramatist Sophocles (1967). After extensive touring in Europe during the 1960s, the Living Theatre was dissolved in 1970.

**Lleras Camargo, Alberto** *(1903–1990)* Colombian politician. Lleras served as president of COLOMBIA (1945–46 and 1958–62). Following the establishment of the ORGANIZATION OF AMERICAN STATES in 1948, he served as the group's first president. He was instrumental in devising a 1957 coalition between his Liberal Party and the Conservative Party that helped end a widespread rural conflict known as "La Violencia." In 1961 he helped organize the Latin American Free Trade Association to help reduce tariffs in the region.

**Llewellyn, Richard (pen name of Richard Dafydd Vivian Llewellyn Lloyd)** *(1907–1983)* Welsh playwright and novelist. Llewellyn's first and best known novel, *How Green Was My Valley* (1939), became an international best seller and was made into an ACADEMY AWARD–winning film (1941) directed by John FORD. It depicted life in a Welsh coal-mining community.

**Llewelyn-Davies, Richard (Lord Llewelyn-Davies)** *(1912–1981)* Welsh architect and city planner. Head of the prominent British architectural firm of Llewelyn-Davies Weeks, he also taught at the University of London, where he was made head of the Bartlett School of Architecture in 1960. However, it was as a designer of NEW TOWNS after World War II that he won international fame. He designed Rushbrooke Village and Milton Keynes, among other new towns in Britain and elsewhere. His other works included London's Stock Exchange and the new wing of the Tate Gallery, and the Atlantic Richfield research complex in Philadelphia. He was made a life peer in 1963.

**Lloyd, Harold** *(1894–1971)* U.S. motion picture actor. Lloyd had already worked for the Edison Company before 1915, when he began appearing as "Lonesome Luke" in a series of one-reel comedies for Hal Roach. His enormous success guaranteed artistic control of his own films, and Lloyd went on to produce longer and feature-length comedies. He portrayed himself as a bumbling young man constantly getting into the most hair-raising situations. He was the highest paid actor of the 1920s, and renowned as one of the silent screen's most innovative performers and directors. Lloyd acted in some 500 films, some of the most popular including *For Heaven's Sake* (1926), *The Kid Brother* (1927) and *Speedy* (1928).

**Lloyd George, David** *(1863–1945)* British statesman, prime minister (1916–22); born in Manchester but raised in Wales. Lloyd George was apprenticed to a solicitor in 1878 and set up his own law practice six years later. He was elected as a LIBERAL PARTY member of Parliament in 1890 and served there for the next 55 years. He became president of the Board of Trade in 1905 and was appointed chancellor of the exchequer by Herbert ASQUITH in 1908. In the latter office, he carried out a number of significant social reforms, including the Old Age Pensions Act (1908) and the National Health Insurance Act (1911), both cornerstones of Britain's WELFARE STATE. In order to finance his pioneering programs, Lloyd George had new land and income taxes enacted in 1909 that proved extremely unpopular with the wealthy, powerful and conservative land-owning members of the House of Lords, who vetoed the tax package. The clash that followed led to the Parliament Act of 1911, which ended the House of Lords' veto power. After the outbreak of WORLD WAR I, Lloyd George remained chancellor until 1915 when he succeeded to the post of minister of munitions and then became minister of war in 1916.

Later in 1916 he joined with Conservatives to form a coalition that ousted Asquith, and Lloyd George succeeded him as prime minister. While frequently quarreling with his generals, he was a forceful and effective wartime leader and was instrumental in unifying Allied military forces under Marshal FOCH. After the war, he led the British delegation at the PARIS PEACE CONFERENCE (1919), where he tried to steer a moderate course between CLEMENCEAU's calls for retribution and WILSON's idealistic programs, and did much to shape the Treaty of VERSAILLES. At home, he dealt harshly with the Irish question but finally set up the Irish Free State in 1922. After the CHANAK CRISIS of that same year, the Conservatives withdrew from the coalition and his ministry fell. From 1926 to 1931 he was head of a severely weakened Liberal Party. Although he sympathized with German grievances and paid a friendly visit to HITLER in 1936, Lloyd George came to strongly oppose the MUNICH PACT and the policy of APPEASEMENT. He was made an earl shortly before his death.

**Lloyd Webber, Andrew** *(1948– )* British composer. Andrew Lloyd Webber has established himself as one of the most successful composers in the modern musical theater. He first won international attention for a string of successes on which he collaborated with British lyricist Timothy Rice—*Joseph and the Amazing Technicolor Dreamcoat* (1968), *Jesus Christ Superstar* (1970), and *Evita* (1976). Webber then went on to compose the acclaimed musicals *Cats* (1981, based on humorous poems by T. S. ELIOT), *Starlight Express* (1984), the phenomenally popular *Phantom of the Opera* (1987), *Aspects of Love* (1989), *Whistle Down the Wind* (1996), and *The Woman in White* (2004). Lloyd Webber founded the London-based Really Useful Company theatrical ensemble. Lloyd Webber's memorable melodies have earned him a fortune in royalties, but some critics charge that his works exploit surface effects and technical gimmickery at the expense of genuine emotional and intellectual depth.

**Locarno Pact** Series of agreements signed on December 1, 1925, by representatives of the governments of Belgium, Great Britain, Czechoslovakia, France, Germany, Italy and Poland, all of whom met at Locarno, Switzerland. As a whole, the treaties dealt with various problems that were unsettled after World War I. The principal agreement, signed by France, Belgium and Germany and guaranteed by Britain and Italy, confirmed the French and Belgian borders with Germany and reaffirmed the demilitarization of the RHINELAND. Arbitration agreements regarding Germany's eastern borders were also signed. A diplomatic triumph for Great Britain's Austen CHAMBERLAIN, France's Aristide BRIAND and Germany's Gustav STRESEMANN, the pact opened the way for Germany's entry into the LEAGUE OF NATIONS. The international harmony embodied in the Locarno Pact was shattered by HITLER's remilitarization of the Rhineland in 1936.

**Lockerbie** See PAN AM 103.

**Lockheed Aircraft Corporation** American firm founded in 1916 by Allan Lockheed (born Loughhead) in Burbank, California, to design and produce airplanes of advanced design. The single-engined, high-wing Lockheed Vega of 1927, designed by John K. NORTHROP, was one of the first truly streamlined airplanes, a monoplane without struts or wires. It was used by Amelia EARHART and Wiley POST in their pioneer flights and made Americans aware of the beauty possible in utilitarian forms. The Sirius of 1929 by the same designer was a low-winged design of similar styling, used by the LINDBERGHS in their early exploratory Arctic flights. The Orion introduced retractable landing gear and may be considered one of the most elegant of pre–World War II aircraft designs. The first Electra, a twin-engined, all-metal transport of 1934, was also an outstanding design, but was overshad-

owed by the success of the larger Douglas DC-3. The postwar Lockheed Constellation and Super-Constellation carried forward the firm's reputation for outstanding design with the remarkably elegant forms of fuselage and the striking triple-rudder tail, destined, however to become obsolete with improving technology. Lockheed continues to produce military aircraft and the 1011 transport jet.

**Lockheed scandal** *(1975)* Scandal involving bribes and kickbacks paid by LOCKHEED Corporation to obtain foreign contracts. In 1975 it was revealed that Lockheed, an aircraft manufacturer, regularly made payments to influence peddlers, foreign politicians and foreign military leaders as part of its sales strategy in marketing its planes overseas. A Senate investigation revealed that the payments were made with the knowledge of the corporation's senior managers. Revelation of the payments had far-reaching consequences. In Japan, Lockheed had made over $12 million in payments, including one to an aide close to Prime Minister TANAKA. In West Germany, Lockheed paid a kickback to the Christian Socialist Party, while in Italy the corporation made payments to members of the military. When it was revealed that Prince Bernhard, husband of Queen Juliana of the Netherlands, had secretly received $1 million, he resigned all his public offices in disgrace. These revelations caused the forced early retirement of a number of senior Lockheed executives.

**Lockwood, Margaret** *(1916–1990)* British actress. Her first well-known role was in the 1938 Alfred HITCHCOCK film *The Lady Vanishes*. She became one of the most popular actresses of the 1940s, appearing in such notable films as *Night Train* (1940), *The Stars Look Down* (1941) and *The Wicked Lady* (1945). In the 1960s and 1970s she appeared with her daughter Julia in the British television series "The Flying Swan." Her last film appearance was in 1976, in *The Slipper and the Rose*.

**Loden, Barbara** *(1934–1980)* American actress-director. Loden was the first woman to write, direct and star in her own feature film. The film, *Wanda* (1970), about a drab, desperate Ap-

palachian housewife, won the International Critics Prize at that year's Venice Film Festival. Loden was married to Elia KAZAN, who directed her on Broadway in a Tony Award–winning performance in Arthur MILLER's play *After the Fall*.

**Lodge, David John** *(1935– )* British critic and novelist. Born in London, Lodge was educated at University College, London. He taught and in 1976 became professor of modern English literature at the University of Birmingham, then retired in the 1980s to write full time. Lodge's critical works *Language of Fiction* (1966), *The Novelist at the Crossroads* (1971), *The Modes of Modern Writing* (1977) and *Working with Structuralism* (1980)—show his familiarity with many literary movements while professing his allegiance to realism. His early fiction, such as *Ginger, You're Barmy* (1962), which drew on his experiences in National Service in the 1950s, were antiestablishment satires. He turned to a more comedic style with *The British Museum is Falling Down* (1965) and *How Far Can You Go* (1980; published in the U.S. as *Souls and Bodies*), which explore the effects of social change on members of the Catholic Church. Other works include the academic satires *Changing Places* (1975); *Small World* (1984); and *Nice Work,* which lampoons both radical academic politics and Thatcherism. Following the publication of *Paradise News* (1991), Lodge has released several additional novels, including *Therapy* (1995), *Home Truths* (1999), *Thinks* (2001), and *Author, Author: A Novel* (2004).

**Lodge, Henry Cabot** *(1850–1924)* U.S. senator. Lodge graduated from Harvard in 1871 and from Harvard Law School in 1874. He received the first Ph.D. granted by Harvard in political science in 1876. Lodge had a successful career as a historian and editor before being elected as a Republican to the U.S. House of Representatives (1887–93), where he championed civil service reform. He served in the U.S. Senate from 1893 until his death. In the upper house Lodge helped draft the Sherman Antitrust Act (1896), the Pure Food and Drug Act (1906) and the Tariff of 1909. He was an ardent protectionist and an opponent of the direct election of senators and woman suffrage. A close friend of Theodore

ROOSEVELT, he welcomed war with Spain in 1898 and supported the development of the armed forces. As chairman of the Senate Committee on Foreign Relations, Lodge bitterly opposed Woodrow WILSON's peace policy and led the successful fight against U.S. entry into the LEAGUE OF NATIONS after WORLD WAR I. Lodge played a major role in the Republican nomination of Warren HARDING in 1920.

**Lodge, Henry Cabot, II** (*1902–1985*) U.S. politician and diplomat. A Massachusetts Republican from a distinguished family, he was elected to the U.S. Senate in 1936 and reelected in 1942. He resigned his seat in 1944 to enter the army in World War II, the first senator since the Civil War to resign to fight in a war. After the war he was reelected (1946). In 1952 he was Dwight D. EISENHOWER's presidential campaign manager; that same year, ironically, he himself was defeated for reelection to the Senate by Democrat John F. KENNEDY. From 1953 to 1960, Lodge headed the U.S. delegation to the UN. In 1960, he was Richard M. NIXON's vice presidential running mate on the losing Republican ticket. He served as U.S. ambassador to VIETNAM (1963–64, 1965–67). After serving briefly as U.S. ambassador to WEST GERMANY, he was chief U.S. representative (1969) to the Paris peace talks on Vietnam. (See also VIETNAM WAR.)

**Lodge, John Davis** (*1903–1985*) American politician. Before entering politics, Lodge was a lawyer and then an actor. His most notable role was as Marlene DIETRICH's lover in *The Scarlet Empress*. He began his political career as a member of the House of Representatives (1947–51). He went on to become governor of Connecticut (1951–55) and U.S. ambassador to Spain (1955–61), Argentina (1969–74) and Switzerland (1983–85). He was the brother of Henry Cabot LODGE II.

**Loeb, William** (*1905–1981*) American newspaper publisher. A maverick ultraconservative, Loeb published New Hampshire's *Manchester Union Leader* and *New Hampshire Sunday News* and printed his editorials on the front page. Although his papers served a small state, from the 1950s through the 1970s he exerted great influence in national

politics because every four years New Hampshire held the first presidential primary. The *Union Leader*, the only statewide paper in New Hampshire, was his forum for evaluating—and usually denouncing—the candidates in the first presidential primary every four years. His black-and-white right-wing views embarrassed many thoughtful conservatives and doomed many liberal causes. Loeb dubbed Dwight D. EISENHOWER "Doppy Dwight" and Gerald FORD "Gerald the Jerk" but staunchly supported Ronald REAGAN. In 1972 he dealt a fatal blow to Edmund MUSKIE's presidential campaign. In spite of his generally reactionary tone, Loeb also supported the labor movement, vigorously attacked waste and corruption, and probably printed more readers' letters than any other paper in the country.

**Loesser, Frank** (*1910–1969*) American lyricist and song writer, best known for his musical *Guys and Dolls* (1950). The fusion of popular and classical traditions was his specialty. Loesser, born in New York into a family of talented artists, struck out on his own, working odd jobs until he was signed by RKO Studios in HOLLYWOOD as staff lyricist. By the mid-1930s he was collaborating with composers Burton Lane, Hoagy CARMICHAEL and Victor Schertzinger on film songs like "Two Sleepy People" (*Thanks for the Memory*, 1938), "See What the Boys in the Backroom Will Have" (*Destry Rides Again*, 1939) and "Jingle, Jangle, Jingle" (*The Forest Rangers*, 1942). During his wartime service, Loesser began writing both lyrics and music; soon thereafter he had two Broadway smash hits, *Where's Charley?* (1948, an adaptation of an old farce called *Charley's Aunt*) and *Guys and Dolls* (1950, based on the underworld characters of Damon Runyan). Few shows could boast a more tuneful score. Critic Brooks ATKINSON wrote: "Every song defined a character . . . There was not a commonplace nor a superfluous song in the score." Perhaps Loesser's greatest achievement was *The Most Happy Fella* (1956), based on Sidney Howard's play *They Knew What They Wanted*, the story of a lovelorn California farmer and his mail-order bride. It was virtually a through-composed opera, juxtaposing arias like "Rosabella" with tuneful ditties like "Standing on the Corner." His last

shows were *Greenwillow* (1960) and the brilliant *How to Succeed in Business Without Really Trying* (1961).

**Loewe, Frederick** (*1904–1988*) Austrian-born composer. Loewe immigrated to the U.S. in 1924, leaving behind a career in European operetta. Popular success eluded him until he teamed with lyricist Alan Jay LERNER in 1942. Their first hit Broadway musical was *Brigadoon* (1947), which was followed by *Paint Your Wagon* (1951). *My Fair Lady*, a musical version of G. B. SHAW's *Pygmalion*, was their biggest success, opening in March 1956 and running for more than 2,700 performances. Their last two major collaborations were the movie musical *Gigi* (1959) and the Broadway musical *Camelot* (1960).

**Loewy, Raymond Fernand** (*1893–1986*) French-born U.S. industrial designer. Loewy came to the U.S. after World War I and embarked on his career in 1929 when he redesigned the Gestetner duplicating machine in three days. That design was unchanged for decades. He was regarded as having pioneered the "streamlined" look that drastically altered the appearance of objects from toothbrushes to airplanes. Perhaps his single best known design was the Coca-Cola bottle, with another the interior of the SKYLAB space orbiter. His company, Raymond Loewy Associates, founded in 1945, was the world's largest industrial design firm.

**Logan, Joshua** (*1908–1988*) American playwright, director and producer. Winner of a PULITZER PRIZE in 1950 for coauthoring the musical play *South Pacific* with Oscar HAMMERSTEIN II, Logan is best known as the director of such plays as *Charley's Aunt* (1940), *Annie, Get Your Gun* (1946), *Mr. Roberts* (1948), *South Pacific* (1949), *Picnic* (1953) and *Fanny* (1954). As a film director, his credits include *South Pacific* (1958), *Fanny* (1961) and *Camelot* (1967). It was Logan who encouraged James STEWART to become an actor.

**Logical Positivism** School of philosophical thought that emerged in Vienna in the late 1920s. A major precursor of the school was Ludwig WITTGENSTEIN. The key figures in the creation of Logical Positivism were the members of what was termed the Vienna Circle—most notably Rudolf CARNAP, Hans Reichenbach, and Moritz Schlick. Philosophers in Berlin, such as Carl HEMPEL, and in England, such as A. J. AYER, also contributed to its development. The Logical Positivists viewed themselves as extending the criteria of science to the entire range of subject matters traditionally analyzed by philosophy. In this effort, statements were to be judged as meaningful only insofar as they were empirically verifiable. As a result, the idealist philosopher's claim of having special insights on issues of metaphysics, ethics and the philosophy of mind were disallowed. Ethical statements, such as "murder is wrong," were viewed as emotive or persuasive rather than verifiable assertions. Many Logical Positivists concluded that traditional philosophy as a whole had become largely meaningless. Logical Positivism had a considerable influence on the linguistic philosophy of later British philosophers such as J. L. AUSTIN.

**Lombard, Carole (Jane Peters)** *(1908–1942)* American film actress. The wife of actor William Powell and, later, of Clark GABLE, Lombard began acting in motion pictures at the Fox Studios in 1926 (see 20TH CENTURY-FOX). She gained fame for her beauty and her performances in "screwball" comedies. She appeared in such films as *No Man of Her Own* (1932), *My Man Godfrey* (1936) and *They Knew What They Wanted* (1940). She was killed in a plane crash while on a war bond sales drive.

**Lombardi, Vince** *(1913–1970)* American football coach. Devoted equally to his players as individuals and to the team as a whole, the Brooklyn-born Lombardi was one of the most successful football coaches of all time. He began his pro career as a coach with the New York Giants in 1954 and joined the Green Bay Packers as head coach and general manager five years later. Often remembered for stating "Winning isn't everything, it's the only thing," he was also devoted to the ideal of equality among men both on and off the field, and refused to tolerate bigotry in any form. In the words of one of his players, "He's not prejudice—He treats us all like dogs." Lombardi led his team, through nine frozen and muddy Wisconsin win-

ters, to six conference championships and five league championships. He retired in 1968, only to reemerge as the coach of the Washington Redskins a year later, leading them to their first winning season in more than a decade. The Super Bowl Trophy is dedicated to his memory.

**Lombardo, Guy** *(1902–1977)* Canadian bandleader. Lombardo was born in London, Ontario. In 1917 he and three brothers formed a band called the Royal Canadians, with Guy as its leader. In 1924 the Royal Canadians began playing in the Midwestern U.S., and by 1928 they had begun to appear in New York City. In 1929 they started their tradition of playing at the Waldorf-Astoria Hotel on New Year's Eve, featuring their theme song "Auld Lang Syne"; these appearances, which were later televised for many years, continued until the time of Lombardo's death.

**London, Artur** *(1915–1986)* Czechoslovakian diplomat and author. He was deputy foreign minister during the early days of the communist regime in CZECHOSLOVAKIA. One of a number of leading officials put on trial for revisionism during a STALINIST-style purge in the early 1950s, he was sentenced to life in prison after confessing his guilt. London was released from prison in 1956 after Nikita KHRUSHCHEV's historic denunciation of STALIN, and moved to France in 1963. In 1969 he published *L'Aveu* (The confession), which gave a graphic account of the tortures inflicted upon him in prison to get him to confess. The book was translated into many languages and made into a 1970 film starring Simone SIGNORET and Yves MONTAND.

**London, Jack** *(1876–1916)* American author. Drawing from his experiences during the Alaskan gold rush, London created several short stories and novels filled with adventure and rugged heroes, both men and dogs, who fight to survive against the forces of nature and civilization. He gained fame with three volumes of short stories, including *The Son of the Wolf* (1900). His novel *The Call of the Wild* (1903) has become an American classic. Other major novels include *White Fang* (1906), *The Sea Wolf* (1904) and *The Iron Heel* (1907), which best re-

veals his social and political beliefs. His most famous short stories are "To Build a Fire" and "The White Silence." London's work has had considerable influence on such American writers as Ernest HEMINGWAY.

**Lone Ranger, The** Riding his horse Silver and accompanied by his Indian companion Tonto, this masked crime-fighter of the Old West was one of the premier heroes of 20th-century popular culture. The Lone Ranger made his debut in early 1933, on radio station WXYZ in Detroit; he was soon heard across America, with 2,596 adventures airing before the show was canceled in 1954. The Lone Ranger was also a syndicated comic strip from September 11, 1938, to April 1, 1984, with a 10-year hiatus from 1971 to 1981. In addition, he starred in movie serials, feature films (including the 1981 release *The Legend of the Lone Ranger*), comic books, novels, his own pulp magazine, a long-running television series and animated cartoons.

**Long, Huey Pierce** *(1893–1935)* U.S. politician. Long was admitted to the Louisiana Bar in 1915 after only seven months of study at Tulane University. His first political victory was his 1918 campaign for the state railroad commission. He won election for state governor in 1928 as a Progressive Democrat. Long survived impeachment on bribery charges his very first year in office. Later, he launched a sweeping campaign to solidify his political

*Louisiana governor Huey Long* (LIBRARY OF CONGRESS, PRINTS AND PHOTOGRAPHS DIVISION)

strength by legislative programs popular with rural voters. Elected to the U.S. Senate in 1930, he retained his governor's seat, at times with the help of the National Guard, until he could turn it over to a loyal supporter. Finally Long claimed his Senate seat in 1932. In 1934 he returned to Louisiana to consolidate his power in the state. He abolished local government, gained total control of the legislature and effectively acted as dictator. He was assassinated by a political opponent in the Louisiana State Capitol.

**"long count" fight** See Jack DEMPSEY.

**Long March** (*1934–1935*) After holding off KUOMINTANG (Guomindang, Chinese Nationalist) troops in mountainous parts of Jiangxi (Kiangsi) in southern CHINA for more than a year, the Chinese communist army of 200,000 men escaped encirclement and started an orderly retreat (October 1934). Fighting along the way, they crossed southeast China to the west and then north to Sha'anxi (Shan-hsi), a 6,000 mile trek over 18 mountain ranges, 24 rivers, a vast swamp and two enemy lines; about 50,000 men survived. The army was joined by about 50,000 along the way. CHU TEH (1886–1976) and MAO ZEDONG (1893–1976) led the Eighth Route Army, the largest force.

**Longo, Luigi** (*1900–1980*) Italian communist politician. Longo was among the founders of the Italian Communist Party (1922). He spent time in prison during MUSSOLINI's rule. During WORLD WAR II he became a guerrilla leader against the Germans. He was considered a superb organizer and rose through the party's ranks to become Communist Party secretary (1964–72). During his tenure the party gained credibility in Italian politics. However, Longo questioned the wisdom of working with the Christian Democrats—ITALY's governing party.

**Longworth, Alice Roosevelt** (*1884–1980*) Elder daughter and last surviving child of President Theodore ROOSEVELT. She was a leading figure in Washington, D.C., society for nearly 80 years and was renowned for her beauty, charm, acerbic wit and influential political connections. Sometimes called

"Washington's other monument," she was acquainted with and held outspoken opinions about virtually every important American political figure from President Benjamin Harrison to President Gerald FORD. Her husband, **Nicholas Longworth,** was Speaker of the House of Representatives (1925–31).

**Lon Nol** (*1913–1985*) President of the Khmer Republic (CAMBODIA, (1972–75). A general who held various ministerial posts under Prince SIHANOUK, including prime minister (1966–67), Lon Nol headed the government after Sihanouk was deposed in 1970. He established close ties with the U.S. and South Vietnam, permitting their forces to operate in Cambodia. He assumed total power in the new republic in 1972 but fled in 1975 as communist KHMER ROUGE rebels marched on the capital.

**Loos, Adolf** (*1870–1933*) Austrian designer and architect. Loos practiced in Vienna where, for a time, he worked with Otto Wagner. He designed a number of houses and shops there, notably the Karntner Bar (1908), the Goldman & Salatsch shop (1910) and the Steiner house. Although his own designs employed some decorative detailing, Loos is well known for his opposition to all decoration which he expressed in theoretical writings such as the essay "Ornament und Verbrechen" (1908; "Ornament and Crime"). Through his works and published writings Loos played an important role in the development of MODERNISM.

**Loos, Anita** (*1893–1981*) American screenwriter, playwright, novelist and social celebrity. Beginning her career as a child actress, Loos began writing plot outlines for films and eventually innovated the practice of writing screen captions for SILENT FILMS. Those she wrote for D. W. GRIFFITH's classic *Intolerance* (1916) were later lauded as classics of the genre. Among her 200-plus filmscripts were the highly acclaimed *San Francisco* (1936) and her adaptation of Clare Boothe LUCE's *The Women* (1939). She wrote several Broadway comedies, including *Happy Birthday* for Helen HAYES; and *Gigi*, an adaptation of the novel by COLETTE. She was probably most famous for the play *Gentlemen Prefer Blondes* (1926), later made into

two movies and two musicals. (The 1953 film version made a star of Marilyn MONROE.) Loos's writing style was characterized by witty dialogue and a tendency to satirize romance.

**López Contreras, Eleazar** (*1883–1973*) President of VENEZUELA (1935–41). Before assuming the presidency, López served as minister of war under the dictator General Juan Vicente GÓMEZ. He stepped in to lead the nation after Gómez's death.

**López Rega, José** (*1916?–1989*) Argentinian politician. A leading right-wing figure, he was regarded as the power behind Isabel PERÓN when she served as president of ARGENTINA following the death of her husband, General Juan D. PERÓN (1974). He was forced to resign as minister of social welfare in 1975, following charges that he had siphoned off millions of dollars from the Argentine treasury and exerted a sinister influence on Isabel Perón, who had consulted him as an astrologer. At the time of his death, he was awaiting trial for his role in organizing Argentina's right-wing death squads in the 1970s.

**Lopokova, Lydia** (*1892–1981*) Russian prima ballerina. While still in her teens Lopokova gained fame dancing with Serge Diaghilev's BALLETS RUSSES, appearing opposite Vaslav NIJINSKY in *Carnival* during her first season (1910). After the RUSSIAN REVOLUTION she emigrated to Britain. Married to the British economist John Maynard KEYNES in 1925, she became a familiar and popular figure in English society.

**Lorca, Federico García** See GARCÍA LORCA, Federico.

**Lorde, Audre** (*1924–1992*) African-American author. Born in New York City, New York, Lorde entered the University of Mexico in 1954. She left that institution the following year to return to New York City, where she lived in Greenwich Village. Lorde attended Hunter College, where she received a B.A. in literature and philosophy in 1959. After obtaining an M.A. in library science in 1961 from Columbia University, Lorde worked as a librarian in Mount Vernon, New York, but later became a head librarian at the New York

Public Library. In 1968 she received a grant from the National Endowment for the Arts that allowed her to leave her job in New York and to become the poet-in-residence at Tougaloo College in Mississippi, where she also taught courses on poetry. While working at Tougaloo, Lorde published her first book of poetry, *The First Cities* (1968), followed later by another book of verse, *Coal* (1976). She also wrote *The Cancer Journals* (1980), which documented her ongoing struggle with breast cancer. Lorde also devoted her time to advancing the political position of lesbians, through such activities as the inaugural 1979 national march for gay and lesbian liberation held in Washington, D.C.

In 1980 she returned to New York City to teach English literature at Hunter College, where she headed the Audre Lorde Poetry Institute. She left that position in 1985 to move to St. Croix in the Virgin Islands. In 1991 New York governor Mario Cuomo awarded Lorde the Walt Whitman Citation of Merit, which made her the New York poet laureate for two years. However, her tenure as laureate ended in 1992 when she died of breast cancer.

**Lord of the Flies** Novel by William GOLDING published in 1954. The story depicts a group of upper-class school boys stranded on an island after an airplane wreck. Initially, they attempt to set up a democratic society, but soon degenerate into cruel savages acting out barbarian rites and rituals that eventually lead to the deaths of two boys. The mythic novel was Golding's response to *The Coral Island* by R. M. Ballantyne, a cheerful, boys' adventure story with the same initial premise, and it reflects Golding's pessimistic belief in the inherent cruelty and evil of man. The *Lord of the Flies* was an immediate success upon its publication in 1954, and is still part of the curricula in many English departments. It was filmed by the British director Peter Brooks in 1963; a second film version was released in 1990.

**Lord of the Rings** A famous trilogy of fantasy novels by philologist and Merton professor of English, J. R. R. TOLKIEN. The *Lord of the Rings* trilogy consists of *The Fellowship of the Ring* (1954), *The Two Towers* (1954), and *The Return of the King* (1955). The story

these novels tell is begun in an earlier Tolkien novel, *The Hobbit* (1937), which introduces Bilbo Baggins, a hobbit who lives in Middle Earth. Hobbits are an ancient people who somewhat resemble humans in form and are by nature unobtrusive and peaceful, albeit capable of heroic valor should the need arise. The need does arise when Bilbo gains hold of a master ring that is sought by the evil Sauron of Mordor as part of his plan to conquer Middle Earth. The *Lord of the Rings* trilogy focuses on the quest of Frodo, Bilbo's heir, to destroy the ring by journeying to the far-off fire mountain Orodruin, where he can throw it into the cracks of doom. Many critics have seen Christian symbolism in the characters and events of the trilogy, although Tolkien himself was careful to disclaim any explicit allegorical interpretation. In 2001 New Line Cinemas released its first adaptation of the Tolkien series, *The Fellowship of the Ring*, followed in 2002 and 2003 by *The Two Towers* and *The Return of the King*, respectively. At the March 2004 Academy Awards ceremony, *Return of the King* received 11 Oscars, tying the record set by *Ben Hur* and *Titanic* for the most Academy Awards received by a single movie.

**Loren, Sophia (Sofia Villani Scicolone)** *(1934– )* A stunning and apparently ageless film star, Loren has appeared on film for almost five decades. Born in Rome, Loren started as a walk-on in Italian films, worked her way to stardom and afterward appeared in many American films, including *The Pride and the Passion* (1957), *Houseboat* (1958), *Desire Under the Elms* (1958) and *Arabesque* (1966). In 1961 she won an ACADEMY AWARD as best actress for her performance in the Italian film *Two Women;* her performance in *A Special Day* (1977) also received critical acclaim. She received an honorary Academy Award in 1990 for her cumulative body of work. In 1996 Loren returned to Hollywood filmmaking with her appearance in the comedy *Grumpier Old Men*. She is married to the producer Carlo Ponti.

**Lorenz, Konrad** *(1903–1989)* German ethnologist. Lorenz was born in Vienna and received his M.D. from the University of Vienna in 1928, followed by a Ph.D. in zoology in 1933. Over the

course of his distinguished academic career, he held a number of positions in European universities and received numerous awards, including the 1973 NOBEL PRIZE for physiology or medicine, which he shared with Karl von Frisch and Nikolaas TINBERGEN. Lorenz is known particularly for his work on individual and group behavior patterns, imprinting (rapid, virtually irreversible learning occurring during a critical period early in life) and aggression, which he believed to be partially innate in some animals, including humans.

**Lorre, Peter (Lazlo Lowenstein)** *(1904–1964)* Hungarian-born film and stage actor. Lorre is widely acknowledged as one of the great character actors in the history of the cinema. He began his career as a stage actor appearing throughout Central Europe— to no great acclaim—in the 1920s. But Lorre won international recognition for his powerful portrayal of a child murderer in the classic German film *M* (1931), directed by Fritz LANG. Lorre fled GERMANY after the NAZIS rose to power and, after a brief time in England during which he appeared in the film *The Man Who Knew Too Much* (1934), directed by Alfred HITCHCOCK, he came to America. In HOLLYWOOD, Lorre achieved fame for his portrayal of the Japanese detective Mr. Moto in a series of B-action films that appeared in the late 1930s. He then achieved film immortality for his supporting roles as Joel Cairo in *The Maltese Falcon* (1941) and Ugarte in *Casablanca* (1943). Lorre's career foundered in the 1950s, due in part to ill health, but he made a comeback in the 1960s through appearances in Roger CORMAN horror films such as *Tales of Terror* (1962) and *The Raven* (1964).

**Losey, Joseph** *(1909–1984)* American film director. Losey was educated at Harvard and devoted his early career to stage direction, most notably the Broadway production of *Galileo Galilei* (1947). He then went to HOLLYWOOD; however, his left-wing political sympathies got him blacklisted during the McCARTHY era (see McCARTHYISM, HOLLYWOOD TEN). As a result, Losey moved to England, where he worked on films for several years under an assumed name before directing *Time Without Pity* (1957) under his real name. In the 1960s, Losey became a preeminent figure in the British film industry as a result of a series of artistic successes, including *The Servant* (1963), *Accident* (1967) and *The Go-Between* (1971), on which he collaborated with writer Harold PINTER. Subsequent films by Losey included *Mr. Klein* (1976) and *Don Giovanni* (1979). *Losey on Losey* (1968) is a selection from his writings on film.

**Loss, Joe** (Joshua Alexander Loss) *(1909–1990)* British band leader. He was one of the most prominent figures in the big band era in Britain in the 1930s and 1940s. He remained popular for more than 50 years, and his band frequently performed on television and for royal social affairs, until the 1980s.

**lost generation** Term coined by Gertrude STEIN that refers to the generation of expatriate American writers who lived and worked in Paris and other European capitals during the post–WORLD WAR I era. Besides Stein herself, other lost generation figures include Sherwood ANDERSON, Ernest HEMINGWAY and F. Scott FITZGERALD. (See also JAZZ AGE.)

**Louganis, Greg(ory)** *(1960– )* American diver. Considered by many to be the greatest diver of all time, Louganis won 47 national and 13 world championships. His first Olympic medal came in 1976, when he won a silver medal in platform diving. He was expected to reach his athletic peak in 1980, when the U.S. boycott of the OLYMPIC GAMES kept him from competition. He won the 3-meter springboard and 10-meter platform gold medals in 1984; his final Olympic victories in 1988 made him the first diver in history to win those medals in successive OLYMPIC GAMES. The 1988 victories were hard-won, as Louganis hit his head on a diving board, then competed the next day with multiple stitches in his head. He retired from diving after the games to pursue an acting career. In 1994 Louganis openly admitted his homosexuality at the Gay Games (an international sports competition). The following year he disclosed that he had AIDS. He has written several books on breeding dogs and continues to promote AIDS awareness.

**Louis, Joe** (Joseph Louis Barrow) *(1914–1981)* American boxer, widely

*World heavyweight boxing champ Joe Louis. 1947*
(LIBRARY OF CONGRESS, PRINTS AND PHOTOGRAPHS DIVISION)

regarded as the greatest heavyweight champion of all time. The son of an Alabama sharecropper, Louis took the heavyweight title from James J. BRADDOCK in 1937 and held it until his first retirement in 1947—the longest reign of any champion in his weight class. Known as the "Brown Bomber" because of his vicious left jab and powerful right straight, Louis entered professional boxing in 1934, after two years as an amateur. His first loss came at the fists of German champion Max SCHMELING in 1936; Nazi propagandists seized on Schmeling's 12th-round knockout of Louis as proof of Aryan superiority over the black race. In their rematch on June 22, 1938, however, Louis knocked Schmeling out in the first round. He successfully defended his title a record 35 times. Besides defeating many second-rate challengers (on his so-called Bum of the Month tour), Louis also vanquished the top heavyweights of his day. After the second Schmeling fight, his most memorable victory came against Billy Conn on June 18, 1941; Louis dropped Conn in the 13th round of that spirited contest. He came out of retirement in 1950 to be beaten by then-champion Ezzard Charles and emerged from his second retirement in 1951, only to fall in his final fight to Rocky MARCIANO. In his 71 pro bouts, Louis had 68 victories, 54 by knockouts. In his later years, he suffered from financial difficulties and from health problems. Louis's triumphs and quiet

dignity made him a national hero, particularly to black Americans.

**Louis, Morris** *(1912–1962)* American painter. A leading figure in COLOR-FIELD PAINTING, he was born in Baltimore and studied at the Maryland Institute (1929–33). During the 1930s he joined other artists in executing projects for the WPA's Federal Arts Project. A resident of Washington, D.C., he taught at the Washington Workshop Center and the Corcoran School of Art (1952–62). Louis is known for his vibrant, stained paintings created by pouring thinned pigment onto unprimed canvases. These large abstract works moved from the "veils" of the early 1950s to bursting "florals" and, in his last works, "stripes" such as *Pillars of Dawn* (1961, Wallraf-Richartz Museum, Cologne).

**Love Canal** Highly publicized toxic waste site in Niagara Falls, New York; it focused public attention on the dangers of hazardous wastes. In 1978 residents in the area around a waterway named Love Canal were experiencing severe health problems. Neighbors brought suit against Hooker Chemical Company, the former owner of the land, and the matter drew national attention. Investigations revealed that the cause of their problems was the residue of the chemicals Hooker had dumped in the neighborhood years earlier. Although the extent of the danger was disputed, President Jimmy CARTER declared a state of emergency in the neighborhood. The inhabitants eventually moved elsewhere after the state of New York bought the majority of their homes, then bulldozed the structures. When Hooker Chemical was merged into Occidental Petroleum, Occidental agreed to compensate the former residents and also agreed to clean up the site.

**Lovecraft, H(oward) P(hillips)** *(1890–1937)* American writer, poet and essayist who was a major figure in 20th-century supernatural fiction. He spent most of his life in Providence, Rhode Island, one of several New England cities that served as a model for his legend-haunted fictional city, Arkham. Poor health and his reclusive nature reinforced his solitary pursuit of reading and writing. Never a prolific contributor to professional publications Lovecraft gained an enthusiastic following from his extensive work for amateur presses and as a consultant for other writers. Contemporary disciples such as Robert Bloch, Henry Kuttner and August Derleth—and later such masters as Brian Lumley and Ramsey Campbell—have all acknowledged his powerful influence. In his best stories—"The Colour Out of Space" (1927), "The Call of Cthulhu" (1928), the novels *At the Mountains of Madness* (1936) and *The Shadow over Innsmouth* (1936)—Lovecraft achieved a unique fusion of evolutionary theory and the type of science that appears in gothic horror tales, especially astronomy. He created a pattern of pseudomyth (the Cthulhu Mythos) that presented the world as a violent intersection of human and cosmic forces locked in a perpetual struggle. His dense and stilted style and rather archaic diction lent these lurid tales a peculiar dignity, elegance and expansiveness. Two years after his death August Derleth and Donald Wandrei established Arkham House, a press devoted to perpetuating Lovecraft's work. Lovecraft's work has been adapted extensively for television and films.

**Lovell, Sir Alfred Charles Bernard** *(1913–   )* British astronomer. Lovell was awarded his Ph.D. from the University of Bristol in 1936. In 1951 he was named director of the Jodrell Bank (now the Nuffield Radio Astronomy Laboratories), where he was instrumental in building the world's first large radio telescope, completed in 1957. In the coming decades, the telescope proved particularly valuable in the investigation of pulsars and quasars. Lovell was knighted in 1961.

**Lovell, James** *(1928–   )* U.S. astronaut. "The moon is essentially gray, no color . . . looks like plaster of Paris, sort of gray sand" is how Lovell described the surface of the moon during the flyby flight of Apollo 8 (December 21–27, 1968). If, in the words of science fiction writer Robert Heinlein, "The moon is a harsh mistress," then we might wonder if such an unflattering description jinxed Lovell's next lunar mission. As commander of Apollo 13 (April 11–17, 1970), Lovell and his crewmates Fred Haise and Jack

Swigert, gave the world some tense moments when an explosion aboard their spacecraft forced the three men into a dangerous and improvised return to Earth aboard the cramped and poorly equipped lunar module. A veteran of 30 days in space, in addition to his two APOLLO missions Lovell also piloted GEMINI 7 (December 4–18, 1965) and Gemini 12 (November 11–15, 1966). After retiring from NASA in March 1973 he entered private industry.

**Lovestone, Jay** *(1898–1990)* Lithuanian-born labor leader. Head of the American Communist Party in the 1920s, Lovestone later became a staunch anticommunist. He had advocated an independent party line in the U.S. and, as a result, was attacked by Soviet leader Joseph STALIN in a well-publicized argument in 1929. By 1940 Lovestone concluded that communism had become nothing more than a totalitarian conspiracy. He later served as international affairs director of the AFL-CIO, where he wielded considerable influence as the American labor movement's representative in international affairs.

**Low, George M.** *(1926–1984)* Vienna-born engineer who was a major force in the APOLLO space program. As a member of the NATIONAL AERONAUTICS AND SPACE ADMINISTRATION (NASA) and its predecessors from 1949 to 1976, Low helped draft the 1960 memo that suggested to President John F. KENNEDY that the U.S. could put a man on the moon by the end of the 1960s. After astronauts GRISSOM, WHITE and CHAFFEE were killed in a launch pad fire (January 27, 1967), Low was charged with redesigning the Apollo spacecraft. He successfully drove the program to meet its end-of-decade deadline. In 1976 he became president of his alma mater, Rensselaer Polytechnic Institute.

**Lowell, Amy** *(1874–1925)* American poet. The Lowell family occupies a special place in the history of American poetry. Amy Lowell was a descendant of the 19th-century poet James Russell Lowell, as well as an ancestor of the famous modern poet Robert LOWELL. Amy Lowell published her first verse at age 36, and soon became one of the most prominent American poets of her era, winning the PULITZER PRIZE in 1925 for her volume *What's O'Clock*. In the

1910s Lowell worked together with Ezra POUND to draw attention to the poetic school of IMAGISM, which Pound soon began to call "Amygism" in wry tribute to Lowell's fervent leadership of the new literary movement. Lowell's other works include a two-volume biography of John Keats (1925). Her *Collected Poems* appeared in 1955. Glenn R. Ruhley has written a biography of Lowell, *The Thorn of a Rose* (1975).

**Lowell, Percival** *(1855–1916)* U.S. astronomer. Wealthy enough to pursue his own interests, Lowell was the world's most famous amateur astronomer, as well as founder of the Lowell Observatory at Flagstaff, Arizona, in 1894. He was also an important force in instituting the search that led to the discovery of the planet Pluto in 1930. Lowell is most famous, however, for his "observations" of "canals" on Mars. Inspired by the writings of Italian astronomer Giovanni Schiaparelli, Lowell believed that he saw a connecting pattern among the shifting patterns of dark and light material on the Martian surface (which we now know to be rock surfaces periodically exposed by wind-driven sand). He convinced himself that he was observing an intricate and elaborate network of artificial canals on the red planet. Not discouraged that other observers failed to report similar findings, Lowell wrote numerous articles and books in support of his observations, putting forth his romantic theories of an arid, dying planet populated by intelligent inhabitants who dug the canals to move water from its poles to the plains. Although Lowell was mistaken in his observations, his enthusiastic writings helped to keep popular interest in astronomy and the solar system alive in the age before spacecraft, and also influenced a generation of science fiction writers (see Edgar Rice BURROUGHS.)

**Lowell, Robert Traill Spence, Jr.** *(1917–1977)* American poet. The scion of a Boston Brahmin line, Lowell was educated at Harvard (1935–37) and Kenyon College (1938–40). He was imprisoned as a conscientious objector during WORLD WAR II (1943–44) and later spent significant periods in mental hospitals. His turbulent marriages to three writers were well known: Jean STAFFORD (1940–48), Elizabeth

HARDWICK (1949–72) and Caroline Blackwood (1972 to his death). *Lord Weary's Castle* (PULITZER PRIZE, 1947) and *The Mills of the Kavanaughs* (1957) focus on his conversion to Catholicism. *Life Studies* (1959) marked a breakthrough into more personal, less rhetorical poetry. *Notebook, For Lizzie and Harriet, The Dolphin* (Pulitzer Prize, 1973) and *Day by Day,* all published in the 1970s, represented an attempt to create a larger work along the lines of POUND's CANTOS or BERRYMAN's *Dream Songs.* Lowell is generally considered the father of the CONFESSIONAL POETS.

**Lowry, Malcolm** *(1909–1957)* English novelist and short story writer. Lowry is best known for his novel UNDER THE VOLCANO (1947), which is an acknowledged classic of 20th-century literature. Lowry, who was educated at St. Catherine's College in England, interrupted his academic studies to go to sea and work for 18 months as a deckhand. This experience formed the basis for his first novel, *Ultramarine* (1933), which appeared when Lowry was 24. Despite this early success, Lowry endured subsequent years of poverty and neglect as a writer. He also battled his own chronic alcoholism. In 1936 Lowry visited Mexico, an important setting for many of his works. In 1939 he settled in Dollarton, British Columbia, where he built for himself a crude squatter's shack in which he lived with his second wife, the novelist Margerie Bonner and wrote in seclusion for more than a decade. Other novels by Lowry include *In Ballast to the White Sea* (1936), the unfinished *Lunar Caustic* (1968) and *Dark Is the Grave Wherein My Friend Is Laid* (1969). His *Selected Letters* were published in 1967.

*loya jirga* A "grand council" called by the head of state in AFGHANISTAN and generally including leaders of the nation's major tribes as well as important bureaucratic, political, military and religious figures. For over a millennium, *loya jirgas* have served to ratify important decisions of state, such as the one that convened in 1941 to confirm Afghanistan's neutrality during WORLD WAR II and the one that met in 1985 to ratify the constitution for the Democratic Republic of Afghanistan. In September 2001, as the U.S. prepared to invade Afghanistan to overthrow the TALIBAN government and eliminate AL-QAEDA, the terrorist group responsible for the terrorist attacks of SEPTEMBER 11, 2001, four *loya jirgas* emerged, each claiming to speak for the Afghani people in the hopes of replacing the Taliban as the country's governing force. Instead, after U.S. forces toppled the Taliban regime, an interim government established by the U.S. coalesced around Hamid KARZAI. In 2002 the former king of Afghanistan, Zahir SHAH, convened a new session of the *loya jirga.* The 1,501 delegates named Karzai president of Afghanistan and designated his cabinet officers.

**LP records** See Carl Peter GOLDMARK.

**LSD** See Timothy LEARY.

**Lubin, Isador** *(1896–1978)* American economist. Lubin was a leading member of President Franklin D. ROOSEVELT's BRAIN TRUST and helped shape the NEW DEAL. As U.S. commissioner of labor statistics (1933–46), he supervised and made famous the CONSUMER PRICE INDEX.

**Lubitsch, Ernst** *(1892–1947)* German-born film director many of whose major works were produced in HOLLYWOOD. Lubitsch was one of the most stylish and sophisticated directors of comedy in the history of cinema. The phrase "the Lubitsch touch" became, in the 1930s and 1940s, synonymous with the subtle and refined handling of adult themes of love and betrayal in the elegant style of drawing room comedy. His best known film is *Ninotchka* (1939), which featured Greta GARBO in her first comedic role as a dour Russian communist agent who is induced to see the charms of Western bourgeois decadence by dapper Melvyn DOUGLAS. *To Be or Not to Be* (1942), starring Jack BENNY and Carole LOMBARD, was a parody of Nazi pretensions set in occupied Poland. Other Lubitsch films include *Monte Carlo* (1930), *Trouble in Paradise* (1932) and *The Merry Widow* (1934).

**Lucas, George** *(1944– )* American film director and producer. Lucas is one of the most popular filmmakers in the history of HOLLYWOOD. He is best known as the creator of the *Star Wars* trilogy— *Star Wars* (1977), which Lucas directed, *The Empire Strikes Back* (1980) and *Return of the Jedi* (1983) which he scripted and produced. The phenomenal box office success of these films, with their pioneering use of computer technology to create elaborate special effects, proved that blockbuster action and storytelling—without reliance on previously established big-name stars could capture the hearts and pocketbooks of audiences. Lucas's first directorial effort was a low-budget science fiction film *THX 1138* (1970). His first critical breakthrough was the acclaimed *American Graffiti* (1973). He has also been associated with director-producer Steven SPIELBERG. Lucas now devotes his primary efforts to producing films. Lucas developed three additional movies for the *Star Wars* saga—*The Phantom Menace* (1999), *Attack of the Clones* (2002), and *Revenge of the Sith* (2005)—which were set in the time before the original *Star Wars.*

**Luce, Clare Boothe** *(1903–1987)* U.S. editor, playwright and politician. Luce's career included the editorship of *Vanity Fair* (1933–34) and the writing of hit plays, most notably *The Women* (1936). Her political career included two terms as a Republican congresswoman from Connecticut (1943–47) and service as U.S. ambassador to ITALY (1953–57). She was married for 32 years to media mogul Henry R. LUCE, the founder of the *TIME* magazine empire. After his death in 1967, she moved to Hawaii, where she lived until she returned to Washington in 1983. Long identified with the conservative wing of the REPUBLICAN PARTY, she served on President REAGAN's Foreign Intelligence Advisory Board.

**Luce, Henry R(obinson)** *(1898– 1967)* American editor and publisher. A titan of the publishing world, Luce founded *TIME,* the first modern news magazine, with Yale classmate Briton Hadden in 1923. He went on to successfully establish the business magazine *Fortune* (1930), the photojournalistic *LIFE* (1936) and *Sports Illustrated* (1954). His magazines reflected his personal views on politics and the free enterprise system. He also acquired radio and television stations and began publishing books under the Time-Life imprint. He was married to diplomat and playwright Clare Boothe LUCE.

**Luciano, Charles "Lucky"** (Salvatore Luciana) *(1897–1962)* American organized crime leader. Born near Palermo, Sicily, he emigrated to the U.S. (1906) and was soon arrested for shoplifting. By 1916 Luciano had become a member of New York's infamous Five Points gang; by the early 1920s he was an important figure in bootlegging. He subsequently assumed second-in-command status in the family of mob chieftain Giuseppe "Joe the Boss" Masseria. During a war (1928–30) between the Masseria factions and the opposing Maranzanos, Luciano solidified relations with younger gangsters in both camps. In 1931 Luciano was responsible for murdering both Masseria and Maranzano. Luciano then became the undisputed head of organized crime in New York and the leading figure in a new national crime syndicate that soon controlled bootlegging, prostitution, drugs, gambling, loanshark activities and labor racketeering. He prospered until 1936, when he was convicted on prostitution charges through the efforts of the crusading prosecutor Thomas E. DEWEY. Sentenced to 30 to 50 years imprisonment, he continued to control organized crime from his cell until his release in 1946, when he was deported to Italy. He wielded power from Cuba for a while but was returned to Italy, where his influence steadily waned.

***Lucky Jim*** Novel by Kingsley AMIS, published in 1954. It earned Amis a reputation as one of the ANGRY YOUNG MEN, and remains his most popular work. The story is set in a provincial British university where its lower-middle-class hero, Jim Dixon, is a lecturer. His radical, anarchist views expressed and reflected the discontent and anger of the young British leftists in the 1950s.

**Ludendorff, Erich** *(1865–1937)* German general. Commissioned in the infantry in 1882, Ludendorff was appointed to the Prussian general staff as a major in 1906. In the early days of WORLD WAR I, he led his troops in the capture of the Belgian citadel at Liège. Thereafter, he was named army chief of staff under HINDENBURG. Both became war heroes after the eastern front victories at Tannenberg and the Masurian Lakes (1914). As the war progressed, the two men made most of GERMANY's important military deci-

*German general Erich Ludendorff* (LIBRARY OF CONGRESS, PRINTS AND PHOTOGRAPHS DIVISION)

sions, and from 1916 to 1918 Ludendorff exercised enormous power in civilian life as well. He was largely responsible for the beginning of unrestricted submarine warfare in 1917 and for the final offensive of 1918. When it failed, Ludendorff insisted on an armistice; after it was concluded, he fled to Sweden. Returning to Germany the following year, he engaged

in antigovernment activity, supporting the KAPP PUTSCH (1920) and HITLER's "BEER-HALL PUTSCH" (1923). He was a National Socialist member of the Reichstag from 1924 to 1928. Although he broke with Hitler, he remained a vociferous supporter of "Aryan" rights and deplored Jews, Catholics and Freemasons alike.

**Ludwigshafen am Rhein** (Ludwigshafen) City on the Rhine River, Germany. A center of German chemical production, it was bombed heavily by the Allies in WORLD WAR II. In 1948 there was a massive explosion that destroyed several chemical plants and killed a number of workers.

**Lugosi, Bela** (Béla Ferenc Dezso) *(1882–1956)* Hungarian-born film and stage actor. Although Lugosi was a working actor for more than four decades, his enduring fame stems from a single role with which he became permanently identified: the evil vampire, Count Dracula. Lugosi's portrayal of the caped count in the classic 1931 film by Tod BROWNING—which followed Lugosi's successful Broadway run in the same role—typecast him forever after in macabre and horrific roles. Prior to his stardom as Dracula Lugosi had been a successful film and stage actor in both Europe and the U.S. to which he had emigrated in 1921. In the 1930s and 1940s, Lugosi appeared almost exclusively in horror films, notably *The Black Cat* (1934), *Mark of the Vampire* (1935) and *The Raven* (1935). Lugosi's career declined in the 1950s, while his increasing psychological identification with the role of Dracula led to his being buried—pursuant to his own instructions—in his vampire cape.

**Lukacs, Gjörgy** *(1885–1971)* Hungarian writer, Marxist philosopher and literary critic. In 1918 Lukacs joined the Hungarian Communist Party. In 1930 he moved to Moscow and from 1933 to 1944 worked at the Institute of Philosophy of the Soviet Academy of Science. He exerted considerable influence on European communist thought and is noted for having formulated a Marxist system of aesthetics that opposes political control of artists and that defends humanism. Having returned to Hungary in 1945, Lukacs twice served as minister of culture. His publications include *Studies on Lenin* (1970) and *Solzhenitsyn* (1970, tr. 1971).

**Lukashenko, Aleksandr Grigoryevich** *(1954–  )* Belarusian politician and president of Belarus (1994–  ). Born in the Byelorussian Soviet Socialist Republic, Lukashenko served in the Soviet armed forces and became the director of a state farm before winning election to the Supreme Soviet of the republic in 1990. He was one of the few members of the parliament to vote against the resolution that ratified the breakup of the Soviet Union and the establishment of the Commonwealth of Independent States, of which the newly independent republic of Belarus became a member. In the following years he became a vocal critic of the widespread corruption in the government of the new state and in 1994 was elected president in the country's first free democratic elections. As president he has presided over impressive economic gains that contrasted sharply with the economic stagnation in the other Slavic republics of the former Soviet Union, Russia and Ukraine. Lukashenko, however, resisted the trend toward privatization and the introduction of free-market economic practices that swept many of Belarus's neighbors and retained close economic ties to Russia. His authoritarian methods, which have included restrictions on freedom of speech, press and assembly, as well as rigged parliamentary and presidential elections and national referenda, have been severely criticized by human rights groups, the European Union, and the United States. In 1996, after forcing through a referendum granting the president additional powers, Lukashenko suspended the elected parliament and replaced it with a hand-picked group of legislators. Two years later he evicted the ambassadors from several Western countries from their residences in the capital to demonstrate his displeasure with their governments' criticism of his undemocratic methods. After winning reelection in 2006 in a contest universally criticized for irregularities, Lukashenko remained one of the last remnants of the old authoritarian tradition in the former Soviet republics in Europe.

**Lula da Silva, Luis Ignacio** *(1945–  )* Brazilian labor leader and politician, president of Brazil (2003–  ). Born to an illiterate peasant family, Lula (a nickname by which he came to be known) left school after the fourth grade and worked as a street vendor and in a steel factory before obtaining his high school equivalency diploma. While working in an auto parts factory he began his career as a radical union activist and in 1978 became the president of the country's steelworkers' union. In 1980 he helped to found the left-wing Workers' Party at a time when Brazil was ruled by a right-wing military dictatorship. In 1986 he was elected to congress on the Workers' Party ticket and in 1989 was defeated in his bid to become president in the first free elections since the end of military rule. After leaving parliament in 1990 Lula became active in the movement that led to the impeachment of President Fernando Collor de Mello for corruption in 1992 and ran unsuccessfully for the presidency twice during the decade of the 1990s.

Although Lula's calls for radical social and economic reforms alarmed the business classes, he was elected president in the 2002 elections and took office on January 1, 2003. Once in power, Lula moderated his radical political rhetoric and pursued pragmatic policies designed to improve the country's difficult economic situation. While attacking the problem of poverty and hunger in Brazil, he pursued relatively moderate fiscal and budgetary policies in order to reassure international financial markets and the International Monetary Fund (IMF). As a result of these policies, the country's high inflation rate was brought under control; it enjoyed a trade surplus after many years of deficits; and Brazil was able to repay its debt to the IMF in 2005, two years ahead of schedule. Under Lula Brazil's foreign policy steered a middle course between radical populism and anti-Americanism of Venezuelan president Hugo Chávez and the free-market policies of the George W. Bush administration in Washington, D.C. In 2005–06 Lula's government was rocked by financial scandals that tarnished its reputation and threatened Lula's chances of reelection to the presidency.

**Lumet, Sidney** *(1924–  )* American motion picture and television director. As a child actor in Philadelphia and New York, Lumet appeared in many radio and Broadway plays. After service in World War II he began directing for some of the early CBS television dramatic anthology series, including *Omnibus, Alcoa Theater, Goodyear Playhouse* and *You Are There* and acquired a reputation for economical, efficient directing. His film career began with an adaptation of Reginald Rose's courtroom drama, *12 Angry Men* (1957). Half of his subsequent film projects derived from the theater—most notably Eugene O'Neill's *Long Day's Journey into Night* (1964), Chekhov's *The Sea Gull* (1968), and *Equus* (1978), *The Wiz* (1979) and *Deathtrap* (1981). Many of his other films probe the gritty streets, tangled lives and police corruption of New York City. *Serpico* (1974) and *Prince of the City* (1981) were about cops who defy their peer groups to maintain their own code of morality; *Q&A* (1990) examined the opposite side of the same issue. Lumet's finest achievement may be *The Pawnbroker* (1965), starring Rod Steiger as Sol Nazerman, a Jew whose CONCENTRATION CAMP memories haunt his daily life. Its uncompromising harshness and brief nudity challenged—and defeated—HOLLYWOOD attempts to censor it. However, many audiences and critics have been put off by Lumet's rather humorless tone and his apparent lack of a consistent style. During the 1990s Lumet directed three films: *A Stranger Among Us* (1992), *Guilty as Sin* (1993), and *Night Falls on Manhattan* (1997). In 1993 Lumet received the Directors Guild of America's D. W. Griffith Award in recognition of his cinematic accomplishments.

**Lumière brothers, the** Auguste (1862–1954) and Louis (1864–1948) Lumière were pioneers of French cinema and the movement known as the documentary. Sons of a photographer, they developed a dry-plate process that made the family's plant in Lyons Europe's leading manufacturer of photographic products. By 1894 they had invented the Cinematographe, which, unlike the Edison Kinetograph, was a portable, hand-cranked mechanism that combined the operations of camera, printer and projector. Within a year Louis had photographed on short lengths of film numerous actualities of French life—the arrival of a train, factory workers at the Lyons plant, fishermen with nets, the demolition of a wall—and shown them to members of the Société d'Encouragement pour l'Industrie Nationale. On December 28, 1895—generally accepted as the birthday of world cinema—these images were projected before a paying audience in the basement of the Grand Café on the Boulevard des Capucines in Paris. This, a full four months before Edison's first projected films in New York City. Soon, the Lumières dispatched an army of skilled photographers ("operators") around the world to shoot what later would be called newsreels showing the coronation of Czar NICHOLAS II in Moscow, the inauguration of President MCKINLEY, etc. After 1900 the brothers sold their film-making interests and devoted their time to invention and the manufacture of photographic processes (including a three-dimensional film process that Louis introduced in his 70s). Today the Lumières, especially Louis, are regarded as founders of cinema.

**Lumumba, Patrice** *(1925–1961)* First prime minister of the Democratic Republic of the CONGO in 1960. In the same year his party emerged as the largest in the national assembly, and the Belgians chose him to be the first prime minister, with KASAVUBU as president. During his four-month incumbency he faced various crises, notably the secession of Katanga province (see KATANGA REVOLT). He was dismissed for seeking Soviet help, arrested by the army and handed over to Katanga rebels, who murdered him in 1961.

**Lunacharsky, Anatoly Vasilyevich** *(1875–1933)* Russian author, literary critic and politician. Deported in 1898 for revolutionary activities, Lunacharsky joined the Bolsheviks and worked on the party's journal *Vperyod*. Imprisoned during the 1905 Revolution, in 1909 he started a school for an elite of Russian factory workers on Capri; he was assisted by Maxim GORKY and Alexander Bogdanov. The three of them broke from LENIN, forming their own left-wing subfaction. In

1917 he joined Lenin and TROTSKY in Russia and was appointed people's commissar for education. A supporter of Bogdanovism during the 1920s, he introduced many innovations into the educational system. In 1933 he was appointed ambassador to Spain but died shortly after the appointment. The author of some 14 plays, Lunacharsky also produced many works of literary criticism.

**Lunt and Fontanne** English-born actress **Lynne Fontanne** (1887–1983) and her husband, American actor **Alfred Lunt** (1892–1977), formed one of the most celebrated couples to act on the American stage in the 20th century. Married in 1922, over the next 40 years Lunt and Fontanne starred together in 27 plays. They scored their biggest hit with *O Mistress Mine*, which opened in New York City in 1946 and completed 451 performances. Among the playwrights with whom Fontanne and Lunt worked were Noel COWARD, Robert E. SHERWOOD, Terence RATTIGAN and Jean GIRAUDOUX; they also acted in G. B. SHAW's *Arms and the Man* and Friedrich DURRENMATT's *The Visit*. The couple won numerous honors, including a Presidential Medal of Freedom from Lyndon B. JOHNSON in 1964 and a special Tony award in 1970. Fontanne was praised for her elegant demeanor, sultry voice and comedic talents.

**Lunts, Lev Natanovich** *(1901–1924)* Soviet essayist and playwright. A member of the SERAPION BROTHERS, Lunts wrote the plays *The Apes Are Coming* and *The City of Truth*, a courageous anti-Bolshevik play. He emigrated and died abroad.

**Luo Ruijing (Lo Jui-ching)** *(1906–1978)* Chinese communist official. Lo took part in the LONG MARCH of 1935. During the 1950s he was minister of public security in the People's Republic of CHINA. He was later army chief of staff. During the CULTURAL REVOLUTION he was purged by the RED GUARDS and disappeared from public view until his rehabilitation in 1975. He returned to the Central Committee of the Chinese Communist Party in 1977.

**Lurcat, Jean** *(1892–1966)* French artist and designer. Lurcat is known

primarily for his important role in stimulating renewed interest in tapestry making in the 20th century. Lurcat created his first tapestry in 1917. By 1939 he had established a tapestry works in Aubusson that attracted international attention. Major tapestries by Lurcat include *Four Seasons* (1940), *Apocalypse Tapestry* (1948) and *The Song of the World* (1957–64). Lurcat was a highly versatile artist who also worked in theatrical set and costume design, lithography and book illustration.

**Luria, Aleksandr R(omanovich)** *(1902–1977)* Russian psychologist and neurologist. Luria was a prodigal figure in Soviet psychology. He earned degrees in medicine, education and psychology and, at an early age, pioneered techniques in the objective, experimental measurement of human emotions. As head of the department of neuropsychology at Moscow University he undertook considerable research on the function of language and how it relates to mental development. During World War II he improved techniques for brain surgery and postoperative recovery for trauma patients. His major works include *Higher Cortical Functions in Man* (1966), *The Mind of a Mnemonist* (1968), *The Working Brain* (1973) and *Basic Problems of Neurolinguistics* (1976).

**Luria, Salvador Edward** *(1912–1991)* Italian-American physician who shared the 1969 NOBEL PRIZE for medicine or physiology with Max DELBRÜCK and Alfred D. Hershey. Luria was a professor at MIT from 1959 to 1978. In awarding the prize, the Nobel Foundation cited Luria's "discoveries concerning the replication mechanism and the genetic structure of viruses," which "set the solid foundation on which modern molecular biology rests." An ardent pacifist, Luria spoke out against the VIETNAM WAR (see ANTIWAR MOVEMENT). His outspokenness was apparently the reason behind his inclusion on a 1969 list of scientists who were barred from participating on advisory panels of the U.S. Department of Health, Education and Welfare.

**Lusaka Accords** A UN-sponsored 1994 agreement between the Angolan government controlled by the Popular Movement for the Liberation of Angola

(MPLA) and the rebel organization known as the National Union for the Total Independence of Angola (UNITA). The Lusaka Accords succeeded the Bicesse Accords of 1991 that had briefly established a cease-fire and arranged for national elections. When UNITA lost the elections to the MPLA, the civil war resumed. The new accords called for a cease-fire in the civil war between the MPLA and UNITA, for the disarmament of the UNITA rebels by February 1998, and for the inclusion of several UNITA members in a government of national unity. They also required the UNITA leader, Jonas Savimbi, to cease his illegal trade of diamonds on UNITA-controlled land, which Savimbi had used to fund his war effort. However, Savimbi did not comply with the UN timetable for disarmament. Instead he seized Congolese territory rich in diamond deposits during the multiparty civil war in the Congo, which he used to provide additional sources of revenue for his rebellion against the MPLA.

***Lusitania*** British passenger ship. Hit by a German submarine torpedo, the *Lusitania* sank in the Atlantic off the south coast of Ireland on May 7, 1915. The Cunard luxury liner was unarmed but carried concealed munitions for the Allies. The sinking resulted in almost 1,200 deaths, among them 128 Americans. There was an immediate large-scale public outcry in the U.S., with some people calling for a declaration of war. President Woodrow WILSON asked GERMANY for reparations, which was denied. This incident caused public opinion to shift in favor of U.S. entry into WORLD WAR I on the side of the Allies.

**Luthuli, Albert John** *(1898–1967)* South African political and civil rights leader. Born near Bulawayo, a descendant of Zulu chiefs, he was educated at a Methodist mission school and taught there for 15 years. Appointed chief in 1936, he advocated the church's policy of nonviolence in the struggle against racial discrimination. In 1945 he joined the AFRICAN NATIONAL CONGRESS, becoming president of the Natal branch in 1951 and head of the organization in 1952. Deposed as chief and restricted by the South African government in his political activities, he nonetheless headed a campaign of passive resist-

ance against APARTHEID. In his efforts, Luthuli was influenced by his religious convictions and by the American CIVIL RIGHTS MOVEMENT. Arrested many times, he was banished to his village in 1959. In 1960 the government outlawed the ANC, and in 1962 Luthuli's statements were banned from publication. Luthuli was awarded the 1960 NOBEL PEACE PRIZE. His autobiography *Let My People Go* was published two years later.

**Lutoslawski, Witold** *(1913–1994)* Polish composer. Lutoslawski was one of the major avant-garde composers of the postwar era. Strongly influenced by the atonal compositional techniques of modernists such as BÉLA BARTÓK and Igor STRAVINSKY, Lutoslawski composed

highly experimental works that occasionally allowed for jazz-like improvisation by orchestral members. His major compositions include *Little Suite* (1951), *Concerto for Orchestra* (1954), *Funeral Music* (1958), *Venetian Games* (1961) and the choral composition *Three Poems by Henri Michaux* (1963).

**Lutyens, Sir Edwin Landseer** *(1869–1944)* English architect. Born in London, Lutyens studied at the South Kensington School of Art. Lutyens started his practice in 1889, designing a number of palatial country homes. Influenced by the Arts and Crafts style, his beautifully crafted houses represent a fusion of traditional English elements with a very personal approach. From domestic to public ar-

chitecture, he executed a number of important projects that merge neoclassicism with mannerism. These include the plan for NEW DELHI, India (1912–14), that city's imposing Viceroy's Palace (1920–31) and Liverpool's monumental Anglican cathedral (1929–41). He is also known for his war memorials, among which are the Cenotaph in London (1920), FRANCE's Thiepval Memorial Arch (1924) and memorials at Manchester, England, and Johannesburg, South Africa.

## Luxembourg, Grand Duchy of

A landlocked country located in the northwest corner of Europe, covering an area of 998 square miles. Luxembourg's link with the Netherlands was severed in 1890, when the accession of a female to the Dutch throne impelled Luxembourg, where Salic Law applied, to choose a male sovereign from the House of Nassau. Salic Law was eventually revoked in 1912 to allow the accession of Grand Duchess Marie-Adelaide, whose sympathies for Luxembourg's German occupiers during WORLD WAR I attracted much criticism. Following an abortive republican coup attempt in early 1919, French pressure obliged Marie-Adelaide to abdicate in favor of her sister CHARLOTTE. Under the 1919 VERSAILLES TREATY Luxembourg was declared perpetually free of all ties with Germany, and in 1922 the Belgium-Luxembourg economic union was formed. Successive interwar governments were dominated by the Christian Social Party (CSV), although in 1937 the Social Democrats joined a coalition that enacted modern social legislation. During WORLD WAR II Luxembourg was again overrun by the Germans (1940) and annexed to the Third Reich (1942). Grand Duchess Charlotte and her ministers escaped to London. Her son, Prince (later, Grand Duke) Jean, was one of the first Allied soldiers to enter liberated Luxembourg in 1944. In the postwar era Luxembourg was a founding member of NATO (1949) and of the WEU (1955). It also joined the BENELUX economic union with Belgium and the Netherlands (1948) and the EUROPEAN COAL AND STEEL COMMUNITY, EUROPEAN ECONOMIC COMMUNITY and EURATOM (1951–58), rapidly achieving renewed prosperity on the basis of its large iron and steel industry. In 1992 Luxembourg, a charter member of the European Economic Community, joined the European Union (EU). In 2000 Prince Henri became grand duke following Grand Duke Jean's abdication. The general election of 2004 returned

| LUXEMBOURG | |
|---|---|
| 1912 | Change in law allows female to succeed to the throne; Grand Duchess Marie-Adelaide becomes sovereign. |
| 1914 | German occupation; Marie-Adelaide is vocally sympathetic to German cause. |
| 1919 | Abortive republican coup; Marie-Adelaide forced to abdicate in favor of her sister, Princess Charlotte; new constitution increases power of the elected government, decreases that of the monarchy; ties with Germany renounced in perpetuity. |
| 1922 | Economic union formed with Belgium. |
| 1940 | Second German occupation. |
| 1944 | (December) Battle of the Bulge; thousands of American soldiers buried on Luxembourg soil. |
| 1948 | "Benelux" economic union with Netherlands and Belgium. |
| 1951 | Membership in European Coal and Steel Community contributes to steel-making boom. |
| 1963 | One-thousandth anniversary as independent state. |
| 1964 | Charlotte abdicates in favor of her son, Prince Jean. |
| 1967 | Compulsory military service abolished; volunteer army under 1,000-strong established. |
| 1968 | "Explosion Scolaire"; rapid increase in school-aged children leads to education reform. |
| 1975 | Slump in steel-making leads government to encourage electronics and other industries. |
| 1992 | Luxembourg became a member of the new European Union. |
| 2000 | Prince Henri becomes grand duke following Grand Duke Jean's abdication. |
| 2002 | The euro becomes the national currency. |
| 2004 | Jean-Claude Juncker, prime minister since 1995, forms a government after his party wins the general election. |

Jean-Claude Juncker of the conservative Christian Social Party to the office of prime minister, which he has held since 1995.

**Luxemburg, Rosa** *(1871–1919)* German revolutionary leader and social theorist. Born in Russian Poland, she was involved in revolutionary activities from the age of 16. Forced to flee Switzerland in 1889, she helped to found the Polish Socialist Party in 1892. Becoming a German citizen by marriage in 1898, she became a leader of the left wing of the German Social Democratic Party. A fiery orator and brilliant writer, she was part of the 1905 revolution in Russian Poland and was active in the Second INTERNATIONAL. Differing with more moderate German socialists, she and Karl Liebknecht founded the radical Spartacus League in 1916. Two years later it became the German Communist Party. Luxemburg was imprisoned during much of World War I (1916–18). After the SPARTACIST uprising in Berlin, she and Liebknecht were again arrested in 1919. While being transported to prison, both were murdered by German soldiers. Luxemburg's best known work is *Accumulation of Capital* (1913, tr. 1951).

**Lvov, Prince Georgi Yevgenevich** *(1861–1925)* Social reformer and statesman. Lvov was active in the ZEMSTVA movement and chairman of the All-Russian Union of Zemstvos. He formed a provisional government at the request of the provisional committee of the state duma in February 1917 following NICHOLAS II's abdication and was prime minister until KERENSKY replaced him in July of that year. He lived in exile in France after the Bolshevik seizure of power.

**Lyautey, Louis-Hubert-Gonzalve** *(1854–1934)* French soldier and colonial administrator. A career officer, educated at Saint-Cyr, he served in Algeria, Madagascar and Indochina before being appointed French resident general in MOROCCO in 1912. He spent the next 13 years (with the exception of 1916–17, when he was war minister) as administrator of the protectorate. Lyautey maintained French control there during World War I and later was successful in a campaign against the Berber tribes of ABD EL-KRIM. As an administrator, he supported Arab traditions, helped to develop the economy, aided in the building of the port of Casablanca and extended the borders of the protectorate. Created a marshal of France in 1921, he resigned his colonial post in 1925.

**lynching of Leo Frank** Infamous case of American ANTI-SEMITISM. In April 1913 Mary Phagan, a 14-year-old employee of the National Pencil Co. in Atlanta, Georgia, was found brutally raped and murdered. Although penciled notes accused a black, suspicions fell on Leo Frank, the 29-year-old, Brooklyn-born Jewish manager of the company. An air of clamorous anti-Semitism pervaded the 30-day trial of Frank, who was found guilty and sentenced to death. For the next two years, the verdict was appealed as far as the U.S. Supreme Court, but rejected by all. In 1915 Georgia governor John M. Slaton, who had been petitioned to save Frank and presented with evidence that he was innocent, commuted his sentence to life imprisonment. On August 17, 1915, a group of men entered the prison in which Frank was incarcerated, and abducted and hanged him.

**Lyons, Joseph Aloysius** *(1879–1939)* Australian statesman, prime minister (1931–39). Born in Tasmania, he taught school there for 13 years before entering the Tasmanian legislature as a Labour member in 1909. Serving as Tasmania's first Labour premier (1923–28), he was elected to the federal Parliament in 1929. He held cabinet posts until 1931, when he broke with the Labour Party over its economic policies and helped found the coalition United Australia Party. As prime minister, he was able to improve the nation's economy and expand its military forces in response to mounting threats from Japan.

**Lysenko, Trofim Denisovich** *(1898–1976)* Soviet agronomist and genetic theorist. Born in Karlovka, Lysenko attended the Kiev Agricultural Institute. During his early years at Odessa's Institute of Selection and Genetics, he worked on the vernalization of spring wheat, a moistening and cold treatment of seed that promotes early flowering. In the course of this work Lysenko became convinced that the acquired effects of vernalization could be inherited. From this faulty assumption, he went on to reject the accepted Mendelian theory of inheritance and to postulate the inheritance of acquired characteristics. This doctrine dovetailed with Marxist dogma regarding social and economic improvement, and Lysenko became a great favorite of STALIN. As president of the Lenin Academy of Agricultural Science (1938–56, 1961–62) and director of the Institute of Genetics of the Soviet Academy of Sciences (1940–65), he quashed all opposition and became the virtual dictator of Soviet genetics, with all teaching and textbooks in the USSR forced to reflect his views. Lysenko's career faltered and his ruinous effect on Soviet biological science lessened after the death of Stalin in 1953. He was completely discredited in 1965 after the retirement of KHRUSHCHEV.

# M

**Ma, Yo-Yo** (*1955–* ) French-born Chinese cellist. Born in Paris, Yo-Yo Ma began to study the violin, the viola and the cello when he was four years old, but soon began to specialize in playing the latter instrument. In 1960 at the age of five, Ma appeared in his first public recital. By 1962, after studying under the renowned cellist Janos Scholz for over a year, Ma enrolled in the prestigious Juilliard School of Music in New York City. For the next 11 years, he studied cello at Juilliard under the tutelage of Leonard Rose. In 1970 Ma gave his first performance in New York City, and shortly afterward made his national debut as a performer in a program organized by American composer Leonard Bernstein. Ma enrolled at Harvard University in 1972, where he studied music and graduated in 1976.

In his professional career, Ma has become well known for both live and recorded performances. Over the past 27 years, he has developed a sterling reputation for his live performances of famous European composers ranging from Bach to Bartók, two of the composers whose works he recorded for Sony Records, the record company with which Ma has an exclusive contract. For his work on some 50 albums of recorded music, Ma has received 13 Grammy Awards.

**Maastricht Treaty** Also known as the Treaty of European Union. This treaty is a December 1991 agreement among the 12 members of the EUROPEAN COMMUNITY (EC) that called for the creation of a common currency and central bank among all EC members, as well as a common approach to defense, environmental and foreign policies. It also provided for the free transit of labor among EC states. It initially encountered some opposition in countries such as France, Germany, Great Britain and Denmark, which had expressed concern over the effect of increasing foreign competition, relative currency devaluation through the creation of a single European currency known as the EURO, and reduced control over their national economies. However, only Denmark voted to reject the treaty in June 1992, before holding a second national referendum in May 1993, that resulted in Denmark's decision to join the EUROPEAN UNION (EU), the new international relationship created among EC members by the Treaty of Maastricht. On November 1, 1993, after all 12 members had ratified the treaty, the EU came into existence and assumed control over all the intergovernmental bodies created by the EC. The replacement of national currencies by the euro occurred in 1999, with the exception of the British, Danish, and Swedish national currencies.

**Maazel, Lorin** (*1930–* ) American conductor. Born in Neuilly, France, Maazel was brought to the U.S. as a child. A musical prodigy, he studied violin, piano and conducting and made his conducting debut at age seven; by the time he was 15, he had conducted most of the major orchestras in the U.S. After studying philosophy, music and fine art at the University of Pittsburgh, he turned to music full-time. He has been director of the Berlin Radio Symphony Orchestra (1965–75), New Philharmonia Orchestra (1970–72, 1976–80), Cleveland Orchestra (1971–82), Orchestre National de France

*Virtuoso cellist Yo-Yo Ma* (PHOTOFEST)

(1977–82), Vienna State Opera (1983–84) and Pittsburgh Symphony Orchestra. In addition, he has served as guest conductor of other major orchestras throughout the world. Maazel is known for his superb baton technique, intellectual approach to music and polished performances. Particularly acclaimed for his interpretations of romantic works, he has an impressive repertoire that extends from Bach to STRAVINSKY, and has made many recordings. In 2002 Maazel became the music director of the New York Philharmonic Orchestra.

**Macao** Macao consists of a peninsula and two islands; the southernmost, Liha de Coloane, is connected to Liha da Taipa by a causeway, and Liha de Taipa is connected to the Chinese mainland of Macao by a bridge. The terrain is flat and essentially urban. There is no land suitable for cultivation. The Portuguese colonized Macao in 1557 and for 200 years the territory flourished as one of the world's major East-West trading posts for silks, gold, spices and opium. Britain's occupation of nearby Hong Kong in the mid-19th century undermined Macao's position as a trading center. In 1848 the Portuguese declared Macao independent from China, an assertion not recognized by the Chinese until 1887. In 1951 Portugal proclaimed Macao an Overseas Province. Macao suffered widespread rioting at the height of the CULTURAL REVOLUTION in China during the mid-1960s. The protests unnerved the Portuguese and served to increase Beijing's influence in the territory.

Shortly after the 1974 Portuguese revolution, the new government offered to return Macao to Chinese rule. China turned the offer down but indicated that it had a comprehensive plan to resume sovereignty over both Macao and HONG KONG. In early 1976 Portugal promulgated an "organic statute" granting Macao greater autonomy and providing for a directly elected minority on the 17-member legislative assembly. In February 1979 Portugal and China established diplomatic relations, with Macao defined as "Chinese territory under Portuguese administration." Sino-Portuguese talks opened in Beijing in June 1986 and ended 10 months later in the signing of a formal agreement on the reversion of Macao to China in 1999. The agreement was based upon the "one country, two systems" principle that had formed the basis of China's negotiated settlement with the United Kingdom in 1984 concerning the future of Hong Kong. In elections in October 1988, three of the six directly elected seats on the legislative assembly were won by a pro-liberal grouping; the remaining seats were retained by the conservative Electoral Union group, which had gained four seats in 1984 elections. In 1999 the Portuguese territory reverted to Chinese rule as a Special Autonomous Region (SAR). Since reuniting with China, Macao's leadership has sought to improve the territory's educational system and to expand its tourist attractions, which include casinos and resorts, in an attempt to compete with fellow SAR Hong Kong for a greater share of the tourist market in Asia.

**MacArthur, Douglas**  *(1880–1964)*
American general, widely considered one of the most brilliant military minds of the 20th century. Born in Little Rock, Arkansas, MacArthur was the son of a general and attended West Point, graduating at the head of his class in 1903. His early assignments took him to the PHILIPPINES and JAPAN, and he was an aide to President Theodore ROOSEVELT from 1906 to 1907. During WORLD WAR I he served with distinction in France: first as chief of staff of the 42nd (Rainbow) Division, then as commander of the 84th Infantry Brigade. After the war, promoted to the rank of brigadier general, he became superintendent of West Point (1919–22), where he raised military and academic standards. He held a variety of field commands from 1922 to 1930, when he was named a full general and appointed army chief of staff, a post he held for the next five years.

MacArthur was appointed adviser to the U.S. military mission in the Philippines in 1935. He retired from the U.S. Army in 1937 and spent four years building the nascent Philippine military. With war imminent, however, he was recalled to active duty in 1941 by President Franklin D. ROOSEVELT as commander of American forces in the Far East. MacArthur valiantly defended the Philippines from Japanese attack until February 1942, when he was forced to retreat but vowed to return. He was awarded the Medal of Honor and immediately posted to Australia as supreme Allied commander in the Southwest Pacific. He masterminded a brilliant campaign in New Guinea and was successful in recapturing the Philippines (October 1944–July 1945), wading ashore with his troops in October 1944. In December of that year, MacArthur became the army's first five-star general; the following April he was appointed commander of the U.S. Army in the Pacific. In this capacity, he accepted Japan's unconditional surrender on the U.S.S. *MISSOURI* on September 2, 1945. From 1945 to 1951 MacArthur directed the Allied occupation of Japan, modernizing and rehabilitating the defeated nation while introducing a new democratic constitution as well as democratic institutions and political practices. He antagonized many people in the U.S., however, with his austere and autocratic style. When fighting broke out in KOREA, he was appointed supreme UNITED NATIONS commander (June 1950). His typical strategic cunning was employed in the amphibious landings at INCHON, but he was surprised by the massive intervention of Chinese troops. Wishing to bomb CHINA and to check the spread of COMMUNISM in the Far East, MacArthur came into direct conflict with President Harry S TRUMAN, who relieved him of command on April 11, 1951. Returning to the U.S., perceived as a farsighted hero by conservatives and a dangerous demagogue by liberals, he gave a dramatic speech to Congress defending his aims and policies. His presidential ambitions were quashed by his failure to

*U.S. Army general Douglas MacArthur*  (LIBRARY OF CONGRESS, PRINTS AND PHOTOGRAPHS DIVISION)

achieve the Republican nomination in 1952, and he then became a successful businessman. MacArthur published *Reminiscences* in 1964.

**MacBride, Sean** *(1904–1988)* Irish lawyer, politician and diplomat. Mac-Bride was the son of the famed Irish beauty and revolutionary Maud Gonne (who inspired much of YEATS's poetry) and Gonne's husband, **Colonel John MacBride,** who was executed for his part in the 1916 EASTER RISING. Following in his parents' footsteps, Sean MacBride was active in the IRISH REPUBLICAN ARMY from 1917 until 1937. He then joined the Irish bar and became Dublin's most successful trial lawyer. In 1946 he founded a radical nationalist party, Clann na Poblachta, which helped oust the FIANNA FÁIL party two years later. From 1948 through 1951, he was the finance minister of the coalition government under which Ireland became an independent republic. He was a cofounder of AMNESTY INTERNATIONAL in 1961 and acted as secretary general of the International Commission of Jurists from 1963 to 1970. From 1974 to 1976 he was the UN commissioner for NAMIBIA. He shared the Nobel Peace Prize with Japanese statesman Eisaku SATO in 1974 and was awarded the Soviet equivalent, the Lenin Prize, three years later.

**MacColl, Ewan (James Miller)** *(1915–1989)* British folk singer and songwriter. He led the folk music revival in Britain in the 1950s and 1960s. He was also a cofounder, with Joan Littlewood, of the touring Theatre Workshop. One of his songs, "The First Time Ever I Saw Your Face," won a Grammy Award for American singer Roberta Flack in 1972.

**MacDiarmid, Hugh (pen name of Christopher Murray Grieve)** *(1892–1978)* Scottish poet and essayist. Mac-Diarmid, one of the greatest Scottish poets of the 20th century, was especially well known for his effort to revive the neglected Scottish language. He was educated in his home town of Langholm, Scotland, as well as in Edinburgh. His earliest writings were journalistic in nature, supporting left-wing political issues and cultural and political independence for Scotland. His first major work was the long poem *A Drunk Man Looks at the*

*Thistle* (1926). Other volumes of MacDiarmid's verse include *To Circumjack Cencrastus* (1930), *First Hymn to Lenin and Other Poems* (1931), *Scots Unbound and Other Poems* (1932) and *In Memoriam James Joyce.* MacDiarmid was awarded the Foyle Poetry Prize and the Fletcher of Saltoun Medal, as well as an honorary doctoral degree from Edinburgh University. *Collected Poems* appeared in 1962; *Selected Essays,* in 1969.

**MacDonald, Dwight** *(1906–1982)* American essayist, critic and editor. He is known for his witty and acerbic writings on culture, politics and film. While a writer for *Fortune* magazine (1929–36), MacDonald became a committed socialist and Trotskyite. (See Leon TROTSKY.) A leading figure in American left-wing intellectual circles during the 1930s and 1940s, he was associated with the PARTISAN REVIEW from 1938 to 1943. A pacifist, he opposed WORLD WAR II, and in the 1960s was an outspoken critic of American involvement in the VIETNAM WAR. He was a longtime staff writer for *The NEW YORKER* (1951–71) and a film critic for *Esquire* (1960–66).

**MacDonald, J(ames) E(dward) H(ervey)** *(1873–1932)* Anglo-Canadian painter and poet. Born in England, he emigrated to Canada in 1887. As a member of Canada's GROUP OF SEVEN, he sought to portray the natural splendors of his new homeland, painting north country panoramas in stylized forms and vivid colors. In his verse, MacDonald was strongly influenced by the 19th-century Americans Henry David Thoreau and Walt Whitman.

**MacDonald, John D(ann)** *(1916–1986)* U.S. author. Over the course of a 40-year writing career, he wrote dozens of books—most of them mysteries. His best-known character was the detective Travis McGee, a tough, cynical expert in salvaging who lived on a Florida houseboat. McGee appeared in 21 books published between 1964 and 1985. Each of those books bore a title that included a color.

**MacDonald, Margaret** *(1865–1933)* British-born artist-designer. She worked closely with her sister Frances MacDonald from 1894 until her marriage to Charles Rennie MACKINTOSH in 1900. MacDonald was educated at the Glas-

gow School of Art, where she met Mackintosh. Her reputation is based primarily on her watercolor paintings and book illustrations, as well as her collaboration in textile design with Mackintosh. After she and Mackintosh relocated to London in 1916, her work as a painter sustained them as his career tapered off in his later years.

**MacDonald, (James) Ramsay** *(1866–1937)* British Labour Party leader, prime minister of the UNITED KINGDOM (1924; 1929–35). MacDonald, born in poverty in the Scottish village of Lossiemouth, settled in England in 1886. An outspoken advocate of socialism, he joined the Independent Labour Party in 1894 and in 1900 became secretary of the newly formed LABOUR PARTY. He was elected Member of Parliament for Leicester in 1906 and then held the seat until 1918. MacDonald ably led the parliamentary Labour Party from 1911 until 1914, when his pacifist views cost him his influence at the outbreak of WORLD WAR I. Elected again in 1922 for Aberavon, he was reelected leader of the parliamentary party, thereby heading the Opposition. In a general election called by Stanley BALDWIN, MacDonald became Britain's first Labour prime minister (January 1924); he also served simultaneously as foreign secretary. Following the publication of the ZINOVIEV LETTER urging a communist overthrow in Britain, the Labour Party was accused of pro-communist sympathies, and the Conservatives were reelected to power in November 1924.

MacDonald again became Labour prime minister from 1929 to 1931. However, the worsening financial situation caused a split in the party (see GREAT DEPRESSION). MacDonald resigned and then formed a coalition with the Conservatives and Liberals, known as the NATIONAL GOVERNMENT, which he headed from 1931 to 1935. Labour Party loyalists viewed MacDonald's formation of the National Government as a betrayal of Labour principles and felt that social ambition had wooed him away from his working-class origins. Although MacDonald maintained a Labour influence in foreign affairs and defense issues, the Conservatives dominated domestic affairs. MacDonald resigned in 1935 and was again succeeded by Baldwin. He remained in the cabinet as Lord President of the Council until his death on a vacation cruise. In his prime MacDonald was a skillful administrator with hopes for world peace through the LEAGUE OF NATIONS. His later years were troubled by declining health and disillusionment.

**MacDowell Colony** In New Hampshire, a permanent summer retreat for writers, composers and artists. Originally a farm, it was purchased in 1896 by composer Edward MacDowell as a retreat. Following his death in 1908, a fund was formed and used to establish the colony. Considered a Mecca for creative artists, it is one of the longest-lasting art colonies in the country. The colony's distinguished roster of fellows includes poet Edwin Arlington ROBIN-SON, novelist Thornton WILDER, composer Leonard BERNSTEIN and artist Milton AVERY.

**Macedonia** Formerly the southern half of YUGOLSAVIA and now an independent republic (1991–   ). After the BALKAN WARS of 1912 and 1913 and the breakup of the OTTOMAN EMPIRE Macedonia was freed from Turkish control and subsequently divided up between Greece, Bulgaria and Serbia. After World War I Serbia joined the Kingdom of Yugoslavia, the southern province including all of what is present-day Macedonia. During World

| MACEDONIA | |
|---|---|
| 1912–13 | After the First Balkan War, Macedonia is partitioned between Bulgaria, Greece and Serbia. |
| 1918 | The Serbian part of Macedonia is included in what will become Yugoslavia. |
| 1941–44 | Macedonia is occupied by Bulgaria. |
| 1945 | Marshal Tito becomes premier of liberated Yugoslavia. Collectivization and mass purges are undertaken by the Communist-dominated government. |
| 1953 | Tito is elected president of Yugoslavia. |
| 1980 | Tito dies. |
| 1991 | Following a referendum, Macedonia proclaims independence and adopts a new constitution. |
| 1992 | Macedonia sees the peaceful withdrawal of the Yugoslav army, making Macedonia the only Yugoslav republic to achieve independence without war. |
| 1993 | The nation becomes a member of the UN. |
| 1995 | The nation becomes a member of the European Council. |
| 1999 | Nearly 250,000 ethnic Albanians from Kosovo seek refuge in Macedonia when NATO begins a campaign of air strikes against Yugoslavia. |
| 2001 | The Albanian National Liberation Army begins an insurgence from Kosovo, soon controlling territory in northern and western Macedonia. A peace agreement is signed in August. |
| 2005 | Macedonia becomes a candidate for membership in the European Union. |

War II the Axis powers occupied the area, and Macedonia was divided between Bulgaria and Italy. At the end of the war Macedonia became a republic within the communist Federal Republic of Yugoslavia, run by Marshal TITO, who ruled the country until his death in 1980. The first noncommunist government since 1945 was elected in 1990, and in 1991 the country peacefully seceded from Yugoslavia and declared independence. In 1993 it joined the UN and in 1995 the Council of Europe. Macedonia managed to remain peaceful through the Yugoslav wars of the early 1990s but was destabilized later in the decade due to the influx into the country of 250,000 Albanian refugees from the conflict in the neighboring Serbian province of KOSOVO. In 2001 an Albanian paramilitary group started an insurgency in Kosovo and soon controlled the north and west portions of Macedonia. The war was ended that same year by the intervention of a NATO peacekeeping force. Macedonia officially became a candidate in 2005 for membership in the European Union.

**MacEntee, Sean** *(1889–1984)* Irish nationalist and politician. MacEntee was a cofounder of the Irish Republic and the last surviving member of the first government established by the FIANNA FÁIL party of Eamon DE VALERA (see IRELAND). He fought against the British in the 1916 EASTER REBELLION and was sentenced to death but reprieved at the last minute and released from prison (with de Valera) under a general amnesty (1917). MacEntee was elected to the parliament of the Irish Free State in 1927. During his career he held a total of 27 posts in Fianna Fail governments, including those of finance minister and deputy prime minister. He retired in 1969.

**Machine Art** Term used in art history and criticism to describe the relationship that developed in the 1920s and 1930s linking many modern artists with the increasing role of industrial machinery in production and its influence on products and the environment. The concept of the house as a machine for living was expressed by LE CORBUSIER, and artists such as Marcel DUCHAMP incorporated machine-made elements into their work. With the inclination of MODERNISM to turn away from ornament, the actual forms of machines and mechanical parts came to be seen as having aesthetic value in their own right. In 1934 the MUSEUM OF MODERN ART, New York City, mounted an exhibit titled *Machine Art* in which such objects as springs, ball bearings and boat propellers were exhibited as art. Also shown were designed objects with strongly mechanistic character such as plumbing components, tools, instruments and utensils, as well as designed items with machinelike qualities such as clocks and furniture. In its effort to find an expressive quality suited to the technological nature of modern life, the Modern movement has had a continuing interest in the machine. The catalog of the *Machine Art* exhibit and the book *The Machine Age in America 1918–1941*—published in connection with an exhibition at the Brooklyn Museum dealing with this subject—are excellent reviews of the way mechanical devices have affected design and art.

**Machito (Frank Grillo)** *(1915–1984)* Cuban-born bandleader. Machito moved to the U.S. in 1937 and pioneered the use of complex Latin rhythms in JAZZ in the early 1940s. His New York–based band, the Afro-Cubans, influenced such jazz greats as Dizzy GILLESPIE and Charlie PARKER. Machito's influence also extended through the Latin dance music known as Salsa, which was popular at the time of his death.

**MacInnes, Helen Clark** *(1907–1985)* Scottish-born novelist known for her stories of intrigue and espionage. MacInnes immigrated to the U.S. in 1937 with her husband, classics scholar Gilbert Highet. She began writing in the early 1940s. Several of her novels are set during WORLD WAR II, while others involve COLD WAR espionage. Her books were translated into 22 languages, and four were made into films, including the bestselling *Above Suspicion* (1941; filmed 1943), *The Venetian Affair* (1963; filmed 1966) and *The Salzburg Connection* (1968; filmed 1972).

**Mack, Connie** *(1862–1956)* American baseball owner-manager. Mack began his 60-year baseball career as a catcher, primarily with the Pittsburgh Pirates. He became player-manager of the team in 1894 and retired from both positions two years later. In 1901 he took on the job of managing the Philadelphia Athletics (known as the A's), an entry in the newly formed American League. They quickly emerged as the team to beat, topping the league in six of its first 14 seasons. He led the A's to five World Series championships in nine fall classic appearances and went on to post a record 3,776 wins—and 4,025 losses. Mack was named to the Baseball Hall of Fame in 1937 and retired 13 years later in 1950, having managed the A's for 50 years.

**Mack, Walter Staunton** *(1895–1990)* U.S. businessman. Mack built Pepsi into the second-most popular soft drink in the U.S. after COCA-COLA. He served as president and chairman of Pepsi-Cola Co. (1951–83), helping to turn the small softdrink firm into a major business through a combination of clever advertising and promotional activities. He resigned from the firm following a series of disputes with the board of directors over his promotional campaigns and went on to head several other companies.

**Macke, August** *(1887–1914)* German painter. Born in the Ruhr Valley, he studied at the Academy of Düsseldorf. He traveled to Paris several times from 1907 on and was deeply influenced by such French movements as CUBISM and FAUVISM and by the orphism of Robert DELAUNAY. In Munich in 1909 Macke met KANDINSKY and MARC; in 1911 he became a founding member of the BLAUE REITER group. A major figure in German EXPRESSIONISM, Macke employed luminous color and linear pattern in defining a very personal view of landscapes, cityscapes and figures. He traveled to Tunisia with Paul KLEE in 1914, producing subtly transparent watercolors in vividly heightened colors. His brilliant career was cut short on a battlefield in France during WORLD WAR I.

**Mackenzie, Compton** *(1883–1973)* British novelist and autobiographer. Mackenzie was one of the most widely read British fiction writers of the first half of the 20th century, and his novels continue to find a readership to this day. Educated at St. Paul's School and at Oxford University, Mackenzie began his writing career in the 1900s as a poet before enjoying success with his first novel, *The Passionate Elopement* (1911). Two other best sellers followed quickly— *Carnival* (1912) and *Sinister Street* (1913–14). Mackenzie served in British naval intelligence during WORLD WAR I, an experience he chronicled in *Athenian Memories* (1931) and which formed the basis of two later novels, *Water on the Brain* (1933) and *Whisky Galore* (1947). Mackenzie was knighted in 1952.

**Mackintosh, Charles Rennie** (*1868–1928*) Scottish architect and designer. Born in Glasgow, he was trained as an architect. In the early 1890s he became one of the first Britons to use the ART NOUVEAU style, employing it in decorative and graphic arts as well as in such architectural works as the Glasgow School of Art (1898–99), where he merged it with native Scottish traditions. Some of the finest of his Art Nouveau efforts are in the architecture, interior decor, furniture and murals of the four Miss Cranston's Tearooms in Glasgow (1896–1901). He is also noted for a number of turn-of-the-20th-century Scottish country houses that updated the 17th-century manor style. These include Windyhill (1899–1901) and Hill House (1902–03). A participant in the Vienna Secession exhibition (1900), he influenced the development of 20th-century European architecture.

**MacLeish, Archibald** (*1892–1982*) American poet, playwright and statesman. Educated at Yale (B.A., 1915) and Harvard (LL.B., 1919), MacLeish gave up his law practice to join the LOST GENERATION of American expatriates in PARIS in 1923. His poems of this period show the influence of POUND, T. S. ELIOT and the symbolists. After his return home in 1928, he became an increasingly public figure, and his poetry reflected this sense of social commitment. A passionate critic of President Herbert HOOVER and an outspoken foe of NAZISM, MacLeish joined President Franklin D. ROOSEVELT's NEW DEAL administration. He was librarian of Congress (1939–44), assistant director of the Office of War Information (1942–43) and assistant secretary of state (1944–45). He represented the U.S. in the organization of UNESCO and from 1949 to 1962 taught at Harvard. MacLeish won three PULITZER PRIZES for his poetry and drama; *Conquistador* (1932), *Collected Poems: 1917–1952* (1953) and *J.B.: A Play in Verse* (1959). *Collected Poems* also won the BOLLINGEN PRIZE and a National Book Award. His screenplay for *The Eleanor Roosevelt Story* received an ACADEMY AWARD in 1966. In his later years he also protested against McCARTHYISM and the VIETNAM WAR.

**MacLennan, (John) Hugh** (*1907–1990*) Canadian writer. A novelist and essayist, he was the author of seven major fiction works. His novel *Two Solitudes* (1945) became a symbol of the conflict between English- and French-speaking Canadians. His other works include *The Watch That Ends the Night* (1959) and *The Colour of Canada* (1967).

**MacLeod, Roderick** (*1892?–1984*) British officer in WORLD WAR II. He organized two top-secret operations to mislead the Germans about Allied invasion plans. Using limited personnel and equipment to simulate large-scale troop movements, and leaking false information about these movements, MacLeod created "phantom armies" in Britain during 1943–44. The first ruse led the Germans to expect an invasion in Norway, where they diverted troops. The second caused the German high troops. The second caused the German high command to expect the D-DAY landings to come at CALAIS rather than NORMANDY as they actually did on June 6, 1944. Both deceptions played a significant rule in the success of the Allied INVASION OF NORMANDY.

**MacLiammoir, Micheal (Micheal Wilmore)** (*1899–1978*) Irish theatrical actor, set designer and playwright. MacLiammoir, one of the major figures in the 20th-century Irish theater, began his acting career as a child. He first achieved renown through founding, with Hilton EDWARDS, the GATE THEATRE in Dublin in the 1920s. MacLiammoir created striking set designs—influenced by the ART DECO style of artists Aubrey Beardsley and Leon BAKST—for more than 300 productions at Dublin Gate. He also appeared there as Romeo, Hamlet and Othello, among other leading roles. MacLiammoir achieved international success with three one-man shows: *The Importance of Being Oscar* (1960), a tribute to Oscar Wilde; *I Must Be Talking to My Friends* (1963); and *Talking about Yeats* (1970).

**Macmillan, (Maurice) Harold** (*1894–1986*) British statesman, prime minister of the UNITED KINGDOM (1957–63). Born in London, Macmillan was the grandson of the founder of the Macmillan publishing house. Educated at Eton and at Balliol College, Oxford, he served in the Grenadier Guards in WORLD WAR I and was wounded three times. A member of the CONSERVATIVE PARTY, he entered politics after the war and was elected to Parliament in 1924 for the constituency of Stockton. Except for two brief periods, he served in the House of Commons for the next 40 years.

In the 1920s Macmillan built a reputation as a leading progressive within the party. In the mid-1930s he joined Winston CHURCHILL in criticizing the foreign policy of the BALDWIN and CHAMBERLAIN governments—particularly Chamberlain's policy of APPEASEMENT toward Adolf HITLER's GERMANY. He served in Churchill's government in 1940 as a junior minister before entering the cabinet in the special post of resident minister in North Africa. Later during WORLD WAR II he was also responsible for Britain's relations with her Allies in the Mediterranean and the Balkans, and served as liaison between Churchill and General Dwight D. EISENHOWER.

Minister of housing from 1951 to 1954, he subsequently served as defense minister (1954–55), foreign secretary (1955) and chancellor of the exchequer (1955–57). He succeeded Anthony EDEN as prime minister following Eden's resignation over the SUEZ CRISIS. Macmillan held office during a period of apparent economic prosperity, although there were some troubling signs in the British economy. In his famous WIND OF CHANGE speech (1960), Macmillan was the first British prime minister to publicly acknowledge and accept the fact that the BRITISH EMPIRE was no longer viable. He presided over the independence of a number of British colonies, mostly in Africa. Widely respected both at home and abroad, Macmillan reestablished good relations with the U.S. after the U.S. rebuke of Britain over the Suez affair. His personal friendships with U.S. presidents and John F. KENNEDY helped maintain British prestige even after it was clear that Britain was no longer a world power. Macmillan resigned after the PROFUMO AFFAIR brought about domestic criticism of his government. In retirement, Macmillan was revered as an elder statesman. After turning down honors on several occasions, he accepted a life peerage as the Earl of Stockton in 1984.

## Macmillan, Kenneth *(1929–1992)*

British dancer, choreographer and ballet director. Macmillan, one of the major choreographers of the 20th century, began his career as a dancer with Sadler's Wells Theatre Ballet (1946) and Sadler's Wells Ballet (1948). After 1952 he worked for both companies and choreographed his first ballet, *Dances Concertantes,* in 1955. In 1958 he began working with ballerina Lynn Seymour, who became the inspiration for such ballets as *Baiser de la Fée* (1960) and the popular *Romeo and Juliet* (1965). Appointed resident choreographer of the Royal Ballet in 1965, he also served as director of the German Opera Ballet in Berlin from 1966 to 1969. He directed the Royal Ballet from 1970 to 1977, creating such works as the innovative *Anastasia* (1971), *Manon* (1974) and *Elite Syncopations* (1974) for that company. He became artistic associate of AMERICAN BALLET THEATRE in 1984 and has choreographed and staged his ballets for many other companies.

## MacNeice, (Frederick) Louis *(1907–1963)* Anglo-Irish poet, playwright and translator. Born in Belfast, the son of an Anglican bishop, MacNeice attended Marlboro public school in England before going to Oxford in the late 1920s. At Oxford he was a prominent member of W. H. AUDEN's circle and briefly shared the left-wing sympathies of Auden, Stephen SPENDER and C. DAY LEWIS. Ultimately, however, he was skeptical of all political systems. After graduating with a first in classics, he taught at Birmingham University and at Bedford College, University of London. From 1941 until his death he wrote and produced features, including numerous radio plays, for the BBC. MacNeice's poems view modern urban life through an introspective and ironic sensibility; the often playful lyricism of his work is matched by formal grace, moral intensity and philosophical seriousness. His translations of Aeschylus and Goethe are highly regarded. Somewhat shy, puritanical and conscious of his Northern Irish roots, MacNeice always felt distanced from the English society in which he moved, despite his success. During his lifetime he was overshadowed by

Auden, but since his death his work has been reevaluated, and he is now regarded as a major literary figure in his own right, especially in Britain and Ireland. MacNeice's unfinished autobiography, *The Strings Are False,* was published posthumously in 1966, and his *Collected Poems* were issued the following year.

## Madagascar (Democratic Republic of Madagascar) Madagascar, which comprises the main island and several

smaller islets, is located in the Indian Ocean, off the southeast coast of Africa. France made Madagascar a colony in 1896, but Malagasy resistance flourished, resulting in brutal French suppression of riots in 1898–1904 and 1947–48. The country achieved autonomy in 1958, full independence in 1960. Philibert Tsirinana was president of the First Republic (1960–72) but resigned after protests and economic problems grew. An interim military

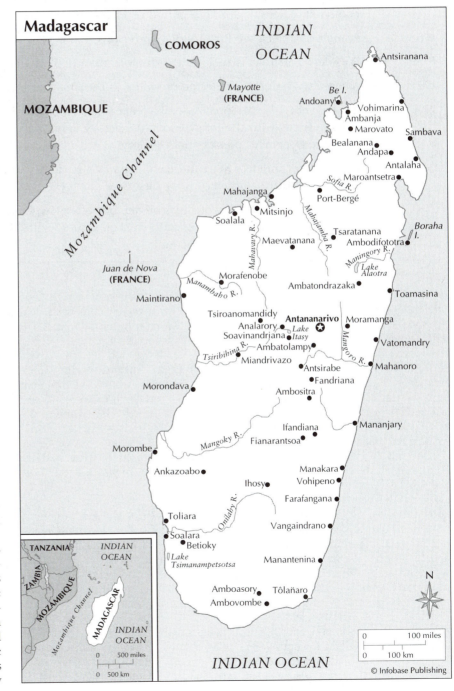

## MADAGASCAR

| | |
|---|---|
| 1960 | Madagascar becomes a sovereign and independent state within the French Community as the Malagasy Republic, with Philibert Tsiranana as president. |
| 1975 | The directorate is superseded by the Supreme Revolutionary Council, headed by Commander Didier Ratsiraka. |
| 1986 | Violent demonstrations take place in Toamasina in response to food shortages and the government austerity program. Student protests erupt at the University of Madagascar in Antananarivo. |
| 1987 | Rioting breaks out. Indian and Pakistani traders are attacked owing to resentment of their comparative wealth during a period of increased poverty. |
| 1988 | Prime Minister Desire Rakotoarijaona resigns and is replaced by Victor Ramahatra. |
| 1989 | President Ratsiraka is reelected with more than 60% of the vote. |
| 1993 | Albert Zafy, a doctor, is elected president in the first free elections under the new constitution. |
| 1996 | In September the National Assembly impeaches President Zafy for failure to renegotiate favorable terms with the International Monetary Fund. Zafy steps down in October. Ratsiraka wins the December presidential elections. |
| 2001 | Opposition candidate Marc Ravalomanana claims victory in presidential elections and charges Ratsiraka with rigging election results. |
| 2002 | Violence between rival protesters breaks out after Ravalomanana declares himself president in February. In April the Constitutional High Court names Ravalomanana as winner of the December elections after a recount. |

regime dissolved parliament and closed foreign military bases. The present Democratic Republic was formed in 1975 with Didier Ratsiraka as president. He has moved the country toward socialism, but economic problems, regional rivalries, coup attempts and brutal suppression of demonstrations have plagued his regime. During the kung fu riots (1984, 1985) several people died as the government suppressed the martial arts cult. In 1987 many Indians and Pakistanis left the country in the face of prejudicial attacks. Although democratic reforms were introduced into the constitution in 1992, Madagascar has remained politically unstable, fluctuating between the control of Ratsiraka and his opponents. In 1993 Ratsiraka was defeated by Albert Zafy in the first multiparty elections. Zafy failed to make improvements and was impeached in 1996. Ratsiraka was reelected in the ensuing elections. The 2001 elections resulted in controversy when opposition leader Marc Ravalomanana's claim to victory was disputed by Ratsiraka. Madagascar's high court ruled in favor of Ravalomanana, who survived a coup attempt in 2003 to continue as president.

**Madariaga, Salvador de** (1886–1978) Spanish author and diplomat. Madariaga was Republican SPAIN's ambassador to the U.S. (1931) and its delegate to the LEAGUE OF NATIONS (1932–34). He was a leading critic of Generalissimo Francisco FRANCO and left Spain at the outbreak of the SPANISH CIVIL WAR.

**Madonna** (1958– ) American musician and actress. Born Madonna Louise Ciccone in Bay City, Michigan, she studied dance on a scholarship at the University of Michigan before leaving the university at the end of her sophomore year to pursue a career in music in New York City, where she performed with a band at clubs. In 1983 she recorded her first album, *Madonna*, which contained the popular singles "Lucky Star," "Borderline," and "Holiday," all of which became popular singles by the end of 1984. Madonna followed the success of her first album with several others, in-

*Pop star Madonna in a poster for her controversial 1991 documentary.* TRUTH OR DARE (PHOTOFEST)

cluding *Like A Virgin* (1984), *True Blue* (1986), *Like A Prayer* (1989), *Bedtime Stories* (1994), *Ray of Light* and *Confessions on a Dance Floor* (2005).

In addition to her music career, Madonna has also regularly appeared in motion pictures. In 1985 she made her on-screen debut in *Desperately Seeking Susan,* a comedy in which she played Susan, a woman attempting to evade her boyfriend (Aidan Quinn). In the 1980s Madonna followed *Susan* with *Shanghai Surprise* (1986) and *Who's That Girl?* (1987). In 1990 she starred in her first major motion picture, *Dick Tracy,* in which she played Breathless Mahoney, a nightclub singer who later proves to be an assassin. Following *Dick Tracy* Madonna appeared in *Shadows and Fog* (1992); *A League of Their Own* (1992); *Body of Evidence* (1993); *Evita* (1996)—for which she won a Golden Globe award in 1996 for best actress in a musical or comedy—*The Next Best Thing* (2000); *Swept Away* (2002) and the James Bond film *Die Another Day* (2002).

**madrassa** Arabic for "school." An Islamic school for Muslim students designed to educate Islamic children in the practices and teachings of their faith. Madrassas separate male and female students into separate class meetings to discuss the Koran and instruct them in Arabic grammar and Islamic law and history. Following the terrorist attacks of SEPTEMBER 11, 2001, the madrassas organized in South Asia by the DEOBANDI sect of Islam were criticized for indoctrinating their students in ISLAMISM, a fundamentalist Islamic movement that required a strict application of Islamic law and the removal of all non-Muslim elements from society. It was also alleged that these Deobandi-sponsored madrassas served as recruiting grounds for the terrorist group AL-QAEDA that arranged the terrorist attacks of September 11, 2001.

**Maeght, Aimé** *(1906–1981)* French printer, art dealer and art promoter. During half a century as an art dealer, Maeght promoted the careers of such leading European artists as Joan MIRO, Alberto GIACOMETTI, Georges BRAQUE and Henri MATISSE. He persuaded many of them to produce lithographs of their work in order to reach a broader public. In 1964 he founded the Foundation Marguerite et Aimé Maeght, an innovative museum.

**Mafia** Secret society of organized crime. Formed in medieval Sicily to fight French oppression of Italians, the name is an acronym of *Morte alla Francia Italia anela!* (Death to the French is Italy's Cry!). The organization evolved into a strongarm group with considerable local autonomy and assumed its criminal identity in 19th-century Sicily. There, in spite of regular campaigns against it (notably by Benito MUSSOLINI), it came to have the tremendous political and social control that it maintains to this day. The Mafia arrived in the U.S. with Sicilian immigrants in the late 1800s. The first killing in the U.S. that is attributed to the Mafia supposedly occurred in Louisiana in 1889 at the beginning of a waterfront war in New Orleans between Sicilian and Neopolitan gangsters. That war is said to have marked the Mafia's entry into big-time U.S. crime. The organization was soon operating in many large cities, often preying on the Italian immigrant community. During PROHIBITION (1920–33) the Mafia grew enormously, controlling the bootleg liquor business and running such enterprises as prostitution, loansharking, gambling and narcotics. As in Sicily, it has over time also taken control of a number of legitimate businesses in America, although their identity remains shadowy. The U.S. Mafia is comprised of a number of regional "families" operating in recognized territories. The American history of the group includes bloody struggles for the control of families as well as a modernization movement, which was largely engineered by "Lucky" LUCIANO, and which brought the Mafia closer to other, non-Italian factions of organized crime. Also referred to as the Cosa Nostra (Our Thing), it comprises an estimated 24 families and remains a dominant force in criminal activities in contemporary America.

**Magic** Code name for material derived from the breaking of the Japanese diplomatic code, a feat accomplished by American cryptographic experts in 1940. The information produced by the Magic operation was vital to Allied success in a number of areas related to Axis activities. These included data on plans for Japanese KAMIKAZE attacks on U.S. warships, intelligence on German coastal defenses in the event of an Allied invasion of Occupied France, information on the development and locations of Germany's lethal V-2 rockets and facts about the spying activities in the U.S. of Spanish diplomats working for Japan.

***Magic Mountain, The*** The most famous novel (1924) of German author Thomas MANN. Its central protagonist, Hans Castorp, is a young German burgher with solidly bourgeois values who has just completed his college studies and is planning, at the outset of the novel, to embark upon an engineering career. But the course of Castorp's life is changed when he goes to visit his tubercular cousin who is residing in a sanatorium high on a mountain—metaphorically, the "Magic Mountain" of the title. While paying his visit, Castorp himself is diagnosed by a physician as suffering from tuberculosis. As a result, his planned visit of three weeks extends on for seven years. In the course of his stay, Castorp grows spiritually as a result of his new, removed perspective of the world. He and his fellow tuberculosis victims, who engage in protracted philosophical dialogues on the declining state of European civilization, come to symbolize the detached helplessness of Western intellectuals confronted with historical forces that they can dissect and judge but never control. Mann's novel is thus a portrait of the conditions in Europe that led to WORLD WAR II.

**magic realism (art)** A style of figurative painting prevalent in the U.S. during the 1930s and, to a limited extent, in the 1940s and 1950s. Considerably influenced by the heightened sensibilities and distortions of SURREALISM, it is characterized by subject matter taken from everyday life. These images are elevated to the extraordinary by their portrayal in minutely precise details and excruciatingly brilliant light. Painters drawn to this style include Ivan Le Lorraine ALBRIGHT, Peter Bloom and Philip EVERGOOD. Among later practitioners of magic realism are the painters George TOOKER and Paul Cadmus.

**magic realism (literature)** Literary movement centered in Latin America. Magic realism is a school of fiction that calls for the narrative intermingling of realistic portrayals of social conditions along with mythic fantasy. A key precursor of magic realism was William FAULKNER, whose novels frequently drew upon the inner dreams and reveries of his characters while providing a detailed and realistic portrait of life in the American South. The generation of Latin American novelists that rose to prominence in the 1960s—notably Miguel Angel ASTURIAS of Guatemala, Julio CORTAZAR of Argentina, Carlos FUENTES of Mexico, Guillermo Cabrera Infante of Cuba and Gabriel GARCÍA MÁRQUEZ of Colombia—became the key proponents of magic realism as a distinct literary school. *One Hundred Years of Solitude* (1970) by García Márquez, with its family chronicle structure overlaid with fantasies and dreams, is perhaps the leading exemplar of the methods of magic realism.

**Maginot Line** French fortification system running for 200 miles along the Franco-German border from Switzerland to Belgium. Consisting mainly of entrenchments and underground forts, it was built from 1930 to 1934 and was named for André Maginot (1877–1932), French minister of war during the first years of its construction. It was built to act as an impregnable barrier to German invasion—built by a militarily and emotionally exhausted France that was intent on using it as a deterrent to avoid another Great War. During WORLD WAR II, this fixed line was easily flanked by German armored forces, which advanced through Belgium in 1940. Its failure led to the fall of FRANCE in June of that year. The Maginot Line has come to be symbolic of fixed defensive positions that are open to mobile attack, and of the false sense of security that such lines can provide.

**Magritte, René** *(1898–1967)* Belgian painter and art theorist. Magritte first won international attention in the 1920s as one of the most original painters in the school of SURREALISM. Heavily influenced by the metaphysical paintings of Giorgio de CHIRICO, Magritte developed a style laden with dreamlike imagery that was quietly poetic in tone, without the violent elements that marked much Surrealist painting of the period. Magritte sometimes painted verbal statements onto his canvases to accompany his pictorial images, as in the case of his famous painting *The Wind and the Song*

(1928–29), which portrays a pipe below which is written *"Ceci n'est pas une pipe"* (This is not a pipe). Other renowned canvasses by Magritte include *The Conqueror* (1925), *The Lovers* (1928) and *The Key of Dreams* (1930).

**Mahathir bin Mohammad, Datuk Seri** *(1925– )* Malaysian politician, member of the Malaysian House of Representatives (1965–69), and Senate (1973–75), minister of education (1974–78) and trade and industry (1978–81), and prime minister of Malaysia (1981–2003). Born in Alur Setar, Mahathir began his political career in 1965 when he was elected to parliament. However, he was defeated when he ran for reelection in 1969. Shortly after those elections, riots broke out in Malaysia protesting the leadership of Prime Minister TUNKU ABDUL RAHMAN. Mahathir soon joined in the public criticism of the Tunku with his book *The Malay Dilemma* (1969). After serving in the Malaysian Senate, Mahathir became minister of education in 1974. In 1978 he became minister of trade and industry, from which post he sought increasing access to foreign markets for Malaysian exports and increased investment in Malaysian facilities.

In 1981 Mahathir became prime minister and was appointed the president of the United Malays National Organization (UNMO). He guided the National Front parliamentary coalition, in which UNMO was the principal party, to successive victories in the 1982, 1986, 1990, 1995 and 1999 national elections. He also became increasingly involved in promoting Malaysia's participation in the Association of Southeast Asian Nations (ASEAN) and the ASIA-PACIFIC ECONOMIC COOPERATION (APEC) forum. When the Asian-Pacific region was plunged into an economic crisis in 1997, Mahathir came under fire for his lavish spending on such projects as the world's tallest building, the Petronas Towers. Additionally, some economists expressed concern that his efforts to insulate the Malaysian currency from attacks from international speculators would lead to a weakened economy. However, the Malaysian currency and domestic market recovered fairly rapidly, compared to other Asian-Pacific countries like Japan. In 2003 after a series of antigovernment protests, and after angering several foreign governments with statements widely interpreted as anti-Semitic, Mahathir left office.

**Mahfouz, Naguib** *(1911–2006)* Egyptian novelist, playwright and screenwriter. A prolific author familiar to the Arab-speaking world, Mahfouz was relatively unknown to Westerners when he became the first Arabic writer to receive the NOBEL PRIZE in literature (1988). He first received acclaim for the novel *Madaq Alley* (1947) but is best known for *The Cairo Trilogy* (1956–57). Mahfouz's novels are realistic works generally portraying the lower and middle classes of Cairo. Mahfouz was criticized in Arabic countries for his moderate stance toward Israel (he received death threats), and his books were banned by religious leaders for what was perceived as his condemnation of Islam.

**Mahler, Gustav** *(1860–1911)* Conductor and composer most famous for his large-scaled, intensely romantic yet intricately crafted symphonic works. In Arnold SCHOENBERG's words, he was "a man in a torment of emotion exerting himself to gain inner harmony." Born in Kalischt, Bohemia (then part of the Austro-Hungarian Empire), Mahler's musical precocity led to his enrollment in the Vienna Conservatory in 1875. Because his early efforts, including his First Symphony (1889), were rebuffed, he began a successful career as an opera conductor in, successively, Laibach, Olmütz, Kassel, Prague, Leipzig, Budapest and Vienna (where he served as artistic director at the Imperial Opera from 1897 to 1907). Driven, often ruthless in his quest for perfection, he virtually revolutionized modern operatic production. However, he seemed to live primarily for those times when he could escape the opera stage and spend his

*Composer Gustav Mahler* (LIBRARY OF CONGRESS, PRINTS AND PHOTOGRAPHS DIVISION)

summers in Steinbach or Maiernigg or Toblach composing his 10 symphonies. These works, in the judgment of historian David Ewen "are the last word in German Romanticism," struggling to convey in tones "the meaning of life and death, of the universe and nature, of eternal love and fate, of suffering, and resignation, and of resurrection." Mahler once told Jean SIBELIUS that "a symphony must embrace the world." His symphonies frequently drew upon songs he had composed to the texts of the Brentano-Arnim German folk poetry collection, *Das Knaben Wunderhorn* (*The Youth's Magic Horn,* 1805–08)—a strange world of talking animals, macabre jests, haunted forests and military marches.

In 1907 fate delivered three hammer blows to Mahler: the death of his daughter Maria, his departure from the Vienna Opera, and the medical diagnosis of a grave cardiac deficiency. He wrote: "At the end of my life, I must go back to living like a beginner and learn again how to stand." He underwent psychoanalysis with Sigmund FREUD, and in 1908 accepted the post of director of the Metropolitan Opera in New York City. During his few years in New York he conducted exceptional performances of operatic and orchestral works, but he returned to Vienna after wearying of disputes with musicians and with the Metropolitan's board.

In his final years Mahler composed a triptych of "farewells" to the world— the Ninth Symphony, fragments of the Tenth Symphony, and the magnificent orchestral song-cycle, *Das Lied von der Erde* (*The Song of the Earth,* 1908). Set to texts by ancient Chinese poets, the work concludes with the famous "Der Abschied" ("The Farewell") to which Mahler penned these lines of his own: "My heart is peaceful, awaiting its hour . . . The beloved earth everywhere flowers and becomes green again." The final page, one of the most astonishing pages in all music, features an endless repetition by the voice of "Ewig" ("Forever") to a diaphanous background of clesta, flute and oboe. Mahler did not live to hear this work; and, according to his wishes, not a word was spoken nor a note sung at his burial.

In the decades after his death, Mahler's music was championed by his main disciple, conductor Bruno WALTER, and by a few others. However, his symphonies did not gain a secure place in the repertory until the 1960s, when Leonard BERNSTEIN's interpretation received wide critical and popular acclaim.

**Mahler, Margaret S.** *(1897–1985)* Hungarian-born American psychiatrist. She was clinical professor of psychiatry at Albert Einstein College of Medicine from 1955 until 1974. Her pioneering research into the psychological development of very young children led her to the conclusion that the foundation for adult character structure was laid in the first three years of life. These ideas were summarized in her 1976 book, *The Psychological Birth of the Human.*

**Mahon, Derek** *(1941– )* Northern Irish poet, editor, screenwriter and translator; widely considered the direct successor to Louis MACNEICE. Born in Belfast, Mahon read classics at Trinity College, Dublin. He was later poetry editor for the *New Statesman* in London. His work reflects a profound awareness of the ironies of 20th-century existence. Technically, his poetry achieves a formal grace and perfection matched by few other poets of this century. Mahon's books include *Poems 1962–1978* (1979), *The Hunt by Night* (1982), *Antarctica* (1985) and *Selected Poems* (1991). Since publishing his *Selected Poems* in 1990, Mahon has released *The Yaddo Letter* (1992), *The Hudson Letter* (1995), *The Yellow Book* (1997), *Collected Poems* (1999), *The Seaside Cemetery* (2001), and *Resistance Days* (2002). He received the Cholmondeley Award for Poets (1991) and *The Irish Times*/Aer Lingus Poetry Prize (1992).

**Mailer, Norman** *(1923– )* American novelist, story writer, essayist and journalist. Mailer is one of the most acclaimed and controversial American writers of the postwar era. Raised in a Jewish family in Brooklyn, Mailer was educated at Harvard University and served in the U.S. Army during World War II. He drew upon his experiences of combat to write his acclaimed first novel, *The Naked and the Dead* (1948). Mailer's next two novels, *Barbary Shore* (1951) and *The Deer Park* (1955), were less successful with the critics and the public, but his essay *The White Negro* (1957) won praise as an astute analysis of race relations and alienation in America; it also revealed Mailer's affinity with the BEAT GENERATION. In the 1960s his most important work was *The Armies of the Night* (1968)—an example of NEW JOURNALISM that earned Mailer a PULITZER PRIZE. His many subsequent works include *The Prisoner of Sex* (1971), an analysis of FEMINISM from the male perspective; *The Executioner's Song* (1979), a study of death-row prisoner Gary Gilmore that garnered Mailer a second Pulitzer Prize; and *Ancient Evenings* (1985), a historical novel set in Dynastic Egypt. Active in the ANTIWAR MOVEMENT during the VIETNAM WAR, Mailer has been involved in other liberal and radical causes. His stormy personal life has brought him much attention in newspaper gossip columns, but whether his work will have lasting literary value is a matter of debate. Mailer has since published *Harlot's Ghost* (1992), a 1,300 page account of CIA activities; *Oswald's Tale* (1995), a biography of Lee Harvey Oswald inspired in part by research Mailer uncovered while writing *Harlot's Ghost*; and *The Gospel According to the Son* (1997). In 2005 Mailer was given an honorary medal for lifetime achievement by the National Book Awards.

**Maillart, Robert** *(1872–1940)* Swiss structural engineer. His work in reinforced concrete structures, particularly bridges, made Maillart one of the very few engineers to become internationally famous for the aesthetic qualities of his work. He was trained at the Zurich Technical College and worked for several established engineering firms before setting up his own practice in 1902. He became a specialist in the design of concrete bridges, designing more than 40 of increasingly elegant modernist form. The most famous of his works, all in Switzerland, are the Val Tschiel Bridge, near Donath (1952); the spectacularly beautiful Salginatobel Bridge with a 295-foot span and three-hinged arch, near Schiers (1929–30); the curving Schwandbach Bridge (1933); the bridge over the Thus, near Felsegg (1933); and the Arve Bridge at Vessy, Geneva (1936). Many of Maillart's bridges are in obscure places where local authorities were willing to accept his dramatically simple designs. Maillart also designed various other structures.

**Maillol, Aristide** *(1861–1944)* French sculptor and graphic artist. He began as a painter, studying at the Ecole des Beaux-Arts in Paris. By 1903 he was associated with the Nabis. Maillol began to sculpt sometime between 1895 and 1900. His first sculptures were small-scale figures in wood or ceramic, but he quickly began much larger projects. His characteristic sculptures are larger-than-life female nudes—massive, idealized and sensuous. Strongly influenced by the classical Greek ideal, his style crystallized during a 1908 trip to Greece. At once strong and langourous, smoothly modeled and beautifully balanced, his nudes are often cast in bronze. Among his typical sculptures are *The River* (c. 1901, Museum of Modern Art, New York City) and *Pomona* (1910, Tuileries, Paris). Maillol is also known for the flowing linear quality of his woodcuts, many of which illustrated classical Greek and Roman poetry.

**Majdanek** Site of a Nazi CONCENTRATION CAMP, located near Lublin, Poland, during WORLD WAR II. Jews, Poles, Russians and other people from Nazi-occupied Europe were sent to Majdanek during the early 1940s; as many as 1.5 million were killed in the camp's gas chambers.

**Major, John** (*1943–   *) British politician, prime minister of the UNITED KINGDOM (1990–97). Born into a lower-middle-class family, Major was raised in Brixton, a run-down district of London. He left school at 16 in order to help support his family and never attended university. He held a variety of odd jobs, including clerk, cement mixer and bus conductor. He also experienced unemployment and spent several months on the dole. Major's fortunes changed when he obtained a job with the district bank; he decided to pursue a career in banking and quickly gained his professional qualifications. He joined Standard Chartered Bank in 1965 and became an assistant to the bank's chairman, who later served as chancellor of the Exchequer in the cabinet of Edward HEATH. Major entered politics in the late 1960s, serving in local government in South London from 1968 to 1971. An unsuccessful candidate for Parliament in 1974, he was elected to the House of Commons in the 1979 general election that swept Margaret THATCHER and the Conservatives into power. As a backbencher, he drew the notice of Thatcher, who made

him a junior minister for social security (1986) and then chief secretary of the Treasury (1987). In June 1989 Major replaced Geoffrey HOWE as foreign secretary. Three months later Thatcher named him chancellor of the Exchequer upon the resignation of Chancellor Nigel Lawson. Conservative members of Parliament elected Major as party leader after Margaret Thatcher announced her resignation in November 1990. Major thus became, at age 47, the youngest British prime minister of the 20th century. He was expected to follow many of Thatcher's policies but to take a more conciliatory view on several major issues, including the controversial community charge (poll tax) and the proposed monetary union with Europe. Major strongly supported the UN coalition action against IRAQ in the PERSIAN GULF WAR. Although Major and the Conservatives staved off defeat in the 1992 national election, the party continued to lose popularity. In the 1997 national election, the Conservatives were voted out of office, and Major was replaced by Labour Party leader Tony BLAIR.

**Makarios III** (*1913–1977*) Archbishop of the Orthodox Church of Cyprus and president of the Republic of CYPRUS. The son of a poor shepherd, he studied theology in GREECE and the United States. Ordained in 1946, he became bishop of Kition in 1948 and archbishop in 1950. A leader in the struggle for ENOSIS (union) with Greece, he was elected president of Cyprus in 1959, 1968 and again in 1973. He survived several assassination attempts and a 1974 coup that resulted in a five-month exile in MALTA and the UNITED KINGDOM. He was unable to prevent Turkish occupation of much of northern Cyprus.

**Makarov, Oleg** (*1933–   *) Soviet cosmonaut and design engineer. Encouraged by the experience of his friend and fellow design-engineer Konstantin Feoktistov in *Voskhod 1,* Makarov, of Sergei KOROLEV's design bureau, also applied to fly in space. As a result, he became one of the steady players in the Soviet program, making four flights in the position of flight engineer between 1973 and 1980. His first flight, aboard *Soyuz 12* (September 1973) with Vasily Lazarev, was the first to follow after the tragedy of *Soyuz 11,* during which three cosmonauts suf-

focated because a valve leaked during reentry (to allow enough room for three they had worn no space suits). Makarov and Lazarev wore space suits in the redesigned *Soyuz* and their brief two-day mission went smoothly. Paired off again with Lazarev, Makarov was to visit Salyut 4 in a 60-day mission two years later. But luck was not with them; their *Soyuz 18-A* booster aborted shortly after launch on April 5, 1975. Their command module separated from the booster and careened back to Earth, landing the two in the mountains near the Chinese border. As the *Soyuz* plunged downward, the cosmonauts endured an agonizing pressure of 18 Gs, which may have caused internal injuries.

Makarov made it back onto the flight docket, and three years later he and Vladimir DZHANIBEKOV took *Soyuz 27* (January 1978) up to the Salyut 6 space station that Makarov had helped design. After their one-week visit with Yuri Romanenko and Georgy Grechko, who were on a 30-day mission there, they returned in Romanenko and Grechko's *Soyuz 26* spacecraft, leaving the fresh vehicle at the space station. November 1980 saw Makarov back at Salyut 6, this time on a repair mission with fellow cosmonauts Leonid Kizim and Gennady Strekalov. After 13 days, they had the station ready for its next long-duration crew, returning aboard their *Soyuz T-3* craft, recently redesigned to accommodate three cosmonauts.

**Makarov, Stepan Osipovich** (*1848–1904*) Russian admiral in charge of defense during the RUSSO-JAPANESE WAR. Makarov went down with his flagship, the *Petropavlovsk,* outside Port Arthur.

**Makarova, Natalia** (*1940–   *) Russian-born ballerina. After studying at the Kirov Ballet School in Leningrad, Makarova joined the Kirov Ballet Company in 1959. She won a gold medal at the Varna Ballet competition in 1965. In 1970 she chose to stay in the West at the conclusion of the Kirov's European tour and joined AMERICAN BALLET THEATRE that same year, making her debut in *Giselle.* Noted for an elegant style and expressiveness, her Giselle is considered the finest of the 1970s and early 1980s. She has been a guest artist with companies worldwide, most especially with the ROYAL BALLET in Britain. She has received acclaim for her dancing in such modern ballets as Antony TUDOR's *Jardin aux Lilas* and *Dark Elegies* as well as for the classical repertory.

**Maki, Fumihiko** (*1928– *) Winner of the 1993 Pritzker Architecture Prize. Born in Tokyo, Maki refined his interest in post-Bauhaus architecture at Tokyo University, where he received his B.A. in architecture in 1952. He then traveled to the U.S. to pursue his graduate education in architecture, first at the Cranbrook Academy of Art in Bloomfield Hills, Michigan, and later at Harvard University's Graduate School of Design, where he served as an apprentice with firms in New York and Boston. After obtaining his M.A. in architecture in 1956, he taught architecture, first while at Washington University and then at Harvard's Graduate School of Design.

In 1965 Maki left Harvard to return to Tokyo and established his own architectural firm, Maki and Associates. He developed a strong interest in constructing the interior layout of business complexes to encourage cooperation and a diversity of viewpoints. To this end, he utilized a synthesis of metal, concrete and glass, as well as more modernist building materials such as anodized aluminum and stainless steel. He also helped found the Metabolists, a group of likeminded young Japanese architects who sought to ensure that their structures emphasized flexibility and could be aesthetically incorporated into the city in which it resided. In the mid-1980s Maki became well known in Japan for his design of the National Museum of Modern Art in Kyoto, which opened in 1987. He has also designed buildings in the U.S., such as Yerba Buena Gardens Visual Arts Center in San Francisco, and in Germany, such as the Isar Buro Office Park in Munich. Maki also designed the Prefectural Sports Center in Osaka, Japan, and the Hillside Terrace Apartment Complex in Tokyo. In 1993 Maki was selected as the recipient of the Pritzker Prize, the most prestigious international architectural award, for his contributions to modern architecture.

**Maklakov, Vasily Alexandrovich** (*1870–1957*) Russian liberal and lawyer. A member of the second, third and fourth dumas, he acted as counsel for the defense for political cases during the 1905 Revolution. A member of the Constitutional Democratic Party, he was appointed ambassador to France by the provisional government in 1917. He subsequently acted as leader of the Russian emigrés in Paris.

**Malamud, Bernard** (*1914–1986*) U.S. author. He was regarded as one of the most distinctive Jewish literary voices in postwar America. His works often reflected a concern with Jewish values and a belief in the nobility of ordinary people. His first novel, *The Natural*—an allegorical tale about the rise and fall of a baseball player—was published in 1952. Later novels included *The Assistant* (1957), *The Fixer* (1966) and *The Tenants* (1971). Some of his best-known short stories appeared in the collections *The Magic Barrel* (1958) and *Idiots First* (1963).

**Malan, Daniel F(rançois)** (*1874–1959*) South African political leader, prime minister of SOUTH AFRICA (1948–54). Trained as a clergyman, Malan was a pastor in the Dutch Reformed Church until World War I, when he became an editor of an Afrikaner nationalist newspaper. He officially entered politics in 1918 as a Nationalist member of Parliament and served as minister of the interior, public health and education in the government of J. B. M. Hertzog (1924–33). When the National Party won the 1940 election Malan became prime minister. In that office he was one of the main architects of APARTHEID. Fighting any movement toward racial integration, he urged the development of segregated black "homelands." Malan retired in 1954.

**Malawi (Republic of Malawi)** Malawi covers an area of 45,735 square miles in southeast Africa. Originally a British colony known as Nyasaland

| MALAWI | |
|---|---|
| 1953 | Malawi becomes part of the white-dominated Central African Federation, which includes South Rhodesia (Zimbabwe) and North Rhodesia (Zambia). |
| 1964 | Nyasaland becomes a fully independent dominion within the Commonwealth under the name Malawi, with Hastings Banda as prime minister. |
| 1966 | Malawi is declared a republic, with Banda as president. |
| 1971 | Banda is made president-for-life. |
| 1988 | Malawi and Mozambique sign an agreement on the repatriation of Mozambican refugees in Malawi. |
| 1992 | About 100,000 people demonstrate against Banda's authoritarian rule. |
| 1994 | Makili Muluzi becomes president. |
| 1997 | Banda dies in South Africa at the age of 99. |
| 1999 | Muluzi is reelected president. |
| 2000 | Muluzi dismisses his entire cabinet after high-ranking officials are accused of corruption, in a move aimed at placating foreign donors. However, his new government includes many of the same people. |
| 2004 | Bingu wa Mutharika is elected president. |

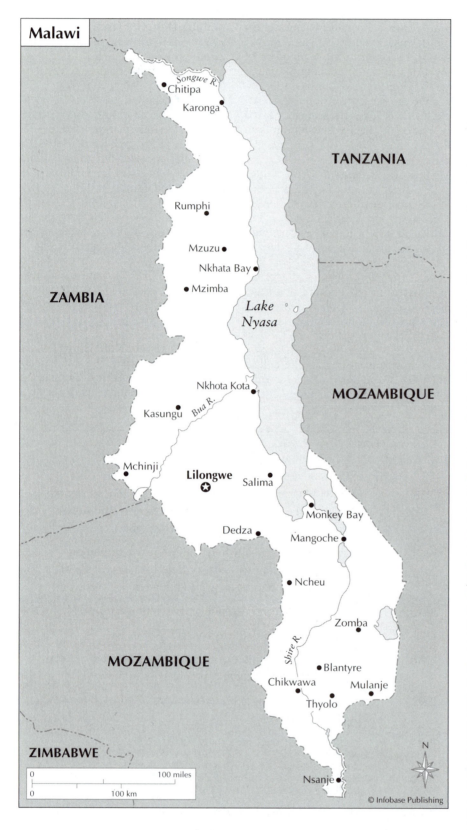

**Malawi**

Songwe R.
Chitipa
Karonga

TANZANIA

Rumphi

Mzuzu
Nkhata Bay
Mzimba

ZAMBIA

*Lake Nyasa*

Nkhota Kota

MOZAMBIQUE

Kasungu    *Bua R.*

Mchinji

**Lilongwe** ☆    Salima

Monkey Bay

Dedza    Mangoche

Ncheu

Zomba

MOZAMBIQUE

*Shire R.*

Blantyre
Chikwawa    Mulanje
Thyolo

ZIMBABWE

N

0        100 miles
0        100 km

Nsanje

© Infobase Publishing

ernment's responsibility for assassinations of opposition leaders living in Zimbabwe, as well as the deaths of possible successors, have been rampant. Tensions with Mozambique over Malawi's supposed aid to Mozambique rebel groups surfaced in the 1980s but were resolved in 1988. In the 1994 presidential elections, the United Democratic Front candidate, Makili Muluzi, defeated Banda and immediately restored some civil liberties at the beginning of his five-year term. In 1999 Muluzi won reelection to a second and final term as president (the Malawi constitution prohibited anyone from serving in office for more than 10 years). Although Muluzi arranged for the World Bank to cancel half of Malawi's foreign debt in 2000, his administration was repeatedly besieged by allegations of corruption surrounding the mismanagement of the country's agricultural resources. In May 2004 he was succeeded by Bingu wa Mutharika.

**Malaysia (Federation of Malaysia)** Comprising a total land area of 127,225 square miles in Southeast Asia, Malaysia consists of two separate sections, East (Sarawak and Sabah on the island of Borneo) and West Malaysia. In 1896 the states of Perak, Selangor, Negri Semilan and Pahang were reunited to form the Federated Malay States under British rule; by 1914 the remaining Malay states came under British control. Invaded by Japan in 1942, Malaysia returned to British control in 1946, then formalized its federation status in 1948. The country achieved independence in 1957 as the Federation of Malaysia. Tensions between the Malay population and the increasing number of Chinese and Indian immigrants led to political and economic unrest, resulting in declarations of a state of emergency in 1948 and again in 1969. Economic and human rights reforms have alleviated some problems, but opposition groups continued to press for more political freedom during the 1980s. In 1997 an Asian economic crisis gripped Malaysia. Six years later, Prime Minister Dr. MAHATHIR BIN MOHAMMAD resigned and was succeeded by Abdullah Ahmad Badawi.

**Malcolm X (Malcolm Little)** *(1925–1965)* American black militant. Born

(1907–53), the country joined Northern and Southern Rhodesia to form the Central African Federation (1953–63), before achieving independence in 1964. The country became a part of the COMMONWEALTH as the Republic of Malawi and elected Dr. Hastings Kamuzu BANDA president in 1966 (became president for life in 1971). Suspicions concerning the Banda gov-

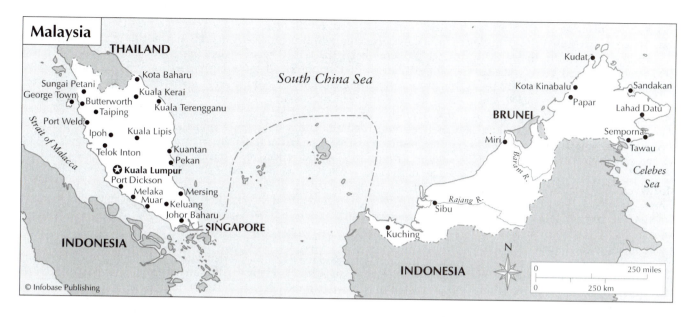

Malaysia

in Omaha, Nebraska, he moved east at 16, settled in New York City and became involved in the crime of Harlem's underworld. In prison from 1946 to 1952, he was impressed with the writings of Elijah MUHAMMAD and, after his release, joined the BLACK MUSLIM movement. Rejecting his "slave name," he changed it to Malcolm X, embraced black separatism and supported armed self-defense. Highly intelligent and a fiery orator, he quickly became the movement's foremost spokesman, winning it a host of new members. When an ideological split between Malcolm and Muhammad caused Malcolm's suspension as a minister in 1963, the firebrand left the Nation of Islam. Making the pilgrimage to Mecca in 1964, he proclaimed his conversion to orthodox Islam and founded a rival group, the Organization for Afro-American Unity.

## MALAYSIA

| | |
|---|---|
| 1914 | Britain gains control of Malay Peninsula. |
| 1942 | (February) Singapore falls to the Japanese. |
| 1957 | (Aug. 31) Malaya granted independence from Britain. |
| 1963 | (September) Malaya, Singapore, Sarawak and North Borneo join together to form the state of Malaysia. |
| 1965 | (Aug.) Singapore leaves the federation. |
| 1969 | (May) Race riots between Chinese and Malays break out and state of emergency is declared. |
| 1981 | Datuk Seri Dr. Mahathir Mohammad of the United Malays National Organization Party is elected prime minister. |
| 1990 | (Oct. 21) Mahathir is reelected. |
| 1997 | The Asian economic crisis strikes hard at Malaysia with markets and currency falling throughout 1997–98. |
| 1998 | Currency and foreign investment controls implemented to combat deepening recession. |
| 1999 | Controls are lifted as economic health returns. Mahathir is reelected prime minister. |
| 2001 | Clashes between Malays and ethnic Indians. Malaysia and Singapore resolve long-standing disputes. |
| 2003 | Mahathir resigns as prime minister and Abdullah Ahmad Badawi assumes the post. |
| 2004 | Prime Minister Badawi wins landslide general election. |

*Malcolm X. a leader of the Black Muslim movement*
(LIBRARY OF CONGRESS. PRINTS AND PHOTOGRAPHS DIVISION)

Forsaking the doctrine of racial separation, Malcolm advocated the struggle for radical social reform. In February 1965 he was shot and killed while addressing a public meeting in New York by assassins alleged to be Black Muslims. His book, *The Autobiography of Malcolm X* (dictated to Alex HALEY, 1964), has become an American literary and sociological classic.

**Maldives** The Maldive archipelago comprises some 1,190 islands (202 of which are inhabited) in a chain of 20 coral atolls, covering an area of 116 square miles; in the Indian Ocean over 400 miles southwest of Sri Lanka. Protected from monsoon devastation by barrier reefs (faros), none of the islands rises above 5 ft. in elevation. Settled by its original Dravidian inhabitants per-

haps as early as the fourth century B.C., the Maldives became a British protectorate in December 1887. The powers of the sultans were circumscribed by provisions of a 1932 constitution, and a short-lived modernizing regime set up a republic (1953–54)—before a coup restored the sultanate. Ibrahim NASIR, prime minister to the last of the sultans (from 1957) and effective leader of the country at the time of independence (July 26, 1965), became president when a referendum approved a republican constitution (November 11, 1968). He strengthened the powers of the presidency (1975) but then stood down and left the country (1978); Maumoon Abdul GAYOOM was elected to succeed him. Reelected for successive presidential terms (1983, 1988), Gayoom survived three

attempted coups (1980, 1981, 1988), in each of which he saw the hand of his predecessor Nasir. The 1988 coup was suppressed only when Indian troops were dispatched to defeat the mercenaries, who apparently came from Sri Lanka. Meanwhile, Gayoom confirmed a nonaligned foreign policy practiced by his predecessor, who in 1957 had rejected a Soviet bid to lease the island of Gan. The Maldives joined the COMMONWEALTH as a special status member (July 1982) and became a full member on June 20, 1985. Al-Gayoom retained his hold on power throughout the 1990s, winning reelection to the presidency in 1993, 1998 and 2003, giving him an unprecedented sixth term as the country's leader.

Since 2002 the Maldives's government has repeatedly voiced concerns

## MALDIVES

| | |
|---|---|
| 1887 | The islands of the Islamic sultunate of the Maldives become an internally self-governing British protectorate, which remains a dependency of Sri Lanka until 1948. |
| 1932 | The sultan becomes an elected position when the Maldives's first constitution is introduced. |
| 1953 | The Maldive Islands become a republic within the Commonwealth, as the ad-Din sultanate is abolished. |
| 1954 | The sultan is restored. |
| 1968 | Following a popular referendum, the Maldives sultanate is replaced with a republican form of government, with Ibrahim Nasir as president. |
| 1978 | President Nasir steps down for health reasons, and Maumoon Abdul Gayoom is elected president. |
| 1983 | President Gayoom is reelected to a five-year term. |
| 1988 | President Gayoom is reelected to another five-year term in September. In November a coup attempt launched by an amphibious force, composed mostly of ethnic Tamil mercenaries from Sri Lanka, is quashed with the assistance of Indian army commandos. |
| 1990 | Two separate international reports warn that global warming could cause the ocean to submerge the Maldives within 100 years. |
| 1993 | President Gayoom runs unopposed for a fourth five-year term as president. |
| 1998 | President Gayoom is reelected to a fifth term as president. |
| 2003 | Crowds riot in the capital city of Male, seeking democratic reforms. President Gayoom is reelected to a sixth term as president. |
| 2004 | In December, a magnitude 9.0 earthquake off the coast of Indonesia creates tidal waves that kill about 100 Maldivians and displace 12,000. Of the country's 199 inhabited islands, 73 are severely damaged or destroyed completely. |

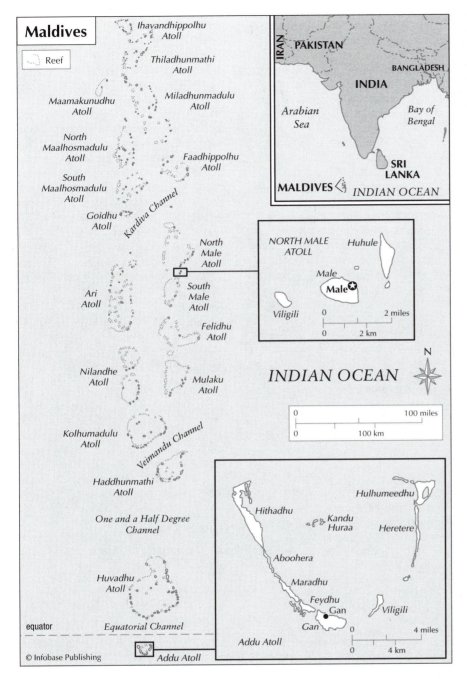

**Maldives**

Reef

Ihavandhippolhu Atoll

Thiladhunmathi Atoll

Maamakunudhu Atoll

Miladhunmadulu Atoll

North Maalhosmadulu Atoll

Faadhippolhu Atoll

South Maalhosmadulu Atoll

Kardiva Channel

Goidhu Atoll

North Male Atoll

Ari Atoll

South Male Atoll

Felidhu Atoll

Nilandhe Atoll

Mulaku Atoll

Kolhumadulu Atoll

Veimandu Channel

Haddhunmathi Atoll

One and a Half Degree Channel

Huvadhu Atoll

equator   Equatorial Channel

© Infobase Publishing   Addu Atoll

IRAN   PAKISTAN

BANGLADESH

INDIA

Arabian Sea

Bay of Bengal

SRI LANKA

MALDIVES   INDIAN OCEAN

NORTH MALE ATOLL   Huhule

Male

Male

Viligili

0   2 miles
0   2 km

INDIAN OCEAN   N

0   100 miles
0   100 km

Hulhumeedhu

Hithadhu

Kandu Huraa

Heretere

Aboohera

Maradhu

Feydhu
Gan

Viligili

Gan   0   4 miles
0   4 km

Addu Atoll

**Malevich, Kazimir** *(1878–1935)* Russian artist, one of the first abstract painters. Influenced by IMPRESSIONISM, FAUVISM and CUBISM, in 1913 Malevich evolved his own abstract geometrical style, known as SUPREMATISM, in which only geometrical elements were used in construction. After teaching painting from 1919 to 1921 in Moscow and Leningrad, he traveled to Weimar, where he met Wassily KANDINSKY, and published his *The Non-Objective World.* Among his best-known paintings is the famous *White Square on a White Background.* Unfortunately his work met with official disapproval, and Malevich died in poverty in 1935.

**Mali (Republic of Mali)** The landlocked country of Mali is located in western Africa and covers an area of 478,640 square miles. A French colony originally known as French Soudan (1920–58), the country was renamed the Sudanese Republic in 1958 and became an autonomous state within the FRENCH COMMUNITY. It united with the Republic of SENEGAL to form the Federation of Mali in 1959. When the federation became independent in 1960, Senegal seceded, and the Republic of Mali was declared. The first president, Modibo Keita, consolidated power in a one-party system but was overthrown in 1968 in a peaceful army coup. The new leader, General Moussa Traoré, has maintained power by suppressing all protests. A brief war (December 25–29, 1985) with BURKINA FASO over a disputed border was resolved in 1986. In 1992 Alpha Konaré won Mali's first free multiparty presidential election. Three years later Konaré participated in government talks with Tuareg tribal leaders in an effort to stave off future conflicts with the indigenous group and to assure the return of several thousand refugees to Mali. In 1999, following the trial and conviction of former Mali president Moussa Traoré, Konaré commuted his death sentence to life imprisonment. After Konaré was succeeded by Amadou Toumani Touré in 2002, Mali was beset by political and civil turmoil. In October 2002 the entire government resigned without explanation, and an interim government of national unity was formed. Additionally, problems within Mali's Islamic community resulted in 10 deaths in August 2003

about the rising sea level and its effect on the archipelago's future. In September 2002 al-Gayoom addressed the World Summit on Sustainable Development in Johannesburg, South Africa, and asked the international community to take all possible measures to reduce the increasing temperatures across the globe that have contributed to rising sea levels in the Indian Ocean.

**Malenkov, Georgi Maximillianovich** *(1902–1988)* Soviet politician. Malenkov succeeded STALIN as premier

in March 1953 and was also, very briefly, first secretary of the COMMUNIST PARTY. He was alleged to have played a key role in the Stalinist purges in which millions of Soviet citizens died. His premiership was marked by a somewhat more conciliatory attitude toward the West and by attempts to increase the production of consumer goods. Nikita KHRUSHCHEV forced him from power in 1955. In 1957 Malenkov was removed from all important posts and banished to remote Kazakhstan in Central Asia to manage a hydroelectric plant.

when opposing Islamic groups briefly fought in the state's western region. In the same year an Islamic group allied with the terrorist organization al-Qaeda came under assault by the Mali army.

**Malik, Charles Habib** (*1906–1987*) Lebanese diplomat. A Greek Orthodox Christian, he helped draft LEBANON's 1943 constitution granting political hegemony to the Christian community. He was one of the last surviving signatories of the UNITED NATIONS Charter, which he helped draft in 1945. In 1958 and 1959 he was president of the United Nations General Assembly and was Lebanese ambassador to the U.S. (1953–55) and foreign minister (1956–58).

**Malik, Yakov A(leksandrovich)** (*1906–1980*) Soviet diplomat. During his career Malik served as the USSR's ambassador to the UNITED NATIONS (1948–52, 1968–76) and deputy foreign minister. He joined the COMMUNIST PARTY in 1938 and played a key

| MALI | |
|------|------|
| 1904 | French Sudan (Soudan) becomes part of the Federation of French West Africa. |
| 1958 | Following a referendum, French Sudan becomes the République Soudanaise (Sudanese Republic) within the French Community. |
| 1959 | Mali Federation is established, with Senegal and the Sudanese Republic as members.  Modibo Keita is elected president of the federation. |
| 1960 | Mali Federation breaks up when Senegal withdraws. |
| 1968 | President Keita is overthrown by a military coup led by General Moussa Traoré, who becomes president. |
| 1985 | Border fighting with Burkina Faso (former Upper Volta) reerupts. |
| 1986 | Burkina Faso and Mali accept World Court settlement of dispute over Agacher Strip. |
| 1992 | Alpha Konaré is elected president, as his party, the Alliance for Democracy, wins 76 of the 116 assembly seats. |
| 1996 | The World Bank praises the economic turnaround headed by Konaré's government. |
| 1999 | Traoré is convicted and sentenced to death on corruption charges, but Konaré commutes the sentence to life imprisonment. Konaré announces that he will not run for a third term as president. |
| 2002 | Amadou Toumani Touré, who overthrew Traoré in 1991, returns to power after winning a landslide victory in presidential elections. |

role in negotiating the terms that ended in the Berlin blockade in 1949 (see BERLIN AIRLIFT). He is best remembered, however, for the decision to boycott the UN Security Council in 1950. When the KOREAN WAR broke out, the U.S. took advantage of his absence to persuade the Security Council to send UN forces to SOUTH KOREA. A year later, Malik proposed a Korean truce; this led to talks between the two sides and an eventual cease-fire in 1953. Malik was regarded as one of his country's leading experts on the West. (See also COLD WAR.)

**Malina, Frank J.** *(1912–1981)* U.S. rocket pioneer and aeronautical engineer; his pioneering work on solid-fuel rockets helped set the stage for early U.S. rocket development. With aerodynamist Theodore von KARMAN, Malina helped found what is now NASA's JET PROPULSION LABORATORY in California in the late 1930s. They researched high-altitude rockets and during WORLD WAR II they worked on jet-assisted takeoff (JATO) for propeller airplanes, using the same rocket principles. In 1945 von Karman and Malina tested the first WAC Corporal rocket, which they had designed for use as a high-altitude sounding rocket. It was one of the early predecessors of space-age rocket power in the U.S. Malina later left JPL to become head of the scientific research division of UNESCO in France, where he died.

**Malinovsky, Rodion Yakovlevich** *(1898–1967)* Soviet marshal. Having served with the French army in WORLD WAR I and having fought in the RUSSIAN CIVIL WAR, Malinovsky joined the party in 1926. In 1930 he graduated from the M. V. Frunze Military Academy. During WORLD WAR II, he proved to be a distinguished commander during the STALINGRAD offensive (1942). He then led the Southwest Army Group (1943) and the Second Ukrainian Army Group (1944), which occupied Romania and Hungary. In 1945 he liberated Czechoslovakia and commanded the Transbaikalian Army Group in the brief war against Japan; in 1945–46 he commanded the Soviet forces in Manchuria. A candidate member of the party's central committee from 1952, in 1957 he was appointed minister of defense.

**Malinowski, Bronislaw** *(1884–1942)* Polish-born British anthropologist. Malinowski studied at the University of Kraców, from which he received a Ph.D. in physics and mathematics in 1908, as well as the University of Leipzig and the London School of Economics. He performed field research in Africa, Melanesia and Mexico, and taught at the University of London from 1924 to 1942, in addition to lecturing at universities in America and throughout Europe. A brilliant descriptive ethnographer, Malinowski originated the theory of "functionalism," that is, that a culture should be studied as a complex whole that functions to satisfy its members' primary biological needs. He also argued against the judgmental 19th-century view that placed various cultures on a developmental ladder ranging from "savagery" to "civilization."

**Malle, Louis** *(1932–1995)* French motion picture director who sprang from the generation of the NOUVELLE VAGUE in the late 1950s. Unlike many of his colleagues—TRUFFAUT, GODARD, CHABROL, Rivette, Vadim—Malle never stopped working and continued to make films of enormous variety and consistent quality. After studying at the Jesuit College at Fontainebleau he turned to filmmaking in 1951–52 and codirected with Jacques COUSTEAU the classic underwater documentary, *Le Monde de Silence* (*The Silent World*, 1956). His *Ascenseur pour l'Echafaud* (*Elevator to the Gallows* [*Frantic*], 1957) and *Les Amants* (*The Lovers*, 1958) are regarded as early expressions of that movement, but Malle's work is difficult to categorize. While his color film *Zazie dans le Metro* (1960) is full of hi-jinks and chases, *Le Feu Follet* (*The Fire Within*, 1963), is a harrowing depiction in black-and-white of the last hours of a suicidal alcoholic. On the one hand, he closely observed contemporary life and poverty in his documentary *Calcutta* (1969), and on the other, lovingly re-created the period charm of the 19th century in *Viva Maria* (1965) and *Le Voleur* (*The Thief of Paris*, 1967). His controversial American film *Pretty Baby* (1978) is full of the lush imagery and sensuality of the New Orleans brothels; *My Dinner with Andre* (1981) explores the tensions between the imagination and reality in a dinner conversation be-

tween an intense theater director and a down-to-earth playwright. Malle's masterpiece is the autobiographical *Au Revoir, les Enfants* (*Goodbye, Children*, 1988), a closely observed, poignant memoir of children growing up in Nazi-occupied Paris during World War II. "Of the New Wave survivors," writes historian John Baxter, "he is the most old-fashioned, the most erotic, and, arguably, the most widely successful."

**Mallet-Stevens, Robert** *(1886–1945)* French designer of furniture and architectural interiors, an important figure in the development of MODERNISM of the 1920s and 1930s. Mallet-Stevens was a student of the Ecole Spéciale d'Architecture from 1905 to 1910 and an admirer of the work of such pioneers as Charles Rennie MACKINTOSH and Josef HOFFMANN. Beginning in 1912 he produced furniture and interiors in an early modern style, and his work gradually moved toward the modernism of the de STIJL movement with similarities to the early efforts of LE CORBUSIER. He designed pavilions for the Paris exhibitions of 1929 and 1937. Mallet-Stevens was a frequent contributor to journals dealing with modern design and wrote a book on modern stained glass.

**Mallett, Jane** *(1899–1984)* Canadian actress and comedienne. Mallett's career spanned nearly 60 years. Mallett played a leading role in the development of Canadian theater, film, radio and television and was active in major theatrical and broadcasting unions. In 1975 she received the Order of Canada and became one of the first to be awarded honorary membership in the newly independent Canadian Actors' Equity.

**Malone, Richard Sankey** *(1909–1985)* Canadian journalist. During his military career, Malone was one of the few members of the Allied forces to serve in all theaters of WORLD WAR II. He created the Canadian Army's public relations service and its newspaper, *The Maple Leaf*. He began as assistant general manager at the *Winnipeg Free Press* (FP) in 1936 and eventually became its publisher and editor in chief. From that base, he built the FP chain, acquiring newspapers throughout CANADA. Malone was publisher and editor in chief of one of FP's purchases, the *Toronto Globe and Mail,* from 1974 to 1978.

**Malraux, André** *(1901–1976)* French novelist, art critic, essayist and government minister. Malraux was a major figure in French letters and culture in the 20th century. He began his career as a world traveler with leftist political leanings. Malraux participated in revolutionary activities in CHINA in the 1920s and fought on the Loyalist side in the SPANISH CIVIL WAR in the 1930s. His experiences in China were reflected in his first novel, *The Conquerors* (1928), as well as in his most famous novel, *Man's Fate* (1933). A subsequent novel, *Man's Hope* (1938), drew from his experiences in Spain. Malraux was a leader of the French RESISTANCE during WORLD WAR II and became a close associate of Charles DE GAULLE, who later named Malraux minister of culture (1959–69). *The Voices of Silence* (1951) is Malraux's major work of art criticism. *Antimemoirs* (1967) is his autobiography.

**Malta (Republic of Malta)** Located in the central Mediterranean Sea, Malta consists of the islands of Malta, Gozo, Comino and the uninhabited islets of Cominotto, Filfa and St. Paul; total land area of 122 square miles. Governed by Great Britain since 1800, the ancient island was claimed by Italy during WORLD WAR II and endured heavy bombing by the Axis powers. Malta was granted self-government by Britain in 1947 and achieved full independence in 1964, though still maintaining defense and economic ties with Britain. The country became a republic within the COMMONWEALTH in 1974. Of strategic importance due to its proximity to the Suez Canal, Malta hosted British and NATO forces (1972–79), then proclaimed its neutrality and nonalignment (1979–80). During the presidency of Dom Mintoff (1971–84) Malta established relations with several communist and Arab countries. In 2004 Malta joined the EUROPEAN UNION (EU).

**Maltese Falcon, The** *(1929)* American detective novel subsequently adapted into three different film versions for HOLLYWOOD. *The Maltese Falcon,* written by the renowned American mystery author Dashiell HAMMETT, has remained immensely popular with readers due to its chiseled, laconic dialogue full of a wit and intelligence that was new to the mystery genre. Hollywood producers were naturally drawn to the novel, but the first two film adaptations—*The Maltese Falcon* (1931) and *Satan Met a Lady* (1936)—are eminently forgettable. The 1941 film version, written and directed by John HUSTON and starring Humphrey BOGART as detective Sam Spade, has become a classic and is regarded as one of the earliest examples of FILM NOIR. The basic plot of *The Maltese Falcon*—as Hammett wrote it and Huston adapted it—concerns the elusive quest for a black statue of a falcon that is filled with priceless jewels. Sam Spade is a tough, worldly-wise cynic who fends off the lies of seductive Brigid O'Shaughnessy (played by Mary Astor in the film) and the evil of the Fat Man (portrayed by Sydney Greenstreet) to solve the paradoxical mystery of the falcon while avenging the murder of his partner.

**Mamet, David** *(1947– )* American playwright. One of the finest contemporary dramatists, Mamet is particularly known for his dialogue. He taught theater at several universities, including the Yale School of Drama (1976–77), and was founder-director of the avant-garde St. Nicholas Theatre Company of Chicago (1973–76). His plays are frequently set in Chicago and focus on the underbelly of society (con artists, drifters) and the crucial interpersonal relationships that hold life together. He was greatly influenced by the improvisational comedy of the Second City Cabaret (in Chicago) where he worked for a while. Major plays include *Sexual Perversity in Chicago* (1975), *American Buffalo* (1976), *A Life in the Theatre* (1977), *Glengarry Glen Ross* (1984), for which he received the PULITZER PRIZE, and *Speed-the-Plow* (1987). Mamet has also made his mark as a screenwriter with such films as *The Verdict* (1982) and *The Untouchables* (1987). In the 1990s Mamet began to focus primarily on screenplay production and composed the scripts for such films as *Hoffa* (1992), *Malcolm X* (1992), *Vanya on 42nd Street* (1994), *Wag the Dog* (1997), and *The Winslow Boy.* (1999). Mamet also directed two films in the 1990s: an adaptation of his play, *Oleanna* (1994), and *The Spanish Prisoner* (1997), a dark espionage film with comedian Steve MARTIN.

**Mamoulian, Rouben Zachary** *(1898–1987)* Russian-born film and stage director. Trained under VAKHTANGOV and STANISLAVSKY at the Moscow Art Theatre, he immigrated to America in 1926 and directed many notable plays for the Theatre Guild, including DuBose Heyward's *Porgy* (1927). He later directed the premiere of George GERSHWIN's operatic version, *Porgy and Bess* (1935). His first talking films for PARAMOUNT PICTURES, *Applause* (1929) and *City Streets* (1931), were acclaimed among the most innovative sound films of the day. In fact, all of his best films were distinguished by the imaginative use of image and sound—especially the horror classic *Dr. Jekyll and Mr. Hyde* (1932), the Jeanette MacDonald–Maurice Chevalier musical *Love Me Tonight* (1932), *Queen Christina* (with Greta GARBO, 1933) and the Technicolor *Becky Sharp* (1935). Mamoulian periodically returned to the Broadway stage, directing the premieres of such landmark productions as *Oklahoma* (1943), *Carousel* (1945) and *Lost in the Stars* (1949). His later films included *Summer Holiday* (1948), a musical version of Eugene O'NEILL's *Ah, Wilderness!;* and *Silk Stockings* (1957), a remake of *Ninotchka* starring Fred ASTAIRE.

**Manchukuo** Name of the Japanese puppet state in Chinese MANCHURIA from 1932 to 1945. The Japanese had long coveted Manchuria, with its rich natural resources and raw materials. They seized the province with little resistance in the early 1930s while CHINA was in political turmoil (see CHINESE CIVIL WAR OF 1930–34). Henry PU-YI, who had been the last Manchu emperor of China, was installed as formal ruler of Manchukuo, but real power rested with the Japanese. Few governments recognized Manchukuo as an independent state, and it was returned to Chinese rule after WORLD WAR II.

**Manchuria** Located in northeastern China, Manchuria became a part of China in 1903 and has been an autonomous area within China since 1924. Both Russia and Japan have dominated Manchuria at various times. In 1931 Japan seized several Manchurian cities and created the puppet state of MANCHUKUO, controlling the region until the end of WORLD WAR II. Soviet troops occupied Manchuria from August 1945 to April 1946. The Chinese communists gained control of Manchuria during the Chinese civil war (1945–49). Since the formation of the People's Republic of China (1949), relations with the Soviet Union have been tense, and both countries continue to keep troops massed along the Manchurian border.

**Mancini, Henry** *(1924–1994)* American composer and arranger. Born in Cleveland, Ohio, Mancini studied music at the Carnegie Institute in Pittsburgh and the Juilliard School in New York City. He then studied composition in Los Angeles and in 1952 became a composer-arranger for Universal-International film studios. Thus began a long, illustrious career creating memorable themes and scores for films and television. In 1958 Mancini won an Emmy for creating the jazzy theme for the *Peter Gunn* TV series. He received ACADEMY AWARDS for his scores for *Breakfast at Tiffany's* (which included song hit "Moon River") (1961) and *Victor/Victoria* (1982). Other well-known film scores Mancini has created include those for the *Pink Panther* films (1963, 1975), *Days of Wine and Roses* (1962), *Charade* (1963) and *Once Is Not Enough* (1976).

**Mandela, Nelson** *(1918– )* Black South African nationalist leader. Mandela practiced law until 1952, when his hostility to APARTHEID led him to join the AFRICAN NATIONAL CONGRESS (ANC). He traveled widely in SOUTH AFRICA in the 1950s, championing his ideal of a free, multiracial society. After the ANC was banned in 1961 he evaded arrest until 1962, when he was jailed for five years. In 1963 he was charged under the Suppression of Communism Act, and after an eight-month trial sentenced to life imprisonment. Although held in prison for over 25 years, he remained an important figure for black South Africans. During this time his wife **Winnie Mandela** continued to take an active part in politics, traveling widely at home and abroad and championing Mandela's causes despite restrictions imposed on her by the South African government.

Many blacks and whites were suspicious of Winnie Mandela's motives and methods, however, especially after she was implicated in the murder of a young black man in the late 1980s. Nelson Mandela was released from prison by Prime Minister F. W. DE KLERK in 1990 and allowed to resume his activities. Following his release Mandela became the leader of the ANC and began negotiations with De Klerk to end the system of apartheid in South Africa and to create a governmental structure that would give voting rights to all South Africans while reassuring white South Africans they would not be the target of reprisals. Mandela and De Klerk eventually created a three-person presidency that would ensure that at least one white South African shared executive authority with the more numerous black political parties. In 1993 Mandela and De Klerk both received the Nobel Peace Prize for their efforts at producing political reconciliation. In 1994 the first free nationwide elections were held in South Africa, which resulted in the ANC's becoming the largest political party in Parliament and the selection of Mandela as president.

Mandela devoted his presidency to improving South Africa's economy and encouraging job growth in the country's industrial sector by encouraging foreign corporations to establish business interests in South Africa following the end of the antiapartheid international boycott. He also sought to improve the quality of public housing available and to create the rudiments of a national health care system. In 1996 Mandela supported the creation of a new constitution for South Africa that strengthened the authority of the central government, further defined the rights of minorities within South Africa, and codified the civil liberties of all citizens. In 1997 he announced he would not seek reelection as president and resigned as leader of the ANC, in order to allow for a smooth transfer of authority. He was replaced by Thabo MBEKI as ANC leader, then the deputy president of South Africa. In June 1999 Mandela's term expired and Mbeki succeeded him as president of South Africa.

**Mandelstam, Osip** *(1891–1938)* Russian poet. One of the foremost Russian poets of the 20th century,

Mandelstam was the son of a Jewish leather merchant and grew up in Warsaw and St. Petersburg. He studied at the Sorbonne and the University of Heidelberg, then returned to St. Petersburg where he allied himself with the poets Anna AKHMATOVA and Nikolai GUMILEV. They christened themselves Acmeists in 1913, espousing the concrete and concise in poetry (see ACMEISM). Mandelstam's first book of poetry was *Stone* (1913). Due to the RUSSIAN REVOLUTION and his reluctance to serve its cause in his writing, his future work went unpublished or was circulated with great circumspection. After the revolution (1917), Mandelstam sought relative political freedom in the Crimea. In 1921 he married Nadezhda Khazina, who courageously preserved much of his poetry after his death. In the late 1920s Mandelstam concentrated on translating Italian poetry, and produced the lyrical prose works *The Noise of Time* (1925) and *The Egyptian Stamp* (1928). He was arrested in 1934 for an anti-STALIN poem and sent into internal exile in the provincial town of Voronezh for three years. In 1938 he was again officially condemned, and died soon after in a transit camp in Siberia. The hallmarks of Mandelstam's poetry are a detached tone, majestic language, an abundance of literary and historical allusions and themes often revolving around art.

**Manhattan Project** *(formally, Manhattan District Project)* Code name for the top secret American project to develop the atomic bomb during WORLD WAR II. During the 1930s, some scientists recognized the theoretical possibility of constructing an atomic bomb. Acting on the belief that Nazi Germany could develop such a bomb, Albert EINSTEIN wrote to U.S. president Franklin D. ROOSEVELT describing the destructive potential of such a weapon and urging a major research program so that the U.S. would be the first nation with the bomb. This letter spurred Roosevelt's decision to institute a crash program, later known as the Manhattan Project. U.S. Army general Leslie R. GROVES was appointed chief administrator. The project was carried out primarily at a facility in Oak Ridge, Tennessee, and, beginning in March 1943, at a "super" laboratory at Los Alamos, New Mexico. American physicist J. Robert

OPPENHEIMER was director of the Los Alamos laboratory and persuaded top nuclear physicists to join the project. Among scientists engaged in the Manhattan Project were Oppenheimer's brother Frank OPPENHEIMER, Enrico FERMI, Edward TELLER, British physicist William George PENNEY and hundreds of others. Shrouded in secrecy, the Manhattan Project culminated in the successful test of the first atomic bomb on July 16, 1945. The atomic age had begun. Although highly controversial, the Manhattan Project is widely regarded as a model for any scientific project requiring the coordination of resources and energy to solve a particular problem.

**Mankiewicz, Herman J.** *(1897–1953)* American film producer and screenplay writer. Mankiewicz, the older brother of screenplay writer and director Joseph MANKIEWICZ, enjoyed considerable success in HOLLYWOOD both as a producer of commercial comedies and as a serious screenplay writer. He began his career as a New York theater critic in the 1920s contributing to the *New Yorker,* among other publications. Mankiewicz came to Hollywood in 1926 and, after a stint of writing titles for SILENT FILMS, came to prominence as the producer of the MARX BROTHERS films *Monkey Business* (1931), *Horsefeathers* (1932) and *Duck Soup* (1933). He also wrote the screenplays for numerous films, including *Dinner at Eight* (1933) and *The Pride of the Yankees* (1942). But Mankiewicz remains best known for his collaboration with Orson WELLES on the ACADEMY AWARD–winning screenplay for the classic film *Citizen Kane* (1941). Controversy continues over the question of whether Mankiewicz or Welles had the major hand in the screenplay.

**Mankiewicz, Joseph L(eo)** *(1909–1993)* American film director, producer and screenwriter. Mankiewicz, the brother of screenwriter and producer Herman J. MANKIEWICZ, became one of the most influential HOLLYWOOD directors of the 1940s and 1950s. He began his career as a journalist, then moved to writing English subtitles for German films, before coming to Hollywood in 1929. His early screenplays include *Million Dollar Legs* (1932) and *Our Daily Bread* (1934), a socially conscious—and

controversial—film directed by King VIDOR. Mankiewicz also produced films, most notably *The Philadelphia Story* (1940). In the 1940s he took up directing his own scripts and, remarkably, won Oscars for Best Director and Best Screenplay in consecutive years for *A Letter to Three Wives* (1949) and *All About Eve* (1950). His career suffered from the commercial disappointment of *Cleopatra* (1963), but he later worked on the acclaimed mystery *Sleuth* (1972), starring Michael Caine and Laurence OLIVIER.

**Manley, Michael** *(1925–1997)* Jamaican prime minister. Manley's father, **Norman Washington Manley,** was Jamaica's first prime minister and the founder of the People's National Party. Michael Manley was appointed to the Senate by his father in 1962. Five years later, he was elected to the House of Representatives. When his father retired in 1969, Manley succeeded him as leader of the People's National Party. In 1972 he began his first term as prime minister and attempted to introduce socialist reforms. He alienated the United States by his overtures to Fidel CASTRO and by the Jamaican government's acquisition of 50 percent of American and Canadian companies' Jamaican interests. He was reelected in 1976 but was unable to curb Jamaica's increasing unemployment. In 1980 Edward P. Seaga of the Jamaica Labor Party became prime minister. With a more moderate platform than he had maintained in the 1970s, Manley returned to power in 1989 when the People's National Party won 44 of the 60 seats in Parliament. Manley upheld the good relations with the U.S. established by Seaga, but also proposed a rebuilding of Jamaica's schools and tax breaks and incentives to small farms and businesses. Manley was forced to resign his office in 1992.

**Mann, Thomas** *(1875–1955)* German novelist, story writer and essayist. Mann, who was awarded the NOBEL PRIZE for literature in 1929, is widely regarded as one of the greatest German writers of the 20th century. Two of his most famous works are the novella *DEATH IN VENICE* (1911) and the novel *THE MAGIC MOUNTAIN* (1924). Mann, whose brother Heinrich also became a renowned novelist, was raised in a

middle-class bourgeois family whose values he depicted in his first novel, *Buddenbrooks* (1901). Over the next two decades, Mann devoted much of his energies to the novella and short story: *Tristan* (1902), *Tonio Kroger* (1903), *Felix Krull* (1911) and *A Man and His Dog* (1918) being prominent examples. In 1933 Mann, an outspoken opponent of the NAZIS, exiled himself from GERMANY and lived in California from 1930 until after the war. Other novels by Mann include the tetralogy *Joseph and His Brothers* (1933–43) and *Doctor Faustus* (1948).

**Mann Act** U.S. law enacted in 1910 and aimed at abolishing the "white slave trade" (prostitution). The federal law bans the transportation of women across state lines for immoral purposes. Little used during the second half of the century, the first recorded prosecution under the act involved a celebrity. Heavyweight boxing champion, Jack JOHNSON, the first black American champion, was prosecuted under the act after he encouraged a white woman whom he later married to leave a brothel where she was working to travel with him to another state. After Johnson was convicted and sentenced to a year in jail, he fled the country but ultimately returned and served his sentence.

**Mannerheim, Carl Gustav Emil** *(1867–1951)* Finnish military and political leader, president of FINLAND. Born of a wealthy and distinguished Finnish-Swedish family in Villnaes—in what was then the Russian province of Finland—he was trained as a soldier and commissioned in the Russian imperial army (1889). He served in the RUSSO-JAPANESE WAR (1904–05) and by the outbreak of WORLD WAR I had attained the rank of general in the czar's army. He was a commander in the war, returning home in 1917, when Finland declared its independence. In 1918, after Finnish BOLSHEVIKS occupied Helsinki, Mannerheim organized a White counterforce and, with German help, drove the communists from Finland. He served briefly as regent of Finland and was defeated in the presidential elections of 1919. He was appointed head of the Finnish defense council in (1931) and built the Mannerheim Line, an unsuccessful attempt to stem Soviet invasion, which occurred in 1940. He commanded Finnish forces in the RUSSO-FINNISH WAR (1939–40) and led his troops against the Soviets again during WORLD WAR II (1941–44). In 1944 he was appointed president of Finland and concluded an armistice with the USSR He retired in 1946.

**Manning, Olivia** *(1908–1980)* British novelist best known for six novels that together compromise a series titled *Fortunes of War,* which Anthony BURGESS has called "the finest fictional record of [WORLD WAR II] produced by a British writer." Born in Portsmouth, England, Manning was raised in Ireland. Just before the outbreak of World War II she accompanied her new husband to Bucharest, Romania, where he lectured for the BRITISH COUNCIL. As German forces invaded the Balkan nations, the couple fled first to Athens, then to Egypt and finally to Jerusalem, in Palestine. Following the war they returned to London, where Manning lived and wrote until her death. Her first novel, *Among the Missing,* was published in 1949, and several others followed during the 1950s. The three books in *The Balkan Trilogy* (the first part of *Fortunes of War*) appeared in 1960, 1962 and 1965, respectively; the six-novel series was completed in *The Levant Trilogy* (1977–80). *Fortunes of War* takes a somewhat feminist view of personal relations during the war, but its scope and richness have earned it comparison with such masterpieces as Tolstoy's *War and Peace* and DODERER's *The Demons.* Manning was awarded a CBE in 1976.

**Manning, Timothy Cardinal** *(1909–1989)* Roman Catholic archbishop of Los Angeles (1970–85). After being appointed to the post in Los Angeles, he worked to heal rifts that had opened between the diocese and the city's black and Hispanic Catholics. He was a liberal on social issues such as the VIETNAM WAR and the 1983 deportation of Salvadoran refugees, but conservative on theological issues such as ABORTION and birth control. He was elevated to cardinal in 1973.

**Man O'War** *(1917–1947)* Thoroughbred racehorse. Until SECRETARIAT, no modern racehorse was mentioned in the same breath as Man O'War. Bred by the Belmont family, the big chestnut made his racing debut in 1919 and won by six lengths. Although handicappers continued to increase the weight he was asked to carry, he knew defeat only once, and that was the result of an inexperienced starter operating the gate. He achieved international celebrity status as he shattered track records wherever he ran. Never a Triple Crown winner, as he was not entered for the Kentucky Derby, he won the Belmont by 20 lengths and set world and American records for the 1 3/8 miles at 2:14 1/5 (2:14:12). After winning 19 of his 20 races, Man O'War was retired as a three-year-old because the higher weights he would be asked to carry as a four-year-old increased the risk of injury. He was an outstanding stud, and many hundreds of successful racehorses can trace back to Man O'War on either side of their pedigree, including the great WAR ADMIRAL. Man O'War died of a colic attack at the age of 30. His memorial service was attended by thousands, and he was mourned by millions throughout the world.

**Mansfield, Katherine (Katherine Mansfield Beauchamp)** *(1888–1923)* British short story writer. Mansfield was born in New Zealand but moved to London in 1908. After a very brief marriage (1909), she became pregnant. Her first collection of stories, *In a German Pension* (1911), reflects her experience of giving birth to a stillborn child in Bavaria. In 1911 Mansfield met John Middleton MURRY, editor of *Rhythm* (to which she contributed short stories), and married him in 1918. They were friends of Frieda and D. H. Lawrence, with whom they founded the short-lived *Signature* magazine. Mansfield's other collections include *Bliss and Other Stories* (1920), *The Garden Party and Other Stories* (1922), and *Something Childish* (1924). Mansfield's original and sometimes ironic stories evidence the influence of Anton CHEKHOV. She died of tuberculosis in a sanitorium in France.

**Mansfield, Mike** *(1903–2001)* U.S. senator. A Democrat from Montana, Mansfield served a record 16 years as the majority leader of the U.S. Senate, from 1961 to 1977. He was particularly known for his influence in foreign affairs, and had a clear vision of the requirements of national security and balance-of-power relationships. He also served 10 years in the U.S. House of Representatives. He carried out foreign diplomatic assignments for Presidents Dwight D. EISENHOWER, John F. KENNEDY and Lyndon B. JOHNSON. He was appointed ambassador to Japan by President Jimmy CARTER, and retained the position under President REAGAN.

**Manship, Paul** *(1885–1966)* American sculptor. Born in St. Paul, Minnesota, he was educated at the St. Paul Institute of Arts, the Pennsylvania Academy of the Fine Arts and the American Academy at Rome, where in 1909 he was awarded the Prix de Rome. Manship used his rigorous academic training and his immersion in the art of ancient Rome and Renaissance Italy as inspiration for his muscular, realistic sculpture of human and animal figures, often drawing on classical mythology for subject matter. Usually working in bronze or marble, he produced many individual sculptures, such as *Dryad, Little Brother* (Metropolitan Museum of Art, New York City) and *Pronghorn Antelope* (Art Institute of Chicago), as well as major public commissions, including *Actaeon* (Brookgreen Gardens, Georgetown, S.C.) and *Prometheus* (Rockefeller Center, New York City).

**Manson, Charles** *(1934– )* American mass murderer. Born in Cincinnati, Ohio, Manson was a habitual criminal who had served a number of terms in prison before setting up his notorious "family" commune in the California desert in the 1960s. His young hippie following, mainly women, believed that Manson was a godlike figure and subscribed to his bizarre, drug-riddled, and satanist-tinged apocalyptic philosophy. His complete control over this cult was exerted in the murders that he masterminded. At his direction, members of his group savagely killed seven people, including actress Sharon Tate, in two houses near Beverly Hills in August 1969. The bloody details of the crimes were front-page news for months—as were the subsequent Los Angeles trials of Manson and four of his accomplices. Manson was found guilty of murder and in 1971 was sentenced to death. When California abolished the death penalty, his sentence was commuted to life imprisonment.

**Manstein, Erich von** *(1887–1973)* German soldier. A general during WORLD WAR II, he engineered the Nazi invasion of Western Europe and led conquering German troops into France. As commander of the 11th German Army, he defeated forces of the USSR in the Crimea in 1941 and in 1942 was unsuccessful in efforts to relieve the troops of General Friedrich von Paulus at STALINGRAD (see WORLD WAR II ON THE RUSSIAN FRONT). A critic of HITLER's Russian campaign, von Manstein was dismissed from duty in 1944. Condemned to an 18-year prison sentence by a British court in 1949, he was freed in 1953.

**Manteuffel, Hasso von** *(1897–1978)* German general who was commander of the Nazi attack during the BATTLE OF THE BULGE in WORLD WAR II.

**Mantle, Mickey Charles** *(1931–1995)* American baseball luminary. Born in Oklahoma, as a boy Mantle was groomed for baseball by his father, who named him in honor of Mickey Cochrane, a great catcher. Signed in high school by the New York Yankees, Mantle played in the minor leagues after graduation. In 1951 he was brought to New York as a centerfielder. Beginning in 1952, he hit over .300 in 10 of his 18 seasons. He was the American League's most valuable player in 1962. He hit 54 home runs in 1961 (the same year his teammate Roger MARIS hit 61 to break Babe RUTH's record by one), and played in 12 World Series. He retired in 1969. His autobiography is titled *The Mick*.

***Man Who Was Thursday, The*** G. K. CHESTERTON's best-known novel, a seminal work in the history of the modern fantastic tale. Published in 1908 it is, by turns, a detective story, allegory, and (according to its subtitle) "nightmare" whose violently bizarre imagery and baffling ambiguity have been compared to Franz KAFKA. A young detective infiltrates a band of anarchists bent on destroying the world only to discover that each member, like him, is also a detective in disguise assigned to the same case. Meanwhile, the group's leader, the diabolically mysterious "Sunday," leads them all on a mad chase ultimately revealing himself to be a godlike entity who mocks their efforts. Man is born to

search but not necessarily to understand, he says: "Since the beginning of the world, all men have hunted me like a wolf—kings and sages, and poets and law-givers, all the churches, and all the philosophers. But I have never been caught yet." Life, while not a sinister conspiracy, may yet turn out to be a cosmic prank. According to his *Autobiography* (1937) Chesterton wanted to vanquish with 20th-century optimism the pessimism and despair of the 19th century. However, this tour-de-force of paradoxes also implies any real meanings in life must remain secrets, hidden behind inscrutable masks.

**Manzu, Giacomo** *(1908–1991)* Italian sculptor. Born in Bergamo, he was apprenticed to a woodcarver in 1919, traveled to Paris in the late 1920s and settled in Milan in 1930. Aware of avant-garde movements in sculpture, he nonetheless chose representational works of classical antiquity and of such masters as Donatello and Rodin as his models. Mainly executed in bronze, his work is figurative, dignified and calm—often with a religious tone or subject matter. Among his many commissioned sculptures are the bronze doors at Salzburg Cathedral (1958) and the bronze *Door of Death* (1962) at St. Peter's Basilica in Rome.

**Maoism** System of communism adopted in CHINA under MAO ZEDONG. Maoism envisions a more flexible political system than Marxism-Leninism and claims that self-reliance is more important than state authority—and that the concept of revolutionary momentum, as expressed in the CULTURAL REVOLUTION, is more important than the state machine. Various terrorist groups in the West professed themselves to be Maoist, but in China Maoism waned under Mao's successors, who were concerned most of all with modernizing the nation's economy.

**Mao Tse-tung** See MAO ZEDONG.

**Maowad, René** *(1925–1989)* Lebanese politician, president of LEBANON (1989). A Maronite Christian from northern Lebanon, the moderate Maowad had been a member of Parliament since 1957 and had served as a cabinet minister three times. After the resignation of President Amin Gemayel in Sep-

tember of 1988, there were two rival interim premiers—General Michel Aoun, head of a military cabinet in Christian east Beirut that claimed to be Lebanon's sole legitimate government, and Selim al-Hoss, a Sunni Moslem in west Beirut. Following Aoun's declaration dissolving Parliament, 30 members of Parliament, most of them Christians, disputed his right to do so. Joining together with 27 deputies (mostly Muslim) they elected Maowad as Lebanon's 9th president in November 1989. Maowad was assassinated after only 17 days in office when a bomb exploded next to his motorcade on November 22, in Muslim west Beirut. No group claimed responsibility for the bombing. Another moderate, Elias Hrawi, was quickly elected president by Parliament on November 24, 1989.

**Mao Zedong** *(1893–1976)* Chinese political leader, founder of the People's Republic of CHINA. Born into a peasant family in Shao-shan, Hunan province, he studied the traditional Chinese classics and also received a modern Western education. He first encountered Marxism while working at Peking University and was soon converted to its doctrine. Mao was a founding member of the Chinese Communist Party (CCP) in 1921 and became its leader in Hunan. In a united effort with the KUOMINTANG, he organized peasant and industrial unions and became (1926) director of the Peasant Movement Training Institute. The CCP and the Kuomintang split in 1927. In the ensuing purge of communists, Mao fled to the countryside and, along with CHU TEH, formed a communist-led guerrilla army that operated in the hinterlands from 1928 to 1931. This stress on the rural areas, with support coming from the peasantry rather than from an urban proletariat, was to be the hallmark of the Chinese brand of communism that Mao pioneered.

In 1931 Mao was named chairman of the newly created Soviet Republic of China, with headquarters in Kiangsi province. Battered by attacks from the Nationalist forces led by CHIANG KAISHEK, Mao led his Red Army in the epic LONG MARCH (1934–35), trekking 6,000 miles before reaching northern Shensi and establishing a new government at Yenan. After the XIAN INCIDENT of 1936, Mao and his communists again collaborated with the Nationalists, this time forming a united front against the Japanese that lasted from 1937 to 1945. After the war, the uneasy alliance again broke and civil war (1946–49) resulted in the rout of the Kuomintang by Mao's forces and the establishment (1949) of the People's Republic of China with Mao as chairman.

His slogan-captioned attempts at making a truly Chinese communist stake began with the Hundred Flowers movement of 1956–57 in which intellectuals were encouraged to criticize the party. The second manifestation was in Mao's GREAT LEAP FORWARD (1958), a failed program that called for rapid industrial development and the total dismantling of private property. At the same time, Mao continued to struggle against domination by the USSR Forced from his chairmanship in 1959, he was replaced by LIU SHAOQI. However, Mao soon regained primacy by means of the CULTURAL REVOLUTION, which peaked in the late 1960s and was spearheaded by his wife, CHIANG CH'ING. During this period, the "little red book" of Mao's maxims became the ultimate authority for political correctness, and Mao and his ideology were the objects of fanatical worship. Liu was ousted in 1968, and in 1969 Mao, who had continued as chairman of the Communist Party, chaired the Ninth Communist Party Congress. The following year he was named supreme commander of the nation and the army.

Mao consolidated his power during the 1970s, drawing further away from the USSR and initiating ties with the U.S. highlighted by a 1972 Peking meeting with President Richard NIXON. Mao is recognized as one of the most important Marxist theoreticians, and his writings have had particular influence throughout the THIRD WORLD. He succeeded in creating an enormous social revolution and in unifying his huge and once-fragmented nation. However, the excesses of Mao's government have caused some diminishing of his stature in his homeland in the years since his death.

**Mapai (Miphlegeth Poalei Israel)** Israeli Workers' Party, founded in PALESTINE in 1930 and usually called the Labor Party. A moderate left-wing party, it dominated Israeli governments until the election of Menachem BEGIN in 1977.

**Mapam** United Workers' Party, an Israeli socialist party far to the left of MAPAI, drawing much of its support from the kibbutzim.

**Mapplethorpe, Robert** *(1946–1989)* American photographer. Mapplethorpe was known for his dramatic, austere black-and-white photos, many with homoerotic or sadomasochistic content. Retrospectives of his work appeared at the Institute of Contemporary Art in Philadelphia, at the Whitney Museum of American Art in New York City, and elsewhere. In June 1989 the Corcoran Gallery of Art in Washington, D.C., announced that it had canceled a retrospective in order to avoid political controversy at a time when Congress was reviewing its annual appropriation for the National Endowment for the Arts, whose funds would have been used to underwrite the exhibit. The Washington Project for the Arts mounted the retrospective instead. In 1990 the Cincinnati Museum of Art and its director were tried but acquitted of obscenity charges after showing the same Mapplethorpe exhibit.

**Maradona, Diego Armando** *(1960– )* Argentine soccer player—the outstanding player of the 1980s. Maradona's hallmark was his phenomenal ball control and goal-scoring abilities. A phenom, Maradona made his professional debut at 15 for Argentinos Juniors in 1975. His goal-scoring rate was astounding, gaining him adulation throughout his homeland. Astonishingly, he was omitted from Argentina's 1978 World Cup winning team, but rebounded from this disappointment to become the focus of the 1982 World Cup side. Following the tournament he joined Spanish giant Barcelona, but after an injury-filled tenure there he was traded to Napoli in Italy, where his career regained its momentum. He led Napoli to its first Italian championship, but his greatest triumph was the 1986 World Cup, where his virtuoso performances gained Argentina the championship. Napoli regained the Italian title in 1990, but injuries and harassment seemed to disenchant Maradona. During the 1990–91 season he missed training and games and in March 1991 was tested positive for drug use. In April the Italian authorities banned him from soccer for 15 months. Following a similar suspension from the 1994 World Cup, Maradona played for Boca Juniors until his retirement in 1997.

**Maravich, Peter "Pistol Pete"** *(1948–1988)* American basketball star. As a college basketball player, he was the greatest scorer in National Collegiate Athletic Association history. From 1968 to 1970, he scored a record 3,667 points for Louisiana State University. During his 10-year NBA career, he averaged 24.2 points per game. He led the league in scoring during the 1977 season and was inducted into the Basketball Hall of Fame in 1987. Throughout his career, he was known for his droopy socks and long hair.

**Marble, Alice** *(1913–1990)* U.S. tennis player. The top woman player of the late 1930s, she was credited with introducing the aggressive serve-and-volley style of play to women's tennis. She won the U.S. women's amateur singles title four times, in 1936, 1938, 1939 and 1940, and dominated the women's doubles championships with her partner Sara Palfrey Fabyan. She won the Wimbledon singles championship in 1939. In 1940 she turned professional, playing in exhibition matches and giving tennis clinics in the U.S. and abroad. In 1945, during the last months of World War II, she worked undercover as a U.S. intelligence agent in neutral Switzerland.

**Marc, Franz** *(1880–1916)* German painter. Born in Bavaria, he studied painting in Germany and became acquainted with modern art during trips to Paris in 1903 and 1909. In 1910 he met Auguste MACKE, who was to influence the expressionistic nature of his work. In 1911 he became a founding member of the BLAUE REITER group. Marc took the figures of animals, usually horses, as his primary subject matter, portraying them in an almost mystically evocative manner in richly vibrant colors and expressively rounded forms. Among his paintings in this genre are *Blue Horses* (Walker Art Center, Minneapolis) and *Yellow Horses* (1912, Staatsgalerie, Stuttgart). His later works depict nature in increasingly abstract shards of form and color, as in *Tyrol* (1913–14, Bavarian State Museum, Munich). Already one of Germany's leading expressionist painters by the beginning of WORLD WAR I, his career was cut short by his death in battle at VERDUN.

**Marceau, Marcel** *(1923–  )* French mime. Marceau has received international acclaim as a mime performer, instantly recognizable in his most famous persona of the amiable, white-faced Bip in such sketches as the "tug-of-war." Influenced by the silent films of Charlie Chaplin, he began using wordless sketches while working as a teacher. As a solo performer he has appeared throughout Europe and the U.S. He established his own mime company in the late 1940s, which tours the world performing complete mime-dramas, such as the well-known drama based on Gogol's *The Overcoat* (1951). In 1998 Marceau was named a Grand Officer of France's National Order of Merit.

**Marcel, Gabriel** *(1889–1973)* French philosopher and playwright. Marcel was one of the leading representatives of Christian existential philosophy. Educated at the Sorbonne, Marcel served in the RED CROSS during WORLD WAR I. The central event of his life was his conversion to Roman Catholicism in 1929—an event he described in his writings as breaking through to true freedom by means of religious faith. Marcel was a philosophical adversary of the atheistic existentialism of fellow French philosopher Jean-Paul SARTRE. His major works include *Metaphysical Journal* (1927), the two-volume *The Mystery of Being* (1951) and *The Existential Background to Human Destiny* (1963). Marcel also wrote a number of plays with Catholic themes that were widely produced in their era.

**"March on Rome"** *(1922)* In the summer of 1922 Italy was in chaos; the government couldn't cope with the fascists, who had seized power in Bologna, Milan and other cities. Benito MUSSOLINI, leader of the National Fascist Party, demanded the government's resignation. Premier Luigi Facta belatedly declared a state of siege when the fascists began to march on Rome (October 28, 1922), but King VICTOR EMMANUEL III refused to sign the martial law decree, dismissing Facta. Mussolini, arriving by railroad sleeping car from Milan, found only 25,000 of his BLACK SHIRTS occupying Rome, but thousands joined them next day, coming on special trains to cheer Mussolini. The king permitted him to form a government to reestablish order.

**March on Washington** Massive civil rights rally held in Washington, D.C., on August 28, 1963. The march, organized by Rev. Martin Luther KING Jr., was attended by more than 200,000 people who gathered to demand immediate equality in jobs and full civil rights for American blacks. The demonstrators gathered in the morning at the Washington Monument, then marched down Constitution and Independence avenues to the Lincoln Memorial. There, almost completely filling the mall, they listened to addresses by the march's leaders, the most significant of which was Dr. King's eloquent speech in which he said "I have a dream."

**Marciano, Rocky (Rocco Francis Marchegiano)** *(1923–1969)* American boxer. An all-around athlete, Marciano gave up a professional baseball career for boxing. As an amateur, he won all but three of his 30 fights. He turned to a professional boxing career in 1947 and began his climb to the heavyweight title. During that struggle, he became only the second person to knock out Joe LOUIS. In 1952 he fought the titleholder, Jersey Joe Walcott, and knocked him out for the title. Over the next four years, Marciano's title was challenged six times, and six times Marciano defended the title successfully. He retired an undefeated champion with 49 wins, 43 of them knockouts. He met an untimely death in a plane crash.

**Marconi, Marchese Guglielmo** *(1874–1937)* Italian electrical engineer and inventor. Marconi, the second son of a prosperous Italian country gentleman and a wealthy Irishwoman, was educated in Livorno and Bologna. He studied physics under several well-known teachers and learned about the work on electromagnetic radiation of Heinrich Hertz, Oliver Lodge, Augusto Righi and others. Marconi became interested in using Hertz's "invisible rays" to signal Morse code and in 1894 began experimenting to this end at his father's estate. Although he was soon able to transmit radio signals over a distance of more than a mile, he received little encouragement to continue his work in Italy and was advised to go to England. Shortly after arriving in London in 1896 Marconi secured the interest of officials from the war office, the Admiralty and the postal service. He spent the next five years in demonstrating and improving the range and performance of his equipment—and in overcoming the prevailing skepticism. In 1897 he helped to form the Wireless Telegraphic and Signal Co. Ltd., which in 1900 became Marconi's Wireless Telegraphy Co. Ltd.

He achieved the first international wireless (i.e., radio) transmission, between England and France, in March 1899; this aroused considerable public interest and attracted attention in the world's press. In the same year the British navy's summer maneuvers, with several ships equipped with Marconi's apparatus, helped to convince the Admiralty and mercantile ship owners of the value of radio telegraphy at sea. In December 1901 Marconi for the first time transmitted radio signals in Morse code across the Atlantic, a distance of some 2,000 miles. Marconi created a sensation, becoming world famous overnight and silencing many of his critics from the scientific world, who had believed that radio waves could not follow the curvature of the Earth. But they did, and this phenomenon was explained by Arthur Kennelly in 1902 as being due to a reflecting layer—the ionosphere—in the Earth's atmosphere. Thus radio telegraphy became a practical system of communication, especially at sea. Marconi spent the rest of his life improving and extending his wireless and managing his companies.

Although a good deal of Marconi's work was based on the ideas and discoveries of others, he was responsible for some notable inventions. He held the first of all radio telegraphy patents based on the use of waves (1896); the elevated antenna (1894); patent 7777, which enabled several stations to operate on different wavelengths without mutual interference (1900); the magnetic detector (1902); the horizontal directional antenna (1915); and the timed-spark system of generating pseudocontinuous waves (1912). From about 1916, Marconi began to exploit the use of radio waves of short wavelength, which allowed a more efficient transmission of radiant energy. In 1924 the Marconi Company obtained a contract to establish shortwave communication between England and British Commonwealth countries; by 1927 a worldwide network had been formed.

Marconi was a plenipotentiary delegate at the 1919 PARIS PEACE CONFERENCE, and in 1923 he joined the Fascist Party and became a friend of MUSSOLINI. Marconi received several honorary degrees and many awards, which included the NOBEL PRIZE for physics jointly with Karl Braun (1909), and was president of the Royal Italian Academy in 1930. At the hour of his state funeral, all post office wireless telegraph and wireless telephone services to the British Isles observed a two-minute silence.

**Marconi Scandal** British political scandal of 1912–13. When Britain's government ordered the British Marconi Company to build wireless stations throughout the British Empire in 1912, cabinet ministers were rumored to have profited from their knowledge of the scheme by buying shares in the company. A committee report (1913) cleared Attorney General Sir Rufus Isaacs, Lord Murray of Elibank and LLOYD GEORGE, then chancellor of the Exchequer, of corruption charges.

**Marco Polo Bridge Incident** Clash between Chinese forces and Japanese troops on July 7, 1937. It occurred at the Marco Polo Bridge that crosses the Yungting River at Wanping in China's northern Hopeh province. This incident marked the beginning of the Second SINO-JAPANESE WAR (1937–45). Provoked by the Japanese, who refused to negotiate, the action provided a convenient pretext for the Japanese occupation of Peking and Tientsin, while Chinese troops were forced to retreat to the south.

**Marcos, Ferdinand Edralin** (1917–1989) President of the PHILIPPINES (1965–86). Marcos was born in Ilocos Norte province. He served in both the Philippine and U.S. armies in WORLD WAR II and emerged from the war as a highly decorated officer. Years later, Marcos dismissed persistent allegations that his war record has been fabricated. He claimed that the documentation of his military exploits had been destroyed in a fire. After spending 15 years in the Philippine legislature, Marcos was elected to his first term as president in 1965. He was reelected in 1969. In 1972 Marcos imposed martial law in the Philippines and adopted a new national constitution under which he became prime minister as well as president. The country remained under martial law until 1981. Marcos's grip on power in the Philippines began to weaken following the assassination in 1983 of Benigno Aquino, the nation's leading opposition figure, who was shot dead upon returning from exile. Marcos blamed the killing on a professional hit-man with ties to the communists, but the country's opposition movement accused the government of masterminding the murder. In the face of increasing unrest at home and new pressure from the U.S. to enact reforms, Marcos decided in November 1985 to call a snap election to test his popularity. The decision backfired when the opposition rallied around the presidential candidacy of Corazon AQUINO, who had assumed the mantle of leadership from her late husband. The subsequent elections, on February 7, 1986, were marred by fraud. Marcos declared himself victorious, but Aquino initiated a nationwide campaign of civil disobedience in an attempt to topple the government. Marcos's fate was sealed when the nation's two top military leaders resigned February 22 and threw their support to Aquino. Marcos left the country for Hawaii February 26 aboard a U.S. Air Force plane.

**Marcuse, Herbert** (1898–1979) German-born political philosopher and social critic. Marcuse taught at the Frankfurt Institute for Social Research before fleeing the Nazis in 1934. He immigrated to the U.S., where, over the next four decades, he taught at Harvard, Yale, Columbia and other universities. Strongly influenced by both Marx and Freud, Marcuse argued that society suffered from psychological and economic repressions that could be alleviated only by revolution. Marcuse was a major influence on the New Left politics of the 1960s. His major works include *Reason and Revolution* (1941), *Eros and Civilization* (1955) and *One-Dimensional Man* (1964).

**Mariana Islands, Northern (Commonwealth of the Northern Mariana Islands)** The Northern Mariana Islands lie in the North Pacific Ocean and cover an area of 184 square miles (see page 957); the southern islands are limestone with fringing coral reefs, while the northern islands are volcanic. The capital is SAIPAN. Inhabited from 1500 B.C., the islands came under Spanish colonial rule in 1668. After losing the Spanish-American War of 1898, Spain ceded GUAM to the U.S. and sold the rest of the Marianas to Germany. With the outbreak of WORLD WAR I, JAPAN took possession of the German islands. In 1920 the LEAGUE OF NATIONS mandated control of Micronesia (which includes the Marianas) to Japan. In August 1944 Japanese forces in the Marianas were defeated by the U.S., and in 1945 the U.S. Navy assumed control of Micronesia. In 1947 the UNITED NATIONS established the Trust Territory of the PACIFIC ISLANDS, a "strategic trust" under U.S. administration. In a plebiscite in June 1975 the people of the Northern Marianas voted to become a self-governing U.S. commonwealth territory separate from the rest of the Micronesian territories. The new status came into force in January 1978, elections for the territory's governorship and bicameral legislature having been held in December 1977. In 1984 the U.S. government entered into negotiations with the landowners on Tinian Island over the use of their land for military purposes. In November 1986 the Northern Mariana islanders were granted U.S. citizenship. The total population in 2004 was just over 78,000.

**Marich, Man Singh Shrestha** (1942– ) Nepalese political leader, selected by King BIRENDRA to be prime minister in 1986. Shrestha was born an illegitimate child in a low-caste family of the Newar clan. At one time a member of the Nepali Communist Party, he was a high school headmaster before winning an uncontested election to the Rashtriya Panchayat. In 1990 Marich was succeeded by LOKENDRA BAHADUR CHAND.

**Mariel Boatlift** Beginning in April of 1980, boatloads of Cuban refugees began leaving Mariel Harbor in CUBA to emigrate to the U.S. These freedom flotillas, as they came to be known, were headed mostly for Florida. The U.S. was having difficulties assimilating the influx of refugees, and U.S. Coast Guard blockades were expensive and largely unsuccessful. Some of the Cubans were contained in refugee and resettlement camps; others were confined in federal prisons to undergo expulsion hearings—a move ordered by President Jimmy CARTER in June. He also announced a plan in September to help Florida with its resettlement efforts, which included federal absorption of the costs of resettlement, prosecution of boat owners who attempted to profit from the refugees and relocation of some to a settlement camp in Puerto Rico. On September 26, the Cuban government closed Mariel Harbor, thus ending the boatlift—but some 125,000 Cubans entered the U.S. during its five-month duration.

**Marin, John** (*1870–1953*) American painter. An important early modernist, he was born in Rutherford, N.J. Marin studied architecture and worked as an architectural draftsman before turning to the study of painting at the Pennsylvania Academy of the Fine Arts from 1899 to 1901. Traveling to Europe in 1905, he was influenced by the work of James McNeill Whistler, and lived a meager existence abroad for five years. After he returned to the U.S. his work was first exhibited by Alfred STIEGLITZ (1909). He soon drew acclaim as a superb watercolorist and was recognized for his powerful use of the medium. Taking for his subject the skyline of New York City, the deserts of Taos, New Mexico, and the seascapes of Maine, he painted with energy and expressiveness, employing bold brushstrokes, colors that are alternately subtle and vivid and an approach that mingled the abstract with the realistic. Marin's oils and watercolors are included in virtually every important collection of modern American art. (See also MODERNISM.)

**Mariner probes** A series of U.S. planetary probes, launched from 1962 to 1973, that greatly expanded our knowledge of the solar system. *Mariner 1* was launched on July 22, 1962, but was destroyed after veering off course following its launch. *Mariner 2* was launched on August 27, 1962, and flew by Venus in December of that year, measuring the Venusian temperature and confirming the existence of the solar wind. *Mariner 3* was launched on November 5, 1964, but failed to obtain the necessary velocity and headed for an unplanned orbit around the sun; communication with the craft was lost 10 hours after launch. *Mariner 4* was launched November 28, 1964, and passed by Mars in July 1965, returning photographs of the planet's surface. *Mariner 5* was launched June 4, 1967, and passed Venus in October of that year, measuring the Venusian temperature, testing its atmosphere and determining the planet's mass and diameter. *Mariner 6* was launched on February 24, 1969, and its twin *Mariner 7* was launched on March 27, 1969; they passed Mars in July and August, respectively, returning photographs and performing experiments testing the planet's temperature, atmosphere and size. *Mariner 9* was launched May 30, 1971, and entered Martian orbit in November of that year, returning more than 7,000 photographs of the planet before losing contact with Earth in October 1972. *Mariner 10* was launched November 3, 1973, flying by Venus in February 1974 and by Mercury in March and September 1974 and again in March 1975; the Mercury flybys resulted in the discovery of the planet's magnetic field. *Mariners 11* and *12* were renamed *Voyager 1* and *Voyager 2*. The latter was launched on August 20, 1977, and flew by Jupiter in July 1979, Saturn in August 1981, Uranus in January 1986 and Neptune in August 1989. *Voyager 1*, which was delayed by technical problems, was launched on September 5, 1977, and passed by Jupiter in March 1979, Saturn in November 1980 and Uranus in December 1985.

**Marinetti, Filippo T(ommaso)** (*1876–1944*) Italian aesthetic theorist, essayist and poet. Marinetti is best remembered as the principal ideologue for the right-wing, Italian segment of the multinational aesthetic movement known as FUTURISM. In his *Foundation and Manifesto of Futurism* (1908) and other writings, Marinetti argued for the aesthetic beauty of modern technology, pitted poetic diction against common language usage and held that nationalism and warfare were worthy of artistic exaltation. In the 1920s and after, Marinetti became a major spokesman for the fascist regime of Benito MUSSOLINI.

**Marini, Marino** (*1901–1980*) Italian sculptor. Beginning his career as a painter, he continued to paint and create prints while becoming an internationally known sculptor. Marini, influenced early in his career by classical Roman statuary, developed an intensely individualistic style that found its finest expression in figures of horses and riders. These powerful equestrian sculptures are exemplified by the monumental *Horse and Rider* (1952–53) in the collection of the Hirshhorn Museum, Washington, D.C.

**Maris, Roger Eugene** (*1934–1985*) American baseball player. In 1961, as an outfielder for the New York Yankees, Maris set an all-time single-season record of 61 home runs, breaking Babe RUTH's record of 60 set in 1927. He received much hostile media and fan attention from those who did not wish to see Ruth's record overturned. There were also those who would have preferred to see Maris's teammate Mickey MANTLE break the record. Maris played with the Yankees until 1966 when he was traded to the St. Louis Cardinals. He retired from baseball in 1968 with a career total of 275 home runs in the major leagues.

**Maritain, Jacques** (*1882–1973*) French philosopher. Educated at the Sorbonne and the University of Heidelberg, Maritain was a Protestant who converted to Roman Catholicism (1906) under the influence of the mystical poet Léon Bloy and an advocate of scientific materialism who was started on a path toward neo-Thomism by the philosophy of Henri BERGSON. He taught at a number of universities in France and the U.S. and was the author of over 50 books of philosophy and numerous scholarly articles. His applications of the philosophy of St. Thomas Aquinas to the contemporary world can be found in his works on metaphysics, politics, religion and aesthetics. Among his books are *The Degrees of Knowledge* (1932, tr. 1937), *True Humanism* (1936, tr. 1938), *Man* *and the State* (1951) and *On the Use of Philosophy* (1961).

**Markelius, Sven** *(1889–1972)* Swedish architect who introduced the vocabulary of MODERNISM through the INTERNATIONAL STYLE to Sweden. Markelius was trained at the Stockholm Technical College and Academy of Fine Arts. The concert hall at Halsingborg (1932) was his first major work. His simple and elegantly modern Swedish Pavilion at the NEW YORK WORLD'S FAIR OF 1939 brought him international notice. He was Stockholm's city architect and planner from 1944 to 1954 and was the primary planner of the satellite town of Vallingby near Stockholm, a much-admired example of advanced concepts in town planning. Markelius also often combined work in architecture with interior design. He was a member of the team that developed the design for the United Nations Headquarters building in New York; the interior of one of the council chambers there is a fine example of his work. Markelius's work combines the ideas of International Style modernism with a certain humane quality that is characteristic of the best of Scandinavian design.

**Markert, Russell** *(1899–1990)* U.S. choreographer. In 1916, he formed the high-kicking chorus line "The 16 Missouri Rockets." They were later billed as "The American Rockets" and were hired by showman Samuel (Roxy) Rothafel for the opening of RADIO CITY MUSIC HALL in 1932. Markert acted as director and choreographer for the troupe, which became known as the Radio City Musical Hall Rockettes, until his retirement in 1971.

**Markham, Beryl** *(1902–1986)* British-born aviator. She grew up in KENYA, where she learned to fly and became a bush pilot. She pioneered the scouting of elephants and other wild game from the air. The first person to fly solo across the Atlantic from east to west, her historic flight took place in September 1936 in bad weather. She took off from Abingdon, England and landed more than 21 hours later in a Nova Scotia bog. New York City, her intended destination, honored her with a ticker tape parade. Her historic flight was described at length in her memoirs, *West with the Night,* first published in 1943. Upon its rerelease in 1983, it was hailed by critics in Britain and the U.S. Also a professional horse trainer, she had six Kenya Derby winners.

**Markievicz, Countess Con(stance) (Constance Gore-Booth)** *(1868–1927)* Irish nationalist. A member of a prominent aristocratic Protestant family in the west of Ireland, Constance Gore-Booth married a Polish count in 1900. She became involved in radical Irish politics and participated in the EASTER REBELLION (1916). She was sentenced to death but pardoned and released from prison in 1917. The following year, as a SINN FÉIN candidate, she became the first woman elected to the British Parliament but (along with the other victorious Sinn Féin candidates) refused to take her seat. Instead, she became a member of the new provisional Irish Parliament. W. B. YEATS celebrated Markievicz and her sister in his poem "In Memory of Eva Gore-Booth and Con Markievicz," although he later condemned her radical politics.

**Mark Morris Dance Group** American dance repertory group (1980–  ). In 1980 American professional dancer Mark Morris formed the Mark Morris Dance Group (MMDG) with several of his friends and colleagues, and premiered a show at the Merce Cunningham Studio in New York City. Since its relatively inauspicious beginning, the MMGG has gone on to perform at the annual Brooklyn Academy of Music's Next Wave festivals (1984–2003) and the Jacob's Pillow Dance Festival in Lee, Massachusetts (1986–2003), and to offer regular shows in touring circuits in major cities and in foreign countries as far afield as Australia. In addition to these touring performances, the MMDG gained great recognition in 1988 when it became the official dance company for the national opera house in Brussels, Belgium, the Théâtre Royal de la Monnaie, where it has staged performances of *L'Allegro, Dido and Aneas* and *Platée.*

**Markova, Alicia (Lillian Alicia Marks)** *(1910–2004)* English dancer. One of the great Giselles of her time, Markova began her career as a member of Serge DIAGHILEV's BALLETS RUSSES (1925–29). From 1930 to 1935 she danced with Ballet Rambert and Vic-Wells Ballet, becoming the first English ballerina to dance the classic roles while creating others in many new ballets, such as Frederick ASHTON's *Facade* (1931). As a ballerina with AMERICAN BALLET THEATRE (1941–46) she created many roles, including Juliet in Antony TUDOR's *Romeo and Juliet* (1943). The Markova-Dolin Company, originally formed with Anton DOLIN in 1935, was re-formed in 1945 and became the London Festival Ballet in 1950. Since her last performance in 1962, Markova served as ballet director of the New York Metropolitan Opera (1963–69), visiting professor of ballet at the University of Cincinnati (1971–74) and first president of the London Festival Ballet.

**Marley, Bob (Robert Nesta Marley)** *(1945–1981)* Jamaican reggae singer. With his group The Wailers, he helped establish the popularity of Reggae music in Britain and the U.S. during the 1970s. An outspoken advocate of Rastafarianism, he survived an assassination attempt in 1976.

**Marne, First Battle of the** *(1914)* In August 1914 German armies invaded Belgium and northeastern France, advancing to the Marne River within 15 miles of Paris. The French staged a desperate counterattack to the German right flank on September 6, 1914, which opened a gap in the German line. British and French troops advanced into the opening, attacking the other flank. The German armies, pushed further apart, retreated to the northern bank of the Aisne River, digging trench defenses and thus initiated the trench warfare of the next four years. The battle quashed German expectations of a quick and easy victory.

The **Second Battle of the Marne** began in late May 1918 when German forces began a powerful offensive against French positions, fighting their way to the Marne. After crossing the Marne on July 15, a German division was trapped and surrendered. On July 18, French, British and American troops under supreme Allied commander Marshal Ferdinand FOCH counterattacked; by mid-August the Germans were in full retreat and back to pre-war German boundaries by September. They were soon to sue for peace.

**Marquand, J(ohn) P(hilips)** *(1893–1960)* American novelist. Born in Wilmington, Delaware, to an aristocratic New England family, he attended Harvard University, where he encountered the Boston Brahmins (who were to be the main subjects of his gently satirical novels). His earliest fiction was in the detective story genre, and he won fame with the character of the Japanese sleuth Mr. Moto. Marquand achieved acclaim as a serious novelist with the publication of *The Late George Apley* (1937), a novel of manners among Boston's best, brightest and richest, which was awarded a Pulitzer Prize. His other novels include *Wickford Point* (1939), *So Little Time* (1943) and *Point of No Return* (1949).

**Marsalis, Wynton** *(1961– )* Celebrated American jazz trumpeter who was a key participant in a series of dynamic events crucial to reenergizing the 1980s jazz scene. Marsalis, the younger brother of noted saxophonist Branford Marsalis and son of venerable pianist Ellis Marsalis, attained initial success at age 19 with Art BLAKEY and the Jazz Messengers. In 1981 his debut album as a leader led to the formation of his own group. Marsalis, like Benny GOODMAN, also won kudos for his classical playing. In 1984, he became the first musician to garner Grammy awards for jazz ("Think of One") and classical (Haydn/Hummel/L. Mozart Trumpet Concertos). Marsalis has been a vigorous spokesman for "authentic" jazz as embodied in the traditions of BEBOP and FUSION JAZZ, rock and rap. Also, Marsalis has insisted that jazz, "America's classical music," be accorded the same kind of respect tendered to European classical music. Through these varied activities, Marsalis has become a well-known media personality; indeed, his success has encouraged the promotion of a number of promising young jazz players, a phenomenon chronicled in a 1990 *TIME* magazine cover story. At the heart of Marsalis's success, though, is a commanding style in which his virtuosic technique and emotional depth are displayed with a neo-bebop vocabulary suggesting the dexterity of Clifford BROWN and the dramatic poignancy of Miles DAVIS. Throughout the 1990s Marsalis has prolifically written, performed and

recorded music. As the director of the Lincoln Center Jazz Orchestra and Artistic Director of the Jazz at Lincoln Center organization, Marsalis has played an integral role in the production of the following performance works—*In This House, On This Morning* (1992), *Six Syncopated Movements* (1993), *At the Octoroon Balls* (1995), *Sweet Release* (1996), *Big Train* (1998), and *Them Twos* (1999). In 1996 he accepted a Peabody Award for his participation in the *Making the Music* series broadcast on National Public Radio. A year later Marsalis received a Pulitzer Prize in recognition for his musical work, *Blood on the Fields*. In 2001 Marsalis was designated a "Messenger of Peace" by UN Secretary-General KOFI ANNAN.

**Marsh, Dame (Edith) Ngaio** *(1899–1982)* New Zealand–born mystery novelist. She wrote 31 thrillers featuring a scholarly and charming detective, Chief Inspector Roderick Alleyn of Scotland Yard. In 1966 she was made a Dame of the British Empire by Queen Elizabeth II.

**Marshall, George C(atlett)** *(1880–1959)* American Army officer, diplomat and statesman. Born in Uniontown, Pennsylvania, Marshall attended the Virginia Military Institute and joined the army in 1902. After service in the Philippines and the U.S., Marshall held high administrative and planning posts in France during WORLD

*U.S. Army general George C. Marshall* (LIBRARY OF CONGRESS, PRINTS AND PHOTOGRAPHS DIVISION)

WAR I and was an aide de camp to General John PERSHING (1919–24). He was stationed in China (1924–27), was assistant commandant of the Army Infantry School (1927–32) and headed several CIVILIAN CONSERVATION CORPS camps during the GREAT DEPRESSION. Having established a reputation for brilliant strategic and organizational skills, Marshall quickly rose to become assistant U.S. Army chief of staff and deputy chief of staff in 1938 and chief of staff in 1939, the year he was promoted to the rank of full general.

Warning of probable armed conflict ahead, he stressed military preparedness, significantly modernizing and enlarging the army, urging the passage (1940) of the Selective Service Act and reorganizing the War Department. After the outbreak of WORLD WAR II, he became Franklin D. ROOSEVELT's military adviser, accompanying the president to the Allied summit conferences and proving himself a consummate diplomat. In military affairs, Marshall directed U.S. operations in both Europe and the Pacific, coordinating the North African and Sicilian campaigns, aiding the besieged USSR, helping to plan the cross-channel invasion of the European continent and urging the dropping of the ATOMIC BOMB on Japan. He was named General of the Army in 1944.

Emerging from the war as a national hero, he retired from army service in 1945. That year he became President TRUMAN's emissary to China, where he failed in an attempt to achieve a settlement of its civil war and a coalition between opposing Nationalists and Communists. In 1947 he was appointed Truman's secretary of state. In this post, he was successful in urging a firmer American policy toward the Soviet Union and in formulating and implementing the European Recovery Program, or MARSHALL PLAN, a comprehensive program of economic and technical assistance aimed at rebuilding war-torn Europe. In recognition of the plan's success, he was awarded the 1953 NOBEL PEACE PRIZE. In poor health, Marshall resigned from office in 1949, but he was recalled to service (1950) after the outbreak of the KOREAN WAR as Truman's secretary of defense. During this period of service, he extended the draft and desegregated the armed forces. Marshall retired permanently in 1951, one of America's most respected military and diplomatic figures.

## Marshall, Thurgood (1908–1993)

First black justice of the U.S. Supreme Court (1967–91). A native of Baltimore and a graduate of Howard University Law School, Marshall became involved with the NAACP before WORLD WAR II and headed the NAACP Legal Defense and Education Fund. In this position, he was at the very center of the U.S. civil rights movement, coordinating the NAACP's legal challenges to segregation in voting rights, education and public accommodations. Marshall was chief counsel in the famous BROWN V. BOARD OF EDUCATION, in which the Supreme Court outlawed separate but equal schools. He was appointed a federal judge by President John F. KENNEDY and in 1967 was elevated to the Supreme Court by President Lyndon JOHNSON, who early in his career had supported segregation. Marshall joined the liberal wing of the Court and helped affirm much of the legislation of the era aimed at protecting minorities. In later years, as the Court grew more conservative, he became known for his liberal dissents and his public criticism of both politicians and potential nominees to the Court.

## Marshall Islands

The Marshall Islands consist of two island chains of 30 atolls and 1,152 islands, including the former U.S. nuclear test sites of BIKINI

*Supreme Court justice Thurgood Marshall* (LIBRARY OF CONGRESS, PRINTS AND PHOTOGRAPHS DIVISION)

and ENIWETOK; total land area is 70 square miles (see map, page 957). The capital is Majuro. An influx of American and European whalers, traders and missionaries in the 19th century caused major social upheaval. Annexed by Spain in 1874, the Marshalls became a German protectorate in 1885. With the onset of WORLD WAR I, JAPAN took possession of the islands. In 1920 the LEAGUE OF NATIONS gave Japan a mandate to administer Micronesia, and in 1945, at the end of WORLD WAR II, the victorious U.S. Navy took control. In 1947 the UNITED NATIONS established the Trust Territory of the Pacific Islands, under U.S. control. From 1946 to 1958 the U.S. used Bikini and other atolls in the Marshalls to test nuclear weapons. Preparations for Micronesian self-government led to a referendum in July 1978 on a common constitution for the whole territory. The Marshallese voted against, and in 1979 the Republic of the Marshall Islands' separate constitution took effect. In 1982 over 1,000 dispossessed landowners from Kwajalein Atoll launched Operation Homecoming, a four-month protest against the U.S. military's use of the atoll as a missile testing range.

In October 1986 a Compact of Free Association between the Marshall Islands and the U.S. government came into effect: The Marshalls would be internally self-governing while the U.S. would retain responsibility for foreign relations and defense. The compact also ensured that the U.S. would maintain its military bases in the islands for at least 15 years and annually provide $30 million in economic aid. U.S. administration of Micronesia formally ended in November 1986. Following the UN's decision to terminate the island's trustee status in 1990, the Marshall Islands were admitted to the world body in 1991. Despite a continued dispute with the U.S. federal government concerning additional compensation payments for the damage caused by the Bikini Atoll nuclear test in the 1950s, the Marshall Islands have sought to improve ties with the U.S. In 2003 U.S. president George W. BUSH agreed to provide the islands with $3.5 billion in aid over a 20-year period.

## Marshall Plan

U.S. plan—formally, the European Recovery Program—for the reconstruction of Europe after WORLD WAR II. The plan was formulated by U.S. secretary of state George C. MARSHALL and his aides, with suggestions from the European nations. At the end of the war Europe lay in ruins. Marshall recognized that, without a comprehensive package of U.S. aid, Europeans—victor and vanquished alike, stateless people and displaced persons—would continue to suffer from hunger, disease, a depressed economy and political instability. Moreover, Marshall was wary of the Soviet Union's intentions and believed that it was necessary to revive western Europe economically and materially in order to prevent COMMUNISM from spreading further. He also believed that a revitalized Western Europe would stimulate U.S. production and trade. Marshall announced the plan during a commencement address at Harvard University (June 1947). "It is logical that the U.S. should do whatever it is able to do to assist in the return of normal economic health in the world, without which there can be no political stability and no assured peace," he said. "Our policy is directed not against any country or any doctrine but against hunger, poverty, depression and chaos." By the spring of 1948 Marshall had persuaded a majority in Congress to support the plan. The Marshall Plan provided $17 billion in assistance to 16 European nations between 1948 and 1952 and was perhaps the most ambitious international peacetime project ever attempted. Immensely successful, it helped restore prosperity to devastated areas of Europe, most notably WEST GERMANY. For his role in developing the European Recovery Program, George C. Marshall was awarded the 1953 Nobel Peace Prize.

## Martin, Frank (1890–1974)

Swiss composer known for his contrapuntal techniques, and his use of harmony and stylized folk songs in his operas, ballets, instrumental and vocal works. A pianist and harpsichordist as well as a composer, Martin also taught at the Institute Jaques-Dalcroze (1927–38), was founder-director of the Technicum Moderne de Musique (1933–39) in Geneva and taught at the Cologne Hochschüle für Musik in Germany (1950–57). His works include the oratorio *In terra pax*, which was specially commissioned to commemorate the end of WORLD WAR II (1945), and his opera *Der Stürm* (1952–54; *The Tempest*).

**Martin, Glenn** (*1886–1955*) U.S. airplane manufacturer. Educated at Kansas Wesleyan University, Martin began to build gliders in 1907 and by 1908 was experimenting with pusher type airplanes. He taught himself to fly and built one of the first airplane factories in the United States in 1909, in Wichita, Kansas. Martin later produced the first American-designed airplanes for Liberty engines and constructed Martin bombers.

**Martin, Graham A(nderson)** (*1912–1990*) U.S. diplomat. Martin, the last U.S. ambassador to South VIETNAM, after the fall of SAIGON (1975), was sharply criticized for having mishandled the evacuation of American personnel. Thousands of Vietnamese who had worked for the U.S. were left behind, together with hundreds of classified documents.

**Martin, Joseph William, Jr.** (*1884–1968*) U.S. politician. He was elected as a Republican to the Massachusetts state legislature (1912–17). In 1925 he won a seat in the U.S. House of Representatives where he served for 42 years. He was elected minority leader in 1939, and he was Speaker of the House from 1947 to 1949 and 1953 to 1955. He created a strong Republican organization in the House, and opposed many of ROOSEVELT's and EISENHOWER's legislative programs.

**Martin, Mary (Virginia)** (*1913–1990*) American musical theater and film actress. She made her Broadway debut in 1938 in the Cole PORTER musical *Leave It to Me,* in which she sang the show-stopping "My Heart Belongs to Daddy." She starred in Richard RODGERS and Oscar HAMMERSTEIN II's *South Pacific* (1949). In 1954 she created on Broadway the role for which she is best known, that of PETER PAN; the musical was presented on television soon afterward. She won a TONY AWARD for her performance in *The Sound of Music* (1959), as well as for *Peter Pan* and *Annie Get Your Gun.* Her son, Larry Hagman, starred in the television series *Dallas.*

**Martin, Steve** (*1945–  *) American comedian, film actor and screenplay writer. Martin is one of the major comedic talents of his generation. He began his show business career in the 1960s as a writer for television and won an Emmy for his scripts for *The Smothers Brothers Comedy Hour.* In the 1970s he turned to stand-up comedy and won national attention for his appearances on SATURDAY NIGHT LIVE. He recorded two Grammy award-winning albums, *Let's Get Small* and *Wild and Crazy Guy.* Martin's famous stand-up image featured a pure white suit, which he sometimes wore along with bunny ears. In the late 1970s Martin turned to comedic film acting, a field in which he became preeminent. While maintaining great box office popularity, Martin is also highly regarded by critics for the genuine pathos he brings to many of his performances and for the diversity of roles and scripts he seeks out. Major films featuring Martin include *The Jerk* (1979), a tribute to Jerry LEWIS comedies; *Pennies from Heaven* (1981), a dark musical scripted by Dennis POTTER; *Dead Men Don't Wear Plaid* (1982), a witty spoof of FILM NOIR detective movies; *All of Me* (1984), for which he won a Best Actor Award from the New York Film Critics Circle; *Roxanne* (1987), a modern adaptation of *Cyrano de Bergerac; Dirty Rotten Scoundrels* (1988), in which he and Michael CAINE play a pair of con men; and *Parenthood* (1989). Martin continues to appear in comedy films such as *Housesitter* (1992) and *Bowfinger* (1999) and dramas such as *The Spanish Prisoner* (1997) as well as writing and directing stage productions, such as the highly acclaimed play *Picasso at the Lapin Agile* (1997). Martin has also written two successful novellas, *Shopgirl* (2000) and *The Pleasure of My Company* (2003).

**Martin du Gard, Roger** (*1881–1958*) French novelist and playwright. Martin du Gard first achieved recognition with his second novel, *Jean Barois* (1913), a fictional portrait of the Dreyfus scandal. It was championed by André GIDE, who was to become a friend and correspondent. Martin du Gard is best known for the eight-volume *roman fleuve, Les Thibault* (the first six volumes were translated as *The*

*Thibaults;* the latter two as *Summer 1914*). Published between 1922 and 1940, the novels depict the degeneration of society prior to WORLD WAR I by following two bourgeois families— one Catholic and one Protestant. Martin du Gard received the NOBEL PRIZE for literature in 1937. Other works include *Confidence Africaine* (*African Secret,* 1931); the play *Un Taciturne* (*A Silent Man* 1932), and the unfinished novel begun in 1940, *Les Souvenirs du colonel Maumort* (*The Memoirs of Colonel Maumort*).

**Martinelli, Giovanni** (*1885–1969*) Italian-American tenor. Born near Padua, Martinelli made his concert and operatic debuts in Milan in 1910. He first achieved recognition when Giacomo PUCCINI selected him as the lead tenor for the premiere of his THE GIRL OF THE GOLDEN WEST in 1911. Martinelli made his American debut in Philadelphia in 1913, and months later he sang for the first time at New York's Metropolitan Opera. For 32 seasons, Martinelli was the Met's principal tenor in the Italian and French repertories, singing some 50 leading roles.

**Martínez Ruis, José (pseudonym: Azorín)** (*1873–1967*) Spanish writer. Born in Manovar, he studied law in Valencia, later becoming a noted and extremely prolific essayist, novelist and playwright. Influenced by ANARCHISM, he began as a leftist writer, but grew increasingly conservative as his career progressed. An important figure in the Generation of 1898, he was especially concerned with defining the nature of Spanish life and character. His compactly written essay collections include *El alma castellana* (1900), *Castilla* (1912) and *Clásicos y modernos* (1913). Among his many novels are the autobiographical *La voluntad* (1902), *Antonio Azorín* (1903) and *Las Confesiones de un pequeño filósofo* (1904), as well as the later experimental and surrealist works *Felix Vargas* (1928) and *Pueblo* (1930). His terse style and his concern with the continuity of Spanish history exercised an important influence on modern Spanish letters.

**Martinique** Martinique is a Caribbean island with a total area of 425 square miles. Its mountainous terrain includes a dormant volcano, while the island's coastline is heavily indented and subject to hurricanes and flooding. The capital is Fort-de-France. Colonized by France in 1635, the island's capital, St. Pierre, was completely destroyed during a volcanic eruption of Mt. Pelée in 1902 that left only one survivor—a resident of the city's jail. In 1947 Martinique became a department of France. Demands for greater autonomy were expressed during the 1950s by the Parti Progressite Martiniquais (OOM), founded and led by Aimé CESAIRE. Rioting in 1959 led to the French government devolving some of its powers in 1960, but a 1962 plebiscite produced a majority in favor of retaining departmental status. In 1974 Martinique also became a region of France and in 1982 was granted more autonomy. The left-wing parties, led by the PPM, succeeded in gaining a small majority on the new regional council, but the general council remained under the control of the right-wing and center parties. In 1986 the left-wing parties maintained their control of the regional council, but in elections to the general council in 1988, although they secured a majority of the seats for the first time, they failed to gain the presidency of the council. Since December 1999 when it signed the Basse Terre Declaration, the government of Martinique, along with the governments of FRENCH GUIANA and GUADELOUPE, has repeatedly sought greater autonomy under French rule. However, the island has retained its legal status as an overseas department of France.

**Martins, Peter** *(1946–  )* Danish dancer, choreographer and ballet master. An outstanding male dancer from the mid-1960s to the mid-1980s, Martins later served as ballet-master-in-chief of the NEW YORK CITY BALLET (NYCB). He joined the ROYAL DANISH BALLET in 1965, then became a principal dancer with NYCB in 1969. He created roles in several ballets, including Jerome ROBBINS's *The Goldberg Variations* (1971) and George BALANCHINE's *Duo Concertant* (1972). Works choreographed for NYCB include *Calcium Light Night* (1978). In 1983 he became joint ballet-master-in-chief of NYCB (with Robbins) and was named sole ballet master in 1989.

**Martinson, Harry** *(1904–1978)* Swedish poet and novelist. Abandoned at an early age, Martinson fled from a number of foster homes before going to sea in his late teens. Forced by illness to return to Sweden in 1929, Martinson began publishing his first poetry, which was strongly derivative of KIPLING. With *Nomad* (1931), a collection of free verse, he began to establish his own voice. Subsequent poetry is steeped in primitivism. Martinson's fiction includes the autobiographical novels *Nässlorna blomma* (*Flowering Nettle,* 1935) and *Vägen ut* (*The Way Out,* 1936). His best-known works are the novel *Vägen till Klockrike* (*The Road,* 1948) and the epic poem *Aniara; En revy on Manniskan i tid och rum* (*Aniara: A Review of Man in Time and Space,* 1956), which some consider to be his masterpiece, blaming the English translation for its lukewarm reception outside of Sweden. Martinson was a joint recipient of the NOBEL PRIZE for literature in 1974, along with Eyvind JOHNSON.

**Martinu, Bohuslav** *(1890–1959)* Czech composer. Martinu, who began his career as a violinist with the Czech Philharmonic (intermittently from 1913 to 1923), is known for his mastery of modern counterpoint and his lyricism inspired by Czech folk traditions. He first gained recognition with the choral/orchestral *Czech Symphony* (1918) and the ballet *Istar* (1921). From 1923 to 1940 he lived in Paris, and his compositions of this period reflect the influence of the French modernists. Martinu fled to the United States in 1941 and became visiting professor of music at Princeton University (1948–51). His best-known works include *Memorial to Lidice* (1943) and numerous chamber works, which were his forte.

*Marvin v. Marvin* *(1976)* Also known as the "palimony case," this 1976 trial established that an unmarried cohabitant could sometimes sue his or her partner after a romantic breakup and receive payments similar to alimony. The case involved the well-known actor Lee Marvin and his companion Michelle Triola, who had obtained the services of the flamboyant matrimonial attorney Marvin Michel-son. The couple had cohabited, essentially as husband and wife, for a number of years, without benefit of wedlock, and later separated—at which point Michelle demanded a monetary settlement from the actor. Although married couples typically divide their marital property, the law at the time had no such provision for unmarried cohabitants: Living together outside marriage was considered to be against public policy. The Marvin case established that an unmarried cohabitant could receive a division of property on the breakup of the relationship on the showing that a formal or informal agreement existed to do so. However, Michelle had failed to prove that any contract to split property ever existed and she ultimately ended up with no damages. Although this was a California case, the concept of "palimony" quickly spread to a number of other states as well. A similar case involving actor William Hurt occurred in 1989.

**Marx Brothers** Comedy stars of vaudeville, stage and screen. The Marx Brothers were five real-life brothers from a New York City tenement: **Chico** (Leonard) (1887–1961), **Harpo** (born Adolph, which later became Arthur) (1888–1964), **Groucho** (Julius Henry) (c. 1890–1977), **Gummo** (Milton) (c. 1893–1977) and **Zeppo** (Herbert) (1901–79). Encouraged by their mother, Minnie, and Uncle Al (Al Shean of the vaudevillian team "Gallagher and Shean"), the brothers toured with their comedy act under various names (including "The Three Nightingales") until they performed on Broadway in *I'll Say She Is* in 1924. This was followed by the Broadway hits *The Coconuts* (1925) and *Animal Crackers* (1928)—filmed in 1929 and 1930, respectively. Moving to HOLLYWOOD with the advent of TALKING PICTURES, for such classic films as *Monkey Business* (1931), *Duck Soup* (1933) and *A Night at the Opera* (1935), the team developed their own hilarious brand of farce, poking fun at convention and confounding audiences with non-sequiturs and double-entendres. Groucho became the leering, wisecracking pseudo-intellectual; Harpo, the mute clown; and Chico, the Italian con-artist. Zeppo appeared in a few early films as straight man but quit to become an agent; Gummo did not work in films. After the act split up in the early 1950s, Groucho went on to write several books and host the TV comedy quiz show *You Bet Your Life*. Spurred by a Marx Brothers revival in the 1970s, Groucho went on a successful one-man tour and recorded the popular album *An Evening with Groucho*.

## Marxism-Leninism, Institute of

Moscow's chief institution of study and research into the history and theory of communism. In 1931 the Marx-Engels Institute and the Lenin Institute merged to form the Marx-Engels-Lenin Institute; it served as a tool of Stalin during his lifetime. From 1953 to 1957 many of the main ideological policies of the party leadership allegedly were based on the findings of the institute.

## Masaryk, Jan *(1886–1948)* Czecho-

slovak diplomat and foreign minister, son of Tomáš MASARYK. Jan Masaryk attended the PARIS PEACE CONFERENCE of 1919–20 and was Czech minister (diplomatic envoy) to London from 1925 to 1928. He resigned after the MUNICH PACT (1938) ceded Czechoslovakia's SUDETENLAND to Germany. He spent WORLD WAR II in London as foreign minister and deputy prime minister of the Czech government-in-exile (1941–45). On the liberation of CZECHOSLOVAKIA he continued as foreign minister. Although unsympathetic to the increasingly pro-Soviet policy, he remained in office after the communist coup in 1948 but died a few days later after falling from a window in the Czech foreign ministry. His death has never been satisfactorily explained; many suspect he either committed suicide under duress or was murdered by the communists.

## Masaryk, Tomáš Garrigue *(1850–*

*1937)* Czech philosopher and political leader, founding president of CZECHOSLOVAKIA (1918–35). Born in Moravia, he received a doctorate in 1876 and was a professor of philosophy at the Czech University, Prague, from 1882 to 1914. An ardent democrat, he served in the Austrian parliament from 1891 to 1913 and again from 1907 to 1914. In 1900 he founded the Progressive (Realist) Party to advance his ideas of social reform, Czech equality and suffrage and the unification and protection of mi-

*Tomáš Masaryk, first president of Czechoslovakia*
(LIBRARY OF CONGRESS, PRINTS AND PHOTOGRAPHS DIVISION)

norities. An early advocate of a federation of self-governing nationalities within the AUSTRO-HUNGARIAN EMPIRE, by the outbreak of WORLD WAR I he was supporting Czech independence. In 1914 he and Eduard BENEŠ fled to London, where he formed a council that was recognized by the Allies in 1918 as Czechoslovakia's de facto government. During the war years, Masaryk traveled throughout Europe and the U.S., winning support and funding for the Czech cause. At the end of the war, the state of Czechoslovakia was established and Masaryk was elected its first president, winning reelection in 1920, 1927 and 1934. He was at least partially successful in creating a multicultural democracy and was revered throughout the world as a democratic leader. He was the father of Jan MASARYK.

## Mason, James *(1909–1984)* British-

born actor. Mason was noted for playing suave aristocrats and refined, romantic villains. His career spanned nearly half a century, and he acted in more than 100 films. He was nominated for ACADEMY AWARDS for his performances in *A Star Is Born, Georgy Girl* and *The Verdict*. Mason's other films include *The Seventh Veil, Odd Man Out, The Desert Fox* and *Lolita*.

## Masood, General Ahmed Shah

*(1953–2001)* Born in Jangalak, Afghanistan, to a local police commissioner and his wife, Masood entered the Kabul Polytechnic Institute for Engi-

neering and Architecture and, later, joined the Jamiat-e Islamic Party.

Following the Soviet invasion of Afghanistan and the installation of a pro-Soviet puppet government in 1979, Masood fought with the MUJAHIDEEN, a diverse group of Islamic freedom fighters, against the Soviet military forces and their allies in the Afghan government. When the Mujahideen captured the capital of Kabul in 1992, Masood became the minister of defense. Soon allegations of corruption within the defense ministry contributed to growing divisions within the mujahideen government and led to its fragmentation and the start of a civil war among the various factions. Heading what became later known as the NORTHERN ALLIANCE, Masood occasionally launched rocket attacks on cities held by his opponents. He soon had to withdraw from Kabul into the northeastern region of Afghanistan on account of the powerful TALIBAN faction that had gained control of the government. In September 2001 Masood was killed by agents of the Taliban in an effort to reduce the effectiveness of the Northern Alliance against the Taliban in the ongoing civil war.

## Massey, Vincent *(1887–1967)* Can-

adian statesman. Born in Toronto, he was a teacher and government official before becoming president of his family business (1921–25). A supporter of the LIBERAL PARTY, he was CANADA's first minister to the U.S. (1926–30) and high commissioner for Canada in Great Britain (1935–46). Massey was chairman of the Royal Commission on National Development in the Arts, Letters, and Sciences (1949–51) and chancellor of the University of Toronto (1947–52). From 1952 to 1959, he served as governor general of Canada, the first native-born Canadian to hold that post. His memoirs were published in 1963.

## Massey, William Ferguson *(1856–*

*1925)* NEW ZEALAND statesman, prime minister (1912–25). Born in Ulster, he emigrated to New Zealand in 1870, farming near Auckland and becoming the political spokesman for local dairy farmers. He entered the New Zealand parliament in 1894. Leader of the conservative Opposition Party (later the Reform Party), he became prime minister in 1912 and held the office until his death. An agrarian conservative, he supported moderate land reforms and suppressed his country's labor unions. A strong supporter of the British Empire, he sent an expeditionary force to Europe at the outbreak of WORLD WAR I and served in the British war cabinet (1917–18). During the war, he participated in the coalition National government of the Reform and Liberal parties (1915–19). After the war, Massey opposed the movement to give New Zealand greater independence by making it a dominion within the empire.

**Massine, Léonide** *(1895–1979)* Russian-born choreographer and dancer whose ideas helped to shape 20th-century ballet. After training at the Imperial Ballet School in St. Petersburg, Massine joined Serge DIAGHILEV's BALLETS RUSSES, winning immediate acclaim in Michael FOKINE's *The Legend of Joseph* (1914). Massine's PARADE (1917), which he choreographed, is considered a milestone in modernist ballet. Other notable works choreographed by Massine include *La Boutique Fantastique, The Three-Cornered Hat, Gaieté Parisienne* and *Jeux d'Enfants.* The 1948 film *The Red Shoes,* which he choreographed and performed in, won Massine wide popularity.

**Massing, Hede** *(1899–1981)* Austrian-born actress who served as a spy for the Soviet intelligence network in the U.S. (1933–37), when she became disillusioned. Massing testified against Alger HISS at his second perjury trial in 1950. She was the only witness to corroborate the allegations by Whittaker CHAMBERS that Hiss, a former State Department official, had been a member of the COMMUNIST PARTY underground in Washington, D.C.

**Masson, André** *(1896–1987)* French painter and graphic artist. Born in Balagny, Masson studied at the Académie des Beaux-Arts, Brussels and Ecole des Beaux-Arts, Paris. His early work was influenced by CUBISM and by the painting of Juan GRIS in particular. After meeting André BRETON, Max ERNST and Joan MIRÓ in 1924, Masson became an exponent of SURREALISM—the style for which he is best known. His exploration of the subconscious led him to experiment with "automatic writing," and spontaneous drawing in which personal imagery is developed. Travel-

ing to Spain in the 1930s, he painted bullfighters and other Catalonian themes, and when he visited the U.S. (1941–45), he explored African-American and American Indian imagery. Masson settled in Aix-en Provence in 1947 and devoted himself to landscape painting. An extremely versatile artist, he is also known for his work as a book illustrator, sculptor, set and costume designer and writer.

**mass production** Widely used term that describes the modern method of industrial production in which a large number of identical items are made by mechanized techniques. "Serial" production is a similar term, also referring to manufacturing based on the concept of the assembly line, where the object is moved (often by mechanized conveyors) past the work stations of individuals who perform particular repetitive tasks. The concept is based on the rationalization of production in which the steps of the manufacturing process are carefully analyzed and equipment is provided (often specially designed) so that each step can be accomplished with a minimum of handwork. Avoiding the delays and constant changes of task that are typical of craftwork increases efficiency and permits a maximum of mechanization that makes the manufacturing process as nearly automatic as possible.

The early enthusiasm for assembly-line production has been somewhat dimmed in recent years by recognition of the unfortunate consequences of monotonous, repetitive tasks for the individual worker. These effects also often lead to a decline in quality since pride in one's skill is negated when the demand for speed is the only significant work criterion. Recent efforts to organize work teams with greater responsibility for a total product and its quality have been introduced in some factories, including the classic assembly-line plant—the automobile factory. At the same time, automation in which human workers are entirely replaced by automatic machinery (robots) makes possible mass production without the costs of human labor. Computer control of automated production also makes possible the efficient manufacture of varied products on a single assembly line.

**Masters, Edgar Lee** *(1869–1950)* American poet. Born in Garnett, Kansas,

Masters attended law school and was a practicing attorney in Chicago from 1892 to 1920. He owes his fame to one volume of poetry, *Spoon River Anthology* (1915), a series of epigrammatic free verse epitaphs that capture the character, triumphs and tragedies of the citizens of a typical American small town. Masters's other volumes of poetry include *Starved Rock* (1919), *Domesday Book* (1920) and *Illinois Poems* (1941). He was also the author of several novels and of such biographies as *Lincoln the Man* (1931), *Whitman* (1937) and *Mark Twain* (1938). His autobiography, *Across Spoon River,* was published in 1936.

**Masters and Johnson** American sex researchers William Howell Masters (1915–2001), a gynecologist, and his wife, Virginia Eshelman Johnson (1925–  ), a psychologist, were pioneers in the field of human sexuality and the testing of various forms of sexual response. In the course of their work, they have exploded a number of widely held misconceptions about the nature of human sexuality. Masters and Johnson detailed their researches in their volumes *Human Sexual Response* (1966), *Human Sexual Inadequacy* (1970) and *Homosexuality in Perspective* (1979). They also did influential work in sex therapy and set up an extensive training program for therapists at the institute they established in St. Louis in 1970. In 1993 Masters and Johnson decided to end their 21-year marriage, and Johnson retired from their jointly run clinic. Masters died in February 2001.

**Mastroianni, Marcello (Vincenzo Domenico)** *(1924–1996)* A charming, handsome film star from Fontana Liri, Mastroianni was generally regarded as the leading Italian screen actor of his generation. On-screen from 1947, the "Italian Cary GRANT" starred in more than 80 (primarily Italian) films, including *White Nights* (1957), *Where the Hot Wind Blows* (1958), *Divorce Italian-Style* (1962) and *Marriage Italian-Style* (1964). In America, he is best recognized in films directed by Federico FELLINI, such as *La Dolce Vita* (1960), *8 1/2* (1963), *City of Women* (1981) and *Ginger and Fred* (1986).

**Masuku, Lookout** *(1939–1986)* African guerrilla leader. He was a leader in the struggle that led to the establishment of the black-ruled nation of ZIMBABWE in 1980. From 1980 to 1982, he was deputy commander of that country's national army. He was arrested in 1982 on charges of conspiring against Prime Minister Robert MUGABE's government. Acquitted in 1983, he was kept under detention until 1986.

**Masursky, Harold** (*1922–1990*) U.S. geologist-astronomer. Working with NASA since the U.S. Ranger series in the early 1960s, Masursky specialized in studies of the surfaces of the moon and the planets of the solar system and has participated in almost every NASA planetary project since that time. As leader of the team that selected and monitored observations of Mars by the *Mariner* spacecraft, he also helped to select the *Viking* landing sites on Mars and is a member of the Venus Orbiter Imaging Radar Science Working Group. A familiar face at NASA press conferences, he was also involved in NASA's Pioneer and Voyager projects. Masursky was a senior scientist with the U.S. Geological Survey. He took his degree from Yale University in 1951 and has received four medals from NASA for exceptional scientific achievement.

**Mata Hari** (*1876–1917*) Dutch spy. Mata Hari was the stage name of Margaretha Geertruida Zelle, a glamorous dancer from the Netherlands who settled in Paris. She entered Germany's secret service in 1907. During WORLD WAR I, she transmitted important military secrets to Germany that had been given to her by her many Allied officer lovers. In 1917 she was arrested, tried, convicted. She was executed by a French firing squad on October 15.

**Mathewson, Christopher "Christy"** (*1880–1925*) American baseball player. Mathewson's fadeaway curve, a forerunner of the screwball, made him one of the most successful and feared right-handers of his era. He spent most of his career with the New York Giants (1900–16), where in 1905 he led the team to a World Series victory by pitching three shutouts in six days. He went to the Cincinnati Reds as a pitcher-manager (1916–18), but his pitching career was ended by WORLD WAR I, when he was gassed in France. He finished with 373 victories and 83 shutouts. Upon his return from the war, he was named president of the Boston Braves, a post he held until his death in 1925. Mathewson was among the first group of players named to the Baseball Hall of Fame, in 1936.

**Mathias, Robert Bruce** (*1930–2006*) American athlete. One of the greatest athletes of all time, Mathias was the only man ever to win the grueling Olympic decathlon twice. In high school, he starred in football and basketball, as well as track. Shortly after his high school graduation, he won his first Olympic gold medal as a decathlete. In the years before his next Olympic triumph, he starred as a fullback for the University of Southern California football team and also won four consecutive U.S. decathlon championships. Mathias went on from his athletic career to pursue his political aspirations and was elected to the U.S. House of Representatives in 1966. (See also OLYMPIC GAMES.)

**Mathieu, Georges** (*1921–* ) French painter. Self-taught, Mathieu began painting in 1942. Two years later, influenced by American ABSTRACT EXPRESSIONISM, he started to paint the large, lyrical and abstract works for which he is known. Extremely calligraphic in nature, his paintings are executed quickly in slashing strokes against a colored ground. A precursor of PERFORMANCE ART, he executed some of his works in front of an audience. Mathieu is also known for his posters and designs for the theater.

**Mathis, Johnny (John Royce Mathis)** (*1935–* ) American popular singer. Born in San Francisco, Mathis joined Columbia Records in New York in 1956. He originally wanted to be a jazz singer, but Mitch Miller persuaded him to concentrate on ballads. A unique and haunting emotional quality made his voice unmistakable in such hits as "Misty" (1959), "The Shadow of Your Smile" (1960) and "The Twelfth of Never" (1961). "When a Child Is Born" was a No. 1 hit in Britain in 1976.

**Matisse, Henri** (*1869–1954*) One of the greatest French painters of the 20th century. After abandoning law studies in Paris, Matisse began to study painting with Gustave Moreau (1892). Soon, in work like the portrait *Green Stripe* (1905), he started working with the vibrant colors, complementary contrasts and spontaneous gestures of FAUVISM, the first real revolution in 20th-century painting. Matisse strove to eliminate all traces of "illusion" in his images for the sake of a greater emphasis upon the two-dimensionality of color and shape. His great works, like *Dance and Music* (1909–10), celebrate the writhing sensuality of color shapes; and *Red Studio* (1911) and *Harmony in Red* (1908) use vibrant color to unify areas of flat, decorative arabesques. Some of his later works, such as the *Bather by a River* (1917), achieve a more monumental grandeur and austerity. He was also a forceful sculptor. His relief bronzes include *Back I-IV* (1909–30). After moving to Nice, where he worked for most of the rest of his life, he turned increasingly to his famous "cut-out" techniques, organizing simple compositions from pieces of brightly colored paper. The culmination of his work came in his decorations for the Chapel of the Rosary at Vence (1949–51), a gift to the nuns who had looked after him during an illness. Despite a crippling arthritis, Matisse continued to work until his death.

**Matisse, Pierre** (*1900–1989*) Internationally known art dealer and younger son of artist Henri MATISSE. Born in France, he moved to the U.S. in 1925 and, with little encouragement from his father, arranged a series of exhibits and eventually established his own gallery in New York City. He helped popularize the works of such artists as Joan MIRÓ, Marc CHAGALL and Jean DUBUFFET.

**Matsuoka, Yosuke** (*1880–1946*) Japanese diplomat and statesman. Born in JAPAN, Matsuoka went to Oregon at the age of 13 and later attended the University of Oregon. He joined the Japanese foreign service and served as JAPAN's chief representative to the LEAGUE OF NATIONS (1932–33), where he expressed his country's expansionist philosophy and withdrew from the organization. He was president of the South Manchurian Railway (1935–39). As Japan's foreign minister (1940–41), he concluded the AXIS Pact with GERMANY and ITALY (1940) and negotiated (1941) a nonaggression agreement with the USSR He was a strong supporter of Japan's entry into WORLD WAR II and opposed negotiations with the U.S. Indicted as a war criminal, he died before his trial.

**Matsushita, Konosuke** *(1894–1989)* Japanese manufacturing magnate, founder of Japan's Matsushita Electrical Industrial Co., the world's largest producer of consumer electrical goods. He rose from poverty to found his own firm (1918) based on his success with a new electric light socket. By the 1980s the company had sales of an estimated $41 billion and produced everything from electric rice cookers to video cassette recorders—many of which were sold under the brand name Panasonic. Matsushita was often regarded as the pioneer of the modern Japanese corporation, with its emphasis on *marugake* (strong social ties between a company and its employees).

**Matta Echuarren, Roberto Sebastián** *(1912–2001)* Chilean painter. Usually known simply as Matta, he was born in Santiago. He moved to Paris, where in the 1930s he studied architecture with LE CORBUSIER. There he met André BRETON and other important figures in French SURREALISM. From 1938 to 1947 Matta painted in a Surrealist style, creating works with a strange otherworldly, almost cosmic aura. In 1939 he traveled to the U.S., where he met and was influenced by Marcel DUCHAMP. His later works were more abstract in nature, taking advantage of the linear designs of controlled spills and the atmospheric effects of deep color.

**Matteotti affair** Giacomo Matteotti (1885–1924), a leader of the Italian Socialist Party and an outspoken opponent of FASCISM, was murdered in June 1924—apparently by fascist thugs. His death triggered antifascist demonstrations in the Italian parliament and pleas for the reestablishment of democracy. Italian leader Benito MUSSOLINI, who claimed ignorance and disapproved of the affair, reacted by banning socialist meetings and censoring the press. In 1926 several fascists were arrested for the murder, but they received little punishment. Antifascists subsequently invoked the affair to rally support. During WORLD WAR II, the Italian RESISTANCE movement formed Matteotti Brigades. A postwar investi-

gation of the affair (1947) found a group of extremists over which Mussolini had little control responsible for the murder.

**Matthews, Burnita Shelton** *(1894–1988)* U.S. judge. Her 1949 appointment as a judge on the U.S. District Court for the District of Columbia reportedly made Matthews the first woman to serve as a federal district judge. By the time of that appointment, she had practiced law in Washington for three decades and had become known as a champion of women's rights. She continued hearing district court cases until 1983.

**Matthiessen, F(rancis) O(tto)** *(1902–1950)* American educator and literary critic. Matthiessen was a professor of history and English at Yale and later at Harvard. His critical works, which show the influence of Van Wyck BROOKS, include *The Achievement of T. S. Eliot: An Essay in the Nature of Poetry* (1935) and *American Renaissance: Art and Expression in the Age of Emerson and Whitman* (1941). He also wrote the biography *Sarah Orne Jewett* (1929).

**Mauchly, John William** *(1907–1980)* American engineer, co-inventor (with J. Presper Eckert Jr.) of the first electronic computer. Working with Eckert, Mauchly built ENIAC (Electronic Numerical Integrator And Computer) for the U.S. War Department in 1946. The computer took up 15,000 square feet and applied electronic speed to mathematical tasks for the first time. The two later designed the more advanced UNIVAC I computer (1951).

**Maudling, Reginald** *(1917–1979)* British politician. A member of the CONSERVATIVE PARTY, Maudling was first elected to Parliament in 1950 and held his seat until his death. He served in the governments of five prime ministers, notably as chancellor of the Exchequer (1962–64) and home secretary (1970–72). He narrowly missed in two bids for party leadership—and the prime ministership—in 1963 and 1965.

**Maugham, Syrie** *(1879–1955)* Noted British interior designer and decorator. She was married for a short time to the writer Somerset MAUGHAM. Her individual style, developed in the

1930s, made use of pale, monochromatic colors and eventually moved toward all- (or nearly all) white schemes. Her firm, Syrie Ltd. established in the 1920s and began by producing work of the traditional eclectic character typical of decorators' taste of the time. As her style developed, Maugham often chose glass, mirror and silvered frames with otherwise largely white finishes. Although her white rooms often included furniture and details of traditional design character, these elements were often finished in white—reflecting her particularly personal way of working.

**Maugham, W(illiam) Somerset** *(1874–1965)* British novelist. Orphaned at the age of 10, Maugham was raised by his aunt and his uncle, a clergyman. He practiced medicine before turning permanently to writing. He recreated his austere childhood in the autobiographical novel *Of Human Bondage* (1915, filmed 1946), his best known work. The protagonist, Philip Carey, suffers from a club foot and later, while a medical student, from an obsessive, unrequited love for a rapacious lower-class woman. Maugham was traumatized by a childhood stutter. He established himself as a writer with his first novel, *Liza of Lambeth* (1897), which reflected his work as an obstetrical clerk in the slums of London and which was considered an example of the "new realism." It was the beginning of a successful and lucrative career, yet Maugham was always troubled by his status as a second-rate writer, a feeling

*British author W. Somerset Maugham* (LIBRARY OF CONGRESS, PRINTS AND PHOTOGRAPHS DIVISION)

he expressed in *The Summing Up* (1938). Other works include the novels *The Moon and Sixpence* (1919), *Cakes and Ale* (1930) and *The Razor's Edge* (1944) and the plays *The Circle* (1921) and *For Services Rendered* (1932). Also notable is the short story "Rain" (1921), which has been staged and was filmed four times.

**Mau Mau** A society formed in 1948 among the Kikuyu tribe in KENYA, then a British colony. The Mau Mau sought the forcible eviction of white farmers from traditional Kikuyu lands by invoking ancient rituals and by murder. In 1952, following a violent Mau Mau uprising, Kenyan authorities responded with military force, declared a state of emergency and arrested Jomo KENYATTA as an instigator. The following year, the Mau Mau was responsible for the massacre of more than 80 people, the majority of whom were African. The Kikuyu and other tribes became disgusted with the rebellion, which was effectively subdued by 1954. The state of emergency was not lifted, however, until 1960. During the Mau Mau uprisings, an estimated 11,000 Kikuyu Mau Mau, 1,800 Africans opposed to them, 167 Kenyan security personnel and 68 Europeans—the original targets of the rebellion—were killed.

**Mauritania (Islamic Republic of Mauritania)** Mauritania covers an area of 397,850 square miles in northwestern Africa. A French protectorate in 1903, Mauritania was incorporated into FRENCH WEST AFRICA in 1904 and became a French colony in 1920. Achieving autonomy within the French Community in

| MAURITANIA | |
|---|---|
| 1903 | The region formally becomes a French protectorate. |
| 1920 | Mauritania becomes a French colony with French West Africa. |
| 1960 | Mauritania gains independence as a member of the French Community. |
| 1968 | Government efforts to abandon French and introduce Arabic as the official language and medium of instruction in schools lead to riots in the black south. |
| 1971 | Riots mark French president Pompidou's state visit to the country. |
| 1978 | Ould Daddh is ousted in a bloodless coup led by army chief of staff Mustapha Ould Mohamed Salek. |
| 1984 | Prime Minister Taya comes to power in a bloodless coup. |
| 1989 | Border dispute with Senegal results in violence. |
| 1993 | U.S. halts aid due to Mauritania's support of Iraq during the 1991 Persian Gulf War. |
| 2005 | Military coup takes place while President Taya is out of the country. Ely Ould Mohamed Vall is named military leader, while Taya is living in exile. |

1958, the country declared its independence as the Islamic Republic of Mauritania in 1960. The resentment of the black African population toward the officially declared Arab identity of the country led to riots in 1966 and 1979. Tensions between Mauritania and MOROCCO over the status of the Saharan Arab Democratic Republic existed from 1976 to 1986, while internal political instability was the result of a series of military coups between 1978 and 1984. A bloodless coup in 1984 brought Colonel Moaouie Ould Sidi Mohamed Taya to power. His government has pursued a democratization policy. In 1989 a dispute with SENEGAL escalated into ethnic violence, resulting in hundreds of deaths and the expulsion of 40,000 black Mauritanians into Senegal. In 1993 the U.S. suspended economic aid to Mauritania because it had supported Iraq in the 1991 Persian Gulf War and because of its mistreatment of its population. In 2005 the military stage a coup while Taya was out of the country. Taya went into exile while the military junta named Ely Ould Mohamed Vall as leader.

**Mauritius** Located east of Madagascar, Mauritius is composed of a main island, 20 adjacent islets and the dependencies of the Agalega and Rodriques Islands and the Cargados Carajos shoals—a total land area of 718 square miles. Mauritius was under

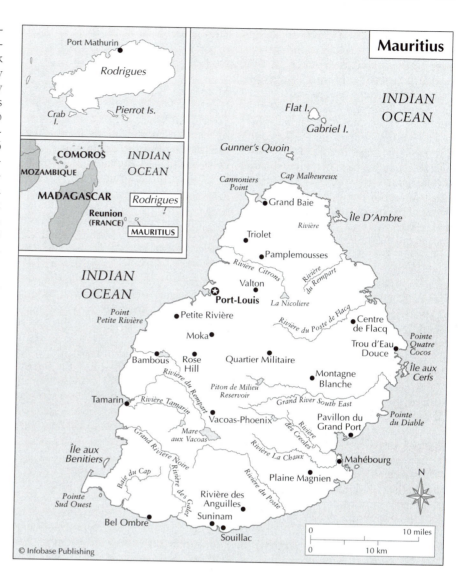

| | MAURITIUS |
|---|---|
| 1968 | Mauritius gains independence from Great Britain and becomes a member of the Commonwealth of Nations. |
| 1982 | Mouvement Militant Mauricien (MMM) gains control of the National Assembly, led by Aneerood Jugnauth. |
| 1983 | Ousted by the MMM, Jugnauth forms the Mouvement Socialiste Mauricien (MSM), whose coalition with the MLP wins a parliamentary majority, making Jugnauth prime minister. |
| 1987 | Jugnauth's coalition is reelected. |
| 1991 | Jugnauth's coalition is reelected. |
| 1992 | Mauritius becomes a republic in the Commonwealth. |
| 1999 | Three days of rioting by Creole youths in February results in damages estimated at $150 million. Discontent among Creoles over their failure to participate in Mauritius's economic progress is cited as a cause. |
| 2000 | Sir Aneerood Jugnauth becomes prime minister. |

British control from 1810 to 1968 when the country achieved independence and became a member of the COMMONWEALTH. Ethnic tensions among the French Creoles, Muslims and immigrant Indian workers have dominated the political scene in Mauritius, resulting in periodic strikes and government crackdowns, a series of unstable coalition governments, and the formation of a left-wing political party. Anerood Jugnauth formed an alliance with several political groups and was elected prime minister in 1983 and again in 1987. Under his leadership the economy has improved, though there have been two attempts to assassinate him (1988, 1989). In March 1992 Mauritius became a republic within the British Commonwealth. Since that time Mauritius has experienced some ethnic tensions and the formation of coalition governments along those divisions.

**Maurois, André (pen name of Emile Herzog)** *(1885–1967)* French novelist, literary critic and biographer. Maurois was successful in a number of literary genres but remains best known for his romantic-style biographies that imaginatively re-created the psyches of his subjects. Maurois's many biographical studies include works on British prime minister Benjamin Disraeli (1924), the English poet Lord Byron (1930), and the French novelists George Sand (1952) and Honoré de Balzac (1965). Maurois also wrote a number of popular novels, such as *The Silence of Colonel Bramble* (1918), and was an influential literary critic who was an early champion of the works of Marcel PROUST. His major autobiographical work is *Memoirs 1885–1967* (1970). He received the NOBEL PRIZE for literature in 1952.

**Maurras, Charles** *(1868–1952)* French political writer and critic. A literary and political conservative, he was a founder of the *École romane*, a neoclassical movement in French letters. A monarchist and nationalist, he disseminated his views as editor of the *Action française* and by writing such book as *Enquête sur la monarchie* (1909) and *Mes idées politiques* (1937). He was elected to the Académie française in 1938. A collaborator during the German occupation, he was expelled from

the Académie and in 1945 was sentenced to life imprisonment. He was pardoned just before his death.

**Maxwell, Robert Ian (Jan Ludwig Hoch)** *(1923–1991)* Czech-born British publisher, head of an information and communications empire that included printing, publishing and cable television companies in 16 countries. His initial publishing success came with Pergamon Press (purchased in 1951), which filled a need for the dissemination of scientific information. Among the companies he owned are the Mirror Group Newspapers in England (since 1984), Macmillan, Inc. (since 1988) and *The New York DAILY NEWS* (since 1991). Maxwell was a LABOUR PARTY member of Parliament (1964–70) and was active in the Czech RESISTANCE during WORLD WAR II. A year after his mysterious drowning off the Canary Islands in 1991, the Mirror Group was forced to file for bankruptcy. It was later discovered that he had taken money from his companies' pension funds to shore up the firms' deteriorating finances.

**May, Elaine (Elaine Berlin)** *(1932– )* American comedic actress, film director and screenplay writer. May first achieved success in show business in the 1950s, when she formed a stage comedy team with Mike NICHOLS. Together they enjoyed a Broadway hit with *An Evening with Mike Nichols and Elaine May* (1960). After the team broke up, May went on to become a pioneering figure in HOLLYWOOD as a woman who wrote, acted in and directed feature films. As an actress, she appeared in the comedies *Luv* (1967) and *Enter Laughing* (1967). One of her finest efforts—which May wrote, directed and costarred in with Walter Matthau—is the comedy *A New Leaf* (1971). Other films directed by May include *The Heartbreak Kid* (1972) and *Ishtar* (1987). She also cowrote the script for the hit comedy *Heaven Can Wait* (1978). May made a Hollywood comeback in the 1990s with her screenplay work on *The Birdcage* (1996) and *Primary Colors* (1998).

**May, Rollo Reese** *(1909–1994)* American psychologist. May studied to be a Congregational minister before turning to psychology and earning a

Ph.D. in clinical psychology at Columbia University (1949). In his books he has explored the relationship between creativity and inner satisfaction. Many of his books, including *The Meaning of Anxiety* (1950), *Love and Will* (1969), *The Courage To Create* (1975) and *Freedom and Destiny* (1981), have become best sellers. His humanistic approach to psychology has had a strong influence on the NEW AGE MOVEMENT.

**Mayakovsky, Vladimir Vladimirovich** *(1894–1930)* Russian poet. In 1908 Mayakovsky joined the Communist Party, and in 1911 he met some of the early FUTURISTS. His first collection of poems, *As Simple as Mooing* (1916), met with success. He wrote many poems about the revolution, including "150,000,000" (1920), in which President WILSON personifies capitalism. He also wrote satirical plays, including *The Bedbug* (1921). He was the leading representative of the Futurist school, and Mayakovsky had considerable influence on subsequent poets. Disenchanted with the party, he committed suicide in 1930; later he was eulogized by Stalin.

**Mayer, Albert** *(1897–1981)* American architect and city planner. Mayer cofounded the firm of Mayer, Whittlesey & Glass (1935) and was its senior partner. His views were influential in the creation of the U.S. Housing Authority (1937). An advocate of rationally planned urban expansion, he was the designer for many housing projects in the U.S. He gained international renown in the 1950s as the master planner for India's NEW TOWN CHANDIGARH.

**Mayer, Arthur Loeb** *(1886–1981)* Legendary American motion picture exhibitor and distributor, onetime head of publicity at PARAMOUNT PICTURES. Mayer would use any gimmick to fill a movie theater. His showings of double-feature horror films at New York's Rialto Theater earned him the epithet The Merchant of Menace. After WORLD WAR II he imported such outstanding Italian films as *Open City* and *The Bicycle Thief* and lectured on film history at colleges across the U.S.

**Mayer, Louis B.** *(1885–1957)* Russian-born motion picture pioneer and celebrated chief executive of MGM. Mayer followed his immigrant father's occupation of junk dealer in Boston until his company failed. In 1907 he took over the management of a theater chain and 10 years later formed his own production company, Louis B. Mayer Pictures. After the merger in 1924 that formed METRO-GOLDWYN-MAYER, he became vice president and general manager of the West Coast operation. At his peak in the 1930s and 1940s, Mayer was the epitome of the HOLLYWOOD mogul—ruthless, hardworking, paternalistic, staunchly conservative, vindictive toward his enemies, loyal to the point of indulgence to his friends—and obsessed with making movies. His annual salary of $1.25 million was the highest in the nation. Mayer's favorite among all his MGM pictures was *The Human Comedy* (1943), written by William SAROYAN. The film reflects Mayer's sentimental ideas, portraying an America of small towns and decent and industrious citizens, who, despite their differences, feel an almost spiritual sense of family. After years of infighting at MGM, Mayer was ousted in 1951 by former aide Dore SCHARY. He refused an opportunity to return as president of the company in 1957.

**May Fourth Incident** Protest of May 4, 1919, by some 3,000 Chinese students in Beijing. They had massed to demonstrate their disapproval of the continuation of internationally sponsored imperialism in CHINA, which was manifested at the PARIS PEACE CONFERENCE with the awarding of Germany's former concessions in Shandong province to Japan. The students marched to the legation quarter to present their grievances and then protested at the home of Ts'Ao Ju-lin (China's minister of communications and former vice foreign minister), where some were arrested. While the incident had little immediate importance, it triggered the MAY FOURTH MOVEMENT, which has been an important factor in the development of Chinese culture in the 20th century.

**May Fourth Movement** Popular reform movement in CHINA that produced a virtual revolution in thought and culture from 1919 to 1921. It was sparked by the MAY FOURTH INCIDENT

and early on resulted in a variety of strikes and anti-Japanese boycotts, which were influential enough to prevent Chinese delegates to the Paris Peace Conference from signing the TREATY OF VERSAILLES. As the movement escalated, it grew to include other aims beyond the elimination of Japanese imperialism in China. These included a program to improve literacy among the populace, an increased popularity of Western liberal ideas, the promotion of a vernacular literature and a widespread refutation of the traditional Confucian social hierarchy. This period of growing modernism also saw the beginnings of Chinese Marxism.

**Mayo Clinic** Noted American medical facility at Rochester, Minnesota. Started in 1889, it is one of the largest and most widely recognized medical centers in the world. Founded by William Worrall Mayo and his two sons to care for surgical patients, the clinic's functions changed to those of a general medical center just before World War I. Over 200,000 patients are treated at the Mayo Clinic annually.

**Mayotte** Island in the Mozambique Channel between Mozambique and Madagascar, forming part of the Comoro Archipelago and covering a total area of 145 square miles; the earliest inhabitants were a Melano-Polynesian people. In 1912 Mayotte was combined with the other Comoro Islands to form a dependency of France's colony of Madagascar. In 1946 the islands became a separate French overseas territory. Internal autonomy was granted in 1961. Elections to the Chamber of Deputies in December 1972 produced a strong majority for the coalition of parties in favor of independence. A referendum on December 22, 1974, resulted in a 96 percent majority throughout the Comoros for independence but not in Mayotte, where 64 percent voted against. In July 1975 the Comoran Chamber of Deputies unilaterally declared the islands independent, despite the protests of Mayotte. FRANCE remained in control of Mayotte and proposed a referendum on the island's future; held on February 8, 1976, it produced a 99 percent vote in favor of retaining links with France. The French government refused to consider making the island a department, but granted it the status of a territorial

collective, a status between that of a department and an overseas territory. Following a Comoran coup in 1978 the new government offered to include Mayotte in a new federal system. Mayotte refused. In March 1987 there were outbreaks of rioting between the local population and illegal immigrants from the Comoros. In a 2001 referendum nearly three-quarters of the populace voted in favor of Mayotte remaining a territory of France, though still claimed by Comoros.

**Mays, Benjamin E.** *(1895–1984)* Black American educator and a champion of the CIVIL RIGHTS movement. Mays gained an international reputation while dean of the Howard University Divinity School (1934–40). From 1940 to 1967 he was president of Morehouse College, where his students included Martin Luther KING Jr. King later called Mays his "spiritual and intellectual leader." Mays also served on the Atlanta Board of Education (1969–81).

**Mays, Willie Howard, Jr.** *(1931– )* American baseball player. Undisputedly one of the greatest baseball players ever, Mays was a major figure during the glory years of New York baseball in the 1950s and 1960s. He was a brilliant fielder, with a career putout total of 7,095, a record that still stands. He led the New York Giants to the National League pennant in 1954 with a .345 batting average, and his outstanding fielding helped them win the World Series. Mays went with the team when they moved to San Francisco after the 1957 season. Although his play continued to sparkle, with another 50-home-run season, Mays was never as happy there as in New York. He finished his career with the New York Mets in 1973, with a career total of 660 home runs. He was named to the Hall of Fame in 1979.

**Maysles, David Peter** *(1933–1987)* U.S. filmmaker. He and his brother **Albert Maysles** (1933– ) played key roles in the development of the documentary genre known as verité, which used handheld cameras, natural sound, and no scripts or staged sets. The best known of the brothers' films were *Salesmen* (1969), *Gimme Shelter* (1970, about the ROLLING STONES) and *Grey Gardens* (1975).

**Maytag, Frederick Lewis** *(1857–1937)* U.S. manufacturer. He converted his small business into a factory at Newton, Iowa, in 1907 to manufacture hand-operated washing machines. Four years later he introduced a motorized washing machine. A leader in the industry by the early 1920s, the company's management was taken over by Frederick's son in 1926. With its ongoing research and promotion, the company produced the first automatic washer in 1948 and continued to be a leading manufacturer of major appliances. The city of Newton still calls itself the "Washing Machine Capital of the World."

**Mazowiecki, Tadeusz** *(1927– )* Polish journalist and political leader, premier of POLAND (1989–90). A leading Catholic intellectual, Mazowiecki was active in the SOLIDARITY movement during the late 1970s and the 1980s and was a trusted adviser to Lech WALESA. In 1989, when the Communist premier resigned under increasing pressure from Solidarity and the noncommunist Polish majority, Mazowiecki was nominated for the post by Communist Party leader and president General Wojciech JARUZELSKI. Confirmed by the Polish parliament in a vote of 378 to 4 (with 41 abstentions), Mazowiecki became the first noncommunist premier in four decades. The momentous vote represented the first known democratic transfer of power away from a ruling communist party. It was an important milestone in the events of 1989 to 1990 that signaled the end both of the communist domination of Eastern Europe and of the COLD WAR. Mazowiecki faced considerable political and economic problems in governing Poland. In 1997 he wrote the preamble to the Polish constitution. In 2005 he was cofounder of the Polish Democratic Party.

**Mazursky, Paul** *(1930– )* American film director, producer, screenplay writer and actor. Mazursky emerged as one of the most prolific directors in HOLLYWOOD during the 1970s and 1980s. His major successes have combined a deft comic touch with a substantive look at social issues of the day. Mazursky began his career in films with minor acting roles in the 1950s but scored a major commercial hit with his first directorial effort, the comedy about wife-swapping, *Bob & Carol & Ted & Alice* (1969). In the ensuing two decades, Mazursky produced, scripted and directed a host of films, most notably *Harry and Tonto* (1974); *An Unmarried Woman* (1978), which was one of the first films to examine the impact of divorce on women; *Moscow on the Hudson* (1984); *Down and Out in Beverly Hills* (1986); and *Moon Over Parador* (1988).

**Mbeki, Thabo** *(1942– )* South African politician, member of the African National Congress (ANC) political party (1956– ), president of the ANC (1997– ) and president of South Africa (1999– ). Born in Idutywa, South Africa, Mbeki joined the ANC's Youth League in 1956 and participated in its efforts to gain followers among black South Africans in secondary schools. In 1959 he was elected secretary of the African Students' Association, which disintegrated the following year after many of its leaders were arrested by the South African police.

In 1962 Mbeki left South Africa for Britain, where he obtained an M.A. in economics at Sussex University in 1966. In 1970 he returned to Africa and became a leader in the struggle against apartheid in his country. As chief of the ANC's Department of Internal Affairs, he headed negotiations with the South African government of F. W. DE KLERK in 1989 for the release of imprisoned ANC activist NELSON MANDELA, and later for the creation of a new constitution giving black South Africans the right to vote in national elections. In 1994 Mandela selected Mbeki as the first deputy president following the ANC's electoral victory. In 1997 Mbeki succeeded Mandela as president of the ANC, and in 1999 Mbeki replaced Mandela as the president of South Africa.

As president, Mbeki attempted to resolve several of the critical issues facing his nation. Foremost among them was the spreading AIDS epidemic. Although earlier in his presidency he had voiced skepticism about the threat of HIV or AIDS, Mbeki agreed in 2003 to accept several millions of dollars in U.S. aid to contain the spread of the virus. He also continued Mandela's efforts to end South Africa's economic recession by encouraging greater foreign investment in the South African economy, to reconcile opposition groups within South African politics, and to improve South Africa's relations with neighboring African states. In 2004 the ANC won the South African general elections in a landslide, ensuring Mbeki's reelection to a second five-year term as president.

**Mboya, Tom** *(1930–1969)* Kenyan politician. A member of the Luo tribe, Mboya was educated at Ruskin College, Oxford, before returning to Kenya to serve as treasurer of the Kenya African Union and as secretary of the Kenya Local Government Workers Union in the 1950s. He was among the first African members elected to the Kenya legislative council (1957), and he distinguished himself as a member of the Kenya African National Union (KANU)—the leading political party. After the country's independence in 1963, Mboya served as minister of labor, minister of justice and minister of economic planning under Jomo KENYATTA. He seemed destined for higher office but was assassinated in Nairobi (1969). Demonstrations following his murder brought Kenya close to civil war. A member of the Kikuyu tribe was found guilty of the killing and was hanged.

**McAdoo, William Gibbs** *(1863–1941)* U.S. politician. He was involved with organizing the Hudson and Manhattan Railways, which built tunnels under the Hudson River between New York and New Jersey. Later, he was appointed to the Woodrow WILSON cabinet as secretary of the treasury (1913–18). Married to Wilson's daughter Eleanor (1914), he was chairman of the Federal Reserve Board and director general of U.S. railroads. McAdoo was elected senator from California and served in that capacity from 1933 to 1938.

**McAuliffe, Anthony C.** *(1898–1975)* McAuliffe was the American general who purportedly sent the reply "Nuts!" to a German ultimatum to surrender during the BATTLE OF THE BULGE (December 1944) in WORLD WAR II. At the time, he was acting commander of the 101st Airborne Division at BASTOGNE. (He was second-in-command to Major General Maxwell D. TAYLOR, who was attending conferences in Washington, D.C., when the battle started.) McAuliffe later commanded the 103d Infantry Division in the European campaign.

**McAuliffe, (Sharon) Christa** *(1948–1986)* American teacher who was killed in the explosion of the SPACE SHUTTLE CHALLENGER (January 28, 1986). She had been selected from more than 10,000 applicants to be the first civilian passenger on a U.S. spaceflight. A high-school social studies teacher from Concord, New Hampshire, she had planned to broadcast lessons from space on the Public Broadcasting Service to school-children throughout the U.S.

**McCain, John Sidney, Jr.** *(1911–1981)* American naval officer. The son of a four-star admiral, during WORLD WAR II he commanded three SUB-MARINES and sank 20,000 tons of Japanese shipping. He was decorated for his accomplishments. During the VIETNAM WAR he served as commander in chief of U.S. forces in the Pacific. McCain was a dedicated advocate of the importance of seapower to the national interest.

**McCain, John** *(1936– )* U.S. naval officer (1958–81), and Republican member of the House of Representatives (1983—86) and the Senate (1987– ) from Arizona. Born in the Panama Canal Zone, McCain followed his father, JOHN SIDNEY MCCAIN JR., and grandfather and entered the U.S. Naval Academy, from which he graduated in 1958. Serving as a naval pilot in the Vietnam War, McCain was captured by the North Vietnamese and remained a prisoner of war (POW) for five years. When he was released by North Vietnam, McCain returned to the U.S. and attended the Naval War College from 1973 to 1974, followed by a tour of duty as the U.S. Senate's naval liaison from 1977 to 1981. McCain moved to Arizona in 1981, where he was elected to the House of Representatives the following year. After two terms in the House, McCain won the U.S. Senate seat vacated by Barry Goldwater in 1986, and was reelected by sizable margins in 1992 and 1998.

In 1999 McCain entered the race for the Republican presidential nomination. After performing well in the New Hampshire, Michigan, and Arizona primaries, McCain's presidential campaign ended soon after he lost the California primary to Texas governor GEORGE W. BUSH. Following Bush's election in December 2000, McCain repeatedly concurred with criticisms expressed by Senate Democrats of President Bush's domestic policies. McCain also cooperated with Democratic senator Russell Feingold to reform campaign finance laws. In foreign affairs, McCain supported the March 2003 invasion of Iraq to overthrow Iraqi dictator Saddam HUSSEIN.

**McCarren-Walter Act** Legislation codifying U.S. immigration laws. Passed in 1952 over the veto of President Harry S TRUMAN, the law maintained the national quota system of the 1924 New Quota Act but ended the earlier legislation's total ban on immigration of Asian and Pacific peoples. Provisions required elaborate screening of immigrants to keep out subversives and authorized the deportation of immigrants for communist and communist-front activities even after they had been naturalized.

**McCarthy, Eugene Joseph** *(1916–2005)* American politician. Born in Watkins, Minnesota, McCarthy later taught at the College of St. Thomas, St. Paul, Minnesota (1946–49). A Democrat, he entered politics in 1948 and served five terms in the U.S. House of Representatives (1949–59). McCarthy became a senator in 1959, establishing a liberal voting record and a reputation

*Senator Eugene McCarthy* (LIBRARY OF CONGRESS. PRINTS AND PHOTOGRAPHS DIVISION)

as a thoughtful, quiet intellectual. In 1966 he began to enunciate his opposition to President Lyndon B. JOHNSON's VIETNAM WAR policy. In 1967 McCarthy announced his candidacy for the Democratic presidential nomination on a platform that supported a negotiated peace. Surrounded by a dedicated army of college students, McCarthy made surprisingly good showings in early primaries. His candidacy was one factor in Johnson's withdrawal from the race. McCarthy lost the nomination to Senator Hubert H. HUMPHREY. Retiring from the Senate in 1971, he returned to teaching. His subsequent attempts to reenter political life, including an independent bid for the presidency in 1976 and a run in a Senate primary in 1982, were unsuccessful.

**McCarthy, Joseph Raymond** *(1908–1957)* American politician. Born in Grand Chute, Wisconsin, McCarthy studied law at Marquette University and, after practicing law in his home state, became a circuit judge (1940). After World War II service in the marines, he entered politics in 1946 by defeating incumbent Wisconsin senator Robert M. LA FOLLETTE Jr. for the Republican nomination and easily besting his Democratic rival. He was little noticed until 1950, when he accused the State Department of harboring communists. When asked for proof, McCarthy simply made new and more virulent accusations, making General George C. MARSHALL a particular object of scorn. Reelected in 1952, McCarthy gathered a loyal following around him and was soon appointed chairman of the Senate Permanent Investigations Subcommittee. Tapping into America's COLD WAR fears and wildly exacerbating them, he assumed great power and was responsible for the relentless pursuit of those he considered communists, subversives or fellow travelers and for the public disgrace of many. His attacks reached new heights in 1954 when his charges of communist infiltration into the U.S. Army provoked hearings that were broadcast on national television (see ARMY-MCCARTHY HEARINGS). As a result of the hearings, the army was cleared and later that year McCarthy was censured by the Senate. After this censure, his influence underwent a steep decline. McCarthy's activities inspired the term MCCARTHYISM, denoting violent and unfounded political attack.

## McCarthy, Joseph Vincent ("Marse Joe") (1887–1978) American baseball manager. McCarthy managed the legendary New York Yankees between 1931 and 1946. In that span, he led the Yankees to eight American League pennants and seven World Series titles. McCarthy was elected to the Baseball Hall of Fame in 1957.

## McCarthy, Mary Therese (1912–1989) American novelist and critic. She was regarded as one of America's preeminent literary figures from the 1930s through the 1970s. Many of her works, including the memoir *Memories of a Catholic Girlhood* (1957) as well as the novel *The Group* (1963), about the lives of eight Vassar College graduates, were autobiographical. Her sharp-edged critical writings and comments often provoked other literary figures. She touched off a feud with Lillian HELLMAN after she declared in a television interview, "Everything she [Hellman] writes is a lie, including 'and' and 'the.'" Hellman sued for libel but died in 1984 before the case could reach trial. In 1984 McCarthy received both the National Medal for Literature and the Edward MacDowell Medal for outstanding contribution to literature.

## McCarthyism Term derived from the behavior of U.S. senator Joseph MCCARTHY in the early 1950s. It refers not only to McCarthy's activities, but also to the atmosphere in which he operated at the height of the COLD WAR. In his crusade against communists and "subversives," McCarthy resorted to a variety of unethical tactics. These included making sensational and unsubstantiated charges against hitherto respectable citizens, claiming to have lists and statistics that supported his charges, and twisting witnesses' words to make them seem guilty or uncooperative. By assuming a patriotic, self-righteous stance, McCarthy made those who denied his charges seem guilty. While McCarthyism originally meant an unthinking right-wing attack against anything that vaguely smacked of COMMUNISM, the term has been expanded to encompass the cynical leveling of any kind of unfair political charges.

## McCartney, Sir (James) Paul (1942– ) British rock and roll songwriter, vocalist, and bassist. Despite a solo career that has now lasted three decades, McCartney remains best known for his songwriting and vocals as a member of THE BEATLES. He and fellow Beatle John LENNON formed what many critics feel was the greatest songwriting team in the history of rock and roll. In 1970, after the breakup of The Beatles, McCartney released a highly successful eponymous solo album, *McCartney* (1970). In 1971 he formed the band Wings, which featured his wife, Linda, on keyboards and as an accompanying vocalist. There resulted a steady stream of singles hits by the ensemble Paul McCartney and Wings, including "My Love" (1973), "Live and Let Die" (1973), "Band on the Run" (1974) and "With a Little Luck" (1978). McCartney has also continued to pursue independent projects, making the hit song "Ebony and Ivory" (1982) in collaboration with Stevie WONDER and another hit, "Say Say Say" (1983), in collaboration with Michael JACKSON. In 1995 the remaining Beatles used a demo tape of John Lennon to release "Free As a Bird"—the band's first new song in twenty-five years. Despite his declining musical production, now primarily focused on producing orchestral and classical pieces for EMI Records (with the exception of the 1999 album *Run Devil Run*), McCartney has continued to receive honors. In 1997 he was knighted by Queen Elizabeth II and in 1999 was inducted into the Rock and Roll Hall of Fame. He was active in fund-raising for the victims of the terrorist attacks in the United States on September 11, 2001, and put in a memorable musical performance at half-time during the Super Bowl in 2005.

## McCay, (Zenas) Winsor (1867–1934) American illustrator, cartoonist and pioneer of motion picture ANIMATION. Born in Spring Lake, Michigan, McCay spent 15 years working as a cartoonist for the *Cincinnati Commercial Tribune*. In New York after 1902, he began his famous comic strips *Dream of the Rarebit Fiend* (*New York Evening Telegram*) and *Little Nemo in Slumberland* (*New York Herald*). Both depicted the nightmares and fantasies of dreamers. These strips were more than just a popular art, writes biographer John Canemaker; they were "an anticipation

of surrealist conceits in juxtapositions of fantastic occurrences in mundane settings, the instability of appearances, and the irrationality of life." Between 1908 and 1911 he hand-colored over 4,000 drawings on 35mm film for *Little Nemo* and in 1911 began touring the vaudeville theater circuits, showing his animated film and illustrating his monologues with hastily drawn sketches of his characters. In 1912 he created *The Story of a Mosquito* and in 1914 *Gertie the Dinosaur,* executing between 6,000 and 10,000 sketches each, on transparent rice paper. Lasting only a few minutes apiece, the films were timed so that the characters seemed to respond to McCay's on-stage "cues." His most ambitious animated film was *The Sinking of the Lusitania* (1918), a fervently anti-German response to the wartime tragedy (see LUSITANIA). After completing several more films, including another *Gertie* picture, McCay returned to newspaper cartooning on the *New York American*. Canemaker claims McCay was the first person to make and exhibit a hand-colored cartoon, the first to base a cartoon on a successful comic strip and the first to use the medium in a highly personal way.

## McCloy, John J(ay) (1895–1989) U.S. lawyer and diplomat. He played key roles in a number of government and business operations. Among his most memorable assignments was that of U.S. high commissioner in Germany (1949–52); during that time he oversaw the creation of a democratic civilian government and supervised the disbursement of $1 billion in aid to the war-ravaged German economy (see MARSHALL PLAN). He also served as assistant secretary of war, president of the WORLD BANK, chairman of Chase Manhattan Bank and of the FORD FOUNDATION, and consultant to presidents KENNEDY, JOHNSON, NIXON and FORD.

## McCormack, John (1884–1943) Irish tenor. McCormack, who enjoyed great success both as an opera performer and as a singer of Irish popular songs, was the favorite vocalist of the great Irish novelist James JOYCE, who proclaimed McCormack to be an artistic genius. McCormack made his operatic debut in Italy (1906) and thereafter enjoyed success in both Europe and America, winning special

*Irish tenor John McCormack* (LIBRARY OF CONGRESS, PRINTS AND PHOTOGRAPHS DIVISION)

praise for his role as Don Ottavio in Mozart's *Don Giovanni*. But while critics loved McCormack's voice, they found him a wooden actor—a verdict that McCormack himself did not dispute. After 1913 McCormack appeared strictly as a concert singer with a repertoire that drew from both opera and popular song; he was a favorite with audiences until his death. McCormack was made a papal count in 1928 and received many other honors. Many of his recordings have been remastered and remain available on LP records and compact discs.

**McCormack, John William** (*1891–1980*) American politician. A Democrat from Boston, Massachusetts, McCormack served in Congress for more than 40 years (1928–70), rising to the powerful position of Speaker of the House (1962–70). He was from an Irish family and was considered a model of the old-style big-city politician who tended to the needs, both great and small, of his home district. In Congress he was noted for his parliamentary skill and shrewd, temperate style, which helped him influence committee selection, shape legislation and control debate. As Speaker he helped formulate and steer through the House the outpouring of domestic legislation in the mid-1960s. (See also Lyndon B. JOHNSON; GREAT SOCIETY.)

**McCovey, Willie Lee** (*1938– *) American baseball player. One of the most fearsome home run hitters of all time, McCovey was one of the few players to have homered in every National League stadium. His career,

which stretched over four decades (1959–80), ended with a total of 521 home runs. He is perhaps best remembered for the hit he didn't get, a 1962 World Series line drive caught by Yankee Bobby Richardson that finished off the Giants' hopes in the bottom of the ninth inning of the seventh game. Traded to the San Diego Padres in 1974, he returned to the Giants for the remainder of his career in 1977. He retired in 1980, and was named to the Hall of Fame in 1986.

**McCracken, James** (*1926–1988*) American dramatic tenor; a mainstay of New York City's Metropolitan Opera Company in the 1960s and 1970s. In 1963 McCracken became the first U.S.-born singer to sing the title role in *Otello,* which remained his most celebrated role.

**McCrea, Joel** (*1905–1990*) U.S. actor. He appeared in more than 80 films, many of them Westerns, and specialized in playing calm, dependable heros. His best known Westerns included *Wells Fargo* (1937), *Union Pacific* (1939) and *Ride the High Country* (1962). He also starred in the Alfred HITCHCOCK thriller *Foreign Correspondent* (1940) and in such comedies as *Sullivan's Travels* (1941), *The Palm Beach Story* (1942) and *The More the Merrier* (1943). With the money he earned from acting, he was able to return to his first love, ranching, and built several large spreads in California.

**McCullers, Carson** (*1917–1967*) U.S. novelist. Partially paralyzed by a series of strokes while in her 20s, she was bound to a wheelchair during her last years. Her major works include *The Heart Is a Lonely Hunter* (1940), *The Member of the Wedding* (1946), *The Ballad of the Sad Cafe* (1951) and *Clock without Hands* (1961).

**McCutcheon, John T.** (*1870–1949*) American cartoonist. His first political cartoon work appeared during the political campaign of 1896. He traveled the world, visiting the Gobi Desert and Amazon River valley, and also covered the Boer conflict and the Mexican revolution of 1914. His cartoons reflected his extraordinary background. He won the PULITZER PRIZE for cartoons in 1931. His writings include *Cartoons by Mc-*

*Cutcheon* (1903) and *Mysterious Stranger and Other Cartoons* (1905). The *Chicago Tribune* has continued to reprint his "Indian Summer" cartoon on an annual basis, believing it to be typical of the Midwest heritage.

**McDivitt, James** (*1929– *) U.S. astronaut. Command pilot of *Gemini 4* (June 3–7, 1965), McDivitt also commanded *Apollo 9* (March 3–13, 1969), which was the first test in space of the lunar module. With David Scott in the command module, McDivitt and Rusty Schweickart moved into the lunar module, nicknamed "Spider," and ran tests in preparation for its future moon excursions. An air force pilot with 145 combat missions to his credit, McDivitt logged nearly 339 hours in space. He retired from NASA in 1972 to enter private industry.

**McDonnell, James S., Jr.** (*1899–1980*) American aircraft manufacturer, known for his innovation in aerospace invention and design. As chairman of the McDonnell Douglas Corporation, McDonnell built the company into one of the world's largest manufacturers of commercial jetliners, military aircraft, spacecraft, and missiles. (See also Donald Wills DOUGLAS.)

**McEnroe, John** (*1959– *) U.S. tennis player. As an 18-year-old amateur, he was the youngest man ever to reach the finals at Wimbledon. He dominated the world of tennis throughout the 1980s, and was only the second player to take the U.S. Open title three consecutive times (1979–81). He also won three Wimbledon singles titles, as well as doubles titles at both events. Known for his hot temper and undisciplined on-court antics, he only rarely let his emotions get the better of his game. He married actress Tatum O'Neal, in 1994 but they divorced. Three years later he married rock musician Patty Smyth.

**McEwen, John** (*1900–1980*) Australian politician who served briefly as prime minister (1967–68). McEwen was known primarily for his leadership in international trade while trade minister. He was the architect of many trade treaties and opened up dozens of new export markets, including the USSR and the People's Republic of

CHINA, for Australian products. He worked to maintain Australia's close agricultural trade relationship with Britain and strongly opposed Britain's entry into the COMMON MARKET.

## McGovern, George S(tanley)
(1922– ) American political leader. Born in Avon, South Dakota, he attended Dakota Wesleyan University, served as a bomber pilot in WORLD WAR II, taught American history (1949–53) and earned his Ph.D. during his last year of teaching. A Democrat, he served in the House of Representatives (1957–61) and was director of President John F. KENNEDY's Food for Peace program (1961–62). Elected to the Senate in 1962, he compiled a liberal record and became an early and outspoken opponent of the VIETNAM WAR. The Democratic Party's nominee for president in 1972, he was overwhelmingly defeated by Richard M. NIXON. McGovern returned to the Senate but was defeated in a bid for re-election in 1980. In August 2000 Mc-Govern received the Presidential Medal of Freedom for his contributions to American political life and for his work as a U.S. ambassador to the United Nations Food and Agricultural Agencies in Rome, Italy, between 1998 and 2001. In 2001 McGovern was appointed United Nations Global Ambassador on World Hunger.

## McGuckian, Medbh (1950– )
Northern Irish poet. Born in Belfast, she was educated at Catholic schools and at Queens University, Belfast, where she was later the first female writer-in-residence (1986–88). She emerged in the 1980s with three collections and won several major prizes. Her work, highly lyrical and often surreal, explores the feminine subconscious. Her books include *The Flower Master* (1982), *Venus and the Rain* (1984), *On Ballycastle Beach* (1988), *Captain Lavender* (1944) and *Drawing Ballerinas* (2001).

## McGwire, Mark (1963– )
American baseball player. Born in Pomona, California, McGwire played baseball in high school as a pitcher, and became a star hitter at the University of Southern California (USC) and played on the U.S. Baseball Team at the 1984 Olympics. After two years in the Oakland Athlet-

Hitter Mark McGwire. playing for the Oakland Athletics (PHOTOFEST)

ics' (A's) minor league system, McGwire joined the A's for 18 games in the 1986 season. In 1987 McGwire won the AL Rookie of the Year because of his record-setting 49 home runs. In part because of his power hitting, the A's made it to the World Series in 1988, 1989, and 1990, and won the Series in 1989. Halfway through the 1997 season Oakland traded him to the St. Louis Cardinals of the National League. The following season, McGwire broke the major league baseball season home run record of 61 set by ROGER MARIS in 1961. After hitting his 62nd home run on September 8, 1998, McGwire ended the season with 70 home runs. His record stood until 2001, when BARRY BONDS hit 73 home runs for the San Francisco Giants. Beset by injuries, McGwire retired in 2001. During a congressional hearing in 2005, Mc-Gwire refused to answer pointed questions about his alleged use of steroids, casting a pall over his record-breaking performance as a home run hitter.

## McIntyre, Oscar Odd (1881–1938)
American newspaper columnist. He began his career in journalism as a feature writer in Missouri, and soon became a political writer and then the managing editor of the Dayton, Ohio, *Herald,* in 1906. His "New York Day by Day" was syndicated in 550 newspapers.

## McIver, Loren (1909–1998)
American painter. Born in New York City, she studied there at the Art Students League. Her pale, misty, poetic canvasses depict forms on the margins of usual attention—such as fallen leaves, chalk scrawls or oil puddle rainbows marking city streets, cracks in the pavement or an ancient window shade. McIver's paintings include *Hopscotch* (1940, Museum of Modern Art, New York City) and *The Street* (Corcoran Gallery of Art, Washington, D.C.).

## McKay, John (1922–1975)
One of the top U.S. test pilots during the 1950s and early 1960s, McKay flew such advanced aircraft as the X-1 rocket plane, the Douglas Skyrocket and the X-15. After growing up in the West Indies, McKay returned to the United States and received his pilot's license at the age of 18. He flew combat missions for the U.S. Navy during World War II and after the war earned his B.S. in aeronautical engineering from Virginia Polytechnic Institute. Rejoining his old employer (NACA—The National Advisory Committee on Aeronautics) after graduation in 1950, he began his career as a test pilot at Edwards Air Force Base in California. McKay flew over 20 flights on the X-15 advanced rocket plane, reaching an altitude of 295,600 feet on one of his flights (September 28, 1965). Although by air force standards this should have qualified him as an astronaut, McKay was not awarded astronaut wings because he was a civilian. A crash landing during an X-15 flight on November 9, 1962, nearly ended his life, but McKay recovered to fly the plane again. His death in April 1975 was attributed to injuries suffered in that crash.

## McKenna, Siobhan (1923–1986)
Irish actress. Her most acclaimed role was as the title character in George Bernard SHAW's play *St. Joan*. Her portrayal of Joan of Arc took London by storm in 1954 and had a similar effect on Broadway two years later. Among landmarks in her later career were her solo show *Here Are Ladies* (1970), an anthology of women as seen by various Irish writers, and her portrayal in 1977 of Sarah BERNHARDT. She began her stage career with Gaelic parts, and Irish audiences saw her in a Gaelic-language version of *St. Joan* that she herself had prepared. She also performed frequently at the ABBEY THEATRE.

**McKinley, William** *(1843–1901)* Twenty-fifth president of the UNITED STATES. After serving with distinction in the Civil War, he returned to Ohio to practice law. After serving in the House of Representatives as a Republican from 1876 to 1891 (except for a brief period), he was elected governor of Ohio in 1891 and 1893. McKinley won the Republican nomination for president in 1896. The early part of his presidency was relatively uneventful, but he later proved to be an able war president during the Spanish-American War (1898). He was the architect of the policies that acquired and governed the new territories coming under U.S. jurisdiction. On July 7, 1898, he signed the bill annexing Hawaii; the Treaty of Paris signed December 10, 1898, freed Cuba and ceded Guam, Puerto Rico and the Philippines to the U.S.; and on December 2, 1899, American Samoa was acquired by treaty. Reelected in 1900, his term had scarcely begun when he was shot in Buffalo, New York, on September 6, 1901; he died after nine days. He was greatly admired for his quiet efficiency, his integrity and a faultless private life. (See also Theodore ROOSEVELT.)

**McLaren, Norman** *(1914–1987)* Scottish-born Canadian filmmaker. He was one of the most inventive figures in the history of film ANIMATION. His career began in his native Scotland and continued in England, the U.S. and Canada. He eventually emerged as Canada's most admired film artist. For most of his career, he was associated with the National Film Board of Canada. His early experimentation at the fledgling NFB in the 1940s included making animation without a camera by drawing directly on clear acetate. Later he developed the technique of **pixillation**—live action seen in staggered single frames—for his cartoon *Neighbors,* about a deadly fight between two men over a flower on their property line. The 1952 ACADEMY AWARD given to the film was but one of more than 500 international awards McLaren won for about 60 short films he created in Canada.

**McLuhan, (Herbert) Marshall** *(1911–1981)* Canadian professor of English at University of Toronto (St. Michael's College). He developed theories about the role of the electronic media in mass popular culture. His books—including *The Mechanical Bride* (1951), *Understanding Media* (1964) and *The Medium Is the Message* (1967)—argue the thesis that print is an outmoded medium, too "linear" in its approach to reality, while television and other visual media override time and distance instantaneously—making the world a "global village." The advertising and broadcasting industries took up McLuhan's ideas with great enthusiasm, since they showed recognition and respect in a way not previously offered to these fields. McLuhan's name and his ideas were widely discussed in the 1960s and 1970s and exerted considerable influence in design fields, where understanding present and future developments is always important. McLuhan's work is now little read and discussed, although its basic message still has validity.

**McMahon, Brien** *(1903–1952)* American politician. Following graduation from Fordham and Yale universities, he practiced law and became a judge in Norwalk, Connecticut. He was elected to the U.S. Senate (1945–56), where he chaired the Joint Committee on Atomic Energy (1945–47) and authored the act that led to the formation of the Atomic Energy Commission.

**McManus, George** *(1884–1954)* American cartoonist. His famous comic strip *Bringing Up Father* appeared in over 700 papers around the world, in 27 languages. His other comic series include *Let George Do It* and *The Newly Weds and Their Baby Snookums.* He was awarded an honorary tribute in the *Congressional Record* of January 26, 1932.

**McMillan, Edwin Mattison** *(1907–1991)* American scientist. McMillan was a professor of physics at the University of California at Berkeley from 1934 to 1973. In 1940, working with Philip ABELSON, he discovered the first element heavier than uranium, element 93, which he named neptunium, after the planet Neptune. McMillan also predicted the discovery of element 94 (plutonium), which was later found by a team working under Glenn SEABORG; McMillan and Seaborg shared the 1951 NOBEL PRIZE in chemistry. In 1945 McMillan conceived the synchrotron, which was 40 times more powerful than the cyclotron developed by Ernest LAWRENCE.

**McNair, Ronald E.** *(1950–1986)* U.S. astronaut, one of seven killed in the explosion of the SPACE SHUTTLE *CHALLENGER* on January 28, 1986. He was a physicist and an expert on lasers. When he flew on a shuttle mission in 1984 he became the second African American in space.

**McNamara, Robert Strange** *(1916– )* U.S. secretary of state. McNamara taught business administration at Harvard (1940–43) and served in the Army Air Corps during World War II. He was an executive of the Ford Motor Company (1946–60), where he was responsible for sweeping reforms in the managerial system and production techniques that led to the modernization of the firm. He became president of Ford in 1960 but resigned shortly thereafter to serve as secretary of defense during the KENNEDY and JOHNSON administrations. McNamara centralized decision making in the hands of the civilian secretary at the expense of the military secretaries and introduced modern management techniques to the department. He also shifted strategy away from nuclear weapons and high technology, strengthening conventional fighting capacity. An early advocate of escalating the VIETNAM WAR, McNamara resigned in 1968 after recommending that the president turn over major responsibility for ground combat to the South Vietnamese. He served as president of the WORLD BANK from 1968 to 1981.

**McPherson, Aimee Semple** *(1890–1944)* American evangelist. A highly flamboyant figure in the 1910s and 1920s, McPherson was one of the most successful of American evangelists. Billing herself as the "World's Most Pulchritudinous Evangelist," she founded the International Church of the Four-Square Gospel in Los Angeles, California, raised $1.5 million from her followers and built the 5,000-person capacity Angelus Temple to house her services, which featured faith healing and baptisms in the faith. In 1926 McPherson was apparently kidnapped, but, during a subsequent criminal obstruction of justice trial, facts emerged indicating that she had been trysting with a married lover during the month in question. While McPherson was ultimately acquitted, she never regained her former popularity.

**McQueen, Steve** (*1930–1980*) American film actor whose portrayal of tough, freewheeling loners made him a national emblem in the 1960s. After training on the stage at the Neighborhood Playhouse and the Actors Studio in New York, he made his Broadway debut in *Hatful of Rain* (1955) and his screen debut in *Somebody Up There Likes Me* (1956). In 1958 he starred in a low-budget horror classic, *The Blob,* and landed the starring role in the television series *Wanted! Dead or Alive.* During a 22-year movie career during which he made more than 24 films, he created an enduring character who lived on the outer fringes of society, surviving by quick wits, sturdy self-reliance and a quirky humor. Among his notable later films were *The Great Escape* (1963), *The Cincinnati Kid* (1965), *The Sand Pebbles* (1966), *The Thomas Crown Affair* (1968), *Bullitt* (1968) and *Papillon* (1973).

**McReynolds, James C.** (*1862–1946*) Associate justice, U.S. Supreme Court (1914–41). A graduate of Vanderbilt University and the University of Virginia Law School, McReynolds established a successful law practice in Nashville, Tennessee. After an unsuccessful run for Congress he was appointed to the Justice Department by President Theodore ROOSEVELT and specialized in prosecuting antitrust cases. After returning to private practice he was appointed U.S. attorney general by President Woodrow WILSON in 1912, and in 1914 he was elevated to the Supreme Court. Although a Democrat, he took conservative positions on the bench. He reputedly would not sit next to either Justice BRANDEIS or CARDOZO, both of whom were Jewish. He retired in 1941.

**McShann, James Columbus "Jay"** (*1916–   *) American jazz pianist and leading exponent of the KANSAS CITY JAZZ sound of the 1930s. Born in Muscogee, Oklahoma, Jay taught himself piano as a child. At the age of 20 he moved to Kansas City, Missouri, where he listened to and played with the emerging jazz greats of the time—Count BASIE, Joe TURNER and Pete Johnson. "When I came to Kansas City, the town was wide open, jumpin', the joints staying open 24 hours a day," McShann told this writer. "I hadn't heard anything like it. I didn't want to go to bed; I was afraid I'd miss somethin'." In 1939 he formed his own big band and took his new discovery, Charlie "Yardbird" PARKER, to the Savoy Ballroom in New York City. But WORLD WAR II intervened; there was a subsequent decline in the popularity of the big bands; and by 1950 McShann was back in Kansas City to study at the Conservatory of Music (now part of the University of Missouri, Kansas City). He maintains an active schedule, still recording frequently for the Capitol, Atlantic, Black and Blue, and Sackville labels; and travels extensively to most of the top international jazz festivals. In 1988 he was the subject and dedicatee of a major Alvin AILEY ballet, *Opus McShann.* Today he is the last major survivor of the legendary Kansas City sound—a distinctive blend of improvisation, uptempo blues and a driving boogie-woogie beat. His signature piece, "Hootie's Blues," derives its name from jazz slang of the 1930s, referring to a state of intoxication, known as "getting hooted."

**Mead, Margaret** (*1901–1978*) American anthropologist. Educated at Barnard College (B.A., 1923) and Columbia University (M.A., 1924; Ph.D., 1929), where she studied with Franz BOAS, Mead began her study of Pacific islands culture in the mid-1920s. *Coming of Age in Samoa* (1928), a best seller that influenced several generations of students to enter the nascent field of anthropology, was followed by *Growing Up in New Guinea* (1930), *Sex and Temperament in Three Primitive Societies* (1935) and, most important, *Male and Female* (1949), an application of anthropological findings to the contemporary urban West. *An Anthropologist at Work* (1959) is a study of close friend and colleague Ruth BENEDICT; *A Rap on Race* (1971) is a dialogue with James BALDWIN; *Blackberry Winter; My Earlier Years* (1972) is her memoir. Although some colleagues criticized her methods, her broad-based, intuitive approach to cross-cultural analysis revolutionized the field. A prolific author and lecturer and a regular contributor to *Redbook* for 17 years, she became a popular celebrity as well as an intellectual and scholar.

**Means, Russell** (*1940–   *) American Indian activist. In 1972 Means participated in the week-long occupation of the offices of the Bureau of Indian Affairs—designed to dramatize grievances against the government's Indian policies. The following year he was one of the leaders of the 71-day armed occupation of Wounded Knee, South Dakota, organized to demand a Senate investigation of Indian treaties. Means continued to participate in feature films throughout the 1990s, including *The Last of the Mohicans* (1992), *Wagons East!* (1994), *Natural Born Killers* (1994), *The Song of Hiawatha* (1997), *Black Cat Run* (1998) and *Thomas and the Magic Railroad* (2000). He also provided the voice for Chief Powhatan in the Disney animated feature film *Pocahontas* (1995).

**Meany, George** (*1894–1980*) American labor leader. Born in New York City, Meaney became a plumber at 16 and began his union career in 1922. He swiftly moved from the Plumbers Union into the Hierarchy of the AMERICAN FEDERATION OF LABOR (AFL), becoming president of the New York federation in 1934 and secretary-treasurer of the national union in 1940. He succeeded William GREEN as the union's president in 1952. Meany was an important force in the merging of the AFL and the CONGRESS OF INDUSTRIAL ORGANIZATIONS (CIO) in 1955. He became the AFL-CIO's first president and was reelected thereafter without opposition. A vocal anticommunist, Meany strongly supported American involvement in the VIETNAM WAR. He broke with the union movement's traditional support of Democrats, refusing to support the candidacy of George MCGOVERN in 1972 and later becoming a critic of the policies of President Jimmy CARTER.

**Medawar, Sir Peter Brian** (*1915–1987*) British zoologist. Born in Rio de Janeiro, Brazil, Medawar immigrated to Great Britain and attended Oxford University. Graduating in 1939, he continued there in research under Howard Florey and as a professor. Later (1947–51) he taught zoology at the University of Birmingham and comparative anatomy at University

College, London (1951–62). Director of the National Institute of Medical Research in London until 1971, he was later affiliated with the Clinical Research Centre and a professor of experimental medicine at the Royal Institution. During WORLD WAR II he became interested in medical biology and he subsequently developed a concentrated fibrinogen used to heal damaged and grafted nerves. The war also precipitated Medawar's experiments on burns and the rejection of skin grafts, and he discovered that grafts were more or less successful depending on the genetic closeness of the donor and recipient. He and Sir Frank Macfarlane BURNET discovered acquired immunological tolerance, which later helped in the development of organ transplantation. For their discovery, Medawar and Burnet were awarded the 1960 NOBEL PRIZE for physiology or medicine.

**Medellín Cartel** A powerful criminal organization of COCAINE producers and traffickers based in Medellín, COLOMBIA, the center of that country's illegal drug trade. Active in the late 1980s and into the 1990s, this violent cartel was believed responsible for about 80 percent of the cocaine smuggled into the U.S. The group assassinated Colombian judges, police officials, newspaper editors and others who opposed them. On August 18, 1989, cartel gunmen assassinated Colombian senator Luis Carlos Galan—a leading presidential candidate and opponent of the drug trade—at a campaign rally near Bogotá. When President Virgilio Barcos announced an all-out war against the cartel, the cartel's paramilitary group, the Extraditables, threatened to escalate the violence and to kill 10 judges for each suspected drug trafficker extradited to the U.S. A total of 550 lower-court judges in Bogotá quit on August 25. After the arrest of a cartel financial adviser, nine bank offices in Medellín were dynamited and other bombings occurred in the days following. On August 30 a curfew was imposed in Medellín and nine other Colombian cities, and the U.S. ordered dependents of American diplomats to leave the country. In subsequent months, several cartel leaders were arrested and their property seized. Although the Medellín cartel suffered setbacks, it remained a dangerous

criminal force. During the 1990s the Medellín Cartel came under increasing assault from U.S. and Colombian military forces in the U.S.'s WAR ON DRUGS, which included American training of Colombian special forces, and joint Colombian-American assaults on cartel airport runways and cocaine plantations. In December 1993, the Medellín Cartel was dealt a substantial blow when its leader, Colombian lord Pablo ESCOBAR was killed in a gunfight with Colombian security forces. The cartel also encountered commercial competition from the Revolutionary Armed Forces of Colombia (FARC), a leftist rebel group that funded its military operations against the Colombian government through profits from the sale of cocaine to the U.S. and other countries.

**Medicaid** American national health insurance for the needy who could not otherwise afford care, including all of those on public assistance. Like MEDICARE, the program was established in 1965. With its costs paid by the federal, state and county governments, it is administered by individual states, each of which must meet federal standards but also has a good deal of latitude in the services it provides. Medicaid plans usually provide for inpatient and outpatient hospital services; nursing home care; services by physicians, dentists and optometrists; X-rays, drugs and other medical necessities. While the Medicare system has proven the focus of many reform attempts since President William Jefferson CLINTON unveiled his own Medicare reform plan in June 1999, Medicaid has neither received the same attention nor benefited from the same type of reform legislation. For instance, the December 2003 Medicare initiative signed by President George W. BUSH permitted Medicare to negotiate for reduced prescription drug costs for senior citizens did not offer the same benefits to Medicaid recipients. However, some legislation has been enacted at the state level, such as the reform passed by the Maine state legislature in 2000.

**Medicare** U.S. national health insurance for those aged 65 and over. Like MEDICAID, it was established in 1965 by amendments to Social Security. Managed by the Health Care Financing

Administration of the Department of Health and Human Services, Medicare provides hospital insurance for most people 65 and over, along with supplementary medical insurance. In addition, it provides certain severely disabled people with health insurance. Medicare pays for a portion of hospital and nursing home care and for some health services administered at home. After paying a certain deductible amount, those covered by Medicare are entitled to 60 days of hospital care and, with a relatively small payment, to 30 more days thereafter. Medicare recipients are also eligible for 100 days of skilled nursing care, the first 20 days at no cost, the following 80 partly paid for by the recipient. Medicare also pays for physicians' services, prescription drugs and a number of other medical costs after a small yearly deductible, picking up 80 percent of "reasonable charges." Medicare is financed by a tax paid by workers and employers as well as by the self-employed as part of their Social Security payments. With the end of the 20th century and the impending retirement of "baby boomers," the federal government began evaluating how best to assure that Medicare could continue to provide adequate assistance to the elderly. In December 2003 President George W. BUSH signed a $400 billion initiative to reform the structure of Medicare through increased subsidies of Health Maintenance Organizations (HMOs) and through offering seniors a plan to reduce the cost on their overall prescription drug purchases by 10 to 25%.

**Medici, Emilio Garrastazu** (1905–1985) Brazilian general and politician. A career army officer, in 1969 he became BRAZIL's third military president since the 1964 overthrow of that country's civilian government. He remained in power until 1974.

**Médecins Sans Frontières (Doctors Without Borders)** International organization of medical professionals providing aid to victims of epidemics, natural disasters, starvation, and wars, and winner of the 1999 Nobel Peace Prize. Founded in Brussels, Belgium, in 1971 by Bernard Kouchner and several other French doctors, Médecins Sans Frontières (MSF) attempted to provide a more rapid response for medical assistance than the International Red Cross. It first intervened following a 1972 earthquake in Nicaragua, following which it offered medical treatment to victims of the Vietnam War as well as Cambodian and Vietnamese refugees in Thailand. During the 1980s, MSF was best known for its efforts to combat famine in Ethiopia and Sudan, as well as to provide food to the war-torn cities of Uganda.

In 1990 MSF opened its first non-European office in New York City. The following year it sent a mission to Kuwait in order to provide medical and food relief following that country's liberation during the Persian Gulf War. Throughout the rest of the 1990s, MSF worked to provide medical and food relief to areas plagued by civil war, such as BOSNIA AND HERZEGOVINA, BURUNDI, RWANDA, and SOMALIA. For its humanitarian missions, MSF received the Nobel Peace Prize in 1999. By 2000 MSF had offered its relief services in over 80 nations, in which it was aided by its over 2,000 volunteers from 20 countries worldwide.

## Medina, Harold Raymond (1888–1990)
American U.S. District Court judge who achieved fame in 1948 when presiding over the trial and conviction of 11 Communist Party members at the height of the anticommunist MCCARTHY era. Born in Brooklyn and educated at Princeton and at Columbia University Law School, Medina was a successful lawyer in private practice when in 1947 he was appointed a federal district court judge in Manhattan. In 1952 he was elevated to the prestigious federal Second Circuit Court of Appeals after the retirement of the Justice Learned HAND. Although Medina wrote hundreds of opinions in a remarkably long 33-year career on the bench, he is best remembered for the 1949 opinion convicting 11 communist leaders. At the time the country was involved in a rage of anticommunist sympathy, and the lengthy trial became a focal point with the judge the center of attention. Although Medina's opinion convicting the communist leaders under the SMITH ACT for advocating the overthrow of the federal government was upheld by the Supreme Court, the dissenting judges roundly criticized Medina's handling of the case as onesided. Medina retired in 1958, although he continued to hear cases until 1980 as a senior judge.

## Meet the Press
NBC public affairs program, the longest-running series on American network television. It was created by Martha Rountree and Lawrence Spivak in 1945 as a radio program. It moved to local television in Washington, D.C. in 1947 and was first telecast over the network later that year. Spivak, who had always appeared as a regular panelist, became the moderator in 1965 and served in that capacity for a decade. Replacements have included Bill Monroe, Marvin Kalb and Chris Wallace. In 1991 NBC journalist Tim Russert became moderator.

## Megawati, Sukarnoputri (1947–  )
President of INDONESIA (2001–2004). Her father, Sukarno, helped lead Indonesia in its struggle for independence from the Dutch after World War II. At age 40 she joined the opposition to the government of her father's successor, Suharto. In 1987 and 1992 she ran unsuccessfully as a congressional candidate of the Indonesian Democratic Party (IDP), and in 1993 became president of the party. In 1996 Megawati's association with opposition to Suharto's presidency prompted Suharto to remove her as leader of the IDP and to prevent her from running in the May 1997 national elections. In response Megawati formed a new political party, the Indonesian Democratic Party of Struggle. In 1999 her popularity as an opponent of the former Suharto regime led to her party becoming the largest in the Indonesian parliament. However, a coalition organized by Abdurrahman Wahid, an Islamic cleric, resulted in Wahid's election as president in October 1999, with Megawati becoming the vice president. When Wahid was impeached after investigations into his alleged mismanagement of government agencies and funds, Megawati succeeded him in July 2001 as president of Indonesia. She was defeated for reelection in 2004 after a relatively mediocre record of dealing with the country's economic problems.

## Meier-Graefe, Julius (1867–1935)
Hungarian-born writer and critic who was influential in encouraging and publicizing the ART NOUVEAU movement in the late 19th and early 20th centuries. Meier-Graefe was trained in engineering at Munich and Zurich and, in 1890, settled in Berlin. In 1893 he traveled in England and there met William Morris. Meier-Graefe later moved to Paris and met Samuel Bing (1895). The two worked together to found the Art Nouveau movement. In 1897 he founded the magazine Dekorative Kunst (published from 1897 until 1929 in Munich), which publicized Germany's Art Nouveau. After 1905 Meier-Graefe became somewhat disillusioned with the ideas of Art Nouveau and turned his attention to art criticism and history. In 1934 he left Germany to escape NAZISM and, in the last year of his life, applied for French citizenship.

## Meiklejohn, William (1903–1981)
HOLLYWOOD talent agent. He discovered such stars as Mickey ROONEY, Judy GARLAND and a young radio sportscaster named Ronald REAGAN. Meiklejohn spent 60 years as a scout, 20 of them as talent chief at PARAMOUNT PICTURES.

## Mein Kampf (My Struggle)
Book (1925–27) by Adolf HITLER, regarded as the bible of NAZISM. Hitler dictated Mein Kampf to his confidant Rudolf HESS while the two were serving a prison sentence for their part in the Munich BEER HALL PUTSCH (1923). Most readers have found Mein Kampf not only distasteful but also dull and unreadable. In a turgid, rambling style, Hitler rants against the JEWS (see ANTI-SEMITISM), the VERSAILLES TREATY and democracy, while extolling the virtues of the "Aryan race." Many, both in Germany and without, dismissed the book as the ravings of a crackpot. However, Hitler was remarkably honest and precise in stating his goals. Historians have speculated that, had the threats in Mein Kampf been taken seriously, the tragic consequences of Hitlerism might have been forestalled. Among other things, Mein Kampf called for the abolition of the WEIMAR REPUBLIC, the rebuilding of German military might, retribution against France and Russia for Germany's defeat in WORLD WAR I, German territorial expansion (see LEBENSRAUM) and the eradication of the Jews and other "inferior" peoples (see FINAL SOLUTION; HOLOCAUST).

**Meir, Golda (Golda Mabovitz)** *(1898–1978)* Israeli political leader, prime minister (1969–74). Born in Kiev, Russia, she and her family immigrated to the U.S. in 1906, settling in Milwaukee. She married Morris Myerson in 1917 and moved to PALESTINE in 1921. She held important posts with the British-run Jewish Agency and the World Zionist Organization before and during World War II. After Israeli independence in 1948, she was ambassador to the USSR, labor minister (1949–56) and foreign minister (1956–66). In 1956 she took the Hebrew name Meir (light-giver). After the death of Levi Eshkol in 1969, she became interim prime minister and was elected to the post later that year. In October 1973, when the Egyptian and Syrian armies combined in a surprise attack, she rallied Israeli forces but was widely blamed for her nation's lack of military preparedness (see YOM KIPPUR WAR). Unable to form a government after Labor Party defeats in 1974, she resigned from office while retaining enormous personal popularity at home and abroad.

**Meitner, Lise** *(1878–1968)* Austrian-Swedish physicist. Meitner entered the University of Vienna in 1901, studied science under Ludwig Boltzmann and obtained her doctorate in 1906. From Vienna she went to Berlin to attend lectures by Max PLANCK on theoretical physics. Here she began to study the new phenomenon of radioactivity in collaboration with Otto HAHN, beginning a partnership that was to last 30 years. At Berlin Meitner met with remarkable difficulties caused by prejudice against women in academic life. She was forced to work in an old carpentry shop and forbidden by Emil FISCHER to enter laboratories in which males were working. In 1914, at the outbreak of WORLD WAR I, she became a nurse in the Austrian army, continuing to work with Hahn during leave periods. In 1918 they announced the discovery of the radioactive element protactinium.

After the war Meitner returned to Berlin as head of the department of radiation physics at the Kaiser Wilhelm Institute. Here she investigated the relationship between the gamma and beta rays emitted by radioactive material. In 1935 she and Hahn began work on the transformation of uranium nuclei under neutron bombardment. Following HITLER's annexation of Austria in 1938 she was no longer safe from persecution and, like many Jewish scientists, left Germany. With the help of Dutch colleagues she found refuge in Sweden, obtaining a post at the Nobel Institute in Stockholm. Hahn, with Fritz Strassman, continued the uranium work and in 1939 published results showing that nuclei were present that were much lighter than uranium. Shortly afterward Meitner, with Otto Frisch (her nephew), published an explanation interpreting these results as fission of the uranium nuclei. For this she received a share in the 1966 Enrico Fermi Prize of the Atomic Energy Commission.

**Melba, Dame Nellie (Helen Porter Mitchell)** *(1859–1931)* Australian operatic soprano. Born in a suburb of Melbourne, Melba studied in Paris with Mathilde Marchesi. She made her European operatic debut in Brussels in 1887 and her American debut at the Metropolitan Opera in 1893. Performing regularly at London's Covent Garden, New York's Metropolitan Opera and various European opera houses, she was acclaimed for such roles as Gilda in Verdi's *Rigoletto* and Violetta in PUCCINI's *La Traviata*. Made a Dame of the British Empire in 1918, she retired from the stage in 1926 and returned to Australia as president of the Melbourne Conservatory. Possessing a superb coloratura, Melba was noted for her pure tone throughout the operatic register, her perfect breath control and her birdlike trill. According to critic Irving Kolodin, her voice was "one of the most precious gifts that heaven ever put in a human throat." One of the leading celebrities of her time, Melba lent her name to such edibles as Melba toast and peach Melba.

**Melchior, Lauritz** *(1890–1973)* Danish opera singer. Melchior was perhaps the greatest interpreter of the *Heldentenor* lead roles that proliferate in the Ring Cycle operas of the 19th-century composer Richard Wagner. Melchior made his debut as Tannhauser in 1918 and followed with portrayals of the Wagnerian heroes Siegfried, Lohengrin, Tristan and Parsifal. Melchior frequently appeared at the Bayreuth Wagnerian festival, as well as at Covent Garden in London and at the Metropolitan Opera in New York. He spent the last 20 years of his life in America, where he taught voice and continued to perform.

**Melen, Ferit** *(1906–1988)* Turkish politician. Melen held the posts of premier (1972–73) and defense minister of TURKEY (1971–72, 1975–77). Melen first became defense minister during one of Turkey's most violent periods, when the military struggled to control what Turks referred to as "the anarchy"—a period of extremist kidnappings, robberies and murders. The draconian countermeasures the military initiated succeeded only after martial law was declared and secretive courts-martial were held, harshly punishing thousands for allegedly attempting to impose a Soviet-style communist regime by terror.

**Méliès, Georges** *(1861–1938)* French stage conjurer and pioneer in the narrative motion picture at the turn of the 20th century. He was the son of a wealthy footwear manufacturer. Although he joined his brothers in the management of the family factory, his ambitions in painting and magic led him to sell his business interests in 1888 and purchase the Théâtre Robert-Houdin. After enthusiastically viewing the program of films by the LUMIÈRE BROTHERS at the Grand Café in Paris in 1895, he developed his own camera and included his films in his stage programs. He utilized cinematic techniques of editing and superimpositions to transfer the effects and transformations of fairy pantomimes and magic shows to celluloid. At first they were simple "illusions," like *Escamotage d'une dame (The Vanishing Lady)* in 1896. By the time he produced *Le Voyage dans la lune (A Trip to the Moon)*, however, they were elaborate story films with painted sets and machinery of his own design. These "artificially arranged scenes," as he called them, were made in his glass-enclosed studio in the garden of his Montreuil home—the first European movie studio—and released under the imprimatur of Star Films. At the peak of his success in 1903, he opened an American studio, where his brother, Gaston, made westerns. After the release of one of George's most ambitious films, *A la* *conquête du Pôle* (*The Conquest of the Pole*) in 1912, he went into decline. Failing fortunes forced him to sell his estate (1913), return to the variety stage (1915), declare bankruptcy (1923) and spend the remainder of his days running a toy concession at the Montparnasse railway station. His relative obscurity was relieved somewhat by the awarding of a Legion of Honor Medal and a pension in 1931. Méliès's importance in the development of the story-film tradition can scarcely be exaggerated. His energies were indefatigable and his imagination unbounded. The motto of his Star Films company was characteristic: "The World Within Reach"—as was his comment on the making of *The Conquest of the Pole*: "Cook and Peary claimed to have reached the Pole. In fact, I don't think either one did. I said to myself, I'm going to go there."

## Mellon, Andrew William (1855–1937)

U.S. financier and cabinet member. Born in Pittsburgh, Mellon joined the family banking firm in 1874. He was active in developing the aluminum, coal and oil industries as well as in consolidating banking. By 1921, when Warren HARDING appointed him secretary of the treasury, Mellon was one of the wealthiest men in the U.S. As secretary, Mellon worked to lower taxes and reduce the national debt. He believed that business would prosper in proportion to a reduction in taxes; prosperity would then filter down to individual workers and farmers. During his tenure (1921–31), Mellon reduced the national debt by over $8 billion despite drastic tax cuts. Mellon did not foresee the GREAT DEPRESSION and emphasized retrenchment as a means to combat it. He resigned in 1932 and served as ambassador to Great Britain until 1933. In 1937 he donated his art collection, valued at $25 million, as well as funds for a museum to house it, to the U.S. The donation was the foundation of the National Gallery of Art, opened in 1941.

## Memel, Insurrection at (1923)

The predominantly German city of Memel (Klaipeda) in western LITHUANIA had been under Allied control since the end of World War I. Despite Lithuanian requests, the Allies established a French garrison in the city. On January 11, 1923, an insurrection engineered by the Lithuanians, whose troops occupied the district, forced out the French. The Allies protested but then decided to make Memel an autonomous region within Lithuania, and passed the Memel Statute on May 8, 1923, ratifying the decision.

## Menchú Túm, Rigoberta (1959– )

Guatemalan humanitarian activist and winner of the 1992 Nobel Peace Prize. Born into a Quiché (an indigenous ethnic group) agrarian community located in a northwestern region in GUATEMALA, Menchú began working to support her family when she was eight years old as a migrant laborer. Eventually, she left her family to work as a maid in the country's capital, Guatemala City. In the late 1970s Menchú began to sympathize with the efforts of revolutionaries in Guatemala to protest the human rights abuses committed by the military-dominated government. In response, Menchú and those members of her family who joined her in the protests became targets of government-sponsored paramilitary forces, leading to Menchú's exile in MEXICO in 1981. While in Mexico, she lectured in an effort to raise international awareness about the troubles caused by the government and military forces in Guatemala. She also dictated *I, Roberta Menchú* (1983), an autobiographical book that also discussed agrarian culture in Guatemala and the ongoing struggle between Guatemalan revolutionaries and the Guatemalan military. As a result of her efforts to raise international condemnation of Guatemala for its treatment of dissident groups, Menchú received the Nobel Peace Prize in 1992. After receiving the Nobel prize Menchú returned to Guatemala, where she began working with dissident groups. In 1998 she released her second book, *Crossing Borders* (1998).

## Mencken, H(enry) L(ouis) (1880–1956)

U.S. author and philologist. He began his career as a reporter in Baltimore. In 1924 he founded the *American Mercury* with fellow critic George Jean Nathan, and served as its editor through 1933. After visiting England Mencken became interested in American linguistics. The outcome of his research was the authoritative *The American Language* (1919), which was revised in 1921, 1923 and 1936; it was followed by *Supplement One* (1946) and *Supplement Two* (1948). Like George Bernard SHAW, Mencken was known for his insistence on correct usage of language. His other works include *Ventures into Verse* (1908) and the series of six collections of satirical essays called *Prejudices* (1919–27).

## Mendelsohn, Erich (1887–1953)

German-born architect associated with the development of MODERNISM through the unique expressionist character of some of his earlier work. Mendelsohn was trained at the Technical High School in Munich and was then active in theater design while coming in contact with artists of the expressionist BLAUE REITER group. After service in WORLD WAR I, he opened an office in Berlin (1919) and began work on a research laboratory for studies relating to EINSTEIN's theory of relativity. This led to his most famous work, the Einstein Tower at Potsdam, completed in 1924. It is an astronomical tower and observatory built in a flowing, sculptural form (intended for concrete construction but actually executed in brick and steel)—which is viewed by critics as expressionistic. Commissions that followed, for houses, industrial and commercial buildings, led to designs that were generally more reserved and related to the INTERNATIONAL STYLE. Mendelsohn's Department Store buildings in Stuttgart and Chemnitz, Germany, for the firm of Schoken are the best-known works of this period (1926–29), while his own house at Rupenhorn in Berlin (1930) is a fine example of his residential work, done in typically international-style terms. Mendelsohn visited the U.S. in 1924, studied the skyscraper architecture of the day and had a meeting with Frank Lloyd WRIGHT, which led to a continuing relationship. The atonal music of Arnold SCHOENBERG was also an ongoing source of stimulation for him.

In 1933 Mendelsohn left Germany for England, where he established a partnership with Serge Chermayeff. Together they designed the De La Ware Pavilion at Bexhill (1934–35). In 1939 Mendelsohn left for Palestine, where he had a number of commissions, but in 1941 he relocated to the U.S. and became a citizen in 1946. He was active as a lecturer and teacher and then designed the Maimonides Hospital

(1946–50) in San Francisco. A number of residential and institutional projects followed; his last major work was the Mount Zion Community Center in St. Paul, Minnesota (1950–54).

In spite of his extensive achievements, Mendelsohn is usually viewed as a secondary figure somewhat outside the main life of modernist development. A recent resurgence of interest in his work has led to exhibition of his striking sketches, with their strongly expressionist qualities, and fresh interest in his unique style. Bruno Zevi's book *Erich Mendelsohn* (1985) is an excellent, compact summary of Mendelsohn's achievement.

**Menderes, Adnan** *(1899–1961)* Turkish statesman. Menderes studied law and entered politics in 1932 as a moderate critic of ATATÜRK. One of the founders of the reformist Democratic Party, Menderes became prime minister in 1950. He strengthened TURKEY's links with the West and sponsored its NATO membership in 1952. He also negotiated the CYPRUS agreement in 1959. Menderes was forced to rule dictatorially in April 1960 because of widespread disorders. His regime was overthrown in May 1960 by army officers under General Gursel. Sentenced to death, Menderes was hanged in September 1961.

**Mendès-France, Pierre** *(1907–1982)* French politician, premier of FRANCE (1954–55). A socialist from a middle-class Jewish family, he served in the National Assembly (1932–40). He was arrested by the Germans shortly after they invaded France (1941) but escaped from a Nazi prison and joined Charles DE GAULLE's FREE FRENCH forces. After the war he again served in the National Assembly (1946–58). He was elected premier in June 1954 but held office for only seven months. During this short tenure he negotiated an end to the FRENCH-INDOCHINA WAR and began negotiations to grant independence to TUNISIA. He resigned in February 1955 after losing a vote of confidence over his policies on France's North African colonies. He remained in the National Assembly until his unpopular opposition to de Gaulle led to his defeat in a general election. He returned to the assembly briefly from 1967 to 1968.

**Menem, Carlos Saúl** *(1930– )* Argentine politician and president of Argentina (1989–1999). Born to a Muslim family of immigrants from Syria in the Argentine town of Anillaco, Menem converted to Catholicism and became a lawyer and political supporter of Argentine populist leader Juan Domingo PERÓN. After his election as governor of La Rioja province in 1973, he was imprisoned by the military government that had overthrown the government of Perón's wife Isabel in 1976. After his release from prison in 1981 and the fall of the military junta in 1983, Menem was again elected governor of La Rioja. Running on a populist Peronist program of wage increases for the working class, Menem was elected president in 1989.

In the early years of his presidency, Menem confronted serious economic problems and, to the surprise of many of his left-wing supporters, introduced a series of free-market reforms (such as the privatization of public utilities) that reduced the hyperinflation that had swept the country. As a result of these reforms, Argentina experienced a long period of economic growth, which was also facilitated by the regional customs union MERCOSUR that Menem played a key role in forming. After Menem's reelection to a second term in 1995, Argentina's impressive growth rate slowed while the country ran up a huge foreign debt and enormous budget deficits. To compound his difficulties with the economy, Menem was criticized for pardoning many of the military leaders of the junta that had ruled the country from 1976 to 1983. He failed in his bid for a third term in 1999 when the Argentine Supreme Court ruled it unconstitutional. In 2001 Menem was indicted for an alleged plot to smuggle arms to Croatia and Ecuador, but charges were eventually dropped for lack of evidence. In the 2003 presidential election Menem withdrew from the second round, when it became clear that his opponent Nestor Kirchner would win in a landslide, and then had to deal with a government investigation of corruption.

**Mengele, Josef** *(1911–1978?)* Nazi war criminal. Known as "the Angel of Death," Dr. Josef Mengele was chief medical officer at AUSCHWITZ concentration camp in Poland, where he was responsible for deciding which prisoners would die immediately and which would be used for slave labor. He also conducted horribly cruel and scientifically worthless "medical experiments" on the camp's inmates. After the war, Mengele escaped to Argentina, where he was granted asylum. In 1960, faced with extradition to West Germany, Mengele escaped to Brazil and then to Paraguay, where he was reported to have drowned in 1978. In 1985 the alleged body of Mengele was exhumed for forensic identification to determine whether it was in fact that of the former Nazi SS official. DNA was extracted from several of the skeleton's bones and compared with blood samples from Mengele's wife and son living in Germany. The examination's results indicated a 99.9 percent probability that the body exhumed was indeed that of Mengele.

**Mengistu Haile Mariam** *(1937– )* President of ETHIOPIA (1977–91). Lt. Col. Mengistu took part in the coup that deposed Emperor HAILE SELASSIE in 1974. He became head of state in 1977 and began to reorganize Ethiopia along Marxist lines. The country was torn by insurrection in ERITREA, war with SOMALIA and a devastating famine in the mid-1980s that cost as many as one million Ethiopian lives. In May 1991, after rebel forces cut supply routes to the capital of ADDIS ABABA, Mengistu fled into exile in Zimbabwe. Since 1991 Mengistu has remained in exile in Zimbabwe. In 1994 an Ethiopian court initiated legal proceedings against the former dictator for alleged acts of genocide committed against Eritreans and Somalis.

**Mennin, Peter** *(1923–1983)* American composer. One of the leading American composers after World War II, he composed nine symphonies and a variety of concertos and chamber works that won high acclaim. In 1962 he became president of the Juilliard School of Music in New York. Under his direction, the size and reputation of Juilliard grew. He established Juilliard's Theater Center in 1968, the American Opera Center in 1970 and a permanent conducting program in 1972.

**Menninger, Karl Augustus** *(1893–1990)* U.S. psychiatrist. In the 1920s, with father **Charles Frederick**

**Menninger** and brother **William Menninger,** he founded the Menninger Clinic and Foundation in Topeka, Kansas. He believed that emotional troubles could be eased by a sufficiently loving, caring environment. He also argued that crime was a result of mental and emotional illness and therefore advocated psychiatric treatment for prisoners. His 13 books and numerous magazine articles helped educate Americans about psychiatry. His books included *The Human Mind* (1930), *Love against Hate* (1959) and *Whatever Became of Sin?* (1988).

**Menninger Family** American psychiatrists. Dr. Charles F. Menninger and sons Drs. Karl and William Menninger founded the Menninger Foundation and Clinic in Topeka, Kansas. Dr. Charles Menninger (1862–1953) led his sons in pioneering the treatment of physical disorders in a community clinic setting. The clinic changed its total emphasis to psychiatry in 1941. William also served as chief consultant on psychiatry to the surgeon general of the United States Army during WORLD WAR II.

**Menninger Foundation Clinic** Medical facility in Topeka, Kansas, established by Dr. Charles F. Menninger and his sons Drs. Karl and William Menninger in 1925 (see MENNINGER FAMILY). One of the world's leading psychiatric centers, it is part of the Menninger Foundation, a nonprofit organization. The clinic includes two psychiatric hospitals, a department of neurology, and internal medicine, neurosurgery, and outpatient and aftercare programs.

**Menotti, Gian Carlo** *(1911–  )* Italian composer. Menotti is considered the foremost composer/librettist of modern, popular American opera. His first success was the one-act comic opera *Amelia Goes to the Ball,* staged at the Philadelphia Academy of Music in 1937. He received the PULITZER PRIZE for his operas *The Consul* (1950) and *The Saint of Bleecker Street* (1954). Menotti's most popular work, AMAHL AND THE NIGHT VISITORS (1951), became an annual Christmas event on television. His non-operatic works include the ballet *Sebastian* (1944), the symphonic poem *Apocalypse* (1951) and

*The Halcyon* symphony (1976). In addition, he founded the Spoleto Arts Festival in Charleston, South Carolina, in 1977 and remained its artistic director until 1991.

**Mensheviks** Russian political party established in August 1917 at a congress of several social democratic groups. The Mensheviks proposed a proletarian party working with the liberals in order to replace the autocracy with a democratic constitution. Before 1917 "Menshevik" referred to the non-Leninist faction of the Russian Social Democratic Labor Party. Although the Mensheviks worked with the BOLSHEVIKS during the 1905 Revolution, and reunited with them the following year, relations were strained. The Mensheviks themselves were divided into the "liquidationalists," the "party-minded Mensheviks" of the center, the followers of Pavel Axelrod and the followers of TROTSKY. In 1922 the Mensheviks were suppressed, and in 1931 a show trial took place in Moscow. In 1920 a group of Mensheviks left Russia and settled in the United States.

**Menuhin, Yehudi** *(1916–1999)* American-born violinist, conductor, teacher and author. Born in New York City, Menuhin first made his mark as a child prodigy. He studied with Louis Persinger and Sigmund Anker and made his debut with the San Francisco

*Violinist and conductor Yehudi Menuhin* (LIBRARY OF CONGRESS, PRINTS AND PHOTOGRAPHS DIVISION)

Orchestra at the age of seven. Continuing his studies in Europe with Adolf Busch and Georges ENESCO, he debuted in Paris at age 10 and in 1929 appeared as a soloist with orchestras in Berlin, Dresden and London to great acclaim. He made a triumphant world tour during the 1934–35 season, then retired briefly to study his art. In subsequent years Menuhin became one of the world's most sought-after violin soloists, famous for his warm tone, intense playing and interpretive depth. A performer both of the classics and of modern music (BARTÓK's "Sonata for Solo Violin" was written for him), Menuhin also explored a number of other musical traditions, such as Eastern music in collaboration with sitarist Ravi SHANKAR and JAZZ with French violinist Stéphane Grappelli. He established a music festival at Gstaad, Switzerland (1959), directed England's annual Bath Festival (1959–68), founded the Menuhin School of Music at Stoke d'Abernon, Surrey (1963) and became president of the Trinity College of Music, London (1972). A gifted conductor, he led his own chamber orchestra and guest-conducted major orchestras in Britain, Europe and the U.S. As a violinist, he often performed chamber pieces with his sister, Hepzibah Menuhin (1920–81), and his son, Jeremy, both pianists. Menuhin made numerous recordings as violin soloist, chamber musician and conductor. He became a British subject in 1985.

**Menzies, Sir Robert Gordon** *(1894–1978)* Australian statesman, prime minister of AUSTRALIA (1949–66). Born in Jeparit, Victoria, he became a barrister in his home province, entered provincial government in 1928 and was elected to the Australian parliament in 1934. He served as attorney general (1935–39) in the Joseph LYONS government, became prime minister upon Lyons's death in 1939 and lost his post in 1941. During his time out of office (1943–49), he led the parliamentary opposition to the Labour Party government and strove to create a coherent Liberal Party ideology. In 1949 a Liberal-Country Party coalition swept the Labor government from power, and Menzies again became prime minister. During his lengthy time in office, from 1949 to 1966, he

*Prime minister of Australia Robert Gordon Menzies*
(Library of Congress, Prints and Photographs Division)

was known for his anticommunist stance, for his development of a thriving Australian economy and for his establishment of strong ties with the U.S. and other Western powers.

**Mercader, Ramón** *(1914–1978)* Spanish laborer who assassinated exiled Soviet leader Leon Trotsky in Mexico City in 1940, using a pickax. Mercader was convicted of the murder and imprisoned until 1961. Although Mercader always insisted that he had acted alone, the assassination was ordered by Soviet dictator Joseph Stalin, and the details were probably planned by Soviet agents of the NKVD.

**Mercer, John Herndon "Johnny"** *(1909–1976)* American lyricist, composer and singer. Born in Savannah, Georgia, Mercer moved to New York in the late 1920s. By the mid-1930s, he had earned a place among the most successful American lyricists. He eventually published more than 1,000 songs, working with the top composers of his day. As a singer, Mercer appeared on film and became popular on radio in the 1930s. He was also a cofounder of Capital Records, in 1942. His songs include: "I'm an Old Cowhand" (1936), "Jeepers Creepers" (1938, with Harry Warren), "Come Rain or Come Shine" (1946, with Harold Arlen), "In the Cool, Cool, Cool of the Evening" (1951, with

Hoagy Carmichael) and "Moon River" (1961, with Henry Mancini).

**Mercer, Mabel** *(1900–1984)* British-American singer. Born in Burton-upon-Trent, Staffordshire, the daughter of an American father and a British music-hall singer, Mercer began performing at an early age. After World War I, she moved to Paris, where she appeared at Bricktop's from 1931 to 1938. Next she went to New York City, where she became popular at the Ruban Bleu. She sang at various clubs throughout the 1950s in New York, eventually opening her own establishment. She continued to perform into the 1980s, and received the American Medal of Freedom in 1983.

**Merchant, Vijay Madhavji** *(1911–1987)* Indian athlete; one of the greatest batsmen in the history of cricket and an elder statesman of the sport in India. In a career that ran from 1929 until 1951, Merchant's first class average of 71.22 ranked second only to that of Sir Donald Bradman's 95.14.

**Merckx, Eddy** *(1945– )* Belgian bicycle-racing champion. The dominant cyclist of the late 1960s and '70s, Merckx won the Tour de France five times (1969–72 and 1974), a record he shares with Jacques Anquetil and Bernard Hinault, both of France. Merckx also holds the record for the most wins in the sport's top events, with a total of 39 victories. He won the world professional road race title three times (in 1967, 1971 and 1974), a record he shares with Alfredo Binda of Italy and Rik van Steenbergen of Belgium. He won the Tour of Italy a record five times (1968, 1970, 1972–74), a mark he shares with Binda and Fausto Coppi of Italy. Merckx also holds the record for most wins in a season, 54, in 1971. In 1996 Merckx was awarded the title of Baron by the Belgian monarchy.

**MERCOSUR (Mercado Común del Sol) ("Southern Cone Common Market")** A customs union among the South American nations of Argentina, Brazil, Paraguay and Uruguay. Created on January 1, 1991, with the signing of the Asuncion Treaty, MERCOSUR has grown to include Bolivia, Chile, Colombia, Peru and Venezuela as associates of the union, making it the

third largest trading bloc in the world with over 240 million consumers. Since its inception MERCOSUR has striven to enhance integration among its members and to improve their economic productivity and development. Its efforts are governed by a Common Market Council (CMC) that organizes the integration of MERCOSUR members' economies. The members of MERCOSUR hope to attract greater foreign investment by collectively stabilizing their economies, as well as producing a fully integrated common market and trade policy and a Common External Tariff (CET) by 2006, a goal stated in the 1997 Protocol of Montevideo signed by its members. Another goal of MERCOSUR is to allow unrestricted travel within the MERCOSUR area by a citizen of each MERCOSUR member. However, a decline in intraunion trade in 2001 and 2002 cast doubt on the ability of MERCOSUR to meet its timetable for integration. In an effort to expand MERCOSUR exports within the Western Hemisphere, the organization's leaders met with representatives from Mexico in 2002 to reduce tariffs between that North American nation and the South American customs union. As a result, Mexican imports of Argentine automotive parts and Uruguayan milk increased substantially in 2003. MERCOSUR also began negotiations with another regional economic organization, the Andean Community, in an effort to create a joint free-trade area between both customs unions. Some have speculated that this effort by MERCOSUR nations to organize an enlarged economic trade bloc will result in its wholesale inclusion in the proposed hemispheric-wide Free Trade Association of the Americas. But some MERCOSUR nations, notably Brazil, have proved reluctant to emphasize trade within the Western Hemisphere at the expense of a more global approach to international trade.

In its efforts to improve its members' economies, MERCOSUR negotiated a 1995 agreement with the European Union (EU), which accounts for almost 30% of MERCOSUR's export trade, to enhance bilateral trade and political cooperation between the two organizations. However, conflicts have emerged over MERCOSUR's desire to gain greater access to the European beef, poultry and sugar markets, and the EU's insistence on providing subsidies to domestic producers of these commodities. To facilitate the growth of MERCOSUR member states' economies and to expand their total trade with the EU, MERCOSUR has reduced its reliance on trade with the U.S. By 2001 most MERCOSUR members had benefited from this arrangement, with export revenue increases of 3.4% (Argentina), 6.9% (Brazil), and 5.9% (Paraguay). But other member states have suffered in the trade transition from a U.S.- to an EU-oriented economy; Uruguay, for example, saw its export revenues decline by 9.5%.

**Mercury program (Project Mercury)** The Mercury program was the first U.S. manned spacecraft program. Seven pilots from the navy, air force and marines were chosen as the first U.S. astronauts; they were popularly known as the Mercury Seven. Several unmanned tests were made in 1960 and early 1961. The cramped quarters of the small Mercury capsule could carry one astronaut, strapped into a seat for the duration of the flight. The capsule was launched atop an Atlas rocket, originally designed as an Intercontinental Ballistic Missile (ICBM). The first two manned flights, in 1961, were short, suborbital flights to test the capsule's controls. Four orbital missions followed. The Mercury astronauts became national heroes; one, John GLENN (the first American to orbit the Earth), later became a U.S. senator. One of the Mercury Seven, Deke SLAYTON, was grounded because of a heart

*Astronaut John Glenn enters the* Mercury-Atlas 6 *spacecraft. 1962.* (LIBRARY OF CONGRESS, PRINTS AND PHOTOGRAPHS DIVISION)

problem and did not go into space during the Mercury program.

**Meredith, James Howard** (*1933– *) American CIVIL RIGHTS activist. Born in Kosciusko, Mississippi, Meredith spent nine years in the air force before returning to his native state in 1960. In 1961 he applied to the all-white University of Mississippi and the following year became the first African American to enter the institution. His court-ordered admission followed months of federal litigation, which ultimately desegregated "Ole Miss" and touched off rioting that brought National Guard and army troops to the campus. Meredith graduated in 1963, attended Columbia Law School and subsequently became a businessman in New York City. Continuing his involvement in the civil rights cause, he participated in demonstrations during the 1960s and was wounded while marching in Mississippi (1966). He unsuccessfully attempted to enter politics in the 1970s.

**Merkel, Angela Dorothea** (*1954– *) German statesperson, the first female chancellor of Germany. Angela Dorothea Kasner was born in Hamburg in 1954 to a Lutheran pastor and his wife, Herlind, a schoolteacher. Shortly after her birth her father accepted a pastorship in a town 50 miles north of Berlin in the German Democratic Republic. Kasner studied at the University of Leipzig and the Central Institute for Physical Chemistry of the Academy of Sciences. After receiving her Ph.D. in physics she became a researcher in quantum chemistry. In 1977 she married physicist Ulrich Merkel, whose surname she took. After her divorce in 1982, she married chemistry professor Joachim Sauer but retained Merkel as her professional name. After the fall of the Berlin Wall she entered politics and was elected to the Bundestag (the lower house of the German parliament) in the first post-reunification election, in December 1990, as a member of an East German party that had merged with the West German Christian Democratic Union. She assumed office as minister for women and youth in the cabinet of Chancellor HELMUT KOHL and in 1994 became minister for the environment, a post that brought her into the public spotlight.

After the Kohl government was voted out of office in 1998, Merkel was

elected secretary-general of the Christian Democratic Union and chair of the party two years later. After the Christian Democratic Party was defeated by the Social Democratic Party of Chancellor Gerhard SCHRÖDER in the elections of 2002, Merkel became the leader of the conservative opposition in the Bundestag. She became a vocal proponent of free-market economic policies and called for an improvement of relations with the United States. She supported the U.S.-led invasion of Iraq in 2003 in the face of strong opposition from the Schröder government and German public opinion. In the national elections of 2005 her party won enough legislative seats to form a "grand coalition" with the Social Democrats. As head of the senior partner in the coalition, Merkel was elected the first female chancellor of Germany since its creation in 1871.

**Merman, Ethel** (*1909–1984*) American musical-comedy star. Merman was known for her booming voice and brash style. Her career spanned 50 years, and her perfect diction and pitch made her a favorite of many of the master composers and lyricists of her time. Her major successes on Broadway included leading roles in Cole PORTER's *Anything Goes,* Irving BERLIN's *Annie, Get Your Gun* and the Jule Styne—Stephen SONDHEIM musical *Gypsy.* She also starred in 14 movies, including *Alexander's Ragtime Band.* In 1972 she received a Tony Award for the entire body of her work.

**Merrill, James** (*1926–1995*) American poet. The son of the founder of the Merrill Lynch brokerage house, Merrill was acknowledged as one of the foremost poets of his time. He established himself as a lyric poet with his earliest volumes, such as *The Black Swan* (1946). With the publication of the volumes *The Fire Screen* (1969) and *Braving the Elements* (1972), Merrill was praised as the finest lyric poet in America, and he received the PULITZER PRIZE. He also excelled as a narrative poet with such poems as *Days of 1971* (1972) and his three-part visionary epic published in one volume as *Changing Lights at Sandover* (1981). In addition, he wrote dramas, such as *The Immortal Husband* (1956), and novels, including *The Seraglio* (1957).

**Merritt, Abraham** *(1884–1943)* American master of science fantasy during the Golden Age of the pulp magazine in the 1920s and 1930s. In contrast to the sober routines of his full-time job editing the popular magazine *American Weekly,* Merritt let his mind run wild in his spare time. His first great success, *The Moon Pool* (published first in *All-Story Magazine,* 1918) told of a gateway into the Earth and the remnants of a Great Race that dwelt there. *The Face in the Abyss* (1923), which depicted a race of Snake Women in the Andes Mountains; *The Ship of Ishtar* (1924), which described a miniature sailing ship encompassing a cosmos of Good and Evil; and one of his finest stories, "Three Lines of Old French" (1918), which took a World War I infantryman back in history for a lesson in human immortality, followed. Two of his stories were adapted into movies—*Seven Footprints to Satan,* (1927) and *Devil Doll* (from *Burn, Witch, Burn!)* (1933)—although he disowned the results. Scorning orthodox religions, and something of a fatalist himself, Merritt questioned man's complacency in an unknowable, even hostile universe. "For in that vast crucible of life of which we are so small a part," he wrote in *The Metal Monster* (1920), "what other Shapes may even now be rising to submerge us?"

**Merritt, H(iram) Houston** *(1902–1979)* Pioneer neurologist and codeveloper (with Dr. Tracy J. Putnam) in 1936 of the anti-epilepsy drug Dilantin (diphenylhydantoin).

**Merton, Thomas** *(1915–1968)* American Trappist monk and spiritual writer. Merton, known as Father Louis once he became a priest, was one of the most important spiritual writers of his time. After teaching English at Columbia University for a brief period, he entered the Catholic Church (1939), joining the Trappist order at Our Lady of Gethsemane monastery in Kentucky (1941). He was ordained a priest in 1949. Among Merton's many spiritual works are *Seeds of Contemplation* (1949), *No Man Is an Island* (1955) and *Mystics and Zen Masters* (1967).

**Messerschmitt, Willy (Wilhelm Messerschmitt)** *(1898–1978)* German aircraft designer, engineer and industrialist. Messerschmitt made and flew his own gliders at age 15. By age 26, he had formed his own aircraft manufacturing company. He was best known for the airplanes he produced for the Luftwaffe in WORLD WAR II. More than 30,000 of his ME-109 single-engine fighter planes were built; these fighters gave the Luftwaffe air supremacy during the early part of the war. Messerschmitt's ME-262 was the first operational combat jet. After the war, Messerschmitt was examined by an Allied denazification court (1948). The court found that he had been forced to build aircraft for the German war effort against his will. For the next 10 years, Messerschmitt and his company manufactured prefabricated houses and sewing machines. They resumed building airplanes in 1958.

**Messiaen, Olivier** *(1908–1992)* French classical music composer and critic. Messiaen was a highly original composer who led a 1930s movement, the Jeune France, that called for greater feeling and flamboyance in classical music, in contradistinction to the technical and intellectual emphases of the LES SIX school of the 1920s. During WORLD WAR II, Messiaen was imprisoned by the Nazis for two years. After the war, he taught at the Paris Conservatory for several decades. His major works include *Quartet for the End of Time* (1941), *Modes of Duration and Loudness* (1950), *Catalog of Birds* (1959) and *The Transfiguration* (1969). Messiaen summarized his compositional methods in the two-volume work *The Technique of My Musical Language* (1944).

**Messter, Oskar** *(1866–1943)* German inventor, producer and motion picture director. His father ran an optical plant, and by 1896 young Oskar was adapting the American kinematograph and the French cinematographe into devices of his own for the recording, printing and projection of filmstrips. Technically, his greatest innovation was the Maltese Cross, a device that made it possible for a filmstrip to move intermittently through camera and projector. He is also credited with the first use in Germany of the close-up—as early as 1897. In 1910 he founded a company to manufacture film equipment, and in 1914 he began producing the German newsreel *Messter Woche* (The Messter weekly), purportedly the first German newsweekly of its kind. Among his many commercial movies were *Salome* (1902), *Verkannt* (1910), *Richard Wagner* (1912) and *Ungarische Rhapsodie* (1913). He retired from active film production in 1917 when his company, Messter-Film, merged with Nordisk-Film and Viennese Sascha-Film to form the giant conglomerate Universum Film Aktien Gesellschaft (UFA).

**metal music** Also known as "heavy metal" or "punk rock." Metal music emerged in the 1970s as a reaction to the more commercialized variants of "rock 'n roll" or "rock" music, such as disco, and popular artists and bands such as ELTON JOHN and FLEETWOOD MAC. Bands such as Black Sabbath, Judas Priest, and LED ZEPPELIN helped develop the distinctive sound and rhythm of metal music, which relied heavily on the use of electric guitars and bass instruments. However, they provoked criticism from fans of more traditional rock because of their occasionally violent and occult lyrics and musical scores (Black Sabbath), and for destroying their hotel rooms while on national or international tours (Led Zeppelin). As a result of this criticism and because of the novel nature of metal albums, bands and singles, the fan base for this genre of rock—predominantly lower-middle-class and working-class males—remained relatively small.

In the late 1970s, metal music began to include a new wave of bands that propelled metal into the foreground of popular music in the U.S. and Great Britain. Led by bands such as AC/DC, Guns N' Roses, Iron Maiden, KISS, Metallica and Van Halen, metal bands regularly released albums that dominated album sales and radio airwaves. These "second generation" metal bands preserved many of the idiosyncrasies of metal music's founders, such as occasional references to occult rituals and singles emphasizing loud use of electric guitars. However, they differed from their predecessors when they began to utilize the relatively new format of the music video featured on networks such as MTV. In these videos, filmed footage of a band playing one of its songs would be interspersed with visual effects or depictions of a fictional storyline related to the content of the song. Also, in their onstage performances and their music videos, the members of such metal bands became known for their unusual outfits, pyrotechnics, and sexually suggestive lyrics and movements. In large part because of the new image projected by the metal bands of the late 1970s and 1980s, metal music began to develop a large fan base among young women. Many of the principal performers in these bands—such as Eddie Van Halen, David Lee Roth, John Bon Jovi and Axl Rose—becoming sex symbols in the American and British markets. Over the course of the 1980s, an estimated 40 percent of album sales on the American market came from metal bands.

In the 1990s, metal music's popularity declined, as the popular music market became increasingly dominated by alternative or "grunge" rock bands such as R.E.M., Smashing Pumpkins, and Nirvana, as well as by "hip-hop" or "rap" music. As a result, metal bands began to produce less popularly oriented music and return to the more traditional styles favored by the genre's white male working-class listeners. However, there have been occasional exceptions to this rule, as bands such as Bon Jovi and AC/DC have maintained a degree of their popularity from the 1980s, and have scored occasional hits with singles such as Bon Jovi's "It's My Life" (2000).

**metaphysical painting** Term coined by the Italian painter Giorgio de CHIRICO to define a kind of pre-SURREALIST painting that placed objects and figures in unexpected and mysterious juxtapositions. Conceived while de Chirico was in Paris from 1910 to 1915, it arose as a reaction against the dynamism of FUTURISM and exalted the stillness of classical antiquity, the architecture of ancient and Renaissance Italy and the validity of the dream world. Influenced by the philosophy of Nietzsche, Schopenhauer and Weininger, metaphysical painting attempted to portray a magically separate reality, defined by a raked perspective and inhabited by dramatic shadows, enigmatic figures, dressmakers' dummies, classical statuary and colonnaded buildings. The other important adherent of the style was the painter Carlo CARRA, with whom de

Chirico founded the magazine *Pittura metafisica* in 1920.

**Metaxas, Joannis** *(1871–1941)* Greek general, statesman, dictator (1936–41). A career soldier commissioned in the army in 1890, he served in the Greco-Turkish War (1897) and the BALKAN WARS (1912–13). Appointed chief of the general staff in 1915, he was exiled to Italy in 1917 when Greece's entry into WORLD WAR I on the Allied side clashed with his pro-German sympathies. Returning in 1920, he led a coup attempt and was again exiled (1923–24). A leading royalist, he held a number of government posts from 1928 to 1936. In 1936, after the reestablishment of the monarchy, Metaxas was appointed prime minister. He assumed dictatorial powers later that year, dissolving parliament and suspending the constitution. When Greece was invaded by Italy in 1940, Metaxas aligned his country with the Allies and directed Greek RESISTANCE.

**Metro-Goldwyn-Mayer** One of Hollywood's "Big Five" production/exhibition motion picture studios (along with WARNER BROS., RKO, TWENTIETH CENTURY-FOX and PARAMOUNT) and, arguably, the most prestigious. The complex history of its formation began with the establishment in 1912 of a theater chain by former nickelodeon and peep-show entrepreneur Marcus Loew. Needing more movie product, Loew acquired the Metro Picture Corporation in 1920 and Goldwyn Pictures Corp. and Louis B. MAYER Pictures in 1924. The new organization, Metro-Goldwyn-Mayer (MGM), was under the control of Louis B. Mayer as studio vice president and Irving THALBERG as vice president in charge of production. The years up to Thalberg's death in 1936 are generally considered MGM's peak period. Popular and prestigious pictures of that time include *Greed* (1924), *The Big Parade* (1926), *Ben Hur* (1927), *Flesh and the Devil* (1928), *Freaks* (1932), *Grand Hotel* (1932), *The Thin Man* (1934), *David Copperfield* (1935), *Mutiny on the Bounty* (1936) and *The Good Earth* (1936). By the mid-thirties MGM had 4,000 employees and 23 sound stages on its 117-acre lot in Culver City. An average of 40 features were made each year, costing approximately $500,000 each.

By the 1940s MGM's boast that it presented "more stars than there are in the heavens" seemed justified. Luminaries included Greta GARBO, Clark GABLE, the BARRYMORES, Jean HARLOW, Joan CRAWFORD, Spencer TRACY, Mickey ROONEY, Elizabeth TAYLOR, Judy GARLAND, William Powell and many others. Popular series included short subjects—such as "Pete Smith Specialties," "Tom and Jerry" cartoons, and Hal Roach comedies—and feature programs—such as the Andy Hardy, TARZAN, and Dr. Kildare series. MGM also released the pictures of its British production company, Denham Studios under Michael Balcon, including *The Citadel* (1938) and *Goodbye, Mr. Chips* (1939), as well as numerous independently made movies—most notably, *GONE WITH THE WIND* (1939). A particularly noteworthy series of musicals appeared in the 1940s and early 1950s under the guidance of producers and filmmakers Arthur Freed, Stanley Donen, Vincente MINNELLI, and Gene KELLY—*Meet Me in St. Louis* (1944), *The Pirate* (1948), *On the Town* (1949), *An American in Paris* (1952), *Singin' in the Rain* (1953), *Seven Brides for Seven Brothers* (1955) and many others. After 1951 many changes affected the studio. The separation of MGM and the Loew's parent company was forced by government antitrust action. Following a bitter dispute between Mayer and Loew's president, Nicholas Schenck, Mayer was forced to resign and was replaced by his former production chief, Dore SCHARY. More corporate turnovers ensued. In 1969 Kirk Kerkorian bought the studio and began selling off the assets, disposing of the British studios and companies such as MGM Records. A public auction sold off many of the costumes and props. In 1979 MGM merged with United Artists, and the amalgamation has produced only sporadic releases, including the successful *Spaceballs* and *Moonstruck* (1988). In 1986 Kerkorian sold the MGM studio to media mogul TED TURNER. Turner subsequently sold the studio back to Kerkorian while retaining MGM's film library, which he would later use for his cable station, Turner Classic Movies (TCM). In 1990 Kerkorian again sold the studio, this time to Italian financier Giancarlo Parretti. Six years later, Kerkorian again repurchased MGM.

*Metropolis* Prototype of the modern science fiction film. Directed by German filmmaker Fritz LANG in 1926 (and premiered in Berlin early in 1927), its futuristic architectural designs and special effects have had a profound effect on the genre. It was the most lavish and expensive film ever shot at the gigantic UFA studio complex in Berlin. Although it led to the virtual bankruptcy of that studio, and its absurd story of the revolt in the year 2000 of underground workers against their "topside" capitalist bosses was poorly received by the critics, there was no denying its spectacular visual and technical work. Cinematographer Karl Freund and set designers Otto Hunte and Karl Vollbrecht served up spectacular images of a divided world—above, the dazzling modern city of towers and flying machines (presided over by the despotic John Frederson), and below, the nightmarish world of gigantic machines and brain-washed workers (terrorized by the mad scientist, Rotwang). The hallucinatory images of the machines transforming into legendary monsters, the panic of the underworld citizens during a flood and the creation in Rotwang's laboratory of a robot remain unforgettable. The cutting of 7 of its original 17 reels for the American release (1927) accounts for the choppy, occasionally incomprehensible storyline of the release-prints available today.

**Mexican Civil War of 1911** Francisco I. Madero (1873–1913), a U.S.-educated lawyer and liberal, called for the ouster of Mexican dictator Porfirio DÍAZ and opposed him in the presidential election of 1910. Díaz had Madero arrested and, after the balloting, proclaimed himself the victor. On November 20, 1910, Madero and his supporters launched an armed revolt. Although the Porfirian army contained most of the outbreaks in 1911, Pascual Orozco maintained resistance in Chihuahua state, and in May 1911 rebel forces under him and Francisco "Pancho" VILLA captured Ciudad Juárez. Thus encouraged, revolutionaries throughout MEXICO took up arms. With his own support crumbling, Díaz was forced to accept the Treaty of Ciudad Juárez stipulating his prompt resignation; Madero was elected president in October. But Madero could not control the forces he had unleashed, and the events of 1911 ushered in two decades of bloodshed. (See also MEXICAN REVOLT OF 1914–15.)

**Mexican Civil War of 1920** Venustiano Carranza tried to dictate who would succeed him as president of MEXICO (see MEXICAN REVOLT OF 1914–15). He chose a little-known diplomat named Ignacio Bonillas, but Alvaro Obregón, who had helped put Carranza in office and served as his minister of war, felt the office should be his. Obregón's former comrade-in-arms, Adolfo de la Huerta, then governor of the state of Sonora, and General Plutarco Elías CALLES, chief of the Sonoran armed forces, called for Carranza's resignation. When Carranza sent federal troops into Sonora to break a labor strike, Huerta declared Sonora an independent republic. Obregón and Calles marched south, collecting arms and volunteer troops as they went. Finding no soldiers willing to oppose Obregón and his rebel army, Carranza fled from the capital, Mexico City, toward Veracruz aboard a train loaded with gold he had taken from the national treasury. En route, he learned that the governor of the state of Veracruz had joined the rebels; he then fled on horseback into the mountains, where he was betrayed and murdered. Obregón entered Mexico City unopposed; Huerta became provisional president and, after a special election, was succeeded by Obregón later in 1920.

**Mexican Insurrections of 1926–29** Mexico's election of 1924 brought to the presidency Plutarco Elías CALLES, who implemented the previously unenforced anticlerical provisions of the 1917 constitution. In early 1926 officials of the Mexican Roman Catholic Church issued a condemnation of the provisions. Calles responded by closing Catholic schools, convents and seminaries; forcing the registration of priests; and accusing the Catholic hierarchy of treason. In mid-1926 Catholic laypersons retaliated by stopping all but their essential purchases, and soon the Catholic clergy ceased performing clerical functions. The *cristeros*, whose cry was *Viva Cristo Rey* ("Long Live Christ the King"), took up arms against the anticlerical government and caused widespread destruction and murder in a dozen Mexican states. Although the Catholic hierarchy disavowed any connection with the *cristeros*, the government ordered the nationalization of church property, the deportation of several bishops, priests and nuns and the execution of a number of Catholics. Government forces crushed most of the *cristeros* by early 1928. Alvaro Obregón was elected president of Mexico on July 1, 1928. (He was assassinated later that month and was succeeded by Emilio Portes Gil, who was appointed provisional president.) The undisputed political power in Mexico still lay with Calles, even though in March 1929 another insurrection erupted under the leadership of politically and religiously discontented generals whose followers ravaged the country for about two months before the government restored order. Calles influenced the election to the presidency of Pascual Ortíz Rubio (1877–1963) in 1929; a half-hearted military insurrection against Ortíz failed; and Ortíz assumed office as Calles's puppet and continued his anticlerical policies.

**Mexican Revolt of 1914–15** By a successful coup d'état, Victoriano Huerta gained the presidency of MEXICO on February 18, 1913, overthrowing Francisco I. Madero, Huerta was opposed by the separate forces of Emiliano ZAPATA in the south, of Venustiano Carranza in the northeast, of Francisco "Pancho" VILLA in the north, and of Alvaro Obregón in the northwest. These four opposing forces increased their military activities until by the spring of 1914 they controlled about three-quarters of Mexico, confining Huerta and his followers to the areas around Mexico City, the capital, and Veracruz. U.S. president Woodrow WILSON refused to recognize Huerta's government, whose hostile acts resulted in American forces seizing and occupying Veracruz (April 21, 1914). When Villa's forces seized Zacatecas and Obregón's took Guadalajara and Querétaro, Huerta resigned as president. The rival leaders, Villa and Obregón, raced for the capital; Obregón arrived first and proclaimed his friend Carranza "First Chief" of Mexico. The leaders met at Aguascalientes to organize a government in late 1914, but Mexico was already torn by anarchy. Villa and Zapata occupied Mexico City, while Carranza and Obregón took control of Veracruz. Although Villa and Zapata had more troops and held about two-thirds of the country, Carranza was recognized by the U.S. and eight other nations in the Western Hemisphere as de facto president of Mexico. Carranza controlled the northeastern border with the U.S., across which he could purchase arms; he also had the expert military assistance of Obregón and the shrewdness to promise the people social reform. In early 1915, Obregón and his troops occupied the capital, forcing Villa to flee to the surrounding countryside. Villa and his forces were pursued to the town of Celaya, where Obregón employed military tactics developed in WORLD WAR I. His troops dug trenches and strung barbed wire around Celaya, and after a three-day battle in April 1915, they won a decisive victory over Villa, who retreated northward. Villa's men pulled up railroad tracks to prevent pursuit by their foes. Both Villa and Zapata continued guerrilla warfare against Carranza, who later became president officially. Obregón was appointed minister of war. (See also MEXICAN CIVIL WAR OF 1911; MEXICAN CIVIL WAR OF 1920; VILLA'S RAIDS.)

**Mexico** North American republic bordered by the U.S. to the north, the Gulf of Mexico and the Caribbean to the east, GUATEMALA and BELIZE to the south and the Pacific Ocean to the west. Its capital is Mexico City. General Porfirio DÍAZ took control of Mexico's government in 1876, and was its effective dictator for the next 34 years. His capitalist government favored the wealthy, and following a revolution, was toppled by Francisco I. Madero in 1910. Madero was himself overthrown and murdered in 1913 when Adolfo de la Huerta took power. The U.S. did not recognize his government, and landed troops in Veracruz in 1914, but ARGENTINA, BRAZIL and CHILE intervened to prevent a war. Following a raid in the U.S. by the revolutionary Francisco "Pancho" VILLA in 1916, the U.S. invaded northern Mexico in his pursuit, but failed to capture him. Venustiano Carranza initiated constitutional reforms in 1917. Following a brief civil war in 1920, a moderate, socialist government prevailed under the governments of presidents Alvaro Obregón and Plutarco Elías CALLES. In 1929 Calles founded the National Revolutionary Party, which was renamed the Institutional Revolutionary Party (PRI) in 1946, and which has peacefully dominated subsequent Mexican politics. Since 1946, internal Mexican policy has stressed industrialization, which, while benefiting the upper and middle classes, did little for most of its rapidly increasing population. In the early 1980s Mexico's economic problems were exacerbated by a drop in oil prices. The peso was devalued in 1982,

## MEXICO

**1911**  Dictator Porfirio Díaz overthrown by Francisco Madero; guerrillas in the north, led by Pancho Villa, and peasants in the south, led by Emiliano Zapata, revolt, calling for social change and land reform.

**1913**  Madero is shot; General Victoriano Huerta seizes power; Madero's followers unite behind Venustiano Carranza, a state governor, to fight Huerta.

**1914**  Backing Carranza, U.S. president Woodrow Wilson sends Marines to occupy the port of Veracruz to prevent arms from reaching Huerta's army.

**1915**  U.S. halts gun supply to Villa and Zapata, who continue to fight Carranza.

**1916**  Villa forces raid Columbus, New Mexico, killing 18 Americans in revenge for U.S. interference in Mexico; American force of 4,000 searches for Villa in Mexico but does not find him.

**1917**  Revolutionary constitution adopted; it curtails the power of Roman Catholic Church, establishes state education, declares mineral and subsoil rights the property of the nation and promulgates social and labor reforms.

**1919**  Emiliano Zapata killed.

**1920**  Venustiano Carranza killed during revolt led by General Alvaro Obregón, who becomes president.

**1923**  Pancho Villa killed; Marxist painter Diego Rivera begins monumental revolutionary murals for the Ministry of Education and the Agricultural School, Chilpancingo.

**1926–29**  Cristero Rebellion led by militant Catholic priests protesting suppression of church.

**1929**  National Revolutionary Party founded (PNR, named Mexican Revolutionary Party in 1938 and Institutional Revolutionary Party, PRI, in 1946).

**1938**  U.S. and British oil companies expelled and their property expropriated during a period of accelerated reform under President Lázaro Cárdenas.

**1940**  Exiled Bolshevik Leon Trotsky murdered in Mexico by Stalin's agent.

**1942–45**  Mexico enters World War II on side of Allies; war supply exports expand economy dramatically.

**1953**  Women receive right to vote.

**1957**  Diego Rivera dies.

**1968**  Summer Olympics held in Mexico City.

**1976**  Economy suffering from worldwide recession, Mexico devalues currency twice to stabilize economy; after discovery of vast new oil deposits, accelerated production is planned.

**1982**  Close to bankruptcy, caused by rising interest rates and falling demand for oil, government announces it can no longer make payments on foreign debt.

**1985**  Earthquakes cause over 7,000 deaths and $4 billion in property damage.

**1990**  Debt-reduction pact is signed to reduce $54 billion debt to commercial banks; Japanese bankers write off 70% of $8.9 billion in loans; magazine *Proceso* prints names and locations of 57 U.S. Drug Enforcement agents working inside Mexico.

**1991**  U.S. president George H. W. Bush and Mexican president Carlos Salinas de Gortari negotiate free trade agreement, pending ratification by U.S. Congress, against opposition of U.S. organized labor and environmental groups; pollution emergency declared in Mexico City, where respiratory illness is number-one cause of death.

*(Table continues)*

## MEXICO (CONTINUED)

| 1994 | Mexico joins the U.S. and Canada in the North American Free Trade Agreement (NAFTA). |
| 1995 | Following the devaluation of the peso in December 1994, the currency crashes. |
| 1996 | Zapatista National Liberation Front representatives and the Mexican government sign the first of six peace accords. Peace talks break off in September. |
| 1997 | In congressional elections in July, the PRI loses its majority for the first time since 1929. |
| 2000 | In July, the PRI loses the presidency for the first time in 71 years to PAN candidate Vicente Fox. The PAN wins 224 seats, the PRI, 209, and the PRD 67 in the lower house of congress. |
| 2001 | A bill is passed increasing the rights of indigenous peoples. |
| 2002 | Millions of security files are released revealing the torture and killing of hundreds of political activists in the 1960s and 1970s by security forces. |
| 2005 | Security and Prosperity Partnership of North America is signed by Mexico, Canada and U.S. |
| 2006 | Results of July 2 presidential elections are disputed, but Felipe Calderón is formally declared the winner. |

but in the following two years Mexico faced extreme unemployment and inability to pay its foreign debt. A devastating earthquake in Mexico City in 1985 worsened the situation. PRI claimed dominance of the 1985 elections, but there were charges of vote fraud. While a PRI candidate won the presidential election, opposition parties prevailed in the 1989 gubernatorial elections. Mexico, the fourth largest oil-producing nation, benefited from the rising oil prices resulting from the IRAQ invasion of KUWAIT in 1990. Mexican foreign policy has traditionally been dominated by the U.S., but Mexico criticized U.S. intervention in Central America, and also maintains ties with CUBA. Mexico's economic union with the U.S. and Canada in the 1994 NORTH AMERICAN FREE TRADE AGREEMENT (NAFTA) failed to produce the economic prosperity envisioned by President Carlos Salinas de Gortari. The resulting economic downturn played a part in the National Action Party's (PAN) victory in the 2000 presidential elections. Results of the July 2, 2006, elections, which gave a narrow victory to the New Action Party's Felipe Calderón, were questioned by Andrés Manuel López Obrador, of the Revolutionary Democratic Party, but Calderón was officially declared the winner.

**Meyer, Hannes** (*1889–1954*) Swiss-born German architect known for his role at the BAUHAUS where he followed Walter GROPIUS as director (1928–30). Meyer was trained at the technical college at Basel and in Berlin. He began teaching at the Bauhaus in 1927 and also submitted an admired but unsuccessful entry to the Palace of the League of Nations competition held that year. After resigning from the Bauhaus, he worked in the USSR (1930–36) and in Mexico (1939–49) where he was director of an institute for town planning. While at the Bauhaus, Meyer was the editor of eight issues of *Bauhaus* magazine published from 1928 to 1929. The 1965 book by Claude Schnaidt, *Hannes Meyer: Buildings, Projects and Writings,* is a comprehensive survey of his work.

**Meyerhof, Otto Fritz** (*1884–1951*) German-American biochemist. Meyerhof devoted the greater part of his academic life to the study of the biochemistry and metabolism of muscle and shared the NOBEL PRIZE for physiology or medicine with Archibald Hill in 1922. He held professorships at Kiel and Heidelberg universities, was director of physiology at the Kaiser Wilhelm Institute for Biology, Berlin, and was director of research at the Paris Institute of Biology. In 1940 he immigrated to America, where he joined the medical faculty of the University of Pennsylvania. Meyerhof demonstrated that the production of lactic acid in muscle tissue, formed as a result of glycogen breakdown, was effected without the consumption of oxygen (i.e., anaerobically). The lactic acid was reconverted to glycogen through oxidation by molecular oxygen, during muscle rest. This line of research was continued by Gustav EMBDEN and Carl and Gerty CORI, who worked out in greater detail the steps by which glycogen is converted to lactic acid—the **Embden-Meyerhof pathway.**

**Meyerhold, Vsevolod Yemilyevich** (*1874–1942*) Russian actor and director. Meyerhold worked with V. I. Nemirovich-Danchenko and Konstantin STANISLAVSKY at the Moscow Art Theater (1898–1902). In 1902 he founded the Society of New Drama in Russia. His method of production known as "biomechanics" involved reducing the actor to the status of a puppet under the control of the producer. He used a bare stage and stylized gestures. In 1920 he became head of theater in the People's Commissariat for Education. He founded his own theater in Moscow. Innovative and modernistic, he worked closely with Vladimir MAYAKOVSKY. In 1915 he made two films, now lost, *The Strong Man* and *Dorian Grey,* which are known to have influenced contemporary filmmakers. From 1920 Meyerhold had a working studio with student directors, including Sergei EISENSTEIN. Accused of Formalism, he was arrested in 1939 and "disappeared."

**MGB** Russian abbreviation for Ministry of State Security. Name of the Soviet security service (1946–53), and responsible for internal security; the MGB replaced the NKVD and NKGB. Under BERIA's leadership and STALIN's orders the MGB became exceedingly powerful. Jewish intellectuals were harassed in 1949, and an operation was led against the former supporters of ZHDANOV. The wave of terror and the powerful position of the MGB reached its zenith with the discovery of the DOCTOR'S PLOT of 1952. Following the death of Stalin the ministry was once again subordinated to party control and was reorganized as the KGB (Committee of State Security).

**MI5** British counterintelligence organization, created in 1909. MI5 was organized to fight subversion in Britain and to undertake counterintelligence operations abroad. During WORLD WAR I and WORLD WAR II, MI5 was successful in countering German spy networks in Britain. However, it was unable to prove that one of the top agents of MI6, Kim PHILBY, had long been a Soviet spy and had passed top secrets to the USSR There were also allegations that MI5's director, Sir Roger Hollis, was a Soviet secret agent.

**MI6** British intelligence agency, also known as the Secret Intelligence Service (SIS), founded in 1911. The British counterpart of the American OSS and, later, the CIA, MI6 operates under the highest secrecy. During the 1940s and 1950s one of MI6's top agents, Kim PHILBY, was a double agent for the Soviet Union.

**Michener, James A(lbert)** *(1907?–1997)* American novelist best known for his historical epics. There is uncertainty about the actual place and date of Michener's birth. He held a number of diverse jobs, including acting and sportswriting before his education and eventual position as a naval historian in the South Pacific. Michener's first work of fiction was *Tales of the South Pacific* (1947), which inspired the Rogers and Hammerstein musical *South Pacific* (1949, filmed 1958). His

later novels are epic, often historical, adventures and include *The Bridges at Toko-Ri* (1953, filmed 1954), *Hawaii* (1959, filmed 1966, and as "The Hawaiians" in 1970), *Centennial* (1974) and *Alaska* (1988), among many others. Michener's nonfiction includes *The Bridge at Andau* (1957), *America vs. America: The Revolution in Middle-Class Values* (1969); he also wrote on Japanese art.

**Mickey Mouse** World-famous animated film character and ambassador for all Walt DISNEY enterprises. "The mouse that built an empire," as Disney described him, was born on a train somewhere between Chicago and Los Angeles in 1927. Disheartened by the failure of his "Alice" series of cartoons and by the loss of rights to the "Oswald Rabbit" character, Disney recalled his days in Kansas City as a youth when he shared his studio with a field mouse. That mouse (dubbed by his wife Lillian as "Mickey" contrary to Walt's wishes to name him "Mortimer") created a sensation at his first public appearance on November 18, 1928, in New York City's Colony Theater. *Steamboat Willie* (1928) not only launched the mouse but was an innovation in the new technique of synchronized-sound TALKING PICTURES. At a rate of 18 cartoons a year, Mickey soon became a national craze. With faithful Minnie and his arch-nemesis, Peg-Leg Pete, Mickey danced, tumbled, flew, and rode through slapstick adventures on screen and, after 1930, in the daily newspapers for King Features Syndicate. With all the trappings of success—an Oscar, the patronage of British aristocracy, his image in Madame Tussaud's—Mickey after 1940 became more of an entrepreneur than a movie star. He presented classical music to the public in FANTASIA (1940), opened the Disneyland theme park in 1955, the Walt Disney World park in 1971, hosted two television shows—*The Mickey Mouse Club* (1955) and *The New Mickey Mouse Club* (1977)—and lent his stature and image to all Disney-related activities. Before his retirement (albeit a temporary one) in 1953, Mickey made 120 cartoons in all. Walt Disney himself provided Mickey with a voice. And it is well known that Walt's mannerisms, sturdy individuality, occasional shyness all were adapted to Mickey's char-

acter. When Walt died in 1966, Mickey lived on, of course. But the edition of *Paris Match* magazine that appeared at the time displayed Mickey on its cover—with a tear in his eye.

**microchip** A small, often microscopic series of electronic circuits composed of as many as several million minute transistors embedded into a thin square piece of silicon measuring approximately one inch per side. Microchips were developed in 1958 by Jack Kilby, an employee of Texas Instruments, to reduce the physical space occupied by computers by performing the central processing unit (CPU) and memory functions previously held by a noticeably larger series of TRANSISTORS. Initially, microchips facilitated the development of computers by serving as CPUs that accelerated the computation and processing power of these machines. Later advances in CPU structure enabled CPUs to regulate audio and visual output on computer monitors and projection screens, as well as in other complex electronic devices, and other consumer goods, such as televisions, alarm clocks, microwaves, hand-held calculators and Personal Digital Assistants (PDAs). Microchips can also function in a memory capacity in such devices as hand-held calculators and computers.

**Micronesia, Federated States of** The Federated States of Micronesia consist of four major island groups in the North Pacific Ocean (see page 957) with a total area of 271 square miles; its 607 islands vary geologically from mountainous terrain to coral atolls. Spain sold the Carolines, where Micronesia is situated, to Germany in 1899. At the outbreak of WORLD WAR I Japan took possession of the German Pacific colonies, and in 1920 the LEAGUE OF NATIONS mandated control of Micronesia to JAPAN. Truk Lagoon in the Carolines was one of Japan's most important bases during WORLD WAR II. The American Navy took command of Micronesia following Japan's defeat in 1945. In 1947 the United Nations established the Trust Territory of the PACIFIC ISLANDS, under U.S. control.

Moves toward preparing Micronesia for self-government began in the 1960s. In a referendum in July 1978, of the six Trust Territory districts only four islands voted in favor of a common constitution. They became the FSM. In October 1982 the FSM and U.S. governments signed a Compact of Free Association, under which the FSM would be internally self-governing while the U.S. maintained responsibility for defense—primarily to deny access to other powers rather than to establish its own bases. U.S. administration of Micronesia formally ended in November 1986. In 1991, following the termination of its UN trusteeship a year earlier, Micronesia was admitted to the UN. Eleven years later, the sovereign nation of Micronesia, working together with the equally sovereign Marshall Islands, renegotiated its relationship with the U.S., and signed a deal worth an estimated $3.5 billion dollars over a 20-year period.

**Microsoft** American software company. In 1975 Bill GATES and Paul Allen created Microsoft in Albuquerque, New Mexico, to develop new versions of BASIC, a computer programming language, for computer manufacturers such as Apple Computer, Commodore Computer and Tandy. Four years later, Microsoft moved its operations to Bellevue, a town in Washington near Seattle. In 1980 Microsoft landed a contract with IBM (INTERNATIONAL BUSINESS MACHINES) to produce an operating system for the line of PERSONAL COMPUTERS (PCs) that IBM was developing for the consumer and business market. Microsoft then purchased the copyright to 86-DOS, an operating system developed by Tim Paterson, adapted its format and licensed it to IBM as Microsoft Disk Operating System (MS-DOS). However, Microsoft's deal with IBM was not exclusive, and Microsoft sold other licenses to similarly designed personal computers, referred to as "clones." Along with MS-DOS, Microsoft also began developing application programs for business and personal computer use, such as its spreadsheet programs Multiplan (1982) and Excel (1984), and its word processing program Microsoft Word (1984).

In 1985 Microsoft began selling an application program known as Windows, a graphical user interface (GUI) program that allowed IBM and IBM-clone PC users to move a cursor on a computer screen to different images or "icons" that represented different com-

puter files or application programs. Microsoft later issued Windows 2.0 in 1987 and Windows 3.0 in 1990 that offered updated GUI features and improved user performance. Microsoft later issued upgrades to Windows 3.0 with Windows 3.1 and Windows 3.11. When Microsoft and IBM ceased to work together in the production of software in 1991, the former continued to produce improved and increasingly complex updates of its Windows software, such as the business-oriented Windows NT (1993), Windows 95 (1995), Windows 98 (1998), Windows 2000 (2000), and Windows XP (2002).

As Windows and DOS became the most commonly used software programs for PCs in their respective genres, allegations began to emerge that Microsoft engaged in unfair business practices, such as the illegal use of copyrighted software designs, and by making it difficult for rival software companies' programs to interact with PCs running on Windows or DOS. In 1993 Microsoft won a substantial legal victory when a judge ruled that its Windows software did not infringe on the copyright held by Apple Computers for a similar and earlier-developed GUI for Apple's computers. In 1997 the Department of Justice renewed its earlier prosecution of Microsoft for antitrust activities, claiming the corporation had breached a previous agreement by seeking to ensure that PC manufacturers to whom they had licensed Windows 95 also installed Microsoft's web browser, Internet Explorer, as the sole software program for accessing the Internet. In 2000 a federal court ruled that Microsoft had indeed violated antitrust laws by the manner in which it promoted Internet Explorer over its competitors and called for the company to be divided into two separate entities. While an appellate court agreed in 2001 that Microsoft possessed a monopoly over the internet browser market, it reversed the ruling that called for the division of Microsoft.

**Midler, Bette** (1945–  ) American actress and singer. Born in Hawaii, Midler received her first motion picture role in the film *Hawaii*, in which she played the wife of a missionary. She later moved to New York City and joined the cast of the Broadway musical *Fiddler on the Roof* and worked as an

entertainer at the Continental Baths, where she entertained the establishment's homosexual male clientele with musical numbers and costumes from the 1920s through the 1960s. In the 1971 rock opera *Tommy*, she played both the Acid Queen and Mrs. Walker. In 1972 she released her first album, *The Divine Miss M*, which included songs from her routines at the Continental Baths, such as the 1940s piece "Boogie Woogie Bugle Boy." In 1979 Midler starred in *The Rose*, a film inspired by the life and death of rock musician Janis Joplin, earning her a Golden Globe Award and an Academy Award nomination for Best Actress. In 1984 Midler signed a long-term contract with Walt Disney Studios. Although she substantially reduced her concert performance schedule in order to concentrate on her film career, she recorded several songs for the soundtrack of *Beaches*, one of which "The Wind Beneath My Wings," became the number-one single in the U.S. in 1988. Since then, her musical and motion picture careers have rarely overlapped. She played a USO entertainer in *For The Boys* (1991) and appeared in the 1993 CBS television production of the musical *Gypsy*. But most of her musical performances, such as her 1993 single "From A Distance" and her stage show in the same year at Radio City Music Hall, focused on songs independent of her career as an actress.

**Midway** Island group in the central Pacific, northwest of the Hawaiian Islands; site of critical WORLD WAR II naval battle between the American and Japanese navies. One of the decisive battles of the war, Midway (June 3–6, 1942) saw the destruction of the main Japanese carrier fleet and forced Japan into a defensive posture in the Pacific. Unaware that U.S. intelligence had broken Japanese military codes and therefore knew of his intentions, Admiral YAMAMOTO pressed ahead with his plans to seize Midway. The Japanese fleet, including four aircraft carriers and about 250 planes, was intercepted by a U.S. force including three carriers and about 350 aircraft, (plus those stationed on Midway itself). In ferocious dive-bomb attacks, American pilots destroyed all four Japanese heavy carriers, two cruisers, three destroyers, and 250 aircraft and killed 3,500 men;

American losses were two ships, including the carrier *Yorktown*, 150 planes and 300 men. (See also WORLD WAR II IN THE PACIFIC.)

**Mies van der Rohe, Ludwig** *(1886–1969)* German architect and designer; one of the most acclaimed of 20th-century architects. His stylistic penchant for simplicity and clean elegance, as evidenced by his famous saying "less is more," shows itself in both his architectural projects and his furniture designs. He is an important figure both in the history of MINIMALISM and in the development of the international design school of architecture. Mies van der Rohe began his architectural career in 1907 without any formal training. In the early 1910s, he worked for the German-based architectural firm of Peter Behrens, a firm that also numbered among its architects Walter GROPIUS and LE CORBUSIER. From 1930 to 1933 Mies van der Rohe served as director of the BAUHAUS. After the Nazis came to power he remained in Germany for several years. In 1938 he fled to the U.S., where he spent most of the remaining years of his life. His most famous architectural works include the BARCELONA PAVILION (1929) in Barcelona, Spain, a largely glass structure without interior walls, and the Lakeshore Drive Apartments (1948–51) in Chicago, Illinois.

**Mifune, Toshiro** *(1920–1997)* Popular Japanese motion picture actor who was frequently associated with the films of Akira KUROSAWA. He was born in Tsingtao, China, to Japanese parents. His appearance as the bandit in Kurosawa's landmark *Rashomon* (1950) led to a list of notable subsequent collaborations—as a psychologically disturbed police detective in *Stray Dog* (1949), a swashbuckling young *ronin* (masterless samurai) in *Seven Samurai* (1954), a murderous feudal king in *Throne of Blood* (1957), and an opportunistic swordsman in *Yojimbo* (1961). Beyond question he was the best known Japanese actor abroad, appearing in American films like *Hell in the Pacific* (1969) and *Midway* (1976), in which he portrayed Admiral YAMAMOTO. His abilities to convey an inner intensity as well as a flamboyant physicality are perhaps best fused in Kurosawa's *Red Beard* (1965), where he portrayed a quiet, dedicated doctor whose work in the ghettos

forces him to dispatch his enemies with some impressive techniques in judo and swordplay.

**migrant labor** Body of transient or nonnational laborers working in a foreign country. The term is usually specifically applied to the black labor force in SOUTH AFRICA, which was housed in barracks or hostels by employers and separated from their families. Elsewhere, Mexican (Chicano) laborers in the southwestern U.S. (generally referred to as **migrant workers**), Algerian workers in France and Turkish workers (called ***Gastarbeiter***) in Germany and Switzerland are also examples of migrant labor.

**Mihailović, Draza** *(1893–1946)* Yugoslav military leader. Born in southern Serbia, he became an officer and served with the Serbian army during WORLD WAR I. After the fall of Yugoslavia (1941) during WORLD WAR II, Mihailović organized the CHETNIKS (Serbian RESISTANCE forces), and was named minister of war by the Yugoslav government-in-exile. Meanwhile, a communist Resistance group under Josip TITO was also fighting the Nazis, for the most part in Bosnia and Montenegro. As the war continued, Mihailović an ardent royalist and Serbian nationalist, opposed and finally fought Tito—and thus gradually lost Allied support. He was captured by Tito's partisan forces in 1946, tried for treason and sentenced to death. Although voices were raised throughout the world to protest his sentence, Tito considered him a threat to the nascent communist regime, and Mihailović was executed.

**Miki, Takeo** *(1907–1988)* Japanese politician; first elected to the Japanese Diet in 1937 and reelected 19 times before his death, making him the parliament's longest-serving member. In the late 1930s, Miki sought to prevent JAPAN from becoming involved in a war against the U.S. After World War II, he rose to become one of the top leaders of the Liberal Democratic Party. When that party needed a candidate to refurbish its image following the 1974 resignation of Premier Kakuei TANAKA, it drafted Miki. He himself resigned from the premiership two years later in reaction to a poor showing by the Liberal Democrats in a parliamentary election.

**Mikoyan, Anastas Ivanovich** *(1896–1978)* Soviet communist official. Mikoyan joined the BOLSHEVIKS in 1915 and became a member of the POLITBURO in 1926. He served under every Soviet leader from LENIN to BREZHNEV and was in the front rank of the Kremlin hierarchy for nearly 50 years. His longevity was remarkable, considering the mortality rate of high-ranking officials during the rule of STALIN. He became deputy prime minister in 1937. He was later first vice chairman of the Council of Ministers (1955–64) and president of the Soviet Union (1964–65).

**Milburn, Jackie (John)** *(1924–1988)* English football (soccer) star and a member of Britain's most famous footballing family. Milburn gained widespread fame as a center-forward for Newcastle United and for England. After retiring from active play, he became a team manager and, later, a sportswriter.

**Milestone, Lewis** *(1895–1980)* Russian-born HOLLYWOOD film director. Milestone directed more than 30 films in a 40–year career and won ACADEMY AWARDS for *Two Arabian Knights* (1928) and *All Quiet On The Western Front* (1930), adapted from Erich Maria REMARQUE's WORLD WAR I novel. His other film credits included *The Front Page* (written by Ben HECHT and Charles MacArthur), *The General Died at Dawn, Of Mice and Men* (adapted from John STEINBECK's novel), *The North Star* (a WORLD WAR II film set in the USSR), and *A Walk in the Sun*, a classic film about American G.I.s in ITALY during World War II. Milestone's directorial style was noted for its fluid camera technique, crisp dialogue, strong characterization, and vivid realism.

**Milhaud, Darius** *(1892–1974)* French composer. Born in Aix-en-Provence, he trained at the Paris Conservatory (1910–15) under Paul Dukas, Vincent d'INDY and others. He was a diplomatic aide to Paul CLAUDEL in Brazil (1917–18), coming into contact with Brazilian folk music, and later visited the U.S. where he became acquainted with JAZZ. Both forms were to influence his music. Returning to France, he became a member of the modernist group known as LES SIX. Milhaud taught composition at Mills

College, Oakland, California, from 1940 to 1947, teaching thereafter at the Paris Conservatory. A prolific composer, he wrote over 400 works. He used polytonality to great effect in compositions noted for their decided rhythmic structure, excellent craftsmanship and expressive instrumentation. Milhaud is especially celebrated for his operas, including *Le Pauvre Matelot* (1930; libretto by Jean COCTEAU), *Christophe Colombe* (1930; libretto by Claudel), *Bolivar* (1943), *David* (1953) and *St. Louis, King of France* (1970–71; libretto by Claudel). His oeuvre also includes 12 symphonies, concertos, orchestral music, incidental music for plays, chamber pieces, choral works and songs.

**Milland, Ray** *(1905–1986)* Welsh-born actor. He was best known for his role as an alcoholic writer in the 1945 film *The Lost Weekend,* a performance that won him an ACADEMY AWARD for best actor. His 56–year career in Britain and the U.S. included numerous television roles and parts in almost 150 films, including *Dial M for Murder* and *Lady in the Dark.*

**Millar, Richard William** *(1899–1990)* American businessman. He was regarded as one of the pioneers in the development of Southern CALIFORNIA's aerospace industry, and helped to forge strong links between the investment and aircraft communities. He served as president of Bankamerica Corp. before joining Northrop as chairman from 1947 to 1949. After a scandal involving illegal payments to political candidates, Millar was returned as chairman for 1975–76. He continued to serve as a board member until 1984.

**Millay, Edna St. Vincent** *(1892–1950)* U.S. poet. Her poem "Renascence" was given a literary prize by the publication *The Lyric Year* in 1912. After graduating from Vassar in 1917, she published the volume *Second April* in 1921. *The Ballad of the Harp-Weaver* (1922) was awarded the PULITZER PRIZE. Influenced by English poets Keats and Hopkins, she has written on a variety of New England subjects.

**Miller, Arthur** *(1915–2005)* American playwright. One of the most acclaimed American dramatists of the

*American playwright Arthur Miller* (LIBRARY OF CONGRESS, PRINTS AND PHOTOGRAPHS DIVISION)

postwar period, he was born in New York City and educated at the University of Michigan, where he began writing plays. A profoundly serious writer, concerned with the morality of ordinary decisions and the tragic elements of everyday life, Miller scored his first big commercial success with *All My Sons* (1947, film 1948). His next box office triumph was the work widely considered his masterpiece, DEATH OF A SALESMAN (1949, film 1952). Winner of the PULITZER PRIZE, it is the story of Willy Loman, an ordinary man betrayed by the shallow values of the American dream. Miller's social conscience is clear in all his work, and is particularly in evidence in his Tony-winning *The Crucible* (1953), a drama set in the 17th-century Salem witch trials that serves as a parable of the effects of MCCARTHYISM. The Pulitzer Prize–winning tragedy *A View from the Bridge* (1955) details the breakdown of a Sicilian-American working-class family and *After the Fall* (1964) is a fictionalized view of Miller's troubled life with his second wife, Marilyn MONROE. His other plays include *Incident at Vichy* (1965), *The Price* (1968) and *The Creation of the World and Other Business* (1972). He is also the author of a novel, *Focus* (1945), the screenplay for *The Misfits* (1961), a short story collection and the television film *Playing for Time* (1980). Miller remained active throughout the 1990s, composing three plays: *The Ride Down Mt. Morgan* (1991), *The Last Yankee* (1993), and *Broken Glass* (1993). *Broken Glass* went on to win the 1993 Olivier Award for Best Play. Miller

also adapted the script for his play *The Crucible* for a feature film production starring Daniel Day-Lewis and Winona Ryder. In 1997 the film *The Crucible* (1996) earned Miller an Academy Award nomination for best adapted screenplay.

**Miller, Glenn** *(1904–1944)* American big band jazz bandleader, trombonist and arranger. Miller began his career as a trombone player and arranger for various 1930s jazz big bands, including the ensemble led by Jimmy and Tommy DORSEY. In 1938 he formed his own big band, which enjoyed a series of hits, including "Chattanooga Choo Choo," "In the Mood," "Moonlight Serenade" and "Tuxedo Junction." In 1942 Miller volunteered to become the leader of the U.S. Army Air Force band, based in Europe, which aired radio broadcasts to entertain the troops during WORLD WAR II. He died in a 1944 plane crash while en route from England to Paris.

**Miller, Henry** *(1891–1980)* American writer. Miller has been acknowledged by fellow writers as diverse as Norman MAILER, Isaac Bashevis SINGER and John UPDIKE as the leading force in the 20th century in widening the boundaries of literature to include frank portrayals of lust and sexuality. Miller created a sensation with the publication of his classic first work, *Tropic of Cancer* (1934), an autobiographical novel that offered a lyric and bawdy portrayal of bohemian life in Paris. *Tropic of Cancer* was banned as obscene in the U.S. for nearly three decades, before a 1964 decision by the U.S. Supreme Court upheld its literary value. *Tropic of Capricorn* (1936) applied a similar approach to Miller's years of coming to manhood in his native Brooklyn. Miller proved himself a gifted literary critic and philosophical essayist in works such as *The Wisdom of the Heart* (1941), *The Time of the Assassins* (1946), and *The Books in My Life* (1952). *The Colossus of Maroussi* (1941) is a stirring account of Miller's travels in Greece just prior to World War II. *Sexus* (1948), *Plexus* (1963) and *Nexus* (1965) are a trilogy of autobiographical novels.

**Miller, Izetta Jewel** *(1884?–1978)* American actress and feminist. In the early 1920s Miller twice ran for the

U.S. Senate from West Virginia, but was unsuccessful. She was the first woman in the American South to be nominated to run for national office by a major party (the DEMOCRATIC PARTY).

**Miller, Jonathan Wolfe** *(1934– )* British director. Although trained as a medical doctor, Miller has spent most of his life as a director in theater, television and opera. His first success was as coauthor and actor in the 1960 revue BEYOND THE FRINGE. He directed his first play, John OSBORNE's *Under Plain Cover,* in 1962. He is particularly noted for his innovative direction of Shakespeare's plays for television during the 1980s. An associate director of Britain's National Theatre from 1973 to 1975, Miller also served as artistic director of London's Old Vic Theatre from 1986 until March 1991. Among his notable productions are *King Lear* (1969), Chekhov's *Three Sisters* (1976) and Racine's *Andromache* (1988). Since 1991 Miller has directed operas among them, *La Fanciulla del West* (1991), *Le Nozze di Figaro* (1991), *Tamerlano* (2001), and *Die Entführung aus dem Serail* (2003). In 2002 Miller was knighted.

**Miller, Johnny** *(1947– )* American professional golfer. Born in San Francisco, Miller developed an interest in golf after being trained in the game's techniques by his father, Larry, and later by golfing coach John Geertson. This training helped Miller win the 1964 U.S. Junior Amateur Open and rank eighth at the 1966 U.S. Open, in which he played as an amateur. After graduating from Brigham Young University in 1969, Miller joined the Professional Golfing Association (PGA). In his fourth year in the association, Miller won his first major golfing tournament on the PGA's schedule, the 1973 U.S. Open. The following year he won eight PGA tournaments, including the Dean Martin–Tucson Open, the World Open and the Kaiser International. Although he did not win a PGA major event, such as the U.S. Open or the Masters' Tournament, in 1974 he earned more prize money than any other golfer. This achievement represented the first time someone had won what is called the "money title" between 1971 and 1980 other than PGA leaders Jack NICKLAUS or Tom Watson. In 1976 Miller captured his second major tournament, the British Open. Since then he

has won seven PGA tour events, giving him a career total of 24 PGA victories. In 1998, in recognition of his accomplishments in the golfing world, Miller was inducted into the World Golf Hall of Fame.

**Miller, Perry** *(1905–1963)* U.S. historian. Miller received his Ph.D. from the University of Chicago in 1931. He joined the Harvard faculty in 1931 and taught at that university until his death. A giant in the field of intellectual history, Miller wrote extensively on American Puritanism. His works argued that religion rather than economics was the primary motive for Puritan settlement in New England. Among his major works are *Orthodoxy in Massachusetts* (1933), *The New England Mind* (1939), *From Colony to Province* (1953) and *Errant into the Wilderness* (1956).

**Miller, Stanley Lloyd** *(1930– )* American chemist who tested the theory, first proposed by the Russian scientist Aleksandr OPARIN, that life on Earth arose out of a "primordial soup." In 1953, while working toward his Ph.D. at the University of Chicago, Miller published the results of an experiment whereby he produced a number of amino acids in an environment that simulated the early atmosphere of the Earth, which was believed to be similar to that of Jupiter and Saturn. To many scholars his famous paper, *A Production of Amino Acids under Possible Primitive Earth Conditions,* was evidence of the spontaneous origin of life. However, subsequent research has shown that for a single protein to develop from simpler amino acids, other principles would have to be involved. Miller has been a professor of chemistry at the University of California in San Diego since 1968.

**Milligan, Spike (Terence Alan Milligan)** *(1918–2002)* British humorist. Best known for his association with the hit radio program THE GOON SHOW. Milligan had a tremendous impact on British humor. He made his radio debut in "Opportunity Knocks" (1949), then, in collaboration with Peter SELLERS, Harry Secombe and Michael Bentine, cowrote and performed in *The Goon Show* (1949–60). Famous for his zany, surrealistic and slightly skewed brand of humor, Milligan appeared in numer-

ous television series and motion pictures and also on stage, most notably in *Treasure Island* (1961, 1973, 1974, 1975). In addition he wrote many humorous works, including *Puckoon* (1963) and *The Looney: An Irish Fantasy* (1987).

**Millikan, Robert Andrews** *(1868–1953)* American physicist. In 1923 Millikan won the NOBEL PRIZE for physics for determining that the electric charge of an electron was always a simple multiple of the same basic electrostatic unit. In conjunction with this project, Millikan also attempted to demonstrate the validity of Albert EINSTEIN's description of the photoelectric effect, which was cited in his own Nobel award of 1905. Following Millikan's crowning achievement of 1923, he began a major study of cosmic rays, which would occupy him for the rest of his career. He argued that these rays were electromagnetic radiation photons, rather than charged particles, but his theory was later disproved by Arthur COMPTON.

**Mills, Irving** *(1894–1985)* U.S. composer and music publisher. In 1919 he cofounded a music publishing company called Mills Music that was to remain under his direction until 1965. He was best known for his association with Duke ELLINGTON, which began in 1926 and lasted until 1939. After discovering Ellington in a Broadway nightclub, Mills became his publisher and manager, as well as collaborating with him on such songs as "Mood Indigo" and "Sophisticated Lady." He also did much to advance the careers of other such well-known artists as Cab CALLOWAY, Hoagy CARMICHAEL and Milton BERLE.

**Mills, Sir John (Lewis Ernest Watts)** *(1908–2005)* British actor. Mills was one of Britain's finest stage and screen actors since the 1930s. His stage career began at the London Hippodrome in 1929 and included leading roles in such varied works as *Charley's Aunt* (1930), Noel COWARD's drama *Cavalcade* (1931), *A Midsummer Night's Dream* (1939) and Brian Clark's *The Petition* (1987). In 1961 he made his New York stage debut in the title role of Terence Rattigan's *Ross*. Mills has also appeared in numerous films, including *Ryan's Daughter* (1971) for which he won an ACADEMY AWARD as best supporting actor.

**Mills, Wilbur Daigh** *(1909–1992)* American politician. Born in Kensett, Arkansas, Mills was trained as a lawyer and was a probate judge before his election as a Democratic member of the House of Representatives in 1938. A protégé of House Speaker Samuel RAYBURN, he was appointed to the prestigious Ways and Means Committee (1943) and assumed its chairmanship (1958). The House's foremost tax expert, he was a budget-balancing fiscal conservative who nonetheless supported various liberal reforms. He was extremely influential in molding the Tax Reform Act of 1969. Mills's distinguished political career ended in disgrace after his affair with a striptease dancer was revealed. Involved in a notorious incident at Washington's Tidal Basin with "the Argentine Firecracker" in 1974, he soon relinquished his post as committee chair. Mills retired from the House in 1977, later admitting his alcoholism.

**Milne, A(lan) A(lexander)** *(1882–1956)* English author. Although he wrote much fiction and drama for adults, Milne is best known for his whimsical portraits of childhood in his various children's books. He worked as a freelance journalist (1903–06), then as assistant editor of the humor magazine *Punch* (1906–14) before becoming a full-time writer. In collaboration with illustrator E. H. Shepard, Milne created the memorable characters of Christopher Robin and Winnie-the-Pooh, among others, in the prose works *Winnie-the-Pooh* (1926) and *The House at Pooh Corner* (1928), and the books of verse *When We Were Very Young* (1924) and *Now We Are Six* (1927), which have become classics of children's literature. His works for adults include the novel *The Red House Mystery.*

**Milošević, Slobodan** *(1941–2006)* President of the Serbian Republic (1989–97) and of YUGOSLAVIA (1997–2000). The son of an Orthodox priest, Milošević graduated from Belgrade University with a degree in law in 1964. After working in the state-run natural gas company and the United Bank of Belgrade, he was named head of the Belgrade Communist Party in

1978. In 1986 he became the leader of the Serbian Communist Party. On April 24, 1987, Milošević delivered a stridently nationalistic speech to a Serbian crowd in the town of Kosovo Polje that was protesting alleged abuse at the hands of the predominantly Albanian population in the Kosovo region of Yugoslavia. He continued to incite pro-Serb demonstrations that forced the leaders of Kosovo and the multiethnic north Serbian province of Vojvodina to leave office. In May 1989 Milošević was elected president of the Serbian republic within the Yugoslav federal state. Milošević oversaw the creation of a new Serbian constitution that called for direct presidential elections and increased the president's authority, although it limited his tenure to two terms in office. The constitution was adopted in mid-1990 and Milošević won the first direct presidential election in December of that year and was reelected in 1992.

Milošević also became involved in the Serbian effort to prevent the secession of the Yugoslav provinces of BOSNIA AND HERZEGOVINA, SLOVENIA and CROATIA from the federated state. When Slovenia, Croatia, and Bosnia-Herzegovina declared their independence, in 1991–92, Milošević launched a Yugoslav invasion of Bosnia and Croatia, to protect the approximately 580,000 ethnic Serbs living in Croatia and the estimated 1.6 million Serbs living in Bosnia. This Yugoslav civil war raged until Milošević met with Croat and Bosnian leaders at the U.S.-sponsored Dayton Conference in 1995, where he signed the DAYTON ACCORDS and recognized Croatian and Bosnian independence in exchange for safeguards for the Serb population in both countries.

Constitutionally barred from running again for Serbia's presidency, Milošević ran for and won the presidency of Yugoslavia in July 1997. As president of Yugoslavia he led the country into war over the secessionist campaign in Kosovo. With a large ethnic Albanian majority, the province sought to emulate Croatia and Bosnia, employing diplomacy and guerrilla tactics to achieve independence (see KOSOVO LIBERATION ARMY). In 1998 Milošević responded to the insurrection in Kosovo by ordering the expulsion of Albanian Kosovars and the

destruction of their villages. Milošević's military operations in Kosovo ended as a result of a NATO air campaign against Yugoslavia in the spring and summer of 1999.

On September 24, 2000, Milošević ran for reelection as president of Serbia. Although the initial tally had him losing to the opposition candidate, Vojislav Koštunica, Milošević insisted that the margin of victory was narrow enough to warrant a runoff election. This led to protests throughout Yugoslavia, which forced Milošević to resign on October 5. In 2001 Milošević was arrested by the Serbian government and transferred to The Hague, Netherlands, where he was tried by the International Criminal Tribunal for Yugoslavia (ICTY) for alleged war crimes committed during Yugoslavia's civil conflicts of the 1990s. He died in his cell of a heart ailment before the end of his trial.

**Milstein, Nathan** *(1904–1992)* Russian-American violinist. Born in Odessa, Milstein studied in his home city and at the St. Petersburg Conservatory with Leopold Auer. He began playing in Odessa at the age of 15 and followed this performance with a recital in Kiev, where he met and impressed the young Vladimir HOROWITZ. Shortly thereafter, the two began to give concerts together, sometimes joined by Gregor Piatigorsky. Given government permission to leave the USSR for two years, Milstein debuted in Berlin in 1925 and made a stunning impact with his first Paris performance shortly thereafter. He made his first American appearance in 1929 and became a U.S. citizen in 1942. An acclaimed virtuoso with a large classical repertoire, Milstein was known for his phenomenal technique, sure yet delicate style and superb musicianship.

**Mindszenty, József** *(1892–1975)* Hungarian Roman Catholic cardinal. He was ordained a priest in 1915, became a monsignor in 1937 and was appointed bishop of Veszprém in 1944 while the Germans occupied HUNGARY. Outspoken in his anti-Nazi views and his opposition to the persecution of Jews, he was arrested by Hungarian Nazis and imprisoned from 1944 to 1945. After World War II, he was named archbishop of Esztergom and primate of Hungary, becoming a cardinal in 1946. As opposed to communism as he was to fascism, he was again arrested in 1948, by the Hungarian government; charged with treason and currency offenses, he was convicted and sentenced to life in prison. Freed during the HUNGARIAN UPRISING of 1956, he took refuge in Budapest's American embassy when the revolt was crushed by the Soviets. He remained there as a symbol of opposition to communism, refusing to recognize the 1964 resumption of relations between the Vatican and Hungary. As stubborn as he was committed, Mindszenty finally left Budapest for Rome in 1971, but he remained anathema to the Hungarian regime. In 1974 Pope PAUL VI, in an attempt to improve relations between Hungary and the Vatican, officially removed Mindszenty as Hungarian primate.

**Mingus, Charles** (*1922–1979*) American bassist-composer, one of jazz history's towering giants. Growing up in Los Angeles, his first notable experiences were with such traditionalists as trombonist Kid ORY, trumpeter Louis ARMSTRONG and vibraphonist Lionel Hampton. After moving to New York, Mingus worked with such bebop giants as trumpeter Dizzy Gillespie and saxophonist Charlie PARKER. As a bassist, Mingus displayed a virtuoso technique and remarkably broad stylistic range; his thorough command of the major jazz styles was a hallmark of his composing as well. And, in works such as "Ysabel's Table Dance" (1957), "Fables of Faubus" (1959) and "Epitaph" (1962), one finds traces of jazzdom's various traditions; also present are dark sonorities (achieved with low-pitched instruments), collective improvisations (an influence on the 1960s "free jazz" movement) and overlapping riff or ostinato figures. Mingus worked out the details of his music, where traditional distinctions between written and improvised sections were often blurred, in various "workshop" situations. His compositions were under constant revision in "performances" resembling rehearsals more than formal concert presentations. A temperamental iconoclast, Mingus lived much of his life in economic and emotional chaos. His sensational autobiography, *Beneath the Underdog,* was published in 1971.

**minimalism** Name for an aesthetic approach that minimizes consciously artistic and illusory effects. Minimalism emerged in the 1960s as a significant force, especially in the visual arts and in music. Painters such as Barnett Newman and Ellsworth KELLY employed flat colors and stark geometrical shapes in their canvasses, while sculptors such as Carl André and Donald Judd displayed basic shapes and structures such as piled bricks and white-painted cubes. In music, minimalism showed itself in the simple melodic and harmonic progressions of composers such as Philip GLASS, Steven Reich and Terry Riley. In addition, minimalism influenced architectural design, although its key exponent in this field—MIES VAN DER ROHE—was a precursor rather than a follower of minimalism. In literature, the minimalist aesthetic played a tangential role in shaping French NOUVELLE ROMAN theory and also influenced the verse of Robert CREELEY and other American poets.

**Minnelli, Vincente** (*1910–1986*) American motion picture director. Recognized for his innovative use of color, he was best known for such film musicals as *Meet Me in St. Louis* and *Gigi,* for which he won an ACADEMY AWARD in 1958. He and his first wife, Hollywood legend Judy GARLAND, were the parents of movie star Liza Minnelli.

**Minton, Sherman** (*1890–1965*) Associate justice, U.S. Supreme Court (1949–56). A graduate of Indiana University and Yale University Law School, Minton served as Indiana public counselor before being elected to the U.S. Senate as a NEW DEAL Democrat in 1934. Defeated for reelection in 1940, he secured a federal post in Washington and was later appointed a justice of the U.S. Court of Appeals for the Seventh Circuit. He was appointed to the Supreme Court in 1949 by President Harry S TRUMAN, with whom he had served in the Senate. Despite his liberal background, Minton proved to be a conservative on the Court, especially in cases involving criminal law. He dissented in many civil liberties decisions in the WARREN Court, but supported the majority decision in *BROWN V. BOARD OF EDUCATION.* He resigned from the Court for health reasons in 1956.

**Minutemen** Members of an extreme right-wing society founded in the U.S. in the 1960s to organize resistance to a feared Communist invasion. The organization had several hundred members, mainly in California and Illinois, and was declared subversive by the U.S. attorney general in 1965.

***Miranda v. Arizona*** (**"right to remain silent"**) (*1966*) Landmark American criminal case that established that criminal suspects must be informed of the constitutional right against self-incrimination when they are arrested. The Fifth Amendment of the U.S. Constitution provides that an individual accused of a crime cannot be compelled to testify against himself: The accused has the right to remain silent. The Supreme Court held that, on arrest, an individual must be informed of this right to remain silent before any interrogation may take place. In *Miranda,* the accused's conviction was reversed because he had been convicted based on a confession he had given without being informed of his rights. The rendition of the defendant's "Miranda rights" on arrest are familiar to viewers of television or motion pictures: "You have the right to remain silent; anything you say may be used in evidence against you in a court of law; you have the right to an attorney."

**Mir Iskusstva (World of Art)** Movement in Russian art at the turn of the 20th century. It took its name from the periodical founded by DIAGHILEV, which appeared from 1898 to 1904 and which published articles on modern Western European painting. At the same time, it also evaluated traditional Russian art. Diametrically opposed to the utilitarian idea that art should serve a socially useful function, the society advocated art for art's sake. It also organized several exhibitions to which the leading Russian artists of the day sent their work. Following the events of 1917, many of the Mir Iskusstva group emigrated. Among their number were Leon BAKST, Alexander BENOIS, Mstislav Dobuzhinsky, Michael LARIONOV and Nicholas ROERICH. Some of them collaborated with Diaghilev's BALLETS RUSSES.

**Miró, Joan** (*1893–1983*) Spanish-born artist. During the 1920s he was one of the leading Surrealist painters in Paris, along with André MASSON, Antonin ARTAUD, and André BRETON. Miró's work combined elements of CUBISM and Catalan primitive art and was often dominated by bright colors and abstract designs. A long collaboration with the potter Joseph Artigas resulted in major works, including the large ceramic murals at Harvard University and at the UNESCO building in Paris. As well as a painter, Miró was also an accomplished sculptor, printmaker, potter and stage designer. His work particularly influenced American ABSTRACT EXPRESSIONIST painters such as Arshile Gorky, Robert MOTHERWELL and Jackson POLLOCK. (See also SURREALISM.)

**Mir space station** Orbiting space station constructed and maintained by the Soviet, and later Russian, space agencies. In 1986 the Soviet space program began launching modules into orbit. When assembled by Soviet cosmonauts, these modules, which served as living quarters and scientific laboratories for the *Mir* crews, formed the *Mir* space station. Although Soviet personnel originally conceived of a five-year lifespan for *Mir,* as indicated by their placing of the space station in a low-earth orbit 250 miles above the earth's surface, *Mir* surpassed their expectations and survived for 15 years. During that time, it held on average three crewmembers, ranging from technical personnel to scientists, and provided the facilities for such experiments as the growth of wheat in outer space. On June 29, 1995, the docking of the U.S. space shuttle *Atlantis* provided a venue for cooperation between Russian and American space agencies to resupply the station and transport personnel. It was also aboard *Mir* that the longest record for a single, continuous stay in space—437 days, 17 hours and 38 minutes—was set by cosmonaut Valeri Polakov. However, *Mir* encountered several problems during its relatively long lifespan. Two of its four science modules, Kvant-2 and Kristall, regularly supplied low yields from their solar blankets as a result of repeated tears in these structures from descending debris. Additional problems included *Mir's* lack of procedures for disposing of waste products such as trash and defunct equipment, and the 1997 incapacitation of the Spektr

module when a supply vehicle collided with it to render it uninhabitable. Because of these continuing structural problems, as well as the Russian space agency's increasing commitment to the *International Space Station,* the Russian government sanctioned *Mir's* destructive reentry into the Earth's atmosphere. After plotting a trajectory that substantially reduced the possibility of space-station debris striking inhabited areas, *Mir* reentered the Earth's atmosphere on March 23, 2001, and proceeded to disintegrate above an uninhabited region of the southern Pacific Ocean.

**Mirza Ali Khan** *(1901?–1960)* Fakir of Ipi, Pashtun tribal leader (on the Pakistan-Afghanistan border). A Muslim religious fanatic, he led violent uprisings in 1931–32. He was later financed by Axis agents to keep an estimated 36,000 British troops occupied with tribal warfare in the region.

**Mishima, Yukio (Kimitake Hiraoka)** *(1925–1970)* Japanese novelist, short story writer, dramatist. The scion of a noble samurai family, after receiving a law degree from Tokyo Imperial University in 1947, Mishima worked briefly in the Finance Ministry. His semi-autobiographical *Confessions of a Mask* (1949) touches on his homosexuality and desire for an early and glorious death. Rejected for service in World War II because of his frailty, Mishima embarked on a regimen of strenuous body-building and samurai training. In 1968 he formed a private army of 83 youths, the goal of which was to return Japan to its prewar non-Western traditions. On November 25, 1970, an hour or two after delivering the final manuscript of his tetralogy to the publisher, Mishima and four of his soldiers took the commander of the Eastern Ground Self-Defense Forces as hostage and in view of 1,200 witnesses committed ritual seppuku (disembowelment) while crying "Long live the Emperor!" Mishima was a prolific, some said facile, writer. Among his works in translation are *Five Modern Noh Plays* (1957), *The Temple of the Golden Pavilion* (1959), *The Sailor Who Fell from Grace with the Sea* (1965), *Death in Midsummer and Other Stories* (1966) and *Thirst for Love* (1969). Mishima himself regarded *The Sea of Fertility: A Cycle of Four Novels*

(1972–74) as the culmination of his work.

**Missouri, USS** U.S. Navy Iowa-class battleship; commissioned on June 11, 1944, it is the last of the super-dreadnoughts built by the U.S. On September 2, 1945, in the presence of General Douglas MACARTHUR and other Allied officers, Japanese officials signed surrender papers aboard the *Missouri* in Tokyo harbor, ending WORLD WAR II. (The papers are now displayed in the Truman Library in Independence, Missouri.) In 1986, in an effort to restore American naval strength, the *Missouri* was re-outfitted and reactivated.

**Mistral, Gabriela (Lucila Godoy Alcayaga)** *(1889–1957)* Chilean poet, educator, stateswoman. Though she won her reputation as a poet with *Sonetos de la muerte,* which received the National Poetry Prize in 1914, Mistral had a parallel vocation first as a rural schoolteacher, later as director of schools throughout Chile and a university professor. The early suicide of her fiancé after discovery of his embezzlement of funds had a profound effect on the tone and themes of her work, which expressed despair and loneliness as well as sympathy with oppressed peoples and sometimes reflected a religious sensibility. Mistral represented Chile as honorary consul in Brazil, Spain, Portugal and the U.S. Between 1922 and 1938 she worked with Mme. CURIE and Henri BERGSON in the LEAGUE OF NATIONS. In 1945 she became the first Latin American to win the NOBEL PRIZE. After World War II she was associated with a number of American universities. She died at her translator's home in Hempstead, New York. Her works include *Desolación* (1922), *Ternura* (1924), *Tala* (1938) and *Lagar* (1954).

**Mitchell, Clarence M.** *(1911–1984)* Black American CIVIL RIGHTS activist. Mitchell was Washington lobbyist for the NATIONAL ASSOCIATION FOR THE ADVANCEMENT OF COLORED PEOPLE (NAACP) (1950–78). During much of the same period, he also lobbied for the Leadership Conference on Civil Rights. He first drew national attention in 1956, when he was arrested for refusing to use a blacks-only entrance to the Florence, South Carolina, railroad station. He was instrumental in the passage of the CIVIL RIGHTS ACT OF 1964, the VOTING RIGHTS ACT OF 1965 and the Fair Housing Act of 1968. Mitchell was so influential among federal lawmakers that he was sometimes called the "101st senator." In 1980 he was awarded the presidential Medal of Freedom by President Jimmy CARTER.

**Mitchell, Edgar** *(1930– )* U.S. astronaut and the sixth person to walk on the Moon; Mitchell was lunar module pilot of Apollo 14 (January 31–February 9, 1971). Mitchell and fellow moonwalker Alan SHEPARD spent over 33 hours investigating the Moon's surface. A Navy pilot, he was one of 19 astronauts selected by NASA in April 1966; he retired from the navy and resigned from NASA in October 1972. Strongly interested in ESP (extrasensory perception) and the paranormal, Mitchell, who had attempted an ESP experiment during his APOLLO flight, founded the Institute for Noetic Studies, in Palo Alto, California. The purpose of the institute is to continue studies into ESP and similar activities. In 1974, Mitchell's coauthored book, *Psychic Exploration: A Challenge for Science,* stirred up a brief flurry of interest among ESP believers.

**Mitchell, Joan** *(1926–1992)* American painter. She was born in Chicago and attended Smith College, Columbia University, the Chicago Art Institute School and New York University. She lived in France since 1959 and was greatly influenced by the work of Claude MONET and Willem DE KOONING. A member of the second generation of ABSTRACT EXPRESSIONISM, Mitchell was known for her large, lush and highly sophisticated canvases.

**Mitchell, John Newton** *(1913–1988)* U.S. attorney general (1969–72) and director of the Committee to Reelect the President in 1972, Mitchell was one of President Richard NIXON's closest and most loyal advisers. The bugging of the offices of the Democratic National Committee in the WATERGATE apartment complex in 1972 and the scandal that followed led to his downfall. Mitchell spent 19 months in a federal prison, from 1977 to 1979, following his conviction for conspiracy, obstruction of justice and perjury.

**Mitchell, Joni (Roberta Joan Anderson)** *(1943– )* Canadian folk and rock and roll songwriter, vocalist, guitarist and painter. Mitchell, who was raised in Alberta, Canada, turned to music while attending the Alberta College of Art. She moved to Detroit in 1965, signed her first record contract in 1967 and soon gained a reputation as a first-rate songwriter after her songs were covered by stars such as Johnny Cash and Judy COLLINS. Mitchell's own debut album, *Song to a Seagull* (1968), was a critical and popular success due in large measure to her emotive and soaring voice. Her third album, *Ladies of the Canyon* (1970), featured her first hit single, *Big Yellow Taxi*. Other noteworthy albums by Mitchell include *For The Roses* (1972), *Court and Spark* (1974), *Mingus* (1979), her tribute to jazz giant Charles MINGUS, and *Dog Eat Dog* (1985). Mitchell continued to record throughout the 1990s, releasing albums such as *Night Ride Home* (1991), *Turbulent Indigo* (1994), *Hits and Misses* (1996), *Taming the Tiger* (1998), and *Both Sides Now* (2002). She was inducted into the Rock and Roll Hall of Fame in 1997. In September 2002, shortly before the release of her latest compilation *Travelogue* (2002), Mitchell announced that *Travelogue* was her last album and that she intended to retire from the industry. A month later Mitchell reversed her decision and announced she would continue recording.

**Mitchell, Margaret** *(1900–1949)* U.S. novelist. Interested in local history from an early age, she began to

*Songwriter and musician Joni Mitchell* (PHOTOFEST)

write for the *Atlanta Journal* in 1922 under the name Peggy Mitchell. In 1926 she started work on a novel based on stories told by family and friends. The outcome was *Gone with the Wind* (1936), which won a PULITZER PRIZE in 1937. It has since become one of the best selling novels of all time and the basis of the immensely popular movie of the same name released in 1939.

**Mitchell, Reginald Joseph** *(1895–1937)* British aircraft designer. Mitchell designed some of the most innovative airplanes of the 1920s. His S-4 Floatplane (seaplane) won the prestigious Schneider Cup in 1927, 1929 and 1931. During the 1930s Mitchell visited GERMANY and witnessed the might of the Luftwaffe, the new German air force created by HITLER and GÖRING. Realizing that war with Germany was probable and that the RAF was unprepared, he worked frantically to design a British fighter plane that could outmaneuver German fighters and shoot down German bombers. The product of his labors was the **Spitfire**, which first flew in 1936. Mitchell was already gravely ill and died the following year, before the fighter could prove itself in combat. The Spitfire helped give the RAF the edge in the BATTLE OF BRITAIN. Referring to "the few" (the Spitfire pilots) to whom so many owed so much, Prime Minister Winston S. CHURCHILL acknowledged Mitchell as the "First of the Few."

**Mitchell, William "Billy"** *(1879–1936)* U.S. Army officer. In 1898, Mitchell dropped out of college and enlisted in the army for the Spanish-American War. In 1915, he joined the aviation division of the Army Signal Corps and the following year was promoted from captain to major. With the U.S. entry into WORLD WAR I, Mitchell became an air officer of the American Expeditionary Forces, and in extensive combat he proved himself a talented air commander. In 1919 Mitchell was named assistant chief of the Air Service, in which capacity he became a vocal proponent of an independent air force and of enhanced air preparedness. By 1925, however, Mitchell's superiors had tired of his hectoring; they demoted him to colonel and transferred him to a much less visible position. That same year, when the navy's dirigible *Shenandoah* was lost in bad weather, Mitchell made a statement to the press charging the navy and the War Department with "incompetence, criminal negligence, and almost treasonable administration of the national defense." For this insubordination, he was court-martialed and given five years' suspension of pay and rank. Mitchell resigned from the army in February 1926 and retired, although he continued to promote the supremacy of air power.

**Mitchum, Robert** *(1917–1997)* American actor. Raised in New York City, Mitchum worked at a number of odd jobs and joined a local theater group. He moved to Southern California and acted in a community theater before making his first film, a western, in 1943. The sleepy-eyed actor became the archetypical HOLLYWOOD tough guy in such movies as *The Big Steal* (1949), *The Racket* (1951), *Cape Fear* (1962), *Farewell, My Lovely* (1975) and *The Big Sleep* (1978), the latter two based on detective novels by Raymond CHANDLER. A versatile actor, he also undertook comedy roles in such motion pictures as *Two for the Seesaw* (1962) and dramatic parts in such films as David LEAN's *Ryan's Daughter* (1970). In the latter part of his career, Mitchum became well known for his performances in such 1980s television miniseries as *North and South, The Winds of War* and *War and Remembrance.*

**Mitford sisters** English authors and daughters—Jessica (1917–1996), Nancy (1904–73), Unity (1914–48), Diana (1910–2003), Pamela (1907–94) and Deborah (b. 1920)—of the second baron Redesdale and his wife, Sydney Bowles. Jessica and Nancy have achieved international recognition as authors. Jessica is known for her journalistic exposés and her books that investigate controversial political and social issues. Her most famous works include *The American Way of Death* (1963); an anthology of her articles titled *Poison Penmanship: The Gentle Art of Muckraking* (1979); and her autobiography, *Daughters and Rebels* (1960). Nancy gained acclaim as a novelist, biographer and essayist. Her witty, often satirical novels about the English upper class include *Love in a Cold Climate* (1949) and *The Blessing* (1959). Her major biographies include *The Sun King* (1966), about Louis XIV of France. As editor of a volume of essays, *Noblesse Oblige: An Inquiry into the Identifiable Characteristics of the English Aristocracy* (1956), she helped to introduce the classification of English locution into "U" (upper class) and "Non-U" (non-upper class). Of the remaining sisters, Unity gained notoriety as a follower and friend of Adolf HITLER, and Diana married the leader of the British fascists, Sir Oswald MOSLEY. Deborah became the duchess of Devonshire, and Pamela ran a large farm.

**Mitterrand, François** *(1916–1996)* President of FRANCE (1981–95). Mitterrand entered politics in 1946 as socialist deputy for the Nièvre department. He was a left-wing candidate against President DE GAULLE in 1965. After disagreement among the French socialist parties in the late 1960s, he recovered his political authority and was accepted as leader of the left throughout the 1970s. Again unsuccessfully contesting the presidency in 1974, in 1981 he defeated Valéry GISCARD D'ESTAING with barely more than 50 percent of the vote. From 1981 to 1986 Mitterrand was backed by a socialist majority in the National Assembly; but, following the parliamentary elections of 1986, he had to share power with a Gaullist majority led by Jacques CHIRAC as prime minister. Mitterrand was reelected president in 1988. Despite his socialist background, he proved a pragmatic leader, at times following an austerity program to deal with economic problems. A strong supporter of the EUROPEAN ECONOMIC COMMUNITY, Mitterrand allied France with the U.S.-led coalition in the 1991 war against Iraq, sending French combat forces to the region. Mitterrand was succeeded by Chirac as president in 1995 and died of cancer a year later amid damaging allegations that he had maintained friendly relations with an official in the Vichy regime during World War II who had been involved in the deportation of Jews to the death camps.

**Mix, Tom** *(1880–1940)* American motion picture actor. Mix claimed to have served in the Spanish-American War (1898), and became a cowboy in Oklahoma in 1906. He got involved in wild west shows, attracted the attention of movie makers and entered movies in 1910. His expert horsemanship made him a HOLLYWOOD star, and during the 1920s he was the leading box office draw. He appeared in more than 100 films, and made his last movie, *The Miracle Rider,* in 1935. During the 1930s he toured the country with his own wild west show. He died in an auto accident in the Southwest in 1940. The Tom Mix Museum is located in Dewey, Oklahoma.

**Miyazawa, Kiichi** *(1919– )* Japanese politician, prime minister (1991–93) and finance minister (1998–2001). Born in Fukuyama to a prominent political family in Imperial Japan, Miyazawa graduated from Tokyo University and then worked for the Japanese Finance Ministry during the U.S. occupation of Japan. In 1953 he ran as a candidate of Japan's Liberal Democratic Party (LDP) for a seat on the House of Councilors, the Upper House of the Japanese parliament. After winning that election he served in that body until 1965. After a two-year absence from politics, Miyazawa was elected to the House of Representatives. He began to serve in several ministerial positions, including minister of international trade and industry (1970–71), foreign minister (1974–76), finance minister (1986–88) and deputy prime minister (1987–88). Because of his success in his various positions, he was elected the party leader of the LDP in 1991, which also resulted in his becoming prime minister. Miyazawa promptly encountered obstacles within the LDP when he attempted to reform the party's structure and enlarge its support base. In the 1993 national elections these conflicts contributed to the LDP's first defeat in 38 years, which prompted Miyazawa to resign as head of the LDP. In 1998 Miyazawa briefly returned to power when he joined a coalition government as minister of finance in an effort to stem the economic recession in which Japan had languished since 1997. Despite his efforts, Japan's economy continued to remain stagnant, leading to his resignation from the Finance Ministry in 2001.

**Mizoguchi, Kenji** *(1898–1956)* Japanese filmmaker. Born in Tokyo, Mizoguchi worked as a textile designer and newspaper illustrator before turning to filmmaking in the early 1920s. In addition to his distinguished body of 85 films—he was acknowledged as Japan's chief filmmaker during the 1940s—he also headed Japan's vast union governing all film production personnel. His reputation in the West was confirmed with *The Life of Oharu,* which won the Grand Prize at the Venice Film Festival in 1952. His post-war films, made with scriptwriter Yoshikata Yoda, actress Kinuyo Tanaka and the Daiei Films Studio, constitute an enduring string of masterpieces. His major themes include the ill-treatment of women (*Saikaku ichaidai onna [The life of Oharu],* 1952) and the samurai epic (*Shin Heike monogatari [New tales of the Taira clan],* 1955). His extraordinary camera technique eschews traditional montage for the choreography of the moving camera and the revelation of the deep-focus shot. The viewer is both involved and distanced at the same time. *Ugetsu* sums up Mizoguchi's artistic and commercial priorities. The potter, Genjuro, abjures his crude wares for the more "artistic" creations inspired by his love for a spirit, the Lady Wakasa; he achieves a compromise between his commercial and elitist concerns. A revival of Mizoguchi's work was led in the 1960s by French NOUVELLE VAGUE artists Jean-Luc GO-DARD and Jacques Rivette.

**Mizrachi** Right-wing political party in ISRAEL; partner of HAPOEL HAMIZRACHI in the National Religious Party.

**Mladić, Ratko** (*1943–* ) Yugoslav and Bosnian Serb military commander, and alleged war criminal. After enrolling in the Yugoslav military-industrial school at Zemun, in 1958, Mladić joined the Yugoslav People's Army. In 1991 he rose to the rank of commander of the 9th Corps of the Yugoslav People's Army, stationed in the Yugoslav province of CROATIA. Soon thereafter, the provinces of Croatia and SLOVENIA declared their independence from the federal state. Mladić headed the abortive campaign to suppress the Croatian independence movement, inflicting serious casualties on the Croat forces and evicting thousands of Croat civilians from their homes. In 1992 Mladić was promoted to command the 80,000-man Yugoslav Army stationed in the Serbian Republic of Bosnia, a political entity created on April 6, 1992, to forestall the independence move-

ment in the former Yugoslav province of BOSNIA AND HERZEGOVINA. In 1995 Mladić led Bosnian Serb militia forces into Srebrenica and Zepa, two areas designated as safe zones by the United Nations, expelling 40,000 Bosnian Muslim refugees and killing as many as 8,000. These acts prompted the International Criminal Tribunal for the Former Yugoslavia (ICTY), located at The Hague, Netherlands, to indict Mladić and the political leader of the Serbian Republic of Bosnia, Radovan Karadžić, for war crimes. In 1996 the ICTY issued a warrant for Karadžić's and Mladić's arrest, prompting the latter's dismissal as the head of the military forces of the Serbian Republic of Bosnia. However, despite the warrant and $5 million reward offered by the U.S. government for information leading to Mladić's arrest, the former military leader remains at large, though he has been occasionally spotted in both Serbia and Bosnia.

**Mobutu Sese Seko (full name Mobutu Sese Seko Kuku Ngbendu Wa Sa Banga; Joseph Desere Mobutu)** (*1930–1997*) President of ZAIRE (formerly the Republic of the Congo, 1965–97). Mobutu was educated at mission schools and later at the Institute of Journalism in Brussels. He served in the Congolese army (1956–58) and worked for the newspaper *L'Avenir* (1956–58). He joined Patrice LUMUMBA's nationalist movement in 1957 and was a delegate at the roundtable conference on the Congo in Brussels (1959–60). During the political crisis surrounding the struggle between Lumumba and Joseph KASAVUBU, Mobuto took power in the name of the army in September 1960 until parliament was recalled in August 1961. Col. Mobutu was promoted to major general in 1961, later rising to lieutenant general and commander in chief of the Congolese armed forces. He supported Moise TSHOMBE's leadership bid in 1964; but after intervening in the ensuing conflict between Tshombe and Kasavubu, Mobutu took power himself, becoming president of the Republic of Congo in November 1965. He remained in power and dominated the public life of Zaire. Mobutu adopted his present name in January 1972 as part of his Africanization policy. He is thought to have amassed enormous wealth; his fortune has been

estimated at $5 billion and includes substantial property in Zaire and Europe. He was chairman of the OAU in 1967. Mobutu was expelled from Zaire in May 1997 by rebel forces. He died later that year in Morocco.

**Moch, Jules** (*1893–1985*) French politician. A Socialist, Moch played a major role in French politics both before and after World War II. During his career he held such posts as minister of public works, minister of the interior and minister of defense. As interior minister, he took measures to crush a series of Communist-led strikes in 1947 and 1948. His actions led to the permanent decline of the French Communist Party. In October 1949 he was premier of FRANCE for three days.

**modal jazz** Popular jazz style originally appearing in the late 1950s. Instead of following the comparatively complex chordal patterns found in the standard tunes of Tin Pan Alley, Broadway and Hollywood that were typically favored by jazz players up to the 1950s, the modal approach employs a limited number of predetermined or modal scales based loosely on the classical modes (dorian, phrygian, etc.) first used by the ancient Greeks. Though providing the system's basic melodic and harmonic building blocks, modal scales are seldom deployed in their pure form; indeed, like the frequent alterations and harmonic "substitutions" found in the traditional diatonic approach, improvisers using modal strategies have added their own contrasting harmonic colors and ornamentations. The broad acceptance of the modal approach can be explained by its relative harmonic simplicity and its exotic and meditative overtones; indeed, some modal approaches are based on various Middle Eastern, Oriental and minor scales. Modality was introduced by pianist Bill EVANS and most significantly because of his widespread visibility, trumpeter Miles DAVIS; Evans's "Peace Piece" (1958), Davis's "All Blues" (1959) and saxophonist John COLTRANE's "Impressions" (1963) are prime examples of modal compositions found in the contemporary jazz repertory.

**modernism** General term to describe certain artistic and cultural movements; used by critics since the mid 20th century. Modernism is a concept that eludes precise definition, most likely because it has been used by so many analysts in such disparate contexts that no precise definition can avoid being overly narrow. Fundamentally, modernism refers to the tendency of 20th-century art, literature and music to value innovation and reformulation over and above received cultural and aesthetic traditions. Artists whose work exemplifies the modernist approach include Pablo PICASSO in painting, James JOYCE in literature, Ezra POUND in poetry, Igor STRAVINSKY in music and Ludwig MIES VAN DER ROHE in architecture. Modernism is regarded by some critics as having reached an end in the 1950s and 1960s, at which time it was superseded by POSTMODERNISM. Other critics argue that modernism is better viewed as a pancultural phenomenon the essentials of which can be discerned in all eras of human civilization.

## Modigliani, Amedeo (1884–1920)

Italian painter. Born in Livorno, Modigliani settled in Paris in 1906 and remained there for the rest of his life. His early work was influenced by CUBISM, by the artists Pablo PICASSO and Paul Cézanne and by African sculpture. His first paintings were characterized by distorted figures and large areas of flat color. Under the influence of his friend, Constantin BRANCUSI, Modigliani produced a number of important sculptures, such as *Caryatid* (1914, Museum of Modern Art, New York City), notable for their stylized vertical forms. From 1915 on, he devoted himself to painting, and his mature work dates from that year until the year of his death. His haunting portraits and languorously sensual nudes are expressively elongated, graceful in line, glowing with rich color; their eyes slanted and almond-shaped, their faces individualized yet simplified and masklike. Unknown to all but his fellow artists, poor and ill with tuberculosis, he died at the age of 35. His works are included in important museum collections throughout the world.

## Modjeski, Ralph (1861–1940)

American engineer, the primary designer for a number of major bridges. Modjeski's best-known work is the Delaware River

suspension bridge between Philadelphia and Camden, New Jersey—now known as the Benjamin Franklin Bridge. Modjeski worked as a partner in several firms over the years, including Modjeski & Cartlidge, designers of a steel railroad bridge over the Ohio River at Metropolis, Illinois (1914–17); Modjeski & Masters; and Modjeski, Masters & Chase. The Philadelphia-Camden bridge (1922–26) is sometimes referred to as the first truly modern suspension bridge, with its two cables and simple, X-braced towers. Paul CRET worked with the engineers as a consulting architect. The nearby Walt Whitman Bridge (1957) is similar but has a conceptually more modern structure and was built by Modjeski & Masters, working together with the firm of Ammann & Whitney.

## Mogadishu raid (1977)

Rescue operation carried out at the airport in Mogadishu, Somalia. Terrorists associated with the West German BAADER-MEINHOF GROUP had hijacked a Lufthansa airliner bound from Majorca to Frankfurt on October 13 in an attempt to extort money and free 13 prisoners. The pilot of the airplane was killed by the hijackers before the raid. A total of 86 passengers and crew members were freed by a squad of 28 West German commandos. Lasting less than a minute, the operation resulted in the death of three hijackers and the wounding of a hijacker, a commando and a hostage. Three imprisoned Baader-Meinhof leaders, including Andreas Baader, committed suicide in a West German prison hours after the rescue.

## Mohammed Nadir Shah (1880–1933)

King of Afghanistan (1929–1933), he quickly abolished most of his predecessor's reforms and began his own by calling together the *loya jirga*—an Afghan "grand council" equivalent to a congress—in 1930 and forming a new constitution in 1931. Although this gave the appearance of shared rule, the government was still very much a royal oligarchy. Nadir Shah did, however, begin many improvements, such as road construction and a banking system, that helped to modernize Afghanistan. In 1933 Nadir Shah was assassinated, and his son Zahir assumed the throne.

## Mohammad Reza Shah Pahlavi (1919–1980)

Shah of IRAN (1941–79); son of Reza Shah, he succeeded to the throne after his father was deposed by British and Soviet pressure. His long rule was interrupted in 1953 after an uprising led by Prime Minister Muhammad MOSSADEQ. He was soon reinstated, with the secret participation of the U.S., and assumed even greater powers of control over the government and the people of Iran. In 1963 the shah began a campaign of modernization that included land reform, the emancipation of women and the promotion of public education. However, as revenue from the nation's oil industries swelled, the shah's government became increasingly corrupt and his own royal extravagance as an ostentatiously uniformed international jet-setter became more extreme. The country suffered from inflation and economic distress, and the shah was opposed both by Muslim fundamentalists and by liberals, all of whom resented the repressive enforcement methods of his brutal secret police, SAVAK. Demonstrations in 1978 led to the full-scale revolution that deposed the shah in 1979 and brought the Ayatollah Ruhollah KHOMEINI to power. Ill with cancer, the shah fled Iran and (after brief stays in Morocco, the Bahamas, Mexico and the U.S.) finally found asylum in Egypt, where he died soon after.

## Mohieddin, Ahmed Fuad (1926–1984)

Prime minister of EGYPT (1982–84). Mohieddin served as deputy prime minister under President Anwar el-SADAT and formed his first cabinet under President Hosni MUBARAK after Sadat's assassination. He was also secretary general of Egypt's ruling National Democratic Party.

## Mohmand, Abdul Ahad (1959– )

The first Afghan cosmonaut in space. Mohmand made his Soyuz TM-6 flight to the Mir space station (docking August 31, 1988) at a time when Soviet troops were withdrawing from his country. His weeklong stay was spent making photographic surveys of Afghanistan and beaming television broadcasts of good will. But the trip home on *Soyuz TM-5* with Soviet veteran Vladimir Lyakhov nearly turned public relations into disaster, when guidance problems left the two cosmonauts stranded for 23 hours orbiting in space, their food and oxygen supply dwindling. Ground efforts to save them paid off, and they landed safely on September 7. Both were given awards for their courage.

**Moholy-Nagy, Lázló** *(1895–1946)* Hungarian painter, sculptor, designer and photographer. Beginning as a law student, Moholy-Nagy became increasingly interested in art. In Berlin, he became a cofounder of CONSTRUCTIVISM, creating geometric sculptures of metal and translucent plastic and experimenting with photograms. In 1921 he met members of the de STIJL group and the bold geometric paintings he created in the early 1920s reveal his affinities with that group and with the Russian disciples of SUPREMATISM. An extremely influential teacher, he was a professor at the BAUHAUS from 1923 to 1928, coediting the school's publications with Walter GROPIUS. Settling in the U.S., he taught at the Chicago Institute of Design from 1938 to 1946. Moholy-Nagy showed his enormous versatility in such other works as films, stage sets and industrial designs. His books include *Painting Photography Film* (1925, tr. 1969) and *Vision in Motion* (1947).

**Moiseiwitsch, Benno** *(1890–1963)* Concert pianist; born in Odessa, Russia. Moiseiwitsch studied at the Black Sea port's Imperial Music Academy and in Vienna with the renowned Theodore Leschetitzky. In 1908 he moved to England, where he settled; he became a British subject in 1937, never returning to Russia. Moiseiwitsch was one of the most traveled virtuosos of his day, giving many concerts throughout Britain; he made his American debut in 1919 and made many recordings during the 1920s, '30s and '40s. His repertoire included music by Beethoven, Schumann and Chopin, as well as such 20th-century composers as POULENC, PROKOFIEV, STRAVINSKY and his friend RACHMANINOFF. During WORLD WAR II Moiseiwitsch was a frequent guest of British prime minister Winston CHURCHILL.

**Moiseyev, Igor Alexandrovich** *(1906–)* Choreographer and founder of the State Folk Dance Ensemble. After graduating from the Choreographic School of the Bolshoi in 1924, from 1924 to 1939 Moiseyev worked as a dancer and choreographer at the Bolshoi Theater. Fascinated by the folk dances of the Soviet republics and wishing to create a national folk ballet, he founded the State Folk Dance Ensemble. The ensemble has toured extensively both abroad and in the Soviet Union, and has won much popularity. Moiseyev's dances include *Three Fat Men* (1935) and *The Snow Storm* (1959). On his 100th birthday in 2006, he received the congratulations of admirers all over the world.

**Mojahedin** Popular name of the Sazman-e Mojahedin-e Khalq-e Iran (Opposition Organization of the Crusaders of the Iranian People), an Iranian leftist political group. It was called the Islamic Marxists by the shah, a name that is still commonly used. It was formed in 1966 by a group of young militants and began military operations five years later. In violent opposition to the shah's regime, group members robbed banks, bombed offices, assassinated American military officials and attempted to hijack an Iranian airliner. The main opposition to the regime of Ayatollah KHOMEINI after it broke with him in 1981, the organization was brutally suppressed by his forces. By 1986 it had ceased to be an important factor in Iranian politics. Nonetheless, it remains the largest leftist group in Iran and continues underground activities in opposition to the ruling regime.

**Moldova** Republic of the Soviet Union (1940–91), and independent republic (1991–   ). Located in the northeast region of the Balkan Peninsula,

## MOLDOVA

| | |
|---|---|
| 1924 | The Moldovan autonomous Soviet Socialist Republic (SSR) is created as part of the Soviet Union, composed of territory east of Dniestr River. |
| 1940 | Romania returns Bessarabia, east of the Prut River, to the Soviet Union, which divides it between the Moldovan SSR and Ukraine, with the Trans-Dniestr region transferred from Ukraine to Moldova. |
| 1941 | The Moldovan SSR is occupied by Romania and its wartime ally, Germany. |
| 1944 | The Red Army reconquers Bessarabia. |
| 1946–47 | Famine becomes widespread as agriculture is collectivized; rich farmers and intellectuals are liquidated. |
| 1950 | Settlers from Russia and Ukraine immigrate as industries develop. |
| late 1980s | An upsurge in Moldovan nationalism is encouraged by the glasnost initiative of reformist Soviet leader Mikhail Gorbachev. |
| 1989 | Nationalist demonstrations occur in Kishinev (now Chisinau). |
| 1990 | Economic and political sovereignty is declared. |
| 1991 | The Republic of Moldova is proclaimed a sovereign state on August 27. Moldova joins the Commonwealth of Independent States. |
| 1992 | Moldova becomes a member of the United Nations. A cease-fire is declared in the Trans-Dniester dispute. |
| 1994 | Multiparty elections are won by former Communists. |
| 1995 | Moldova is admitted to the Council of Europe. |
| 1998 | The Communist Party of Moldova wins the most seats in parliament. |
| 2001 | A pro-Russian Communist Party wins 70 of the 101 seats in parliament and a Communist is elected president. |
| 2006 | Russia energy company cuts the gas supply off when Moldova refuses to pay twice the previous price. A compromise is soon worked out. |

Moldova was under the control of ROMANIA from 1918 to 1940. During this time, it was referred to as BESSARABIA. However, in 1939 the Soviet Union signed the GERMAN-SOVIET NONAGGRESSION PACT with Nazi Germany, which secretly authorized the Soviet Union to absorb this territory. Following the Nazi invasion of Poland in September 1939, the Soviet government sent military forces into Bessarabia (Moldova) in June 1940 to ensure the region's transfer to Soviet control. On August 2, 1940, the area became the Moldovan Soviet Socialist Republic within the USSR. A year later, Romania reclaimed Moldavia when it joined in Hitler's invasion of the Soviet Union and liberated the region from Soviet control. It continued to rule Moldova until 1944, when Soviet forces reentered the territory and reattached it to the USSR. In 1947 the Moldavian S.S.R. was reestablished as a result of the peace treaty between the Communist government of Romania and the USSR. Between 1947 and 1953, Soviet leader Joseph STALIN sought to reduce the ethnic ties between Moldova and Romania by resettling a large portion of Moldova's population throughout the USSR, and by introducing many ethnic Russians to take their place. Additionally, the Soviet Union made efforts to incorporate Moldova into its economic infrastructure by building industrial centers throughout the region, which in turn provided jobs for the recently arrived Russians. The Soviets also required Moldavian citizens to use the Cyrillic alphabet and the Russian language rather than the Latin alphabet and the Romanian language that had been previously used.

When Soviet leader Mikhail Gorbachev introduced the political reforms termed GLASNOST (or "openness") into the Soviet Union in the second half of the 1980s, the Popular Front of Moldova emerged to celebrate the unique history and heritage of the province. In November 1989 the followers of the Popular Front of Moldova engineered the replacement of Semyon Grossu, the first secretary of the Communist Party of Moldavia with the reformist Petru Lucinschi. In June 1990 the Moldavian Supreme Soviet declared the sovereignty of its own constitution above that of the USSR stipulating that Moldavian law superseded Soviet law.

The Moldavian legislature subsequently ended the Communist Party's monopoly on political power and began introducing economic reforms that sought to create a free-market economy. After the defeat of the reactionary coup against Gorbachev in August 1991 that the Moldavian Supreme Soviet declared the province's independence on August 27, 1991, and assumed full control of military and political institutions of the renamed state of Moldova. Other SSRs within the Soviet Union soon followed Moldova's example, which led to the Soviet Union's disintegration on December 25, 1991.

Since independence, Moldova has maintained relations with the former Soviet republics by joining the COMMONWEALTH OF INDEPENDENT STATES (CIS), an organization that has sought to encourage the preservation of strong economic, military and political ties among the former SSRs. Moldova has also sought integration within the political and economic framework of Western Europe. By 1994 it had gained admission into such European-oriented organizations as the European Bank for Reconstruction and Development, the Organization for Security and Cooperation in Europe, and (in conjunction with NATO members) the Partnership for Peace Program. Along with its efforts to strengthen relations with CIS members with its initiatives toward Europe, Moldova ended the separatist agitation in the self-proclaimed DNIESTER REPUBLIC, a short-lived ethnic Russian entity between Moldova and Ukraine. With the start of the 21st century the Communist Party was swept back into power, based on promises to help improve the living standards of one of Europe's poorest nations.

**Moley, Raymond** (1886–1975) Adviser to President Franklin D. ROOSEVELT and the leader of Roosevelt's BRAIN TRUST. It was Moley who coined the term NEW DEAL to describe Roosevelt's sweeping social reform program for dealing with the GREAT DEPRESSION. Moley broke with the President in 1936 when he could not reconcile himself with what he considered a radical trend in the New Deal.

**Molina, Mario** (1943– ) Mexican-American chemist and winner of the 1995 Nobel Prize in chemistry. Born in Mexico City, Molina enrolled in the chemical engineering program at the National University of Mexico. In 1972 Molina received his Ph.D. from the University of California at Berkeley and remained at the institution to study the effects of certain industrial chemicals known as chlorofluorocarbons (CFCs) on the atmosphere and the environment. A year later, his research on CFCs, in conjunction with that of F. Sherwood Rowland, helped develop the "CFC-ozone depletion theory," which held that CFCs released into the atmosphere as a by-product of industrial production rapidly decomposed, producing chlorine atoms that degraded the ozone layer's integrity.

Teaching at the University of California at Irvine, Molina continued to conduct research on the effect on the ozone layer of compounds released into the upper atmosphere. In 1982 he left the University of California at Irvine and joined the Molecular Physics and Chemistry division of the Jet Propulsion Laboratory (JPL), where he focused his CFCs research on the chlorine-ozone reactions that occurred in polar stratospheric clouds. In 1989 he left the JPL to accept a position at the Massachusetts Institute of Technology (MIT), where he continued his research on the impact of chemical compounds on the upper levels of the Earth's atmosphere. In 1995 he, Paul Crutzen and F. Sherwood Rowland shared the Nobel Prize in chemistry for their research on the influence CFCs have on the degradation of the ozone layer.

**Mollet, Guy** (1905–1975) French statesman, premier (1956–57). A teacher and trade union leader, he took an active part in the RESISTANCE during the German occupation of France in WORLD WAR II. He was elected to the Chamber of Deputies in 1945 and served as secretary-general of the French Socialist Party (1946–69). During the Léon BLUM government, he was minister of state (1946–47) and vice premier (1951). While premier, he supported the unity of western Europe, sent French troops into Algeria to suppress a revolt (1956) and joined with Great Britain and Israel in invading Egypt during the SUEZ CRISIS (1956). Mollet subsequently served as minister of state under Charles DE GAULLE (1958–59).

**Molotov, Vyacheslav Mikhailovich** (1890–1986) Soviet communist official, a close aide of Joseph STALIN and a member of the Soviet leadership from 1921 to 1957. A nephew of composer Alexander SCRIABIN, he took the name Molotov ("The hammer") as a young revolutionary. As premier (1931–41), Molotov oversaw industrial and agricultural development. He helped implement Stalin's policy of forced COLLECTIVIZATION of farms, which led to famine in the UKRAINE. He also played a key role in the GREAT PURGE. As foreign minister (1939–49), he negotiated the GERMAN-SOVIET NONAGGRESSION PACT with Joachim von RIBBENTROP (August 1939). After the German invasion of the USSR in 1941, Molotov helped strengthen the Soviet alliance with the West. An opponent of Nikita KHRUSHCHEV, Molotov was expelled from the Politburo in 1957 after his failed attempt to oust Khrushchev. He was expelled from the COMMUNIST PARTY in 1962 but reinstated in 1984.

**Molucca Islands** Small island chain in the Pacific Ocean and territory of the Dutch Empire (1600s–1949) and INDONESIA (1949– ). From the 17th century until 1949, these islands were administered as a separate imperial possession of the Netherlands. In that year, the Dutch government turned over control of this territory to the newly independent state of Indonesia, another former Dutch imperial possession in Southeast Asia. Originally the Molucca Islands were to be part of a federal governing structure in Indonesia, in which the indigenous peoples of the hundreds of islands comprising the country had a notable degree of autonomy. However, in 1950, Indonesian president Achmed Sukarno abandoned the federal structure in favor of a strongly centralized government that greatly reduced the autonomy in the Molucca Islands. In response, a secessionist movement among the predominantly Christian population in the southern half of the islands, called the Republic of the South Moluccas (RMS), began to stage sporadic attacks on the Indonesian central authority. This low-intensity counterinsurgency did not adversely affect the amicable relationship between Christians and Muslims in the southern islands. But these relatively subdued assaults intensified in January 1999 when the southern region—in which Muslims and Christians had achieved rough numerical parity—exploded in a spate of violence between members of the two religions. The violence was fueled by both Muslim resentment at the efforts of the largely Christian RMS to gain foreign support for its cause and Christian resentment at the increased presence of Muslims in local positions of power. The violence quickly spread to the northern half of the island chain through the use of guerrilla tactics by both sides. In response to the efforts of the RMS to protect Christians and attack Muslims in the Moluccas, Islamic extremists formed the Laskar Jihad, an organization dedicated to using similar terrorist tactics to eradicate the RMS's efforts to establish an independent state, as militants in EAST TIMOR had done in 1999. The clashes between these two extremist groups have led to over 6,000 deaths since 1999.

**Molyneux, Edward** *(1891–1974)* London-born Irish fashion designer. His career was based in Paris, where he catered to an elegant society of celebrities of the social and theatrical worlds. Molyneux was an art student in London when his fashion sketches were seen by Lady Duff Gordon (Lucile, as she was known in the world of fashion), who hired him as an artist and then as a designer for her Paris shop. After service in World War I, he opened his own house of fashion in Paris in 1919, beginning a long career of supplying simple elegance to such figures as Gertude LAWRENCE, whose Molyneux costumes in *Private Lives* made his work widely known and admired. He closed his firm in 1950 when he faced declining health, but, after a period of retirement in Jamaica, he recovered sufficiently to introduce a ready-to-wear line (1965) mass-produced under the name *Studio Molyneux*. His fame rests mainly on his simple, elegant designs of the 1930s.

**Monaco, Principality of** Tiny principality on the Mediterranean Sea coast of southeastern France in the hills fronting the Côte d'Azur; it is the second smallest independent state in the world. Princely absolutism gave way to constitutional rule in 1911. France recognized Monaco's sovereignty in 1918 and 1919, subject to its acting "in

complete conformity" with French interests. Occupied by the Italians (1940) and then by the Germans (1943), postwar Monaco reestablished itself as a major tourist center and, by virtue of economic union with France, became an integral part of the EUROPEAN COMMUNITY in the 1950s. Prince Rainier III succeeded to the throne in 1949 and on April 19, 1956, married U.S. film star GRACE Kelly.

In the face of growing pressure for increased powers from the elected National Council (in particular, following the collapse in 1955 of Monaco's leading bank, the Société Monegasque de Banque) Prince Rainier asserted his sovereign powers in 1959 by suspending the council. However, a revised constitution promulgated in 1962 guaranteed representative government and renounced royal divine right. Tensions with France over the principality's role as a tax haven were eased in 1963 by a convention placing certain Monaco-based companies under French fiscal law. Since 1963 the pro-Rainier National and Democratic Union group has dominated the National Council and won all 18 seats in the National Council in elections in 1978, 1983 and 1988. Monaco joined the UN in 1993. Prince Rainier died in 2005 and was succeeded by his son Albert, who became Prince Albert II.

**Mondale, Walter F.** *(1928– )* Vice president of the UNITED STATES (1977–81). A graduate of the University of Minnesota (1951) and of Minnesota Law School (1956), Mondale served as attorney general of Minnesota from 1960 to 1964. Active in the Democratic–Farmer-Labor Party of Minnesota, he gained national attention when he supported the cause of free legal counsel for indigent defendants in the case of GIDEON V. WAINWRIGHT (1963). When Mondale's mentor Hubert H. HUMPHREY vacated his U.S. Senate seat to run for vice president in 1964, Mondale was appointed as his replacement. Mondale was elected on his own in 1972. In 1976 Jimmy CARTER chose Mondale as the Democratic nominee for vice president. Mondale served as vice president of the U.S. from 1977 to 1981. The Democratic candidate for president in 1984, Mondale was the first candidate of a major party to choose a woman (Geraldine FERRARO) as his running mate. Advocating traditional liberal De-

mocratic policies, they lost in the landslide reelection of President Ronald REAGAN and Vice President George BUSH. In 1993 Mondale was appointed to a four-year term as the U.S. ambassador to Japan by President Bill Clinton.

**Mondrian, Piet** *(1872–1944)* Dutch painter. One of the foremost geometric modernists, he was born in Amersfoort, the Netherlands, and studied at the Amsterdam Academy. His early work consisted of naturalistic landscapes. He became aware of avant-garde movements in art around 1908 and traveled to Paris in 1910, discovering the Cubist works of PICASSO and BRAQUE. In Paris (1912–14), Mondrian struggled with his own interpretation of Cubism and, returning to Holland, began to create the rigorous geometrical work for which he is famous. In 1917 he and a number of other Dutch artists founded DE STIJL magazine and, with it, the movement that bears its name. Three years later, Mondrian explained his theories in the book *Neoplasticism*. The artist sought a plastic perfection through the use of intersecting straight lines meeting in right angles on vertical and horizontal axes and through a limitation of his palette to the primary colors of red, yellow and blue—along with black, white and gray. Through these purposely austere abstract means, he sought to express universal truths and to indicate the spiritual harmony of humankind and nature. Mondrian emigrated to the U.S. in 1940 and settled in New York City. Some of his finest compositions, such as *Broadway Boogie-Woogie* (1942–45), can be found in New York's Museum of Modern Art, as well as in the Gemeente Museum, The Hague, and the Art Institute of Chicago. (See also MODERNISM.)

**Monet, Claude** *(1840–1926)* French painter. The paragon of Impressionism and a founder of the movement, Monet was born in Paris and spent his youth in Le Havre. There he struck up a friendship with the painter Eugène Boudin, who encouraged the young artist to paint in the open air—a practice that was central to his later style. Moving to Paris in 1859, Monet studied at the Académie Suisse and, after two years in the army, returned to the city to study painting. Living in appalling poverty, he persevered as a painter. At the same time, he became friendly with such artists as Camille Pissarro, Pierre Renoir,

Paul Cézanne and Alfred Sisley. In the late 1860s Monet began to paint landscapes that reflected what were to be his lifelong concerns: the changing effects of light and color caused by variations in time and season. Studying the laws of optics, he developed a unique manner of capturing the phenomena of light as it is expressed in the forms, textures and hues of the landscape by breaking it down into its color components.

In 1872 Monet painted *Impression, Sunrise* (Musée Marmotton, Paris), a work whose title was soon assumed by the Impressionist movement. From 1872 to 1875, he painted river and garden scenes in which the forms of objects begin to dissolve in a shimmer of color and a flurry of brushstrokes. From 1876 on, he concentrated on a number of single subjects, such as the Parisian Gare

Saint-Lazare. When his financial fortunes improved in the 1880s, Monet set about traveling through France, again painting the same subject in a series of views. These luminous, semi-abstract works are the culmination of his nature style. They include poplars, haystacks, the facade of Rouen Cathedral (1892–94) and the celebrated waterlilies (1899, 1904–25), which are lyrical masterpieces painted in his garden at Giverny. Among these *Nympheas* is the monumental triptych (c. 1920) in the Museum of Modern Art, New York City.

**monetarism** A macroeconomic theory that arose in the 1960s; it views the money supply as central to understanding price levels and the economy's performance. Monetarists argue that although monetary policy cannot influ-

ence either output or employment in the long run, it does determine price levels, and accordingly affects both output and employment in the short-term. Accordingly, monetary policy has a direct affect on the stability of the economy. Monetarism was a reaction to Keynesian economics, which downplayed the role of the money supply in explaining the operation of the economy (see John Maynard KEYNES). In the U.S., economist Milton FRIEDMAN was a leading monetarist. Monetarist principles were followed by the FEDERAL RESERVE under Paul Volcker and Alan Greenspan during the REAGAN administration in the U.S. They were also applied by Margaret THATCHER's government in the U.K.

**Mongolia (Mongolian People's Republic)** Mongolia comprises an area of

| MONGOLIA | |
|---|---|
| 1911 | Independence is proclaimed by Mongolian nationalists after the Chinese "republican revolution"; czarist Russia helps Mongolia to secure autonomy, under a traditionalist Buddhist monarchy in the form of a reincarnated lama, or "Living Buddha." |
| 1919 | Chinese sovereignty is reasserted. |
| 1921 | Chinese rule is overthrown with Soviet help. |
| 1924 | A People's Republic is proclaimed after the death of the Living Buddha, and the monarchy is abolished; a defeudalization program is launched, entailing collectivization of agriculture and suppression of lama Buddhism. |
| 1932 | An armed antigovernment uprising is suppressed with Soviet assistance; 100,000 are killed in political purges. |
| 1957 | Railway line from Ulaanbaatar to Beijing is opened. |
| 1960 | New constitution is promulgated. |
| 1961 | Mongolia is admitted to the United Nations. |
| 1962 | Frontier agreement is concluded between Mongolia and China. |
| 1987 | Mongolia and the United States establish diplomatic relations. |
| 1990 | The ruling Communist Party gives up power after peaceful demonstrations. |
| 1992 | Mongolia adopts a more democratic and market economy–oriented constitution. |
| 1993 | First presidential elections in 50 years take place. |
| 1996 | The Democratic Union Coalition wins parliamentary elections, marking the first time in 75 years that the Communists have not held power. |
| 2000 | Election of the former communist Mongolian Peoples Revolutionary Party (MPRP). |
| 2005–2006 | Both MPRP candidates for president and prime minister are elected. |

604,090 square miles in north-central Asia. With the support of czarist Russia Mongolia broke from Chinese control and declared itself an independent monarchy in 1911, naming Jebtsun Damba Khutukhtu, the Living Buddha, of Urga as head of state. China occupied Mongolia (1919–20) after the Russian Revolution, but the Mongolians again declared independence in 1921, gaining military support from the newly formed USSR The death of the Living Buddha brought a new Soviet-inspired constitution and the establishment of the Mongolian People's Republic (1924). The movement toward a socialist state brought slow collectivization of the economy (1928–1950s) and political purges (1922, 1939). During the presidency of Jambyn Batmonh Mongolia slowly initiated some reforms, paralleling those taking place in the Soviet Union. In addition, peaceful demonstrations occurred and new political organizations formed (1989–90). These demonstrations, together with the dissolution of the Soviet Union, resulted in the 1992 reform of Mongolia's constitution to allow for free multiparty elections. In 1993 the country held its first presidential election, and in 1996 the first non-Communist government in 75 years came to power. In 2005–06 two members of the former communist Mongolian People's Revolutionary Party were elected president and prime minister.

**Monk, Thelonius Sphere** (*1917–1982*) American jazz pianist and composer. His original style—dissonant and rhythmically innovative—created a mu-

sical bridge between 1930s SWING and the BEBOP style of the 1940s. He became popular in the 1950 when he began recording his compositions, including "Round Midnight," "Ruby My Dear," "Well, You Needn't" and "Blue Monk." After 1957 he appeared regularly in New York nightclubs.

**Monnet, Jean** (*1888–1979*) French statesman and financier. At the age of 31, Monnet was assistant secretary general of the LEAGUE OF NATIONS. During WORLD WAR II he conceived the idea for LEND-LEASE. The Monnet Plan, which he authored in 1947, led to France's postwar economic recovery through participation in the MARSHALL PLAN. An architect of the EUROPEAN COAL AND STEEL COMMUNITY (1952), he also played a major role in the formation of the EUROPEAN ECONOMIC COMMUNITY (EEC, 1957), and later worked to establish a European monetary reserve fund with a single European currency. Monnet never sought or held elective office, but was a behind-the-scenes, moving force in European political life for much of the 20th century.

**Monod, Jacques Lucien** (*1910–1976*) French biochemist. Monod graduated from the University of Paris in 1931 and became assistant professor of zoology there in 1934, having spent the years immediately following his graduation investigating the origin of life. After World War II, in which he served in the RESISTANCE, he joined the Pasteur Institute, becoming head of the cellular biochemistry department in 1953. In 1958 Monod began working with François

Jacob and Arthur Pardee on the regulation of enzyme synthesis in mutant bacteria. This work led to the formulation, by Monod and Jacob, of a theory explaining gene action and, particularly, how genes are switched on and off as necessary. In 1960 they introduced the term "operon" for a closely linked group of genes, each of which controls a different step in a given biochemical pathway. The following year they postulated the existence of a molecule, messenger RNA, that carries the genetic information necessary for protein synthesis from the operon to the ribosomes, where proteins are made. For this work Monod and Jacob were awarded the 1965 NOBEL PRIZE in physiology or medicine, which they shared with André Lwoff, who was also working on bacterial genetics. In 1971 Monod became director of the Pasteur Institute and in the same year published the best seller *Chance and Necessity,* in which he argued that life arose by chance and progressed to its present level as a necessary consequence of the pressures exerted by natural selection.

**Monroe, Harriet** (*1860–1936*) American poetry editor and publisher. One of the most influential figures in the publication and development of modern poetry, she began as an art and drama critic for various CHICAGO newspapers and also wrote her own verse. Her greatest fame came as editor of *Poetry: A Magazine of Verse,* which she founded in 1912. Its contributors included almost every major American poet of the period, including T. S. ELIOT, Marianne MOORE and Ezra POUND, whose reputations were largely made through appearance in the magazine. Monroe particularly favored IMAGISM but included a wide variety of work in the magazine. With Alice Henderson she edited *New Poetry: An Anthology of Twentieth-Century Verse in English* (1917, rev. 1923, 1932). *Poetry* continues today with substantial but lessened influence. (See also MODERNISM.)

**Monroe, Marilyn (Norma Jean Mortenson)** (*1926–1962*) American motion picture actress who became a sex symbol in the 1950s. After surviving abuse and neglect as a child, an unhappy first marriage (she was divorced in 1945) and tedious work in a wartime defense plant, she was discovered by

*International sex symbol Marilyn Monroe, in a scene from* THE SEVEN YEAR ITCH. *1955 (LIBRARY OF CONGRESS, PRINTS AND PHOTOGRAPHS DIVISION)*

pin-up photographers and HOLLYWOOD scouts. She changed her name and was in and out of the Fox and Columbia studios in a succession of bit parts. Finally, Fox signed her to a long-term contract in 1950, and by the time she married baseball hero Joe DIMAGGIO in 1954, she had made a thriller, *Niagara* (1952), a musical, *Gentlemen Prefer Blondes* (1953), and an adventure story, *River of No Return* (1954). At the height of her fame, when she had become the most sensational "sex goddess" in the movies, Monroe turned her back on Hollywood and, in a much publicized move, went to New York to study the famous "Method" with Lee and Paula STRASBERG. Her subsequent work in *Bus Stop* (1956), *Some Like It Hot* (1959) and her last film (scripted by playwright Arthur MILLER, her third husband), *The Misfits* (1961), showed greater range and subtlety. However, illness, depression, drug abuse and psychiatric problems cut short her promising career. She died in 1962 while filming *Something's Got to Give,* the victim of an apparent overdose of barbiturates.

**Monroe, Marion** *(1898–1983)* American child psychologist. With Dr. WILLIAM GRAY, she was coauthor of the famous Dick and Jane series of school books that from the 1940s to the early 1970s introduced millions of American schoolchildren to reading. The books fell out of favor with educators in the late 1960s and early 1970s because of their perceived racist and sexist attitudes and stereotypes.

**Montagu, Ewen** *(1901–1985)* British espionage agent. Montagu led the British counterespionage unit responsible for a WORLD WAR II hoax to deceive the Nazis over landings in the Mediterranean. Code named Operation Mincemeat, the hoax (1943) involved floating ashore on the Spanish coast what seemed to be the dead body of a British officer. The body bore faked documents, indicating that Sardinia and GREECE were to be the targets for the next main Allied effort in the Mediterranean, providing cover for the real invasion in Sicily. The operation remained secret until 1953, when Montagu wrote about it in the book *The Man Who Never Was.* That account of the operation sold more than two million copies and was made into a film in 1956.

**Montale, Eugenio** *(1896–1981)* Italian poet, critic, editor, translator and journalist. Although Montale produced only five volumes of poetry in 50 years, his citation for the 1975 NOBEL PRIZE for literature declared him to be "one of the most important poets of the contemporary West." He supported his poetry as an editor, translator, literary journalist and music critic. In the 1930s he was forced to resign his position as curator of a rare book collection because he refused to join the Fascist Party (see FASCISM). In 1947 he began a long association with the Milan daily newspaper *Corriere della sera.* His most important works are *Ossi di seppia* (1925, Cuttlefish bones), *Le occasioni* (1939, The occasions), *La bufera e altro* (1956, The storm and other things). His poetry is marked by profound pessimism; it is highly subjective and symbolic. Along with UNGARETTI and QUASIMODO, he is associated with the movement known as **Hermeticism.** He is also a distinguished translator of HARDY, Dickinson, Melville, T. S. ELIOT and Eugene O'NEILL.

**Montana, Joe** *(1956– )* American football player, considered by many sports aficionados to be the greatest quarterback of all time. Montana quarterbacked the San Francisco 49ers during their domination of the National Football League (NFL)—and the Super Bowl—in the 1980s. Winner of four Super Bowls, in 1982, 1985, 1989 and 1990, Montana was named most valuable player of the championship game three times. He holds the Super Bowl career passing record with 1,142 yards and 83 completions, as well as the single game mark of 357 yards. After his trade to the Kansas City Chiefs, Montana started at quarterback on that team for the 1993 and 1994 seasons. Although he led the Chiefs to the NFL playoffs in both years, including the AFC Championship game in January 1994, Montana failed to win a fifth Super Bowl title in his new home. At the end of his second season in Kansas City, Montana announced his retirement from professional football.

**Montand, Yves (Ivo Livi)** *(1921–1991)* Italian-born French actor and singer. Montand began his career performing in vaudeville and in the Paris music halls before gaining fame in Marcel Carne's film *Les Portes de la Nuit* (1946). International acclaim and stardom came with his performance in *Le Salaire de la Peur* (1953). He worked with several great directors, but his most important collaboration was with Costa-Gavras in the films *Z* (1968), *L'Aveu* (1970) and *Etat de Siège* (1973). He made a few Hollywood films, most notably Vincente Minnelli's *On a Clear Day You Can See Forever* (1970) with Barbra STREISAND.

**Montecassino** See CASSINO.

**Montenegro** Independent kingdom (1910–15), province of YUGOSLAVIA (1915–92), and constituent member of the Federal Republic of Yugoslavia (1992–2003). In 1910 after having established a liberal parliamentary constitution five years earlier, Prince Nicholas I Petrović became the first king of Montenegro. During the 1912–13 Balkan Wars, Montenegro allied with SERBIA, GREECE and BULGARIA, to expel the OTTOMAN EMPIRE from the Balkan Peninsula. Upon the outbreak of WORLD WAR I (1914–19), Montenegro supported SERBIA and RUSSIA in their war against the Central Powers. When Austria-Hungary and Germany occupied Serbia and Montenegro in 1915, several bands of Montenegrin partisans united with similar groups of Serbians, Croats and Slovenes on the Greek island of Corfu. There they declared the union of their peoples under a single kingdom. After the victory of the Allies in 1918, this pact led to the establishment of the Kingdom of the Serbs, Croats, and Slovenes (later renamed Yugoslavia), of which Montenegro became and remained a province. On the establishment of the Communist regime at the end of WORLD WAR II, Montenegro became one of Yugoslavia's six constituent republics.

In 1992 following the declarations of independence by four Yugoslav republics—BOSNIA AND HERZEGOVINA, CROATIA, MACEDONIA, and SLOVENIA—the provincial government of Montenegro held a referendum to determine whether its citizens wished to remain united with the Serbian remnant of Yugoslavia, or whether they wished to declare independence. More than 66% chose to support a continued union with Serbia. Following this vote, Serbia and Montenegro formed a new political entity on April 27, 1992, the Federal Republic of Yugoslavia, in which both states would elect their own presidents and parliaments in addition to voting for leaders and presidential candidates for the federal government. However, Montenegro's amicable relationship with Serbia was subsequently strained, both by continuing developments in the Balkans and by changes in Montenegrin leadership. In 1997 Milo Djukanović, a businessman-turned-politician, won election as president of Montenegro, unseating Momir Bulatović, who had grown unpopular because of his continued support of the policies of SLOBODAN MILOŠEVIĆ designed to repress ethnic Albanians in the Serbian province of KOSOVO and non-Serbs in the portion of Bosnia under Serb control. In 1998 the crackdown by Serbian and Yugoslav military forces on these ethnic Albanians resulted in intensified NATO-sponsored sanctions on Montenegro. When Serbia expanded its operations in Kosovo, prompting a series of NATO air-strikes to deter Milošević, thousands of Kosovo Albanians fled their homes and sought sanctuary in Montenegro. In 2001 Filip Vojanović was elected president of Montenegro. In 2003 the Federal Republic of Yugoslavia was officially restructured and renamed Serbia and Montenegro and a new constitution was approved. Svetozvar Marović was elected president of Serbia and Montenegro. A referendum on May 21, 2006, determined that the union of the two nations would be disolved, and Montenegro declared its independence on June 3, 2006. Montenegro sided with NATO against Milošević, who was subsequently turned over to the International War Crimes Tribunal at the Hague, where he died.

## Montessori, Maria *(1870–1952)*

Italian educator. The first Italian woman to receive an M.D., Montessori graduated from the University of Rome in 1894. In 1907 she became head of the new Casa dei Bambini in the Roman slums of San Lorenzo, and here Montessori put to work her revolutionary educational theories, which stressed light discipline, spontaneity and child-directed learning. In 1909 Montessori began to train others in her techniques, which became known as the Montessori Method, and in 1911, the first American Montessori school opened, in Tarrytown, New York. Soon similar institutions were established through the U.S. and Europe. Although Montessori was a controversial figure, many of her educational concepts have been incorporated into traditional schools throughout the world.

## Monteux, Pierre *(1875–1964)* The

foremost French conductor of his generation. He was trained at the Paris Conservatory and became conductor in Paris of Serge DIAGHILEV's BALLETS RUSSES (1912). During the next few years he conducted world premieres of some of the most important new music of this century, including Igor STRAVINSKY's *Petrouchka*, LE SACRE DU PRINTEMPS and *Rossignol*; Maurice RAVEL's *Daphnis et Chloe* and Claude DEBUSSY's *Jeux*. Subsequently, he held numerous appointments in the U.S., including conducting at the Metropolitan Opera (1917–19), the Boston Symphony Orchestra (1917–19) and the San Francisco Symphony (1936–52). Rivaling Arturo TOSCANINI and Pablo CASALS in longevity, Monteux became music director of the London Symphony at the age of 86. Few conductors have been as universally beloved. Dapper and elegant, he was a superb technician and the most amiable of men. Critic Virgil THOMSON described his famous transparent sound as possessing "perfect balance" and "translucency." A model of tact, restraint and economy, Monteux insisted a conductor must not "overconduct" or make "unnecessary noises or gestures"; certainly he must never "worry" or "annoy" his players. A protean figure, he led an all-embracing life in opera, ballet and symphony.

## Montgomery, Bernard Law (first Viscount Montgomery of Alamein)

*(1887–1976)* British field marshal. Educated at Sandhurst, Montgomery was commissioned in the Royal Warwickshire Regiment in 1908 and served with distinction on the western front during most of WORLD WAR I. In the years between the world wars, he held various staff and command posts in Britain and India. Probably the most important and popular British military commander in WORLD WAR II, "Monty" led an Expeditionary Force division in France from 1939 to 1940, and was involved in the evacuation of DUNKIRK. He was subsequently in charge of the commando raid at DIEPPE (1942) before being posted soon after to North Africa as commander of the Eighth Army. His military fame was assured there, as he commanded his troops in the spectacular victory over ROMMEL's Afrika Korps at EL ALAMEIN (1942) and pursued the retreating German forces across Libya and Tunisia into Sicily and southern Italy. Commanding the Allied ground forces in the invasion of NORMANDY, Montgomery and his troops swept through France and into Germany during 1944

*British field marshal Bernard Law Montgomery* (LIBRARY OF CONGRESS, PRINTS AND PHOTOGRAPHS DIVISION)

and 1945. His successes, however, were somewhat marred by his strategic disagreements with the Allied supreme commander Dwight D. EISENHOWER. Promoted to the rank of field marshal in 1944, he was created a viscount in 1946. In postwar Europe, Montgomery was commander of Great Britain's occupation forces in Germany (1945–46), chief of the British general staff (1946–48) and deputy supreme commander of NATO (1951–58). He was the author of a number of books on military history and published *Memoirs* in 1958.

**Montgomery bus boycott** Struggle to end SEGREGATION on the public buses of Montgomery, Alabama. It took place from December 1955 until December 1956 and began when Rosa Parks, a black seamstress, was ordered to give up her seat on a bus to a white person. She refused and was arrested and jailed. Her action led to a boycott of the bus system by the black citizens of Montgomery. The boycott, led by the Rev. Martin Luther KING Jr., disrupted business as usual in the city. After a protracted struggle, it resulted in the desegregation of public transportation in Montgomery. This landmark event was one of the earliest victories of the CIVIL RIGHTS movement in the South.

**Montherlant, Henri(-Marie-Joseph-Milon) de** *(1896–1972)* French novelist, playwright and essayist. Born in Paris, by the time of World War II de Montherlant had become one of France's leading men of letters. He won the 1934 Grand Prix for *The Bachelors*. His 17 plays won popular acclaim and became part of the standard French theatrical repertoire. In 1960 he was elected to the French Academy. Like the American writer Ernest HEMINGWAY, early in his life de Montherlant was an active sportsman (and a bullfighter), and his works celebrate physical courage. Also like Hemingway, he committed suicide by shooting himself, apparently out of despondency over his failing health.

**Montreux International Jazz Festival** The Montreux International Jazz Festival, established in 1967, continues to be one of jazzdom's most broad-based and significant forums. Presided over until the late 1980s by Claude Nobs, the jazzfest has typically pre-sented a wide variety of jazz stylists over a 17-day period in July of each year. In the mid-1970s, the inclusion of popular music groups led to the deletion of "Jazz" in the event's title; by the late 1970s, "Jazz" was back in the festival's title and its center ring. In addition to featuring internationally known jazz groups playing everything from BEBOP to fusion, and big band to dixieland, the festival has spotlighted student groups, many from the U.S. It has enjoyed sponsorship from a variety of recording companies, a productive relationship that through the years has yielded a number of excellent recordings, especially those issued by the Pablo and Atlantic labels. There is a cooperative arrangement with a "sister" event in the U.S., the Montreux-Detroit Kool Jazz Festival.

**Montserrat** A Caribbean island with a total land area of 39 square miles; it is a United Kingdom dependent territory. Between 1871 and 1956 Montserrat was administered as part of Britain's Federal Colony of the Leeward Islands, and between 1958 and 1962 it participated in the Federation of the West Indies. In 1960 a new constitution was granted, providing greater autonomy for the island. In 1978 the ruling Progressive Democratic Party (PDP) was defeated in elections by the opposition People's Liberation Movement (PLM), which won all seven seats in the Legislative Council. John Osborne, the leader of the PLM, became chief minister. The PLM won elections in 1983, and Osborne stated that he would be in favor of eventual independence for the territory. In June 1984 a state of emergency was declared after a strike by public service employees disrupted services. An early general election was held in August 1987 and again won by the PLM, which defeated the PDP and the more recent National Development Party. As a result of a severe volcanic eruption that began on July 18, 1995, two-thirds of Montserrat's population was evacuated and much of the island's surface was destroyed. By July 2004 only a few of those who left the island in 1995 had returned.

**Monty Python's Flying Circus** British comedy troupe and television show of the same name, noted for its bizarre sense of humor, ranging from surreal farce to sophisticated satire. The troupe was formed by a group of students at Cambridge University in the early 1960s as an amateur stage entertainment revue; the members were **Graham Chapman, John Cleese, Eric Idle, Terry Jones, Michael Palin** and **Terry Gilliam** (the only American-born member). They turned professional, and the show was broadcast by the BRITISH BROADCASTING CORPORATION (BBC) from 1969 to 1974. It was also repeated on public television in the U.S. and was a huge hit in both countries. The group also made several irreverent but good-natured films, including *Monty Python and the Holy Grail* (1978) and *The Life of Brian* (1979). Several of the members—notably Cleese, Idle and Palin—went on to successful careers in other films and television shows. Gilliam launched a spectacular career in the movies, directing *Time Bandits* (1981) and *Brazil* (1985, cowritten by Palin). Chapman died in 1989.

**Moody, Helen Newington Wills** *(1905–1998)* American tennis player. Combining thoughtful play with power, Moody dominated women's tennis throughout the 1920s and 1930s, winning her first U.S. championship at the age of 17 in 1923. She would win that title six more times, as well as an astonishing eight Wimbledon championships and four French championships. In 1928 and 1929, she took the women's Grand Slam, winning all three titles. She was named to the International Tennis Hall of Fame in 1959.

**Moody, William H.** *(1853–1917)* Associate justice, U.S. Supreme Court (1906–10). A native of Massachusetts, Moody graduated from Harvard University and briefly attended its Law School, leaving to read law in a law office in Boston. He became a prosecutor and is remembered for the unsuccessful prosecution of Lizzie Borden. He was elected to Congress in 1895 and was selected by President Theodore ROOSEVELT as secretary of the navy and later as attorney general. Roosevelt appointed Moody to the Supreme Court. His nomination ran into opposition from business interests because, as attorney general, Moody had vigorously enforced the antitrust laws. In a highly unusual move he had personally argued in the antitrust case *Swift and*

*Company v. United States*. Moody was forced to resign from the Court after only four years because of ill health.

**Moody Blues, The** British rock and roll band, founded in 1964. The Moody Blues are best known for their successful blending of rock rhythms, orchestral string overlays and pop philosophy lyrics. The band enjoyed its greatest success with the album *Days of Future Passed (Dream)* (1967), which it recorded with the London Symphony Orchestra. the album featured the enduring hit single "Nights in White Satin." The personnel for this album were Graeme Edge, drums; Justin Hayward, vocals and guitar; John Lodge, bass; Mike Pinder, vocals; and Ray Thomas, flute and vocals. With occasional personnel changes, the band has remained together to the present day. Noteworthy albums include *In Search of the Lost Chord* (1968), *On the Threshold of a Dream* (1969) and *Octave* (1978). In 2002 Ray Thomas left the band.

**Moon, Keith** (*1947–1978*) British drummer who played in the rock group The WHO. Moon was one of the wild figures of the ROCK AND ROLL scene during the late 1960s and the 1970s. On one occasion, during a concert tour, he reportedly paid $400,000 to a hotel for damages caused by his antics. Another time, he drove his Rolls-Royce into a swimming pool. He died of a drug overdose.

**Moon, Sun Myung** (*1920–  *) South Korean evangelist. Moon is best known as the founder and spiritual leader of the Unification Church (1954). Between 200,000 and 2 million people belong to the church worldwide. Most recruits are young people (derogatorily called "Moonies") who are encouraged to leave families and jobs in order to live in communes and work for the church. Due to conflicts with his business enterprises, Moon moved church headquarters from South Korea to the U.S. in 1973. He was convicted of income tax evasion in 1984 and sentenced to a prison term. In the 1990s Moon became an avid supporter of the Republican Party in the U.S., often siding with it on cultural issues.

**Moore, Archie (Archibald Lee Wright)** (*1913–1998*) American boxer. Moore began boxing in 1936, but it wasn't until 1952 that he defeated Joey Maxim for the light-heavyweight title. In 1955 he sought the heavyweight title but was defeated by Rocky MARCIANO. The following year he tried again and was defeated by Floyd Patterson. He was able to successfully defend his light-heavyweight title until 1962. Moore registered 136 knockouts during his 220-bout career. Moore also appeared in films—*The Adventures of Huckleberry Finn* (1959)—and written an autobiography, *Any Boy Can* (1971).

**Moore, Brian** (*1921–1999*) Irish-born novelist. Although he had written some early novels under the pseudonym Michael Bryan, Moore is best known for *The Lonely Passion of Judith Hearne* (1956; originally published in Britain as *Judith Hearne*, 1955; filmed 1987). This work depicts a lonely spinster who, thwarted in her last attempt for companionship, seeks solace in alcohol; it is typical of Moore's work with its themes of alienation and despair. Moore often called upon his experiences as an emigré to Canada and later the U.S. in his subsequent fiction, which includes *The Luck of Ginger Coffey* (1960), *I Am Mary Dunne* (1968), *The Mangan Inheritance* (1979) and *Lies of Silence* (1990).

**Moore, Colleen (Kathleen Morrison)** (*1902–1988*) American actress who was a popular star of HOLLYWOOD silent films and early talkies. In a career that extended from 1917 to 1934, Moore achieved stardom through her portrayal of a flapper in *Flaming Youth* (1923), helping to touch off a craze for bobbed hair and short skirts; probably her greatest success was *Lilac Time* (1928). One of Hollywood's highest paid stars in the silent era, her personal favorite of her 100 or so films was *The Power and the Glory* (1933), in which she appeared opposite Spencer TRACY.

**Moore, Dudley** (*1935–2002*) British composer-songwriter, comedian and actor. Moore first gained notice in the revue BEYOND THE FRINGE (1960), for which he also wrote the songs. He went on to a second career as an accomplished jazz pianist and also formed a memorable partnership with Peter COOK in such classic films as *Bedazzled* (1967). In the U.S. he is best known for his starring roles in the hit film comedies *10* (1979) and *Arthur* (1981), in which he cultivated a bumbling but charming persona.

**Moore, George Augustus** (*1852–1933*) Anglo-Irish novelist. Moore studied painting in Paris, and his works show the influence of such French writers as Balzac and Zola. After returning to England he published *A Modern Lover* (1883). The novel's Bohemian subject matter caused it to be banned by circulating libraries in England, and Moore became an adamant opponent of censorship. Moore's other early novels include *A Mummer's Wife* (1885) and *Esther Waters* (1894), his best known work, which evokes his childhood home in County Mayo. Moore's later novels are of more epic proportions and include *The Brook Kerith* (1916) and *Heloise and Abelard* (1921). Moore was instrumental, along with W. B. YEATS, in the forming of the Irish National Theatre. Moore has also written the autobiographical *Confessions of a Young Man* (1888), *Memoirs of My Dead Life* (1906) and the three-volume *Hail and Farewell* (1911–14).

**Moore, G(eorge) E(dward)** (*1873–1958*) British philosopher. Moore, who was educated at Cambridge University and taught there for most of his adult life, was a highly influential philosopher who had a special fascination for the BLOOMSBURY GROUP. In his major work, *Principia Ethica*, Moore argued that ethical decisions hinged on a blend of idealism and utilitarianism. The idea of absolute good was an appropriate guide to right action in daily life. But right action, in turn, hinged upon moral obligations to others as well as the special value one assigned to aesthetic beauty and to personal joys such as friendship and love. Moore analyzed a variety of epistemological and ethical questions in *Philosophical Studies* (1922), in which his basic approach was to defend common sense as opposed to technical language analysis. Moore edited the influential British philosophical journal *Mind* from 1921 to 1947.

**Moore, Henry Spencer** (*1898–1986*) British sculptor. During WORLD WAR II he became widely known in Britain for his drawings of people huddled together taking shelter in the London Underground during the blitz. He went on to become one of the most successful public sculptors of his age, and hundreds of his works came to grace parks, public squares and buildings throughout the world. His most characteristic subject was the reclining female. Many of his human figures had holes in them and small heads atop massive bodies. Among the best known of his works are the six-ton bronze sculpture completed in 1964 that decorated a fountain at Lincoln Center and the marble sculpture that decorates the headquarters of the UNITED NATIONS Educational, Scientific and Cultural Organization in PARIS.

**Moore, Marianne** *(1887–1972)* American poet. An indifferent student at Bryn Mawr (1905–09), where she was denied an English major, Moore burst onto the literary scene in 1915, when her first poems were accepted by the *Egoist* and *Poetry* magazines. Her originality, precise language, sharp and idiosyncratic vision and concentration of thought so impressed her literary peers that she was soon regarded as one of the leaders of the modernist movement in literature (see MODERNISM). Her position as editor of the *Dial* (1925–29) made her arguably the most powerful figure in modernist poetry in the 1920s. Her *Collected Poems* (1951) received the Bollingen Award, the PULITZER PRIZE and the NATIONAL BOOK AWARD. She went on to win virtually every prize and accolade offered to a poet in the U.S. In later years, her public image as a charming white-haired eccentric who appeared at Brooklyn Dodgers baseball games wearing a black tricorne hat overshadowed her reputation as a major poet.

*American poet Marianne Moore* (LIBRARY OF CONGRESS, PRINTS AND PHOTOGRAPHS DIVISION)

**Morales Ayma, Juan Evo** *(1959– )* Bolivian coca farmer and president of Bolivia (2005– ). Born to a poor family of the indigenous Quechua people, Morales became the leader of a coalition of coca leaf–growing farmers who opposed the government campaign financed by the U.S. to eradicate coca leaf production in Bolivia. He also formed a political party, the Movement for Socialism, that called for sweeping socioeconomic reforms in this impoverished South American country. Morales's movement won a notable victory in 2000 when it forced the government to back down from a plan to privatize the waterworks of a Bolivian city and hand it over to a multinational corporation. But it was peasant resistance to the U.S. backed coca-eradication campaign that brought Morales into the international spotlight. In 2001 he placed second in the presidential elections, surprising and alarming the traditional parties, and became an outspoken critic of the government. In the presidential elections of 2005, Morales ran on a campaign calling for the nationalization of key industries, price freezes on certain essential goods, an increase in taxation for the wealthy, and land redistribution. He also endorsed the legalization of the production of coca leaves for chewing as a dietary supplement, a habit indulged in by most indigenous peasants in Bolivia. Amid growing unrest in rural areas and political instability in the capital, Morales won a majority of the votes and became the country's first president of indigenous descent. He promptly aligned himself with Cuba's Fidel CASTRO and Venezuela's Hugo Chávez in opposition to the economic policies promoted by the U.S. and its supporters in Latin America. In 2006 Morales announced the nationalization of the natural gas industry and expressed hopes of nationalizing mining, forestry and other sectors of Bolivia's economy. Morales raised some eyebrows by visiting foreign heads of state (including the king of Spain) dressed in a striped sweater. On taking office he reduced his salary by half and led a very spartan life as president of Bolivia.

**Moral Majority** See Jerry FALWELL.

**Moral Re-Armament** See Frank BUCHMAN.

**Morandi, Giorgio** *(1890–1964)* Italian painter. Born in Bologna, he lived in that city for most of his life, never leaving his native country. Early in his career (1918–20) he was associated with the METAPHYSICAL PAINTING of the painter Giorgio de CHIRICO. In the early 1920s he created his own style of still-life painting. In these quietly poetic compositions, Morandi portrayed humble bottles, vases and jars in simplified shapes and in a severely limited palette, mainly earth tones. He was also a skilled etcher, again using still lifes for his subject matter.

**Morante, Elsa** *(1918–1985)* Italian novelist. Morante is one of the most highly regarded Italian novelists of the post–WORLD WAR II era. Her novels reflect a deep sense of historical awareness and a sensitivity to the need for love and to the ultimate fragility of the human psyche. While not prolific, Morante has so carefully crafted each of her novels as to gain them the status of modern classics. Morante first gained international attention with *Arturo's Island* (1957), an examination of the relationship between individualism and societal demands. *History: A Novel* (1974) is a penetrating study of the impact of World War II upon European culture. *Aracoeli* (1983) is a moving depiction of the difficulties of homosexual existence and the depth of a mother's love. Morante was at one time married to the Italian novelist Alberto MORAVIA.

**Moravia, Alberto** *(Alberto Pincherle)* *(1907–1990)* Italian author. Moravia was perhaps the best known and most widely read Italian writer of his time. His books explored sex, alienation and other contemporary social issues. His first novel, *The Time of Indifference* (1929), was published when he was 21 years old. His subsequent works include *The Women of Rome* (1949; filmed 1956), *The Conformist* (1951) and *Two Women* (1958; adapted for the screen by Vittorio DE SICA and starring Sophia LOREN).

**Moreau, Jeanne** *(1928– )* French actress and director. Moreau, who is known for her sultry eroticism and wry humor, achieved international acclaim, particularly for her work in the films of Louis MALLE, François TRUFFAUT, and Luis BUÑUEL. She began her career as a member of the Comedie Française (1948–52), then became the star of the Théâtre National Populaire. Her first screen success came in Malle's *L'Ascenseur pour l'échafaud* (1957). Her performance in Roger Vadim's *Les Liaisons Dangereuses* (1959) made her a star. Other famous roles were in Truffaut's *Jules et Jim* (1961), Buñuel's *Le Journal d'une femme de chambre* (1964) and Malle's *Viva Maria!* (1965) with Brigitte BARDOT. She has also written, sung and recorded her own songs. In the 1990s Moreau made only four film appearances: *Until the End of the World* (1991), *The Lover* (1992), *Beyond the Clouds* (1995), and *Ever After* (1998). During that decade Moreau also received several awards in recognition of her contributions to the silver screen, most notably a Golden Lion at the 1991 Venice Film Festival and a 1997 European Film Academy Lifetime Achievement Award.

**Morgan, J(ohn) P(ierpont)** *(1837–1913)* U.S. financier. Morgan was born in Hartford, Connecticut, and educated at the University of Göttingen. In 1856 he entered his father's banking firm and by the end of the century had made the firm (known as J. P. Morgan & Co. after 1895) one of the most powerful banking houses in the world. Morgan was a major force in the centralization of industry and credit around the turn of the 20th century. He also played a central role in the reorganization of U.S. railroads and in the marketing of government bonds. Morgan's personal influence helped stabilize financial conditions during the Panic of 1907. The financier was a target of the progressive Trust Busters. In 1904 the Supreme Court dissolved his Northern Securities Company, formed to control Western railroads, for violation of the Sherman Antitrust Act. The chief target of the 1912 Pujo investigation of the "Money Trust," Morgan emerged with his reputation and prestige unimpaired. A great philanthropist, he was a major benefactor of the Metropolitan Museum of Art. Morgan bequeathed his personal library to the public.

**Morgan, J(ohn) P(ierpont), Jr.** *(1867–1943)* U.S. businessman. The son of J. P. MORGAN, young Morgan became head of the house of Morgan after his father's death in 1913. As American agent for Great Britain in 1914, Morgan's banking firm raised huge amounts of money for the purchase of military supplies. The firm was not important in financing the war but handled most of the postwar loans, including those associated with reparations, while also sponsoring billions of dollars in domestic securities. A philanthropist, Morgan made large gifts to education and the arts.

**Morgan, Thomas Hunt** *(1866–1945)* American geneticist. Born in Lexington, Kentucky, Morgan earned his Ph.D. from Johns Hopkins in 1890. While a professor of experimental zoology at Columbia University (1904–28), he amended Mendel's laws of inheritance and developed the chromosome theory of genetics; he mapped individual genes, demonstrated genetic linkage and described the process of "crossing over," by which linkages are broken. In 1933, in recognition of his pioneering role as one of the founders of modern genetics, Morgan received the NOBEL PRIZE in medicine or physiology.

**Morgenstern, Christian** *(1871–1914)* German poet. Morgenstern contracted tuberculosis from his mother at an early age; due to his illness, he was forced to withdraw from the university. He moved to Scandinavia, where he translated the works of HAMSUN, STRINDBERG and Ibsen. His popular nonsense verse appeared as *Galgenlieder* (1905) and *Palmstroem* (1910). However, he was strongly influenced by Rudolf Steiner and anthroposophism and thus regarded his serious mystical verse as his greatest achievement. He also published lyric love poems in *Ein Sommer* (1899) and *Ich und Du* (1911), but he is best remembered as a master of wordplay and nonsense whose inventiveness rivals that of Edward Lear and Lewis Carroll.

**Morgenthau, Hans Joachim** *(1904–1980)* German-born political scientist, author and teacher. A Jewish exile from Nazi GERMANY, Morgenthau taught at the University of Chicago for 17 years. There he became one of America's most respected foreign policy analysts, known for writings that stressed national interest rather than world opinion in policy making. He was an early critic of American involvement in the VIETNAM WAR. He was also an outspoken critic of the USSR's treatment of JEWS and a strong advocate of nuclear arms control and DÉTENTE with the USSR

**Morgenthau, Henry, Jr.** *(1891–1967)* U.S. secretary of the Treasury (1933–45). Born into a wealthy family, Morgenthau was a gentleman-farmer and a Hyde Park, N.Y., neighbor of Franklin ROOSEVELT. He assisted FDR's political comeback after Roosevelt was stricken with polio; and, after FDR became governor of New York, Roosevelt appointed his friend to a state post. Despite Morgenthau's lack of experience Roosevelt appointed him secretary of the Treasury when FDR went to the White House. Although a fiscal conservative, Morgenthau proved an active secretary and a major NEW DEAL figure. He was instrumental in financing the New Deal spending programs and in establishing a scheme to stabilize the world's monetary system. Toward the end of World War II his MORGENTHAU PLAN advocated a "pastoralized" Nazi Germany. After Harry S. TRUMAN became president on FDR's death in 1945, Morgenthau's influence waned and he resigned. He was critical of Truman for abandoning FDR's policy of cooperation with the USSR In later years Morgenthau devoted himself to philanthropy, especially the United Jewish Appeal. He died at the age of 75 in 1967.

**Morgenthau plan** Plan advanced toward the end of World War II by U.S. secretary of the Treasury Henry MORGENTHAU to "pastoralize" Nazi GERMANY after the war. German industry would be dismantled, and Germany would be turned into an agricultural nation. Industrial areas would be annexed by FRANCE and POLAND, and the nation itself would be split into separate northern and southern states. The plan also proposed separating German children from their parents by sending them to special Allied boarding schools. Proposed by Secretary Morgenthau at the QUEBEC CONFERENCE in 1944, the plan was originally accepted by U.S. president Franklin ROOSEVELT and British prime minister Winston CHURCHILL. However, they both dropped their support of the plan after the U.S. State Department and British Foreign Office rejected it as unworkable because it would require heavy subsidies from the Allies. The Nazi propaganda office used the plan to encourage Germans to resist the Allied invasion to the bitter end.

**Morison, Samuel Eliot** (*1887–1976*) U.S. historian. He started his teaching career in 1915 at Harvard and became a full professor there in 1925. Two of his books, *Admiral of the Ocean Sea* (1942) and *John Paul Jones* (1959), won PULITZER PRIZES. He was commissioned by President Franklin ROOSEVELT to write the 15-volume *History of United States Naval Operations in World War II* (1946–62).

**Morley, Christopher** (*1890–1957*) American author and editor. A Rhodes scholar, Morley began his career in publishing. He helped found *The Saturday Review of Literature* in 1924, for which he wrote until 1941, and served in an editorial capacity for many other journals and periodicals. Morley is best known for his popular novels which include *Parnassus on Wheels* (1917), *The Haunted Bookshop* (1919), *Kitty Foyle* (1939, filmed 1940) and *The Man Who Made Friends with Himself* (1949). Morley was also a poet, playwright and essayist; he also wrote the autobiography *John Mistletoe* (1931).

**Moro, Aldo** (*1916–1978*) Italian political leader. A prominent lawyer and Christian Democrat, he entered the constituent assembly in 1946, was elected to the Chamber of Deputies in 1948 and served as minister of justice from 1955 to 1957. Moro was also foreign minister (1965–66, 1969–72 and 1973–74) and prime minister (1963–68 and 1974–76). Considered an elder statesman in the Christian Democratic Party, he became its president in 1976, advocating rapprochement with the Communist Party. Moro was kidnapped on March 16, 1978, by the terrorist RED BRIGADES and was found shot to death on May 9, 1978. (See also ITALY.)

**Moroccan War of 1907–12** The AL-GECIRAS Conference (1906) stipulated that Moroccan territorial integrity was to be enforced by France and Spain although these two powers agreed to partition MOROCCO between them eventually. In 1907 Moroccans rioted against foreign workers in Casablanca and were crushed by French troops; but native opposition reemerged in 1908 when Sultan Abd-al Azziz IV was deposed by his brother. The new sultan requested help to maintain order; in consequence Spanish troops suffered defeat by Rif tribesmen who attacked Fez, which the French then occupied (1909). Germany, protesting French actions, sent a gunboat to Morocco. War was averted when France ceded Congolese territory to Germany to gain recognition of French authority in Morocco. By the Treaty of Fez (March 30, 1912), the sultan agreed to a French protectorate, and France and Spain then split Morocco into four zones with French rule over three of them.

**Morocco** Coastal African nation, bordering the Mediterranean Sea on the north, the Atlantic Ocean on the west; it is north of Mauritania and west of Algeria.

In 1912 Morocco was made wholly a French protectorate, with the exception of a small Spanish territory in the north. The 1920s saw a period of almost constant revolt, but Moroccan independence did not come about until 1956, when Mohammed V established an independent monarchy. Absolute power was consolidated by his successor, Hassan II. In 1976 the oil-rich region of the Spanish Sahara in the southwest was taken over jointly with MAURITANIA (which renounced its claim in 1979 after fierce guerrilla opposition), and Morocco regained full control of the territory. In 1991 Morocco agreed to a UN-monitored ceasefire in Western Sahara that called for a referendum on the territory's future. However, that vote has yet to occur. The following year King Hassan II inaugurated a new constitution that allowed for the election of a prime minister independent of the monarchy. In 1998 this led to the first government controlled by the opposition party. Following the death of King Hassan II in

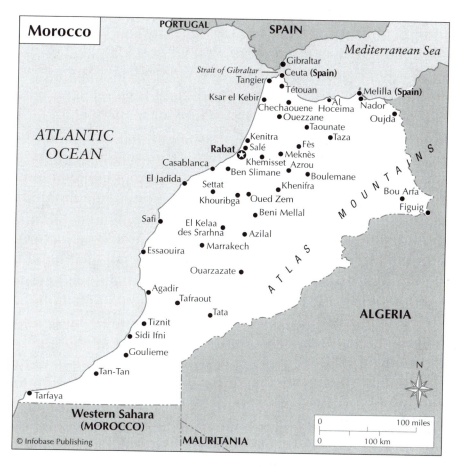

## MOROCCO

| 1904 | Secret agreement between France and Spain divides control of Morocco. |
|------|------|
| 1912 | Rebellion against the sultan; French seize opportunity to send troops and proclaim protectorate; flood of French immigration begins. |
| 1921 | Abd el-Krim proclaims republic in the Rif Mountains; begins bitter five-year defense against French and Spanish. |
| 1947 | King Mohammed V leads independence struggle through Istiqlal Party. |
| 1953 | Mohammed exiled; terrorists fight French and Spanish. |
| 1956 | Independence granted by French; Mohammed returns; Spanish follow suit. |
| 1961 | Mohammed dies; his son crowned Hassan II; Morocco becomes world's leading source of phosphates. |
| 1979 | Polisario guerrillas wage independence struggle in Western Sahara; Hassan begins military buildup; price of phosphates drops; economy suffers. |
| 1988 | UN organizes peace talks with guerrilla forces. |
| 1989 | Polisario mounts new offensive; "Arab Maghreb" economic union joins countries of northwest Africa. |
| 1991 | Morocco agrees to a UN-monitored cease-fire in Western Sahara that endorsed a referendum on the territory's future. |
| 1992 | A new constitution is ratified, providing for a prime minister as the head of the government, to be appointed by the king. |
| 1996 | A national referendum approves creation of a second chamber in the legislature and direct election of members of the existing Chamber of Representatives. |
| 1999 | King Hassan dies and is succeeded by his son, who is crowned as King Mohammed VI. |
| 2003 | Casablanca court jails three Saudi citizens, members of al-Qaeda, for 10 years for plotting to attack British and U.S. warships in the Strait of Gibraltar in 2002. |
| 2004 | Earthquake in northern Morocco kills more than 500. A free trade agreement is signed with the U.S. |
| 2005 | Truth Commission claims more than 500 people were killed during King Hassan II's rule. |

1999 and the ascension of his son, Mohammed VI, to the throne, Morocco has striven to resolve the disputed status of Western Sahara. King Mohammed VI has also personally engaged in talks with Spain to resolve the jointly disputed status of the island of Perejil. After deadly suicide bombings in Casablanca in 2003, Morroco launched a crackdown on suspected Islamic militants. King Mohammed's Truth Commission began to uncover possible human rights violations that occurred during King Hassan's reign.

**Moro Wars** (*1901–1913*) The Moros, Muslim tribespeople of central and western Mindanao in the PHILIPPINES, traditionally had lived apart from Christian Filipinos. The Spanish, rulers until driven out by Americans in 1898, had left them alone. The Americans, however, wished them to be assimilated; the Moros resisted with sporadic outbreaks beginning in 1901. In 1903 they attacked American troops in central Mindanao; in 1906, 600 Moro rebels, taking refuge inside a volcanic crater in Jolo, were slaughtered by U.S. troops under General Leonard Wood, resulting in

public indignation. The fighting ended after June 1913 and the Moros were left in peace.

**Morrison, Herbert** (*1906–1989*) U.S. radio reporter. His emotional broadcast of the crash of the German airship *HINDENBURG* at Lakehurst, New Jersey, in 1937 was recorded and made his voice familiar to millions.

**Morrison, Herbert Stanley** (*1888–1965*) British politician. The son of a London policeman, Morrison held a variety of jobs as he became involved in the London LABOUR PARTY, becoming its general secretary in 1915. He entered the London County Council in 1922 and through his abilities as an organizer became its leader (1934–40). Morrison was a member of Parliament (1923–24, 1929–31 and 1935–45). He also served as minister of transport (1931), and as minister of supply in Winston CHURCHILL's coalition government (1940), after which he served as home secretary until the end of the coalition. Morrison was instrumental in creating the National Fire Service and was involved in the development of the social services adopted after Clement ATTLEE came to power in 1946. Morrison was deputy prime minister and lord president of the council from 1945 to 1951 when he served briefly as foreign secretary. He attempted to succeed Attlee as party leader in 1955 but was defeated by Hugh GAITSKELL.

**Morrison, Toni (Chloe Anthony Wofford)** *(1931–  )* American novelist. Beginning with *The Bluest Eye* (1969), which examines black self-hatred, Morrison's original fiction has explored the black experience in a racist culture, as well as universal themes of human interrelations. Subsequent novels, include *Sula* (1973) and *Tar Baby* (1981). Morrison's work is both highly popular and critically esteemed. She was awarded the 1977 National Book

*Nobel Prize–winning author Toni Morrison. 1977*
(LIBRARY OF CONGRESS, PRINTS AND PHOTOGRAPHS DIVISION)

Critics Circle Award for *Song of Solomon* (1977) and the 1988 PULITZER PRIZE for *Beloved* (1987). Educated at Howard University and Cornell University, Morrison has been a member of the faculties of many American universities, including Princeton and Yale. In 1993 Morrison received the Nobel Prize in literature.

**Morro Castle** On September 8, 1934, the passenger liner *Morro Castle* caught fire off the coast of New Jersey and beached at Asbury Park. One-hundred-thirty passengers were killed in the disaster, which, because of its proximity to New York, was thoroughly covered by newsreel camera crews.

**Morse, David Abner** *(1907–1990)* U.S. labor leader. He was acting U.S. secretary of labor in 1948, and director general of the UNITED NATIONS' INTERNATIONAL LABOR ORGANIZATION from 1948 to 1970. He was an advocate of an eight-hour working day, child labor laws, maternity leave, workers' compensation and improved safety regulations. In 1969, Morse accepted the NOBEL PEACE PRIZE in behalf of the ILO.

**Mortimer, John Clifford** *(1923– )* British novelist and playwright. Mortimer trained and worked as a barrister before turning to writing. He is best known for the series "Rumpole of the Bailey," which centers on an eccentric barrister and his cases. These include *Rumpole and the Age of Miracles* (1989); early Rumpole books have been published in collections, such as *The Second Rumpole Omnibus* (1987). The series was successfully televised by the BBC. Mortimer's acute observations of life enrich his novels, which include *Summer's Lease* (1989), *Paradise Postponed* (1985) and its sequel *Titmus Regained* (1990). He is also known for his libertarian views and his stand against censorship. Other works include *A Voyage Round My Father* (1970), a biography of his father, and *Clinging to the Wreckage* (1982), an autobiography. Mortimer was formerly married to the novelist Penelope Mortimer.

**Morton, Jelly Roll (La Menthe Morton)** *(1890–1941)* American pianist-composer, ranks among jazzdom's

true innovators by dint of his unique amalgamation of the different black musical styles he learned and performed in his native New Orleans—namely, ragtime, instrumental blues, gospel songs, field hollers and minstrel show tunes. As a pianist, Morton is credited with "opening up" the through-composed ragtime of W. C. HANDY by interpolating sections designated for improvisation; Morton's "Grandpa's Spells" and "Kansas City Stomp" encapsulate the expanded ragtime approach that would be taken up in the 1930s by such piano virtuosos as Earl "Fatha" HINES. In ensemble works such as "Black Bottom Stomp" and "The Pearls," Morton proved that meticulous arrangements could include improvised sections without sacrificing clarity of form; the most significant examples of his group concept were recorded in 1926–27 by Morton's well-rehearsed and disciplined Red Hot Peppers. By the 1930s, given the whimsical nature of society's ever fickle and shifting musical tastes, Morton was considered passé. However, recordings made by folklorist Alan Lomax in 1938 revived Morton's career until ill health forced his retirement in 1940. Other classic Morton compositions include "Wolverine Blues," "Milenberg Joys" and the eponymous "Jelly Roll Blues."

**Moscow Art Theater** Founded in 1898 by Konstantin STANISLAVSKY and Vladimir NEMIROVICH-DANCHENKO, the Moscow Art Theater achieved worldwide acclaim for its theatrical naturalism. Stanislavsky, who was in charge of stage direction, strove to strip the theater of commercialism and stereotyped mannerisms by concentrating on inner moods and emotions; in this he was influenced by the German Meiningen Company. The original ensemble was composed of amateur actors from the Society of Art and Literature. The theater performed plays by GORKY, ANDREYEV, Maeterlinck and HAUPTMANN, and in particular the works of CHEKHOV. The theater continued to flourish after the revolution. It has undertaken several international tours and has influenced theaters all over the world.

**Moser, Koloman (Kolo Moser)** *(1868–1918)* Viennese artist, graphics and furniture designer. He was a founding member of the Vienna Secession movement. Moser had studied painting before becoming acquainted with Josef HOFFMANN, Gustav Klimt and Josef Olbrich. In 1898 he designed a stained-glass window for Olbrich's Secession Gallery. In 1899 Moser began to teach at the Vienna School of Applied Arts—a post he held until his death. During his career he designed furniture—often using decorative inlays—jewelry, toys and bookbindings. He also designed stained glass for Otto Wagner's Vienna Kirche am Steinhof (1904), posters, and other graphics items, including an Austrian postage stamp of 1908. He was, with Josef Hoffmann, a founder of the Wiener Werkstätte. In his later years, Moser was chiefly active as a painter.

**Moser-Proell, Annemarie** *(1953– )* Austrian skiing champion. Known for her aggressive, risk-taking style, Moser-Proell joined the Austrian national ski team at age 15. Over the course of her career, she won 62 individual World Cup victories, more than any other woman. She also won a record seven World Cup downhill titles (1971–75, 1978–79) and won the overall World Cup title a record six times, in 1971–75 and again in 1979. From December 1972 to January 1974, she won 11 consecutive World Cup downhill races, a record. In the 1980 Winter OLYMPIC GAMES in Lake Placid, New York, Moser-Proell won a gold medal in the downhill. She announced her retirement from World Cup events that year.

**Moses, Robert** *(1888–1981)* American urban planner who transformed the landscape of NEW YORK CITY from the 1920s through the 1960s. A shrewd and aggressive bargainer known for his single-minded determination, he gained power within the state's public works system—at one point holding 12 positions simultaneously. He entered public service in 1919 under Governor Alfred E. SMITH. For various periods between 1924 and 1968 his titles included, among others, New York City parks commissioner, head of the State Parks Council and chairman of the Triborough Bridge and Tunnel Authority and of the New York State Power Authority. Although he was never elected to any

public office (he was an unsuccessful candidate for governor in 1934), behind the scenes he wielded more actual power than many of the governors and mayors under whom he served. During his reign he oversaw the construction of 75 state parks, 11 bridges and 481 miles of highway around New York City. He was also responsible for the development of massive housing complexes, tunnels, playgrounds, beaches, zoos, civic centers and exhibition halls. Among his projects were Lincoln Center, the New York Coliseum, Shea Stadium, the Robert Moses Niagara Power Plant and the 1964–65 World's Fair grounds. He held on to his power until the age of 80, when Governor Nelson ROCKEFELLER forced him to retire.

Moses exemplified the bigger-is-better approach to urban development in the 20th century. His monumental plans—often carried out at the expense of neighborhoods, tradition and human needs—contributed to the impersonality of the city. His projects in New York set an example that was repeated throughout the U.S. and in other parts of the world.

**Mosley, Sir Oswald Ernald** *(1896–1980)* British fascist leader. He began his political career as a Conservative member of Parliament in 1918, becoming an independent from 1922 to 1924, when he joined the Labour Party. A junior cabinet minister (1929–30), he resigned in a dispute over economic policies, and in 1931 founded the socialist New Party. Soon his views took a decidedly right-wing turn, and in 1932 he dissolved the New Party and founded the British Union of Fascists. When his first wife, Lady Cynthia Curzon died, he married (1936) Diana Guinness—a member of the MITFORD family, many of whom were active supporters of Adolf HITLER. Mosley began to stage fascist rallies and marches and to make violently anti-Semitic speeches. Mosley and his wife were interned in 1940 due to their espousal of the Nazi cause. They were released three years later. After the war, Mosley unsuccessfully attempted to revive his movement and his political career. His autobiography, *My Life,* was published in 1968.

**Mosquito Coast (Miskito Coast, Mosquitia; Costa de Mosquitos)** *(Honduras and Nicaragua)* A 40-mile-wide region extending from the San Juan River in the north into northeast HONDURAS, its name having been derived from the Mosquito (Misketto) Indians. In 1894 it was made part of NICARAGUA under the dictatorship of José Santos Zelaya, an issue that was not settled until 1960, when the International Court of Justice awarded the northern coastal region to Honduras. In the early 1980s, the Sandinista regime in Nicaragua was accused of having massacred the Indian population occupying both sides of the border with Honduras.

**Mossadeq, Mohammed** *(1881–1967)* Iranian political leader, prime minister of IRAN (1951–53). Born in Tehran, Mossadeq entered politics in 1914 and served as foreign minister from 1922 to 1924. When the shah assumed dictatorial powers in 1925, Mossadeq protested by retiring from political life. He returned to governmental affairs as a member of the Iranian parliament in 1942. A militant nationalist who objected to foreign interference in Iran's affairs, he opposed Soviet attempts to exploit the country's oil resources and spearheaded the movement to nationalize the British-owned Anglo-Iranian Oil Company. A fiery reformer and powerful speaker who was extremely popular with the Iranian people, he was appointed prime minister in 1951 after the passage of the oil nationalization act. Thereafter, Western technology experts withdrew from the country, rendering Iran powerless to produce the oil on which the country's economy and Mossadeq's promised social reforms rested. With the nation in political crisis, Mossadeq was dismissed by the shah in 1953 and was subsequently arrested. Imprisoned for three years, he spent the rest of his life under house arrest.

**Motherwell, Robert** *(1915–1991)* American painter. Born in Aberdeen, Washington, he was educated at Stanford University and pursued graduate studies in philosophy and art history at Harvard and Columbia. He later taught art at a number of colleges. An articulate exponent of ABSTRACT EXPRESSIONISM, Motherwell edited the 15-volume series *Documents of Modern Art* from 1944 to 1961. His abstract works have titles that often allude to philosophical or political ideas. Motherwell paints large bold forms in strongly contrasting colors with slashing brushstrokes. Created as a reaction to the SPANISH CIVIL WAR, his best-known works are a series of more than 100 powerful paintings entitled *Elegy to the Spanish Republic* (1947–76).

**Mothopeng, Zephania Lekoane** *(1913–1990)* South African political activist. He joined the AFRICAN NATIONAL CONGRESS in his youth but split with the organization in 1959 to form the more militant Pan-African Congress. The group opposed power-sharing with whites and refused to join negotiations proposed by government President F. W. DE KLERK. Mothopeng was jailed several times between 1964 and 1988 for his activities.

**Motown** American record company that was the wellhead of much of the important music of the 1960s. Motown artists included Smokey Robinson, the Temptations, Martha Reeves and the Vandellas, the Jackson 5, Stevie WONDER, the Four Tops and innumerable others. Founded in Detroit by paternal despot Berry Gordy, Motown became one of the most prominent black-owned corporations in the world. Gordy dictated artists' behavior on-and off-stage, including clothes, hair and choice of companions. Gordy was also reluctant to share financial information with the artists who were bringing in the revenue, and the label lost many artists in later years. Gordy's mark on the label's music is unmistakable, however, and the Motown sound instantly recognizable.

**Mott, John Raleigh** *(1865–1955)* American humanitarian and religious leader. Born in Livingston Manor, New York, he became an active member of the YMCA while an undergraduate at Cornell University, serving as national secretary of the organization's Intercollegiate Committee from 1888 to 1915. In 1888 he also became the director of the Student Volunteer Movement for Foreign Missions. In 1895 Mott founded the World's Student Christian Federation. As national executive of the American YMCA (1915) and general secretary of the National War Work Council (1916), he helped to raise some $200 million for WORLD WAR I relief efforts.

Mott became chairman of the International Missionary council in 1921 and president of the World YMCA in 1926. During WORLD WAR II he worked on numerous fund-raising campaigns to support the YMCA's many humanitarian programs. In 1946 he shared the NOBEL PEACE PRIZE with Emily Greene BALCH. A leading Methodist layman and advocate of ecumenical efforts, he was named honorary president of the newly formed World Council of Churches in 1948.

**Mott, Sir Nevill Francis** *(1905–1996)* British physicist; studied at Cambridge University, gaining his bachelor's degree in 1927 and master's in 1930. Mott never pursued a doctorate but from 1930 until 1933 was a lecturer and fellow of Granville and Caius College, Cambridge. Subsequently he moved to Bristol University as a professor of theoretical physics. In 1948 he became director of Bristol's physics laboratories but returned later to Cambridge as Cavendish Professor of Experimental Physics, where he served from 1954 until his retirement in 1971. Mott's work in the early 1930s was on the quantum theory of atomic collisions and scattering. With H. S. W. Massey he wrote the first of several classic texts, *The Theory of Atomic Collisions* (1934). Other influential texts that followed were *The Theory of the Properties of Metals and Alloys* (with H. Jones, 1936) and *Electronic Processes in Ionic Crystals* (with R. W. Gurney, 1940). Each marked a significant phase of active research. Mott also began to explore the defects and surface phenomena involved in the photographic process (explaining latent-image formation) and did significant work on dislocations, defects and the strength of crystals. By the mid-1950s, Mott was able to turn his attention to problems of disordered materials, liquid metals, impurity bands in semiconductors, and the glassy semiconductors. His models of the solid state became more and more complex and included an analysis of electronic processes in metal-insulator transitions, often called "Mott transitions." In 1977 Mott shared the NOBEL PRIZE in physics with Philip ANDERSON and John Van Vleck for their "fundamental theoretical investigations of the electronic structure of magnetic and disordered systems." Mott was knighted in 1962.

**Moulin, Jean** *(1899–1943)* Leader of the French RESISTANCE. A civil prefect in the French department of Eure-et-Loire when the Germans occupied France in 1940 during WORLD WAR II, Moulin was an active opponent of the Nazis, who imprisoned him. Released, he fled to London but returned to France and, from 1942 to early 1943, organized Resistance efforts, coordinated Resistance fighters in the north and south of France and united representatives of political movements, trade unions and political parties into a national Resistance council. Betrayed to the Germans, Moulin was captured on June 21, 1943, and, after nearly a month of torture by the GESTAPO, died on July 8, 1943.

**Mountbatten, Lord Louis** (Earl Mountbatten of Burma) *(1900–1979)* British naval officer, colonial administrator, member of the royal family; born Louis Francis Albert Nicholas Battenberg. As the last viceroy of INDIA, he guided that country's transition from Britain's largest colony to an independent nation and member of the COMMONWEALTH. A grand-nephew of Queen Victoria, Mountbatten trained as a naval officer and served as a midshipman in WORLD WAR I. Early in WORLD WAR II he commanded a Royal Navy destroyer. He rose rapidly to become Allied Chief of Combined Operations in Southeast Asia, coordinating the Allied recapture of Burma from the Japanese. He also planned commando raids on German-held Europe before D DAY. In 1947, as part of Britain's plan to grant India independence, Prime Minister ATTLEE appointed him viceroy. Mountbatten accomplished his task in five months, negotiating successfully with NEHRU and JINNAH despite many obstacles. Following independence, he was India's first governor-general. He later held the posts of commander in chief of NATO forces in the Mediterranean, first sea lord (head of the British navy) and chief of the British defense staff. In his later years he was an influential adviser to his grandnephew, Prince CHARLES. While vacationing in Ireland Mountbatten was killed by a bomb planted aboard his boat by IRA terrorists. After his death his cousin Queen ELIZABETH II changed the name of the royal family to Windsor-Mountbatten in his honor.

**Moureu, Henri** *(1899–1978)* French scientist and patriot. During WORLD WAR II Moureu foiled German plans to develop an ATOMIC BOMB by keeping the French supply of heavy water out of Nazi hands. He also foiled a German plan to destroy Paris with *V-2* rockets. This he did by calculating the location of the German *V-2* launching bases and passing this information to the U.S. Air Force, which destroyed them. Moureu was a member of the French Academy of Sciences.

**Moynihan, Daniel Patrick** *(1927–2003)* American politician. Moynihan gained prominence as a member of Governor Averell HARRIMAN's staff in the 1950s. He served as assistant secretary of labor (1963–65) in the KENNEDY and JOHNSON administrations. During the 1970s he was ambassador to India and to the UN. As urban affairs adviser to President NIXON he caused a furor by proposing a policy of "benign neglect" toward welfare recipients. Elected to the U.S. Senate as a New York Democrat in 1978, he supported a strong defense, criticized President REAGAN's Latin American policies and took a liberal approach to domestic issues. Moynihan decided not to run for reelection in 2000 and was succeeded by First Lady Hillary Rodham Clinton.

**Mozambique (formerly: Portuguese East Africa)** East coastal African nation south of Tanzania, bordering Zimbabwe, Malawi and Zambia to the west, South Africa to the south. Until recent times, the Portuguese dominated Mozambique for nearly 400 years, during which it had been used as a dumping ground for convicts, when Portugal's power waned in the 18th century, and later for slave trading, owing to heavy labor demands from Brazil in the late 18th and early 19th centuries. Actual control of the colony was wrested from Portugal for the most part, by renegade settler and native rebellions during the 19th century; the interior of Mozambique was not to be fully regained until 1920. The economy of the colony was

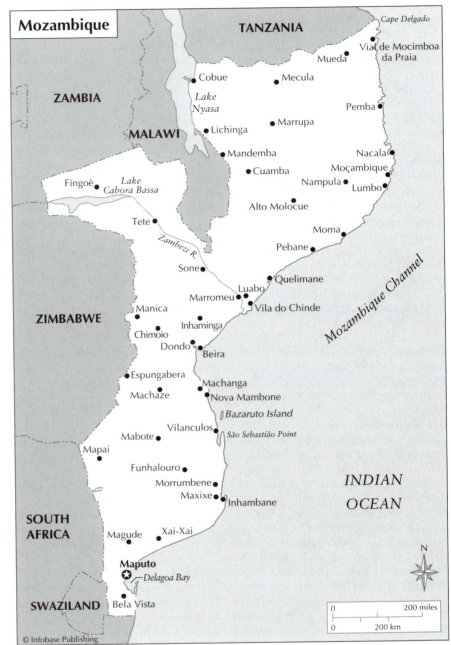

successfully developed, by Portugal's utter exploitation of Mozambique's native population. Its capital, the town of Mozambique, was replaced in 1907 by Lourenço Marques, renamed Maputo in 1976.

After the outbreak of guerrilla warfare in ANGOLA in 1961, PORTUGAL begrudged the colony token reforms, but not until 1964 did the Mozambique National Liberation Front, FRELIMO, openly declare war against the colonial government, which mired Portugal in a rapidly escalating, costly war. In 1974 the government in Lis-

bon was overthrown, and the new regime moved quickly to negotiate with the rebels. In 1975 Mozambique became an independent nation, with Samora MACHEL, Frelimo's former leader, as the new socialist head of state. War was declared with RHODESIA, where border clashes were frequent in 1976, and ZIMBABWE guerrillas operated out of Mozambique until 1979, when Rhodesia gained independence and emerged as the nation of Zimbabwe. It is estimated that 600,000 people died in the war. President Machel died in a suspicious

## Mozambique

| | |
|---|---|
| 1951 | Mozambique becomes a province of Portugal. |
| 1964 | Armed struggle against Portuguese commences. |
| 1975 | Mozambique gains independence from Portugal; Samora Machel becomes ruler. |
| 1976 | Mozambique closes its border to Rhodesia in support of that country's guerrilla movement; the Rhodesian intelligence service forms and fosters the Mozambique National Resistance, which institutes terror campaign. |
| 1986 | Machel dies in mysterious plane crash and is succeeded by his foreign minister, Joaquim Chissano. |
| 1989 | Joint UNICEF/Mozambican report estimates that 600,000 have been killed in the civil war and 494,000 have died of malnutrition. |
| 1990 | Mozambique legislature adopts new constitution designed to establish a Western-style democracy. |
| 1992 | President Chissano signs peace accord with the anticommunist movement Renamo. |
| 1994 | President Chissano is elected president in the first ever multiparty elections, and Frelimo wins a narrow majority in the assembly. |
| 1995 | UN peacekeepers leave the country. |
| 1999 | Frelimo candidates win a majority of seats in elections to the assembly. Chissano is reelected president. |
| 2000 | The worst floods in 50 years ravage the country; international donors pledge $453 million in relief. |
| 2004 | Frelimo's Armando Guebuza defeats Afonso Dhlakhama of Renamo in presidential elections. |

plane crash (Oct. 1986) and was succeeded by Foreign Minister Joaquim CHISSANO. In 1992 Chissano signed a peace accord with the anticommunist rebel organization Renamo. In 1995, a year after Chissano's reelection, UN troops departed because it appeared that the country's political situation had stabilized. However, subsequent developments—including allegations of corruption in the 1999 presidential election in which Chissano won a third term; the deaths of several imprisoned opposition supporters in November 2000; and the November 2002 allegations that Chissano was involved in the 2000 murder of jour-

nalist Carlos Cardoso—revealed serious political problems for the country. Chissano declined to run for another term in the 2004 elections, in which Armando Guebaza was elected president.

**MPLA (People's Movement for the Liberation of Angola)** A socialist movement that fought alongside UNITA and FNLA between 1961 and 1975 to secure Angolan independence from Portuguese rule (see ANGOLAN WAR OF INDEPENDENCE). After independence (November 10, 1975) it fought a civil war with UNITA and FNLA for control of the country; it was aided by CUBA.

Its People's Republic was eventually recognized as the true government of ANGOLA. (See also ANGOLAN CIVIL WAR.) In the 1990s the MPLA attempted to resolve its disputes with UNITA through diplomatic negotiations, such as the BICESSE ACCORD (1991), and the LUSAKA ACCORDS (1994). However, UNITA failed to abide by either agreement until its leader, Jonas Savimbi, was killed in 2002.

**Mravinsky, Yevgeny Alexandrovich** (1903–1988) Soviet conductor renowned for his interpretations of the Russian classics, particularly the symphonies of Tchaikovsky. Mravinsky led the Leningrad Philharmonic from 1938 until his death and was credited with transforming it into one of the world's great orchestras. Outside the USSR, he was known largely through his many recordings. He led the first performances of Dmitri SHOSTAKOVICH's fifth, sixth, eighth, ninth and tenth symphonies.

**MTV** A cable-based television network originally devoted to broadcasting music videos. Created in 1981, the network's original list of investors included Warner Communications and American Express, but was soon purchased by Viacom, Inc. Originally, MTV's programming schedule was dominated by the broadcast of music videos of various artists in the popular music genre of "soft rock," interspersed with commercials purchased by advertisers. However, by 1985 it became clear that more and more music fans of Generation X, the original target audience of MTV, were developing an interest in the genres of "heavy metal" or "METAL MUSIC," and "HIP-HOP" or rap music, and so MTV began to broadcast music videos from heavy metal groups like Van Halen and Metallica, and rap artists like Run DMC and Jam Master Jay. In 1985 MTV Networks launched Video Hits 1, a network designed to appeal to a more adult music audience. In 1989 MTV began to experiment with its programming lineup by reducing the number of music videos the network aired and introducing more programming it produced, such as the Cindy Crawford–hosted fashion show *House of Style* (1989), the animated series *Beavis and Butthead,* and the reality television series *The Real World* (1992).

Throughout the 1990s MTV continued this trend with additional original programs like *Total Request Live* (TRL), *Road Rules*, *MTV Cribs* and its annual *Video Music Awards*. During the 1990s, MTV also began to encourage greater voter registration among its audience. In 1992 it created Rock the Vote!, an organization dedicated to registering young adults 18 to 25 years old for local, state and national elections.

**Mubarak, Hosni** *(1928– )* President of EGYPT (1981– ). Mubarak began his career in the Egyptian air force, rising through the ranks to become a squadron and then fighter brigade commander. After Egypt's defeat by ISRAEL in the SIX-DAY WAR (1967), Mubarak was appointed director of the Egyptian Air Academy. President NASSER appointed him air force chief of staff in 1969; in 1972 he was made commander in chief of the air force by President Anwar el-SADAT. In October 1973, during the ARAB-ISRAELI WAR OF 1973, he was promoted to lieutenant general; in 1975 Mubarak was appointed vice president of Egypt. He headed Egyptian delegations to the ORGANIZATION OF AFRICAN UNITY conferences in 1975 and 1976 and in 1981 was elected vice chairman and then secretary general of Egypt's ruling National Democratic Party. In October 1981, following the assassination of Sadat, Mubarak was elected president of Egypt in a national referendum. Although lacking the charisma of his predecessors, Mubarak has proved a capable leader. Faced with serious economic and political problems at home and in the region, he has generally continued Sadat's pro-Western policies and is the leading Arab moderate in seeking peaceful coexistence rather than confrontation with Israel. Mubarak supported the U.S. coalition against IRAQ during the PERSIAN GULF WAR. Mubarak survived a November 1995 assassination attempt masterminded by Islamist enemies. With the dawn of a new millennium, Murbarak has maintained an active role in international affairs. In 2000 he involved himself in the Israeli-Palestinian peace process, and attempted to broker an accord between PALESTINIAN AUTHORITY president Yasir ARAFAT and Israeli prime minister Ehud BARAK. In 2005 Egypt permitted multiparty elections for the first time, but Mubarak's control of the electoral machinery assured his reelection despite allegations of fraud by rival candidates.

**muckrakers** Name applied to American social and political critics writing during the first decade of the 20th century. The writers, most of whom wrote for mass circulation magazines such as *Colliers*, *McClure's* and *Everybody's*, attempted to expose political and business corruption as well as problems such as child labor and prostitution. The term was derived from a 1906 speech by Theodore ROOSEVELT in which he criticized the writers for an interest in turning up only filth. Among the most famous muckrakers were Lincoln STEFFENS, Ida TARBELL and Upton SINCLAIR. The muckrakers prepared the way for many of the social and political reforms of the Progressive period including child labor and pure food legislation, greater regulation of business and direct election of senators. The public lost interest in the writers after 1912, but their influence was long-lasting.

**Muddy Waters** *(1915–1983)* American musician. The acknowledged king of the Chicago BLUES style of music, he was credited with having led the first electric blues-rock band using few players and maximum amplification. He began singing and playing guitar in the Mississippi Delta around 1930, and continued performing into the 1960s. He exerted a significant influence on modern popular musicians, including the ROLLING STONES.

**Mugabe, Robert** *(1924– )* African rebel leader, prime minister of ZIMBABWE (1980– ). A member of the Shona tribe, Mugabe was educated at the University of South Africa and the University of London. He began his professional career as a teacher in the 1950s and his political career as a member of a group that opposed Rhodesia's white rule and favored independence. Detained by Rhodesian authorities in 1962, he fled to Tanzania and was a cofounder (1963) of the Zimbabwe African National Union (ZANU). Imprisoned by the Ian SMITH government from 1964 to 1974, he joined with Joshua NKOMO in 1976 and became joint leader of the Patriotic Front (PF).

Mugabe became ZANU's sole leader in 1975, and, as head of the Zimbabwe African National Liberation Army, he led a guerrilla war (1976–79) against the Rhodesian regime and the government of Abel Muzorewa. After the cease-fire, Mugabe and the ZANU-PF were victorious in the new nation's elections; and he became Zimbabwe's first prime minister. In 1987 a merger was negotiated between his ZANU-PF and Nkomo's opposition party, ZAPU. That same year, Mugabe engineered the passage of a new constitution under which he was appointed executive president and head of state. In August 2002 Mugabe ordered the seizure of farmland belonging to nearly 3,000 white commercial farmers, as the economy declined drastically.

**Muggeridge, Malcolm** *(1903–1990)* British journalist, author, social critic and television personality. Muggeridge was known for his caustic wit and iconoclastic views that frequently offended both the right and the left. Initially an admirer of Soviet COMMUNISM, he changed his mind after spending time there in the early 1930s as a journalist for the *Manchester Guardian*. He subsequently became a committed Christian. During WORLD WAR II, Muggeridge worked for British intelligence in Africa. From 1953 to 1957 he served as editor-in-chief of *Punch* and was credited with helping to sharpen the magazine's humor. After leaving *Punch* he turned to television journalism and book reviewing. His 1957 article, "Does England Really Need a Queen?" provoked a national controversy in Britain; he also ruffled feathers with his outspoken opinions on U.S. presidents EISENHOWER and KENNEDY. In the 1960s Muggeridge became a leading voice of traditional CONSERVATISM and denounced the COUNTERCULTURE. His book *Jesus Reconsidered* (1969) described his spiritual journey. His other books include *Something Beautiful for God: Mother Teresa of Calcutta*, *Confessions of a Twentieth-Century Pilgrim* and *Chronicles of Wasted Time: An Autobiography*.

**Muhammad, Elijah (Elijah Poole)** *(1897–1975)* American Black Muslim leader. Son of a Baptist minister, in 1923 he moved with his family to Detroit to find work. He experienced unemployment and welfare, and developed a bitter hostility to public assistance. In 1931, Wali Farad, the founder of Nation of Islam, renamed Poole as Muhammad. He was named Messenger of Allah in 1934 at Farad's disappearance. The Muslim faith grew under Muhammad's leadership and, after his death, continues to grow under the leadership of his son, Wallace.

**Muir, Edwin** *(1887–1959)* Scottish poet, essayist, novelist and translator. Muir is regarded by such critics as T. S. ELIOT as one of the finest English-language poets of the 20th century. Born on Orkney Island off the north coast of Scotland, Muir never received a university education, working instead at a series of dreary factory jobs through his 20s. By dint of self-education and his passion to write, he succeeded in establishing himself as an author of eminence. His most notable volumes of poetry are *Journeys and Places* (1937), *The Narrow Place* (1943), *One Foot in Eden* (1956) and the posthumous *Collected Poems* (1960). Muir's poignant *Autobiography* (1954) remains a classic of that genre. As a literary critic, he produced the influential *Structure of the Novel* (1928) and was invited to give the Charles Eliot Norton Lectures at Harvard University (1955–56), which were subsequently published as *The Estate of Poetry* (1962). Muir's best novel is *The Marionette* (1927). He and his wife Willa Muir were the first to translate the works of Franz KAFKA into English.

**Muir, John** *(1838–1914)* American naturalist and conservationist. Born in Dunbar, Scotland, he immigrated to the U.S. in 1849, studied at the University of Wisconsin and moved to California in 1868. Devoted to the American wilderness, he traveled throughout the U.S., spending years studying the flora and geology of the Yosemite Valley and Alaska, where he discovered the Muir glacier. He also traveled extensively in Australia, India and Russia. Muir's love and respect for America's wild places helped to convince President Theodore ROOSEVELT to preserve wilderness areas in an extended national park system. Roosevelt also established (1908) the Muir Woods National Monument in California to honor the naturalist's achievements. Among Muir's books are *The Mountains of California* (1894), *Steep Trails* (1918) and the posthumously published journals of *John of the Mountains* (1938).

**mujahideen** Radical Islamic guerrilla fighters. In December 1979, following the assassination of Afghani leader Hafizullah Amin, Soviet forces entered AFGHANISTAN and imposed a pro-Soviet government upon the country under the leadership of Babrak Karmal. In response to this Soviet invasion, small bands of guerrilla fighters composed of men from Afghanistan and other countries in the Middle East (such as the Saudi-born Osama BIN LADEN) organized an insurgency against the Soviet-supported government and the Soviet forces in Afghanistan that ensured the government's hold on power. Calling themselves mujahideen ("Islamic fighters"), these loosely coordinated bands received military support and training from both the Carter and Reagan administrations, both of which sought to deny the SOVIET UNION a greater presence in Central Asia. For 10 years the mujahideen waged a ceaseless war against the Soviet forces, creating a situation for Moscow that many observers equated with the experience of the U.S. in the Vietnam War. In 1989 Soviet president Mikhail GORBACHEV decided that the military operation in Afghanistan was too costly, and announced the withdrawal of Soviet forces by the end of the year. Between 1989 and 1992 the mujahideen continued their efforts to overthrow the Soviet-installed government in Kabul. In 1992 they succeeded in entering the capital city, deposing the government and declaring an Islamic republic headed by Burhanuddin RABBANI. Following their victory, conflicts among the various mujahideen factions led to infighting. In 1994 a group of young Islamic fundamentalists called the TALIBAN began to gain the support of mujahideen such as bin Laden's AL-QAEDA, by calling for the strict application of Islamic law throughout the country. By 1996 the Taliban and their mujahideen supporters had captured Kabul and gained control of most of Afghanistan; the new regime waged a relentless campaign against rival factions of mujahideen, which had regrouped as the NORTHERN ALLIANCE. Even after the expulsion of the Taliban from power following the U.S.-led invasion of Afghanistan in October 2001, mujahideen continue to operate in Afghanistan, frustrating the efforts of Afghan president Hamid KARZAI to establish a strong central authority throughout the country.

**Mujica Lainez, Manuel** *(1910–1984)* Argentine novelist. Mujica was a leading figure in the Latin American school of MAGIC REALISM. His historical and fantastic novels were based on South American myths. Mujica Lainez's *Bomarzo*, banned by the Argentine government, made him known internationally and became a worldwide sensation as an opera with music by Alberto GINASTERA. He won Argentina's national prize for his 1957 novel *Invitados en el paraíso*.

**Mukden (Chinese: Shen-Yang)** Capital of China's province of Liao-ning, northeast on the Hun River, controlling north-south routes along the plain of south Manchuria. During the Russo-Japanese struggle for control of MANCHURIA it became a stronghold, first conquered by the Russians and then taken by the Japanese between February 19 and March 10, 1905, after the battle of Mukden. In 1924 the warlord Chan Tso-Lin made it his headquarters during the CHINESE CIVIL WAR, he was assassinated there in 1928. On September 18, 1931, a railroad was blown up, the so-called Mukden or Manchurian Incident, used by Japan to justify the invasion of Manchuria and the setting up of its puppet regime, MANCHUKUO. Under Japanese occupation from that time until 1945, Mukden was returned to Nationalist Chinese authority only to become a major battle site during the CHINESE CIVIL WAR OF 1945–49. In 1947–48, after 10 months of heavy fighting and severe casualties, where thousands starved and the Nationalist force was annihilated, Mukden fell to communist forces on November 1, 1948. It continued as a base for further conquest.

**Mulder, Cornelius Petrus "Connie"** *(1925–1988)* South African politician. Mulder almost defeated P. W. BOTHA for the prime ministership of SOUTH AFRICA in 1978. Shortly thereafter, his career in the ruling National Party was ruined by the exposure of his involvement in a secret influence-buying campaign. This scandal, known as "Muldergate," forced his resignation as minister of information. Later, he was forced to resign as leader of the National Party, and, finally as a member of the parliament. Mulder reentered politics in May 1987, when he was returned to Parliament as a candidate of the extreme right-wing Conservative Party.

**Muller, Hermann Joseph** *(1890–1967)* American geneticist. Muller is considered by some the most influential geneticist of the 20th century. Born in New York City, he earned his Ph.D. from Columbia University in 1916. He began to study mutations at a number of institutions, including the Rice Institute in Houston, Texas, the Berlin Institute for Brain Research, and the Moscow Institute of Genetics, before becoming in 1945 a professor of zoology at Indiana University, where he worked for the rest of his career. Among Muller's important contributions to genetics was his discovery in 1926 that X RAYS are capable of causing genetic mutations, which furthered research by allowing investigators to create mutations in the laboratory. Muller was awarded the 1946 NOBEL PRIZE for physiology or medicine.

**Mullin, Willard** *(1902–1978)* American sports cartoonist. Mullin's distinctive pen-and-ink drawings appeared in the *New York World-Telegram* (1934–66), *Life*, *Look*, the *Saturday Evening Post*, and many other publications. His best-known creation was probably the character "the Brooklyn Bum," who symbolized the Brooklyn Dodgers baseball team and their fans. In 1971 the National Cartoonists Society voted Mullin "The Sports Cartoonist of the Century."

**Mullis, Kary B.** *(1944–   )* Recipient of the 1993 Nobel Prize in chemistry. Born in Lenoir, North Carolina, Mullis received his B.S. degree in chemistry from the Georgia Institute of Technology in 1966 his Ph.D. in biochemistry at the University of California at Berkeley in 1972. He joined the University of Kansas Medical School in 1973 as a postdoctoral fellow in pediatric cardiology, and specialized in pulmonary vascular physiology, and then did two years of postdoctoral work at the University of California at San Francisco in pharmaceutical chemistry.

Two years later he accepted a position at the Cetus Corporation in Emeryville, California. Between 1979 and 1986 he worked on issues related to the chemical structure and nature of DNA, where he developed and patented the process known as a polymerase chain reaction (PCR), a method for exponentially increasing the duplication of DNA, producing billions of copies of single strands of DNA within a few hours. In addition to facilitating great advances in the fields of biotechnology, forensic science and genetic engineering, PCR also provided the scientific basis for Michael Crichton's novel, *Jurassic Park*. In 1986 Mullis left Cetus to become the director of molecular biology at Xytronyx, Inc. At Xytronyx Mullis focused his efforts on advancing the company's DNA technology and photochemistry divisions. In 1993 he won the Nobel Prize in chemistry for his development of PCR. Her other honors include the California Scientist of the Year (1992), the Thomas A. Edison Award (1993) the Japan Prize (1993), and membership in the National Inventors Hall of Fame (1998).

**Mulroney, (Martin) Brian** *(1939–   )* Prime Minister of CANADA (1984–93). Born in Quebec, Mulroney received his law degree from Laval University in 1963. He became active in the PROGRESSIVE CONSERVATIVE PARTY while in college, after which he became a labor lawyer. He received national attention when he assumed presidency of the troubled Iron Ore Company in 1976, settled its labor disputes and turned a profit. He left the company in 1983 when he became leader of the Progressive Conservative Party. His party won the elections (1984) and he became prime minister. Mulroney had never held an elected office before and was the first leader of Canada to come from Quebec in 90 years. In 1988 Mulroney signed a trade agreement with President REAGAN that aimed to reduce trade barriers between the U.S. and CANADA; the Liberal Party opposed it. In the elections later that year, the Progressive Conservatives maintained a majority, and Mulroney remained prime minister. In 1989 he proposed a budget targeting reduction in Canada's deficit by half by the year 1994. Mulroney resigned as prime minister in 1993 as a result of declining popularity

due to the introduction of a new sales tax and the failed separatist referendum in Quebec in October 1992.

**Mumford, Lewis** *(1895–1990)* American cultural critic, urban planner, historian, political commentator and self-described social philosopher. Born in New York City, Mumford attended City College (but did not graduate) and later took graduate classes at Columbia University and the New School for Social Research. In his writings and lectures, Mumford examined almost every facet of modern life, including architecture, science, technology, literature and city planning. Humanistic and antitechnocratic in his outlook, Mumford was an outspoken critic of architectural congestion and its dehumanizing influence. He published his first book, *The Story of Utopias*, in 1922 while also contributing to various journals. His writing led to his teaching an innovative course on American architecture at the New School. In 1923 Mumford helped found the Regional Planning Association of America. Beginning in the 1930s, he wrote a column, "Sky Line," for *The NEW YORKER*, reviewing architecture and discussing the urban landscape of New York and other cities. Mumford is perhaps best known for the "Renewal of Life" series, which consists of *Technics and Civilization* (1933), *The Culture of Cities* (1938), *The Condition of Man* (1944) and *The Conduct of Life* (1951). These works follow the history of cities from the 10th century and set forth Mumford's ideas on the betterment of city life. Other important works include *The City in History* (1961), *Technics and Human Development* (1967) and *The Pentagon of Power* (1971). In 1986 Mumford was awarded the National Medal of Arts.

**Munch, Charles** *(1891–1968)* The most important French conductor of his generation, excepting only Pierre MONTEUX. Although he was born in Strasbourg, most of his early training and performing (as a violinist) was in Germany, where he was concertmaster of the Leipzig Gewandhaus Orchestra under Wilhelm FURTWÄNGLER. After refusing to become a German national, he moved to Paris and began to conduct the Straram Orchestra in 1932.

Other positions followed—principal conductor with the Paris Philharmonic Orchestra and conductor of the Paris Conservatoire Orchestra. During WORLD WAR II he declined the directorship of the Paris Opera, refusing to collaborate with the Nazis. He was awarded the Legion of Honor after the war for his efforts on behalf of the French RESISTANCE. In 1948 he succeeded Serge KOUSSEVITZKY as conductor of the Boston Symphony Orchestra, remaining for the next 14 years. Not as temperamental as Koussevitzky or as authoritarian as George SZELL, Munch was most noted for his performances of the French repertoire—the ballets of RAVEL, POULENC and HONEGGER—and for his characteristic gentle humility and temperament. He conducted without a baton and usually from memory. "I came to conducting rather late," he said with whimsical candor in his book, *I Am a Conductor* (1954), "only because I am too stupid to do anything else."

**Munch, Edvard** (1863–1944) Norwegian painter; one of the most striking and influential painters of the 20th century. Munch stands alongside Paul Cézanne, Vincent Van Gogh and James Ensor as one of the key founders of the artistic school of EXPRESSIONISM. He held that painting should go beyond the depiction of nature and render visible the intense states of the soul, thereby illuminating the nature of human existence. Munch's most famous painting, *The Cry* (1893), illustrates the expressionist method by its utilization of line and color to underscore the fear and terror experienced by an isolated, screaming woman on a bridge over swirling water. Munch produced large numbers of portraits and landscapes and was also a gifted woodcut artist.

**Muni, Paul** (**Muni Weisenfreund**) (1896–1967) Austrian-born character actor who was a major HOLLYWOOD star in the 1930s. Muni came to America with his family and first appeared in Yiddish theater in New York City. He debuted on Broadway in 1926 and soon moved into film, where he was quickly nominated for an ACADEMY AWARD as best actor for his performance in *The Valiant* (1929). His film career was established with *Scarface*

(1931), in which he played a gangster resembling Al CAPONE. Muni subsequently gave notable performances in *The Story of Louis Pasteur* (1936), for which he won an Academy Award for best actor; *The Life of Emile Zola;* and *Juarez* (1939). He played a Chinese in the 1937 film adaptation of Pearl BUCK's *The Good Earth* and starred in the classic *I Am a Fugitive from a Chain Gang* (1933). After the 1930s he acted mainly on Broadway and made few films; his final film appearance was in *The Last Angry Man* (1959).

**Munich Olympics massacre** On September 5, 1972, during the 1972 summer OLYMPIC GAMES in Munich, West Germany, Palestinian guerrillas of the BLACK SEPTEMBER organization attacked and occupied the Israeli athlete quarters. They killed two Israelis and took nine others hostage. German security forces subsequently attempted to rescue the hostages as they were being taken out of the country at Munich's airport. During the attempt, the remaining nine Israelis were killed, as were two Germans and five Palestinians.

**Munich Pact** Agreement reached at the Munich Conference of September 29–30, 1938, by the heads of state of Germany (HITLER), Great Britain (CHAMBERLAIN), France (DALADIER) and Italy (MUSSOLINI). The agreement acceded to Hitler's demands by providing for Germany's occupation of the SUDETENLAND, a strategically important German-speaking region of Czechoslovakia. It also stipulated that plebiscites were to be held, which would have given residents a voice in the change, but the votes never took place. No Czech representative was present at the conference. Coming at a time of increased aggressive activity by Germany, the agreement was hailed by Chamberlain as a step toward peace in our time, and was simultaneously condemned by Winston CHURCHILL. The Munich Pact did not serve to halt, or even to slow Germany's march on Europe, and it is widely considered a blatant act of prewar APPEASEMENT—one that pushed Europe even closer to the brink of WORLD WAR II.

**Muñoz Marín, Luis** (1898–1980) Governor of PUERTO RICO (1948–64). An early believer in Puerto Rican inde-

pendence, Muñoz later advocated economic association with the U.S. He helped found the Popular Democratic Party in 1938. As Puerto Rico's first elected governor, he implemented Operation Bootstrap. This program brought roads and schools to backward rural areas and helped diversify the island's economy.

**Munsey, Frank Andrew** (1854–1925) U.S. magazine and newspaper publisher. *Munsey's Magazine* (1889) was the nation's first illustrated general-circulation magazine. He also pioneered the publication of mass-market, all-fiction magazines, printed on rough, wood-pulp paper and aimed at the general reading public; his editorial innovations and development of new writers and genres, like science fiction, drove the circulation of his magazines, like *Argosy* and *All-Story,* to unheard-of figures, creating a media form that splashily dominated U.S. newsstands for the first half of the 20th century. He eventually acquired a host of large-circulation newspapers in major U.S. cities. His practice of buying out competing newspapers made him a pioneer in newspaper consolidation.

**Munson, Thurman** (1947–1979) American baseball player. A star catcher, he was captain of the New York Yankees. He was the only Yankee ever to be named both American League rookie of the year (1970) and most valuable player (1976). An amateur pilot, he died when the private jet he was flying crashed near Canton, Ohio.

**Muppets** See Jim HENSON.

**Murder, Inc.** Popular name for a group of professional killers who worked on assignment for organized crime during the 1930s. It originated as a gang in Brooklyn, New York, and came to be controlled by the labor racketeer Louis (Lepke) Buchalter, who expanded the organization's activities to cover the entire nation. Known to organized crime as the Troop, the group was also led by mobster Albert Anastasia. During its 10 years of operation, Murder, Inc., was responsible for somewhere between 100 and 500 killings of underworld figures—the most prominent of whom was probably "Dutch" SCHULTZ. Its activities were brought to light and ended in the early 1940s by the investigations of special prosecutor Thomas E. DEWEY, and many of the group were either convicted or killed. Later mob hits, which have continued to this day, have been executed on a less organized basis.

**Murdoch, Iris (Alice Irene Murdoch)** *(1922–1999)* British author, widely regarded as one of the most important English-language novelists of the 20th century. Born to an Anglo-Irish family in Dublin, she studied philosophy at Sommerville College, Oxford. After World War II she worked briefly for the UNITED NATIONS Relief Agency (UNRA). She later became a lecturer in philosophy at St Anne's College, Oxford, and has published a study of Jean-Paul SARTRE and several works of philosophy. In the early 1950s she began writing fiction that explored such philosophical issues as good and evil, randomness and choice, and freedom and responsibility. Her plots are simultaneously gothic and witty; they usually involve a cast of eccentric characters in complex relationships. In Murdoch's world, love is both a disruptive and a healing force that has unforeseen dramatic consequences. Although Murdoch professed to be an agnostic, her more than 25 novels often reflect consciously religious concerns. Among her books are *Under the Net* (1954), *The Bell* (1958), *The Unicorn* (1963), *The Black Prince* (1973), *The Good Apprentice* (1984) and *The Message to the Planet* (1990).

**Murdoch, Keith Rupert** *(1931– )* Australian-American communications magnate. Educated at Oxford, Murdoch began his career in Adelaide, Australia, in 1953 when he inherited two modest-sized newspapers from his father. Returning to England in 1968, he started his British newspaper empire with the acquisition of *The News of the Week* (1968). His newspaper holdings grew to include London's three largest dailies, and he became famous for his shrill and often sleazy tabloids. In 1976 he began building his American holdings with the acquisition of *New York* magazine and the *New York Post* (later sold). He became a U.S. citizen in 1985. By the 1990s Murdoch controlled the world's first global media business encompassing television, publishing and entertainment. In Australia, he owned an airline, nine magazines and more than 100 newspapers; in Great Britain, five national newspapers, eight magazines and Sky T.V. (a four-channel satellite system); in the U.S., he had 10 magazines, seven television stations, two magazines, a book publishing house (Harper-Collins, formerly Harper & Row) and the Fox television and motion picture conglomerate. Immensely successful yet beset by debt, Murdoch turned increasingly to innovations in electronic journalism. In October 1996 Murdoch launched FOX News Channel, a 24-hour competitor to Cable News Network (CNN). As majority shareholder and managing director of News Corporation, one of the world's largest media conglomerates, Murdoch has exercised great influence on the dissemination of news across the globe.

**Murphy, Audie** *(1924–1971)* American WORLD WAR II hero and movie actor. Attacked with his unit near Colmar, France, on January 26, 1945, Murphy used the machine gun on a burning tank destroyer to hold off six tanks and 250 enemy troops, killing about 50. Awarded more decorations during World War II than any other individual, including the Medal of Honor, Murphy later turned to acting and appeared in such films as *To Hell and Back* (1955). He made about 40 films, but by 1960 his popularity had faded. Turning to business he was unsuccessful and declared bankruptcy. He was killed in a light plane crash.

***Murphy Brown*** American television series (1988–98). On November 14, 1988, CBS introduced the situation comedy *Murphy Brown* in its Monday night fall lineup. Starring Candice Bergen as the title character, a journalist and coanchor on the fictional network new program, *FYI* (For Your Information). The show revolved around Brown's private life and professional career. In 1992 *Murphy Brown* briefly became an important issue in the reelection campaign of President George H. W. BUSH and his vice president, Dan Quayle. Quayle publicly criticized one of the plot developments in the 1991–92 season of *Murphy Brown,* in which Brown became pregnant and decided to raise her child as a single mother. Quayle argued that the character's belief that she could raise her child independent of a father represented a sad commentary on the destruction of the American family and traditional "family values." The controversy and attention surrounding Brown's single motherhood helped make the sitcom the fourth most popular television program in the 1992–93 season. However, after the defeat of the Bush-Quayle ticket, *Murphy Brown* entered a slump of its own, falling from the number four television program in 1993 to number 20 in 1996. The series finale of Murphy Brown was aired on May 18, 1998. During its 10 seasons, *Murphy Brown* won 18 Emmy Awards.

**Murray, Sir (John) Hubert** *(1861–1940)* Australian colonial administrator. Born in Sydney, the brother of Gilbert Murray, he was educated there and at Oxford University. He served in the BOER WAR and later practiced law in Australia. Appointed a colonial officer in Papua New Guinea in 1907, he became known for his humane treatment of the Papuans; the following year he was named the territory's lieutenant governor, a post he held until his death. His administration allowed economic development of the area without the enormous toll on its native population that was taken in many other colonial enterprises. Murray was knighted in 1925.

**Murray, Les(lie Allan)** *(1938–    )* Widely considered the foremost Australian poet of his generation and one of the leading English-language poets of his time. Raised on a farm in New South Wales, in his mid-30s Murray began devoting himself solely to his writing. His interests are exceptionally wide-ranging, and his catholic tastes and knowledge are reflected in poems that are both intimate and all-encompassing. His books include *Poems against Economics* (1972), *The Vernacular Republic* (1976) and *Dog Fox Field* (1990). Murray continued to publish throughout the 1990s, and released such works as *A Working Forest* (1997), which contained several pieces of his prose, and *Translations from the Natural World* (1992), *Subhuman Redneck Poems* (1996), *Freddy Neptune* (1998), and *Conscious & Verbal* (2000), all of which included original poems that Murray authored.

**Murray, Phillip** *(1886–1952)* American labor leader. A Scot by birth, Murray was a coal miner who rose to the presidency of the United Mine Worker's Union (UMW). The position was a powerful one because at the time coal was a vitally important fuel in the U.S. As head of the umbrella labor organization, the Congress of Industrial Organizations (CIO), he successfully led the drive to organize the steelworkers and later became president of the steelworker's union—the United Steelworkers of America.

**Murrow, Edward R.** *(1908–1965)* American radio and television newsman, war correspondent, and federal administrator. In the words of historian Daniel J. Leab, Murrow's verbal abilities "were coupled with a superb and dramatic sense of delivery as well as with a breadth and humanity of thought." He was born in Greensboro, North Carolina, traveled extensively as a young man in academic-related activities for the National Student Federation, and joined CBS in 1935. Soon after his assignment to Europe, war broke out. He was everywhere—flying combat missions, reporting from the concentration camps, and transmitting from the rooftops during the London Blitz: "It's a bomber's moon tonight . . ." After the war with partner Fred Friendly he developed the television investigative news program, SEE IT NOW. He was not afraid of controversy, and in a landmark *See It Now* broadcast he attacked the red-baiting tactics of Senator Joseph MCCARTHY in 1954: "We must not confuse dissent with disloyalty," he declared at the end of the show, glowering into the camera through a trail of cigarette smoke; "this is no time for men who oppose Senator McCarthy's methods to be silent." Al-

though there were other television shows after the demise of *See It Now*— PERSON TO PERSON, for example, a live series of interviews by two-way hookup between Murrow in the studio and celebrities in their own homes—Murrow grew increasingly disenchanted with CBS. He left in 1961 to serve as director of the U.S. Information Agency in the KENNEDY administration. After a prolonged battle with lung cancer, he died in April 1965. Ironically, just 10 years before, June 7, 1955, the chain-smoking Murrow had narrated a two-part television series on the relationship between cigarettes and cancer.

**Murry, John Middleton** *(1889–1957)* British author and critic. While still a student at Oxford, Murry began editing *Rhythm,* a modernist magazine (see MODERNISM). He was later to serve as editor for *The Athenaeum* (1919–21) and *The Adelphi* (1923–30). In his editorial capacity he was to gain an influence over British literary life, publishing the authors Katherine MANSFIELD (whom he married in 1918); D. H. LAWRENCE (with whom Murry and Mansfield would publish the short-lived magazine, *Signature*); Virginia WOOLF; T. S. ELIOT; and VALERY—among others. Murry was an outspoken critic of the GEORGIAN pets, and his critical works include *Dostoevski* (1916), *The Problem of Style* (1922) and *Son of Woman, the Story of D. H. Lawrence* (1931). Following Mansfield's death in 1923, Murry— who married three more times—edited her works and wrote her biography in 1932. He also wrote the autobiography *Between Two Worlds* (1935).

**Musa Dagi (Musa Dagh)** (Turkey) West of Antakya, rising from the Mediterranean Sea, this southern mountain peak became a battleground for the Armenians' heroic struggle against the Turks during WORLD WAR I; depicted by Franz WERFEL in his novel *The Forty Days of Musa Dagh.*

**Museum of Broadcasting, The** A nonprofit, public-access repository of more than 25,000 American television and radio programs located in midtown New York City. Sensing a need for a broadcasting archive, William S. PALEY, founder and longtime chairman of CBS Inc., conceived and funded the museum in 1976. As of the early 1990s it operates on a $2 million annual budget deriving mostly from corpora-

tions, foundations, individual philanthropists and the small contributions of people using the facilities. Three-thousand hours of additional TV programming are added each year. Dozens of private viewing/listening cubicles enable visitors to review a wide range of fare, including HALLMARK HALL OF FAME, the ARMY-MCCARTHY HEARINGS, the Nixon-Kennedy Debates and the work of pioneering figures in broadcasting, such as Edward R. MURROW, Ernie KOVACS, Orson WELLES, Leonard BERNSTEIN, Lucille BALL, Sid CAESAR and others. All materials at the museum have been transferred to video tape, and the originals are preserved in fireproof, climate-controlled vaults. Activities include mounting traveling exhibitions, beaming seminars by satellite to college campuses, taping seminars for the permanent collection, presenting programs at the Manhattan location and sponsoring festivals at the Television Academy of Arts and Sciences in Los Angeles. A worldwide search continues for many lost television programs and newscasts, particularly material from the TRUMAN administration—the first administration to use television broadcasts. "What we have to do is come to terms with television as a creative force," said the museum's president Robert Batscha. "It has been a rich part of our lives and needs to be shared with future generations."

**Museum of Modern Art** Museum located in New York City that houses one of the world's premier collections of modern paintings, sculpture and other works of art. It was founded in 1929 by a group of prominent collectors in the city and was directed by Alfred H. BARR Jr. until his retirement in 1967. At first housed in rented facilities, the collection moved to its present location in 1945. Its building, designed in 1939 by Philip Goodwin and Edward Durell STONE, was enlarged by a new wing designed by Philip JOHNSON (1962–63). The nucleus of the museum's impressive collection is the Lillie P. Bliss bequest of 1934, which included a number of important Cézannes as well as other significant modern works. The museum's present permanent collection includes works from all of the major movements in European and American art during the late 19th and 20th centuries. The museum includes departments of painting and sculpture, architecture, film, prints and drawings. It also maintains an extensive

*Journalist Edward R. Murrow* (LIBRARY OF CONGRESS. PRINTS AND PHOTOGRAPHS DIVISION)

reference library, as well as educational programs, loan and circulating exhibitions and programs for film and video.

**Musharraf, Pervez** *(1943– )* Pakistani military officer, and head of state of Pakistan (1999– ). Born in India, in 1943, Musharraf and his family moved to Karachi, Pakistan, in 1947 following the partition of British India into INDIA and PAKISTAN. In 1964 Musharraf entered the Pakistani army and gradually moved up its ranks. In 1998 Prime Minister Nawaz Sharif selected Musharraf to become the new head of the armed forces. Soon after his elevation, renewed fighting erupted between Indian and Pakistani forces in the disputed territory of KASHMIR. Soon after the conflict started, Musharraf publicly acknowledged that Pakistan had deployed troops in the disputed region, which hurt Sharif's efforts to achieve a diplomatic solution to the conflict. In October 1999, not long after Sharif fired Musharraf for his actions during the conflict with India, Musharraf organized the overthrow of the Sharif government in a bloodless coup that established martial law and made him the chief executive of Pakistan. By June 2001 Musharraf appointed himself president and promised he would restore civilian rule by October 2002.

Musharraf drew ire from Islamic fundamentalists for his support of the U.S. campaign against the terrorist group AL-QAEDA as well as the TALIBAN, the Islamic fundamentalist group that ruled Afghanistan from 1996 to 2001 with the support of Pakistan. In April 2002 Musharraf organized a national referendum in which Pakistani voters supported an extension of his executive rule for another five years. Seven months later, Musharraf honored his pledge to restore democratic rule to Pakistan when the National Assembly, Pakistan's national legislature, was permitted to reconvene and assume some of its earlier duties.

**Musial, Stan(ley Frank) ("Stan the Man")** *(1920– )* American baseball player. A St. Louis Cardinal for 22 seasons, Musial was one of the few athletes beloved by fans in every city. A three-time Most Valuable Player, he also led the National League in batting average seven times. He batted over .300 16 times. When he retired, he held more than 25 major league records. Upon his retirement in 1964, he began working for the Cardinals in an administrative capacity and continued to do so for over 25 years. Musial was named to the Hall of Fame in 1969, and in 1972 became the first non-Pole to be awarded Poland's Merited Champions Medal.

**Musil, Robert** *(1880–1942)* Austrian novelist. Trained first for the military and then as an engineer, Musil later studied philosophy, psychology and mathematics, earning a Ph.D. from the University of Berlin in 1908. The success of his first novel, *Young Torless* (1906), caused him to reject an academic career and to devote himself to writing. In this short fictional work, as well as in his long, unfinished novel, *The Man without Qualities* (3 volumes, 1930–42), Musil reveals profound psychological and philosophical concerns in a style of great analytic subtlety. He was also the author of short stories, plays, essays and literary criticism. When the Nazis entered Vienna in 1938, Musil and his Jewish wife fled to Switzerland, where he spent his last years in poverty and obscurity.

**Muskie, Edmund Sixtus** *(1914– 1996)* U.S. politician. After practicing law, he was elected to the Maine House of Representatives (1947–51), and in 1955 became the first Democratic governor of Maine in two decades. He served in the U.S. Senate from 1959 to 1980. He also served briefly as secretary of state in 1980–81.

**Mussolini, Benito** *(1883–1945)* Italian political leader who established FASCISM in ITALY; as Il Duce ("the leader"), he was the supreme authority in Italy from 1922 to 1943. Born in Predappio in Emilia Romagna, Mussolini was originally a journalist and a socialist and was active in the left-wing Italian opposition movement around the turn of the 20th century. He spent several years in exile in Switzerland. Returning to Italy, he became a well-known figure in left-wing journalistic circles, editing a leading journal and writing articles in favor of left-wing causes. At the outbreak of WORLD WAR I (1914) he professed pacifism but soon after abruptly changed his views and urged Italy's entry into the war on the side of the Allies. He was immediately expelled from the Socialist Party. However, his editorials and speeches

*Italian Fascist leader Benito Mussolini* (LIBRARY OF CONGRESS, PRINTS AND PHOTOGRAPHS DIVISION)

helped sway Italy to enter the war on May 24, 1915. He fought in World War I and was wounded.

After the war, Mussolini continued to espouse Italian nationalism and patriotism. He built a base of support among the working class and lower middle class, and organized a paramilitary group, known as the BLACK SHIRTS. During a period of domestic violence between socialist and fascist groups, Mussolini made a bold bid for power. He led his Black Shirts in the MARCH ON ROME and demanded that King VICTOR EMMANUEL III appoint him prime minister in order to restore order (1922); to his surprise, the king agreed. Mussolini subsequently consolidated his authority and on January 3, 1925, he proclaimed Italy a fascist state, with himself as dictator. His authority was confirmed by a plebiscite in March 1929.

Mussolini was driven by visions of himself as a new Caesar who would restore Italy's greatness. In numerous speeches and decrees, he called on Italians to devote themselves to his national goals; at the same time, he quietly eliminated all political opposition. He also desired an overseas empire. On his orders Italy invaded and conquered ETHIOPIA (1935–36), now without resistance from the poorly armed Ethiopians. Although initially suspicious of German chancellor Adolf HITLER, Mussolini met with the Führer and formed an alliance with him—the Rome-Berlin AXIS, a term coined by Mussolini. The following year Mussolini joined Hitler and the Japanese government in the Anti-Comintern

Pact; shortly thereafter he formally withdrew Italy from the LEAGUE OF NATIONS. When Hitler threatened CZECHOSLOVAKIA in 1938, Mussolini played the statesman and arranged a conference among Germany, France and Britain—the conference at which Neville CHAMBERLAIN signed the MUNICH PACT.

Mussolini brought Italy into WORLD WAR II on the side of his German ally—a disastrous move for Mussolini and Italy. Despite his long insistence on military glory and discipline, the Italian forces were ill-prepared for the world war and lacked Germany's armaments, organization and fighting will. After conquering ALBANIA, Italy suffered embarrassing reversals in its invasion of GREECE and in the NORTH AFRICAN CAMPAIGN in Libya. In both cases, Mussolini relied on German aid to salvage the situation. Following the Allied invasion of Sicily, Mussolini's Grand Fascist Council deposed Il Duce (July 24, 1943) and arrested him. On September 12, 1943, he was rescued by a German ss commando team acting on Hitler's orders. He subsequently declared a new fascist republic in northern Italy, but this was little more than a puppet government beholden to Nazi Germany. As the Allies drove northward, Mussolini attempted to flee in disguise but was captured by anti-fascist Italian partisans and executed (April 27, 1945).

**Mustard, Dr. William Thornton** *(1914–1987)* Canadian surgeon. A pioneer in pediatric surgery, he was best known for an operation called the Mustard Procedure. This procedure involved rerouting the blood flow in hearts of children born with major blood vessels on the wrong side. He retired as chief of vascular surgery at Toronto's Hospital for Sick Children in 1976.

**Muthesius, Hermann** *(1861–1927)* German design theorist, writer and spokesman for design causes of the early Modern movement. Muthesius studied philosophy before training as an architect at the Berlin technical college. He worked for several architects before becoming an official architect for the Prussian government in 1893. In 1896 he was sent to the German embassy in London to study and report on English design developments of the time. In articles published in

Germany, Muthesius reported on the ideas and work of William Morris and the Arts and Crafts movement and on Charles Rennie MACKINTOSH. Back in Germany (1904 to 1905), he published the three-volume *Das Englishe Haus,* which brought the concepts of British domestic architecture and design to a German readership. Muthesius was an important figure in the formation of the DEUTSCHER WERKBUND (1907) and continued to encourage design quality through various roles in that organization. He exerted significant influence not only on the development of design and taste in Germany by introducing MODERNISM to that country in the 1920s but also on the character of German work since World War II.

**mutual assured destruction (MAD)** Theory and strategy used to maintain the balance of power between the U.S. and the USSR during the COLD WAR. The MAD theory held, paradoxically, that the large number of nuclear weapons in each nation's arsenal would prevent these weapons from ever being used, because both nations would be destroyed in any nuclear war.

**Muzorewa, Abel** *(1925– )* Zimbabwean churchman and political leader. Bishop of the United Methodist Church in Southern Rhodesia in 1968, he was founder and president of the African National Council in 1971. Muzorewa mobilized African opinion against the proposed Rhodesia settlement of 1971–72. A member of the executive council of the transitional government in Zimbabwe-Rhodesia (1978–80), he was considered by the British government and Rhodesian whites to be more conciliatory than his rivals. However, he was heavily defeated by Robert MUGABE in the 1980 election. Muzorewa's autobiography is *Arise and Walk.*

**Myanmar** See BURMA.

**Myer, Dillon S.** *(1891–1982)* American government administrator. As director of the **War Relocation Authority** (1942–46), Myer supervised the internment of more than 100,000 Japanese-Americans during WORLD WAR II. However, he advocated the abolition of the agency and the return of Japanese

Americans to their homes. He was later cited by the Japanese-American Citizens League as a champion of human rights and common decency. After the war he served as commissioner of Indian affairs and as head of the Federal Public Housing Authority.

**My Lai massacre** Atrocity that took place on May 16, 1968, in the South Vietnamese hamlet of My Lai during the VIETNAM WAR. A U.S. platoon headed by **Lt. William L. Calley** invaded the town, a supposed VIET CONG stronghold, rounded up its civilian population and shot to death 347 unarmed men, women and children. The incident came to light in 1969 and was then investigated by the Army. Although 13 officers and enlisted men were eventually charged with war crimes, only Lt. Calley was found guilty. Convicted on March 29, 1971, he was sentenced to life imprisonment. The verdict caused a great deal of controversy, and the incident helped to fuel the ANTIWAR MOVEMENT. Calley's sentence was eventually reduced to 10 years, and he was paroled in March 1974.

**Myrdal, Alva** *(1902–1986)* Swedish diplomat. A cowinner of the 1982 Nobel Peace Prize, she first became known in the 1930s as a feminist, educator and sociologist. Later in her career, she held two major posts at the UNITED NATIONS. She also served as Sweden's ambassador to India, was a member of the Swedish parliament and a cabinet minister. Her husband, Gunnar Myrdal, was Nobel laureate in economics (1974).

**Myrdal, (Karl) Gunnar** *(1898–1987)* Swedish economist and social scientist. His seminal work *An American Dilemma: The Negro Problem and Modern Democracy* (1944) left a deep mark on the history of race relations in the U.S. He helped draft many social and economic programs in Sweden and was also a vigorous advocate of land reform in South Asia. As a UNITED NATIONS official he was an early promoter of East-West détente, and as an economist he criticized orthodox ways of thinking and pioneered new ones. He was cowinner of the NOBEL PRIZE in economics in 1974. His wife, Swedish diplomat Alva Myrdal, was cowinner of the 1982 NOBEL PEACE PRIZE.

# N

**NAACP** See NATIONAL ASSOCIATION FOR THE ADVANCEMENT OF COLORED PEOPLE.

**Nabokov, Vladimir Vladimirovich** *(1899–1977)* Russian author. An important and original voice in fiction and literary criticism, Nabokov left Russia in 1919, studying at Cambridge, in Berlin and in Paris before settling in the U.S. in 1940. Nabokov was a lecturer at Wellesley College and a professor of Russian Literature at Cornell University. Nabokov is perhaps best known for the controversial novel *Lolita* (1958), which depicts a middle-aged man's sexual obsession with a young girl. His writing is characterized by linguistic resourcefulness and perceptive narrative. His later works were written in English, which he translated to his native Russian. His other fiction includes *Mary* (1926). *Pale Fire* (1962) and *Look at the Harlequins!* (1974). Nabokov also wrote volumes of short stories and literary criticism, such as *Lectures on Literature* (1980) and his memoirs *Speak, Memory* (1967).

**Nadelman, Elie** *(1882–1946)* Polish-American sculptor. Born in Warsaw, he studied art in his native city and in Paris, where he lived from 1904–14. His work was exhibited in the U.S. at the Armory Show in 1913, and he emigrated to the U.S. the following year. Working mainly in metal or wood, he employed a number of styles in portraying the human form as simplified and often symbolic. His best known work is probably the elegantly

*Russian novelist Vladimir Nabokov* (LIBRARY OF CONGRESS)

jaunty bronze *Man in the Open Air* (c. 1915, Museum of Modern Art, New York City).

**Nader, Ralph** *(1934–  )* American consumer advocate. Born in Winsted, Connecticut, Nader attended Princeton University and Harvard Law School. His role as a consumer activist began with his book *Unsafe at Any Speed* (1965), a study of defective automobile design and its relationship to accidents. This book and Nader's testimony before Congress (1966) were instrumental in bringing about the passage of the National Traffic and Motor Vehicle Safety Act of 1966. Two years later, the young lawyer organized a group of college in-

terns in Washington, dubbed Nader's Raiders, into an investigative team. This group formed the nucleus of the Center for Study of Responsive Law—the first of many Nader-affiliated organizations that studied consumer problems and advocated various reforms. Other Nader organizations include the Center for Auto Safety, the Public Interest Research Group, Public Citizen, Congress Watch and various groups specializing in litigation, health research and tax reform. Nader was an important figure in the passage of the Wholesome Meat Act (1967), and he has been an outspoken critic of nuclear power and the abuses of private industry and public institutions. A hero to many and a villain to some, Nader maintains a spartan lifestyle and a selfless devotion to social and political causes. In 2000 Nader ran as a candidate for U.S. president under the banner of the Green Party. By attracting votes that might otherwise have gone to Democrat Al GORE, he contributed to the victory of Republican candidate George W. BUSH.

**Nagaland** A state of northeastern INDIA, bordered by Burma to the east, Manipur to the south and Assam to the north and west. A setting for missionary activity since 1840, British posts in Nagaland were raided by the Japanese during WORLD WAR II, who failed in their attempt to capture Kohima, its capital. Since the 1940s the spirited Naga people violently opposed Indian statehood, and in 1956–57 they fought viciously against government troops. In 1961 Nagaland was incorporated into India. Yet, the Nagas remain in favor of independence.

**Nagano, Shigeo** *(1900–1984)* Japanese industrialist and diplomat who helped shape JAPAN's post–WORLD WAR II foreign policy, domestic politics and economy. Nagano brought about the merger (1970) that made the Nippon Steel Corp. the world's largest steelmaker. Although a political conservative, he helped persuade Japanese businessmen to support the establishment of relations with CHINA and to cooperate with the USSR on development projects in Siberia. He was president of the Japanese chamber of commerce from 1969 until his death.

**Nagasaki** Port capital of Nagasaki prefecture, approximately 590 miles southwest of Tokyo. Nagasaki was the second Japanese city obliterated by the new ATOMIC BOMB, dropped by the U.S. on August 9, 1945, near the end of WORLD WAR II.

**Nagorno-Karabakh** A region in southwestern of AZERBAIJAN with a predominantly Armenian population. During the period of Soviet control of Armenia and Azerbaijan (1920–91), the Soviet government regularly altered the status of the region. In 1923 the territory was transformed into an autonomous region under Azerbaijani jurisdiction despite its 70 percent Armenian population. Seven years later JOSEPH STALIN ended the region's autonomy and made it a fully integrated

*Mushroom cloud over Nagasaki, 1945* (LIBRARY OF CONGRESS, PRINTS AND PHOTOGRAPHS DIVISION)

province of Azerbaijan. When Soviet leader MIKHAIL GORBACHEV introduced his political reform of GLASNOST (or "openness") in the mid-1980s, the long-suppressed Armenian-Azerbaijani conflict exploded in this region. Because GLASNOST allowed the right to form nonpolitical groups, independent of government control—Armenian movements emerged in Nagorno-Karabakh that emphasized the common cultural background shared with inhabitants of the Armenian S.S.R. By the end of the 1980s, these groups had begun to demonstrate for the province's union with the Armenian S.S.R., which led to bloody conflicts with Azerbaijanis. This conflict escalated following the secession of Armenia and Azerbaijan from the defunct Soviet Union at the end of 1991. In November 1991 a month before the dissolution of the Soviet Union, Azerbaijan abolished the vestiges of autonomy possessed by Nagorno-Karabakh. In response, the predominantly Armenian population declared its independence a month later and launched a guerrilla war against Azerbaijani rule. Over the next three years, these rebel forces in Nagorno-Karabakh received support from Armenia in their rebellion against Azerbaijan and their efforts to unite with Armenia. In 1994, after more than 15,000 deaths, the civil war was halted by a truce accepted by the Azerbaijani and Armenian governments and the two contending forces within Nagorno-Karabakh. Neither this armistice nor subsequent negotiations among parties concerned has produced a definitive settlement of the dispute.

**Nagurski, Bronislau "Bronko"** *(1908–1990)* American football player. Nagurski became a legendary running back and tackler with the University of Minnesota and the Chicago Bears in the 1920s and '30s. He helped lead the Bears to championships in 1932 and 1933, and by the time he retired, his name had become synonymous with gritty, dedicated play. In 1963 he was named a charter member of the Pro Football Hall of Fame.

**Nagy, Imre** *(1896–1958)* Hungarian political leader. Born in Kaposvár in southern HUNGARY, Nagy became a communist during WORLD WAR I. From 1930 to 1944 he lived in the

USSR, where he became an agricultural specialist. Returning to Hungary in 1945, he was responsible for a number of major land reforms. Becoming premier in 1953, he moderated the harsh communist policies of his predecessors, placing greater emphasis on agriculture and less on heavy industry, eliminating forced collectivization and initiating a more liberal political climate. Nagy was removed from office in 1955 for his criticism of Soviet influence and his growing independence, and he was expelled from the Communist Party in 1956. He was reinstated (1956) as premier during the HUNGARIAN UPRISING as head of a coalition government. After Soviet forces quelled the rebellion, Nagy took refuge in the Yugoslav embassy. He later left under a false promise of safe conduct, was arrested·and taken to Romania, where he was secretly tried for treason. In 1958 Janos KADAR announced that Nagy had been executed. Many Hungarians regard Nagy a national hero. In 1989 the Hungarian Socialist Workers (Communist) Party declared that Nagy's trial had been unlawful; on June 16, 1989, Nagy was reburied in a solemn nine-hour ceremony in Budapest, attended by an estimated 250,000 Hungarians.

**Naipaul, Shiva** *(1945–1985)* Author and journalist born in Trinidad. Like his older and better-known brother, V. S. NAIPAUL (also a writer), Shiva Naipaul made London his home base. He journeyed widely in the THIRD WORLD and wrote about it in a critical and often satirical manner. Among his half-dozen books were *North of South* (1978), dealing with Africa; and *Journey to Nowhere* (1980), an account of the mass suicide in JONESTOWN, GUYANA, of the followers of Rev. Jim Jones.

**Naipaul, V(idiadhar) S(urajprasad)** *(1932– )* British novelist and essayist. Born in Trinidad, of Indian descent, Naipaul was educated at University College, Oxford, and settled in Great Britain in 1955. Naipaul's early fiction, most notably *A House for Mr. Biswas* (1961), takes place in Trinidad and depicts, in a sometimes comic, almost Dickensian fashion, the dissolution of a traditional way of life. His later works are darker and more political. They have been compared to the works of Joseph CONRAD because of their pessimistic portrayal of human nature and because of Naipaul's themes of exile and alienation. These include *In a Free State* (1971, Booker Prize), *A Bend in the River* (1979) and *Among the Believers* (1985). His fictional memoir, *The Enigma of Arrival* (1987), depicts the uneasy attempt of a West Indian to come to grips with English life. Naipaul has drawn considerable criticism from left-wing writers for his blunt criticisms of third-world social and political attitudes and for his disdain of fashionable left-wing ideologies. Naipaul's brother Shiva NAIPAUL was also a distinguished writer. Naipaul received the Nobel Prize in literature in 2001.

**Najibullah, Mohammed** (1947–1996) Afghan Communist leader and president of AFGHANISTAN (1987–92). In April 1978, following a coup that brought the Communist Party into power, Najibullah, a longtime Communist activist, served in the communist government established by Hafizullah Amin. But he remained aligned with the faction led by Babrak Karmal, who favored closer alignment with the Soviet Union. In 1979 Soviet forces entered Afghanistan, overthrew Amin and replaced him with Karmal. The following year Karmal orchestrated his election as president of Afghanistan and made Najibullah one of his key subordinates. In 1986 Najibullah obtained Soviet support and replaced Karmal as Afghanistan's leader in large part because of Karmal's failure to end the civil war between the pro-Soviet government of Afghanistan and the various bands of MUJAHIDEEN supplied and partly trained by the U.S. Najibullah's regime came under threat when in 1989 the Soviet Union ended its 10-year military occupation of the country in support of the pro-Soviet government in Kabul. In 1992 Najibullah's regime completely collapsed when mujahideen, dominated by the Islamic Council of Mujahideen (which later became the NORTHERN ALLIANCE), entered Kabul. Najibullah fled to a UN compound in Kabul, where he resided for four and a half years. In September 1996 the TALIBAN, a political-religious group espousing ISLAMISM (the rigid application of Islamic law to all aspects of Afghanistan society), seized power in Kabul, took Najibullah from UN-sponsored protective custody, and executed him.

**Nakasone, Yasuhiro** (1918– ) Japanese statesman, and prime minister of Japan (1982–87). Born in Takasaki, Japan, Nakasone served as a naval officer during WORLD WAR II (1939–45) before entering the Japanese Ministry of Home Affairs in 1945 and working there for two years. In 1947 Nakasone won election to the Japanese Diet, the national legislature, as a member of the Liberal Democratic Party (LDP), a conservative party that dominated Japanese politics. In 1982 he became prime minister and won reelection to that position in 1984. Nakasone's tenure in office was atypical of Japanese leaders because of his flair, eloquence and forcefulness in dealing with foreign leaders, particularly with the U.S. president, Ronald REAGAN, with whom he worked to strengthen and maintain Japanese-American relations. In 1987 he resigned from the premiership and picked Noboru Takeshita as his successor, and continued to exert great political influence as a leader of one faction within Japan's ruling Liberal Democratic Party. Following his retirement from public office, Nakasone has functioned as an intermediary between successive LDP governments and Asian countries with which Japan has unresolved diplomatic issues, such as the continuing dispute between Japan and Russia over the KURILE ISLANDS.

**Namath, Joseph William** (1943– ) American football player. The most outstanding quarterback of the 1960s at both the college and the professional levels, the charismatic, green-eyed Namath was as well known for his taste in nightclubs as for his athletic ability. During his career at the University of Alabama, the Crimson Tide dominated college football, achieving a rare undefeated record in 1964. Signing with the New York Jets of the American Football League, he set into motion the process by which the NFL and the competing AFL would become one by giving the AFL the credibility it had lacked. Hobbled by serious knee injuries, Namath led the Jets to the AFL championship in 1969 and shocked the football world by "guaranteeing" a Jets win over the NFL champion Baltimore Colts. In a victory as memorable as Babe Ruth's called shot, the cool and confident Namath led the Jets to a stunning 16-7 victory over the Baltimore Colts and the forces of sports conservatism. He has gone on to a career as a commercial spokesman and sports commentator.

**Namibia** Former German colony, mandated to SOUTH AFRICA by the LEAGUE OF NATIONS on December 17, 1920. In October 1966 the South-West Africa People's Organization (SWAPO) launched a guerrilla campaign, which was stepped up in 1978 from bases in Angola and Zambia. In spite of the 1973 United Nations designation of SWAPO as the "sole authentic representative of the Namibian people," South Africa carried out a series of attacks on SWAPO camps in Angola. Despite a nonaggression pact signed by Angola and South Africa on February 16, 1984, SWAPO guerrilla activity in Namibia continued. In 1988 Angola, Cuba and South Africa signed an agreement providing for Namibian independence. Despite some preelection violence, UN-supervised elections were held in November 1989. Namibia formally gained independence on March 21, 1990. SWAPO held a majority of seats in the new government. President Sam NUJOMA and SWAPO retained their power in the 1994 and 1999 national elections, but President Nujoma announced he would step down at the end of his term in 2004. In 2004 Nujoma's political protégé Hifikepunye Pohamba won the presidential election.

**Nanchang Uprising** Revolt (1927) against China's KUOMINTANG (KMT) government that occurred in the city of Nanchang, capital of Kiangsi province. After communist members of the KMT were expelled in July, a garrison of some 30,000 communist soldiers under the leadership of CHU TEH rose against the government on August 1, 1927. They briefly founded a Chinese republic, before losing control of the city and fleeing west to eventually join MAO ZEDONG's forces. The Nanchang Uprising marked the birth of the People's Liberation Army—the military arm of what would become China's Communist government.

**Nanking (Nanjing), Rape of** Common term for the brutal treatment meted out to the inhabitants of the Chinese city of Nanking by the invading Japanese army during the SINO-JAPANESE WAR. Beginning on December

Namibia

11, 1937, the terrible orgy of murder, torture and rape resulted in the death of hundreds of thousands of Chinese civilians and caused worldwide condemnation of the Japanese.

***Nanook of the North*** Classic American documentary film by Robert J. FLAHERTY. Its combination of ethnological documentation, poetic expression, and entertainment values has influenced generations of documentarists. An experienced explorer and cartographer for the Canadian railroads, Flaherty began taking portable cameras and developing equipment on his expeditions to Eskimo country around Hudson Bay. In 1916 he prepared a film documenting Eskimo life, but it was destroyed in a fire. Undaunted, he worked for another five years to finance a new film. In 1920, subsidized by Revillon Frères, he spent 16 months shooting the lifestyle and hunting activities of Nanook, the celebrated hunter of the Itivimuit tribe. Not only did the tribesmen willingly re-create their customs (some of them already outmoded) for the camera, but they became accomplished technicians in developing the film and servicing the equipment. Despite some manipulations and

| NAMIBIA | |
|---|---|
| 1920 | South-West Africa (as Namibia was known) is mandated to South Africa by the League of Nations (later, the United Nations [UN]), with the goal of eventual independence. |
| 1966 | South Africa ignores UN action and extends apartheid laws to South-West Africa. SWAPO begins armed struggle. |
| 1973 | The UN recognizes SWAPO as the sole legitimate representative of the Namibian people. |
| 1978 | The Democratic Turnhalle Alliance wins elections boycotted by SWAPO, and a South African–backed internal government is established. |
| 1988 | An agreement between Angola, Cuba, and South Africa for Namibian independence. |
| 1989 | UN-sponsored elections are held. SWAPO wins majority in Constituent Assembly, which drafts a new constitution. |
| 1990 | Namibia becomes independent. Sam Nujoma becomes the first president. |
| 1994 | Nujoma and SWAPO reelected. |
| 1999 | Nujoma wins a third presidential term. |
| 2001 | Nujoma says he will not run for another term in 2004. |
| 2004 | Hifikepunye Pohamba, President Nujoma's nominee, wins the presidency. |

distortions—the natives had to learn anew how to build igloos, for example—the results were an impressive reaffirmation of a vanishing lifestyle threatened by industrial incursion. HOLLYWOOD, of course, had no idea what to do with such a film, so Pathé Distributors released it in July 1922—to immediate success and acclaim. *Nanook,* according to John Grierson, "first drew world-wide attention to the film's power of imaginative natural observation." Meanwhile, Nanook himself died of starvation two years later while deer hunting in the Ungava interior; years later, Flaherty's wife, Frances, recalled that once in Berlin she bought an "eskimo pie" confection depicting Nanook's face on the wrapper.

**Nansen, Fridtjof** *(1861–1930)* Norwegian explorer, scientist, diplomat and humanitarian. Born near Oslo, Nansen studied at Christiania (now Oslo) University and embarked on his first expedition to the Arctic in 1882 while still a student. In 1888 he skied across GREENLAND, a journey chronicled in *First Crossing of Greenland* (1890). In order to prove his theory about the flow of ocean currents, he and his crush-resistant vessel, the *Fram,* anchored in the polar ice pack in 1893 and drifted, reaching Norway in 1896. In hopes of reaching the NORTH POLE, Nansen and a companion

*Norwegian polar explorer and oceanographer Fridtjof Nansen* (LIBRARY OF CONGRESS, PRINTS AND PHOTOGRAPHS DIVISION)

left the ship and traveled by sledge and skis to the northernmost point ever reached at that date. This expedition provided much useful scientific data about the Arctic Ocean and made Nansen a heroic figure at home and abroad. Named a professor at Christiania University in 1897, he also headed (1901) an International Commission for Study of the Sea and made a series of explorations in the North Atlantic from 1910 to 1914.

Nansen also launched a career as a statesman, working for the separation of NORWAY and SWEDEN in 1905. The following year, he was appointed Norway's first minister to Great Britain, serving until 1908. After WORLD WAR I, Nansen became Norway's representative to the LEAGUE OF NATIONS. At the League, he was instrumental in providing relief to the victims of famine in Russia and in repatriating war prisoners. Becoming high commissioner for refugees in 1921, Nansen received the 1922 NOBEL PEACE PRIZE for his humanitarian work. He was the author of many books both on the Arctic and on international relations.

**napalm (acronym for naphthenic and palmitic acids)** A jellied gasoline used in flamethrowers and bombs. Napalm was used by both sides in the VIETNAM WAR—by the U.S. and South Vietnam primarily in the form of aerial bombs. The North Vietnamese and VIET CONG used it in flamethrowers, as in their massacre of the Montagnard villagers at Dak Son. Although fire has been used as a weapon since prehistoric times, napalm came into widespread use in WORLD WAR II, especially in flamethrowers used to destroy entrenched Japanese positions in the Pacific war. It was used extensively in the form of aerial bombs in the KOREAN WAR against Chinese and North Korean entrenchments. A favorite of television war coverage because of its vivid and awful display, use of napalm touched a primordial nerve among many Americans and aroused considerable controversy, including demonstrations against chemical companies that manufactured napalm.

**Napster** Online Web site that allowed users to exchange digitally recorded music files. In 1999 Napster made available computer software that al-

lowed individual Napster users both to make their digitally recorded music files available to other users and to download songs themselves that had been converted and compressed into the Moving Picture Experts Group Audio Layer 3 (MP3) format from the online files made available on other users' PERSONAL COMPUTERS (PCs). When Napster began operation in December 1999, the Recording Industry Association of America (RIAA) quickly filed a lawsuit against the music-swapping service, claiming that it facilitated music piracy. In 2001 the 9th Circuit Court of Appeals ruled that, despite its denials, Napster did indeed know that numerous users were using its network to violate copyright law, but that the RIAA and its members could not sue Napster until they had informed the company of specific MP3 files present on its servers that violated copyright law. In March 2001 Napster installed a filtering software to detect copyrighted material and prevent users from making MP3 downloads of such material available through Napster's servers. By mid-2001 it had made arrangements to license music files from AOL Time Warner, BMG Entertainment and EMI Group and make them available for download on its Web site, upon payment of a fee. The transformation of Napster from a free service to a paid service led to a 90 percent decline in the number of files available through its service, indicating a reduced consumer interest in its facilities. In 2002 Napster filed for bankruptcy and was sold to Roxio Inc. A year later, after improving its software and resolving issues with RIAA members, Napster returned to the online music scene and resumed operations.

**Narain, Raj** *(1917–1986)* Indian Socialist Party leader. His suit against then prime minister Indira GANDHI for electoral fraud (1975) precipitated a constitutional crisis that lasted nearly two years. When new elections were called in 1977, Gandhi was turned out of office and lost her parliamentary seat in Utar Pradesh State to Narain. Narain was briefly health minister in the administration of Prime Minister Morarji DESAI. He later led a fierce political revolt that toppled Desai in the summer of 1979 and replaced him with Charan Singh. After Gandhi swept back into power in 1980, Narain fell out with Singh and founded his own socialist party, which had few followers.

**Narayan, Jayaprakash** *(1902–1979)* Indian statesman. An early disciple of Mohandas K. GANDHI, he worked with Gandhi to free India from British colonial rule through nonviolent means. He founded the Congress Socialist Party (1934), organized strikes against the British and served several long prison terms for his actions. After India achieved independence (1947) he helped found the Indian Socialist Party. He was a leader of the coalition that temporarily toppled Prime Minister Indira GANDHI from power in 1977. Although Narayan never held elective office, he wielded great moral and political influence as a result of his campaigns for social justice.

**Narayan, R(asipuram) K(rishnaswami)** *(1906–2001)* Anglo-Indian novelist. Narayan wrote in English, and his fiction explored the clash between Western ideology as imported by the British and the traditions of India. His first novel, *Swami and Friends* (1935), introduced the fictional town of Malgudi, which he developed and peopled in subsequent works such as *The Financial Expert* (1952), *The Painter of Signs* (1977) and the short story collection *Malgudi Days* (1982). Other works included his memoir, *My Days* (1975), and *The World of Nagaraj* (1990).

**NASA** See NATIONAL AERONAUTICS AND SPACE ADMINISTRATION.

**NASDAQ** U.S.-based stock exchange market for the purchase, sale and trade of shares in publicly held companies. In 1971 the National Association of Securities Dealers formed the National Association of Securities Dealers Automated Quotation (NASDAQ), with the goal of regulating the trading of over-the-counter stocks. Unlike the New York Stock Exchange, in which the purchase and sale of stock certificates occurs in a single central location, the trading of over-the-counter stocks was done over telephone lines. NASDAQ's creators hoped that the regulation of over-the-counter trade through NASDAQ would enable investors to purchase shares at better prices than was possible with unregulated individual stock brokers who managed the trade of over-the-counter stocks.

Because many companies whose stocks traded over-the-counter were new to the market, such as computer-related firms, NASDAQ began to acquire a reputation as a barometer of the high-technology industries in the U.S. In 1990 NASDAQ changed its name to the Nasdaq Stock Market. Eight years after this change in title, it merged operations with the American Stock Exchange (AMEX), though both Nasdaq and AMEX continue to function as separate stock exchanges. During the 1990s, as companies began to invest heavily in computer and Internet-related technology, the value of stocks traded on the Nasdaq increased dramatically, and more investors bought into the companies on the young stock exchange. In 2001 the period in which these stocks had skyrocketed in value came to an end, as the stock market began a dramatic decline. It had become clear that many companies trading on Nasdaq were trading at inflated prices far out of proportion to their actual earnings.

**Nash, Ogden** *(1902–1971)* American poet. Nash is known for his stylish light verse, in which he employed puns and other verbal antics as well as unconventional rhymes and irregular meter. His verse began appearing in *The NEW YORKER* and other publications in 1931. His collections include *The Private Dining Room* (1953), *You Can't Get There from Here* (1957) and *The Untold Adventures of Santa Claus* (1965).

**Nash, Paul** *(1889–1946)* British painter, designer and photographer. Educated at the Slade School of Art in London, Nash served in the British army during WORLD WAR I. After being invalided by a wound, he became an official war artist and earned praise for his sketches at the front lines. In the 1920s and 1930s, Nash worked as a painter and wood engraver, as well as in applied arts such as upholstery and glass design and photography. In all these areas, Nash provided a unique blending of symbolic and surrealistic elements. In the 1930s he was a principal founder of "Unit One," an avant-garde group of British artists and architects. Nash again served as an official war artist during WORLD WAR II.

*Outline: An Autobiography* (1949) was posthumously published.

**Nashua** *(1952–1982)* Thoroughbred racehorse. Bred at Claiborne Farm, Nashua was champion two-year-old of 1954, champion three-year-old and Horse of the Year the following year. Nashua's rivalry with his contemporary, the California-bred Swaps, began in the 1955 KENTUCKY DERBY, with Swaps taking the race by 1 1/2 lengths. Swaps returned home as Nashua went on to win the Preakness and Belmont. The two then met in a 1 1/4-mile match race at Washington Park, a race Nashua won by 6 1/2 lengths. As a four-year-old, he had an uneven campaign carrying heavy weights, but won the prestigious Jockey Club Gold Cup by 2 1/4 lengths, setting a 3:20 2/5 record in the process. He finished his career with 22 wins, four places, one show, finishing out of the money only three times. He retired to Spendthrift Farm, where he went on to become a successful sire, his progeny including the outstanding Damascus.

**Nasir, Amin Ibrahim** *(1926– )* Nasir became the first president of the independent Republic of MALDIVES in 1968. He had served as prime minister under Sultan Muhammad Amin Didi from 1957 to 1968, when the sultanate was abolished for the second time. Nasir eliminated the post of prime minister in 1975 and strengthened his powers; the following year he signed an agreement formally terminating the British military presence on the islands. After Nasir declined to stand for reelection in 1978, he left the country. He was later charged in absentia with misappropriation of government funds.

**Nassau Agreement** *(December 18, 1962)* An agreement between U.S. president John F. KENNEDY and U.K. prime minister Harold MACMILLAN on nuclear cooperation. Under the agreement, the U.S. would supply Britain with Polaris missiles for its submarines. The move antagonized French president DE GAULLE, who interpreted it as Britain's reassertion of its American rather than European loyalties. A month later, France vetoed Britain's entry into the EUROPEAN ECONOMIC COMMUNITY.

**Nasser, Gamal Abdel** *(1918–1970)*
Egyptian political leader, first president
of EGYPT (1956–70). Nasser was born
near Asyut and educated at the Cairo
Military Academy, graduating in 1938.
A revolutionary from his youth, he was
devoted to driving the British from
Egypt. Nasser fought in the ARAB-IS-
RAELI WAR OF 1948 and was shocked
by the Egyptian armed forces' ineffi-
ciency and corruption. He organized
and led the anti-British republican
group known as the FREE OFFICERS
Movement that succeeded in ousting
King FAROUK in 1952. In 1954 he toppled General Muhammad Naguib, a
relative figurehead, becoming Egypt's
premier and, two years later, its president. Instituting a system called "Arab
Socialism," Nasser confiscated the nation's great estates and nationalized
(1956) the SUEZ CANAL. This action
provoked the SUEZ CRISIS, a brief
Anglo-French invasion of the canal and
an Israeli invasion of the Sinai. The ensuing ARAB-ISRAELI WAR OF 1956 was
halted by a UNITED NATIONS cease-fire,
which left Nasser with increased prestige and popularity in the Arab world
for his stand against Israel and the
West. Nasser was the head of the short-
lived UNITED ARAB REPUBLIC (1958–61).
He again came into conflict with Israel
in 1967, during the SIX-DAY WAR. Taking responsibility for the humiliating
defeat, Nasser resigned but popular
support quickly returned him to office.
In 1968 Nasser succeeded in obtaining

*Egyptian president Gamal Abdel Nasser at the
United Nations* (LIBRARY OF CONGRESS. PRINTS AND
PHOTOGRAPHS DIVISION)

Soviet support for the massive ASWAN
DAM project, for which the U.S. and
Britain had refused to pay in 1956; it
marked the apex of his career. Although increasingly dependent on Soviet support, he nonetheless was an
important pan-Arabist and a hero to
much of the THIRD WORLD. He died of
a heart attack in 1970 while attempting
to mediate a dispute between Jordan
and the PALESTINE LIBERATION ORGANI-
ZATION. Nasser is widely considered
one of the preeminent Arab leaders of
the 20th century.

**Nasser, Lake** Lake in southeastern
Egypt and northern Sudan created by
the ASWAN High Dam, built in the
1960s for the production of hydroelectric power. Having flooded such important archaeological sites as ABU-SIMBEL,
whose temple had to be elevated above
the waters, nearly 90,000 people, mostly
Sudanese, were relocated when the lake
was formed.

**Nast, Condé** *(1873–1942)* American magazine publisher. Nast achieved
success as advertising manager for *Col-
lier's Weekly* between 1898 and 1905.
In 1909 he acquired *Vogue,* then a
small society periodical, and turned it
into America's leading fashion magazine. He established a British edition of
*Vogue* in 1916 and a French edition in
1920. By 1922 Nast's holdings included *Vanity Fair* and *House and Garden,* and he formed Condé Nast
Publications, which continues to publish many periodicals. Nast also
founded the Vogue Pattern Company
in 1914 and published the *Vogue Pattern Book* in 1925. Nast was known as
a lavish host to New York society.

**Nation, The** American periodical
founded in 1865. *The Nation,* a liberal
weekly covering politics, philosophy
and literature, has maintained its left-
leaning, humanitarian stance throughout the shifts in American political
thought. Frederick Law Olmsted, the
architect of Central Park, proposed the
formation of *The Nation,* which was established by Edwin Lawrence Godkin,
who served as its editor from 1865 to
1881. *The Nation* was then owned by
the *Saturday Evening Post* until 1918,
when new editor Oswald Garrison Villard, son of the *Evening Post's* late editor, severed *The Nation's* ties with the

paper. Villard was a founder of the NA-
TIONAL ASSOCIATION FOR THE ADVANCE-
MENT OF COLORED PEOPLE, and *The
Nation* was an early supporter of that
organization as well as the AMERICAN
CIVIL LIBERTIES UNION. It also espoused
pacifism, opposed the TREATY OF VER-
SAILLES, backed the strikers and Wobblies and was sympathetic to the
Russian revolutionaries. In the 1930s,
*The Nation* advocated sanctions against
the Nazi-Fascist AXIS, supported the
Loyalists in the SPANISH CIVIL WAR and
Franklin D. ROOSEVELT and his NEW
DEAL. *The Nation* fought MCCARTHYISM
in the '50s, opposed American intervention in VIETNAM in the '60s, and rallied against the conservative trend of
the REAGAN administration. *The Nation*
has rarely broken even—its circulation
hovers around 25,000—and it is supported by patrons committed to the
liberal cause.

**National Aeronautics and Space
Administration (NASA)** U.S. government agency that oversees advanced aeronautics; lunar, planetary
and interplanetary spaceflights; and
space probes, rockets and satellites. It
was founded as an independent agency
in 1958 and maintains headquarters in
Washington, D.C. It has 10 major installations, including the John F.
Kennedy Space Center, Cape
Canaveral, Florida; the Johnson Space
Center, Houston, Texas; the Goddard
spaceflight Center, Beltsville, Maryland; the Marshall Space Flight Center,
Huntsville, Alabama and the Jet
Propulsion Laboratory, Pasadena, California. NASA has a staff of some 21,000
scientists, engineers and technicians.
The agency grew rapidly in the 1960s
and scored a triumph with its lunar-
landing APOLLO missions. In 1973 it
created America's first manned orbiting
space lab, and in 1981 it launched the
U.S.'s first manned space shuttle. After
the explosion of the *CHALLENGER* shuttle
in 1986, NASA's policies were widely
investigated. Once held in the highest
esteem, the agency was subjected to
scrutiny and criticism, and its activities
were to a large degree halted for two
years. After management and safety reforms, NASA resumed manned spaceflight with the launch of the space
shuttle *Discovery* in 1988. Following
the disintegration of the space shuttle
*Columbia* during reentry in 2003,

NASA suspended all shuttle launches, pending investigation. The shuttle resumed flight in 2005.

**National Association for the Advancement of Colored People (NAACP)** American CIVIL-RIGHTS organization. The oldest and largest organization of its kind, with a 1990 membership of some 400,000, it strives to eliminate discrimination against blacks and other minorities. Its membership is mainly black but also includes many whites and others. It was founded in 1910 by the merging of the NIAGARA MOVEMENT formed by W. E. B. DU BOIS and a group of prominent white liberals. With lawyer Moorfield Storey as its first president, much of the group's power was wielded by Du Bois, who edited its magazine *Crisis* from 1910 to 1934. During its early years, the organization worked successfully to pass antilynching laws and to stop lynching in the U.S. Its main thrust has always been change through legal and legislative action, a moderate stance that brought it criticism by more radical civil rights advocates. The NAACP played an important role in many legal battles, most memorably the landmark school desegregation case *BROWN V. BOARD OF EDUCATION* of Topeka (1954). Led by Roy WILKINS from 1955 to 1977, it also was important in obtaining passage of the CIVIL RIGHTS ACTS of 1957 and 1964 and the VOTING RIGHTS ACT OF 1965 and in winning extensions of the latter in the 1970s and '80s. In 2000 the NAACP organized protests to force the South Carolina state government to stop flying the Confederate battle flag over its capitol. In addition to litigation and lobbying, the NAACP runs voter registration drives, promotes education, acts to reduce poverty and hunger in the black community and protects the rights of black prison inmates. It is headquartered in Baltimore, Maryland.

**National Education Association (NEA)** An organization of professional educators in the U.S., the NEA is the largest group of its kind in the world with a membership (2004) of 2,700,000. Founded in 1857 as the National Teachers Association, it received a congressional charter in 1906. Its goals include the improvement of public education and the increase of salaries and benefits for teachers, administrators and other educators—from elementary school through college. It promotes these aims through professional activities, judicial and legislative efforts and collective bargaining. The NEA is headquartered in Washington, D.C., but has branches in every state and Puerto Rico and facilities for representing U.S. teachers abroad.

**National Endowment for the Arts (NEA)** Arts funding arm of the National Foundation on the Arts and the Humanities founded in 1965. The NEA's stated purpose is to encourage the development and preservation of the arts in the U.S. It consists of a chairperson and 26 presidentially appointed members, who award grants to individual artists, state and local arts agencies and nonprofit organizations. The NEA became embroiled in controversy in the late 1980s when its funding of a photography exhibit by Robert MAPPLETHORPE (which included homoerotic images) drew criticism from the right, led by Senator Jesse Helms. After much debate about obscenity, censorship and federal funding of the arts, Congress established an Independent Commission to determine if the NEA should be restructured or perhaps even abolished. In October of 1990, the House of Representatives passed a bill that included the requirement that artists funded by the NEA and convicted of violating local obscenity laws must return their grant money. By 2003 the NEA had awarded over than 119,000 grants.

**National Enquirer, The** Published by Generoso P. Pope Jr., who converted the paper in 1952 to a tabloid featuring the bizarre and the gory. By the mid-1960s, the paper had a circulation of nearly one million and was making huge profits. Pope again changed the formula in the late 1960s, putting the paper into supermarkets and featuring celebrities, UFOs and predictions by clairvoyants. In 1988, the paper had a circulation of over 4.5 million. Due to several libel lawsuits in 1980s, the *Enquirer* was forced to tighten its reporting standards with regards to actual people and events. Despite this the *Enquirer* is often regarded as sensationalist. In recent years the circulation of the *Enquirer* has slumped below 1 million.

**National Geographic Society** Scientific and educational organization. Popularly known through its monthly publication *The National Geographic Magazine,* the National Geographic Society also sponsors expeditions and research projects in a broad range of fields, including anthropology, geography and oceanography. The Society was founded in 1888 and now has more than 10 million members worldwide. Its notable projects include sponsorship of Richard BYRD and Robert PEARY's polar expedition and the first U.S. trek to the peak of Mount Everest. Its other publications include *National Geographic World, National Geographic Research, National Geographic Traveler,* maps and other educational support materials. It also produces popular television specials on nature, science and exploration.

**National Health Service** The British National Health Service Act became law in 1946. Based on the recommendations of the BEVERIDGE REPORT, the act's intent was to provide free, comprehensive "cradle-to-grave" medical, dental and ophthalmological services to all Britons. The National Health Service came into being during the Labour government of Clement ATTLEE and had been a long-term goal of the LABOUR PARTY and then minister of health, Ernest BEVIN. The program was an expensive one, and subsequent governments began imposing fees for some services. Margaret THATCHER's call for more private care and cutbacks in the Health Service in the 1980s resulted in real and threatened strikes by nurses and other health-care workers. In 1988 she fired the minister of health; created a new Cabinet position, secretary of state for health; and named Kenneth Clarke to the post. She planned a proposal by which doctors would operate within a budget and allot health services to their patients without exceeding it. The budget of the National Health Service in 2005–2006 was £80 billion.

**National Industrial Recovery Act** Major NEW DEAL program, designed to regulate and revive industry; it was declared unconstitutional in 1935. When President Franklin ROOSEVELT assumed office at the height of the Depression, economic activity was at a standstill. The National Industrial Recovery Act was passed to revive the industrial sector. Modeled after the War Industries Board of World War I, it established industry codes designed to increase capital investment, end destructive competition and create jobs. The antitrust laws were suspended for two years, and trade, prices and labor practices were controlled by industry codes, while workers were guaranteed collective bargaining rights. To ensure job creation the NATIONAL RECOVERY ADMINISTRATION (NRA) and the Work Projects Administration (WPA) were created to carry out the act's provisions and to put people to work. In practice the system was not as successful as planned. Little new investment actually occurred and the law was criticized by a wide array of groups. While unions found the act harmful, so did the small business community, which feared the growth of government-supported monopolies. In 1935 in *Schechter v. United States,* which involved interstate commerce provisions of the act, the Supreme Court held the National Industrial Recovery Act to be unconstitutional. The Court reasoned that the act went far beyond the scope of Congress's power to regulate interstate commerce.

## National Institutes of Health (NIH)

An agency in the Public Health Service division of the U.S. Department of Health and Human Services. Originally started in 1887 as the Hygienic Laboratory at the U.S. Marine Hospital in Staten Island, New York, NIH took its present name in 1948; its laboratories are now located in Bethesda, Maryland. NIH conducts biomedical research, supports the training of research scientists and funds approximately 40 percent of health research in the U.S. It is comprised of 11 institutes, each specializing in health fields, such as aging, child health and human development and cancer research. It also includes the National Library of Medicine, the Fogarty International Center for Advanced Study in the Health Sciences and its research hospital—the Clinical Center.

**nationalization** The process of assuming control and ownership of an industry on a national scale by a national government. This has happened in a number of countries and for a variety of purposes. Some governments, especially those in the THIRD WORLD, have nationalized vital industries to gain local control and keep profits in their own country. Other governments have tried nationalization to promote efficiency or to promote social goals such as increased employment or subsidization of certain goods. Utilities such as airlines, electric and gas generation and distribution, postal services and communication companies are commonly nationalized. Although FRANCE and the UNITED KINGDOM nationalized many industries, they later sought to divest these holdings to private ownership. Forced nationalization without compensation is known as "expropriation."

## National Labor Relations Act (aka the Wagner Act) (1935)

Landmark NEW DEAL legislation, sponsored by Senator Robert Wagner of New York, that established the right to collective bargaining and set up the **National Labor Relations Board,** a federal agency to oversee union elections. Although Congress legalized union membership and the right to peaceful picketing in the 1932 NORRIS-LAGUARDIA ACT, unions were still at a distinct disadvantage. The Wagner Act shifted this balance by providing a mechanism that enabled unions to hold certification elections under government supervision. The act also created the National Labor Relations Board (NLRB) with power to supervise elections and police "unfair labor practices"—such as interference with union organizing efforts, discrimination against union members and refusal to bargain in good faith with a duly-elected union representing workers.

## National Labor Relations Board v. Jones & Laughlin Steel Corp. (1937)

U.S. Supreme Court decision upholding a major NEW DEAL program. President Franklin D. ROOSEVELT's New Deal had run into a substantial roadblock when the Supreme Court overturned a number of the president's programs as unconstitutional. The Court had objected to New Deal programs as unwarranted governmental interference with private business. The NATIONAL LABOR RELATIONS ACT was a cornerstone of the New Deal, recognizing the right of workers to collectively bargain and establishing the National Labor Relations Board to supervise union elections. In a surprise decision, the conservative Supreme Court closely approved the legislation by a 5-4 margin. This marked the end of the Supreme Court's resistance to FDR's reform plans.

## National Liberation Front (NLF)

The National Liberation Front was appropriately named, for it was a classic communist-front organization. Formed in Hanoi in December 1960, the NLF was designed to disguise its communist control and thus draw support from noncommunist South Vietnamese disaffected with their government. Many noncommunist members of the NLF though they were working for southern independence, and the ANTIWAR MOVEMENT in the U.S. championed the NLF as the true representative of the South Vietnamese people. The NLF stressed land reform, expulsion of foreigners, unfairness of South Vietnam's tax system and other issues.

After the war the North Vietnamese freely admitted that the NLF was their own creation, totally controlled and directed from Hanoi. Betrayed and disillusioned, many southern NLF leaders were purged or imprisoned or fled into exile. (See also VIET CONG.)

## National Missile Defense (NMD)

A missile defense program initiated by the United States. Fulfilling one of his campaign promises in 2002, U.S. president George W. BUSH withdrew the U.S. from the 1972 Anti-Ballistic Missile Treaty in order to pursue a small-scale missile defense system designed to prevent "rogue" states from launching a small number of nuclear-armed ballistic missiles at American targets. Unlike earlier missile defense program designs, such as the multilayered system known as the Strategic Defense Initiative begun in 1983 by President Ronald Reagan, the NMD program proposed by President Bush would be incapable of preventing a massive nuclear strike by Russian or Chinese intercontinental ballistic missiles (ICBMs). President Bush also offered to make the technology developed under the NMD program available to Russia, the other signatory state to the ABM Treaty that the U.S. had unilaterally abrogated. However, this NMD program raised concerns in other nuclear weapon states, such as Russia,

France, and China. These governments, as well as critics of the NMD program within the U.S., voiced concerns that this missile defense system could lead to a new nuclear arms race as countries might rush to devise means of defeating the proposed U.S. missile shield. In 2002 President Bush signed a directive to begin deployment of operational ballistic missile systems by 2004.

## National Party (New Zealand)
New Zealand political party formed in 1935. During the GREAT DEPRESSION there were three conservative, anti-LABOUR parties in New Zealand: the Reform Party, the United Party and the Democratic Party. Their lack of unification contributed to Labour's stunning victory in 1935, after which the three parties' leadership called a convention to organize the National Party. It came to power in 1949 under the leadership of Sir Sidney Holland, who was prime minister until 1957, and again under Sir Keith HOLYOAKE (1960–72). From 1974 to 1984, National leader Robert Muldoon was prime minister. After the party's defeat (1984), Muldoon was succeeded by Jim McClay (1945–   ) as its leader.

## National Party (South Africa)
South African political party (1914–2000). Created in 1914, the National Party (NP) became the political vehicle of the Afrikaners. These were descendants of Protestant Dutch and French settlers who had emigrated to South Africa in the 17th century to escape the religious wars in Europe. Its leaders favored the strict social, political and economic separation between the privileged white settlers and the other inhabitants of the newly created British dominion called the Union of South Africa (1910). In the white-only national elections in 1948, the NP ran on a platform of APARTHEID ("apartness" in the language of Afrikaans). This policy would segregate white South Africans from the three other racial categories the party identified—coloured (those of mixed racial ancestry), Asian (predominantly Indian), and Bantu (those of African ancestry)—and ensure the political, social and economic superiority of white South Africans.

In 1982 the party sought to reduce domestic and foreign pressure against its apartheid policies by amending the South African constitution to create separate legislatures for coloured and Asian citizens. Five years later dissident elements in the NP began clamoring for reform, and in a few cases, the elimination of apartheid. When the party ignored their petitions, this produced a wave of resignations from the party.

In 1989 the NP launched a major campaign to reform apartheid. That year, South African president F. W. DE KLERK began to allow greater civil liberties for black dissident groups like the ANC. The following year, de Klerk released the ANC militant leader Nelson MANDELA from prison and announced his intention to end apartheid. Although he fell under increasing criticism from the more hard-line members of the NP, de Klerk's policies obtained the approval of the white electorate in a March 1992 national referendum. De Klerk also opened the NP to all races and entered into negotiations with the ANC and the Inkatha Freedom Party (an organization representing the Zulus) to create a new, multiparty and multiracial South Africa. These talks resulted in a November 1993 constitution that called for a tripartite presidency and permitted free elections for the first time in the country's history. In April 1994 the NP lost control of the government after winning the second highest number of delegates to the National Assembly. De Klerk began serving as deputy president under the ANC's leader, Nelson Mandela. Although the reforms undertaken by deKlerk did expand the NP's base of support to include the more affluent and urban members of the "Cape Coloured"—an ethnic group descended from Dutch, Khoisan and Indian ancestors—it continued to recede in political importance, especially after deKlerk retired from politics in 1997. In 2000, following the June 1999 national elections in which the NP's membership in the National Assembly had shrunk to 28 delegates, the NP united with the Democratic Party to form the Democratic Alliance.

## National Public Radio
Based in Washington, D.C., National Public Radio provides programming to its noncommercial radio station members nationwide. Its news programming includes the acclaimed *All Things Considered* and *Morning Edition*. It initially relied on the Corporation for Public Broadcasting for the majority of its funding; in 1981 they provided two-thirds of its $21 million budget. By 1983 NPR was close to bankruptcy but recovered by successfully seeking institutional donations. It then stopped depending on the Corporation for Public Broadcasting for support. The corporation now gives federal money directly to member stations, which pay higher rates to NPR for programming. By 1989 NPR had become solvent. In 2003 NPR was given $200 million from the estate of the late Joan B. Kroc, widow of Ray Kroc, founder of McDonald's Corporation.

## National Radio Astronomy Observatory (NRAO)
The largest radio-astronomy observatory in the U.S. It is used by scientists throughout the country, funded by the National Science Foundation and operated by Associated Universities Inc. Founded in 1956, NBAO's many radio telescopes have detected radio waves given off by a huge number of objects in space—from the planets of our solar system to vastly distant quasars. With headquarters, scientific offices and computer facilities in Charlottesville, Virginia, the NRAO is responsible for radio telescopes in Socorro, New Mexico; Kitt Peak, Arizona, and Green Bank, West Virginia. Its Socorro facility is the home of the Very Large Array, the world's most powerful radio telescope. It consists of 27 large mirrored reflectors, each 82 ft. in diameter and all operating as a single instrument. The Kitt Peak telescope, designed expressly to deal with extremely short radio waves, measures 39 ft. in diameter. The large Green Bay telescope, which with a diameter of 300 ft. was long the world's largest movable instrument of its kind, collapsed in 1988 and was completely destroyed. The other six smaller radio telescopes at the facility remain in operation. The NRAO constructed another instrument, the Very Long Baseline Array Telescope, which was completed in 1993 at a cost of $85 million, which operates from Socorro, with 10 reflectors situated throughout the U.S. and in the Virgin Islands.

## National Recovery Administration (NRA)
U.S. government administrative bureau established in June 1933 under the NATIONAL INDUSTRIAL

RECOVERY ACT. One of President Franklin D. ROOSEVELT's earliest NEW DEAL creations, the NRA drew up and oversaw codes relating to fair competition in business and industry. These codes regulated prices, wages, working conditions, the construction of facilities and terms of credit. Administered by Hugh S. Johnson, it gained the cooperation of major industries throughout the U.S. The NRA was declared unconstitutional in May 1935 by a U.S. Supreme Court decision and it was subsequently abolished. A number of its provisions were enacted in later labor legislation.

*National Review.* Biweekly political magazine noted for its conservative outlook. The *National Review* was founded by William F. BUCKLEY Jr. in 1955, and has maintained its status as a leading journalistic forum for conservative political viewpoints. Buckley has edited the magazine since its inception, although in 1990 he announced his intention of turning over the primary editorial responsibilities to other hands in the near future. The *National Review* has frequently expressed opposition to government deficit spending, welfare programs and DÉTENTE with the USSR and other communist regimes. The magazine has won a loyal following of subscribers and regular readers and has achieved commercial as well as critical success. Buckley remained an editor-at-large with the magazine until his June 2004 decision to divest himself of his shares in the *National Review*, but the chief editorial duties have been exercised since 1997 by Rich Lowry.

**National Rifle Association of America (NRA)** Organization that promotes the shooting of rifles and pistols as a sport, in sharpshooting, hunting and other activities. Established in 1871, it sponsors competitions and chooses participants in international shooting events. With a membership that reached 3,000,000 by the early 1990s, the NRA also maintains a powerful lobby in Washington. The NRA opposes gun control and any other acts that it believes to provide unnecessary restrictions on the rights of gun owners and enthusiasts. From 1998 to 2003 acclaimed Hollywood film actor Charlton Heston served as the NRA's president. As of 2004 the NRA has 4 million members.

**National Urban Coalition** American organization that works to solve urban problems. Founded in 1970 through the merger of the Urban Coalition and Urban America, it attempts to identify and publicize serious urban problems and to take steps to begin dealing with these problems. With representatives from business and labor as well as leaders from civic, community, religious and minority-rights groups, the organization deals with issues of employment, housing, education, economic well-being and health care for urban Americans. The National Urban Coalition is headquartered in Washington, D.C.

**Native Dancer** *(1950–1967)* Thoroughbred racehorse. Known as "the Gray Ghost," Native Dancer was an imposing gray colt who won all but one of his 22 races over the course of his brief career. Lightly raced but undefeated as a two-year-old, in his second season he lost only the Kentucky Derby, in which he was fouled. He went on that year to win the Preakness, Belmont, Arlington Classic and Dwyer and Travers Stakes. Asked to carry extraordinary weights as a four-year-old, his already weak ankles began to suffer and he was retired to stud. Among his outstanding descendants were Kauai King, NORTHERN DANCER and the brilliant Majestic Prince.

**NATO** See NORTH ATLANTIC TREATY ORGANIZATION.

**Nauru (*formerly* Pleasant Island)** Independent island state west of KIRIBATI in the west Pacific Ocean (see map, page 957), discovered in 1798.

In 1888 it was claimed by Germany, and was made an Australian LEAGUE OF NATIONS mandate at the end of WORLD WAR I. From August 1942 through WORLD WAR II Nauru was occupied by the JAPANESE, and in 1947 became a trust territory of AUSTRALIA, UNITED KINGDOM, and NEW ZEALAND, gaining independence in 1968. In 1999 Nauru joined the UN. Since joining the UN, Nauru has encountered domestic and international difficulties because of its 2001 agreement with Australia to act as a holding station for asylum seekers caught trying to enter Australia illegally, its alleged involvement in money laundering schemes and its ongoing efforts to honor its national debt.

*Nautilus* The world's first atomic-powered submarine, the USS *Nautilus* was launched in January 1954 and had its first sea trials a year later. It was developed largely through the advocacy of Admiral Hyman RICKOVER, who began supporting the idea of the nuclear-powered craft in the late 1940s. The 2,800-ton vessel was completed at a cost of some $55 million. It measures 323 feet long, can attain a speed of over 20 knots per hour when submerged and carries a crew of 105. In August 1958 the submarine made the first undersea crossing of the North Pole; later that month it set an east-west transatlantic record for submarines traveling from Portland, England, to New York.

**Navarre, Henri** *(1898–1983)* French general. Navarre was commander in chief of the French forces in INDOCHINA from 1953 to 1954, when the VIET MINH defeated the French at the Battle of DIEN

*The* USS Nautilus (LIBRARY OF CONGRESS, PRINTS AND PHOTOGRAPHS DIVISION)

BIEN PHU, which marked the end of the French attempt to maintain control in Indochina.

**Navratilova, Martina** *(1956–   )* Czechoslovakian-born U.S. tennis player. The daughter of avid tennis players, she won the Czech singles title three times from 1972 to 1974. In 1974 she defected to the U.S. From 1978 to 1984 she won five Wimbledon singles titles, in addition to her six doubles titles. A two-time winner of the French Open, she did not win the U.S. Open until 1983, a feat she repeated in 1984. In 1993 Navratilova won the Paris Open, the last major tennis tournament she would win on the World Tennis Association tour. The following year she retired from professional tennis. However, she later returned to tournament tennis, and in July 2003 won the Wimbledon mixed doubles tournament with Leander Paes. This tied Navratilova with Billie Jean King's record of 20 Wimbledon titles. At Wimbledon in 2004, Navratilova played and won her first singles match in 10 years, beating her 24-year-old opponent in straight sets.

**Nazism** An ideology and a political movement that arose in GERMANY during the 1920s. Led by Adolf HITLER, crystallized in his National Socialist German Workers' Party (or Nazi Party), and at least partially defined in his book *MEIN KAMPF,* the movement ruled Germany from 1933 to 1945. The name "Nazi" was originally a derogatory abbreviation of the first word of the party's German name. Nazi ideology combined the pseudoscientific racism of such figures as the Comte de Gobineau (1816–82), Houston Stewart CHAMBERLAIN and the Nazis' own Alfred Rosenberg, with a powerful nationalism and sense of national destiny that demanded the unification of all German-speaking peoples. Violently anti-Semitic, it elevated the Germanic or "Aryan" race and placed the JEWS at the lowest end of the racial spectrum. A kind of FASCISM, it was authoritarian and totalitarian in character, allowing private property while suppressing individual rights.

Nazism arose as a result of the political, social and economic crises that befell Germany after the humiliation of its defeat in WORLD WAR I. Its ex-

*Nazi propaganda before the outset of the Holocaust reading. "Germans! Defend yourselves! Do not buy from Jews!"* (LIBRARY OF CONGRESS, PRINTS AND PHOTOGRAPHS DIVISION)

tremist positions appealed to a people exhausted by war and disillusioned with the performance of postwar democracy. Promising order and prosperity to the German people and exalting discipline and power, Nazism condemned democracy, socialism and communism with equal fervor. The movement drew adherents from the military, the farmers, the urban middle class and the wealthy industrialist classes, and by the mid-1920s the party had some 20,000 members. It became more appealing and more powerful with the GREAT DEPRESSION, holding out promises of economic stability and glory for the German nation. By 1929 the Nazi Party had some 176,000 members, and in the 1932 elections it emerged as Germany's most powerful political party.

In 1933 Hitler was named chancellor, and Nazism became Germany's ruling ideology (with the Nazi Party as the nation's only legal political party). The Nazis took control of all aspects of German life, abolishing freedom of the press and speech and severely limiting civil liberties. Having established a private army in the 1920s, the Nazis expanded their military strength by creating a fearsome secret police force, the GESTAPO. They also established CONCENTRATION

CAMPS, where they imprisoned Jews and other "enemies" of the Third Reich. Over the years, they murdered some six million Jews (see HOLOCAUST) and killed about five million others, including Gypsies, Slavs, homosexuals, communists and other political opponents of Nazism. In an attempt to build a German empire, the Nazis achieved ANSCHLUSS with Austria in 1938 and used strong-arm political tactics and intimidation that same year against Czechoslovakia, annexing its German-speaking SUDETENLAND. When the Nazis entered Poland in 1939, WORLD WAR II was launched and Germany entered on a course that was to see its utter defeat in the war, marking the disintegration of Nazism. The Nazi Party was officially banned by WEST GERMANY's postwar constitution. Nonetheless, the movement and its ideology reappeared in neo-Nazi groups that occasionally sprang up in Europe and the U.S.

**Nazi-Soviet Pact** See GERMAN-SOVIET NON-AGGRESSION PACT.

**NBC (National Broadcasting Company)** One of the three major U.S. radio and television networks. The National Broadcasting Company was established in 1926; its stock was owned by RCA (Radio Corporation of America), Westinghouse and General Electric. RCA bought out the other two in 1930 to assume full ownership of the company. NBC established two national radio networks, the Red Network (with 25 stations) and the Blue Network (with six stations). During the GREAT DEPRESSION, NBC and its rival CBS provided news and entertainment programs to millions of radio listeners across the U.S. In 1943, the Federal Communications Commission ordered NBC to sell its Blue Network, which subsequently became ABC (the American Broadcasting Company). In the late 1940s and early 1950s, NBC pioneered programming in the new medium of television. NBC was especially known for its live drama and variety programs. In the 1960s, the network's news and documentary programs were noteworthy; NBC also programmed many new situation comedies and drama series. Live comedy returned to television in the 1970s via NBC's popular SATURDAY NIGHT LIVE program. By the 1980s, the NBC television network consisted of five NBC-owned stations plus some 210 affiliated stations; the NBC radio network included eight NBC-owned stations and about 300 affiliated stations. NBC was purchased by General Electric in 1986. Under GE the television network began to dominate the Nielsen ratings with programs like *Friends, Seinfeld, ER* and *THE WEST WING*.

**NBC White Paper** A notable series of investigative television documentaries. In its first real challenge to programs like CBS's *SEE IT NOW*, NBC lured Irving Gitlin from CBS to head the "creative projects" unit in NBC News. These network specials began with "The U-2 Affair" in November 1961 and included such other contemporary news subjects as "Angola: Journey to a War" (1961), "The Death of Stalin" (1963) and "Cuba: Bay of Pigs" (1964). Filmmakers like Robert Young and Albert Wasserman developed lightweight, portable 16mm cameras and sound equipment. This "cutting edge" technology enabled them to penetrate areas, from Angola to American slums, more easily and less obtrusively than had been possible with the old-fashioned 35mm camera equipment. By contrast to these probing contemporary investigations were programs like

"The Real West" (1961), narrated by Gary COOPER, which used historic photographs to re-create a vanishing aspect of American culture.

**Neagle, Dame Anna (Florence Marjorie Robinson)** *(1904–1986)* British actress. She was regarded as the first lady of British cinema from the late 1930s through the early 1950s. She was Britain's number one box-office draw throughout most of the 1940s. From 1943 until his death in 1977, she was married to Irish-born producer Herbert Wilcox, who produced and directed nearly all her films. Among her most successful performances were two as Queen Victoria in *Victoria the Great* and in *Sixty Glorious Years*. Her portrayal of a WORLD WAR II heroine of the French Resistance in *Odette* (1950) was regarded as her finest performance. Also active in the theater, she came to be listed in the GUINNESS BOOK OF RECORDS for her 2,062 performances in the London musical *Charlie Girl*.

**Nearing, Scott** *(1883–1983)* American pacifist and radical of the early 1900s. He had a doctorate in economics and taught at several universities early in his career but encountered difficulty because of his Marxist, anti-establishment views. In 1915 he lost his teaching post at the University of Pennsylvania when he spoke out against child labor. He lost another job when he was indicted for opposing U.S. participation in WORLD WAR I. He later became a leading environmentalist, dedicated to simple, rural living. His ideas about the environment, which he and his wife, Helen, put into practice on their farm in New England, attracted a large following in the 1960s. The Nearings wrote *Living the Good Life* (1954); Scott Nearing's autobiography is *The Making of a Radical* (1972).

**Neave, Airey** *(1916–1979)* British WORLD WAR II hero and politician. An RAF flier during the war, Neave was shot down over Germany and held as a PRISONER OF WAR in Germany's notorious Colditz Castle but managed to make a daring escape. After the war he was on the British prosecution team in the NUREMBERG TRIALS. He was elected to Parliament in 1953. A supporter of,

and leading adviser to, Margaret THATCHER, he helped engineer her election to the leadership of the CONSERVATIVE PARTY in 1975. Neave took a particular interest in the problems of NORTHERN IRELAND, and it was widely assumed that he would become secretary of state for Northern Ireland in a Thatcher government. However, he was killed by a car bomb as he was leaving Parliament on March 30, 1979. The radical Irish National Liberation Army claimed responsibility for Neave's death.

**Neel, Alice** *(1900–1984)* American painter. The Pennsylvania-born expressionist painter spent most of her life in New York City. Highly individualistic in her style, she is noted for her psychologically acute and physically candid portraiture. Largely neglected during the postwar heyday of ABSTRACT EXPRESSIONISM, she was rediscovered in the late 1960s and 1970s and won a good deal of critical praise.

**Negritude** Literary movement among black writers from French colonies in Africa that originated in Paris during the 1930s. Founded by the Guianan poet Léon Damas, it championed and celebrated the uniqueness of black experience and talent. Léopold SENGHOR, later the founding father and first president of independent SENEGAL, was also a leader of the movement. Negritude was a consciousness-raising phenomenon that strongly influenced the black social and political revolution in the U.S. during the 1960s.

**Negro leagues** American baseball leagues formed in the era when black players were banned from major league teams. The Negro National League was formed in 1920; the Negro American League followed in 1937. After Jackie ROBINSON joined the Brooklyn Dodgers in 1947, breaking baseball's color bar, many other black players began to play for major league teams, and the Negro leagues declined in importance. The last, the Negro American League, was disbanded in 1960. Stars of the Negro leagues included pitcher Satchel PAIGE; outfielder Cool Papa BELL; and catcher Josh Gibson, who held the Negro leagues' home run record.

**Nehru, Pandit Jawaharlal** *(1889–1964)* Indian statesman and national-

*Jawaharlal Nehru, first prime minister of India*
(LIBRARY OF CONGRESS, PRINTS AND PHOTOGRAPHS
DIVISION)

ist, first prime minister of INDIA
(1947–64). The son of attorney and
journalist Motilal Nehru, Jawaharlal
Nehru was born in Allahabad and educated in England at Cambridge University. After the AMRITSAR MASSACRE of
1919, he became active in the Indian
Congress movement; with the support
of Mohandas K. GANDHI, he assumed
the presidency of the movement in
1929. In this position, Nehru was the
chief architect of India's independence
from Britain. Beginning in 1947, he
served as the country's first prime minister, until his death in 1964. During
his tenure, the pragmatic Nehru introduced industrial and social advances,
guiding India to a role of leadership in
the developing world. He was succeeded as prime minister by Lal SHAS-
TRI, who was in turn succeeded by
Nehru's daughter, Indira GANDHI.

**Neill, A(lexander) S(utherland)**
*(1883–1973)* Scottish educator. A revolutionary, progressive educator, Neill
is best known for establishing the independent, self-governing Summerhill
School which was based on the premise of making "the school fit the child."
A teacher at various schools
(1903–21), he first founded a school
near Salzburg, Austria, but moved it to
Leiston in Suffolk, England, and called
it the Summerhill School (1927). The
school was coeducational and catered
to children from higher-income families, mostly American. He published
many books on education, and his

ideas influenced the direction of education in both Britain and America.

**Nelson, George "Baby Face"
(Lester, J. Gillis)** *(1908–1934)* American gangster. Born in Chicago, the
diminutive bankrobber and killer
began his recognized criminal career at
the age of 14, when he was sent to a juvenile home for auto theft. By 1929 he
was working as a strong-arm man for
Al CAPONE's gang. Arrested during a
bank robbery in 1931, he escaped
prison the following year and joined
DILLINGER's gang. Nelson quickly af-
firmed his violent reputation by indiscriminately killing bank guards and
bystanders. After Dillinger's death at
the hands of the FBI in July 1934, Nelson succeeded to the title of public
enemy number one. He was killed by
FBI agents during a shootout in Illinois
four months later.

**Nelson, Nate** *(1932–1984)* Lead
singer for the Flamingos (1954–62)
and the Platters (1964–82). With the
Flamingos he recorded the hit "I Only
Have Eyes for You." His hits with the
Platters included "Only You" and
"Smoke Gets in Your Eyes."

**Nelson, Ricky (Eric Hillard Nel-
son)** *(1940–1985)* Ricky Nelson became a teenage singing idol for fans of
ROCK AND ROLL during the 1950s. He
appeared with his family on the long-
running television show *The Adventures
of Ozzie and Harriet*. By the time the
show went off the air (1966), he had
sold millions of records. Two of his
biggest hits were "Mary Lou" and
"Travellin' Man." In later years, he had
a more modest career as a country rock
musician.

**Nemerov, Howard Stanley** *(1920–
1991)* American poet. Nemerov's first
book of poetry, *The Image and Law*
(1947), was critically acclaimed but derivative of T. S. ELIOT and other modernist poets. It was with *The Salt Garden*
(1955) that he found his own voice. His
realistic, romantic poetry often reflects
an increasing concern with nature. Subsequent poetic works include *Inside the
Onion* (1984) and *War Stories: Poems
about Long Ago and Now* (1987). Nemerov's fiction, which shares with some
of his poetry an ironic wit, includes *The
Melodramatists* (1949) and *Stories, Fa-*

*bles and Other Diversions* (1971). Other
works include *Figures of Thought: Speculations on the Meaning of Poetry and Other
Essays* (1978) and *The Oak in the Acorn:
On Remembrance of Things Past and on
Teaching Proust, Who Will Never Learn*
(1987). In 1988 he became the third
poet laureate of the U.S. His sister was
the photographer Diane ARBUS.

**Nemirovich-Danchenko, Vasily
Ivanovich** *(1848–1936)* Author
and journalist. He wrote prolifically,
producing a vast number of narratives
and novels directed at the general
reader. Although superficial, his
works are versatile and entertaining.
They include *Personal Reminiscences of
General Skobeleff* (1884), *The Prices of
the Stock Exchange* (1914) and *Peasant
Tales of Russia* (1917).

**Nemon, Oscar** *(1905–1985)* One
of Britain's most accomplished sculptors, he was famed for his portrait
busts and full-size sculptures. Nemon's
subjects included Queen ELIZABETH II,
Margaret THATCHER, Dwight D. EISEN-
HOWER and Sigmund FREUD. He was
best known for his more than 50 like-
nesses of Winston CHURCHILL, one of
which was in the members' lobby of
the House of Commons.

**Nemtchinova, Vera** *(1899–1984)*
Russian-born ballerina. Nemtchinova
became a star of Serge DIAGHILEV's BAL-
LETS RUSSES in the 1920s and went on
to lead several other dance companies.
Her most famous role was as the an-
drogynous "Girl in Blue" in *Les Biches*,
Bronislava NIJINSKA's 1924 ballet about
French sexual and social mores.
Nemtchinova was hailed both for her
abilities as a classical dancer and as an
experimental performer in the modern
mold.

**Nenni, Pietro** *(1891–1980)* Italian
socialist politician. Nenni's political career spanned seven decades. In 1922
he succeed Benito MUSSOLINI (who was
then still a socialist) as editor of *Avanti*,
a leading socialist newspaper. Strongly
opposed to FASCISM, he was later imprisoned several times by Mussolini
and spent a period in exile. He fought
for the Loyalists in the SPANISH CIVIL
WAR. After WORLD WAR II, he helped
found the new Italian republic and
served in its first government as

deputy prime minister and foreign minister. He led ITALY's Socialist Party from 1949 to 1969. His political alliance with the Italian Communist Party and his opposition to the NORTH ATLANTIC TREATY ORGANIZATION (NATO) earned him a Stalin Prize for Peace in 1952. He broke with the communists, however, and renounced the award after the Soviet invasion of Hungary (1957; see HUNGARIAN UPRISING). In 1962 he allied his party with the Christian Democrats in a coalition that ruled Italy until 1976.

**neoexpressionism** Term used for a revival and reinterpretation of 20th-century EXPRESSIONISM that flourished worldwide in the late 1970s, throughout the 1980s and into the 1990s. Rejecting passionless minimalist abstraction, the movement draws its subject matter from the contemporary world in figurative images that are often violent, brutal, childlike and erotic. Among the many different artists who have been attracted to elements of the style are the Americans David Salle and Julian Schnabel and the Spaniards Sandro Chia and Francesco Clemente.

**neorealism** Italian literary movement that began in the late 1920s and came to dominate Italian literature in the 1930s, 1940s and 1950s. Its major figures included Alberto MORAVIA, Cesare PAVESE and Ignazio SILONE. A major precursor in Italian letters was the 19th-century novelist and story writer Giovanni Verga. Neorealism saw itself as a liberating impulse that could enable writers to abandon pseudo-sophistication and ornate literary stylings in favor of a more direct vision of life that encompassed the hopes and sorrows of everyday men and women. The neorealists frequently set their works in smaller Italian towns and villages as opposed to such cosmopolitan centers as Rome. In their blunt vision of the social and economic hardships of the Italian people, they were antifascist and a source of concern to MUSSOLINI's government. Neorealism had a great influence on Italian film directors of the 1940s, such as Roberto ROSSELLINI and Vittorio DE SICA.

**Nepal** Isolated central Asian kingdom bordering India in the northeast, Tibet and China in the north, landlocked by

| NEPAL | |
|---|---|
| 1923 | Full independence is formally recognized by Britain. |
| 1945 | Rana Padma Shamsher becomes prime minister. |
| 1946 | The Nepali Congress Party is founded. |
| 1950 | Ranas family is in open conflict with the monarch, Tribhuvan. Tribhuvan, implicated in Nepali Congress Party conspiracy against Rana power, seeks and is granted asylum in India. |
| 1951 | King Tribhuvan is restored to the throne. Elections and the formation of a constituent assembly are promised. Interim constitution, the Government of Nepal Act, is promulgated. |
| 1955 | Tribhuvan dies and is succeeded by Mahendra as king. Nepal joins the United Nations. |
| 1960 | All political parties are banned. The king takes over direct control of government. |
| 1972 | Mahendra dies and is succeeded as king by his son Birendra. |
| 1980 | In national referendum, people vote for continuance of the current form of "partyless" government and against the reintroduction of political parties. |
| 1990 | Nepal adopts a new constitution providing for the king as head of state. Executive power is to be exercised by a prime minister, who leads the majority party in the legislature. |
| 1991 | Nepal hold its first election in 50 years. |
| 1996 | Maoist rebels, wishing to end the monarchy and replace it with a "people's democratic republic," attack government forces and gain control of certain parts of the country. |
| 2001 | King Birendra and all members of the royal family are murdered by Crown Prince Dipendra in a drunken rage. The king's brother Gyanendra assumes the throne. |
| 2005 | In the face of the rebel insurgency Gyanendra dismisses the government and assumes full power. |
| 2006 | Supporters of the multiparty system stage protests in Kathmandu. King Gyanendra announces the reinstatement of the parliament. |

the Himalayan mountains. It was recognized as independent by GREAT BRITAIN in 1923. Nepal's Rana family held power as prime ministers from 1846 to 1950, and until 1956 Nepal exacted tribute from TIBET. After a successful democratic revolt in 1950, autocratic rule was replaced by constitutional government, later modified under the regime of King Mahendra in the 1960s. After his death

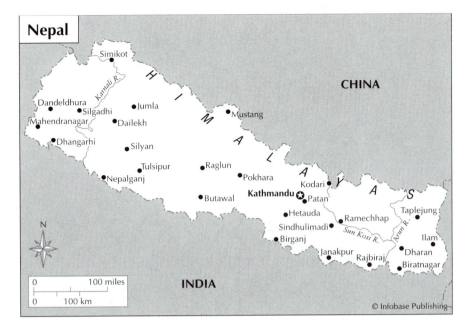

**Nepal**

in 1972 the king's son, Prince BIRENDRA, ascended the throne, and in May 1980 his monarchy and a parliament were ratified in Nepal's first election. Having aided BRITAIN during WORLD WAR I, Nepal over the years accepted financial aid from the USSR, China, and the U.S., though it remained essentially isolationist. In 1990 a Maoist people's movement party forced King Birenda to allow a multiparty government, and in 1991 Nepal held its first elections in 50 years. In 1996, in what has become known as the Nepal Civil War, Maoist rebels battled government forces and claimed several areas of Nepal to be under their rule. Birendra remained king until June 2001, when he, Queen Aiswarya, Prince Nirajan, and Princess Shruti were shot and killed by Crown Prince Dipendra over the latter's future marriage prospects. Dipendra promptly committed suicide, and Prince Gyanendra was crowned king of Nepal on June 4, 2001. A parliamentary system was established shortly after the regicide. In the face of an insurgency launched by Maoist rebels, however, Gyanendra assumed full powers in 2005. In 2006, facing widening protests, King Gyanendra announced he would reinstate parliament, which he dissolved more than a year before.

**Neruda, Pablo (Neftalí Ricardo Reyes)** *(1904–1973)* Chilean poet and diplomat. Neruda, who won the NOBEL PRIZE in literature in 1971, is one of the most widely read poets of modern times. His works are popular in all parts of the world, including China and the USSR. Neruda uses a variety of free verse forms—from short, epigrammatic poems to longbreath lines reminiscent of Walt Whitman. Born in Chile, the son of a railroad worker, Neruda studied for a career as a teacher. But his book of lyric poems, *Twenty Love Poems and a Song of Despair* (1924), proved a phenomenal success and set him on a career as a writer. Neruda also served in the Chilean diplomatic corps for many years, including stints as a consul in Burma, Singapore, Argentina (where he met Federico GARCÍA LORCA) and Spain. A member of the Chilean Communist Party, Neruda ran as its candidate for the presidency of Chile in 1969 but then stepped aside in favor of Salvador ALLENDE. Other books of verse by Neruda include *Crepusculario* (1923), *Residence on Earth* (1933), *Canto General* (1950), *Elemental Odes* (1954) and *Extravagaria* (1958).

**Nervi, Pier Luigi** *(1891–1979)* Italian architect. Nervi was educated as a civil engineer, graduating in 1913. He had no formal training as an architect. Nonetheless, he went on to become an influential architect and winner of the 1965 gold medal of the American Institute of Architects. A pioneer in the structural and design use of concrete, in the mid-1940s he developed ferroce-

mento, a blend of mortar and steel-wire mesh. Using this material, he designed intricate buildings with soaring buttresses and swooping ceilings. Among his best-known buildings are the Turin Exhibition Hall (1949–50), the UNESCO building in Paris, the Palazzetto della Sport and other buildings for the 1960 OLYMPIC GAMES in Rome, and the Vatican Audience Hall.

**Ness, Eliot** *(1902–1957)* American law enforcement officer. Ness attended the University of Chicago and later joined the Justice Department. In 1928 he was put in charge of a hand-picked 10-man squad of incorruptible lawmen. Popularly known as the Untouchables, they were charged in general with fighting organized crime and in particular with eliminating Al CAPONE and his mob. They conducted a series of highly publicized brewery raids and distracted Capone while other agents ferreted out evidence of his income tax evasion, which led to his downfall. Ness was later named the Justice Department's chief investigator of PROHIBITION violations, first in Chicago, then in Appalachian moonshine territory. From 1935 to 1941 he was public safety director for crime-ridden Cleveland, Ohio and was credited with ridding the city of violence and corruption. He was federal director of the Division of Social Protection for the Office of Defense during WORLD WAR II, becoming a private businessman after the war. Ness's exploits were the subject of the popular television series *The Untouchables* during the 1950s and 1960s, and of a film by the same title (1989).

**Netanyahu, Binyamin** *(1949– )* Born in Tel Aviv, Israel, Netanyahu spent his childhood in Jerusalem and his adolescence in the U.S., where his father, Benzion Netanyahu, was a professor of history. In 1967 Binyamin Netanyahu entered a commando unit of the Israeli Defense Forces (IDF) for his obligatory military service, participating in several counterterrorism operations. After his discharge from the IDF in 1972, Netanyahu obtained a B.S. in architecture and a M.S. in management studies from the Massachusetts Institute of Technology in 1974. After working as a business consultant for several years, Netanyahu joined the foreign service and became Israeli ambassador to the UN in 1984. In 1988 Netanyahu returned to Israel, where he was elected to the Knesset, the Israeli parliament, as a member of the right-wing Likud Party. In October 1991 he served as a senior member of the Israeli mission to the Madrid Peace Conference, which represented the first attempt at establishing a dialogue between Israel and the Arab countries of SYRIA and LEBANON, as well as with Palestinian delegates. In 1993 Netanyahu was elected chairman of the Likud Party and became prime minister in 1996, the year in which Israel held its first direct elections for that office. To ensure that Jerusalem would remain under Israeli rule, Netanyahu increased the number of Jewish settlements erected in the predominantly Arab districts of eastern Jerusalem. He also clashed repeatedly with the head of the Palestinian Authority Yasir Arafat. In the 1999 Israeli elections, Netanyahu lost the premiership to the new Labor candidate, Ehud BARAK, leading Netanyahu to resign his position in the Knesset and briefly retire from Israeli politics. Three years later, following the defeat of Barak by the Likud candidate, Ariel Sharon, Netanyahu returned to politics as Israeli foreign minister, a post he held for one year. Following national elections a year later, Netanyahu left the Foreign Ministry to become minister of finance. He resigned in 2005 in protest against the Sharon government's removal of Israeli settlements from the Gaza Strip.

**Netherlands, The (Kingdom of the Netherlands)** The Netherlands, popularly called Holland, lies on the North Sea coast of Western Europe and is bordered on the east by Germany and on the south by Belgium; the capital is Amsterdam but the seat of government is The Hague. A constitutional monarchy with a bicameral parliament, the sovereign is Queen Beatrix Wilhelmina Armgard (1938–   ), who became queen when her mother Queen Juliana, who had reigned since 1948, abdicated in 1980. Queen Beatrix was married in 1966 to Claus von Amsberg, a former West German diplomat, and gave birth to a son, Willem-Alexander Claus George Ferdinand in 1967—the first male heir to the throne since 1884. The monarch appoints a prime minister who is head of state and who chooses

the cabinet; Prime Minister Ruud Lubbers was appointed in 1982.

The Netherlands had a firm tradition of neutrality and remained so during WORLD WAR I, but in WORLD WAR II it was invaded in 1940 by Nazi Germany. During the occupation, 104,000 Dutch Jews were deported and killed, but many were hidden and saved by other citizens. Following liberation in 1945, the Netherlands became a founder-member of the NORTH ATLANTIC TREATY ORGANIZATION (NATO), a member of the Western European Union and of the BENELUX customs union.

In 1949 the Netherlands granted independence to its East Indies colony after a four-year war. The new Republic of INDONESIA expanded in 1963 when the Netherlands ceded its western half of New Guinea to Indonesia, finally ending 300 years of Dutch presence in Asia. In 1975 SURINAME, on the northeast coast of South America, became independent. The independence of its former colonies resulted in some economic instability at home due to increased immigration homewards and resulting unemployment. In 1953 the Netherlands' economic problems were exacerbated by destructive flooding. The autonomous NETHERLANDS ANTILLES is the sole Dutch territory outside of the Netherlands. A new constitution, based on the constitution of 1815, was introduced in 1983. In 1985, after much controversy, Prime Minister Lubbers agreed to accept the deployment of U.S. CRUISE MISSILES on Dutch soil. In 1994 Wim Kok, the leader of the country's Labor Party, became prime minister and led a three-party coalition into power. Wim Kok retained his premiership as the result

## NETHERLANDS

| 1904 | Dutch kill 541 Achinese in Sumatra; divide Timor island with Portuguese. |
|---|---|
| 1914–18 | Maintain neutrality during World War I. |
| 1920 | Permanent Court of Justice opens at The Hague. |
| 1940 | German troops invade, bomb Rotterdam; Dutch army surrenders, most of navy escapes to help Allies. |
| 1945 | Joins United Nations. |
| 1947 | Receives $1 billion in Marshall Plan aid. |
| 1948 | Queen Wilhelmina abdicates in favor of daughter Juliana; nationalist revolts intensify in Netherlands Indies (Indonesia); Dutch circle Jakarta, arrest Sukarno in defiance. |
| 1949 | Netherlands recognizes Indonesian independence. |
| 1954 | Suriname and Netherlands Antilles made self-governing, equal members of Dutch kingdom. |
| 1990 | Nearly completed Oosterscheldedam, world's most advanced sea barrier, holds off highest flood waters in 37 years. |
| 1991 | Lends noncombat support to Operation Desert Storm in Persian Gulf. |
| 1994 | Wim Kok of the Labor Party is named prime minister. |
| 1998 | Kok's coalition wins reelection to parliament. |
| 2000 | Euthanasia is legalized based on strict procedures; national legislation permits homosexual couples to marry and adopt children. |
| 2002 | The government resigns following release of a report critical of its role in the Srebrenica massacre in Bosnia in 1995. Anti-immigration party leader Pim Fortuyn is shot dead by a lone gunman. In elections in May, CDA and List Pim Fortuyn form a new government under Jan Peter Balkenende. The Netherlands adopts the euro. |
| 2003 | Christian Democrats win a narrow victory in general elections and a center-right coalition with Balkenende as premier secures a second term. |
| 2004 | Massive protests in Amsterdam against public spending cuts and welfare reforms. Filmmaker Theo Van Gogh is murdered after receiving death threats for his controversial film on women's position in Islamic society. |
| 2005 | A radical Islamist is jailed for life for the murder of Van Gogh. Voters reject a proposed EU constitution. |

of the 1998 national elections. He pushed through legislation in 2001 allowing homosexual couples to marry and adopt children. Since 1993 the Netherlands has become a vanguard state in the effort to permit euthanasia administered by physicians. The Dutch parliament formally authorized the procedure in 2000. In 2004 filmmaker Theo Van Gogh was murdered by a Dutch-Moroccan youth with radical Islamic beliefs, sparking debate about immigration and radical Islam in the Netherlands.

**Netherlands Antilles** Overseas territory containing the islands of Curaçao, Bonaire, and Aruba off the coast of South America, as well as several northern Leeward Islands, in the West Indies, in the Caribbean Sea. Formerly a colony, it became a territory of the Netherlands in 1954, with Willemstad, on Curaçao, as its capital. In 1969 it was the scene of civil strife, on Curaçao. In 1999 the Netherlands Antilles came under investigation for alleged money laundering, drug trafficking, and human rights violations on the five islands that make up the archipelago. In 2005 an agreement was signed that would make Curaçao and Sint Maarten associate states within the Kingdom of the Netherlands, while Bonaire, Saba and Sint Eustatius would become directly part of the kingdom.

**Neto, Agostinho António** (1922–1979) Angolan physician and revolutionary leader, president of ANGOLA (1975–79). Born in a village near Luanda, Neto was the son of a white Methodist missionary and a black Angolan woman. He studied medicine in Portugal and received his degree in 1958. As a student in Lisbon, he became active in the movement to depose Portuguese dictator Antonio SALAZAR and was imprisoned several times. Escaping from house arrest in 1962, he assumed leadership of the Popular Movement for the Liberation of Angola (MPLA), a Soviet-backed independence group. The MPLA emerged victorious, not only in its guerrilla war against Portugal, but also (with the aid of Cuban troops) in a subsequent civil war against two other nationalist organizations—Jonas SAVIMBI's National Union for the Total Independence of Angola (UNITA) and Holden Roberto's National Front for the Liberation of

Angola (FNLA). Neto was proclaimed president of an independent Angola in 1975. He established a one-party state that favored the USSR but sought ties with the West. Neto died in Moscow following surgery for cancer and was succeeded by José Eduardo DOS SANTOS.

**Neuilly, Treaty of** Post–WORLD WAR I agreement concluded in 1919 between the Allies and BULGARIA. Part of western Thrace was ceded to Greece and small border areas were ceded to Yugoslavia. In addition, southern Dobrudja, acquired after the BALKAN WARS, was confirmed as Romanian territory. Reparations were imposed, as was the restriction of the Bulgarian army to 20,000 men.

**Neumann, John von (János von Neumann)** (*1903–1957*) German mathematician who studied at the University of Berlin, the Berlin Institute of Technology and the University of Budapest, from which he obtained his doctorate in 1926. Von Neumann was Privatdozent at Berlin (1927–29) and taught at Hamburg (1929–30). He left Europe in 1930 to work in Princeton, first at the university and later at the Institute for Advanced Study. From 1943 he was a consultant on the ATOMIC BOMB project. Von Neumann may have been one of the last men able to span the fields of pure and applied mathematics. His first work was in set theory (the subject of his doctoral thesis), but in 1928 he published his first paper in the field for which he is best known, the mathematical theory of games. This work culminated in 1944 with the publication of *The Theory of Games and Economic Behavior,* which von Neumann had coauthored with Oskar Morgenstern. Not all the results in this work were novel, but it was the first time the field had been treated in such a large-scale and systematic way. Apart from the theory of games von Neumann did important work in the theory of operators. Dissatisfied with the resources then available for solving the complex computational problems that arose in hydrodynamics, von Neumann developed a broad knowledge of the design of COMPUTERS and, with his interest in the general theory of automata, became one of the founders of a whole new discipline. He was much interested in the general role of science and technology

in society, and this led to his increasing involvement with high-level government scientific committees.

**Neutra, Richard Josef** (*1892–1970*) Austrian-born American architect, a pioneer in introducing modern architecture and design in the U.S. Neutra studied in Vienna with Adolf LOOS, and from 1921 to 1922 worked with Erich Mendelsohn before coming to the U.S. in 1923, where he met Louis Sullivan and worked briefly for Frank Lloyd WRIGHT. In 1926 Neutra moved to California where he established a successful practice designing houses in the INTERNATIONAL STYLE vocabulary of MODERNISM when such work was otherwise virtually unknown in the U.S. His Lovell ("Heath") house of 1927–29, with its white walls and bands of windows, established his style. It was included in New York's MUSEUM OF MODERN ART 1932 exhibition entitled *The International Style.* The desert house near Los Angeles for film director Josef Von STERNBERG, with walls of gleaming steel and large windows looking into a courtyard with a pool and curving walls (1936), is a striking example of the work that made him famous. Later work included schools and housing projects, such as the Channel Heights housing of 1946 at San Diego and the house of the same year for Edgar Kaufmann Sr. near Palm Springs, California. The massive Los Angeles County Hall of Records (1958), with automatically adjusting louvers for sun control, is an example of his later, large-scale work. Neutra's philosophy and design theories are set forth in his 1954 book *Survival Through Design.*

**Nevelson, Louise** (*1900–1988*) American sculptor. Born Louise Berliawsky in Kiev, Russia, she came to the U.S. with her family at the age of five. She studied at the Art Students League in New York (1929–30) and at the Hans Hoffmann School in Munich (1931), subsequently serving as an assistant to Diego RIVERA in Mexico City (1932–33). She traveled widely in Europe and Latin America, returned to the U.S. and had her first one-woman show in New York in 1941. Her abstract sculptures are often composed of found objects, mainly planks, chair legs, balusters and other turned pieces of wood. Assembled into boxes painted in uniform

tones of black, white or gold, they have a compelling and enigmatic presence. These compositions grew larger and more environmental as her career progressed. In the work of the 1960s and 1970s, Nevelson also made use of metals and Plexiglas. Her work is particularly well represented in the collections of New York's MUSEUM OF MODERN ART and Whitney Museum of American Art.

**Nevins, Allan** (*1890–1971*) American historian. Nevins earned a master's degree from the University of Illinois in 1913, after which he worked in New York City as a journalist. In 1928 he joined the history department of Columbia University, where he remained for three decades. During his long and fruitful career, Nevins wrote widely on American history, including his biographies of Grover Cleveland and Hamilton Fish, which won PULITZER PRIZES in 1932 and 1936, respectively, and his eight-volume history of the Civil War, *Ordeal of the Union* (1947–71). Nevins was also one of the founders of *American Heritage* magazine.

**New Age movement** The New Age movement, which first won attention during the intense social change of the 1960s with its proclamations of a new Age of Aquarius, emerged in the 1980s and 1990s as a loosely defined but highly cherished label for a broad variety of spiritual, social and personal concerns. Basically, New Age refers to an open attitude toward such belief systems as pagan, occult, oriental and modern syncretistic movements; it considers them to be valid spiritual alternatives to the Judeo-Christian tradition. The New Age also posits the end of a past historical epoch dominated by war, nationalism and materialism; points to a new planetary union of peoples that will combine benign development with ecological awareness. Key, albeit disparate, figures in the development of New Age thinking include Joseph CAMPBELL, TEILHARD DE CHARDIN, Aleister CROWLEY, Fritz PERLS, E. F. Schumacher, D. T. Suzuki and Alan Watts.

**Newbery Medal** American children's literature award. The John Newbery Medal was established in 1922 and is awarded annually by the Children's Librarians Sections of the American Library Association to notable works of literature for children. It is named after John Newbery (1713–67), one of the earliest publishers of children's books. The medal itself was designed by the American sculptor, Rene Chambellan and is contributed by Frederic G. Melcher, the editor of *Publisher's Weekly.* The first medal was presented to Hendrik Willem Van Loon for *The Story of Mankind* (1922).

**New Britain (*German:* Neu-Pommern)** (Papua New Guinea). Largest of the islands of the BISMARCK ARCHIPELAGO, in the southwest Pacific Ocean, first discovered by the British in 1700. In 1884 it was colonized by Germany, and during WORLD WAR I was taken by AUSTRALIA and retained as a LEAGUE OF NATIONS mandate from 1920 to 1941. In January 1942 it was claimed by the Japanese, whose positions here subjected it to heavy U.S. air raids and follow-up invasions from late 1943 to March 1944, and it remained the scene of intense conflict until the end of WORLD WAR II.

**New Criticism** A term coined by poet and critic John Crowe RANSOM in *The New Criticism* (1941), which addresses the works of I. A. RICHARDS, T. S. ELIOT and William EMPSON, among others. The term's meaning has been stretched and blurred but generally it refers to literary interpretation based on close attention to the text and its nuance as well as emphasis on thematic organization. It rejects analysis of a work's background or its creator's motivation, focusing instead on each poem, story or novel as a self-contained work of art. Others associated with the New Criticism (not always willingly) include Robert Penn WARREN, R. P. Blackmur and F. R. LEAVIS. The New Criticism was dominant in the academic study of literature from the 1940s through the 1960s but has since been largely supplanted by other critical approaches such as FEMINISM, DECONSTRUCTION and STRUCTURALISM.

**New Deal** Economic and social reform program instituted by President Franklin ROOSEVELT in 1933. When Roosevelt assumed the presidency, the U.S. was in the depths of the GREAT DEPRESSION. Nearly one-quarter of the workforce had lost their jobs, and thousands of people, unable to pay their bills, had been thrown out of their homes and farms. FDR was elected with a mandate to deal with the crisis. His program was radical for its day: The government established social programs and became involved in the economy in an unprecedented manner. Programs like the Civil Works Administration (CWA), CIVILIAN CONSERVATION CORPS (CCC) and WORKS PROGRESS ADMINISTRATION (WPA) used borrowed money to put the unemployed back to work. FDR also established the Social Security system to provide a universal, social safety net. Many feared this massive expansion of government power, and the Supreme Court initially struck down many of the programs. Although the New Deal helped many, it was the mobilization for World War II that decisively brought the U.S. out of the Depression. However, the legacy of the New Deal endures—an expanded federal government that continues to play an active role in the social and economic life of the country.

**New Democratic Party (Canada)** The third major Canadian political party behind the Liberals and Progressive Conservatives. The New Democratic Party is left-of-center and was formed in 1933 out of the United Farmers Party, the Socialist Party of Canada and various immigrant groups. Until 1961 the party was known as the Cooperative Commonwealth Federation. Its support has traditionally come from western farmers and working people in Ontario. To date, the party has been most successful at the provincial rather than the national level. During the 1970s the NDP controlled governments in the provinces of British Columbia and Saskatchewan. In 1990 the NDP shocked the nation as it took control of the government of Ontario, Canada's wealthiest and most populous province. However, the party has suffered from lack of support at the polls in the early years of the 21st century.

**New Economic Policy** Economic policy practiced by the Soviet government in 1921–28, replacing the policies of WAR COMMUNISM (1918–21). It aimed at revitalizing the economy by allowing greater freedom in agriculture, industry and trade. In this, the government was successful and raised the national income above that of 1913. The NEP was followed by the first FIVE-YEAR PLAN.

**Newfoundland** Province of eastern CANADA. Although Newfoundland had been an independent British colony since 1855, France did not cede its fishing rights until 1904. With fishing, paper production and iron ore, Newfoundland's economy was strong until the end of WORLD WAR I, when demand for its exports declined. After squabbling between Quebec and Newfoundland over Labrador, the British Privy Council established the current boundaries of the provinces in 1927. During the GREAT DEPRESSION, Britain responded to an appeal for help by suspending Newfoundland's internal government and reassuming control in 1934. In 1948 Newfoundland elected to become a part of Canada, and in 1949 Newfoundland and Labrador became Canada's 10th province.

**New Georgia** See Solomon Islands.

**Newhouse, Samuel Irving** (1895–1979) American publishing and broadcasting magnate. Described as "America's most profitable publisher," Newhouse began with a single newspaper in 1922 and went on to build a multimillion-dollar communications empire. By the 1970s his properties included 31 newspapers in 22 American cities, seven magazines, six television stations, five radio stations, and 20 cable television stations. His son S(amuel) I(rving) "Sy" Newhouse II inherited the business and added the distinguished publishing firm Random House to the Newhouse empire in 1980.

**Ne Win, U** (1911–2002) Ne Win was by far the dominant figure in the political life of independent Myanmar (formerly BURMA). He was chief of the armed forces from 1948, deputy prime minister from 1948 to 1950, prime minister from 1958 to 1960, chairman of the Revolutionary Council from 1962 to 1974, president from 1974 to 1981 and chairman of the Burmese Socialist Program Party from 1962 to 1988. Ne Win had a retiring, self-effacing public persona; paradoxically, he exerted a most powerful charisma. It is widely believed that Ne Win corruptly acquired vast wealth.

This belief, allied to severely deteriorating economic conditions, fueled the unrest in mid-1988 that drove Ne Win to resign as chairman of the BSPP on July 12. He remained a powerful figure, and it is thought that he was the guiding hand behind the army coup of September 18, 1988.

**New Journalism** Style of journalistic writing that first won wide popularity in the U.S. in the 1960s. New Journalism is a blending of factual reporting and imaginative interpretation that first flourished in such magazines as *Esquire* and *Rolling Stone* and weekly urban tabloids, such as the *Village Voice*—rather than in traditional daily newspapers. The best New Journalism pieces brought a freshness of style and an impassioned mode of analysis to subject matter—such as presidential elections—that had long been handled in a strictly objective format. Among the key practitioners of New Journalism during its emergence were Joan DIDION, Norman MAILER, Gay Talese, Hunter S. THOMPSON and Tom WOLFE. The style has remained a staple of magazine writing ever since.

**newly industrialized countries (NICS)** Nations in the developing world that possess high-growth industrial centers, but which have not yet risen to the status of the G8 nations, (such as the U.S., Britain, France or Germany). An example of an NICs is Singapore, which has accumulated substantial reserves of foreign capital over several decades through its production of inexpensively produced, labor-intensive export products, such as clothing and toys. The economic development of such NICS generally follows what some economists have termed the "law of comparative advantage." According to this principle, NICS will tend to produce goods that capitalize on the economic factor of production (land, raw materials, capital or labor) that the country possesses in abundance. For example, most NICS in East Asia originally had a large surplus of low-wage labor, which facilitates the production of labor-intensive goods.

**Newman, Arnold** *(1918–2000)* American photographer. Born in New York City, Newman is highly acclaimed for his portraits of famous writers, ac-

tors, artists and political leaders. His photographic style is probing and sharply focused. He often poses his sitters in a setting that reflects their personalities and professions. Newman has continued to organize exhibitions of his work, such as his 1992 presentation at the National Portrait Gallery titled *Arnold Newman's Americans* and the 2000 exhibition at the Corcoran Museum of Art titled *Arnold Newman: Breaking Ground.*

**Newman, Barnett** *(1905–1971)* American painter. Born in New York City, he studied at City College, Cornell University and the Art Students League. In the mid-1940s, he began to paint canvases that exploded spatial convention by interrupting flat fields of pure color with one or more narrow vertical stripes. *Stations of the Cross*, a series of paintings he did from 1958 to 1966, are severe black-and-white compositions in which vertical bands interact with a raw ground in completely two-dimensional space. Newman's later paintings, such as *Blue Midnight* (1970), contrast large areas of color on huge canvases, again separated and intensified by narrow stripes. Newman bridged the gap between ABSTRACT EXPRESSIONISM and COLOR-FIELD PAINTING—and was active in both movements. His works proved extremely influential on abstract painters of the 1960s and 1970s.

**Newman, Paul** *(1925– )* American movie actor. Born in Shaker Heights, Ohio, he attended Kenyon College and was trained as an actor at the Yale School of Drama and the Actors Studio. His meteoric rise to fame began with his stage role in *Picnic* (1953). He achieved HOLLYWOOD stardom in *The Long Hot Summer* (1958). Handsome, gifted and possessed of extraordinary blue eyes, Newman gained fame for roles as ironic and self-reliant antiheroes in such movies as *The Hustler* (1961), *Hud* (1963), *Cool Hand Luke* (1967), *Butch Cassidy and the Sundance Kid* (1969), *The Sting* (1973), *Absence of Malice* (1981), *The Verdict* (1982) and *Blaze* (1989). He gave memorable performances in two dramas by Tennessee WILLIAMS: *Cat on a Hot Tin Roof* (1959) and *Sweet Bird of Youth* (1962). Newman received an ACADEMY AWARD for his reprise of *The*

*Hustler's* Fast Eddie in *The Color of Money* (1986). He is also a successful director whose credits include *Rachel, Rachel* (1968), starring his wife, actress **Joanne Woodward.** The couple are also active in social causes. In the 1990s Newman appeared sparingly in Hollywood films, such as *Message in a Bottle* (1999). He also appeared on Broadway in a limited engagement as the Stage Manager in a revival of *Our Town* by Thorton Wilder. In 2005–6 he won an Emmy and a Golden Globe for his work in the miniseries *Empire Falls.*

**Newport Jazz Festival** One of the oldest jazz festivals in virtually continuous operation; first appeared in 1954 in Newport, Rhode Island, as a nonprofit community event. Pianist-night club owner George Wein was its first artistic director, a position he still holds. From the start, the NJF has attracted loyal followings by featuring internationally known jazz stars; it also helped revive the jam session, an "institution" that had faded appreciably because of the music's growing sophistication and stylistic diversification. In 1958 a documentary film *Jazz on a Summer's Day* brought even greater fame. In 1961 the NJF was canceled by Newport's City Council because of riotous crowds in previous years; it was resumed in 1962 but in 1971 was again cut short because of unruly crowds. In 1972 it was moved to New York City where it became known as the Newport Jazz Festival/New York. Corporate sponsorship, an extended 10-day schedule and a host of venues ranging from Carnegie and Avery Fisher Halls to the Roseland Ballroom and Staten Island Ferry, have made the NJF America's premier jazz festival. Impresario Georg Wein has produced a number of "satellite" concert events around the world under the Newport banner; the NJF has also been the source of a large number of excellent "live" recordings. In 1986 the NJF changed its name to the JVC Jazz Festival/New York to acknowledge its prime sponsor, the Japanese Victory Corporation.

**New Republic, The** American periodical founded in 1914. A liberal weekly, *The New Republic* was founded by William Straight, who married the wealthy Dorothy Whitney; the two financed the magazine and absorbed its losses. Under the editorship of Herbert Croly from 1914 until 1930, the magazine supported labor unions, woman suffrage and prison reform. It reluctantly abandoned its neutrality in WORLD WAR I but opposed the TREATY OF VERSAILLES, espousing "Peace without victory." Croly was succeeded by Bruce Bliven in 1930, and the magazine maintained its left-leaning stance, first supporting the socialist presidential candidate but later embracing Franklin D. ROOSEVELT. It accepted U.S. participation in WORLD WAR II. Henry A. WALLACE, former vice president to Roosevelt, became editor in 1946, and the magazine's circulation soared to nearly 100,000. In 1954 Dorothy Straight sold the magazine to Gilbert A. Harrison, and it went on to support the presidential bids of Adlai STEVENSON and John F. KENNEDY and later to assail the corruption of WATERGATE. In 1974, the magazine was sold again, to Martin Peretz, a lecturer at Harvard University, and has continued to uphold a moderate, liberal stance. Contributors to *The New Republic* have included Malcolm COWLEY, Margaret SANGER, Thomas WOLFE, John STEINBECK, Mary MCCARTHY and Delmore SCHWARTZ.

**Newton, Huey P(ercy)** (*1942–1989*) American black activist. In the late 1960s he cofounded the BLACK PANTHER Party, which advocated black self-reliance and self-defense against police racism and brutality. A charismatic symbol of black anger, Newton was dogged by frequent trouble with the law. When he was convicted in 1968 of voluntary manslaughter in the death of an Oakland, California, policeman, "Free Huey" became a rallying cry among radicals and many college students. The conviction was overturned in 1970, and the charges were dismissed after two subsequent trials ended in hung juries. Later troubles stemmed from charges that he had murdered a prostitute, charges that were ultimately dropped. He was convicted in the early 1980s for weapons possession. In the meantime, he earned a Ph.D. in social psychology (1980) and entered a drug-abuse program in 1984. He was shot to death on a street in Oakland.

**New Wave** Loosely defined and loosely organized movement in rock music that emerged in the 1970s. The New Wave, which became popular in both Britain and the U.S., embraced a number of highly disparate musical talents. It was united, however, by a reaction against both the superstar syndrome that had come to dominate rock and roll as well as the heavy-metal emphasis that had emerged in the early 1970s (with bands such as LED ZEPPELIN). Instead, the New Wave musicians sought to pare rock down to its basic 1950s rhythm forms and to introduce new sounds, such as Reggae and minimalist electronic music. Major New Wave musicians and bands include The B-52s, The Cars, Elvis COSTELLO, Dave Edmunds, Nick Lowe, Graham Parker, The POLICE and Jonathan Richman.

**New Wave** French film movement that began in the late 1900s. (See also NOUVELLE VAGUE.)

**new world order** Term coined by U.S. president George H. W. BUSH to describe a post–COLD WAR realignment in international relations among the world's nations. Among the main tenets of the new world order is the assumption that the U.S. and the USSR are no longer ideological enemies or military rivals; rather, the U.S. and the USSR would cooperate to assure that other nations (notably those formerly under communist rule in Eastern Europe) achieve self-determination. The ideals of the new world order were first put to the test during the PERSIAN GULF WAR. In that conflict, the USSR supported UNITED NATIONS resolutions to oust IRAQ from KUWAIT. Moreover, the USSR did not oppose U.S. military efforts in the conflict.

**New York City Ballet** One of the great dance companies in the world, it emerged under its present name in 1948 as the resident company of New York City Center after 14 years of development, during which time it was known variously as American Ballet, Ballet Caravan and Ballet Society. With George BALANCHINE as artistic director, Jerome ROBBINS as artistic codirector and Lincoln KIRSTEIN as general manager, the company developed a classical style that is distinctly American.

The company presented the first original full-length ballet created in America, Balanchine's *Midsummer Night's Dream* (1963), and staged a triumphant Stravinsky Festival in 1972 in honor of Balanchine's longtime musical collaborator, Igor STRAVINSKY. The repertory is dominated by the works of Balanchine, such as *Agon* (1957) and *Liebeslieder Walzer* (1960), and of Robbins, such as *Dances at a Gathering* (1969) and *The Goldberg Variations* (1971). Outstanding dancers associated with the company include Edward Villella, Maria TALLCHIEF, Suzanne FARRELL, Patricia McBride and Peter MARTINS. In 1964 the company took up residence at the New York State Theatre at Lincoln Center. After the death of Balanchine in 1983, Martins and Robbins became ballet masters in chief. In 2001 Christopher Wheeldon became the first individual to hold the title of Resident Choreographer for the New York City Ballet.

*New Yorker, The* American magazine founded by Harold Ross in 1925. The magazine established itself as a sophisticated, satirical weekly notable not only for its humor but also for its intelligent reporting. The many legendary American authors associated with the magazine's early days include Dorothy PARKER, James THURBER, E. B. WHITE, John HERSEY and the cartoonist Charles ADDAMS. The magazine maintains its literary standing, publishing fiction by John UPDIKE and Mavis GALLANT, among others. Since the editorial changes in the mid-1980s, however, when many longtime staffers left, some readers feel that its editorial quality has diminished. In 1985 *The New Yorker* was acquired by the publishing magnate S. I. NEWHOUSE.

*New York Herald Tribune, The* American newspaper begun in 1924 and folded in 1966. The *Herald Tribune* was formed by the merger of *The New York Herald* and *The New-York Tribune,* whose owners, Ogden M. and Helen Rogers Reid, bought the *Herald* from Frank A. Munsey for $5 million. In its prime, the *Herald Tribune* was noted for its typographical excellence, quality writing and incisive political and foreign reporting and commentary. Its reporters were considered the best in the country, and its political columnists included Walter Lippmann, Joseph Alsop and Roscoe Drummond. Its politics were consistently Republican except in 1964, when it supported Democratic presidential candidate Lyndon B. Johnson over Republican Barry Goldwater. The paper began to flounder following Ogden Reid's death in 1947 when his wife became president and their elder son, Whitelaw, editor. Mrs. Reid later withdrew, and her younger son Ogden became publisher and editor. In 1957 the *Herald Tribune* was bought by John Hay Whitney, head of Whitney Communications Corporation, but his attempts to revive the paper were of little avail. The 114-day newspaper strike of 1962–63 proved disastrous; the paper steadily lost money and was forced to shut down three years later.

**New York Times, The** American newspaper founded in 1851. Perhaps America's most venerated newspaper, the *Times* established its current reputation at the turn of the 20th century under the leadership of Adolph S. Ochs, who had been appointed publisher and general manager in 1896. Ochs adopted the motto "All the News That's Fit to Print," installed the paper's vast, worldwide network of correspondents, emphasized international news and established the paper's policy of printing important speeches, papers and news conferences in their entirety. The *Times* was the only paper to publish the complete Treaty of Versailles, and it won a Pulitzer Prize in 1918 for its comprehensive publication of wartime documents. It received another Pulitzer in 1972 for printing the Pentagon Papers. The *Times* and its staff have won more Pulitzer Prizes than any other American daily. The *Times* pioneered the use of the wireless in news gathering, and on election night, 1928, its famous electronic bulletin board began circling the Times Tower in Manhattan's Times Square. This building, to which the paper had moved in 1904, was sold in 1961.

Following World War I, the paper characterized its editorial policy as independent and Democratic, yet it upheld a fairly conservative stance. It backed Republican presidential candidates in the '40s and '50s yet denounced McCarthyism. In the 1960s, under executive editor A. M. Rosen-

thal, it endorsed Democratic candidates and published the entire Warren Commission Report following John F. Kennedy's assassination. But it was unsympathetic to the student uprisings in 1968, and Columbia University students picketed the home of publisher Arthur Ochs "Punch" Sulzberger. While its revelation of the Pentagon Papers helped bring about an end to the Vietnam War, the *Times* was second to the Washington Post in its coverage of the Watergate break-in. In the mid-1970s, though, it led the way in exposing abuses in the Central Intelligence Agency.

In 1978 it began running a four-section daily, with the third section devoted to a different topic each day. The *Times* has been criticized from both the right and the left for its political views and its economic position. In the 1980s, its shift toward more entertainment and "soft" news incurred censure; however, it retains its worldwide reputation with a nationwide circulation of approximately 1,100,000 daily and 1,700,000 Sunday, and also owns other papers, magazines, radio and television stations and book publishers. In 2003 the newspaper became the center of controversy following revelations that one of its reporters, Jayson Blair, had plagiarized other periodicals in his work for the *Times*. Two years later another one of the paper's reporters, Judith Miller was jailed for several months for refusing to identify a confidential source to a grand jury. The newspaper staunchly defended her right to remain silent to protect her source. But after her release from jail, the reporter was forced to resign from the paper when evidence surfaced that she had misled her editors while filing stories alleging Iraq's possession of weapons of mass destruction that were based on unreliable sources.

**New York Times v. Sullivan** (1964) Landmark U.S. Supreme Court decision defining libel law and the right of the press under the First Amendment. In 1960 the *New York Times* ran a civil rights group's ad charging the Montgomery, Alabama, police with misconduct. Several statements in the ad were inaccurate, and a Montgomery court awarded the local police commissioner a $500,000 libel award against the newspaper. The *Times* appealed, and

the case went to the Supreme Court. The Court absolved the *Times,* holding that if a public official or a "public figure" is libeled by a false report, the injured party must show that the press acted with actual malice in publishing the statement. Malice would consist of knowledge that the statement was false or reckless disregard of its falsity. A public figure is one who, although not a public official, is a party who has jumped or been thrust into the public limelight by news events.

**New York Times v. United States** Popularly known as the Pentagon Papers case; the Supreme Court refused to halt the publication of stories in the *New York Times* and *Washington Post* based on material from a classified Pentagon study of the origins of the Vietnam War. The Nixon administration had attempted to halt publication of these stories, claiming that their publication during the continuing Vietnam conflict would be detrimental to national security. The Supreme Court rejected this argument and held that, under the First Amendment, suppression of the material would be an illegal prior restraint of freedom of the press.

**New York World's Fair of 1939** Held in Flushing Meadows, Queens (1939–40), this exposition included a number of American exhibits as well as national exhibits from various countries around the world. It took for its theme "Building the World of Tomorrow." Costing nearly $160 million, the Fair was symbolized by a 700 ft.-tall Trylon and a 200 ft.-diameter Perisphere. Among the better-known U.S. designers and architects who created sleek and streamlined exhibits for the 1939 World's Fair were Norman Bel Geddes, Henry Dreyfuss, Raymond Loewy and Walter Dorwin Teague. It was the last major World's Fair held until the Brussels Exposition of 1958.

**New Zealand** Country in the South Pacific, 1,000 miles south of Australia. Formerly a British colony, New Zealand became a dominion in 1907 and was granted independence by the Statute of Westminster in 1931. Its full independence as a commonwealth was confirmed by its parliament in 1947. New Zealand aided Britain and fought with the Allies in both World War I and World War

## NEW ZEALAND

| | |
|---|---|
| 1907 | New Zealand made a dominion under the British Crown. |
| 1910 | Refrigeration makes it possible for Britain to buy huge quantities of New Zealand meat and dairy products. |
| 1914 | Almost 10% of population volunteers to fight in World War I; almost 2% killed. |
| 1926 | Granted self-government within British Commonwealth. |
| 1935 | Labour Party creates world's first welfare state in response to Great Depression. |
| 1936 | National Party formed in opposition. |
| 1944 | Wartime conditions encourage self-sufficiency in manufacturing. |
| 1947 | Granted full independence. |
| 1949 | National Party wins elections. |
| 1951 | ANZUS alliance formed with Australia and U.S. |
| 1952 | New Zealand grants independence to Western Samoa. |
| 1953 | One of history's worst train wrecks kills hundreds at Tangiwai. |
| 1967 | Decimal currency adopted. |
| 1984 | Effectively leaves ANZUS alliance by refusing to allow nuclear-powered or -armed ships to enter its harbors. |
| 1985 | *Rainbow Warrior*, a ship belonging to Greenpeace environmentalist group, is blown up in Auckland harbor by French Secret Service; government begins programs to aid Maoris, islands' indigenous population. |
| 1987 | Maori recognized as an official language. |
| 1990 | Recession creates dissatisfaction with Labour government; National Party wins elections in landslide. |
| 1993 | National Party wins a slight majority. In a referendum, voters approve a mixed, member-proportional representation and an increase in the number of seats in parliament from 99 to 120. |
| 1995 | Parliamentary agreement offers cash and land compensation to the Tainui on the North Island and a statement of regret and apology for past Maori-settler hostilities. |
| 1996 | The New Zealand First Party forms an alliance with the National Party. |
| 1999 | A Labor-Alliance coalition secures 59 of the 120 seats in national elections; its leader, Helen Clark, becomes prime minister. |
| 2002 | Clark wins a second term. |
| 2004 | A fierce debate over a bill in parliament to nationalize the seabed. Maori protesters affirm enactment of the bill would infringe their ancestral rights. The government survive a no-confidence vote. A law is enacted recognizing civil unions of gay couples. |
| 2005 | Prime Minister Clark wins a narrow election over the National Party. |

II. New Zealand troops joined the UNITED NATIONS forces in KOREA in the 1950s, and a smaller contingent fought in VIETNAM in the 1960s. New Zealand has a history of progressive social reform, having passed legislation on the vote for women and on social security in the late 19th century. Beginning in 1935 under Prime Minister M. J. SAVAGE, the

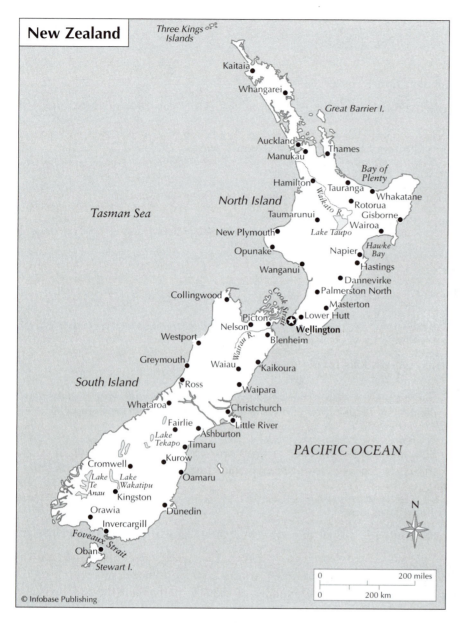

**New Zealand**

Three Kings Islands

Kaitaia

Whangarei

Great Barrier I.

Auckland
Manukau
Thames

Bay of Plenty

Hamilton
Tauranga
Whakatane

North Island
Rotorua
Taumarunui
Gisborne
Wairoa

New Plymouth

Lake Taupo

Opunake
Napier
Hawke Bay

Wanganui
Hastings

Dannevirke
Palmerston North

Collingwood
Masterton

Picton
Lower Hutt

Nelson
Wellington

Westport
Blenheim

Greymouth
Waiau
Kaikoura

South Island
Ross
Waipara

Whataroa
Christchurch

Fairlie
Little River

Lake Tekapo
Ashburton
Timaru

Kurow

Cromwell

Lake Te Anau
Lake Wakatipu
Oamaru

Kingston

Orawia
Dunedin

Invercargill

Foveaux Strait

Oban

Stewart I.

Tasman Sea

Waikato R.

Cook Strait

Wairau R.

PACIFIC OCEAN

N

0          200 miles
0          200 km

© Infobase Publishing

LABOUR PARTY introduced public works programs, aid to farmers as well as health care and social security enhancements to mitigate the effects of the worldwide GREAT DEPRESSION.

In the early 1970s under the administration of Labour Party prime minister Norman Kirk, New Zealand experienced some economic instability due to the energy crisis and GREAT BRITAIN's decision to enter the EEC. New Zealand began withdrawing what troops it had in Southeast Asia at this time. Kirk died in 1974 and was succeeded by his finance minister, Wallace Rowling. The economy worsened and the National Party was voted into power in 1975 with Robert Muldoon as prime minister.

The Labour Party returned to power in 1984, led by David LANGE, who proposed an antinuclear defense policy. Lange's government strained relations with the UNITED STATES by refusing entry into New Zealand's ports of any nuclear-powered vessel or vessel bearing nuclear arms. In 1985 *Rainbow Warrior,* a vessel of the GREENPEACE environmental organization that was monitoring nuclear tests in the area, was mined in Auckland Harbor—arousing much indignation. French prime minister MITTERRAND later admitted the French secret service was responsible. New Zealand's relations with the U.S. improved in 1987 when the National Party supported a bipartisan non-nuclear policy. Although the

National Party continued its rule of New Zealand with a narrow victory in 1993, the Labour Party won the 1999, 2002 and 2005 elections, and Helen Clark became and remained prime minister.

**Ngala, Ronald G.** *(1923–1972)* Kenyan political leader. A moderate nationalist, Ngala was involved in the movement for Kenyan independence in the late 1950s and early '60s. In 1960 with Daniel Arap Moi, he formed the Kenyan African Democratic Union, which was a rival to Jomo KENYATTA's more militant Kenya African National Union (KANU). Ngala led a coalition government in the early 1960s before independence. In 1964, following independence (December 12, 1963), Ngala announced that the KANU would support Kenyatta as president of the new republic. (See also KENYA.)

**Ngoyi, Lillian** *(1911–1980)* Black nationalist South African leader known as "the mother of the black resistance." From the mid-1960s until her death, Ngoyi was declared a "banned person" by the South African government. Under the banning order, the government restricted her movements and contacts and forbade her to be quoted by newspapers. She was also one of the first persons to be confined under a 90-day detention law, spending 71 days in prison without charge or trial in 1963. (See also SOUTH AFRICA, APARTHEID.)

**Nguyen Van Linh (Nguyen Van Cuc)** *(1915–1998)* Vietnamese communist leader. Nguyen Van Linh was elected secretary general of the Vietnamese Communist Party in 1986. He joined the students' union of the Vietnam Revolutionary Youth Association in 1929 and was imprisoned in 1930 by the French for his resistance activities. He joined the ICP upon his release from prison in 1936 and founded a provisional party organization and many party bases in Haiphong. He was arrested again in 1941 after conducting revolutionary activities in central VIETNAM. After his release in 1945 he became secretary of the Saigon Party Committee and led the resistance against the French. From 1957 until 1960 he was acting secretary of the Central Party Commission for the South. In 1960 he was elected to the party central committee. Linh's party positions made him a major leader in southern resistance to the U.S.-backed regimes. He was appointed secretary of the Ho Chi Minh City Party Committee after reunification. He was reelected to the party central committee and appointed to the political bureau. Though origi-nally a northerner, Linh spent much time in the south. He followed a reform policy and showed a willing-ness to experiment with free-market principles.

**Niagara Movement** Pioneering or-ganization formed by black Ameri-cans whose aim was to fight racial discrimination in the U.S. Led by W. E. B. DU BOIS, it was founded in 1905 and disbanded in 1910. The group was not particularly influential, but its ideas and programs were adopted by the NA-TIONAL ASSOCIATION FOR THE ADVANCE-MENT OF COLORED PEOPLE (NAACP), an interracial group cofounded by Du Bois in 1909 that supplanted the Nia-gara Movement.

**Nicaragua** Largest Central American nation, bordered by EL SALVADOR and

---

### NICARAGUA

|  |  |
|------|-------|
| 1911 | Nicaragua becomes a U.S. protectorate under the Knox-Castillo Treaty. |
| 1934 | Gen. Anastasio Somoza García, head of national guard, becomes dictator under National Liberal Party. |
| 1956 | General Somoza is shot and dies and is succeeded by his son Col. Luis Somoza Debayle. |
| 1961 | The Sandinista National Liberation Front (FSLN) is formed. |
| 1967 | General Anastasio Somoza, the younger brother of Luis, is elected president. |
| 1972 | Earthquake virtually destroys Managua; Somoza's control of foreign aid increases his power. |
| 1979 | FSLN overthrows Somoza. Daniel Ortega Saavedra is later named as coordinator of the "provisional junta of national reconstruction." |
| 1982 | Contra attacks begin; financial support for the contras is approved by the U.S. Congress. |
| 1984 | Ortega is elected president. |
| 1990 | Ortega is soundly defeated by Violeta Chamorro, the candidate sponsored by the 14-party National Opposition Union. |
| 1990 | The Chamorro government negotiates an end to hostilities with the contras. |
| 1991 | An economic stabilization plan announced; Former contras start to rearm. |
| 1993 | Hostile actions by Sandinistas and contras flare up. |
| 1996 | The National Assembly places the police under civilian authority. Violeta Chamorro is succeeded by Arnoldo Alemán. |
| 1998 | Hurricane Mitch kills approximately 4,000. |
| 2000 | The constitution is amended giving more power to the two largest political parties. |
| 2001 | Liberal Party candidate Enrique Bolaños Geyer elected president. |
| 2002 | Daniel Ortega is reelected leader of the opposition Sandinista Party. |
| 2003 | Nicaragua negotiates a free trade agreement with the U.S. Alemán is convicted of corruption. Vice President Bolaños is made president. |
| 2004 | World Bank forgives 80 percent of Nicaragua's debt to the organization. |
| 2005 | Fuel price and cost of living rises trigger weeks of violent protests. The government and an alliance of main opposition parties become embroiled in a power struggle, creating a political crisis, which eases when congress agrees to delay constitutional reforms. |
| 2006 | Daniel Ortega is elected president, returning to power after 16 years. |

## Nicaraguan Civil War of 1909–12

In 1909 conservatives rebelled against the liberal dictator-president José Santos Zelaya; two U.S. citizens aiding the rebels were executed, causing angry U.S. protests. Zelaya was forced to resign (December 16, 1909), and NICARAGUA was reduced to near anarchy. After a power struggle between conservative and liberal factions, the conservative Adolfo Diaz became provisional president (May 11, 1911), and requested U.S. aid. A treaty, to retire debts through U.S. customs collection and provide loans from New York banks, was rejected by the U.S. Senate. It was, however, enacted by President William Howard TAFT as an executive order. A revolt by Nicaraguan liberals in July 1912 was suppressed with aid from 2,500 U.S. Marines, who supervised elections; Diaz was elected. A U.S. legation guard of 100 remained in Nicaragua for 13 years.

## Nicaraguan Civil War of 1925–1933

In 1925 a coalition government was elected; conservative Carlos Solarzano (fl. 1920s) became president, and liberal Juan Bautista Sacasa vice president, allowing U.S. Marines to depart after having been in the country for 13 years. On October 25, 1925, conservatives (General Emiliano Chamorro Vargas and Adolfo Díaz) seized power, ousting liberal Sacasa. Chamorro became president, despite U.S. disapproval, after Solarzano resigned in January 1926. But when liberal rebels under General Augusto Cesar SANDINO seized U.S. property, U.S. forces intervened. Chamorro resigned in October 1926, and Diaz was elected by the Nicaraguan congress, while Sacasa returned to establish a rival liberal government.

The resulting civil war was joined by Sandino when Díaz received the help of 2,000 U.S. Marines. U.S. mediator Henry L. STIMSON induced rival leaders Díaz and liberal general José María Moncada to disarm, while the U.S. supervised elections. Moncada was elected president on November 4, 1928, but Sandino vowed to continue guerrilla warfare until the U.S. Marines departed. When Sacasa was elected president in 1932, he persuaded Sandino to surrender after the marines withdrew (1933), but Sandino was assassinated by national guardsmen in 1934.

HONDURAS to the north, by the Caribbean Sea on the east, by COSTA RICA on the south and the Pacific Ocean to the west. In 1909 a revolution broke out against the harsh presidency of José Santos Zelaya, and with help of the UNITED STATES, drove him from office. In 1912 U.S. Marines landed in Nicaragua to help quell rebellion against President Adolfo Díaz and to protect American investments, thus beginning an almost unbroken U.S. military presence in the country, which would continue until 1933. General Augusto César SANDINO led rebels who were resentful of U.S. intervention. The U.S. helped establish a National Guard, which was led by Anastasio SOMOZA García. After the departure of the U.S. Marines, Somoza had Sandino assassinated and later forced President Juan Sacasa out of office and assumed power. The Somoza family led a repressive and corrupt regime, aided by the U.S., toward whose interests they were friendly. In 1979 the Sandinista National Liberation Front (FSLN), with broad-based popular support, toppled the government of Major General Anastasio SOMOZA DEBAYLE, who fled the country.

The Sandinistas established a junta to run the government. Initially moderate, the junta became increasingly left-leaning. In 1981 President REAGAN, charging that the Sandinistas had communist ties and were supplying arms to EL SALVADOR, revoked U.S. economic aid and set out to overthrow the government of Daniel ORTEGA, the revolutionary leader who became president in 1984. The CIA began covert operations, including mining Nicaraguan harbors, and the U.S. backed the counterrevolutionary CONTRAS, initially with the approval of Congress and later illegally. In 1985 Reagan declared a trade embargo on Nicaragua, further destabilizing the economy. In 1988 the Sandinistas and the contras negotiated a cease-fire, and elections were scheduled for 1990, when Violeta Barrios de CHAMORRO, a former publisher of La Prensa and a member of a prominent political family, was elected president. In 1996 Chamorro was succeeded by Arnoldo Alemán (1996–2001). In 2003 Alemán was convicted of embezzlement; Vice President Enrique Bolaños became president. Daniel Ortega was elected president in November 2006.

**Nicholas, Grand Duke** *(1856–1929)* Son of Grand Duke Nicholas and grandson of Czar Nicholas I. An army officer, commissioned in 1872, he introduced major military reforms while serving in the Russo-Turkish War of 1877–78 and as inspector general of the cavalry (1895–1905). In 1905 he was appointed commander of the military district of St. Petersburg and first president of the imperial committee for national defense. He was commander in chief at the beginning of WORLD WAR I and then was sent to the Caucasus as viceroy of NICHOLAS II. He remained there until 1917. He was then reappointed commander in chief by the czar, but Prince Georgy LVOV, head of the provisional government, canceled the appointment. Nicholas then settled in France.

**Nicholas II** *(1868–1918)* Last czar of Russia (1894–1917). The eldest son of Alexander III, he assumed the throne in 1894, the same year he married Princess Alix of Hesse (ALEXANDRA FEDOROVNA). Dedicated to maintaining autocratic powers but possessing a limited understanding of the forces at work in his country, Nicholas suppressed all opposition. He refused pleas by moderates for political change in a Russia that was seething with discontent. His aggressive policies in the Far East were met with humiliating defeat in the RUSSO-JAPANESE WAR (1904–05), causing the monarch even greater unpopularity. This, coupled with domestic corruption, resulted in the RUSSIAN REVOLUTION OF 1905. Urged by Count Sergei WITTE, Nicholas agreed to set up a constitutional government and provide an elective DUMA. He soon reneged on his promises (1906), fired Witte and dissolved the Duma. His downfall began with the outbreak of WORLD WAR I. Taking command of the army in 1915, he all but abandoned domestic affairs to the superstitious czarina and her fanatical adviser Gregory RASPUTIN. Severe economic distress, food shortages and war weariness worsened the situation. Strikes and rioting erupted in Petrograd (St. Petersburg) in February 1917, and Nicholas was forced to abdicate in March 1917 (see FEBRUARY REVOLUTION). Exiled first to Siberia and then to the Urals, the czar and his family were executed by the BOLSHEVIKS on July 16, 1918.

**Nichols, Mike (Michael Igor Peschowsky)** *(1931–  )* American comedian and theatrical and film director. Nichols is one of the leading current-day directors, having achieved triumphs both on the Broadway stage and in Hollywood films. After dropping out of the University of Chicago in the 1950s, Nichols briefly pursued a solo career as a standup comedian in New York City before returning to Chicago to join the renowned *Second City* comedy troupe. There, in 1957, he met fellow comedienne Elaine MAY. They teamed up for the Broadway hit *An Evening with Mike Nichols and Elaine May* (1960). Thereafter, Nichols turned his attention to directing on Broadway, winning Tony Awards for his work on *Barefoot in the Park* (1963) and *The Old Couple* (1965). Other Broadway directorial efforts by Nichols include *The Real Thing* (1984) and a solo show by Whoopi Goldberg (1984). Nichols's films include *The Graduate* (1967), which launched the career of Dustin HOFFMAN; *Catch-22* (1969); *Carnal Knowledge* (1971), which starred Jack NICHOLSON; and *Working Girl* (1988). Nichols received numerous honors in the 1990s, such as his 1994 nomination for the Academy Award for Best Picture for *The Remains of the Day* (1994) and his two Emmy Awards for the Home Box Office (HBO) production, *Wit* (2000). In 2004 he was nominated for a Golden Globe Award for best director for his film, *Closer.* In 2005 he achieved another Broadway success as the producer of *Monty Python's Spamalot.*

**Nicholson, Ben** *(1894–1982)* British painter. Nicholson was internationally renowned for his abstract paintings, which were heavily influenced by CUBISM. At the same time, his canvasses reflected the softer tones and representational techniques of the English landscape painting tradition. In the 1930s, Nicholson produced a series of all-white geometric "reliefs" carved out of wood that combined cubist montage techniques with pure abstract shapes. Nicholson, by virtue of both his technical excellence and his eclecticism, has remained a key influence on subsequent generations of British painters.

**Nicholson, Jack** *(1937–  )* American film actor and director; one of the preeminent actors in HOLLYWOOD,

*Jack Nicholson as Frank Chambers in The Postman Always Rings Twice. 1981* (PHOTOFEST)

renowned for both the diversity of his roles and the intensity and intelligence that he brings to their portrayal. Raised in New Jersey and California, he took his first job in Hollywood—errand boy at Metro-Goldwyn-Mayer—at age 17. His first screen role came in the Roger CORMAN cheapie *The Cry Baby Killer* (1958). After a decade of B-movie work with Corman and others, Nicholson emerged as a star in the Sixties cult hit *Easy Rider* (1969). Over the following decades, Nicholson consolidated his status as a great actor despite appearing in a fair number of box-office failures. His major successes include *Five Easy Pieces* (1970), *The Last Detail* (1973), *Chinatown* (1974), *One Flew Over the Cuckoo's Nest* (1975), for which he won an ACADEMY AWARD as best actor, *Terms of Endearment* (1983), for which he won a best supporting actor Oscar, *Prizzi's Honor* (1985) and *Batman* (1989). Nicholson also directed *Drive He Said* (1971) and *Goin' South* (1978). *The Two Jakes* (1990), a sequel to *Chinatown* that Nicholson starred in, won mixed reviews. In 1998 Nicholson won another Academy Award for Best Actor for his performance in *As Good As It Gets* (1997).

**Nicklaus, Jack William** *(1940–  )* U.S. golfer. In 1988 Nicklaus was named "Player of the Century," a title that few would dispute. After winning the U.S. Amateur championship in 1959 and 1961, he turned professional in 1961. He won the U.S. Open in 1962. Five times PGA player of the year, from 1967 to 1976, he was named athlete of the decade for the Seventies.

Golf's all-time money winner, among his 18 international titles are three British Opens, six Australian Opens and six Masters tournaments. Nicklaus has become an active competitor on the PGA Senior Tour, winning the Tradition tournament four times.

**Niebuhr, Reinhold** *(1892–1971)* American theologian, philosopher and social critic. Niebuhr was the foremost American Protestant theologian of the 20th century. He exercised a considerable influence not only in church circles but also in the fields of domestic and foreign governmental policy. Niebuhr earned a degree in divinity from Yale University in 1914 and subsequently spent 13 years as a minister for a Detroit church. During this period, his numerous books and journalistic pieces advocated social activism on the part of the church and a left-wing approach to political issues. From 1928 to 1960, Niebuhr taught at the Union Theological Seminary in New York and became friends with many of the American political leaders of the era. After WORLD WAR II, Niebuhr became more conservative; during the COLD WAR, he championed an expansion of American power on the grounds of its relative moral superiority to communism. President Jimmy CARTER cited Niebuhr as a major influence on his own thought. Niebuhr's major works include *Moral Man and Immoral Society* (1932) and the two-volume *Nature and Destiny of Man* (1941–43).

**Niemoeller, Martin** *(1892–1984)* German Protestant minister and theologian. After serving as a U-boat commander in WORLD WAR I, Niemoeller became a Lutheran pastor in Berlin. At first sympathetic to Adolf HITLER and National Socialism, he quickly became a leader of the anti-Hitler movement in GERMANY. In 1933 he formed the pastors' Emergency League against Hit-lerism, a forerunner of the evangelical German Confessing Church. Arrested in 1937, he spent eight years in Nazi CONCENTRATION CAMPS. After his release at the end of the war (1945), he declared that the German people bore collective guilt for the war. He criticized the creation of the NORTH ATLANTIC TREATY ORGANIZATION (NATO) and the rearmament of WEST GERMANY. In 1948 he was one of the founders of the WORLD COUNCIL OF CHURCHES and served as one of its six presidents from 1961 to 1968. A pacifist, Niemoeller actively opposed the VIETNAM WAR and visited HANOI in 1967 to express his opposition to U.S. policies. Several months later he received the USSR's Lenin Peace Prize. In 1971 he was awarded Germany's highest honor, the Grand Cross of Merit.

**Niger** Country in west-central Africa, landlocked by Libya and Algeria on the north, Benin and Nigeria on the south,

| NIGER | |
|---|---|
| 1890 | French occupy Niger. |
| 1958 | Niger becomes an autonomous republic within the French Community. |
| 1960 | Niger proclaims its independence as a republic, with Hamani Diori as president. |
| 1973 | Drought of unprecedented severity ravages Niger, decimating the national herds and wrecking the economy. |
| 1974 | The chief of staff, Lieutenant General Seyni Kountché, seizes power in a bloody coup. Diori is placed under house arrest, the National Assembly is suspended, and all political parties are banned. |
| 1987 | Kountche dies and is succeeded by Ali Saibou. |
| 1990 | Demonstrators are killed by police. Saibou tries to calm the situation by announcing plans for democratization. |
| 1992 | Multiparty elections are held; no clear winner emerges. |
| 1995 | The Tuaregs of the Armed Resistance Organization engage in guerrilla activity in the north, seeking autonomy. |
| 1996 | A military coup led by Colonel Ibrahim Baré Maïnassara takes control of the government. Maïnassara is elected president in a highly controversial election. |
| 1999 | Maïnassara is assassinated by military dissidents. Mamadou Tandja is elected president. |
| 2003 | U.S. President George W. Bush claims that Iraq was attempting to buy uranium from Niger, though this report later prove to be false. |
| 2005 | Severe drought and a plague of locusts threatens the population with starvation. |

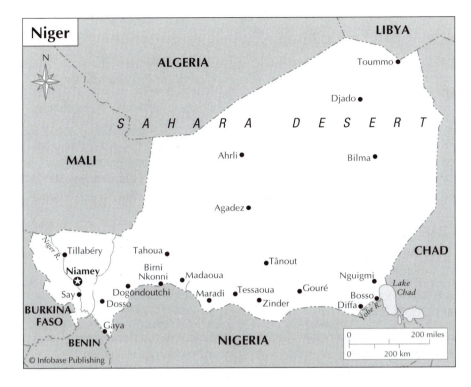

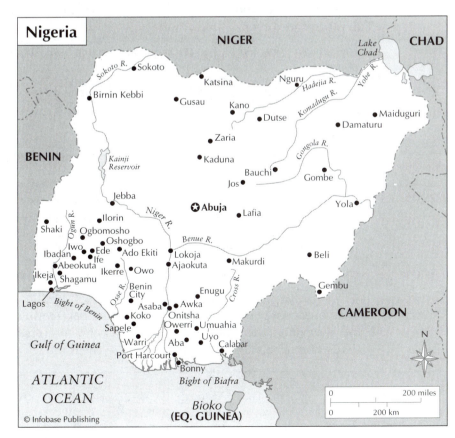

called in 1995 to help settle disputes over the structure of the government. Meanwhile the Taureg insurgency continued in the northeast of the country, where the government imposed martial law. In 1996 the country experienced yet another military coup when army chief of staff Ibrahim Baré Maïnassara became head of state. In 1999 Mainassara was assassinated by his bodyguards, and a military junta took control of the country. That same year Mamadou Tandja was elected president; he was reelected in the 2004 elections. In 2003 U.S. president George W. BUSH claimed that Iraqi leader Saddam HUSSEIN had attempted to purchase uranium from Niger, a claim that was subsequently demonstrated to be erroneous. In 2005 a food crisis emerged in the wake of drought and a locust plague

**Nigeria** West African country. The Federal Republic of Nigeria is bordered by Niger and Chad to the north, Cameroon to the east, the Gulf of Guinea to the south and Benin to the west. At the turn of the 20th century, Nigeria consisted of two British protec-

Upper Volta on the southeast, Mali on the west, and Chad on the east. Modern Niger did not become unified politically until late in the 19th century, when FRANCE made it part of its colonial African empire. Previously, the territory had been constantly under siege by warring tribes and rival states who competed for control of the region. Having overcome resistance by the Tuareg Arabs centered around Agadez, the French made Niger a territory in 1900, as part of their holdings in Upper Senegal–Niger.

In 1922 it was made a separate colony of FRENCH WEST AFRICA and remained under colonial rule until the end of WORLD WAR II, after which it was swept up in a great wave of African nationalism. It gained autonomy in 1958, and achieved complete independence under President Hammani DIORI. His leadership endured until the great Sahel drought brought famine and illness to his country from 1968 to 1974. That year, a coup led by Lt. Col. Senyi Kountche toppled the Diori government, and the military took power. Kountche himself survived several coup attempts. After his death in 1987 Army Chief of Staff col. Ali Saibou became president. After several people were killed during protests against austerity measures in 1990, the government was restructured. In 1992 a constitution

was signed, and elections were held in 1994, yet with no clear majority by any party. Several short-lived governments followed, with international mediators

## NIGERIA

| | |
|---|---|
| 1914 | British protectorate of Northern Nigeria and British protectorate of Southern Nigeria are joined to form colony of Nigeria. |
| 1960 | Independence. |
| 1966 | Ibo-led coup overthrows central government and kills regional premiers in the northern and western, non-Ibo regions; Ibo leader General Johnson Aguiyi-Ironsi abolishes federal system, establishes central government with mostly Ibo advisers; northern, Hausa-Fulani, army officers kill Aguiyi-Ironsi and seize government, making army chief of staff Yakuba Gowan head of state. |
| 1967 | Gowan divides country into 12 states to dilute power of larger tribes; the eastern Ibo tribal region refuses to be divided and attempts to secede as the independent nation of Biafra; three years of brutal civil war follow. |
| 1985 | Major General Ibrahim Babangida comes to power by internal military coup and promises return to civilian rule by 1992. |
| 1989 | Babangida overrules registration applications for 50 different political parties and creates a two-party system to dilute regional factionalism as a step toward civilian government. |
| 1990 | In advance of talks on reducing Nigeria's huge debt to Western commercial interests, President Babangida calls for reparations from Western countries for slave trade. |
| 1990 | Coup attempt fails. Nigeria leads a multinational African peacekeeping force to Liberia. |
| 1991 | Nigeria send troops to Sierra Leone, which is fighting rebels from Liberia. |
| 1993 | Babangida voids the results of the 1992 elections, which would have placed opposition candidate Moshood Abiola in office. Babangida resigns and his handpicked successor is ousted in a November coup. |
| 1994 | The government, led by former defense minister Sani Abacha, continues arresting political opponents. |
| 1998 | Abacha dies and is replaced by General Abdulsalami Abubaker. |
| 1999 | Military government is replaced as democratically elected president Olusegun Obasanjo is sworn in. |
| 2001 | Nigeria, South Africa and Algeria launch the New Partnership for African Development (NEPAD), a plan to revive Africa. |
| 2003 | The first legislative elections since the end of military rule: President Obasanjo's People's Democratic Party wins a parliamentary majority; Obasanjo is reelected to a second term; Opposition parties reject the results and international observers say there were serious irregularities in the polling. |
| 2004 | UN brokers talks between Nigeria and Cameroon over their disputed border. Religious clashes between Muslims and Christians in central Plateau State. |
| 2005 | A national conference to introduce constitutional reform opens in Abuja, opposition boycotts the gathering saying the delegates have too few powers. Paris Club of lenders forgives two-thirds of Nigeria's $30 billion debt owed to them. |

torates: Northern and Southern. The two were joined in 1914 when Nigeria became Britain's largest African colony. Through the 1920s and '30s many Nigerians sought self-government, and in 1946 the country was divided into three regions—each with an advisory assembly consisting of Nigerian and British members. In 1954 a new constitution was adopted increasing the powers of the assemblies and making Nigeria a federation. It became a constitutional monarchy within the Commonwealth in 1960, and later an independent republic (1963). Dr. Nnambi AZIKIWE, formerly governor-general, was its first president; his political rival Abubakar Tafawa Balewa had been prime minister since 1957. In 1966 Tafawa Balewa was assassinated in a military coup led by Ibo officers from the oil-rich eastern region. Major General Johnson Aguiyi-Ironsi took power and attempted to abolish the federal system of government, but he was killed months later in a counter-coup led by Colonel Yakuba GOWON, who assumed command. Following the massacre of thousands of Ibo in northern Nigeria, the military governor of the eastern region, Colonel Chikwuemeka OJUKWU, rejected Gowon's leadership and involved him in a dispute over oil revenues. In 1967 Odumegwu-Ojukwu declared the eastern region a separate Ibo state, BIAFRA, and a bloody civil war broke out. Biafra surrendered three years later.

Extensive reconstruction based on anticipated oil income ran aground, and in 1975, while Gowon was out of the country attending a meeting of the Organization of African Unity, a bloodless coup put Brigadier Murtala Mohammad in to power. He attempted some constitutional reforms and increased the number of states to 19, but he was killed in 1976 during an unsuccessful coup attempt. He was succeeded by General Olusegun OBASANJO, who announced a return to free elections and civilian government. In 1979 Shehu Shagari, leader of the National Party of Nigeria, was elected president, but the falling oil prices of the early 1980s destabilized his government. He was unseated in another bloodless coup and Major General Muhammadu Buhari assumed power. In 1985 Buhari was deposed by yet another nonviolent coup, and Major General Ibrahim Babangida, the army chief of staff, became head of the military government. Babangida quickly thwarted an attempted coup and announced a gradual return to a civilian, democratic government by 1992. Nigeria was ruled by General Sani ABACHA from 1993 until his death in 1998. After an interim government headed by Major-

General Abdulsalami Abubakar, Olusegun Obasanjo won the 1999 national elections and was reelected in 2003. Since 2004 Nigeria has been plagued by religious strife between Christians and Muslims. A group of rich lenders known as the Paris Club forgave Nigeria's foreign debt. That, in addition to record oil prices, allowed Nigeria to be debt-free in 2006.

**Nightline** Late-night weeknight television news program on the ABC (1980–   ). In November 1979 during the Iranian hostage crisis, in which personnel stationed at the U.S. embassy in Tehran, Iran, were taken hostage by Islamic fundamentalist followers of the AYATOLLAH KHOMEINI, ABC's news division decided to offer nightly updates of the evolving situation of the Americans in Iran in a program called *America Held Hostage,* anchored by Frank Reynolds. As these late-night broadcasts began to generate a regular audience, ABC News president Roone Arledge decided to make the improvised program permanent and replaced Reynolds with ABC's diplomatic correspondent Ted KOPPEL. The new program, named *ABC News Nightline* debuted. In addition to covering the standoff between Iran and the U.S., *Nightline* served as an encapsulation of the day's international and national news events, often featuring live interviews with ABC correspondents and dignitaries from around the world through the network's satellite technology. Because of an agreement with the BRITISH BROADCASTING CORPORATION (BBC) to share video recordings of interviews and news segments, *Nightline* regularly aired segments produced by the BBC, thereby amplifying the amount of news media available to its producers. In 1987 the program achieved its highest ratings when Koppel interviewed Christian televangelist Jim Bakker and his wife, Tammy Faye, who at the time were embroiled in sexual and financial scandals relating to his affair with a church secretary and the misuse of funds raised through their television ministry. Koppel retired from *Nightline* in 2005.

**Nijinska, Bronisława** (*1891–1972*) Dancer, choreographer and teacher and sister of Vaslav NIJINSKY. She studied at the Imperial Theater School, in St. Pe-

tersburg, and appeared with Nijinsky in the first season of the BALLETS RUSSES. She enjoyed the distinction of being the first woman choreographer and was called "La Nijinska" by DIAGHILEV. The most important ballets in her varied and brilliant career were *Les Noces* (1923), *Les Biches* (1924), *Les Comediens Jaloux* (1932) and *Pictures from an Exhibition* (1944). Her work as a teacher has been of the greatest significance.

**Nijinsky, Vaslav** (*1890–1950*) Ballet dancer and choreographer. Nijinsky trained at the Imperial Ballet School, in St. Petersburg, from 1900. His performance in *Le Pavilion d'Armide* by Fokine in 1907 attracted attention, and from 1909 he was the leading dancer in DIAGHILEV'S BALLETS RUSSES in Paris, where he enjoyed enormous popularity, especially in *Le Spectre de la Rose* and *Pétroucha*. Dismissed by Diaghilev, who was angered by Nijinsky's unexpected marriage in 1913, Nijinsky unsuccessfully attempted to form his own company. He continued to perform until 1919, when he suffered a nervous breakdown that permanently ended his career. He spent the remainder of his life in asylums in Switzerland and Britain. His unique powers of dancing earned him the title of *le dieu de la danse*, and he is remembered as one of the greatest male dancers.

**Nikisch, Arthur** (*1855–1922*) Hungarian violinist, pianist and conductor. A child prodigy, Nikisch began performing on the violin and the piano at age 8 and entered the Vienna Conservatory at 11. He started to conduct in 1878, later serving as the conductor of the Boston Symphony (1889–93), musical director of the Budapest Opera (1893–95), conductor of the Leipzig Opera (1879–89, 1905–06) and conductor of the Berlin Philharmonic (1895–1922). A frequent guest conductor throughout Europe and the U.S., Nikisch also made many appearances as a piano accompanist of lieder singer Elena Gerhardt. Noted for his superb technique and extraordinary expressive hands, he excelled in interpretations of such German and Austrian masters as Beethoven, Brahms, Schubert and Schumann. In 1913 he made the first complete recording of a symphony (Beethoven's Symphony No. 5).

**Nikolayev, Andrian** *(1929–2004)*
Soviet cosmonaut. The son of a farmer,
Nikolayev attended the Marinsky-
Posad Forestry Institute and worked as
a lumberjack before being drafted into
the Soviet army in 1950. Earning his
wings as a pilot, he graduated from the
Chernigov Higher Air Force School in
1954. After becoming a cosmonaut in
1960, he set an endurance record, of
four days in space aboard *Vostok 3*
(August 1962). As commander of the
Soyuz 9 mission (June 1970), he set a
new record of 18 days in space, along
with fellow cosmonaut Vitaly Sev-
astyanov. Nikolayev, who later married the world's first woman to travel
in space, Valentina TERESHKOVA, has
written two books, *Meeting in Orbit*
(1969) and *Space, A Road without End*
(1979).

**Niles, John Jacob** *(1892–1980)*
American folklorist, folksinger and
collector of ballads and carols. His career spanned more than 70 years,
from before WORLD WAR I until his
death. He composed more than 1,000
ballads and carols and performed
throughout the U.S. and Europe. He
was credited with contributing to the
revival of interest in American folk
music.

**Nilsson, Birgit** *(1918–2005)* Swedish
operatic soprano known for the clarity

*Folksinger and balladeer John Jacob Niles.* 1937

and power of her voice and for her brilliant interpretations of the heroines of
Richard Wagner. Born on a farm near
Malmö, Nilsson studied at Stockholm's
Royal Academy of Music, graduating in
1946, the year she made her first operatic appearance. Nilsson sang at the
Stockholm Opera from 1947 to 1951,
in 1950 undertaking the first of the
roles that would make her the most celebrated Wagnerian soprano of her generation. Her first important appearance
outside Sweden was at England's GLYN-
DEBOURNE FESTIVAL in 1951, and she
made her debut at the BAYREUTH FESTI-
VAL in 1954. She was widely acclaimed
for her performance as Brunnhilde in
Wagner's *Siegfried* at the Florence May
Music Festival in 1956 and had a triumphant American debut with the San
Francisco Opera as Brunnhilde in *Die
Walküre* that same year. Nilsson also became known for her performance of the
title role in *Turandot*, a part she first sang
at her La Scala debut in 1958. Her first
Metropolitan Opera performance was as
Isolde in 1959. Nilsson was a guest
soloist with many of the world's major
opera companies and music festivals.

**Nimitz, Chester William** *(1885–
1966)* U.S. naval commander. Nimitz
graduated from the United States
Naval Academy at Annapolis in 1905,
and served as chief of staff to the commander of the United States Atlantic
submarine force during WORLD WAR I.
After the Japanese PEARL HARBOR attack, he was promoted to commander
in chief of the Pacific Fleet. He planned
the successful battles of Midway and
the Coral Sea. The Japanese surrender
was signed on his flagship, the USS MIS-
SOURI, in Tokyo Bay on September 2,
1945. He was promoted to field admiral.
From 1945 to 1947 he was chief of
naval operations. After leaving government service he was a consultant on defense matters and edited, with E. B.
Potter, *Sea Power, a Naval History* (1960).

**Nin, Anais** *(1903–1977)* American
author. Nin was born in Paris and became an American citizen in 1914. She
later returned to France and was associated with the Villa Seurat group,
which included Henry MILLER, when
she began writing fiction in the 1930s.
She is best known for her many published journals, beginning with *The
Diary of Anais Nin, Volume I 1931–1934*

(1966) and ending with the posthumously published Volume VII (1980).
Their feminist perspective and search
for self-knowledge and freedom
caused her to be a much requested lecturer in universities across the U.S.
There is much critical dispute about
her fiction, although Edmund WILSON
was an early champion of it in the U.S.
Fictional works include *Winter of Arti-
fice* (1939), *A Spy in the House of Love*
(1954) and the erotic short story collection *The Delta of Venus* (1977).

**1984** Novel by George ORWELL, written in 1948 and published in 1949.
An impassioned warning about the
dangers of totalitarianism and dehumanization, it depicts a bleak futuristic society headed by a mysterious
and all-knowing dictator called "Big
Brother" (believed to be modeled on
Josef STALIN). In the world of the book,
the state is all-important; all privacy
and individual freedom have been
abolished and all human activities are
directed by the "thought police." The
hero, Winston Smith, is a weak but decent man who yearns for a better existence. He finds brief happiness in a love
affair with a young female member of
the underground. However, they are
discovered and arrested, and Smith is
tortured, brainwashed and crushed.
The book had an enormous impact on
intellectuals around the world, and
many of its catchwords—including
"Big Brother," "Newspeak" (the Party's
attempt to control thought by manipulating language) and "Doublethink"
(the ability to cease to know what the
Party has condemned)—became part of
the vocabulary of the late 20th century.

**Nineteenth Amendment** Enacted
in 1920, it gave the vote to women in
the U.S. Although nonwhites had been
given the right to vote by the Fifteenth
Amendment (1870), women did not
gain that same right until much later.
The woman suffrage movement arose
in the late 19th century with the goal
of universal woman suffrage. Although
individual states had earlier allowed
women to vote, it was not until 1920
that all states and the federal government were constitutionally required to
allow women the vote.

**Nirenberg, Marshall Warren**
*(1927–   )* American biochemist. Niren-

berg earned his Ph.D. from the University of Michigan in 1957, after which he began work at the National Institutes of Health in Bethesda, Maryland. Using Severo Ochoa's technique for producing artificial RNA, Nirenberg took a vital step in breaking the "genetic code" when he discovered that a uracil triplet in RNA was the code for the amino acid phenylalanine. For this work, Nirenberg shared the 1968 NOBEL PRIZE in physiology or medicine with Har Gobind Khorana and Robert Holley.

**Nisei** Term for second-generation Japanese Americans. (See also internment of JAPANESE AMERICANS.)

**Nishio, Suehiro** *(1891–1981)* Japanese politician, founder of Japan's Democratic Socialist Party (1960). A left-wing activist, he was a labor leader in the early 1920s. In 1938 he was expelled from the Japanese parliament because of his criticisms of the government's militarist policies. After the war he served as a member of the Japan Socialist Party but broke with the party when it opposed the security treaty with the U.S. in 1960.

**Nixon, Richard M(ilhous)** *(1913–1994)* Thirty-seventh president of the UNITED STATES (1969–74). Richard Nixon—the only U.S. president to resign from office—is perhaps the most complex and controversial American

*Richard Nixon. 37th president of the United States* (LIBRARY OF CONGRESS, PRINTS AND PHOTOGRAPHS DIVISION)

political figure of the postwar era. Born into a modest Quaker family in Yorba Linda, California, he developed a reputation as a brilliant debater in high school and was class president. He received a B.A. from Whittier College, graduating second in his class (1934); then earned a law degree from Duke University Law School (1937), where he placed third in his class. He returned to Whittier to start his own practice. At the outset of WORLD WAR II he worked for eight months in the Office of Price Administration (OPA), an experience that left him distrustful of government bureaucracy. From 1942 to 1945 he served as a noncombat navy officer in the South Pacific.

Upon his return he entered REPUBLICAN PARTY politics and in 1946 won election to the House of Representatives from his California district. Nixon gained a national reputation as a strong anticommunist while a member of the HOUSE UN-AMERICAN ACTIVITIES COMMITTEE (HUAC). He was a prominent figure in the HISS-CHAMBERS case (1948–49), accusing State Department official Alger HISS of having been a communist agent. In 1950 he ran for the Senate against Helen Gahagan DOUGLAS. Portraying Douglas as pro-communist, he defeated her by a 680,000-vote margin. Regarded as a rising star in the Republican Party, Nixon became a national spokesman against the domestic and foreign policies of the TRUMAN administration. After Dwight D. EISENHOWER's presidential nomination, Thomas DEWEY successfully recommended Nixon for the vice presidency. Nixon's youth, his anticommunist reputation and his internationalist outlook were all considered assets. During the fall 1952 campaign, a political fund-raising scandal briefly jeopardized Nixon's fortunes, and some Republicans urged him to step down from the campaign. However, he survived the crisis after making an emotional half-hour appeal on national television—the so-called **Checkers speech,** in which he denied taking any gifts except one, a cocker spaniel named Checkers that had become the family pet. The Checkers speech gave a new boost to Nixon; moreover, it signaled the first significant use of television in national election campaigning. In November the Eisenhower-Nixon ticket won by a landslide.

Nixon was a highly visible vice president. He assumed many of Eisenhower's obligations as leader of the Republican Party and represented the administration in many overseas trips. During a tour of South America in May 1958 he was confronted by left-wing rioters in Lima, Peru, and Caracas, Venezuela. His fortitude and calmness in facing physical danger earned him considerable admiration throughout the Western Hemisphere. Throughout his two terms he advocated a hard-line policy toward communist expansion. In July 1959 Nixon went to Moscow to open the American National Exhibition. The day after his arrival, Nixon and Soviet premier Nikita KHRUSHCHEV engaged in an impromptu debate over the respective merits of capitalism and communism. The discussion took place in the model kitchen of the exhibition and became known as the **kitchen debate.** Many Americans believed that Nixon had bested the Soviet leader.

Nixon was the Republican presidential candidate in 1960, choosing UN ambassador Henry Cabot LODGE as his running mate; their Democratic opponents were Massachusetts senator John F. KENNEDY and Texas senator Lyndon B. JOHNSON. Nixon was better known and hoped to take advantage of his greater experience in national and international affairs. Believing it would be to his advantage, he agreed to debate Kennedy on national television—the first televised presidential debates in history. Four debates were scheduled. However, Nixon failed to come across well in the first debate (September 26, 1960). He appeared haggard—he had recently been ill, and did not wear makeup; Kennedy, by contrast, looked healthy and confident. Television viewers gave Kennedy a clear edge in the debate, while radio listeners believed Nixon had done better. Many people believed that Nixon won the final three debates, but his candidacy had already been damaged. Kennedy's popularity surged, and he defeated Nixon—by only 113,000 votes out of 69 million, the smallest percentage difference in history.

Nixon retired to private life, joining a California law firm and publishing his autobiographical *Six Crises* (1962). Later that year he ran for governor of California but lost to the incumbent, Pat Brown. Following this defeat, Nixon announced his withdrawal from politics and told reporters "you won't have Richard Nixon to kick around any more." He subsequently joined a New York law firm but campaigned for Republican candidates in other elections. Nixon made a triumphant return to politics when he won the 1968 Republican presidential nomination and then defeated Democratic candidate Hubert H. HUMPHREY and third-party candidate George WALLACE. Nixon's campaign platform called for an honorable end to the VIETNAM WAR and for a return to law and order at home.

His first priority as president was the "Vietnamization" of the war, shifting more responsibility for the ground fighting to the South Vietnamese while stepping up U.S. air bombings of North Vietnam and of Vietcong bases in LAOS and CAMBODIA. From 1969 to 1972 Nixon gradually withdrew 555,000 U.S. soldiers from Vietnam. However, mass protests against the war continued in the U.S. (see ANTIWAR MOVEMENT). Domestically, Nixon instituted "revenue sharing," a plan whereby the federal government directly transferred revenues to the states and localities. He also dealt with inflation through a multi-phase economic strategy that included wage and price controls. Nixon regarded foreign affairs as his main strength. During his presidency, he pursued a policy of DÉTENTE with the USSR Nixon's greatest international triumph was a breakthrough in relations with the People's Republic of CHINA. His national security advisor, Henry KISSINGER, secretly flew to Beijing in July 1971 to begin negotiations with the Chinese. Nixon himself visited China in Feb. 1972 for an historic meeting with MAO ZEDONG and ZHOU ENLAI that laid the groundwork for formal relations between the two nations. Despite these successes, Nixon was frustrated by his inability to end the Vietnam War. On the eve of the 1972 presidential elections, Kissinger returned from talks with the North Vietnamese in Paris and announced that "peace is at hand." However, fighting continued until a formal cease-fire was announced on January 23, 1973.

Nixon easily defeated his Democratic rival, George McGOVERN, and was reelected in 1972. However, the WATERGATE scandal would cripple Nixon's administration and force the president

to resign. Nixon and his staff were tied to a June 1972 break-in at the Democratic campaign headquarters in the Watergate apartment complex in Washington. The media and Congress began a highly publicized investigation of the break-in and the White House's role in a possible coverup. Nixon continued to deny any knowledge of the break-in, despite mounting evidence to the contrary, and his popularity plunged. Facing impeachment and a Senate trial Nixon resigned in disgrace on August 9, 1974. Nixon later acknowledged that he had made mistakes regarding the break-in but continued to deny any wrongdoing.

Nixon has been the subject of much personal and political analysis. His opponents cite what they see as his contempt for the Constitution and the democratic political process. His defenders point to his accomplishments in foreign affairs and claim that he was the victim of political persecution. After a period in relative seclusion, Nixon reemerged as something of an elder statesman. He wrote several volumes of memoirs and political commentary before his death in 1994. (See also Spiro AGNEW.)

**NKGB** Abbreviation for Norodny Komitet Gosudarstvennoy Bezopasnosti (People's Commissariat for State Security), which was the Soviet security force from 1943 to 1946. It was mainly concerned with "unreliable elements," many of whom were deported or sent to corrective labor camps. In 1946 the NKGB was renamed the MGB and, after the death of Stalin, the KGB.

**Nkomati Accord** An agreement of March 1984 between SOUTH AFRICA and MOZAMBIQUE. South Africa promised not to support the Mozambique's rebel National Resistance Movement in return for Mozambique's undertaking not to back the outlawed AFRICAN NATIONAL CONGRESS's activities in South Africa. By 1986 the agreement had effectively disintegrated with the resistance group Renamo resuming its offensives. In 1992 the signing of a peace accord between Mozambique president Joaquim CHISSANO and Renamo leader Afonso Dhaklama helped revitalize the Nkomati Accord.

**Nkomo, Joshua** *(1917–1999)* Zimbabwean nationalist and guerrilla leader. A member of the Kalanga tribe, Nkomo was educated in South Africa. He began as a worker in the Rhodesian Railways and became active in the railroad union. A dedicated nationalist and opponent to white rule of RHODESIA, Nkomo was president of the AFRICAN NATIONAL CONGRESS (ANC) from 1957 to 1959. In exile from 1959 to 1960, he became president of the Zimbabwe African People's Union (ZAPU) in 1961 and was imprisoned from 1964 to 1974. After failed negotiations with Ian SMITH, Nkomo joined his ZAPU with Robert MUGABE's ZANU, and the two became joint leaders of the Patriotic Front (PF) in its guerrilla warfare against the Rhodesian government (1976–79). After Zimbabwean independence and ZANU's victory in the subsequent elections, Nkomo joined Mugabe's cabinet. He was ousted in 1982 after allegations that he had attempted to lead a coup against the Mugabe regime. In 1987 the two leaders merged ZAPU and ZANU-PF, and the following year Nkomo rejoined Mugabe's cabinet. Nkomo advanced to vice president of Zimbabwe, a post that he held until his death.

**Nkrumah, Kwame** *(1909–1972)* Ghanaian statesman, president (1960–66). Born in what was then the western Gold Coast, he attended Achimota College in Accra, Lincoln University in Pennsylvania and the London School

*Ghanaian president Kwame Nkrumah* (LIBRARY OF CONGRESS, PRINTS AND PHOTOGRAPHS DIVISION)

of Economics. A dedicated African nationalist and anticolonialist, he was active in student groups and soon founded (1949) the Convention's People's Party (CPP), which advocated self-government for the colony. Although he was imprisoned by the British from 1950 to 1951, his party won the colony's first general election (1951). Nkrumah then gained his freedom to become a member of parliament (1951) and then prime minister of Gold Coast (1954 to 1957) and of the newly renamed dominion of GHANA (1957 to 1960). When Ghana attained independence as a republic within the British Commonwealth (1960), Nkrumah became its first president. A respected pan-African leader, he opposed direct Western influence on the continent and was a participant (1961) in the Casablanca Conference, which codified African opposition to neocolonialism in the African Charter. He was a supporter of Patrice LUMUMBA in the Congo and an opponent of the government of SOUTH AFRICA. Becoming increasingly dictatorial at home, he quashed dissenters and established a one-party state. This, coupled with economic policies that led to a wild inflationary spiral and financial chaos (1965 to 1966), led to Nkrumah's increased unpopularity and to the military coup that deposed him in 1966. He fled, first to Guinea and then to Romania, where he sought medical treatment in 1972 and died later that year.

**NKVD** Abbreviation for Norodny Komitet Vnutrennykh Del (People's Commissariat of Internal Affairs), which was from 1934 to 1943 the Soviet security service in charge of police and civil registry offices and of the corrective labor camps. It was one of STALIN's main tools during the GREAT PURGE. In 1943 it was divided into two commissariats, the NKVD and the NKGB.

**Nobel Prize** Established in the will of Alfred Nobel (1833–96), the Swedish chemist who made his fortune in the development of explosives, the yearly Nobel prizes go to individuals who have made outstanding contributions in the fields of physics, chemistry, physiology or medicine, literature and world peace. Nobel had stipulated that the winners in the fields of physics and

chemistry be determined by the Royal Swedish Academy of Sciences; in medicine by the Karolinska Institute in Stockholm; for literature by the Swedish Academy in Stockholm; and for champions of peace by a committee of five elected by the Norwegian Storting (Parliament). He further asked that candidates of all nationalities be considered for the prizes. In 1900 the Nobel Foundation was established to carry out the intent of the will. The first Nobel Prizes were awarded on December 10, 1901. In 1968 the Bank of Sweden made a donation to establish an additional prize in economics. Called the Prize in Economic Sciences in Memory of Alfred Nobel, it was first awarded in 1969 and is presented on the same day as the other awards in a ceremony following their presentation in Oslo. The amount of the prize money has grown over the years, from a relatively small amount in 1901 to $700,000 in 1990. Apart from the monetary award, the Nobel Prize bestows the highest recognition of intellect and achievement on the recipient and commands worldwide attention and respect. The prize has often been criticized, however, because of the secrecy of the selection committees. In some years, the peace and literature awards have reportedly been influenced by political considerations. By 2003 the Nobel Prize monetary award had risen to over $1.3 million.

**Nobile, Umberto** (1885–1978) Italian aviator and aeronautical engineer. General Nobile became the second person to fly over the NORTH POLE when he piloted the dirigible *Norge* over the spot two days after Admiral Richard BYRD made his historic flight (May 9, 1926). Nobile's passengers on this expedition included the Norwegian polar explorer Roald AMUNDSEN and the American explorer Lincoln ELLSWORTH. Two years later, Nobile attempted another such flight in a smaller airship, the *Italia*. However, he crashed in the Arctic. Amundsen quickly organized a rescue attempt, but his plane was lost at sea. Meanwhile, Nobile managed to survive and returned to Italy. The incident caused an international controversy. Nobile was accused of cowardice and recklessness and blamed for the deaths of Amundsen and 17 others, and his military career ended in disgrace. He

spent the 1930s and early 1940s in the U.S. and the USSR His rank of general was restored in 1945, and he lived to the age of 93.

**Noel-Baker, Philip (Philip John Baker)** (1889–1982) British diplomat, statesman and pacifist. He was born into a British family from Canada; his parents were Quakers, and his father later became a Liberal member of Parliament (1905). Educated in England and the U.S., he won honors in history (1910) and economics (1912) from King's College, Cambridge, receiving his M.A. in 1913. He was a conscientious objector to WORLD WAR I, but organized and commanded the Friend's Ambulance Corps and won awards for valor while serving in France and Italy. After the war he was an assistant to Robert CECIL at the PARIS PEACE CONFERENCE (1919) and helped draft the covenant of the LEAGUE OF NATIONS. He also worked with Fridtjof NANSEN on behalf of war refugees. In 1926 he published two books, *The League of Nations at Work* and *Disarmament*, which established him as an authority on disarmament. He was elected to Parliament for the LABOUR PARTY in 1929 and became parliamentary private secretary to the foreign secretary, Arthur HENDERSON. Defeated in the general election of 1931, he won another seat in 1936 and held it until his retirement in 1970.

During the 1930s Noel-Baker advocated sanctions against ITALY because of MUSSOLINI's invasion of ETHIOPIA (see ITALO-ETHIOPIAN WAR OF 1935–36). He also joined Winston CHURCHILL in warning of the dangers of NAZISM and militarism in HITLER's Germany. During WORLD WAR II he held posts in Churchill's coalition government. He continued as an influential member of Parliament after the war and helped negotiate the independence of INDIA. He also played an important role in establishing the UNITED NATIONS. He was awarded the 1959 NOBEL PEACE PRIZE for his work in the League of Nations and the United Nations and for his commitment to international disarmament. Not only was Noel-Baker a distinguished statesman, he was also an outstanding athlete, competing in four OLYMPIC GAMES (1912, 1920, 1924, 1928) and winning a silver medal in the 1,500-meter run (1920). He changed his name to Noel-Baker in

1923, adding his wife's family name to his. He was made a life peer as Baron Noel-Baker of Derby in 1977.

**No Exit** Play (1944) by French author Jean-Paul SARTRE. *No Exit,* written during the German occupation of FRANCE, is a dark portrayal of the limitations of human goodness and the difficulties of collective resistance to evil. The play illustrates the existential outlook of Sartre in the 1940s, as exemplified in more abstract terms in his philosophical magnum opus *BEING AND NOTHINGNESS.* The straightforward plot of *No Exit* concerns a group of randomly chosen persons who find themselves in Hell, which has taken the form of a comfortable room from which exit is impossible. The tortures of Hell are seen to be of these people's own devising, as each in turn seeks futilely to manipulate the others for the sake of selfish personal needs.

**Noguchi, Isamu** *(1904–1988)* American sculptor. Born in Los Angeles, he lived in Japan from the age of two to 14. Returning to the U.S., he was a premedical student before studying at New York City art schools and apprenticing with Gutzon BORGLUM. He traveled to Paris on a Guggenheim grant and studied with Constantin BRANCUSI from 1927 to 1929. During the 1940s Noguchi designed a variety of striking sets and costumes for the Martha GRAHAM dance company and developed his sculptural style in various free-standing abstract pieces. He is best known for the sculptures he created from the 1950s on—large abstract works, often in stone, that are designed in conjunction with architecture. Smooth, still and graceful presences, his works are elegant blends of Eastern and Western traditions, many designed for outdoor sculpture gardens and playgrounds. Among his public projects are the Garden of Peace at the UNESCO building, Paris (1956 to 1958), the Billy Rose Art Garden, Jerusalem (1965) and the entrance to the Museum of Modern Art, Tokyo (1969).

**Noland, Kenneth** *(1924– )* American painter. Born in Asheville, North Carolina, he studied at Black Mountain College and at the Zadkine School in Paris. Associated with both COLOR-FIELD and HARD-EDGE PAINTING, Noland ex- perimented with the use of stained colors of equal pictorial value on unprimed canvas. He is particularly noted for his huge images of vividly colored targets and chevrons, painted in the late 1950s and early 1960s. Later works employed large horizontal stripes or plaid designs in a more muted tonal range.

**Nolde, Emil** *(1867–1956)* German painter. Born Emile Hansen, he was trained as a furniture craftsman, studied art in Munich, Dachau and Paris and changed his name to Nolde, the town in which he was born. An early exponent of EXPRESSIONISM, he exhibited with DIE BRÜCKE from 1906 to 1907. A solitary and deeply individualistic painter, he soon left the group to pursue his own singular imagery. Nolde is known for expressionistically distorted paintings filled with violent color combinations. He was particularly brilliant in capturing religious images that mingle the demonic with the mystical. Typical of these paintings are *The Last Supper* (1909, Statens Museum, Copenhagen) and *The Prophet* (1912, National Gallery, Washington, D.C.). Nolde also used his expressionist technique to great effect in powerful landscapes, still lifes, figure paintings and portraits. He was also a master of the watercolor and of graphic arts, executing many important etchings, lithographs and woodcuts. Like many other modernists, Nolde was condemned by the Nazis. Forbidden to paint, he retired to his farm and executed a monumental series of watercolors entitled *Unpainted Pictures* (1938 to 1945).

**nongovernmental organization (NGO)** A national or international organization that represents the concerns of individuals on economic, environmental, military, political, religious and/or social issues, but which is not controlled by any particular government or group of governments. Examples of NGOs include the American Association of Retired Persons (AARP), the environmentalist group Greenpeace and the humanitarian medical organizations International Red Cross/ Red Crescent. NGOs operate by championing particular national and international policies, issues, or developments concerning issues they consider important. They observe the actions of companies, governments and inter-governmental organizations (IGOs) in order to inform their members and the general public about activities that agree or disagree with interests of the NGOs.

**Nono, Luigi** *(1924–1990)* Italian composer. Born in Venice, Nono was a student of Bruno Maderna and learned twelve-tone technique from Hermann SCHERCHEN (see SERIAL MUSIC). Married to the daughter of Arnold SCHOENBERG, whose compositions strongly influenced him, Nono became an important figure in contemporary music during the 1950s. A leader of the Italian Communist Party in Venice, he composed a number of extremely political pieces, such as *Intolerance* (1960) and *A Specter Rises over Europe* (1971). Nono also experimented with taped sounds and electronic music.

**Noordung, Hermann Potocnik** *(1892–1929)* Austrian army captain. Writing under the pen name "Hermann Noordung," Captain Potocnik of the Austrian reserve was a graduate engineer. Little else is known about his personal life, but his visionary writings about space, published in 1928, explored the concept of space stations from an engineering perspective in a way no one else had. He envisioned a 164-foot long wheel-shaped craft that would spin on its axis to produce artificial gravity. Noordung inspired many more recent concepts, including Gerard K. O'Neill's wheel-shaped "space colony." The Noordung space station also included a bowl-shaped power station and a cylinder-shaped observatory.

**Noriega Morena, Manuel Antonio** See PANAMA.

**Norman, Jessye** *(1945– )* American opera singer. An impressive interpreter of both soprano and mezzo-soprano roles in the French, German and Italian repertories, Norman is famous for her rich, powerful voice and precise diction. She made her debut as Elisabeth in Richard Wagner's *Tannhäuser* with the Deutsche Opera in Berlin in 1969. Her New York Metropolitan Opera debut, first as Cassandra then as Dido in Berlioz's *Les Troyens,* was a triumph (1983). Other major roles include Aida and Ariadne in *Ariadne auf Naxos.* In addition, Norman is well known as a *lieder* singer, especially for her interpretations of songs by Wagner and Richard Strauss.

**Normandie** French ocean liner designed to be the largest, fastest and most beautiful passenger ship in the world. The *Normandie*'s maiden voyage in 1935 established a transatlantic speed record but created even more interest through its extraordinary design, both technical and visual, external and internal. The *Normandie* incorporated innovations in turboelectric propulsion machinery and hull design developed by Russian-born architect and engineer Vladimir Yourkevitch. It presented an unusual and striking visual appearance, with streamlined forms for portions of its superstructure and its three giant funnels. It was widely viewed as outstandingly beautiful externally. Internally, the passenger accommodations were a lavish showcase of French ART DECO design of the 1930s. Jean Dupas, René LALIQUE, Emile-Jacques Ruhlmann, Raymond Subes and Louis SUE were among the distinguished artists and designers whose work was represented on the *Normandie,* although many others with lesser-known names also had major roles. Although larger and faster ships were built after the *Normandie,* she captured the imagination of the public in a way that has made her the ultimate example of the ocean liner. Early in 1942 the vessel was at one of New York City's Hudson River piers, being converted into a troopship for World War II duty, when a fire broke out; after burning for several days, the ship capsized when too much water was pumped into the wrong compartments. Years later it was revealed that the fire had been set by Mafia hitman Albert Anastasia in an effort to shake down the U.S. government into appealing for organized crime's aid in keeping Nazi saboteurs out of New York Harbor.

**Normandy, invasion of** On June 6, 1944, the Allies, directed by supreme Allied commander General Dwight D. EISENHOWER, invaded the European mainland across the English Channel. Thousands of troop ships, amphibious craft and warships transported British, French, American, Canadian and other Allied troops across the stormy English Channel to NORMANDY in northwestern

*General Eisenhower talks to American paratroopers before the Allied invasion of Normandy. 1944.*
(LIBRARY OF CONGRESS, PRINTS AND PHOTOGRAPHS DIVISION)

France. Before the invasion, the Allied air forces and navies had bombarded strong German fortifications along the French coast. Nonetheless, U.S. forces encountered stiff resistance on Utah and Omaha beaches; to the east, British and Canadian troops fought resolutely for the German-defended port of Caen. The hedgerow terrain of Normandy was fairly easy to defend, and the Germans made the most of it. By the end of July 1944, however, after seven weeks of intense fighting, Allied bridgeheads were established and the invasion had succeeded. The Allied armies were united along the coast. In early August 1944, the U.S. Third Army broke through German lines in the west into Brittany, south to the Loire River, and then east toward Paris. A German attempt to split the American forces failed, and instead a British force driving from the south trapped the German Seventh Army and wiped it out. (See also WORLD WAR II ON THE WESTERN FRONT.)

**Norodom Sihanouk** (1922– ) Prince and later king of CAMBODIA. Son of the late king Norodom Suramarit and Queen Kossamack Nearireath, Sihanouk has been on-and-off head of the CGDK coalition government of Democratic Kampuchea since it was formed in 1982. He was educated in Saigon and Paris and in 1941 became king. Frustrated at restrictions on the monarchy's power, he abdicated in 1955 and assumed the positions of prime minister and minister of foreign affairs. He was elected head of state after the death of his father in 1960. His conservative government followed a neutralist path throughout the 1960s, seeking to avoid becoming embroiled in the Vietnam conflict. In 1970 Sihanouk was deposed by Marshal LON NOL and took up residence in Beijing, where he formed the FUNC in alliance with the Khmer Rouge. He was restored as head of state when the KHMER ROUGE captured PHNOM PENH in 1975 but resigned a year later and spent four years under house arrest in the capital. In 1982 he became head of the CGDK; known for his volatile personality, he has since resigned several times. Sihanouk's resignation on Janu-

*American soldiers land on the Normandy shore. 1944.* (LIBRARY OF CONGRESS, PRINTS AND PHOTOGRAPHS DIVISION)

ary 30, 1988, was interpreted as a ploy to strengthen his position in negotiations with the Phnom Penh government. After the end of the Cambodian civil war in 1991, Sihanouk returned as king with only ceremonial powers. In 2004 he abdicated the throne in favor of his son Norodom Sihamoni.

**Norris, George William** *(1861–1944)* U.S. politician. In 1912 Norris began a 30-year career as Republican U.S. senator from Nebraska, and prided himself on his independence from party domination. He supported Franklin D. ROOSEVELT in his four presidential campaigns, and worked tirelessly for the establishment of the TENNESSEE VALLEY AUTHORITY. Norris secured appropriation for a series of dams for conservation and power in the Platte Valley in Nebraska, creating what became known as the "Little TVA." He led the fight in the Senate for passage of the NORRIS-LAGUARDIA Anti-Injunction Act (1932).

**Norris, Kathleen** *(1878–1966)* American novelist. Norris is best known for her more than 80 works of romantic fiction, beginning with *Mother* in 1911, and her numerous short stories originally published in women's magazines. Norris described her fiction as depicting conventional heroines with simple virtues. Other novels include *Certain People of Importance* (1922), which is considered her best work, and *Family Gathering* (1959). Norris was also a feminist and pacifist dedicated to worldwide disarmament. She spoke at a rally for world peace in Madison Square Garden in 1932.

**Norrish, Ronald George Wreyford** *(1897–1978)* British chemist. Norrish was educated at Emmanuel College, Cambridge. His studies were interrupted by WORLD WAR I, in which he served in the Royal Artillery in France. In 1918 he was captured by the Germans and spent a year as a PRISONER OF WAR. He received his undergraduate degree in 1921 and his Ph.D. in 1924. He was later a professor and director of physical chemistry (1937–65) at Cambridge. During WORLD WAR II he headed government research on the suppression of gun flash. From 1949 to 1965 he worked with his former student George Porter on flash photolysis

and kinetic spectroscopy. These methods allowed researchers to observe and investigate very fast chemical reactions for the first time. For this work, Norrish and Porter shared the 1967 NOBEL PRIZE in chemistry with Manfred EIGEN.

**Norris-LaGuardia Act** Anti-injunction act of 1932 that was a major advance for organized unions in the U.S. During the infancy of the American labor movement, unions were viewed with mistrust—and by the courts as conspiracies and illegal restraints of trade under the Sherman Antitrust Act. Employers could seek an injunction in federal court to ban even peaceful strikes, picketing and boycotts. The anti-injunction act was named after its cosponsors in Congress, Fiorello LA-GUARDIA and George NORRIS. The act restricts federal courts in issuing injunctions against a union that is engaged in a peaceful strike against an employer. It was the first step in establishing organized labor's right to organize, strike and collectively bargain.

**Norstad, General Lauris** *(1907–1988)* American air force officer. A West Point graduate, Norstad was assistant chief of intelligence for the U.S. Army Air Corps during WORLD WAR II. He helped coordinate air support for the Allied landings in North Africa and Sicily; later in the war he helped direct the bombing campaign against Japan, including the dropping of the ATOMIC BOMB on HIROSHIMA and NAGASAKI. After the war, Norstad helped establish the air force as a separate branch of the U.S. armed forces. Commander of the NORTH ATLANTIC TREATY ORGANIZATION from 1956 to 1963, he headed Allied forces in Europe during the BERLIN crisis of 1961, when East Germany built the BERLIN WALL. As NATO commander, he urged organization members to strengthen conventional forces as a defensive "ground shield" while holding nuclear retaliatory power in reserve. Norstad resigned from the air force in January 1963 over a policy dispute with President John F. KENNEDY.

**North African Campaign** In North African (1940–43) during WORLD WAR II, the AXIS sought to seize the SUEZ CANAL to control the Mediterranean. Large tank battles occurred along Egyptian and Libyan shores. In Septem-

ber 1940 Italian forces penetrated Egyptian territory but were repulsed and later destroyed. The German Afrika Korps, under General Erwin ROMMEL replaced the Italians in March 1941, forcing the British out of Libya. The British Eighth Army counterattacked in November, driving the Germans westward. In May 1942 Rommel took the offensive, routing the British in the battle of Gazala-Bir Hakim (May 28–June 13, 1942), pushing them 250 miles into Egypt. The British established a defensive line from El Alamein on the coast of the Qattara Depression, which Rommel was unable to breach. On October 23, 1942, the British Eighth Army under General Bernard L. MONTGOMERY attacked, broke through German lines and forced Rommel on a long retreat into Tunisia. The battle of El Alamein was decisive, boosted Allied moral and led to the surrender of Axis forces in North Africa on May 12, 1943.

**North American Air Defense Command (NORAD)** Coordinator of air defenses of the United States and Canada. NORAD, headquartered deep within Cheyenne Mountain near Colorado Springs, Colorado, controls all American and Canadian air defense forces through a $65 million combat operations center completed in 1965.

**North American Free Trade Agreement (NAFTA)** A comprehensive trade agreement among Canada, Mexico and the United States designed to remove all tariffs and other barriers to trade and investment among the three North American countries. Unlike regional organizations, such as the EUROPEAN UNION (EU), NAFTA did not create a supranational political body that could nullify economic policies conducted by each member nation. In 1992 following negotiations among American, Canadian and Mexican trade representatives, the leaders of all three nations signed NAFTA and agreed to seek ratification of the agreement by their national legislatures. Although many Americans, such as Texas billionaire H. Ross Perot, opposed NAFTA on the grounds that it would lead to the closing of American factories and the loss of American jobs to low-wage Mexican workers, the U.S. Senate ratified the agreement in October 1993, and NAFTA went into effect on January 1,

1994. Although NAFTA did not end all barriers to trade among the three nations, such as restrictions on the transportation of certain agricultural goods across international boundaries, it prescribed the gradual elimination of these barriers by 2008.

While the absence of any international authority facilitated NAFTA's rapid acceptance by all three member nations, the resulting economic integration created difficulties in trade and labor matters. In 2001 the U.S. Senate imposed more stringent safety regulations on companies employing Mexican trucking firms to transport goods into the U.S., claiming that many drivers hired by Mexican firms possessed driving skills and qualifications below U.S. standards. Also, as NAFTA did not address the issue of the free exchange of labor among its members, the issue of illegal immigration from Mexico into the U.S., and the U.S.'s continued efforts to prevent this influx has repeatedly generated tensions between the two countries, which has in turn impeded efforts by certain American manufacturing firms to obtain unfettered access to Mexico's consumer market.

**North Atlantic Treaty Organization (NATO)** Military alliance established under the terms of the North Atlantic Treaty, signed in Washington, D.C., on April 4, 1949, to provide for the mutual defense of member nations—originally, Belgium, Canada, Denmark, France, Iceland, Italy, Luxembourg, the Netherlands, Norway Portugal, the U.K. and the U.S. They were joined by Greece and Turkey in 1952, West Germany in 1955 and Spain in 1982. NATO's principal goal is to develop individual and collective capacity among Atlantic Community nations to resist armed attack and, re-

garding an attack on one as an attack on all, to take whatever action is deemed necessary under Article 51 of the UN Charter. It also aimed at settling disputes by peaceful means and at promoting various kinds of political, social and economic ties among its members. Aimed mainly at protecting Western nations from the Soviet bloc, which came to be represented by the WARSAW PACT, it was the most important Western military organization formed in response to the COLD WAR.

With headquarters in Brussels, Belgium, NATO is run under the auspices of the North Atlantic Council (its policy-making and coordinating body), headed by a secretary general. NATO's military force was formed in 1950 under its first commander, General Dwight D. EISENHOWER; its headquarters, the Supreme Headquarters Allied Powers in Europe (SHAPE), is also located in Brussels. NATO's Military Committee recommends defense actions to the council's military arm, the Defense Planning Committee (DPC). Consisting of military representatives from each member country (except France, which withdrew from the Military Committee in 1966 while remaining a member of the council), the DPC has its headquarters in Washington, D.C. NATO maintains three separate commands: the Atlantic Ocean Command, the European Command and the Channel Command. In addition, North American questions are handled by the Canada-U.S. Regional Planning Group. With the disbanding of NATO's rival organization, the communist WARSAW PACT, in 1991, NATO announced it would halve its forces.

With the end of the cold war and the dissolution of the WARSAW PACT, NATO expanded its membership to include the former Communist states of Poland, Hungary, and the Czech Re-

public. In 2004 Bulgaria, Estonia, Latvia, Lithuania, Romania, Slovakia, and Slovenia were admitted.

**Northcliffe, Viscount (Lord Alfred Charles William Harmsworth)** (1865–1922) British journalist and newspaper publisher. Born near Dublin, he was raised in London. His journalistic efforts started in boyhood, and by 1880 he had founded *Answers to Correspondents*, a successful weekly magazine featuring information, puzzles and games. In 1894 he and his brother Harold Harmsworth (later Viscount Rothermere), with whom he had collaborated on *Answers*, purchased the London *Evening News*, thus launching his career in newspapers. In 1896 he founded the morning *Daily Mail*, selling it at a halfpenny—half the price of other newspapers—and thus beginning the modern British daily. The *Daily Mirror*, an illustrated tabloid, followed in 1903 and the *Continental Daily Mail* was founded in Paris in 1905. In 1908 he gained control of the failing *Times*, restoring it to journalistic eminence. During WORLD WAR I, he pressed for vigorous leadership in England's conduct of the war, and his support of LLOYD GEORGE in 1916 helped to topple the ASQUITH government. Northcliffe transformed English popular journalism by introducing the blaring headline and the brightly written story and by initiating such features as the gossip column, serial and women's page. In addition, his publicity-seeking led him to finance Arctic exploration, automobile driving and aviation. Through his newspapers, Northcliffe exercised enormous influence on British public opinion and public policy.

**Northern Alliance** A confederation of MUJAHIDEEN (Islamic fighters) in AFGHANISTAN that regularly fought for control of the country and an offshoot of the United National and Islamic Front for the Salvation of Afghanistan, which ruled the country from 1992 to 1996. Following the withdrawal Soviet military forces from Afghanistan in 1989, the Northern Alliance, which included a diverse ethnic array of Hazaras, Tajiks and Uzbeks, led the opposition to the formerly pro-Soviet regime of Mohammed NAJIBULLAH. In

*French, U.S. and British NATO representatives* (LIBRARY OF CONGRESS. PRINTS AND PHOTOGRAPHS DIVISION)

1992 the Northern Alliance toppled Najibullah and took power in Kabul, but it failed to win the support of fervent Islamic militants who advocated IS-LAMISM and the rigid application of Islamic law in all aspects of Afghanistan society. Such fundamentalists supported the efforts of the TALIBAN, a political-religious group espousing the cause of Islamism in Afghanistan, to establish an Islamic state. In 1996 the Taliban forced the Alliance to withdraw from Kabul and retreat to the mountainous regions in the northern part of the country (hence the title "northern alliance").

In October 2001, U.S. military forces entered Afghanistan to destroy training camps operated in Taliban-controlled territory by the terrorist organization AL-QAEDA (a mujahideen band allied with the Taliban) to capture al-Qaeda's leader, Osama BIN LADEN, and to overthrow the Taliban regime because of its support of al-Qaeda. Northern Alliance military leaders seized on the opportunity to coordinate operations with U.S. forces and provided American units with translators and guides familiar with the terrain of Afghanistan. Upon the removal of the Taliban from power, officials of the Northern Alliance worked with interim Afghanistan president Hamid KARZAI in an effort to establish a strong unitary government. Several Alliance officials also occupied key posts in the central government that was established in Kabul. However, rivalries and conflicts within the Northern Alliance led to some of its most powerful members to establish control over portions of Afghanistan as their personal fiefdoms and challenge the authority of the national government.

**Northern Dancer** *(1961–1990)* Canadian thoroughbred racehorse. Northern Dancer enjoyed an outstanding racing career, posting wins in the Kentucky Derby and the Preakness, and winning 14 of his 18 starts. Northern Dancer's career as an athlete, however, was far overshadowed by his career as one of the greatest sires in thoroughbred history. Three of his colts won the Epsom Derby in England—the most famous being Nijinsky II, who went on to a brilliant career at stud that rivaled that of his sire. A grandson of NATIVE DANCER, Northern Dancer sired 635 offspring who won nearly 500 stakes races—primarily in Europe—by the time of his death at

the age of 29 from colic. Certainly the greatest Canadian-bred horse in history, he was returned to his native land for burial.

**Northern Expedition** *(1926–1928)* To reunify CHINA, Kuomintang (Guomindang) forces under CHIANG KAI-SHEK (Jiang Jieshi) set out northward from their capital, Canton (July 1926). By spring 1927 they controlled all provinces south of the Yangtze River, and Honan north of it. Kuomintang success came in part from having soldiers who were trained not to prey on civilians and in part from propaganda. A widening rift within the movement, however, caused Chiang to resign his command, while dismissing Russian advisers and expelling the communists. Chiang resumed command in the spring of 1928, and the northward push continued. Northern armies were defeated, a sympathetic general captured Beijing, the capital, and China was reunited (June 1928). The capital was then moved south to Nanking (Nanjing).

**Northern Ireland** A part of the UNITED KINGDOM of Great Britain and Northern Ireland; often called Ulster, it is made up of six of the nine counties of that historic province in northeastern IRELAND: Antrim, Armagh, Down, Fermanagh, Londonderry and Tyrone. BELFAST is the capital. In recent years Northern Ireland has been torn by violence between the Protestant majority (wishing to remain a part of the United Kingdom) and the Catholic minority (demanding union with the Republic of Ireland). Thousands of British troops maintain, or attempt to maintain, the public peace, while the Catholics' illegal IRISH REPUBLICAN ARMY (IRA) and the Protestants' Ulster Defence Force both disrupt public order with acts of terrorism.

In the late 19th century proposals were made for Irish self-government via HOME RULE, an early slogan of Irish nationalists. But Northern Ireland feared that this would lead to domination by the island's Catholic majority. Northern Ireland was by then more industrialized than the perennially depressed south and so had more economic ties with England. The threat of civil war simmered for decades, until in 1920 Great Britain enacted the Government of Ireland Act, which gave Home Rule separately to the two

sections and thus officially created Northern Ireland. But the Irish Free State, established in the south in 1922, refused to recognize this partition. Violence began and has continued, off and on, ever since.

In 1968, Bernadette Devlin and others organized a protest movement (modeled on the U.S. CIVIL RIGHTS MOVEMENT) calling for equal rights for Northern Irish Catholics. Protestants responded with violence, and British troops arrived specifically to protect the Catholic minority. However, relations between the British army and the Catholics soon soured. The BLOODY SUNDAY Massacre occurred in January 1972, when British troops killed 13 Catholics demonstrating in Londonderry. This led in March to the suspension of the Protestant-ruled Northern Irish government by the London authorities. A coalition government of Protestants and Catholics was formed in 1973, but it collapsed in May 1974, after a general strike called by Protestant extremists. London once again took direct control. In the late 1970s Mairead CORRIGAN and Betty WILLIAMS attempted to bring about a peaceful solution; they received little more than the 1977 Nobel Peace Prize for their efforts at reconciliation. The 1985 HILLSBOROUGH ACCORD, signed by the U.K. and Ireland, gave the Irish Republic an advisory role in the governing of Northern Ireland. Many viewed the accord as the most promising and constructive step toward peace in Northern Ireland, but extremist unionist leaders (notably Ian PAISLEY) denounced it. In 1998 a joint-governing settlement was reached with Irish Protestant and Catholic political leaders in the Good Friday Accords, brokered in part by British and American officials. However, the government that was created by the accords has been plagued with uncertainties in its leadership (see David TRIMBLE) and British prime minister Tony BLAIR suspended the agreement in October 2002.

**North Pole** Northernmost end of the Earth's axis, and one of the great conquests of explorers and adventures. American admiral Robert E. PEARY reached it first on April 6, 1909, after a series of unsuccessful attempts in the race to the North Pole. In 1926 Admiral Richard E. BYRD and Floyd BENNETT were the first to reach it by air, and in

1958 the atomic-powered *Nautilus* submarine was the first to reach the North Pole underwater. In 1960 another U.S. submarine, the *Skate*, arrived at the surface of the pole following the *Nautilus* route. The first successful foot dogsled expedition crossed over the pole in 1968 and 1969, and in 1971 Italy's Guido Monzino faithfully retraced Peary's footsteps. Naomi Uemura of Japan was the first men ever to reach the North Pole alone by dogsled in 1978, and in 1977 the Soviet icebreaker *Arktika* arrived here, followed in 1979 by a Soviet team on skis. An international expedition led by Will Stegner traveled to the pole in the 1980s.

**Northrop, John Howard** *(1891–1987)* American chemist. Between 1930 and 1935, Northrop and several colleagues at the Rockefeller Institute of Medical Research succeeded in isolating a number of enzymes, crystallizing them and revealing their protein nature. These experimental findings confirmed James B. Sumner's 1926 report that the enzyme urease also appeared to be a protein, a theory that had been rejected in favor of the assertion by the influential German chemist Richard Willstatter that enzymes were unlike any known organic compound. Building on Northrop's findings, another Rockefeller Institute colleague, Wendell Stanley, would be the first to isolate a bacterial virus, in 1939. For their preparation of enzymes and virus proteins in pure form, Northrop and Stanley shared the 1946 NOBEL PRIZE in chemistry.

**Northrop, John Knudsen** *(1895–1981)* American pioneer aircraft designer, cofounder of the Lockheed Corp. (1927) and founder of the Northrop Corp. (1939). He designed and built the Lockheed Vega (1927), the aircraft used by Amelia EARHART in her historic solo transatlantic flight in 1932. He also designed several important military airplanes. Among these were the A-17 attack plane, early navy dive bombers, the WORLD WAR II P-61 night fighter (known as the Black Widow) and the boomerang-shaped Flying Wing.

**North Trial** *(1989)* Trial of Oliver North, a Marine colonel and member of President Ronald REAGAN's National Se-

curity Council who was implicated in the IRAN-CONTRA SCANDAL. The Reagan administration supported a rebel group, dubbed the CONTRAS, who opposed the leftist Sandinista regime in NICARAGUA. When Congress cut off all funding of the contras, individuals in the Reagan administration arranged for the sale of arms to Iran and the diversion of the profits to the contras. At the time the Iranian regime was unpopular because it had seized several hundred U.S. hostages during the fundamentalist revolution that had deposed the shah of IRAN. (See IRAN HOSTAGE CRISIS.)

North was implicated in the arms deal. North became a national celebrity when his secretary revealed that he had shredded numerous incriminating documents during a congressional in-

vestigation of the matter. Although North was convicted on three of 12 criminal counts, two of these were later thrown out. North was viewed by both the jury and a large segment of the public as a scapegoat for high administration officials who may have participated in the arms transfer and subsequent diversion of funds to the contras. North's critics viewed him as a maverick who considered himself above the law; his supporters claimed that North had acted out of patriotism.

**Norway** Northern European country on the Scandinavian Peninsula, bordered on the north by the Barents Sea, the northeast by Finland and the Soviet Union, the east by Sweden and the west by the Atlantic Ocean. Norway

## NORWAY

| | |
|---|---|
| 1901 | First Nobel Peace Prize awarded in Christiania. |
| 1905 | Norway demands its own foreign service to handle affairs of world's leading merchant fleet; union with Sweden dissolved; Haakon VII is king. |
| 1913 | Suffrage for women. |
| 1914 | Economic boom as neutral Norway supplies Allies with food and raw materials. |
| 1918 | Merchant fleet at half of prewar level due to sinkings by Germany. |
| 1925 | Christiania reverts to original name—Oslo. |
| 1928 | Prince Olav wins Olympic gold medal in sailing. |
| 1935 | Labor government, elected in the face of 25% to 33% unemployment, begins 30-year hold on government; creation of a welfare state. |
| 1940 | Germans invade; Haakon VII leads government-in-exile from London; Olav organizes armed resistance. |
| 1945 | Vidkun Quisling, leader of puppet government during occupation, is executed; border with USSR created. |
| 1949 | Joins NATO but rejects bases and nuclear arms to avoid angering Soviets; Trygve Lie is first secretary-general of UN. |
| 1957 | Haakon VII dies; prince crowned Olav V. |
| 1965 | Non-socialist coalition assumes control of government. |
| 1970 | Norway's second university founded at Bergen. |
| 1972 | Voters reject membership in European Economic Community. |
| 1975 | North Sea oil and gas fields stimulate economy. |
| 1981 | Government-owned computer company implicated in scandal for selling equipment to USSR |
| 1990 | Brundtland elected for third time as voters again reject EEC membership. |
| 1991 | Kaci five assumes leadership of Conservatives; leaders of three out of four major parties, one-third of Storting (parliament) and one-half of cabinet, are women. |
| 1991 | King Olaf V dies; his son succeeds him as King Harald V. |
| 1993 | Norwegian government sponsors the Oslo Accords between Israel and the PLO. |
| 1994 | Voters again reject membership in the European Union. |
| 1996 | Brundtland resigns and is replaced by Thorbjørn Jagland, head of the Labor Party since 1992. |
| 1997 | Christian Democratic Party leader Kjell Magne Bondevik becomes prime minister. |
| 2000 | Bondevik loses a vote of no confidence in parliament; Jens Stoltenberg of the Labor Party becomes prime minister. |
| 2001 | In parliamentary elections, the Labor Party loses more than a third of its seats; Bondevik, leading a center-right coalition, becomes prime minister again. |
| 2003 | A proposal to explore for oil and gas in the Barents draws criticism from environmentalists and the fishing industry. |
| 2005 | A center-right alliance led by Stoltenberg wins a majority of seats in parliamentary elections. |

entered the 20th century under the Swedish Crown, but with its own Storting, or Parliament. In 1905 a peaceable agreement was reached by which Norway would become independent under its own monarch. Prince Carl of DENMARK was elected King Haakon VII, and he ruled until his death in 1957 when he was succeeded by his son, OLAV V. Norway remained neutral during WORLD WAR I and attempted to do so during WORLD WAR II, but it was invaded by Germany in 1940 and occupied until 1945. Norway made its merchant fleet available to the Allies during the war. The experience of the occupation led Norway away from its neutral stance, and it joined NATO in 1949 but refused to allow NATO bases or nuclear weapons on its territory. During the years of the COLD WAR, Norway managed to maintain amicable relations with the USSR without alienating its Western allies. Norway joined the EUROPEAN FREE TRADE ASSOCIATION (EFTA) in 1960 and was accepted into membership of the EUROPEAN COMMUNITY in 1972, but Norwegian voters rejected the referendum. Norway began exploiting North Sea oil fields in the 1970s and has been prosperously producing petroleum and natural gas. In 1993 Norway was responsible for brokering the Oslo Accords between Israel and the **Palestine Liberation Organization** (PLO), which created a timetable for the transfer of authority over the West Bank and Gaza Strip from Israel to the PALESTINIAN AUTHORITY. The following year the country rejected participation in the EUROPEAN UNION (EU) by a margin of 5 percent and has remained out of the union ever since. Since the start of the 21st century the government has been a coalition of several parties, with no clear majority by any one party.

**Norway, German invasion of** Although Norway had proclaimed its neutrality at the beginning of WORLD WAR II, the Germans invaded on April 9, 1940. Their warships seized control of the major harbors, while the Luftwaffe bombed airfields and radio stations, and troops swiftly occupied the cities—aided by Nazi sympathizers (see Vidkun QUISLING). Norwegians resisted, British submarines sank Nazi warships, a landing force temporarily drove the Germans out of Narvik and

an Anglo-French force aided in fighting Germans around Oslo, Norway's capital. The Germans responded with blitzkrieg tactics. Norway's King Haakon VII (1871–1957) and his cabinet escaped to London, along with many Norwegian ships and Norwegians who later joined the RESISTANCE movement. (See also Lief LARSEN.)

**nouveau roman ("new novel")** French literary movement that gained prominence in the 1950s and 1960s. Major writers associates with the Nouveau Roman movement included Michael BUTOR, Alain ROBBE-GRILLET, Nathalie SARRAUTE and Claude SIMON. The major critical text produced by the movement was Robbe-Grillet's *For A New Novel: Essays on Fiction* (1963). Writers in the nouveau roman movement declared that the traditional mainstays of fictional technique—dramatic plotting, moral and psychological analysis of character and elegant style—were out of date and inappropriate for the modern consciousness. Writers, they said, ought not to invent dramatic significance for the events of life but should rather depict them in a matter-of-fact style that reflected their essentially random sequence. Fiction could thus become a means of pointing the reader toward the possibility of freely construction one's individual life out of the dictates of one's own taste or conscience.

**Nouvelle Vague (New Wave)** Term for a French film movement inspired by a "new wave" of directors of the late 1950s and early 1960s; now used to characterize any new movement in any national cinema. Given its initial impetus by the film writer for the journal *CAHIERS DU CINÉMA*, the movement generally espoused an admiration for American cinema, a personal style in direction and an informal approach to filmmaking, with a preference for shooting out in the streets or in real houses, often using a hand-held camera. The first important film of the *nouvelle vague* was Claude CHABROL's *Le Beau Serge* (1959). Several critically acclaimed as well as commercially successful new wave films followed, including François TRUFFAUT's *Les Quatre Cents Coups* (*The 400 Blows,* 1959), Alain RESNAIS's *Hiroshima, Mon Amour* (1959) and Jean-Luc GODARD's *À bout de souffle* (*Breathless,* 1960).

**Novaes, Guiomar** *(1896–1979)* Brazilian concert pianist. A child prodigy, Novaes gave her first public performance at age eight and later won a scholarship to study in Paris (1909). Her debuts in London (1912) and New York (1915) established her as one of the finest pianists of her generation. She was especially known for her performances of works by Chopin and Schumann. Her final New York appearance was in 1972.

**Novaya Zemlya** Two USSR islands between the Barents and Kara seas in the Arctic Ocean, north of the Arctic Circle. In the late 1970s these large islands were the site of Soviet thermonuclear testing, and contained scientific stations and other settlements.

**Novello, Ivor (David Ivor Davies)** *(1893–1951)* British composer, author and actor. A matinee idol on stage and screen during the 1920s, Novello first gained fame with his 1914 song "Keep the Home Fires Burning" (composed to a poem by Lena Guilbert Ford), which became one of the most popular songs of WORLD WAR I. After that war he appeared in movies and on stage; he turned to writing for the theater in the 1930s and '40s. Among his successful musicals are *Glamorous Night* (1935) and *Perchance to Dream* (1945). In 1955 the Songwriter's Guild for Great Britain initiated the Ivor Novello Awards to honor achievement in popular and light music.

**Novotný, Antonín** *(1904–1975)* First secretary, Czechoslovak Communist Party (1953–68) and president of CZECHOSLOVAKIA (1957–68). Novotný joined the Czechoslovak Communist Party shortly after it was formed in 1921. When the communists won key government positions after WORLD WAR II, Novotný organized the communist control of the Czech police. A hard-line Stalinist, he played a key role in crushing opposition to the communist takeover of the government in 1948 (see STALINISM). He took a prominent part in the spy trial and execution of Rudolf SLÁNSKÝ and was made a member of the Politburo. THE Slánský Trial was held in 1952. Novotný was a major ally of Klement GOTTWALD, and after Gottwald's death he became the leader of the Czech communist hardliners and of the party itself. In 1957 he also succeeded the more reform-minded Antonín Zápotocký as president of Czechoslovakia. Thus he held the two top positions in Czechoslovakia until he was deposed during the PRAGUE SPRING (1968) by Alexander DUBČEK and reformers. Novotný failed to regain his prestige even after the SOVIET INVASION OF CZECHOSLOVAKIA ousted the reformers and restored a more orthodox communist regime.

**Novy Mir** (New world) Monthly literary magazine, first published in January 1925 in Moscow. Many well-known works, such as A. Tolstoy's *Peter the First* (1929–45) and Mikhail SHOLOKHOV's four-volume *The Quiet Don* (1937–40), and numerous sketches by Leonid Leonov, Alexander Tvardovsky, Konstantin Simonov, Konstantin Fedin, Fedor Gladkov and Yury Trifonov have been serialized in *Novy Mir*—as was SOLZHENITSYN's *One Day in the Life of Ivan Denisovich.*

**Noyce, Robert Norton** (1927–1990) American inventor. In 1957 he founded the Fairchild Camera and Instruments Corp. in what was to become CALIFORNIA's Silicon Valley. Two years later, with Jack Kilby, he was awarded a patent for the integrated circuit. In the 1970s and 1980s, the device, also known as the silicon microchip, became the basis for such products as the personal COMPUTER, the pocket calculator and the programmable microwave oven.

**Noyes, Alfred** (1880–1959) British poet. Noyes firmly resisted MODERNISM, embracing the traditional style in his poetry, which includes *Drake* (1908) and *Tales of the Mermaid Tavern* (1913). Life at sea is a recurring theme in Noyes's work, but in the ambitious *The Torchbearers,* a trilogy appearing between 1922 and 1930, he celebrates men of science. Noyes, who taught at Princeton from 1914 to 1923, also wrote plays, novels and an autobiography, *Two Worlds for Memory* (1953).

**nuclear magnetic resonance (NMR)** Medical diagnostic technique in which radio waves are passed through a body in an electromagnetic field. First used in 1973 and widely employed since the early 1980s, the test allows researchers to create images of interior organs and to detect and an-alyze changes in the structure and function of those organs. Since it does not rely on X RAYS, like the CAT SCAN, NMR imaging has been considered a safe procedure for the patient.

**Nuclear Non-proliferation Treaty** Treaty, signed in 1968 by over 60 nations, that was designed to stop the spread of nuclear weapons. The agreement provided that nuclear-weapons states signing the treaty would act immediately through the United Nations to provide or support immediate assistance to any non-nuclear-weapon signatory of the treaty that came under nuclear attack or threat of nuclear attack. The declared nuclear states that signed the treaty pledged not to help non-nuclear states to develop nuclear weapons, and non-nuclear signatories pledged not to acquire nuclear weapons. In 1994 North Korea agreed to abide by the treaty and cease production of weapons-grade plutonium at its nuclear reactors, provided the U.S. would supply it with oil for its power plants. However, in 2003 North Korean leader KIM JONG IL revealed that he had resumed production of the plutonium and in 2005 announced that his country possessed nuclear weapons. In the meantime, Iran, although a signatory of the treaty, was suspected of conducting a program to develop nuclear weapons in violation of the treaty. Three nations—India, Pakistan and Israel—have declined to sign the treaty. India and Pakistan joined the nuclear club in 1974 and 1998, respectively. Israel is widely suspected of possessing nuclear weapons or at least the capability of producing them on short notice.

**Nuclear Test Ban Treaty** A U.S., Soviet and British agreement (August 5, 1963) to end nuclear tests in the atmosphere, in space and underwater; concluded after five years of negotiations. Underground testing was permitted to continue. France and China refused to accept the treaty, but over 90 other nations signed in the following two years. The nuclear test ban treaty was the first major international treaty of its kind between the superpowers in the nuclear age.

**Nujoma, Sam** (1929–  ) President of Namibia (1990–  ). Born in 1929 to Namibian farmers in the village of Etunda in what was then South-West Africa (a former German colony administered by SOUTH AFRICA as a mandate under the League of Nations), Nujoma spent much of his youth herding cattle and cultivating crops for his family. In 1959 Nujoma became involved in the workers movement in the capital city of Windhoek and was elected leader of the Owambo People's Organization (OPO). In 1962 OPO was reorganized as the SOUTH-WEST AFRICA PEOPLE'S ORGANIZATION (SWAPO) to unite all the residents of South-West Africa against continued South African rule. As head of SWAPO Nujoma led the organization in a struggle to terminate South Africa's control of the country and to abolish the practice of APARTHEID there. His high profile in the independence movement made Nujoma a regular target of South African security forces, and prompted him to leave his country throughout much of the 1960s. In 1966 Nujoma arranged for the purchase of weapons from Algeria, which SWAPO used to conduct an insurgent guerrilla campaign against continued South African rule. After 11 years of strife, South African officials finally agreed to meet with Nujoma and representatives from the five permanent members of the UN Security Council in UN sponsored negotiations to end the civil war and bring about South West Africa's independence. In 1978 these negotiations resulted in the passage of UN Security Council Resolution 435, which established a five-stage plan for independence. However, this resolution was not enacted until 1988, when all parties involved in the conflict had implemented a cease-fire. This led to free multiparty democratic elections in late 1989, in which SWAPO candidates won a majority of seats in the national legislature.

In February 1990, following the independence of South-West Africa (which was renamed Namibia), Nujoma became the country's first elected president. He subsequently won reelection to that office in 1994 and 1999. As president of Namibia Nujoma dealt with numerous domestic and international issues in an effort to bring peace, stability and prosperity to his country. In his efforts to reform the distribution of arable farm land, Nujoma arranged the government's confiscation of farmland owned by white residents.

Nujoma has also attempted to educate Namibia's citizens about the threat passed by the transmission of the HIV/AIDS virus. In foreign affairs, Nujoma cooperated with the leaders of UGANDA, MOZAMBIQUE and RWANDA to end the civil war in the Democratic Republic of the CONGO. He retired from the presidency in 2005.

**Nuremberg Rallies** Series of annual Nazi party meetings held each September from 1933 through 1938 near the Bavarian city of Nuremberg. Organized by Joseph GOEBBELS and other Nazi chiefs, they were highly theatrical PROPAGANDA exercises. Each rally featured athletic events, impressive torchlight processions and inflammatory speeches—and ended with a speech by Adolf HITLER at the Nuremberg stadium designed by Albert SPEER. During the 1935 rally, Hitler announced the so-called **Nuremberg laws,** which deprived JEWS of civic rights, closed professions to them and forbade the marriage of Jews to non-Jews. The German filmmaker Leni RIEFENSTAHL documented the 1934 Nuremberg Rally in her spectacular film *The Triumph of the Will* (1936).

**Nuremberg Trials** Trials in 1946 of high-ranked Nazi politicians and German military officers following WORLD WAR II. After the Nazi defeat U.S., Soviet, British and provisional French leaders decided to try Nazi leaders for crimes against peace, for planning and waging the war, for war crimes, including needless killing of civilians, the use of slave labor and the destruction of cities, towns and villages, and for crimes against humanity—the deportation and genocide of the Jews and

other groups in Europe. The individual defendants included 24 top Nazis; among them were Hermann GÖRING, Rudolf HESS, Joachim von RIBBENTROP, Albert SPEER, Field Marshal Wilhelm KEITEL and Martin BORMANN, who was tried in absentia. Adolf HITLER, Joseph GOEBBELS and Heinrich HIMMLER were not tried, as they had all committed suicide in the closing days of the war.

The trial judges included Francis Biddle (U.S.), Henri Donnedieu de Vabre (France), General Nikitchenko (USSR) and Lord Justice Lawrence (U.K.). U.S. Supreme Court justice Robert JACKSON was one of the prosecutors. The defendants argued that they were merely following lawful orders. Most but not all of the defendants were found guilty; several, including Göring, were sentenced to death. Hess was given life imprisonment and others received lesser terms.

**Nureyev, Rudolph** (*1938–1993*) Russian-born dancer, choreographer and ballet director. Internationally acclaimed as the greatest male dancer of the 1960s and early 1970s, Nureyev showed astounding virtuosity and a charismatic stage presence in more than 100 roles in the classical and modern dance repertory. After studying at the Kirov Ballet School in Leningrad, he joined the Kirov Ballet in 1958 and scored a personal triumph during its Paris visit in 1961. He was granted political asylum in 1961 and danced with many companies worldwide. As a guest artist with Britain's ROYAL BALLET (1962 to mid-1970s) he formed a legendary partnership with Margot FONTEYN. He is famous for his interpretation of heroic roles in such ballets as *Petrushka, Marguerite and Armand*

and Kenneth MACMILLAN's *Romeo and Juliet,* as well as for creating roles in such modern works as Rudi van DANTZIG's *The Ropes of Time* (1970) and Martha GRAHAM's *Lucifer* (1975). He choreographed and staged many works, including *Nutcracker* (1967) and *Don Quixote* (1966; film version, 1973) and starred in the television film *I Am a Dancer* (1972). He became an Austrian citizen in 1982. In 1983 he became director of the Paris Opera Ballet. He was inducted, as a knight, into the Ordre des Arts et des Lettres, France's most prestigious award for cultural achievement.

**Nurmi, Paavo** (*1897–1973*) Finnish athlete. Popularly known as the Flying Finn, Nurmi was one of the greatest track stars of the 20th century. He set 20 world records from 1920 to 1932 and won nine gold and three silver medals in the OLYMPIC GAMES of 1920, '24 and '28. He set records in runs of from 1 to 10 miles and from 1,500 to 20,000 meters. His running career was effectively ended in 1932 when he was barred from the Olympics for accepting expense money and compromising his amateur standing.

**Nye, Gerald Prentice** (*1892–1971*) U.S. senator. After a newspaper editing career in Wisconsin and North Dakota, Nye became involved in populist politics. In 1926 he was elected a Republican senator from North Dakota. He served in the U.S. Senate until 1944 where he opposed corruption in politics, monopolies, price-fixing and banking, and worked for farm interests. He generally defended President Franklin D. ROOSEVELT's NEW DEAL. As the chief spokesman for the Peace Lobby in Congress, his efforts had revealed the profiteering of munitions makers during WORLD WAR I. He was most instrumental in passage of the Neutrality Act of 1935 and in opposing LEND-LEASE.

**Nyerere, Julius Kambarage** (*1922–1999*) Tanzanian political leader, president (1964–85). The son of a Butiama chief, he was born at a village on Lake Victoria and attended Makerere University College in Uganda, and Edinburgh University. He taught at various mission schools and founded the Tanganyika African National Union (1954) to promote self-rule. After the party's overwhelming victory in the 1960 election, Nyerere became the colony's chief

*The Nuremberg Rallies* (LIBRARY OF CONGRESS, PRINTS AND PHOTOGRAPHS DIVISION)

minister and pursued a Christian socialist agenda. When Tanganyika achieved independence in 1961, he became its first prime minister and, after it became a republic the following year, he was elected its first president. Nyerere engineered the union of Tanganyika and Zanzibar into the Republic of TANZANIA (1964). He won reelection in Tanzania's subsequent presidential elections.

**Nyswander, Marl** *(1919–1986)* American psychiatrist. In the 1950s she became one of the first members of her profession to advocate treating drug addiction as a medical problem. She and Dr. Vincent Dole, whose research group she joined in 1964 and whom she married in 1965, were credited with developing the methadone maintenance method for treating heroin addiction.

**Oak Ridge** City in Anderson County in the east-central part of Tennessee. Located on a 59,000-acre tract of federal land, it was built to accommodate the WORLD WAR II Atomic Energy Program (the MANHATTAN PROJECT); its personnel reached a wartime high of 70,000. The site was chosen for its seclusion and also because it provided the necessary resources and transportation via the Louisville & Nashville, and Southern Railroads. Government engineers started construction of Oak Ridge (originally named the Clinton Engineer Works) in 1942 and completed it in two-and-a-half years under tight security. In 1944 its plants began to process uranium. By the early 1950s, although activity had been greatly reduced from wartime, Oak Ridge still had processing plants, an atomic energy field office and an atomic laboratory where training and research was carried on. The government began offering its land and homes for private purchase in 1956, and Oak Ridge was incorporated as a city in 1959. Present manufactures include tools, dies, metal fabrication and electroplating. The city is the home of the American Museum of Science and Energy and the Oak Ridge Associated Universities.

**O.A.S. (Organisation de l'Armée Secrète)** A secret army made up of dissident members of the French army in ALGERIA (1961–62). Led by General Raoul SALAN and supported by French settlers in Algeria, the group launched a terrorist campaign aimed at preventing DE GAULLE's Algerian policy, thwarting Algerian independence and, ultimately, bringing down France's Fifth Republic. The O.A.S. engaged in terrorist activities against Algeria's Muslims, and it was unsuccessful in a variety of attempts to assassinate de Gaulle. It ceased to pose a threat after the capture of Salan and other leaders, and the revolt was ended. (See also ALGERIAN WAR OF 1954–62.)

**Oates, Joyce Carol** *(1938– )* American novelist. Oates's naturalistic fiction often explores deviance and violence in contemporary American settings. Such works include, *Them* (1969), *Wonderland* (1971) and *Because It Is Bitter and Because It Is My Heart* (1990)—the title of which was taken from a poem by Stephen Crane. An extremely prolific author, Oates has also written several neo-gothic novels, such as *A Bloodsmoor Romance* (1982), and mystery fiction under the pseudonym Rosamond Smith. She has written nonfiction, short stories, and edited the *Ontario Review* with her husband, Raymond J. Smith. Oates continues her prolific publishing activities. Recent titles are: *What I Lived For* (1994), *My Heart Laid Bare* (1998), *Blonde* (2000) and *I'll Take You There* (2002).

**Obasanjo, Olusegun** *(1937– )* Officer in the Nigerian army (1958–79), military ruler of Nigeria (1976–79), and president of Nigeria (1999– ). Born in Abeokuta in the province of Ogun, Obasanjo was born into the Yoruba ethnic group in Nigeria. After joining the Nigerian army in 1958, Obasanjo was sent to Great Britain, India and Ghana for advanced military training. He was promoted to the rank of general in 1976 because of his effective service during the Biafran civil war (1967–70) and with the UN peace keeping forces dispatched to the Congo (1960–61). In 1976 following the assassination of General Murtala Muhammad, Obasanjo succeeded him as the ruler of Nigeria. After three years of military rule, Obasanjo oversaw the Nigerian national elections in 1979 that resulted in the election of Shehu Shagari, a civilian from northern Nigeria, as president. Following the transfer of power to civilian control, Obasanjo resigned from the Nigerian army, and returned to Ogun, where he became a poultry and pig farmer. Because of his continued criticism of the Nigerian military junta that had seized power in 1993, Obasanjo was arrested in 1995 on charges of conspiracy to overthrow the government. Although sentenced to life imprisonment, Obasanjo was released in 1998 after the ascension to power of Gen. Abdulsalami Abubakar. In the national elections that were held the following year, Obasanjo won election as the presidential candidate of the People's Democratic Party (PDP), in large part because of his successful efforts (although he was a Christian) to win the support of the Muslim regions in the north of Nigeria.

As president Obasanjo attempted to reduce the violence between Christians and Muslims in Nigeria, to improve the country's infrastructure

*Nigerian president Olusegun Obasanjo* (NIGERIAN INFORMATION SERVICE)

(particularly in relation to the nation's large oil reserves), to allow greater civil liberties for Nigerian citizens, and to remove authoritarian elements within the ruling elite. The most difficult issue Obasanjo faced was the renewal of tensions between the Muslim north and the Christian south, such as the conflict that broke out when the adoption of *sharia* (Islamic law) by several northern states prompted their Christian residents to flee their homes. In foreign affairs, Obasanjo joined with South African president THABO MBEKI and Algerian president Abdelaziz Bouteflika to create the New Partnership for African Development (NEPAD), a trilateral organization that seeks to promote democratization throughout Africa, to encourage greater economic development, to advance foreign investment in Africa and to reduce barriers to trade. In April 2003, Obasanjo won reelection as Nigerian president with over 60% of the popular vote, although European Union (EU) election observers took note of "serious irregularities" during the voting.

## Oberth, Hermann *(1894–1989)*
Hungarian mathematician, rocket theorist and experimenter. Rocket pioneer, Oberth never left as big a mark as his two contemporaries, Konstantin TSIOLKOVSKY and American Robert GODDARD. The son of a physician, he became interested in astronautics while recuperating from wounds suffered while serving in the Austro-Hungarian army during WORLD WAR I. The government wasn't interested in listening to his ideas; and after the war, in 1922, his attempt to obtain his Ph.D. with a dissertation on rocket design was also rejected. Turning to his own greatly limited resources, he published *The Rocket into Interplanetary Space,* partly at his own expense. The book, which also included one of the first detailed discussions of orbiting space stations, was a popular success, and in 1929 he published his major work *The Road to Space Travel.* A theorist rather than a hands-on engineer or inventor, Oberth nevertheless began to build up a following in Germany, and in 1938 he joined the faculty of the Technical University of Vienna and became a German citizen. Although he worked for a while with VON BRAUN and for the Nazis at PEENEMÜNDE, the association was uneasy, as were his later years spent with von Braun in the United States. In 1958, after three years in the U.S., he retired and returned to Germany.

## Obote, Milton *(1924–2005)* Ugandan political leader. Obote was a member of the Uganda National Congress from 1950 to 1962. When UGANDA became independent in 1962, Obote, head of the majority Uganda People's Congress (UPC), became prime minister. He soon suspended the constitution, deposed the president, assumed all executive power himself and used the military to quell opposition. In 1971 military commander Idi AMIN seized control. After a nine-year exile in Tanzania, Obote returned (1980) and, in a disputed election, became president. In 1985 he was deposed by a military coup and exiled to Zambia.

## O'Brien, Conor Cruise *(1917– )*
Irish critic, playwright and diplomat. O'Brien's first critical work, *Maria Cross: Imaginative Patterns in a Group of Modern Catholic Writers* (written under the pseudonym Donat O'Donnell, 1952) was much admired by Dag HAMMARSKJÖLD, to whom O'Brien became a special representative. A leading member of the FINE GAEL Party, he also served as IRELAND's representative at the UNITED NATIONS (1955–61) and as minister of posts and telegraphs (1973–77) in the cabinet of Prime Minister Liam Cosgrave. He was also editor of the British Sunday newspaper, the *Observer.* O'Brien has written widely on politics and the arts. His plays, perhaps best known of which is *Murderous Angels: A Political Tragedy and Comedy in Black and White* (1970), present the world political arena as drama. He addressed issues of international diplomacy in *To Katanga and Back: A UN Case* (1962) and *The United Nations: Sacred Drama* (1968). Among his other varied works are *The Idea of the Modern in Literature and the Arts* (1968), *Literature in Revolution* (1972) and *God Land: Reflections on Religion and Nationalism* (1988). O'Brien remained professionally active throughout the 1990s, releasing *The Great Melody: A Thematic Biography of Edmund Burke* (1993), *On the Eve of the Millennium: The Future of Democracy through an Age of Unreason* (1995), and *The Long Affair: Thomas Jefferson and the French Revolution, 1785–1800* (1996). In 1998 he published his *Memoir: My Life and Themes.*

## O'Brien, Edna *(1932– )* Irish author. Born in the west of Ireland, she attended the Pharmaceutical College in Dublin. After marriage at age 20 and the birth of two sons, she moved to London, *The Country Girls* (1960) is her first novel and the first of a trilogy (completed with) *The Lonely Girls,* 1962, and *Girls in Their Married Bliss,* (1963) that follows the lives of two convent-bred Irish girls, Cathleen Brady and Bridget Brennen, who escape to Dublin and eventually move to London. O'Brien's writing reflects her rejection of the constraints of her Catholic upbringing. Though she is cynical about relations between the sexes, her fiction is exuberantly sensual. Other works include *A Pagan Place* (1971), *Johnny I Hardly Knew You* (1977) and *Tales for the Telling: Irish Folk and Fairy Tales* (1986). O'Brien has also published collections of short stories and has written plays and television scripts. O'Brien remained a prolific writer throughout the 1990s, publishing such fictional works as *Time and Tide* (1992), *House of Splendid Isolation* (1994), *Down by the River* (1997), and a biographical work, *James Joyce* (1999). Her latest books are *Wild December* (2000) and *In the Forest* (2002).

## O'Brien, Flann **(pen name of Brian Ó Nualláin)** *(1912–1966)* Irish novelist, widely considered one of the

greatest and most original comic writers of the 20th century. Nolan worked for the Irish civil service and wrote a brilliant satirical column in the *Irish Times* for 27 years under the pseudonym Myles na gCopaleen (literally, "Myles of the Little Horses"). His first novel, *At Swim-Two-Birds* (1939), was largely ignored at the time of its publication but has since come to be regarded as a masterpiece. The book shows the influence of James JOYCE, who championed it, and is an innovative pastiche of Irish culture and folklore. *The Third Policeman* (written in 1940 but not published until 1966), in which the central character is dead and in which a policeman's molecules become intermixed with those of his bicycle—so that each takes on some characteristics of the other—is also highly regarded. His other fiction includes *An Beal Bocht* (1941), written in Gaelic and published in English as *The Poor Mouth* (1973); *The Dalkey Archive* (1964); and *The Hard Life* (1962). Few other writers have matched O'Brien's ear for dialogue, his brilliant wordplay, philosophical outlook and sense of the absurd.

## O'Brien, Lawrence Francis, Jr.
(1917–1990) U.S. political strategist. A Democrat, he directed the successful senatorial and presidential campaigns of John F. KENNEDY. He was Kennedy's liaison to Congress and helped win passage of many of Kennedy's New Frontier programs, such as the CIVIL RIGHTS ACT of 1964 and MEDICARE. He went on to serve as postmaster general (1965–68) and as chairman of the Democratic National Committee (1968–69 and 1970–72). It was his office at the WATERGATE building that was broken into in 1972 by burglars seeking to wiretap his conversations, an event leading to the eventual resignation of President Richard M. NIXON. He left politics to serve as commissioner of the National Basketball Association, overseeing its merger with the American Basketball Association.

## O'Casey, Sean (1880–1964) Irish
playwright. Born into a lower-middle-class Protestant family, O'Casey described himself as educated in the streets of Dublin. In his early years he held a number of menial jobs, was involved in James Larkin's labor move-

ment and joined the Irish Citizen Army. O'Casey's early dramas realistically portrayed lower-class life in Dublin and the violence that can spring from it; they also explore themes of patriotism. In 1923 his first mature play, *The Shadow of a Gunman,* was staged at the ABBEY THEATRE; it was followed by *Juno and the Paycock* (1924), perhaps his greatest play. *The Plough and the Stars* (1926), set during the EASTER RISING, provoked rioting when it was performed at the Abbey because it portrayed Irish republican revolutionaries as less than noble. He moved to England in 1927. After his antiwar play *The Silver Tassie* (1928) was rejected by W. B. YEATS, O'Casey ended his association with the Abbey. He experimented with EXPRESSIONISM in such later plays as *Within the Gates* (1933) and *The Bishop's Bonfire* (1955). These works were never as well received as his earlier, realistic plays. O'Casey also wrote six acclaimed volumes at autobiography beginning with *I Knock at the Door* (1939); *Sunset and Evening Star* (1954) is the last.

## ocean liners The 20th century saw
the rise, glory and eventual decline of the great ocean liners. The North Atlantic route between Northern Europe and North America was the most popular and glamorous. But ocean liners also plied other seas and traveled to other destinations. Some ships sailed regularly between Europe and South America, Africa or Australia. For the first part of the century, ocean liners were the only way to travel across oceans. But these ships were not just a means of travel; they were expressions of national pride and prosperity. The industrial nations of Europe vied with one another to build the largest, fastest and most luxurious liners. The British White Star liner *TITANIC* (launched 1912) was to be not only the greatest ship of its time but also the embodiment of a new technological age. When it struck an iceberg and sank on its maiden voyage (April 14–15, 1912) with the lost of some 1,500 lives, it was a stark lesson in the limits of technology. However, the *Titanic* disaster led to new safety regulations and improved designs for ships.

In 1921 new U.S. immigration laws restricted the number of immigrants who could enter the U.S. The new law had a profound effect on the interna-

tional shipping business. Despite their much-publicized luxury, ocean liners had been designed to capitalize on the immigrant trade, carrying huge numbers of European immigrants westward to the U.S. in small, cramped third-class quarters ("steerage"). After the new law came into effect, shipping lines modified their vessels and changed their appeal. Instead of concentrating on transporting immigrants to the U.S., liners began carrying large numbers of well-to-do American tourists to Europe. The 1930s was the heyday of the ocean liner. The two great liners of the day were Cunard's *QUEEN MARY* (launched 1936; 80,774 tons) and CGT's (French Line) *NORMANDIE* (launched 1935; 79,280 tons). Both ships vied for the "Blue Riband," representing the speed record for the fastest voyage across the Atlantic. The *Queen Mary* and the *Normandie* were the first ships able to cross the Atlantic in less than four days.

During WORLD WAR II, many ocean liners (including the *Queen Mary* and her newer sister ship, *Queen Elizabeth* [launched 1940]), were pressed into service as troop ships. Some of these liners survived the war; others were torpedoed or otherwise sunk by the enemy. A few were accidentally destroyed while being converted, either at the beginning of the war or after the war.

Ocean liners remained the primary means of intercontinental travel throughout the 1950s. *Queen Mary, Queen Elizabeth* and many smaller ships regularly carried thousands of passengers between Europe and North America, and between these continents and destinations in South America, Africa, Asia and Australia. In 1958, however, transatlantic passenger jet service was introduced, and more and more passengers began to fly rather than take the liners. Regular ocean liner service continued through the 1960s and into the 1970s, and new ships were introduced, but the passenger shipping companies began to feel the pinch of increased competition from the airlines and increased operating costs. By 1990 there was no regular year-round transatlantic passenger ocean liner service. New cruise liners thrived by carrying passengers to the West Indies and other vacation destinations. In the 1990s and until 2004, the *Queen Elizabeth II* was the lone ship providing frequent trans atlantic service. In January 2004 the *Queen Mary II* was launched into transatlantic service to replace Cunard's *Queen Elizabeth II* on that route. The *Queen Mary II* is currently the largest, longest, tallest and widest of the ocean liners.

**Ochab, Edward** *(1906–1989)* Polish communist official. He served as party leader for seven months in 1956, a time of intense anti-Soviet feeling. In 1964 he became chairman of the Polish Council of State, the collective presidency of POLAND. He resigned four years later in protest against a communist-led ANTI-SEMITISM campaign that forced some 20,000 Polish Jews to emigrate.

**Ochoa, Severo** *(1905–1993)* Spanish-American biochemist. Ochoa was one of the first to demonstrate the role of high-energy phosphates in the storage and release of the body's energy. Of great significance was his isolation of the bacterial enzyme polynucleotide phosphorylase in 1955, while investigating the process of oxidative phosphorylation. He then used this enzyme to catalyze the formation of ribonucleic acid (RNA) from appropriate nucleotides. This procedure was later used in the synthesis of artificial RNA. His pivotal achievement enabled subsequent researchers to decipher the genetic code. In 1959 Ochoa shared the NOBEL PRIZE in physiology or medicine with Arthur Kornberg, who synthesized deoxyribonucleic acid.

**O'Connor, Donald** *(1925–2003)* Hollywood actor-dancer. O'Connor was born into a family of circus performers and worked as a child in VAUDEVILLE. He made his film debut at age 11 in *Melody for Two* (1937). Although he made many low-budget musicals during the 1940s, it was a nonmusical role playing opposite a talking mule named *Francis* that boosted his career and lead to a starring role in the classic musical film *Singin' In the Rain* (1952) with Debbie Reynolds and Gene KELLY. During the 1950s O'Connor appeared in the musicals *Call Me Madam* (1953) and *There's No Business Like Show Business* (1954). He also starred in five films and a TV series featuring Francis, the talking

mule. After the 1950s O'Connor made few film and TV appearances.

**O'Connor, (Mary) Flannery** *(1925–1964)* American author. After graduating from Georgia College (B.A., 1945), O'Connor went to the University of Iowa Writer's Workshop (M.F.A., 1947). She published her first story, "The Geranium" (1946), and first novel, *Wise Blood* (1953). Despite constant illness, there followed *A Good Man Is Hard to Find and Other Short Stories* (1955), her acclaimed *The Violent Bear It Away* (1959) and other stories, including "Judgment Day" and "Parker's Back." O'Connor's highly polished fiction, often comic and misunderstood, presented characters tortured over the meaning of their lives.

**O'Connor, Frank (Michael O'Donovan)** *(1903–1966)* Irish author. O'Connor is perhaps best known for his short stories, which include the collections *Bones of Contention* (1936), *Traveller's Samples* (1951) and *Domestic Relations* (1957), and which present the middle and lower middle classes of IRELAND, often situated in his native County Cork. O'Connor was also a champion of Irish literature and wrote *A Short History of Irish Literature: A Backward Look,* translated many Gaelic works into English and edited the anthology *A Book of Ireland* (1959). Other works include the novel *The Big Fellow* (1937) and the autobiographies *An Only Child* (1961) and *My Father's Son* (1969). In the latter part of his life, O'Connor lived mostly in the U.S. and taught at Harvard and Northwestern universities. His critical works include *The Lonely Voice: A Study of the Short Story* (1962).

**O'Connor, Sandra Day** *(1930– )* O'Connor is the first woman to serve on the U.S. Supreme Court. A native of west Texas, she graduated from Stanford University and its law school. Although graduating at the top of her class, O'Connor was rejected by a number of large law firms and first worked as a deputy county attorney in California, and was later in private practice, before becoming an Arizona assistant attorney general. A Republican active in politics, O'Connor was appointed and then elected to the Arizona state senate, eventually rising to the position of majority leader. She was

*Supreme Court justice Sandra Day O'Connor* (LIBRARY OF CONGRESS, PRINTS AND PHOTOGRAPHS DIVISION)

next elected a local judge and later appointed to the Arizona Court of Appeals. In 1981 O'Connor was a surprise appointment to the Supreme Court by President Ronald REAGAN. On the bench O'Connor was generally a member of the conservative bloc, sometimes voting against legislation favoring women and minorities. She proved a champion of STATES' RIGHTS against the federal government. Throughout the 1990s, however, O'Connor proved part of a swing vote coalition with Justices David Souter and Anthony Kennedy on several cases. In 2005 she retired from her seat on the Court to care for her husband, who suffered from Alzheimer's disease.

**October (November) Revolution** After an abortive attempt by the BOLSHEVIKS (a radical Marxist party) to seize power from the Provisional Government in Petrograd, later Leningrad (now Saint Petersburg), in July 1917, Bolshevik leader Vladimir I. LENIN fled to Finland, and Russian socialist Alexander F. KERENSKY succeeded the liberal Prince LVOV as premier (see RUSSIAN REVOLUTION; FEBRUARY REVOLUTION). A reactionary coup attempt failed (see KORNILOV'S REVOLT) but weakened Kerensky's power; support for the Bolsheviks increased as the Russians, exhausted and suffering severe privations from WORLD WAR I, grew suspicious of military and governmental leaders. In early November 1917 (late October by the Old Style calendar), soviets, or revolutionary councils, throughout RUSSIA voted to form a Soviet government that would end the war and establish citizen-run industries and farms.

Bolshevik leader Leon TROTSKY took over the military revolutionary committee at Petrograd, where the troops voted to obey only the committee's orders. Kerensky demanded rescission of the vote and sent soldiers on November 6, 1917 (October 24, O.S.), to shut down the Bolshevik press in Petrograd. The Bolsheviks, along with sympathetic troops and the workers' Red Guards, marched upon and peacefully took over the government buildings and public utilities. While Kerensky gathered his forces to oust the Bolsheviks, his ministers at the Winter Palace surrendered in the face of Bolshevik armed might. Then Kerensky's troops marched to Gatchina near Petrograd, and there the pro-Kerensky committee of public defense ordered the military-school trainees to arrest the military revolutionary committee and to attack Bolshevik or Soviet-held areas. The Bolsheviks withstood this assault and took charge of the military schools. Trotsky moved to Gatchina, where his troops defeated government forces in two days; Kerensky then fled abroad. Lenin became president of a Council of People's Commissars, the name of the new government, in which Trotsky and Joseph STALIN (1879–1953) were chief commissars. The Bolsheviks soon took Moscow after bloody street fighting, and within a month they controlled the country. In January 1918, Lenin dissolved the freely elected, socialist-dominated national assembly, thereby ending Russia's only attempt at democracy. (See also RUSSIAN CIVIL WAR.)

**Octobrists** Members of the "Union of October 17," a political party founded in November 1905 with the aim of ensuring the implementation of the promises made in NICHOLAS II's manifesto of 1905, which granted a constitution. The party was led by Alexander Ivanovich GUCHKOV and Michael Vladimirovich RODZYANKO, and the party won 12 seats in the first duma, 32 in the second, 150 in the third and 97 in the fourth. In the third and fourth dumas the Octobrists had an overall majority. They joined the

"progressive bloc" in 1915 and took part in the provisional government of 1917.

**Ó Dalaigh, Cearbhall** (1911–1978) President of the Republic of IRELAND (1974–76). A noted lawyer, Ó Dalaigh became a judge in 1953, and was chief justice of Ireland's Supreme Court from 1961 to 1973.

**Oder-Neisse Line** Boundary along the Rivers Oder and Neisse between POLAND and GERMANY; provisionally agreed upon by the U.S., U.K. and USSR at the YALTA and POTSDAM conferences. The new boundary gave Poland a fifth of Germany's 1938 territory and a sixth of its population. WEST GERMANY did not officially recognize the Oder-Neisse line until November 18, 1970, as a part of Chancellor Willy BRANDT's OSTPOLITIK reconciliation policy.

**Odets, Clifford** (1906–1963) American playwright. Known for his social protest dramas of the 1930s, Odets was born in Philadelphia, became an actor and joined the GROUP THEATER (1931). Turning from acting in plays to writing them, he created the short, working-class drama *Waiting for Lefty* (1935). Immediately acclaimed for his powerful play, Odets followed it with his first full-length drama, *Awake and Sing!* (1935)—a tale of travail and rebellion in an impoverished Jewish family; it is widely considered his best work. His most popular play, *Golden Boy* (1937), tells of a young man who gives up the violin for a more lucrative career in the brutal world of prizefighting. His other plays include *Clash by Night* (1942), *The Big Knife* (1949), *The Country Girl* (1950) and *The Flowering Peach* (1954). Odets spent the latter part of his life as a HOLLYWOOD screenwriter.

**O'Donnell, Peadar** (1893–1986) Irish author and political activist. He fought for Irish independence with the IRISH REPUBLICAN ARMY and later helped organize the small Irish group that joined the International Brigade to fight in the SPANISH CIVIL WAR. He co-founded *The Bell,* a major literary magazine during WORLD WAR II, with Sean O'FAOLAIN. Early in his career he wrote such acclaimed novels as *Islanders* and *The Knife,* chronicling the lives of Irish

peasants. *The Big Window* (1954) is widely regarded as his finest novel.

**Odum, Howard Washington** (1884–1954) Sociologist and author. Odum developed regional analysis to reflect the social life of the Southern Negro. At the University of North Carolina (1920) he began pioneer work in social science, founding the departments of public welfare and sociology, establishing the journal *Social Forces* and developing the university's research institute. Under President Herbert HOOVER he prepared the influential report *Recent Social Trends* (1933). Author of many books, including *Rainbow Round My Shoulder* (1928) and *Southern Regions of the United States* (1936), Odum also earned a Master Breeders Award for work with cattle.

**Oe, Kenzaburo** (1935– ) Japanese author and recipient of the 1994 Nobel Prize in literature. Born in the forested regions of the Japanese island of Shikoku, Oe spent much of his childhood hearing the women of his village recite the legends and history of the region. During WORLD WAR II (1939–45), Oe's mother fostered her son's interest in the style and content of literature when she gave him two books: *The Adventures of Huckleberry Finn,* and *The Strange Adventures of Nils Holgersson.* In 1953 Oe enrolled in Tokyo University, where he studied French literature under Professor Kazuo Watanabe, specializing in the symbolism in the works of François Rabelais. Oe also began composing his own fictional narratives, such as the Akutagawa Award–winning short story, *The Catch* (1957), and his first novel, *Bud-Nipping, Lamb Shooting* (1958). In general these works explored the "loss of innocence" among Japanese youths after World War II during the U.S. occupation of Japan. After composing *Hiroshima Notes* (1965), an essay that explored the memories of Japanese victims of the atomic bomb, Oe began to study the history of the island of Okinawa, how it was integrated into Japanese society, how it fared in the U.S. occupation and how its inhabitants remained culturally separate from Japanese society. His experiences in Okinawa led him to write *The Silent City* (1967), in which he examined the relationship between the culturally different legends of his native village and contemporary Japanese society. In addition to these works on the presence of mythology within Japan, Oe was inspired to write novels that described his experiences with his mentally handicapped son, Hikari, such as *Teach Us to Outgrow Our Madness* (1969), *My Deluged Soul* (1973) and *Rouse Up, O, Young Men of the New Age!* (1983). In 1993 Oe released *Until the 'Savior' Gets Socked*, the first book in *The Flaming Green Tree* trilogy, a series that Oe was inspired to write by the metaphorical poetry of William BUTLER YEATS. In 1994 in recognition of his contribution to the development of literature, Oe was awarded the Nobel Prize in literature.

**Oerter, Al (Alfred Adolph)** *(1936– )* American athlete. Oerter won the OLYMPIC gold medal for the discus throw in 1956, 1960, 1964 and 1968. This is an Olympic record—he is the only individual to have won four consecutive titles in the same event. In 1962 he broke the 200–foot barrier by throwing the discus 200 feet 5 inches. He was also national Amateur Athletic Union (AAU) champion six times.

**O'Faolain, Sean** *(1900–1991)* Irish novelist and short story writer. O'Faolain was a member of the IRISH REPUBLICAN ARMY and studied at Harvard University prior to the publication of his first collection of short stories, *Midsummer Night Madness and Other Stories* (1932). His fiction affectionately satirizes his Irish characters, and laments the lost cause of Irish nationalism. O'Faolain wrote three novels, *A Nest of Simple Folk* (1934), *Bird Alone* (1936) and *Come Back to Erin* (1940), many biographies, and the nonfiction, *The Irish* (1947). His autobiography, *Vive Moi!* (1964), recounts his experiences in the IRA and contains lyrical descriptions of the Irish countryside. *Collected Stories* was published in 1981.

**Office of Strategic Services** American intelligence agency during WORLD WAR II; forerunner of the peacetime CIA. On June 13, 1942, President Franklin D. ROOSEVELT replaced the Office of Coordinator of Information with the OSS. William "Wild Bill" DONOVAN

was named head of the new civilian agency, whose mission was to direct intelligence operations and related covert activities. During the war, the OSS proved extremely useful to the Allies. Its activities in North Africa were credited with ensuring the success of the Allied landings there. OSS agents also worked extensively with RESISTANCE groups throughout Europe, fought behind enemy lines and provided Allied planners with a steady stream of invaluable intelligence on enemy troop movements, battle plans and other topics of vital concern. The OSS was disbanded on September 20, 1945; it was succeeded in early 1946 by the Central Intelligence Group, which in July 1947 became the Central Intelligence Agency (CIA).

**Ó Fiaich, Cardinal Tomás** *(1923–1990)* Irish religious leader. As Roman Catholic primate of all Ireland since 1977, he headed the Catholic Church both in the Republic of IRELAND and in predominantly Protestant NORTHERN IRELAND. He was an outspoken critic of the IRISH REPUBLICAN ARMY's attempt to end British rule in Northern Ireland and, at times, of Britain's administration there.

**O'Flaherty, Liam** *(1897–1984)* Irish author and nationalist. A political influence as well as a literary one, O'Flaherty helped form the Irish Communist Party before writing his first novel, *The Neighbor's Wife* (1923). His fiction often depicts rural life in Ireland and reflects his own political struggles. O'Flaherty's writing generally lacks subtlety. His stories are often overwritten and crudely constructed. Nonetheless, they made a powerful impact. Perhaps his best-known novel is *The Informer* (1925), which was filmed by John FORD in 1935, but critics point to *Famine* (1937) as his most important book. In Ireland he is equally lauded for his short stories, which include *Spring Sowing* (1924) and *Two Lovely Beasts* (1948). He has also written three lively volumes of autobiography, *Two Years* (1930), *I Went to Russia* (1931) and *Shame the Devil* (1934).

**Ogaden** Region in ETHIOPIA's Harar province, bordering SOMALIA. Claimed by ITALY as a protectorate in 1891, Ogaden was recaptured by Menelik II

in the same year. Coveted by MUSSOLINI, he contrived a 1934 dispute at Walwal as a pretext for invading Ethiopia. (See also ITALO-ETHIOPIAN WAR OF 1935–36.) In 1948 Ogaden was restored to Ethiopia and remained the subject of boundary disputes between Somalia and Ethiopia since 1960. After a major Ethiopian offensive with the aid of CUBA and the Soviet Union in 1978, Somali troops were withdrawn, but Ethiopian forces continued to be opposed by the rebels. The territory has remained the scene of various anti-Ethiopian actions by Somali nationalists, prompting some humanitarian organizations, such as MÉDECINS SANS FRONTIÈRES (Doctors Without Borders) to leave the region in 2000.

**Ogdon, John** *(1937–1989)* British pianist. A champion of 20th-century and late Romantic-era works, he was praised for his virtuosic technique and his unusual programming. He won the Liszt Prize in BUDAPEST in 1961 and shared first place in the 1962 Tchaikovsky Competition with Vladimir ASHKENAZY. His career was curtailed by acute schizophrenia.

**O'Hara, John Henry** *(1905–1970)* American author. O'Hara is best known for his short stories, a great many of which were first published in *The NEW YORKER* and later published in various collections, including *The Doctor's Son* (1935). O'Hara's tone was tough and sophisticated, and his works were noted for their frank treatment of sexuality. His novels include *Appointment in Samarra* (1934); *Butterfield 8* (1935, filmed 1960); *Pal Joey* (1940), which was adapted into a musical that was filmed in 1957; and *A Rage to Live* (1949). His subsequent works lacked the impact of his early fiction.

**O. Henry (William Sydney Porter)** *(1862–1910)* O. Henry was the pen name of the American short story writer William Sydney Porter. Born in Greensboro, North Carolina, he settled in Texas in 1882, working at a number of jobs and becoming the editor of a humor magazine. Accused of embezzling while a teller at an Austin bank, he protested his innocence but fled to Honduras and South America to avoid arrest. Returning in 1897, he was tried and convicted and served three years in a federal penitentiary. There he began writing and selling his short stories. After his release, he moved to New York City (1902), where he flourished as an author, contributing pieces to many popular magazines. Intricately plotted, his famous stories usually involve everyday people and situations subjected to ironic twists and surprise endings. Often artificial and sentimental, they are nonetheless beautifully drafted, colorful and often deeply felt. Over 700 in number, his stories were collected in such volumes as *Cabbages and Kings* (1904), *The Four Million* (1906), *The Voice of the City* (1908) and *Opinions* (1909).

**Ohno, Talichi** (*1912–1990*) Japanese engineer. Ohno developed the just-in-time manufacturing system, which Toyota adopted in the 1950s. The system, in which inventories of parts were kept intentionally low in order to reduce costs and increase flexibility, helped transform the company into the third-largest auto manufacturer in the world. Ohno's system was widely adopted by manufacturers in many other industries around the world.

**oil embargo, Arab** In October 1973, the Arab oil-producing states imposed an oil embargo against the UNITED STATES because of its support of ISRAEL in the ARAB-ISRAELI WAR OF 1973. LIBYA ordered a complete halt in shipments of crude oil and petroleum products to the U.S. on October 19; SAUDI ARABIA followed suit the following day, and BAHRAIN, Dubai, KUWAIT and QATAR cut off their exports to the U.S. on October 21. U.S. oil companies estimated that by October 26, shipments of oil from the Arab countries had been cut by about 4 million barrels per day, or about 20 percent of the prewar flow. The NETHERLANDS was also targeted by the embargo, and on October 30 imposed a ban on Sunday pleasure driving. Gasoline prices rose significantly in the U.S. The crisis continued into 1974 but was eased as the Arab nations resumed oil shipments. The embargo and its effects showed the danger of U.S. dependence on imported oil and the necessity for conservation. This lesson was reinforced during the energy crisis of 1979 and

again during the PERSIAN GULF WAR (1990–91).

**Oistrakh, David** (*1908–1974*) Soviet violinist. A graduate of the Odessa Conservatory (1926), he first won international attention during the 1930s when he won several important competitions and began to make recordings. He began teaching at the Moscow Conservatory in 1934 and from 1937 until his death held the rank of professor. He received the Stalin Prize in 1942. He first performed in the U.S. in 1955 and thereafter appeared frequently there and in Western Europe. Oistrakh was considered not only the finest Soviet violinist of his generation but was also widely regarded as one of the top half-dozen players in the world. He excelled in the violin concertos and sonatas of the great classical and romantic composers and made many recordings.

**O. J. Simpson murder trial** (*People v. Simpson*) 1995 trial of O(renthal) J(ames) SIMPSON, National Football League legend, for the murders of his ex-wife, Nicole Brown Simpson, and her friend, Ronald Goldman, in June 1994. Beginning on January 24, 1995, the prosecution, led by Marcia Clark and assisted by Christopher Darden, began their efforts to convict Simpson of both murders. In this task they were opposed by the Simpson defense team, which was eventually headed by Johnnie Cochran and included specialists on the legal ramification of evidence drawn from samples of DNA. During the pretrial phase, Simpson's defense team attempted to suppress much of the evidence against him, arguing that the Los Angeles Police Department (LAPD) had attempted to frame Simpson for the two murders. Although the trial judge, Lance Ito, agreed that the LAPD had been reckless in its efforts to obtain a search warrant for Simpson's home, he declared the evidence obtained during the search admissible in the trial. Simpson's defense team then centered its efforts on proving that one of the LAPD's detectives on the case had planted evidence against Simpson because of his racist attitudes toward African Americans, producing witnesses who had heard the detective make anti–African-American state-

ments prior to the two murders. The defense also benefited greatly when, on the witness stand, Simpson proved unable to put on the black gloves he allegedly used when he killed his ex-wife and Goldman, because the gloves themselves fitted his hands too tightly. On October 3, 1995, after nearly 10 months of hearing arguments in the case, the largely African-American jury reached a verdict of not guilty on both counts of murder. The trial was carried live by the major television stations in the United States and became one of the most closely watched trials in American history.

**Ojukwu, Chukwuemeka Odumegwu** (*1933–  *) President of BIAFRA (1967–70). An army officer who served in the UN peacekeeping force in the Congo in 1962, Ojukwu became military governor of Eastern Nigeria in 1966. The following year he proclaimed the province as the independent Republic of Biafra. He led Biafra's rebellion against federal NIGERIA from 1967 until Biafra's defeat in 1970. He then fled to the Ivory Coast (now CÔTE D'IVOIRE). Ojukwu returned to Nigeria in 1980 after the government pardoned him for his separatist activities. He later founded a political party dedicated to the protection of the predominantly Christian Ibo ethnic group within Nigeria.

**O'Keeffe, Georgia** (*1887–1986*) U.S. artist. O'Keeffe was a leading figure in American art for seven decades. Her paintings were noted for their stunning use of color and the subtle eroticism with which she invested such objects as flowers, skyscrapers and animal skulls. Her first major exposure as an artist came in 1916, with a one-woman show mounted by pioneer photographer Alfred STIEGLITZ, whom O'Keeffe married eight years later. He continued to present her work in one-woman shows until his death in 1946. O'Keeffe drew inspiration from New Mexico, which she first visited in 1929 and made her permanent home after her husband's death.

**Okinawa** Agricultural island in the Ryukyu Islands chain, 350 miles southwest of Kyushu in the north Pacific Ocean. From April 1 to June 21,

1945, U.S. Marines staged a successful amphibious assault to establish air bases here during WORLD WAR II. Close to mainland JAPAN, costly damages were inflicted on U.S. ships by KAMIKAZE air attacks in one of the bloodiest campaigns of the war. In 1972 the U.S. returned Okinawa to Japan but retained several military bases.

*Oklahoma!* Landmark American musical show by RODGERS and HAMMERSTEIN. It opened at the St. James Theatre on March 31, 1943, and ran for 2,248 performances. It was directed by Rouben MAMOULIAN, choreographed by Agnes DE MILLE, and starred Alfred Drake as Curly. This first collaboration between Rodgers and Hammerstein was not, as has been claimed, the first "serious" musical on Broadway (*Show Boat* achieved that distinction), or the first to feature a ballet (*On Your Toes,* 1936, had the "Slaughter on 10th Avenue" ballet), or the first to achieve literary distinction (*Of Thee I Sing,* 1931, had won a PULITZER PRIZE as a drama); but it was a revolutionary integration of songs, dance and action that signalled, in historian Abe Laufe's words, "the change in the whole concept of musical theater." The source materials were Lynn Riggs's comedy, *Green Grow the Lilacs* (1931), a folksy play about ranchers and cowboys set in Indian territory (now called Oklahoma) in 1907. When the musical version opened in New Haven it was entitled *Away We Go.* There were predictions of failure: no musical had ever opened so quietly, or had a character killed on stage, or had waited 45 minutes before bringing on the chorus girls, etc. But with some revisions and a new title, *Oklahoma!* (the exclamation point was added during a tryout in Boston), it was a smash on Broadway. Hit songs included "Oh, What a Beautiful Mornin'," "Surrey with the Fringe on Top," "People Will Say We're in Love," the mournfully satiric "Pore Jud," and, of course, the title song (which became Oklahoma's state song in 1953). The motion picture version, starring Gordon McCrae as Curly, was directed in 1955 by Fred Zinneman.

**Oklahoma City Bombing** 1995 terrorist attack against the Murrah Federal Building in Oklahoma City, Oklahoma. On the morning of April 9, 1995, an enormous explosion occurred in the on-site parking lot of the Murrah Federal Building, killing 168 men, women, and children. After determining that the explosion was caused by a bomb, the FEDERAL BUREAU OF INVESTIGATION (FBI) centered its investigation on Timothy McVeigh, a discharged sergeant in the U.S. Army, who had been arrested 90 minutes after the explosion for driving without a license plate. On April 21, shortly before he was set to be released from jail, McVeigh was arrested and charged with terrorism, murder and conspiracy to commit murder. Shortly afterward a friend of McVeigh, Terry Nichols, was also arrested and charged by the FBI as an accomplice in the Oklahoma City bombing. In February 1996, a federal judge ruled that McVeigh's and Nichols's separate trials would be moved to Denver, Colorado.

On May 29, the jury in McVeigh's trial began four days in deliberations before finding McVeigh guilty of murder on all counts. Nine days later, the same jury sentenced McVeigh to death by lethal injection. After his appeal was rejected by a federal appellate court, McVeigh announced he would no longer appeal his conviction. On June 11, 2001, he was executed by lethal injection in a federal prison in Terre Haute, Indiana.

Although a jury found Nichols guilty of one count of conspiracy to commit murder and eight counts of involuntary manslaughter on December 24, 1997, a deadlocked jury caused the presiding judge to impose a life sentence on the convicted conspirator.

**Olav V** (*1903–1991*) King of NORWAY (1957–91), son of King Haakon VII. Olav was born at the British royal estate in Sandringham, England, and attended the Norwegian Military Academy and Oxford. In 1929 he married Princess Martha of Sweden. When Hitler's troops invaded Norway in 1940, Crown Prince Olav, the king and parliamentary leaders held out in the Norwegian forests before fleeing to exile in England. He took an active part in the RESISTANCE movement, helping to build and commanding (1944) a free Norwegian army. A national symbol of resistance to Nazi occupation, he aided in the Allied liberation of his country and returned home in triumph in 1945. Olav became regent in 1955 and king in 1957.

He was succeeded by his son, Crown Prince Harald.

**Oldenburg, Claes** (*1929– *) American sculptor. Born in Stockholm, he spent his childhood in Chicago, graduated from Yale University (1950) and attended the Chicago Art Institute School (1952–55). In 1956 he settled in N.Y.C. and began to create sculptures of objects from the everyday world in plaster or papier-mâché. A leader of the POP ART movement, Oldenburg is noted for his witty versions of the commonplace in unexpected materials and sizes. He is best known for his soft sculptures, such as *Soft Typewriter* (1963) and *Soft Toilet* (1966), and for his jumbo-sized renditions of common objects, such as the *Lipstick Monument* (1969) at Yale University.

**Oldfield, Sir Maurice** (*1915–1981*) British intelligence officer. Oldfield spent four decades in the British intelligence service and worked under Kim PHILBY, the Soviet double agent who betrayed the West's secrets for 20 years. Known for his reserved manner and dry wit, Oldfield is believed to have been the inspiration for George Smiley in John LE CARRÉ's spy novels and also of the spy chief "M" in Ian FLEMING's James Bond books.

**Olduvai Gorge** East African ravine 150 miles northwest of TANZANIA's Mt. Kilimanjaro, where the ancient fossil skull of *Homo habilis,* 1.75 million years old, was discovered by British anthropologist L.S.B. Leakey in 1959. The site of rich fossil beds, discoveries have since been made, and anthropological explorations continue.

**Oliver, Joe "King"** (*1885–1938*) Like the best of jazzdom's first generation of innovators, King Oliver received his first important experiences in various New Orleans brass and dance bands. In 1918, after winning fame as a distinctive Dixieland cornet stylist in his native New Orleans, Oliver moved upriver to Chicago, where he attained even greater success at the helm of King Oliver's Creole Jazz Band and Dixie Syncopaters. During this productive Chicago period (1920–27), Oliver nurtured the talents of such jazz notables as reedmen Barney Bigard and Albert Nicholas, trombonist Kid ORY, pianist

Lil Harden (Armstrong) and most prominently, fellow cornetist Louis ARMSTRONG, who named Oliver his idol and mentor. Celebrated stints at venues such as the Royal Garden Café and Lincoln Gardens enabled aspiring white musicians to "study" Oliver's approach firsthand. In 1923 Oliver's influence was further extended through a series of landmark recordings, the first such series by a black group, regardless of genre. Significant Oliver compositions include "Sugar Foot Stomp" and "West End Blues"; as a cornetist, Oliver's approach was noted for its wa-wa-effects, mute tricks and clipped, syncopated style.

**Olivier, Giorgio Borg** *(1911–1980)* Prime Minister of MALTA (1966–71). He was a dominant figure in Maltese life for more than 30 years. A nationalist, he guided the island to independence from Britain in 1964. Under his government, Malta began a program to change its economy from one based on revenue earned from British military bases to one that relied mostly on manufacturing and tourism.

**Olivier, Laurence** *(1907–1989)* British actor, widely considered the most distinguished actor of his generation. Olivier began acting professionally as a teenager and by the 1930s was regarded as one of the foremost classical theater actors of the day, along with John GIELGUD and Ralph RICHARDSON.

*British stage and screen actor Laurence Olivier. 1931* (PHOTOFEST)

His appearance in such HOLLYWOOD films as *Wuthering Heights* (1939) and Alfred HITCHCOCK's *Rebecca* (1940) made him a movie star as well. He also directed and starred in film adaptations of Shakespeare's *Henry V* (1945), *Hamlet* (1948) and *Richard III* (1956), remarkable for his physical energy and his psychological insight. Returning to the stage, he broke new ground in 1958 by playing the second-rate vaudeville performer Archie Rice in John OSBORNE's drama *The Entertainer*—a role he re-created on film two years later. As a veteran theater actor-manager, he was the obvious choice to head Britain's ROYAL NATIONAL THEATRE following its official opening in 1963; he served as artistic director until he was replaced by Sir Peter HALL in 1973. In failing health in his later years, he returned to movie roles and television productions in order to earn money. His later projects included the films *Marathon Man* (1976) and *The Boys from Brazil* (1978), as well as television adaptation of Evelyn WAUGH's *Brideshead Revisited*. An early marriage (to Jill Esmond) had broken up when he began a widely publicized but scandalous affair with the actress Vivien LEIGH in the late 1930s; the couple married in 1940, but the marriage gradually disintegrated due to Leigh's advancing mental illness. Olivier later married the actress Joan Plowright. He was knighted in 1947 and elevated to a life peerage in 1970.

**Olson, Charles** *(1910–1970)* American poet, essayist and educator. Olson, one of the most influential American poets of the postwar era, was educated at Wesleyan, Yale and Harvard. After working for a time as a government bureaucrat, Olson shifted his energies, in the 1940s, to writing and teaching. He first received literary acclaim for *Call Me Ishmael* (1947), a study of Herman Melville that blended history, geography and economics with more standard forms of literary analysis. As a poetic theorist, Olson was markedly influenced by Ezra POUND. This influence showed in Olson's essays *Projective Verse* (1950) and *Human Universe* (1951), which called for a spoken, direct language in poetry, with lines to be measured by the natural rhythms of human breathing. Olson was a key founder of the Black Mountain School of poetry, which also included, among others,

Robert CREELEY and Robert DUNCAN. The movement took its name from Black Mountain College in North Carolina, where Olson taught from 1948 to 1956. *The Maximus Poems* (1960) is Olson's major volume of poetry.

**Olympic Games** In ancient Greece, the Olympic Games were a celebration of amateur sportsmanship, held from 776 B.C. to A.D. 393. Resumed on an international basis in 1896, the first modern games were held in Athens. A host of events—including archery, equestrian competitions and canoeing—were gradually added to the traditional track and field contests. Women were allowed to compete in the games beginning in 1912, and winter sports were added with the Chamonix games in 1924. Despite the avowed spirit of amateur and individual, not national, competition, the games have always had political overtones. From Nazi objections to the American team's Jewish and black competitors (particularly Jesse OWENS) in 1936, to the tragedy of Israeli athletes murdered by terrorists in 1972, security—and nationalism—has seemingly increased with each round of games. In the selection process for the 2000 Summer Olympic Games, political considerations, particularly allegation of human rights abuses in China, contributed to the narrow decision to award the games to Sydney, Australia, instead of Beijing, China. In 2004 the Olympic Games returned to Athens, Greece, the birthplace of Olympic competition. (See also MUNICH OLYMPICS MASSACRE.)

**Omaha Beach** Code name for the west central coastal region of France's NORMANDY during WORLD WAR II. On D-Day, June 6, 1944, U.S. troops landed here under intensive air and naval cover, opening a major invasion of Nazi-held Europe. After prolonged and bitter fighting, the Allies eventually gained a foothold on the European continent.

**O'Malley, Walter F.** *(1903–1979)* U.S. baseball executive. The colorful O'Malley owned the Brooklyn (and Los Angeles) Dodgers from 1950 until his death, building the team into one of major league baseball's most successful franchises. During his tenure, the Dodgers won 10 National League pennants and four World Series. However, the team's New York fans never forgave him for moving the Dodgers from Brooklyn to the West Coast (making it the first major league team in California) in 1958.

**Oman (Sultanate of Oman)** Oman covers an area of 82,008 square miles on the southeastern coast of the Arabian Peninsula, and includes the islands of Masirah, Kuria Maria, and Daymaruyat plus the tip of the Musandam Peninsula. Though Oman was ostensibly a British protectorate since 1798, power struggles based on the geographical and religious divisions between the coastal region governed by Hindu sultans and the interior ruled by Muslim imams occurred until a 1920 agreement, which ushered in three decades of peaceful coexistence. In the mid-1950s the imam, with support from Saudi Arabia, started a revolt, but was defeated by the British-backed sultan. Sultan Said bin Taimur (ruled 1932–70) was replaced in 1970 during a palace coup by his son, Sultan Qabus, who changed the country's name to the Sultanate of Oman. Rebellion in the province of Dhofar (1960s–1975) was quelled, resulting in the province being governed as a separate entity. A founding member of the Gulf Cooperation Council (1981), Oman has promoted peace among the Gulf states. In 1997 Sultan Qaboos decreed that women within his country could vote and run for office. Five years later he lowered the voting age to 21.

**Omar, Mullah Mohammed** (c. 1962– ) Leader of the TALIBAN, a political-religious movement that controlled most of AFGHANISTAN from 1996 to 2001. In 1979 Omar joined in the guerrilla campaign of the loosely organized MUJAHIDEEN, or Islamic freedom fighters, to overthrow the pro-Soviet government of Afghanistan and evict the Soviet military forces that kept it in power. It was during this insurgent effort that Omar met and befriended OSAMA BIN LADEN, a young Saudi Islamic militant who had also joined the mujahideen. In 1994 two years after mujahideen factions from the northern part of the country had ousted the Soviet-installed government and taken power in Kabul, Omar led the Taliban from its base in the southern city of KANDAHAR in an effort to depose the new rules in the capital. After two years of struggle, Taliban forces entered Kabul in 1996, and forced the former rulers to retreat to the northern mountainous regions and regroup as the "NORTHERN ALLIANCE." Omar became the new leader of Afghanistan. Between 1996 and 2001, Omar used his position to ensure a strict application of Islamic law to all aspects of Afghanistan life, such as ending educational opportunities for women, stoning women for adultery, burying homosexuals under brick walls, and amputating thieves' hands. In 2001 Omar also approved the destruction of two ancient and giant carved statues of Buddha in the city of Bamyan, denouncing them as repellant symbols of idolatry.

In the aftermath of the terrorist attacks on SEPTEMBER 11, 2001, when Omar failed to surrender bin Laden (the organizer of the attacks) to U.S. custody, American forces invaded the Taliban-controlled segments of Afghanistan in

## OMAN

| 1951 | The Sultanate of Muscat and Oman achieves full independence from Britain. A Treaty of Friendship with Britain is signed. |
|---|---|
| 1955 | Imam Ghalib ibn Ali rebels against the sultan of Muscat and Oman, Said bin Taimur. |
| 1956 | With the aid of the British-led Muscat and Oman Field Force, the sultan occupies the capital. The imam's brother Talib ibn Ali escapes to Cairo and, with Egyptian and Saudi help, sets up an imamate in exile. |
| 1959 | The civil war ends with the complete rout of the rebel imam. |
| 1970 | Sultan Said bin Taimur is overthrown in a palace coup led by his son Qabus ibn Said. Tariq ibn Ali is named new prime minister. |
| 1975 | The 11-year civil war ends, as the Dhofar insurgents are crushed and their leaders surrender. |
| 1981 | Oman becomes a founding member, in addition to six other Middle East states, of the Gulf Cooperation Council. |
| 1997 | Law is passed that women can vote and hold political office. Omani elections bring two women to the Consultative Council, an advisory body. |
| 1999 | Oman and the United Arab Emirates sign an agreement defining a portion of their common border. |
| 2002 | Voting rights are given to all citizens over the age of 21, whereas previously voters were chosen from tribal leaders and businessmen. |

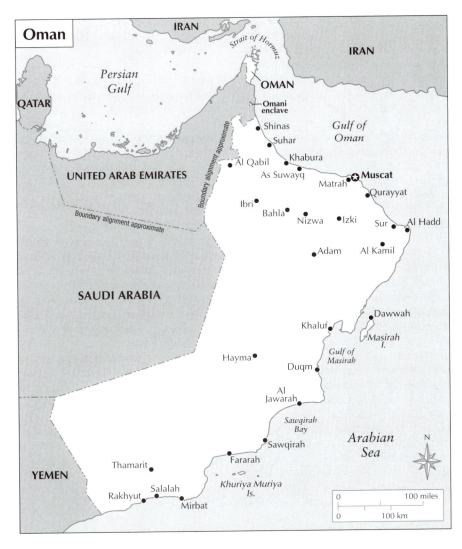

**Oman**

October 2001 and toppled Omar's government. U.S. military forces failed to capture Omar or bin Laden, both of whom (it is believed) took refuge among the nomadic communities along the Afghanistan-Pakistan border.

**Omega workshops** British effort of 1913–21 to re-create in a 20th-century context some of the design-craft philosophy of the arts and crafts movement. Leading spirit Roger FRY drew into it such personalities as Vanessa BELL, Duncan GRANT and Wyndham LEWIS. The workshops produced various items of furniture, pottery, textiles, stained glass and a few complete interiors, but the effort appears to have been handicapped by an amateurish, dilettante level of performance that kept its productions decorative and trivial. Dissension among the participants led to its collapse in the 1920s.

**Onassis, Aristotle** (1906–1975) Greek shipping magnate. Onassis's early business dealings left him in control of the Allied tanker fleet when WORLD WAR II broke out, thus giving him a golden edge in profits. The closing of the SUEZ CANAL and the SUEZ CRISIS (1956) also proved a bonanza for Onassis, whose fleet of supertankers were most profitable in the longer route around Cape Horn. Onassis gained worldwide attention in 1968 when he married Jacqueline KENNEDY, the widow of President John F. KENNEDY. At the time of his death, Onassis's holdings were valued at $500 million. He had controlling interest in about 100 interlocking companies in a dozen countries, including 30 shipping concerns. His holdings included hotels, banks, piers, Olympic Airways and real estate—including the island of Scorpios in the Ionian Sea, where he was buried.

**Onassis, Jacqueline** See Jacqueline KENNEDY.

**O'Neill, Eugene Gladstone** (1888–1953) America's first modern playwright of international stature. Before he began writing in the mid-teens, realism on the American stage was confined to several tentative efforts by such playwrights as James A. Herne, David BELASCO, Clyde FITCH and William Vaughn Moody. Modern European movements in EXPRESSIONISM and Symbolism had yet to make an appearance. With O'Neill, however, they all merged in a unique theatrical aesthetic, which was to become the model for later American playwrights, such as Tennessee WILLIAMS, Arthur MILLER, and Edward ALBEE. O'Neill was born in New York to a theatrical family. His father spent most of his career touring in the lead role of the popular melodrama *The Count of Monte Cristo*. Eugene's early life was restless and dissipated: He prospected for gold in Honduras, worked as a seaman and a journalist and, during a stay in a sanitorium for treatment of tuberculosis began writing his first plays (most of them derivative of the style of melodrama popularized by his father). From 1913 to 1917 he wrote more than 24 plays. Most important in this group were the four short plays collectively entitled *S.S. Glencairn*, produced by the PROVINCETOWN PLAYERS in 1916. With *Beyond the Horizon* (1918) he moved from little theaters in GREENWICH VILLAGE to Broadway and a growing popularity. A remarkably fertile period ensued throughout the decade of the 1920s. *Anna Christie* (1921) won a PULITZER PRIZE. He experimented with Expressionist techniques in *The Emperor Jones* (1920) and *The Hairy Ape* (1921); with the masks and choruses of the Greek Theater in *The Great God Brown* (1928) and *Lazarus Laughed* (1928); and with devices of the stock melodrama, like the aside, in *Strange Interlude* (1928). However, his subsequent work in the 1930s—the trilogy *Mourning Becomes Electra* (1929–31), the nostalgic comedy of *Ah, Wilderness!* (1933), *The Iceman Cometh* (1930) and *Long Day's Journey into Night* (1939)—subsumed experimental techniques, melodrama and realism into a unified vision. Characters and situations were frankly autobiographical, drawing extensively from O'Neill's own family. The themes of displaced persons, dysfunctional families, dreams as mechanisms for coping with sordid life and alienation from history predominated. He called his method supernaturalism, by which he meant going beyond realism by using symbolism in a realistic way. (He detested what he called the photographic plays of his contemporaries.) Thus, for example, the character of Yank in *The Hairy Ape* is both a man and a representation of mankind; the site of Harry Hope's saloon in *The Iceman Cometh* becomes, in Act 2, an evocation of The Last Supper; and so forth. After a failed production of *A Moon for the Misbegotten* (1943), O'Neill wrote no new plays. He died in 1953 of a lifelong nervous disorder, which brought about a loss of motor control.

**O'Neill, Terence Marne (Baron O'Neill of the Maine)** *(1914–1990)* Irish politician. From 1963 to 1969, he served as prime minister of NORTHERN IRELAND. While in office, he worked to improve relations between the Roman Catholic minority and the Protestant majority. He offered important concessions to Catholics, including the establishment of an ombudsman to oversee the fairness of government policies. In 1965 he became the first prime minister of Northern Ireland to meet with a prime minister of the Republic of IRELAND. Their efforts were criticized both by Catholics and his own Unionist Party. He was forced to resign in 1969, and was made a life peer in 1970.

**Onizuka, Ellison** *(1946–1986)* U.S. astronaut, one of seven killed in the explosion of the SPACE SHUTTLE *CHALLENGER* on January 28, 1986. The Hawaiian-born aerospace engineer became the first Asian American in space when he flew on a shuttle mission in 1985.

**Oparin, Alexander Ivanovich** *(1894–1976)* Soviet biochemist. Oparin studied plant physiology at the Moscow State University, where he later served as professor. He helped found the Bakh Institute of Biochemistry, which the Soviet government established in 1935. Oparin became director of the institute in 1946. As early as 1922, Oparin was speculating on how life first originated; he made the then

controversial suggestion that the first organisms must have been heliotropic—that is, they could not make their own food from inorganic materials but relied upon organic substances. This questioned the prevailing view that life originated with autotropic organisms that (like present-day plants) could synthesize their food from simple inorganic materials. Oparin's view gradually gained acceptance in many circles. Oparin did much to stimulate research on the origin of life and organized the first international meeting to discuss the problem in Moscow in 1957.

**op art (abbreviation for optical art)** Op art was a movement and a style that developed in Europe and the U.S. during the 1960s. Its guiding principle was the exploitation of various phenomena of visual perception in color or black and white. Op art images appear to vibrate with violently contrasting but tonally similar color, move backward and forward from the picture plane in geometric constructs, pulsate in concentric circles or shimmer with moire patterns. Much op art attempted to re-create the effect of psychodelic trips. Artists who were active in the movement include Victor de Vasarely, Richard Anusziewicz and Bridget Riley.

**OPEC** See ORGANIZATION OF PETROLEUM EXPORTING COUNTRIES.

**Open University** An experimental university for adults opened in January of 1971 and located in Milton Keynes, Buckinghamshire, England. Its goal was to provide access to higher education to a broad range of people; there were no academic prerequisites for admission. To extend its reach, courses were conducted by correspondence, supplemented by television, and by seminars and study groups held at various locations across the country.

**Operation Barbarossa** See BARBAROSSA.

**Operation Bootstrap** See Luis MUÑOZ MARIN.

**Operation Coronet** See OPERATION OLYMPIC.

**Operation Desert Shield** See PERSIAN GULF WAR; H. Norman SCHWARZKOPF.

**Operation Desert Storm** See Saddam HUSSEIN; PERSIAN GULF WAR; H. Norman SCHWARZKOPF.

**Operation Dynamo** See Sir John FISHER.

**Operation Mincemeat** See Ewen MONTAGU.

**Operation Olympic** Code name for a planned U.S. invasion of JAPAN (at the island of Kyushu) in WORLD WAR II. Operation Olympic was scheduled for November 1945; a second invasion near Tokyo (**Operation Coronet**) on the island of Honshu was planned for March 1946. It was widely reported that U.S. analysts had estimated that perhaps 1 million American lives would be lost in the invasions. Japan's surrender on September 2, 1945, following the destruction of HIROSHIMA (August 6) and NAGASAKI (August 9), made the invasions unnecessary. Later historical research revealed that no U.S. Army estimate ever suggested that 1 million American casualties would result. Instead figures have ranged from 100,000 to 500,000 estimated casualties.

**Operation Overlord** Code name for the Allied invasion of NORMANDY (June 6, 1944) in WORLD WAR II.

**Operation Paperclip** U.S. plan that brought German scientists to the United States at the end of WORLD WAR II. Fearing that German military and scientific secrets would fall into the hands of the USSR, the joint chiefs of staff ordered General Dwight D. EISENHOWER to "preserve from destruction and take under your control records, plans, documents, papers, files and scientific, industrial and other information belonging to . . . German organizations engaged in military research." The plan was supervised by U.S. chief of technical intelligence Holger N. TOFTOY. Among the Germans brought to the U.S. in this sensitive and controversial operation were many who had worked on the V-2 rocket at PEENEMÜNDE. American critics were incensed that those who had helped HITLER develop weapons of war used

German scientists brought to the United States under Operation Paperclip. 1945 (LIBRARY OF CONGRESS, PRINTS AND PHOTOGRAPHS DIVISION)

against the Allies were suddenly part of the U.S. scientific establishment. Ironically, these engineers came to play a crucial role in developing the U.S. space program. They included Walter DORNBERGER and Wernher von BRAUN.

**Ophüls, Marcel** *(1927– )* German-born film director. Ophüls, who is the son of the renowned film director Max OPHÜLS, accompanied his father to the U.S. in 1941 and ultimately became an American citizen. But in 1950 Ophüls returned to France, where he worked as an assistant to numerous directors, including his father and John HUSTON. After directing features for French television, Ophüls achieved international recognition for *The Sorrow and the Pity* (1969), a powerful documentary on French ANTI-SEMITISM and collaboration with the Nazis during WORLD WAR II. Subsequent political documentaries by Ophüls include *A Sense of Loss* (1972), on NORTHERN IRELAND and *Memory of Justice* (1976)—which portrayed military atrocities in Europe during WORLD WAR II, during the 1950s in ALGERIA, and in VIETNAM.

**Ophüls, Max (Max Oppenheimer)** *(1902–1957)* German-born film director. Ophüls was a brilliant and well-traveled director who made films throughout Europe and in HOLLYWOOD. He began his career as a theatrical actor and director in Germany before becoming a French citizen in 1934. After making films in Italy and the Netherlands, Ophüls evaded the Nazis by going to Hollywood in 1941, where his greatest successes were *Letter*

*from an Unknown Woman* (1948) and *The Reckless Moment* (1949). Ophüls then returned to France, where he made a number of films, including *La Ronde* (1950), *The Earrings of Madame de . . .* (1953) and *Lola Montez* (1955), a sweeping and sentimental historical epic on the life of a 19th-century romantic adventuress that is regarded as Ophüls's masterwork.

**Oppenheimer, Frank** *(1912–1985)* U.S. nuclear physicist. During WORLD WAR II he worked on the development of the ATOMIC BOMB in the MANHATTAN PROJECT, headed by his older brother, J. Robert OPPENHEIMER. At the time, his left-wing views aroused concern in the government that he and his brother were security risks. In 1949 after testifying before the HOUSE UN-AMERICAN ACTIVITIES COMMITTEE that he had been a member of the American Communist Party in the 1930s, he was fired from his teaching position at the University of Minnesota. He later became a cattle rancher in Colorado. In 1969 he founded the Exploratorium, a San Francisco museum with exhibits that help even young children grasp the basic principles of science.

**Oppenheimer, J(ulius) Robert** *(1904–1967)* American physicist, best known as the father of the ATOMIC BOMB. Born in New York City, he attended Harvard (B.A., 1925), Cambridge and the University of Göttingen (Ph.D., 1927). Collaborating with Max BORN, he did significant work on the quantum theory of molecules. From 1929 to 1942, Oppenheimer taught theoretical physics at the University of California (Berkeley) and the California Institute of Technology (Pasadena). At both schools, he studied quantum theory and nuclear physics and did experimental research on the positron, while

Leslie Groves (r) and Dr. J. R. Oppenheimer examine an atomic test site. 1945. (NEW YORK WORLD TELEGRAM AND THE SUN NEWSPAPER COLLECTION, LIBRARY OF CONGRESS, PRINTS AND PHOTOGRAPHS DIVISION)

winning a reputation as a brilliant and inspirational teacher and acquiring a corps of dedicated assistants. Oppenheimer first became interested in the possibility of an atomic bomb in 1939, and in 1941 he began research into the problems of nuclear fission at the Lawrence Radiation Laboratory, Berkeley. This work was continued during WORLD WAR II, when he acted (1942–45) as director of the top-secret atomic energy research program known as the MANHATTAN PROJECT—at a remote site in LOS ALAMOS, New Mexico. Gathering around him some of the greatest minds in nuclear physics, Oppenheimer and his colleagues worked tirelessly in a successful effort to create the bomb. In 1945 he was one of a panel of scientists who advised its use against Japan. After the bomb was dropped, he became a strong adherent of the international control of atomic energy.

In 1947 Oppenheimer returned to academia as director of the Institute for Advanced Study at Princeton. At the same time, he remained an adviser to the State Department and the Pentagon, and that same year he was appointed chairman of the General Advisory Committee (GAC) to the Atomic Energy Commission (AEC). In this capacity, Oppenheimer at first opposed research on a HYDROGEN BOMB but reversed his position in 1951. However, his early opposition to the fusion bomb, his stand on arms control, his left-wing political connections and his sometimes lofty attitude soon brought him into conflict with the MCCARTHYISM of the 1950s. Faced with allegations that the scientist was a security risk, President EISENHOWER suspended Oppenheimer's security clearance in a controversial 1953 decision. After an appeal failed to restore the clearance, Oppenheimer devoted himself to his Princeton activities and to work on the spiritual and intellectual ramifications of nuclear physics. A man of undoubted integrity and loyalty, he was the most notorious scientific victim of McCarthyism. In 1963 Oppenheimer was awarded the government's prestigious Enrico Fermi Award.

**Orangemen** Members of the **Orange Order,** an Irish society formed in Ulster in 1795 to uphold Protestantism. The name is taken from William III, Prince of Orange, who defeated James II at the Battle of the Boyne in 1690.

The society is bitterly anti-Catholic. It maintains the Ulster Unionist Party and has branches outside NORTHERN IRELAND, particularly in Liverpool and Glasgow. The society organizes annual summer marches—notably the march in Belfast on July 12—to celebrate William's victory at the Boyne and to demonstrate the Protestant and LOYALIST presence in Northern Ireland.

**Orbison, Roy** (*1936–1988*) U.S. singer-songwriter. In the early 1960s, Orbison was one of the world's most popular recording artists. He favored an introspective musical style that wedded rockabilly and dramatic ballads. His career first took off in 1960 with a recording of "Only the Lonely." Between 1960 and 1964 he was the top-selling male singer in the world, with such songs as "Running Scared," "Crying," "Blue Bayou" and "Oh, Pretty Woman." The death of his first wife in 1966, followed by the deaths of two of his children in 1968 and by problems with alcohol and drugs, temporarily ended Orbison's performing career. He began a successful comeback effort in 1987, the year he was inducted into the Rock and Roll Hall of Fame.

**Oren Affair** In 1952, while visiting CZECHOSLOVAKIA, prominent Israeli leftist Mordechai Oren was arrested and summoned to testify against Rudolf SLÁNSKÝ, the Communist Party secretary general who was on trial for treason. Accused of treason himself, Oren was sentenced to 15 years in prison in 1953. He was released in 1956 during Czechoslovakia's de-Stalinization period. (See STALIN; STALINISM.) After returning to ISRAEL, he claimed that he had been forced to confess what never happened. In the 1960s the Czechoslovak government formally cleared Oren.

**Orff, Carl** (*1895–1982*) German composer and music educator. Born in Munich, he attended the city's Academy of Music and was cofounder (1924) and teacher at its Güntherschule. Fascinated by the primitive in music and with the combination of music, dance and text, he initiated an influential teaching method that mixed rhythmic games, melodic exercises, chant, gymnastics and dance. Orff's method was outlined in his popular

text *Das Schulwerk.* Extremely interested in early music, he incorporated its lively rhythms and monodic forms into his own compositions. His most popular work is *Carmina Burana* (1937), a vigorous setting of secular medieval texts for choir and vocal soloists. It forms the first part of a trilogy that also includes *Catulli Carmina* (1943) and *Trionfo di Afrodite* (1953). Prior to 1937, Orff composed a variety of orchestral, chamber and vocal music. After that date, he composed exclusively for the theater in such works as the operas *Die Kluge* (1941–42), *Prometheus* (1968) and *Play from the End of Time* (1973). From 1961, he was head of the Orff Institute at the Mozarteum Music Academy in Salzburg.

**Organisation de l'Armée Secrète** See O.A.S.

**Organization for Economic Cooperation and Development (OECD)** International organization that succeeded the ORGANIZATION FOR EUROPEAN ECONOMIC COOPERATION (OEEC) in 1960. With headquarters in Paris, it is an attempt by the leading industrial nations to promote high economic growth in member states and to assist in the economic growth of the developing countries. The OECD is an important research organization, studying and debating such international questions as balance of payments, agriculture, energy and technology. Headed by a secretary-general, its organizational structure employs a council and an executive committee.

**Organization for European Economic Cooperation (OEEC)** International organization established in 1948 as a coordinating group for MARSHALL PLAN aid. It aimed at reconstructing Europe and at achieving a sound European economy through the cooperation of its members. Its original 16 member states were Austria, Belgium, Denmark, France, Greece, Iceland, Ireland, Italy, Luxembourg, the Netherlands, Norway, Portugal, Sweden, Switzerland, the U.K. and Turkey. They were joined by West Germany in 1955 and Spain in 1958. The U.S. and Canada later became associate members. This organization provided a framework for the EUROPEAN ECONOMIC

COMMUNITY or Common Market. In 1960 it was superseded by the ORGANIZATION FOR ECONOMIC COOPERATION AND DEVELOPMENT.

## Organization of African Unity

An international group of African states founded in Addis Ababa, Ethiopia, in 1963. Its goals included promoting the unity and solidarity of African nations; guaranteeing the independence and territorial integrity of its members; coordinating political, economic, cultural, health, scientific and defense policies among its members and eliminating colonialism. Heads of the member states met on an annual basis, the Council of Ministers met every six months and separate commissions concentrated on varying subjects. The organization was successful in mediating border disputes between Algeria and Morocco (1965) and between Somalia and Ethiopia and Somalia and Kenya (1965–67) but failed in an attempt to settle the Nigeria-Biafra civil war (1968–70). While it had a membership of 50 in the early 1990s, it failed to command the respect it had in its earlier days. On September 9, 1999, the 53 members of the Organization for African Union transformed it into the African Union, a structure dedicated to achieving the same degree of political and economic cooperation as the EUROPEAN UNION (EU).

## Organization of American States (OAS)

Regional organization of Western Hemisphere states formed to promote peace, justice and solidarity; to strengthen political cooperation among its members; to encourage hemispheric economic development and to defend the sovereignty and independence of its member nations. It was established by treaty at a meeting in Bogotá, Colombia, in April 1948 and was officially founded in 1951. With a membership of 32 countries, it has headquarters in Washington, D.C. The OAS is built on the earlier International Bureau of American Republics, established in 1890, and its successor, the Pan-American Union, founded in 1910, which became the Secretariat of the OAS. It is made up of a General Assembly, which meets annually in member nations, a Permanent Council and a Meeting of Consultation of Ministers of Foreign Affairs. Four other councils consider such issues as economic and social conditions, education, legal matters and human rights. The organization is overseen by a secretary general, elected by the assembly for a five-year term. The OAS has taken stands against Cuba, which was expelled from active membership in 1962 and boycotted by the OAS from 1964 to 1975. In more recent years, the organization has rebelled against the strong role traditionally played by the U.S. in Latin American affairs. Despite the anti-American stance of some of its members, the OAS has largely supported U.S. efforts to increase hemispheric trade through the proposed Free Trade Act of the Americas (FTAA).

## Organization of Petroleum Exporting Countries (OPEC)

Organization established in 1960 to coordinate oil policies in member states, all Third World petroleum-producing nations; original members were Iran, Iraq, Kuwait, Saudi Arabia and Venezuela. Qatar joined in 1961, Indonesia and Libya in 1962, Algeria in 1969, Abu Dhabi (now in the U.A.E.) in 1967, Nigeria in 1971 and Ecuador and Gabon in 1973. The original intent of OPEC was to guard against oil price cuts and overproduction by companies in the U.S. and Europe. In the 1970s it pressed for petroleum rate increases and succeeded in raising oil prices by more than 100 percent before the end of the decade, thus creating severe oil shortages. At the beginning of the 1980s, large-scale production of oil by Saudi Arabia and energy-preserving policies initiated by many oil-importing nations caused an oil surplus and led to problems in OPEC. As widely varying prices for oil held sway, the organization strove to maintain a standardized pricing structure.

## Original Dixieland Jazz Band

The Original Dixieland Jazz Band, often considered the first white jazz band, was formed during WORLD WAR I in New Orleans by cornetist-leader Nick LaRocca, clarinetist Larry Shields, trombonist Eddie Edwards, drummer Tony Sbarbaro and pianist Henry Ragas (later replaced by J. Russell Robinson). Achieving success in Chicago in 1916, the ODJB was brought to New York in 1917 for a sensational stand at Reisenweber's Restaurant, where it successfully capitalized on the wartime vogue for jazz dancing; the group continued as a major attraction until breaking up in 1925. The ODJB is also significant for being the first jazz band to record phonograph records. As for its historical significance, the ODJB is the subject of still heated controversy. Some experts dismiss it as derivative of black New Orleans music; others, including La-Rocca, argue that the ODJB deserves greater credit for its "innovations." The truth, as Gunther Schuller eloquently chronicles in *Early Jazz* (1968), lies at some point between these extremes. What is incontrovertible, however, is the significant role played by the ODJB in popularizing the Dixieland style throughout the U.S. and Europe.

## Orkin, Ruth (1921–1985)

American photographer. Orkin's work on celebrities and street life regularly appeared in *LIFE, Look* and other major magazines during the 1940s, 1950s and 1960s. In the early 1950s, she and her husband Morris Engel made *The Little Fugitive,* a film that was credited with influencing the French NOUVELLE VAGUE (new wave) cinema.

## Orlando, Vittorio Emmanuele (1860–1952)

Italian statesman, premier (1917–19). A law professor in Palermo, he was elected to parliament in 1897 and held several cabinet posts from 1903 to 1917. Appointed premier after Italy's defeat at Caporetto, he helped to rally his nation for ultimate victory in WORLD WAR I. Orlando was one of the "Big Four" (with Georges CLEMENCEAU, David LLOYD GEORGE and Woodrow WILSON) at the 1919 PARIS PEACE CONFERENCE. He quarreled bitterly with Wilson over Italy's territorial demands, dramatically leaving the conference only to return a month later. Failing in his efforts, Orlando resigned the premiership. An opponent of MUSSOLINI's fascist government, he resigned from parliament in 1925. After the defeat of the fascists, he became a leader of the Democratic Union and served as president of the constituent assembly (1946–47) and as a senator from 1948 until his death.

## Orlov, Yuri Alexandrovich (1893–1966)

Soviet paleontologist and member of the Academy of Sciences from 1960. Having graduated from Petrograd

University in 1917, Orlov taught at Perm, Leningrad (now St. Petersburg) and Moscow. He was named head of Moscow's department of paleontology in 1942. He edited the *Paleontology Journal* (1959–66) and was chief editor of the 15-volume *Basic Paleontology*. He was awarded the Order of Lenin and various other medals.

**Ormandy, Eugene (Jeno Blau)** *(1899–1985)* Hungarian-born American conductor. Trained in BUDAPEST as a violinist, Jeno Blau came to the U.S. in 1921 on the liner *Normandie,* from which he took his new name. He played briefly in a theater orchestra before becoming its conductor and made guest appearances with other orchestras. He conducted the Minneapolis Symphony (1932–36). In 1936 he became co-director of the Philadelphia Orchestra with Leopold STOKOWSKI and was named sole musical director in 1938. Under his guidance, the orchestra retained the celebrated richness of sound that Stokowski had done much to cultivate. Over the years, Ormandy led the orchestra on numerous foreign tours, including a historic visit to China in 1973. Between 1936 and 1986 he made almost 600 recordings. When he retired in 1980, he had been head of a single orchestra longer than any other conductor in the 20th century. Although critics sometimes complained that his interpretations were slick, Ormandy was an extremely knowledgeable musician. He had a wide repertoire but was best known for his performances of music of the romantic period.

**O'Rorke, Brian** *(1901–1974)* English designer known for his work on boat and airplane interiors. Trained in engineering and architecture, O'Rorke established his own design firm in London in 1929. His most distinguished work was the interior design of the Orient Line passenger vessels *Orion* and *Orcades* of the 1930s. These ships were remarkable for their sensibly functional, handsome interiors at a time when the more excessive ART DECO was the norm for ocean-liner interior design. O'Rorke also worked on railroad and airplane interiors, providing straightforward and appropriate design for a number of transport projects, including the interior of the Vickers Viking airplane of 1946.

**Orpen, Sir William (Newenham Montague)** *(1878–1931)* Irish portrait, landscape and genre painter. Born in County Dublin, he studied art at Dublin's Metropolitan School, where he later taught (1902–14), and at London's Slade School. Perhaps the most influential and popular Irish painter of his day, he was knighted in 1918. He is best known for his sketches of everyday life in Ireland, scenes of WORLD WAR I (being an official war artist from 1917–18) and portraits of prominent Irish figures. His works are in major Irish museums as well as such collections as the Tate Gallery, London; Metropolitan Museum, New York City and Carnegie Institute, Pittsburgh.

**Orr, Robert Gordon "Bobby"** *(1948– )* Canadian hockey player. In many ways, Orr was the artist who put the finishing touches on the modern game of hockey. While there had been earlier rushing defensemen, Orr orchestrated his team's movements from the blueline when he was not carrying the puck across himself, as he won the league's scoring title three times. The Boston Bruins of the early 1970s became known as the "Big Bad Bruins" as they dominated the league with their explosive scoring and their fists. Plagued throughout his career by bad knees, Orr was an All-Star throughout that career and won the Norris Trophy as best defenseman eight times. He was named to the Hockey Hall of Fame in 1979.

**Ortega Saavedra, Daniel** *(1945– )* Nicaraguan guerrilla and political leader, president of NICARAGUA (1945–90, 2007– ). Active in various underground resistance movements against the regime of Anastasio SOMOZA, Ortega was a member of the National Directorate of the FSLN (Sandinista Liberation Front), 1966–67, and imprisoned from 1967 to 1974. He resumed his position with the FSLN and became involved in further revolutionary activities. He fought a two-year military offensive that overthrew the Somoza regime in 1979. He was subsequently a member of the Junta of National Reconstruction and became president in 1981. Ortega developed close relations with CUBA. As he became increasingly intolerant of those who did not follow his party line and espoused Marxist revolutionary doctrine, the noncommunist members of the junta either resigned or were forced out. Many of his onetime associates denounced his rule, and some joined the CONTRAS, who were attempting to overthrow Ortega. Ortega was also denounced by the U.S. REAGAN administration, which gave support to the contras. In the late 1980s Ortega agreed to hold free elections under a plan that called for the contras to lay down their arms. Ortega was predicted to win easily, but he was upset on February 25, 1990, by Violeta CHAMORRO, the candidate of the 14-party National Opposition Union. Ortega remained the leader of the Sandinista Party and served repeatedly as its presidential candidate 1996 and 2001, but lost both times to Liberal Party candidates Arnoldo Alemán (1996) and Enrique Bolanos (2001). He won, however, in 2006.

**Ortega y Gasset, José** *(1883–1955)* Spanish philosopher, sociologist, literary critic and politician. Ortega was one of the preeminent Spanish men of letters of the 20th century. He held the chair of metaphysics at the University of Madrid for several decades and served as a member of the Spanish parliament. After the SPANISH CIVIL WAR and the rise of FRANCO's fascist regime in the 1930s, Ortega went into exile, ultimately settling in Portugal. Ortega was known for his ardent defense of classicism and the humanities, as well as for his fear that the working class, in gaining political power, would threaten the ultimate values of Western civilization. His major works include *Meditations on Quixote* (1914), *The Dehumanization of Art and Other Essays* (1925) and *Revolt of the Masses* (1930).

**Ortiz, Peter J(ulien)** *(1913–1988)* U.S. military hero. He was a highly decorated U.S. Marine Corps veteran whose exploits were the subject of two films: *13 Rue Madeleine* (1946) and *Operation Secret* (1952).

**Orton, Joe (Kingsley Orton)** *(1933–1967)* British playwright and actor. Orton left school to begin acting at 16. His dark comedies, starting with *Entertaining Mr. Sloane* (1964), frequently focused on sexual perversion, corruption and violence and created a sensation based partly on shock value. Other works include *Loot* (1965), *The Ruffian* *on the Stair* (1967) and *What the Butler Saw* (1969), which was performed posthumously. Orton was beaten to death by his lover and companion, who then committed suicide.

**Orwell, George (pen name of Eric Arthur Blair)** *(1903–1950)* British novelist, essayist and journalist. Born to a middle-class English family in Bengal (then part of Britain's Indian empire), he was educated at Eton and afterward spent five years with the Indian Imperial Police in Burma—an experience that later provided the background for his first novel, *Burmese Days* (1934). During the GREAT DEPRESSION he worked at a variety of jobs, often leading a hand-to-mouth existence. His experiences of this time, which gave him a profound sympathy with the poor and unemployed and intensified his commitment to socialism, are recounted in his nonfiction works *Down and Out in Paris and London* (1933) and *The Road to Wigan Pier* (1937). In 1936 he went to Spain to report on the SPANISH CIVIL WAR; he soon joined the fight against the Fascists (see FASCISM). He described his experience and perceptions in *Homage to Catalonia* (1939), an incisive account of the war that criticized the infighting amongst the various Republican factions. The war confirmed Orwell's hatred of TOTALITARIANISM and increased his distrust of COMMUNISM. These attitudes are apparent in his two most important novels, ANIMAL FARM (1945), an allegorical satire of the RUSSIAN REVOLUTION; and *1984* (1949), a warning about the bleak outcome of totalitarianism. These two political works have had an enormous influence on other writers and thinkers and have been subject to much literary and political analysis.

During WORLD WAR II, Orwell served as literary editor for the British LABOUR PARTY journal, *Tribune* (1943–45), and broadcast for the BRITISH BROADCASTING CORPORATION. He wrote numerous essays and articles, many of which can be found in *Collected Essays, Journalism and Letters* (1968). His other, more conventional novels include *A Clergyman's Daughter* (1935), *Keep the Aspidistra Flying* (1936) and *Coming Up for Air* (1939). A complex and often contradictory figure, Orwell stands as one of the most original and uncompromising writers of his time—and as a champion of human liberty and decency.

**Ory, Edward "Kid"** *(1886–1973)* Kid Ory is the most famous exponent of the New Orleans "tailgate" trombone style, with its roughhewn syntax of growls, glissandi and other "vocalizations," the latter often achieved with various mutes. Between 1912 and 1919, Ory led one of the most influential bands in New Orleans; among his sidemen were noted trumpeters King OLIVER and Louis ARMSTRONG, as well as clarinetists Johnny Dodds, Sidney Bechet, Jimmie None and George Lewis. Ory was also a key figure in the prolific Chicago jazz scene of the 1920s, where he participated in the landmark "Hot Five" recordings with Louis Armstrong. After retiring to run a successful California chicken ranch in the 1930s, his career was revived due to a 1944 radio broadcast with Orson WELLES. In 1954 his Dixieland standard, "Muskrat Ramble," attained hit status with newly fitted lyrics; he also had an acting and playing role in *The Benny Goodman Story* (1955). Ory's pioneering style exerted profound influence both in his early years in New Orleans and during the post–World War II traditional jazz revival.

**Osborne, John James** *(1929–1994)* British playwright and actor. Osborne, who began his career acting in provincial repertory companies, was best known for the play *Look Back in Anger* (1956). Its domestic realism and its lower-class antihero caused Osborne to be categorized as one of the ANGRY YOUNG MEN. His early work, which also includes *The Entertainer* (1957, filmed 1960), *The World of Paul Slickey* (1959) and *Luther* (1961), is credited with changing the course of British drama. *A Patriot for Me* (1966) was originally censored because of its homosexual theme but was revived successfully in 1983. Many critics felt that Osborne's later works, such as *West of Suez* (1971) and *Watch It Come Down* (1975), were increasingly cranky in tone and lacked the impact of his early plays.

**OSS** See OFFICE OF STRATEGIC SERVICES.

**Ossietzky, Carl von** *(1889–1938)* German author and pacifist. Born in Hamburg, he was a fledgling poet when distaste for German militarism led him to cofound the German Peace Society in 1912. Service in WORLD WAR I deepened his antiwar sentiments, and in 1920 he became the secretary of the German Peace Society. Settling in Berlin, he became the editor in chief of the antimilitarist weekly *Weltbühne* in 1927. Jailed briefly for publishing an article that criticized the government for allowing the development of paramilitary organizations, he was again imprisoned in 1932 for printing a piece that exposed Germany's secret rearmament. After the REICHSTAG FIRE (1933), Ossietzky was again imprisoned—this time by the Nazis: first in Berlin, then in two CONCENTRATION CAMPS. Suffering from a heart condition and tuberculosis, he was transferred to a prison hospital in 1936—the same year he was awarded the NOBEL PEACE PRIZE. Subsequently, the German government decreed that no citizen could accept a Nobel Prize. Ossietzky died two years later in the prison hospital.

***Ostpolitik*** **(German, "eastern policy")** Policy of the German Federal Republic (WEST GERMANY) developed by Willy BRANDT and others as an attempt to normalize relations with communist countries, including the German Democratic Republic (GDR). With the reunification of GERMANY in 1990, West Germany seemed to have far surpassed the original goals of *Ostpolitik*.

**Oswald, Lee Harvey** *(1939–1964)* Presumed assassin of U.S. president John F. KENNEDY. Born in New Orleans and raised in poverty, he was by all accounts a loner. He served in the U.S. Marine Corps but received an undesirable discharge (1959). He then lived in the USSR for two and half years, marrying a Soviet woman, Marina Nicholaevna. Apparently disillusioned with the USSR, he returned to the U.S. in June 1962 with his wife and infant daughter and became involved in pro-CASTRO activities. He separated from his wife in 1963 and moved to Dallas, where he found a low-paying job in the **Texas School Book Depository**, from where, as far as can be determined, he fired the shots that killed President Kennedy. Shortly after leaving the building, he also shot and killed a

Dallas police officer, **J. D. Tippitt,** who had stopped him for questioning. Oswald was captured soon thereafter. He met his own death two days later on November 24 as police were taking him through the basement of Dallas's municipal building to be transferred from the city jail to the county jail. As millions watched on television, Jack RUBY, a Dallas nightclub owner, sprang from a crowd of reporters and fired a .38-caliber revolver point blank at Oswald, who died within hours. From the time of his arrest until his own death, Oswald never admitted any connection with the Kennedy assassination; his defiant words upon his arrest were "Mister, I shot nobody." Because of Oswald's death, the evidence against him could not be presented in court. Although the Warren Commission later reported that Oswald acted alone in the assassination, conspiracy theories claiming Cuban and Mafia involvement in the assassination persisted.

**Oświęcim**  See AUSCHWITZ.

**Ott, Mel(vin Thomas)**  *(1909–1958)* American baseball player. Ott became a regular with the New York Giants at the age of 19, and remained with the club throughout his 22-year career. A perennial All-Star, he was the first player in the National League to reach the 500-home-run plateau. His popularity in New York led to his being named player-manager of the Giants in 1942. He retired from the managerial post in 1948, one year after the end of his playing career. He was named to the Hall of Fame in 1951.

**Ottoman Empire**  The once powerful Ottoman Empire lasted for hundreds of years until it met its fate in the first quarter of the 20th century. By the turn of the 20th century, its size, power, wealth and stability had declined greatly from its height in the 1500s. It was widely regarded as "the sick man of Europe." At this time, its territory had been reduced to present-day TURKEY and regions mainly in the Middle East and on the Arabian Peninsula under Turkish rule. The Sublime Porte was threatened by Russia, by Arab independence movements and by the YOUNG TURKS, who demanded modernization and reform. In 1908 the Young Turks forced Sultan ABDUL HAMID II to restore constitutional rule. The empire was allied with GERMANY in WORLD WAR I. During the war, the British occupied much of the Ottoman territory in PALESTINE and present-day IRAQ. This occupation, combined with Arab uprisings (assisted by Colonel T. E. LAWRENCE, "Lawrence of Arabia") ended Turkish domination of the region. The Treaty of SÈVRES (1920) recognized the independence of the non-Turkish peoples of the Middle East. Meanwhile, the Turkish nationalist Kemal ATATÜRK assumed power (1920), abolished the sultanate (1922) and declared Turkey a republic (1923), thus formally dissolving the Ottoman Empire.

**Outerbridge, Paul, Jr.**  *(1891–1959)* American photographer whose work ranged from rather sentimentalized commercial images to still lifes with an abstract and documentary quality and powerful design impact. Outerbridge became involved in photography during his military service in WORLD WAR I. In 1921 he entered the school operated by Clarence H. White in New York to learn pictorial and commercial photography. *Collar,* produced on his first commercial assignment in 1922, is a still life showing a man's collar resting on a checkerboard background in a way that makes the image abstract and elegant while still totally realistic. Other work included city scenes, details of mechanical parts, and such common objects as a wine glass or tin box, beautifully contact-printed on platinum paper, making each image an expressive design. His role in the history of modern photography points toward the work of Berenice ABBOTT and Walker EVANS, whose work gave documentary photography a place in both design and art.

**Ovando Candia, Alfredo**  *(1918–1982)* President of BOLIVIA (1969–70) and co-president (1965–66). Ovando organized the 1967 military offensive against Ernesto "Che" GUEVARA, in which the revolutionary was killed.

**Owen, David Anthony Llewellyn, Baron**  *(1938– )* British politician. Educated at Cambridge, Owen practiced as a neurologist before entering Parliament as a Labour member in 1966. As foreign secretary (1977–79) in the government of James CALLAGHAN, he was instrumental in negotiating an agreement with Rhodesian leader Ian SMITH, Bishop Abel MUZOREWA, Robert MUGABE and Joshua NKOMO to bring about the peaceful transfer of power to the black majority (see ZIMBABWE). A leading moderate in the LABOUR PARTY, Owen was one of the GANG OF FOUR who left the party in 1981 to found the SOCIAL DEMOCRATIC PARTY (SDP). In 1983 Owen succeeded Jenkins as party leader. Owen opposed the SDP's decision to merge with the LIBERAL PARTY in 1987 and stepped down from his post. In 1992 Owen worked with former U.S. secretary of state Cyrus Vance to create the VANCE-OWEN PLAN, a proposal that sought in vain to end the Yugoslav conflict over BOSNIA AND HERZEGOVINA. He was made a life peer in 1992 and in 1994 appointed as a Companion of Honour by Queen Elizabeth for his service to government. Owen is the author of *Face the Future* (1981), *Time to Declare* (1992) and *Balkan Odyssey* (1995).

**Owen, Wilfred**  *(1893–1918)* British poet and military hero. Owen, who was killed in action on the western front one week before the end of WORLD WAR I, is regarded by many critics as the finest poet to have written of that war, as well as one of the greatest elegiac poets in the history of the English language. Educated at the University of London, Owen enlisted in the British army in 1915 despite ill health. Invalided in 1917 and suffering from shattered nerves, Owen met fellow British poet Siegfried SASSOON while in a hospital in Scotland. Sassoon, who saw to the publication of Owen's posthumous *Poems* (1920), was a major influence on Owen, as was Robert GRAVES. Owen returned to active service, won the Military Cross for combat bravery in October 1918 and was killed the following month. His notable poems include "Strange Meeting" and "Anthem for Doomed Youth." Owen's *Collected Poems* (1931) featured an introduction by Edmund Blunden.

**Owens, Jesse**  *(1913–1980)* African-American track and field star. Jesse Owens is considered one of the greatest athletes of the 20th century and ranks as one of the all-time greats in track and field events. When in his early 20s, he had achieved fame as a sprinter, hurdler and longjumper of unsurpassing grace. In his sophomore

*American track and field star Jesse Owens* (LIBRARY OF CONGRESS, PRINTS AND PHOTOGRAPHS DIVISION)

year at Ohio State University, he broke five world records and tied a sixth, all within 45 minutes of competition. He was best known for his memorable performance at the 1936 OLYMPIC GAMES in BERLIN, where he won four gold medals (in the 100- and 200-meters dashes, the broad jump and the 400-meter relay). The feat was made more dramatic by the presence of Adolf HITLER in the stadium. Before the games, Hitler had proclaimed Aryan racial superiority and mocked American black athletes as members of an inferior race. Despite his Olympic triumphs, Owens did not receive official U.S. recognition of his feats until 1975, when he was awarded the Presidential Medal of Freedom. After his career as an amateur runner, he became a well-known public speaker and operated his own public relations and marketing firms.

**OXFAM (Oxford Committee for Famine Relief)** Privately funded British relief agency founded in Oxford, England, in 1942, to feed the children in GREECE during WORLD WAR II. Its scope broadened as it aided refugees worldwide following the war. In the 1960s OXFAM changed its focus to improving agriculture and food production in developing and THIRD WORLD countries, providing staff, equipment and training to people so that they could control their own production. In the 1970s OXFAM organizations were formed in the U.S., CANADA, BELGIUM and AUSTRALIA. In addition to continued agricultural support, OXFAM provides emergency assistance in areas stricken by natural disasters.

**Oxford Group** Established at Oxford in the 1920s, the Oxford Group was the British equivalent of Frank BUCHMAN's MORAL RE-ARMAMENT in the U.S. This evangelical movement aimed at changing social conditions through personal religious action.

**Özal, Turgut** *(1927–1993)* Turkish statesman. After graduating in electrical engineering, Özal taught at the Middle East Technical University at ANKARA. A member of the right-wing Motherland Party, Özal was formerly a member of the religious National Salvation Party. In 1967 he became undersecretary of the State Planning Organization. Özal also worked for the WORLD BANK. He served as the minister of state (1980–82) and became prime minister in 1983. With strong background in economic policy, he sponsored TURKEY's application for membership in the EUROPEAN COMMUNITY in 1987. He survived an assassination attempt in 1988, and a defeat in a March 1989 referendum regarding local elections. He strongly supported the UNITED NATIONS actions against IRAQ after Iraq's 1990 invasion of KUWAIT.

**Ozawa, Seiji** *(1935– )* Japanese-born conductor known for his sensitivity to tempo, tone and balance. Ozawa was influenced by his mentors, KARAJAN and BERNSTEIN. He made his Western conducting debut at New York's CARNEGIE HALL in 1961. From 1970 to 1976 he was musical director of the San Francisco Symphony Orchestra. He has appeared at the SALZBURG FESTIVAL and at Covent Garden and conducted operas at La Scala and Paris. Since 1968 he has been principal conductor of the New Japan Philharmonic Orchestra, and from 1973 to 2002 he served as musical director of the Boston Symphony Orchestra. In 2002 he was named music director of the Vienna State Opera.

**Ozu, Yasujiro** *(1903–1963)* Japanese filmmaker. Ozu is ranked with Kenji MIZOGUCHI and Akira KUROSAWA as the greatest of modern Japanese filmmakers. He has been called "the most Japanese" of all directors. The Tokyo-born filmmaker has won the Japanese equivalent of six ACADEMY AWARDS. By contrast with the more flamboyant work of his famous protégé, Kurosawa, Ozu reveals character primarily through dialogue, not action. His main subject is the strain of contemporary life upon the integrity of the family. He began in the movies as an assistant cameraman for the great Japanese studio, Shochiko Motion Picture Company (with which he was associated for the rest of his life). His "home dramas," such as *Ochazuke no aji* (*The Flavor of Green Tea over Rice,* 1952), *Tokyo monogatari* (*Tokyo Story*), and *Ukigusa* (*Floating Weeds*), display a fascinating formal design. He places his camera in the *tatami* position, approximately the point-of-view from a kneeling position three feet above the floor. He eschews such transitional devices as fades and dissolves. Dialogue and action are intercut with shots of static views—trees, hallways, windows, street signs, etc. The entire effect is a spare simplicity, serene calm and repose. Yet the emotional charge of those lingering shots through doorways—such as the last view of an old man abandoned by his family in *Samma no aji* (*An Autumn Afternoon,* 1962)—is overwhelming. "What remains after an Ozu film is the feeling that, if only for an hour or two, you have seen the goodness and beauty of everyday things and everyday people," says biographer Donald Richie. Ozu's tombstone displays the single character for *mu*—a term translated as "nothingness"—which in Zen philosophy also means "everything."